A Thematic Access-Oriented Bibliography of Jesus's Resurrection

A Thematic Access-Oriented Bibliography of Jesus's Resurrection

MICHAEL J. ALTER

RESOURCE *Publications* • Eugene, Oregon

A THEMATIC ACCESS-ORIENTED BIBLIOGRAPHY OF JESUS'S RESURRECTION

Copyright © 2020 Michael J. Alter. All rights reserved. Except for brief quotations in critical publications or reviews, no part of this book may be reproduced in any manner without prior written permission from the publisher. Write: Permissions, Wipf and Stock Publishers, 199 W. 8th Ave., Suite 3, Eugene, OR 97401.

Resource Publications
An Imprint of Wipf and Stock Publishers
199 W. 8th Ave., Suite 3
Eugene, OR 97401

www.wipfandstock.com

PAPERBACK ISBN: 978-1-7252-5273-8
HARDCOVER ISBN: 978-1-7252-5274-5
EBOOK ISBN: 978-1-7252-5275-2

Cataloguing-in-Publication data:

Names: Alter, Michael J., 1952–

Title: A thematic access-oriented bibliography of Jesus's resurrection / Michael J. Alter.

Description: Eugene, OR: Resource Publications, 2020 | **Includes bibliographical references and index.**

Subjects LCSH: Jesus Christ—Resurrection. | Jesus Christ—Historicity. | Jesus Christ—Bibliography

Identifiers: ISBN 978-1-7252-5273-8 (paperback) | ISBN 978-1-7252-5274-5 (hardcover) | ISBN 978-1-7252-5275-2 (ebook)

Classification: BT 481 2020

Manufactured in the U.S.A.   12/31/19

To libraries,

librarians,

and their support staff

Contents

Preface | IX
Acknowledgments | XIII

CATEGORY I—***Books Dealing with Jesus's Resurrection***

CHAPTER 1
Entire books Dealing with Jesus's Resurrection: Pro | 3

CHAPTER 2
Entire Books Dealing with Jesus's Resurrection: Con | 43

CHAPTER 3
Partial Books Dealing with Jesus's Resurrection: Con—Agnostics, Atheists, Detractors, Humanists, Liberal Christians, Rationalists, Skeptics, Gnostic Texts, and Controversial Literature | 47

CHAPTER 4
Books Fewer than 47 Pages Dealing with Jesus's Resurrection: Pro and Con | 61

CHAPTER 5
Juvenile Books Dealing with Jesus's Resurrection | 65

CATEGORY II—***The Bodily Resurrection of the Dead***

CHAPTER 6
The Bodily Resurrection of the Dead | 75

CATEGORY III—***Apologetics and Anti-Apologetics***

CHAPTER 7
Apologetics: Pro Resurrection | 85

CHAPTER 8
Agnostics, Atheists, Detractors, Humanists, Liberal Christians, Rationalists, and Skeptics: Con Resurrection | 127

CATEGORY IV—*Miracles and Science*

CHAPTER 9
Miracles and Science: Pro Resurrection | 147

CHAPTER 10
Miracles and Science: Con Resurrection | 156

CATEGORY V—*Jesus's Life: Biographies and Historicity of Christ*

CHAPTER 11
Jesus's Life: Biographies and Historicity of Christ: Pro Resurrection | 161

CHAPTER 12
Jesus's Life: Biographies and Historicity of Christ: Con Resurrection | 204

CATEGORY VI—*Jesus's Life: General Works and the Person of Jesus, the History of the Early Church, and the Shroud of Turin*

CHAPTER 13
Jesus's Life: General Works the Person Jesus, the History of the Early Church, and the Shroud of Turin: Pro Resurrection | 211

CHAPTER 14
Jesus's Life: General Works the Person Jesus, the History of the Early Church, and the Shroud of Turin: Con Resurrection | 235

CATEGORY VII—*Excerpts from Edited Books*

CHAPTER 15
Excerpts from Edited Books: Pro Resurrection | 241

CHAPTER 16
Excerpts from Edited Books: Con Resurrection | 267

CATEGORY VIII—*The New Testament*

CHAPTER 17
The Gospel of Mark | 275

CHAPTER 18
The Gospel of Matthew | 294

CHAPTER 19
The Gospel of Luke | 313

CHAPTER 20
The Gospel of John | 328

CHAPTER 21
The Acts of the Apostles | 350

CHAPTER 22
1 Corinthians 15 | 365

CATEGORY IX—*Creeds, Religion, Doctrinal, Sermons, Commentaries*

CHAPTER 23
The Apostles' Creed | 383

CHAPTER 24
Philosophy, Psychology, Religion e.g., Catholic, Protestant, Mormon | 398

CHAPTER 25
Doctrines, Dogmatics, and Systematic Theology | 405

CHAPTER 26
Jesus Christ Resurrection Sermons | 439

CHAPTER 27
New Testament Commentaries and Annotations
by One Person | 450

CATEGORY X—*Islamic Interpretations of the Crucifixion*

CHAPTER 28
Jesus's Crucifixion: Pro Resurrection | 463

CHAPTER 29
Jesus's Crucifixion: Con Resurrection | 475

CATEGORY XI—*Judaic Interpretations of Jesus's Resurrection*

CHAPTER 30
Jewish Converts: Pro Resurrection | 483

CHAPTER 31
Jewish Detractors: Con Resurrection | 485

CATEGORY XII—*Reference Sources, Dissertations and Theses, and Introduction to the New Testament*

CHAPTER 32
Dictionaries, Encyclopedia, and Glossaries | 493

CHAPTER 33
Dissertations, Theses, and Papers | 511

CHAPTER 34
Introduction to the New Testament and Biblical Criticism | 529

Name Index | 535

Preface

PRESENT-DAY SCHOLARS CAN BE significantly challenged as they forage through voluminous documents on the resurrection of Jesus. The literature measures well over 7,000 sources in English-language books alone. This makes finding specific sources that are most relevant for specific scholarly purposes an arduous task. Even when a specific book is relevant, finding the parts of the book that are most relevant to the resurrection rather than other topics often requires additional effort.

This access-oriented bibliography addresses these challenges in several ways. First, the bibliography organizes more than 7,000 English sources into twelve main categories and then subcategories, which are designed to help you find the most relevant literature quickly and efficiently. Embedded are pro and con arguments which support efficient access through brief annotations and then annotate the diversity and complexity of the field of religion by including sources that represent a diverse range of views: theistic (e.g., Christian, Jewish, Muslim, etc.), agnostic, and nontheistic. The objective of this bibliography is to provide convenient access to relevant sources from a variety of perspectives allowing you to browse or find the one source with ease, and accurately.

Each of the twelve categories will be summarized briefly:

I: Books Dealing with Jesus's Resurrection
The keystone of Christianity is Jesus's physical, bodily resurrection. The centrality of Jesus's resurrection in Christianity is confirmed by the publication of over one thousand English texts written on that topic. The vast majority of these works, written by believers, assert that Jesus's body rose from the dead. In contrast, relatively few books have been penned that refute his resurrection.

II: The Bodily Resurrection of the Dead
The resurrection of the dead and the resurrection of the body is a fundamental core belief of Christianity, extensively discussed in 1 Corinthians 15. Significantly, Paul wrote in verse 16, "For if the dead are not raised, then Christ has not been raised either." Approximately one hundred sources are identified that interact with this important topic.

III: Apologetics and Anti-Apologetics

The resurrection of Jesus is claimed to be a historical fact. Category III identifies over eight hundred works that support and defend belief in Jesus's physical, bodily resurrection, and, over two hundred writings that challenge, question, or refute his resurrection.

IV: Miracles and Science

Miracles comprise an inordinate role in the New Testament; chief among them is Jesus's resurrection. Science has a history of mixed assessments on the topics of miracles, and Jesus's resurrection. This category identifies sources from both sides of the religious aisle on these important topics.

V: Jesus's Life: Biographies and Historicity of Christ

Christian apologists maintain that Jesus's life is the most significant in the history of mankind. Over eight hundred books, pro and con, have been written on the topics of his biography and historicity.

VI: Jesus's Life: General Works and the Person of Jesus, the History of the Early Church, and the Shroud of Turin

Christians assert that Jesus's life is the most momentous and meaningful in the history of humankind. Reflecting that impact, over four hundred sources have been published, devoted to general works about the person of Jesus, the history of the early church, and the Shroud of Turin.

VII: Excerpts from Edited Books

Paul wrote in 1 Corinthians 15:16, "For if the dead are not raised, then Christ has not been raised either." Almost five hundred articles from edited texts have been written about the resurrection, representing interpretations from both sides of the religious aisle.

VIII: The New Testament

The New Testament is the foremost source available to researchers that details the life of Jesus. This category identifies over two thousand works, primarily New Testament commentaries that cover Mark 16, Matthew 28, Luke 24, John 20 and 21, Acts 1, and 1 Corinthians 15.

IX: Creeds, Religion, Doctrinal, Sermons, Commentaries

A creed (also known as a confession, symbol, or statement of faith) is a statement of the shared beliefs of a religious community in the form of fixed formula summarizing core tenets. This significant category examines creeds including the Apostles' Creed, and doctrinal statements, sermons, and material representative of several Christian denominations such as Protestant, Catholic, Mormon, etc.

X: Islamic Interpretations of the Crucifixion
There are an estimated 1.7 billion Muslim adherents whose tradition rejects the New Testament narrative that Jesus died on the cross. If Jesus did not die on the cross, no resurrection occurred. This category identifies an abundant collection of sources that support and reject, the Islamic interpretation of Jesus's crucifixion.

XI: Judaic Interpretations of Jesus's Resurrection
Christianity is a product of Judaism; yet, "traditional" Judaism rejects belief in Jesus. In contrast, a small portion of the Jewish population has accepted Jesus, and presumably, the historicity of Jesus's resurrection. Category XI identifies literature from these two divergent groups.

XII: Reference Sources, Dissertations and Theses, and Introduction to the New Testament
The final category in this text identifies and locates useful reference sources that deal with Jesus's resurrection and ascension. These sources include religious encyclopedias and dictionaries, dissertations, and introductory works to the New Testament.

Choices reflected in this bibliography. Producing this bibliography required considering a number of issues related to organizing over 7,000 sources that touch many topics related to the resurrection.

Pairing of topics. Subcategories are often paired, as where one subcategory contains sources supporting Jesus's resurrection and another subcategory challenges, questions, or refute it.

Same source in several categories. Sources are listed under several categories or subcategories in cases where they contain significant information that belongs in several different places. Ideally that approach will help researchers find the sources they need.

Relationship to Library of Congress (LoC) classifications. LoC call numbers (such as BT482 .A47 2015) provided important guidance for the organization of much of this bibliography but did not cover all situations. Many older sources and self-published sources lack a LoC call number. Other sources have multiple call numbers. The related challenge in producing the bibliography was to create a set of useful categories and subcategories and to classify each source in a way that would be as useful as possible for users. That goal applied to all sources, regardless of whether they had LoC call numbers.

Format. The bibliography employs an alphabetical-by-author format within subcategories. When the author or editor is not known, the entry is alphabetized by title.

List of authors. A separate name list that accompanies the bibliography includes only the first author for each source.

Bibliographic limitations. Many of the bibliography entries identify the title, author, date, and publisher for each source, but do not include other bibliographic information such as the LoC call number, multiple editors, additional places of publication, and so on. The rationale was three-fold: (1) to keep the text at a reasonable length, (2) the additional information can be easily accessed online from a variety of venues: WorldCat, OPAC, the Library of Congress, the National Union Catalog, ProQuest Dissertations & Theses Global, etc., and (3) in lieu of that information, additional important details are provided. Several of these enhanced details include the part/chapter/section number and name, its author(s), the respective pages, identification if the work is available online at Archive.org, Google book, Gutenberg.org, HathiTrust.org, etc., and for some entries a brief annotated comment.

Omissions. This bibliography covers only sources in the English language. Many sources in other languages are not included.

Even within sources in English, the number of sources is voluminous and constantly growing. I visited many seminaries and university libraries in my attempt to make this bibliography as complete as possible. I hope that I succeeded well enough to make this bibliography useful to a wide range of users.

Acknowledgments

I WISH TO THANK the many libraries that granted me permission to access their collections. In addition, I want to thank the numerous librarians and the members of the library support staff for their assistance.

Most important, I want to acknowledge the assistance of Matt Wimer, the project manager for *A Thematic Access-Oriented Bibliography of Jesus's Resurrection*. His responsibility included serving as my liaison with other departments at Wipf and Stock providing updates on the project, and addressing any of my concerns or questions throughout the publication process. Significantly, Matt was also responsible for the coordination, direction, and management of the production schedule.

Last, I want to acknowledge the efforts of all members of the Wipf and Stock staff for their helpfulness throughout the production of this text. In particular, I wish to acknowledge the contribution of Ian Creeger, the typesetter. Together, by phone, we spent several hours working on this project. Ian's attention to the details is appreciated. I also wish to recognize the efforts of Shannon Carter, the text's cover designer and Daniel Lanning, Editorial Administrator. And, a final big thank you to the publishers, John Wipf and Jon Stock.

Category I

Books Dealing with Jesus's Resurrection

CHAPTER 1

Entire books Dealing with Jesus's Resurrection: Pro

Aldrich, J. K. *A Critical Examination of the Question in Regard to the Time of Our Saviour's Crucifixion Showing that He was Crucified on Thursday, the Fourteenth Day of the Jewish Month Nisan, AD 30*. Boston, Printed by Rand, Avery, 1882. [262 pages; N.B. Archive.org, Google book, and HathiTrust. This important, dated source advocates a Thursday crucifixion.]

Alkier, Stefan. *The Reality of the Resurrection: The New Testament Witness*. Waco, Texas: Baylor University Press, 2013. [335 pages; N.B. Alkier's work should be explored.]

Allberry, Sam. *Lifted: Experiencing the Resurrection Life*. Phillipsburg, NJ: P&R, 2012. [144 pages; N.B. The author does not explore the resurrection narratives.]

Allen, O. Wesley. *Preaching Resurrection*. St. Louis: Chalice, 2000. [131 pages; N.B. In four separate chapters, the author explores the four gospel narratives.]

Allison, Dale C. *The End of the Ages Has Come: An Early Interpretation of the Passion and Resurrection of Jesus*. Philadelphia: Fortress, 1985. [194 pages; N.B. This book was based on his PhD Thesis.]

———. *Resurrecting Jesus: The Earliest Christian Tradition and Its Interpreters*. New York: T&T Clark, 2005. [404 pages; N.B. This text critically analyzes Jesus's resurrection and it is a must read.]

Alsup, John E. *The Post-Resurrection Appearance Stories of the Gospel Tradition: A History-of-Tradition Analysis with Text-Synopsis*. Stuttgart: Calwer Verlag, 1975. [307 pages; N.B. This detailed, often cited work should be examined.]

Anderson, Don. *Joy Comes in the Morning*. Neptune, NJ: Loizeaux, 1990. [246 pages; N.B. Besides the resurrection narratives, the author explores Isaiah 53 and Psalm 22.]

Anderson, Kevin L. *'But God Raised Him from the Dead': The Theology of Jesus' Resurrection in Luke-Acts*. Eugene, OR: Wipf & Stock, 2006. [353 pages; N.B. Anderson's detailed analysis is a slight revision of his dissertation.]

Andrewes, Lancelot. *Two Sermons of the Resurrection*. 1932. Repr., Cambridge: Cambridge University Press, 2013. [56 pages]

Ankerberg, John, and John Weldon. *Do the Resurrection Accounts Conflict? and What Proof Is There That Jesus Rose from the Dead?* Chattanooga, TN: Ankerberg Theological Research Institute, 1990. [191 pages; N.B. This work is a recommended read.]

———. *Knowing the Truth About the Resurrection*. Eugene, OR: Harvest House, 1996. [48 pages]

———. *The Passion and the Empty Tomb*. Eugene, OR: Harvest House, 2005. [217 pages; N.B. Two apologists wrote this text.]

Archer-Shepherd, E. H. *The Nature and Evidence of the Resurrection of Christ*. London: Rivingtons, 1910. [100 pages; N.B. This book consists of two lectures.]

Armstrong, William Park. *The Place of the Resurrection Appearances of Jesus*. New York: Scribner's Sons, 1912. [355 pages; N.B. Google book]

Arraj, Jim. *The Bodily Resurrection of Jesus*. Chiloquin, OR: Inner Growth, 2007. [110 pages]

Atkins, Peter. *Ascension Now: Implications of Christ's Ascension for Today's Church*. Collegeville, MN: Liturgical Press, 2001. [154 pages; N.B. This work also discusses liturgical, preaching, and theological implications of Jesus's ascension.]

Augsburger, Myron S. *The Resurrection Life: The Power of Jesus for Today*. Nappanee, IN: Evangel Publishing House, 2005. [196 pages]

Austin, B. F., ed. *The Crucifixion and The Resurrection of Jesus by an Eye-Witness*. Los Angeles: Austin Publishing, 1919. [94 pages; N.B. Google book. Austin claims that Jesus did not die upon the cross but six months later.]

Austin, E. L. C. *Earth's Greatest Day*. Grand Rapids: Baker, 1980. [127 pages; N.B. Not very useful.]

Avis, Paul D. L., ed. *The Resurrection of Jesus Christ*. London: Darton, Longman & Todd, 1993. [186 pages; N.B. Ten contributors to this work.]

Bacchiocchi, Samuele. *The Time of the Crucifixion and the Resurrection*. Berrien Springs, MI: Biblical Perspectives, 1985. [119 pages; N.B. Bacchiocchi, a Seventh-day Adventist author and theologian, "supports the traditional Friday-Crucifixion and Sunday-Resurrection of Christ."]

Balsiger, David W., and Michael Minor. *The Case for Christ's Resurrection*. Orlando, FL: Bridge-Logos, 2007. [310 pages; N.B. Companion book to the TV specials "The Case for Christ's Resurrection" and "Fabric of Time: Secrets of the Universe."]

Balthasar, Hans Urs von, and Aidan Nichols. *Mysterium Paschale: The Mystery of Easter*. Edinburgh, Scotland: T&T Clark, 1990. [312 pages]

Banks, William L. *Three Days and Three Nights: The Case for a Wednesday Crucifixion Date*. West Conshohocken, PA: Infinity, 2005. [167 pages; N.B. This work is useful to understand the position of Wednesday advocates.]

Bannerman, James. *Inspiration, the Infallible Truth and Divine Authority of the Holy Scriptures*. 1865. [See. 127, 129, 197–99, 204–5, 273, 380, 391; N.B. Google book. Not useful.]

Baring-Gould, S. *The Death and Resurrection of Jesus: Ten Lectures for Holy Week and Easter*. New York: James Pott, 1888. [85 pages; N.B. Archive.org and Google book. Only three of ten essays directly relate to Jesus's resurrection.]

Barker, Margaret. *The Risen Lord: The Jesus of History as the Christ of Faith*. Valley Forge, PA: Trinity Press International, 1996. [166 pages; N.B. Minimal discussion about the resurrection narratives.]

Barnett, Henry C. *The Evidence of the Resurrection of Jesus Christ*. St. Louis: Christian Board of Publication, 1921. [107 pages; N.B. An interesting, dated source.]

Barnhouse, Donald Grey. *The Cross Through the Open Tomb*. Grand Rapids: Eerdmans, 1961. [152 pages; N.B. Not useful.]

Barth, Markus, and Verne H. Fletcher. *Acquittal by Resurrection*. New York: Holt, Rinehart & Winston, 1964. [178 pages; N.B. Not very useful.]

Entire books Dealing with Jesus's Resurrection: Pro

Bartlett, David Lyon. *Fact and Faith: Coming to Grips with Miracles in the New Testament.* Valley Forge, PA: Judson, 1975. [144 pages. Republished by Wipf & Stock, 2007; N.B. The author provides an overview of the resurrection narratives.]

Barton, John. *Love Unknown: Meditations on the Death and Resurrection of Jesus.* London: SPCK, 1990. [82 pages; N.B. Nothing substantial.]

Barton, Stephen C., and Graham Stanton, eds. *Resurrection: Essays in Honour of Leslie Houlden.* London: SPCK, 1994. [233 pages; N.B. This edited work consists of nineteen essays.]

Barton, William E., et al. *His Last Week: The Story of the Passion and Resurrection of Jesus in the Words of the Four Gospels.* Chicago: Hope Publishing, 1905. [64 pages; N.B. Archive.org. A superficial overview of Jesus's last week.]

Bast, David. *Easter Hope: How Jesus' Resurrection Changes Life.* Grand Rapids: Words of Hope, 1996. [88 pages]

Bayer, Hans F. *Jesus' Predictions of Vindication and Resurrection: The Provenance, Meaning, and Correlation of the Synoptic Predictions.* Tübingen: Mohr Siebeck, 1986. [267 pages; N.B. Bayer's work should be examined.]

Beard, Arthur. *Bar-Jonah: The Son of the Resurrection.* London: George Bell, 1887. [91 pages; N.B. Not useful.]

Beasley-Murray, George Raymond. *Christ Is Alive!* London: Lutterworth, 1947. [178 pages]
———. *The Resurrection of Jesus Christ.* London: Oliphants, 1964. [48 pages]

Beasley-Murray, Paul. *The Message of the Resurrection: Christ is Risen!* Downers Grove, IL: InterVarsity, 2001. [269 pages; N.B. This work should be explored.]

Belknap, Jeremy. *Dissertations on the Character, Death & Resurrection of Jesus Christ, and the Evidence of His Gospel: With Remarks on Some Sentiments Advanced in a Book Entitled "The Age of Reason."* Boston: From the Apollo Press in Boston by Joseph Belknap, 1795. [140 pages; N.B. Google book. Only Dissertation 7, about 25 pages (96–119) directly discusses the actual resurrection narratives.]

Belser, Joh Evang. *History of the Passion, Death, and Glorification of Our Saviour, Jesus Christ: An Exegetical Commentary.* Edited by Arthur Preuss. Translated by F. A. Marks. St. Louis: Herder, 1929. [658 pages; N.B. Only the last seventy pages discuss the resurrection narratives.]

Benedict XVI, Pope. *Jesus of Nazareth. Holy Week: From the Entrance into Jerusalem to the Resurrection.* London: Catholic Truth Society, 2011. [362 pages; N.B. Not useful!]

Benesch, Friedrich. *Easter.* Translated by Robin Alexander and Sibylle Alexander. Edinburgh: Floris, 1981. [79 pages; N.B. Not useful.]

Benoit, Pierre. *The Passion and Resurrection of Jesus Christ.* Translated by Benet Weatherhead. New York: Herder & Herder, 1969. [342 pages; N.B. This source is a text that should be examined.]

Benson, George. *A Summary View of the Evidences of Christ's Resurrection.* London: Printed and Sold by J. Waugh, 1754. [59 pages; N.B. Google book]

Benson, Richard Meux. *The Life Beyond the Grave: A Series of Meditations Upon The Resurrection and Ascension of Our Lord Jesus Christ.* J. T. Hayes: London, 1885. [682 pages; N.B. Google book. This book provides a general overview plus answers to six objections to Jesus's resurrection.]

Bernard, Pierre R. *The Mystery of Jesus.* Vol. 2. Translated by Francis V. Manning. New York: Alba House, 1996. [Chapter 11 The Resurrection of the Lord, See. 449–519 for a discussion of the resurrection narratives.]

Bevan, William. *The Coming of Christ the Resurrection and Judgment as They Affect Believers, with Short Notes on the Church and Ministry.* Toronto: W. Briggs, 1889. [60 pages; N.B. Google book. Nothing substantial about the gospel narratives.]

Bewes, Richard. *The Resurrection: Fact or Fiction?* Tring, Herts, England: Lion Book, 1989. [48 pages; N.B. Minimal information.]

Bible, Andrew F. *Jesus and the Resurrection: The Glad News of Our Lord and Saviour Jesus Christ.* London: Simpkin, Marshall, Hamilton, Kent, &, 1890. [212 pages; N.B. Located in the British Library and Cambridge University Library.]

Bieringer, Reimund, and Jan Lambrecht, eds. *Resurrection in the New Testament: Festschrift J. Lambrecht.* Leuven: Leuven University Press, 2002. [549 pages. This work contains twenty-six essays.]

Bigland, John. *Reflections on the Resurrection and Ascension of Christ: And of the Probable Consequences of a Public Exhibition of His Ascension; Which Some Think Necessary to the Credibility of the Fact.* London: T. Williams, 1803. [108 pages; N.B. Google book. Not useful.]

Binz, Stephen J. *The Passion and Resurrection Narratives of Jesus: A Commentary.* Collegeville, MN: Liturgical Press, 1989. [127 pages; N.B. The author, in four chapters reviews each of the gospels.]

———. *The Resurrection & The Life.* New London, CT: Twenty-Third Publications, 2006. [120 pages; N.B. Not useful.]

Biser, Eugen. *The Light of the Lamb.* Translated by William Kramer. Chicago: H. Regnery, 1961. [111 pages; N.B. No substantial details about the resurrection narratives.]

Bishop, Hugh. *The Easter Drama.* London: Hodder & Stoughton, 1958. [60 pages; N.B. Not useful.]

Bligh, John. *The Sign of the Cross: The Passion and Resurrection of Jesus According to St John.* Slough: St Paul Publications, 1975. [112 pages]

Blunt, John J. *Principles for the Proper Understanding of the Mosaic Writings Stated and Applied; Together with an Incidental Argument for the Truth of the Resurrection of Our Lord.* London: John Murray, 1833. [246 pages; N.B. Archive.org. Only Lecture 8, See. 212–46 discusses Jesus's resurrection and it is not useful.]

Boardman, George Dana. *Epiphanies of the Risen Lord.* New York: Appleton, 1879. [289 pages; N.B. Google book. Not useful.]

———. *Our Risen King's Forty Days.* Philadelphia: Lippincott, 1902. [214 pages; N.B. Not useful.]

Bode, Edward Lynn. *The First Easter Morning: The Gospel Accounts of the Women's Visit to the Tomb of Jesus.* Rome: Biblical Institute Press, 1970. [217 pages; N.B. This book should be examined.]

Body, George. *The Appearances of the Risen Lord: Practical Readings.* London: Wells Gardner, Darton, 1889. [93 pages; N.B. Google book. Not useful.]

Boff, Leonardo. *The Question of Faith in the Resurrection of Jesus.* Translated by Luis Runde. Chicago: Franciscan Herald Press, 1971. [65 pages; N.B. Not useful.]

Boice, James Montgomery. *The Christ of the Empty Tomb.* Chicago: Moody, 1985. [126 pages; N.B. Not useful.]

Bold, T. A. *New Testament Evidence for the Resurrection.* London: Arthur H. Stockwell, 1925? [56 pages; N.B. The author provides only a minimal overview of the resurrection narratives.]

Bombaro, John J., and Adam S. Francisco, eds. *The Resurrection Fact: Responding to Modern Critics*. Irvine, CA: New Reformation, 2016. [248 pages; N.B. This work is an edited book with eight essays.]

Bonnke, Reinhard. *Explosion of Life: The World Drama of Resurrection*. London: Hodder & Stoughton, 1994. [57 pages; N.B. Not useful.]

Bookhart, C. Franklin. *Living the Resurrection: Reflections After Easter*. New York: Morehouse, 2012. [148 pages]

Borg, Marcus J., and John Dominic Crossan. *The Last Week: What the Gospels Really Teach About Jesus's Final Days in Jerusalem*. San Francisco: HarperCollins, 2007. [227 pages; Chapter 8 Easter Sunday, See. 189–215. Not useful.]

Bornhäeuser, Karl. *The Death and Resurrection of Jesus Christ: The Only Attempt so Far at an Adequate Exegesis of These Supreme Facts of the Christian Truth as Recorded in the Gospels, Made by the Author with Consummate Scholarship and Reverence for the Inspired Word of God*. Translated by A. Rumpus. Bangalore: C.L.S. Press, 1958. [264 pages; N.B. Only pages 173–264 deal with the resurrection.]

Bounds, Edward McKendree. *The Ineffable Glory: Thoughts on the Resurrection*. London: Hodder & Stoughton, 1921. [142 pages; N.B. Archive.org and Google book. This work is primarily focused on the resurrection of the dead.]

———. *The Resurrection*. Nashville: Publishing House of M.E. Church South, 1907. [172 pages; N.B. Archive.org and Google book. This work primarily discusses the resurrection of the dead.]

Bourgy, Paul. *The Resurrection of Christ and of Christians*. Translated by Raymond E. Married. Dubuque, IA: Priory Press, 1963. [88 pages; N.B. Not useful since it does not substantially interact with the resurrection narratives.]

Bowen, Clayton Raymond. *The Resurrection in the New Testament an Examination of the Earliest References to the Rising of Jesus and of Christians from the Dead*. New York: G. P. Putnam, 1911. [492 pages; N.B. Archive.org, Google book, and HathiTrust. This dated source is a must read.]

Brookes, James H. *Did Jesus Rise? A Book Written to Aid Honest Skeptics*. St. Louis: Gospel Book & Tract Depository, 1945. [151 pages; N.B. Archive.org. This is a good, dated work to examine. It was originally published in the 1800s.]

———. *He is Not Here: The Resurrection of Christ*. Philadelphia: Presbyterian Board of Publication and Sabbath-School Work, 1896. [170 pages; N.B. Brookes presents a general overview of Jesus's resurrection.]

Broughton, William P. *The Historical Development of Legal Apologetics: With an Emphasis on the Resurrection*. Longwood, FL: Xulon, 2009. [164 pages; N.B. This work is recommended to examine.]

Brown, James Baldwin. *The Risen Christ, the King of Men*. London: T. F. Unwin, 1890. [368 pages; N.B. Google book and Haititrust.org. Not useful because Brown does not analyze the resurrection narratives.]

Brown, Raymond E. *A Risen Christ in Eastertime: Essays on the Gospel Narratives of the Resurrection*. Collegeville, MN: Liturgical Press, 1991. [95 pages; N.B. Brown devotes one chapter each to Mark, Matthew, and Luke; and two chapters to John.]

———. *The Virginal Conception and Bodily Resurrection of Jesus*. New York: Paulist, 1973. [136 pages; N.B. Pages 69–129 actually deal with Jesus's resurrection.]

Bruce, David. *The Resurrection of History: History, Theology, and the Resurrection of Jesus*. Eugene, OR: Wipf & Stock, 2014. [162 pages; N.B. Bruce interacts with several writers:

Marcus Borg, Amy-Jill Levine, Gerd Lüdemann, etc. There is little discussion about the narratives.]

Brumback, Carl. *Accent on the Ascension!* Springfield, MO: Gospel Publishing House, 1955. [151 pages]

Brundrit, Daniel Fernley. *Is the Resurrection True?* London: P. Allan, 1934. [173 pages; N.B. The author provides a good overview of the topic.]

Bryan, Christopher. *The Resurrection of the Messiah*. New York: Oxford University Press, 2011. [432 pages; N.B. Bryan offers a healthy reading.]

Bryan, David W., and David W. Pao, eds. *Ascent into Heaven in Luke-Acts*. Minneapolis: Fortress, 2016. [287 pages; N.B. This work contains eight essays with a selected bibliography on the Ascension in Luke-Acts (1995–2015).]

Bryan, Lyman. *The Easter Story: The Story of Jesus from His Triumphal Entry into Jerusalem to His Ascension into Heaven as Related in the Four Gospels and Woven Together into One Continuous Narrative*. Philadelphia: Judson, 1941. [80 pages; N.B. Only pages 67–80 deal with the resurrection narratives.]

Bryant, Robert A. *The Risen Crucified Christ in Galatians*. Atlanta: Society of Biblical Literature, 2001. [272 pages; N.B. Virtually no interaction with the resurrection narratives.]

Buck, D. D. *Our Lord's Great Prophecy and Its Parallels throughout the Bible, Harmonized and Expounded Comprising a Review of the Common Figurative Theories of Interpretation, with a Particular Examination of the Principal Passages Relating to the Second Coming of Christ, the End of the World, the New Creation, the Millennium, the Resurrection, the Judgment, the Conversion and Restoration of the Jews: And a Synopsis of Josephus' History of the Jewish War*. New York and Auburn: Miller, Orton & Mulligan, 1856. [484 pages; N.B. Archive.org. No interaction with the resurrection narratives.]

Budd, Leonard H., and Roger G. Talbott. *Resurrection Promises: Sermons, Worship Resources, and Group Discussion Questions for the Easter Season*. Lima, OH: C.S.S. Publishing, 1987. [84 pages; Chapter 1 Resurrection: Temporal to Eternal Luke 24:13–35, See. 13–21]

Bürgener, Karsten. *The Resurrection of Christ from the Dead*. Bremen: K. Bürgener, 1978. [130 pages; N.B. This work was not accessed.]

Burgess, Andrew R. *The Ascension in Karl Barth*. Aldershot: Ashgate, 2004. [209 pages]

Burrell, David James. *The Resurrection and the Life Beyond*. New York: American Tract Society, 1920. [241 pages; N.B. Not useful.]

Bush, George. *The Resurrection of Christ in Answer to the Question Whether He Rose in a Spiritual and Celestial or in a Material and Earthly Body*. New York: J.S. Redfield, 1845. [92 pages; N.B. Archive.org and Google book; N.B. This is an interesting, dated work.]

Butcher, John Beverley. *Telling the Untold Stories: Encounters with the Resurrected Jesus*. Harrisburg, PA: Trinity Press International, 2000. [163 pages; N.B. Not useful.]

Butler, Samuel. *The Evidence for the Resurrection of Jesus Christ as Given by the Four Evangelists: Critically Examined*. Edited by Robert Johnstone. London: Colin Smythe, 1980. [64 pages; N.B. Reprint of 1865 original. An interesting, dated source.]

Buttrick, David G. *The Mystery and the Passion: A Homiletical Reading of the Biblical Traditions*. Philadelphia: Fortress, 1992. [Part 1: The Mystery of the Resurrection, See. 15–91; N.B. Pages 66–91 interact with the resurrection narratives.]

Entire books Dealing with Jesus's Resurrection: Pro

Candler, Warren Akin. *Easter Meditations*. Nashville: Cokesbury, 1930. [116 pages; N.B. The Fact and Force of Christ's Resurrection, See. 7–32. Virtually no interaction with the resurrection narratives.]

Cantalamessa, Raniero. *Easter: Meditations on the Resurrection*. Translated by Demetrio S. Yocum. Collegeville, MN: Liturgical Press, 2006. [48 pages; N.B. Not useful because there is no content about the resurrection narratives.]

Capt, E. Raymond. *The Resurrection Tomb*. Thousand Oaks, CA: Artisan Sales, 1988. [80 pages; N.B. Analysis of Gordon's Garden Tomb. Identifies it to the satisfaction of the author as the most probable site of the tomb from which the resurrection of Jesus Christ took place.]

Carnley, Peter. *The Structure of Resurrection Belief*. Oxford: Clarendon, 1987. [394 pages; N.B. This work is a recommended read. It is often discussed in other texts.]

Carpenter, Boyd. *Forty Days of the Risen Life*. New York: Dodd, Mead, 1898. [104 pages; N.B. Archive.org. Not useful because it lacks content.]

Carson, D. A. *Scandalous: The Cross and Resurrection of Jesus*. Wheaton, IL: Crossway, 2010. [173 pages; N.B. Only Chapter 5, Doubting the Resurrection of Jesus: John 20:24–31 is relevant. That chapter is totally refuted in Michael J. Alter's *The Resurrection: A Critical Inquiry*. 2015, 591–96.]

Catchpole, David. *Resurrection People: Studies in the Resurrection Narratives of the Gospels*. London: Darton, Longman & Todd, 2000. [236 pages; N.B. Catchpole presents fourteen parallels of the Emmaus travellers and Tobit.]

Cattermole, R., and Henry Stebbing, eds. 1835. *Sacred Classics: or, Cabinet Library of Divinity: Sermons on the Resurrection*. Vol. 16. London: John Hatchard. [Sermon 8, See. 179–208 (by Donne); Sermon 10, See. 239–56 (Bishop Horne); N.B. Google book]

Cecilia, Madame. *From the Sepulchre to the Throne*. New York: Benziger, 1914. [427 pages; N.B. Archive.org and Google book; N.B. The author provides an overview of the resurrection narratives.]

Chaffey, Tim. *In Defense of Easter: Answering Critical Challenges to the Resurrection of Jesus*. Hebron, KT: Midwest Apologetics, 2014. [213 pages; N.B. This book is a must read. It is divided into three sections: The Case for the Resurrection, Alternative Theories, and Other Relevant Questions.]

Chalakkal, Sebastian. *Resurrection Appearances in Contemporary Christology*. Kottayam: Oriental Institute of Religious Studies, 2009. [158 pages; N.B. This work should definitely be examined. It includes an apologetic to nine topics.]

Chandler, Samuel. *The Witnesses of the Resurrection of Jesus Christ Re-Examined: And their Testimony Proved Entirely Consistent*. London: Printed for J. Noon, at the White-Hart, near Mercer's-Chappel in Cheapside, and R. Hett, at the Bible and Crown in the Poultry, 1744. [170 pages; N.B. Google book. A good, dated text.]

Chapman, Raymond. *Stations of the Resurrection: Meditations on the Fourteen Resurrection Appearances*. Harrisburg, PA: Morehouse, 1998. [66 pages; N.B. Not useful because it lacks content.]

Chappell, Wallace D. *When Jesus Rose*. Nashville: Broadman, 1972. [127 pages; N.B. The author presents a series of addresses. Not useful.]

Charles, Elizabeth Rundle. *By Thy Glorious Resurrection and Ascension: Easter Thoughts*. London: SPCK, 1888. [144 pages; N.B. Not useful because the discussion is superficial.]

Charlesworth, James H. *Resurrection: The Origin and Future of a Biblical Doctrine.* New York: T&T Clark, 2006. [250 pages; N.B. This work consists of input from six contributors writing primarily about the resurrection of the dead.]

Chevrot, Georges. *On the Third Day: The Resurrection in the Gospel and in the Liturgy.* Chicago: Scepter, 1961. [208 pages; N.B. The first half of the text interacts with the resurrection narratives.]

Chojnacki, Stanislaw. *Christ's Resurrection in Ethiopian Painting.* Roma: Pontificio Istituto Orientale, 2009. [104 pages; N.B. Not useful.]

Chrispin, Gerald. *The Resurrection: The Unopened Gift.* Epsom: Day One, 1999. [176 pages; N.B. Only the first forty pages interact with the resurrection narratives.]

Clark, Daniel. *Dead or Alive? The Truth and Relevance of Jesus' Resurrection.* Nottingham: Inter-Varsity, 2007. [160 pages; N.B. The last forty pages interact with the resurrection narratives.]

Clark, Neville. *Interpreting the Resurrection.* 2nd ed. Philadelphia: Westminster, 1967. [128 pages; N.B. Only pages 81–101 interact with the narratives.]

Cleveland, Rich. *The Words of the Risen Christ: A Bible Study on Jesus' Resurrection.* Ijamsville, MD: Word Among Us Press, 2007. [108 pages]

Clifford, Ross. *Leading Lawyers Look at the Resurrection.* Claremont, CA: Albatross, 1991. [143 pages; N.B. The author presents the opinions of eight contributors from the legal field.]

Clifford, Ross, and Philip Johnson. *The Cross Is Not Enough: Living as Witnesses to the Resurrection.* Grand Rapids: Baker, 2012. [311 pages]

Collins, Anthony. *Risen as He Said.* Boston: St. Paul Editions, 1959. [59 pages]

Collins, Thomas. P. *The Risen Christ in the Fathers of the Church.* Glen Rock, NJ: Paulist, 1967. [118 pages; N.B. The author "provides a modest survey of patristic materials on the resurrection . . ." p. vii.]

Comblin, Joseph. *The Resurrection in the Plan of Salvation.* Notre Dame, IN: Fides, 1966. [176 pages; N.B. Almost no interaction with the resurrection narratives. Not useful.]

Conner, W. T. *The Resurrection of Jesus: A Message of Hope and Cheer.* Nashville: Sunday School Board of the Southern Baptist Convention, 1926. [139 pages; N.B. Only the first fifty pages interact with the resurrection narratives.]

Cook, George. *An Illustration of the General Evidence Establishing the Reality of Christ's Resurrection.* Edinburgh: Printed for Peter Hill, 1808. [323 pages; Cook's dated work is worth examining.]

———. *An Illustration of the General Evidence Establishing the Reality of Christ's Resurrection.* Edinburgh: Printed for Peter Hill, 1826. [199 pages; N.B. Cook's dated work is worth examining.]

Cooper, Thomas. *The Verity of Christ's Resurrection from the Dead: An Appeal to the Common-Sense of the Peoples.* London: Hodder & Stoughton, 1875. [176 pages; N.B. Google books. An interesting, dated source to examine.]

Cox, Samuel. *The Resurrection: Twelve Expository Essays on the Fifteenth Chapter of St. Paul's First Epistle to Corinthians.* London: R.D. Dickinson, 1881. [348 pages; N.B. Google book; N.B. The first sixty pages directly relate to Jesus's resurrection.]

Craig, William Lane. *Assessing the New Testament Evidence for the Historicity of the Resurrection of Jesus.* Lewiston, NY: Mellen, 1989. [442 pages. An absolute must read. Perhaps the most detailed analysis on the topic.]

———. *The Historical Argument for the Resurrection of Jesus During the Deist Controversy.* Lewiston, NY: Mellen, 1985. [677 pages. N.B. Craig's work is a lengthy, important text to examine.]

———. *Knowing the Truth about the Resurrection: Our Response to the Empty Tomb.* Ann Arbor, MI: Servant, 1988. [153 pages. N.B. This book is a short, but detailed reading.]

———. *The Son Rises: The Historical Evidence for the Resurrection of Jesus.* Chicago: Moody, 1981. [156 pages; N.B. The first of many works by Craig on this subject. A definite read.]

Craig, William Lane, and John Dominic Crossan. *Will the Real Jesus Please Stand Up? A Debate Between William Lane Craig and John Dominic Crossan.* Edited by Paul Copan. Grand Rapids: Baker, 1998. [192 pages; N.B. This is an interesting text to read.]

Craig, William Lane, and Gerd Lüdemann. *Jesus' Resurrection: Fact or Figment? A Debate Between William Lane Craig & Gerd Lüdemann.* Edited by Paul Copan and Ronald K. Tacelli. Downers Grove, IL: InterVarsity, 2000. [206 pages; N.B. This debate should be examined.]

Cranfield, Thomas. *An Harmony of the Gospels, from the Resurrection to the Ascension of Our Lord and Saviour Jesus Christ: In Which the English Narrations of the Four Evangelists Are Orderly Exhibited in Appropriate Columns, Observations Are Subjoined, Tending to Investigate the True Evangelical Sense, Reconcile Seeming Discrepances, and Defend the Order of the Facts as Laid down in the Harmony.* Dublin: Printed by William Sleater, 1795. [79 pages; N.B. English Short Title Catalog, T166684; Eighteenth Century Collections Online.]

Crawford, Dan R. *Church Growth Words From the Risen Lord.* Nashville: Broadman, 1990. [176 pages; N.B. Not useful.]

Cromie, Richard M. *Sometime Before the Dawn: Responses to the Resurrection.* Mount Lebanon, PA: Southminster Extended Ministries, 1982. [111 pages; N.B. This work consists of a series of sermons; not useful.]

Crossan, John Dominic, and N. T. Wright. *The Resurrection of Jesus: John Dominic Crossan and N. T. Wright in Dialogue.* Edited by Robert B. Stewart. Minneapolis: Fortress, 2006. [220 pages; N.B. This work has eight contributors.]

Croswell, Laurence. *It Is Finished: Passion, Death, and Resurrection of Jesus Christ.* Belleville, ON: Essence, 2002. [88 pages]

Crowder, Bill. *Windows on Easter.* Grand Rapids: Discovery House, 2010. [124 pages; N.B. No content.]

Culver, Robert Duncan, and Murray J. Harris. *A Wakeup Call: Is Serious False Doctrine about the Resurrection of Christ, the Soul of Man and the Believing Dead Propagated in the Writings of a Tenured Professor at Trinity Evangelical Divinity School and Is It Being Disregarded, Protected & Defended There?* Clayton, CA: Witness, 1993. [123 pages; N.B. This is a very interesting and must read work that discusses the controversy between the late Norman Geisler and Murray J. Harris.]

Cummings, Brad. *Resurrection of the Divine: Compelling Evidence for the Risen Christ.* West Conshohocken, PA: Infinity, 2008. [364 pages; N.B. This work is a recommended read.]

D'Costa, Gavin, ed. *Resurrection Reconsidered.* Oxford, England: Oneworld Publications, 1996. [227 pages. This work consists of thirteen essays; several that are very interesting.]

Davies, J. G. *He Ascended into Heaven: A Study in the History of Doctrine.* London: Lutterworth, 1958. [224 pages; N.B. No interaction with the gospel narratives.]

Davis, Stephen T. *Risen Indeed: Making Sense of the Resurrection*. Grand Rapids: Eerdmans, 1993. [220 pages; N.B. This work is a definite, must read.]

Davis, Stephen T., et al., eds. *The Resurrection: An Interdisciplinary Symposium on the Resurrection of Jesus*. Oxford: University Press, 1997. [368 pages. This work contains thirteen essays written by many distinguished scholars.]

Dawe, Donald G. *Jesus: The Death and Resurrection of God*. Atlanta: John Knox, 1985. [205 pages]

Dawson, Gerrit Scott. *Jesus Ascended: The Meaning of Christ's Continuing Incarnation*. T&T Clark Limited, 2004. [255 pages; N.B. The author provides detailed information about Jesus's ascension.]

Dawson, Ralph. *Was There a Resurrection? The Challenge to Reason and Belief*. New York: Vantage, 1977. [116 pages]

Dawson, R. Dale. *The Resurrection in Karl Barth*. Aldershot, England: Ashgate, 2007. [246 pages; N.B. This book attempts to elaborate on the writings of Karl Barth.]

Day, E. Hermitage. *On the Evidence for the Resurrection: With Reference Especially to the Emmaus Narrative of St. Luke's Gospel, and to Recent Criticism*. London: SPCK, 1906. [64 page; N.B. Google book. This dated book provides an overview of Jesus's resurrection.]

Derrett, J. Duncan M. *The Anastasis: The Resurrection of Jesus as an Historical Event*. Shipston-on-Stour, Warwickshire, England: P. Drinkwater, 1982. [166 pages. This book is a must read. It discusses the possibility that Jesus's body was cremated.]

Dhanis, Édouard [prepared]. *Resurrexit: Actes du Symposium International sur la Résurrection de Jésus*, Rome 1970. Città del Vaticano: Libreria Editrice Vaticana, 1974. [766 pages; N.B. This work has essays written in multiple languages. It includes a bibliography with 1,500 sources.]

Dickinson, Richard William. *The Resurrection of Jesus Christ Historically and Logically Viewed*. Philadelphia: Presbyterian Board of Publication, 1865. [142 pages; N.B. Google book; Dickinson provides a healthy, dated source to examine.]

Ditton, Humphry. *A Discourse Concerning the Resurrection of Jesus Christ: In Three Parts . . .* 3rd ed. London: Printed by S. Palmer, 1722. [432 pages; N.B. Google book. Part 3 deals with proofs of the fact of Jesus's resurrection.]

Divine of the Church of England. *The History of the Incarnation, Life, Doctrine, and Miracles: The Death, Resurrection, and Ascension, of Our Blessed Lord and Saviour Jesus Christ . . .* London: Printed for T. Cooper, 1737. [875 pages]

Doane, William Croswell. [Introduction]. *The Book of Easter*. New York: MacMillan, 1910. [246 pages; N.B. Useless due to no content.]

———. *The Manifestations of the Risen Jesus Their Methods and Their Meanings*. Oxford: University Press, 1898. [189 pages; N.B. Google book; no content.]

Dobson, Cyril Comyn. *The Empty Tomb and the Risen Lord*. London: Marshall, Morgan & Scott, 1934. [160 pages; N.B. Dobson attempts to harmonize the resurrection narratives.]

———. *The Risen Lord and His Disciples: A Continuation of The Empty Tomb and the Risen Lord*. London: Stanley Martin, 1935. [110 pages; N.B. This work is a continuation of *The Empty Tomb and the Risen Lord*.]

———. *The Story of the Empty Tomb as If Told by Joseph of Arimathaea*. London: C. J. Thynne, 1920. [50 pages]

Dodson, Jonathan K., and Brad Watson. *Raised? Finding Jesus by Doubting the Resurrection*. Grand Rapids: Zondervan, 2014. [112 pages]

Donne, Brian K. *Christ Ascended: A Study in the Significance of the Ascension of Jesus Christ in the New Testament*. Exeter: Paternoster, 1983. [98 pages; N.B. This work presents an overview of topics related to Jesus's ascension.]

Dore, James. *An Essay on the Resurrection of Christ: In Which Proofs of the Fact Are Adduced, Its Import Is Explained, and Its Beneficial Influence Illustrated*. London: Printed for M. Gurney, 1797. [96 pages; N.B. This work is from the Bodleian Libraries and was scanned by Google. The author discusses the evidence and importance of the resurrection.]

Dowse, Edgar. *Christian Doctrine: The Virgin Birth and the Resurrection of Jesus Christ*. Penrith: Fort House Publications, 1986. [69 pages]

———. *The Resurrection Appearances of Our Lord*. London: Avon, 1996. [131 pages]

Drinkwater, F. H. [Francis Harold]. *The Fact of the Resurrection*. Beccles, UK: W. Clowes, 1978. [80 pages]

Du Bose, Horace M. *The Bodily Resurrection of Jesus Christ*. Nashville: Publishing House of the M.E. Church, South, 1924. [533 pages; N.B. No. 12 of the Aftermath Series.]

Durrwell, F.-X. *Christ Our Passover: The Indispensable Role of Resurrection in Our Salvation*. Ligiori, MO: Liguori, 2004. [194 pages; N.B. No interaction with the resurrection narratives.]

———. *The Resurrection: A Biblical Study*. Translated by Rosemary Sheed. New York: Sheed & Ward, 1960. [371 pages; N.B. Minimal interaction with the resurrection narratives.]

Dyer, Keith D., and David J. Neville, eds. *Resurrection and Responsibility: Essays on Theology, Scripture, and Ethics in Honor of Thorwald Lorenzen*. Eugene, OR: Pickwick, 2009. [275 pages; N.B. This work is a collection of twelve essays with virtually no interaction with the resurrection narratives.]

Dymski, J. Daniel. *Stations of Joy: Meditations on the Scriptural Events from Resurrection to Pentecost*. Villa Maria, PA: Center for Learning, 2004. [94 pages; N.B. Not useful.]

Eaton, Robert. *The Forty Days: Chapters on the Risen Life of Our Lord*. London: Sands, 1927. [140 pages]

Eckman, George P. *When Christ Comes Again*. 2nd ed. New York: Abingdon, 1918. [372 pages; N.B. Google book. N.B. No interaction with the resurrection narratives.]

Edgar, R. McCheyne. *The Gospel of a Risen Saviour*. Edinburgh: T&T Clark, 1892. [376 pages; N.B. Edgar's work is an important, dated source.]

Edmunds, Albert J. *The Oldest Resurrection Documents: Showing that Event to have been a Series of Apparitions*. York, PA: Albert J. Edmunds, 1917. [49 pages; N.B. This work is also called "Resurrection Studies 1917"; Google book.]

Edwards, Mark J., ed. *We Believe in the Crucified and Risen Lord*. Downers Grove, IL: InterVarsity, 2009. [194 pages; N.B. Ancient Christian Doctrine Series v. 3. This is a useful work to examine ancient sources.]

Elliott, E. K. *From Death to Resurrection, or, Spiritual Teachings Respecting the Departed in Christ*. London: Simpkin, Marshall, Hamilton, Kent, 1907? [131 pages]

Ellis, Eric Kent. *The Power of His Resurrection*. London: Faith Press, 1962. [87 pages; No interaction with the resurrection narratives.]

Elson, Edward L. R. *And Still He Speaks: The Words of the Risen Christ*. Westwood, NJ: Revell, 1960. [124 pages; N.B. Nothing useful because of a lack of substance.]

Endsjø, Dag Øistein. *Greek Resurrection Beliefs and the Success of Christianity*. New York: Palgrave Macmillan, 2009. [274 pages; N.B. The Absence of Jewish Parallels to the Resurrected Jesus, See. 134–40; Chapter 6 The Challenge of Immortal Flesh, See. 141–79]

Evans, C. F. *Resurrection and the New Testament*. London: SCM, 1970. [190 pages; N.B. This book is worth examining.]

Evans, Craig A., and N. T. Wright. *Jesus, the Final Days: What Really Happened*. Edited by Troy A. Miller. Louisville: Westminster John Knox, 2009. [126 pages; Chapter 3 The Surprise Resurrection, See. 75–107 (N. T. Wright).]

Evans, William. *From the Upper Room to the Empty Tomb*. Grand Rapids: Eerdmans, 1934. [294 pages]

Évely, Louis. *Joy*. Translated by Brian and Marie-Claude Thompson. New York: Herder & Herder, 1968. [96 pages; N.B. Not useful.]

Ewen, Pamela Binnings. *Faith on Trial: An Attorney Analyzes the Evidence for the Life, Death & Resurrection of Jesus of Nazareth*. Nashville: Broadman & Holman, 1999. [210 pages; N.B. Ewen's work is an apologetic that defends the resurrection.]

Fairleigh, John. *The Passion and Glorious Resurrection of Our Lord and Saviour Jesus Christ: According to the Authorized Version of the New Testament*. London: Herbert Joseph, 1937. [92 pages]

Farrow, Douglas. *Ascension and Ecclesia: On the Significance of the Doctrine of the Ascension for Ecclesiology and Christian Cosmology*. Grand Rapids: Eerdmans, 1999. [340 pages; N.B. This work is a detailed analysis of the ascension.]

Faunce, Daniel Worcester. *Advent and Ascension: or, How Jesus Came and How He Left Us*. New York: Eaton & Mains, 1903. [215 pages; N.B. Google books. This work is primarily concerned with the ascension.]

Fenton, J. C. *Preaching the Cross: The Passion and Resurrection According to St. Mark. With an Introduction and Notes*. London, SPCK, 1958. [80 pages; N.B. Virtually no interaction with the resurrection narratives.]

Fernando, Mark. *Questions You Always Wanted to Ask about Easter Answered*. Cheltenham, PA: Hermit Kingdom, 2005. [101 pages; N.B. Question 1 Did Jesus Really Rise from the Dead?, See. 13–22; Question 5 What Happened to Jesus' Body?, See. 61–74]

Filson, Floyd V. *Jesus Christ, the Risen Lord*. Nashville: Abingdon, 1956. [288 pages; N.B. No interaction with the resurrection narratives.]

Fishel, Kent M., and John W. Rayls. *Resurrection Evidences: A Bible Study*. Grand Rapids: Zondervan, 1985. [105 pages; N.B. Nothing useful. It presents questions for students.]

Flood, Edmund. *The Resurrection*. New York: Paulist, 1973. [55 pages; N.B. The book provides a general overview of the resurrection.]

Flynn, Leslie B. *Day of Resurrection*. Nashville: Broadman, 1965. [96 pages; N.B. The book offers a minimal overview.]

Ford, D. W. Cleverley. *Preaching the Risen Christ*. London: Mowbray, 1988. [128 pages; N.B. Nothing useful.]

Ford-Grabowsky, Mary. *Stations of the Light: Renewing the Ancient Christian Practice of the via lucis as a Spiritual Tool for Today*. New York: Doubleday, 2005. [214 pages; N.B. Meditations]

Foster, Charles A. *The Jesus Inquest: The Case for and Against the Resurrection of the Christ*. Nashville: Nelson, 2010. [304 pages; N.B. This book is a recommended Christian apologetic.]

Entire books Dealing with Jesus's Resurrection: Pro

Fraser, Neil McCormick. *The Glory of His Rising; a Closer Look at the Resurrection.* Neptune, NJ: Loizeaux, 1963. [127 pages; N.B. Not useful because it does not interact with the resurrection narratives.]

Frederick, William. *Infallible Proof by Three Immutable Witnesses Proving Wednesday Crucifixion by the Literal Fulfillment of Many Types and Prophesies, in the Death and Resurrection of Jesus, and the Science of Astronomy.* Clyde, OH: Author. [336 pages; N.B. Google book. This is a dated, recommended text to read.]

Frick, Philip Louis. *The Resurrection and Paul's Argument: A Study of First Corinthians, Fifteenth Chapter.* Cincinnati: Jennings and Graham, 1912. [348 pages; N.B. An excellent dated source.]

Frye, Edwin Gibson. *Breakfast with the Risen Lord: Devotional Talks on the Resurrection of Jesus.* Harrisburg, PA: Evangelical Press, 1938. [111 pages; N.B. Not useful because it lacks substance.]

Fudge, Edward, ed. *Resurrection! Essays in Honor of Homer Hailey.* Athens, AL: C.E.I. Publishing 1973. [131 pages; N.B. This book is a collection of seven essays.]

Fuller, Daniel P. *Easter Faith and History.* Grand Rapids: Eerdmans, 1965. [279 pages; N.B. This work is a definite text to read.]

Fuller, Reginald H. *The Formation of the Resurrection Narratives.* New York: Macmillan, 1971. [225 pages; N.B. This often-cited text is a definite work to read.]

Fullmer, Paul M. *Resurrection in Mark's Literary-Historical Perspective.* London: T&T Clark, 2007. [256 pages; N.B. This book is a recommended reading.]

Furness, William Henry. *The Story of the Resurrection of Christ Told Once More: With Remarks upon the Character of Christ and the Historical Claims of the Four Gospels.* Philadelphia: Lippincott, 1885. [151 pages; N.B. Archive.org. Only pages 5–51 deal with the resurrection narratives.]

Gaddy, C. Welton. *Easter Proclamation: Remembrance, and Renewal.* Nashville: Broadman, 1974. [95 pages; N.B. Nothing useful because it lacks substance.]

Gansky, Alton. *40 Days: Encountering Jesus between the Resurrection and Ascension.* Nashville: B&H, 2007. [278 pages; N.B. This work presents a general overview.]

Garbutt, Richard, Nathaniel Jackson, and Christopher Cartwright. *A Demonstration of the Resurrection of Our Lord and Saviour Jesus Christ; And therein of the Christian Religion. Very Useful for the Further Satisfaction and Confirmation of All Good Christians; as Likewise for the Confutation and Conviction of Those That Have a Jewish or Atheistical Spirit in Them.* London: Printed for Samuel Gellibrand, at the Ball in Paul's Churchyard, 1657. [250 pages; N.B. This Google book is a 1669 printing. At times, difficult to read.]

Gardner-Smith, Percival. *The Narratives of the Resurrection: A Critical Study.* London: Methuen, 1926. [196 pages; N.B. This dated book provides a good overview of the topic.]

Garrott, John. *The Unseen Presence: Encounters on the Emmaus Road.* AR: Selah, 2003. [72 pages]

Gault, C. W. *Indebted to Christ's Resurrections.* New York: Pageant, 1956. [237 pages; N.B. The author collected commentaries from numerous writers.]

Geering, Lloyd. *Resurrection: A Symbol of Hope.* London: Hodder & Stoughton, 1971. [256 pages; N.B. Perhaps, this text should belong to Category 2. It presents an honest and critical discussion about Jesus's resurrection. It is a recommended text to read.]

Geis, Robert J. *The Christ from Death Arisen*. Lanham: University Press of America, 2008. [250 pages; N.B. See pages 139–155 that deal with Jesus's resurrection.]

Geisler, Norman L. *The Battle for the Resurrection*. Eugene, OR: Wipf & Stock, 2004. [256 pages; updated edition. The late Geisler was a prolific writer in defense of Jesus's resurrection.]

———. *The Battle for the Resurrection*. Nashville: Nelson, 1989. [256 pages; N.B. This work is a recommended read.]

———. *In Defense of the Resurrection*. Lynchburg, VA: Quest, 1991. [131 pages]

Gibbins, Ronald C. *The Stations of the Resurrection: Devotions for Use at Easter*. Collegeville, MN: Liturgical Press, 1988. [87 pages; N.B. Useless.]

Gilchrist, J. M. *Jesus! What Was That? A Critical Look at the Resurrection*. Walsall: Blue Ocean, 2007. [208 pages]

Goergen, Donald. *The Death and Resurrection of Jesus*. Wilmington, DE: M. Glazier, 1988. [292 pages; N.B. Chapter 4 Jesus is Raised from the Dead, See. 117–59.]

Gooder, Paula. *Journey to the Empty Tomb*. Minneapolis: Fortress, 2015. [176 pages; Chapter 5 The Empty Tomb and Resurrection Appearances, See. 132–63.]

———. *This Risen Existence: The Spiritual Easter*. Minneapolis: Fortress, 2015. [130 pages; N.B. The author presents a general overview of the resurrection narratives.]

Goodier, Alban. *The Risen Jesus: Meditations*. London: Burns Oates & Washbourne, 1948. [161 pages; N.B. Nothing useful.]

Goodwin, Thomas. *Christ Set Forth, in His Death, Resurrection, Ascension, Sitting at God's Right Hand, and Intercession*. London: The Religious Tract Society, 1846. [Originally London: Printed by J. G. for R. Dawlman, 1651; N.B. Google book. See. Volume 10 July 1, 51–91]

———. *The Glories of Christ Set Forth: In His Mediatorial Character, under the Several Offices in His Death, Resurrection, Ascension, Sitting at God's Right Hand, and Intercession*. Plymouth: Printed for and Published by J. Bennett, 1817. [430 pages; N.B. Google book, Book 3. Faith Supported by Christ's Resurrection, See. 61–97.]

Goppelt, Leonhard, et al. *The Easter Message Today: Three Essays*. Translated by Salvator Attanasio and Darrell Likens Guder. New York: Nelson, 1964. [156 pages]

Green, Michael. *The Day Death Died*. Downers Grove, IL: InterVarsity, 1982. [119 pages; N.B. Green provides a minimal overview of the topic.]

———. *The Empty Cross of Jesus*. Downers Grove, IL: InterVarsity, 1984. [247 pages; N.B. See. 91–123.]

———. *Man Alive!* Downers-Grove, IL: Inter-Varsity, 1968. [96 pages; N.B. Green provides a minimal overview of the topic.]

Greenhalgh, John, and Elizabeth Russell, eds. *'If Christ Be Not Risen . . .': Essays in Resurrection and Survival*. San Francisco: Collins Liturgical, 1986. [110 pages. This edited book contains eight essays.]

Grey, Mary C. *The Resurrection of Peace: A Gospel Journey to Easter and Beyond*. London: SPCK, 2012. [129 pages; N.B. Not useful.]

Grierson, Herbert, ed. *And the Third Day . . . A Record of Hope and Fulfilment*. New York: Macmillan, 1948. [348 pages; N.B. This work is a collection of numerous essays.]

Grierson, James. *Heaven on Earth; or, Interviews with the Risen Saviour, Including His Ascension*. Edinburgh: Johnstone & Hunter, 1856. [353 pages; N.B. Google book]

———. *Scenes and Interviews with the Risen Saviour, Including His Ascension.* 2nd ed. Edinburgh: J. Maclaren, 1869. [370 pages; N.B. Originally published in 1856 under title: *Heaven on Earth, or, Interviews with the Risen Saviour.*]

Grieve, Val. *Your Verdict.* Carlisle: OM Publishing, 1996. [112 pages]

Griffin, James A. *Easter Joy.* New York: Alba House, 2007. [52 pages]

Grove, Henry. *The Evidence for Our Saviour's Resurrection Consider'd: With the Improvement of This Important Doctrine.* London: Printed for John Gray, 1730. [72 pages]

Guinness, Howard. *Call the Witnesses: St. Paul on Trial: A Dramatic Representation of the Evidence for the Resurrection of Jesus Christ.* Vaucluse, N.S.W., Australia: Omega Press, 1969. [69 pages; N.B. Located only in two Australian libraries.]

Gunter, W. Stephen. *Resurrection Knowledge: Recovering the Gospel for a Postmodern Church.* Nashville: Abingdon, 1999. [104 pages; N.B. This text does not interact with the resurrection narratives.]

Gurney, T. A. *Alive for Evermore: Studies in the Manifestations of the Risen* Lord. London: The Religious Tract Society, 1930. [254 pages; N.B. Most of this text does not interact with the resurrection narratives.]

Habermas, Gary R. *The Resurrection: Heart of the New Testament.* Vol. 1. Joplin, MO: College Press, 2000. [239 pages; N.B. Most of this text does not interact with the resurrection narratives.]

———. *The Resurrection: Heart of the Christian Life.* Vol. 2. Joplin, MO: College Press, 2000. [118 pages; N.B. Most of this text does not interact with the resurrection narratives.]

———. *The Resurrection of Jesus.* Grand Rapids: Baker, 1980. [187 pages; reprinted Lanham, MD University Press of America. N.B. Most of this text does not interact with the resurrection narratives.]

———. *The Risen Jesus & Future Hope.* Lanham, MD: Rowman & Littlefield, 2003. [239 pages; N.B. Most of this text does not interact with the resurrection narratives.]

Habermas, Gary R., and Antony Flew. *Did the Resurrection Happen? A Conversation with Gary Habermas and Antony Flew.* Edited by David Baggett. Downers Grove, IL: InterVarsity, 2009. [184 pages; N.B. This work presents an interesting discussion.]

———. *Did Jesus Rise from the Dead? The Resurrection Debate.* Edited by Terry L. Miethe. San Francisco: Harper & Row, 1987. [190 pages; N.B. This work offers an interesting debate.]

———. *Resurrected? An Atheist and Theist Dialogue.* Edited by John Ankerberg. Lanham, MD: Rowman & Littlefield, 2005. [112 pages; N.B. This work presents an interesting dialogue.]

Habermas, Gary R., and Michael R. Licona. *The Case for the Resurrection of Jesus.* Grand Rapids: Kregel, 2004. [352 pages; N.B. This noteworthy work explains the Minimal Facts strategy.]

Hailey, O. L. *The Three Prophetic Days of Matt. 12:40; or, Jesus and Jonas, Jesus in the Grave Three Full Days, a Suggested Harmony of All the Scriptures Concerning the Death, Burial and Resurrection of Jesus Christ.* Boston: Stratford, 1931. [96 pages; N.B. This work attempts to prove that Jesus was crucified on a Wednesday.]

Hales, B. D. *Walking in Newness of Life: An Answer to the Resurrection.* Chessington: Bible and Gospel Trust, 2012. [245 pages]

Hall, A. W. *Resurrection of Christ and What It Stands For.* Syracuse, NY: Wesleyan Methodist Publishing Association, 1905. [51 pages]

Hall, Francis J. *The Passion and Exaltation of Christ*. New York: Longmans, Green, 1918. [323 pages; N.B. HathiTrust. This is a dated, but good work to examine. See Chapter 6 The Fact of the Resurrection (164–235).]

Hall, Jean. *Out of Easter, the Gospels*. Minneapolis: Winston Press, 1979. [110 pages]

Hallett, Joseph. *Christ's Ascension into Heaven Asserted and Practically Improved in Several Sermons*. London: Printed for John Salusbury and Robert Osborne, 1693. [106 pages; N.B. Early English Books, 1641–1700, 1463:10]

Han, Cheon-Seol. *Raised for Our Justification: An Investigation on the Significance of the Resurrection of Christ within the Theological Structure of Paul's Message*. Kampen: Kok [South Korea], 1995. [387 pages; N.B. This work is a published doctoral dissertation on theology rather than the resurrection narratives.]

Hanegraaff, Hank. *Resurrection*. Nashville: Word, 2000. [281 pages. N.B. This work written by a Christian apologist should be examined.]

———. *The Third Day: The Reality of the Resurrection*. Nashville: W Publishing Group, 2003. [118 pages; N.B. This text was excerpted and revised from *Resurrection*.]

Hanna, William. *The Forty Days After Our Lord's Resurrection*. Edinburgh: Edmonston & Douglas, 1863. [271 pages; N.B. Google book. A classic, dated source.]

Hanson, George. *The Resurrection and the Life: A Study of the Resurrection and Ascension Narratives in The Gospels, and of the Threefold Version in the Acts of Christ's Appearance to Saul on the Way to Damascus*. New York: Revell, 1912. [372 pages; N.B. This work is a classic, dated source.]

Hanson, Richard S. *Journey to Resurrection: The Drama of Lent and Easter in the Gospel of John*. New York: Paulist, 1986. [81 pages; N.B. Just three pages are devoted to the resurrection narratives.]

Harden, Ralph William. *The Evangelists and the Resurrection*. London: Skeffington, 1914. [240 pages; N.B. This text is a dated, good read.]

Hare, Augustus, and Hare, Julius. *Letters to the Editor of The New Trial of the Witnesses: By an Oxford Layman*. London: Richard Taylor, 1824. [111 pages; N.B. Google book. This anonymous work consists of five essays. The authors are identified in *Guesses at the Truth by Two Brothers*, 1867, (p. xviii).]

Harmony of the Gospel Narratives of Holy Week: Also of the Resurrection, the Ascension, and the Descent of the Holy Ghost, A. Edited by F. D. Huntington. New York: E. & J. B. Young, 1889. [136 pages; N.B. Archive.org. This anonymous text lists in chronological order the narratives of the Holy Week.]

Harries, Richard. *Christ Is Risen*. London: A. R. Mowbray, 1988. [131 pages; N.B. Not very helpful.]

Harris, Greg. *The Darkness and the Glory: His Cup and the Glory from Gethsemane to the Ascension*. Woodlands, TX: Kress Christian Publications, 2008. [209 pages]

Harris, Murray J. *From Grave to Glory: Resurrection in the New Testament: Including a Response to Norman L. Geisler*. Grand Rapids: Academie, 1990. [493 pages; N.B. This detailed analysis of Jesus's resurrection is a definite must to read.]

———. *Raised Immortal: Resurrection and Immortality in the New Testament*. Grand Rapids: Eerdmans, 1985. [304 pages; N.B. This work is a definite must to read.]

Hartill, Isaac. *The Ascension of Our Lord Jesus Christ*. London: A.H. Stockwell, 1902. [64 pages]

Harvey, Nicholas Peter. *Death's Gift: Chapters on Resurrection and Bereavement*. Grand Rapids: Eerdmans, 1995. [See. 58–64]

Hayes, Doremus A. *The Resurrection Fact.* Nashville: Cokesbury, 1932. [355 pages; N.B. This source is a good text to examine.]

Hays, Steve. *This Joyful Eastertide a Critical Review of the Empty Tomb.* n.p.: Steve Hays, 2006. [494 pages; N.B. This work is an important text to carefully read and it is available online.]

Head, E. D. *Burning Hearts.* Nashville: Broadman, 1947. [102 pages]

Head, Peter M., ed. *Proclaiming the Resurrection: Papers from the First Oak Hill College Annual School of Theology.* Carlisle: Paternoster, 1998. [130 pages; N.B. This edited book contains five essays.]

Heath, Dale E. *The Risen-Christ Scriptures: A Data-based View of the Evidence.* Lake City, FL: Heath, 1994. [124 pages; N.B. Heath's book is a useful read.]

Hendrickx, Herman. *The Resurrection Narratives of the Synoptic Gospels.* London: G. Chapman, 1984. [158 pages; N.B. This source is a recommended read.]

Heuschen, J. *The Bible on the Ascension.* Translated by F. Vander Heijden. De Pere, WI: St. Norbert Abbey, 1965. [104 pages; N.B. This work deals exclusively with Jesus's ascension.]

Hewson, John. *Christ Rejected, or, the Trial of the Eleven Disciples of Christ in a Court of Law and Equity as Charged with Stealing the Crucified Body of Christ out of the Sepulchre . . .* Philadelphia: Printed for the Author by Joseph Rakestraw, 1832. [444 pages; N.B. Google book. The book was written by a believer in Christ under the assumed named of Captain Onesimus.]

Hickling, S. Ross. *An Evidentiary Analysis of Doctor Richard Carrier's Objections to the Resurrection of Jesus Christ.* Eugene, OR: Wipf & Stock, 2018. [380 pages; N.B. This work is a modified version of his PhD thesis available online. It emphasizes the principals of evidence and canons of criminal law; it should be read!]

Hill, William Bancroft. *The Resurrection of Jesus Christ: A New Study of an Old Problem.* New York: Revell, 1930. [160 pages; N.B. The author also analyzes six alternative theories.]

Hindmarsh, Robert. *An Essay on the Resurrection of the Lord: Being an Humble Attempt to Answer the Question, With What Body Did the Lord Rise from the Dead? with an Appendix, Containing the Authorities Consulted in Relation to That Subject . . .* London: J. S. Hodson, 1833. [283 pages. N.B. The author attempts to answer the much-discussed question, "With what Body did the LORD rise from the Dead?" After reviewing exhaustively the different opinions on this profound subject, he states, as his own conclusion from the Doctrines, "that the material body was dissipated in the sepulchre, at or before the time of the Lord's resurrection in and with a Divinely-substantial body, perfectly distinct from the former." Google book]

Hoadley, Burton James. *Two Mornings.* Portland, OR: Metropolitan Press, 1925. [92 pages; N.B. HathiTrust. Not useful due to minimal content.]

Hoare, Rodney. *Testimony of the Shroud.* New York: St. Martin's Press, 1978. [128 pages]

Hobbs, Herschel H. *Messages on the Resurrection.* Grand Rapids: Baker, 1959. [87 pages; N.B. Not useful due to minimal content.]

Holding, James Patrick, ed. *Defending the Resurrection: Did Jesus Rise from the Dead?* US: Xulon, 2010. [410 pages. N.B. This forty-four-chapter text has several contributors.]

Hollis, Gertrude. *But Chiefly. A Help to Easter Gladness.* London: SPCK, 1920. [92 pages; N.B. Not useful.]

Holloway, David. *Where Did Jesus Go? The Meaning and Truth of the Resurrection.* Basingstoke: Marshalls, 1983. [160 pages; N.B. Not useful.]

Holzapfel, Richard Neitzel. *A Lively Hope: The Suffering, Death, Resurrection, and Exaltation of Jesus Christ.* Salt Lake City, UT: Bookcraft, 1999. [214 pages; N.B. Not helpful. Written from a Mormon perspective that includes material from Joseph Smith.]

Hooke, S. H. *The Resurrection of Christ as History and Experience.* London: Darton, Longman & Todd, 1967. [209 pages; N.B. This work discusses numerous aspects of the resurrection: interpretation, meaning, theology, etc.]

Hornsby, Sarah. *Jesus Reigns in Me! Living Daily in the Power of His Resurrection.* Grand Rapids: Chosen Books, 1996. [230 pages]

Horsley, Samuel. *Nine Sermons, on the Nature of the Evidence by Which the Fact of Our Lord's Resurrection Is Established . . .* New York: T&J Swords, 1816. [250 pages; N.B. Google book. Not useful.]

Hoskyns, Edwyn Clement, and Francis Noel Davey. *Crucifixion—Resurrection: The Pattern of the Theology and Ethics of the New Testament.* London: SPCK, 1981. [383 pages; esp. 270–95 interact with the resurrection narratives.]

Houlden, J. Leslie. *Backward into Light: The Passion and Resurrection of Jesus According to Matthew and Mark.* London: SCM, 1987. [84 pages; N.B. Virtually no interaction with the resurrection narratives.]

Houselander, Caryll. *The Risen Christ: The Forty Days after the Resurrection.* New York: Scepter, 2007. [92 pages; reprinted from Sheed & Ward, 1958; N.B. No interaction with the gospel narratives.]

Howe, Fisher. *The True Site of Calvary: And Suggestions Relating to the Resurrection.* New York: A. D. F. Randolph, 1871. [68 pages. See. Twilight; or Suggestions Relating to the Resurrection of Our Lord, 55–62; N.B. Archive.org, Google book, and HathiTrust. There is virtually no interaction with the resurrection narratives.]

Hutson, Curtis, comp. *Great Preaching on the Resurrection.* Murfreesboro, TN: Sword of the Lord, 1984. [245 pages; N.B. This work is a collection of nineteen sermons (preachings) by at least fifteen people.]

Ide, Arthur Frederick. *The Resurrection: An Analysis of the Gospels, Writings of St. Paul, and Historical Records.* Chicago: Sepore, 1999. [125 pages]

———. *Resurrection, Sex, and God: Essays on the Foundations of Faith.* Dallas: Minuteman, 1990. [101 pages; N.B. Only one essay by John R. Rogers discusses Jesus's resurrection.]

Ingram, Joseph Edward. *On the Witness Stand, He Who Was and Now Is.* Los Angeles: Hoffman, 1931. [101 pages; N.B. Useless, a question and answer format.]

Ireson, Gordon W. *Strange Victory: The Gospel Resurrection.* New York: Seabury, 1970. [128 pages; N.B. Not useful because there is virtually no interaction with the resurrection narratives.]

Jacob, of Serug. *Jacob of Sarug's Homilies on the Resurrection.* Translated by Thomas Kollamparampil. Piscataway, NJ: Georgias Press. [71 pages; N.B. Not useful.]

Jacobovici, Simcha, and Charles Pellegrino. *The Jesus Family Tomb: The Evidence Behind the Discovery No One Wanted to Find.* New York: HarperOne, 2007. [218 pages; N.B. This controversial book deals with the alleged family tomb of Jesus's family.]

Jaki, Stanley L. *Resurrection.* Pinckney, MI: Real View, 2004. [80 pages; N.B. There is no interaction with the narratives.]

Jansen, John Frederick. *No Idle Tale.* Richmond: John Knox, 1967. [106 pages; N.B. Five of the six chapters deal with Luke's witness to the resurrection.]

———. *The Resurrection of Jesus Christ in New Testament Theology*. Philadelphia: Westminster, 1980. [187 pages; N.B. The book attempts to discuss the significance of Jesus's resurrection.]

Jennings, A. G. *The Last Days of Jesus Christ, or, The Gospel Account of the Great Atonement: Including the Betrayal, Trial, Sufferings and Death of Our Lord and His Resurrection and Ascension*. Philadelphia: American Sunday-School Union, 1893. [112 pages; N.B. Archive.org, Google book, and HathiTrust. Only pages 83–112 interact with the resurrection narratives.]

Jensen, Matthew D. *Affirming the Resurrection of the Incarnate Christ: A Reading of 1 John*. Cambridge: Cambridge University Press, 2012. [227 pages; N.B. Virtually no interaction with the resurrection narratives.]

John-Charles, Peter. *When Was Christ's Death and Resurrection?* West St. Paul, MN: Bible Search, 2001. [63 pages; N.B. This book is exclusively concerned with chronology.]

John Paul II, Pope. *Rising in Christ: Meditations on Living the Resurrection*. Edited by Jo Garcia-Cobb and Keith E. Cobb. Ijamsville, MD: Word Among Us Press, 2004. [63 pages; N.B. Not useful.]

Johnson, Cliff R. *Every Moment An Easter*. Alexandria, VA: Author, 1962. [125 pages; N.B. Not useful. An overview of the Apostles' Creed.]

Johnson, Kim Allan. *The Morning: His Empty Tomb Means More than You Ever Dreamed*. Nampa, ID: Pacific Press 2002. [159 pages]

Johnson, Timothy Luke. *Living Jesus: Learning the Heart of the Gospel*. San Francisco: HarperSanFrancisco, 1998. [210 pages; N.B. Not useful because he does not interact with the resurrection narratives.]

Judson, Albert. *Scripture Questions Concerning the Life, Death Resurrection and Ascension of the Lord Jesus Christ*. London: Religious Tract Society, 183? [148 pages]

Kadlecek, Jo. *A Desperate Faith: Lessons of Hope from the Resurrection*. Grand Rapids: Baker, 2010. [185 pages; N.B. Not useful.]

Kankaanniemi, Matti. *The Guards of the Tomb: (Matt 27:62–66 and 28:11–15); Matthew's Apologetic Legend Revisited*. Åbo: Åbo Akad. Förl., 2010. [340 pages; N.B. This work is a recommended read.]

Kartsonis, Anna D. *Anastasis: The Making of an Image*. Princeton: Princeton University Press, 1986. [263 pages; See. 15–22; N.B. Not useful since it deals with art.]

Kee, Alistair. *From Bad Faith to Good News: Reflections on Good Friday and Easter*. London: SCM, 1991. [147 pages]

Keigwin, John. *Mount Calvary, or, The History of the Passion, Death, and Resurrection, of Our Lord and Saviour Jesus Christ*. Edited by Davies Gilbert. London: Printed for Nichols & Son, Simpkin & Marshall, 1826. [98 pages; N.B. Archive.org. Written in Cornish.]

Kelly, Anthony. *The Resurrection Effect: Transforming Christian Life and Thought*. Maryknoll, NY: Orbis, 2008. [205 pages; N.B. This text is primarily concerned with theology and doctrine.]

———. *Upward: Faith, Church, and the Ascension of Christ*. Collegeville, MN: Liturgical Press, 2014. [174 pages; N.B. This text is primarily concerned with the ascension and theology.]

Kelsey, Morton T. *The Drama of the Resurrection*. New York: New City Press, 1999. [140 pages; N.B. No useful content.]

Category I—Books Dealing with Jesus's Resurrection

———. *Resurrection, Release from Oppression*. New York: Paulist, 1985. [201 pages; N.B. Not useful because it does not interact with the resurrection narratives.]

Kena, Kwasi Issa. *The Resurrected Jesus*. Nashville: Abingdon, 2001. [96 pages; N.B. Very superficial.]

Kennedy, D. James. *Who Is This Jesus, Is He Risen?* Fort Lauderdale, FL: Coral Ridge Ministries, 2002. [103 pages]

Kennedy, John. *The Resurrection of Jesus Christ: An Historical Fact with an Examination of Naturalistic Hypotheses*. London: Religious Tract Society, 1871. [176 pages; N.B. Google book. This dated source, at its time, was often cited in the literature. It is a recommended read.]

Kepler, Thomas S. *The Meaning and Mystery of the Resurrection*. New York: Association Press, 1963. [188 pages; N.B. This work is primarily concerned with theology.]

Kerr, Hugh Thomson. *After He Had Risen*. New York: Revell, 1934. [95 pages; N.B. No interaction with the resurrection narratives.]

Kesich, Veselin. *The First Day of the New Creation: The Resurrection and the Christian Faith*. Crestwood, NY: St. Vladimir's Seminary Press, 1982. [206 pages; N.B. Pages 75–122 interact with the resurrection narratives,]

Kessler, William Thomas. *Peter as the First Witness of the Risen Lord: An Historical and Theological Investigation*. Rome: Editrice Pontificia Università Gregoriana, 1998. [237 pages; N.B. This book is a recommended read.]

King, Geoffrey R. *The Forty Days: Studies in the Last Six Weeks of Our Lord's Earthly Life, From Calvary and Easter to the Ascension*. Grand Rapids: Eerdmans, 1962. [105 pages; N.B. The author providence an overview of the resurrection narratives.]

Kirkland, Winifred. *The Continuing Easter*. New York: Scribner's Sons, 1943. [60 pages; N.B. No useful content.]

Kirkpatrick, Kathy Newell. *He Is Risen! He Is Risen Indeed! The Post-Resurrection Ministry of Jesus*. Prescott, AZ: Educational Ministries, 1994. [64 pages; N.B. The author tersely reviews twelve appearance scenes.]

Klopstock, Friedrich Gottlieb. *The Messiah: Descriptive of the Principal Events Attending the Passion, Crucifixion, Resurrection, and Ascension, of Our Lord and Saviour Jesus Christ*. Edited by Joseph Collyer and Mary Collyer. London: Printed for R. Evans, 1817. [559 pages; N.B. This work is a prose translation of the poem "Der Messiah," begun by Mary Collyer. After Mary's death her husband, Joseph Collyer, completed it. First published in 1763.]

Knowles, Archibald Campbell. *The Triumph of the Cross: A Devotional Study of the Passion, Crucifixion and Resurrection of Our Blessed Lord and Redeemer Jesus Christ*. Skeffington: London, 1900. [281 pages; N.B. Only pages 244–68 interact with the resurrection.]

Koester, Craig R., and R. Bieringer, eds. *The Resurrection of Jesus in the Gospel of John*. Tübingen, Germany: Mohr Siebeck, 2008. [358 pages; N.B. This book contains a series of essays.]

Krummacher, Friedrich W. *The Risen Redeemer: The Gospel History from the Resurrection to the Day of Pentecost*. Translated by John T. Betts. New York: Robert Carter, 1863. [298 pages; N.B. Google book. This book is a classic, dated source that was often cited in the literature.]

Künneth, Walter. *The Theology of the Resurrection*. St. Louis: Concordia, 1965. [302 pages; N.B. This work is a recommended read.]

Kuyper, Abraham. *The Death and Resurrection of Christ: Messages for Good Friday and Easter*. Translated by Henry Zylstra. Grand Rapids: Zondervan, 1960. [160 pages; N.B. Not useful due to a lack of substance.]

Ladd, George Eldon. *I Believe in the Resurrection of Jesus*. Grand Rapids: Eerdmans, 1975. [156 pages; N.B. Ladd's work is a recommended read.]

Lake, Kirsopp. *The Historical Evidence for the Resurrection of Jesus Christ*. London: Williams & Norgate, 1907. [291 pages; N.B. Archive.org, Google book, and HathiTrust. Lake postulated that the women went to the wrong tomb.]

Lampe, G. W. H., and Donald M. MacKinnon. *The Resurrection: A Dialogue Arising From Broadcasts by G. W. H. Lampe and D. M. MacKinnon*. Edited by William Purcell. London: Mowbray, 1966. [112 pages; N.B. This work consists of a dialogue between two men.]

Landels, William. *The Sepulchre in the Garden, or, The Buried and Risen Saviour*. London: James Nisbet, 1867. [355 pages; N.B. Google book; N.B. An interesting, dated source.]

Lange, Reinhold. *The Resurrection*. Translated by Hans Hermann Rosenwald. Recklinghausen: Aurel Bongers; London: Distributed by Universal-Tandem, 1967. [74 pages; N.B. Not useful because it deals with art.]

La Potterie, Ignace de. *The Hour of Jesus: The Passion and the Resurrection of Jesus According to John*. Translated by Georg Murray. New York: Alba House, 1989. [233 pages; N.B. Only pages 193–233 interact with John's resurrection narrative.]

Latham, Henry. *The Risen Master: A Sequel to Pastor Pastorum*. Cambridge: Deighton Bell, 1901. [488 pages; N.B. Google book. This often-referenced work is a classic, dated source.]

Laurie, Greg. *Why the Resurrection? A Personal Guide to Meeting the Resurrected Christ*. Wheaton, IL: Tyndale House, 2004. [77 pages; N.B. Simplistic and minimal content.]

Lavoie, Gilbert R. *Resurrected: Tangible Evidence That Jesus Rose from the Dead: Shroud's Message Revealed 2000 Years Later*. Allen, TX: Thomas More, 2000. [173 pages]

Layton, Bentley, editor and translator. *The Gnostic Treatise on Resurrection from Nag Hammadi*. Missoula, MT: Scholars Press, 1979. [See. 11–19]

Lee, Robert Greene. *A Grand-Canyon of Resurrection Realities*. Grand Rapids, Eerdmans, 1935. [172 pages; N.B. Useless.]

Leeper, Wayne D. *Prelude to Glory: Insights into the Death, Burial and Resurrection of Jesus Christ*. Nashville, TN: Christian Communications, 1987. [247 pages; N.B. especially Chapter 9 The Rising of the Son, See. 173–193; Chapter 10 The Last Forty Days, See. 194–208]

Léon-Dufour, Xavier. *Resurrection and the Message of Easter*. Translated by R. N. Wilson. New York: Holt, Rinehart & Winston, 1975. [330 pages; N.B. This source is a recommended read.]

Lewis, Alan E. *Between Cross and Resurrection: A Theology of Holy Saturday*. Grand Rapids: Eerdmans, 2001. [477 pages; N.B. This work primarily focuses on theology.]

Licona, Michael R. *Paul Meets Muhammad: A Christian-Muslim Debate on the Resurrection*. Grand Rapids: Baker, 2006. [175 pages; N.B. This source is an interesting book.]

———. *The Resurrection of Jesus: A New Historiographical Approach*. Downers Grove, IL: InterVarsity, 2010. [718 pages; N.B. This work is mostly Licona's dissertation that must be examined. His interaction with several scholars is interesting.]

Liddon, H. P. *Easter in St. Paul's: Sermons Bearing Chiefly on the Resurrection of Our Lord*. 2nd ed. London: Rivingtons, 1877. [288 pages; N.B. Google book. Not useful]

Category I—Books Dealing with Jesus's Resurrection

Lilley, James Samuel. *Was the Resurrection a Fact? And Other Essays.* Boston: Richard G. Badger, 1916. [61 pages; N.B. Archive.org and Google book. Five essays and only pages 9–18 are relevant to the resurrection.]

Linton, Henry. *"Jesus and the Resurrection:" Being an Exposition, in Twelve Sermons, of 1 Corinthians 15.* London, 1865. [204 pages; N.B. This work is part of the Bodleian Library collection scanned by Google. See. Sermons 2–4.]

Lipscomb, A. A. *Studies in the Forty Days between Christ's Resurrection and Ascension. A Series of Essays for the Times.* Nashville: Southern Methodist Publishing House, 1884. [362 pages; N.B. Google book. This dated source should be explored.]

Little, Sophia L. *The Birth, Last Days, and Resurrection of Jesus: Three Poems.* Pawtucket, RI: Published by the author, 1841. [156 pages; N.B. Google book. A poem.]

Loane, Marcus L. *It Is The Lord.* Edinburgh: Marshall, Morgan & Scott, 1965. [126 pages; N.B. The author provides an overview of selected portions of the resurrection narratives.]

———. *Jesus Himself: The Story of the Resurrection— From the Garden Tomb to the Mount of Olives.* Edinburgh: Banner of Truth, 2007. [126 pages; N.B. This book primarily retells the resurrection narratives.]

———. *Our Risen Lord.* Grand Rapids: Zondervan, 1968. [119 pages; N.B. The author presents a general overview of Jesus's resurrection.]

———. *The Prince of Life.* London: Marshall, Morgan & Scott, 1947. [142 pages; N.B. The author presents an overview of selected portions of the resurrection narratives.]

———. *Then Came Jesus.* London: Oliphants, 1967. [111 pages; N.B. The author presents an overview of selected portions of the resurrection narratives.]

Lockton, W. *The Resurrection and Other Gospel Narratives; And, the Narratives of the Virgin Birth: Two Essays.* London: Longmans, Green, 1924. [184 pages; N.B. This is an interesting, honest work that should be examined (See. 1–120). Archive.org]

Loken, John. *The Shroud Was the Resurrection: The Body Theft, the Shroud in the Tomb, and the Image That Inspired a Myth.* Ann Arbor, MI: Falcon, 2006. [176 pages]

Longenecker, Richard N. ed. *Life in the Face of Death: The Resurrection Message of the New Testament.* Grand Rapids: Eerdmans, 1998. [314 pages; N.B. This book consists of essays by twelve contributors.]

Lopez, René A. *The Jesus Family Tomb Examined: Did Jesus Rise Physically?* Springfield, MO: 21st Century Press, 2008. [384 pages]

Lorenzen, Thorwald. *Resurrection and Discipleship: Interpretive Models, Biblical Reflections, Theological Consequences.* Maryknoll, NY: Orbis Books, 1995. [358 pages; N.B. Part 2: Foundations The Resurrection of the Crucified Christ as a Foundational Event, See. 115–87]

———. *Resurrection, Discipleship, Justice: Affirming the Resurrection Jesus Christ Today.* Macon, GA: Smyth & Helwys, 2003. [186 pages]

Lorimer, William. *A Discourse of the Death and Resurrection of Christ: As They Are to Be Affectionately Remembered and Considered in Their Mutual Respect to One Another.* London: Printed by J. H. for R. Ford, 1718. [95 pages; N.B. Google book. This book is a healthy, dated source.]

Loughry, J. N. *Christology: or, The Resurrection, as Taught by Our Lord and Savior Jesus Christ, Who Said of Himself, I Am the Resurrection and the Life.* Nashville: Cumberland Presbyterian Publishing House, 1888. [187 pages; N.B. Chapter 5 Our Lord's Resurrection, See. 76–130]

Ludington, James. *Various Revelations: With an Account of the Garden of Eden, and the Settlement of the Eastern Continent, as Related by the Leaders of the Wandering Tribes. From the age of Enoch, Seth, and Noah, to the birth of Jesus of Nazareth, as related by Mary his mother, and Joseph the foster-father; with a confirmation of his crucifixion and resurrection, as related by Pilate and the different apostles.* Boston: 1876. [See. 34–35, 105, 109, 113; N.B. Archive.org. His novel, offers a history of the Lost Tribes of Israel, with Lost Race elements, ending in a description of the Second Coming.]

Lunn, Arnold. *The Third Day: A Defence of the Miracle of the Resurrection of Jesus Christ.* Westminster, MD: Newman Book Shop, 1945. [145 pages; N.B. See. 90–116]

Lunny, William J. *The Sociology of the Resurrection.* SCM, 1989. [146 pages; N.B. Lunny interacts with four writers.]

Luther, Martin. *The Martin Luther Easter Book.* Translated by Roland H. Bainton. Philadelphia: Fortress, 1983. [87 pages]

Macan, Reginald Walter. *Resurrection of Jesus Christ: An Essay in Three Chapters.* London: Williams & Norgate, 1877. [168 pages; N.B. Google book. This is a classic, dated work.]

MacArthur, John. *The Resurrection of Jesus Christ.* Chicago: Moody, 1989. [101 pages; This work is a healthy read.]

Maclaren, Alexander. *The Post-Resurrection Ministry of Christ.* Minneapolis: Klock & Klock. [300 pages; Reprint (1st work). Originally published: *After the Resurrection.* London: Hodder and Stoughton, 1902. Reprint (2nd work). Originally published: *The Appearances of Our Lord After the Passion.* London: Macmillan, 1912.]

Maclaren, Alexander, et al. *The Empty Tomb: Resurrection Realities Made Plain.* Chicago: Moody, 1896. [122 pages; N.B. The text has five contributors with eight essays. Revell first published it in 1896 under the title, *Resurrection*. Later reprinted, 1963, by Baker.]

———. *Great Sermons on The Resurrection.* Grand Rapids: Baker, 1963. [127 pages; N.B. This book contains eight sermons.]

MacMunn, Vivian Charles. *Resurrectio Christi: An Apology Written from a New Standpoint and Supported by Evidence, Some of Which Is New.* London: Kegan, Paul, Trench, Trübner, 1909. [127 pages; N.B. The author interacts with numerous non-scriptural works.]

———. *The Vision of the Young Man Menelaus: Studies of Pentecost and Easter.* London: Kegan Paul, Trench, Trübner, &, 1910. [210 pages; N.B. Author of "Resurrectio Christi."]

MacPherson, Robert, and David Friedrich Strauss. *The Resurrection of Jesus Christ: With an Examination of the Speculations of Strauss in His 'New Life of Jesus'. An Introductory View of the Present Position of Theological Inquiry in Reference to the Existence of God and the Miraculous Evidence of Christianity.* Edinburgh: William Blackwood, 1867. [467 pages; N.B. Google book; This work is a classic, dated source.]

Mahoney, Robert. *Two Disciples at the Tomb: The Background and Message of John 20.1–10.* Bern: H. Lang, 1974. [344 pages; N.B. The text focuses in on John 20:1–10.]

Maloney, George A. *The First Day of Eternity: Resurrection. Now.* New York: Crossroad, 1982. [126 pages; N.B. The text's focus is on theology.]

Marchant, James. *Theories of the Resurrection of Jesus Christ.* London: Williams & Norgate, 1899. [122 pages; N.B. Google book. This work reviews and refutes several resurrection theories.]

Marsh, F. E. *The Resurrection of Christ: Fact or Fiction?* London: Pickering & Inglis, 1923. [216 pages]

———. *What Does the Resurrection of Christ Mean?* London: Marshall, 1901. [216 pages; N.B. This work emphasizes theology.]

Marsh, Gideon W. B. *The Resurrection of Christ. Is It a Fact?* St. Louis: Herder, 1905. [55 pages; N.B. Microsoft digitized this text.]

Marshall, Peter. *The First Easter.* New York: McGraw-Hill, 1959. [137 pages; N.B. Juvenile.]

Martelet, Gustave. *The Risen Christ and the Eucharistic World.* London: Collins, 1976. [252 pages; N.B. Useless.]

Martin, James. *Did Jesus Rise from the Dead?* New York: Association Press, 1956. [91 pages; N.B. This work offers a healthy overview of the topic under investigation.]

Martin, J. Walter. *A Critique on the Criticism of the Resurrection of Jesus Christ.* Newport News, VA: Author, 1973. [106 pages]

Marxsen, Willi. *Jesus and Easter: Did God Raise the Historical Jesus from the Dead?* Translated by Victor Paul Furnish. Nashville: Abingdon, 1990. [92 pages; N.B. This work should be examined. Its emphasis is on theology.]

———. *The Resurrection of Jesus of Nazareth.* Translated by Margaret Kohl. Philadelphia: Fortress, 1970. [191 pages; N.B. Marxsen's work should be examined.]

Marxsen, Willi, and C. F. D. Moule. *The Significance of the Message of the Resurrection for Faith in Jesus Christ.* London: SCM, 1968. [142 pages; N.B. This work should be examined.]

Massee, J. C. *After His Passion: Lessons from the Resurrection Appearances of Jesus.* New York: Revell, 1929. [128 pages; N.B. Massee offers a general overview.]

Massie, Edward. *The Risen Saviour: And Other Sermons.* London: James Nisbet, 1894. [267 pages; N.B. Google book. Useless.]

Matera, Frank J. *Resurrection: The Origin and Goal of the Christian Life.* Collegeville, MN: Liturgical Press, 2015. [149 pages; N.B. The author provides a general overview of the topic.]

Mathewson, Steven D. *Risen: 50 Reasons Why the Resurrection Changed Everything.* Grand Rapids: Baker, 2013. [143 pages; N.B. There is little interaction with the resurrection narratives.]

McAllister, Dawson. *A Walk with Christ Through the Resurrection: A Discussion Manual.* Englewood, CO: Shepherd Productions, 1981. [222 pages]

McCasland, S. Vernon. *The Resurrection of Jesus: A New Study of the Belief That Jesus Rose from the Dead, of Its Function as the Early Christian Cult Story, and of the Origin of the Gospel Literature.* New York: T. Nelson, 1932. [219 pages; N.B. An interesting text.]

McDonald, James I. H. *The Resurrection: Narrative and Belief.* London: SPCK, 1989. [161 pages; N.B. This source is a healthy work to examine.]

McDowell, Josh. *The Resurrection Factor.* San Bernardino, CA: Here's Life, 1981. [211 pages; N.B. One of the early, simplistic, apologetic texts penned by this writer.]

McDowell, Josh, and Sean McDowell. *Evidence for the Resurrection: What It Means for Your Relationship with God.* Ventura, CA: Regal, 2009. [254 pages; N.B. This work should be read to understand often asserted Christian apologetics for Jesus's resurrection.]

———. *Jesus: Dead or Alive?* Teen Edition. Ventura, CA: Regal, 2009. [126 pages]

———. *Resurrection and You.* Grand Rapids: Baker, 2017. [60 pages]

McDowell, Josh, et al. *Jesus Is Alive! For Kids: Evidence for the Resurrection.* Singapore: IMprint Edition, 2009. [128 pages. N.B. See. 82–123]

McDowell, Josh, and Dave Sterrett. *Did the Resurrection Happen— Really? A Dialogue on Life, Death, and Hope.* Chicago: Moody, 2011. [145 pages; N.B. This book is an easy to read source.]

McDowell, Josh, and David A. Stoop. *Resurrection Growth Guide.* San Bernardino, CA: Here's Life, 1982. [79 pages; N.B. This non-technical guide provides questions for its reader to respond.]

McGarvey, J. W. *Jesus and Jonah.* Cincinnati: Standard Publishing, 1896. [72 pages; N.B. Archive.org. This book should be explored to better understand the three day prophecy recorded in Matthew 12:40.]

McGee, J. Vernon. *After His Resurrection.* Pasadena, CA: Thru the Bible Books, n.d. [79 pages]

———. *The Empty Tomb: Proof of Life After Death.* Glendale, CA: Regal, 1968. [128 pages; N.B. Not useful.]

McGrath, Alister E. *Resurrection.* Minneapolis: Fortress, 2008. [70 pages; N.B. The author provides a simple overview of the resurrection.]

McKay, Johnston R. *Through Wood and Nails.* Glasgow Bellahouston Steven Parish Church, Glasgow: J. R. Mackay, 1983. [48 pages]

McKenna, Megan. *And Morning Came: Scriptures of the Resurrection.* Lanham, MD: Sheed & Ward, 2003. [229 pages; N.B. The author presents an overview of the resurrection narratives.]

McKenzie, Leon. *Pagan Resurrection Myths and the Resurrection of Jesus: A Christian Perspective.* Charlottesville, VA: Bookwrights, 1997. [160 pages; N.B. McKenzie refutes the claim that Jesus did not die, was not resurrected, and derived from pagan resurrection myths.]

McKenzie, Robert A. *The First Day of the Week: The Mystery and Message of the Empty Tomb of Jesus.* New York: Paulist, 1985. [87 pages; N.B. The author presents an overview of the resurrection narratives.]

McKibbon, W. Stan. *The Anointed One.* Pensacola, FL: Sonshine Publishing House, 1994. [140 pages]

McKinley, J. L. *Jesus and the Resurrection: The Catalyst of Historical Christianity.* n.p.: Xulon, 2005. [124 pages; N.B. The author presents an overview of the resurrection narratives.]

McLeman, James. *The Birth of the Christian Faith.* Edinburgh: Oliver & Boyd, 1962. [82 pages; N.B. Nothing useful]

———. *Resurrection Then and Now.* London: Hodder & Stoughton, 1965. [Part 3 The Resurrection Narratives, See. 127–72; N.B., Reprinted in 1995. This work is a useful read.]

Meadows, W. S. H. *Alive from the Dead.* [Reflections on 1 Cor. 15. 35–58.] London, 1869. [1 Volume]

Merton, Thomas. *He Is Risen.* Niles, IL: Argus Communications, 1975. [59 pages; N.B. Not useful, poetry.]

Michaelis, Johann David. *The Burial and Resurrection of Jesus Christ: According to the Four Evangelists.* London: J. Hatchard, 1827. [352 pages; N.B. Google book. This book is a classic, dated source.]

Miller, Calvin. *The Christ of Easter: Readings for the Season of Resurrection: 48 Days of Devotions.* Nashville: Broadman & Holman, 2004. [160 pages; N.B. Not useful.]

Miller, Laurence W. *Jesus Christ Is Alive.* Boston: W. A. Wilde, 1949. [89 pages; N.B. This work refutes seven natural explanations for the empty tomb.]

Category I—Books Dealing with Jesus's Resurrection

Miller, Richard C. *Resurrection and Reception in Early Christianity*. New York: Routledge, 2015. [206 pages; N.B. This work is an important reading!]

Miller, Thomas A. *Did Jesus Really Rise From the Dead? A Surgeon-Scientist Examines the Evidence*. Wheaton, IL: Crossway, 2013. [176 pages; N.B. This work is a Christian apologetic.]

Milligan, William. *The Ascension and Heavenly Priesthood of Our Lord*. London: Macmillan, 1892. [374 pages; N.B. Google book. This work does not interact with the resurrection narratives.]

———. *The Resurrection of Our Lord*. London: MacMillan, 1881. [304 pages; N.B. Google book. This publication is a classic, dated text.]

Mills, Watson E. *Bibliographies on the Life and Teachings of Jesus*. Vol. 8. *The Resurrection*. Lewiston, NY: Mellen, 2002. [88 pages; N.B. This work contains 1204 references that are primarily journals.]

Minear, Paul S. *To Die and to Live: Christ's Resurrection and Christian Vocation*. New York: Seabury, 1977. [162 pages; N.B. Little interaction with the resurrection narratives.]

Mishkin, David. *Jewish Scholarship on the Resurrection of Jesus*. Eugene, OR: Wipf & Stock, 2017. [256 pages. N.B. Essentially, this work is a copy of his dissertation, available online.]

M'Neile, Hugh. *Lectures on the Sympathies, Sufferings, and Resurrection of The Lord Jesus Christ Resurrection of the Lord Jesus*. London: John Hatch, 1843. [Lectures 7 and 8, See. 167–231; N.B. Google book]

Moberly, George. *The Sayings of the Great Forty Days: Between the Resurrection and Ascension, Regarded as the Outlines of the Kingdom of God: In Five Sermons*. 3rd ed. London: Francis & John Rivington, 1846. [396 pages; N.B. Google book]

Mohler, J. S. *The Resurrection*. Elgin, IL: Brethren Publishing House, 1901. [128 pages; N.B. Google book. This book primarily deals with the resurrection of the dead.]

Molnar, Paul D. *Incarnation and Resurrection: Toward a Contemporary Understanding*. Grand Rapids: Eerdmans, 2007. [418 pages; N.B. The author of this theological book interacts with several writers.]

Moloney, Francis J. *The Resurrection of the Messiah: A Narrative Commentary on the Resurrection Accounts in the Four Gospels*. New York: Paulist, 2013. [203 pages; N.B. The book should be examined.]

Montefiore, Hugh. *Womb and the Tomb: Mystery of the Birth and Resurrection of Jesus*. Fount, 1992. [189 pages; N.B. Pages 111–66 deal with the resurrection.]

Moore, T. V. *The Last Day of Jesus: or, The Appearance of Our Lord During the Forty Days Between the Resurrection and Ascension*. Philadelphia: Presbyterian Board of Publication, 1858. [300 pages; N.B. Archive.org and Google book. This work is a classic, dated source.]

Morison, Frank [pseud.]. *Who Moved the Stone?* London: Faber & Faber, 1930. [294 pages; N.B. The name of the author was Albert Henry Ross. This popular work is perhaps one of the most cited apologetics for Jesus's resurrection.]

Morrison, Charles R. *The Proofs of Christ's Resurrection: From a Lawyer's Standpoint*. Andover: W.F. Draper, 1882. [155 pages; N.B. Google book. This work is a classic, dated source.]

Mortimer, Alfred G. *Jesus and the Resurrection; Thirty Addresses for Good Friday and Easter*. New York: Longmans, Green, 1898. [298 pages; N.B. Google book]

Moss, Charles, and William Bowyer. *The Evidence of the Resurrection Cleared: From the Exceptions of a Late Pamphlet, Entitled, the Resurrection of Jesus Considered by a Moral Philosopher, in Answer to the Tryal of the Witnesses, &c.* London: Printed for John and Henry Pemberton at the Golden Bush against St. Dunstan's Church in Fleetstreet, 1744. [164 pages; N.B. Archive.org and Google book. The author interacts with Peter Annet.]

Motter, Alton M., ed. *Preaching the Resurrection: Twenty-Two Great Easter Sermons.* Philadelphia: Muhlenberg, 1959. [186 pages; N.B. Not useful]

Moule, C. F. D., ed. *The Significance of the Message of the Resurrection for Faith in Jesus Christ.* London: SCM, 1968. [142 pages; N.B. The essays of the four contributors should be examined.]

Moule, H. C. G. *Emmaus.* London: Samuel Bagster & Sons, 1912. [63 pages; N.B. Not useful.]

———. *Jesus and the Resurrection: Expository Studies on St. John 20. 21.* London: Seeley, 1893. [213 pages; N.B. Google book. This work should be examined.]

Mumaw, John R. *The Resurrected Life.* Scottdale, PA: Herald Press, 1965. [160 pages; N.B. No interaction with the resurrection narratives.]

Muncaster, Ralph O. *What Is the Proof for the Resurrection?* Eugene, OR: Harvest House, 2000. [48 pages; N.B. This brief work is an apologetic.]

Murphy, Richard Thomas Aquinas. *Days of Glory: The Passion, Death, and Resurrection of Jesus Christ.* Ann Arbor, MI: Servant, 1980. [198 pages; N.B. See. 141–72]

New Trial of the Witnesses; or, The Resurrection of Jesus Considered, The . . . London: Printed for John Hunt, 1823. [89 pages; largely as a reply to Thomas Sherlock's *The Trial of the Witnesses.* "With an Enquiry into the Origin of the Gospels, and the Authenticity of the Epistles of Paul." N.B. Google book. This work is a classic, dated source.]

Neyrey, Jerome H. *The Resurrection Stories.* Wilmington, DE: M. Glazier, 1988. [109 pages; N.B. This publication is a recommended read.]

Niebuhr, Richard R. *Resurrection and Historical Reason: A Study of Theological Method.* New York: Scribner's Sons, 1957. [184 pages; N.B. This work does not interact with the resurrection narratives.]

Noble, Samuel. *The Rev. Samuel Noble on the Glorification of the Lord's Humanity: And the Nature of His Resurrection-Body; with Articles, or Statements, on the Same Subjects.* London: William White, 1856. [226 pages; N.B. HathiTrust. Noble interacts with six authors.]

Nott, Eliphalet. *The Resurrection of Christ: A Series of Discourses.* New York: Scribner, Armstrong, 1872. [157 pages; N.B. Google book. The author presents common apologetics for the resurrection.]

Nouet, Jacques. *The Life of Jesus Christ, in Glory on Earth: A Series of Meditations, for each Day, from Easter to Ascension Day: Adapted for Members of the Church of England.* London: James Burns, 1846. [292 pages; N.B. Google book. Not useful]

Novakovic, Lidija. *Raised from the Dead According to Scripture: The Role of Israel's Scripture in the Early Christian Interpretations of Jesus' Resurrection.* London: Bloomsbury, 2012. [269 pages; N.B. The text does not interact with the resurrection narratives.]

———. *Resurrection: A Guide for the Perplexed.* London: Bloomsbury T&T Clark, 2016. [208 pages; N.B. This source is a recommended read.]

Nseka, Christian Kita. *The Messiahship of the Lord: Introducing a New Perspective on the Resurrection of Jesus Christ.* Salt Lake City, UT: Millennial Mind, 2009. [198 pages]

Ochsenford, S. E. *The Passion Story: Being a Connected Narrative of the Passion, Death, and Resurrection of the Lord Jesus Christ, as Recorded by the Four Evangelists, Matthew, Mark, Luke and John.* Philadelphia: G. W. Frederick, 1889. [N.B. Google book. See. 100–14; Not useful.]

O'Collins, Gerald. *Believing in the Resurrection: The Meaning and Promise of the Risen Jesus.* New York: Paulist, 2012. [225 pages; N.B. Chapter 3 The Appearances of the Risen Jesus, See. 61–99]

———. *Easter Faith: Believing in the Risen Jesus.* London: Darton Longman & Todd, 2003. [122 pages; N.B. This work is useful to read.]

———. *The Easter Jesus.* 2nd ed. London: Darton, Longman & Todd, 1980. [142 pages; N.B. This source is a useful work to examine.]

———. *Interpreting the Resurrection: Examining the Major Problems in the Stories of Jesus' Resurrection.* New York: Paulist, 1988. [88 pages; N.B. This short work should be examined.]

———. *Jesus Risen: An Historical, Fundamental, and Systematic Examination of Christ's Resurrection.* New York: Paulist, 1987. [233 pages; N.B. This text is a recommended read.]

———. *The Resurrection of Jesus Christ.* Valley Forge, PA: Judson Press, 1973. [142 pages; English edition published under the title *The Easter Jesus*.]

———. *The Resurrection of Jesus Christ: Some Contemporary Issues.* Milwaukee, WI: Marquette University Press, 1993. [50 pages; N.B. No interaction with the resurrection narrative, primarily theological concerns.]

———. *Saint Augustine on the Resurrection of Christ: Teaching, Rhetoric, and Reception.* New York: Oxford University Press, 2017. [128 pages]

———. *What Are They Saying about the Resurrection?* New York: Paulist, 1978. [120 pages; N.B. This book offers little interaction with the resurrection narratives.]

Olshausen, Hermann. *The Last Days of the Saviour, or, History of the Lord's Passion.* Boston: J. Munroe, 1839. [248 pages; N.B. Google book and HathiTrust. See. 187–247. The author provides a general review of the relevant texts.]

Olson, Carl E. *Did Jesus Really Rise from the Dead? Questions and Answers about the Life, Death, and Resurrection of Jesus Christ.* San Francisco: Ignatius Press, 2016. [201 pages]

Onesimus, Captain. [pseud.]. *Christ Rejected: or, The Trial of the Eleven Disciples of Christ, in a Court of Law and Equity, as Charged with Stealing the Crucified Body of Christ out of the Sepulchre . . .* Philadelphia: Printed for the Author by Joseph Rakestraw, 1832. [444 pages; N.B. Google book. His name is a pseudonym for John Hewson.]

Ordal, Z. J. *The Resurrection of Jesus: An Historical Fact.* Minneapolis: Augsburg, 1923. [128 pages; N.B. This work is worth examining.]

Orr, James. *The Resurrection of Jesus.* London: Hodder & Stoughton, 1908. [292 pages; N.B. Google book. A classic, dated text that is often cited in the literature.]

Osborne, Grant R. *The Resurrection Narratives: A Redactional Study.* Grand Rapids: Baker, 1984. [344 pages; N.B. This is a solid, detail text.]

Osborne, Kenan B. *The Resurrection of Jesus: New Considerations for Its Theological Interpretation.* New York: Paulist, 1997. [194 pages; N.B. Virtually no interaction with the resurrection narratives.]

Oxford Layman, An. *Letters to the Editor of The New Trial of the Witnesses.* London: Printed for John & H. L. Hunt, 1824. [107 pages; N.B. Google book. Not useful.]

Palmer, Joseph. *The Central Event of Universal History: A Study of the Resurrection of Jesus Christ from the Dead*. Sydney: Christian World Print, 1918. [111 pages; N.B. Palmer's book is an interesting read.]

Parsons, Elmer E. *Witness to the Resurrection*. Grand Rapids: Baker, 1967. [131 pages; N.B. The author provides a good general, overview.]

Parsons, Mikeal C. *The Departure of Jesus in Luke-Acts: The Ascension Narratives in Context*. Sheffield: JSOT, 1987. [301 pages; N.B. The author presents an important reading on Jesus's ascension.]

Paternoster, Michael. *Stronger than Death*. London: SPCK, 1972. [82 pages; N.B. No interaction with the resurrection narratives.]

Paton, James. *The Glory and Joy of the Resurrection*. New York: American Tract Society, 1902. [227 pages; N.B. Google book; N.B. Only the first thirty pages directly interact with the resurrection narratives.]

Patrick, Simon. *Jesus and the Resurrection Justified by Witnesses in Heaven and in Earth. In Two Parts. The First Shewing, That Jesus Is the Son of God; the Second, That in Him We Have Eternal Life*. Dublin: Printed by A. Rhames, for J. Hyde, R. Gunne, R. Owen, & E. Dobson, 1723. [504 pages; N.B. Google book]

———. *The Works of Symon Patrick*. Vol. 3 Oxford: At the University Press, 1858. [*Jesus and the Resurrection Justified by Witnesses in Heaven and Earth; or the Witnesses to Christianity*, Chapters 1—14, See. 8–346; N.B. Google book. Not useful.]

Pawson, David. *Explaining the Resurrection*. Tonbridge: Sovereign World, 1993. [80 pages]

Paxy, Alumkal Jacob. *Death and Resurrection of Jesus Christ Implied in the Image of the Paschal Lamb in 1 Cor 5:7 : An Intertextual Exegetical and Theological Study*. Bern, Lang, 2014. [416 pages; Chapter 1 Death and Resurrection of Jesus Christ in the Teachings of Paul, See. 25–73; N.B. The text does not interact with the resurrection narratives.

Paynter, H. M. *The Holy Resurrection: A Critical Exposition of All That Is Told Us in the New Testament Narratives Concerning the Resurrection and Ascension of Jesus*. Chicago: C. H. Whiting, 1884. [222 pages; N.B. Archive.org. This source is an interesting read.]

Pearce, Zachary. *The Miracles of Jesus Vindicated: In Four Parts*. 5th ed. London: Printed for J. Watts, 1749. [86 pages; N.B. Google book. Part 1 covers the proofs of the resurrection and objections to it are answered, See. 4–31.]

Perkins, Pheme. *Resurrection: New Testament Witness and Contemporary Reflection*. Garden City, NY: Doubleday, 1984. [504 pages. N.B. This text is a solid read.]

Perkins, Rufus Lord. *One Story: Four Parts of the Several Narratives of Events on the Day of Our Lord's Resurrection*. Erie: Ashby, 1892. [61 pages; N.B. Google book. This book is a superficial read.]

Perrin, Norman. *The Resurrection According to Matthew, Mark, and Luke*. Philadelphia: Fortress, 1977. [85 pages; N.B. This work is a good, easy read.]

Perry, Charles Austin. *The Resurrection Promise: An Interpretation of the Easter Narratives*. Grand Rapids: Eerdmans, 1986. [139 pages; N.B. Perry's work offers a good overview.]

Perry, John M. *Exploring the Resurrection of Jesus*. Kansas City, MO: Sheed & Ward, 1993. [145 pages; N.B. Perry's work is an easy read with questions for review at the end of each chapter.]

Perry, Michael C. *The Easter Enigma: An Essay on the Resurrection with Special Reference to the Data of Psychical Research*. London: Faber & Faber, 1959. [264 pages; N.B. This work should definitely be examined.]

Category I—Books Dealing with Jesus's Resurrection

Peters, Ted, et. al, eds. *Resurrection: Theological and Scientific Assessments*. Grand Rapids: Eerdmans, 2002. [344 pages; N.B. This work contain eighteen essays.]

Peterson, Eugene H. *Living The Resurrection: The Risen Christ in Everyday Life*. Colorado Springs, CO: NavPress, 2006. [151 pages; N.B. Peterson does not interact with the resurrection narratives.]

Peterson, Paul K., ed. *Voices at the Crossroads: First-person, Dramatic Portrayals of Witnesses to Jesus' Death and Resurrection*. Minneapolis: Augsburg, 1991. [71 pages; N.B. Juvenile in nature and therefore not useful.]

Petty, Daniel W. ed. *Of First Importance: He Was Raised and Appeared Studies in the Resurrection of Jesus*. Temple Terrace, FL: Florida College Press, 2013. [259 pages; N.B. This work is a collection of fifteen essays.]

Phillips, Forbes Alexander. *What Was the Resurrection?* London: F. Griffiths, 1910. [177 pages; N.B. This work is an interesting, dated source.]

Pine, Thomas. *Reflections on the Principles and Evidences of Christianity; in Which the Resurrection of Our Saviour to Everlasting Life Is Shown to Be the Pattern of a Corresponding Blessing to Be Extended to Mankind, According to the Order of Their Moral Proficiency*. London: R. Hunter, 1835. [219 pages; N.B. Google book. The first seventy pages interact with the resurrection narratives.]

Pöelzl, Franz Xaver. *The Passion and Glory of Christ: A Commentary on the Events from the Last Supper to the Ascension*. Translated by Anna Maud Buchanan. Edited by C. C. Martindale. New York: Joseph F. Wagner, 1919. [371 pages; N.B. Google book. Pages 267–358 interact with the resurrection and ascension.]

Pollard, George Frederick. *On the Third Day: Evidences for the Bodily Resurrection of Our Lord and Saviour Jesus Christ*. London: Wells Gardner, Darton, 1900. [120 pages; N.B. The author provides his input about the resurrection.]

Pollock, A. J. *The Resurrection of the Lord Jesus Christ*. London: Central Bible Truth, 1930? [56 pages; N.B. Online at BibleTruthPublishers.com. The author provides a general overview of the relevant chapters in the New Testament.]

Porter, Stanley E., et al., eds. *Resurrection*. Sheffield: Sheffield Academic, 1999. [376 pages. N.B. This text contains eighteen essays.]

Poteat, Edwin McNeill. *These Shared His Power: Studies in the Days following the Resurrection of Jesus*. New York: Harper & Brothers, 1941. [180 pages; N.B. Useless.]

Power, Philip Bennett. *The Feet of Jesus: In Life, Death, Resurrection, and Glory*. London: Hamilton, Adams, 1872. [315 pages; N.B. Google book; N.B. Useless.]

Price, Nelson L. *The Destruction of Death*. Nashville: Broadman, 1982. [127 pages; N.B. Juvenile.]

Priceless Pearls for All Christians, Etc. London: Willoughby, 1850. [Pearl 7 The resurrection, See. 118–28; N.B. Google book from the Bodleian Library.]

Priestley, Joseph. *The Evidence of the Resurrection of Jesus Considered: In a Discourse First Delivered in the Assembly-Room, at Buxton, on Sunday, September 19, 1790. To Which Is Added, An Address to the Jews*. Birmingham, Eng: Printed by J. Thompson for J. Johnson, 1794. [56 pages; N.B. Google book: Reprinted as Discourse 11 in *Discourses on the Evidence of Revealed Religion*. London, 1794. AC901 .M5 vol. 801, no. 13 Misc Pam. Useless!]

Pritchard, John. *Living Easter Through the Year: Making the Most of the Resurrection*. Collegeville, MN: Liturgical Press, 2005. [133 pages; N.B. Easter meditations. Useless.]

Proctor, William. *The Resurrection Report*. Nashville: Broadman & Holman, 1998. [212 pages; N.B. This work is presented as if by a modern day newspaper reporter.]

Purves, Andrew. *The Resurrection of Ministry: Serving in the Hope of the Risen Lord*. Downers Grove, IL: InterVarsity, 2010. [158 pages; N.B. Not useful.]

Quarles, Charles L., ed. *Buried Hope or Risen Savior: The Search for the Jesus Tomb*. Nashville: B&H Academic, 2008. [243 pages; N.B. Essays by six contributors. Not useful.]

Quenot, Michel. *The Resurrection and the Icon*. Translated by Michael Breck. Crestwood, NY: St. Vladimir's Seminary Press, 1997. [264 pages; N.B. Not useful.]

Queripel, John Henry. *On the Third Day: Re-looking at the Resurrection*. Eugene, OR: Wipf & Stock, 2018 [136 pages; N.B. Previously published by Morning Star Publishing, 2017.]

Ramsey, A. Michael. *The Resurrection of Christ: An Essay in Biblical Theology*. Philadelphia: Westminster, 1946. [123 pages; N.B. Only pages 59–74 deal with evidence of Jesus's resurrection.]

Randolph, B. W. *The Empty Tomb: Being Thoughts on the Resurrection of Our Lord*. London: Longmans, Green, 1906. [56 pages; N.B. Google book. Randolph offers a general discussion of the resurrection.]

Reeves, Keith Howard. *The Resurrection Narrative in Matthew: A Literary-critical Examination*. Lewiston, NY: Mellen, 1993. [113 pages]

Rex, H. H. *Did Jesus Rise from the Dead?* Auckland, N.Z.: B&J Paul, 1967. [93 pages; N.B. The author provides a general discussion on the topic.]

Rice, John R. *The Resurrection of Jesus Christ: Glorious, Heart-Warming Truth from the Bible on the Importance of Christ's Resurrection to the Christian Faith, and the Many Infallible Proofs of the Resurrection*. Wheaton, IL: Sword of the Lord, 1953. [60 pages]

Richards, Hubert J. *The First Easter: What Really Happened?* Mystic, CT: Twenty-Third Publications, 1986. [126 pages; N.B. The author provides a good overview on the topic.]

Riddle, T. Wilkinson. *The Gospel of the Resurrection: And Other Addresses*. London: Marshall, Morgan & Scott, 1939. [117 pages; N.B. Not useful.]

Riga, Peter J. *The Redeeming Christ*. Washington: Corpus Books, 1969. [124 pages; N.B. Only pages 86–113 interact with the resurrection narratives.]

Riggenbach, Eduard. *The Resurrection of Jesus*. New York: Eaton & Mains, 1907. [74 pages; N.B. Google book. This dated source is not very useful.]

Riggs, Ollie L. *Three Days and Three Nights in the Heart of the Earth*. Durham, NC: Author, 1928. [176 pages]

Riley, Gregory J. *Resurrection Reconsidered: Thomas and John in Controversy*. Minneapolis: Fortress, 1995. [222 pages; N.B. This is an interesting source to examine.]

Ring, T. P. *The Most Certain Fact in History: Addresses on the Resurrection*. 2nd ed. London: Skeffington, 1892. [101 pages; N.B. Pages 51–67 discuss natural explanations of Jesus's resurrection.]

Riper, David Van. *The Resurrection of Christ: Reconciling the Gospel Accounts*. Bloomington, IN: WestBow Press, 2016. [108 pages; N.B. Those interested in apologetics should examine this work. It discusses nine controversies.]

Riss, Richard M. *The Evidence for the Resurrection of Jesus Christ: Legal, Historical, and Eyewitness Evidence for the Resurrection!* Minneapolis: Bethany Fellowship, 1977. [106 pages; N.B. Riss presents a general overview of apologetic arguments.]

Roberts, Griffith. *Why We Believe that Christ Rose from the Dead.* London: SPCK, 1914. [112 pages; N.B. Roberts provides a general overview.]

Roberts, Robert. *The Trial of the Most Notable Lawsuit of Ancient or Modern Times: The Incorporated Scientific Era Protection Society v. Paul Christman and Others, in the Court of Common Reason, before Lord Penetrating Impartiality and a Special Jury: Issue, Did Christ Rise from the Dead? Verbatim Report.* Birmingham, Eng: C. C. Walker, 1908. [339 pages; N.B. Archive.org and Google book. Not useful.]

Robinette, Brian DuWayne. *Grammars of Resurrection: A Christian Theology of Presence and Absence.* New York: Crossroad, 2009. [144 pages; N.B. Portions of the text are interesting.]

Robinson, Charles H. *Studies in the Resurrection of Christ: An Argument.* London: Longmans, Green, 1909. [169 pages; N.B. Google book. Primarily theological with some interaction with the resurrection narratives.]

Robson, John. *The Resurrection Gospel: A Study of Christ's Great Commission.* Edinburgh: Oliphant Anderson & Ferrier, 1908 [N.B. Google book, 311 pages; N.B. Almost no interaction with the actual resurrection.]

Rollock, Robert. *Lectures, Upon the History of the Passion, Resurrection, and Ascension of Our Lord Jesus Christ. Beginning at the Eighteenth Chapter of the Gospel, According to S. John, and from the 16. Verse of the 19. Chapter Thereof, Containing a Perfect Harmony of All the Four Evangelists, for the Better Understanding of All the Circumstances of the Lords Death, and Resurrection.* Edinburgh: Printed by Andro Hart, 1616. [576 pages; Lectures 42–54 Of the Resurrection of Christ, See. 409–554; Lectures 55–56 The Ascension, See. 555–76; N.B. Google book.]

Roper, Albert L. *Did Jesus Rise From the Dead? A Lawyer Looks at the Evidence.* Grand Rapids: Zondervan, 1965. [54 pages; N.B. Provides a minimal overview.]

Roth, Timothy Dean. *The Week that Changed the World: The Complete Easter Story.* New York: Seabury, 2009. [113 pages; Saturday—Ascension, See. 88–106; N.B. Not useful.]

Ruch, Velma. *Transformation: A New Creation in Christ: The Journey from Easter to Pentecost.* Independence, MO: Herald Publishing House, 2006. [141 pages]

Runcorn, David. *Rumours of Life: Reflections on the Resurrection Appearances.* London: Darton, Longman & Todd, 1996. [134 pages; N.B. Not useful.]

Rutland, Mark. *Resurrection: Receiving and Releasing God's Greatest Miracle.* Lake Mary, FL: Creation House, 2005. [116 pages; N.B. Deals with Christian life.]

Sadler, I. A. *The Love of God: As Displayed in the Life, Death and Resurrection of the Lord Jesus Christ.* Chippenham: I. A. Sadler, 2006. [84 pages]

Sancken, Joni S. *Stumbling Over the Cross: Preaching the Cross and Resurrection Today.* Eugene, OR: Cascade, 2016. [208 pages; N.B. Not useful.]

Sawicki, Marianne. *Seeing the Lord: Resurrection and Early Christian Practices.* Minneapolis: Fortress 1994. [375 pages; N.B. Primary theological, little interaction with the resurrection narratives.]

Sayers, Stanley E. *He Is Risen.* Delight, AR: Gospel Light, 1990. [240 pages]

Scarborough, Lee Rutland. *After the Resurrection—What?* Grand Rapids: Zondervan, 1942. [121 pages; N.B. Not useful.]

Schlier, Heinrich. *On the Resurrection of Jesus Christ.* Translated by Michael Sullivan. Rome: 30Giorni, 2008. [79 pages; N.B. Primarily theological.]

Schneiders, Sandra Marie. *Jesus Risen in Our Midst: Essays on the Resurrection of Jesus in the Fourth Gospel.* Collegeville, MN: Liturgical Press, 2013. [206 pages; N.B. The book offers some essays of interest.]

Schutte, Flip. *Jesus' Resurrection in Joseph's Garden: A Postmodern Revisit.* Pretoria: Protea Book House, 2008. [207 pages; N.B. See. 96–136]

Schwartzkopff, Paul. *The Prophecies of Jesus Christ Relating to His Death, Resurrection, and Second Coming, and Their Fulfilment.* Translated by Neil Buchanan. Edinburgh: T&T Clark, 1897. [328 pages; N.B. Google book. No interaction with the resurrection narratives.]

Schwarzwäller, Klaus. *Cross and Resurrection: God's Wonder and Mystery.* Minneapolis: Fortress, 2012. [164 pages; N.B. Focused on the cross.]

Selby, Peter. *Look for the Living: The Corporate Nature of Resurrection Faith.* Philadelphia: Fortress, 1976. [212 pages; N.B. Theological, not useful.]

Shafto, G. R. H. *The Reality of the Resurrection.* New York: Revell, 1930. [100 pages; N.B. Shafto presents a general overview.]

Shaw, John Mackintosh. *The Resurrection of Christ: An Examination of the Apostolic Belief and Its Significance for the Christian Faith.* Edinburgh: T&T Clark, 1920. [N.B. Google book, 215 pages. An informative, dated text.]

Shepherd, William H. *If a Sermon Falls in the Forest–: Preaching Resurrection Texts.* Lima, OH: CSS Pub., 2002. [253 pages; N.B. Not useful.]

Sherlock, Thomas. *The Trial of the Witnesses of the Resurrection of Jesus, to Which Is Added the Sequel of the Trial.* Philadelphia: Presbyterian Board of Publication, 1800? [128 pages; N.B. Google book. This source is a classic text.]

———. *Proofs of Christianity: From The Resurrection of Jesus, by Dr Sherlock, Late Bishop of London . . .* Edinburgh: Printed by J. Robertson, for W. Gray, 1769. [250 pages; N.B. Google book. A classic, dated source.]

Silvester, Tipping. *The Evidence of the Resurrection of Jesus Vindicated, Against the Cavils of a Moral Philosopher.* 2nd ed. London: Printed and sold by T. Gardner, 1744. [129 pages; N.B. Google book]

Simon, Ulrich E. *The Ascent to Heaven.* London: Barrie & Rockliff, 1961. [181 pages; N.B. Not useful.]

Simpson, A. B. *The Christ of the Forty Days: What Jesus Taught Between His Resurrection and Ascension.* New York: Christian Alliance, 1890. [322 pages; N.B. Archive.org. This book is a recommended reading.]

Singleton, Richard O. *The Last Words of the Resurrected Christ.* Winona, MN: Saint Mary's Press, 1997. [91 pages; N.B. Not useful.]

Sirr, Joh D'Arcy. *The First Resurrection Considered in a Series of Letters: Occasioned by a Treatise of the Late Rev. H. Gipps.* Dublin: Richard M. Tims, 1833. [330 pages; N.B. Google book; N.B. Nothing useful.]

Skinner, Andrew C. *The Garden Tomb.* Salt Lake City, UT: Deseret Book, 2005. [218 pages; N.B. "This work is not an official publication of The Church of Jesus Christ of Latter-day Saints."]

Skrine, John Huntley. *Miracle and History: A Study in the Virgin Birth and the Resurrection.* London: Longmans, Green, 1912. [48 pages; N.B. Google book. Nothing useful.]

Sleeman, Matthew. *Geography and the Ascension Narrative in Acts.* Cambridge: Cambridge University Press, 2009. [300 pages; N.B. This text only interacts with Acts.]

Sloan, Harold Paul. *He Is Risen*. New York: Abingdon-Cokesbury, 1942. [186 pages; N.B. Not useful.]

Smith, Daniel Alan. *The Post-Mortem Vindication of Jesus in the Sayings Gospel Q*. London: T&T Clark, 2006. [206 pages; N.B. This is an interesting work to examine.]

———. *Revisiting the Empty Tomb: The Early History of Easter*. Minneapolis: Fortress, 2010. [267 pages; N.B. This work should be examined.]

Smith, Graeme. *Was the Tomb Empty? A Lawyer Weighs the Evidence for the Resurrection*. Monarch, 2014. [224 pages; N.B. Not useful.]

Smith, Robert H. *Easter Gospels the Resurrection of Jesus According to the Four Evangelists*. Minneapolis: Augsburg, 1963. [254 pages; N.B. Smith separately analyzes the four gospel narratives.]

Smith, Wilbur M., ed. *A Great Certainty in This Hour of World Crisis*. Wheaton, IL: Van Kampen, 1951. [48 pages; N.B. Not useful.]

———. *Great Sermons on the Resurrection of Christ*. Natick, MA: W.A. Wilde, 1964. [289 pages; N.B. Eighteen sermons by various theologians.]

Snowden, James Henry. *A Wonderful Morning; an Interpretation of Easter*. New York: Macmillan, 1921. [155 pages; See. 48–97; N.B. Google book. Snowden provides a general overview.]

Söderblom, Nathan. *The Death and Resurrection of Christ; Reflections on the Passion*. Translated by A. G. Herbert and Gene J. Lund. Minneapolis: Augsburg, 1968. [87 pages; N.B. This book offers a minimal overview.]

Sparrow-Simpson, W. J. *Our Lord's Resurrection*. London: Longmans, Green, 1909. [320 pages; N.B. Google book. This dated work is a recommended read.]

———. *The Resurrection and Modern Thought*. London: Longmans, Green, 1915. [462 pages; N.B. Google book; N.B. This dated work is a recommended read.]

Spencer, Bonnell. *They Saw the Lord*. New York: Morehouse-Gorham, 1947. [225 pages; N.B. Minimal use.]

Spencer, Claudius B. *Easter Reflections*. Cincinnati: Jennings & Graham, 1909. [274 pages; N.B. Minimal use.]

Spurgeon, C. H. *Jesus Rose for You*. New Kensington, PA: Whitaker House, 1998. [207 pages]

———. *Spurgeon's Sermons on the Death and Resurrection of Jesus*. Compiled by Patricia Klein. Peabody, MA: Hendrickson, 2005. [597 pages]

———. *Spurgeon's Sermons on the Resurrection*. Grand Rapids: Kregel, 1993. [207 pages]

———. *Twelve Sermons on the Resurrection*. London: Marshall, Morgan & Scott, 1937. [204 pages]

Stanback, C. Foster. *The Resurrection: A Historical Analysis*. Spring, TX: Illumination Publishers International, 2008. [88 pages]

Stanford, Charles. *From Calvary to Olivet: Being a Sequel to Voices from Calvary*. London: Religious Tract Society, 1893. [256 pages; N.B. Google book; Not useful.]

Stanford, Shane. *The Seven Next Words of Christ: Finding Hope in the Resurrection Sayings*. Nashville: Abingdon, 2006. [98 pages; N.B. Not useful.]

Stanley, David Michael. *Christ's Resurrection in Pauline Soteriology*. Rome: E Pontificio Instituto Biblico, 1961. [313 pages; N.B. No interaction with the resurrection narratives.]

Stecher, Richard C., and Craig L. Blomberg. *Resurrection : Faith or Fact? A Scholars' Debate Between a Skeptic and a Christian*. Durham, North Carolina: Pitchstone Publishing,

2019. [This work is perhaps, one of the finest debates about Jesus's resurrection. It is an absolute must reading! Craig Blomberg presents the Christian apologetic.]

Steinmeyer, F. L. *The History of the Passion and Resurrection of Our Lord: Considered in the Light of Modern Criticism*. Translated by Thomas Crerar and Alexander Cusin. Edinburgh: T&T Clark, 1879. [398 pages; N.B. Google book. This book is a classic, dated source.]

Stephenson, William. *Days of Joy; Thoughts for all Times*. Westminster, MD: Newman Press, 1955. [176 pages]

Stevenson, Kenneth E., and Gary R. Habermas. *Verdict on the Shroud: Evidence for the Death and Resurrection of Jesus Christ*. Ann Arbor, MI: Servant, 1981. [224 pages; N.B. This book should be compared to the work by Joe Nickell.]

Stewart, George. *The Resurrection in Our Street*. Garden City, NY: Doubleday, Doran &, 1928. [294 pages; N.B. Not useful.]

Stewart, John J. *The Eternal Gift: The Story of the Crucifixion and Resurrection*. 3rd ed. Bountiful, UT: Horizon Publishers & Distributors, 1978. [94 pages]

Stoffel, Ernest Lee. *The Apocalyptic Resurrection of Jesus*. Macon, GA: Smyth & Helwys, 1999. [104 pages; N.B. Not useful.]

Stone, James S. *The Glory After the Passion: A Study of the Events in the Life of Our Lord from His Descent into Hell to His Enthronement in Heaven*. London: Longmans, Green, 1913. [393 pages; N.B. Stone's book should be examined.]

Strobel, Lee. *The Case for Easter: A Journalist Investigates the Evidence for the Resurrection*. Grand Rapids: Zondervan, 2003. [95 pages; N.B. Not recommended.]

———. *The Case for the Resurrection: A First-century Reporter Investigates the Story of the Cross*. Grand Rapids, MI: Zondervan, 2009. [91 pages; N.B. Not recommended.]

Sullivan, James. *The Risen Lord*. Dublin: M. H. Gill and Son, 1963. [121 pages]

Surgy, Paul De., et al. *The Resurrection and Modern Biblical Thought*. Translated by Charles Quinn. New York: Corpus Books, 1970. [162 pages; N.B. This book contains five essays.]

Swain, Lionel. *Reading the Easter Gospels*. Collegeville, MN: Liturgical Press, 1993. [131 pages; N.B. The author presents an overview of the four gospels.]

Swete, Henry Barclay. *The Appearances of Our Lord After the Passion: A Study in the Earliest Christian Tradition*. London: Macmillan, 1915. [151 pages; N.B. Archive.org and Google book; N.B. This source is a classic, dated work.]

———. *The Ascended Christ: A Study in the Earliest Christian Teaching*. London: Macmillan, 1911. [168 pages; N.B. Google book. This work is concerned with Jesus's ascension.]

Swinburne, Richard. *The Resurrection of God Incarnate*. Oxford: Clarendon, 2003. [224 pages; N.B. This often-referenced book is an interesting work to examine.]

Tait, Arthur J. *The Heavenly Session of Our Lord: An Introduction to the History of the Doctrine*. London: R. Scott, 1912. [247 pages; Especially Chapter 1 The Heavenly Session of Our Lord, 1–50.]

Tatham, C. Ernest. *He Lives: Seven Studies of the Resurrection Appearances of the Lord Jesus Christ*. Chicago: Moody, 1938. [80 pages; N.B. Not useful.]

Taylor, John V. *Weep Not For Me Meditations on the Cross and the Resurrection*. Geneva: World Council of Churches, 1986. [57 pages; N.B. Not useful.]

Taylor, Myron J. *Proclaiming the Risen Lord*. Johnson City, TN: Emmanuel School of Religion Press, 2006. [149 pages; N.B. This work is a collection of sermons.]

Tenney, Merrill C. *The Reality of the Resurrection*. New York: Harper & Row, 1963. [221 pages; N.B. This work provides a good overview.]

———. *Resurrection Realities: "Now is Christ Risen."* Los Angeles, CA: Bible House of Los Angeles, 1945. [96 pages]

Thatcher, Floyd W., ed. *The Gift of Easter*. Waco, TX: Word, 1976. [165 pages; N.B. This text is a collection of fifteen essays that Thatcher compiled.]

Thayer, E. W. *The Bloody Sacrifice*. Springfield, IL: H.W. Rokker, 1898. [183 pages; N.B. Google book and HathiTrust; N.B. Not useful.]

Theisz, George Elmer. *The Eight First Words of the Risen Saviour. John 20-21*. Chicago: Moody, 1950. [124 pages; N.B. Not useful.]

Thomas, George Ernest. *The Meaning of the Resurrection in Christian Experience*. Nashville: Tidings, 1964. [84 pages; N.B. Not useful.]

Thompson, Alan J. *The Acts of the Risen Lord Jesus: Luke's Account of God's Unfolding Plan*. Downers Grove, IL: InterVarsity, 2011. [232 pages; N.B. Not useful.]

Thompson, Gordon G. *Living the Easter Faith: The Power of the Resurrection in the Modern World*. Decatur, GA: Looking Glass, 2004. [239 pages; N.B. Not useful.]

Thompson, K. C. *Received up into Glory: A Study of the Ascension*. London: Faith Press, 1964. [108 pages; N.B. Not useful.]

Thomson, Alexander. *Did Jesus Rise from the Dead?* Grand Rapids: Zondervan, 1940. [144 pages]

Thorburn, Thomas James. *The Resurrection Narratives and Modern Criticism: A Critique Mainly of Professor Schmiedel's Article "Resurrection Narratives" in the Encyclopædia Biblica*. London: Kegan Paul, Trench, Trübner, 1910. [217 pages; N.B. Google book. Thorburn's work is an important, dated text to read.]

Thorogood, Bernard. *Risen Today*. London: SCM, 1986. [113 pages; N.B. Not useful.]

Toon, Peter. *The Ascension of Our Lord*. Nashville: Nelson, 1984. [153 pages; N.B. One of the better works on Jesus's ascension.]

Torrance, Thomas F. *Space, Time, and Resurrection*. Grand Rapids: Eerdmans, 1976. [196 pages; N.B. This text focuses primarily on Jesus's ascension.]

Torrey, R. A. *Is the Bible the Inerrant Word of God, and Was the Body of Jesus Raised From the Dead*. New York: George H. Doran, 1922. [Chapter 7 Is It Absolutely Certain that the Body of Jesus that was Nailed to the Cross, that Really Died, and that was Laid in Joseph's Tomb, was Raised from the Dead?, See. 121–66; Chapter 8 What One Gains by Believing in the Christ Who Rose from the Dead, See. 167–85; N.B. Google book. This book is a classic text.]

Tóth, Tihamér, Newton Wayland Thompson, and Violet Grace Jenkins Ágotai. *The Risen Christ; Sermons on the Resurrection and on the Blessed Virgin*. St. Louis: B. Herder, 1938. [213 pages; N.B. Not useful.]

Townson, Thomas. *A Discourse on the Evangelical History: From the Interment to the Ascension of Our Lord and Saviour Jesus Christ*. Oxford: Sold by J. Fletcher and T. Payne, London, 1793. [210 pages; N.B. Google book; N.B. Not useful.]

Trench, George Henry. *The Crucifixion and Resurrection of Christ by the Light of Tradition*. London: J. Murray, 1908. [192 pages; N.B. Google book; N.B. This book is an interesting dated work.]

Trull, Joe E. *The Seven Last Words of the Risen Christ*. Grand Rapids: Baker, 1985. [110 pages; N.B. Not useful.]

Entire books Dealing with Jesus's Resurrection: Pro

Trumper, Peter. *Breakfast on the Beach: The Empty Tomb and the Subsequent Glory.* Darlington: Evangelical Press, 1999. [304 pages; N.B. Trumper pens a general overview.]

Tulga, Chester E. *The Case for the Resurrection of Jesus Christ.* Chicago: Conservative Baptist Fellowship, 1951. [59 pages; N.B. Tulga sources provides a general overview.]

Upham, Francis W. *The First Words from God, or, Truths Made Known in the First Two Chapters of His Holy Word; Also, the Harmonizing of the Records of the Resurrection Morning.* New York: Hunt & Eaton, 1894. [159 pages; After the Appendix on page 131 examine 1–28 The Harmonizing of the Four Records of the Resurrection Morning, N.B. Google book. The author attempts to harmonize potential contradictions.]

Van Daalen, David H. *The Real Resurrection.* London: Collins, 1972. [191 pages; N.B. The authors provides a general overview.]

Vander, Ray Laan. *Death and Resurrection of the Messiah Discovery Guide.* Grand Rapids: Zondervan, 2009. [301 pages; N.B. Volume 4 of The Faith Lessons Series; N.B. Not useful.]

Varley, Henry. *The Evangel of the Risen Christ His Resurrection Triumphs.* London: Alfred Holiness, 1901? [400 pages; N.B. Not useful.]

Vinzent, Markus. *Christ's Resurrection in Early Christianity and the Making of the New Testament.* Surrey, England: Ashgate, 2011. [276 pages; N.B. No interaction with the resurrection narratives.]

Violette, E. E. *In Palestine at the Empty Tomb.* New York: George H. Doran, 1923. [89 pages; N.B. Not useful.]

Wace, Henry. *The Story of the Resurrection.* London: J. Murray, 1923. [254 pages; N.B. Bodleian Libraries, a Google book. This book is a useful source to examine.]

Wade, George. *Two Discourses: The First, an Appeal to the Miracles of Jesus as Proofs of His Messiahship. The Second, a Demonstration of the Truth and Certainty of His Resurrection . . .* London: Printed for George Strahan, 1729. [54 pages]

Walker, Peter W. L. *The Weekend That Changed the World: The Mystery of Jerusalem's Empty Tomb.* Louisville: Westminster John Knox, 2000. [220 pages; N.B. This book provides a general overview.]

Wansbrough, Henry. *The Resurrection.* Staten Island, NY: Alba House, 1975. [109 pages; N.B. The author provides a general overview.]

———. *Risen From the Dead.* Slough: St. Paul Publications, 1978. [107 pages; N.B. This book is a good, easy read.]

Ward, Nelson W. *"The Master Key" . . . to the Problems of Passion Week . . . and . . . the Resurrection, According to the Scriptures.* Long Beach, CA: Author, 1915. [179 pages; N.B. Google book. See. 152–70. Not useful.]

Ware, Augustus William, and Julius Ware. *Letters to the Editor of The New Trial of the Witnesses.* London: Richard Taylor, 1824. [N.B. Google book. The anonymous author is identified as by "An Oxford Layman"; however the two authors are identified in WorldCat and elsewhere. Not useful.]

Warnock, Adrian. *Raised with Christ: How the Resurrection Changes Everything.* Wheaton, IL: Crossway, 2010. [272 pages; N.B. Primarily theological. Not useful.]

Warren, Elizabeth. *The Great Forty Days (following the Resurrection of . . . Jesus Christ). Designed to Be a Help to Sunday School Teachers.* Dublin: Hodges, Foster, 1876. [97 pages; N.B. Google book. Not useful.]

Water, Mark. *Understanding the Resurrection of Jesus Made Easy*. Ropley: John Hunt, 2004. [64 pages]

Waterman, Mark M. W. *The Empty Tomb Tradition of Mark: Text, History, and Theological Struggles*. Los Angeles, CA: Agathos Press, 2006. [255 pages; N.B. This book is a good reading.]

Watson, John. *Children of the Resurrection*. New York: Dodd, Mead, 1912. [190 pages; N.B. Google book; N.B. Not useful.]

Watson, Nigel, ed. *The Heart of the Matter Reflections on the Resurrection Faith*. Melbourne: Joint Board of Christian Education, 1980. [80 pages; N.B. Eleven essays.]

Weatherhead, Leslie D. *The Manner of the Resurrection in the Light of Modern Science and Physical Research*. New York: Abingdon, 1959. [92 pages; N.B. Weatherhead provides a general overview.]

———. *The Resurrection and the Life*. New York: Abingdon-Cokesbury, 1953. [60 pages; N.B. Not useful.]

———. *The Resurrection of Christ in the Light of Modern Science and Physical Research*. London: Hodder & Stoughton, 1959. [92 pages.]

Weaver, Jonathan. *Discourses on the Resurrection*. Dayton, OH: United Brethren Publishing House, 1871. [157 pages. See. 37–55; N.B. Not useful.]

Webb, Guilford Polly. *Jesus on Trial To Day: An Examination into the Evidence of the Death, the Resurrection and the Ascension of Jesus of Nazareth . . .* Dallas: Texas Presbyterian Print, 1914. [85 pages; N.B. Google book. This work is a general overview in the form of an apologetic.]

Wedderburn, A. J. M. *Beyond Resurrection*. Peabody, MA: Hendrickson, 1999. [320 pages; N.B. This book is a recommended read.]

Wenham, John William. *Easter Enigma*. 2nd ed. Grand Rapids: Baker, 1993. [168 pages. This book is a popular apologetic. Its weaknesses are the numerous assumptions that it attempts to rationalize.]

Weren, Wim, H. Van De Sandt, and Joseph Verheyden, eds. *Life Beyond the Death in Matthew's Gospel: Religious Metaphor or Bodily Reality?* Leuven: Peeters, 2011. [284 pages; N.B. This book consists of twelve essays.]

West, Gilbert. *A Defence of the Christian Revelation on Two Very Important Points: As Contained in One Treatise Entituled, Observations on the History and Evidences of the Resurrection of Jesus Christ*. London: Printed by Voluntary Subscription, 1748. [246 pages; N.B. Google book. This work is a classic, dated source.]

———. *Observations on the History and Evidences of the Resurrection of Jesus Christ*. London: Printed for R. Dodsley, 1749. [455 pages; N.B. Google book. This work is a classic, dated source.]

West, J. R. *Parish Sermons on the Ascension of Our Lord*. London: Masters, 1871. [190 pages; N.B. Google book. This work consists of twenty-one sermons.]

Westcott, Brooke Foss. *The Gospel of the Resurrection: Thoughts on Its Relation to Reason and History*. London: Macmillan, 1891. [210 pages; N.B. Google book. This classic, dated and often referenced book is a must read.]

Whatmore, Leonard E. *The Resurrection Under Attack: (AD 33–1978)*. n.p., 1979. [71 pages]

White, Ellen Gould Harmon. *The Great Controversy Between Christ and Satan: The Death, Resurrection and Ascension of Our Lord Jesus Christ*. Battle Creek, MI: Steam Press of the Seventh-day Adventist Pub. Association, 1878. [392 pages; N.B. Archive.org; N.B. White provides a general overview.]

———. *Message from Calvary: The Day God Died for You.* Mountain View, CA: Pacific Press Publication Association, 1981. [64 pages; N.B. Originally published as Chapters 78–81 of the author's *The Desire of the Ages*. She founded the Seventh-day Adventist Church.]

———. *Redemption: or the Resurrection of Christ and His Ascension.* Battle Creek, MI: Steam Press of the Seventh-day Adventist Pub. Association, 1877. [80 pages; N.B. Archive.org; N.B. General overview.]

Whiton, James Morris. *The Gospel of the Resurrection.* 3rd ed. Boston: Houghton, Mifflin, 1881. [284 pages; N.B. Google book. This work does not interact with the narratives; it is more theological.]

Wiebe, Phillip H. *Visions of Jesus: Direct Encounters from the New Testament to Today.* New York: Oxford University Press, 1997. [279 pages; N.B. This source is an interesting book to examine.]

Wiersbe, Warren W., comp. *Classic Sermons on the Resurrection of Christ.* Peabody, MA: Hendrickson, 1991. [155 pages; N.B. This work is a collection of twelve sermons.]

Wilckens, Ulrich. *Resurrection: Biblical Testimony to the Resurrection: An Historical Examination and Explanation.* Translated by A. M. Stewart. Atlanta: John Knox, 1978. [134 pages; N.B. This book is a recommended read.]

Williams, Isaac. *The Gospel Narrative of Our Lord's Resurrection, Harmonized.* 2nd ed. London: Rivington, 1855. [430 pages; N.B. Archive.org and Google book; N.B. This is a classic, dated source that should be examined.]

———. *Our Lord's Resurrection: Devotional Commentary on the Gospel Narrative.* London: Longmans, Green, 1904. [210 pages; N.B. Google book. This is a classic, dated source that should be examined.]

Williams, N. P. *The First Easter Morning A Suggested Harmony of the Gospel.* London: SPCK, 1920. [91 pages; N.B. An interesting attempted harmonization.]

Williams, Rowan. *Resurrection: Interpreting the Easter Gospel.* London: Darton, Longman & Todd, 1982. [129 pages; N.B. This work does not interact with the resurrection narratives.]

Wilson, William. *A Discourse of the Resurrection Showing the Import and Certainty of It.* London: Printed by J.H. for William Rogers, 1694. [236 pages; N.B. Early English books, 1641–1700—1244:20]

Wingeier, Douglas E. *Jesus Christ: Resurrection.* Nashville: Graded Press, 1985. [64 pages; N.B. Not useful.]

Wise, Robert L. *The Son Rises: Resurrecting the Resurrection.* Ventura, CA: Regal, 2008. [224 pages; N.B. Not useful because it focuses on theology.]

Witcher, W. C. *Legal Proof: Being an Answer to Thomas H. Huxley and Other Sceptics Demands for Legal Proof of the Resurrection of Christ from the Dead, and Containing Pilate's Official Verification of the Same . . .* Fort Worth, TX: Christian Forum, 1937. [123 pages.]

Wolfe, Charles E. *The Post Resurrection Appearances: A Commentary.* Honolulu, HI: Pulpit Resource, 1988. [78 pages; N.B. This work is located in only one library.]

Wolfe, Rolland. *How the Easter Story Grew from Gospel to Gospel.* Lewiston, NY: Mellen, 1989. [244 pages; N.B. This logical book is a must read.]

Wood, William. *The Antichrist Identified, or The Resurrection of Jesus Christ from the Dead: Was It Fact, Fancy, Fable or Fiction, Which?* Lexington, KY: Quo Warranto, 1918. [99 pages.]

Woodrow, Ralph. *Three Days and Three Nights: Reconsidered in Light of Scripture: Woodrow versus Woodrow.* Riverside, CA: R. Woodrow Evangelistic Association, 1993. [54 pages; N.B. Woodrow's text is only located in the Library of Congress.]

Wright, N. T. *The Challenge of Easter.* Downers Grove, IL: InterVarsity, 2009. [64 pages [N.B. Not useful.]

———. *The Resurrection of the Son of God.* Minneapolis: Fortress, 2003. [817 pages; N.B. Perhaps one of the most highly praised books by Christian apologists and theologians.]

Wuellner, Bernard J. *Graces of the Risen Christ.* Milwaukee: Bruce, 1960. [138 pages; N.B. Useless.]

Yarnold, Greville Dennis. *Risen Indeed: Studies in the Lord's Resurrection.* New York: Oxford University Press, 1959. [134 pages; N.B. This source provides a general overview.]

Yarrington, W. H. H. *The Resurrection of Jesus Christ and Kindred Subjects: A Book for Easter.* Sydney, Australia, 191-? [84 pages]

Zwemer, Samuel Marinus. *The Glory of the Empty Tomb.* New York: Revell, 1947. [170 pages; N.B. This book was written in the form of an apologetic.]

Zwiep, Arie W. *The Ascension of the Messiah in Lukan Christology.* Leiden: Brill, 1997. [291 pages; N.B. Zweip has penned a detailed work on Jesus's ascension that is a must read.]

Chapter 2

Entire Books Dealing with Jesus's Resurrection: Con

Allen, Don [pseud. for Hiram L. True]. *The Resurrection of Jesus: An Agnostic's View*. New York: Truth Seeker, 1893. [164 pages; Hiram L. True, 1845–1912, was the real author; N.B. Google book. This interesting, dated book suggests that Pilate ordered Jesus's body to be secretly buried elsewhere.]

Alter, Michael J. *The Resurrection: A Critical Inquiry*. US: Xlibris, 2015. [912 pages. N.B. This book is the most extensive work that critically analyzes Jesus's resurrection. This text discusses 120 contradictions and 217 speculations.]

Annet, Peter. *The Resurrection Defenders Stript of All Defence*. London: Printed for the Author, 1745. [95 pages; N.B. Archive.org]

———. *The Resurrection of Jesus Considered in Answer to the Trial of the Witnesses*. London: Print for the Author, 1744. [98 pages; N.B. Google book. ["By a Moral Philosopher."]

———. *The Resurrection of Jesus Demonstrated to Have No Proof: In Answer to a Late Pamphlet Call'd, The Resurrection of Jesus Cleared & C*. London: Printed for J. Jackman, 1744. [52 pages; Annet responds to Charles Moss.]

———. *The Resurrection Reconsidered: Being an Answer to the Clearer and Others: By Way of Dialogue between the Considerer and His Friend*. London: Printed for the Author and Sold by M. Cooper in Paternoster Row, and the Booksellers of London and Westminster, 1744. [84 pages; N.B. Google book]

———. *Supernaturals Examined: In Four Dissertations on Three Treatises: Viz. 1. On the Observations of the History and Evidence of the Resurrection of Christ . . . 2. and 3. On Miracles and Prophecies, Showing the Impossibility of the One, and the Falsity of the Other . . . 4. On the Defence of the Peculiar Institutions and Doctrines of Christianity*. London: Printed for F. Page, 1750. [100 pages; N.B. Archives.org]

Aus, Roger David. *The Death, Burial, and Resurrection of Jesus, and the Death, Burial, and Translation of Moses in Judaic Tradition*. Lanham, MD: University Press of America, 2008. [318 pages; N.B. This work employs Jewish sources i.e., the midrash and haggadah to better understand the narratives from a different perspective.]

Bell, William S. *The Resurrection of Jesus*. New York: Truth Seeker, 1910? [49 pages]

Berna, Kurt (pseud.). *Inquest on Jesus Christ*. Translated by Wilkli Frischauer. London: Frewin, 1967. [208 pages]

———. *A World Discovery: Christ Did Not Perish on the Cross: Christ's Body Buried Alive.* Zurich: International Foundation for the Holy Shroud; Hicksville, NY: Distributed by Exposition Press, 1975. [253 pages; N.B. Kurt Berna a.k.a. John Reban are pseudonyms for Hans Naber. He claims that Jesus did not die on the cross.]

Clarke, John. *A Critical Review of the Life, Character, Miracles, and Resurrection of Jesus Christ.* 2nd ed. Leeds: Printed by Joshua Hobson, 1839. [450 pages; N.B. Google book. This dated book critically analyzes aspects of Jesus's life and it should be read.]

Conner, Robert. *Apparitions of Jesus: The Resurrection as Ghost Story.* Valley, WA: Tellectual Press, 2018. [189 pages; N.B. Conner's book is an easy and interesting read.]

Covington, Nicholas. *Extraordinary Claims, Extraordinary Evidence, and the Resurrection of Jesus.* CreateSpace, 2012. [62 pages]

Docker, Ernest Brougham. *If Jesus Did Not Die on the Cross: A Study in Evidence.* London: Robert Scott Roxburghe House, 1920. [78 pages; N.B. Archive.org. This short work is an interesting, dated read.]

Furneaux, Rupert. *The Empty Tomb: The World's Greatest Mystery.* London: Panther, 1963. [191 pages; N.B. This book is an outstanding work that is an absolute must read. It presents a frank and honest investigation of Jesus's resurrection.]

Gorham, Charles T. *The First Easter Dawn: An Inquiry into the Evidence for the Resurrection of Jesus.* London: Watts, 1908. [320 pages; N.B. Google book. This is one of the best dated sources that challenges the resurrection.]

Hallquist, Chris. *UfOs, Ghosts, and a Rising God: Debunking the Resurrection of Jesus.* Reasonable Press, 2009. [216 pages; N.B. Available free online. Hallquist's book should be examined. It objectively examines various issues related to the resurrection.]

Hanhart, Karel. *The Open Tomb: A New Approach: Mark's Passover Haggadah.* Collegeville, MN: Liturgical Press, 1995. [865 pages. N.B. This is an interesting book that must be examined.]

Hegemann, Werner. *Christ Rescued.* Translated from the German by Gerald Griffin. London: Skeffington, 1933. [223 pages]

Kent, Jack A. *The Psychological Origins of the Resurrection Myth.* London: Open Gate, 1999. [132 pages; N.B. The author advocates that the disciples experienced grief-related hallucinations and the apostle Paul suffered a conversion disorder.]

Kersten, Holger, and Elmar Gruber. *The Jesus Conspiracy: The Turin Shroud and the Truth about the Resurrection.* Shaftesbury, Dorset: Element, 1994. [373 pages. N.B. The authors espouse the idea that Jesus survived the crucifixion and moved to India. See the Wikipedia entry on the author for extra details.]

Komarnitsky, Kris D. *Doubting Jesus' Resurrection: What Happened in the Black Box?* 2nd ed. Drapper, UT: Stone Arrow, 2014. [236 pages; N.B. Komarnitsky has penned a good and interesting book to examine.]

Lapide, Pinchas. *The Resurrection of Jesus: A Jewish Perspective.* Minneapolis: Augsburg, 1983. [160 pages; N.B. Lapide was the first Jewish rabbi to write an entire book on this topic.]

Lüdemann, Gerd. *The Resurrection of Christ: A Historical Inquiry.* Amherst, NY: Prometheus, 2004. [248 pages. N.B. This book is an important text to read by a New Testament scholar.]

———. *The Resurrection of Jesus: History, Experience, Theology.* Translated by John Bowen. Minneapolis: Fortress, 1994. [261 pages]

———. *What Really Happened to Jesus: A Historical Approach to the Resurrection*. Edited by Alf Özen. Translated by John Bowen. Louisville: Westminster John Knox, 1995. [147 pages]

McCabe, Joseph. *The Myth of the* Resurrection. Little Blue Book No. 1104. Girard, KS: Haldeman-Julius, 1925. [63 pages; N.B. McCabe was a former monk who turned apostate.]

Mirsch, David. *The Open Tomb: Why and How Jesus Faked His Death and Resurrection*. Banger, US: Booklocker, 2011. [500 pages.]

Nickell, Joe. *Inquest on the Shroud of Turin*. Buffalo, NY: Prometheus, 1983. [178 pages; N.B. This book totally refutes the use of the Shroud of Turin to serve as a proof of the resurrection.]

Price, Robert M. *Jesus is Dead*. Cranford, NJ: American Atheist Press, 2007. [279 pages; N.B. This book critically analyzes and refutes the arguments of many leading apologists.]

———. *Night of the Living Saviour*. Cranford: New Jersey, American Atheist Press, 2011. [239 pages; N.B. This book critically debunks the belief that Jesus actually lived.]

Price, Robert M., and Jeffery Jay Lowder, eds. *The Empty Tomb: Jesus Beyond the Grave*. Amherst, NY: Prometheus, 2005. [545 pages; N.B. This substantial work consists of fifteen essays. It should be in everyone's library. Significantly, apologists have written numerous responses to this text. They too, should be examined.]

Prokofieff, Sergei O. *The Mystery of the Resurrection in the Light of Anthroposophy*. Forrest Row: Temple Lodge, 2010. [214 pages; N.B. This text does not specifically analyze the resurrection narratives. The author was influenced by the writings of Rudolf Steiner.]

Rhys, Jocelyn. *Shaken Creeds: The Resurrection* Doctrines. London: Watts, 1924. [268 pages; N.B. Part 1 The Resurrection Story, Chapter 1 The Evidence From The New Testament, See. 3–47; Chapter 4 The Ascension, See. 102–18; Chapter 6 Modern Scepticism, See. 144–69]

Saladin. *Did Jesus Christ Rise from the Dead?* London: W. Stewart, 1887. [64 pages; N.B. Saladin is a pseudonym for William Stewart Ross.]

Sandoval, Chris. *Can Christians Prove the Resurrection? A Reply to the Apologists*. Victoria, BC: Trafford On Demand, 2010. [364 pages; N.B. "This book is a skeptic's critique of the most popular and persuasive Christian arguments for the Resurrection."]

Schonfield, Hugh J. *After the Cross*. San Diego: A.S. Barnes, 1981. [117 pages]

———. *The Passover Plot*. New York: Bantam, 1966. [N.B. According to Schonfield, Jesus's plans went unexpectedly wrong e.g., he was to be on the cross for only a few hours and then taken down alive to be nursed back to health.]

Scott, Bernard Brandon, ed. *The Resurrection of Jesus: A Source Book*. Salem, OR: Polebridge, 2009. [N.B. This work consists of seven articles and it should be examined.]

———. *The Trouble With the Resurrection From Paul to the Fourth Gospel*. Salem, OR: Polebridge, 2010. [N.B. This is a well-written fifteen chapter work that critically analyzes numerous troubles with Jesus's resurrection.]

Sheehan, Thomas. *The First Coming: How the Kingdom of God Became Christianity*. New York: Random House, 1986. [287 pages; 2000 electronic edition available online; N.B. This work provides a rational explanation for the resurrection narratives.]

Sigal, Gerald. *The Resurrection Fantasy: Reinventing Jesus*. US: Xlibris, 2012. [289 pages; N.B. This is a hard-hitting work by a significant contributor of JewsforJudaism and it is a must read.]

Spong, John Shelby. *The Easter Moment*. New York: Seabury Press, 1980. [240 pages; N.B. The author is convinced the Jesus's resurrection was real, however he challenges a literal reading of the text.]

———. *Resurrection: Myth or Reality? A Bishop's Search for the Origins of Christianity*. San Francisco, CA: HarperSanFrancisco, 1994. [320 pages; N.B. Authored by an Episcopalian Bishop, he questions the historical validity of the literal narrative concerning the resurrection.]

Stecher, Richard C., and Craig L. Blomberg. *Resurrection: Faith or Fact? A Scholars' Debate Between a Skeptic and a Christian*. Durham, North Carolina: Pitchstone Publishing, 2019. [This work is perhaps, one of the finest debates about Jesus's resurrection. It is an absolute must reading!]

Thiering, Barbara. *Jesus & the Riddle of the Dead Sea Scrolls: Unlocking the Secrets of His Life Story*. San Francisco: HarperSanFrancisco, 1992. [Chapters 26–35, See. 121–60; The author postulates that Jesus did not die on the cross.]

Twyman, Tracy R. *The Judas Goat/The Substitution Theory of the Crucifixion*. Amazon Digit Services LLC, 2011. [47 pages and 745 KB; N.B. This source was originally published by Dagobert Revenge Magazine (2003).]

Unitheist. *The Theological Bee-hive; or, Book of Dogmas, Comprising an Inquiry into the Reality of the Death and the Nature of the Resurrection of Jesus Christ, Together with a Concise View of the Several Dogmas of Inspiration, Faith, Mystery . . .* Boston: n.p., 1847. [124 pages; Resurrection, See. 64–71; Appearances, See. 71–73; Ascension, See. 74–78; N.B. Archive.org; This dated book critically investigates the resurrection and it is a must read.]

Wolfe, Rolland. *How the Easter Story Grew from Gospel to Gospel*. Lewiston, NY: Mellen, 1989. [244 pages; N.B. This logical and well thought out work is a must read.]

CHAPTER 3

Partial Books Dealing with Jesus's Resurrection: Con—Agnostics, Atheists, Detractors, Humanists, Liberal Christians, Rationalists, Skeptics, Gnostic Texts, and Controversial Literature

Acharya, S. [pseud.]. *Suns of God: Krishna, Buddha and Christ Unveiled*. Kempton, IL: Adventures Unlimited, 2004. [Chapter 12 The Historical Jesus, See. 372–445; especially 439–40. This book challenges the existence of a historical Jesus. N.B. Archive.org]

Aletheia, M. D. [pseud.]. *A Rationalist Catechism of Subjects Concerning Man, His Gods and Superstitions*. London: Watts, 1897. [Jesus, his crucifixion, ascension, etc.—Heaven, See. 7–9; N.B. Google book]

———. *The Rationalist's Manual: In Two Parts*. London: Watts, 1897. [The Resurrection and Ascension, See. 46–47; N.B. Google book]

Allen, Ethan. *Reason, The Only Oracle of Man: or, A Compendious System of Natural Religion*. New York: G.W. & A.J. Matsell, 1836. [Chapter 6 Remarks on the Testimony Concerning Christ's Resurrection, His Appearance After It, and His Ascension, See. 57–66; also See. 55–56; N.B. Google book]

Annet, Peter. *A Collection of the Tracts of a Certain Free Enquirer*. London: Routledge, 1995. [Supernaturals Examined In Four Dissertations on Three Treatises. Dissertation 1. On the Observations of History and Evidence of the Resurrection of Jesus Christ by Gilbert West, Esq. See. 1–29; The Resurrection of Jesus Considered; In Answer to The Tryal of the Witnesses, See. 265–326; The Resurrection Reconsidered. Being An Answer to the Clearer and others, See. 327–78; The Sequel of the Resurrection of Jesus Considered In Answer to Sequel of the Trial of the Witnesses, See. 379–401; The Resurrection Defenders Stript of all Defence, See. 403–60]

———. *Supernaturals Examined In Four Dissertations on Three Treatises*. London: Printed for F. Page, 1747. [Dissertation 1. On the Observations of History and Evidence of the Resurrection of Jesus Christ by Gilbert West, Esq. See. 1–29; N.B. Archive.org]

Atwill, Joseph. *Caesar's Messiah: The Roman Conspiracy to invent Jesus: Flavian Signature*. Charleston, SC: CreateSpace, 2011. [The author of this book believes that Jesus was a fictional character and the invention of a Roman emperor.]

Avalos, Hector. *The End of Biblical Studies.* Amherst, NY: Prometheus, 2007. [Chapter 4 The Unhistorical Jesus, Resurrecting the Resurrection, See. 185–90; Marian Apparitions and the Resurrection, See. 191–94]

Baigent, Michael. *The Jesus Papers: Exposing the Greatest Cover-up in History.* San Francisco: HarperSan Francisco, 2006. [Chapter 7 Surviving the Crucifixion, See. 115–32; Chapter 8 Jesus in Egypt, See. 133–58]

Balfour, Frederic H. *The Higher Agnosticism.* London: Greening, 1907. [See. 108; N.B. Google book. Balfour states that the resurrection and other events of Jesus's life are "explained by the astronomical and solar myths which lie at the root of so many of the mystical religions."]

Ballou, Robert O. *The Other Jesus: A Narrative Based On Apocryphal Stories Not Included in the Bible.* New York: Doubleday, 1972. [Chapter 6 The Resurrection, See. 91–119; Chapter 7 The Later Appearances of Jesus, See. 121–36]

Barker, Dan. *Godless: How an Evangelical Preacher Became One of America's Leading Atheists.* Berkeley, CA: Ulysses Press, 2008. [Chapter 16 Did Jesus Really Rise From the Dead?, See. 277–304; N.B. Barker marshals numerous rationales to refute Jesus's resurrection.]

Baring-Gould, S. *The Lost and Hostile Gospels: An Essay on the Toldedoth Jeschu, and the Petrine and Pauline Gospels of the First Three Centuries of Which Fragments Remain.* London: Williams & Norgate, 1874 [Rev. Baring-Gould was not an atheist or detractor. His work includes a translation *Toledothe Jeschu* that challenges the gospel narratives; N.B. Google book]

Bell, William S. *A Handbook of Freethought: Containing in Condensed and Systematized Form a Vast Amount of Evidence Against the Superstitious Doctrines of Christianity, Selected from the Writings of the following Named Distinguished Writers and Others.* San Francisco: W. S. Bell, 1890. [Jesus Christ. The Resurrection of Jesus, See. 91–118; N.B. Archive.org and Gutenberg.org]

Benjamin, Joshua M. *The Mystery of Israel's Ten Lost Tribes and the Legend of Jesus in India.* New Delhi: Mosaic, 2001. [Chapter 4 Life of Jesus and the Mystery of His Crucifixion, See. 50–49; Chapter 5 Jesus and Thomas Go to India, See. 60–64; etc.]

Bennett, D. M. *The Gods and Religions of Ancient and Modern Times.* New York: Liberal & Scientific Publishing House, 1881. [See. 720–21, 834–35; N.B. Google book]

———. *An Open Letter to Jesus Christ.* New York: Truth Seeker, n.d. [See. 14–15; N.B. HathiTrust]

———. *The World's Sages, Thinkers and Reformers: Being Biographical Sketches of Leading Philosophers, Teachers, Skeptics, Innovators, Founders of New Schools of Thought, Eminent Scientists, etc.* 2nd ed. New York: Truth Seekers, 1876. [See. 236; N.B. Google book]

Bentham, Jeremy. *Not Paul, But Jesus.* London: Printed for John Hunt, 1823. [Chapter 12 Section 1 Resurrection-Witnesses Multiplied, See. 277–81; N.B. Archive.org. The title page states that the work was by Gamaliel Smith, a pseudonym.]

Besant, Annie. *Esoteric Christianity; or, The Lesser Mysteries.* 2nd ed. London: Theosophical Publishing House, 1905. [Chapter 8 Resurrection and Ascension, See. 231–52; N.B. Google book]

———. *The Freethinker's Text-Book: Part 2. Christianity: Its Evidences. Its Origin. Its Morality. Its History.* London: R. Forder, 1893. [See. 220, 228, 295, 339; N.B. Google book]

———. *The Myth of the Resurrection*. London: Freethought, 1886. [16 pages; N.B. Lecture 9. JSTOR archives]

Blackford, Russell, and Udo Schüklenk. *50 Great Myths About Atheism*. Malden, MA: Wiley Blackwell, 2013. [Myth 47 Atheists Can't Explain the Resurrection, See. 171–75]

Blatchford, Robert. *God and My Neighbour*. London: Clarion, 1903. [The Resurrection, See. 85–89; The Gospel Witnesses, See. 90–100; N.B. Archive.org]

Bradlaugh, Charles. *Humanity's Gain From Unbelief: And Other Selections From The Works Of Charles Bradlaugh*. London: Watts, 1929. [Who Was Jesus Christ and What Did He Teach?, See. 71–73; N.B. Google book]

Bradlaugh, Charles, and Robert Roberts. *Is the Bible Divine? A Six Nights' Discussion Between Mr. Charles Bradlaugh and Mr. Robert Roberts*. London: F. Pitman, 1876. [See. 25–26, 28, 35–47, 63, 72, 80, 82, 96–98, 135, 141–42; N.B. Google book]

Browne, Sylvia. *The Mystical Life of Jesus: An Uncommon Perspective on the Life of Christ*. New York: Dutton, 2006. [Chapter 7 The Resurrection—A Plan for Christ's Survival, See. 165–94; N.B. Browne claims, with the help of her spiritual guide, to deliver the truth about Jesus.]

Burr, William Henry. *Revelations of Antichrist: Concerning Christ and Christianity*. Boston: D. M. Bennett (Truth Seeker), 1879. [Chapter 8 The Resurrection of Christ, See. 20–26; N.B. Archive.org.]

———. *Self-Contradictions of the Bible*. NY: Prometheus, 1987. [Theological Doctrines #79–91, See. 62–67; First published 1860 by A. J. Davis, New York]

Cadoux, Cecil John. *The Case for Evangelical Modernism: A Study of the Relation Between Christian Faith and Traditional Theology*. Chicago: Clark, 1939. [See. 154–59]

Campbell, Douglas. *New Religious Thoughts*. 2nd ed. London: William & Norgate, 1865 [Chapter 19 The Resurrection, See. 109–20; N.B. Google book. Campbell, in almost a sarcastic manner points out numerous contradictions in the gospel narratives.]

Campbell, Steuart. *The Rise and Fall of Jesus: The Ultimate Explanation for the Origin of Christianity*. Edinburgh: Explicit, 1996. [Chapter 9 Aftermath, See. 154–73]

Campbell, William A. *The Crucifixion and Resurrection of Jesus*. London: Pioneer Press, 1933. [The Resurrection 2, See. 63–99; Issued for the Secular Society Limited. *Idem. Did the Jews Kill Jesus? And the Myth of the Resurrection* with different pagination.]

———. *Did the Jews Kill Jesus? And the Myth of the Resurrection*. New York: Peter Eckler, 1927. [112 pages; N.B. Only pages 65–111 deal with the resurrection myth.]

Cannon, Delores. *Jesus and the Essenes*. Huntsville, AR: Ozark Mountain, 2000. [Chapter 25 The Crucifixion and Resurrection, See. 249–64; Chapter 26 The Purpose of the Crucifixion and Resurrection, See. 265–69; N.B. The text declares "Eyewitness accounts of the missing years of Jesus, the portions that have been removed from the Bible, and the community of the Essenes at Qumran. The information was gained through regressive hypnosis, conducted by Delores Cannon."]

Carotta, Francesco. *Jesus Was Caesar: On the Julian Origin of Christianity An Investigative Report*. Translated by Tommie Hendriks, Joseph Horvath, and Manfred Junghardt. The Netherlands: Aspekt, 2005. [Jesus' Entombment and Resurrection, See. 313–16; Appearances of the Resurrected One—Ascension, See. 317–23]

Carrier, Richard. *Not The Impossible Faith: Why Christianity Didn't Need A Miracle To Succeed*. United States: Lulu.com, 2009. [Chapter 8 Who Would Want to be Persecuted?, See. 219–45; N.B. An interesting chapter to read.]

Category I—Books Dealing with Jesus's Resurrection

———. *On the Historicity of Jesus: Why We Might Have Reason for Doubt*. Sheffield: Sheffield Phoenix, 2014. [Multiple entries; See. What Happened to the Body?, See. 368–71; The Mysterious Vanishing Acts, See. 371–75]

Cassels, Walter R. *A Reply to Dr Lightfoot's Essays*. London: Longmans, Green, 1889. [See. 165–67; N.B. Google book]

———. *Supernatural Religion: An Inquiry Into the Reality of Divine Revelations*, Popular edition, carefully revised. London: Watts, 1902. [Part 6 The Resurrection and Ascension, See. 801–901; N.B. Google book and Archive.org. This book is an important, dated work frequently discussed in the literature.]

Cavin, Robert Greg, and Carlos A. Colombetti. Casper, WY: RandomNPC LLC, 2008. *The Doubting Thomas Guide to Logic and Religion*, 2008. [Chapter 9 The Argument for the Revivification of Jesus, See. 56–75. N.B. This is a good read.]

Celsus [See. Origen].

Chubb, Thomas. *A Collection of Tracts on Various Subjects*. London: T. Cox, 1730. [See. 80, 133, 161, 186; N.B. Google book]

———. *Four Tracts*. London: T. Cox, 1732. [Tract 2. Some Short Remarks on Britannicus's Letters, See. 51–82; N.B. Google book]

Clarke, James Freeman. *Orthodoxy: Its Truth and Errors*. Boston: American Unitarian Association, 1890. [Chapter 4 Truths and Errors as Regards Miracles, §8. Miracle of the Resurrection. Sceptical Objections, See. 80–85; N.B. Google book. The author is a Unitarian.]

Clarke, John. *A Critical Review of the Life, Character, Miracles, and Resurrection of Jesus Christ*. 2nd ed. Leeds: Printed by Joshua Hobson, 1839. [450 pages; N.B. Google book; See. Letters 15 and 16. The author presents a must read, critical analysis of Jesus's resurrection and ascension]

Collins, Anthony. *A Discourse of the Grounds and Reasons of the Christian Religion: In Answer to Mr. Green's Letters, &c. with a Postscript*. London: 1737. [Preface. See. i–xii; N.B. Google book]

Columbine, William Brailsford. *Mr. Balfour's Apologetics Critically Examined*. Watts: London, 1902 [Jesus, resurrection of, See. 134–37; N.B. Google book and HathiTrust]

Cooper, Robert. *The Bible and its Evidences*. London: E. Truelove, 1858. [The Resurrection, See. 258–260; The Ascension, See. 260–61; N.B. Google book]

———. *Classified Biblical Extracts, or The Holy Scriptures Analyzed; Showing Its Contradictions, Absurdities and Immoralities*. Cincinnati: J. Cooper, 1860. [See. #254–257, See. 57–58; #431–438, See. 80–81; N.B. Archive.org]

Craig, William Lane, and Walter Sinnott-Armstrong. *God? A Debate Between a Christian and an Atheist*. New York: Oxford University Press, 2004. [Chapter 2 There Is No Good Reason to Believe in God (Walter Sinnott-Armstrong), See. 31–52; N.B. Refuted in Chapter 3 Reason Enough by William Lane Craig, See. 53–78]

Cresswell, Peter. *Censored Messiah: The Truth about Jesus Christ*. Winchester, UK: O Books, 2005. [See. 144, 154–56,

Crooker, Joseph Henry. *Different New Testament Views of Jesus*. Boston: American Unitarian Association, 1891. [See. 42–43; N.B. Archive.org, Google book, and HathiTrust]

Crossan, John Dominic. *The Birth of Christianity*. New York: HarperSanFrancisco, 1998. [Chapter 25 The Other Passion-Resurrection Story, See. 481–525; N.B. This work is a definite read.]

———. *The Historical Jesus the Life of a Mediterranean Jewish Peasant.* San Francisco: HarperSanFrancisco, 1991. [Chapter 14 Death and Burial, See. 391–94; Chapter 15 Resurrection and Authority, See. 395–426; N.B. Another important work by Crossan to examine.]

Cruz, Arthur. *Death Conspiracy Theories.* Lulu.com, 2017. [The Stolen Body Hypothesis, See. 248–51; The Substitution Hypothesis, See. 267]

Cutner, Herbert. *Jesus: God, Man Or Myth? An Examination of the Evidence.* New York: Truth Seeker, 1950. [Resurrection, See. 18, 21–24, 142, 218, 269]

Daleiden, Joseph L. *The Final Superstition: A Critical Evaluation of the Judeo-Christian Legacy.* Amherst: Prometheus, 1994. [The Resurrection, See. 118–24]

Daniels, Kenneth W. *Why I Believed: Reflections of a Former Missionary.* Duncanville, TX: Author, 2009. [Chapter 11 The Resurrection of Jesus, See. 225–36. N.B. The title speaks for itself. Available online at The Secular Web.]

Dawes, Gregory W. *The Historical Jesus Quest: Landmarks In The Search For The Jesus Of History.* Louisville: Westminster John Knox, 2000. [Chapter 2 History and Myth. David Friedrich Strauss (1808–74) From *The Life of Jesus Critically Examined*, See. 54–111; N.B. Contains extracts from *Fragments*.]

Deedat, Ahmed. *Crucifixion or Crucifiction: Resurrection or Resuscitation; The God that Never Was.* 2nd ed. [Doha, Qatar: Dar El-Ulum Foundation; Doha, Qatar: Distributed by Ministry of Awqaf and Islamic affairs] 1993. [88 pages. This well-known Muslim theologian refutes Jesus's crucifixion. N.B. His material is available online.]

Doane, T. W. *Bible Myths And Their Parallels In Other Religions Being a Comparison of the Old and New Testament Myths and Miracles with Those of Heathen Nations of Antiquity Considering Also Their Origin and Meaning.* 4th ed. New York: Truth Seeker, 1882. [Chapter 23 The Resurrection and Ascension of Christ Jesus, 215–32; N.B. Archive.org, Google book, and Gutenberg.org]

Docker, Ernest Brougham. *If Jesus Did Not Die on the Cross: A Study in Evidence.* London: Robert Scott Roxburghe House, 1920. [78 pages; N.B. Archive.org]

Doherty, Earl. *Jesus: Neither God Nor Man: The Case for a Mythical Jesus.* Ottawa: Age of Reason, 2009. [Resurrection of Jesus, See. 72, 75–77, 79, 81, 86, 134–37, 189, n.62; N.B. Doherty postulates that Jesus never existed.]

Drake, Durant. *Problems of Religion: An Introductory Survey.* Boston: Houghton Mifflin, 1916. [See. 72, 82 84, 287, 288, 291; N.B. Google book]

Draper, George Otis. *Searching For Truth.* New York: Peter Eckler, 1902. [Chapter 5 Was Christ Divine?, See. 126–27; N.B. Google book]

Drews, Arthur. *The Christ Myth.* 3rd ed. Translated by C. Delisle Burns. London: T. Fischer Unwin, 1910. [N.B. This famous, classic work advocates the Christ Myth; N.B. Archive.org, Gutenberg.org, and HathiTrust. If Jesus did not exist, he could not have been a resurrection.]

Drohan, Francis Burke. *Jesus Who? (The Greatest Mystery Never Told).* New York: Philosophical Library, 1985. [Chapter 16 He Is Risen, See. 191–200]

Duke, Doyle E. *The Amazing Deception: A Critical Analysis of Christianity.* 2nd ed. US: Doyle E. Duke, 2009. [Chapter 6 The Verdict and the Resurrection, See. 87–97]

Ehrman, Bart D. *How Jesus Became God: The Exaltation of a Jewish Preacher From Galilee.* New York: HarperOne, 2014. [Chapter 4 The Jesus of Jesus: What We Cannot Know, See. 129–69; Chapter 5 The Resurrection of Jesus: What We Can Know, See. 171–210; N.B. This work is a must reading by a leading scholar.]

———. *Jesus, Apocalyptic Prophet of the New Millennium*. Oxford: Oxford University Press, 1999. [Chapter 12 The Last Days of Jesus, See. 224-25]

———. *Jesus, Interrupted: Revealing the Hidden Contradictions in the Bible (And Why We Don't Know About Them)*. New York: HarperCollins, 2010. [Chapter 2 A World of Contradictions. The Resurrection Narratives, See. 47-49; also See. 173-78]

———. *The New Testament: A Historical Introduction to the Early Christian Writings*. 2nd ed. New York: Oxford University Press, 2000. [See. 72-74, 133, 135, 183-84, 188, 253-55, 270-72, 294-97, 324-31]

———. *Peter, Paul, and Mary Magdalene: The Followers of Jesus in History and Legend*. Oxford: Oxford University Press, 2006. [Peter and the Resurrection, See. 49-57; Paul and the Resurrection of Jesus, See. 111-13; The Women at the Tomb, See. 227-39; N.B. This work is an interesting read.]

Ellegård, Alvar. *Jesus—One Hundred Years Before Christ: A Study in Creative Mythology*. Woodstock, NY: Overlook Press, 1999. [Paul's life and his revelations, See. 14-19; Resurrection, See. 76-78]

English, George Bethune. *The Grounds of Christianity Examined by Comparing the New Testament With The Old*. Printed for the Subscribers, 1839. [Chapter 16 Examination of the Evidence, External and Internal, in Favor of the Credibility of the Gospel History, See. 132-43; N.B. Archive.org, Google book, Gutenberg.org, and HathiTrust]

Evans, Elizabeth Edson. *The Christ Myth*. New York: Truth Seeker, 1900. [See. 69-74; N.B. Google book]

Fida, Ahtisham, et al. *Jesus Lived in Japan*. Srinagar, Kashmir, India: Dastgir Publications Trust, 1996. [134 pages; N.B. Fida postulates that Jesus survived the crucifixion.]

Fitzgerald, David. *Jesus: Mything in Action*. Vol. 1. US: Create Space, 2016. [Chapter 12 Jesus is Dead, See. 313-34]

Fodor, James. *Unreasonable Faith: How William Lane Craig Overstates the Case for Christianity*. US: Hypatia Press, 2018. [Chapter 5 The Christological Arguments, See. 231-334; N.B. This book presents a detailed rebuttal of William Lane Craig's historical argument for the resurrection of Jesus. An important text to examine!]

Frede, Victoria. *Doubt, Atheism, and the Nineteenth-Century Russian Intelligentsia*. Madison, WI: University of Wisconsin Press, 2011. [Resurrection of Christ at Easter, See. 130-31, 156, 160-61]

Funk, Robert W., and the Jesus Seminar. *The Acts of Jesus: The Search for the Authentic Deeds of Jesus*. San Francisco: HarperSanFrancisco, 1998. [Empty Tomb, Appearances & Ascension, See. 449-95. N.B. This work chronologically analyzes in detail the stories of the empty tomb, appearances of the risen Jesus, and the ascension. It must be examined.]

Gardner, James. *Jesus Who? Myth vs. Reality in the Search for the Historical Jesus*. Bangor, ME: Booklocker, 2006. [Was Jesus Resurrected?, See. 213-22]

Gardner, Laurence. *Bloodline of the Holy Grail: The Hidden Lineage of Jesus Revealed*. Shaftesbury: Element, 1997. [This book asserts that Jesus did not die on the cross and Mary Magdalene had Jesus's child.]

Graham, Lloyd. *Deceptions and Myths of the Bible*. New York: Bell, 1979. [The Resurrection, See. 356-62]

Graves, Kersey. *The World's Sixteen Crucified Saviors, or Christianity before Christ: Containing New, Startling, and Extraordinary Revelations in Religious History, Which Disclose the Oriental Origin of All the Doctrines, Precepts, and Miracles of the*

Christian New Testament . . . 2nd ed. New York: Freethought Press, 1875. [Chapter 19 Resurrection of the Saviors, See. 144–51; Chapter 20 Reappearance and Ascension of the Saviors, See. 152–55; N.B. Google book and Gutenberg.org. A dated and classic text.]

Graves, Robert, and Joshua Podro. *Jesus In Rome: A Historical Conjecture.* London: Cassell, 1957. [Chapter 1 The Crucifixion and Resurrection, See. 1–15; Chapter 5 The Tomb of Jesus, See. 68–87; N.B. This work speculates that Jesus survived his crucifixion.]

Guerber, H. A. *Legends of the Virgin and Christ with Special Reference to Literature and Art.* New York: Dodd, Mead And Company, 1901. [Chapter 10 Death, Burial, and Resurrection of Christ, See. 208–41; N.B. Archive.org]

Guild, E. E. *The Pro and Con of Supernatural Religion, or, an answer to the question—have we a supernaturally revealed, infallibly inspired, and miraculously attested religion in the world.* New York: D. M. Bennett, 1876. [See. 72–78; N.B. Archive.org]

Harpur, Tom. *For Christ's Sake.* Toronto: McClelland & Stewart, 1993. [The Resurrection of Jesus, See. 97–103]

Harris, Sam. *The End of Faith: Religion, Terror, and the Future of Reason.* New York: W. W. Norton, 2004. [See. 74–77, 87–88, 97]

Heinz-Werner, Kubitza. *The Jesus Delusion. How the Christians Created Their God: The Demystification of a World Religion Through Scientific Research.* US: Tectum Verlag, 2016. [The Legends of the Resurrection, See. 134–53]

Helms, Randel. *Gospel Fictions.* Amherst, NY: Prometheus, 1988. [Chapter 7 Resurrection Fictions, See. 129–54]

Hennell, Charles C. *An Inquiry Concerning the Origin of Christianity.* London: Smallfield, 1838. [See. 35–37; N.B. Google book]

Hernandez, David. *The Greatest Story Ever Forged: Curse of the Christ Myth.* Pittsburgh: Red Lead Press, 2009. [See. 6, 60–61, 76–77, 319–20]

Holbach, Paul Henri Thiry. *Christianity Unveiled: Being An Examination of the Principles and Effects of the Christian Religion.* New York: B.W. Johnson, 1895. [Chapter 3 Sketch of the History of the Christian Religion, See. 29; Chapter 6 Of the proofs of the Christian Religion, Miracles, Prophecies, and Martyrs, See. 52; Chapter 10 Of the Inspired Writings of the Christians, See. 80; N.B. Archive.org, Google book, and Gutenberg.org]

Hopkins, Keith. *A World Full of Gods: The Strange Triumph of Christianity.* New York: The Free Press, 2000. [Chapter 4 Jesus And His Twin Brothers, See. 136–76]

Horbury, William. *Jews and Christians: In Contact and Controversy.* London: T&T Clark, 2005. [Resurrection—denial of Jesus, See. 18, 103, 104, 177, 178–79]

Humphreys, Kenneth. *Jesus Never Existed: An Introduction to the Ultimate Heresy.* Nine-Banded Books, 2014. [140 pages; N.B. If Jesus never existed, there was no resurrection.]

Ingersoll, Robert G. *The Works of Robert G. Ingersoll.* Vol. 2. New York: The Ingersoll League, 1929. [The Resurrection, See. 400–401; The Ascension, See. 401–4]

John, Paul. *The Misconception Trilogy Christianity The Ultimate Urban Legend Book 2.* Victoria, BC: Trafford, 2006. [After the Death of Jesus, See. 207–9]

Johnson, B. C. *The Atheist Debater's Handbook.* Buffalo, NY: Prometheus, 1981. [Chapter 14 God and Jesus, See. 119–22]

Kearney, Milo, and James Zeitz. *World Saviors and Messiahs of the Roman Empire, 28 BCE—135 CE: The Soterial Age.* Lewiston, NY: Mellen, 2009. [Chapter 8 See. Jesus of

Nazareth, See. 195–200; Chapter 11 Why Jesus' Followers Prevailed, See. Victory Over Death, See. 323; Ascension to Heaven, See. 323–25]

Kennedy, Ludovic. *All In The Mind: A Farewell To God*. London: Hodder & Stoughton, 1999. [Chapter 4 Judaeo-Christian Mythologies. 3. Alleged Miracles, See. 64–69]

Kersten, Holger, and Elmar Gruber. *The Jesus Conspiracy: the Turin Shroud and the Truth about the Resurrection*. New York: Barnes & Noble, 1995. [See. 254–75]

Kryvelev, Iosif Aronovic. *Christ: Myth Or Reality?* Moscow: USSR Academy of Sciences, "Social Sciences Today," 1987. [See. 69]

Kuhn, Alvin Boyd. *Who is this King of Glory? A Critical Study of the Christos-Messiah Tradition*. Elizabeth, NJ: Academy Press, 1944. [See. 235–36, 294, 295, 368–69, 395–400]

Kurtz, Paul. *The Transcendental Temptation: A Critique of Religion and the Paranormal*. Buffalo, NY: Prometheus, 1986. [Chapter 7 The Jesus Myth. See. The Resurrection: What is the Evidence?, See. 153–61]

Lane Fox, Robin. *The Unauthorized Version: Truth and Fiction in the Bible*. New York, Knopf, 1991. [See 143–45, 388, 390]

Lee, William. *The Inspiration of Holy Scripture: Its Nature and Proof: Eight Discourses, Preached Before the University of Dublin*. New York: Robert Carter, 1857 [See. 346. N.B. Google book]

Leland, John. *A View of the Principal Deistical Writers That Have Appeared in England in the Last and Present Century*. London: Printed for T. Tegg, 1837. [Letter 8. See. 81–90; Letter 12, See. 136–57; N.B. Archive.org, Google book, and HathiTrust]

Leslie, Rolla J. *Was the Bible Inspired*. New York: Broadway, 1915. [The Resurrection?, See. 157–73; The Ascension?, See. 174–80; N.B. Google book]

Levett, Arthur. *A Martian Examines Christi*anity. London: Watts, 1934. [See. 91–92; N.B. This work employs humor and sarcasm.]

Lewis, Abram Herbert. *Paganism Surviving in Christianity*. New York: G.P. Putnam's Sons, 1892. [Chapter 8 Sunday Directly Referred to but Three Times— It is Never Spoken of as a Sabbath, nor as Commemorative of Christ's Resurrection— The Bible does Not State that Christ Rose on Sunday— Christ and His Disciples Always Observed the Sabbath— The Change of the Sabbath Unknown in the New Testament, See. 171–84; N.B. Google book]

Lewis, H. Spencer. *The Mystical Life of Jesus*. San Jose, CA: Rosicrucian Press, 1929. [Chapter 16 The Secret Facts of the Resurrection, See. 269–81; Chapter 17 The Unknown Life of Jesus, See. 283–92. N.B. Jesus survived the crucifixion.]

Lockhart, Douglas. *Jesus the Heretic: Freedom and Bondage in a Religious World*. Shaftesbury: Element, 1997. [Jesus after crucifixion, See. 82–86, 100–101, 103, 247–48, 258, 265, The Spirit of truth, See. 277–88, 285; The Importance of the Resurrection, See. 87–89; Paul's Heavenly Vision, See. 89–93]

Loftus, John W. *Why I Became an Atheist: A Former Preacher Rejects Christianity*. Amherst, NY: Prometheus, 2008. [Chapter 20 Did Jesus Bodily from the Dead?, See. 344–82; N.B. Loftus presents a solid overview for rejecting Jesus's resurrection.]

Loftus, John, W., and Randal D. Rauser. *God or Godless? One Atheist. One Christian. Twenty Controversial Questions*. Grand Rapids: Baker, 2013. [Chapter 19 Jesus Was Resurrected, So Who Do You Think Raised Him?, See. 157–63; N.B. Arguing the Affirmative: Randal the Christian and Arguing the Negative: John the Atheist.]

Lunn, Arnold, and C. E. M. Joad. *Is Christianity True? A Correspondence Between Arnold Lunn and C. E. M. Joad.* London: Eyre & Spottiswoode, 1933. [Correspondence 29 Miracles and the Resurrection, See. 281–93 (A. L.); Correspondence 30 Protests Against Discussing The Resurrection, But Discusses It, See. 294–304 (C. E. M. J.); [N.B. Lunn was a Catholic apologist and Joad an agnostic philosopher.]

MacDonald, Dennis R. *Mythologizing Jesus: From Jewish Teacher to Epic Hero.* Lanham, MD: Rowman & Littlefield, 2015. [Chapter 23 Living Dead, See. 129–34; Chapter 24 Disappearing into the Sky, See. 135–43]

Madison, David. *Ten Tough Problems in Christian Thought and Belief: A Minister-Turned Atheist Shows Why You Should Ditch the Faith.* Valley, WA: Tellectual Press, 2016. [Chapter 7 Why the Resurrection Isn't Worth Believing, See. 219–40]

Mangasar M. M. *The Bible Unveiled.* Chicago: Independent Religious Society, 1911. [See. 178–80; N.B. HathiTrust]

———. *The Truth About Jesus: Is He A Myth?* Chicago: Independent Religious Society, 1909. [See. 34–40, 116–17, 121, 254–57; N.B. Google book]

Martin, Michael. *Atheism: A Philosophical Justification.* Philadelphia: Temple University Press, 1990. [See. 162, 188, 189, 217, 255, 503]

———. *Atheism, Morality, and Meaning.* Amherst, NY: Prometheus, 2002. [Chapter 18 The Meaning of Life and the Resurrection, See. 291–318; N.B. Martin presents a five step plan to demonstrate the improbability of the resurrection.]

May, Joseph. *The Myth of the Resurrection of Jesus.* 2nd ed. Philadelphia: Edward J. Bicking, 1893. [20 pages]

Maylone, W. Edgar. *Thrown at the Atheist's Head.* Philadelphia: Dorrance, 1973. [See. 545–51]

McCabe, Joseph. "The Resurrection." In *A Rationalist Encyclopedia.* London: Watts, 1950. [See. 496–97]

McComas, E. W. *A Rational View of Jesus and Religion.* New York: J. W. Lovell, 1880. [Chapters 19–23, See. 588–706; N.B. HathiTrust]

McConnachie, James, and Robin Tudge. *The Rough Guide to Conspiracy Theories.* London: Rough Guides, 2005. [Jesus the Myth, See. 160–63]

McCormick, Matthew S. *Atheism and the Case Against Christ.* Amherst, NY: Prometheus, 2012. [Chapters 2–4, See. 37–105; N.B. This required book to read presents a logically compelling case that refutes the claim that Jesus was resurrected.]

McKinsey, C. Dennis. *Biblical Errancy: A Reference Guide.* Amherst, NY: Prometheus, 2000. [Jesus, Resurrection, See. 445–57]

Meredith, Evan Powell. *The Prophet of Nazareth; or A Critical Inquiry Into the Prophetical, Intellectual and Moral Character of Jesus Christ.* London, 1864. [Chapter 6 Sections 1–4, See. 245–91; N.B. Google book]

Meslier, Jean. *Superstition in all Ages: A Dying Confession.* Translated by Anna Knoop. New York: Peter Eckler, 1920. [See. 303–5; The first part, "Common Sense," is a translation of "Le bon sens, ou Idées naturelles," by Baron Holbach, also published with title: *Le bon sens du curé J. Meslier.* The second part, "Abstract of the Testament of John Meslier," was first published by Voltaire in 1761. cf. Voltaire, par G. Bengesco; Le libertinage, par F. Lachèvre, v. 7, See. 227–46; Baron Holbach, by M. P. Cushing, etc. N.B. Google book, Gutenberg.org, and HathiTrust]

———. *Testament: Memoir of the Thoughts and Sentiments of Jean Meslier.* Translated by Michael Shreve. Amherst: Prometheus, 2009. [Chapter 17 Contradictions Among the Gospels, See. 110–12]

Miles, W. J. *The Myth of the Resurrection of Jesus, the Christ.* Sydney: F.E. Moore/W. J. Miles, 1914. [36 pages]

Miller, Robert J. *The Jesus Seminar and Its Critics.* Santa Rosa, CA: Polebridge, 1999. [Chapter 8 Apologetics and the Resurrection, See. 125–46; N.B. Miller offers important insights about the Gospels, their relation to faith, and Jesus's resurrection.]

Mills, David. *Atheist Universe: The Thinking Person's Answer to Christian Fundamentalism.* Berkeley, CA: Ulysses Press, 2008. [Resurrection of Christ, See. 38]

Mongar, Thomas M. *Only with Marx and Jesus.* Lanham, MD: University Press of America, 1997. [Chapter 14 How the Resurrection Story May Have Evolved, See. 79–86]

Mountcastle, William W. *The Secret Ministry of Jesus: Pioneer Prophet of Interfaith Dialogue.* Lanham, MD: University Press of America, 2008. [See. 1–2, 27–50, etc. The author suggests that Jesus survived the crucifixion and made his way to Srinagar and India. He is an ordained United Methodist Minister, and a member of the Unitarian Universalist Church.]

Newton, Michael. *The Encyclopedia of Conspiracies and Conspiracy Theories.* New York: Checkmark, 2006. [Jesus Christ, See. 187–88]

Notovitch, Nicolas. *The Unknown Life of Jesus Christ.* Translated by Alexina Loranger Donovan. Chicago: Rand, McNally, 1894; N.B. Archive.org, Google book, and Gutenberg.org. This work asserts that Jesus survived the crucifixion and moved to India. Modern scholars consider his work to be a hoax.]

Origen. *The Writings of Origen. Vol. 2. Origen Contra Celsum, Books 2–8.* Edited by Alexander Roberts and James Donaldson. Translated by Frederick Crombie. Edinburgh: T&T Clark, 1894. [Against Celsus, Book 2, Chapters. 55–70, See. 58–75; N.B. Google book]

Osman, Ahmed. *The House of the Messiah: Controversial Revelations on the Historical Jesus.* London: HarperCollins, 1992. [Chapter 32 Evidence From the Tomb, See. 169–74; N.B. The author, Egyptian born, proposes that Jesus and Joshua were one and the same.]

———. *Jesus in the House of the Pharaohs: The Essene Revelations On the Historical Jesus.* Rochester, VT: Bear, 2004. [N.B. The author proposes that Jesus and Joshua were one and the same. Originally published in 1992 in Great Britain under the title *The House of the Messiah*.]

Owen, John Pickard [pseud.]. *The Fair Haven: A Work in Defense of the Miraculous Element in Our Lord's Ministry Upon Earth, Both as Against Rationalistic Impugners and Certain Orthodox Defenders.* 2nd ed. London: Trübner, 1873. [This work, actually written by Samuel Butler is an "ironical defense of Christianity, which under the guise of orthodox zeal undermines its miraculous foundations." According to Robert Johnstone, editor of Butler's 1980 edition of *The Evidence for the Resurrection of Jesus Christ*, "In this work Butler presented his own heretical conclusions in a highly convincing manner and pretended to refute them by the weakest of conventional arguments." See. 9–10; N.B. Archive.org]

Paassen, Pierre van. *Why Jesus Died.* New York: Dial Press, 1949. [Chapter 7 What Happened To The Body Of Jesus, See. 176–206]

Pagels, Elaine. *The Gnostic Gospels.* New York: Random House, 1979 [Chapter 1 The Controversy over Christ's Resurrection: Historical Event or Symbol?, See. 3–27]

Paine, Thomas. *The Age of Reason*. London: Freethought, 1860. [See. 5–6, 124–36; N.B. Archive.org and Gutenberg.org. Paine's work is an often-cited classic source.]

Powys, Llewelyn. *The Pathetic Fallacy: A Study of Christianity*. London: Longmans, Green, 1930. [Chapter 4 The Legend of the Resurrection, See. 30–36]

Price, Robert M. *The Case Against the Case for Christ: A New Testament Scholar Refutes Lee Strobel*. Cranford, NJ: American Atheist Press, 2010. [Part 3. Rationalizing the Resurrection, See. 205–54; N.B. This work totally defeats apologist Lee Strobel with a bit of humor and sarcasm.]

———. *Deconstructing Jesus*. Amherst, NY: Prometheus, 2000. [See. 9, 10, 27, 34, 35, 43, 47, 54, 55, 56, 61, 93, 148, 149, 179, 215, 224, 228, 251, 260, 264; N.B. Chapter 7 The Cruci-fiction?, See. 215–26]

———. *Jesus is Dead*. Cranford, NJ: American Atheist Press, 2007. [279 pages. N.B. Significantly, Price interacts with numerous writers. This work should be definitely read.]

———. *Killing History: Jesus in the No-Spin Zone*. Amherst, NY: Prometheus, 2014. [The Missing Chapter. Raising Jesus, See. 205–14]

Ranke Heinemann, Uta. *Putting Away Childish Things*. San Francisco: HarperSanFrancisco, 1994. [Chapter 9 Easter, See. 130–40; Chapter 10 The Ascension, See. 141–49]

Reimarus, Hermann Samuel. *Fragments From Reimarus: Consisting of Brief Critical Remarks on the Object of Jesus and His Disciples as Seen in the New Testament*. Edited by Charles Voysey. Translated by Gotthold Ephraim Lessing. London: Williams & Norgate, 1879. [See. 30, 31, 33, 34, 44, 45, 46, 47, 69, 76, 82, 95–98, 110; N.B. Archive.org]

———. *The Goal of Jesus and His Disciples*. Translated by George Wesley. Buchanan. Leiden: Brill, 1970. [Part Two. 54–60, See. 126–43]

Remsburg, John E. *The Christ A Critical Review and Analysis of the Evidences of His Existence*. New York: Truth Seeker, 1909. [Chapter 7 Resurrection of Christ, See. 296–339; N.B. Google book and Gutenberg.org. This work is a classic, dated source.]

Renan, Ernest. *Renan's Life of Jesus*. Translated by William G. Hutchison. London: Scott, 1897. [Chapter 26 Jesus In The Tomb. See. 271–72; N.B. Google book; various translations are available.]

Rhys, Jocelyn. *Shaken Creeds: The Resurrection Doctrines*. London: Watts, 1924. [Part 1 The Resurrection Story, Chapter 1 The Evidence From The New Testament, See. 3–47; Chapter 4 The Ascension, See. 102–18; Chapter 6 Modern Scepticism, See. 144–69]

Robertson, J. M. *Studies in Religious Fallacy*. London: Watts, 1900. [See. 62, 121, 158, 175, 199; N.B. Google book]

Robinson, Neil. *Why Christians Don't Do What Jesus Tells Them to Do: And What They Believe Instead*. CreateSpace, 2012. [Part 1: Failed Prophecies, See. 25–27]

Rylands, L. Gordon. *The Christian Tradition: An Examination of Objections to the Opinion that Jesus was Not An Historical Person*. London: Watts, 1937. [Paul's Vision and the Belief in the Resurrection, See. 46–52]

Schlagel, Richard H. *The Vanquished Gods: Science, Religion, and the Nature of Belief*. Amherst, NY: Prometheus, 2001. [The Christos Legend, See. 157–67]

Schonfield, Hugh J. *The Passover Plot: New Light on the History of Jesus*. London: Hutchinson of London, 1966. [Chapter 13 He is not Here, See. 170–82]

Scott, Thomas. *The Tactics and Defeat of the Christian Evidence Society*. Ramsgate: Thomas Scott, 1871. [See. 6, 14–15, 21, 22, 26–27, 32–33; N.B. Google book]

Sheehan, Thomas. *The First Coming: How the Kingdom of God Became Christianity*. New York: Random House, 1986. [N.B. This book is a good read.]

Sheldon, Henry C. *Unbelief in the Nineteenth Century: A Critical History*. New York: Eaton & Mains, 1907. [See. 162–63; 177–80, 315, 320; N.B. Archive.org]

Sinnott-Armstrong, Walter. *God? A Debate Between A Christian And An Atheist. William Lane Craig and Walter Sinnott-Armstrong*. Oxford: Oxford University Press, 2004. [Chapter 2 There Is No Good Reason to Believe in God. See. 2. Miracles, See. 36–38]

Smart, J. J. C., and J. J. Haldane. *Atheism and Theism*. Oxford: Blackwell, 1996. [Jesus, life of, See. 63–65, 73, 88, 205–9]

Smith, George H. *Atheism The Case Against God*. Amherst, NY: Prometheus, 1989. [See. 117, 123, 205]

Spong, John Shelby. *Jesus For The Non-Religious*. New York: HarperOne, 2007. [Chapter 11 The Eternal Truth Inside the Myths of Resurrection and Ascension, See. 117–29]

Spooner, Lysander. *The Deist's Reply to the Alleged Supernatural Evidences of Christianity*. Boston, 1836. [Chapter 5 See. 50–62; N.B. Archive.org. An excellent reading!]

Stansbury, Hubert. *In Quest of Truth; a Study of Religion and Morality*. London: Watts, 1913. [See. 85–87; N.B. HathiTrust]

Steele, David Ramsey. *Atheism Explained: From Folly to Philosophy*. Chicago: Open Court, 2008. [See. 147–49]

Steiner, Rudolf. *The Easter Festival: Four Lectures given in Dornach, Switzerland, 19th to 22nd April, 1924*. London: Rudolf Steiner Press, 1968. [80 pages; N.B. Reprint from 1924 lectures.]

———. *The Fifth Gospel: Seven Lectures given in Oslo, 1st–6th October, 1913 and Cologne, 17th and 18th December, 1913*. London: Rudolf Steiner Press, 1978. [Lecture 2, October 2, 1913; N.B. Available online]

Stitt, Frederick H. *Myths, Dreams, and Theology in Early Christianity*. Charleston, SC: BookSurge Publishing, 2006. [Chapter 3 An Analysis of the Resurrection Stories, See. 35–50]

Strauss, David Friedrich. *The Life of Jesus: Critically Examined*. Translated by George Eliot. 4th ed. London: Swan Sonnenschein, 1902. [Third Part. Chapter 4 The Death and Resurrection of Jesus, See. 691–744; Chapter 5 The Ascension, See. 745–56; N.B. Archive.org and Google book. This classic work is often cited in the literature.]

Sweeley, John W. *Jesus in the Gospels: Man, Myth, or God*. Lanham: University Press of America, 2000. [Chapter 7 The Resurrection of Jesus: Myth, Magic, or Miracle?, See. 163–94]

Tacey, David J. *Religion As Metaphor: Beyond Literal Belief*. New Brunswick: Transaction Publishers, 2015. [Chapter 9 Resurrection: Ascending to Where?, See. 167–186]

Talbot, George F. *Jesus, His Opinions and Character: The New Testament Studies*. Boston: G. H. Ellis, 1883. [Chapter 12 The Legend of the Resurrection, See. 382–86; N.B. Google book]

Taylor, Robert. *The Diegesis; Being a Discovery of the Origin, Evidences, and Early History of Christianity*. Boston: Abner Kneeland, 1834. [See. 103–5, 130, 139, 163–64, 235, 293, 299, 310, 374–75, 382, 384; N.B. Archive.org]

———. *Syntagma of the Evidences of the Christian Religion*. Boston: J. P. Mendum, 1828. [See. 129, 131, 157, 163–64, 168, 179, 189; N.B. Archive.org]

Templeton, Charles. *Farewell to God: My Reasons for Rejecting the Christian Faith*. Toronto, ON: McClelland & Stewart, 1996. [The Resurrection, See. 117–22; The Ascension, See. 123–24]

Tertullian. *Apology. De Spectaculis*. Translated by T. R. Glover. Cambridge, MA: Harvard University Press, 1927. [30.6; See. 299. N.B. Archive.org. This excerpt details "The Lettuce Theory."]

Thiering, Barbara. *Jesus & the Riddle of the Dead Sea Scrolls: Unlocking the Secrets of His Life Story*. San Francisco: HarperSanFrancisco, 1992. [Chapters 26–35, See. 121–60; Postulates that Jesus did not die.]

Thomson, James. *Satires And Profanities*. London: Progress, 1844. [The Resurrection and Ascension of Jesus, See. 110–15; N.B. Google book. Written with a sarcastic tone.]

Thorburn, Thomas James. *The Mythical Interpretation of the Gospels: Critical Studies in the Historic Narratives*. New York: Scribner's Sons, 1916. [Chapter 15 The Descension to Hades. The Resurrection and Ascension to Heaven, See. 302–29; N.B. Archive.org]

Tobin, Paul. *The Rejection of Pascal's Wager: A Skeptics Guide to the Bible and the Historical Jesus*. Sandy: Authors OnLine, 2009. [Chapter 15 Burial and Resurrection, See. 539–79; N.B. This is an interesting book to examine.]

Vaiden, Thomas J. *America Vindicated From European Theologico-Political and Infidel Aspersions*. New York: Morgan, 1855. [See. 267–68; N.B. Archive.org]

Waite, Charles B. *History of the Christian Religion to the Year Two Hundred*. Chicago: C. V. Waite, 1881. [See. 13, 26–27, 41, 206–12, 218, 220, 229, 251, 263, 312, 334–36, 354, 363, 374–76, 433, 434; N.B. Archive.org]

Washburn, Lemuel K. *Is the Bible Worth Reading, and Other Essays*. New York: Truth Seeker, 1911. [What Does It Prove?, See. 58; N.B. Archive.org and Gutenberg.org]

Watts, Charles. *The Claims of Christianity Examined from a Rationalist Standpoint*. London: Watts, 1896. [Section 6 The Resurrection of Christ; N.B. Available online at The SecularWeb]

Weigall, Arthur. *Paganism in our Christianity*. New York, London, G. P. Putnam's Sons, 1928. [Chapter 9 The Resurrection, See. 91–101; Chapter 10 The Ascension. See. 102–13]

Wells, George Albert. *Did Jesus Exist?* London: Pemberton, 1986. [on third day, See. 30–34, 67, 115, 165; of Jesus his appearances after, See. 21, 26, 30, 37, 67, 124, 144]

———. *The Historical Evidence for Jesus*. Buffalo, NY: Prometheus, 1982. [Section 1. Chapter 8 Paul and the Resurrection, See. 43–45]

———. *The Jesus Legend*. Chicago: Open Court, 1996. [Chapter 3 See. 5. A Modern Jewish Scholar Concedes the Historicity of the Resurrection, See. 56–63]

———. *The Jesus Myth*. Chicago, Open Court, 1999. [Chapter 2 Miracles in the New Testament and Beyond. (2). The Resurrection, See. 123–42; N.B. Wells presents a critical analysis of pertinent texts.]

———. *The Jesus of the Early Christians: A Study in Christian Origins*. London: Pemberton, 1971. [Part One: The Historical Jesus. Chapter 1 The Gospel Miracles. (2) The Resurrection, See. 40–49]

———. *Who Was Jesus?: A Critique of the New Testament Record*. La Salle, IL: Open Court, 1989. [Chapter 2 The Resurrection, See. 25–52]

Wells, H. G. *Outline of History: Being a Plain History of Life and Mankind*. London: Cassell, 1920 [Book 6, Christianity and Islam. Chapter 28 The Rise of Christianity, §4, The Crucifixion of Jesus of Nazareth, See. 534–36; N.B. Archive.org and Gutenberg.org]

Whitney, Loren Harper. *A Question of Miracles: Parallels in the Lives of Buddha and Jesus: A Critical Examination of the So-called Miracles Surrounding the Birth, Life and Death of Buddha and Jesus and the Achievements of Other Miracle-workers* . . . Chicago: Library Shelf, 1908. [Chapter 24 Was It A Resurrection or Was It Resuscitation?, See. 281–91; Chapter 25 The Miracles of Jesus' Appearance to the Disciples, See. 292–99; Chapter 29 Examination of Luke Resumed, See. 331–39; N.B. Archive.org]

Worth, Roland H. *Alternative Lives of Jesus: Noncanonical Accounts Through the Early Middle Ages*. Jefferson, NC: McFarland, 2003. [Chapter 10 Triumph Over Death, See. 157–70]

Chapter 4

Books Fewer than 47 Pages Dealing with Jesus's Resurrection: Pro and Con

Bard, Andreas. *Is the Resurrection a Fact or a Fable? Is Death a Wall or a Door? Two Sermons*. Kansas City, MO: Mr. & Mrs. J. Frank Witwer, 1927. [15 pages]

Barnett, Paul, et al. *Resurrection: Truth and Reality*. Sydney South, Australia: Aquila, 1994. [45 pages]

Beck, William F. *He Died and Rose for Me: The Story of Lent, Easter, and the Ascension from the New Testament in the Language of Today*. St. Louis: Concordia, 1966. [32 pages]

Blanchard, John. *Jesus: Dead or Alive?* Faverdale North, Dalington, England: EP, 2009. [40 pages]

Bottome, Margaret. *Our Lord's Seven Questions After Easter*. New York: E. Scott, 1889. [30 pages]

Bourke, Myles M. *Passion Death and Resurrection of Christ*. Glen Rock, NJ: Paulist, 1963. [30 pages]

Boyse, Christopher. *The Certainty and Necessity of our Lord's Resurrection from the Dead*. Exon: Printed by Sam. Farley and Jos. Bliss, for Edward Score, 1707. [32 pages; N.B. Google book, Primary Source Microfilm, an imprint of Thomson-Gale, 2006. 1 reel; 35 mm. (The Eighteenth Century; reel 16316, no. 07). Unit 467.]

Chapman, Raymond. *The Way of Resurrection—Fourteen Devotional Stations for Easter and Other Occasions*. London & Oxford: Mowbray, 1986. [35 pages]

Chase, Frederick Henry. *The Ascension of Jesus Christ*. London: SPCK, 1916. [19 pages]

Clarke, Richard F. *The Glorious Resurrection and Ascension of Jesus Christ*. New York: Benziger, 1889. [46 pages; N.B. Meditations]

Considine, Thomas. *The Resurrection of Jesus Christ: An Historical Fact*. Colorado Springs: Seraphim Company, 1955. [32 pages; N.B. Archive.org]

Cook, George. *An Illustration of the General Evidence Establishing the Reality of Christ's Resurrection*. Edinburgh: Printed for Peter Hill, 1808. [34 pages]

Deedat, Ahmed. *Resurrection or Resuscitation*. Deedat, 1978. [18 pages; N.B. Written by a Muslim who rejects the crucifixion.]

Erlandson, E. J. *The Resurrection of Christ*. n.p. n.d. [19 pages]

Falconer, Thomas. *The Resurrection of Our Saviour Asserted from an Examination of the Proofs of the Identity of His Character after that Event, in a Letter to the Reverend L. R.* London: Printed by R. Cruttwell and Sold by C. Dilly, 1798. [21 pages]

Findlow, Bruce. *I Question Easter*. London: Lindsey Press, 1966. [19 pages; N.B. Written by a Unitarian.]

Foster, James. *The Resurrection of Christ Proved and Vindicated, Against the Most Important Objections of the Ancient Jews, or Modern Deists; and His Disciples Shown to be Sufficient Witnesses of the Fact: A Sermon*. London: Printed for John Clark, 1720. [31 pages; N.B. Google book]

Gere, George W. *Did Jesus Rise the Resurrection from the View-Point of a Lawyer*. Winona Lake, IN: Winona Publishing, 1903. [27 pages; N.B. Archive.org and Google book]

Ginder, Richard. *The Facts Behind the Resurrection*. New York: Catholic Information Society, 1944. [15 pages; N.B. Archive.org]

Girdlestone, Robert Baker. *The Resurrection of Christ: An Examination of the Testimony*. London: Evangelical Alliance, n.d. [20 pages]

Gordon, A. J. *Risen With Christ: An Address on the Resurrection*. New York, Revell, 1895. [18 pages]

Haldeman, I. M. *On What Day Did Our Lord Rise from the Dead?* New York: I. M. Haldeman, 1900z. [38 pages; N.B. This brief work advocates a Thursday crucifixion.]

Harmon, George Milford. *Fact or Fiction in the New Testament Narratives of the Resurrection*. Boston: Universalist Publishing House, 1894. [26 pages]

Harris, Murray J. *Easter in Durham: Bishop Jenkins and the Resurrection of Jesus*. Exeter: Paternoster, 1985. [32 pages]

Hart, Levi. *The Resurrection of Jesus Christ Considered and Proved: And the Consequent Truth and Divinity of the Christian System Briefly Illustrated*. Providence: John Carter, 1786. [21 pages; N.B. Newport Collection at Digital Commons @ Salve Regin. Newport Book. Book 14.]

Hodgetts, Albert William. *Call the Witnesses: The Fact of the Resurrection*. Epworth, 1950. [24 pages]

Holland, Henry Scott. *The Resurrection of Jesus Christ*. London: SPCK, 1916. [16-page tract]

Horsley, John. *An Enquiry into the Force of the Objection Made Against the Resurrection of Christ*. London, Printed for J. Watts, 1730. [40 pages]

Hunkin, J. W. *The Resurrection*. London. In *Liberal Evangelicalism*; pamphlets 1–27. London: Hodder & Stoughton, 1923–1926. [16 pages]

Impartial Examination and Full Confutation of the Argument Brought by Mr. Woolston's Pretended Rabbi. 2nd ed. London: Printed for J. Roberts, 1730. [23 pages; N.B. Google book]

Jaimson, David Lee. *The Resurrection of Jesus Considered from the Lawyer's Viewpoint*. Philadelphia: Sunday School Times, 1923. [32 pages]

Kates, Frederick Ward, ed. *The Sources of the World's Joy: The Resurrection of Jesus Christ*. Cincinnati: Forward Movement. 1986. [23 pages]

Kevan, Ernest F. *The Resurrection of Christ*. Glasgow: Pickering & Inglis, 1961. [16-page pamphlet]

Layman, A. *A Sermon on the Resurrection*. London: Printed by J.W. 1738. [15 pages]

Lee, Robert Greene. *Buried and Alive*. Grand Rapids: Zondervan, 1938. [13 pages]

Luckhoo, Lionel. *The Question: Did Jesus Rise From the Dead?* 19?? [29 pages]

Lushington, Thomas. *The Resurrection of our Saviour Vindicated and the Soldiers Calumnies Against it Fully Answered, in a Sermon Preached at St. Mary's in Oxford. Formerly printed under the signed name of Robert Jones*. London: Printed for T. Davis, 1741.

[26 pages; N.B. Google book. Originally preached in 1624 and published in 1659. Reproduction of the original from the British Library]

Maltby, William Russell. *The Meaning of the Cross and the Resurrection.* Nashville: Publishing House M.E. Church, South, 1920. [44 pages; N.B. Also printed in London: Epworth.]

Manning, Samuel. *The Resurrection of Christ Proved by Friends and Foes.* London: Religious Tract Society, 1882? [20 pages; N.B. Book tracts, no. 3. Only located in two libraries in Britain.]

Mardon, Benjamin. *The Truth of the Resurrection of Jesus Christ Proved Upon the Principle of Human Testimony, Considered as a Branch of Moral Evidence.* Glasgow: Printed by James Hedderwick, 1822. [24 pages; N.B. Google book]

Martin, Aleck. *Aleck Martin's Difficulties about the Resurrection.* London: London Tract Society, 1883.

McGee, J. Vernon. *Appearances of Jesus After His Resurrection.* Grand Rapids: Zondervan, 1955. [32 pages]

McNaughter, John. *The Resurrection of Jesus Christ.* Pittsburgh: United Presbyterian Board of Publication and Bible School Work, 1938. [33 pages]

Miles, W. J. *The Myth of the Resurrection of Jesus.* Sydney: Author, 1914. [36 pages; Australia]

Newcome, William. *A Review of the Chief Difficulties in the Gospel-History Relating to our Lord's Resurrection.* Dublin: Printed by R. Marchbank, 1791. [17 pages; N.B. Google book]

Newton, Benjamin Wills. *Scriptural Proof of the Doctrine of the First Resurrection.* London: Houlston & Wright, 1858. [36 pages; N.B. Google book]

Panton, D. M. *Christ Risen: A Fact.* London: Alfred Holiness, 1918. [36-page pamphlet]

———. *The First Resurrection.* London: Alfred Holiness, 1918. [16-page pamphlet]

Phelps, William Lyon. *Easter: The World's Best News.* New York: Fleming, 1933. [41 pages]

Pries, Mitchell Peter. *A Physician Looks at the Death.* Summerland, CA: Harbor House (West), 1994. [38 pages]

Prince, Nathan. *An Essay to Solve the Difficulties that Attend the Several Accounts Given by the Evangelists of our Saviour's Resurrection and His Appearances to His Followers on the Day He Rose.* Boston, in New England: Printed and sold by S. Kneeland & T. Green, 1734. [30 pages; N.B. Early American Imprints: Evans 1639–1800 (Series I) / EAI I]

Ramsay, D. M. *The Resurrection of our Lord: A Sermon Preached* by the Rev. D. M. Ramsay, pastor of Knox Church, Ottawa, on Sunday, the 2nd April, 1899 (Easter Sunday). Ottawa: Printed by James Hope & Sons, 1899. [12 pages; N.B. Archive.org]

Reynell, Carew. *The Resurrection of our Saviour Rightly Timed, and Duly Evidenced: A Sermon Preached at White-Hall on Easter Day April 10th. 1726 in Answer to Some Objections Lately Revived by Mr. Woolston.* London: Printed for Tho. Combes, 1726. [35 pages]

Rogers, Clement F. *Non-Christian Theories of the Resurrection of Christ.* London: SPCK, 1937. [32 pages, *Little Books on Religion* no. 121]

Sandlin, P. Andrew. *Easter Every Sunday: The Great Resurrection Victory.* La Grange, CA: Center for Cultural Leadership, 2003. [18 pages]

Sayers, Dorothy L. *The Greatest Drama Ever Staged and the Triumph of Easter.* London: Falcon, 1964. [16 pages]

Category I—Books Dealing with Jesus's Resurrection

Scott, Thomas. *Dean of Ripon on the Physical Resurrection of Jesus.* London: Thomas Scott, 1873. [40 pages; N.B. Google book]

Seabury, William Jones. *The Power of the Witness of the Resurrection: A Sermon.* New York: E & J B Young, 1891. [19 pages]

Selwyn, E. Gordon. *The Risen Lord and His Church: Four Lectures.* Delivered June 14 and 15, 1928. Washington, DC: n.p., 1928. [43 pages]

Singh, Bakht. *The Greatest Secret: (Power of His Resurrection)* India: Hebron, 1975. [20 pages]

Smith, Elias. *A Discourse on the Resurrection: Containing an Account of the Resurrection of Christ.* Windsor, VT: Spooner, 1806. [19 pages]

Smith, Wilbur M. *Glorious Deliverance by Resurrection.* Chicago: Moody, 1941. [32 pages; The Fact of Christ's Resurrection, See. 19–22; The Body Not in the Tomb, See. 22–25]

———. *The Man Who Lived Again.* Chicago: Inter-Varsity Christian Fellowship, 1944. [22 pages]

Some Doubts Respecting the Death, Resurrection, and Ascension of Jesus Christ. New York: Printed for John Fellows, 1797. [42 pages; N.B. American Imprint Collection (Library of Congress). The Library of Congress holds the only known copy.]

Stevens, A. T. *The Resurrection of Jesus Christ: Fact or Fiction?* Brighton, Victoria: C. D. & E. Cutler, 1999. [38 pages]

Webster, William. *The Fitness of the Witnesses of the Resurrection of Christ consider'd in . . .* London: Printed for James Lacy, 1731. [26 pages, N.B. Google book]

Wharton, Edward C. *The Resurrection of Jesus Christ, Historical or Mythological? A Study in Historical Evidences.* Lubbock, TX: Wharton? n.d. [17 pages]

Wright, John J. *The Resurrection: Fact or Myth? An Easter Pastoral Addressed to the Diocese of Pittsburgh.* Washington, DC: United States Catholic Conference, 1969. [9 pages; N.B. Archive.org]

Yoho, Walter Allan. *Who Moved the Stone? Reassuring Reasons for the Resurrection.* Winston-Salem, NC: Piedmont Bible College Press, 1989. [14 pages]

Chapter 5

Juvenile Books Dealing with Jesus's Resurrection

Adams, Michelle Medlock. *What Is Easter?* Illustrated by Amy Wummer. Nashville, CandyCane Press, 2006. [Unpaged]

Amery, Heather. *The Easter Story*. Illustrated by Norman Young. London: Usborne Publishing, 2006 [16 pages]

Anders, Isabel. *Easter ABCs: Matthew 28:1–28; Mark 16:1–8; Luke 24:1–12; John 20:1–18*. Illustrated by Shelly Rasche. St. Louis: Concordia, 1999. [Unpaged]

Avant, John. *Authentic Power*. Sisters, OR: Multnomah, 2006. [235 pages]

Bachelard, Sarah. *Resurrection and Moral Imagination*. Farnham, Surrey, England; Burlington, VT: Ashgate, 2014. [209 pages]

Baden, Robert. *Thomas, the Doubting Disciple: John 20:19–29 for Children*. Illustrated by Andy Willman. St. Louis: Concordia, 1997. [Unpaged]

Bader, Joanne. *He's Risen! He's Alive! The Story of Christ's Resurrection: Matthew 27:32—28:10 for Children*. St. Louis: Concordia, 2003. [16 pages]

Barsness, Todd. *Only God Would've Planned it That Way!* Illustrated by Shelly Hehenberger. St. Louis: Concordia, 2002. [34 pages]

Beckman, Beverly Ann. *From, Understanding the Resurrection*. Illustrated by Kathy Counts. St. Louis: Concordia, 1980. [50 pages]

Beers, V. Gilbert. *The Toddlers Bible Easter Book*. Illustrated by Carole Boerke. Wheaton, IL: Victor, 1996. [27 pages]

Bergt, Carolyn S. *Something Wonderful! The Easter Story*. Illustrated by Michelle Dorenkamp. St. Louis: Concordia, 1998. [Unpaged]

Biffi, Inos, and Franco Vignazia. *The Way of the Cross: Holy Week, the Stations of the Cross, and the Resurrection*. Grand Rapids: Eerdmans, 1997. [47 pages]

Billington, Rachel. *The First Easter*. Illustrated by Elisa Trimby. London: Fount Paperbacks, 1988. [32 pages]

Binder, Amy, and Kim Freeberg. *He is Risen: Activity Book*. Irving, TX: Family Entertainment Network, 1993. [46 pages]

Blackaby, Henry T., and Melvin Blackaby. *Experiencing the Resurrection: The Everyday Encounter that Changes Your Life*. Colorado Springs, CO: Multnomah, 2008. [211 pages]

Blythe, Catherine, et al. *The Easter Story*. Illustrated by Bill Wood. North Shore, NZ: Pearson, 2009. [16 pages]

Category I—Books Dealing with Jesus's Resurrection

———. *Holy Week and Easter.* Illustrated by Jenny Hale and Sarah Jolly. North Shore, NZ: Pearson, 2009. [20 pages]

Blyton, Enid. *The Story of Easter.* Illustrated by Penny Horne. London: Grafton, 1986, [24 pages]

Bohnet, Eric C. *Mary's Easter Story: The Story of Easter: Matthew 21:1–11 and John18:1— 20:31 for Child*ren. Illustrated by Elizabeth Swisher. St. Louis: Concordia, 2002. [16 pages]

Boon, Fiona, and Dawn Machell. *The Story of Easter.* Hertfordshire, UK: Make Believe Ideas, 2017. [Unpaged]

Bowden, Joan Chase. *Something Wonderful Happened: The First Easter for Beginning Readers: Matthew 28:1–10, for Children Mark 16:1–11, Luke 24:1–12, John 20:1–18.* Illustrated by Aline Cunningham. St. Louis: Concordia, 1977. [46 pages]

Brundage, George. *The Story of Easter.* NJ: Catholic Book Publishing, 2007. [Unpaged]

Buck, Deanna Draper. *Easter.* Illustrated by Jerry Harston. Salt Lake City, UT: Deseret Book, 2008. [Unpaged]

Buehner, Caralyn. *In the Garden.* Illustrated by Brandon Dorman. Salt Lake City, UT: Deseret Book, 2007. [Unpaged]

Burgess, Beverly Capps. *Is Easter Just for Bunnies?* Illustrated by Nancy Titolo. Broken Arrow, OK: Burgess, 1985. [Unpaged]

Burkart, Jeffrey E. *A Surprise in Disguise: Luke 24:13–35 for Children.* Illustrated by Michelle Dorenkamp. St. Louis: Concordia, 1999. [16 pages]

Butcher, Geoffrey. *Peter and the Resurrection of Jesus.* Vero Beach, FL: Rourke Publications, 1984. [29 pages]

Chambers, Catherine. *Easter.* London: Evans, 2010. [30 pages]

Chew, J. A. *The Easter Story.* Athena Press, 2006. [47 pages]

Chung, Chi. *That Easter Morn.* St. Louis: Concordia, 2007. [Unpaged]

Coleman, Sheila Schuller. *The Best Story About Jesus.* Illustrated by John Ham. Cincinnati: Standard Publishing, 1989. [31 pages]

Courtney, Claudia. *Rise and Shine: The Story of Easter, Matthew 28:1–8.* Illustrated by Bill Clark. St. Louis: Concordia, 1999. [16 pages]

Cowley, Joy. *The Easter Story.* Illustrated by Donald Morrison. Otane, NZ: Pleroma , 2011. [Unpaged]

Dale, Alan T. *Jesus is Really Alive Again!* Wilton, CN: Morehouse-Barlow, 1976. [Unpaged]

David, Juliet. *The Easter Story.* Illustrated by Elina Ellis. Oxford, England: Candle, 2014. [40 pages]

Davidson, Alice Joyce. *Mary & the Empty Tomb.* Illustrated by Tammie Lyon. Grand Rapids: Zondervan, 1998. [Unpaged]

———. *The Story of Easter.* Illustrated by Victoria Marshall. Pasay City: Paulines Publishing House, 1998. [Unpaged]

Davis, John. *The Story of the Empty Tomb: John for Children.* Illustrated by Len Ebert. St. Louis: Concordia, 1998. [Unpaged]

Davis, Joy Morgan. *God's Love at Easter.* Illustrated by Marion Eldridge. St. Louis: Concordia, 2002. [Unpaged]

Davis, Robert. *Great day in the Morning!* Illustrated by Douglas Keller. Richfield, OH: Davis, 1986. [Unpaged]

Daybell, Chad. *Through the Eyes of John: The Beloved Apostle Watches the Savior's Final Days on the Earth.* Provo: Spring Creek Book, 2004. [27 pages]

Doyle, Christopher, and John Haysom. *The Story of Easter*. St. Louis: Concordia, 2008. [29 pages]

Draper, Deanna. *My First Story of the First Easter*. Illustrated by Jerry Harston. Salt Lake City, UT: Deseret Book, 2013. [Unpaged]

Dreyer, Nicole E. *The Easter Stranger: The Easter Story, Luke 24:1-35, for Children*. Illustrated by Len Ebert. St. Louis: Concordia, 2009. [Unpaged]

Elder, Karen Childs, et al. *Rejoice! The Story of Easter Morning from the Gospel of Matthew*. Illustrated by Karen Childs Elder. Rochester: Fountain, 2009. [Unpaged]

Elliot, Rachel. *The Easter Story*. Illustrated by Xuân Thanh Lê. New York: Parragon, 2016. [Unpaged]

Ellis, Gwen. *The Story of Easter: Read and Share*. Illustrated by Steve Smallman. Nashville: Thomas Nelson, 2007. [Unpaged]

Engelbrecht, Edward A., and Gail E. Pawlitz, eds. *The Easter Story: Drawn Directly from the Bible*. Saint Louis: Concordia, 2011. [26 pages]

Erickson, David. *He is Risen, Indeed!* Saint Louis: Concordia, 2006. [25 Unpaged]

Erickson, Mary E. *Miracle in the Morning: The Wonderful Story of Easter*. Illustrated by Jenny Williams. Elgin, IL: Chariot, 1994. [32 pages]

Everard, Elizabeth. *The Easter Story*. Melbourne: Book Depot, 1946. [12 pages]

Fisher, Aileen. *The Story of Easter*. Illustrated by Stefano Vitale. New York: HarperCollins, 1997. [Unpaged]

Flinn, Lisa, and Barbara Younger. *Easter A to Z: Every Letter Tells a Story*. Nashville: Abingdon, 2002. [Unpaged]

Frank, Penny. *The First Easter*. Illustrated by John Haysom. Tring, Herts, England; Belleville, MI: Lion, 1986. [22 pages]

French, Fiona. *Easter: With Words From the King James Bible*. New York: HarperCollins, 2002. [Unpaged]

Friedrich, Elizabeth. *Jesus is Alive*. Illustrated by Karen Pauls. St. Louis: Concordia, 1987. [32 pages]

Fryar, Jane L. *The Easter Day Surprise*. St. Louis: Concordia, 2008. [25 pages]

Ganeri, Anita. *The Easter Story*. Illustrated by Rachael Phillips. North Mankato, MN: Smart Apple Media, 2005. [23 pages]

Glaser, Rebecca Stromstad. *Jesus Ascends and Other Bible Stories*. Illustrated by Bill Ferenc and Emma Trithart. Minneapolis: Sparkhouse Family, 2016. [32 pages]

Godfrey, Jan, and Marcin Piwowarski. *The Road to Easter Day*. Boston: Pauline Books & Media, 2008. [29 pages]

Gooding, Christina. *My Little Easter Story*. Illustrated by Claudine Gévry. Oxford: Lion Children's, 2011. [29 pages]

Greene, Carol. *The Easter Women: Luke 7:36-8.3; 23:55—24:12; John 20:1-18 for Children*. Illustrated by Betty Wind. St. Louis: Concordia, 1987. [24 pages]

Grimes, Nikki. *At Jerusalem's Gate: Poems of Easter*. Woodcuts by David Frampton. Grand Rapids: Eerdmans, 2005. [Unpaged Poetry]

Haidle, Helen. *He is Alive: A Picture Book on the Last Week of Jesus' Life & His Resurrection*. Illustrated by Joel Spector. Grand Rapids: Zonderkidz, 2001. [Unpaged]

Hardesty, Susan. *A Child's Story of Easter*. Illustrated by Kristina Stephenson & Terry Julien. Cincinnati: Standard Publishing, 2011. [Unpaged]

Harrast, Tracy L. *The Easter Story*. Illustrated by Terry Workman. Grand Rapids: Zonderkidz, 2000. [Unpaged]

Hartman, Bob. *Easter Angels*. Illustrations by Tim Jonke. Oxford: Lion Children's, 2005. [98 pages]

———. *Easter Stories*. Illustrated by Nadine Wickenden. St. Louis: Arch, 2005. [Unpaged]

Hartman, Sara. *Mary Magdalene's Easter Story: Mary Magdalene Visits the Empty Tomb, John 20:10–18: for Children*. Illustrated by Ed Koehler. St. Louis: Arch, 2005. [Unpaged]

Heyer, Carol. *The Easter Story*. Nashville: Ideals Children's Books, 1990. [32 pages]

Holmes, Andy. *Bible for Me: Easter*. Illustrated by Ralph Voltz. Nashville: Tommy Nelson, 2006. [Unpaged]

Howie, Vicki, and Honor Ayres. *On Easter Day in the Morning*. Abingdon: Bible Reading Fellowship, 2011. [29 pages]

Howie, Vicki, and Moira Maclean. *Easter Surprise*. St. Louis: Concordia, 2006. [18 pages]

Huffaker, Alice. *Resurrection Day*. Chicago, IL: Moody, 1990. [30 pages]

Ingalls, Marilyn F. *Welcome Easter: Teacher Guide : A Four-Session Unit for Grade 1*. Edited by R. Harold Terry. Philadelphia: Parish Life, 1976. [24 pages]

Jackson, Antonia. *Easter Story*. Lion Hudson, 2015. [32 pages]

Jeffs, Stephanie. *The Easter Story*. Illustrated by John Haysom and Milton Keyes, Bucks: Tamarind, 1997. [Unpaged]

Johnson, Alice W., and Allison H. Warner. *When the Stone Was Rolled Away*. Illustrated by Jerry Harston. Salt Lake City, UT: Deseret Book, 2008. [82 pages]

Johnson, Cathy Ann. *The Easter Story: From the Gospels of Matthew, Mark, Luke and John*. Nashville: Tommy Nelson, 2003. [18 pages]

Jones, Dennis G. *The First Easter Ever*. Grand Rapids: Zondervan, 2015. [Unpaged]

Joslin, Mary. *On that Easter Morning*. Illustrated by Helen Cann. Intercourse, PA: Good Books, 2006. [Unpaged]

Kean, Leah. *Jesus Has Risen: A First Book for Little Catholics*. Pictures by Julian Paul. New York: Guild Press, 1962. [Unpaged]

Keffer, Lois. *Peter Tells the Easter Story*. Loveland, CO: Group Pub., 1995. [8 pages]

Koestler-Grack, Rachael A. *Easter*. Illustrations by Constanza Droop; translation by Linda M. Maloney. Collegeville, MN Liturgical Press, 2001. [24 pages]

Kovcs, Victoria. *Easter Story*. Illustrated by Mike Krome. United Kingdom: GoldQuill, 2013. [Unpaged]

Krenzer, Rolf. *Jesus is Risen*. Illustrated by Constanza Droop and translated by Linda M. Maloney. Collegeville, MN: Liturgical Press, 2001. [24 pages]

Kueker, Donald. *The Easter Story: According to Matthew*. St. Louis: Concordia, 2006. [32 pages]

Langley, Andrew. *The Story of Easter*. New York: Gallery, 1989. [16 pages]

Lee, Laurel. *My Jesus Pocketbook of God's Greatest Day*. Illustrated by Lindy Burnett. Decatur, GA: Stirrup Associates, 1985. [32 Unpaged]

Leigh, Susan K. *Happy Easter*. St. Louis: Concordia, 2006. [Unpaged]

Lewis, Lorna. *Jesus is Risen*. Illustrated by Arthur Baker. Bury St Edmunds: Kevin Mayhew, 1993. [31 pages]

Lloyd, Mary Edna. *Glad Easter Day*. Pictures by June Goldsborough. New York: Abingdon, 1961. [Unpaged]

Loots, Barbara Kunz. *The Story of Easter: Adapted from the Gospel of Mark Chapters 11–16*. Illustrated by Tammy Haddix. Kansas City, MO: Hallmark Cards, 1996. [Unpaged]

Mackall, Dandi Daley. *Journey, Easter Journey!* Illustrated by Gene Barretta. Nashville: Nelson, 2004. [Unpaged]

Mackenzie, Carine. *Jesus is Alive*. Ross-shire, Scotland: Christian Focus, 1998. [32 pages]

———. *Long, Long Ago in Jerusalem: The Life and Resurrection of Jesus*. Illustrated by Fred Apps. Tain: Christian Focus, 2001. [Unpaged]

Maier, Paul L. *The Very First Easter*. Illustrated by Francisco Ordaz. St. Louis: Concordia, 2004. [Unpaged]

Marshall, Martha. *The Wonderful Surprise*. Illustrated by James Conaway. Elgin, IL: Dandelion House, 1983. [31 pages]

Marshall, Peter. *The First Easter*. New York: McGraw-Hill, 1959. [See. 102–34]

Matthews, Leonard. *Wonderful Easter*. Illustrated by Clive Uptton. Vero Beach, FL: Rourke Publications, 1984. [24 pages]

McDonough, Andrew. *Mary and the Gardener*. Unley, S. Aust. Lost Sheep Resources, 2018. [Unpaged]

Miller, Calvin. *My Lord & My God: Thomas' Incredible Account of Jesus' Resurrection*. Illustrated by Ron DiCianni. Colorado Springs, CO: ChariotVictor, 1998. [31 pages]

Miller, Jean. *The Story of Easter*. Illustrated by Debbie Pinkney-Davis. New York: Golden, 1999. [Unpaged]

Moser, Julie. *Death and Resurrection of Jesus*. Vancouver: Effective Youth Ministry, 2010. [42 pages]

Murphy, Elspeth Campbell. *Happy Easter, God*. Illustrated by Jim Lewis. Bloomington, MN: Bethany Backyard, 2001. [Unpaged]

Nederveld, Patricia L. *The Best Day Ever! The Story of Easter*. Illustrations by Patrick Kelley. Grand Rapids: CRC Publications, 1998. [24 pages]

———. *Goodbye, for Now: The Story of Jesus' Return to Heaven*. Illustrated by Patrick Kelley. Grand Rapids: CRC Publications, 1998. [24 pages]

Neff, LaVonne. *Jesus is Risen!* Illustrated by Toni Goff. Wheaton, IL: Tyndale House, 1993. [Unpaged]

Odor, Ruth Shannon. *The Happiest Day*. Illustrated by Helen Endres. Elgin, IL: Child's World, 1979. [30 pages]

Pawlitz, Gail. *Thomas Believes: John 20 for Children*. Illustrated by Bill Clark. St. Louis: Concordia, 2005. [Unpaged]

Peterson, Eugene H. *The Easter Story*. Illustrated by Rob Corley and Tom Bancroft. Colorado Springs, CO: NavPress, 2009. [32 pages]

Pingry, Patricia A. *Story of Easter*. [S.I.] : Worthykids, 2016]

Pipe, Rhona. *The Easter Story*. Illustrated by Annabel Spencely. Alresford, Hants: Hunt & Thorpe, 1993. [Unpaged]

Piper, Sophia. *The First Easter*. Illustrated by Estelle Corke. Oxford: Lion Children's, 2014. [Unpaged]

Poole, Susie. *Easter Journey*. Manchester: Pupfish, 2004. [48 pages]

Pulley, Kelly. *Jesus is Risen!* Oxford Candle, 2006. [Unpaged]

Punter, Russell. *Easter Story*. Illustrated by John Joven. London: Usborne, 2016. [Unpaged]

Quattlebaum, Mary. *The Story of Easter*. Illustrated by Richard Murdock. Alexandria, VA: Time-Life for Children, 1997. [Unpaged]

Ramsbottom, B. A. *The Resurrection of Jesus*. Harpenden (Herts.): Gospel Standard Trust, 1997. [31 pages]

Rawson, Christopher. *The Easter Story*. Illustrated by Victor Ambrus. Tulsa: Hayes/Usborne, 1981. [31 pages]

Rayburn, Cherie. *A Child's Story of Easter*. Illustrated by Rebecca Farley. Colorado Springs, CO: Current, 1993. [12 pages]

Robertson, Cindy. *He is Risen*. Illustrated by Emily Owens. Franklin, TN: Dalmation, 2001. [Unpaged]

Robertson, Jenny. *The Easter Story*. Illustrated by Alan Parry. Grand Rapids: Zondervan, 1980. [29 pages]

Robinson, Sandra E. *Easter Celebrations: A Four-Session Unit for Grades 2 and 3*. Edited by R. Harold Terry. Philadelphia: Parish Life Press, 1976. [2 volumes]

Rock, Lois. *The First Easter*. Oxford: Lion Children's, 2013. [Unpaged]

Rodriguez, K. S. *The Easter Story*. Illustrated by Jan Gregg-Kelm. New York: GT Pub., 1999. [19 pages]

Rottmann, Erik. *The Easter Victory: The Story of Easter : Matthew 26—28 for Children*. Illustrated by Paige Billin-Fry. St. Louis: Concordia, 2006. [Unpaged]

Sanders, Nancy I. *Easter*. New York: Children's Press, 2003. [47 pages]

Sayers, Dorothy L. *The Story of Easter*. The pictures painted by B. Biro. London: Hamish Hamilton, 193-? [Unpaged]

Schidlovsky, Dimitry. *The First Easter Day*. Mill Neck, NY: The Mill Neck Family of Organizations, 2011. [23 pages]

Simon, Mary Manz. *My Easter Basket: And the True Story of Easter*. Illustrated by Linda Clearwater. Cincinnati: Standard Pub., 2002. [Unpaged]

———. *Where is Jesus? : Matthew 27:62-66; 28:1-9 : Easter*. Illustrated by Dennis Jones. St. Louis: Concordia, 1991. [Unpaged]

Simonson, Louisie, et al. *The Easter Story*. New York: Marvel Comics : Distributed to the religious market exclusively by Thomas Nelson, 1993. [32 pages]

Skarmeas Nancy J. *The First Easter*. Paintings by Leslie Benson. Nashville: CandyCane Press, 1998. [31 pages]

Smith, Martina. *The Story of Easter*. Illustrated by Peter Grosshauser and Ed Temple. Minneapolis: Sparkhouse Family, 2015. [32 pages]

Smith, Terrell D. *The Miracle of Easter*. Illustrated by Arvis L. Stewart. Alexandria, VA: Time-Life for Children, 1997. [Unpaged]

Stiegemeyer, Julie. *Bright Easter Day*. Illustrated by Susan Spellman. St. Louis: Concordia, 2005. [Unpaged]

———. *My Little Easter Book*. Pictures by Dana Regan. St. Louis: Concordia, 2008. [Unpaged]

St. John, Patrica. *A King is Risen*. Chicago: Moody, 1991. [Unpaged]

Strong, Cynda. *The Resurrection: Isaiah 53:4-6 and Matthew 21:1-11; 26; 27:27-66; 28:1-10 for Children*. Illustrated by Helen Cann. St. Louis: Concordia, 2010. [Unpaged]

Storr, Catherine. *The First Easter*. Pictures by Chris Molan. Milwaukee: Raintree Children's Books; London: Belitha Press, 1984. [31 pages]

Stowell, Gordon. *Jesus Lives!* London: Scripture Union, 1982. [23 pages]

Taylor, Mark A. *Breakfast with Jesus: John 21:1-14*. Illustrated by Andy Stiles. Cincinnati: Standard, 1993. [26 pages]

Tebo, Mary Elizabeth, and Patricia Edward Jablonski. *The Very First Easter*. Illustrated by Anna Winek-Leliwa. Boston: Pauline Books & Media, 2002. [31 pages]

Tess, Fries. *He is Risen*. Illustrated by Emily Owens. Franklin, TN: Dalmation Press, 2000. [Unpaged]

Thomason, Jean, and Nancy Gordon. *The Story of the Resurrection Eggs in Rhyme and Song: Opens up the Wonder of the Easter Story*. Nashville: Integrity. [Unpaged]

Toast, Sarah. *The Easter Story*. Illustrated by Thomas Gianni. Lincolnwood, IL: Publications International, 1995. [Unpaged]

Truitt, Gloria A. *My Happy Easter Book: Matthew 27:57—28:10 for Children*. Illustrated by Len Ebert. St. Louis: Concordia, 1996. [Unpaged]

Tuttle, Emily. *Baby's First Easter*. Illustrated by Moira MacLean. St. Louis: Concordia, 1996. [Unpaged]

Vischer, Phil. *What is Easter?* Illustrated by Heath McPherson. n.p.: Jellyfish One, 2015.

Walker, Joni. *Tell Me the Easter Story*. St. Louis: Concordia, 2004? [Unpaged]

Ward, Verlie. *The Unexpected Guest*. Illustrated by Steven Butler. Siloam Springs, AR: Concerned Group, 2006. [24 pages]

Watson, Rhonda, and Sue Aiken. *Easter for Kids*. Sydney South: Christian Education Publications, 2006. [160 pages]

Wedeven, Carol. *The Easter Cave*. Illustrated by Len Ebert. St. Louis: Concordia, 2001. [28 pages]

Wildsmith, Brian. *The Easter Story*. Grand Rapids: Eerdmans Books for Young Readers, 2000. [Unpaged]

Williamson, Karen. *The First Easter*. Illustrated by Sarah Conner. Oxford, England: Candle, 2016. [Unpaged]

Willoughby, R. *Three Easter Journeys*. Illustrated by David Miller. Nashville: Abington, 2001. [24 pages]

Wilson, Etta. *The Miracle of Easter*. Illustrated by Thomas Gianni. Lincolnwood, IL: Publications International, 1993. [Unpaged]

Winthrop, Elizabeth. *He is Risen: The Easter Story*. Illustrated by Charles Mikolaycak. New York: Holiday House, 1985. [30 pages]

Wolf, Beth Rowland. *The Miracle of Easter*. Illustrated by Jennifer Schneider. Loveland, CO: Group Pub., 1996. [8 pages]

Yenne, Bill. *The Story of the First Easter*. Nashville: Nelson, 1994. [Unpaged]

Yohe, Lou. *Mommy, Why Do We Have Easter?* Shippensburg, PA: Destiny Image, 1996. [16 pages]

Youd, Pauline. *Thomas Becomes a Believer: An Easter Story*. Illustrated by Reg Sandland. Boston: Pauline Books & Media, 2000. [13 pages]

Zimmermann, Eleanor. *How Easter Began?* Illustrated by D. K. Stone. Philadelphia: Lutheran Church Press, 1967. [Unpaged]

Zobel-Nolan, Allia. *The Easter Story*. Illustrated by Tracey Moroney. New York: Scholastic, 2007. [Unpaged]

Category II

The Bodily Resurrection of the Dead

Chapter 6

The Bodily Resurrection of the Dead

Alger, William Rounseville. *The Destiny of the Soul: A Critical History of the Doctrine of a Future Life*. 10th ed. Boston: Roberts, 1880. [Chapter 7 Resurrection of Christ, See. 346–73; N.B. Archive.org, Google book, and HathiTrust. This dated work is an interesting read that surveys various thoughts concerning a future life.]

Aurelio, John. *Returnings: Life-after-Death Experiences: A Christian View*. New York: Continuum, 1995. [Chapter 8 He Is Not Here, See. 55–59; Chapter 11 A Pattern In Resurrection, See. 67–76; N.B. Only a few pages directly deal with the resurrection narratives.]

Barth, Karl. *The Resurrection of the Dead*. Translated by Henry James Stenning. London: Revell, 1933. [Chapter 3 Explanation of 1 Corinthians 15, See. 125–62; N.B. This dated work has been subject to much investigation.]

Bloesch, Donald G. *The Last Things: Resurrection, Judgment, Glory*. Downers Grove: InterVarsity, 2004. [The Resurrection of Jesus, See. 115–20; N.B. Chapter 6 exclusively deals extensively with Jesus's resurrection.]

Boismard, Marie-Emile. *Our Victory Over Death: Resurrection?* Translated by Madeleine Beaumont. Collegeville, MN: Liturgical Press, 1999. [Part 3: The Rise Christ, See. 123–30; N.B. Just seven pages deal with the resurrection narratives.]

Bourgy, Paul. *Christ's Resurrection*. Translated by J. Holland Smith. London: Challoner, 1961. [73 pages; N.B. This book has virtually no interaction with the resurrection narratives.]

Bowen, Clayton Raymond. *The Resurrection in the New Testament: An Examination of the Earliest References to the Rising of Jesus and of Christians from the Dead*. New York: G. P. Putnam's Sons. [514 pages; N.B. Archive.org, Google book, and HathiTrust. This must read text extensively analyzes all aspects of Jesus's resurrection.]

Brown, Paul J. *Bodily Resurrection and Ethics in 1 Cor 15: Connecting Faith and Morality in the Context of Greco-Roman Mythology*. Tübingen: Mohr Siebeck, 2014. [Chapter 4 The Bodily Resurrection of Jesus (1 Cor 15:1–11), See. 108–38; Chapter 5 The Veracity of the Bodily Resurrection and the Resulting Ethical Imperatives (1 Cor 15:12–34), See. 139–40; N.B. Brown's work should be examined.]

Burgess, George. *The Last Enemy; Conquering and Conquered*. Philadelphia: H. Hooker, 1850. [Chapter 61 Resurrection of Christ, See. 291–94; Chapter 62 Resurrection of Man in Christ, See. 295–98; Chapter 63 Body of Christ after his Resurrection,

See. 299–302; N.B. Google book; Approximately twelve pages interact with Jesus's resurrection.]

Bush, George. *Anastasis: or, The Doctrine of the Resurrection of the Body, Rationally and Scripturally Considered.* New York: Wiley & Putnam, 1845. [Chapter 7 The Resurrection of Christ, See. 151–67; N.B. Archive.org and Google book. This is a classic, often cited dated source. Only the seventh chapter is relevant to Jesus's resurrection.]

Bynum, Caroline Walker. *The Resurrection of the Body in Western Christianity, 200–1336.* New York: Columbia University Press, 1995. [Jesus, ascension of, See. 168; bodily resurrection of, See. 4–5, 26–27, 72, 264. N.B. An interesting book but not useful in analyzing the resurrection narratives.]

Camp, Norman Harvey. *The Resurrection of the Human Body.* Chicago: Bible Institute Colportage Association, 1937. [Chapter 4 Was the Body of Christ Raised?, See. 28–50. N.B. The author merely cites the witnesses reported in the New Testament as proof that Jesus's body was raised.]

Cochrane, James. *The Resurrection of the Dead: Its Design, Manner, and Results. In An Exposition of the Fifteenth Chapter of First Corinthians.* Edinburgh: W. Blackwood, 1869. [Discourse 2 The Resurrection of Christ the Grand Proof of the Truth of Christianity, See. 33–51; N.B. Google book and HathiTrust. Only one chapter interacts with the resurrection narratives.]

Cooke, Richard Joseph. *Outlines of the Doctrine of the Resurrection Biblical, Historical, and Scientific.* New York: Philips & Hunt, 1884. [Chapter 12 The Resurrection of Our Lord—Pledge and Pattern, See. 289–316; N.B. Google book. Only Chapter 12 is relevant to Jesus's resurrection.]

Cornélis, H., et al. *The Resurrection of the Body.* Translated by Sister M. Joselyn. Notre Dame, IN: Fides, 1964. [Chapter 2 Scriptural Sources of Faith and the Resurrection of the Body (by J. Guillet), 2. The New Testament, See. 113–19; N.B. Not useful due to a lack of content.]

Cox, Jennifer Anne. *Jesus the Disabled God.* Eugene, OR: Wipf & Stock, 2017. See. 44–49]

Dale, Robert William. *Christ and the Future Life.* London: Hodder & Stoughton, 1895. [The Resurrection, See. 137–60; N.B. Archive.org and HathiTrust. This book has virtually no interaction with the resurrection narratives.]

Darlison, Bill. *The Gospel and the Zodiac: The Secret Truth About Jesus.* London: Duckworth Overlook, 2007. [See. 211, 216; N.B. This study suggests that Jesus never existed historically. Instead he was, in fact, a representation of the zodiac sign Aquarius.]

Davis, Singleton Water. *A Future Life? A Critical Inquiry into the Scientific Value of the Alleged Evidences that Man's Conscious Personality Survives the Life of the Body.* Los Angeles: Humanitarian Review, 1907. [Chapter 2 The Resurrection Theory, See. 23–32; N.B. Google book. Not useful due to a lack of content.]

Dean, David A. *Resurrection, His and Ours.* Charlotte, NC: Advent Christian General Conference of America, 1977. [159 pages]

Downie, Robert Mager. *The Resurrection and Its Implications: An Examination of the Reasons Why So Many Consider It A Thing Incredible that God Should Raise the Dead.* Boston: Roxburgh, 1924. [Chapter 9 The Resurrection and the Return of Christ, See. 197–215; N.B. Not useful due to a lack of substance.]

Dryden, D. A. *They Rise: Suggestive Inquiries Concerning The Resurrection of the Dead As Taught In the New Testament.* Cincinnati: Hitchcock & Walden, 1872. [Chapter 7 The

Resurrection Of Jesus, See. 130–50; N.B. Archive.org and HathiTrust. Only twenty pages directly discuss Jesus's resurrection.]

Endsjø, Øistein Dag. *Greek Resurrection Beliefs and the Success of Christianity.* New York: Palgrave: Macmillan, 2009. [The Pierced Resurrection Body of John, See. 178–80. N.B. Carefully read the author's explanation why Jesus's bones were not broken while on the cross: interesting!]

Fysh, Frederic. *An Examination of 'Anastasis,' The Late Work of Professor Bush; Exposing The Fallacy of The Arguments Therein Advanced and Proving the Doctrine of The Resurrection of The Body To Be Scriptural and a Rational Doctrine.* London: Seeley, Burnside, and Seeley, 1847. [Section 22 The Resurrection of Christ, See. 247–307; N.B. Google book. The author interacts with Professor Bush's text, *Anastasis*.]

George, N. D. *Annihilationism Not of the Bible: Being an Examination of the Principal Scriptures in Controversy Between Evangelical Christians and Annihilationists.* Boston: For Sale by J. P. Magee, 1870. [See. 31–32, 47–48, 59–60, 129, 170–78; N.B. Google book]

Gerhard, Calvin S. *Death and the Resurrection: An Inquiry Into Their True Nature.* C. G. Fischer: Philadelphia, 1895. [Chapter 6 The Resurrection of Christ, See. 151–65; Chapter 7 The Forty Days, See. 166–77; N.B. Google book. Not useful due to a lack of substance.]

Goulburn, Edward Meyrick. *The Doctrine of the Resurrection of the Body, as Taught in Holy Scripture. Eight Sermons.* Oxford: Printed and Published by J. Vincent, 1850. [Lecture 5 The Resurrection of Our Lord Jesus Christ, See. 149–91; N.B. Archive.org, Google book, and HathiTrust]

Gray, James M. *A Picture of the Resurrection: An Exposition of the Fifteenth Chapter of First Corinthians.* New York: Revel, 1917. [Chapter 2 The Resurrection of Christ, See. 12–17; N.B. Google book]

Gutzke, Manford George. *Plain Talk on the Resurrection.* Grand Rapids: Baker, 1974. [Chapter 12 Was Christ's Resurrection Real?, See. 44–46]

Habermas, Gary R., and J. P. Moreland. *Beyond Death Exploring the Evidence for Immortality.* Eugene, OR: Wipf & Stock, 1998. [Chapter 5 The Resurrection of Jesus, See. 111–35; Chapter 6 Some Recent Objections to Jesus' Resurrection, See. 136–54; N.B. This work provides a solid analysis of Jesus's resurrection and objections to it.]

Hall, John. *How Are the Dead Raised: And with What Body Do They Come?* Hartford: Brown & Gross, 1875. [Chapter 2 See. Resurrection of Christ's body, Ascension of Christ, See. 32–43; Chapter 6 Translation of 1 Cor. 15. 12–57.—Remarks on the First Ten of these Verses, See. 124–36; N.B. Google book]

Hanna, William. *The Resurrection of the Dead.* New York: Robert Carter, 1874. [See. 7–47; N.B. Archive.org and Google book]

Hardman, Oscar. *The Resurrection of the Body.* London: SPCK, 1934. [Chapter 3 The Fact and Significance of the Empty Tomb, See. 39–52]

Harris, Henry. *Death and Resurrection: With An Introduction on the Value of External Evidence.* Oxford: James Parker, 1880. [Chapter 7 Two Witnesses, See. 38–44; Chapter 11 Dead and Risen, See. 67–73; Chapter 17 The Road to Glory, See. 104–10; N.B. Google book. Nothing substantial.]

Heikkinen, Jacob W. *To This We Are Witness Studies on the Contexts of Resurrection.* Gettysburg, PA: Lutheran Theological Seminary, 1971. [See. 17, 20–27]

Herbert, Albert J. *Raised From the Dead: True Stories of 400 Resurrection Miracles*. Rockford, IL: Tan, 1986. [Chapter 31 The Resurrection of Christ, The Basis of Our Faith, See. 289–308; N.B. Nothing substantial due to a lack of substance.]

Hodgson, George. *The Human Body at the Resurrection of the Dead*. London, 1853. [Error Relative to "Flesh and Blood," See. 20–24; N.B. Google book]

Hoyland, Geoffrey. *The Resurrection*. London: Gerald Duckworth, 1947. [Chapter 8 The Resurrection Pattern, See. 96–107]

Hughes-Games, Joshua. *On The Nature of the Resurrection Body*. London: James Nisbet, 1898. [Chapter 5 The Nature of Christ's Resurrection Body, See. 73–98]

Humphry, William Gilson. *The Doctrine of a Future State in Nine Sermons*. London: John W. Parker, 1850. [Lecture 6 The Evidence of Christ's Resurrection; An Objection Considered, See. 160–84; N.B. Google book. Nothing useful due to a lack of substance.]

Hutchinson, Samuel. *Scriptural Exhibition of the Mighty Conquest, and Glorious Triumph of Jesus Christ, Over Sin, Death, and Hell: and His Exaltation, His Second Coming, the Day of Judgment, and the Capacity, Equality, and Success of His Reign; and Ultimate Triumph*. Norway, ME: Printed at the Observer Office, by A. Barton, 1828. [144 pages]

Johnston, Robert Dougall. *Resurrection: Myth or Miracle*. Kilmarnock, Scotland: J. Ritchie, 1934. [Chapter 8 Internal Evidence of the Resurrection, See. 63–71; Chapter 9 External Evidence of the Resurrection, See. 73–80; Chapter 10 Further External Evidence of the Resurrection, See. 81–90; Chapter 11 Fruits of the Resurrection, See. 91–98; N.B. Nothing substantial due to a lack of substance.]

Killingworth, Grantham. *On the Immortality of the Soul: The Resurrection of the Body, The Glorious Millennium, The Most Glorious Kingdom Of God, and the Prophet Daniel's Numbers*. London: Printed for Geo. Kearsley & T. Piety, 1761. [See. 26–27, 66–67, 79; N.B. Google book]

Kingsley, Calvin, and George Peck. *The Resurrection of the Dead: A Vindication of the Literal Resurrection of the Human Body*. New York: Lane & Tibbett, 1848. [Part 2. Scriptural Argument—The Resurrection of Our Saviour Considered, See. 45–79; N.B. Archive.org, Google book, and HathiTrust. Nothing substantial due to a lack of substance.]

Küng, Hans. *Eternal Life? Life After Death as a Medical, Philosophical, and Theological Problem*. Translated by Edward Quinn. Garden City, NY: Doubleday, 1984. [Difficulties with the Resurrection of Jesus, See. 96–118]

Landis, Robert W. *The Doctrine of the Resurrection of the Body: Asserted and Defended; in Answer to the Exceptions Recently Presented by Rev. George Bush*. Philadelphia: Perkins & Purves, 1846. [Chapter 3 The New Testament Doctrine of the Resurrection. Section 3.— Examination of Passages in 1 Corinthians, See. 188–93; also See. 31, 32, 114, 115, 236, 332, 341, 344; N.B. Archive.org]

Lehtipuu, Outi. *Debates over the Resurrection of the Dead: Constructing Early Christian Identity*. Oxford, England: Oxford University Press, 2015. [Chapter 1 What Is Resurrection?, See. 23–65 (especially, The Resurrection of Jesus and Its Relationship to the General Resurrection; Christ's Appearance to Paul; The Gospel Tradition: The Empty Tomb and the Tangible Body; Jesus as a Prototype of the Believers?); N.B. His book is primarily about the early Christian debates over the resurrection of the dead.]

Levering, Matthew. *Jesus and the Demise of Death: Resurrection, Afterlife, and the Fate of the Christian*. Waco, TX: Baylor University Press, 2012. [Chapter 2 The Resurrection of

Jesus Christ, See. 27–42; N.B. Only Chapter 2 directly interacts with the resurrection narratives.]

Lewis, Jason. *The Anastasis of the Dead: or, Philosophy of Human Immortality, As Deduced from the Teaching of the Scripture Writers, in Reference to "the Resurrection."* Boston: A. Tompkins, 1860. [Chapter 33 Our Savior's Resurrection, &c, See. 293–300; Chapter 34 Christ's Ascension, See. 301–3; N.B. Google book]

Madigan, Kevin J., and Jon D. Levenson. *Resurrection: The Power of God for Christians and Jews.* New Haven: Yale University Press, 2008. [See. 1–4, 21–23, 24–27, 42]

Mattison, Hiram. *The Resurrection of the Dead: Considered in the Light of History, Philosophy, and Divine Revelation.* Philadelphia: Perkinpine & Higgins, 1866. [Chapter 7 The Resurrection of Christ, See. 100–30; Chapter 8 The Resurrection of Christ and the "New Church" Theory, See. 131–44; N.B. Google book. Mattison presents a basic review of the arguments in support of Jesus's resurrection. He does not ask any hard questions that challenge that resurrection.]

Maxwell-Stuart, P. G. *Ghosts A History of Phantoms, Ghouls and Other Spirits of the Dead.* Great Britain: Tempus, 2006. [See. 35]

McCann, Justin. *The Resurrection of the Body.* New York: Macmillan, 1928. [Chapter 5 The Testimony of Holy Scripture in General, See. 34–36]

McLeman, James. *Resurrection Then and Now.* London: Hodder & Stoughton, 1965. [Part 3 The Resurrection Narratives, See. 127–72; N.B. Reprinted in 1995. A good read.]

Mettinger, Tryggve N. D. *The Riddle of Resurrection: "Dying and Rising Gods" in the Ancient Near East.* Stockholm: Almqvist & Wiksell, 2001. [See. 221]

Mitchell, Thomas. *Non Spiritus: The Philosophy of Spiritualism.* Albany: Weed, Parsons & Co., 1872. [Chapter 15 That Spiritualism Supersedes the Bible, See. 141–46; N.B. Archive.org]

Mott, George Scudder. *The Resurrection of the Dead.* New York: N. Tibbals, 1866. [Chapter 3 Resurrection of Jesus Christ, See. 51–70; N.B. Archive.org. Nothing substantial due to a lack of substance.]

Mullowney, John James. *I Believe.* Tampa, FL: Florida Grower Press, 1944. [The Narrative of the Resurrection, See. 44–55; N.B. Not useful due to a lack of content.]

Nisbet, E. *The Resurrection of the Body: Does the Bible Teach It?* New York: Authors' Publishing, 1877. [Chapter 10 Christ's Resurrection Body, See. 84–90; N.B. Nothing substantial due to a lack of substance.]

Perry, Michael. *The Resurrection of Man: Christian Teaching on Life after Death.* London: Mowbrays, 1975. [The Resurrection of Jesus, See. 40–47]

Peters, Ted, ed. *Resurrection Theological and Scientific Assessments.* Grand Rapids: Eerdmans, 2002. [This edited book consists of eighteen essays. Most of this text does not deal with Jesus's physical, bodily resurrection.]

Pilcher, Charles Venn. *The Hereafter in Jewish and Christian Thought: With Special Reference to the Doctrine of Resurrection.* London: SPCK, 1940. [Lecture 6 Resurrection in Christian Thought, See. 157–90; N.B. This work does not directly discuss Jesus's resurrection.]

Rahner, Karl. *The Resurrection of the Body.* Derby, NY: St. Paul Publications, 1967. [Chapter 1 The Resurrection of Christ, See. 13–18]

Reichenbach, Bruce R. *Is Man the Phoenix? A Study of Immortality.* Grand Rapids: Christian University Press, 1978. [Chapter 8 The Historical-Theological Argument, See. 135–62; N.B. Only Chapter 8 interacts with the resurrection narratives.]

Rolt, C. E. *The Spiritual Body.* SPCK: London, 1920. [Chapter 4 The Appearances of the Risen Christ, See. 81–105; N.B. Archive.org]

Schep, J. A. *The Nature of the Resurrection Body: A Study of the Biblical Data.* Grand Rapids: Eerdmans, 1964. [Chapter 4 The Resurrection-Body of Jesus Christ, See. 107–44; Chapter 5 The Body of Our Exalted Lord, The Life-Giving Spirit, See. 145–81; N.B. This text explores different aspects of Jesus's resurrection.]

Schmisek, Brian. *Resurrection of the Flesh or Resurrection from the Dead: Implications for Theology.* Collegeville, MN: Liturgical Press, 2013. [Chapter 2 Biblical Data, See. 49–92; Attestations to the Risen Christ, See. 56–72; N.B. The author discusses the strength of many metaphors, including Jesus's resurrection. This chapter should be examined.]

Sears, Edmund H. *Athanasia, or, Foregleams of Immortality.* 10th ed. Boston: American Unitarian Association, 1858. [382 pages; N.B. Google book. This is a classic, dated source. Of interest, Part 2, The Excarnation of the Son of Man, See. 169–225]

Setzer, Claudia. *Resurrection of the Body in Early Judaism and Early Christianity: Doctrine, Community, and Self-definition.* Boston: Brill Academic, 2004. [Chapter 3 Resurrection Among Believers in Jesus. See. 53–70]

Sherman, Loren Albert. *Science of the Soul: A Scientific Demonstration of the Existence of the Soul of Man as his Conscious Individuality Independently of the Physical Organism; of the Continuity of Life and the Actuality of Spirit Return.* Fort Huron, MI: Sherman, 1895. [Part 3 The Soul Decarnate, Chapter 41, See. 180–95; N.B. Archive.org and Google book. Sherman does not extensively interact with the narratives.]

Slattery, Charles Lewis. *Life Beyond Life: A Study of Immortality.* London: Longmans, Green, 1907. [Chapter 3 The Christian Revelation, See. 29–47; N.B. Google book. Nothing substantial in this source.]

Staudt, Calvin Klopp. *The Idea of the Resurrection in the Ante-Nicene Period.* Chicago: University of Chicago Press, 1909. [Chapter 2 The New Testament, See. 17–25; N.B. Google book]

Swete, Henry Barclay. *The Life of the World to Come: Six Addresses.* London: SPCK 1918. [Address 3 The Resurrection of Christ, See. 37–56; N.B. Google book. Swete's essay presents a traditional argument in support of the resurrection.]

Tenney, Merrill C. *Resurrection Realities; "Now Christ Is Risen."* Los Angeles: Bible House of Los Angeles, 1945. [Chapter 1 Resurrection Facts, See. 11–24]

Thomas, Reuen. *Through Death to Life: Discourses on St. Paul's Great Resurrection Chapter.* 2nd ed. Boston: Silver, Burdett, 1891. [N.B. Archive.org; No substantial interaction with the narratives.]

Turrentine, Charles P. *Examination of the Doctrine of the Resurrection and Other Subjects Therewith Connected.* Louisville: Morton & Griswold, 1849. [See. 143–50; N.B. Google book. No substantial interaction with the narratives.]

Villars, I. *The Resurrection Life or "Beyond the Grave" Examined.* Cincinnati: Walden & Stowe, 1881. [Chapter 2 (1) the argument from the resurrection body of Christ, See. 164–65]

Westcott, Brooke Foss. *The Gospel of the Resurrection: Thoughts on its Relation to Reason and History.* London: Macmillan, 1879. [Chapter 1 The Resurrection and History, See. 44–119, The Special Evidence for the Resurrection, See. 92–118. The author's book is often cited in the literature.]

White, Wilbert W. *The Resurrection Body "according to the Scriptures."* New York: Doran, 1923. [Chapter 4 Why is the Resurrection Judged Credible?, See. 45–79; N.B. The author presents a review of the gospel narratives.]

Whiton, James Morris. *Beyond the Shadow, or, The Resurrection of Life.* 4th ed. New York: Thos. Whittaker, 1898. [Chapter 3 The Resurrection Exemplified In the Risen Christ, See. 49–77; N.B. Google book and originally published in 1881 under the title, *The Gospel of the Resurrection.*]

———. *The Gospel of the Resurrection.* Boston: Houghton, Mifflin, 1881. [Chapter 3 The Resurrection Exemplified in the Risen Christ, See. 56–82; N.B. Archive.org. The author advocates a bodily resurrection.]

Whitworth, John F. *Legal and Historical Proof of the Resurrection of the Dead: With an Examination of the Evidence in the New Testament.* Harrisburg, PA: Publishing House of the United Evangelical Church, 1912. [Chapter 4 An Examination of the Evidence in the New Testament, See. 39–70]

Wong, John B. *The Resurrected Body—Y2K and Beyond: A New Concept of the Resurrected Body from Biblical, Theological, Philosophical, and Scientific Perspectives.* Lanham, MD: University Press of America, 2000. [Chapter 3 The Resurrected Body — Biblical Perspective. See. 55–87; N.B. Wong's work is interesting and a recommended read.]

Wright, N. T. *Surprised By Hope: Rethinking Heaven, the Resurrection, and the Mission of the Church.* New York: HarperCollins, 2008. [Chapter 4 The Strange Story of Easter, See. 53–76; N.B. Wright discusses seven mutations of the Jewish resurrection belief and its association with messiahship.]

Category III

Apologetics and Anti-Apologetics

CHAPTER 7

Apologetics: Pro Resurrection

Abanes, Richard. *Defending the Faith: A Beginner's Guide to Cults and New Religions.* Grand Rapids: Baker, 1997. [Chapter 9 Death's Defeat, See. 133–49]

Abbott, Lyman. *The Kernel and the Husk: Letters on Spiritual Christianity.* London: MacMillan, 1886. [Letter 21 The Development of Imagination and its Bearing on the Revelation of Christ's Resurrection, See. 233–39; Letter 22 Christ's Resurrection Regarded Naturally, See. 240–45; Letter 23 Faith in the Spiritual Resurrection is Better than So-Called Knowledge of the Material Resurrection, See. 246–57; N.B. Archive.org, Google book, and HathiTrust]

Abell, Dave. *Common Sense Apologetics: One God, One Book, One Way.* Bloomington, IN: West Bow Press, 2010. [Chapter 12: A World Changer: The Resurrection of Jesus Christ, See. 132–35]

Adams, Alice Dana. *Young Christian's Bible Class Questions & Answers on the Old and New Testaments.* Philadelphia: Holman, 1931. [100. The Resurrection Days, See. 87–88, 101; The Acts of the Apostles, See. 88–89]

Adams, Hannah. *The Truth and Excellence of the Christian Religion Exhibited in Two Parts.* Boston: David Carlisle, 1804. [Part 2, Section 4. The Resurrection of Christ Evinces the Certainty of Revealed Religion, See. 259–63 N.B. Archive.org, Google book, and HathiTrust]

Addison, Joseph. *The Evidences of the Christian Religion.* 2nd ed. London: Printed for J. Tonson, 1733. [See. 18, 43, 47, 74, 216–19, 259–60; N.B. Archive.org and Google book]

Aiken, Charles Augustus. *Christian Apologetics: The Lectures Constituting the Course in Ethics and Apologetics.* Princeton: Press Printing Establishment, 1879. [See. 63, 64, 65, 69, 82, 108; N.B. Archive.org]

Aikman, David. *The Delusion of Disbelief: Why the New Atheism is a Threat to Your Life, Liberty, and Pursuit of Happiness.* Carol Stream, IL: Tyndale House, 2008. [Appendix, Assertion #6: The Gospels differ in their accounts of the resurrection of Jesus, See. 208–11]

Alden, Joseph. *Outlines of Christian Evidences.* New York: Nelson & Phillips, 1887. [Chapter 6 The Miracles of the Gospel, See. 18–21]

Alexander, Archibald. *A Brief Outline of the Evidences of the Christian Religion.* Philadelphia: American Sunday School Union. 1829. [Section 5 The Miracles of the Gospels are Credible, See. 69–120, esp. 76–109; N.B. Google book]

———. *Evidences of the Authenticity, Inspiration, and Canonical Authority of the Holy Scriptures.* Philadelphia: Presbyterian Board of Publication, 1836. [Chapter 7 The Miracles of the Gospel are Credible, See. 95, 96, 100, 107, 108, 162, 230; N.B. Google book]

Alexander, William. *Christ and Christianity: A Vindication of the Divine Authority of the Christian Religion Grounded on the Historical Verity of the Life of Christ.* New York: Carlton & Philips, 1854. [Christ, resurrection of, See. 98, 111–17, 162–63, 180; N.B. Google book]

———. *Primary Convictions.* London: Osgood, McIlvaine, 1893. [Discussion 4 A Literary Proof of the Resurrection of Jesus Christ, See. 93–128; N.B. Google book]

Allix, Pierre. *Reflections Upon the Books of the Holy Scripture: To Establish the Truth of the Christian Religion.* Oxford: Clarendon, 1822. [Part 4 Chapter 21 That the Messiah was Soon After to Rise Again, See. 331–34; Part 4 Chapter 13 That Jesus Christ was Raised Again the Third Day, according to the Prophets, and Afterwards Ascended into Heaven, See. 429–39; N.B. Google book]

Anderson, J. N. D. *The Evidence for the Resurrection.* Downers Grove, IL: InterVarsity, 1966. [N.B. pamphlet]

Anderson, Norman. *A Lawyer Among the Theologians.* London: Hodder & Stoughton, 1973. [Chapter 3 The Resurrection—Its Basic Historicity, See. 66–104; Chapter 4 The Resurrection—The Biblical Evidence, See. 105–47]

Andrews, Thomas. *Thoughts on Faith and Scepticism.* London: James Nisbet, 1894. [See. 39, 40, 100, 119; N.B. Google book]

Ankerberg, John, and Dillon Burroughs. *Taking a Stand for the Bible: Today's Leading Experts Answer Critical Questions About God's Word.* Eugene, OR: Harvest House, 2009. [Jesus Physically Rose from the Dead as Proof of His Claim, See. 184–86]

Ankerberg, John, and Emil Caner. *The Truth About Islam and Jihad.* Eugene, OR: Harvest House, 2009. [See. 66–67]

Ankerberg, John, and John Weldon. *The Facts on Islam.* Eugene, OR: Harvest House, 2003. [Islam teaches that Jesus Christ was neither crucified nor resurrected; therefore, salvation cannot possibly be had through faith in Christ, See. 27–29]

———. *Fast Facts on Defending Your Faith.* Eugene, OR: Harvest House, 2002. [See. Issue 25. Did Jesus Actually Rise From the Dead?, See. 109–11; Section 5: The Resurrection of Christ, Issues 28–36. See. 121–74; N.B. These issues should be examined.]

———. *The Fast Facts on Islam.* Eugene, OR: Harvest House, 2001. [See. Denial of Resurrection, See. 30–32]

———. *Handbook of Biblical Evidences.* Eugene, OR: Harvest House, 2002. [Chapter 6 Resurrection on Trial, See. 99–109; Chapter 7 Alternate Theories to the Resurrection, See. 111–29; Chapter 8 Did He Rise? The Resurrection Debate, See. 131–39]

———. *Ready with an Answer.* Eugene, OR: Harvest House, 1997. [Chapter 6 Resurrection on Trial, See. 99–110; Chapter 7 Alternate Theories on the Resurrection, See. 111–30; Chapter 8 Did He Rise? The Resurrection Debate, See. 131–39]

Archer, Gleason L. *Encyclopedia of Bible Difficulties.* Grand Rapids: Zondervan, 1982. [Do not the many discrepancies in the four Resurrection narratives cast doubt on the historicity of the resurrection itself?, See. 347–56]

Armstrong, C. B. *Creeds and Credibility.* Oxford: Mowbray, 1969. [Chapter 7 The Resurrection, See. 101–7]

Baggott, L. J. *The Faith for the Faithful*. London: Nisbet, 1928. [Chapter 6 Dead. Buried. Risen. See. 128–43]

Bahnsen, Greg L. *Van Til's Apologetic: Readings and Analysis*. Phillipsburg, NJ: P&R, 1998. [Jesus Christ resurrection, See. 35, 272, 580–87, 642n.193, 645–47, 650–51, 652–53]

Bailie, Gil. *Violence Unveiled: Humanity at the Crossroads*. New York: Crossroad, 2001. [The Empty Tomb, See. 228–32; The Resurrection, See. 232–33]

Ballard, Frank. *The Miracles of Unbelief*. Edinburgh: T&T Clark, 1904. [Chapter 5 Facts of History and Their Explanation, See. 107–74; Chapter 4, See. 135–73; N.B. Archive.org and HathiTrust]

———. *The People's Religious Difficulties*. London: Robert Culley, 1909. [Questions 660–62. See. 413–16]

Barclay, Oliver R. *Reasons for Faith*. Downers Grover, IL: InterVarsity, 1974. [Chapter 12 God is not dead, See. 113–16]

Barclay, Robert. *Barclay's Apology for the True Christian Divinity as Professed by the People Called Quakers*. 2nd ed. Abridged by George Harrison. London: Printed for Harvey & Darton, 1822. [See. 76, 96, 104, 109, 203, 209; N.B. HathiTrust]

Barclay, William, and Iain Reid. *Arguing About Christianity: Seven Discussions between William Barclay and Iain Reid*. Edinburgh: Saint Andrew Press, 1980. [See. 28–29: N.B. Barclay opines that Jesus never said that he was God.]

Barnett, Paul. *Is the New Testament Reliable? A Look at the Historical Evidence*. Downers Grove, IL: InterVarsity, 2003. [The Resurrection of Jesus, See. 111–35]

———. *Jesus and the Logic of History*. Grand Rapids: Eerdmans, 1997. [Excursus The Resurrection of Jesus From the Dead, See. 128–31]

Barry, Alfred. *The Manifold Witness for Christ*. London: J. Murray, 1880. [Chapter 7 The Spirituality of Man and the Resurrection of Christ, See. 123–44; N.B. Archive.org. Not useful.]

Barry, F. R. *Questioning Christian Faith*. New York: Seabury, 1966. [Resurrection of Jesus, See. 15, 77, 90, 111, 127, 129, 131, 135, 145, 147, 155, 169, 176, 177, 178, 179, 184]

Bartholomew, David J. *Uncertain Belief: Is it Rational to be a Christian?* Oxford: Clarendon, 2000. [Jesus resurrection of, See. 67–68, 105, 110–12, 205]

Bate, George. *Heathen, Jewish, and Infidel Testimony to Bible Facts, Christianity, Etc.* London: Hamilton Adams, 1883. [Lecture 5 Has Christ Risen From The Dead?, See. 101–21; N.B. Google book]

Baxter, Batsell Barrett. *I Believe Because . . . A Study of the Evidence Supporting Christian Faith*. Grand Rapids: Baker, 1971. [Chapter 27 Evidence of the Resurrection, See. 223–32]

Baxter, Richard. *The Reasons of the Christian Religion*. London: Pr. by R. White, for Fran. Titon, 1667. [See. 278–79, 305, 326, 335–36, 423; N.B. Google book]

Beard, J. R. *Illustrations of the Divine in Christianity: A Series of Discourses Exhibiting Views of the Truth, Spirit, and Practical Value, of the Gospel*. London: Simpkin, Marshall, 1849. [Chapter 16 The Divine in Attestation, See. 107–14; N.B. Google book]

———. *A Manual of Christian Evidence: Containing as an Antidote to Current Materialistic Tendencies, Particularly as Found in the Writings of Ernest Renan, an Outline of the Manifestation of God in the Bible, in Providence, in History, in the Universe, and in the Lord and Saviour Jesus Christ*. London: Simpkin, Marshall, 1868. [Chapter 8 (12). The Resurrection of Lazarus and the Resurrection of Jesus, See. 427–45; N.B. HathiTrust]

Category III—Apologetics and Anti-Apologetics

Beattie, James. *Evidences of the Christian Religion: Briefly and Plainly Stated.* Volume First. Edinburgh: Printed for A. Strahan & T. Cadell, London and W. Creech, Edinburgh, 1786. [See. 63–64, 79, 122, 163–64; N.B. Google book]

Beauchamp, William. *Essays on the Truth of the Christian Religion.* Marietta: Joseph Israel, 1811. [Essay 26 The Miracles Recorded in the New Testament, See. 159–66; N.B. Google book]

Beckwith, Francis J. *David Hume's Argument Against Miracles: A Critical Analysis.* Lanham, MD: University Press of America, 1989. [See. 50–51, 62–63, 98–100]

Beet, Joseph Agar. *The Credentials of the Gospel: A Statement of the Reason of the Christian Hope.* New York: Hunt & Eaton, 1891. [Section 6 The Historical Argument, See. 122–26; N.B. Archive.org and Google book]

———. *The Firm Foundation of the Christian Faith: A Handbook of Christian Evidences for Sunday School Teachers.* 2nd ed. London: Wesleyan Methodist Sunday School Union, 1896. [Chapter 10 The Resurrection of Christ, See. 66–76; N.B. Google book]

Beisner, E. Calvin. *Answers for Atheists, Agnostics, and Other Thoughtful Skeptics: Dialogs About Christian Faith and Life.* Wheaton, IL: Crossway, 1985. [Chapter 5 Did Jesus Really Rise from the Dead?, See. 73–81]

Bell, B. Clayton. *Moorings in a World Adrift: Answers for Christians Who Dare to Ask Why.* San Francisco: HarperSanFrancisco, 1990. [Chapter 5 Where Was Jesus While His Body Was in the Graves?, See. 43–50; Chapter 6 What Does Easter Have To Do With Christmas?, See. 51–58; Chapter 7 What Is Jesus Doing Now?, See. 59–65]

Benson, C. *On Evidences of Christianity.* 4th ed. London: Baldwin, Cradock & Joy, 1826. [See. 126, 153, 154, 155, 156; N.B. Google book]

Bergen, John Tallmadge. *Old and New Evidences of Christianity.* New York: Broadway 1916. [Chapter 11 Authenticity of the Resurrection of Jesus, See. 99–108]

Bickel, Bruce, and Stan Jantz. *Evidence for Faith 101.* Eugene, OR: Harvest House, 2008. [The Resurrection of Jesus, See. 157–68; 224–26]

Blaiklock, E. M. *Layman's Answer: An Examination of the New Theology.* London: Hodder & Stoughton, 1968. [The Resurrection in History, See. 70–81]

———. *Still a Christian.* London: Hodder & Stoughton, 1980. [Chapter 6 Unless Christ be Risen, See. 79–92]

Blaiklock, E. M., and David A. Blaiklock. *Is It-or Isn't It? Why We Believe in the Existence of God.* Grand Rapids: Zondervan, 1968. [Chapter 7 That Empty Tomb, See. 64–71]

Blanchard, John. *Does God Believe in Atheist?* Auburn, MA: Evangelical Press, 2000. [Man alive!, See. 578–84; N.B. Blanchard reviews and shoots down various naturalistic resurrection theories.]

———. *Right with God: A Straightforward Book to Help Those Searching for a Personal Faith in God.* London: Banner of Truth Trust, 1971. [Thirdly, the Death of Jesus was Victorious, See. 77–81]

Blomberg, Craig. *The Historical Reliability of the Gospels.* 2nd ed. Leicester, London: Inter-Varsity Press, 2007. [The Resurrection, See. 136–51]

———. *The Historical Reliability of John's Gospel: Issues & Commentary.* Downers Grove, IL: InterVarsity, 2002. [Part Two: Commentary, See 258–81]

———. *The Historical Reliability of the New Testament: Countering the Challenges to Evangelical Christian Beliefs.* Nashville: B&H Academic, 2016. [Resurrection, See. 695–715]

———. *Making Sense of the New Testament: Three Crucial Questions*. Grand Rapids: Baker, 2004. [Resurrection, See. 68–70]

Boa, Kenneth, and Robert M. Bowman. *Faith Has Its Reasons: Integrative Approaches to Defending the Christian Faith*. 2nd ed. Waynesboro, GA: Paternoster, 2005. [Presenting Evidence that Demands a Verdict. See. Miracles As Evidence For God, See. 191–98]

———. *20 Compelling Evidences That God Exists: Why Believing in God Makes So Much Sense*. Colorado Springs, CO: Victor, 2005. [Evidence 16 The Evidence of Jesus' Empty Tomb, See. 217–27; Evidence 17 The Evidence of Jesus' Resurrection Appearances, See. 247–61]

Bomford, Rodney. *The Symmetry of God*. London: Free Association, 1999. [The Resurrection—Miracle Or Myth?, See. 120–22]

Bond, B. W. *The Positive Evidences of Christianity*. Edited by Thomas O. Summers. Nashville: Southern Methodist Publishing House, 1880. [Part 2 The Weight of the Evidence, 5. (2) The Evidence of the Miracle of the Resurrection of Christ, in Particular, See. 231–53; Bond presents a good overview from the point of view of a traditional apologist; N.B. Archive.org and Google book]

Bonnet, M. Charles. *Interesting Views of Christianity*. Boston: Bradford & Read, 1813. [Section 6 The Resurrection of the Founder, See. 30–44; N.B. Google book]

———. *Philosophical and Critical Inquiries Concerning Christianity*. Translated by John Lewis Boissier. Philadelphia: Printed and Published by W. W. Woodward, 1803. [Book 2 Chapter 6 The Resurrection, See. 136–46; N.B. Google book 1787 printing.]

Boomsma, Clarence. *Why I Still Believe the Gospel*. Grand Rapids: Eerdmans, 2007. [Chapter 2 The Resurrection of Jesus, See. 25–41; Chapter 3 Modern Denial of the Resurrection of Jesus, See. 43–69; Chapter 4 Christ Has Been Raised from the Dead, See. 71–106]

Bose, Ram Chandra. *The Truth of the Christian Religion as Established by the Miracles of Christ*. London: R. K. Burt, 1882. [Lecture 15, See. 333–63; N.B. Google book]

Boully, James. *The Oxford Declaration and the Eleven Thousand Biblical Truths and Bishop Colenso*. London: Frederick Farrah, 1864. [See. 57, 86, 89, 90, 92, 95, 99, 100, 101, 102; N.B. Google book]

Bourn, Samuel. *A Series of Discourses on the Principles and Evidences of Natural Religion and the Christian Revelation*. Vol. 1. London: Printed for R. Griffiths, 1760. [Discourse 11, See. 259–84; N.B. Google book]

Bowman, S. L. *Historical Evidence of the New Testament: An Inductive Study in Christian Evidences*. Cincinnati: Jennings & Pye, 1903. [Chapter 10 The Resurrection of Jesus Christ, See. 233–95; Chapter 11 The Ascension of Jesus Christ, See. 296–311; N.B. HathiTrust. This work is a significant reading.]

Boyd, Gregory A., and Paul Eddy. *Lord or Legend? Wrestling with the Jesus Dilemma*. Grand Rapids: Baker, 2007. [Jesus resurrection of, See. 45, 59, 131]

Boyd, Robert T. *Boyd's Handbook of Practical Apologetics: Scientific Facts, Fulfilled Prophecies, and Archaeological Discoveries That Confirm the Bible*. Grand Rapids: Kregel, 1997. [The Resurrection of Christ, See. 90–91, and 183, 195]

Braaten, Carl E. *Who Is Jesus? Disputed Questions and Answers*. Grand Rapids: Eerdmans, 2011. [Chapter 3 Did Jesus Really Rise from the Dead?, See. 49–57]

Braden, Clark. *Ingersoll Unmasked: A Scathing and Fearless Expose of His Real Life*. Lexington, KT: Blue Grass, 1900. [See. 106–7; N.B. Archive.org]

Category III—Apologetics and Anti-Apologetics

Brierley, Justin. *Unbelieveable?—Why After Ten Years of Talking with Atheists, I'm Still a Christian.* SPCK, 2017. [Chapter 6 Facts that only fit the resurrection]

Brown, John. *A Compendious View of Natural and Revealed Religion.* 2nd ed. Philadelphia: Published and Sold by David Hogan, 1819. [Book 4 Chapter 2 Of Christ's States: His Humiliation and Exaltation, 302–20; N.B. Google book]

Brown, Raymond E. *Responses to 101 Questions on the Bible.* New York: Paulist, 2010. [#52, 53, 76; See. 72–76, 103–5]

Brown, William E. *Making Sense of Your Faith.* Wheaton, IL: Victor, 1989. [The Grand Miracle: The Resurrection of Jesus, See. 95–97]

Brownson, O. A. *Charles Elwood or the Infidel Converted.* Boston: Charles C. Little & James Brown, 1890. [See. 160–61, 163, 240–41; N.B. Google book]

Bruce, Alexander Balmain. *Apologetics: or, Christianity Defensively Stated.* New York: Scribner's Sons, 1892. [Chapter 4 Jesus Risen, See. 383–97; V. Jesus Lord. See. The Resurrection, See. 402–3; N.B. Google book]

———. *The Miraculous Element in the Gospels: A Course of Lectures on the "Ely Foundation."* New York: C. Armstrong, 1886. [Chapter 9 The Great Moral Miracle. Birth From a Virgin and Resurrection Denied, See. 351–53; N.B. Google book]

Bryan, William Jennings. *Seven Questions in Dispute.* New York: Revell, 1924. [Chapter 5 The Bodily Resurrection of Our Lord, See. 85–102]

Bulfinch, Stephen G. *Manual of the Evidences of Christianity, for Classes and Private Reading.* Boston: W. V. Spencer, 1866. [Section 10. Death and Resurrection of Jesus, See. 29–32; N.B. Google book and Archive.org]

———. *Studies in the Evidences of Christianity.* Boston: William V. Spencer, 1869. [See. 5, 14, 151–52, 160–61, 165, 223, 227–28, 260; N.B. Google book]

Busenitz, Nathan. *Reasons We Believe: 50 Lines of Evidence that Confirm the Christian Faith.* Wheaton, IL: Crossway, 2008. [Part 2. Reasons We Believe in Jesus: He Died and Rose Again, See. 193–212]

Butt, Kyle. *Out With Doubt: A Look at the Evidence for Christianity.* Montgomery, Alabama: Apologetics Press, 2001. [The Resurrection of Jesus Christ]

Buttrick, George Arthur. *The Christian Fact and Modern Doubt.* New York: Scribner's Sons, 1935. [See. 272–76]

Cairns, John. *Christ the Central Evidence of Christianity, and other Present Day Tracts.* London: Religious Tract Society, 1893. [See. 4, 8, 16–20, 31–43; N.B. Google book]

Campbell, Archibald. *The Authenticity of the Gospel History Justified and the Truth of the Christian Revelation Demonstrated.* Edinburgh: Hamilton, Balfour & Neill, 1759. [Section 3, See. 99; N.B. Google book]

Campbell, Charlie. *One-Minute Answers to Skeptics.* Eugene, OR: Harvest House, 2010. [Question 19 How can you be sure Jesus rose from the dead?, See. 55–56; Question 28 Isn't there evidence that the New Testament authors borrowed their idea for Jesus' resurrection from ancient pagan religions that were around long before the time of Christ?, See. 73–74]

Candler, Warren A. *Christus Auctor: A Manual of Christian Evidences.* Nashville: Publishing House of the M.E. Church, 1900. [Chapter 6 Has God Appeared Among Men? Did Jesus Rise from the Dead? St. Paul's Testimony, See. 69–88; Chapter 8 Has God Appeared Among Men? Did Jesus Rise from the Dead? The Testimony of the Evangelists, See. 105–24; N.B. Google book]

Caner, Ergun Mehmet, and Emir Fethi Caner. *Unveiling Islam: An Insider's Look at Muslim Life and Beliefs*. Grand Rapids: Kregel, 2009. [Chapter 15 Jesus According to the Qur'an. See. Christ's Death and Ascension, See. 219–20]

Carey, P. M. *A Concise View of the Evidences and Corruptions of Christianity*. London: Smallfield, 1838. [Appendix C. On the Resurrection, See. 277–83; N.B. Google book]

Carnell, Edward John. *An Introduction to Christian Apologetics: A Philosophic Defense of the Trinitarian-Theistic Faith*. 3rd ed. Grand Rapids: Eerdmans, 1948. [Chapter 14 See. Natural Law and the Resurrection of Christ, See. 253–60]

———. *The Kingdom of Love and the Pride of Life*. Grand Rapids: Eerdmans, 1960. [Chapter 4 Hope of the Resurrection, See. 97–105]

Chalmers, Thomas. *On the Miraculous and Internal Evidences of the Authority of its Records*. Vol. 1. New York: Robert Carter, 1850. [See. 103–4, 125, 136, 164, 221, 253, 268, 277, 286–87; N.B. Google book]

Chamberlain, Paul. *Why People Stop Believing*. Eugene, OR: Cascade, 2018. [See. 112, 118–20, 135, 177–80]

Chapman, Colin. *Christianity on Trial*. Wheaton, IL: Tyndale House, 1975. [Did Jesus Rise From The Dead?, See. 505–50]

———. *Cross and Crescent: Responding to the Challenges of Islam*. Downers Grove, IL: InterVarsity, 2008. [Jesus was not crucified, See. 253–54]

Christlieb, Theodore. *Modern Doubt and Christian Belief: A Series of Apologetic Lectures Addressed to Earnest Seekers after Truth*. Translated by H. U. Weitbrecht and T. I. Kingsbury. New York: Scribner's Sons, 1878. [Seventh Lecture. Modern Denials of the Resurrection of Christ, See. 448–503; N.B. Google book]

Clark, Mark. *The Problem of God: Answering a Skeptic's Challenges to Christianity*. Grand Rapids: Zondervan, 2017. [The Resurrection]

Clark, William R. *Witnesses to Christ, a Contribution to Christian Apologetics*. Chicago: A. C. McClurg, 1888. [Lecture 7 The Resurrection of Jesus Christ Part 1: See. 216–54; Lecture 8 The Resurrection of Jesus Christ Part 2, See. 255–85; N.B. Google book]

Clarke, James Freeman. *Orthodoxy: Its Truths And Errors*. Boston: American Unitarian Association, 1876. [Chapter 4 Truths and Errors as Regards Miracles. §8. Miracle of the Resurrection. Skeptical Objections, See. 80–86; N.B. Archive.org and Google book]

———. *Steps of Belief or, Rational Christianity Maintained Against Atheism, Free Religion, and Romanism*. Boston: American Unitarian Association, 1880. [See. 26, 114, 170; N.B. Google book and HathiTrust]

Clergy Centre (London). *A Reason For the Hope: A Short Course of Apologetic on the Apostles' Creed, etc*. London: A. R. Mowbray, 1955. [See. The Risen Christ, See. 53–65]

Clifford, Ross. *John Warwick Montgomery's Legal Apologetic: An Apologetic for All Seasons*. Eugene, OR: Wipf & Stock, 2016. [Numerous places; especially The Resurrection and Circumstantial Evidence, See. 189–211, The Resurrection and Direct Evidence—Montgomery and the Place of Story, See. 217–23]

Clifford, Ross, and Philip Johnson. *The Cross Is Not Enough Living as Witness to the Resurrection*. Grand Rapids: Baker, 2012. [Chapter 11 The New Testament, See. 225–51]

Cogitans, John. *The Spiritual Mustard Pot: Containing a Demonstration of the Existence of God, Answers to Three Objections to the Divine Origin of the Scriptures*. Troy, NY: 1824. [See. 150–51; N.B. Google book]

Coles, George. *The Antidote, or Revelation Defended, and Infidelity Repulsed; in a Course of Lectures.* Hartford: Printed by P. Canfield, 1836. [Lecture 13 On the Resurrection of Christ, See. 368–86; N.B. Google book]

Colgrave, Bertram, and A. J. Rendle Short. *The Historic Faith in the Light of Today.* 2nd ed. London: Marshall Brothers, 1921. [The Evidence for the Resurrection, See. 98–107]

Colquhoun, Frank, ed. Hard Questions. Downers Grove, IL: InterVarsity, 1977. [Chapter 10 Did Jesus really rise from the dead?, See. 41–44 (A. P. Waterson); Chapter 11 Can anyone today believe that Jesus 'ascended into heaven'?, See. 45–47 (D. M. Mackay)]

Conversations on the Evidences of Christianity: In Which the Leading Arguments of the Best Authors Are Arranged, Developed, and Connected with Each Other. London: Longman, Rees, Orme, Brown, & Green, 1826. [See. 258, 268–71, 279; N.B. Google book]

Conway, Bobby, and J. Warner Wallace. *Does God Exist? And 51 Other Compelling Questions.* Eugene, OR: Harvest House, 2016. [Question 50 Resurrection: Fact or Fiction, See. 145–47; Question 51 Is There Evidence for the Resurrection?, See. 148–51]

Cook, David. *Thinking About Faith: An Introductory Guide to Philosophy & Religion.* Grand Rapids: Academie, 1986. [See. 20, 87, 89, 90, 91, 106]

Cooper, Thomas. *The Bridge of History Over the Gulf of Time: A Popular View of the Historical Evidence for the Truth of Christianity.* London: Hodder & Stoughton, 1871. [See. 79–84; N.B. Google book]

Copan, Paul. *"True for You but Not for Me": Overcoming Objections to Christian Faith.* 2nd ed. Minneapolis: Bethany House 2009. [Chapter 28 People Claim JFK and Elvis Are Alive, Too!, See. 172–82]

———. *When God Goes to Starbucks: A Guide to Everyday Apologetics.* Grand Rapids: Baker, 2008. [Chapter 5 Miracles Are Unscientific. See. 58–60]

Cornish, Rick. *5 Minute Apologist: Maximum Truth in Minimum Time.* Colorado Springs, CO: NavPress, 2005. [Part 6. The Resurrection, Chapters 44–50, See. 150–73]

Courduan, Winfried. *Reasonable Faith: Basic Christian Apologetics.* Nashville: Broadman & Holman, 1993. [See. 220–30]

Cowan, Steven B., and Terry L. Wilder, eds. *In Defense of the Bible: A Comprehensive Apologetic for the Authority of Scripture.* Nashville: B&H, 2013. [The Resurrection, See. 250–54]

Craig, William Lane. *Apologetics: An Introduction.* Chicago: Moody, 1984. [The Resurrection of Jesus, See. 167–206; N.B. The first of many solid works by Craig.]

———. *On Guard: Defending Your Faith with Reason and Precision.* Colorado Springs, CO: David C. Cook, 2010. [Chapter 9 Did Jesus Rise From the Dead? See. 219–64; N.B. This work is a must read.]

———. *Reasonable Faith: Christian Truth and Apologetics.* 3rd ed. Wheaton, IL: Crossway, 2008. [Chapter 8 The Resurrection of Jesus, See. 333–404; N.B. This work is an absolute must read.]

———. *Reasonable Faith: Christian Truth and Apologetics.* Revised ed. Wheaton, IL: Crossway, 1994. [Chapter 8 The Resurrection of Jesus, See. 255–98; N.B. This work is a must read.]

Craig, William Lane, and Joseph E. Gorra. *A Reasonable Response: William Lane Craig Answers to Tough Questions on God, Christianity and the Bible.* Chicago: Moody, 2013. [On Assessing Independent Sources for Jesus' Burial and Empty Tomb, See. 297–300; On the Significance of the Witness of the Pre-Pauline Tradition to the Empty Tomb,

See. 301–3; Can One Justifiably Infer Jesus' Resurrection on the Basis of Empirical Evidence, See. 304–9]

Crean, Thomas. *God is No Delusion: A Refutation of Richard Dawkins*. San Francisco: Ignatius Press, 2007. [The Resurrection, See. 73–79]

Cree, Robert. *Lectures on the Evidences of Christianity: With an Introductory Lecture on Religion in General, and One on the Authenticity of the Jewish Scriptures*. London: Sold by Messrs. Sherwood . . . Mr. Hunter . . . and Messrs. Fox and Eaton, 1827. [Evidence of Miracles Part 2, See. 237–70; N.B. Google book]

Crooll, Rabbi Joseph, and Thomas Scott. *Restoration of Israel by R. Joseph Crooll and an Answer by Thomas Scott*. London: Printed by B. R. Goakman, 1814. [Crooll's work spans pages 1–104. The 318-page response by Thomas Scott, *Answer to the Restoration of Israel* immediately follows Crooll's work. See. 139–41. This dated work is a solid presentation by both contributors. N.B. Archive.org]

Crosse, Charles H. *An Analysis of Paley's Evidences of Christianity in the Form of Question and Answer*. London: Macmillan, 1855. [Chapter 8 Of the History of the Resurrection, See. 85–86; 97; N.B. Archive.org]

Davis, J. D. *Handbook of Christian Evidences*. Kyoto: n.p., 1889. [Chapter 7 Christ's resurrection, See. 173–83; N.B. Google book]

Davis, Stephen T. *Disputed issues: Contending for Christian Faith in Today's Academic Setting*. Waco, TX: Baylor University Press, 2009. [Chapter 5 Have the Infidels Refuted the Resurrection?, See. 49–75]

———. *Rational Faith: A Philosopher's Defense of Christianity*. Oxford: Lion Hudson, 2016. [Chapter 4 Was Jesus Raised from the Dead?, See. 68–80]

Davis, Will. *Why Faith Makes Sense: Reasons You Can Believe God is Real*. Grand Rapids: Revell, 2008. [The Resurrection, See. 153–54]

Dean, Robert James. *How Can We Believe?* Nashville: Broadman, 1978. [What About the Resurrection?, See. 55–59]

De Candole, H. L. C. V. *Christian Assurance*. London: SPCK, 1919. [Assurance Through the Resurrection, See. 50–61]

Defence of Natural and Revealed Religion Being An Abridgment of the Sermons Preached at the Lecture Founded by the Honorable Robert Boyce, A. Vol. 1. London: Printed for Arthur Bettersworth, 1737. [See. 74, 81, 93–96, 154, 341, 382, 399, 421–22, 424–25, 428, 438, 480, 483; N.B. Google book]

Dell, J. A. *I Still Believe in God*. Columbus. OH: Wartburg Press, 1942. [Chapter 9 The Claims of the Christ, The Resurrection of Jesus, See. 173–85]

Devivier, Walter, and Sebastian G. Messmer. *Christian Apologetics: A Defense of the Catholic Faith*. New York: Benziger, 1903. [Article 3 Second Proof. The Resurrection of Jesus Christ, See. 187–99; N.B. Google book]

Dewar, Daniel. *The Evidences of Divine Revelation*. Edinburgh: Oliver & Boyd, 1838. [Book 5 Chapter 3, On the Resurrection of Jesus, See. 373–89; Chapter 4 On the Resurrection of Jesus, See. 390–405; N.B. Google book]

De Wohl, Louis. *Adam, Eve and the Ape*. Chicago: Henry Regnery, 1960. [The Miracle of Miracles, See. 81–83; N.B. Not useful.]

Dibble, Charles Lemuel. *A Grammar of Belief: A Revaluation of the Bases of Christian Belief in the Light of Modern Science and Philosophy*. Milwaukee, WI: Morehouse, 1922. [See. 58–59; N.B. Not useful]

Category III—Apologetics and Anti-Apologetics

Dix, Morgan. *Three Guardians of Supernatural Religion: The Bedell Lectures for 1899*, New York: Gorham, 1901. [Lecture 2; N.B. Internet, Anglicanhistory.org]

Dodd, Thomas J. *Miracles: Were They or Were They Not Performed by Jesus? A Question of Fact, Not of Science or Theology.* Cincinnati: Curts & Jennings, 1899. [See. 168–86]

Dodge, Ebenezer. *The Evidences of Christianity: With an Introduction on the Existence of God and the Immortality of the Soul.* Boston: Gould & Lincoln, 1869. [The Sceptical Theories (No room for mistake or deception in regard to the fact) . . . See. 72–77; N.B. Google book]

Dudley, Thomas Underwood. *A Wise Discrimination: The Church's Need.* New York: Thomas Whittaker, 1881. [See. 103–11; N.B. Archive.org]

Dulles, Avery. *Apologetics and the Biblical Christ.* London: Burns & Oates, 1964. [Chapter 4 The Resurrection: History and Confession, See. 45–60]

———. *A History of Apologetics.* Eugene, OR: Wipf & Stock, 1999. [Resurrection, doubts about, See. 43–46, 360]

Duncan, Alexander. *A Preservative Against the Principles of Infidelity.* Edinburgh: Printed for W. Creech, 1774. [Chapter 4 Sect 1 From the Resurrection of Jesus from the dead, See. 93–117; N.B. Google book]

Ebrard, Johannes Heinrich August. *Apologetics: or, The Scientific Vindication of Christianity.* Vol. 1 Translated by John MacPherson. Edinburgh: T&T Clark, 1886. [See. 351–53; N.B. Google book]

Edwards, Martin Luther. *The Bible and Reason Against Atheism in a Series of Letters to a Friend.* Chicago: M. L. Edwards, 1881. [Letter 9 The Crucifixion and Resurrection, See. 79–87; also See. 45, 46, 48, 49, 118, 152; N.B. Google book]

Ellicott, C. J. *Modern Scepticism: A Course of Lectures Delivered at the Request of the Christian Evidence Society.* London: Hodder & Stoughton, 1871. [See. 181, 209, 216, 320, 337–42; 372–83, 388–89, 396–408; N.B. Google book]

Essay on the Evidence of the Truth of Christianity, An. Oxford: Printed by W. Baxter, 1840. [Section 3 On the Evidences of Christianity, See. 104–6, 113–14; Section 4 On the Fundamental Doctrines of Christianity, See. 137–56, also 161, 163, 166, 175, 194, 195; N.B. Google book]

Estborn, Sigfrid. *Our Christian Faith: A Brief Account for Inquirers and Beginners.* Madras: The Christian Literature Society for India, 1939. [See. 34–36]

Evans, C. Stephen. *Why Christian Faith Still Makes Sense: A Response to Contemporary Challenges.* Grand Rapids: Baker Academic, 2015. [The Miracle of the Resurrection, See. 124–30]

Everest, Harvey W. *The Divine Demonstration: A Text-Book of Christian Evidence.* St. Louis: Christian Publishing, 1884. [Of Objections. Discussion, See. 246–48; The Resurrection, Ascension and Coronation of the Messiah, See. 336–39]

Faber, George Stanley. *The Difficulties of Infidelity.* New York: D. Cooledge, 1829. [See. 99, 142–45, 150, 173, 174; N.B. Google book]

Faid, Robert W. *A Scientific Approach to Christianity.* Forrest, AZ: New Leaf Press, 1990. [Chapter 7 The Resurrection! Hoax or Reality, See. 57–68]

Farrelly, John. *Faith in God Through Jesus Christ.* Collegeville, MN: Liturgical Press, 1997. [The Resurrection of Jesus, and Early Christian Understanding of Salvation and Revelation, See. 162–207]

Faust, David. *Honest Questions, Honest Answers: How to Engage in Compelling Conversations About Your Christian Faith.* Cincinnati: Standard Publishing, 2012.

[Appendix L. Jesus' Resurrection—Why do Christians believe Jesus literally rose from the dead?, See. 200–202]

Feinberg, John S. *Can You Believe It's True? Christian Apologetics In a Modern and Postmodern Era.* Wheaton, IL: Crossway, 2013. [Chapter 12 The Resurrection of Jesus Christ, See. 405–42]

Fell, John, and Henry Hunter. *Lectures on the Evidences of Christianity.* London: Printed by Bye & Law, 1798. [Lecture 2 Luke 24 Ver. 44, See. 29–64 (John Fell); N.B. Google book]

Fenton, Joseph Clifford. *Laying the Foundation: A Handbook of Catholic Apologetics.* 2016. [Chapter 16 The Resurrection; N.B. This source should be examined. It was originally published in 1942 under the title *We Stand with Christ an Essay in Catholic Apologetics.*]

Ferbeck, Guillaume. *Jesus Christ and His Church: A Manual of Christian Apologetics.* Translated by Ralph C. Giorno. Flavigny-sur-Ozerain: Traditions Monastiques, 2000. [By the Miracle of His Own Resurrection, See. 76–81]

Fernandes, Phil. *Contend Earnestly for the Faith: A Survey of Christian Apologetics.* Baltimore: PublishAmerica, 2008. [Chapter 26 Did Jesus Rise From The Dead?, See. 280–92]

Fernando, Ajith. *The Supremacy of Christ.* Wheaton, IL: Crossway, 1995. [Chapter 15 The Resurrection Is Proof, See. 225–59]

Feuerbach, Ludwig. *The Essence of Christianity.* Translated by Marianne Evans. 2nd ed. New York: Calvin Blanchard, 1855. [Chapter 24 The Mystery of the Resurrection and of the Miraculous Conception, See. 181–86; N.B. Archive.org]

Fichter, Joseph Henry. *Textbook in Apologetics.* Milwaukee: Bruce, 1947. [Chapter 8 Miracles Prove the Divinity of Christ. See. The Supreme Miracle: the Resurrection, See. 72–78]

Figgs, John Neville. *The Gospel and Human Needs.* London: Longmans, Green, 1917. [See. 57–59]

Fisher, George Park. *The Christian Religion.* New York: Chautauqua Press, 1886. [See. 15, 32, 33, 41; N.B. Google book]

———. *Essays on the Supernatural Origin of Christianity, with Special Reference to the Theories of Renan, Strauss, and the Tübingen School.* New York: Scribner's Sons 1870. [Essay 8 The Legendary Theory of Renan: Supplementary Note: Renan on the Resurrection of Jesus, See. 433–48; N.B. Google book]

———. *Grounds of Theistic and Christian Belief.* New York: Scribner's Sons, 1903. [Proof of the Crowning Miracle of Christianity, See. 192–99; N.B. Archive.org, Google books, and HathiTrust]

———. *Manual of Christian Evidences.* New York: Scribner's Sons, 1890. [Chapter 7 Proof of the Resurrection of Jesus from Statements by the Apostle Paul, See. 41–46; Chapter 10 The Proofs of the Resurrection of Jesus from the Evangelists, See. 82–84; N.B. Google book]

Footman, Henry. *Reasonable Apprehensions and Reassuring Hints: Being Papers Designed to Attract Attention to the Nature of Modern Unbelief, and to Meet Some of its Fundamental Assumptions.* London: Field & Tuer, Ye Leadenhalle Presses, 1883. [See. 30–33, 126–28, 132–33; N.B. Google book]

Foster, Chad. *How Firm a Foundation: A Handbook on the Historical Reliability of the New Testament and the Resurrection.* Longwood, FL: Xulon, 2004. [The Bodily Resurrection of Jesus, See. 69–86]

Foster, Randolph S. *Studies in Theology: Evidences of Christianity: The Supernatural Book.* New York: Hutton & Eaton, 1890. [The Argument From Miracles, See. 244–47; N.B. Google book]

Fowle, T. W. *A New Analogy Between Revealed Religion and the Course and Constitution of Nature.* London: Macmillan, 1881. [Chapter 10 On the Self-Sacrifice of Christ to Death and His Resurrection to Life, See. 228–58; Cellarius, pseud.; N.B. Google book and HathiTrust]

Frame, John M. *Apologetics to the Glory of God: An Introduction.* Phillipsburg, NJ: P&R, 1994. [Miracle and Resurrection, See. 143–47]

Franks, James Clarke. *Hulsean Lectures for 1821: On the Evidences of Christianity, as They Are Stated and Enforced in the Discourses of Our Lord.* Cambridge, J. Smith, 1821. [Lecture 17 The Method in which our Lord Evidenced the Reality of his Resurrection, and His Reasoning on Prophecy after that Event, See. 417–46]

Franzmann, Majella. *Jesus in the Nag Hammadi Writing.* Edinburgh: T&T Clark, 1996. [See. 156–61]

Freemantle, W. H. *Natural Christianity.* London: Harper & Brothers, 1911. [Resurrection 75–79; N.B. Archive.org.]

Frey, Joseph Samuel C. F. *A Course of Lectures on the Messiahship of Christ.* New York: Joseph Samuel C. F. Frey, 1844. [Lecture 13 The Resurrection of the Messiah, 267–82; Lecture 13 Second Part, The Resurrection of the Messiah, See. 283–99; N.B. Google book]

———. *Joseph and Benjamin: A Series of Letters on the Controversy between Jews and Christians.* New York: Published by Peter Hill. D. Fanshaw, Printer. 1837. [Letter 18 The Burial of Christ, 392–99; N.B. Google book]

Fry, Thomas Charles. *Why We Christians Believe in Christ: Bishop Gore's Bampton Lectures Shortened for Popular Use.* London: John Murray, 1904. [Chapter 3 The Supernatural Christ Historical, See. 24–32; N.B. Google book]

Furches, Joel. *Christ-Centered Apologetics: Sharing the Gospel with Evidence.* Rapid City, ND: Crosslink, 2014. [Chapter 16 The Minimal Facts Argument, See. 161–76]

Garbett, C. F., and F. O. T. Hawkes. *Can We Believe? Reasonable Words for Reasonable Men.* London: Masters, 1905. [The Resurrection, See. 141–59]

Garnett, Nathan. *5 Answers for Christians Today: Biblical Lessons for Living in Christ.* Bloomington, IN: WestBow Press. 2016. [Question 3: Do I Have to Believe in the Resurrection of Christ?, See. 48–66]

Garvie, Alfred Ernest. *Handbook of Christian Apologetics.* Scribner's Sons, 1913. [See. 104, 133, 173, 226; N.B. Google book]

Geisler, Norman L. *Baker Encyclopedia of Christian Apologetics.* Grand Rapids: Baker, 1999. [Resurrection, Alternate Theories of, See. 644–51; Resurrection, Evidence for, See. 651–56; Resurrection, Objections to, See. 657–64; Resurrection, Physical Nature of, See. 664–70; N.B. This detailed work is a solid and must reading!]

———. *The Big Book of Christian Apologetics: An A to Z Guide.* Grand Rapids: Baker, 2012. [Miracles, False. See. 343–46; Resurrection, Alternate Theories of, See. 487–90; Resurrection, Evidence for, See. 490–96; Resurrection, Objections to, See. 496; Resurrection, Physical Nature of, See. 496–501; Resurrection Claims in Non-Christian Religions, See. 501–3; Resurrection of Christ, See. 503–6; N.B. Geisler's work is a solid and must reading!]

———. *Christian Apologetics*. 2nd ed. Grand Rapids: Baker, 2013. [Resurrection, the historicity of, See. 72–75, 80–82, 86; Chapter 20 See. Jesus's Resurrection as Evidence of His Deity, See. 406–18; N.B. This work is a solid and must reading.]

Geisler, Norman L., and Peter Bocchino. *Unshakable Foundations*. Minneapolis: Bethany House, 2001. [His Resurrection From The Dead, See. 305–8]

Geisler, Norman L., and Ronald M. Brooks. *When Skeptics Ask: A Handbook on Christian Evidences*. Grand Rapids: Baker, 2008. [Chapter 6 Questions About Jesus Christ. Jesus Rose Bodily from the Grave, See. 123–25; Jesus Appeared in a Resurrected Body, See. 125–28]

Geisler, Norman L., and Thomas A. Howe. *When Critics Ask: A Popular Handbook on Bible Difficulties*. Wheaton, IL: Victor, 1992. [Matthew, See. 361–67; Mark, See. 377–79; Luke, See. 395–401; John, See. 422–25]

Geisler, Norman L., and Ronald Rhodes. *Conviction Without Compromise: Standing Strong In the Core Beliefs of the Christian Faith*. Eugene, OR: Harvest House, 2008. [See. The Bodily Resurrection of Christ, See. 109–20; The Bodily Ascension of Christ, See. 145–56; N.B. This is a good reading.]

———. *When Cultists Ask: A Popular Handbook on Cultic Misinterpretations*. Grand Rapids: Baker, 1997. [Matthew 27:53 What Resurrection Happened at the Cross?, See. 400–402; Luke 23:43, See. 488–89; John 20:1–8, See. 506–8]

Geisler, Norman L., and Abdul Saleeb. *Answering Islam: The Crescent in Light of the Cross*. Grand Rapids: Baker, 1993. [See. 247–54]

Geisler, Norman L., and Patty Tunnicliffe. *Reasons for Belief: Easy-to-Understand Answers to 10 Essential Questions*. Minneapolis, MN: Bethany House, 2013. [Chapter 10 Jesus' Resurrection, Challenge #8: Jesus Did Not Rise From The Dead, See. 151–70]

Geisler, Norman L., and Frank Turek. *I Don't Have Enough Faith to be an Atheist*. Wheaton: Crossway, 2004. [Chapter 12 Did Jesus Really Rise from the Dead?, See. 299–324]

Geisler, Norman L., and Patrick Zukeran. *The Apologetics of Jesus: A Caring Approach to Dealing with Doubters*. Grand Rapids: Baker, 2009. [Chapter 3 Jesus' Apologetic Use of the Resurrection, See. 47–63]

Getty, George Albert. *Foundations of Faith: A Manual of Christian Evidences*. Philadelphia: United Lutheran Publication House, 1925. [Section 4 The Argument From the Resurrection of Christ, See. 77–80]

Ghattas, Raouf G., and Carol B. Ghattas. *A Christian Guide to the Qur'an: Building Bridges in Muslim Evangelism*. Grand Rapids: Kregel, 2009. [Jesus' Crucifixion: Verse 157, See. 66–67]; Jesus' Death and Resurrection: Verse 33, See. 174–75]

Gibbons, James. *Our Christian Heritage*. Baltimore: J. Murphy, 1889. [Chapter 16 Our Lord's Divinity Confirmed by His Miracles, and Especially by His Resurrection, See. 240–51; N.B. Google book]

Gibson, John Monro. *The Foundations a Series of Lectures on the Evidences of Christianity*. Chicago: Jansen, McClurg, 1880. [Lecture 7 The Resurrection, See. 104–22; N.B. Google book]

Gift of the Holy Ghost to the Apostles and First Christians: A Demonstration of the Resurrection of Jesus: And an Answer to All the Objections That Are Made against It. London: Printed for J. and J. Rivington, 1749. [66 pages; N.B. Google book and Eighteenth Century Collections Online. Reproduction of original from the British Library.]

———. *Rock versus Sand; or, The Foundations of the Christian Faith.* London: Nisbet, 1883. [The Resurrection, See. 77–88; N.B. Google book]

Gillmore, Hiram. *Lectures on Christianity: Wherein Its Necessity, Authenticity, and Utility Are Supported by Evidences Historical, Philosophical, Experimental, and Miscellaneous; with an Affectionate Appeal to Those Who Have Been Entangled in the Same Snare of Infidelity.* Cleveland: Printed by Francis B. Pennman, 1837. [Lecture 8 Authenticity of Christianity shown from the Miracles of Scripture, See. 192–213; N.B. Google book]

Girdlestone, A. G. *Christianity and Modern Scepticism.* London: Hodder & Stoughton, 1882. [See. 51, 64, 102–13, 135, 156, N.B. Google book]

Glenn, Paul J. *Apologetics: A Class Manual in the Philosophy of the Catholic Religion.* St. Louis: B. Herder Book, 1948. [Jesus Christ Proved Himself God by His Wondrous Works, b) The Resurrection of Christ, See. 215–26]

Godbey, J. E. *Foundations of Faith: Being a Consideration of the Grounds of Religious Belief, and Especially of the Evidences of Divine Revelation in the Religion of the Bible.* Nashville: Publishing House of the M.E. Church, South, Bigham & Smith, 1903. [Chapter 20 Jesus of Nazareth—The Resurrection, See. 238–51]

Godet, Frédéric Louis. *Lectures in Defence of the Christian Faith.* 3rd ed. Translated by W. H. Lyttelton. Edinburgh: T&T Clark, 1895. [The Resurrection of Jesus Christ, See. 1–52; N.B. Google book]

Goodchild, Frank M. *Can We Believe? Popular Discussions of Fundamental Christian Truths.* New York: Revell, 1926. [Chapter 8 Can We Believe in the Resurrection of Christ?, See. 123–34]

Gore, Charles. *Belief in God.* London: Murray, 1921. [The Resurrection, See. 262–72; The Ascension, See. 272–82]

———. *Can We Then Believe?* London: Murray, 1926. [The Supposed Incredibility of the Ascension, See. 206–9]

———. *The Holy Spirit and the Church.* New York: Scribner's Sons, 1924. [Appended Note D. The Commission in St. John 20, See. 21–23, 70–71]

———. *The Reconstruction of Belief.* New York: Scribner's Sons, 1926. [The Resurrection, See. 262–72; The Ascension, See. 272–82]

Grant, Malcolm. *A New Argument for God and Survival and a Solution to the Problem of Supernatural Events.* London: Faber & Faber, 1934. [See. 77, 337, 339]

Gray, Arthur R. *An Introduction to the Study of Christian Apologetics.* Sewanee, TN: The University Press at the University of the South Sewanee, 1912. [See. 209]

Green, Michael. *You Must Be Joking? Popular Excuses for Avoiding Jesus Christ.* London: Hodder & Stoughton, 1976. [Chapter 9 When You're Dead, You're Dead!, See. 114–30]

Green, Michael, and Gordon Carkner. *Ten Myths about Christianity.* Batavia, IL: Lion, 1989. [Myth 8: There is No Evidence that Jesus Christ Rose From the Dead, See. 56–62]

Greene, Oliver B. *Bible Truth.* Downers Grove, IL: InterVarsity, 1968. [Chapter 4 Bible truth concerning the bodily resurrection of Jesus, See. 247–316]

Greg, William R. *The Creed of Christendom: Its Foundations Contrasted with Its Superstructure* Vol. 2. 3rd ed. London: Trübner, 1874. [Chapter 14 Resurrection of Jesus, See. 140–62]

Gregory, Olinthus. *Letters on the Evidences, Doctrines, and Duties, of the Christian Religion. Addressed to a Friend.* 6th ed. London: Bohn, 1851. [Letter 8 On the Resurrection of Jesus Christ, See. 57–176; N.B. Google book]

Griffin, George. *The Gospel: Its Own Advocate*. New York: D. Appleton, 1850. [Chapter 9 The Miracles of the Gospel, See. 177–200; N.B. Google book]

Groothuis, Douglas R. *Christian Apologetics: A Comprehensive Case for Biblical Faith*. Downers Grove, IL: InterVarsity, 2011. [Chapter 22 The Resurrection of Jesus, See. 527–66]

Grotius, Hugo. *The Truth of the Christian Religion: In Six Books*. Translated by John Clarke. 9th ed. London: Printed for J. & J. Knapton, 1729. [Book 2 Sect. 6 The Resurrection of Christ Proved From Credible Testimony, See. 94–99; Sect. 7 The Objection drawn from the seeming impossibility of a Resurrection, answered, See. 98–100; The Truth of Jesus' Doctrine proved from his Resurrection, See. 100; N.B. Archive.org]

Grubb, Edward. *The Religion of Experience: An Examination of Some of the Difficulties of Christian Faith*. London: Swathmore Press, 1918. [Chapter 7 The Christ Experience, See. 83–86]

Guest, John. *In Search of Certainty: Answers to Doubt When Values are Eroding and Unbelief is Fashionable*. Ventura, CA: Regal, 1983. [Chapter 7 The Evidence of the Resurrection, See. 121–31]

Guinness, H. Grattan. "On This Rock," or, the Certainties of Faith. London: Morgan S. Scott, 1909. [See. 88–92; N.B. Archive.org]

Guitton, Jean. *The Problem of Jesus: A Free-Thinker's Diary*. New York: P. J. Kenedy, 1955. [Part 3. Resurrection, See. 120–239; N.B. This work is a definite book to explore.]

Gurney, Joseph John. *Four Lectures on the Evidences of Christianity Delivered in Southwark, 1834, to the Junior Members of the Society of Friends*. London: Hamilton, Adams &, Etc., 1835. [First Lecture: on the Genuineness and Authenticity of the New Testament, See. 1–50; N.B. Google book]

Gutteridge, Don J. *The Defense Rests Its Case*. Nashville: Broadman, 1975. [Chapter 4 Did Christ Really Rise from the Dead?, See. 33–50]

Habermas, Gary R. *The Investigator: Finding the Truth Is All That Matters*. n.p.: Bridegroom Press, 2017. [Chapter 5 Did Jesus Rise from the Dead?; N.B. This workbook serves as a companion piece to the feature film, "The Investigator."]

Hadnut, Robert K. *A Thinking Man and the Christ*. Philadelphia: Fortress, 1971. [A Thinking Man and the Resurrection, See. 78–83]

Hall, Joseph. *Contemplations on the Historical Passages of the Old And New Testament* Vol. 3. London: A. J. Valpy, 1832. [Contemplation 33— The Resurrection, See. 421–42; Contemplation 24—The Ascension, See. 442–51; N.B. Google book]

Haller, Karl Ludwig von. *Letters from Baron Haller to His Daughter: On the Truths of the Christian Religion*. London: J. Murray, 1780. [Letter 9 The Resurrection of Jesus Christ, See. 154–82; N.B. Google book]

Hamilton, Edward John. *Rational Orthodoxy: Essays on Mooted Questions*. New York: Funk & Wagnalls, 1917. [Chapter 3 The Virgin Birth and the Resurrection of Our Lord: Credible Occurrences which Accord with all other Events of Gospel History, See. 42–76; Chapter 4 The Resurrection of Christ Explained: It Included a Miraculous Transformation of His Body, See. 77–106; N.B. Google book]

Hamilton, Floyd Eugene. *The Basis of Christian Faith: A Modern Defense of the Christian Religion*. New York: Harper & Brothers, 1946. [Chapter 16 The Resurrection of Jesus Christ, See. 283–95]

Hamilton, Frank. *Evidences that Jesus is the Messiah*. Ventnor, NJ: Frank Hamilton, 1939? [Evidence 123 The Resurrection, See. 39; Evidence 124 The Ascension, See. 39]

Hanegraaff, Hank. *The Bible Answer Book*. Nashville: J. Countrymen, 2004. [Answer 56. How can we be sure about the resurrection of Christ?, See. 192–96; 58. What does it mean to Say that Jesus Ascended into Heaven?, See. 200–202]

———. *The Bible Answer Book for Students*. Nashville: Nelson, 2007. [See. How Can We Be Sure about the Resurrection of Christ?, See. 102–5]

Hanson, Delbert James. *The Place of Miracles in a Biblical Apologetic*. Master's thesis, Wheaton College, 1955. [Chapter 5 The Resurrection of Christ, See. 99–119]

Hare, Augustus, and Hare, Julius. *Letters to the Editor of The New Trial of the Witnesses: By an Oxford Layman*. London: Richard Taylor, 1824. [This anonymous 111-page work consists of five essays. The authors are identified in *Guesses at the Truth by Two Brothers*, 1867, [p. xviii]. N.B. Google book]

Harkness, Georgia Elma. *The Modern Rival of Christian Faith: An Analysis of Secularism*. New York: Abingdon-Cokesbury, 1952. [Jesus Christ resurrection, See. 19, 23, 48, 54, 61–62, 157, 165]

Harris, Charles. *Pro Fide: A Defence of Natural and Revealed Religion: Being a Text-Book of Modern Apologetics for Students of Theology and Others*. London: John Murray, 1905. [Chapter 22 The Resurrection of Jesus, See. 463–94; N.B. Google book]

Harrison, John, of the Inner Temple. *A Vindication of the Holy Scriptures. Or the Manifestation of Jesus Christ the True Messiah Already Come. Being the Christians antidote against the poysons of Judaisme and atheisme of this present age. Proved out of sacred scripture, ancient historians, and Jewish Rabbins*. London: Printed by J. M., 1656. [His Resurrection, See. 93–95; N.B. EEBO]

Hay, William. *Religio Philosophi: or, The Principles of Morality and Christianity Illustrated From a View of the Universe, and of Man's Situation on It*. London: Printed for the Editors, 1831. [See. 95–101; N.B. Not useful.]

Hebblethwaite, Brian. *In Defence of Christianity*. Oxford: Oxford University Press, 2005. [resurrection, See. 35, 39, 50, 51, 85, 97, 98, 99, 100–101, 103–4, 106–7, 120, 149]

Heffern, Andrew Duff. *Apology and Polemic in the New Testament: The Bohlen Lectures, 1915*. New York: Macmillan, 1922. [See. Resurrection, Jesus', See. 52, 55, 60, 64, 72, 94; N.B. Archive.org and Google book]

Hellen, John. *The Bible Is No Fairy Tale! The Compelling Evidence Proving the Bible to Be God's True and Inspired Word*. Mustang, MO: Tate, 2009. [Fulfillment of Prophecies of Jesus being Buried in a Rich Man's Grave, Resurrected, and Sitting at the Right Hand of God, See. 125–50]

Henderson, Timothy P. *The Gospel of Peter and Early Christian Apologetics: Rewriting the Story of Jesus' Death, Burial, and Resurrection*. Tübingen: Mohr Siebeck, 2011. [See (especially). 123–220]

Hennell, S. S. *Christianity and Infidelity: An Exposition of the Arguments on Both Sides*. London: Arthur Hall, Virtue, 1857. [Part 1 Infidelity Against Christianity. Answer 25 As is Seen in their Accounts of the Resurrection, See. 38–43; N.B. Google book]

Hetherington, William M. *The Apologetics of the Christian Faith*. Edinburg: T&T Clark, 1867. [Chapter 3 Sec. 7 Great Special Instance: The Resurrection of Christ, See. 302–13; N.B. Google book]

Hick, John. *Christianity at the Centre*. London: SCM, 1968. [Chapter 1 God Is Alive. 4. The Meaning of Jesus' Death and Resurrection, See. 40–49]

———. *The Second Christianity*. London: SCM, 1983. [Chapter 1 Jesus—the Centre or Christianity?, 2. Jesus' Death and Resurrection, See. 20–26]

Hill, George. *Lectures in Divinity*. Edited by Alexander Hill. Philadelphia: Herman Hooker, 1844. [Chapter 8 Resurrection of Christ, See. 180–92; N.B. Archive.org and Google book; edited by his son]

Holden, Joseph M., and Norman Geisler. *The Popular Handbook of Archaeology and the Bible*. Eugene: OR, Harvest House, 2013. [Chapter 12 Criticism of the Resurrection Account and the Epistles, See. 159–65]

Holding, James Patrick. *Blowing the Doors Off! A Defense Manual for Christian Students*. US: Xulon, 2008. [Tomb on Empty: Did the Resurrection of Jesus Really Happen?, See. 331–36]

———. *The Impossible Faith: Why Christianity Succeeded When It Should Have Failed*. US: Xulon, 2007. [Chapter 9 Body Snatchers, See. 95–105]

Holloway, Richard. *Let God Arise*. London: A. R. Mowbray, 1972. [Chapter 12 Resurrection, See. 119–31]

Holy Bible Explained; or the Old and New Testament Digested and Illustrated by the Way of Question and Answer, The. Baltimore: Printed for Henry S. Keatinge, 1808. [Chapter 8 The Burial and Resurrection of Jesus Christ, See. 424–31; N.B. Google book]

Hoover, Arlie J. *The Case of Christian Theism: An Introduction to Apologetics*. Grand Rapids: Baker, 1980. [Chapter 16 The Resurrection of Jesus Christ, See. 227–46; N.B. Also called *Dear Agnos: A Defense of Christianity* in the first edition.]

Hopkins, Mark. *Evidences of Christianity Before the Lowell Institute Revised as a Text-Book*. Boston: T. R. Marvin, 1909. [See. 194–96, 272, 279, 353, 362, 371; N.B. Google book]

Hopp, Kenneth Harvey. *A Troubled Modern Man Discovers that Christianity Makes Sense*. Mountain View, CA: Pacific Press, 1983. [The Resurrection, Facts or Myth?, See. 57–58]

Horne, Thomas Hartwell. *Deism Refuted: or, Plain Reasons for Being a Christian*. 3rd ed. London: Printed for T. Cadell, 1826. [Chapter 9 Particularly of the Resurrection of Jesus Christ, See. 97–110; N.B. Google book]

Hort, Fenton John Anthony. *The Way The Truth The Life*. London: Macmillan, 1897. [See. 62–63; N.B. Archive.org and HathiTrust]

Horváth, Tibor. *Faith Under Scrutiny*. Notre Dame, IN: Fides, 1975. [How do you explain the contradictions in the resurrection story?, See. 52–53; The Resurrection of Jesus, See. 199–241]

Hosking, John. *The Elements of Christian Theology, Philosophy, Morals, & History; or, Christianity Stated and Defended*. Christchurch: H. J. Weeks, 1894. [See. 38–39, 45–47, 55, 93, 113, 126, 316, 336, 531, 552; N.B. Google book]

Houdmann, S. Michael. *Got Questions Bible Questions Answered—Answers to the Questions People*. Bloomington, IN: WestBow Press, 2010. [Question: Is the Resurrection of Jesus Christ True?, See. 51–53]

House, H. Wayne, and Joseph M. Holden. *Charts of Apologetics and Christian Evidences*. Grand Rapids: Zondervan, 2006. Chart 55 Theories on the Resurrection of Jesus; Chart 56 Early Church Fathers on the Nature of the Resurrection Body; Chart 57 Three Modern Views of Christ's Resurrection Body; Chart 58 Which Resurrection Theory Best Fits the Facts?; Chart 59 Comparing Resurrection, Resuscitation, and Reincarnation]

House, Wayne H., and Dennis W. Jowers. *Reasons for Our Hope: An Introduction to Christian Apologetics*. Nashville: B&H Academic, 2011. [Chapter 24 The Meaning and Importance of the Physical Resurrection of Christ, See. 331–41]

Howard, Thomas. *Once Upon A Time, God . . .* Philadelphia: A. J. Holman, 1974. [See. 118–28]

Howe, Frederic R. *Challenge and Response, a Handbook of Christian Apologetics*. Grand Rapids: Zondervan, 1982. [Chapter 10 The Problem of History and Christianity. Historical Validity Tested, See. 123–31; Chapter 11 Some Challenges Concerning Christ, See. 142–47]

Hudnut, Robert K. *A Thinking Man and the Christ*. Philadelphia: Fortress, 1971. [A Thinking Man and the Resurrection, See. 78–83]

Hunt, David. *In Defense of the Faith*. Eugene, OR: Harvest House, 1996. [Evidences of Authenticity and Inspiration, See. 169–72]

Hunter, Henry. "Lecture 13." In *Lectures on the Evidences of Christianity 1798, Four by John Fell and Eight by Henry Hunter*, See. 333–76. London: Bye & Law, 1798. [N.B. Google book]

Ing, Paul Tan Chee. *"In Defence of . . . "* Kuala Lampur: Catholic Research Centre, 1991. [Did Jesus Die on the Cross and Rise from the Dead?, See. 75–77]

Ingram, Chip. *Why I Believe Straight Answers to Honest Questions about God, the Bible, and Christianity*. Grand Rapids: Baker, 2017. [Chapter 1 Why I Believe in the Resurrection, See. 17–32; Chapter 2 Did Jesus Really Died?, See. 33–54]

Instone-Brewer, David. *The Jesus Scandals: Why He Shocked His Contemporaries (and Still Shocks Today)*. Oxford: Monarch, 2012. [Embarrassing Resurrection, See. 76–80]

Inwagen, Peter Van. *The Possibility of Resurrection and Other Essays in Christian Apologetics*. Boulder, CO: Westview, 1999. [Chapter 3 The Possibility of Resurrection, See. 45–51]

Ireland, John. *Paganism and Christianity Compared, in a Course of Lectures*. London: John Murray, 1825. [See. 19–21; N.B. Google book]

Jabbūr, Nabīl. *The Crescent Through the Eyes of the Cross: Insights from an Arab Christian*. Colorado Springs, CO: NAV Press, 2008. [See. 168–69]

Jackson, John. *An Address to Deists, Being a Proof of Reveal'd Religion from Miracles and Prophecies. In Answer to a Book, Entitled, The Resurrection of Jesus Consider'd by a Moral Philosopher*. London: Printed for J. & P. Knapton, 1744. [See. Especially 124–50; N.B. Google book]

Jacoby, Douglas A. *Compelling Evidence for God and the Bible: Finding Truth in an Age of Doubt*. Eugene, OR: Harvest House, 2010. [Chapter 10 Many Convincing Proofs: The Resurrection, See. 147–62]

———. *Your Bible Questions Answered: Clear, Concise Compelling*. Eugene, OR: Harvest House, 2011. [See. 159, 171, 182–84]

Jefferson, Charles Edward. *Things Fundamental: A Course of Thirteen Discourses in Modern Apologetics*. New York: T.Y. Crowell, 1903. [Chapter 8 The Miracles, See. 191–221]

Jeffrey, Grant R. *Unveiling Mysteries of the Bible*. Toronto, ON: Frontier Research, 2002. [Chapter 20 The "Three Days ands Three Nights" Between Christ's Crucifixion and Resurrection, See. 181–85; Chapter 23 The Mystery of the 153 Fish, See. 207–17]

Jenkin, Robert. *The Reasonableness and Certainty of the Christian Religion*. 3rd ed. Vol. 1. London: Richard Sare, 1708. [Chapter 13 The Prophecies concerning . . . those concerning his Resurrection and Ascension, See. 240–46; Chapter 14 Of the Resurrection of our Blessed Savior, See. 246–61; N.B. Archive.org and Google book]

Jenkins, David E. *God, Jesus, and Life in the Spirit*. Philadelphia: Trinity Press International, 1989. [Chapter 9 Easter, See. 105–21]

Jersild, Paul T. *Invitation to Faith: Christian Belief Today*. Minneapolis: Augsburg, 1978. [Chapter 4 Jesus and His Resurrection. See. The Cross and the Resurrection, See. 85–90]

Jesse, William. *Lectures Supposed to have been delivered by the Author of a View of the Internal Evidence of the Christian Religion*. Boston: I. Thomas and E. T. Andrews, 1793. [Lecture 4 The Ascension of Christ, See. 103–22; N.B. Google book]

Johnson, G. Timothy. *Finding God in the Questions: A Personal Journey*. Waterville, ME, Walker Large Print, 2007. [The Resurrection, See. 127–30]

Johnson, John J. *Currents in Twenty-First-Century Christian Apologetics: Challenges Confronting the Faith*. Eugene, OR: Wipf & Stock, 2008. [Part 2 What can We Believe about the Resurrection of Jesus? Chapter 6 Were the Resurrection Appearances Hallucinations? Some Psychiatric and Psychological Considerations, See. 99–110; Chapter 7 Hans Frei as Unlikely Apologist for the Historicity of the Resurrection, See. 111–29]

Johnston, Howard Agnew. *Scientific Faith*. Chicago: Winona Publishing, 1904. [Christ's resurrection of the victory over sin, See. 187; N.B. Archive.org, Google book, and HathiTrust]

Jones, J. D. *Things Most Surely Believed*. London: J. Clarke, 1908. [Chapter 5 The Resurrection, See. 84–104]

Jones, John. *A Series of Important Facts Demonstrating the Truth of the Christian Religion drawn from the Writings of its Friends and Enemies in the First and Second Centuries*. London: Printed For Rowland Hunter, 1820. [See. 6, 11, 21, 35, 47, 71, 78, 82, 110, 113, 147, 155, 177, 206; N.B. Google book]

Jones, John Benjamin. *A Defence of Christianity, or Conferences on Religion*. Vol. 2. London: Printed for the Author by Gilbert & Rivington, 1836. [Chapter 20 The Resurrection of Jesus Christ, See. 170–203; N.B. Google book]

Jortin, John. *Discourses Concerning the Truth of the Christian Religion and Remarks on Ecclesiastical History*. Vol. 2. London: Richard Taylor, 1805. [See. 5, 6, 12, 13, 90–93, 118, 392; N.B. Archive.org and Google book]

Juster, Daniel C. *The Biblical World View: An Apologetic*. San Francisco: International Scholars, 1995. [Chapter 14 The Historicity of the Gospels and the Resurrection of Jesus, See. 245–64]

Kallenbach, Walter D. *The Higher Significance of the Gospel*. Saint Paul: Bruce, 1938. [The Significance of the Virgin Birth and the Resurrection, See. 137–38]

Kamecke, Fred von. *Busted! Exposing Popular Myths about Christianity*. Grand Rapids: Zondervan, 2009. [Chapter 9 Jesus Never Rose from the Dead, See. 121–34]

Kedney, John Steinfort. *Christian Doctrine Harmonized and Its Rationality Vindicated*. New York: G.P. Putnam's Sons, 1889. [Chapter 24 Eschatology, —The Resurrection and Glorification of Jesus Christ, See. 79–85; N.B. Google book]

Keener, J. C. *Studies of Bible Truths*. Nashville: Publishing House of the M.E. Church, South, 1899. [Chapter 5 The Ascension, See. 214–39; N.B. Archive.org]

Keith, Alexander. *Demonstration of the Truth of the Christian Religion*. New York: Harper & Brothers, 1839. [See. 90, 208, 221, 259, 282, 320, 374, 375, 426; N.B. Archive.org and Google book]

Keller, Timothy. *The Reason for God: Belief in an Age of Skepticism*. New York: Dutton, 2008. [Chapter 13 The Reality of the Resurrection, See. 201–12]

Kennedy, John. *A Popular Handbook of Christian Evidences*. London: Sunday School Union, 1880. [Chapter 6 The Jesus Christ of the Gospels Certified By His Resurrection From the Dead, See. 224–46; N.B. Archive.org]

Kephart, Ezekiel Boring. *Apologetics or, A Treatise on Christian Evidences*. Dayton, OH: United Brethren Publishing House, 1913. [See. 24, 62, 64, 65, 95, 100, 102; N.B. Archive.org]

Keyser, Leander S. *The Rational Test: Bible Doctrine in the Light of Reason*. Philadelphia: Lutheran Publication Society, 1908. [Chapter 10 Christ's Resurrection: Its Ultimate Purpose, See. 157–74; N.B. Archive.org and Google book]

———. *A System of Christian Evidence*. 2nd ed. Burlington, IA: Lutheran Literary Board, 1922. [Chapter 8 Internal Proofs Continued. 2. Internal Proofs Continued, 9. The Apostles and Evangelists as Witnesses, See. 91–95; Chapter 9 Continuation of the Internal Proofs. 2. Internal Proofs (continued), See. 95–102; N.B. Archive.org and Google book]

Kidder, Richard. *A Demonstration of the Messias In Which the Truth of the Christian Religion Is Proved, against all the Enemies thereof, But especially against the Jews*. London: Printed for John Osborn, 1726. [Part 1 Chapter 8 Of the Resurrection of Christ, See. 92–105; Chapter 9 Of the Ascension into Heaven, See. 106–11; Part 2. Chapter 2 The Various Accounts of the Resurrection Reconciled, See. 43–48; N.B. Google book and HathiTrust]

Kindī, Muḥammad ibn Yūsuf [Muḥammad ibn Yūsuf al-Kindī]. *The Apology of al Kindy, Written at the Court of al Mâmûn (circa AH 215; AD 830), in Defence of Christianity against Islam*. 2nd ed. [Translated by William Muir. SPCK, 1911. [The Life of Christ. See. 118–22; N.B. Archive.org and HathiTrust. This is a polemical work against Islam and it is attributed to an unknown person, Al-Kindi.]

Knechtle, Cliffe. *Give Me an Answer That Satisfies My Heart and My Mind: Answers to Your Toughest Questions about Christianity*. Downers Grove, IL: InterVarsity, 1986. [Question 27 Isn't the Resurrection a Myth?, See. 113–17]

Knox, John. *Limits of Unbelief*. New York: Seabury, 1970. [Jesus, resurrection, See. 61, 70, 75, 77–79, 102]

Koch, Franz Xavier Jos. *A Manual of Apologetics*. Edited by Charles Paul Bruehl. Translated by Anna Maud Buchanan. New York: J.F. Wagner, 1915. [Chapter 6 The Divinity of Christ Proved by His Miracles, See. 133–35; the Divinity of Christ Proved by His Resurrection, See. 135–39; N.B. Archive.org and Google book]

Komoszewski, J. Ed, et al. *Reinventing Jesus: How Contemporary Skeptics Miss the Real Jesus and Mislead Popular Culture*. Grand Rapids: Kregel, 2006. [Chapter 18 Osiris, Frankenstein, and Jesus Christ. See. Christ's Resurrection, See. 249–58]

Köstenberger, Andrea J., et al. *Truth in a Culture of Doubt: Engaging Skeptical Challenges to the Bible*. Nashville: B&H Publishing, 2014. [Conclusions: Reasons to Believe, See. 168–78]

Kreeft, Peter. *Fundamentals of the Faith: Essays in Christian Apologetics*. San Francisco: Ignatius Press, 1988. [Essay 23. The Apostles' Creed: The Resurrection and Life Everlasting, See. 149–52]

———. *Socrates Meets Jesus*. Downers Grove, IL: InterVarsity, 1987. [Chapter 9 Look Out! It's Alive, See. 147–79. N.B. An interesting read.]

———. *Yes or No? Straight Answers to Tough Questions about Christianity*. San Francisco: Ignatius Press, 1991. [Dialogue 7 The Resurrection, See. 67–72]

Kreeft, Peter, and Ronald K. Tacelli. *Handbook of Catholic Apologetics: Reasoned Answers to Questions of Faith.* San Francisco: Ignatius Press, 2009. [Chapter 8 The Resurrection, See. 185–210; N.B. This work presents a good overall review of the topic.]

———. *Handbook of Christian Apologetics: Hundreds of Answers to Crucial Questions.* Downers Grove, IL: InterVarsity, 1994. [Chapter 8 The Resurrection, See. 175–98]

Kreeft, Peter, and Ronald Tacelli. *Pocket Handbook of Christian Apologetics.* Downers Grove, IL: InterVarsity, 2003. [Chapter 9 The Resurrection, See. 69–78]

Kumar, Steve. *Christianity for Skeptics.* Hendrickson, 2000. [See. 94–96; 172–74; N.B. First published 1987 under the title *Christianity for Skeptics*]

Küng, Hans. *On Being a Christian.* Garden City, NY: Image Books, Doubleday, 1984. [Chapter 5 The New Life, See. 343–410]

Lake, James E. *Bishop Foster's Heresy.* Bordentown, NJ: Gazette Press, 1889. [Chapter 3 In Light of the Resurrection, See. 54–98, especially 84–98; N.B. Google book. This work criticizes Randolph Foster.]

Laney, J. Carl. *Answers to Tough Questions From Every Book of the Bible: A Survey of Problem Passages and Issues.* Grand Rapids: Kregel, 1997. [See. 211, 216–18, 222–23, 238–40, and 241–42]

Lang, J. Stephen. *The Complete Book of Bible Secrets and Mysteries.* Carol Stream, IL: Tyndale House, 2005. [See. 42–44]

———. *1,001 Things You Always Wanted to Know About the Bible.* Nashville: Thomas Nelson, 1999. [See. #427, 428, 626, 627]

Lanier, W. Mark. *Christianity On Trial: A Lawyer Examines the Christian Faith.* Downers Grove, IL: InterVarsity, 2014. [Chapter 10 The Audacity of the Resurrection, See. 186–210]

La Touche Boesnier, Pierre de. *A Preservative Against Atheism and Infidelity Proving the Fundamental Principles of Natural Religion.* London: Printed for Tho. Osborne, 1706. [See. 228, 238, 241; N.B. Google book. The book's author is identified as P.L.T.]

La Touche, Digges E. *Christian Certitude: Its Intellectual Basis.* Boston: Pilgrim Press, 1910. [Chapter 5 Whom God Hath Raised Up, See. 165–206; Chapter 6 He Hath Ascended Up On High, See. 209–16; N.B. Google book]

Lawrence, John J. *The Christian Credentials: An Appeal of Faith to Doubt.* New York: Fleming, 1923. [Chapter 4 The Divine Element in Christian Origins, See. Resurrection of Jesus, See. 99–110]

Leathes, Stanley. *Grounds of Christian Hope: A Sketch of the Evidences of Christianity.* London: Religious Tract Society, 1877. [Chapter 13 Steps in Divine Revelation, See. His Resurrection, 230–32]

———. *The Religion of the Christ: Its Historic and Literary Development Considered as an Evidence of its Origin.* New York: Pott, Young, 1874. [See. xxxi, xxxvii, xxxix, xl, ilx, xlv, xlvi, 208–16, 226, 243–57, 260, 270, 278–80, 286–87, 291, 298, 302, 305, 322, 323, 330, 337–40; N.B. Google book]

Leavitt, John McDowell. *Reasons for Faith in Christianity with Answers to Hypercriticism.* New York: Eaton & Mains, 1900. [Chapter 15 Proofs of the Resurrection, See. 202–16; Chapter 16 Narratives of the Resurrection, See. 217–30; Chapter 17 Consequences of the Resurrection, See. 231–40; N.B. Google book and HathiTrust]

———. *Reasons for Faith in This Nineteenth Century.* New York: James Pott, 1884. [Chapter 10 Proofs of the Resurrection, See. 131–44; Chapter 11 Narratives of the Resurrection,

See. 145–60; Chapter 12 Consequences of the Resurrection, See. 161–70; N.B. Google book]

Leitch, Ian. *Life Before Death: A Restored, Regenerated, and Renewed Life.* Larkspur, CO: Grace Acres Press, 2007. [The Significance of the Resurrection, See. 45–54]

Leland, John. *A View of the Principal Deistical Writers That Have Appeared in England: In the Last and Present Century; with Observations upon Them, and Some Account of the Answers That Have Been Published against Them: In Several Letters to a Friend.* London: Printed for Benj. Dod, 1757. [Letter 12 The Resurrection of Jesus considered, See. 167–92; N.B. Archive.org and Google book]

Lennox, John C. *Gunning for God: Why the New Atheists Are Missing the Target.* Oxford: Lion, 2011. [Chapter 8 Did Jesus Rise from the Dead?, See. 187–225]

Leslie, Charles. *The Case of the Jews Considered with Respect to Christianity.* London: 1755. [See. 88, 98, 120, 134–35, 139; N.B. Google book]

———. *The Sceptic's Manual, or Christianity Verified: Being a New Method of Appeal to the Understandings and Consciences of Deists, Jews, Sceptics, and Formal Professors.* Philadelphia: J. F. Walton, 1811. [See. 48, 51–52, 115, 169–72, 259; N.B. Archive.org and Google book; states "By the Author of Deism Refuted."]

Lewis, Edwin. *A Manual of Christian Belief.* New York: Scribner's Sons, 1927. [See. 75, 125]

Lewis, Gordon R. *Testing Christianity's Truth Claims: Approaches to Christian Apologetics.* Lanham, MD: University Press of America, 1990. [Resurrection of Christ, See. 60, 64, 92–94, 106–7, 110, 117, 140, 142, 154–55, 194–98, 202, 251, 281]

Lewis, Paul. *A Final Call to the Jews: or An Explanation of the Original Promise; Being a Full and Satisfactory Answer to all Objections that ever have, shall, or may be, Raised against Christianity.* London: Printed for the author; and sold by M. Cooper, at the Globe in Paternoster-Row, 1744. [Chapter 15 See. 172, 177, 178, The Probability of a Recovery, etc. See. 195–257; N.B. Google book]

Lewis, W. S. *The Great Problem; or, Christianity as It Is. By a Student of Science.* Religious Tract Society: London, 1881. [Part 4— Proofs: See. 201–399; Part 5—Results, See. 400–45; N.B. Google book. The author is identified in WorldCat, not in the text.]

Lindberg, Conrad Emil. *Apologetics or A System of Christian Evidence.* Rock Island, IL: Augustana Book Concern, 1917. [The Resurrection of Christ, See. 117–25]

Linton, Irwin H. *A Lawyer Examines the Bible: An Introduction to Christian Evidences.* Boston: W.A. Wilde, 1943. [Appendix "H" Trial of the Witnesses, See. 262–97]

Lisle, Lionel. *The Two Tests: The Supernatural Claims of Christianity Tried by Two of Its Own Rules.* London: Williams & Norgate, 1877. [Chapter 5 The Resurrection and Ascension of Jesus, See. 76–105; N.B. Google book and Gutenberg.org]

Little, Paul E. *Know Why You Believe.* Downers Grove, IL: InterVarsity, 2008. [Did Christ Rise from the Dead?, See. 60–73]

———. *Paul Little's Why & What Book.* Wheaton, IL: Victor, 1981. [Christ Left the Grave, See. 169–70; Resurrection Implications, See. 170–72]

Locke, John. *Vindications of the Reasonableness of Christianity.* Edited by Victor Nuovo. Oxford: Oxford University Press, 2012. [Messiah, resurrection of, great demonstrative proof, See. 161–63, 165–69, 172, 187; N.B Google book. Originally published in 1695.]

Lord, Charles E. *Evidences of Natural and Revealed Theology.* Philadelphia: J. B. Lippincott, 1869. [Chapter 6 Birth, Resurrection, and Ascension of Christ, and Miracles of His Apostles, See. 341–47; N.B. Google book]

Lorimer, George Claude. *The Argument for Christianity*. Philadelphia: American Baptist Publication Society, 1894. [See. 46, 52, 56, 58, 60, 100, 106, 122, 125, 160–63, 171, 174, 177, 194, 201, 202, 252, 253, 255, 306, N.B. Archive.org and Google book]

Lowber, James William. *The Highest Culture and Christianity*. Cincinnati: Standard Publishing, 1915. [See. The Resurrection of Christ, See. 162–69; also 274, 361; N.B. Archive.org]

Loysen, Jacobus A. St. Morilyon. *True to Life: Genuine Christian Belief for Western and Eastern Modern Man*. London: Regency, 1977. [Chapter 15 See. 83–87]

Lunn, Arnold. *The Third Day: A Defence of the Miracle of the Resurrection of Jesus Christ*. Westminster, MD: Newman Book Shop, 1945. [145 pages]

Lunny, W. J. *The Sociology of the Resurrection*. SCM, 1989. [146 pages]

Luthardt, Chr Ernst. *Apologetic Lectures on the Saving Truths of Christianity*. Translated by Sophia Taylor. 3rd ed. Edinburgh: T&T Clark, 1873. [Lecture 7 Revelation. See. The Resurrection of Christ, See. 203–6; N.B. Google book and HathiTrust]

Macartney, Clarence Edward. *Christianity and Common Sense: A Dialogue of Faith*. Chicago: John C. Winston, 1927. [Chapter 7 Common Sense and the Resurrection, See. 161–91]

———. *The Faith Once Delivered*. New York: Abingdon-Cokesbury, 1952. [Chapter 10 The Resurrection, See. 92–103]

MacGregor, James. *Studies in the History of Christian Apologetics: New Testament and Post-Apostolic*. Edinburgh: T&T Clark, 1894. [See. General Aspect, with a reference to Christ's resurrection, See. 67–73; The Miracle of Christ's Resurrection, See. 73–76; N.B. Google book]

Mackintosh, Robert. *A First Primer of Apologetics*. London: Elliot Stock, 1900. [Chapter 8 The Narratives Of Our Lord's Resurrection, See. 57–66; N.B. Google book]

Madgett, A. Patrick. *Christian Origins*. Cincinnati: Xavier University, 1939. [Chapter 8 Miracles: The Resurrection. 2. The Resurrection of Christ, See. 215–41]

Madigan, Kevin J., and Jon D. Levenson. *Resurrection: The Power of God for Christians and Jews*. New Haven: Yale University Press, 2008. [See. 1–4, 21–27]

Mair, Alexander. *Studies in the Christian Evidences*. Edinburgh: T&T Clark, 1889. [Chapter 9 The Resurrection of Christ, and What It Implies, See. 223–47; N.B. Archive.org and Google book]

Malham, John. *A Word for the Bible Being a Serious Reply to the Declarations and Assertions of the Speculative Deists and Practical Atheists of Modern Times, Particularly The Age of Reason, Part the Second, by Thomas Paine*. London: Printed for Allen and West, 1796. [See. 91–100; N.B. Google book]

Maltby, Edward. *Illustrations of the Truth of the Christian Religion*. 2nd ed. Cambridge: Printed at the University Press, 1803. [Chapter 3 On the Conduct of Disciples. See. 127–35; N.B. Archive.org, Google book, and HathiTrust]

Markos, Louis. *Apologetics for the Twenty-First Century*. Wheaton, IL: Crossway, 2010. [Chapter 18 The Case for the Resurrection of Christ, See. 165–73]

———. *Atheism on Trial: Refuting the Modern Arguments Against God*. Eugene. OR: Harvest House, 2018. [Christian Cross-Examination #2 The Resurrection Can Withstand Scrutiny, See. 82–86]

Martin, Cecil. *The Decline of Religion*. London: George Allen & Unwin, 1941. [Resurrection of Christ, See. 51, 174–78, 219, 222]

Martin, James Alfred, Jr. *Fact, Fiction, & Faith*. New York: Oxford University Press, 1960. [What about the Resurrection, See. 54–57; N.B. Archive.org]

Martin, Walter R. *The Kingdom of the Cults*. Bloomington, MN: Bethany House, 2003. [Jehovah's Witness, See. 119–21; Theosophical Society, See. 295–96; Buddhism, See. 317–18; New Agers, See. 424–25; See. Worldwide Church of God, See. 507–8; N.B. This work is a definite must read.]

Masson, Robert. *The Charmed Circle: Theology for the Head, Heart, Hands, and Feet*. Kansas City, MO: Sheed & Ward, 1987. [The Man Who God Raised from the Dead, See. 143–49; also See. 103–4, 192, 194, 195, 219, 221]

McBurnie, David. *Errors of Infidelity*. London: A. Hall, Virtue, 1854. [Section 13 The Resurrection—Immateriality of Mind—Future Life, See. 103–13]

McCosh, James. *Christianity and Positivism: A Series of Lectures to the Times on Natural Theology and Apologetics*. New York: Robert Carter, 1874. [See. 161, 242, 288; N.B. Archive.org and Google book]

McDowell, John. *Christian Essentials: What We Believe about Christianity and Why We Believe It*. New York, Chicago: Revell, 1928. [Chapter 4 The Essential Fact: The Resurrection of Jesus Christ, See. 47–57]

McDowell, Josh. *Christianity: Hoax or History*. Wheaton, IL: Tyndale House, 1989. [Chapter 1 Back from the Grave, 13–28; Chapter 2 Consider the Facts, See. 29–44]

———. *Evidence for Christianity*. Nashville: Nelson. 2006. [Chapter 7 The Resurrection—Hoax or History, See. 245–349]

———, comp. *Evidence that Demands a Verdict: Historical Evidences for the Christian Faith*. San Bernardino: Campus Crusade for Christ International, 1972. [Chapter 10 The Resurrection—Hoax or History?, See. 185–273; N.B; This popular work is often cited in internet articles.]

———. *Josh McDowell Answers Five Tough Questions*. Wheaton, IL: Tyndale House, 1991. [Jesus Christ Died and Rose Again, See. 345–55]

———. *The New Evidence That Demands a Verdict*. Nashville: Nelson, 1999. [Chapter 9 Support of Deity—The Resurrection—Hoax or History?, See. 203–84]

———. *A Ready Defense the Best of Josh McDowell*. Compiled by Bill Wilson. Nashville: Nelson, 1993. [Chapter 20 The Resurrection of Jesus, See. 215–40]

McDowell, Josh, and Bob Hostetler. *Beyond Belief to Convictions*. Wheaton, IL: Tyndale House, 2002. [Part 4 The Resurrection: God Wants Us To Trust Him, No Matter What, especially Chapter 13 The Case of the Empty Tomb, See. 259–76]

McDowell, Josh, and Kevin Johnson. *The Awesome Book of Bible: Answers for Kids*. Eugene, OR: Harvest House, 2011. [Questions 31–34, See. 59–62]

McDowell, Josh, and Sean McDowell. *The Bible Handbook of Difficult Verses: A Complete Guide to Answering the Tough Questions*. Eugene, OR: Harvest House, 2013. [See. 202–6]

———. *77 FAQs about God and the Bible*. Eugene, OR: Harvest House, 2012. [Chapter 44 Is There Proof that Jesus Rose from the Dead?, See. 124–26; Chapter 46 Why Is Jesus' Resurrection So Central To Christianity?, See. 130–31]

———. *The Unshakable Truth*. Eugene, OR: Harvest House, 2010. [33. The Evidence that Jesus Literally Rose from the Dead, See. 281–96]

McDowell, Josh, and Don Stewart. *Answers to Tough Questions Skeptics Ask about the Christian Faith*. San Bernardino, CA: Here's Life, 1980. [How do we know that Jesus rose from the dead?, See. 47–49; How could Jesus have remained in the tomb three days and three nights if He was crucified on Friday and rose on Sunday?, See. 50–51; How do you explain the contradictions in the resurrection story?, See. 52–53]

McDowell, Josh, and Jim Walker. *Understanding Islam & Christianity*. Eugene, OR: Harvest House, 2013. [New Testament Christians Say That Jesus Was Crucified, See. 137–46]

McDowell, Josh, and Bill Wilson. *The Evidence for the Historical Jesus*. Eugene, OR: Harvest House, 2011. [Chapter 14 The Reliability of the Resurrection Reports, See. 265–76]

McFarland, Alex. *10 Answers for Atheists: How to have an Intelligent Discussion about the Existence of God*. Ventura, CA: Regal, 2012. [Question #6 How can Christians believe that Someone who was dead rose and came back to life?, See. 171–72]

McFarland, Alex, and Elmer Towns. *10 Questions Every Christian Must Answer: Thoughtful Responses to Strengthen Your Faith*. Nashville: B&H Academic, 2011. [Chapter 6 Are the Claims of Jesus' Physical Resurrection from the Dead Valid? (Alex McFarland), See. 93–107]

McGarvey, J. W. *Evidences of Christianity: Parts 3 and 4*. Cincinnati, OH: Standard Publishing, 1912. [Chapter 10 The Direct Evidence for the New Testament Miracles: The Resurrection of Jesus, See. 116–31; Chapter 11 The Resurrection of Jesus: Adverse Theories Considered, See. 132–45; Chapter 12 The Resurrection of: The Testimony of the Witnesses, See. 146–62]

McGrath, Alister E. *Bridge Building Effective Christian Apologetics*. Leicester: Inter-Varsity Press, 1993. [Part 2 Overcoming Barriers to Faith, 4 The Resurrection, See. 160–65]

———. *Explaining Your Faith*. Grand Rapids: Baker, 1996. [Chapter 5 Intellectual Barriers to Faith. D. The Resurrection, See. 65–85]

———. *Intellectuals Don't Need God & Other Modern Myths: Building Bridges to Faith Through Apologetics*. Grand Rapids: Zondervan, 1993. [Part 2 Overcoming Barriers to Faith 5. Intellectual Barriers to Faith D. The Resurrection, See. 119–22]

McIlvaine, Charles Pettit. *The Evidences of Christianity; in their External, or Historical, Division: Exhibited in a Course of Lectures*. Philadelphia: Smith & English, 1859. [See. 252, 280, 382; N.B. Archive.org, Google book, and HathiTrust]

McLeskey, James Meadows. *Is Christianity the Only True Religion?* Nashville: Cumberland Presbyterian Publishing House, 1923. [The Resurrection, a Test of His Claims, See. 34–73]

McRoberts, Kerry D. *A Letter from Christ: Apologetics in Cultural Transition*. Lanham, MD: University Press of America, 2012. [Chapter 4 The "Sign of Jonah": Beyond Reasonable Doubt?, See. 59–70]; Appendix Three: The "Sign of Jonah": An Unbroken Chain of Testimony, See. 104–9]

McWhinney, Thomas M. *Reason and Revelation, Hand in Hand*. New York: Fords, Howard, & Hulbert, 1886. [Chapter 24 Christ's Resurrection, See. 566–87; N.B. Archive.org and Google book]

Mead, Charles Marsh. *Supernatural Revelation: An Essay Concerning the Basis of the Christian Faith*. New York: A. D. F. Randolph and, 1889. [Chapter 7 Proof of the Christian Miracles, See. 196–228; N.B. Archive.org, Google book, and HathiTrust]

Meighan, Thomas (Londres), ed. *The True Church of Christ, Showed by Concurrent Testimonies of Scripture and Primitive Tradition*. Part 3. London, 1715. [See. 14, 15, 17–18, 22, 59, 163, 202, 215, N.B. Google book and HathiTrust]

Meister, Chad V. *Building Belief: Constructing Faith from the Ground Up*. Eugene, OR: Wipf & Stock, 2009. [Chapter 8 The Resurrection of Jesus: Fact or Fiction?, See. 157–75]

Meldau, Fred John. *The Miracle Man and the Wonder Book.* Chicago: Bible Institute Colportage Assn., 1923. [Proof of the Deity of Christ from His Resurrection, See. 57–61]

Mendon Associates. *Evidences of Revealed Religion.* Northampton: Printed by William Butler, 1798. [Section 8 The Prophecies, which Christ Uttered, Concerning His Own Resurrection, See. 142–53; N.B. Google book and HathiTrust]

Miall, Edward. *Bases of Belief: An Examination of Christianity as a Divine Revelation by the Light of Recognised Facts and Principles.* 3rd ed. London: Arthur Hall, Virtue, 1861. [§18. Christian Miracles Sustained by Evidence. The Resurrection of Christ, See. 163–74; N.B. Google book]

Micklem, Nathaniel. *Ultimate Questions (The Cole Lectures, 1954.).* New York: Abingdon, 1955. [Chapter 4 The Resurrection, See. 78–103]

Micou, Richard Wilde. *Basic Ideas in Religion or Apologetic Theism.* Edited by Paul Micou. New York: Association Press, 1916. [Christ, Resurrection, See. 287, 444, 448, 449, 451; N.B. Archive.org and Google book]

Miethe, Terry L., and Gary R. Habermas. *Why Believe? God Exists! Rethinking the Case for God and Christianity.* Joplin, MO: College Press, 1998. [Chapter 26 The Resurrection, See. 261–74]

Miller, Calvin. *A Hunger for Meaning.* Carmel: NY, Guideposts, 1984. [Chapter 8 The Miracle of Life, See. 84–90]

Miller, Herbert Sumner. *The Christian Workers' Manual.* New York: George H. Doran, 1922. [The Resurrection of the Lord Jesus, See. 89–97; The Ascension and Exaltation of the Lord Jesus, See. 97–100; N.B. Archive.org]

Miller, Randolph Crump. *This We Can Believe.* New York: Hawthorn, 1976. [Jesus, resurrection, See. 74, 75, 76, 82, 91–92, 93, 101]

Minton, Henry Colin. *Christianity Supernatural: A Brief Essay on Christian Evidence.* Philadelphia: Westminster, 1900. [See. 41–43]

Moltmann, Jürgen. *Sun of Righteousness, Arise! God's Future for Humanity and the Earth.* Minneapolis: Augsburg, 2010. [Chapter 5 The Raising of Jesus, See. 43–57]

Molyneux, Reginald E. *Reasonable Faith and Hope.* London: Longmans, Green, 1895. [See. 48, 49, 90, 94, 111, 133, N.B. Archive.org and Google book]

Montgomery, John Warwick. *Defending the Gospel in Legal Style: Essays on Legal Apologetics & the Justification of Classical Christian Faith.* Eugene, OR: Wipf & Stock, 2017. [A New Approach to the Apologetic for Christ's Resurrection by Way of Wigamore's Judicial Analysis of Evidence, See. 55–67; N.B. This is an important work to read.]

———. *Faith Founded on Fact: Essays in Evidential Apologetics.* Nashville: Nelson, 1978. [Chapter 3 Are You Having A Fuddled Easter?, See. 75–79]

———. *History and Christianity.* Minneapolis: Bethany House, 1986. [Appendix: Faith, History & The Resurrection, See. 83–110; Reprint, 1971]

———. *How Do We Know There is a God? And Other Questions Inappropriate in Polite Society.* Minneapolis: Bethany Fellowship, 1973. [Question 8 Did Jesus Rise from the Dead? If So, How Do We Know He Is Alive Today?, See. 21]

———. *Tractatus Logico-Theologicus.* Bonn, Ger: Verlag für Kultur und Wisenschaft, 2005. [3.6, See. 97–109; 3.7, See.109–16; 3.87, See. 125–26; N.B. This work should be examined.]

Montizambert, Eric. *This We Believe: A Brief Study of the Foundations of Faith*. New York: Morehouse-Gorham, 1951. [Chapter 8 The Resurrection and After, See. 95–102; N.B. Not Useful.]

Moore, Aubrey Lackington. *Science and the Faith, Essays on Apologetic Subjects, With an Introduction*. London: Kegan Paul, Trench, Trübner, 1905. [See. 97–98, 226; N.B. Archive.org, Google book, and HathiTrust]

Moreland, J. P. *The God Question: An Invitation to a Life of Meaning*. Eugene, OR: Harvest House, 2009. [The Resurrection of Jesus from the Dead, See. 121–25]

———. *Scaling the Secular City: A Defense of Christianity*. Grand Rapids: Baker, 1987. [Chapter 6 The Resurrection of Jesus, See. 159–84; N.B. This book presents a concise and similar presentation of William Lane Craig.]

Moreland, J. P., and Tim Muehlhoff. *The God Conversation: Using Stories and Illustrations to Explain Your Faith*. Downers Grove, IL: InterVarsity, 2007. [Chapter 6 The Resurrection: Conspiracy Theory or Fact?, See. 78–88; Chapter 7 The Resurrection: Conspiracy Theory or Fact? (Part 2), See. 89–101]

Morgan, Robert J. *Beyond Reasonable Doubt!* Wheaton, IL: Evangelical Training Association, 1997. [Exhibit A: The Resurrection of Christ, See. 5–18]

———. *Evidence and Truth: Foundations for Christian Truth*. Wheaton, IL: Crossway, 2003. [Exhibit A: The Resurrection of Christ, See. 9–26]

Morison, John. *Counsels to Young Men, on Modern Infidelity and the Evidences of Christianity*. New York: American Tract Society, 1834. [The Resurrection of Christ, See. 112–22; N.B. Google book and HathiTrust]

———. *The Rock of Faith: In Contrast with the Quicksands of Modern Skepticism*. Philadelphia: American Baptist Publication Society, 1853. [The External Evidences of Christianity 2. The Resurrection of Christ, See. 123–34; N.B. Google book and HathiTrust]

Morley, Brian. *Mapping Apologetics: Comparing Contemporary Approaches*. Downers Grove, IL: InterVarsity, 2015. [Chapter 12 Evidentialism. Gary Habermas: Christianity can be proved by widely accepted crucial facts, See. 334–50]

Morris, Henry M. *The Bible Has the Answer: Practical Biblical Discussions of 100 Frequent Questions*. Grand Rapids: Baker, 1971. [The Work of Christ. See 4. How do we know Christ rose from the dead?, See. 46–47]

———. *The God Who Is Real: A Creationist Approach to Evangelism and Missions*. Grand Rapids: Baker, 1988. [The Resurrection of Christ, See. 66–71]

———. *Many Infallible Proofs: Practical and Useful Evidences of Christianity*. San Diego, CA: Creation-Life, 1974. [The Resurrection of Christ, See. 88–97]

Morris, Henry M., and Martin E. Clark. *The Bible Has the Answer*. El Cajon, CA: Master Books, 1987. [Chapter 4 The Work of Christ #4 How do we know Christ rose from the dead?, See. 46–48]

Morrison, John Douglas. *Has God Said? Scripture, the Word of God, and the Crisis of Theological Authority*. Eugene, OR: Pickwick, 2006. [Jesus Christ, resurrection, See. 21, 57, 153, 162, 166, 207, 237, 257, 269, 275]

Morrow, Jonathan. *Welcome to College: A Christ-Follower's Guide for the Journey*. Grand Rapids: Kregel, 2008. [Chapter 17 Jesus Rise from the Dead?, See. 135–42]

Moucarry, Chawkat. *The Prophet & the Messiah: An Arab Christian's Perspective on Islam & Christianity*. Downers Grove, IL: InterVarsity, 2002. [Chapter 12 Evidence for the death and resurrection, See. 157–66]

Moule, Arthur Evans. *Reasons for the Hope that is In Us / Brief Essays on Christian Evidences*. London: Hodder & Stoughton, 1891. [Chapter 2 The Fact of the Resurrection, See. 17–43; N.B. Google book and HathiTrust]

Mowat, Oliver. *Christianity and Some of its Evidences: An Address*. Toronto: Williamson, 1890. [See. 17, 43–49, 58–62, 69; N.B. Archive.org, Google book, and HathiTrust]

Mudge, Zachariah Atwell. *Towers of Zion; or, The Evidences of Christianity Illustrated*. New York: Protestant Episcopal Society for the Promotion of Evangelical Knowledge, 1856. [Section 4 The Resurrection of Christ, See. 72–77. WorldCat identified the author, not in the text. N.B. Archive.org and Google book]

Mullins, Edgar Young. *Why Is Christianity True? Christian Evidences*. Chicago: Christian Culture Press, 1905. [Chapter 13 The Resurrection of Jesus, See. 188–203; N.B. Archive.org, Google book, and HathiTrust]

Muncaster, Ralph O. *Examine the Evidence*. Eugene, OR: Harvest House, 2004. [Part 4 Evidence of the Resurrection of Jesus, See. 373–442]

Munk, Arthur W. *Perplexing Problems of Religion*. St. Louis: Bethany Press, 1954. [See. 148]

Muzzey, Artemas Bowers. *Man a Soul; or, The Inward, and the Experimental, Evidences of Christianity*. Boston: William Crosby, 1842. [Chapter 7 The Soul the Test of External Evidence. See. 69–70; N.B. Google book]

Nairne, Charles Murray. *Paley's Evidences of Christianity. With Notes and Additions*. New York: Robert Carter, 1882. [Chapter 8 Of the History of the Resurrection, See. 376–79]

Nash, Ronald H. *World-Views in Conflict: Choosing Christianity in a World of Ideas*. Grand Rapids: Zondervan, 1992. [Chapter 9 The Incarnation and the Resurrection, See. 147–63]

Newcomb, Harvey. *The Four Pillars: or the Truth of Christianity Demonstrated. In Four Distinct and Independent Series of Proofs: Together with an Explanation of the Types and Prophecies Concerning the Messiah*. Boston: Goldsmith, Crocker & Brewster, 1842. [Concerning his resurrection and ascension, See. 217–19; the burial and resurrection of Christ, See. 257; N.B. Google book]

Nichols, Ichabod. *Hours with the Evangelists*. Vol. 2. Boston: Crosby & Nichols, 1864 [Chapter 21 The Resurrection, See. 357–73; Chapter 22 Appearances to the Disciples—The Ascension, See. 374–88; N.B. Google book and HathiTrust]

Noble, S. *Important Doctrines of the True Christian Religion, Explained, Demonstrated, and Vindicated from Vulgar Errors*. New York: J. Allen, 1848. [Lecture 8 The Resurrection of the Lord Jesus Christ, and the Divine Nature of his Resurrection-Body, See. 113–29; N.B. Archive.org and Google book]

O'Brien, John A. *Truths Men Live By: A Philosophy of Religion and Life*. New York: Macmillan, 1946. [Confirmed by Miracles, See. 345–46]

Origen. *The Writings of Origen*. Vol. 2. Origen Contra Celsum, Books 2.-8. Edited by Alexander Roberts and James Donaldson. Translated by Frederick Crombie. Edinburgh: T&T Clark, 1894. [Against Celsus, Book 2, Chapters 55–70, See. 58–75; N.B. Google book]

Orr, James. *The Faith of a Modern Christian*. London: Hodder & Stoughton, 1910. [Chapter 7 The Cross and the Resurrection, See. 121–38; N.B. Archive.org]

Orr, J. Edwin. *The Faith that Persuades*. New York: Harper & Row, 1977. [Birth, Life, Death, Resurrection, See. 132–33]

Osborne, Cecil G. *The Joy of Understanding Your Faith*. Nashville: Abingdon, 1983. [Chapter 9 Death and the Resurrection, See. 127–37]

Owen, Robert and Alexander Campbell. *The Evidences of Christianity: A Debate Between Robert Owen, and Alexander Campbell, Containing an Examination of the "Social System," and All the Systems of Skepticism of Ancient and Modern Times.* 4th ed. Cincinnati: E. Morgan, 1852. [Mr. Campbell's Twenty-Second Reply, See. 259–404; especially 277–319; N.B. Archive.org, Google book, and HathiTrust. This 1829 debate spanned eight days. Alexander Campbell defended Christianity.]

Paley, William. *Paley's Evidences of Christianity: With Notes and Additions by Charles Murray Nairne.* New York: Robert Carter, 1882. [Part 2 Of the Auxiliary Evidences of Christianity, See. 8. Of the History of the Resurrection, See. 376–79]

———. *The Works of William Paley: In Five Volumes. Volume 2. Containing A View of the Evidences of Christianity.* Boston: Joshua Belcher, 1810. [Chapter 8 Of the History of the Resurrection, See. 312–16; N.B. Google book]

Parsons, Lawrence (Earl of Rosse). *An Argument to Prove the Truth of the Christian Revelation.* London: John Murray, 1834. [Chapter 46 See. 396–408; N.B. Google book and HathiTrust]

Parton, Craig A. *Religion on Trial.* Cambridge, UK: Lutterworth, 2010. [Don't Both Philosophy and Science Make the Resurrection Story the Stuff of Primitive Myth?, See. 74–78]

Pascal, Blaise. *Pascal's Pensées or, Thoughts on Religion.* Edited and translated by Gertrude Burfurd Rawlings. New York: Peter Pauper Press, 1900. [See. 23, 27, 28, 51; N.B. Archive.org]

Paterson, Andrea C. *Three Monotheistic Faiths—Judaism, Christianity, Islam: An Analysis and Brief History.* Bloomington, IN: AuthorHouse, 2009. [Jesus, resurrection, See. 48, 72, 112]

Patey, Edward H. *All in Good Faith.* London: Mowbrays, 1978. [Chapter 9 Jesus Christ: Resurrection, See. 86–95]

Patrick, John. *The Apology of Origen in Reply to Celsus: A Chapter in the History of Apologetics.* Edinburgh: W. Blackwood, 1892. [Resurrection of Christ, See. 33–34; 70; 216–24; N.B. Archive.org and Google book]

Patterson, Robert. *Fables of Infidelity and Facts of Faith: A Series of Tracts on the Absurdity of Atheism, Pantheism and Rationalism.* Cincinnati: American Reform Tract & Book Society, 1859. [See. 19, 85, 89, 91, 105, 106, 113, 114, 116, 119, 120, 127, 159, 177; N.B. Archive.org, Google book, Gutenberg.org, and HathiTrust]

Peabody, Andrew P. *Christianity and Science a Series of Lectures.* New York: R. Carter, 1874. [Lecture 6 Paul's Testimony to Christ's Resurrection the Earliest Extant, 118–42; N.B. Archive.org and Google book]

Petty, Daniel W., ed. *Of First Importance: He Was Raised and Appeared: Studies in the Resurrection.* Temple Terrace, FL: Florida College Press, 2013. [258 pages; N.B. This book contains fifteen essays.]

Philip, Robert Kemp. *The Biblical Reason Why: A Family Guide to Scripture Readings.* 1859. London: Houlston & Wright, 1859. [#1127–1160, See. 244–53; N.B. Google book]

Pickering, David. *Lectures in Defence of Divine Revelation.* Providence: Samuel W, Wheeler, 1830. [See. 49, 174, 175, 193, 198, 204, 209, 211; N.B. Archive.org, Google book, and HathiTrust]

Pictet, Bénédict. *True and False Religion Examined the Christian Religion Defended and the Protestant Reformation Vindicated.* Translated by A. Bruce. Edinburgh: Sold by Ogle, Robertson & Constable, 1797. [Third Discourse, See. 65–74; N.B. Google book]

Pierson, Arthur Tappan. *Many Infallible Proofs: A Series of Chapters on the Evidences of Christianity*. Chicago: Revell, 1886. [See. 22, 73, 98, 187, 188, 190, 204, 242; N.B. Archive.org, Google book, and HathiTrust]

Pieters, Albertus. *The Facts and Mysteries of the Christian Faith*. Grand Rapids: Eerdmans, 1926. [Chapters 28–33, See. 114–41]

Pinnock, Clark H. *Reason Enough: A Case for the Christian Faith*. Downers Grove, IL: InterVarsity, 1980. [Chapter 4 The Historical Basis for Faith, See. 83–89]

———. *Set Forth Your Case: Studies in Christian Apologetics*. Nutley, NJ: Craig Press, 1968. [Chapter 11 On The Third Day, See. 63–68.]

Plantinga, Alvin. *Warranted Christian Belief*. New York: Oxford University Press, 2000. [Jesus Christ, resurrection of, See. 275–77, 400–401, 405–6, 413]

Poling, Judson. *What Difference Does Jesus Make?* Grand Rapids: Zondervan, 2003. [Discussion Five. Isn't the Resurrection of Jesus a Myth?, See. 57–66]

Poole, Garry, and Judson Poling. *Tough Questions Leader's Guide*. Rev. ed. Grand Rapids: Zondervan, 2003. [Discussion 5 Isn't the Resurrection of Jesus Myth?, See. 45–53]

Poole, Michael. *The 'New' Atheism: Ten Arguments that Don't Hold Water*. Oxford, England: Lion Hudson, 2009. [See. 36–39, 42]

Porteus, Beilby. *A Summary of the Principal Evidences for the Truth and Divine Origin of the Christian Revelation*. 3rd ed. Charlestown: Samuel Etheridge, 1800. [Proposition 12 The Resurrection of Our Lord from the Dead, See. 135–53; N.B. Archive.org, Google book, and HathiTrust. This work also appears in Google book *In The Christian Armed Against Infidelity. A Collection of Tracts in Defense of Divine Revelation*, edited by Thomas Jackson, London: John Mason, 1837, See. 148–63]

Potts, James Henry. *Faith Made Easy, or, What to Believe and Why a Popular Statement of the Doctrines and Evidences of Christianity in the Light of Modern Research and Sound Biblical Interpretation*. Cincinnati: Cranston & Stowe, 1889. [Part 9 What to Believe Concerning the Future State, 7. (1.) The Resurrection, See. 471–78; N.B. Archive.org and Google book]

Powell, Doug. *Holman QuickSource Guide to Christian Apologetics*. Nashville: Holman, 2006. [Chapter 11 The Resurrection, See. 265–306]

Poynter, William. *Christianity; or, The Evidences and Characters of the Christian Religion*. London: Keating and Brown, 1827. [Part 1 Chapter 6 The Fact of the Divine Revelation of the Christian Religion, See. 25–28; N.B. Archive.org and Google book. Nothing useful.]

Priestley, Joseph. *A Continuation of the Letters to the Philosophers and Politicians of France on the Subject of Religion and of the Letters to a Philosophical Unbeliever; In Answer to Mr. Paine's Age of Reason*. Northumerland-Town, 1794. [Letter 3 Of the Object of Christianity, and of the History of Jesus, See. 57–60; N.B. This brief letter refutes Thomas Paine. Kraus Reprint Co. Millwood, NY, 1977. This work is also online at Archive.org, Google book, and HathiTrust]

———. *Discourses on the Evidence of Revealed Religion*. London: Printed for J. Johnson, 1794. [Discourse 11 On the Resurrection of Jesus, See. 300–54; N.B. Archive.org, Google book, and HathiTrust]

———. *Letters to the Jews Inviting Them to an Amicable Discussion of the Evidences of Christianity*. Birmingham: Pearson & Rollason, 1787. [Letter 2, See. 9; Letter 3, See. 25, 33, 34, 35; Letter 4, See. 42; N.B. Google book and HathiTrust]

Prior, Kenneth Francis William. *The Gospel in a Pagan Society: A Book for Modern Evangelists*. Downers Grove, IL: InterVarsity, 1975. [Chapter 5 Jesus and the Resurrection, See. 46–54]

Pritchard, John. *How to Explain Your Faith*. Collegeville, MN: Liturgical Press, 2006. [Chapter 13 He Did What?, See. 89–96]

Protestant Episcopal Society for the Promotion of Evangelical Knowledge. *Towers of Zion; or, The Evidences of Christianity Illustrated*. New York: Protestant Episcopal Society for the Promotion of Evangelical Knowledge, 1856. [Section 4 The Resurrection, See. 72–77; N.B. Archive.org and Google book]

Quackenbos, John D. *Enemies and Evidences of Christianity: Thoughts on Questions of the Hour*. New York: Eaton & Mains, 1909. [What is Christianity More than Agnosticism? Modern Doubt and Christian Conviction, See. 294–332 especially pages 316–32; N.B. Archive.org, Google book, and HathiTrust]

Quick, Oliver Chase. *The Grounds of Faith and the Chaos of Thought*. London: Nisbet, 1932. [Resurrection, See. 126]

Quist, Allen. *Many Convincing Proofs: A Biblical Approach to Christian Apologetics*. Mankato, MN: Lutheran Synod Book Co., 2008. [Chapter 3 The Resurrection of Jesus (1), See. 9–22; Chapter 4 The Resurrection of Jesus (2), See. 23–30; N.B. Originally *The Marks of the Nail: A Survey of the Evidence for Christianity*. Milwaukee: Northwestern Publishing House, 1985.]

———. *The Marks of the Nail: A Survey of the Evidence for Christianity*. Milwaukee: Northwestern Publishing House, 1985. [Chapter 3 The Resurrection of Jesus (1), See. 9–21; Chapter 2 The Resurrection of Jesus (2), See. 22–29, 39]

Ragg, Lonsdale. *Evidences of Christianity*. 2nd ed. New York: Edwin S. Gorham, 1909. [Chapter 5 The Risen Christ, See. 89–101; N.B. Google book and HathiTrust]

Rahner, Karl, and Karl-Heinz Weger. *Christian Faith: Answers for the Future*. New York: Crossroad, 1981. [Chapter 7 Redemption and Resurrection, See. 105–23]

Ramm, Bernard L. *The God Who Makes a Difference: A Christian Appeal to Reason*. Waco, TX: Word, 1972. [Section 34: Evil and the Resurrection, See. 149–51]

———. *Protestant Christian Evidences: A Textbook of the Evidences of the Truthfulness of the Christian Faith for Conservative Protestants*. Chicago: Moody, 1953. [Supernatural Verification Through the Resurrection of Christ, See. 184–207]

Ramsay, D. M. *The Resurrection of Our Lord A Sermon Preached by the Rev. D. M. Ramsay*. Ottowa: James Hort, 1899. [See. 32]

Rauser, Randal. *Faith Lacking Understanding: Theology "Through a Glass, Darkly."* Paternoster: Milton Keyes, 2008. [Chapter 6 On Not Understanding the Ascension, See. 113–35]

Raymond, Bradford Paul. *Christianity and the Christ: A Study of Christian Evidences*. New York: Hunt & Eaton, 1894. [Chapter 6 Christ and the Resurrection, See. 125–44; N.B. Google book and HathiTrust. The author interacts with Reimarus and Renan.]

Real Dialogues on the Evidences of Christianity: From "Death Bed Scenes." New York: Leavitt, Lord, 1835. [Chapter 2 The Main Argument, See. 119–29; By A Clergyman of the Church of England; N.B. Google book. The Library of Congress states that John Warton authored the text. WorldCat reports this name is a pseudonym of William Wood. The name Wm. Wood is handwritten on the Google book scan.]

Category III—Apologetics and Anti-Apologetics

Redford, R. A. *The Christian's Plea Against Modern Unbelief: A Handbook of Christian Evidence*. 2nd ed. London: Hodder & Stoughton, 1883. [See. 10, 207, 210, 228, 246, 247, 255, 258, 350, 408, 420, 441, 444, 445. 487–96; N.B. Google book and HathiTrust]

———. *Primer of Christian Evidence*. London: Sunday School Union, 1884. [The Credentials of Christianity as the Religion of Jesus Christ. 3 (vii) But the One Chief Credential of a Miraculous Kind is the Resurrection of Jesus Christ Himself from the Dead, See. 22–24; N.B. Archive.org and Google book]

Reed, Elizabeth A., and H. L. Hastings. *The Bible Triumphant: Twelve Dozen Sceptical Arguments Refuted: A Reply to an Infidel Work Entitled 144 Self-Contradictions of the Bible*. London: S. Bagster, 1882. [See. 89–91; N.B. Google book and Haititrust.org]

Reid, Louis Arnaud. *Preface to Faith*. London: George Allen & Unwin, 1939. [Chapter 6 The "Divinity" of Christ and Some Historical Considerations. See. (4) Resurrection, See. 87–94]

Reiss, Robert. *Sceptical Christianity: Exploring Credible Belief*. London: Jessica Kingsley, 2016. [Chapter 5 The Resurrection, See. 83–91]

Reymond, Robert L. *Faith's Reasons for Believing: An Apologetic Antidote to Mindless Christianity*. Fearn, Ross-shire: Mentor: Christian Focus, 2008. [Chapter 4 Faith's Reasons for Believing in the Bodily Resurrection and Ascension to Heaven of Jesus Christ, See. 131–66]

———. *The Justification of Knowledge: An Introductory Study in Christian Apologetic Methodology*. Nutley, NJ: Presbyterian and Reformed Pub., 1976. [Montgomery's Historical Apologetic for Christ's Claims, See. 93–99. N.B. Available online]

Rhodes, Ron. *Answering the Objections of Atheists, Agnostics, & Skeptics*. Eugene, OR: Harvest House, 2006. [Chapter 11 The Evidence for the Resurrection, See. 205–24]

———. *The Big Book of Bible Answers: A Guide to Understanding the Most Challenging Questions*. Eugene, OR: Harvest House, 2013. [The Resurrection of Christ, See. 143–50]

———. *The Complete Book of Bible Answers*. Eugene, OR: Harvest House, 1997. [Chapter 14 The Resurrection, See. 131–39]

———. *5-Minute Apologetics for Today: 365 Quick Answers to Key Questions*. Eugene, OR: Harvest House, 2010. [Day 197 The Resurrection: The Heart of Biblical Christianity; Day 198 Evidence for the Resurrection; Day 199 Jesus Rose Physically; Day 200 The Resurrection—a Conspiracy?; Day 201 The Wrong Tomb?; Day 202 Did Jesus Swoon on the Cross?; Day 203 Jesus' Body Was Not Stolen; Day 204 The Disciples' Memories and Jesus' Resurrection; Day 205 Mass Hallucinations?; N.B. No pagination.]

———. *Reasoning From the Scriptures with Muslims*. Eugene, OR: Harvest House, 2002. [Jesus was Not Crucified, but was Taken into Heaven by Allah, See. 136–39]

———. *What Does the Bible Say About Easy-to-Understand Answers to the Tough Questions*. Eugene, OR, 2007. [Chapter 14 The Resurrection, See. 131–33]

Richardson, Alan. *Christian Apologetics*. London: Harper & Brothers, 1947. [Resurrection of Christ, See. 167–68, 172, 209, 216–17]

Rishell, Charles W. *The Foundations of the Christian Faith*. New York: Eaton & Mains, 1899. [Section 5 The Resurrection of Jesus and the Validity of His Claims, See. 523–58; N.B. Google book and HathiTrust]

Robbins, Wilford L. *A Christian Apologetic*. 2nd ed. London: Longmans, Green, 1903. [Chapter 6 The Resurrection of Jesus Christ, See. 88–115; N.B. Archive.org, Google book, and HathiTrust]

Roberts, A. Wayne. *Assumptions and Faith: You Have to Begin Somewhere.* Broadview, IL: Gibbs, 1974. [See. 85–86]

Robinson, Edward. *A Harmony of the Four Gospels in Greek.* Boston: Crocker & Brewster, 1845. [Part 9 Our Lord's Resurrection, His Subsequent Appearances, and His Ascension. §159–173. See. 228–35; N.B. Archive.org, Google book, and HathiTrust]

Robinson, Ezekiel Gilman. *Christian Evidences.* New York: Silver, Burdett, 1895. [Chapter 2. Section 1 The Resurrection of Jesus, See. 36–43; N.B. Google book and HathiTrust]

Robinson, John A. T. *Can We Trust the New Testament?* Grand Rapids: Eerdmans, 1977. [The Resurrection, See. 120–29]

Rogers, Clement F. *The Case for Christianity: An Outline of Popular Apologetics.* New York: Harper & Brothers, 1928. [Chapter 3 The Trustworthiness of the Records (2) The Resurrection of Christ, See. 86–89]

———. *Non-Christian Theories of the Resurrection of Christ.* London: SPCK, 1937. [N.B. Little Books on Religion, No. 121; 32 pages]

Rolfe, Eugene. *The Intelligent Agnostic's Introduction to Christianity.* London: Skeffington, 1959. [The Road to Emmaus, See. 157–65]

Roop, Hervin Ulysses. *The Fundamentals of Christianity.* Wheaton: Wheaton College, 1926. [Lesson 18 The Crowning Miracle: The Resurrection of Jesus, See. 236–44]

Row, C. A. *Christian Evidences Viewed in Relation to Modern Thought.* 2nd ed. Frederic Norgate, 1879. [Lecture 7 The Theory of Visions Considered and Refuted, See. 358–400; Supplement 1. See. 400–10; Supplement 2. Dr. Carpenter's Objections to the Evidence of the Christian Miracles Considered, See. 410–27; N.B. Google book and HathiTrust]

———. *A Manual of Christian Evidences.* 11th ed. New York: T. Whittaker, 1901. [Chapter 10 The Resurrection of Jesus Christ: An Objective Fact, See. 171–87; N.B. Archive.org and Google book]

———. *Reasons for Believing in Christianity Addressed to Busy People.* New York: Thomas Whittaker, 1881. [Chapter 13 The Testimony which they Give to the Chief Facts of Christianity, and Especially to the Resurrection of Jesus Christ, See. 108–16; Chapter 14 The Theories Propounded by Unbelievers as the Alternative to the Resurrection of Jesus Christ . . . See. 117–36; Chapter 15 The Theory that Jesus Christ Did Not Actually Die, See. 137–40; N.B. Google book and HathiTrust]

———. *The Supernatural in the New Testament: Possible, Credible and Historical: or, An Examination of the Validity of Some Recent Objections Against Christianity as a Divine Revelation.* London: Frederic Norgate, 1875. [Chapter 19 The Evidence Furnished by the Epistles to the Facts of Our Lord's Life, and to the Truth of the Resurrection, See. 423–46; Chapter 20 The Resurrection of Jesus Christ: An Historical Fact, See. 447–72; N.B. Google book. This is a classic work.]

Rowe, Samuel. *An Epitome of Paley's Evidences of Christianity.* 2nd ed. London: Baldwin & Cradock, 1828. [Chapter 8, See. 126–27; N.B. Archive.org]

Russell, Jeffrey Burton. *Exposing Myths about Christianity: A Guide to Answering 145 Viral Lies and Legends.* Downers Grove, IL: InterVarsity, 2012. [Myth 124. The Resurrection of Jesus has been Disproved, See. 307–9; Myth 125; The Resurrection of Jesus was a "Resurrection Experience" Rather than a Physical Resurrection, See. 309–10]

Sagebeer, Joseph Evans. *The Bible in Court: The Method of Legal Inquiry Applied to the Study of the Scriptures.* Philadelphia: J. B. Lippincott, 1900. [See. 108, 130–32, 142–43; N.B. Archive.org]

Category III—Apologetics and Anti-Apologetics

Salmon, Edgar Frank. *Why I Believe*. Philadelphia: H. M. Jacobs, 1942. [Chapter 4 The Resurrection of Christ, See. 39–50]

Sanders, Phil. *Evangelism Handbook of New Testament Christianity*. Edmond, OK: In Search of the Lord's Way, 2009. [Chapter 3 Christian Evidences. See. Some Positive Evidence of the Resurrection, See. 36–39]

Sandison, Geo H. *Difficult Bible Questions Answered: Scriptural Knowledge for the Layman*. New York: World Syndicate, 1916. [See. #237, 239, 243, 244]

Satta, Ronald F. *True and Reasonable: In Defense of the Christian Faith*. Eugene, OR: Wipf & Stock, 2009. [See. 68–70]

Saunders, Daniel J. *Reason to Revelation*. New York: Herder, 1949. [Resurrection, See. 202–20]

Sayers, Dorothy L. *Letters to a Diminished Church: Passionate Arguments for the Relevance of Christian Doctrine*. Nashville: Nelson, 2004. [The Triumph of Easter, See. 117–24]

Scepticism Credulity: Socinianism Irreconciliable with Reason and the Simplicity of the Gospel. Birmingham: Printed and Sold by W. Suffield, 1814. [See. 98, 109, 132, 141, 151; N.B. Google book]

Schanz, Paul. *A Christian Apology God and Revelation*. Vol. 2: *God and Revelation*. 5th ed. Translated by Michael F. Glancey and Victor J. Schobel. New York: Frederick Pustet, 1891. [Chapter 16 The Life of Jesus, See. 501–16; N.B. Archive.org and Google book]

Scheffczk, Leo. *On Being Christian: The Hans King Debate*. Translated by Peadar Mac Seumais. Dublin: Four Courts, 1982. [Chapter 6 The Emptied Cross and the Resurrection, See. 66–70]

Schermerham, Martin Kellogg. *Renascent Christianity: A Forecast of the Twentieth Century in the Light of Higher Criticism of the Bible, Study of Comparative Religion and of the Universal Prayer for Religious Unity*. New York: G. P. Putnam, 1898. [Chapter 37 The Resurrected Jesus, See. 56–57; also Rose From The Dead And Ascended To Heaven, See. 71; The Corporeal Resurrection and Ascension, See. 192–93; N.B. Archive.org, Google book, and HathiTrust. Title page reads "By a Clergyman."]

Schmidt, Austin G. *Guidance*. Chicago: Loyola University Press, 1958. [Chapter 5 The Death and Resurrection of Christ, See. 178–80]

Schultz, Emil. *Impartial Investigation into the Reasonableness of the Doctrines of Christianity*. Philadelphia: Lutheran Publication Society, 1892. [See. 166–67, 172, 178; N.B. Google book]

Schultz, Hermann, and Alfred Bull Nichols. *Outlines of Christian Apologetics: For Use in Lectures*. 2nd ed. New York: Macmillan, 1905. [Christianity the Perfect Revelation, See. 279–81; N.B. Google book]

Scott, Ernest Findlay. *The Apologetic of the New Testament*. London: Williams & Norgate, 1907. [Resurrection Christ, See. 42, 47, 115, 129; N.B. Archive.org and Google book]

Scott, Kevin F. *Hazard of Faith*. London: Mowbray, 1987. [Chapter 5 Is Jesus Risen from the Dead?, See. 62–75]

Scott, Martin J. *The Credentials of Christianity*. New York: P.J. Kenedy, 1920. [Chapter 6 The Resurrection, See. 105–31; N.B. Archive.org and HathiTrust]

Scott, Robert. *Questions Muslims Ask: What Christians Actually Do (and don't) Believe*. Downers Grove, IL: InterVarsity, 2011. [Chapter 3 What Sort of God Can Be Murdered?, See. 51–67]

Scott, Thomas (1747–1821). *The Restoration of Israel by E Joseph Crooll and An Answer by Thomas Scott*. London: B. R. Goakman, 1814. [See. 11, 43, 84, 125–26, 134, 139, 140–41, 172, 306, 308; N.B. Archive.org]

Seaver, Richard W. *To Christ Through Criticism*. Edinburgh: T&T Clark, 1906. [Lecture 6 The Resurrection Fact, See. 119–36; Chapter 7 The Resurrection Form, 137–56; N.B. Google book]

Seber, G. A. F. *Can We Believe It? Evidence for Christianity*. Eugene, OR: Resource Publications, 2016. [He Had an Extraordinary Death and Resurrection, See. 201–18]

Selecman, Charles C. *Christ or Chaos*. Nashville: Cokesbury, 1923. [Chapter 5 The Resurrection—Did Jesus Rise from the Dead?, See. 75–88]

Sewall, Frank. *Reason in Belief or Faith for an Age of Science: An Examination into the Rational and Philosophic Content of the Christian Faith*. London: Elliot Stock, 1906. [See. 6, 22, 112, 113, 125; N.B. Google book and HathiTrust]

Sexton, George. *Biblical Difficulties Dispelled: Being an Answer to Queries Respecting So-Called Discrepancies in Scripture; Misunderstood and Misinterpreted Texts*. Toronto: William Briggs, 1885. [Question 11 The Three Days and Three Nights that the Body of Jesus was in the Grave, See. 17–18; Number of Women Who Visited the Tomb on the Occasion of the Resurrection of the Lord, See. 18–19]

Shannon, Foster H. *God Is Light: A Case for Christianity Today*. Campbell, CA: Green Leaf, 1981. [Chapter 7 The Resurrection of Jesus Christ, See. 76–86]

Sheehan, Michael. *Apologetics and Catholic Doctrine*. Edited by Peter M. Joseph. 6th ed. London: Saint Austin Press, 2001. [Second Proof: The Resurrection of Jesus Christ Proves that He was God, See. 110–19; 406–14. The Resurrection and Ascension: Completion of the Redemption. Christ's Risen Body and the Import of the Resurrection. Sunday, the New Sabbath. Pentecost; N.B. This text is worth examining.]

Shelly, Rubel. *Prepare to Answer: A Defense of the Christian Faith*. Grand Rapids: Baker, 1991. [Chapter 10 I Confess—He's the One! See. The Bodily Resurrection, See. 201–7]

Sheppard, John. *The Divine Origin of Christianity, Deduced from some of Those Evidences Which are Not Founded on the Authenticity of Scripture*. Vol. 2. London: Whittaker, Treacher & Arnot, 1829. [Chapter 9 On Some Parts of the Proof for Christ's Resurrection, See. 1–74; N.B. Google book]

Shields, Charles Woodward. *The Scientific Evidences of Revealed Religion: The Bishop Paddock Lectures*. New York: Scribner's Sons, 1900. [See. 204, 221, 222; N.B. Google book]

Shorrosh, Anis A. *Islam Revealed: A Christian Arab's View of Islam*. Nashville: Nelson, 2003. [Chapter 4 The Crucifixion: Fact or Fiction?, See. 107–37]

Short, Frank B. *Christianity is it True? Foundations and Facts Simply Stated*. London: Hodder & Stoughton, 1917. [Chapter 7 Miracles, See. 136–43]

Sieker, Adolphus Theodore. *555 Difficult Bible Questions Answered: A Book of Reference for All Denominations*. New York: Christian Herald Bible House, 1914. [#237–244; N.B Archive.org and Google book]

Simpson, John. *Internal and Presumptive Evidences of Christianity: Considered Separately and as Uniting to Form One Argument*. Bath, England: Printed by R. Cruttwell, 1801. [Resurrection of Jesus from the Dead, See. 558–89; N.B. Google book]

Siniscalchi, Glenn B. *Retrieving Apologetics*. Eugene, OR: Pickwick, 2016. [Chapter 9 Resurrecting Jesus and Critical Historiography, See. 149–68; Chapter 10 Assessing the Evidence for Jesus' Resurrection, See. 169–94]

Sinkinson, Chris. *Christian Confidence: An Introduction to Defending the Faith*. Downers Grove: IVP, 2012. [Dead man walking, See. 189–93]

Sire, James W. *Apologetics Beyond Reason: Why Seeing Really is Believing*. Downers Grove, IL: InterVarsity, 2014. [Resurrection of Jesus, See. 110, 116, 127, 130, 133, 135–36, 139]

———. *Why Should Anyone Believe Anything at All?* Downers Grove, IL: InterVarsity, 1994. [Part 2 Why Should Anyone Believe Christianity?, Chapter 11 The Resurrection of Jesus, See. 150–64]

Sleigh, W. W. *The Christians Defensive Dictionary: Being an Alphabetical Refutation of the General Objections to the Bible*. Philadelphia: Edward C. Biddle, 1837. [Resurrection, See. 333–36; Resurrection of Christ, See. 338–42; N.B. Google book]

Smith, George Williamson. *A Short Apology for Being a Christian in the XXth Century*. New York: Longmans, 1916. [Chapter 16 The Resurrection, See. 104–14; N.B. HathiTrust]

Smith, Graeme. *Was the Tomb Empty? A Lawyer Weighs the Evidence for the Resurrection*. Oxford, UK: Monarch, 2014. [224 pages]

Smith, Samuel. *The Credibility of the Christian Religion: or, Thoughts on Modern Rationalism*. London: Hodder & Stoughton, 1872. [Part 2 Rationalism and Miracles. Chapter 2 The Chief Miracle of All—The Resurrection of Christ—The Foundation of Christianity, See. 82–95; N.B. Google book]

Smith, Samuel Stanhope. *Lectures on the Evidences of the Christian Religion: Delivered to the Senior Class, on Sundays, in the Afternoon, in the College of New Jersey*. Philadelphia: Hopkins & Earle, 1809. [Lecture 4 The Credibility of the Witnesses of the Miracles and Resurrection of Christ, See. 50–62; N.B. Google book and HathiTrust]

Smith, Wilbur M. *The Supernaturalness of Christ, Can We Still Believe in It?* Boston: W. A. Wilde, 1940. [Chapter 6 The Historical Reality of Christ's Resurrection, See. 189–228]

———. *Therefore, Stand: A Plea for a Vigorous Apologetic in the Present Crisis of Evangelical Christianity*. Boston: W. A. Wilde, 1959. [Chapter 8 The Resurrection of Christ from the Dead: The Apologetic for An Age Demanding Historical Certitude, See. 359–437]

Smyth, William. *Evidences of Christianity*. 2nd ed. London: William Pickering, 1848. [See. 108, 125–33, 149–50, 275, 287–89; N.B. Google book]

Snow, Eric V. *A Zeal for God Not According to Knowledge: A Refutation of Judaism's Arguments against Christianity*. 2nd ed. New York: iUniverse, 2005. [The Problems of the Empty Tomb and the Resurrection, See. 187–206]

Sproul, R. C., and Abdul Saleeb. *The Dark Side of Islam*. Wheaton, IL: Crossway, 2003. [Chapter 6 Islam and Christianity on the Death of Jesus, See. 65–71]

Sproul, R. C., et al. *Classical Apologetics: A Rational Defense of the Christian Faith and a Critique of Presuppositional Apologetics*. Grand Rapids: Zondervan, 1984. [Resurrection, See. 20, 193, 283, 307]

Stackhouse, John G. *Can God Be Trusted?: Faith and the Challenge of Evil*. Downers Grove, IL: InterVarsity, 1998. [Chapter 6 The Fork in the Road, See. 88–153]

Steele, James. *A Manual of the Evidences of Christianity: Chiefly Intended for Young Persons*. Edinburgh: Johnstone & Hunter, 1860. [Miracles, See. 40–59; N.B. Google book]

———. *The Philosophy of the Evidences of Christianity*. Edinburgh: William Whyte, 1834. [Chapter 3 The Evidence Furnished by Jesus Christ of his Messiahship, See. 30–76; Chapter 4 Media through which Evidence Furnished by Jesus Christ of his Messiahship, and the Collateral Evidences of Christianity, have been Transmitted to Use, See. 77–127; N.B. Google book]

Sterrett, James Macbride. *The Freedom of Authority Essays in Apologetics*. New York: MacMillan, 1905. [Chapter 3 Abbe Loisy, See. 111–12; N.B. Archive.org and Google book]

Stewart, Alexander. *Handbook of Christian Evidences*. New York: Anson D. F. Randolph, 1895. [Chapter 6 The Resurrection of Christ, See. 66–74; N.B. Google book]

Stillingfleet, Edward. *Origines Sacræ: or A Rational Account of the Grounds of Natural and Revealed Religion*. Vol. 1. Oxford: At the Clarendon Press, 1797. [See. 161, 271–73, 295, 326, 329–30, 340–41, 366; N.B. Archive.org, Google book, and HathiTrust]

Stone, David Reuben. *The Loftus Delusion: Why Atheism Fails and Messianic Israelism Prevails*. Lulu, 2010. [Resurrection. See. 148]

Storrs, Richard S. *The Divine Origin of Christianity Indicated by Its Historical Effects*. New York: A.D.F. Randolph, 1884. [Notes to Lecture 10 Appendix 19 The Resurrection, See. 636; N.B. Archive.org and Google book]

Story, Dan. *The Christian Combat Manual: Helps for Defending Your Faith*. Chattanooga, TN: AMG, 2007. [Chapter 24 Resurrection: Fraud, Fantasy, or Fact, See. 198–213]

———. *Defending Your Faith: Reliable Answers for a New Generation of Seekers and Skeptics*. Grand Rapids: Kregel, 2004. [Chapter 7 Is the Resurrection a Fraud, Fantasy, or Facts?, See. 87–98]

Sweis, Khaldoun A., and Chad V. Meister, eds. *Christian Apologetics: An Anthology of Primary Sources*. Grand Rapids: Zondervan, 2012. [Part 7 The Resurrection of Jesus. See. 335–77. This text contains excerpts: Thomas Aquinas, The Resurrection of Jesus, See. 335–38; John Warwick Montgomery, A Judicial Defense of Jesus' Resurrection, See. 339–53; Gary R. Habermas, Experiences of the Risen Jesus, See. 354–61; and William Lane Craig, The Bodily Resurrection of Jesus, See. 362–76]

Sykes, Arthur Ashley. *An Essay Upon the Truth of the Christian Religion: Wherein Its Real Foundation Upon the Old Testament Is Shown. Occasioned by the Discourse of the Grounds and Reasons of the Christian Religion*. London: Printed for James & John Knapton, 1725. [Chapter 9 On the Resurrection of Jesus, See. 146–58; N.B. Google book and HathiTrust]

Tabor, Britton H. *Skepticism Assailed*. New York: S. S. Wood, 1895. [Chapter 6 It Is Evidentially Clear that the "Resurrection," The Greatest of Alleged Miracles, Is A Sacred Reality, See. 241–66; N.B. Google book]

Taggart, Samuel. *A View of the Evidence of Christianity, and of the Inspiration of the Scripture of the Old and New Testaments, Collected Principally from the Scripture Themselves. In Nine Discourses*. Greenfield: Printed by John Denio, 1811. [Discourse 4 Particular Evidences of the Divine Authority and Inspiration of the New Testament, See. 126–76; N.B. Google book and HathiTrust]

Tasker, John Greenwood. *Spiritual Religion: A Study of the Relation of Facts to Faith*. London: Charles H. Kelly, 1901. [See. 114–22; N.B. Google book]

Taylor, David Bruce. *Elements of Christian Belief*. London: Constable, 1967. [Chapter 4 The Resurrection, See. 132–70]

Taylor, H. B. *A Comprehensive View of the Evidences of Divine Revelation: To which is Annexed, Some of the Results of Paganism and Christianity*. Philadelphia: Wm. S. Young, 1848. [See. 24–26, 36–39, 46–47; N.B. Google book]

Taylor, James E. *Introducing Apologetics: Cultivating Christian Commitment*. Grand Rapids: Baker Academic, 2006. [Chapter 15 He Is Risen Indeed! The Resurrection of Jesus, See. 199–211]

Category III—Apologetics and Anti-Apologetics

Terry, Milton Spencer. *The New Apologetic: Five Lectures on True and False Methods of Meeting Modern Philosophical and Critical Attacks Upon the Christian Religion.* New York: Eaton & Mains, 1897. [See. 18, 186, 188, 189, 195; N.B. Google book]

Tertullian. *Apology. De Spectaculis.* Translated by T. R. Glover. Cambridge, MA: Harvard University Press, 1927. [30.6; See. 299. N.B. Archive.org. This work discusses "The Lettuce Theory."]

Thayer, Thomas B. *Christianity Against Infidelity; or, the Truth of the Gospel History.* 2nd ed. Cincinnati: John A. Gurley, 1849. [See. 110, 214, 230–31, 236–40, 246–47, 272, 274, 277, 333, 336, 353, 355, 384, 385; N.B. Google book]

Thielicke, Helmut. *The Evangelical Faith: Volume Two: The Doctrine of God and of Christ.* Edited by G. W. Bromiley. Grand Rapids: Eerdmans, 1977. [The Resurrection of Christ, See. 423–52]

———. *The Faith Letters.* Translated by Douglas Crow. Waco, TX: Word, 1978. [Letter 9 Resurrection—The Meaning of Easter and the New Life, See. 87–96]

Thompson, Edward. *Evidences of Revealed Religion.* Cincinnati: Hitchcock & Walden, 1872. [Lecture 13 Miracles, See. 295; N.B. Google book]

———. *Prophecy, Types, and Miracles, the Great Bulwarks of Christianity: or, A Critical Examination and Demonstration of Some of the Evidence, by Which the Christian Faith Is Supported.* London: Hatchard, 1838. [Miracles. See. The Resurrection of Christ, See. 364–70; N.B. Archive.org and Google book]

Thornton, Norman. *Searching for Christianity.* Arena, 2011. [Chapter 26 The Resurrection and Ascension, See. 191–97; N.B. Superficial chapter]

Tobey, Alvan. *Christianity From God.* Boston: American Tract Society, 1868. [Chapter 10 The Resurrection of Christ, See. 176–93; N.B. Google book]

Torrey, R. A. *Difficulties and Alleged Errors and Contradictions in the Bible.* New York: Revell, 1907. Chapter 17 Jonah and "The Whale." See. 74–77; Chapter 18 Some Important "Contradictions" in the Bible, See. The Resurrection of Jesus, See. 83–85; [Chapter 21 Was Jesus Really Three Days and Three Nights in the Heart of the Earth?, See. 101–6]

———. *Is the Bible the Inerrant Word of God, and Was the Body of Jesus Raised from the Dead.* New York: George H. Doran, 1922. [Chapter 7 Is It Absolutely Certain That The Body of Jesus that was Nailed to the Cross, That Really Died, and That was Laid in Joseph's Tomb, Was Raised from the Dead?, See. 121–66; N.B. Google book and HathiTrust]

Touche, Everard Digges la. *Christian Certitude. Its Intellectual Basis.* London: James Clarke, 1910. [Chapter 5 Whom God Hath Raised Up, See. 167–206]

Treffry, Richard. *Lectures on the Evidences of Christianity.* London: J. Mason, 1839. [Lecture 6 The Evidence of Miracles to the Inspiration of Scripture. Especially examine that of the Resurrection of Jesus, See. 123–44; N.B. Google book]

Trice, Rico, and Barry Cooper. *Christianity Explored: Study Guide.* New Malden, Surrey: Good Book Company, 2003. [Jesus—His Resurrection, See. 62–75]

Tuck, Robert. *A Handbook of Biblical Difficulties: or, Reasonable Solutions of Perplexing Things in Sacred Scripture.* London: Elliot Stock, 1889. [Section 3 Difficulties Relating to the Miraculous, See. Open Graves at the Crucifixion, See. 530–31; Our Lord's Resurrection Body, See. 533–34; N.B. Archive.org and Google book]

Tullidge, Henry. *Triumphs of the Bible, with the Testimony of Science to its Truth*. New York: Scribner's Sons, 1863. [See. 237, 243, 245, 410, 412; N.B. Archive.org, Google book, and HathiTrust]

Turton, William Harry. *The Truth of Christianity: Being an Examination of the More Important Arguments For and Against Believing in That Religion*. 9th ed. London: Wells Gardner, Darton, 1919. [Chapter 17 That Therefore the Resurrection of Christ Is Probably True, See. 301–48; N.B. Archive.org, Google book, and HathiTrust]

Tymms, T. Vincent. *The Mystery of God: A Consideration of Some Intellectual Hindrances to Faith*. 2nd ed. New York: Anson D.F. Randolph, 1887. [Chapter 9 The Resurrection of Christ, See. 292–326; N.B. Google book and HathiTrust]

Uhlhorn, Gerhard. *The Modern Representations of the Life of Jesus*. Translated by Charles E. Grinnell. Boston: Little, Brown, 1868. [Fourth Discourse: Miracles, See. 126–36; N.B. Archive.org and Google book]

Vanderlaan, Eldred Cornelius, ed. *Fundamentalism versus Modernism*. New York: H. W. Wilson, 1925. [The Bodily Resurrection, See. 333–50; N.B. This work has five contributors.]

Van Kempen, Case. *Hard Questions People Ask About the Christian Faith*. Grand Rapids: Faith Alive Christian Resources, 2002. [Chapter 4 "Is there more to Easter than the Easter Bunny?" Who Is Jesus Christ, and Did He Really Rise from the Dead?, See. 35–42]

Van Til, Cornelius. *Christian Apologetics*. Phillipsburg, NJ: P&R, 2003. [Jesus Christ, resurrection of, See. 149]

Vaughan, David James. *Christian Evidences and the Bible: Being Sermons*. London: Macmillan, 1865. [Sermon 3 External Evidence of Christianity. Acts 1.3, See. 44–47]

Vaughan, Edward T. *Some Reasons of Our Christian Hope*. London: Macmillan, 1876. [See. vii, 50–52, 92–95, 97, 110, 115, 122, 128, 135–36; N.B. Google book]

Vining, Teresa. *Making Your Faith Your Own: A Guidebook for Believers with Questions*. Downers Grove, IL: InterVarsity, 2001. [Grave Issues: Did Jesus Really Rise from the Dead?, See. 75–86]

Waldie, Lance. *A Christian Apologetic For Christian Apologists*. Lulu, 2013. [Chapter 13 The Resurrection of Jesus from the Dead, See. 225–37]

Wallace, J. Warner. *Cold-Case Christianity: A Homicide Detective Investigates the Claims of the Gospels*. Colorado Springs, CO: David C. Cook, 2013. [This text discusses numerous tactics often employed by apologists in support of Jesus's resurrection without specifically analyzing that subject.]

Walsh, Chad. *Stop Looking and Listen: An Invitation to the Christian Life*. New York: Harper & Brothers, 1948. [See. 48, 53–56]

Walshe, Thomas Joseph. *The Principles of Christian Apologetics: An Exposition of the Intellectual Basis of the Christian Religion, Specially Written for Senior Students*. London: Longmans, Green, 1919. [Chapter 15 The Divinity of the Christian Faith. See. 3 Attestation of the Resurrection of Christ—Christ predicted His Resurrection in Confirmation of His Mission—Witnesses to His Resurrection, See. 200–203]

Walton, Alfred Grant. *This I Can Believe: An Outline of Essentials of the Christian Faith*. New York: Harper & Brothers, 1935. [Chapter 6 Did Jesus Rise From The Dead, See. 112–29]

Warburton, William. *The Divine Legation of Moses Demonstrated*. Vol. 2. London: R. Griffin, 1837. [See. 481, 499, 673–75; N.B. Archive.org, Google book, and HathiTrust]

Ward, Keith. *God, Faith and the New Millennium: Christian Belief in an Age of Science.* Oxford: OneWorld, 1999. [Chapter 14 The Life of Jesus, See. 182–84]

Ward, William Hayes. *What I Believe and Why.* New York: Scribner's Sons, 1915. [Chapter 21 Jesus the Christ, See. 272–79; N.B. Google book. Not useful.]

Ware, Augustus William, and Julius Ware. *Letters to the Editor of The New Trial of the Witnesses.* London: Richard Taylor, 1824. [N.B. Google book. The anonymous author is identified as by "An Oxford Layman"; however the two authors are identified in WorldCat and elsewhere.]

Warschauer, J. *The New Evangel: Studies in the 'New Theology.'* London: J. Clarke, 1907. [Chapter 10 the Resurrection, See. 165–91; N.B. Archive.org and Google book]

Watson, David C. K. *My God Is Real.* New York: Seabury, 1970. [Chapter 5 The Resurrection: Christ Our Contemporary, See. 55–67]

Watson, Richard, bishop. *An Apology for the Bible, In a Series of Letters, Addressed to Thomas Paine.* New York: John Bull, 1796. [Letter 8 "The Tale of the Resurrection," See. 162–89; N.B. Google book]

Watson, Richard, bishop, and William H. Ellison. *Evidences of the Authenticity of the Holy Scriptures*, Abridged from R. Watson. Philadelphia: Sorin & Ball, 1848. [Chapter 14 The Resurrection of our Lord, See. 69–76]

Watson, Richard, bishop, and Charles Leslie. *An Apology for the Bible: In a Series of Letters Addressed to Thomas Paine, Author of the Age of Reason.* New York: Published by J. Emory & B. Waugh, for the Methodist Episcopal Church, at the Conference Office, 1832. [Letter 8, See. 121–41; N.B. Archive.org and Google book]

Watson, Thomas. *Popular Evidences of Natural Religion and Christianity.* London: Printed for Longman, Hurst, Rees, & Orme, 1805. [Part 2. Chapter 1 Reflections on the Evidences of Christianity, 254–73; Chapter 10 Evidence from Prophecy, See. 388–90; N.B. Google book]

Watt, William Montgomery. *A Christian Faith for Today.* London: Routledge, 2002. [The Resurrection, See. 81–83]

Webster, Douglas D. *Second Thoughts for Skeptics.* Vancouver, BC: Regent College Publishing, 2010. [Chapter 7 The Empty Tomb and the New Biology, See. 125–45]

Weghe, Rob Van de. *Prepared to Answer: A Step-by-Step Guide to Bring the Power of Christian Evidences to Your Life.* Port Hadlock, WA: Windmill Ministries, 2007. [Chapter 21 Did the Resurrection Really Happen?, See. 233–60]

Weir, John Ferguson. *The Way. The Nature and Means of Revelation.* London: A. P. Watt, 1889. [Chapter 5 The Risen Christ, See. 265–310; N.B. Google book]

Weir, Wilbert Walter. *How Real Is Religion.* New York: Vantage, 1956. [Resurrection, See. 36, 236, 237]

Wellman, Jack. *Blind Chance or Intelligent Design Empirical Methodologies and the Bible.* Belle Plain, KS, 2009. [Chapter 3 Evidence of the Resurrection, 32–36; N.B. Available online]

Wells, James. *Christ in the Present Age.* New York: American Tract Society, 1903. [Chapter 5 The Risen Christ, See. 77–93; N.B. Google book]

Welsh, Robert Ethol. *In Relief of Doubt.* Cincinnati: Jennings & Graham, 1907. [See. 101, 102, 103, 129, 176; N.B. Archive.org and HathiTrust]

West, Steven D. *Philosophical Dialogues on the Christian Faith: Discussions on the Arguments, Evidence, and Truth of Christianity.* Eugene, OR: Wipf & Stock, 2007. [Chapter 6 Truth and the Resurrection, See. 71–83]

———. *Resurrection, Scripture, and Reformed Apologetics: A Test for Consistency in Theology and Apologetic Method*. Eugene, OR: Pickwick, 2012. [227 pages]

Whately, Richard. *Introductory Lessons on Morals, and Christian Evidences*. Cambridge. John Bartlett, 1857. [See. 188, 228, 326; N.B. Archive.org, Google book, and HathiTrust]

Whatmore, George Bernard. *A Scientist Looks at Religion: Based on Evidence Plus Logic*. 3rd ed. Haverford, PA: Infinity, 2002. [Chapter 12 Determining the Probably Truth or Falsity of the One Most Basic Belief Upon Which All of Christianity Stands or Falls: The Belief in the Resurrection of Jesus Christ, Examine Chapter 12.1–18; Chapter 23:6–7; and Chapter 24:2–3; no pagination]

Whiston, William. *A Defence of Natural and Revealed Religion: Being a Collection of the Sermons Preached at the Lecture Founded by the Honourable Robert Boyle, Esq. (From the Year 1691 to the Year 1732)*. Vol. 2. London: Printed for D. Midwinter, 1739. Print. [The Accomplishment of Scripture Prophecies in Eight Sermons, See. 343–48; N.B. Google book]

Whitbie, Daniel. *Logos tēs pisteōs, or, An Endeavour to Evince the Certainty of Christian Faith in Generall: and of the Resurrection of Christ in Particular*. Oxford: Printed at the Theater in Oxford, 1671. [Chapter 11 Of the Resurrection of our Saviour Christ, See. 388–400; N.B. First three words of title transliterated from the Greek. Google book]

White, James Emery. *A Search for the Spiritual: Exploring Real Christianity*. Grand Rapids: Baker, 1998. [Why The Resurrection of Jesus Matters, See. 56–63]

White, James R. *What Every Christian Needs to Know About the Qur'an*. Minneapolis: Bethany House, 2013. [Chapter 6 The Qur'an and the Cross, See. 129–43]

Willett, Herbert Lockwood. *Basic Truths of the Christian Faith*. Chicago: Christian Century, 1903. [Chapter 7 The Resurrection, See. 71–77; N.B. Google book]

Williams, A. Lukyn. *Adversus Judaeos: A Bird's-Eye View of Christian Apologiae until the Renaissance*. Cambridge: At the University Press, 1935. [Resurrection of Christ, See. 88]

Williams, Rheinallt Nantlais. *Faith, Facts, History, Science, and How They Fit Together*. Wheaton, IL: Tyndale House, 1974. [The Message of the Resurrection, See. 87–91]

Williams, Roy. *God, Actually: Why God Probably Exists, Why Jesus was Probably Divine, and Why the "Rational" Objections to Religion are Unconvincing*. Oxford: Monarch, 2009. [Chapter 6 The Resurrection, See. 186–213]

Williams, Stephen Douglas. *The Bible in Court; or, Truth vs. Error; a Brief for the Plaintiff*. Dearborn, MI: Dearborn Book Concern, 1925. [Division 8 Proof of the Resurrection of Jesus, See. 212–35]

Williams, Stephen Joseph. *What Your Atheist Professor Doesn't Know (But Should)*. Amazon Digital Services LLC, 2013. [Chapter 7 The Argument from the Resurrection of Jesus Christ; N.B. Kindle edition]

Williamson, I. D. *An Argument for the Truth of Christianity: In a Series of Discourses*. New York: P. Price, 1836. [Discourse 10 Proofs of the Resurrection, See. 163–80; N.B. Archive.org and Google book]

Wilmers, W. *Handbook of the Christian Religion for the Use of Advanced Students and the Educated Laity*. 2nd ed. Edited by James Conway. New York: Benziger, 1902. [#23. The divine mission of Christ is proved in particular by His resurrection from the dead, See. 41–44; N.B. Archive.org and HathiTrust]

Category III—Apologetics and Anti-Apologetics

Wilson, Clifford A. *The Passover Plot Exposed: Wilson Challenges Schonfield.* San Diego, CA: Creation Life, 1977. [Chapter 10 Swoons, Hallucinations, and Reality, See. 170–87]

Wilson, Daniel. *The Evidences of Christianity Stated in a Popular and Practical Manner.* Vol. 1. Boston: Crocker & Brewster, 1830. [See. 13, 93, 98, 102, 106, 108, 109, 114, 118, 119, 131–34, 141, 181, 221, 231, 265; N.B. Google book]

———. *The Evidences of Christianity Stated in a Popular and Practical Manner.* Vol. 2. Boston: Crocker & Brewster, 1833. [See. 284, 351; N.B. Google book]

Winchester, Elhanan. *A Defence of Revelation in Ten Letters to Thomas Paine; being an answer to his first part of The Age of Reason.* London: T. Gillet, 1796. [100 pages; Letter 2, See. 14–19; Letter 3, See. 20–30; N.B. Early American imprints—no. 29909 Evans 2990]

Winnington-Ingram, A. F. *Popular Objections to Christianity.* London: SPCK, 1899. [Chapter 3 The Resurrection, See. 16–22]

Witcher, W. C. *Legal Proof: Being an Answer to Thomas H. Huxley and Other Sceptics Demands for Legal Proof of the Resurrection of Christ from the Dead, and Containing Pilate's Official Verification of the Same: Together with a Discussion of the Kingdom of Heaven: How We Know Our New Testament Contains the Words of Jesus: Chronology of the Apostolic Fathers and the Testimony of H. G. Wells.* Fort Worth, TX: Christian Forum, 1937. [123 pages]

Wrangham, Francis. *The Pleiad: A Series of Abridgements from Seven Distinguished Writers on the Evidences of Christianity.* Edinburgh: J. Hutchinson. Constable; London, Hurst, Chance, 1828. [See. 158–65; N.B. Archive.org and Google book]

Wright, Charles James. *Miracle in History and in Modern Thought; or, Miracle and Christian Apologetic.* New York: H. Holt, 1930. [Chapter 7 The Resurrection of Christ and Miracle, See. 344–65]

Wright, G. Frederick. *The Logic of Christian Evidence.* Andover: W. F. Draper, 1883. [Chapter 5 Were Jesus and His Immediate Disciples Either Imposters or Deluded Enthusiasts?, See. 252–85; See. 13 The Resurrection of Christ Is the Great Miracle, See. 263–64; N.B. Google book and HathiTrust]

———. *Scientific Aspects of Christian Evidences.* New York: D. Appleton, 1898. [Chapter 9 See. The Freedom of the Gospels from Comments by the Writers, See. 285–89; N.B. Archive.org and Google book]

Wright, N. T. *Simply Good News: Why the Gospel is News and What Makes it Good.* New York: HarperOne, 2015. [What the Resurrection Reveals, See. 46–52]

Young, John. *The Case Against Christ.* London: Hodder & Stoughton, 1986. [Chapter 16 Dead Men Don't Rise, See. 158–71]

Zacharias, Ravi K. *The End of Reason: A Response to the New Atheists.* Grand Rapids: Zondervan, 2008. [Jesus, resurrection of, See. 74–75]

Zaka, Anees and Diane Coleman. *The Truth about Islam: The Noble Qur'an's Teachings in Light of the Holy Bible.* Phillipsburg, NJ: P&R Publishing, 2004. [The Islamic View of Jesus Christ, See. 59–63]

Zukeran, Patrick. *Unless I See: Is There Enough Evidence to Believe?* Bloomington, IN: CrossBooks, 2011. [Chapter 8 See. The Risen Savior, 111–23]

Chapter 8

Agnostics, Atheists, Detractors, Humanists, Liberal Christians, Rationalists, and Skeptics: Con Resurrection

Allen, Ethan. *Reason, The Only Oracle of Man: or, A Compendious System of Natural Religion. To which is added, Critical Remarks on the Truth and Harmony of the Four Gospels with Observations on the Instructions Given By Jesus Christ, and the Doctrines of Christianity*. New York: G. W. & A. J. Matsell, 1836. [Chapter 6 Remarks on the Testimony Concerning Christ's Resurrection, His Appearance After It, and His Ascension, See. 57–66; N.B. Google book has a different pagination. This reading is anonymously penned By A Free Thinker, presumably Ethan Allen. This book is an important, dated work to examine.]

Amberley, John Russell, viscount. *An Analysis of Religious Belief*. New York: D. M. Bennett, 1877. [See. 269–77; N.B. Archive.org]

Andrews, Richard, and Paul Schellenberger. *The Tomb of God: The Body of Jesus and the Solution to a 2000-year-old Mystery*. Great Britain: Little, Brown, 1996. [N.B. This 500 plus page book asserts that Jesus was reburied in the 12th century in France!]

Annet, Peter. *Supernaturals Examined In Four Dissertations on Three Treatises*. London: Printed for F. Page, 1747. [Dissertation 1. On the Observations of History and Evidence of the Resurrection of Jesus Christ by Gilbert West, Esq. See. 1–29; N.B. Archive.org]

Asimov, Isaac. *Asimov's Guide to the Bible*. Vol. 2. New York: Random House, 1981. [See. 897–902; N.B. Archive.org. Not useful.]

Atrott, Hans. *Jesus' Bluff: "The Universal Scandal of the World."* Frederick, MD: American Star, 2009. [604 pages]

Avalos, Hector. *The End of Biblical Studies*. Amherst, NY: Prometheus, 2007. [Chapter 4 The Unhistorical Jesus, Resurrecting the Resurrection, See. 185–90; Marian Apparitions and the Resurrection, See. 191–94; N.B. This book is a must read. Avalos refutes Craig's usage of C. Behan McCullagh's best evidences (*Justifying Historical Descriptions*).]

Baigent, Michael. *The Jesus Papers: Exposing the Greatest Cover-up in History*. San Francisco: HarperSan Francisco, 2006. [Chapter 7 Surviving the Crucifixion, See. 115–32; Chapter 8 Jesus in Egypt, See. 133–58; N.B. Jesus survived his crucifixion and moved to Egypt along with his wife, Mary Magdalene! Later, they moved to France. Ridiculous!]

Category III—Apologetics and Anti-Apologetics

Balfour, Frederic H. *The Higher Agnosticism.* London: Greening, 1907. [See. 108; N.B. Google book. Balfour states that the resurrection and other events of Jesus's life are explained by the astronomical and solar myths which lie at the root of so many of the mystical religions.]

Ballou, Robert O. *The Other Jesus: A Narrative Based On Apocryphal Stories Not Included in the Bible.* New York: Doubleday, 1972. [Chapter 6 The Resurrection, See. 91–119; Chapter 7 The Later Appearances of Jesus, See. 121–36; N.B. The title tells it all.]

Barker, Dan. *Godless: How an Evangelical Preacher Became One of America's Leading Atheists.* Berkeley, CA: Ulysses Press, 2008. [Chapter 16 Did Jesus Really Rise From the Dead?, See. 277–304; N.B. Barker identifies numerous contradictions and discrepancies in the New Testament accounts of Jesus's resurrection.]

———. *Losing Faith In Faith: From Preacher To Atheist.* Madison, WI: FFFR, 2006. [Chapter 24 Leave No Stone Unturned: An Easter Challenge for Christians. [N.B. This interesting, thought provoking challenge first appeared in Freethought Today (March 1990) and it can be found online.]

Baring-Gould, S. *The Lost and Hostile Gospels: An Essay on the Toldedoth Jeschu, and the Petrine and Pauline Gospels of the First Three Centuries of Which Fragments Remain.* London: Williams & Norgate, 1874. [Rev. Baring-Gould was not an atheist or detractor. His work includes a translation of *Toledothe Jeschu* that challenges the gospel narratives; N.B. Google book]

Bell, William S. *A Handbook of Freethought: Containing in Condensed and Systematized Form a Vast Amount of Evidence Against the Superstitious Doctrines of Christianity, Selected from the Writings of the following Named Distinguished Writers and Others, Ingersoll.* San Francisco: W. S. Bell, 1890. [Jesus Christ. The Resurrection of Jesus, See. 91–118; N.B. Archive.org and Gutenberg.org. Similar to other detractors, Bell shows numerous contradictions and discrepancies in the New Testament accounts of Jesus's resurrection.]

Bennett, D. M. *The Gods and Religions of Ancient and Modern Times.* Vol. 1 New York: Liberal & Scientific Publishing House, 1881. [See. 600–601; N.B. Google book and HathiTrust]

———*The Gods and Religions of Ancient and Modern Times.* Vol. 2 New York: Liberal & Scientific Publishing House, 1881. [See. 720–21, 834–35; N.B. Google book and HathiTrust]

———. *An Open Letter to Jesus Christ.* New York: Truth Seeker, n.d. [See. 14–15; N.B. HathiTrust]

———. *The World's Sages, Thinkers and Reformers: Being Biographical Sketches of Leading Philosophers, Teachers, Skeptics, Innovators, Founders of New Schools of Thought, Eminent Scientists, etc.* 2nd ed. New York: Truth Seekers, 1876. [See. 236; N.B. Archive.org and Google book]

Bentham, Jeremy. *Not Paul, But Jesus.* London: John Hunt, 1823. [Chapter 1 Paul's Conversion, See. 1–20; Chapter 2 Paul Disbelieved, See. 89–90; Chapter 12 More Falsehoods—Resurrection, See. 277–81; Chapter 14 Acts . . . Time between Resurrection and Ascension, See. 339–46; N.B. Archive.org and Guternberg.org; Gamaliel Smith, Esq. is a fictitious name.]

Besant, Annie. *Esoteric Christianity; or, The Lesser Mysteries.* 2nd ed. London: Theosophical Publishing House, 1905. [Chapter 8 Resurrection and Ascension, See. 231–52; N.B. Archive.org, Google book, and Gutenberg.org]

———. *The Freethinker's Text-Book: Part 2. Christianity: Its Evidences. Its Origin. Its Morality. Its History*. London: R. Forder, 1893. [See. 220, 228, 295, 339; N.B. Archive.org and Google book]

———. *The Myth of the Resurrection*. London: Freethought, 1886. [Lecture 9; N.B. JSTOR archives]

Blackford, Russell, and Udo Schüklenk. *50 Great Myths About Atheism*. Malden, MA: Wiley Blackwell, 2013. [Myth 47 Atheists Can't Explain the Resurrection, See. 171–75]

Blatchford, Robert. *God and My Neighbour*. London: Clarion, 1903. [The Resurrection, See. 85–89; The Gospel Witnesses, See. 90–100; N.B. Archive.org and Gutenberg.org; N.B. This text shows contradictions, discrepancies, and omissions of details.]

Boynton, Richard W. *Beyond Mythology: A Challenge to Dogmatism in Religion*. Boston: Beacon, 1951. [Chapter 10 The Christian Mythology, See. 148–64; N.B. Boyton's chapter is logical.]

Bradlaugh, Charles. *Humanity's Gain From Unbelief: And Other Selections From The Works of Charles Bradlaugh*. London: Watts, 1929. [Who Was Jesus Christ and What Did He Teach?, See. 71–73; N.B. Archive.org and Google book]

Bradlaugh, Charles, and Robert Roberts. *Is the Bible Divine? A Six Nights' Discussion Between Mr. Charles Bradlaugh and Mr. Robert Roberts*. London: F. Pitman, 1876. [See. 25–26, 28, 35–47, 63, 72, 80, 82, 96–98, 135, 141–42; N.B. Archive.org, Google book, and HathiTrust]

Browne, Sylvia. *The Mystical Life of Jesus: An Uncommon Perspective on the Life of Christ*. New York: Dutton, 2006. [Chapter 7 The Resurrection—A Plan for Christ's Survival, See. 165–94; N.B. Useless.]

Burr, William Henry. *Revelations of Antichrist: Concerning Christ and Christianity*. Boston: D. M. Bennett (Truth Seeker), 1879. [Chapter 7 The Resurrection of Christ, See. 20–26; N.B. Archive.org, Google book, and HathiTrust. The author shows contradictions, discrepancies and inconsistencies in the resurrection narratives.]

———. *Self-Contradictions of the Bible*. NY: Prometheus, 1987. [Theological Doctrines #79–91, See. 62–67; First published 1860 by A. J. Davis, New York; N.B. Archive.org. N.B. The author lists numerous contradictions, discrepancies and inconsistencies in the resurrection narratives.]

Cadoux, Cecil John. *The Case for Evangelical Modernism: A Study of the Relation Between Christian Faith and Traditional Theology*. Chicago: Clark, 1939. [See. 154–59; N.B. The author acknowledges a number of beliefs about Jesus are historically untenable.]

Campbell, Douglas. *New Religious Thoughts*. 2nd ed. London: William & Norgate, 1865. [Chapter 19 The Resurrection, See. 109–20; N.B. Google book. Campbell, in almost a sarcastic manner points out numerous contradictions in the gospel narratives.]

Campbell, Steuart. *The Rise and Fall of Jesus: The Ultimate Explanation for the Origin of Christianity*. Edinburgh: Explicit, 1996. [Chapter 9 Aftermath, See. 154–73; N.B. This work should be read.]

Campbell, W. A. [William A.] *The Crucifixion and Resurrection of Jesus*. London: Pioneer Press, 1933. [The Resurrection 2, See. 63–99; N.B. Issued for the Secular Society Limited. Idem. Did the Jews Kill Jesus? And the Myth of the Resurrection with different pagination.]

———. *Did the Jews Kill Jesus? And the Myth of the Resurrection*. New York: Peter Eckler, 1927. [112 pages; N.B. Only pages 65–111 deal with the resurrection myth.]

Cannon, Delores. *Jesus and the Essenes*. Huntsville, AR: Ozark Mountain, 2000. [Chapter 25 The Crucifixion and Resurrection, See. 249–64; Chapter 26 The Purpose of the Crucifixion and Resurrection, See. 265–69; N.B. The text declares "Eyewitness accounts of the missing years of Jesus, the portions that have been removed from the Bible, and the community of the Essenes at Qumran. The information was gained through regressive hypnosis, conducted by Delores Cannon."]

Carotta, Francesco. *Jesus Was Caesar: On the Julian Origin of Christianity An Investigative Report*. Translated by Tommie Hendriks, Joseph Horvath, and Manfred Junghardt. The Netherlands: Aspekt, 2005. [Jesus' Entombment and Resurrection, See. 313–16; Appearances of the Resurrected One—Ascension, See. 317–23; N.B. The book's title says it all.]

Carrier, Richard. *Not The Impossible Faith: Why Christianity Didn't Need A Miracle To Succeed*. United States: Lulu, 2009. [Chapter 8 Who Would Want to be Persecuted?, See. 219–45; N.B. Carrier's book is a recommended read.]

———. *On the Historicity of Jesus: Why We Might Have Reason for Doubt*. Sheffield: Sheffield Phoenix, 2014. [Multiple entries; See What Happened to the Body?, See. 368–71; The Mysterious Vanishing Acts, See. 371–75; N.B. Carrier's book is a recommended read.]

———. *Sense and Goodness Without God: A Defense of Metaphysical Naturalism*. US: AuthorHouse, 2005. [Resurrection of Jesus, See. 224, 242–45; N.B. Carrier discusses categories of evidence.]

Cassels, Walter R. *Supernatural Religion: An Inquiry Into the Reality of Divine Revelations, Popular edition, carefully revised*. London: Watts, 1902. [Part 6 The Resurrection and Ascension, See. 801–901; N.B. Archive.org and Google book. This work is a classic, dated text often cited in the literature must be examined.]

Celsus [See. Origen].

Chubb, Thomas. *A Collection of Tracts on Various Subjects*. London: T. Cox, 1730. [See. 80, 133, 161, 186; N.B. Archive.org and Google book]

———. *Four Tracts*. London: T. Cox, 1732. [Tract 2 Some Short Remarks on Britannicus's Letters, See. 51–82; N.B. Google book]

Clarke, James Freeman. *Orthodoxy: Its Truth and Errors*. Boston: American Unitarian Association, 1890. [Chapter 4 Truths and Errors as Regards Miracles, §8 Miracle of the Resurrection. Sceptical Objections, See. 80–86; N.B. Google book]

Clarke, John. *A Critical Review of the Life Character, Miracles, and Resurrection of Jesus Christ in a Series of Letters to Dr. Adam Clarke*. London: J. Clarke, 1825. [Letter 15, See. 262–85; Letter 16, See. 286–315; N.B. Archive.org, Google book, and Gutenberg.org; N.B. This important critical and dated work is a must read.]

Columbine, William Brailsford. *Mr. Balfour's Apologetics Critically Examined*. Watts: London, 1902 [Jesus, resurrection of, See. 134–37; N.B. Google book and HathiTrust]

Conner, Robert P. *Jesus The Sorcerer Exorcist & Prophet of the Apocalypse*. Oxford: Mandrake of Oxford, 2006. [Chapter 4 The Resurrection as Ghost Story, See. 63–72]

Cooper, Robert. *Classified Biblical Extracts, or The Holy Scriptures Analyzed; Showing Its Contradictions, Absurdities And Immoralities*. Cincinnati: J. Cooper, 1860. [#254–257, See. 57–58; #431–438, See. 80–81; N.B. Archive.org and HathiTrust]

Coyne, Jerry A. *Faith Versus Fact: Why Science and Religion Are Incompatible*. New York: Penguin, 2015. [Falsifiability, See. 44–45, 72–74, 76]

Craig, William Lane, and Walter Sinnott-Armstrong. *God? A Debate Between a Christian and an Atheist.* New York: Oxford University Press, 2004. [Chapter 2 There Is No Good Reason to Believe in God (Walter Sinnott-Armstrong), See. 31–52; N.B. Refuted in Chapter 3 Reason Enough by William Lane Craig, See. 53–78]

Cresswell, Peter. *Censored Messiah: The Truth about Jesus Christ.* Winchester, UK: O Books, 2005. [248 pages; especially 150-63; N.B. Cresswell postulates that Jesus had an audacious plan to survive his execution.]

Crooker, Joseph Henry. *Different New Testament Views of Jesus.* Boston: American Unitarian Association, 1891. [See. 42-43; N.B. Archive.org, Google book, and HathiTrust]

Crossan, John Dominic. *The Birth of Christianity.* New York: HarperSanFrancisco, 1998. [Chapter 25 The Other Passion-Resurrection Story, See. 481–525; N.B. This work is a must read.]

———. *The Historical Jesus the Life of a Mediterranean Jewish* Peasant. San Francisco: HarperSanFrancisco, 1991. [Chapter 14 Death and Burial, See. 391–94; Chapter 15 Resurrection and Authority, See. 395–426; N.B. This work is a must read.]

Cutner, Herbert. *Jesus: God, Man Or Myth? An Examination of the* Evidence. New York: Truth Seeker, 1950. [Resurrection, See. 18, 21–24, 142, 218, 269]

Daleiden, Joseph L. *The Final Superstition: A Critical Evaluation of the Judeo-Christian Legacy.* Amherst: Prometheus, 1994. [The Resurrection, See. 118–24]

Daniels, Kenneth W. *Why I Believed: Reflections of a Former Missionary.* Duncanville, TX: Kenneth W. Daniels, 2009. [See. 62, Chapter 11 The Resurrection of Jesus, See. 225–36; N.B. This work is an interesting text to read.]

Dawes, Gregory W. *The Historical Jesus Quest: Landmarks In The Search for the Jesus of History.* Louisville: Westminster John Knox, 2000. [Chapter 2 History and Myth. David Friedrich Strauss (1808–74) From The Life of Jesus Critically Examined, See. 54–111; N.B. Contains extracts from *Fragments*.]

Delos, Andrew C. *Myths We Live By From the Life and Times of Jesus and Paul.* 2005. US: BookSurge, 2005. [He is Alive!, See. 56–69; His Ascension, See. 69–71]

Doane, T. W. *Bible Myths And Their Parallels In Other Religions Being a Comparison of the Old and New Testament Myths and Miracles with Those of Heathen Nations of Antiquity Considering Also Their Origin and Meaning.* 4th ed. New York: Truth Seeker, 1882. [Chapter 23 The Resurrection and Ascension of Christ Jesus, See. 215–32 N.B. Archive. org, Google book, and Gutenberg.org. Reprint. A classic, dated source.]

Docker, Ernest Brougham. *If Jesus Did Not Die on the Cross: A Study in Evidence.* London: Robert Scott Roxburghe House, 1920. [78 pages; N.B. Archive.org]

Doherty, Earl. *Challenging the Verdict: A Cross-Examination of Lee Strobel's "The Case for Christ."* Ottowa, Canada: Age of Reason, 2001. [Part 3: Did Jesus Rise from the Dead?; N.B. This part contains four chapters.]

———. *Jesus: Neither God Nor Man: The Case for a Mythical Jesus.* Ottawa: Age of Reason, 2009. [Resurrection of Jesus, See. 72, 75–77, 79, 81, 86, 134–37, 189, n.62; N.B. The author postulates that Jesus never existed. This work should be examined.]

———. *The Jesus Puzzle: Did Christianity Begin with a Mythical Christ? Challenging the Existence of an Historical Jesus.* Ottowa: Age of Reason, 2005. [390 pages; N.B. Doherty advocates the Christ Myth. This book should be explored.]

Drake, Durant. *Problems of Religion: An Introductory Survey.* Boston: Houghton Mifflin, 1916. [See. 72, 82 84, 287, 288, 291; N.B. Archive.org and Google book]

Drange, Theodore. *Nonbelief & Evil*. Amherst, NY: Prometheus, 1998. [The Resurrection, See. 356–58]

Draper, George Otis. *Searching For Truth*. New York: Peter Eckler, 1902. [Chapter 5 Was Christ Divine?, See. 126–27; N.B. Archive.org and Google book]

Drohan, Francis Burke. *Jesus Who? (The Greatest Mystery Never Told)*. New York: Philosophical Library, 1985. [Chapter 16 He Is Risen, See. 191–200]

Duke, Doyle E. *The Amazing Deception: A Critical Analysis of Christianity*. 2nd ed. US: Doyle E. Duke, 2009. [Chapter 6 The Verdict and the Resurrection, See. 87–97]

Dupuis, Charles. *The Origin of all Religious Worship*. New Orleans, 1872. [N.B. Google book. The author was one of the early advocates the Christ Myth. The text does not specifically discuss Jesus's resurrection.]

Ehrman, Bart D. *How Jesus Became God: The Exaltation of a Jewish Preacher From Galilee*. New York: HarperOne, 2014. [Chapter 4 The Jesus of Jesus: What We Cannot Know, See. 129–69; Chapter 5 The Resurrection of Jesus: What We Can Know, See. 171–210. N.B. This work should be read.]

———. *Jesus, Apocalyptic Prophet of the New Millennium*. Oxford: Oxford University Press, 1999. [Chapter 12 The Last Days of Jesus, See. 224–25]

———. *Jesus, Interrupted: Revealing the Hidden Contradictions in the Bible (And Why We Don't Know About Them)*. New York: HarperCollins, 2010. [Chapter 2 A World of Contradictions. The Resurrection Narratives, See. 47–49; also See. 173–78]

———. *The New Testament: A Historical Introduction to the Early Christian Writings*. 2nd ed. New York: Oxford University Press, 2000. [See. 72–74, 133, 135, 183–84, 188, 253–55, 270–72, 294–97, 324–31]

———. *Peter, Paul, and Mary Magdalene: The Followers of Jesus in History and Legend*. Oxford: Oxford University Press, 2006. [Peter and the Resurrection, See. 49–57; Paul and the Resurrection of Jesus, See. 111–13; The Women at the Tomb, See. 227–39; N.B. This work is an easy and interesting read.]

Ellegård, Alvar. *Jesus—One Hundred Years Before Christ: A Study in Creative Mythology*. Woodstock, NY: Overlook Press, 1999. [Paul's life and his revelations, See. 14–19; Resurrection, See. 76–78]

English, George Bethune. *The Grounds of Christianity Examined by Comparing the New Testament with the Old*. Printed for the Subscribers, 1839. [Chapter 16 Examination of the Evidence, External and Internal, in Favor of the Credibility of the Gospel History, See. 132–43; N.B. Archive.org, Google books, Gutenberg.org, and HathiTrust]

Evans, Elizabeth Edson Gibson. *The Christ Myth*. New York: Truth Seeker, 1900. [See. 69–74; N.B Archive.org, Google book and HathiTrust. Not useful.]

Feurerbach, Ludwig. *The Essence of Christianity*. 2nd ed. Translated by Marian Evans. New York: Calvin Blanchard, 1855. [Chapter 14 The Mystery of the Resurrection and of the Miraculous Conception, See. 182–86; N.B. Google book]

Fida, Ahtisham, Masto Oki, and Yoshiaki Soro. *Jesus Lived in Japan*. Srinagar, Kashmir, India: Dastgir Publications Trust, 1996. [134 pages. N.B. The authors postulate that Jesus survived the crucifixion.]

Fleming, Caleb. *True Deism the Basis of Christianity or Observations on Mr. Thomas Chubb's Posthumous-Works*. London: Printed for the author, 1749. [See. 85–88; N.B. Google book. Not useful.]

Fodor, James. *Unreasonable Faith: How William Lane Craig Overstates the Case for Christianity*. US: Hypatia Press, 2018. [Chapter 5 The Christological Arguments,

See. 231–334; N.B. This chapter presents a detailed rebuttal of William Lane Craig's historical argument for the resurrection of Jesus.]

Foote, G. W. *Bible Romance*. 4th ed. London: Pioneer Press, 1922. [The Resurrection, See. 205–24; N.B. Archive.org, Google book, Gutenberg.org, and HathiTrust]

———. *Flowers of Freethought*. London: R. Forder, 1893. [Did Jesus Ascend?, See. 134–37; The Rising Son, See. 137–40; N.B. Archive.org and Google book]

Frede, Victoria. *Doubt, Atheism, and the Nineteenth-Century Russian Intelligentsia*. Madison, WI: University of Wisconsin Press, 2011. [Resurrection of Christ at Easter, See. 130–31, 156, 160–61]

Freud, Sigmund. *The Standard Edition of the Complete Psychological Works of Sigmund Freud: Translated from the German. 23. 1937–1939. Moses and Monotheism. An Outline of Psycho-Analysis and Other Works*. London: Hogarth Press; Institute of Psychoanalysis, 1939. [Essay 3 Part 1 D. Application, See. 89–90; N.B. *The Origins of Religion*. Penguin, 1960. See. 334]

Funk, Robert and the Jesus Seminar. *The Acts of Jesus: The Search for the Authentic Deeds of Jesus*. San Francisco: HarperSanFrancisco, 1998. [Empty Tomb, Appearances & Ascension, See. 449–95; N.B. This important work should be examined.]

Gardner, James. *Jesus Who? Myth vs. Reality in the Search for the Historical Jesus*. Bangor, ME: Booklocker, 2006. [Was Jesus Resurrected?, See. 213–22; N.B. The author provides a good overview.]

Gardner, Laurence. *Bloodline of the Holy Grail: The Hidden Lineage of Jesus* Revealed. Shaftesbury: Element, 1997. [N.B. Gardner asserts that Jesus did not die on the cross and Mary Magdalene had his child!]

Gauvin, Marshall J. *Fundamentals of Freethought*. New York: Peter Eckler, 1923. [Did Jesus Christ Rise from the Dead?, See. 73–104; N.B. This chapter is a recommended read.]

Graham, Lloyd. *Deceptions and Myths of the* Bible. New York: Bell, 1979. [The Resurrection, See. 356–62; N.B. The author discusses several interesting ideas.]

Graves, Kersey. *The World's Sixteen Crucified Saviors, or Christianity before Christ: Containing New, Startling, and Extraordinary Revelations in Religious History, Which Disclose the Oriental Origin of All the Doctrines, Precepts, and Miracles of the Christian New Testament . . .* 2nd ed. New York: Freethought Press, 1875. [Chapter 19 Resurrection of the Saviors, See. 144–51; Chapter 20 Reappearance and Ascension of the Saviors, See. 152–55; N.B. Google book and Gutenberg.org. A classic, dated source.]

Graves, Robert, and Joshua Podro. *Jesus In Rome: A Historical* Conjecture. London, 1957. [Chapter 1 The Crucifixion and Resurrection, See. 1–15; Chapter 5 The Tomb of Jesus, See. 68–87; N.B. This book speculates that Jesus survived his crucifixion.]

Guerber, H. A. *Legends of the Virgin and Christ with Special Reference to Literature and Art*. New York: Dodd, Mead And Company, 1901. [Chapter 10 Death, Burial, and Resurrection of Christ, See. 208–41; N.B. Archive.org and HathiTrust. Not useful.]

Guild, E. E. *The Pro and Con of Supernatural Religion, or, an Answer to the Question—have we a supernaturally revealed, infallibly inspired, and miraculously attested religion in the world*. New York: D. M. Bennett, 1876. [See. 72–78; N.B. Archive.org. The author provides a general overview of contradictions.]

Hallquist, Christopher. *UFOs, Ghosts, and a Rising God: Debunking the Resurrection of Jesus*. 2009. Cincinnati: Reasonable Press. [N.B. The entire e-book is available free online and should be definitely read.]

Category III—Apologetics and Anti-Apologetics

Harden, William Dearing. *An Inquiry Into the Truth of Dogmatic Christianity: Comprising a Discussion with a Bishop of the Roman Catholic Church*. New York: G. P. Putnam's, 1893. [See. 170–74; N.B. Google book]

Harpur, Tom. *For Christ's Sake*. Toronto: McClelland & Stewart, 1993. [The Resurrection of Jesus, See. 97–103. N.B. These few pages should be examined.]

Helms, Randel. *Gospel Fictions*. Amherst, NY: Prometheus, 1988. [Chapter 7 Resurrection Fictions, See. 129–54; N.B. Helm's work must be examined.]

Hernandez, David. *The Greatest Story Ever Forged: Curse of the Christ Myth*. Pittsburgh: Red Lead Press, 2009. [See. 6, 60–61, 76–77, 319–20; N.B. Not useful.]

Hittell, John S. *The Evidences Against Christianity*. 2nd ed. Vol 1. New York: Calvin Blanchard, 1857. [See. 188–191; N.B. Archive.org. This work discusses discrepancies of the reports.]

Holbach, Paul Henri Thiry. *Christianity Unveiled: Being An Examination of the Principles and Effects of the Christian Religion*. New York: B. W. Johnson, 1895. [Chapter 3 Sketch of the History of the Christian Religion, See. 29; Chapter 6 Of the proofs of the Christian Religion, Miracles, Prophecies, and Martyrs, See. 52; Chapter 10 Of the Inspired Writings of the Christians, See. 80; N.B. Archive.org, Google book, and Gutenberg.org]

Hopkins, Keith. *A World Full of Gods: The Strange Triumph of Christianity*. New York: The Free Press, 2000. [Chapter 4 Jesus and His Twin Brothers, See. 136–76; N.B. Hopkins discusses the ridiculous theory that Jesus had a twin brother.]

Horbury, William. *Jews and Christians: In Contact and Controversy*. London: T&T Clark, 2005. [Resurrection—denial of Jesus, See. 18, 103, 104, 177, 178–79]

Houston, George [?]. An Israelite. *Israel Vindicated; Being a Refutation of the Calumnies Propagated Respecting the Jewish Nation; in which the Objects and Views of the American Society for Ameliorating the Condition of the Jews, are Investigated*. New York: Abraham Collins, 1823 [Letter 22 Death and Resurrection of Jesus, See. 71–73; Letter 23, Same Subject Continued, See. 74–77; N.B. Google book. The assumed author's name is subject to debate. See. Jonathan D. Sarna, *AJS Review*, Vol. 5, 101–14, 1980.]

Humphreys, Kenneth. *Jesus Never Existed: An Introduction to the Ultimate Heresy*. Charleston, WV: Nine-Banded Books, 2014. [126 pages; N.B. If Jesus never existed, there could not be a resurrection.]

Hurst, John F. *History of Rationalism*. New York: Charles Scribner, 1865. [See. 213, 248, 266–269, 277; N.B. Google book. The pages dealing with the resurrection primarily discusses the work of David Frederic Strauss, *The Life of Jesus*, not very useful.]

Indian Officer (G. J. Berwick). *The True Source of Christianity: or A Voice from the Ganges*. London: Freethought, 1881. [Chapter 24 Prophecies of the Resurrection, See. 97–98; Chapter 31 Resurrection, See. 110–12; Chapter 33 Did Jesus Die on the Cross?, See. 112–14; N.B. Archive.org and Google book. The author's name does not appear in the text; however, WorldCat identifies it.]

Ingersoll, Robert G. *The Works of Robert G. Ingersoll*. Vol. 2. New York: The Ingersoll League, 1929. [The Resurrection, See. 400–401; The Ascension, See. 401–4; N.B. Not useful.]

John, Paul. *The Misconception Trilogy Christianity The Ultimate Urban Legend Book 2*. Victoria, BC: Trafford, 2006. [After the Death of Jesus, See. 207–9]

Johnson, B. C. *The Atheist Debater's Handbook*. Buffalo, NY: Prometheus, 1981. [Chapter 14 God and Jesus, See. 119–22; N.B. Not useful.]

Joshi, S. T. *God's Defenders: What They Believe and Why They Are Wrong*. Amherst, NY: Prometheus, 2003. [See. 144–48; N.B. Not useful.]

Jung, C. G. "Psychology and Religion." In *Collected Works of C. G. Jung*, Vol. 18. Princeton University Press, 1976. [On Resurrection, See. 904. (p. 692–96) N.B. Jung writes: "It is funny that the Christians are still so pagan that they understand spiritual existence only as a body and as a physical event.")]

Kearney, Milo, and James Zeitz. *World Saviors and Messiahs of the Roman Empire, 28 BCE—135 CE: The Soterial Age*. Lewiston, NY: Mellen, 2009. [Chapter 8 See. Jesus of Nazareth, See. 195–200; Chapter 11 Why Jesus' Followers Prevailed, See. Victory Over Death, See. 323; Ascension to Heaven, See. 323–25]

Keim, Theodor. *The History of Jesus of Nazara*. Vol. 6. Translated by Arthur Ransom. London: Williams & Norgate, 1883. [Part 3 Burial and Resurrection, See. 250–83; N.B. Google book and HathiTrust. This book is an important, and must read dated work from a liberal-rationalist point of view.]

Kennedy, Ludovic. *All In The Mind: A Farewell To God*. London: Hodder & Stoughton, 1999. [Chapter 4 Judaeo-Christian Mythologies. 3. Alleged Miracles, See. 64–69]

Kersten, Holger, and Elmar Gruber. *The Jesus Conspiracy: the Turin Shroud and the Truth about the Resurrection*. New York: Barnes & Noble, 1995. [See. 254–75; N.B. Kersten postulates that Jesus survived the crucifixion and moved to India. In addition, he asserts that the Vatican interfered with the carbon 14 dating of the Shroud of Turin.]

Komarnitsky, Kris D. *Doubting Jesus' Resurrection: What Happened in the Black Box?* 2nd ed. Drapper, UT: Stone Arrow, 2014. [236 pages; N.B. This work must be read.]

Kryvelev, Iosif Aronovic. *Christ: Myth Or Reality?* Moscow: USSR Academy of Sciences, "Social Sciences Today." 1987. [See. 69]

Kuhn, Alvin Boyd. *Who is this King of Glory? A Critical Study of the Christos-Messiah Tradition*. Elizabeth, NJ: Academy Press, 1944. [See. 235–36, 294, 295, 368–69, 395–400]

Kurtz, Paul. *The Transcendental Temptation: A Critique of Religion and the Paranormal*. Buffalo, NY: Prometheus, 1986. [Chapter 7 The Jesus Myth. Examine. The Resurrection: What is the Evidence?, See. 153–61; N.B. Kurtz concludes that "we cannot say with certainty that he [Jesus] ever existed." This conclusion is based on the contradictions and inconsistencies of the recorded records.]

Landers, Caleb Marshall. *The Skeptic's Defense Against All Christian or Other Priests: Being a Series of Miscellaneous Writings having for their Main Object a Comparison of the Value of Science Over Religion*. Rochester, NY: Author, 1895. [See. 28–29, 43, 53, 346–47, 431–32, 440–41; N.B. Google book. Not useful.]

Lane Fox, Robin. *The Unauthorized Version: Truth and Fiction in the Bible*. New York, Knopf, 1991. [See 143–45, 388, 390]

Leedom, Tom C., ed. *The Book Your Church Doesn't Want You to Read*. San Diego: Truth Seeker, 1993. [The Resurrection: What is the Evidence (Tovia Singer), See. 219–22; No Stone Unturned (Dan Barker), See. 223–26]

Lee, William. *The Inspiration of Holy Scripture: Its Nature and Proof: Eight Discourses, Preached Before the University of Dublin*. New York: Robert Carter, 1857. [See. 346. N.B. Archive.org and Google book]

Leidner, Harold. *The Fabrication of the Christ Myth*. Tampa, FL: Survey, 1999. [N.B. Leidner was an American patent attorney and advocate of the Christ Myth. If Jesus did not exist, there was no resurrection.]

Leland, John. *Remarks On a Late Pamphlet Entitled Christianity not Founded on Argument: In a Letter to a Friend.* London: Printed for R. Hett, 1744. [Letter 2 Remarks On a Late Pamphlet Entitled Christianity not Founded on Argument, See. 43–47; N.B. Google book]

———. *A View of the Principal Deistical Writers That Have Appeared in England in the Last and Present Century.* London: Printed for T. Tegg, 1837. [Letter 8, See. 81–90; Letter 12, See. 136–57; N.B. Google book]

Leslie, Rolla J. *Was the Bible Inspired.* New York: Broadway, 1915. [The Resurrection?, See. 157–73; The Ascension?, See. 174–80; N.B. Google book and HathiTrust. Similar to other skeptics, Leslie points out contradictions and inconsistencies with the New Testament records.]

Levett, Arthur. *A Martian Examines Christianity.* London: Watts, 1934. [See. 91–92; N.B. Sarcastic and humorous.]

Lewis, Abram Herbert. *Paganism Surviving in Christianity.* New York: G. P. Putnam's Sons, 1892. [Chapter 8 Sunday Directly Referred to but Three Times— It is Never Spoken of as a Sabbath, nor as Commemorative of Christ's Resurrection— The Bible does Not State that Christ Rose on Sunday— Christ and His Disciples Always Observed the Sabbath— The Change of the Sabbath Unknown in the New Testament, See. 171–84; N.B. Archive.org, Google book, and Gutenberg.org]

Lewis, H. Spencer. *The Mystical Life of Jesus.* San Jose, CA: Rosicrucian Press, 1929. [Chapter 16 The Secret Facts of the Resurrection, See. 269–81; Chapter 17 The Unknown Life of Jesus, See. 283–92; N.B. The author speculates that Jesus survived the crucifixion.]

Lockhart, Douglas. *Jesus the Heretic: Freedom and Bondage in a Religious World.* Shaftesbury: Element, 1997. [Jesus after crucifixion, See. 82–86, 100–101, 103, 247–48, 258, 265, The Spirit of Truth, See. 277–88, 285; The Importance of the Resurrection, See. 87–89; Paul's Heavenly Vision, See. 89–93]

Loftus, John W. *The Outsider Test for Faith: How To Know Which Religion is True?* Amherst, NY: Prometheus, 2013. [What Then of the Resurrection of Jesus?, See. 180–84]

———. *Why I Became an Atheist: A Former Preacher Rejects Christianity.* Amherst, NY: Prometheus, 2008. [Chapter 20 Did Jesus Bodily from the Dead?, See. 344–82; N.B. This is a recommended text to read.]

Loftus, John, W., and Randal D. Rauser. *God or Godless? One Atheist. One Christian. Twenty Controversial* Questions. Grand Rapids: Baker, 2013. [Chapter 19 Jesus Was Resurrected, So Who Do You Think Raised Him?, See. 157–63; N.B. Arguing the Affirmative: Randal the Christian and Arguing the Negative: John the Atheist]

Lunn, Arnold, and C. E. M. Joad. *Is Christianity True? A Correspondence Between Arnold Lunn and C .E .M. Joad.* London: Eyre & Spottiswoode, 1933. [Chapter 29 Miracles and the Resurrection, See. 281–93 (Lund); Chapter 30 Protests Against Discussing The Resurrection, But Discusses It, See. 294–304 (C. E. M. J.); N.B. Lunn was a Catholic apologist and Joad an agnostic philosopher.]

MacDonald, Dennis R. *Mythologizing Jesus: From Jewish Teacher to Epic* Hero. Lanham, MD: Rowman & Littlefield, 2015. [Chapter 23 Living Dead, See. 129–34; Chapter 24 Disappearing into the Sky, See. 135–43; N.B. An interesting book to examine.]

Mangasar M. M. *The Bible Unveiled.* Chicago: Independent Religious Society, 1911. [See. 178—80; N.B. Archive.org, Google book, and HathiTrust; N.B. Not useful.]

———. *The Truth About Jesus: Is He A Myth?* Chicago: Independent Religious Society, 1909. [See. 34–40, 116–17, 121, 254–57; N.B. Google book and HathiTrust; N.B. Not useful.]

Martin, Michael. *Atheism: A Philosophical* Justification. Philadelphia: Temple University Press, 1990. [See. 162, 188, 189, 217, 255, 503]

———. *Atheism, Morality, and* Meaning. Amherst, NY: Prometheus, 2002. [Chapter 18 The Meaning of Life and the Resurrection, See. 291–318; N.B. This is a logical presentation that should be examined.]

May, Joseph. *The Myth of the Resurrection of Jesus.* 2nd ed. Philadelphia: Edward J. Bicking, 1893. [20 pages]

Maylone, W. Edgar. *Thrown at the Atheist's Head.* Philadelphia: Dorrance, 1973. [See. 545–51]

McCabe, Joseph. *The Myth of the Resurrection.* Little Blue Book No. 1104. Girard, KS: Haldeman-Julius, 1925. [63 pages]

———. "The Resurrection." In *A Rationalist Encyclopedia.* London: Watts, 1950. [See. 496–97]

McComas, E. W. *A Rational View of Jesus and Religion.* New York: J. W. Lovell, 1880. [Chapters 19–23, See. 588–706; N.B. HathiTrust. This interesting, dated source should be examined. McComas postulates that Jesus survived his crucifixion!]

McConnachie, James, and Robin Tudge. *The Rough Guide to Conspiracy Theories.* London: Rough guides, 2005. [Jesus the Myth, See. 160–63]

McCormick, Matthew S. *Atheism and the Case Against Christ.* Amherst, NY: Prometheus, 2012. [Chapters 2–4, See. 37–105; N.B. This work is a must read.]

McKinsey, C. Dennis. *Biblical Errancy: A Reference* Guide. Amherst, NY: Prometheus, 2000. [Jesus, Resurrection, See. 445–57; N.B. McKenzie identifies twenty contradictions in his reference guide.]

Meredith, Evan Powell. *The Prophet of Nazareth; or A Critical inquiry Into the Prophetical, Intellectual and Moral Character of Jesus Christ.* London, 1864. [Chapter 6 Sections 1–4, See. 245–91; N.B. Archive.org, Google book, and HathiTrust]

Miles, Leland Weber. *The Hijacking of Jesus: How the Greeks Stole Jesus from the Jews and Made Him a Second Christian God.* Edited by Kathleen Ober. Charleston, SC: Createspace, 2012. [Chapter 6 The Miracle Worker: Jesus at the Heart of the Gospels, See. 107–15]

Miles, W. J. *The Myth of the Resurrection of Jesus, the Christ.* Sydney: F. E. Moore, 1914. [36 pages]

Miller, Robert J. *The Jesus Seminar and Its Critics.* Santa Rosa, CA: Polebridge, 1999. [Chapter 8 Apologetics and the Resurrection, See. 125–46; N.B. This chapter is an excellent, thoughtful, must read.]

Mills, David. *Atheist Universe: The Thinking Person's Answer to Christian Fundamentalism.* Berkeley, CA: Ulysses Press, 2008. [Resurrection of Christ, See. 38]

Mongar, Thomas M. *Only with Marx and Jesus.* Lanham, MD: University Press of America, 1997. [Chapter 14 How the Resurrection Story May Have Evolved, See. 79–86]

Mountcastle, William W. *The Secret Ministry of Jesus: Pioneer Prophet of Interfaith Dialogue.* Lanham, MD: University Press of America, 2008. [See. 1–2, 27–50, etc. N.B. The author suggests that Jesus survived crucifixion and made his way to Srinagar and India.]

Newton, Michael. *The Encyclopedia of Conspiracies and Conspiracy Theories.* New York: Checkmark, 2006. [Jesus Christ, See. 187–88]

Niemojewski, Andrzej. *God Jesus: The Sun, Moon and Stars as Background to the Gospel Stories. Abridged by Violet MacDermot and translated from the German by Anna Meuss and Violet MacDermot.* London: Janus, 1996. [N.B. This work asserts that the gospel stories are astral myths.]

Nietzsche, Friedrich W. *The Antichrist.* Translated by H. L. Mencken. New York: Alfred A. Knopf, 1931. [Section, 42, See. 118–21; N.B. Archive.org, Gutenberg.org, and HathiTrust]

Notovitch, Nicolas. *The Unknown Life of Jesus Christ.* Translated by Alexina Loranger Donovan. Chicago: Rand, McNally, 1894. [N.B. Archive.org, Google book, and Gutenberg.org; N.B. This work claims that Jesus survived his crucifixion and later moved to India.]

Origen. *The Writings of Origen. Vol. 2. Origen Contra Celsum, Books 2–8.* Edited by Alexander Roberts and James Donaldson. Translated by Frederick Crombie. Edinburgh: T&T Clark, 1894. [Against Celsus, Book 2, Chapters 55–70, See. 58–75; N.B. Google book]

Osman, Ahmed. *The House of the Messiah: Controversial Revelations on the Historical Jesus.* London: HarperCollins, 1992. [Chapter 32 Evidence From the Tomb, See. 169–74]

———. *Jesus in the House of the Pharaohs: The Essene Revelations On the Historical Jesus.* Rochester, VT: Bear, 2004. [N.B. Osman proposes that Jesus and Joshua were one and the same. Originally published in 1992 in Great Britain under the title *The House of the Messiah.*]

Paassen, Pierre van. *Why Jesus Died.* New York: Dial Press, 1949. [Chapter 7 What Happened to the Body of Jesus, See. 176–206; N.B. The author proposes that Jesus's body was thrown into a pit and that over a period of many years the resurrection accounts developed and evolved.]

Pagels, Elaine. *The Gnostic Gospels.* New York: Random House, 1979. [Chapter 1 The Controversy over Christ's Resurrection: Historical Event or Symbol?, See. 3–27; N.B. This work discusses Gnostic texts.]

Paine, Thomas. *The Age of Reason.* London: Freethought, 1860. [See. 5–6, 124–36; N.B. Archive.org and Gutenberg.org]

Perakh, Mark. *Unintelligent Design.* Amherst, NY: Prometheus, 2004. [Is the Gospel Logical?, See. 237–43]

Pfeiffer, C. Boyd. *No Proof At All: A Cure for Christianity.* Algora, 2015. [See. 85–87; N.B. The author merely shows a few contradictions in the resurrection narratives.]

Philipse, Herman. *God in the Age of Science? A Critique of Religious Reason.* Oxford: Oxford University Press, 2012. [10.3 The Resurrection of Jesus: The Testimony, See. 170–75; 10.4 Explaining the Existing Testimony, See. 175–78; 10.5 Cognitive Dissonance and Collaborative Storytelling, See. 178–82; N.B. This is an excellent text to read.]

Porcupine, Peter. *Christianity Contrasted with Deism: Or The Present Religion of France. To which is added, an address to the Society for Promoting Christian Knowledge and Piety.* 2nd ed. Philadelphia: Printed for the Booksellers, 1796. [See. 33–38; N.B. The author ridicules numerous aspects of Christianity. This work is available online, the Evans Early American Imprint Collection.]

Powys, Llewelyn. *The Pathetic Fallacy: A Study of Christianity.* London: Longmans, Green, 1930. [Chapter 4 The Legend of the Resurrection, See. 30–36]

Price, R. G. *Deciphering the Gospels: Proves Jesus Never Existed*. Lulu, 2018. [370 pages; N.B. If Jesus never existed, there was never a resurrection.]

Price, Robert M. *The Case Against the Case for Christ: A New Testament Scholar Refutes Lee Strobel*. Cranford, NJ: American Atheist Press, 2010. [Part 3 Rationalizing the Resurrection, See. 205–54; N.B. This book is a definite read.]

———. *Deconstructing Jesus*. Amherst, NY: Prometheus, 2000. [See. 9, 10, 27, 34, 35, 43, 47, 54, 55, 56, 61, 93, 148, 149, 179, 215, 224, 228, 251, 260, 264; N.B. Chapter 7 The Cruci-fiction?, See. 215–26]

———. *The Incredible Shrinking Son of Man: How Reliable Is the Gospel Tradition?* Amherst, NY: Prometheus, 2003. [Chapter 14 Resurrection, See. 333–48; N.B. This work should be examined.]

———. *Jesus is Dead*. Cranford, NJ: American Atheist Press, 2007. [279 pages; N.B. This book is another of Price's works to checkout.]

———. *Killing History: Jesus in the No-Spin Zone*. Amherst, NY: Prometheus, 2014. [The Missing Chapter. Raising Jesus, See. 205–14]

Pullman, Philip. *The Good Man Jesus and the Scoundrel Christ*. Edinburgh: Canongate, 2010. [N.B. This work is a historical novel that reports Jesus had a twin brother named Christ. After Jesus is dead and buried, Christ masquerades as the dead brother and deceives people into believing that Jesus rose from the dead. This hypothesis is utterly unbelievable.]

Ranke Heinemann, Uta. *Putting Away Childish Things*. San Francisco: HarperSanFrancisco, 1994. [Chapter 9 Easter, See. 130–40; Chapter 10 The Ascension, See. 141–49]

Reimarus, Hermann Samuel. *Fragments From Reimarus: Consisting of Brief Critical Remarks on the Object of Jesus and His Disciples as Seen in the New Testament*. Edited by Charles Voysey. Translated by Gotthold Ephraim Lessing. London: Williams & Norgate, 1879. [See. 30, 31, 33, 34, 44, 45, 46, 47, 69, 76, 82, 95–98, 110; N.B. Archive.org]

———. *The Goal of Jesus and His Disciples*. Translated by George Wesley. Buchanan. Leiden: Brill, 1970. [Part 2. #54–60, See. 126–43; N.B. This work is a classic, dated source.]

Remsburg, John E. *The Christ A Critical Review and Analysis of the Evidences of His Existence*. New York: Truth Seeker, 1909. [Chapter 7 Resurrection of Christ, See. 296–339; N.B. Google book and Gutenberg EBook. This is a classic, dated source.]

Renan, Ernest. *Renan's Life of Jesus*. Translated by William G. Hutchison. London: Scott, 1897. [Chapter 26 Jesus In The Tomb. See. 271–72; N.B. Google book; various translations are available.]

Rhys, Jocelyn. *Shaken Creeds: The Resurrection Doctrines*. London: Watts, 1924. [Part 1 The Resurrection Story, Chapter 1 The Evidence From The New Testament, See. 3–47; Chapter 4 The Ascension, See. 102–18; Chapter 6 Modern Scepticism, See. 144–69]

Robertson, J. M. *Studies in Religious Fallacy*. London: Watts, 1900. [See. 62, 121, 158, 175, 199; N.B. Google book and HathiTrust]

Robinson, Frank B. *Crucified Gods Galore or Christianity Before Christ*. Moscow, IO: Review Publishing, 1933. [Chapter 19 Resurrection of Saviors, See. 137–44; Chapter 20 Reappearance and Ascension of the Saviors, See. 145–48; N.B. Very Similar to Kersey Graves's work *The World's Sixteen Crucified Saviors or Christianity Before Christ*.]

Robinson, Neil. *Why Christians Don't Do What Jesus Tells Them to Do: And What They Believe Instead*. CreateSpace, 2012. [Part 1: Failed Prophecies, See. 25–27]

Category III—Apologetics and Anti-Apologetics

Ross, William Stewart. *Did Jesus Christ Rise From The Dead?* London: W. Stewart, 1887. [64 pages; N.B. Saladin is a pseudonym and this is the name that appears on the title page.]

Rylands, L. Gordon. *The Christian Tradition: An Examination of Objections to the Opinion that Jesus was Not An Historical person.* London: Watts, 1937. [Paul's Vision and the Belief in the Resurrection, See. 46–52]

Schlagel, Richard H. *The Vanquished Gods: Science, Religion, and the Nature of Belief.* Amherst, NY: Prometheus, 2001. [The Christos Legend, See. 157–67]

Schonfield, Hugh J. *The Passover Plot: New Light on the History of Jesus.* London: Hutchinson of London, 1966. [Chapter 13 He is not Here, See. 170–82; N.B. This ludicrous work postulates that Jesus and his followers conspired to stage the crucifixion but their plans went wrong.]

Scott, Thomas. *Errors, Discrepancies, Contradictions, of the Gospel.* Record. Mount Pleasant, Ramsgate: Thomas Scott, 1869. [See. 28–42; N.B. Google Book]

———. *The Tactics and Defeat of the Christian Evidence Society.* Ramsgate: Thomas Scott, 1871. [See. 6, 14–15, 21, 22, 26–27, 32–33; N.B. Google book]

Sheaffer, Robert. *The Making of the Messiah: Christianity and Resentment.* Buffalo, NY: Prometheus, 1991. [Chapter 5 The Making of the Messiah, Part Three: The Post-Resurrection Appearances, See. 127–46]

Sheehan, Thomas. *The First Coming: How the Kingdom of God Became Christianity.* New York: Random House, 1986. [287 pages; 2000 electronic edition at infidels.org. N.B. This book is a good read.]

Sheldon, Henry C. *Unbelief in the Nineteenth Century: A Critical History.* New York: Eaton & Mains, 1907. [See. 162–63; 177–80, 315, 320; N.B. Archive.org and HathiTrust]

Sinnott-Armstrong, Walter. *God? A Debate Between A Christian And An Atheist. William Lane Craig and Walter Sinnott-Armstrong.* Oxford: Oxford University Press, 2004. [Chapter 2 There Is No Good Reason to Believe in God. See. 2. Miracles, See. 36–38]

Smart, J. J. C., and J. J. Haldane. *Atheism and Theism.* Oxford: Blackwell, 1996. [Jesus, life of, See. 63–65, 73, 88, 205–9]

Smith, Christian. *Atheist Overreach: What Atheism Can't Deliver.* New York: Oxford University Press, 2019. [See. 96]

Smith, Homer W. *Man and His Gods.* New York: Grosset & Dunlay, 1956. [Resurrection of Jesus, See. 187–89].

Spong, John Shelby. *The Easter Moment.* New York: Seabury Press, 1980. [240 pages]

———. *Jesus for the Non-Religious.* New York: HarperOne, 2007. [Chapter 11 The Eternal Truth Inside the Myths of Resurrection and Ascension, See. 117–29]

———. *Resurrection: Myth or Reality? A Bishop's Search for the Origins of Christianity.* San Francisco, CA: HarperSanFrancisco, 1994. [320 pages]

Spooner, Lysander. *The Deist's Reply to the Alleged Supernatural Evidences of Christianity.* Boston. 1836. [Chapter 5 The Resurrection, See. 50–62; N.B. Archive.org and Google book. N.B. This is an interesting, dated work.]

Stansbury, Hubert. *In Quest of Truth; a Study of Religion and Morality.* London: Watts, 1913. [See. 85–87; N.B. HathiTrust]

Stecher, Richard C., and Craig L. Blomberg. *Resurrection : Faith or Fact? A Scholars' Debate Between a Skeptic and a Christian.* Durham, North Carolina: Pitchstone Publishing, 2019. [This work is perhaps, one of the finest debates about Jesus's resurrection. It is an absolute must reading!]

Steele, David Ramsey. *Atheism Explained: From Folly to Philosophy*. Chicago: Open Court, 2008. [See. 147–49]

Stenger, Victor J. *God: The Failed Hypothesis— How Science Shows That God Does Not Exist*. Amherst, NY: Prometheus, 2008. [See. 179–80]

Steiner, Rudolf. *The Easter Festival: Four Lectures given in Dornach, Switzerland, 19th to 22nd April, 1924*. London: Rudolf Steiner Press, 1968. [80 pages; N.B. This work is a reprint from the 1924 lectures.]

Stitt, Frederick H. *Myths, Dreams, and Theology in Early Christianity*. Charleston, SC: BookSurge Publishing, 2006. [Chapter 3 An Analysis of the Resurrection Stories, See. 35–50]

Strauss, David Friedrich. *The Life of Jesus: Critically Examined*. Translated by George Eliot. 4th ed. London: Swan Sonnenschein, 1902. [Third Part. Chapter 4 The Death and Resurrection of Jesus, See. 691–744; Chapter 5 The Ascension, See. 745–56; N.B. Archive.org and Google book. This book is a classic, dated source that should be examined.]

Sweeley, John W. *Jesus in the Gospels: Man, Myth, or God*. Lanham: University Press of America, 2000. [Chapter 7 The Resurrection of Jesus: Myth, Magic, or Miracle?, See. 163–94]

Tacey, David J. *Religion As Metaphor: Beyond Literal* Belief. New Brunswick: Transaction Publishers, 2015. [Chapter 9 Resurrection: Ascending to Where?, See. 167–86]

Talbot, George F. *Jesus, His Opinions and Character: The New Testament Studies*. Boston: G. H. Ellis, 1883. [Chapter 12 The Legend of the Resurrection, See. 382–86; N.B. Google book]

Tarico, Valerie, and Dale McGowan. *Trusting Doubt: A Former Evangelical Looks at Old Beliefs in a New Light*. 2nd. ed. Independence, VA: Oracle Press Institute, 2017. [Appendix B. Father Dan's Easter Quiz, See. 262–64]

Taylor, Robert. *The Diegesis; Being a Discovery of the Origin, Evidences, and Early History of Christianity*. 3rd ed. London: W. Dugdale, 1845. [See. 96, 121, 130, 153, 221, 253, 277, 286, 294, 355–56, 364; N.B. Archive.com and HathiTrust]

Templeton, Charles. *Farewell to God: My Reasons for Rejecting the Christian Faith*. Toronto, Ont.: McClelland & Stewart, 1996. [The Resurrection, See. 117–22; The Ascension, See. 123–24]

Thiering, Barbara. *Jesus & the Riddle of the Dead Sea Scrolls: Unlocking the Secrets of His Life Story*. San Francisco: HarperSanFrancisco, 1992. [Chapters 26–35, See. 121–60; Jesus did not die.]

Thomson, James. *Satires and Profanities*. London: Progress, 1844. [The Resurrection and Ascension of Jesus, See. 110–15; N.B. Google book and Gutenberg.org]

Thorburn, Thomas James. *The Mythical Interpretation of the Gospels: Critical Studies in the Historic Narratives*. New York: Scribner's Sons, 1916. [Chapter 15 The Descension to Hades. The Resurrection and Ascension to Heaven, See. 302–29; N.B. Archive.org and HathiTrust]

Tobin, Paul. *The Rejection of Pascal's Wager: A Skeptics Guide to the Bible and the Historical Jesus*. Sandy: Authors OnLine, 2009. [Chapter 15 Burial and Resurrection, See. 539–79]

Unitheist. *The Theological Bee-Hive: or Book of Dogmas Comprising an Inquiry into the Reality of the Death and Nature of the Resurrection of Jesus Christ, Together with a Concise View of the Several Dogmas*. Boston, 1847. [The Resurrection, See. 64–71;

Appearances, See. 71–73; The Ascension, See. 74–78; N.B. Archive.org. The writer asserts that Jesus survived his crucifixion and suggests that Jesus was possibly the angel at the tomb in white grave clothes. He also rejects the ascension. This book is a must read.]

Vaiden, Thomas J. *America Vindicated From European Theologico-Political and Infidel Aspersions*. New York: Morgan, 1855. [See. 267–68; N.B. Archive.org, Google.org, and HathiTrust]

Vivian, Philip. *The Churches and Modern Thought: An Inquiry into the Grounds of Unbelief and an Appeal for Candor*. London: Watts, 1906. [Chapter 2 The Extraordinary State of Apologetics with Regard to Miracles, The Resurrection, See. 64–75; The Ascension, See. 75–77; N.B. Archive.org, Google book, and Gutenberg.org]

Volney, C. F. *The Ruins or Meditation on the Revolutions of Empires and the Law of Nature*. New York: Peter Eckler, 1890. [Chapter 22 #13 Christianity, or the Allegorical Worship of the Sun under the cabalistic names of Chrish-en or Christ and Yesus or Jesus, See. 153–62; N.B. Google book. The author was an early founder of the Christ Myth.]

Vredenburgh, Charles Edwin. *The Case Against the Church: A Summary of the Arguments Against Christianity*. New York: Charles P. Somerby, 1876. [See. 59–61; N.B. Archive.org]

Waite, Charles B. *History of the Christian Religion to the Year Two Hundred*. Chicago: C. V. Waite, 1881. [See. 13, 26–27, 41, 206–12, 218, 220, 229, 251, 263, 312, 334–36, 354, 363, 374–76, 433, 434; N.B. Archive.org and HathiTrust]

Warne, Floyd Lawrence. *Christianity: A Critique of Religious Doctrine*. New York: Vantage Press, 1956. [See. 37–39]

Washburn, Lemuel K. *Is the Bible Worth Reading, and Other Essays*. New York: Truth Seeker, 1911. [What Does It Prove?, See. 58; N.B. Archive.org and Gutenberg.org]

Weigall, Arthur. *Paganism in Our Christianity*. New York, London, G. P. Putnam's Sons, 1928. [Chapter 9 The Resurrection, See. 91–102; Chapter 10 The Ascension and the Messiahship, See. 103–13]

Wells, George Albert. *Cutting Jesus Down to Size: What Higher Criticism Has Achieved and Where It Leaves Christianity*. Chicago: Open Court, 2009. [Chapter 4 The Resurrection, See. 113–77; N.B. Wells presents a detailed challenge to the resurrection accounts found in the New Testament. A must read.]

———. *Did Jesus Exist?* London: Pemberton, 1986. [on third day, See. 30–34, 67, 115, 165; of Jesus his appearances after, See. 21, 26, 30, 37, 67, 124, 144]

———. *The Historical Evidence for Jesus*. Buffalo, NY: Prometheus, 1982. [Paul and the Resurrection, See. 43–45]

———. *The Jesus Legend*. Chicago: Open Court, 1996. [A Modern Jewish Scholar Concedes the Historicity of the Resurrection, See. 56–63]

———. *The Jesus Myth*. Chicago, Open Court, 1999. [Chapter 2 Miracles in the New Testament and Beyond. ii. The Resurrection, See. 123–42; N.B. This critical text is a recommended read.]

———. *The Jesus of the Early Christians: A Study in Christian Origins*. London: Pemberton, 1971. [Part 1 The Historical Jesus. Chapter 1 The Gospel Miracles. (2) The Resurrection, See. 40–49]

———. *Religious Postures Essays on Modern Christian Apologists and Religious Problems*. La Salle, IL: Open Court, 1988. [See. 36–37, 43–44, 51–53, 69–70, 73, 76–77, 127, 220;

N.B. The author states his concern in this text is with "the methods of apologists, both fundamentalists and liberal . . . "]

———. *Who Was Jesus?: A Critique of the New Testament Record*. La Salle, IL: Open Court, 1989. [Chapter 2 The Resurrection, See. 25–52]

Whitney, Loren Harper. *A Question of Miracles: Parallels in the Lives of Buddha and Jesus: A Critical Examination of the So-called Miracles Surrounding the Birth, Life and Death of Buddha and Jesus and the Achievements of Other Miracle-workers . . .* Chicago: Library Shelf, 1908. [Chapter 24 Was It A Resurrection or Was It Resuscitation?, See. 281–91; Chapter 25 The Miracles of Jesus' Appearance to the Disciples, See. 292–99; Chapter 29 Examination of Luke Resumed, See. 331–39; N.B. Archive.org]

Wolfe, Rolland. *How the Easter Story Grew from Gospel to Gospel*. Lewiston, NY: Mellen, 1989. [244 pages; N.B. This book is a must read.]

Wood, James. *Leaving Jesus*. Midland, VA: New Dominion Publishing, 2013. [Chapter 10 Crucifying the Resurrection. N.B. This is a free e-book available online. Wood was a committed Christian for twenty-five years before rejecting that faith and becoming a believer in YHVH and the Hebrew Bible.]

Worth, Roland H. *Alternative Lives of Jesus: Noncanonical Accounts Through the Early Middle Ages*. Jefferson, NC: McFarland, 2003. [Chapter 10 Triumph Over Death, See. 157–70]

Zepa. *Eye-opener: Citateur, par Pigault : Le Brun, Doubts of Infidels : Embodying Thirty Important Questions to the Clergy : also, Forty Close Questions to the Doctors of Divinity*. Boston: William White, 1871. [See. 129–31; N.B. Archive.org]

Zindler, Frank R. *The Jesus the Jews Never Knew*. Cranford, NJ: American Atheist Press, 2003. [567 pages; N.B. This lengthy book asserts that the ancient Jews never heard of Jesus of Nazareth. If there was no Jesus, there could not be a resurrection.]

Category IV

Miracles and Science

CHAPTER 9

Miracles and Science: Pro Resurrection

Albro, John A. *The Miracles of Christ*. Boston: Massachusetts Sabbath School Society, 1848. [Lesson 58 The Miraculous Draught of Fishes after the Crucifixion John 21:1–17, See. 107–8. N.B. Not useful.]

Alexander, Dennis. *Rebuilding the Matrix: Science and Faith in the 21st Century*. Grand Rapids: Zondervan, 2003. [Resurrection of Jesus, See. 261, 268, 311, 317, 438, 443, 446, 449, 451, 453–55]

Aradi, Zsolt. *The Book of Miracles*. New York: Farrar, Strauss & Cudahy, 1956. [See. 143–50; N.B. Not useful.]

Ballard, Frank. *The Miracles of Unbelief*. Edinburgh: T&T Clark, 1901. [See. Resurrection of Jesus Christ, 135–51; Varying theories of unbelief concerning, 322; The only rational explanation, of 323; N.B. Archive.org and HathiTrust. Ballard presents a good overview.]

Barclay, William. *And He had Compassion on Them: A Handbook on the Miracles of the Bible*. Edinburgh: Church of Scotland Youth Committee, 1955. [Chapter 26 The Resurrection, See. 278–92; N.B. Barclay's work presents a superficial read.]

Bartlett, David L. *Fact and Faith*. Valley Forge, PA: Judson Press, 1975. [Chapter 4 The Miracle of the Resurrection, See. 85–91; Chapter 5 Resurrection Traditions in the New Testament, See. 93–124; Chapter 6 The Significance of the Resurrection for Christian Faith, See. 125–32; N.B. Not useful.]

Beardsley, Frank Grenville. *The Miracles of Jesus*. New York: American Tract Society, 1926. [Chapter 5 The Resurrection of Jesus, See. 101–24; N.B. Beardsley presents a general overview.]

Beckwith, Francis J. *David Hume's Argument Against Miracles: A Critical Analysis*. Lanham: University Press of America, 1989. [See. 50–51, 62–63, 98–100]

Best, John H. *The Miracles of Christ: In Light of Our Present-Day Knowledge*. London: SPCK, 1937. [Chapter 5 The Miracles of the Resurrection and Ascension, See. 133–72; N.B. This source should be examined.]

Bragge, Francis. *On the Miracles of Our Lord*. Volume 1 of The Works of Francis Bragge in 5 Volumes. Oxford: University Press, 1833. [Chapter 11 Our Saviour's miraculous resurrection from the dead, See. 557–79; Chapter 12 Our Saviour's glorious ascension into heaven, See. 580– 601; N.B. Google book. Bragge emphasizes the importance of Jesus's resurrection.]

Brown, Colin. *Miracles and the Critical Mind*. Grand Rapids: Eerdmans, 1984. [Resurrection of Jesus, See. 43, 50, 57–58, 63, 88, 89, 96, 108, 113, 114, 152, 156, 166–67, 176, 180, 182, 190, 191, 201, 202, 203, 207, 208, 212, 214, 220, 227, 228, 235, 287–90, 336n, 354n, 357–358n, 371n, 373n]

———. *That You May Believe: Miracles and Faith Then and Now*. Grand Rapids: Eerdmans, 1985. [Miracles and the Resurrection, See. 104–7. Not useful.]

Bruce, Alexander Balmain. *The Miraculous Element in the Gospels*. 4th ed. London: Hodder & Stoughton, 1899. [See. 21, 70, 80, 351–54, 358–59, 388; N.B. Archive.org]

Burge, Ted. *Science and the Bible Evidenced Christian Belief*. West Conshohocken, PA: Templeton Foundation Press, 2005. [Chapter 13 Evidence for the Resurrection of Jesus, See. 109–17; N.B. Chiefly, the author reviews the post-resurrection appearances.]

Cairns, D. S. *The Faith That Rebels: A Re-Examination of the Miracles of Jesus*. New York: Harper & Brothers, 1954. [Resurrection of Jesus, See. 168–72; Modern Views of, See. 44–46, 100, 170; the Supreme sign of, See. 172; Modern scientific speculations on, See. 174]

Campbell, George. *A Dissertation On Miracles: Containing An Examination of the Principles Advanced By David Hume In An Essay On Miracles; With A Correspondence On The Subject By Mr. Hume, Dr. Campbell & Dr. Blair; To Which Are Added Sermons and Tracts*. Edinburgh: Printed for Bell & Bradfute . . . etc., 1823. [See. 98, 101, 131, 291, 310, 325; N.B. Archive.org and Google book]

Clayton, Philip, and Steven Knapp. *The Predicament of Belief Science, Philosophy, Faith*. Oxford: Oxford University Press, 2011. [Chapter 5 The Scandal of Particularity, Part 1 The Resurrection Testimony, See. 79–92; Chapter 6 The Scandal of Particularity, Part 2 Jesus and the Ultimate Reality, See. 93–110; N.B. This work is a recommended read.]

Clowes, J. *The Miracles of Jesus Christ: Explained According to Their Spiritual Meaning, in the Way of Question and Answer*. Manchester: Published by the Manchester Printing Society of the New Jerusalem Church, 1817. [Miracle 35. The Resurrection and Ascension of Jesus Christ, See. 307–29; N.B. Archive.org, Google book, and HathiTrust. The author employs a question and answer format.]

Collins, Francis S. *Language of God: A Scientist Presents Evidence for Belief*. New York: Free Press, 2006. [See. 221–24; N.B. Not useful.]

Collyer, William Bengo. *Lectures on Scripture Miracles*. London: J. G. Barnard, 1812. [Lecture 12 Miracles Attending the Death of Christ—And His Own Resurrection, See. 503–29; N.B. Google book and HathiTrust]

Corner, David. *The Philosophy of Miracles*. London: Continuum, 2007. [Resurrection of Jesus, See. 76, 92, 93, 152]

Corner, Mark. *Signs of God: Miracles and Their Interpretation*. Aldershot: Ashgate, 2005. [Chapter 10 Jesus' Resurrection and the Nature of God. See. 149–62; N.B. Perhaps, of interest.]

Crawford, Robert G. *Is God a Scientist? A Dialogue Between Science and Religion*. New York: Palgrave Macmillan, 2005. [The Resurrection of Christ, See. 144–48; N.B. The author interacts with a few writers.]

Davies, E. O. *The Miracles of Jesus: A Study of the Evidence, Being the Davies Lecture for the Year 1913*. London: Hodder & Stoughton, 1913. [See. 15, 94; N.B. Google book]

Deigloriam, A. M. *Miracles Beyond Our Comprehension*. Eugene, OR: Resource, 2016. [The Resurrection of Jesus Christ, See. 63–66; The Miracle of Catching Fish After the

Resurrection, See. 66–68; The Ascension, See. 68–69; N.B. The author's presentation is very superficial.]

Dockeray, Norman R. C. *The Power of Miracle*. Sussex, UK: Book Guild, 1991. [The Resurrection, See. 213–26]

Dodd, Thomas J. *Miracles: Were They or Were They Not, Performed by Jesus? A Question of Fact, Not of Science or Theology*. Cincinnati: Jennings & Pye, 1899. [Chapter 5 General Review of the Adverse Argument, See. 168–86; N.B. Dodd interacts with Renan and Strauss to lend credence to the resurrection.]

Duff, Edward Macomb, and Thomas Gilchrist. Allen. *Psychic Research and Gospel Miracles: A Study of the Evidences of the Gospel's Superphysical Features in the Light of the Established Results of Modern Psychical Research*. New York: Thomas Whittaker, 1902. [Chapter 1 Old Verification of History, See. 18–22; Chapter 2 Christ's "Mighty Works" In the Light of Psychic Law; Including His Birth and Resurrection, See. 280–89; N.B. Archive.org]

Earman, John. *Hume's Abject Failure: The Argument Against Miracles*. Oxford: Oxford University Press, 2000. [See. 7–8, 15–20]

Felder, Hilarin. *Christ and the Critics: A Defence of the Divinity of Jesus Against the Attacks of Modern Sceptical* Criticism. Translated by John L. Stoddard. Vol. 2. London: Burns Oates & Washbourne, 1924. [Chapter 3 Science and Christ's Resurrection, See. 370–432; N.B. This dated source should be examined.]

Fuller, Reginald H. *Interpreting the* Miracles. London: SCM, 1963. [The Miraculous Draft of Fishes, See. 120–23; N.B. This miracle parallels John 21:1–11.]

Gaskill, Alonzo L. *Miracles of the New Testament: A Guide to the Symbolic Messages*. Springville, UT: CFI, 2014. [Great Haul of Fishes John 21:1–14, See. 259–66; N.B. The author does not specifically discuss Jesus's resurrection.]

Geisler, Norman L. *Miracles and the Modern Mind: A Defense of the Biblical Miracles*. Eugene, OR: Wipf & Stock, 2004. [See. 11, 16, 17, 69–74, 132–38; Originally in Baker, 1992]

Geisler, Norman L., and R. C. Sproul. *Miracles and Modern Thought*. Grand Rapids: Zondervan, 1982. [Cross-Examining the Witnesses for the Resurrection, See. 146–52; The Identity of the Resurrection as a Miracle, See. 152–54; N.B. Geisler's work should be examined.]

Geivett, R. Douglas, and Gary R. Habermas, eds. In *In Defense of Miracles: A Comprehensive Case for God's Action in History*. Downers Grove: InterVarsity, 1997. [Chapter 10 The Empty Tomb of Jesus, See. 247–61 (William Lane Craig), Chapter 16 The Resurrection Appearances, See. 262–75 (Gary R. Habermas); N.B. Both essays should be carefully read.]

Gerdtell, Ludwig von. *Miracles Under Fire: A Treatise For Modern Thinkers*. Translated by S. H. Wilkinson. Edited by Byrdine Akers Abbott and Willard E. Shelton. St. Louis: Bethany Press, 1930. [Chapter 3 The Resurrection of Jesus, See. 47–118; N.B. This work is a recommended read.]

Gilliom, James O. *Walking on Water: Sermons on the Miracles of Jesus*. Nashville: Abingdon, 1995. [The Empty Tomb, See. 66–70; The Walk to Emmaus, See. 83–89; N.B. Not useful.]

Goddard, Jerome. *Faith Vs. Science: The Unnecessary Dichotomy*. 2nd ed. Lee's Summit, MO: Father's Press, 2012. [Chapter 21 Wasn't Jesus Just an Ordinary Teacher Who was Later Deified by His Followers?; Was There Really a Resurrection?, no pagination]

Category IV—Miracles and Science

Gordon, George A. *Religion and Miracle*. Boston: Houghton Mifflin, 1909. [Chapter 3 Jesus Christ and Miracle, See. 94, 107–9; 112–31; N.B. Archive.org. Nothing substantial.]

Grant, Malcolm. *A New Argument for God and Survival and a Solution to the Problem of Supernatural* Events. London: Faber & Faber, 1934. [See. 77]

Grant, Robert M. *Miracle and Natural Law in Graeco-Roman and Early Christian Thought*. Amsterdam: North Holland, 1952. [Chapter 14 Resurrection in the Bible, See. 221–34, Chapter 15 Resurrection in Apologetics, See. 235–45; Chapter 16 Resurrection in Theology, See. 246–63; N.B. An interesting read.]

Habershon, Ada R. *The Study of the Miracles*. London: Morgan & Scott, 1961. [Chapter 10 The Miracles in the New Testament, See. 118–34; N.B. Nothing useful.]

Hargreaves, Cecil. *The Miracles of Jesus*. Madras: Published for the Senate of Serampore College by the Christian Literature Society, 1964. [John No. 6. The Catch of Fish John 21:1–14), See. 232–36; N.B. Not useful.]

Harpur, James, and Marcus Braybrook. *The Miracles of Jesus*. London: Reader's Digest, 1997. [An Encounter with the Risen Christ, See. 86–89]

Hayes, Patrick J., ed. *Miracles: An Encyclopedia of People, Places, and Supernatural Events from Antiquity to the Present*. Santa Barbara, CA: ACC-CLIO, 2016. [Resurrection/Resuscitation, See. 343–44]

Headlam, Arthur C. *The Miracles of the New Testament: Being the Moorhouse Lectures for 1914 Delivered in S. Paul's Cathedral, Melbourne*. London: Scribner's Sons, 1915. [Lecture 6 The Resurrection, See. 244–68; N.B. Archive.org and Google book. Headlam reviews the evidence from 1 Corinthians 15 and the Gospels.]

Hitchcock, F. R. Montgomery. *The Present Controversy on the Gospel Miracles*. London: SPCK, 1915. [See. iv, viii, 24, 29, 43, 47, 57, 58, 60, 68, 69, 70, 74, 102, 107, 108, 114, 115, 128, 130, 131, 136, 141, 143, 148, 154, 161, 162, 172, 193, 207; N.B. Archive.org]

Holloway, Gary. *A Miracle Named Jesus*. Joplin, MO: College Press, 1997. [Chapter 13 An Unexpected Return. Luke 24:13–35, See. 133–41; N.B. Useless.]

Houston, J. *Reported Miracles: A Critique of Hume*. Cambridge: Cambridge University Press, 1994. [Chapter 12 Reported Miracles in Theology, See. 208–55]

Hovey, Alvah. *The Miracles of Christ as Attested by the Evangelists*. Boston: Graves & Young, 1864. [Third Part. Miracles on His Own Body. 2. The Resurrection of Jesus from the Dead, See. 271–300; N.B. Google book and HathiTrust]

Howick, E. Keith. *The Miracles of Jesus the Messiah*. St. George, UT, WindRiver, 2003. [Part 5 It Is I., See. 159–64; N.B. Useless.]

Hubbard, George Henry. *Spiritual Messages of the Miracle Stories*. Boston: Pilgrim Press, 1922. [Chapter 39 The Crowning Miracle. The Resurrection of Jesus, See. 325–32; N.B. Google book and HathiTrust. Not useful.]

Huelster, A. *Miracles in the Light of Science and History*. Chicago: Author, 1900. [Chapter 7 Miracles are Historical Facts, See. 117–64; N.B. Archive.org. Consider examining this chapter.]

Hutchison, John. *Our Lord's Signs in St. John's Gospel: Discussions Chiefly Exegetical and Doctrinal on the Eight Miracles in the Fourth Gospel*. Edinburgh: T&T Clark, 1892. [Chapter 8 The Second Miraculous Draught of Fishes, See. 213–34; N.B. Google book and HathiTrust]

Illingworth, J. R. *The Gospel Miracles; An Essay with Two Appendices*. London: Macmillan, 1915. [Chapter 2 The Resurrection, See. 19–39; N.B. Google book and HathiTrust]

John, Jeffrey. *The Meaning in the Miracles*. Grand Rapids: Eerdmans, 2004. [Chapter 19 Two Miraculous Catches of Fish, See. 228–38; N.B. Not useful]

Johnson, Timothy Luke. *Miracles God's Presence and Power in Creation*. Louisville: Westminster John Knox, 2018. [The Resurrection Experience, See. 149–56; N.B. Not useful.]

Johnston, Howard Agnew. *Scientific Christian Thinking for Young People*. New York: George H. Doran, 1922. [Chapter 13 The Program of Christ, See. 190–92; N.B. Not useful]

Kaye, Bruce. *The Supernatural in the New Testament*. Guildford: Lutterworth, 1977. [Chapter 2 Selected Passage 9. The Resurrection of Jesus, See. 39–44]

Kaye, Bruce, and John Rogerson. *Miracles and Mysteries in the Bible*. Philadelphia: Westminster, 1977. [The Resurrection of Jesus, See. 107–11]

Keener, Craig S. *Miracles: The Credibility of the New Testament Accounts*. Grand Rapids: Baker Academic, 2011. [resurrection of Jesus in Christian understanding, See. 110n14, 111n20, 120n61, 133n148, 140, 145n, 222, 148n239, 159n315, 160, 181n71, 182n77, 213n11, 538, 581n493, 607n16, 611nn34–35; in Hume and others who reject supernaturalism, 111nn19, 21, 162n337, 635; N.B. Keener's work is an absolute must read.]

Kidder, Daniel P. *The Miracles of Christ: With Explanatory Observations, and Illustrations from Modern Travels*. Philadelphia: Presbyterian Board of Publication, 1880. [Chapter 13 Resurrection and Ascension of Christ, See. 249–52; N.B. Google book and HathiTrust; N.B. This work only discusses the draught of fishes in John 21.]

Kim, Stephen S. *The Miracles of Jesus According to John: Their Christological and Eschatological Significance*. Eugene, OR: Wipf & Stock, 2010. [See. 195]

Kistemaker, Simon. *The Miracles: Exploring the Mystery of Jesus's Divine Works*. Grand Rapids: Baker, 2006. [Miracles of Jesus. The Resurrection, See. 228–31; Postresurrection Appearances, See. 232–37; The Ascension, See. 238–41; N.B. This book primarily reviews the appearances.]

Laidlaw, John. *Miracles Of Our Lord: Expository and Homiletic*. New York: Funk & Wagnalls, 1892. [Second Miraculous Draught of Fishes John xxi. 1–14, See. 373–84; N.B. Archive.org and Google book]

Lamb, Francis Jones. *Miracle and Science: Bible Miracles Examined by the Methods, Rules and Tests of the Science of Jurisprudence as Administered Today in Courts of Justice*. Oberlin: Bibliotheca Sacra, 1909. [Section 5 . . . Apostles' Faith Awakened, not Perfected, by Resurrection of Jesus; Resurrection of Jesus etc. See. 267–95; Section 6 See. Ascension and Pentecost, See. 296–97; N.B. Archive.org and HathiTrust. Nothing substantial.]

Larmer, Robert A., ed. *Questions of Miracle*. Montreal & Kingston: McGill-Queen's University Press, 1996. [Authenticating Biblical Reports of Miracles (Philip Wiebe), See. 102–20, especially 113–14]

———. *Water into Wine? An Investigation of the Concept of Miracle*. Kingston: McGill-Queen's University Press, 1988. [Resurrection of Jesus, See. 8, 28, 29, 54, 116, 127, 128, 129]

Latourelle, René. *The Miracles of Jesus and the Theology of Miracles*. Translated by Matthew J. O'Connell. New York: Paulist, 1988. [The Miraculous Catch, See. 161–65]

Lawton, John Stewart. *Miracles and Revelation*. New York: Association Press, 1960. [Resurrection, appearances, See. 49, 157–58, 176–79, 183, 197–200; empty tomb, See. 177, 179, 183, 197–98, 200, 202, 254; fraud theory, See. 49–51 Jesus' predictions, See. 50,

199; narratives, See. 49, 176, 196–98, 200, nature and significance of, See. 164–65, 174–80, 188–91, 196–97, 200–205, 227, 254; Paul's evidence, See. 178; witness of, See. 50]

Lewis, C. S. *Miracles: A Preliminary Study*. New York: Macmillan, 1947. [Chapter 17 Miracles of the New Creation, See. 171–96; N.B. This book, written by an often mentioned apologist, is a must read.]

Lias, J. J. *Are Miracles Credible?* London: Hodder & Stoughton, 1883. [Chapter 11 What is the Evidence For the Scripture Miracles!, See. 198–211; N.B. Google book. This chapter should be inspected.]

Litton, E. A. *Miracles*. London, SPCK, 1868. [Chapter 5 The Foregoing Remarks Applied to the Resurrection of Christ, See. 134–64; N.B. Google book and HathiTrust. This worked should be examined.]

Lockyer, Herbert. *All the Miracles of the Bible: The Supernatural in Scripture, Its Scope and Significance*. Grand Rapids: Zondervan, 1961. [The Miracles in the Gospel, See. 237–396; The Miracle of His Resurrection, See. 381–85; The Miracles in the Acts, See. 397–454; The Miracle of Christ's Resurrection (1:3), See. 398–99; The Miracle of the Ascension (2:9–11), See. 399. Lockyer's text should be explored.]

Lodge, Oliver. *Man and the Universe: A Study of the Influence of the Advance in Scientific Knowledge Upon Our Understanding of Christianity*. London: Methuen, 1908. [The Resurrection of Christ, See. 287–92; N.B. Haithitrust.org and Google book]

London Religious Tract Society. *Magic, Pretended Miracles, and Remarkable Natural Phenomena*. London: London Religious Tract Society, 1855. [See. 181–82; N.B. Archive.org]

Loos, H. Van Der. *The Miracles of Jesus*. Leiden: Brill, 1968. [Chapter 17 The Miraculous Catches of Fish, See. 670–79]

Lunn, Arnold and J. B. S. Haldane. *Science and the Supernatural: A Correspondence Between Arnold Lunn and J. B. S. Haldane*. New York: Sheed & Ward, 1935. [See. 379]

Lyttelton, A. T. *The Place of Miracles in Religion*. London: J. Murray, 1899. [Chapter 3 Miracles in the New Testament, See. 42–80; See. 65–73; N.B. Archive.org and Google book. This work explores the miraculous catch of fishes.]

MacDonald, George. *The Miracles of Our Lord*. London: Strahan, 1870. [Chapter 11 The Resurrection, See. 260–71; N.B. Google book. Nothing substantial.]

Mackenzie, Mary Jane. *Lectures on Miracles Selected from the New Testament*. London: Printed for T. Cadell, 1823. [Lecture 11 The Resurrection of Christ, See. 246–73; N.B. Google book. Nothing substantial.]

Maitland, Brownlow. *Miracles*. London: Cassell, 1886. [See. 18, 19, 57, 79, 103, 110, 123; N.B. Google book]

McInerny, Ralph M. *Miracles: A Catholic View*. Huntington, IN: Our Sunday Visitor, 1986. [The Resurrection, See. 57–59]

Meldau, Fred John. *The Miracle Man and the Wonder Book*. Chicago: Bible Institute Colportage Assn., 1923. [Proof of the Deity of Christ from His Resurrection, See. 57–61]

Metaxas, Eric. *Miracles: What They Are, Why They Happen, and How They Can Change Your Life*. New York: Plume, 2014. [Chapter 8 The Resurrection, 95–111. N.B. The author analyzes and refutes three naturalistic explanations of Jesus's resurrection.]

Miller, Calvin. *Miracles and Wonders: How God Changes His Natural Laws to Benefit You*. New York: Warner, 2003. [Chapter 4 The Resurrection: The Queen of Miracles, See. 68–84; N.B. Nothing useful.]

Montefiore, Hugh. *The Miracles of Jesus*. London: SPCK, 2005. [Chapter 12 Resurrection Appearances, See. 105–14; N.B. Nothing substantial.]

Mountford, William. *Miracles, Past and Present*. Boston: Fields, Osgood, 1870. [Jesus and the Resurrection, See. 452–77; N.B. Google book. Nothing substantial.]

Mullin, Robert Bruce. *Miracles and the Modern Religious Imagination*. New Haven: Yale University Press, 1996. [See. 228, 235, 254]

Mundt, Phil. *A Scientific Search for Religious Truth*. Austin, TX: Bridgeway, 2007. [See. The Resurrection, 127–31; The First Century, See. 131–35]

Nash, Ronald. *Christianity and the Hellenistic World*. Dallas: Probe, 1991. [See. 265]

Newman, John Henry Cardinal. *Two Essays on Biblical and On Ecclesiastical Miracles*. London: Pickering, 1881. [See. 80, 88, 92, 351; N.B. Archive.org and Google book]

Nicholson, William R. *The Six Miracles of Calvary Unveiling the Story of the Resurrection*. Grand Rapids: Discovery House, 2001. [Chapter 5 The Undisturbed Grave Clothes of Jesus, See. 89–108; Chapter 6 Revivals to Life in the Calvary Graveyard, See. 109–27]

Padgett, Alan G. *Science and the Study of God: A Mutuality Model for Theology and Science*. Grand Rapids: Eerdmans, 2003. [See. 48, 49, 63–64, 144]

Palmer, Francis B. *The Supernatural Revealed by Nature*. Boston: Richard G. Badger, 1917. [Chapter 2 The Possibility of the Supernatural Birth and Resurrection of Jesus Not Now to be Disputed, See. 32–39; Chapter 11 The Resurrection of Jesus, 139–48. Nothing useful.]

Peacocke, Arthur. *All That Is A Naturalistic Faith for the Twenty-First Century*. Minneapolis: Fortress, 2007. [Chapter 6 Jesus of Nazareth A Naturalistic Interpretation, Jesus' Resurrection, See. 33–35]

Pearce, Zachary. *The Miracles of Jesus Vindicated: In Four Parts*. London: Printed for J. Watts In Four Parts, 1749. [Part 1 The Truth of Jesus's Resurrection from the Dead Shown from the following Arguments, See. 1–14; N.B. Google book]

Penrose, John. *A Treatise on the Evidence of the Scripture Miracles*. London: G. Woodfall, 1826. [See. 79, 98–99, 110–17, 123, 130, 46–47, 49, 57–59, 66, 263, 67–70; N.B. Archive.org and Google book]

Perry, M. C. *The Miracles and the Resurrection: Some Recent Studies*. Edited by Ian T. Ramsey, G. H. Boobyer, F. N. Davey, M. C. Perry, and Henry J. Cadbury. London: SPCK, 1964. [Chapter 4 Believing the Miracles and Preaching the Resurrection, See. 64–78. Consider examining this chapter.]

Peters, Ted. *Science, Theology, and Ethics*. Burlington, VT: Ashgate, 2002. [Resurrection of Jesus, See. 42, 89, 242, 305, 306, 309, 317]

Phipps, William E. *Paul Against Supernaturalism: The Growth of The Miraculous In Christianity*. New York: Philosophical Library, 1987. [Chapter 3 The Growth of A Materialized Resurrection, See. 73–101; N.B. This chapter should be examined.]

Polkinghorne, John. *Exploring Reality The Intertwining of Science and Religion*. 2005. New Haven: Yale University Press, 2005. [Jesus Christ, Resurrection, See. 82–88, 101, 124–25, 171–74]

———. *Science and Religion in Quest of Truth*. New Haven: Yale University Press, 2011. [Jesus Christ, appearance stories after resurrection of, See. 121–27]

———. *Serious Talk: Science and Religion in Dialogue*. Valley Forge, PA: Trinity Press International, 1995. [Chapter 7 Resurrection, See. 91–103; N.B. This chapter should be examined.]

Category IV—Miracles and Science

———. *Theology in the Context of Science.* New Haven: Yale University Press, 2009. [Resurrection, See. xxvi, 133–42; N.B. This chapter should be examined.]

Poythress, Vern S. *The Miracles of Jesus: How the Savior's Mighty Acts Serve as Signs of Redemption.* Wheaton: Crossway, 2016. [Part 4 The Resurrection of Christ and Its Applications, See. 231–37]

Religious Tract Society, The. *The Miracles of Christ: With Explanatory Observations, and Illustrations from Modern Travels.* London: Religious Tract Society. 1843. [Chapter 13 See. Miraculous Draught of Fishes John 21, See. 1–14, 206–9; N.B. Google book].

Richardson, Alan. *The Miracle Stories of the Gospels.* London: SCM, 1941. [Chapter 7 The Historical and Religious Value of the Miracle-Stories, See. 132–33]

Roberts, Michael Symmons. *The Miracles of Jesus.* Oxford: Lion Hudson, 2006. [Chapter 12 The Greatest Miracle of All?, See. 116–26; Chapter 13 Was the Tomb Empty?, See. 127–33; Chapter 14 Did the Reporters Make It All Up?, See. 136–44, Chapter 15 Did the Eyewitnesses Make It All Up?, See. 145–57; N.B. This chapter should be examined.]

Rogers, Clement F. *The Case for Miracle.* London: Society for Promoting Christian Knowledge, 1936. [Chapter 3 Non-Christian Theories of the Resurrection of Christ, See. 69–98; N.B. Rogers has collected an interesting array of non-Christian theories.]

Rogerson, John, and Bruce Kaye. *Miracles and Mysteries in the Bible.* Philadelphia: Westminster, 1978. [See. The Resurrection of Jesus]

Ross, Hugh, Kenneth R. Samples, and Mark Clark. *Lights in the Sky & Little Green Men: A Rational Christian Look at UFOs and Extraterrestrials.* Colorado Springs, CO: NavPress, 2002. [Chapter 10 The Interdimensional Hypothesis; N.B. Hugh Ross wrote this chapter.]

Rota, Michael. *Taking Pascal's Wager: Faith, Evidence, and the Abundant Life.* Downers Grove, IL: InterVarsity, 2016. [Chapter 12 Miracle or Myth, See. 165–77; N.B. Rota discusses the Minimal Facts Approach and refutes several natural explains for the reported resurrection.]

Schaaffs, Werner. *Theology, Physics, and Miracles.* Translated by Richard L. Tenfold. Washington: Canon Press, 1974. [Chapter 8 Biblical Theology Evaluated in the Light of Physics, 4. The Resurrection, See. 87–93]

Sharpe, Kevin. *Science of God Truth in the Age of Science.* Lanham, MD: Rowman & Littlefield, 2006. [Resurrection, Jesus', See. 2, 88, 227]

Smalbroke, Richard. *A Vindication of the Miracles of Our Blessed Saviour in which Mr. Woolston's Discourses on them are Particularly Examin'd, . . . By . . . Richard, Lord Bishop of St. David's. Vol. 2. In which the Three Last Discourses of Mr. Woolson are Considered.* London: Printed for James and John Knapton, 1731. [Chapter 3, See. 428–578; N.B. Google book. This work is a dated, but recommended read.]

Stackhouse, Thomas. *Fair State of the Controversy Between Mr. Woolston and his Adversaries—Containing the Substance of What He Asserts in His Six Discourses Against the Literal Sense of Our Blessed Saviour's Miracles.* London: Printed for Edward Symon, 1730. [Section 16 Of Christ's Own Resurrection, See. 251–87; N.B. Archive.org]

Stevenson, William. *A Conference Upon the Miracles of Our Blessed Saviour.* London: Printed for J&J Knapton, 1730. [Section 6 The Resurrection of Jesus Fulfilled, 295–310; N.B. Google book]

Taylor, William Francis. *Miracles: Their Physical Possibility, Moral Probability, and Historical Reality.* Liverpool: Edward Howell, 1868. [See. 28–35; N.B. Google book]

Taylor, William M. *The Gospel Miracles in Their Relation to Christ and Christianity*. New York: Anson D. F. Randolph, 1880. [Lecture 3 The Credibility of Miracles, See. 92–97; N.B. Archive.org]

———. *The Miracles Helps to Faith, Not Hindrances*. Edinburgh: William Oliphant, 1865. [Credibility of Miracles, See. 67–72; N.B. Archive.org and Google book]

———. *The Miracles of Our Savior Expounded and Illustrated*. 3rd ed. New York: C. Armstrong, 1893. [Chapter 32 The Second Miraculous Draught of Fishes (John xxi–1–16), See. 438–49; N.B. Google book]

Thompson, J. M. *Notes on Miracles in the New Testament*. London: Edward Arnold, 1912. [See. 75–76, 89–90, 110, 118, Chapter 10 The Resurrection, 161–206; N.B. Archive.org and Google book. A dated, but recommended book to examine.]

Torrance, T. *Expository Studies in St. John's Miracles*. London: James Clarke, 1938. [Chapter 10 The Second Miraculous Draught of Fishes, See. 186–205]

Trench, Richard Chenevix. *Notes on the Miracles of Our Lord*. 2nd ed. New York: D. Appleton, 1862. [Miracle 33 The Second Miraculous Draught of Fishes, See. 361–75; N.B. Archive.org and Google book]

Twelftree, Graham H. *Jesus the Miracle Worker: A Historical & Theological Study* Downers Grove, IL: InterVarsity, 1999. [Chapter 7 The Miracles of Jesus in the Fourth Gospel: The Stories, See. 215–19]

Valentine, Mary Hester. *Miracles: Guidelines For Contemporary Catholics*. Chicago, Thomas More Press, 1988. [The Great Miracle: The Resurrection, See. 55–71]

Ward, Keith. *The Big Questions in Science and Religion*. West Conshohocken, PA: Templeton Foundation Press, 2008. [Chapter 4 Do the Laws of Nature Exclude Miracles? (Are the Laws of Nature Absolute?), The Resurrection of Jesus as a Paradigmatic Miracle, See. 101–3]

Wardlaw, Ralph. *On Miracles*. New York: R. Carter, 1853. [Chapter 4 Concentration of the Principles of Our Argument on the One Great Miracle of the Resurrection of Jesus from the Dead, See. 127–66; N.B. Google book. A dated, but recommended read.]

Wendland, Johannes. *Miracles and Christianity*. Translated by H. R. Mackintosh. London: Hodder & Stoughton, 1911. [Chapter 8 Miracle and History, See. 235–40; N.B. Archive.org. Not useful.]

Whiton, James Morris. *Miracles and Supernatural Religion*. New York: Macmillan, 1903. [Chapter 8 See. 115–17; N.B. Archive.org and Gutenberg.org]

Williams, Horace Blake. *Fundamentals of Faith in the Light of Modern Thought*. New York: Abingdon, 1922. [Chapter 12 The Risen Lord, See. 167–81; N.B. Google book. A good dated source.]

Williams, T. C. *The Idea of the Miraculous: The Challenge to Science and* Religion. London: Macmillan, 1990. [Resurrection, See. 39, 207–8; 209–10]

Willits, A. A. *The Miracles of Jesus and Their Moral Lessons*. Philadelphia: Hubbard Brothers, 1881. [Chapter 24 The Second Miraculous Draught of Fishes, See. 517–28; N.B. Archive.org]

Wilson, W. D. *Miracles in Nature and in Revelation: And Especially the Great Miracle of Our Lord's Resurrection from the Dead*. New York: Thomas Whittaker, 1890. [#7 The Miracle of the Resurrection, See. 28–29; cont. 30–41; N.B. Google book]

Wright, C. J. *Miracle in History and in Modern Thought: or, Miracle and Christian Apologetic*. London: Constable, 1930. [Chapter 7 The Resurrection of Christ and the Miracle, See. 344–65; N.B. This work is a recommended read.]

Chapter 10

Miracles and Science: Con Resurrection

Bennett, James. *The Impossibility of Imposture in the Miracles of Scripture*. London: Westley & Davis, 1831. [See. 31–33, 200–201, 207, 215–16; N.B. Google book. Nothing useful.]

Brooke, John Hanley. *Science and Religion: Some Historical Perspectives*. Cambridge: Cambridge University Press, 1991. [See. 264–70]

Cassels, Walter R. *Supernatural Religion . . . Popular edition, carefully* revised. London: Watts, 1902. [Part 6 The Resurrection and Ascension, See. 801–901; N.B. Archive.org and Google book. *Supernatural Religion* is a significant, dated source that was subject to much discussion after it was published.]

Chubb, Thomas. *A Discourse of Miracles: Considered as Evidence to Prove the Divine Original of a Revelation. In Which Several Mistakes are Rectified, and Deficiencies Supplied, in Mr. Tho. Chubb's Late Discourse on the Same Subject . . .* London: Printed for J. Noon, 1742. [See. 64, 67, 73, 79–85; N.B. Google book and HathiTrust. An interesting discourse.]

Clements, Tad S. *Science versus Religion*. Buffalo: Prometheus, 1990. [Resurrection of Christ, See. 192–95; N.B. Not useful.]

Coyne, Jerry A. *Faith Versus Fact: Why Science and Religion Are Incompatible*. New York: Penguin, 2015. [Falsifiability, See. 44–45, 72–74, 76]

Darrow, Floyd L. *Miracles, A Modern View*. Indianapolis: Bobbs-Merrill, 1926. [Chapter 4 Miracles of the New Testament, See. The Resurrection and the Ascension, See. 128–35; Pagan Parallels to the Resurrection, See. 135–40; The Testimony of Paul, See. 140–42; One Thing Certain, See. 142–45]

Edis, Taner. *The Ghost in the Universe: God in Light of Modern Science*. Amherst, NY: Prometheus, 2002. [Chapter 5 God Incarnate. Myth Making, See. 155–65; The Risen Lord, See. 166–78; N.B. Interesting.]

Emerton, Ephraim. *Unitarian Thought*. New York: Macmillan, 1911. [Chapter 2 Miracle, See. 29–58; especially 52; N.B. Archive.org, Google book, and HathiTrust. Not useful.]

Harwood, Philip. *German Anti-Supernaturalism: Six Lectures on Strauss's "Life of Jesus."* London: Charles Fox, 1841. [Lecture 5 . . . History of the Death and Resurrection of Jesus, See. 71–92; N.B. Archive.org, Google book, and HathiTrust. Not helpful]

Hume, David. *Philosophical Essays Concerning Human* Understanding. London: Printed for M. Cooper, 1751. [Section 10 Of Miracles, See. 69–82; N.B. This work does not specifically discuss Jesus's resurrection. However, it discusses material that directly relates to the claims of that event.]

Huxley, Thomas H. *The Evidence of the Miracle of the Resurrection*. January 11, 1876. [This seven page paper was presented before the Metaphysical Society; N.B. Google book. Not useful.]

Hyslop, James H. *Psychical, Research and the Resurrection*. Boston: Small, Maynard, 1908. [Chapter 12 Psychical Research and the Resurrection, See. 352–409; N.B. Google book]

May, Joseph. *The Miracles and Myths of the New Testament with Other Essays and Sermons*. Boston: George H. Ellis, 1901. [Chapter 3 The Myth of the Resurrection of Jesus, See. 58–90; N.B. Google book and HathiTrust]

Nickell, Joe. *The Science of Miracles: Investigating the Incredible*. Amherst, NY: Prometheus, 2013. [Chapter 33 Jesus' Resurrection Apparitions, See. 225–32]

Perakh, Mark. *Unintelligent Design*. Amherst, NY: Prometheus, 2004. [Chapter 7 Show Me Proof: A Preacher in a Skeptic's Court, See. 238–41]

Powell, Baden. *The Order of Nature Considered in Reference to the Claims of Revelation*. London: Longman, 1859. [Resurrection of Christ, Naturalistic view, See. 329–31; The Mythic Theory of Strauss, See. 345–48; Other Views, See. 362, 370, 431, 457; N.B. Google book]

Schapiro, Lawrence A. *The Miracle Myth: Why Belief in the Resurrection and the Supernatural Is Unjustified*. New York City: Columbia University Press, 2016. [Chapter 6 Jesus's Resurrection, See. 109–36; N.B. Gary Habermas (2018), in *The Journal of Theological Studies* 69 critically reviewed this book.]

Schlagel, Richard H. *Seeking the Truth: How Science Has Prevailed over the Supernatural Worldview*. Amherst, NY: Humanity, 2010. [The Gospel's Authenticity and the Quest for the Historical Jesus, See. 174–91; N.B. The author emphasizes the numerous discrepancies found throughout the NT narratives and how little we actual know about the historical Jesus.]

———. *The Vanquished Gods: Science, Religion, and the Nature of Belief*. Amherst, NY: Prometheus, 2001. [The Christos Legend, See. 157–67]

Spooner, Lysander. *The Deist's Reply to the Alleged Supernatural Evidences of Christianity*. Boston: [sn], 1836. [Chapter 5, See. 50–62; N.B. Archive.org. An excellent reading!]

Tuckett, Ivor. *The Evidence for the Supernatural: A Critical Study Made with "Common Sense."* London: Kegan Paul, Trench Trübner, 1911. [Chapter 6 Miracles, See. 170–75; N.B. Archive.org]

Washburn, Lemuel K. *The Miracles of Jesus: And Other Essays*. New York: Truth Seeker, 1917. [See. 13–15; N.B. Google book and HathiTrust]

Whitney, Loren Harper. *A Question of Miracles: Parallels in the Lives of Buddha and Jesus: A Critical Examination of the So-Called Miracles Surrounding the Birth, Life and Death of Buddha and Jesus and the Achievements of Other Miracle-Workers . . .* Chicago: Library Shelf, 1908. [Chapter 24 Was It A Resurrection or Was It Resuscitation?, See. 281–91; Chapter 25 The Miracles of Jesus' Appearance to the Disciples, See. 292–99; Chapter 29 Examination of Luke Resumed, See. 331–39; N.B. Archive.org, Google book, and HathiTrust. The author employs a question and answer format. The text is not very useful.]

Woolston, Thomas. *A Discourse on the Miracles of Our Saviour, in View of the Present Controversy between Infidels and Apostates*. 2nd ed. London: Printed for the Author, and Sold by Him . . . and by the Booksellers of London and Westminster, 1727. [See. A Sixth Discourse on the Miracles of Our Saviour, &c. N.B. Google book, 71 pages]

———. *A Sixth Discourse on the Miracles of Our Saviour, in View of the Present Controversy Between Infidels and Apostates.* London: Printed for the Author, 1729. [71 pages; N.B. Google book. Woolston, a deist, died in prison because of this book.]

Young, Matt. *No Sense of Obligation Science and Religion in an Impersonal Universe.* Bloomington, IN: 1st Books Library, 2001. [See. 138–47]

Category V

Jesus's Life: Biographies and Historicity of Christ

CHAPTER 11

Jesus's Life: Biographies and Historicity of Christ: Pro Resurrection

Abbott, Lyman. *Jesus of Nazareth: His Life and Teachings; Founded on the Four Gospels, and Illustrated by Reference to the Manners, Customs, Religious Beliefs, and Political Institutions of His Times.* New York: Harper, 1882. [Chapter 36 See. 499–509; N.B. Archive.org, Google book, and HathiTrust]

Adams, Charles C. *The Life of our Lord Jesus Christ.* New York: C. F. Roper, 1878. [Chapters 44–49, See. 349–407; N.B. Google book]

Alden, Isabella McDonald. *The Prince of Peace: or, The Beautiful Life of Jesus . . . from the Manger to the Throne.* Boston: Lothrop, 1890. [Chapters 69–72, See. 526–61; N.B. Google book]

Alexander, Gross. *The Son of Man: Studies in His life and Teachings.* Nashville: Publishing House of the M.E. Church, South, 1900. [Chapter 14 The Resurrection of Jesus, See. 327–71; N.B. Google book]

Allard, Daniel. *War Against War or The Joys of Peace.* Boston: Stratford, 1926. [Chapters 50–53, See. 141–56]

Allen, Charles Livingstone. *The Life of Christ.* Old Tappan, NJ: Revell, 1962. [Chapter 6 The Forty Days, See. 150–57]

Allen, Charlotte. *The Human Christ: the Search for the Historical Jesus.* New York: Free Press, 1998. [Resurrection of Jesus, See. 50, 55, 73, 76, 78, 79, 107–8, 134–35, 137, 139, 142, 145, 156, 167, 169, 175, 231, 277]

Allen, David M. *The Historical Character of Jesus: Canonical Insights from Outside the Gospels.* Minneapolis: Fortress, 2014. [Exaltation of, See. 39, 78–79, 83, 90, 108, 118; resurrection of, See. 8, 16–17, 25–27, 29, 38–39, 44, 47, 49, 54–55, 75–76, 79–80, 84, 86, 89–90, 108–10, 113, 118 126, 135, 147, 158]

Allen, Ronald J. *The Life of Jesus for Today.* Louisville: Westminster John Knox, 2008. [Chapter 9 The Resurrection: Definitive Sign of the Realm, See. 74–81]

Allen, Thomas. *The Travels of Our Lord and Saviour Jesus Christ from His Infancy to His Ascension into Heaven.* London: Printed for A. Bettesworth & C. Hitch, 1735. [Resurrection of Christ, See. 83–84; The Ascension of Our Savior, See. 85–87; N.B. Google book]

Allison, Dale C. *Constructing Jesus: Memory, Imagination, and History.* Grand Rapids: Baker Academic, 2013. [God Raised Jesus from the Dead, See. 55–59; Function of the

Resurrection, See. 240–44; Christ Jesus, Who Died . . . Is at the Right Hand of God, See. 247–51; N.B. This work is a scholarly, well-referenced text to read.]

Anderson, Charles C. *The Historical Jesus: A Continuing Quest*. Grand Rapids: Eerdmans, 1972. [Chapter 4 The Resurrection of Jesus, See. 156–78]

Anderson, Hugh. *Jesus and Christian Origins: A Commentary on Modern Viewpoints*. New York: Oxford University Press, 1964. [Chapter 5 The Resurrection of Jesus Christ, See. 185–240; N.B. Anderson presents a healthy, overview of the literature.]

Anderson, Norman. *Jesus Christ: the Witness of History*. Downers Grove, IL: InterVarsity, 1985. [Chapter 4 The Empty Tomb: What Really Happened?, See. 111–57]

Andrews, Samuel J. *The Life of Our Lord Upon the Earth: In Its Historical, Chronological and Geographical Relations*. New York: Scribner's Sons, 1903. [Part 108 From the Resurrection to the Ascension, See. 589–639; N.B. Archive.org, Google book, and HathiTrust]

Angus, Joseph. *Christ Our Life: In its Origin, Law, and End*. London: James Nisbet, 1853. [The Resurrection of Our Lord, and Lessons Connected With It, See. 275–83; N.B. Google book]

Angus, William. *The Life of Our Lord and Saviour, Jesus Christ, from Campbell's Translation of the Gospels*. 2nd ed. Glasgow: Printed by James Hedderwick, 1814. [Chapter 28 The Resurrection, See. 156–65; N.B. Google book]

Armstrong, Garner Ted. *The Real Jesus*. Mission, KS: Sheed Andrews & McMeel, 1977. [Chapter 20 A Step Through Stone, See. 256–80]

Atwater, John Birdseye. *The Real Jesus of the Four Gospels*. Minneapolis: n.p., 1922. [The Resurrection, See. 54–61; N.B. Google book and Gutenberg.org]

Aurelio, John. *Myth Man: A Storyteller's Jesus*. New York: Crossroad, 1991. [Chapter 6 The Resurrection of Jesus, See. 190–218]

Austin, Mary. *The Man Jesus: Being a Brief Account of the Life and Teaching of the Prophet of Nazareth*. New York: Harper & Brothers, 1915. [See. 173–91; N.B. Google book]

Baker, Septina. *Life of Our Master Christ Jesus*. San Francisco: California Press, 1925. [Chapter 34 Resurrection, See. 226–31; Chapter 35 Re-appearance of Jesus, See. 232–37; Chapter 36 Ascension, See. 238–43]

Baldwin, Louis J. *Jesus of Galilee: His Story in Everyday Language*. Valley Forge, PA: Judson Press, 1979. [Chapter 8 Victory, See. 125–32]

Barclay, William. *Crucified and Crowned*. London: SCM, 1961. [Chapter 11 The Resurrection, See. 137–70; Chapter 12 The Ascension, See. 171–78]

———. *Discovering Jesus*. Louisville: Westminster John Knox, 2000. [Chapter 5 Triumph, See. 60–71]

———. *Jesus of Nazareth*. London: Collins, 1977. [The Prophecy Fulfilled, See. 233–49]

———. *The Life of Jesus for Everyman*. New York: Harper & Row, 1965. [Chapter 5 Triumph, See. 69–80]

———. *The Mind of Jesus*. SanFrancisco: HarperSanFrancisco, 1994. [Chapter 11 The Resurrection, See. 137–70; Chapter 12 The Ascension, See. 171–78]

———. *The Mind of Jesus*. New York: Harper, 1961. [Chapter 28 The Resurrection, See. 287–314; Chapter 29 The Ascension, See. 315–21]

———. *We Have Seen the Lord!: The Passion and Resurrection of Jesus Christ*. Louisville: Westminster John Knox, 1998. [See. 112–23]

Barker, Gregory A., and Stephen E. Gregg, eds. *Jesus Beyond Christianity: The Classic Texts*. Oxford: Oxford University Press, 2011. [See. 43–44, 61–62, 93–94, 237–38, 247]

Barnett, Paul. *Finding the Historical Christ*. Grand Rapids: Eerdmans, 2009. [Chapter 1 The Postresurrection Church and the Preresurrection Christ, See. 1–10]

———. *Jesus and the Logic of History*. Leicester: Apollos, 1997. [Excursus The Resurrection of Jesus from the Dead, See. 128–31]

Barnett, Walter. *Jesus The Story of His Life*. Chicago: Nelson-Hall, 1975. [Chapter 11 The Resurrection, See. 203–14]

Barrows, Charles H. *The Personality of Jesus*. Boston: Houghton Mifflin, 1906. [Chapter 10 The Personality of the Risen Lord, See. 231–47; N.B. Google book]

Bartlett, Clarence. *As a Lawyer Sees Jesus: A Logical Analysis of the Scriptural and Historical Record*. New York: Greenwich Book, 1960. [Part 2 The Evidence, See. 114–29; Part 3 Weighing the Evidence, See. 130–69; Part 4 Witnesses Corroborated by Collateral Facts, See. 170–97]

Barton, George A. *Jesus of Nazareth: A Biography*. New York: Macmillan, 1924. [Book 6 The Passion and Resurrection Chapter 62 The Resurrection, See. 390–92; N.B. Archive.org, Google book, and HathiTrust]

Barton, William E. *Day By Day With Jesus: A Book for Holy Week*. Oak Park, IL: Puritan Press, 1913. [See. 303–48; N.B. Archive.org]

———. *Jesus of Nazareth: The Story of His Life and the Scenes of His Ministry, with a Chapter on the Christ of Art*. Boston: Pilgrim Press, 1903. [Chapter 41 Easter, See. 416–29; Chapter 42 The Forty Days and the Future, See. 43–43; N.B. Archive.org]

Barton, William E., et al. *His Life: A Complete Story in the Words of the Four Gospels*. Chicago: Hope, 1906. [Chapter 7 His Resurrection, See. 216–26; N.B. Archive.org, Google book, and Gutenberg.org]

———. *The Week of Our Lord's Passion*. Chicago: Hope, 1906. [Easter Sunday, See. 205–10; After the Resurrection, See. 211–14; N.B. Google book, Gutenberg.org, and HathiTrust]

Bass, John. *The Light of Men: An Interpretation*. Cedar Rapids, IA: Torch Press, 1916. [See. 180–89; N.B. Archive.org]

Battenhouse, Henry Martin. *Christ in the Gospels: An Introduction to His Life and Its Meaning*. New York: Ronald Press, 1952. [Chapter 29 The Living Christ . . . The Story of the Resurrection, See. 307–12]

Bauman, Edward W. *The Life and Teaching of Jesus*. Philadelphia: Westminster, 1960. [Chapter 8 Resurrection, See. 109–21]

Baxter, Margaret. *Jesus Christ: His Life and His Church*. Philadelphia: Westminster, 1987. [Chapter 4 The Central Events. See. Resurrection and Ascension, See. 52–57]

Beck, William F. *The Christ of the Gospels*. Saint Louis: Concordia, 1959. [Chapter 12 Our Risen Saviour, See. 202–12]

Beiler, Irwin Ross. *Studies in the Life of Jesus*. New York: Abingdon-Cokesbury, 1936. [Chapter 28 Not Dead, But Alive, See. 276–82]

Belser, J. E. *History of the Passion, Death, and Glorification of Our Saviour Jesus Christ: An Exegetical Commentary*. St Louis: B. Herder, 1929. [Part 3 The Resurrection and Manifestations of the Risen Lord, and His Ascension Into Heaven, See. 573–658]

Benedict XVI, Pope. *Jesus of Nazareth: Part Two: Holy Week From the Entrance into Jerusalem to the Resurrection*. San Francisco: Ignatius Press, 2011. [Chapter 9 Jesus' Resurrection From the Dead, See. 241–77; Epilogue, He Ascended into Heaven, See. 278–93; N.B. Joseph Ratzinger Pope Benedict XVI.]

Bennett, James. *Lectures on the History of Jesus Christ.* 2nd ed. Vol. 2. London: Published by F. Westley & A. H. Davis, 1825. [Lectures 93–97, See. 513–84, 597–98; N.B. Archive.org and Google book]

Benson, C. *The Chronology of Our Saviour's Life: or An Inquiry into the True Time of the Birth, Baptism, and Crucifixion, of Jesus Christ.* Cambridge: Printed at the University Press, 1819. [Section 2, See. 293–338; N.B. Archive.org and Google book]

Berguer, Georges. *Some Aspects of the Life of Jesus from the Psychological and Psychoanalytic Point of View.* Translated by Eleanor Stimson Brooks and Van Wyck Brooks. New York: Harcourt, Brace, 1923. [Chapter 9 The Resurrection, See. 270–94; N.B. Archive.org]

Bernard, Henry Norris. *The Mental Characteristics of the Lord Jesus Christ.* New York: Thomas Whittaker, 1888. [Chapter 14 The Manifestations of the Risen Christ, See. 272–310; N.B. Archive.org and Google book]

Bernard, Pierre R. *The Mystery of Jesus.* Vol. 2. Translated by Francis V. Manning. Staten Island, NY: Alba House, 1966. [Chapter 11 The Resurrection of the Lord, See. 447–520]

Berthe, Augustin. *Jesus Christ, His Life, His Passion, His Triumph.* Translated by Ferreol Girardey. St. Louis: Herder, 1914. [Book Eighth. The Triumph, Chapters 1–4, See. 426–58]

Bessler, Joseph A. *A Scandalous Jesus: How Three Historic Quests Changed Theology for the Better.* Salem, OR: Polebridge, 2013. [Resurrection, See. 31, 37, 39, 55–58, 65–67, 69, 83, 84, 113, 132, 134, 150, 151, 180, 216, 227]

Bethune-Baker, J. F. *Early Traditions About Jesus.* New York: Macmillan, 1930. Chapter 8 The Crucifixion and the Resurrection, See. 157–70]

Bird, Michael F. *The Gospel of the Lord: How the Early Church Wrote the Story of Jesus.* Grand Rapids: Eerdmans, 2014. [See. 16–20, 23–25]

Bird, Robert. *Jesus, the Carpenter of Nazareth . . . By a Layman.* 2nd ed. Glasgow: Scribner's Sons, 1891. [See. 466–83; N.B. Robert Bird's name does not appear in this text. His name appears in the 7th edition, 1892 published by Kegan Paul, Trench, Trübner available on Archive.org, Google book, and HathiTrust]

Bisset, William. *The Entire History of Our Lord Jesus Christ; or the Gospel by the Four Evangelists, Given in Their Own Words, According to the English Version; and Digested into One Narrative.* Dublin: Porter, 1807. [Part 7 The Transactions of Forty Days from the Resurrection to the Ascension, See. 313–29, N.B. Google book]

Blomfield, Ezekiel. *The Life of Jesus Christ with a History of the First Propogation of the Christian Religion, and the Lives of the Most Eminent Persons Mentioned in the New Testament.* Bungay, 1809. [Chapter 15, See. 362–89; N.B. Google book]

Blunt, Henry. *Lectures Upon the History of Our Lord and Saviour Jesus Christ.* Philadelphia: Willis P. Hazard, 1857. [Lecture 8 St. John xx. 13, See. 356–60; N.B. Archive.org, Google book, and HathiTrust]

Bock, Darrell L. *Jesus According to Scripture: Restoring the Portrait from the Gospels.* Grand Rapids: Baker Academic, 2002. [Chapter 11 The Passion Week: Controversy, Prediction of Judgment and Return, Trial, Death and Resurrection, See. 394–405; Chapter 14 The Book of Glory, See. 542–57]

———. *Studying the Historical Jesus: A Guide to Sources and Methods.* Grand Rapids: Baker Academic, 2002. [The Year of Jesus' Death, See. 75–77]

———. *Who is Jesus? Linking the Historical Jesus with the Christ of Faith.* New York: Howard, 2012. [Chapter 13 The Women Discover an Empty Tomb: Fabrication, Metaphor, or Something More?, See. 190–210]

Bock, Darrell L., and Daniel B. Wallace. *Dethroning Jesus: Exposing Popular Culture's Quest to Unseat the Biblical Christ.* Nashville: Nelson, 2008. [Claim 6 Jesus' Tomb Has Been Found, and His Resurrection and Ascension Did Not Involve a Physical Departure, See. 193–213; also See. 220–23]

Bock, Emil. *The Three Years: the Life of Christ Between Baptism and Ascension.* Edinburgh: Floris, 1987. [See. 233–85]

Bockmuehl, Markus N. A. *This Jesus: Martyr, Lord, Messiah.* Edinburgh: T&T Clark, 1994. [Chapter 4 Conclusion. Resurrection and the Aims of Jesus, See. 96–97; Chapter 7 Why Was Jesus Exalted to Heaven?, See. 145–63]

Bonaventure. *The Life of Christ.* Translated by W. H. Hutchings. London. Rivingtons, 1881. [Chapters 86–97 Of the Lord's Resurrection—The Ascension of Our Lord, See. 296–327; N.B. Google book]

———. *Meditations on the Life of Christ; an Illustrated Manuscript of the Fourteenth Century.* Edited by Rosalie Green. Translated by Isa Ragusa. Princeton: Princeton University Press, 1961. [Chapters 87–97, See. 359–84]

Bond, Helen K. *The Historical Jesus: A Guide for the Perplexed.* London: T&T Clark, 2013. [Chapter 13 Resurrection, See. 166–74]

Bonforte, John. *The Rebellious Galilean.* New York: Philosophical Library, 1982. [Chapter 44 The Resurrection, See. 310–19]

Bovon, François. *The Last Days of Jesus.* Translated by Kristin Hennessy. Louisville: Westminster John Knox, 2006. [Chapter 5 Conclusion, See. 61–69]

Bornhäeuser, Karl. *The Death and Resurrection of Jesus Christ: The Only Attempt so far at an Adequate Exegesis of these Supreme Facts of the Christian Truth as Recorded in the Gospels, Made by the Author with Consummate Scholarship and Reverence for the Inspired Word of God.* Translated by A. Rumpus. Bangalore: C.L.S. Press, 1958. [264 pages]

Bornkamm, Günther. *Jesus of Nazareth.* Translated by Irene McLuskey and Fraser McLuskey. New York: Harper & Brothers, 1960. [The Resurrection, See. 180–86]

Bosley, Harold A. *The Character of Christ.* Nashville: Abingdon, 1967. [Chapter 7 Triumph, See. 125–43]

———. *The Mind of Christ.* Nashville: Abingdon, 1966. [Chapter 7 Why Did He Live Again? Scripture: 1 Corinthians 15:1–20, See. 124–42]

Bosworth, Edward I. *The Life and Teaching of Jesus According to the First Three Gospels.* New York: Macmillan, 1926. [Chapter 38 The Resurrection of Jesus, See. 395–406; N.B. HathiTrust]

———. *Studies in the Life of Jesus Christ.* New York: International Committee of Young Men's Christian Associations, 1909. [Study 23 The Resurrection, See. 186–94; Study 30 See. 256–58; N.B. Archive.org, Google book, and HathiTrust]

Bourgeault, Cynthia. *The Wisdom Jesus: Transforming Heart and Mind— A New Perspective on Christ and His Message.* Boston: Shambhala, 2008. [Part 2 The Mysteries of Jesus. Chapter 11 The Great Easter Fast, See. 125–37]

Bowen, Clayton Raymond. *The Gospel of Jesus: Critically Reconstructed from the Earliest Sources.* Boston: Beacon, 1916. [Appendix. Mark's Resurrection Story, Matthew's

Resurrection Story, Luke's Resurrection Story, See. 127-33; N.B. Archive.org and Google book. This source is a dated, but good reading.]

Bowie, Walter Russell. *The Master: A Life of Jesus Christ*. New York: Scribner's Sons, 1958. [Chapter 17 Victory, See. 307-22]

Boyd, Gregory A. *Jesus Under Siege*. Wheaton, IL: Victor, 1995. [Chapter 5 Devoured by Dogs? What Became of the Crucified One?, See. 63-85]

Braden, Clark. *The Gross Errors of Popular Teaching in Regard to the Dates of the Birth of Christ and of Events Connected with His Early History, and in Regard to the Dates of his Arrest; the Trials; the Crucifixion; the Burial; the Resurrection, and the Ascension of Christ*. Cairo, IL: Author, 1902. [See. 104-66; N.B. Archive.org]

Bradley, Samuel Carlyle. *Jesus of Nazareth: A Life*. Sherman, French: Boston, 1908. [Chapter 71 The Resurrection, See. 561-65; Chapter 71 Obdurate, See. 566-72; Chapter 72 Faithful, See. 573-75; N.B. Archive.org and Google book]

Briggs, Charles Augustus. *New Light on the Life of Jesus*. New York: Scribner's Sons, 1904. [Chapter 10 The Forty Days of the Risen Jesus, See. 110-24; N.B. Archive.org and HathiTrust]

Brot, Keith A. La. *The Nazarene*. New York: Vantage Press, 1992. [Chapter 8 Jesus Lives!, See. 139-51]

Brouwer, Sigmund. *Can the Real Jesus Still Be Found?* Eugene, OR: Harvest House, 2000. [The Resurrection, See. 83-93]

Brown, John. *The Self-Interpreting Bible, Containing the Old and New Testaments*. Edinburgh: Hutchison & Brookman, 1831. [See. 994-95; 1015-16; 1052-54; 1086-88; 1088-89; 1170-71; N.B. Google book]

Brown, S. Kent, et al. *Beholding Salvation: The Life of Christ in Word and Image*. Salt Lake City, UT: Deseret Book, 2006. [Chapter 14 Resurrection, See. 95-102; Chapter 15 The First Vision, See. 103-8]

Brown, Thomas (ca. 1820). *The Self-Explanatory History and Life of our Blessed Lord and Saviour Jesus Christ*. London: T. Kelly, 1830. [Chapter 9 The Transactions of Forty Days, from the Day of the Resurrection of Jesus till his Ascension into Heaven, See. 424- 47; N.B. Google book]

Brown, Thomas, Gent. of Blackheath (ca.1770). *The Evangelical History of Our Lord and Saviour Jesus Christ*. London: Printed for J. Buckland, 1807. [See. 587-612; N.B. Google book]

Browne, Sylvia. *The Mystical Life of Jesus: An Uncommon Perspective on the Life of Christ*. New York: Dutton, 2006. [Chapter 7 The Resurrection—A Plan for Christ's Survival, See. 165-94]

Bruckberger, R. L. *The History of Jesus Christ*. New York: Viking, 1965. [Part 4 Chapter 24 The Resurrection, See. 389-448; Chapter 25 The Ascension, See. 449-59]

Bruggen, Jakob van. *Christ on Earth: The Gospel Narratives as History*. Translated by Nancy Forest-Flier. Grand Rapids: Baker, 1998. [Chapter 17 Burial, Resurrection, and Ascension, See. 267-87]

Bryan, William Jennings. *Christ and His Companions, Famous Figures of the New Testament*. New York: Revell, 1925. [Chapter 26 Christ Risen!, See. 218-26; Chapter 27 Christ After Resurrection, See. 227-35; Chapter 28 Christ and the Great Commission, See. 236-44]

Bryant, Wilbur Franklin. *The Historical Man of Nazareth*. Lincoln, NE, J. North, 1908. [See. 82-85; N.B. Archive.org and HathiTrust]

Buck, D. D. *The Closing Scenes of the Life of Christ*. Philadelphia: Lippincott, 1869. [Part Eighth Time: Forty Days—from the Resurrection to the Ascension, See. 230–52; N.B. Archive.org and HathiTrust]

Buckham, Allan, et al. *Life of Christ*. Part 2. Kisumu, Kenya: Evangel Publishing House, 1978. [See. 221–42]

Burgess, Isaac B. *The Life of Christ: For the Use of Classes in Secondary Schools and in the Secondary Division of the Sunday School*. Chicago: University of Chicago Press, 1908. [Part 9 The Forty Days From the Resurrection Until the Ascension, See. 280–300; N.B. Google book and HathiTrust]

Burkitt, F. C. *Jesus Christ: An Historical Outline*. London: Blackie, 1932. [Crucifixion and Resurrection, See. 55–59]

Burns, J. *The Christian's Sketch Book*. 2nd ed. London: Simpkin & Marshall, 1829. [The Resurrection of Christ, See. 104–8; The Ascension of Christ, See. 108–19; N.B. Google book]

Burton, Ernest DeWitt, and Shailer Mathews. *Constructive Studies in The Life of Christ: An Aid to Historical Study and a Condensed Commentary on the Gospels*. 3rd ed. Chicago: University of Chicago Press, 1900. [Part 9 The Forty Days. Chapter 35 The Appearances of Jesus After His Resurrection, See. 273–95; N.B. Archive.org, Google book, and HathiTrust]

Businger, L. C. *The Life of Our Lord and Saviour Jesus Christ*. Edited by John E. Mullett. New York: Benziger, 1913. [Sixth Part. The Triumph of Jesus Christ. His Mysterious and Miraculous Life in His Church, See. 402–39; N.B. Google book]

Butler, J. Glentworth. *The Fourfold Gospel: The Four Gospels, Consolidated without Alteration in a Continuous Narrative, Presenting the Life of Christ in the Order of Its Events. The Text, Arranged in Sections, Taken from "The Bible Work,"* Vol. 1. New York: Butler Bible-Work, 1892. [Sections 160–66; See. 189–98; N.B. Google book]

Buttrick, David. *The Mystery and the Passion*. Minneapolis: Fortress, 1992. [The Reality of the Resurrection, See. 15–91; N.B. This book is worth examining.]

Byung-Mu, Ahn. *Jesus of Galilee*. Hong Kong: Christian Conference of Asia, 2004. [Chapter 12 Minjung Arise: The Story of the Resurrection, See. 247–60]

Cable, John H. *Christ in the Four Gospels*. New York: Christian Alliance, 1926. [Forty Days, See. 349–66]

Cadman, Jas P. *Christ in the Gospels, or, The Life of Our Lord in the Words of the Evangelists*. 5th ed. Chicago: American Publication Society of Hebrew, 1886. [Part 10 Christ's Resurrection: His Subsequent Appliances And Ascension. The Great Forty Days, See. 341–58; N.B. Archive.org, Google book, and HathiTrust]

Cadoux, Cecil John. *The Life of Jesus*. West Drayton, Moddlesex: Penguin, 1948. [The Resurrection, See. 206–7]

Cahill, Thomas. *Desire of the Everlasting Hills: The World Before and After Jesus*. New York: Nan A. Talese, 1999. [Post-resurrection appearances, See. 111, 220–21, 245; resurrection, See. 108–11, 123, 124, 131, 132, 192, 208, 217–19, 247, 260, 323]

Campbell, R. J. *The Life of Christ*. New York: Appleton, 1921. [He Is Risen, See. 396–417; N.B. Archive.org and HathiTrust]

Campbell, Robert Allen. *The Four Gospels in One, Containing Every Statement in Matthew, Mark, Luke and John, in Exactly the Words of the Authorized Version*. 2nd ed. St. Louis: H. W. Brand, 1875. [Chapter 10 Christ's Resurrection, His Subsequent Appearances and Ascension, See. 269–83; N.B. Archive.org, Google book, and HathiTrust]

Category V—Jesus's Life: Biographies and Historicity of Christ

Cannon, Delores. *Jesus and the Essenes.* Huntsville, AR: Ozark Mountain, 2000. [Chapter 25 The Crucifixion and Resurrection, See. 249–64; Chapter 26 The Purpose of the Crucifixion and Resurrection, See. 265–69; N.B. This text declares "Eyewitness accounts of the missing years of Jesus, the portions that have been removed from the Bible, and the community of the Essenes at Qumran. The information was gained through regressive hypnosis, conducted by Delores Cannon."]

Card, Michael. *Immanuel: Reflections on the Life of Christ.* Nashville: Nelson, 1990. [See. 195–97]

Carey, S. Pearce. *Jesus.* London: Hodder & Stoughton, 1939. [Chapter 5 The New Beginnings, See. 225–46; also See. 15, 44, 104, 111, 170, 193]

Carrington, Philip. *Our Lord and Saviour: His Life and Teachings.* Greenwich, CT: Seabury, 1958. [Chapter 12 Easter Day, See. 126–35]

Carroll, Patrick J. *The Man-God: A Life of Jesus.* Chicago: Scott, Foresman, 1927. [Chapter 30 The Resurrection and Afterwards, See. 323–35]

Cartledge, Samuel A. *Jesus of Fact and Faith: Studies in the Life of Christ.* Grand Rapids: Eerdmans, 1968. [Chapter 11 The Resurrection, See. 145–56]

Case, Shirley Jackson. *The Historicity of Jesus.* Chicago: University of Chicago Press, 1912. [See. 6, 15, 16, 17, 52, 55, 129, 144, 146, 149, 155, 160, 165, 174, 175, 194, 224, 226, 229, 234, 235, 239, 240, 257, 265, 266, 275, 276, 277, 278, 279, 280, 311, 334, 335; N.B. Archive.org and Google book]

———. *Jesus: A New Biography.* Chicago: University of Chicago Press, 1927. [See. 49–50]

Casey, Maurice. *Jesus: Evidence and Argument or Mythicist Myths?* London: Bloomsbury Academic, 2014. [See. 94, 115, 116, 134, 141, 142, 230–32]

Caspari, Charles Edward. *A Chronological and Geographical Introduction to the Life of Christ.* Translated by Maurice J. Evans. Edinburgh: T&T Clark, 1876. [Chapter 10 History of the Resurrection of Christ, See. 235–428; Chapter 11 Critical Review of the History of the Resurrection, See. 248–55; N.B. Google book and Archive.org]

Cassels, Louis. *This Man is Good News— A Newsman Reports on Jesus Christ.* Guildford: Lutterworth, 1974. [Chapter 12 A mighty act!, See. 85–90]

———. *The Real Jesus: How He Lived and What He Taught.* Garden City, NY: Doubleday, 1968. [The Resurrection, See. 111–17]

Cell, Charles W. *Jesus the Divine Layman: God's Gift to Humanity.* Riverside, CA: Quinn & Boden, 1941. [Chapter 16 The Resurrection and Ascension of Jesus, See. 179]

Chadwick, John White. *The Man Jesus: A Course of Lectures.* Boston: Roberts Brothers, 1881. [Chapter 6 The Resurrection, See. 187–221; N.B. Archive.org, Google book, and HathiTrust]

Chapman, Edwin. *Life of Our Lord and Savior Jesus Christ.* London: J. Green, 1840. [Chapter 27 The Resurrection, See. 127–30; Chapter 28 Further Manifestations of Christ, See. 130–33; Chapter 29 The Ascension, See. 134; N.B. Google book]

Charlesworth, James H. *The Historical Jesus: An Essential Guide.* Nashville: Abingdon, 2008. [Chapter 9 Jesus' Crucifixion and Resurrection, See. 105–18]

———. *Jesus Within Judaism: New Light from Exciting Archaeological Discoveries.* New York: Doubleday, 1988. [See. 11, 12, 14, 20, 21, 24, 33–34, 92, 94, 125, 159n.27]

Cheney, Johnston M. *The Life of Christ in Stereo: The Four Gospels Combined as One.* Portland, OR: Western Baptist Seminary Press, 1969. [Chapter 21 Risen Victorious, See. 204–14]

Church, Leslie F. *The Life of Jesus: His journeying and His Triumph*. London: Epworth, 1956. [Part 10 The Victory, See. 235–46]

Church of Jesus Christ of Latter-Day Saints, The. *The Life and Teachings of Jesus and his Apostles: Course Manual (Rel. 211-212)*. Salt Lake City: Church of Jesus Christ of Latter-day Saints, 1979. [Chapter 27 "He Is Risen!," See. 190–96; Chapter 28 "I Know That He Lives," See. 198–205]

Clark, Braden. *The Gross Errors of Popular Teaching in Regard to the Dates of the Birth of Christ and of Events Connected with His Early History, and in Regard to the Dates of the Arrest, the Trials, the Crucifixion, the Burial, the Resurrection, and the Ascension*. Cairo, IL: Author, 1902. [See. 210–20, 224–25, 253–63; N.B. Archive.org]

Clark, Dennis E. *The Life and Teaching of Jesus Christ*. Elgine, IL: Dove, 1977. [Part 11 The Conquest of Death, See. 291–306; Part 12 Implications of the Resurrection of Jesus, See. 307–12]

Clark, Horace. *Life of Jesus Christ as by the Apostles Matthew, Mark, Luke, and John*. Hartford, CT: Hartford Press, 1906. [Chapter 6 From The Last Supper To Resurrection. See. 158–64; N.B. Archive.org]

Clarke, Adam, et al. *Life of Christ and His Apostles*. Baltimore: A. Colby, 1867. [Chapter 23 Resurrection of Christ, See. 292–304; Chapter 24 The Walk to Emmaus, See. 305–17; Chapter 25 Christ's Ascension, See. 318–30; N.B. Published in 1855 under title: *Life Scenes of the Messiah*; 1859]

Clarke, Laurence. *A Compleat History of the Life of Our Blessed Lord and Saviour Jesus Christ with the Lives, Travels and Sufferings of the Apostles and Evangelists . . .* London: Printed for the Author, and Sold by the Booksellers in Town and Country, 1737. [Chapters 15–16, See. 564–72; N.B. Google book]

Clow, W. M. *The Five Portraits of Jesus*. New York: Doran, 1957. [Chapter 5 The Risen Lord, See. 107–32]

Cockin, George S. *Some Difficulties in the Life of Our Lord*. London: Elliot Stock, 1904. [Chapter 8 The Resurrection and Ascension, See. 165–85; N.B. Google book and HathiTrust]

Coleridge, Henry James. *The Passage of Our Lord to the Father: Conclusion of The Life of Our Life*. London: Burns & Oates, 1892. [Chapter 14 Easter Day, See. 326–60; Chapter 15 Last Words by the Lake, See. 361–79; Chapter 16 Before the Ascension, See. 380–96; Chapter 17 The Ascension, See. 397–426; N.B. Google book and HathiTrust]

Conaty, Thomas James. *New Testament Studies: The Principal Events in the Life of Our Lord*. New York: Benziger, 1898. [The Days of Triumph, See. 229–39; N.B. Archive.org]

Conder, Eustace Rogers. *Outlines of the Life of Christ: A Guide to the Study of the Chronology, Harmony, and Purpose of the Gospels*. London: Religious Tract Society, 1887. [Part 4 Section 2 The Resurrection, See. 176–91; Section 3 From Easter to Pentecost, See. 192–203; N.B. Google book]

Connick, C. Milo. *Jesus: The Man, the Mission, and the Message*. Englewood Cliffs, NJ: Prentice-Hall, 1963. [Chapter 22 The Resurrection, See. 405–21]

Cook, Michael L. *Responses to 101 Questions About Jesus*. New York: Paulist, 1993. [Part 4 The Resurrection of Jesus: The Decisive Theological Event (Questions 67–74), See. 81–90]

Cook, Richard B. *The Story of Jesus: Being an Account of the Life and Work, the Walks and Talks of Christ*. Baltimore: R.H. Woodward, 1889. [Book 9, See. 513–32; N.B. Google book and HathiTrust]

Cooke, Greville. *The Light of the World: A Reconstruction and Interpretation of the Life of Christ*. Indianapolis: Bobbs-Merrill, 1950. [Chapter 11 The Aftermath, See. 424–27; Postlude, See. 431–49]

Cooley, William Forbes. *The Story of the Messiah*. New York: Dodd, Mead, 1889. [See. 529–46; N.B. Archive.org. This book depicts Jesus's life in a narrative form.]

Cooper, Charles D. *The Last Days of Our Saviour: The Life of Our Saviour*. Philadelphia: Lippincott, 1867. [Chapter 7 The Tomb –The Resurrection—The Ascension, See. 89–105; N.B. Google book]

Cordelier, John, and Evelyn Underhill. *The Spiral Way: Being Meditations upon the Fifteen Mysteries of the Soul's Ascent*. London: John M. Watkins, 1912. [First Triumphant Mystery: The Resurrection, See. 125–34; Second Triumphant Mystery: The Ascension, See. 135–43]

Cornell, George W. *Behold the Man: People, Politics, and Events Surrounding the Life of Jesus*. Waco, TX: Word, 1974. [Part 6 The Waiting and the Wind 1. Encounter on a Road, See. 187–90]

Cornfeld, Gaalyahu. *The Historical Jesus: A Scholarly View of the Man and His World*. New York: Macmillan, 1982. [Chapter 9 The Crucifixion . . . Visiting the Tomb Within the First Three Days, See. 176–78; Chapter 10 The Explanations the Evidence, See. 179–86; Chapter 11, See. 187–93; Chapter 12 Historic Records and the Resurrection, See. 194–98; Chapter 13 Archaeological Evidence, See. 199–217]

Counts, Bill. *Once a Carpenter*. Irvine, CA: Harvest House, 1975. [Chapter 20 O Death, Where Is Your Victory?, See. 244–54; N.B. Later published under the title *The Incredible Christ*]

Cowgill, Frank Brooks. *Jesus the Patriot*. Boston: Christopher Publishing House, 1928. [Victory Through Death, See. 112–13; N.B. Archive.org]

Cowley-Brown, George James. *Daily Lessons on the Life of Our Lord on Earth: In the Words of the Evangelists*. Vol. 2. London: George Bell, 1880. [Chapters 560–587, See. 445–81; N.B. Google book]

Cox, Harvey. *When Jesus Came to Harvard: Making Moral Choices Today*. Boston: Houghton Mifflin, 2004. [Chapter 26 The Easter Story, See. 267–85]

Cox, Ronald J. *The Gospel of Jesus: The Story in Modern English*. Huntington, IN: Our Sunday Visitor, 1976. [Chapters 66–70, See. 155–65]

Craveri, Marcello. *The Life of Jesus*. Translated by Charles Lam Markmann. New York: Grove Press, 1967. [Chapter 21 Death and Resurrection, See. 410–35]

Crooker, Joseph Henry. *The Supremacy of Jesus*. Boston: American Unitarian Association, 1904. [See. 74–75; N.B. Google book and HathiTrust]

Crosby, Howard. *Jesus: His Life and Work as Narrated by the Four Evangelists*. New York: University Pub., 1871. [Chapter 30 The Resurrection, See. 533–31; N.B. Google book and HathiTrust]

Croscup, George E. *The Gospel History of Our Lord Made Visible: Historical Charts of the Life and Ministry of Christ, with an Outline Harmony of the Gospels*. Philadelphia: Sunday School Times, 1912. [Table 6 The Resurrection Period, See. 29; N.B. Google book]

Culver, Robert Duncan. *The Life of Christ*. Grand Rapids: Baker, 1976. [Chapter 13 Denouement: His Resurrection and Ascension, See. 265–84]

Cumo, Christopher. *A Skeptic's Guide to Jesus*. New York: Algora, 2016. [See. 125–25, 127–28, 130–32; 135–53]

Cunningham, Phillip J. *A Believer's Search for the Jesus of History*. New York: Paulist, 1999. [Chapter 12 The Aftermath, See. 125–34]

Curtis, Arthur Herbert. *The Vision and Mission of Jesus: A Literary and Critical Investigation Based Specially Upon the Baptismal and Temptation Narratives and Their Old Testament Background*. Edinburgh: T&T Clark, 1954. [Part 1. Chapter 21 The Nature of the Resurrection-witness, See. 103–7; Chapter 22 On the third day, See. 108–12; Chapter 23 The Resurrection as Kingdom, See. 113–15; Chapter 24 The Ascension as Kingdom, See. 116–18]

Cutts, Edward Lewes. *A Devotional Life of Our Lord and Saviour Jesus Christ*. London: Society for Promoting Christian Knowledge, 1882. [Part 5 The Risen Life; Chapter 42 The Resurrection, See. 473–538; Chapter 43 The Risen Life; See. 539–46; Chapter 44 The Ascension, See. 547–63; N.B. Archive.org, Google book, and HathiTrust]

Dale, Alan T. *Portrait of Jesus*. Oxford: Oxford University Press, 1979. [See. 108–10]

Dallas, H. A. *Gospel Records: Interpreted by Human Experience*. London: Longmans, 1903. [Chapter 21 The Resurrection of Jesus, See. 247–68]

Dallmann, William. *Jesus, His Words and His Works: According to the Four Gospels*. Milwaukee: Northwestern Publishing House, 1914. [Chapter 70 Jesus Rose and Ascended, See. 462–81; N.B. Google book and HathiTrust]

Damon, Louis A. *A Story of Jesus the Christ*. Chicago: Rand McNally, 1916. [See. 120–27; N.B. Google book and HathiTrust]

Daniel-Rops, Henri. *Jesus and His Times*. New York: Dutton, 1954. [Chapter 12 Victory Over Death, See. 420–41]

———. *The Life of Our Lord*. New York: Hawthorn, 1964. [Chapter 20 Death, Where is Thy Victory?, See. 164–71]

Darden, Bob. I. *Jesus: Stories from the Savior*. Arlington, TX: Summit, 1997. [Epilogue: A New Beginning, See. 241–66]

Davis, Noah K. *The Story of the Nazarene in Annotated Paraphrase*. New York: Revell, 1903. [Chapter 31 The Resurrection Day, See. 389–98; Chapter 32 The Forty Days, See. 399–406; Chapter 33 The After Days, See. 407–14; N.B. Archive.org and Google book]

Dawes, Gregory W. *The Historical Jesus Quest: Landmarks in the Search for the Jesus of History*. Louisville: Westminster John Knox, 2000. [Unreliability of the Resurrection accounts, See. 77–78]

———. ed. *The Historical Jesus Question: The Challenge of History to Religious Authority*. Louisville: Westminster John Knox, 2001. [Resurrection appearances, See. 73–74, 83–84, 163 n.21, 196–97, 232 n.146, 333–35; empty tomb, See. 84, 335; evidence for, See. 89, 281, 332–35]

Dawson, William J. *The Life of Christ*. Philadelphia: G. W. Jacobs, 1901. [Chapter 30 The Resurrection and After, See. 428–47; N.B. Google book]

Deane, Anthony C. *Jesus Christ*. Garden City, NY: Doubleday, Doran, 1928. [Chapter 8 The End—And The Beginning, See. 214–26]

Deems, Charles F. *Who Was Jesus?* New York: J. H. Brown, 1880. [Part 8 Resurrection of Jesus and Subsequent Events, See. 686–710; N.B. Google book]

Denney, James. *The Death of Christ*. London: Hodder & Stoughton, 1911. [See. 48–54; N.B. Google book]

Denny, Walter Bell. *The Career and Significance of Jesus*. New York: T. Nelson, 1934. [Chapter 26 The Experience of the Resurrection, See. 313–24]

Dickens, Charles. *The Life of Our Lord*: Written for His Children During the Years, 1846–1849. New York: Simon & Schuster, 1999. [See. 112–22]

Dickson, John P. *The Christ Files: How Historians Know What They Know About Jesus.* Grand Rapids: Zondervan, 2010. [See. 42–46]

———. *A Doubter's Guide to Jesus: An Introduction to the Man from Nazareth for Believers and Skeptics*. Grand Rapids: Zondervan, 2018. [Chapter 11 Adam: The Promise of His Resurrection, See. 182–207]

———. *Jesus: A Short Life*. Oxford, Lion, 2008. [Chapter 11 Resurrection, See. 119–28]

Didon, père (Henri). *Jesus Christ: Our Saviour's Person, Mission and Spirit*. Vol. 2 New York: D. Appleton, 1891. [Chapter 12 Jesus Risen From the Dead, See. 364–88; Appendix U. The Situation of Emmaus, See. 462–64; N.B. Archive.org and Google book]

Dietz, Thos G. *The Gospel: The Unification of the Four Gospels: from the American Standard Edition of the Revised Bible*. Grand Rapids: Eerdmans, 1951. [Part 6 Forty Days of Resurrection Life, See. 170–79]

Dirksen, Aloys. *A Life of Christ: Together with the Four Gospels*. New York: Holt, Rinehart & Winston, 1962. [Chapter 27 Easter, the Forty Days, and Pentecost, See. 300–306]

Dougherty, Robert Lee. *Jesus the Pioneer: The Christ of the Gospels*. Boston: Christophe, 1952. [Chapter 20 The Man Who Came Back, See. 134–36]

Dow, John. *Jesus and the Human Conflict*. London: Hodder & Stoughton, 1927. [See. 296–302]

Drane, John William. *Son of Man: A New Life of Christ*. Grand Rapids: Eerdmans, 1993. [Chapter 5 Crucifixion & Resurrection, See. The Resurrection, See. 147–53; Ascension and Glory, See. 153–54]

Drummond, Richard Henry. *A Life of Jesus the Christ: From Cosmic Origins to the Second Coming*. San Francisco: Harper & Row, 1989. [Chapter 13 The Resurrection and the Ascension, See. 132–45]

Duncan, George Simpson. *Jesus, Son of Man: Studies Contributory to a Modern Portrait*. New York: Macmillan, 1949. [Chapter 13, See. 172–86]

Du Pin, Louis Ellies. *The Evangelical History: Or, the Life of Our Blessed Saviour Jesus Christ*. London: Printed for Abel Swall and T. Childe, 1694. [Book 4 The Resurrection, See. 178–88; The Ascension of Jesus Christ, See. 189–92; N.B. Google book]

Duquesne, Jacques. *Jesus: An Unconventional Biography*. Translated by Catherine Spencer. Liguori, MO: Triumph, 1997. [Chapter 15 The Death and Resurrection, See. 230–47]

Duriez, Colin. *The Year That Changed the World*. Downers Grove, IL: InterVarsity, 2006. [Resurrection, See. 33, 34, 112, 124, 125–26, 127–28, 129–31, 210, 215]

Eddy, Sherwood. *A Portrait of Jesus: A Twentieth Century Interpretation of Christ*. New York: Harper & Brothers, 1943. [Chapter 9 The Resurrection and Its Consequences, See. 128–45]

Eddy, Zachary, and Richard S. Storrs. *Immanuel, or The Life of Jesus Christ Our Lord: From His Incarnation to His Ascension*. Springfield, MA: W. J. Holland, 1868. [Part 10 Our Risen Lord, See. 729–52; N.B. Archive.org, Google book, and HathiTrust]

Edersheim, Alfred. *The Life and Times of Jesus the Messiah*. Grand Rapids: Eerdmans, 1953. [Chapter 16 On the Resurrection of Christ from the Dead, See. 1422–28; Chapter 17 On The Third Day He Rose Again From The Dead; He Ascended Into Heaven, See. 1429–45; N.B. Archive.org; An interesting work to examine. Originally published in 1883.]

Edinger, Edward F. *The Christian Archetype: A Jungian Commentary on the Life of Christ.* Toronto, Canada: Inner City, 1987. [Chapter 12 Resurrection and Ascension, See. 113–22]

Edwards, F. Henry. *Life and Ministry of Jesus.* Independence, MO: Herald Publishing House, 1982. [Chapter 42 The Resurrection, See. 319–27; Chapter 43 The Forty Days, See. 328–36; Chapter 44 The Ascension, See. 337–42]

Eggleston, Edward. *Christ in Literature: Being a Treasury of Choice Readings, in Prose and Verse, from Writers of all Ages, Illustrative of the Acts and Words of Jesus Christ, Together with the Four Gospels, Arranged in One Continuous Narrative, for Convenient Reference.* New York: J. B. Ford, 1875. [Chapter 41 The Resurrection, See. 360–68; Chapter 42 Last Appearance and Ascension, See. 369–72; N.B. Google book and HathiTrust]

Eikamp, Arthur R. *Jesus Christ: A Study of the Gospels.* Anderson, IN: Warner Press, 1963. [Chapter 17 Crucifixion and Resurrection, See. 173–76]

Eisler, Robert. *The Messiah Jesus and John the Baptist According to Flavius Josephus' Recently Rediscovered 'Capture of Jerusalem' and the Other Jewish and Christian Sources.* New York: Dial Press, 1931. [Chapter 15 Ecce Homo . . . Josephus on the Bodily Appearance of Jesus, See. 393–96]

Ellicott, C. J. *Historical Lectures on the Life of Our Lord Jesus Christ, Being the Hulsean Lectures for the Year 1859. With Notes, Critical, Historical and Explanatory.* 2nd ed. London: Parker, Son and Bourn, 1861. [Lecture 8 The Forty Days, See. 367–417; N.B. Google book]

Elliott, Walter. *The Life of Jesus Christ: Embracing the Entire Gospel Narrative, Embodying the Teachings and the Miracles of Our Savior, Together with His Foundation of the Christian Church.* New York: Columbus Press, 1905. [Book 4 The Resurrection, See. 723–59; N.B. Google book and HathiTrust]

Emerson, William A. *The Jesus Story.* New York: Harper & Row, 1971. [Epilogue, See. 132–33]

Emmerich, Anna Catherine. *The Lowly Life and Bitter Passion of Our Lord Jesus Christ.* Vol. 4. Edited by K. E. Schmöger, New York: Sentinel Press, 1914. [The Resurrection. The Ascension. The Descent of the Holy Ghost, See. 359–423; N.B. Reprinted as *The Life of Jesus Christ, and Biblical Revelations*, Rockford, IL: Tan, 1986]

Endō, Shūsaku. *A Life of Jesus.* Translated by Richard A. Schuchert. New York: Paulist, 1973. [Chapter 13 The Question, See. 156–79]

Erdman, Charles R. *The Lord We Love: Devotional Studies in the Life of Christ.* New York: Doran, 1924. [Chapter 13 The Day He Arose, See. 123–30; Chapter 14 The Ascension, See. 131–38]

Erskine, John. *The Human Life of Jesus.* New York: Morrow, 1945. [Chapter 19 The Resurrection, See. 236–40]

E. S. A. (Earnest S. Appleyard). *A History of Our Lord's Life on Earth, from the Four Gospels. For the Use of Children.* Edited by W. E. Heygate. London: Bell & Daldy, 1871. [Part 7 The Resurrection, See. 215–22; The Great Forty Days, See. 223–27; The Ascension, See. 228–29; N.B. Google book]

Evans, Craig A., and N. T. Wright. *Jesus, The Final Days: What Really Happened.* Edited by Troy A. Miller. Louisville: Westminster John Knox, 2009. [Chapter 3 The Surprise of Resurrection (N. T. Wright), See. 75–107]

Evans, William. *Epochs in the Life of Christ*. New York: Revell, 1916. [Chapter 6 The Resurrection of Jesus Christ—The Crux of Christianity, See. 153–85; N.B. Archive.org and Google book]

———. *From The Upper Room to the Empty Tomb*. Grand Rapids: Eerdmans, 1934. [Chapter 9 The Resurrection of Jesus, See. 273–94]

Evanson, Edward. *The Dissonance of the Four Generally Received Evangelists, and the Evidence of their Respective Authenticity*. 2nd ed. Gloucester: D. Walker, 1805. [See. 68, 90, 94, 97–98, 151–52, 231, 258–59, 281, 288; N.B. Google book.]

Ewald, H. *The Life of Jesus Christ*. Translated by Octavius Glover. Cambridge: Deighton, Bell, 1865. [Chapter 40 The Eternal Exaltation, See. 337–48; N.B. Archive.org and Google book]

Fahling, Adam. *The Life of Christ*. St. Louis: Concordia, 1936. [Chapter 37 The Risen and Exalted Savior, See. 687–712]

Fairbairn, A. M. *Studies in the Life of Christ*. 2nd ed. London: Hodder & Stoughton, 1881. [Chapter 18 The Resurrection, See. 331–58; N.B. Archive.org, Google book, and HathiTrust]

Farley, Benjamin Wirt. *Jesus as Man, Myth, and Metaphor: Beyond the Jesus of History* Eugene, OR: Wipf & Stock, 2007. [Chapter 10 The Resurrection, See. 119–30]

Farrar, F. W. *The Life of Christ*. New York: R. P. Dutton, 1891. [Chapter 62 The Resurrection, See. 452–64; N.B. Archive.org, Google book, and HathiTrust]

———. *The Life of Lives; Further Studies in the Life of Christ*. New York: Dodd, Mead, 1900. [Chapter 41 The Resurrection, See. 529–43; Chapter 42 The Ascension, See. 544–48; N.B. Google book]

———. *The Sweet Story of Jesus: The Life of Christ*. New York City: Commonwealth, 1891. [Chapter 62 The Resurrection, See. 515–30; N.B. Google book]

Farrell, Walter. *Only Son*. New York: Sheed & Ward, 1953. [Chapter 12 the Conquest of Death, See. 229–44]

Faunce, D. W. *Advent and Ascension: or, How Jesus Came and How He Left Us*. New York: Eaton & Mains, 1903. [Chapter 4 Questions About the Lord's Departure, See. 151–67; Chapter 5 The Witnesses To the Lord's Resurrection and Ascension, See. 167–82; Chapter 6 The Testimony of these Witnesses to the Resurrection and Ascension, See. 183–213; N.B. Archive.org, Google book, and HathiTrust]

Feeney, Robert. *The Rosary: "The Little Summa."* 4th ed. Marysville, WA: Aquinas Press, 1991. [Chapter 25 The Resurrection of Jesus, See. 292–99; Chapter 26 The Ascension, See. 300–303]

Fernández, Andrés. *The Life of Christ*. Translated by Paul Barrett. Westminster, MD: Newman Press, 1958. [Chapter 29 The Glorified Life, See. 752–88]

Ferris, Theodore Parker. *The Story of Jesus*. New York: Oxford University Press, 1953. [Chapter 14 The Resurrection, See. 107–14]

Field, Frank McCoy. *Where Jesus Walked: Through the Holy Land with the Master*. New York: Exposition Press, 1951. [Chapter 20 Calvary and the Garden of the Resurrection, See. 225–36]

Fillion, L.-Cl. *The Life of Christ: A Historical, Critical, and Apologetic Exposition*. Translated by Newton Wayland Thompson. Vol. 3. St. Louis: B. Herder, 1939. [Part 6—The Glorified Life of Christ. Chapter 1 The Resurrection, See. 565–602; Chapter 2 The Ascension, See. 603–8; Appendices. The Glorified Life of Christ, See. The Resurrection, See. 684–99; The Ascension, See. 699–701]

Finegan, Jack. *Jesus, History, and You*. Richmond: John Knox, 1964. [Chapter 19 The Empty Tomb, See. 130–34; Chapter 20 The Reality of the Resurrection, See. 134–40]

Fischer, M. Hadwin. *The Story of Jesus with Suggestions for Further Study: A Text for Classes in Christian Training Schools*. Philadelphia: The United Lutheran Publication House, 1924. [Chapter 20 Crucified—Buried—Risen—Ascended, See. 166–74]

Fiske, Charles. *The Christ We Know: Son of Man and Son of God: Master, Lord and Saviour*. New York: Harper & Brothers, 1927. [Chapter 23 The Victorious Issue, See. 228–44; Chapter 24 His Tremendous Claims, See. 245–58]

Fleetwood, John. *The Life of Our Blessed Lord and Savior Jesus Christ: And the Lives and Sufferings of His Holy Apostles and Evangelists*. Philadelphia: Bradley, Garretson, 1874. [Chapter 38, See. 446–58; Chapter 39, See. 459–71; Chapter 41, See. 472–80; N.B. Archive.org, Google book, and HathiTrust]

Flood, Edmund. *The Jesus Story*. Kansas City, MO: Sheed & Ward, 1991. [Chapter 1 The Resurrection, See. 83–94]

Forward, Martin. *Jesus: A Short Biography*. Oxford, England: Oneworld, 1998. [Chapter 3 The Kingdom of God Has Come Near. Resurrection, See. 91–94]

Foster, R. C. *The Final Week*. Grand Rapids: Baker, 1966. [Chapters 19–22, See. 251–313]

Fouard, Constant. *The Christ, the Son of God: A Life of Our Lord and Saviour Jesus Christ*. Vol. 2. London & Dublin: Longmans, Green, 1908. [Chapter 8 The Resurrection, See. 350–65; Chapter 9 The Forty Days, See. 366–78; Chapter 11 Harmony of the Four Gospels in the Narratives of the Resurrection, See. 395–98; N.B. Archive.org and HathiTrust]

Frame, Hugh Fulton. *Wonderful, Counsellor: A Study in the Life of Jesus*. Hodder & Stoughton: London, 1935. [Part 5 Chapter 6 God Raised Him From The Dead, See. 289–98]

France, R. T. *I Came to Set the Earth on Fire: A Portrait of Jesus*. Downers Grove, IL: InterVarsity, 1976. [Chapter 11 Vindication, See. 160–72]

Fredriksen, Paula. *Jesus of Nazareth, King of the Jews: A Jewish Life and the Emergence of Christianity*. New York: Knopf, 1999. [post-Resurrection appearances, See. 21, 23, 252, 262–66; post-Resurrection movement of, See. 9–11, 23, 39, 61, 75–78, 93–94, 106, 146–47, 203, 215, 236–37, 245–46, 261–70]

Furness, William Henry. *Jesus and His Biographers, or, The Remarks on the Four Gospels*. Philadelphia: Carey, Lea & Blanchard, 1838. [Chapter 13 The Resurrection, See. 406–30; N.B. Archive.org, Google book, and HathiTrust]

———. *The Power of Spirit Manifest in Jesus of Nazareth*. Philadelphia: Lippincott, 1877. [Easter, See. 53–74; N.B. Google book and HathiTrust]

———. *Remarks on the Four Gospels*. London: Charles Fox, 1837. [Chapter 12 The Death and Resurrection of Jesus, See. 246–88; N.B. Archive.org, Google book, and HathiTrust]

———. *The Unconscious Truth of the Four Gospels*. Philadelphia: Lippincott, 1868. [Chapter 4 The Resurrection of Jesus, See. 76–113; N.B. Google book]

Furst, Jeffrey, comp. *Edgar Cayce's Story of Jesus*. New York: Coward-McCann, 1969. [Chapter 10 Crucifixion and Resurrection, See. 218–428]

Garbett, C. F. *We Would See Jesus*. London: Longmans, Green, 1941. [Chapter 8 The Risen Christ, See. 77–84]

Gardiner, Frederic. *Diatessaron: The Life of Our Lord; in the Words of the Gospels.* Andover: W. F. Draper, 1878. [Chapter 24 The Day of the Resurrection, See. 246–53; Chapter 25 The Forty Days to the Ascension, See. 254–53; N.B. Google book]

Gardner, James. *Jesus Who? Myth vs. Reality in the Search for the Historical Jesus.* Bangor, ME: Booklocker, 2006. [Was Jesus Resurrected?, See. 213–22]

Gardner-Smith, P. *The Christ of the Gospels: A Study of the Gospel Records in the Light of Critical Research.* Cambridge: W. Heffer, 1938. [Chapter 19 The Resurrection, See. 219–28; Chapter 20 The Johannine Account, See. 229–38]

Garman, W. O. H. *The Life and Teachings of Christ.* Wilkinsburg, PA: Author, 1942. [Part 9 The Forty Days, See. 139–52]

Garvie, Alfred E. *Studies in the Inner Life of Jesus.* New York: A. C. Armstrong, 1907. [Chapter 23 The Risen Lord, See. 426–46; N.B. Archive.org and Google book]

Geikie, Cunningham. *The Life and Words of Christ.* New York: D. Appleton, 1883. [Chapter 64 The Resurrection and the Forty Days, See. 580–608; N.B. Archive.org and Google book]

Geil, William Edgar. *The Man of Galilee.* New York: International Committee of Young Men's Christian Association, 1906. [Chapter 10 The Final Forty Days, See. 189–98; N.B. Archive.org. Useless.]

Genesis Project, Inc. *Jesus, His Life and Times.* New York: Morrow, 1979. [The Empty Tomb, See. 187–204]

Gestefeld, Ursula N. *The Master of the Man.* Chicago: Exodus, 1907. [Chapter 29 Resurrection, See. 375–87; Chapter 30 Ascension, See. 391–95; N.B. Archive.org, Google book, and HathiTrust]

Gibson, Joseph Thompson. *Jesus Christ, the Unique Revealer of God.* Chicago: Revell, 1915. [Chapter 65 The Resurrection, See. 485–508; N.B. Archive.org, Google book, and HathiTrust]

Gibson, Shimon. *The Final Days of Jesus: The Archaeological Evidence.* New York: HarperCollins, 2009. [Chapter 8 Who Moved the Stone?, See. 149–65]

Gigot, Francis E. *Outlines of the Life of Our Lord.* Brighton, MA: St. John's Boston Ecclesiastical Seminary, 1896. [Chapter 35 The Risen Life, See. 208–15; N.B. Archive.org and Google book]

Gilbert, George Holley. *Jesus.* New York: Macmillan, 1912. [Part 3 Chapter 3 The Legend of a Material Resurrection, See. 275–307; N.B. HathiTrust]

———. *Jesus for the Men of Today: When Science Aids Religion.* New York: Hodder & Stoughton, 1917. [Chapter 12 The Triumph of Jesus Over Death, See. 163–76; N.B. Archive.org and Google book]

———. *The Student's Life of Jesus.* 3rd ed. New York: Macmillan, 1900. [Chapter 17 The Resurrection and the Risen Christ, See. 314–34; N.B. Archive.org and Google book]

Gilbert, Levi. *Visions of the Christ.* Cincinnati: Jennings & Pye, 1903. [Chapter 10 Christ's Character in Relation to His Resurrection, See. 101–13]

Gillie, R. C. *The Story of Stories.* 2nd ed. London: A&C Black, 1907. [See. 388–428; N.B. HathiTrust]

Gilmore, Albert Field. *Who Was This Nazarene? A Challenging and Definitive Biography of the Master.* New York: Prentice-Hall, 1940. [Chapter 27 The Resurrection and Ascension, See. 287–301]

Girzone, Joseph F. *Jesus: A New Understanding of God's Son.* New York: Doubleday, 2009. [Chapter 43 The Resurrection of Jesus, See. 332–43]

Glover, T. R. *The Jesus of History*. New York: Doran, 1917. [The Resurrection, See. 178; N.B. Archive.org and Gutenberg.org]

Gnilka, Joachim. *Jesus of Nazareth: Message and History*. Peabody, MA: Hendrickson, 1997. [Chapter 12 Easter Epilogue, See. 319–20]

Goguel, Maurice. *Jesus the Nazarene: Myth or History?* Translated by Frederick Stephens. New York: D. Appleton, 1926. [Chapter 11 The Origin of the Faith in the Resurrection and Its Function in Primitive Christianity, See. 279–313; N.B. The author presents a balanced analysis of the texts.]

Goodspeed, Edgar J. *A Life of Jesus*. New York: Harper, 1950. [Chapter 18 The Crucifixion and the Resurrection, See. 216–28]

Goodwin, Thomas. *Christ Set Forth in His Death, Resurrection, Ascension, Sitting at God's Right Hand, Intercession, as the Cause of Justification. Object of Justifying Faith. Together with a Treatise Discovering the Affectionate Tenderness of Christ's Heart Now in Heaven, Unto Sinners on Earth . . .* London: Printed for Robert Dawlman, 1645. [Chapter 3 Faith Supported By Christ's Resurrection, See. 51–91; Chapter 4 Faith Supported By Christ's Ascension, And Sitting At God's Right Hand, See. 92–116; N.B. Google book]

Gordon, George Angier. *The Great Assurance* Boston: Pilgrim Press, 1910. [N.B. Google book; 31 pages]

Gore, Charles. *Jesus of Nazareth*. London: T. Butterworth, 1929. [Chapter 6 The Risen Jesus and the Faith of the Apostles, See. 212–48]

Goudge, Elizabeth. *God So Loved the World*. New York: Coward-McCann, 1951. [Chapter 12 Victory, See. 289–311]

Grant, Michael. *Jesus: An Historian's Review of the Gospels*. New York: Scribner's Sons, 1977. [Part 3 Chapter 10 From Disaster to Triumph. See. 176–78]

Grassi, Joseph A. *Rediscovering the Jesus Story: A Participatory Guide*. New York: Paulist, 1995. [See. Mark, See. 51–52; Matthew, See. 107–9; Luke, See. 161–64; John, See. 210–15]

Greg, Samuel. *Scenes From the Life of Jesus*. Edinburgh: Edmonston & Douglas, 1869. [Chapter 33 The Evening of the Day of Resurrection, See. 298–307; Chapter 34 A Cloud Receives Him From Our Sight, See. 308–9; N.B. Google book]

Griffith, Gwilym O. *St. Paul's Life of Christ*. New York: Doran, 1925. [Chapter 6 Christ Risen and Exalted, See. 153–91]

Grimbol, William R. *The Complete Idiot's Guide to the Life of Christ*. Indianapolis, IN: Alpha, 2001. [Chapter 19 It Is All About Appearances, See. 167–71]

Grist, William Alexander. *The Historic Christ in the Faith of To-day*. New York: Revell, 1911. [Book 9 The Finished Work; Chapter 3 Jesus Rises and Appears, See. 485–98; N.B. Archive.org]

Griswold, Rufus W., ed. *Scenes in the Life of the Saviour: By the Poets and Painters*. Philadelphia: Lindsay & Blakiston, 1846. [See. 171–97; N.B. Google book and HathiTrust]

Groothuis, Douglas R. *Jesus in an Age of Controversy*. Eugene, OR: Harvest House, 1996. [Chapter 8 Did Jesus Travel to India?, See. 133–51]

Grubb, Edward. *Notes on the Life and Teaching of Jesus*. London: James Clarke, 1910. [Chapter 12 The Resurrection, See. 92–97; N.B. HathiTrust. Grubb was an influential English Quaker.]

Guardini, Romano. *The Lord*. London: Longmans, Green, 1956. [Part 6. Resurrection and Transfiguration, See. 403–9]

Guignebert, Charles. *Jesus*. Translated from the French by S. H. Hooke. New York: University Books, 1966. [Part 3 The Death of Jesus and the Easter Faith. Chapter 5 The Resurrection, See. 490–512; Chapter 6 The Easter Faith, See. 513–36]

Guinness, Paul Grattan. *The Christ of All Nations*. New York: Association Press, 1950. [Chapter 7 He Rises to Re-Make the World, See. 245–60]

Gunsaulus, Frank Wakeley. *The Man of Galilee: A Biographical Study of the Life of Jesus Christ*. Chicago: Monarch, 1899. [Chapter 60 The Risen And Ascended Lord, See. 667–82]

Guthrie, Donald. *Jesus the Messiah: An Illustrated Life of Christ*. Grand Rapids: Zondervan, 1972. [Chapter 25 From Golgotha to the Empty Tomb, See. 347–60; Chapter 26 The Risen Lord, See. 361–74]

Guy, Harold A. *The Life of Christ: Notes on the Narrative and Teaching in the Gospels*. London: Macmillan, 1951. [See. 177–81]

Habermas, Gary R. *Ancient Evidence for the Life of Jesus*. Nashville: Nelson, 1984. [Part One. Chapter 3 Popularistic Lives of Jesus, See. 53–84; Primary Sources: Creeds and Facts, See. 119–34]

———. *Evidence for the Historical Jesus: Is the Jesus of History the Christ of Faith?* Lynchburg, VA: Gary R. Habermas, 2015. [N.B. This volume is a transcribed and expanded version of six television programs that appeared originally on "The John Ankerberg Show." This is a free e-book, downloadable from Habermas's homepage.]

Hall, G. Stanley. *Jesus, the Christ, In the Light of Psychology*. Vol. 1. Garden City, NY: Doubleday, Page, 1917. [See. x, xi, xii, xiii, 26, 50, 51, 61, 136, 139, 144, 145, 149, 150, 154, 186, 187, 193, 196; N.B. Archive.org and HathiTrust]

Halsey, Leroy J. *The Beauty of Immanuel: His Name Shall Be Called Wonderful*. Philadelphia: Presbyterian Board of Publication, 1860. [Chapter 9 His Resurrection and Ascension, See. 117–37; N.B. Archive.org and Google book]

Hamilton, James. *A Morning Beside The Lake of Galilee*. London: J. Nisbet, 1863; [N.B. Archive.org and Google book]

———. *Lessons From the Great Biography*. New York: Robert Carter, 1857. [Final Glimpses. The Risen Redeemer, See. 295–318; N.B. Archive.org]

Hammer, Bonaventure, adaptor. *Cochem's Life of Christ*. New York: Benziger, 1897. [Chapter 32 The Resurrection of Jesus, See. 286–95; Chapter 33 Jesus appears repeatedly to His Disciples, See. 296–306; Chapter 34 The Ascension of Jesus, See. 307–9; N.B. Archive.org]

Hanna, William. *The Life of Christ: Last Day of Our Lord's Passion and Forty Days After the Resurrection*. Vol. 3. New York: Robert Carter, 1873. [The Forty Days After Our Lord's Resurrection, See. 1–316; N.B. Archive.org and HathiTrust]

Harington, Joy. *Jesus of Nazareth*. Leicester: Brockhampton, 1956. [Part 9: I Am With You Always, See. 165–91]

Harmony of the Gospel Narratives of Holy Week, A. Also of the Resurrection, The Ascension and the Decent of the Holy Ghost. New York: E & J B Young, 1889. [See. 109–26; N.B. Archive.org]

Harrington, Wilfrid J. *The Jesus Story*. Dublin, Ireland: Columba Press, 1991. [See. 61–63, 95–96, 130–31, 157–59]

Harrison, Everett F. *A Short Life of Christ*. Grand Rapids: Eerdmans, 1968. [Chapter 16 The Resurrection, See. 231–46; Chapter 17 The Ascension, See. 247–55]

Harvey, A. E. *Jesus and the Constraints of History.* Philadelphia: Westminster, 1982. [See. 138, 139, 150–51, 166, 167]

Harwood, Philip. *German Anti-Supernaturalism: Six Lectures on Strauss's "Life of Jesus;" Delivered at the Chapel in South Place,* Finsbury. London: C. Fox, 1841. [Lecture 5, See. 79–92; N.B. Archive.org, Google book, and HathiTrust]

Hase, Karl von. *Life of Jesus: A Manual for Academic Study.* Translated by James Freeman Clarke. 4th ed. Boston: Walker & Wise, 1860. [#118–122; See. 230–41; N.B. Google book]

Helm, Nellie Lathrop. *When Jesus was Here Among Men.* Chicago: Fleming H. Revell, 1902. [Chapter 19 The Risen Lord, See. 194–205; N.B. Google book. Useless.]

Henry, A. M. *The Triumph of Christ: The Word Made Flesh.* Notre Dame, IN: Fides, 1962. [Chapter 2 See. The Resurrection of Christ, See. 48–53; The Ascension, See. 54–56]

Herzog, William R. *Jesus, Justice and the Reign of God: A Ministry of Liberation.* Louisville: Westminster John Knox, 2000. [Chapter 11 A Concluding Unhistorical Postscript, See. 247–56]

Hession, Brian. *More Than A Prophet: The Life of Jesus.* London: P. Davies, 1959. [Chapter 24 The third day, See. 196–214; Chapter 25 The dawn of a new age, See. 215–18]

Hill, William Bancroft. *Introduction to the Life of Christ.* New York: Scribner's Sons, 1911. [See. 12, 13, 14, 22, 23, 26, 27, 39, 80, 190, 191, 192, 216, 217; N.B. Archive.org and HathiTrust]

———. *The Life of Christ.* New York: Revell, 1917. [Chapter 19 The Resurrection, See. 299–326: N.B. Archive.org and HathiTrust]

———. *Mountain Peaks in the Life of Our Lord.* New York: Revell, 1925. [Chapter 11 The Mount of the Ascension, See. 174–89]

Hillard, A. E. *A Continuous Narrative of the Life of Christ in the Words of the Four Gospels.* 2nd ed. New York: James Pott, 1895. [Part 6, See. 177–84; N.B. Google book]

Hitchcock, Albert Wellman. *The Psychology of Jesus: A Study of the Development of His Self-Consciousness.* Boston: Pilgrim Press, 1907. [Chapter 11 The Death and Resurrection of Jesus as He Regarded Them, See. 218–45; N.B. Archive.org, Google book, and HathiTrust. Not useful.]

Hobbs, Herschel H. *The Life and Times of Jesus: A Contemporary Approach.* Grand Rapids: Zondervan, 1966. [Chapter 11 The Resurrection and Ascension of Jesus Christ, See. 205–18]

Hodge, Richard Morse. *Historical Atlas and Chronology of the Life of Jesus Christ: A Text Book and Companion to a Harmony of the Gospels.* Wytheville, VA: D. A. St. Clair, 1899. [See. 39, N.B. Archive.org]

Hodgson, Ch. *An Evangelical Summary of Corroborative Testimonies Concerning the Birth, Life, Death, Resurrection and Ascension, of Jesus Christ to which are also Prefixed the Prophecies Relative to the Same Events . . . London:* Printed for the author, and sold by T&J Evans, J. Matthews, 1788. [The Resurrection of Jesus Christ, See. 42–59; The Ascension of Jesus Christ, See. 62–67; N.B. The author's name does not appear in the text: "By a member of the University of Cambridge."]

Hoehner, Harold W. *Chronological Aspects of the Life of Christ.* Grand Rapids: Zondervan, 1977. [Chapters 4–5, See. 65–114]

Hoffman, Reuben F. *From Manger to Mansion.* New York: Vantage, 1977. [Chapter 8 The Resurrection of Jesus, See. 55–59]

Hosie, Lady. *Jesus and Woman: Being a Study of the Four Gospels with Special Reference to the Attitude of the Man, Jesus Christ Towards Women*. London: Hodder & Stoughton, 1946. [The Women on Christ's Resurrection Morning, See. 303–4]

Houghton, Louise Seymour. *The Life of Christ in Picture and Story*. New York: American Tract Society, 1890. [He Arose From The Dead— He Ascended Into Heaven, See. 282–95; N.B. Google book]

Hunt, T. W. *The Mind of Christ: The Transforming Power of Thinking His Thoughts*. Nashville: Broadman & Holman, 1995. [Chapter 10 Raised from the Dead, See. 121–42]

Hunter, Archibald Macbride. *The Work and Words of Jesus*. Philadelphia: Westminster, 1973. [Chapter 15 The Resurrection, See. 155–64]

Hurlbut, Jesse Lyman. Hurlbut's *Life of Christ for Young and Old: A Complete Life of Christ Written in Simple Language, Based on the Gospel Narrative*. Philadelphia: Winston, 1915. [Chapters 98–103, See. 469–96; N.B. Archive.org and Gutenberg.org]

Hutchinson, Robert J. *Searching for Jesus: New Discoveries in the Quest for Jesus of Nazareth*. Nashville: Nelson, 2015. [Chapter 10 Do We Have Proof for the Resurrection?, See. 219–52]

Hutton, Vernon Wollaston. *The Mind of Christ: Thoughts Derived from the History of Our Lord's Temptation and Passion, Arranged as Aids to Meditation*. London: E. Longhurst, Church Bookseller, 1879. [Chapters 99–104, See. 198–209; N.B. Google book.]

Irvine, Alexander. *The Carpenter and His Kingdom*. New York: Scribner's Sons, 1922. [Chapter 16 Conspiracy and Murder. Paragraph 150, The First Easter Morn, See. 236–37; N.B. Archive.org, Google book, and HathiTrust]

James, C. C., ed. *The Gospel History of Our Lord and Saviour Jesus Christ*. London: Clay, 1890. [Sections 175–87, See. 167–76; N.B. Google book and HathiTrust]

James, Rick. *Jesus Without Religion*. Downers Gove, IL: IVP, 2007. [The Rise of Jesus, See. 109–20]

Jarvis, F. Washington. *And Still Is Ours Today: The Story of Jesus*. New York: Seabury, 1980. [Chapter 17 The Resurrection, See. 1, 158–66; Chapter 18 The Resurrection, See. 2, 167–72; Chapter 19 I Am With You Always, See. 173–83]

———. *Come and Follow: An Introduction to Christian Discipleship*. New York: Seabury, 1972. [Chapter 16 The Resurrection, See. 1, 115–21; Chapter 17 The Resurrection, See. 2, 122–29]

Jarvis, Samuel Farmar. *A Chronological Introduction to the History of the Church: Being a New Inquiry into the True Dates of the Birth and Death of our Lord and Saviour Jesus Christ*. London: W. J. Cleaver, 1844. [See. 103, 376, 377, 381, 420–21, 460–61, 481, 491, 513, 522–23; N.B. Archive.org]

Jennings, A. G. *The Last Days of Jesus Christ: or the Gospel Account of the Great Atonement*. Philadelphia: American Sunday-School Union, 1893. [See. 83–112; N.B. Google book]

Jensen, Irving L. *The Life of Christ: A Bible Correspondence Course*. Chicago: Moody, 1986. [The Resurrected Christ, See. 11/1–11/9]

Jeon, Paul S. *A New King Encountering the Risen Son*. Eugene, OR: Wipf & Stock, 2018. [Chapter 3 The King Rises (Luke 23:50–24:12), See. 30–42; Chapter 4 The King Accompanies (24:13–35), See. 43–56; Chapter 5 The King Appears (Luke 24:36–53), See. 57–69]

Johnson, Ben Campbell, and Brant D. Baker. *The Jesus Story*. Louisville, KY: Geneva Press, 2000. [The Risen Lord, See. 150–62]

Johnson, Harry. *The Humanity of the Saviour: A Biblical and Historical Study of the Human Nature of Christ in Relation to Original Sin, with Special Reference to Its Soteriological Significance.* London: Epworth, 1962. [Part 2 The New Testament Evidence (f) The Resurrection Appearances, See. 63–67]

Johnson, Paul. *Jesus: A Biography from a Believer.* New York: Viking, 2010. [Chapter 9 The Resurrection and the Birth of Christianity, See. 209–26]

Johnson, Sherman E. *Jesus and His Towns.* Wilmington, DE: Glazier, 1989. [Chapter 17 The Resurrection and Ascension, See. 160–65]

Johnstone, T. Boston. *The Life of Jesus Christ: Arranged from the Four Gospels into One Consecutive Narrative.* London: Andrew Elliot, 1874. [Part 7 Christ's Resurrection and Ascension, See. 193–201, N.B. Google book]

Jones, Joel. *Jesus and the Coming Glory: or, Notes on Scripture.* Philadelphia: James S. Claxton, 1865. [Chapter 12 The Resurrection, See. 446–90; Chapter 13 Walk to Emmaus, See. 490–517; Chapter 14 Events that Followed the Lord's Resurrection, See. 517–75; N.B. Archive.org]

Joyce, Donovan. *The Jesus Scroll.* New York: Dial, 1973. [Chapter 19 Escape from the Tomb, See. 148–55]

Kähler, Martin. *The So-Called Historical Jesus and the Historic Biblical Christ.* Translated by Carl E. Braaten. Philadelphia: Fortress, 1977. [See. 14–15, 24, 35, 66, 89, 103; N.B. This book is a translation of the first and second essays from the 1896 edition of *Der sogenannte historische Jesus und der geschichtliche, biblische Christus.*]

Kallas, James G. *Jesus and the Power of Satan.* Philadelphia: Westminster, 1968. [Chapter 14 The Resurrection and Promised Return, See. 194–201]

Keener, Craig S. *The Historical Jesus of the Gospels.* Grand Rapids: Eerdmans, 2009. [Chapter 22 The Resurrection, See. 330–49; N.B. This work is a concise reading.]

Kent, Charles Foster. *The Life and Teachings of Jesus: According to the Earliest Records.* New York: Scribner's Sons, 1913. [Chapter 144 The Living Christ, See. 297–310; N.B. Archive.org, Google book, and HathiTrust]

Kephart, Cyrus Jeffries. *Jesus, Lord and Teacher.* Dayton, OH: Otterbein, 1913. [The Tragedy and the Triumph, See. 155–64]

———. *Jesus the Nazarene: A Brief Life of Our Savior, with a Parallel Harmony.* Dayton, OH: W. J. Shuey, 1894. [Chapter 8 Resurrection, Appearances, and Ascension, See. 63–66; N.B. Archive.org and HathiTrust]

Kiehl, Erich H. *The Passion of Our Lord.* Grand Rapids: Baker, 1990. [Chapter 15 Epilog: Jesus' Resurrection, See. 153–58]

Kingsland, John P. *The Man Called Jesus.* New York: Thomas Whittaker, 1903. [Chapter 12 The Resurrection, See. 246–80; N.B. Archive.org and Google book]

Kirke, Edmund [pseud.]. *The Life of Jesus According to His Original Biographers.* Lee & Shepard: Boston, 1867. [Part Ninth, See. 287–97; N.B. Google book. James Roberts Gilmore wrote under the name, Edmund Kirke]

Kirkland, Winifred. *The Great Conjecture: Who Is This Jesus?* New York: Henry Holt, 1929. [Chapter 4 The Jesus of the Resurrection, See. 105–32]

Kitto, John F. *Illustrated History of the Bible: . . . Including the Life of Christ and His Apostles.* Norwich, CT: Henry Brill, 1872. [See. 547–48; N.B. Google book and HathiTrust]

Klein, Felix. *Jesus and His Apostles.* Translated by W. P. Baines. London: Longmans, Green, 1932. [Chapter 30 The Resurrection, See. 341–52; Chapter 31 Farewell. The Invisible Presence, See. 353–63]

Klopstock, Frederich Gottlieb. *The Messiah: Descriptive of the Principal Events Attending the Passion, Crucifixion, Resurrection, and Ascension of Our Lord and Saviour Jesus Christ.* London: For R. Evans, 1824. [Book 14 See. 385–425; N.B. The Google book is a 1780 translation by Joseph and Mary Collyer.]

Knox, John. *The Church and the Reality of Christ.* New York: Harper & Row, 1962. [Chapter 3 The Church and the Resurrection, See. 60–77]

Komroff, Manuel. *The Story of Jesus.* Philadelphia: John C. Winston, 1955. [Part 5 Resurrection, See. 143–50]

Kopp, Clemens. *The Holy Places of the Gospels.* New York: Herder & Herder, 1963. [See. 389–90, 395–400, 402–5]

Köstenberger, Andreas J., and Justin Taylor. *The Final Days of Jesus: The Most Important Week of the Most Important Person Who Ever Lived.* Wheaton: Crossway, 2014. [Sunday (April 5, AD 33), See. 173–94; Epilogue: Later Appearances of Jesus and the Ascension, See. 195–202]

Krummacher, Friedrich W. *Christ and His People.* Translated by Samuel Macauley Jackson. London: Seeley, Jackson, & Halliday, 1855. [Part 2 The Messiah, 20. The Walk to the Sepulcher, See. 244–64; 21. Christ Appearing to Thomas, See. 264–71; 22. The Ascension, See. 271–79; N.B. Google book and HathiTrust]

Kuhn, Clyde L. *The Problem of Jesus.* Boston: Stratford, 1928. [Chapter 19 The Resurrection, See. 327–51]

Lacey, T. A. *The Historic Christ.* London: Longmans, Green, 1905. [Chapter 7 The Resurrection—The Historic Fact, See. 97–114; Chapter 8 The Resurrection—The Object of Faith, See. 115–30; Chapter 9 The Ascension, See. 131–49; N.B. Archive.org and Google book]

Lagrange, Marie-Joseph. *The Gospel of Jesus Christ.* Vol. 2. London: Burns, Oates & Washbourne, 1938. [Chapter 7 The Resurrection, Apparitions, and Ascension of Christ, See. 282–305]

Lamsa, George M. *The Man From Galilee: a Life of Jesus.* Garden City, NY: Doubleday, 1970. [Chapter 29 The Resurrection and the Ascension, See. 287–93]

Lange, Johann Peter, and Robert Smith, trans. *The Life of the Lord Jesus Christ: A Complete Critical Examination of the Origin, Contents, and Connection of the Gospels.* Edited by Marcus Dods. Vol. 6. Edinburgh: T&T Clark, 1864. [Section 22 The Resurrection of the Lord, See. 238–47; N.B. Archive.org (1872) and Google book]

Larned, C. W. *The Great Discourse of Jesus the Christ, the Son of God: A Topical Arrangement and Analysis of All His Words Recorded in the New Testament Separated from the Context.* New York: Revell, 1899. [Ministry and Passion. Death, Resurrection, and Ascension, See. 122–26; Chapter 11 Utterances After Resurrection, See. 127–30; N.B. Archive.org, Google book, and HathiTrust]

Laubach, Frank Charles. *The Greatest Life: Jesus Tells His Story.* Westwood, NJ: Revell, 1956. [See. 181–92]

Lawson, McEwan. *Understanding Jesus Christ.* Greenwich, CT: Seabury, 1955. [Chapter 11 Christ Still Alive, See. 157–71]

Layman, A. *The Life of our Saviour Jesus Christ by Question and Answer: Intended as a Reading Book for Schools . . . By a Layman.* Huntington: Thomas Lovell, 1826. [See. 161–83; N.B. Google book]

Laymon, Charles M. *Christ in the New Testament.* New York: Abingdon, 1958. [Resurrection of, See. 13–14, 44, 46, 58, 60, 69, 74, 132–34]

———. *The Life and Teachings of Jesus*. New York: Abingdon, 1958. [Chapter 25 The Resurrection, See. 305–15]

———. *Luke's Portrait of Christ*. New York: Abingdon, 1959. [Chapter 10 The Resurrected Life, See. 147–58]

Leask, William. *The Footsteps of the Messiah: A Review of Passages in the History of Jesus Christ*. New York: W. S. Martien, 1847. [Chapter 22 The First Day of the Week—Resurrection, See. 308–21; Chapter 23 Galilee—The Evidence Complete, See. 322–36; Chapter 24 Mount Olivet—The Ascension, See. 337–51; N.B. Archive.org]

Lebreton, Jules. *The Life & Teaching of Jesus Christ Our Lord*. New York: Macmillan, 1950. [Chapter 7 The Resurrection. The Appearances. The Ascension, See. 398–432]

Le Camus, Émile. *The Life of Christ*. Translated by William A. Hickey. New York: The Cathedral Library Association, 1906. [Book 2, Life, See. 412–92; Book 3, Glory. See. 493–501; N.B. Google book and HathiTrust]

Lee, John David. *From Bethlehem To Olivet*. New York: Abingdon-Cokesbury, 1942. [Chapter 6 The Crucifixion and Resurrection, See. 114–20]

Lee, Umphrey. *The Life of Christ: A Brief Outline for Students*. Nashville: Cokesbury Press, 1930. [Chapter 12 The Risen Christ, See. 164–75]

Lees, G. Robinson. *The Life of Christ*. New York: Dodd, Mead, 1920. [Chapter 42 The Resurrection and Ascension, See. 432–46; N.B. HathiTrust]

Le Feuvre, Amy. *The Most Wonderful Story in the World: A Life of Christ for Little Children*. New York: Revell, 1922. [See. 199–219; N.B. Archive.org. For children.]

Lemcio, Eugene E. *The Past of Jesus in the Gospels*. Cambridge: Cambridge University Press, 1991. [Matthew, See. 72–73; Luke, See. 74–90; John, See 95–106]

Léon-Dufour, Xavier. *The Gospels and the Jesus of History*. Translated by John McHugh. New York: Desclée, 1967. [Chapter 13 The Quest of the Historical Jesus. 4. The Resurrection: God's Final Word, See. 254–58]

Lessing, Erich. *Jesus History and Culture of the New Testament: A Pictorial Narration*. Translated by Kevin Smyth. New York: Herder & Herder, 1971. [See. 96–102]

Lester, Charles Stanley. *The Historic Jesus: A Study of the Synoptic Gospels*. New York: G. P. Putnam's Sons, 1912. [The Synoptic Gospels, See. 373–404; N.B. Archive.org]

Lewis, F. Warburton. *Jesus of Galilee*. 5th ed. London: Ivor Nicholson & Watson, 1933. [The First Day of the Week, See. 223–29; When It Was Evening, See. 230–34; Ascension, See. 235–40]

———. *Jesus of Galilee: Saviour of Men*. London: Epworth, 1954. [See. 425–61]

Liderbach, Daniel. *The Jesus of History as the Christ of Faith*. New York: Paulist, 2009. [Chapter 12 The Resurrection of Jesus, See. 80–83]

Life of Christ and his Apostles: From the Writings of Dr. Adam Clarke, Rev. Rufus W. Clark, and other Eminent Divines, and from the Bible . . . including Writers of the New Testament, Religious Creed and History of the Jews, and the True Christian Religion. Baltimore: A. Colby, 1867. [Chapter 23 Resurrection of Christ, See. 292–304; Chapter 24 The Walk To Emmaus, See. 305–17; Chapter 25 Christ's Ascension, 318–30]

Life of Our Saviour Jesus Christ, By Question and Answer, The: Adapted to the Comprehension of Young Persons, Intended as a Reading Book for Schools and Families . . . By a Layman. Huntingdon: Thomas Lovell, 1826. [See. 161–83; N.B. Google book]

Ligny, François de. *The History of the Life of Our Lord Jesus Christ, from His Incarnation until His Ascension, Denoting and Incorporating the Words of the Sacred Text from the Vulgate. Also the History of The Acts of the Apostles. Connected, Explained, and Blended with Reflections*. Translated by J. Sadlier. New York: D. & J. Sadlier, 1853. [Chapter 69 The Resurrection . . . See. 544–50; Chapter 70 Divers Apparitions . . . See. 551–58; Chapter 71 Apparition By the Sea-Side-Conclusion, See. 558–66; N.B. Archive.org and HathiTrust]

Limbaugh, David. *The True Jesus: Uncovering the Divinity of Christ in the Gospels*. Washington, SC: Regenery, 2017. [Chapter 12 From the flogging of Jesus to his ascension]

Lindvall, Michael L. *What Did Jesus Do? A Crash Course in His Life and Times*. New York: Sterling, 2006. [Life—The Last Word, See. 114–19]

Lockhart, Douglas. *Jesus the Heretic: Freedom and Bondage in a Religious World*. Shaftesbury: Element, 1997. [See. 86–91]

Lockyer, Herbert. *The Man Who Died For Me Meditations on the Death and Resurrection of Our Lord*. Waco, TX: Word, 1979. [Chapter 14 Who Saw Him Die? (Luke 24:46, 48), See. 110–20; Chapter 16 Visiting the Grave (Matt. 28:6), See. 130–36]

Lohfink, Gerhard. *Jesus of Nazareth: What He Wanted, Who He Was*. Translated by Linda M. Maloney. Collegeville, MN: Liturgical Press, 2012. [Chapter 18 The Easter Events, See. 288–307]

Longford, Frank Pakenham. *The Life of Jesus Christ*. Garden City, New York: Doubleday, 1975. [Chapter 12 Jesus Rises from the Dead, See. 163–74]

Longking, Joseph. *Notes, Illustrative and Explanatory, on the Holy Gospels: Arranged According to Townsend's Chronological New Testament*. Vol. 4. New York: Published by G. Lane & P. P. Sandford, for the Sunday School Union of the Methodist Episcopal Church, 1844. [Lessons 24–26, See. 456–510; N.B. Google book]

Lorimer, George C. *The Galilean, or Jesus, the World's Savior*. New York: Silver, Burdett, 1892. [Chapter 23 The Resurrection, See. 350–69; Chapter 24 The Ascension, See. 370–89; N.B. Archive.org]

———. *Jesus the World's Savior: Who He Is, Why He Came, and What He Did*. Chicago: S. C. Griggs, 1883. [Chapter 19 The Resurrection of Jesus, See. 284–97; N.B. Google book and HathiTrust]

Losch, Henry. *The God-Man: or, The Life and Works of Jesus, the Christ and Son of God: A Poem in Fifteen Parts*. Philadelphia: Ferris & Leach, 1904. [Part 10 Christ's Resurrection From the Dead, See. 106–22; N.B. Google book]

Lowrie, Walter. *The Short Story of Jesus*. New York: Scribner's Sons, 1943. [The Resurrection, See. 219–24]

Lucado, Max. *His Name Is Jesus: the Promise of God's Love Fulfilled*. Nashville: Nelson, 2009. [His Resurrection, See. 154–75]

Ludwig, Emil. *The Son of Man: The Story of Jesus*. Translated by Eden and Cedar Paul. New York: Boni & Liveright, 1928. [See. 313–15; N.B. Originally Emil Cohn, he was raised as a non-Jew but he was not baptized.]

Maas, A. J. *The Life of Jesus Christ According to the Gospel History*. 4th ed. St. Louis: Herder, 1904. [Part 4 The Resurrection and Ascension of Jesus, See. 554–91]; N.B. Google book and HathiTrust]

MacArthur, John. *One Perfect Life: The Complete Story of the Lord Jesus*. Nashville: Nelson, 2012. [Part 10, See. 470–99]

Macbride, John David. *Lectures of the Diatessaron, or The History of Our Lord and Saviour Jesus Christ, Collected from the Four Gospels, in the Form of a Continuous Narrative*. Oxford: John Henry Parker, 1838. [Part 7 See. 526–52; N.B. Google book]

Mackenzie, W. Douglas. *The Revelation of the Christ: Familiar Studies in the Life of Jesus.* London: Sunday School Union, 1896. [Chapter 34 The Resurrection, See. 277–85; Chapter 35 The Walk to Emmaus, See. 287–95]

Mackinnon, James. *The Historic Jesus.* London: Longmans, Green, 1931. [Chapter 9 The Resurrection of Jesus, See. 276–300]

MacMunn, Vivian. *Neglected Galilee: An Attempt to Read Between the Lines of the Gospels.* London: George Allen & Unwin, 1922. [94 pages; N.B. Archive.org]

Madden, Richard C. *Father Madden's Life of Christ.* Milwaukee: Bruce, 1960. [Chapter 32 He Is Risen, See. 158–61]

Maier, Paul L. *First Easter: The True and Unfamiliar Story in Words and Pictures.* San Francisco: Harper & Row, 1982. [Chapter 11 The Evidence: An Empty Tomb, See. 114–22]

———. *In the Fullness of Time: A Historian Looks At Christmas, Easter, and the Early Church.* New York: HarperSanFrancisco, 1991. [Chapter 22 The Unanticipated: Eastern Dawn, See. 179–88; Chapter 23 Explanations: Doubts and Skepticism, See. 189–96; Chapter 24 The Evidence: An Empty Tomb, See. 197–205]

Malleson, Frederick Amadeus. *Jesus Christ: His Life and His Work.* London: Ward, Lock & Bowden, 1880. [Chapters 41–43, See. 344–68; N.B. Google book]

Mann, C. S. *The Man For All Time.* New York: Morehouse-Barlow, 1971. [Chapter 20 Resurrection, See. 118–24]

Manson, T. W. *The Beginning of the Gospel.* London: Oxford University Press, 1950. [§72–85 The Empty Tomb, See. 104–8]

March, Daniel. *Days of the Son of Man.* Philadelphia: J. C. McCurdy, 1882. [Chapter 24 After His Passion, See. 643–76; N.B. Google book]

Marchant, James, ed. *Anthology of Jesus.* New York: Harper & Brothers, 1926. [Chapter 32 His Resurrection, See. 212–31; Chapter 33 The Ascension, See. 232–43]

Marnas, Mélanie. *Who Is Then This Man?* Translated by Henry Longan Stuart. New York: Dutton, 1929. [Chapter 21 Marvel On Marvel, See. 312–23]

Marsh, Clive, and Steve Moyise. *Jesus and the Gospels: An Introduction.* London: Cassell, 1999. [Resurrection stories, See. 15, 25, 27, 32, 40–41, 56, 68, 105]

Marsh, Gideon W. B. *Messianic Philosophy: An Historical and Critical Examination of the Evidence for the Existence, Death, Resurrection, Ascension, and Divinity of Jesus Christ.* London: Sands, 1908. [197 pages; N.B. Google book]

Marsh, John. *Jesus in His Lifetime.* London: Sidgwick & Jackson, 1981. [The Epilogue, See. 227–34; The Resurrection: A Supplementary Study, See. 235–45]

Martin, A. D. *A Plain Man's Life of Christ.* London: George Allen & Unwin, 1941. [Chapter 23 Resurrection, See. 197–208]

———. *Aspects of the Way: Being Meditations and Studies in the Life of Jesus Christ.* Cambridge: Cambridge University Press, 1924. [Chapter 10 His Ascension, See. 138–54]

Martin, Alfred W. *The Life of Jesus: In the Light of Higher Criticism.* New York: D. Appleton, 1913. [Chapter 6 The Resurrection, See. 209–49; N.B. Archive.org and Google book]

Martin, Hugh. *Luke's Portrait of Jesus.* London: SCM, 1949. [Chapter 9 The Risen Jesus, See. 98–105]

Martin, James. *The Empty Tomb: The Disappearance of Jesus as Related in the Letters of Caiphais the High Priest.* New York: Harper & Brothers, 1960. [93 pages; N.B. Fiction. Published in Great Britain under the title of "Letters of Caiaphas to Annas."]

Category V—Jesus's Life: Biographies and Historicity of Christ

Martin, James J. *Jesus: A Pilgrimage.* HarperCollins, 2014. [Chapters 22–25, See. 395–459]

Martin, von Cochem. *Cochem's Life of Christ.* Edited by Bonaventure Hammer. New York: Benziger, 1897. [Chapter 32 The Resurrection of Jesus, See. 286–95; Chapter 33 Jesus appears repeatedly to His Disciples, See. 296–306; Chapter 34 The Ascension of Jesus and the Descent of the Holy Ghost, See. 307–14; N.B. Archive.org]

Matheson, George. *Studies of the Portrait of Christ.* Vol. 2. London: Hodder & Stoughton, 1901. [Chapter 24 The Meaning of Easter Morning, See. 327–41; N.B. Archive.org]

Mathews, Basil Joseph. *A Little Life of Jesus.* New York: Richard R. Smith, 1931. [Chapter 65 The Prince of Life, See. 479–89; Chapter 66 Follow Me, See. 490–93]

Mauriac, François. *Life of Jesus.* Translated by Julie Kernan. New York: Longmans, Green, 1937. [Chapter 27 Resurrection, See. 239–45]

McAteer, Michael R., and Michael G. Steinhauser. *The Man in the Scarlet Robe: Two Thousand Years of Searching for Jesus.* Etobicoke, ON: United Church Publishing House, 1996. [Chapter 7 The Empty Tomb, See. 107–23]

McBirnie, William Steuart. *Preaching on the Life of Christ (Sermons on the Epochs in the Life of Christ).* Grand Rapids: Zondervan, 1958. [Chapter 6 The Risen Redeemer, See. 91–107]

McCasland, S. Vernon. *The Pioneer of Our Faith: A New Life of Jesus.* New York: McGraw-Hill, 1964. [The Resurrection, See. 181–88]

McClelland, Adam. *The History of Our Lord; Specially Adapted as a Textbook for Bible Classes and Institutions of Learning.* Dubuque, IA: Presbyterian Pub., 1898. [Chapter 17 From the Open Tomb to the Throne, i.e., April 9 to May 18, See. 338–46]

McConaughy, James. *The Great Events in the Life of Christ: In Twenty-Five Studies.* New York: Young Men's Christian Association Press, 1909. [See. 175–88; N.B. Google book]

———. *The Life Story of the Lord Jesus as Mark Tells It: A Bible Course for Older Boys and Girls.* Philadelphia: American Sunday-School Union, 1929. [Lesson 10 At the Right Hand of God, See. 60–63]

McConnell, T. M. *The Last Week with Jesus.* Nashville, Southern Methodist Publishing House, 1886. [See. 208–19; N.B. Google book]

McCrum, Michael. *The Man Jesus: Fact and Legend.* London: Janus, 2002. [Chapter 22 The Resurrection: Introduction, See. 118–26; Chapter 23 Ascension, See. 127–29]

McDonald, Lee Martin. *The Story of Jesus in History and Faith.* Grand Rapids: Baker Academic, 2013. [Part 3 Chapter 6 Easter: The Story of Jesus Within History and Faith, See. 271–332; N.B. This work should be examined carefully.]

McDowell, Josh, and Bill Wilson. *The Evidence for the Historical Jesus.* Nashville: Nelson, 1993. [Chapter 14 The Reliability of the Resurrection Reports, See. 278–90]

McFarland, John Thomas. *Etchings of the Master.* New York: Eaton & Mains, 1909. [See. 228–44; N.B. Google book]

McGrath, James. *The Burial of Jesus: History & Faith.* Charleston, SC: BookSurge, 2008. [Chapter 4 Jesus Beyond the Tomb: Matters of Death and (After)life, See. 99–127; Chapter 5 Conclusion: Beyond History, See. 129–42]

McKnight, Edgar V. *Jesus Christ in History and Scripture: A Poetic and Sectarian Perspective.* Macon, GA: Mercer University Press, 1999. [Jesus Christ resurrection, See. 8, 20, 40, 48, 67, 70, 81, 161, 174, 181, 186, 187, 192, 204, 207, 208, 213, 219, 233, 236, 239, 240, 247, 301]

McLaren, Robert Bruce. *What's Special About Jesus?* New York: Association Press, 1963. [Chapter 8 What Do You Mean . . . Arose From The Dead?, See. 112–14]

McLennan, William E. *In His Footsteps: A Record of Travel to and in the Land of Christ with an Attempt to Mark the Lord's Journeyings in Chronological Order from His Birth to His Ascension.* New York: Eaton & Mains, 1896. [Chapter 10 The Forty Days, See. 215–22; N.B. 1911 revised edition; Google book]

McNabb, Vincent. *A Life of Jesus God Our Lord.* New York: Sheed & Ward, 1938. [The Risen Life of Jesus, See. 181–97]

McWherter, Leroy. *The King of Glory—or—The Most Important Events—In—The Life of Jesus Christ—with—Their Precious and Practical Lessons to Humanity.* Nashville: Southwestern Publishing House, 1900. [Chapter 9 The Resurrection of the King, See. 215–45; Chapter 10 The Ascension of the King, See. 246–56; N.B. Google book and HathiTrust]

Meagher, Jas L. *The Tragedy of Calvary.* 2nd ed. New York: Christian Press, 1905. [Chapter 19 Three Days in the Tomb, the Resurrection and Ascension, See. 455–78; N.B. Archive.org]

Men, Alexander. *Son of Man.* Translated by Samuel Brown. Torrance, CA: Oakwood Publications, 1998. [Chapter 21 Victory Over Death, See. 203–12; Chapter 22 I Send You . . . , See. 213–17]

Meredith, Evan Powell. *The Prophet of Nazareth or A Critical Inquiry into the Prophetical, Intellectual, and Moral Character of Jesus Christ.* London: F. Farrah, 1864. [Chapter 6 Sections 3–4, See. 250–91; N.B. Archive.org, Google book, and HathiTrust]

Merezhkovsky, Dmitry Sergeyevich. *Jesus Manifest.* Translated by Edward Gellibrand. New York: Scribner's Sons, 1936. [Chapter 11 The Resurrection, See. 544–67; Chapter 12 He Is Risen Indeed, See. 568–86]

Merrick, Mary Virginia. *The Life of Christ: Course of Lectures Combining the Principal Events in the Life of Our Lord with the Catechism.* St. Louis: B. Herder, 1909. [Lessons 30–33, See. 53–64; N.B. Archive.org and HathiTrust]

Merrill, George E. *The Reasonable Christ: A Series of Studies.* New York: Silver, Burdett, 1893. [Chapter 13 The Risen Lord, See. 186–97; N.B. HathiTrust]

Messori, Vittorio. *Faith's Answer: The Mystery of Jesus.* Translated by Kenneth D. Whitehead. Edited by Eugene M. Brown. New Rochelle, NY: Don Bosco, 1986. [Jesus, resurrection of, See. 8, 10–11, 26, 27, 29, 99, 100, 114, 118, 120, 137, 138, 146–48, 150, 167, 171, 173–74, 180–81, 185, 188, 192, 199, 209–10, 239, 240, 274]

Meyer, Ben F. *The Man for Others.* New York: Bruce, 1970. [Chapter 7 The Stunning Reversal, See. 129–44]

Meyer, F. B. *Calvary to Pentecost.* New York: Fleming, 1894. [Chapter 2 The Resurrection, See. 25–43; Chapter 3 Ascension Day, See. 47–58; Chapter 10 The Supreme Gift of the Ascension, See. 145–60; N.B. Archive.org and Google book]

Meyer, Frank Herman. *The Crux of Chronology: An Essay to Establish the Life-Time of Jesus Christ and to Stabilize the Date of Easter.* Boston: B. Humphries, 1942. [Conclusion. The Crucifixion and Resurrection of Jesus Christ, See. 546]

Micklem, E. R. *The World's Ransom.* London: SCM, 1946. [Chapter 27 Jesus Lives, See. 141–44; Chapter 28 A Picture Suggested By John 21. 3, See. 145–49; Chapter 29 He Ascended Into Heaven, See. 150–55]

Miller, J. R. *Come Ye Apart: Daily Readings in the Life of Christ.* London: Nelson, 1890. [No pagination. See. Dec. 20—Dec. 31]

———. *Personal Friendships of Jesus.* New York: Thomas Y. Crowell, 1897. [Chapter 14 Jesus' Friendship After He Rose, See. 228–47; N.B. Google book]

Moffatt, James, ed. *Everyman's Life of Jesus: A Narrative in the Words of the Four Gospels.* New York: Doran, 1925. [Chapter 17 After Death, See. 221–29]

More, Paul Elmer. *The Christ of the New Testament.* Princeton: Princeton University Press, 1924. [Miracles and the Resurrection, See. 256–80]

Morell, Thomas. *Sacred Annals, or The Life of Christ, as Recorded by the Four Evangelists: With Practical Observations: Compiled from the Works of Bp. Taylor, Locke, Cradock, Whiston, Le Clerc, Lamy, Macknight, and Other Harmonizers of the Gospels, Principally Dr. Dodderidge. Designed for General Use: But Particularly for the Sunday-Exercise of the Young Gentlemen Educated at Eton School.* Second Edition. London: Longman, 1784. [Sect. 69, See. 428–52; N.B. Google book]

Morgan, G. Campbell. *The Crises of the Christ.* New York: Revell, 1903. [Book 6—The Resurrection, See. 345–84; Book 7—The Ascension, See. 385–97; N.B. Google book]

Morgan, Richard. *The Christ of the Cross: Dare Christians Follow Him?* New York: R. R. Smith, 1950. [Chapter 6 Jesus the Risen Lord, See. 137–56]

Morison, John Hopkins. *Scenes from the Life of Jesus.* Boston: Crosby, Nichols, 1854. [Chapter 30 The Morning Of the Resurrection, See. 130–34; Chapter 31 The Ascension, See. 134–37; N.B. Google book and HathiTrust]

Muggeridge, Malcolm. *Jesus: The Man Who Lives.* New York: Harper & Row, 1975. [Part 3 The Man Who Lives, See. 188–91]

Muncaster, Ralph O. *Evidence for Jesus.* Eugene, OR: Harvest House, 2004. [Chapter 16 Prophecies About Jesus' Crucifixion and Resurrection, See. 188]

Murphy, Catherine M. *The Historical Jesus for Dummies.* Hoboken, NJ: Wiley, 2008. [Part 4 Witnessing Jesus's Execution and Resurrection. Chapter 15 The Resurrection: From the Messiah to the Son of God, See. 239–56]

Murphy, John. *An Evangelical Life of Our Lord and Saviour Jesus Christ: Forming a Harmony of the Four Gospels: Together with the History of the Church, Until the Promulgation of the Decrees of the Council of Jerusalem: Carefully Compiled . . . in an Appendix . . .* Dublin: Printed by J.J. Nolan for John Murphy, 1820. [Third Part. Chapters 1–8, See. 194–204; N.B. Google book]

Murry, J. Middleton. *The Life of Jesus.* London, Jonathan Cape, 1926. [Epilogue, See. 311–17]

Nappa, Mike. *God in Slow Motion: Reflections on Jesus and the 10 Unexpected Lessons You Can See in His Life.* Nashville: Nelson, 2013. [Chapter 10 Bloodied Hope, See. 183–202]

Neander, August. *The Life of Jesus Christ in Its Historical Connexion and Historical Development.* Translated from the Fourth German Edition. New York: Harper, 1849. [Chapter 8 The Resurrection, See. 422–35; Chapter 9 The Ascension, See. 436–38; N.B. Archive.org and HathiTrust]

Nelson, W. H. *A Walk With Jesus.* Cincinnati: Jennings & Pye, 1901. [Chapter 8 Words and Acts of Jesus from the Resurrection to the Ascension, See. 445–62; N.B. Archive.org]

Neufeld, Thomas R. Yoder. *Recovering Jesus: The Witness of the New Testament.* Grand Rapids: Brazos, 2007. [Chapter 12 Resurrection of Jesus, See. 267–90]

Neumann, Arno. *Jesus.* Translated by Maurice A. Canney. London: Black, 1906. [Chapter 17 The Resurrection Faith, See. 164–70; N.B. Google book]

Newcome, William. *Observations on Our Lord's Conduct as a Divine Instructor: And on the Excellence of His Moral Character . . .* Oxford: At The University Press, 1853. [See. 111–12, 138, 146, 147, 155, 260, 302, 303, 327, 340, 368, 418, 419, 424; N.B. Google book]

Newton, Richard. *The Life of Jesus Christ for the Young*. Philadelphia: Gebbie & Barrie, 1880. [Chapter 35 The Resurrection, See. 825-46; Chapter 36 The Ascension, See. 847-66; N.B. Archive.org and Google book]

Nicoll, W. Robertson. *The Church's One Foundation: Christ and Recent Criticism*. New York: Armstrong, 1902. [Chapter 6 The Resurrection of Our Lord from the Dead, See. 130-50; N.B. Archive.org and HathiTrust]

———. *The Incarnate Saviour: A Life of Jesus Christ*. Edinburgh: T&T Clark, 1897. [Chapter 20 The Burial and Resurrection of Christ, See. 267-81; Chapter 21 The Resurrection Life of Christ, See. 283-93; Chapter 22 The Ascension of Christ, See. 295-306; N.B. Google book]

Niles, Daniel T. *Living with the Gospel*. New York: Association Press, 1957. [Chapter 8 Whom God Raised Up, See. 84-92]

Nodet, Etienne. *The Historical Jesus? Necessity and Limits of an Inquiry*. Translated by J. Edward Crowley. New York: T&T Clark, 2008. [Resurrection, See. 13-14]

Noel, Conrad. *The Life of Jesus*. New York: Simon & Schuster, 1937. [Chapter 39 The Mighty Resurrection, See. 514-27; Chapter 40 The Glorious Ascension, See. 528-31]

Nolloth, Charles Frederick. *The Person of our Lord and Recent Thought*. Macmillan: London, 1908. [Chapter 11 The Resurrection, See. 237-53; N.B. Archive.org and Google book]

Norborg, C. Sverre. *Christ on Main Street*. Minneapolis: Denison, 1959. [The Third Day, See. 387-400]

O'Brien, John A. *The Life of Christ*. New York: J. J. Crawley, 1957. [Chapter 40 The Risen Christ, See. 565-90]

O'Collins, Gerald. *Experiencing Jesus*. New York: Paulist, 1994. [Resurrection, See. 102-9]

———. *Jesus: A Portrait*. Maryknoll, NY: Orbis Books, 2008. [Chapter 11 Jesus The Lord of Glory, See. 183-200]

O'Connell, John P., and Jex Martin, eds. *The Life of Christ: Our Lord's Life with Lessons in His Own Words for Our Life Today*. Chicago: Catholic Press, 1954. [Part 10 The Risen Christ, See. 289-304]

Olmstead, A. T. *Jesus in the Light of History*. New York: Scribner's Sons, 1942. [Chapter 13 The Risen Messiah, See. 247-61; Chapter 14 The Christ Triumphant, See. 262-74]

Orchard, Bernard. *Born to Be King: The Epic of the Incarnation*. London: Ealing Abbey Scriptorium, 1993. [Chapter 2 From Resurrection to Pentecost, See. 317-35]

Osborn, Edwin Faxon. *The Vanishing of the Prince: A Narrative of the Life of Christ From the Triumphal Entry to the Ascension*. 5th ed. Kalamazoo, MI: Prince, 1898. [Chapters 9-14, See. 178-303; N.B. Archive.org]

Our Saviour: or, A Brief Exposition of the Birth, Teaching, Miracles, Death, Resurrection and Great Commission, of Jesus Christ. Philadelphia: American Baptist Publishing Society, 1844. [144 pages; juvenile; N.B. Google book and HathiTrust. The work is anonymously identified "By A Teacher."]

Paassen, Pierre van. *Why Jesus Died*. New York: Dial, 1949. [Chapter 7 What Happened to the Body of Jesus, See. 176-206]

Page, Charles R. *Jesus & the Land*. Nashville: Abingdon, 1995. [Epilogue: The Resurrection of Jesus, 165-71]

Page, Kirby. *The Personality of Jesus: Pathways by Which He Climbed the Heights of Life*. New York: Association Press, 1932. [Chapter 12 The Resurrection, See. 128-35]

Page, Nick. *The Longest Week*. London: Hodder & Stoughton, 2009. [Chapter 7 Day Seven: The Silence—Saturday 4 April, See. 250–53; Day Eight: The Return—Sunday 5 April, See. 254–66]

Pagola, Jose Antonio. *Jesus: An Historical Approximation*. Miami, FL: Convivum Press, 2011. [Chapter 14 Raised by God, See. 387–412]

Papini, Giovanni. *Life of Christ*. Translated by Dorothy Canfield Fisher. New York: Harcourt, Brace, 1923. [He Is Not Here, See. 380–408; N.B. Archive.org]

Paradise, Frank Ilsley. *Jesus Christ and the Spirit of Youth*. Boston: Small, Maynard, 1923. [Chapter 18 The Resurrection, See. 227–36]

Parini, Jay. *Jesus: The Human Face of God*. Boston: Houghton Mifflin Harcourt, 2013. [Chapter 7 Resurrection, See. 118–35]

Pate, C. Marvin. *40 Questions About the Historical Jesus*. Grand Rapids: Kregel, 2015. [Part 4 Questions About Jesus' Crucifixion and Resurrection, See. 343–69]

Patterson, Alexander. *The Greater Life and Work of Christ: As Revealed in Scripture, Man, and Nature*. Chicago: Revell, 1896. [Chapter 4 Christ In His Earthly Life, See. 196–212; N.B. HathiTrust]

Patterson, Stephen J. *Beyond the Passion: Rethinking the Death and Life of Jesus*. Minneapolis: Fortress, 2004. [Epilogue: The Resurrection of a Nobody, See. 103–21]

———. *The God of Jesus: The Historical Jesus and the Search for Meaning*. Harrisburg, PA: Trinity Press International, 1998. [Chapter 7 Was Jesus Right? On the Meaning of Resurrection, See. 211–40]

Patton, William. *Jesus of Nazareth: Who Was He? and What Is He Now?* London: Religious Tract Society, 1878. [Chapter 11 The Resurrection, See. 229–82; Chapter 12 The Ascension, See. 285–92; N.B. Google book]

Paul, Leslie Allen. *Son of Man*. New York: E. P. Dutton, 1961. [Chapter 18 The Epilogue Which was a Prologue, See. 254–68]

Pax, Wolfgang E. *In the Footsteps of Jesus*. New York: Putnam, 1970. [The Empty Tomb—The Ascension, See. 212–20]

Pearson, Charles William. *The Carpenter Prophet: A Life of Jesus Christ and a Discussion of His Ideals*. Chicago: H. S. Stone, 1902. [Chapter 25 The Resurrection, See. 218–30; Chapter 26 The Ascension, See. 231–37; N.B. Archive.org and Google book]

Pentecost, J. Dwight. *The Words and Works of Jesus Christ: A Study of the Life of Christ*. Grand Rapids: Zondervan, 1981. [Chapter 10 The Resurrection of the King, See. 495–513]

Peters, F. E. *Jesus & Muhammad: Parallel Tracks, Parallel Lives*. New York: Oxford University Press, 2011. [Chapter 8 A New Dawn: The Aftermath, the Legacy, See. 143–51]

Peters, G. M. *The Master, or, The Story of Stories Retold*. New York: Revell, 1911. [Chapter 31 Victory, See. 429–48; Chapter 32 Glory, See. 449–61; N.B. Google book and HathiTrust]

Phelps, Elizabeth Stuart [pseud.]. *The Story of Jesus Christ: An Interpretation*. Boston: Houghton, Mifflin, 1897. [Chapter 27 The Resurrection and the Life, See. 396–413; N.B. In most writings the author used her mother's name "Elizabeth Stuart Phelps" as a pseudonym, both before and after her marriage in 1888 to Herbert Dickson Ward. The name "Ward" is handwritten after "Phelps" in the Google book.]

Phillips, Wendell. *An Explorer's Life of Jesus*. New York: Two Continents Pub. Group, 1975. [Chapters 18–24, See. 415–89]

Piatt, Christian., ed. *Banned Questions About Jesus*. St. Louis: Chalice Press, 2011. [See. 95–97, 106–7]

Pickl, Josef. *The Messias*. Translated by Andrew Green St Louis: Herder, 1946. [Chapter 11 Sequel to the Passion, See. 306–27]

Piepenbring, Charles. *The Historical Jesus*. Translated by Lilian A. Clare. Macmillan: New York, 1924. [Chapter 7 Jesus' Passion and Resurrection, See. 154–71; N.B. Archive.org]

Pitre, Brant James. *The Case for Jesus: The Biblical and Historical Evidence for Christ*. New York: Image, 2016. [Chapter 12 The Resurrection, See. 173–91]

Plumptre, E. H. *Christ and Christendom*. London: A. Strahan, 1867. [Chapter 8 The Resurrection, See. 285–314; N.B. Google book and HathiTrust]

Poling, Daniel A. *Between Two Worlds: The Romance of Jesus*. New York: Harper & Brothers, 1931. [Chapter 39 He Is Risen! See. 217–20; Chapter 40 What the Stranger Said, See. 221–24; Chapter 41 The Light on the Shore, See. 225–28; Chapter 42 Home Coming, See. 229]

Pollock, John. *The Master: A Life of Jesus*. Wheaton, IL: Victor, 1985. [Part 3 Glorious Morning, See. 215–40]

Ponsonby, Reginald G. *The Life and Teaching of Christ: In the Very Words of Scripture*. London: Simpkin Marshall, 1928. [Part 9 The Resurrection and Ascension, See. 233–52]

Porter, J. R. *Jesus Christ: The Jesus of History, the Christ of Faith*. New York: Oxford University Press, 1999. [Aftermath, See. 128–34; Jesus In Art: The Resurrection, See. 218–19; Christ Triumphant, See. 220]

Porter, Stanley E., and Stephen J. Bedard. *Unmasking the Pagan Christ: An Evangelical Response to the Cosmic Christ Idea*. Toronto: Clements, 2006. [Chapter 4 The Birth, Death and Resurrection of Jesus: Did It Happen Before?, See. 66–69]

Potin, Jacques. *Jesus in His Homeland*. Maryknoll, NY: Orbis Books, 1997. [See. 108–11]

Power, Philip Bennett. *The Feet of Jesus: In Life, Death, Resurrection, and Glory*. London: Hamilton, Adams, 1872. [Chapters 12–14 See. 196–303; N.B. Archive.org]

Prat, Ferdinand. *Jesus Christ: His Life, His Teaching, and His Work*. Translated by John J. Heenan. Vol. 2. Milwaukee: Bruce, 1950. [Note X The Apparitions of the Risen Christ, See. 528–31; Note Y. The Question of Emmaus, See. 532–35]

Pressensé, Edmond de. *Jesus Christ: His Times, Life and Work*. Translated by Annie Harwood. London: Hodder & Stoughton, 1872. [Chapter 6 The Resurrection of Jesus Christ, See. 485–509; N.B. Google book]

Puig i Tàrrech, Armand. *Jesus: A Biography*. Waco, TX: Baylor University Press, 2011. [Chapter 6 From Death to Life, See. 607–28; N.B. This work is worth exploring.]

Puiseux, J. *Life of Our Lord and Saviour Jesus Christ*. Translated by Roderick McEachen. New York: D. H. McBride, 1900. [Part Third. Chapter 5 The Resurrection, See. 185–93; Chapter 6 The Ascension, See. 194–95; N.B. Archive.org and HathiTrust. Not useful.]

Pulsford, W. Hanson. *Scenes in the Life of Jesus: Thirty-Six Lessons for Advanced Classes*. Boston: Unitarian Sunday-School Society, 1895. [Lesson 36 The Resurrection, no pagination; N.B. Google book. Pulsford opines " . . . the gospels and Acts do not warrant our thinking of a bodily, resurrection of the crucified teacher."]

Purinton, Herbert R., and Sadie Brackett Costello. *The Achievement of the Master*. New York: Scribner's Sons, 1926. [Chapter 24 Victory Over Death, See. 190–95; N.B. Useless.]

Rall, Harris Franklin. *The Life of Jesus*. New York: Abingdon, 1917. [Chapter 24 The Risen Christ, See. 188–93; N.B. Google book. Not useful.]

Ramsey, Russ. *Behold the King of Glory: A Narrative of the Life, Death, and Resurrection of Jesus Christ*. Wheaton. IL: Crossway, 2015. [Chapters 36–40, See. 210–35]

Randolph, Thomas. *A View of Our Blessed Saviour's Ministry and the Proofs of His Divine Mission Arising from Thence Together with a Charge, Dissertations, Sermons, and Theological Lectures*. Oxford: Printed for J&J Fletcher & Mess. Rivington, London, 1784. [Chapter 6 See. 260–380; N.B. Google book]

Rankin, John Chambers. *A Believer's Life of Christ*. Natick, MA: Wilde, 1960. [Chapter 25 Resurrection and Ascension, See. 166–74; Chapter 26 Humiliation and Exaltation, See. 175–83; N.B. Not useful.]

Reading, William. *The History of Our Lord and Saviour Jesus Christ In Three Parts*. London: Printed for J. Watts, 1716. [Part 3 Containing the Occurrences of the Great Week, or Last Passover of Christ's Ministry; with the account of his Resurrection and Ascension, See. 264–351; N.B. Google book]

Reams, William. *The Whole Man: Meditations on the Life of Christ*. Conyers, GA: Our Lady of the Holy Spirit Abbey, 1996. [Chapter 14 He Is Risen—He Is Not Here, See. 223–36; N.B. Useless.]

Reardon, Patrick Henry. *The Jesus We Missed: The Surprising Truth About the Humanity of Christ*. Nashville: Nelson, 2012. [Chapter 12 Risen In Flesh, See. 191–201; N.B. Not useful.]

Reumann, John. *Jesus in the Church's Gospels: Modern Scholarship and the Earliest Sources*. Philadelphia: Fortress, 1968. [Chapter 5 God Raised Him from the Dead, See. 110–41]

Rhees, Rush. *The Life of Jesus of Nazareth: A Study*. New York: Scribner's Sons, 1921. [Chapter 9 The Resurrection, See. 201–16; N.B. Google book]

Rhymer, Joseph. *The Illustrated Life of Jesus Christ*. New York: Grove Weidenfeld, 1991. [The Resurrection and Ascension, See. 172–81; Useless.]

Ricciotti, Giuseppe. *The Life of Christ*. Translated by Alba I. Zizzamia. Milwaukee: Bruce, 1947. [Chapter 26 The Second Life, See. 648–68]

Roberson, Carroll. *The Christ: His Miracles, His Ministry, His Mission*. Green Forrest, AZ: New Leaf, 2005. [See. 255–72]

Robertson, A. T. *Epochs in the Life of Jesus: A Study of Development and Struggle in the Messiah's Work*. New York: Scribner's Sons, 1907. [Chapter 8 The Final Triumph of Jesus, See. 169–90; N.B. Archive.org and HathiTrust]

Robinson, Donald F. *Jesus, Son of Joseph: A Re-Examination of the New Testament Record*. Boston: Beacon, 1964. [Chapter 2 The Resurrection Experience, See. 5–22; N.B. Worthy examining.]

Rogers, Arthur Kenyon. *The Life and Teachings of Jesus: A Critical Analysis of the Sources of the Gospels, Together with a Study of the Sayings of Jesus*. New York, London: Putnam, 1894. [Chapter 9 The Resurrection of Jesus, See. 326–35; N.B. Archive.org and Google book]

Rogers, James Edwin Thorold. *Rabbi Jeshua: An Eastern Story*. London: C. Kegan Paul, 1881. [See. 150; N.B. Google book. Useless.]

Rollins, Wallace Eugene, and Marion Benedict Rollins. *Jesus and His Ministry*. Greenwich, CT: Seabury, 1954. [Chapter 15 The Resurrection, See. 266–84; N.B. This chapter is useful to examine.]

Roscamp, R. G. *The Life of Jesus Christ: A Systematic Arrangement of the Principal Events in the Life of "the great Nazarene," especially adapted to the Youth of the Age*. New York: Abbey Press, 1902. [See. 227–55; N.B. Archive.org]

Ross, Alexander Wendell. *The Christ*. New York: Revell, 1938. [Chapter 12 Jesus and Tomorrow, See. 202–22]

Roth, Timothy Dean. *The Week That Changed the World: The Complete Easter Story*. New York: Seabury, 2009. [Chapter 9 Saturday, See. 88–92; Chapter 10 Easter Sunday, See. 93–100; Chapter 11 Ascension, See. 101–6; N.B. Not useful.]

Row, C. A. *The Jesus of the Evangelists: His Historical Character Vindicated; or, An Examination of the Internal Evidence of Our Lord's Divine Mission with Reference to Modern Controversy*. London: Williams & Norgate, 1868. [See. 412–19; N.B. Google book]

Rowlingson, Donald Taggart. *The Gospel-Perspective on Jesus Christ*. Philadelphia: Westminster, 1968. [Resurrection of Jesus, See. 19, 48, 51–53, 63, 70, 84, 87, 90, 93, 95, 98, 136, 139, 154–56, 168, 172, 177, 180, 183, 185, 208, 213; Ascension, See. 51, 139–40, 210]

Rustomjee, Framroz. *An Interpretation of the Life of Jesus the Christ*. Colombo: Rustomjee, 1976. [Chapter 52 The Physical Body of Jesus, See. 164–70; Chapter 53 Ascension of Jesus, See. 170; N.B. The author advocates a spiritual resurrection.]

Ryland, John. *The Life and Actions of Jesus Christ by Way of Question and Answer: For the Edification of Children and Youth in Four Parts*. London: T & J W. Pasham, 1767. [See. 78–82; N.B. Google book. Juvenile.]

Sackman, Lana, and Rasmus Alsaker. *Behold the Man: A Revelation of Christ the Master*. New York: Grafton, 1928. [The Resurrection, See. 197–205]

Sadler, J. *Sacred Records, of the History of Our Lord and Saviour Jesus Christ*. 2nd ed. London: Printed for the Author; and Published by W.H. Hyde, Newcastle-under-Lyne, 1836. [Chapter 12 AD 33. —Tiberius, 19, 20. The Day of Our Lord's Resurrection, Commonly called Easter Sunday, See. 395–417; The Miracle of Christ's Resurrection, See. 428–34; N.B. Google book]

Sailhamer, John H. *The Life of Christ*. Grand Rapids: Zondervan, 1998. [The Resurrection and Appearances of Jesus, See. 121–25]

Sallmon, William H. *Studies in the Life of Jesus: For Bible Classes and Private Use*. New York: International Committee of Young Men's Christian Associations, 1907. [Study 25, See. 136–42; N.B. Archive.org]

Salmond, S. D. F. *The Life of Christ*. Edinburgh: T&T Clark, 18??. [Chapter 6 The Resurrection and Ascension, See. 105–7]

Sanday, William. *The Life of Christ in Recent Research*. New York: Oxford University Press, 1907. [Resurrection, The, See. 73, 75–76, 132; N.B. Google book]

———. *Outlines of the Life of Christ*. 2nd ed. Edinburgh: T&T Clark, 1906. [Chapter 6 The Messianic Crisis. See. The Resurrection, See. 178–86; The Ascension, See. 186–90; N.B. Google book]

Sanders, E. P. *The Historical Figure of Jesus*. London: Allen Lane, 1993. [Chapter 17 Epilogue: The Resurrection, See. 276–81]

Sanders, Frank Knight. *Historical Notes on the Life of Christ*. New York: Scribner's Sons, 1905. [Chapter 50 The Risen Christ, See. 191–94; Chapter 51 The Last Instructions, See. 195–98; N.B. Google book]

Santucci, Luigi. *Meeting Jesus: A New Way to Christ*. Translated by Bernard Wall. New York: Herder & Herder, 1971. [Resurrection and Ascension, See. 207–22; N.B. Not useful.]

Saunders, Ernest W. *Jesus in the Gospels*. Englewood Cliffs, NJ: Prentice-Hall, 1967. [Chapter 12 The Easter Gospel, See. 292–312]

Savage, Minot Judson. *Out of Nazareth*. Boston: American Unitarian Association, 1903. [Appendix 3 The Empty Tomb, See. 355–78; N.B. Google book; Savage was a Unitarian with a very liberal interpretation of the recorded events.]

Schauffler, William G. *Meditations on the Last Days of Christ: Together with Three Meditations on the Thirty Years of Silence and One on Daniels Rest*. New York: American Tract Society, 1853. [See. 193–340; N.B. Archive.org. This work consists of ten sermons.]

Schleiermacher, Friedrich. *The Life of Jesus*. Edited by Jack C. Verheyden. Translated by S. MacLean Gilmour. Philadelphia: Fortress, 1975. [Third Period: B. The Story of Christ's Resurrection Until His Ascension, See. 431–81; N.B. This work is a must read.]

Schlink, Edmund. *Victor Speaks*. Translated by Paul F. Koehneke. St. Louis: Concordia, 1958. [Chapters 9–17, See. 52–126]

Schmidt, Nathaniel. *The Prophet of Nazareth*. London: Macmillan, 1905. [Excursus C. The Resurrection, See. 392–98; N.B. Google book]

Schnabel, Eckhard J. *Jesus in Jerusalem: The Last Days*. Grand Rapids: Eerdmans, 2018. [The Empty Tomb and Jesus' Appearances to the Women, See. 350–62; Excursus 13: The Ending of Mark, 362–66; Jesus' Appearances to the Disciples, See. 366–75; N.B. Schnabel's text is an excellent work that is a required reading.]

Schröter, Jens. *Jesus of Nazareth: Jew From Galilee, Savior of the World*. Translated by Wayne Coppins and S. Brian. Pounds. Baylor University, 2014. [Resurrection, Empty Tomb, and Appearances: Death and No End, See. 203–11]

Schwartzkopff, Paul. *The Prophecies of Jesus Christ: Relating to His Death, Resurrection, and Second Coming, and Their Fulfilment*. Translated by Neil Buchanon. Edinburgh: T&T Clark, 1897. [Chapter 3 Jesus' Predictions of His Resurrection, See. 61–155; N.B. Google book]

Schweitzer, Albert. *The Quest of the Historical Jesus . . .* 2nd. English edition. Translated by William Montgomery. Adam & Charles Black: London, 1911. [See. 3, 15, 20, 21, 25, 43, 54, 55, 60, 64, 66, 83, 84, 86, 95, 102, 106, 11, 113–15, 130, 131, 136, 145, 153, 165, 167, 169, 170, 176, 198, 232, 233, 241, 256, 257, 260, 261, 267, 306, 312, 316, 327, 331, 332, 334, 337, 343, 344, 345, 364, 370, 372, 379, 380, 381, 384; N.B. Archive.org and Google book]

Schweitzer, Don. *Jesus Christ for Contemporary Life: His Person, Work, and Relationships*. Eugene, OR: Cascade, 2012. [Part 1 Jesus' Resurrection, See. 27–44; From Risen Christ to Second Person of the Trinity, See. 45–51]

Schweizer, Eduard. *Jesus: The Parable of God: What Do We Really Know about Jesus?* Allison Park, PA: Pickwick, 1994. [Chapter 5 Jesus the Resurrected, See. 71–92]

Scott, Joseph John. *The Life of Christ: A Continuous Narrative in the Words of the Authorised Version of the Four Gospels*. New York: E. P. Dutton, 1905 [Chapter 14 The Resurrection, See. 294–303; Chapter 15 The Ascension, See. 304–6]

Scott, Thomas. *The English Life of Jesus*. Mount Pleasant, Ramsgate: Thomas Scott, 1872. [Chapter 6 The Crucifixion, Resurrection, and Ascension of Jesus, See. 316–44; N.B. Google book]

Scrymgeour, William. *Lessons on the Life of Jesus.* Edinburgh: T&T Clark, 1883. [Lesson 31 The Resurrection of Our Lord, See. 211–19; Lesson 32 From the Resurrection to the Ascension, See. 220–27; N.B. Ebscohost.com]

Seaver, Richard W. *To Christ Through Criticism: Containing the Substance of the Donnellan Lectures Delivered before the University of Dublin, 1905–6.* Edinburgh: T&T Clark, 1906. [Chapter 6 The Resurrection Fact, See. 119–36; Chapter 7 The Resurrection Form, See. 137–56; N.B. Google book]

Séché, Alphonse. *The Radiant Story of Jesus.* Translated by Helen Davenport Gibbons. New York: Century, 1927. [Chapter 6 Hell and Heaven, See. 356–81; N.B. Archive.org]

Segundo, Juan Luis. *The Historical Jesus of the Synoptics.* Maryknoll, NY: Orbis Books, 1985. [Appendix 1. The Resurrected Jesus, See. 167–77]

Selbie, W. B. *The Life & Teaching of Jesus Christ.* New York: Hodder & Stoughton, 1909. [Chapter 11 The Resurrection and Ascension, See. 147–56; N.B. Google book]

Sell, Henry T. *Bible Studies in the Life of Christ: Historical and Constructive.* New York: Revell, 1902. [Chapter 8 The Resurrection, See. 145–60; N.B. Archive.org and Google book]

Shaw, Elton Raymond. *The Man of Galilee: A Short Sketch of Christ's Three Years of Ministry.* Grand Rapids: Shaw, 1912. [Chapter 12 The Trial —The Crucifixion—The Resurrection, See. 153–59; N.B. Google book]

Shearer, James W. *The Pictured Outline of the Gospel Narrative.* St. Louis; 1900. Part 10 Resurrection Appearances, See. 207–22; N.B. Archive.org]

Shearer, J. B. *Studies in the Life of Christ.* Richmond: Presbyterian Committee of Publication, 1907. [Chapter 16 The Resurrection and Ascension, See. 143–54; N.B. Archive.org and Google book]

Sheed, F. J. *To Know Christ Jesus.* New York: Sheed & Ward, 1962. [Chapter 44 Resurrection and Ascension, See. 356–63]

Sheen, Francis J. *The Book of the Saviour.* New York: Sheed & Ward, 1952. [Life Victorious, See. 394–95]

———. *The Eternal Galilean.* New York: Appleton, 1934. [See. 133–47]

———. *Life of Christ.* New York: McGraw-Hill, 1958. [Chapters 54–61, See. 480–533]

Shepard, John Watson. *The Christ of the Gospels. An Exegetical Study.* 4th ed., revised. Grand Rapids: Eerdmans, 1947. [Chapter 34 The Resurrection, See. 608–35]

Shorto, Russell. *Gospel Truth: The New Image of Jesus Emerging from Science and History and Why It Matters.* New York: Riverhead, 1997. [Chapter 11 Resurrection, See. 213–30]

Sinclair, Upton. *A Personal Jesus: Portrait and Interpretation.* New York: Evans, 1952. [Book 3: Spirit, See. 131–39]

Slack, Elvira J. *Jesus, the Man of Galilee: Studies in the Life of Jesus Arranged for Secondary School Students—Adapted both to Class Use and to Personal Study.* New York, National Board of the Young Women's Christian Associations of the United States of America, 1911. [Chapter 11 The Upper Room. Section 6. The Wonderful Fact of the Resurrection, See. 207–8; Section 7. The Last Wish of Our Lord, See. 209–10; N.B. Google book]

Sloyan, Gerard S. *Christ the Lord.* New York: Herder & Herder, 1962. [See. 220–31]

———. *Jesus In Focus: A Life In Its Setting.* Mystic, CT: Twenty-Third Publications, 1983. [Chapter 20 The Man Raised from the Dead, See. 145–52]

Smith, David. *The Days of His Flesh: The Earthly Life of Our Lord and Savior Jesus Christ.* 2nd ed. Hodder & Stoughton: London, 1905 [Chapter 50 The Resurrection, See. 505–26; N.B. Archive.org and Google book]

———. *Our Lord's Earthly Life.* New York: Doran, 1926. [The Resurrection, See. 466–94]

Smith, Paul. *Jesus: Meet Him Again for the First Time.* Gresham, OR: Vision House, 1994. [Coming to Believe (John 19:38–20:31), See. 149–56; Feed My Sheep (John 21:1–19), See. 157–61; Where In The World Is Jesus (Acts 1:1–11), See. 163–70]

Smith, Robert Ora. *A Biography of Jesus Christ.* New York: Vantage Press, 1987. [Chapter 38 The Resurrection of Jesus, See. 200–203; Chapter 39 The Appearances of Jesus after His Resurrection, See. 204–13; Chapter 40 Promises that Jesus Made to His Followers, See. 214–18; Chapter 41 Jesus Makes a New Covenant with His Followers, See. 219–20; N.B. Useless.]

Smith, William A. M. *The History of the Holy Jesus Containing a Brief Account of the Birth and Life, the Death, Resurrection, & Ascension of Our Blessed Saviour.* 5th ed. London: Printed for Eben Tracy, 1708. [The Resurrection of our Blessed Lord and Savior Jesus Christ, See. 103–27; N.B. Google book]

Smyth, John Paterson. *A People's Life of Christ.* London: Hodder & Stoughton, 1921. [Book 6 Jerusalem, Chapter 10 The Resurrection, See. 403–7; Chapter 11 An Old Man's Easter Memories, See. 408–15; Chapter 12 The Training of the Forty Days, See. 416–22; N.B. Google book]

Snowden, James H. *Scenes and Sayings in the Life of Christ.* New York: Revell, 1904. [Chapter 47–50, See. 338–65]

Soelle, Dorothee, and Luise Schottroff. *Jesus of Nazareth.* Translated by John Bowden. Louisville: Westminster John Knox, 2002. [Chapter 18 Resurrection, See. 129–38]

Soltau, George. *Four Portraits of the Lord Jesus Christ.* New York: Charles C. Cook, 1905. [Chapter 13 The Resurrection and Ascension, See. 231–54; N.B. Archive.org]

South, James T. *Just Jesus: The Evidence of History.* Chillicothe, OH: Deward, 2012. [Chapter 7 Did Jesus Really Rise From the Dead?, See. 117–36; N.B. The author presents eight rationales that suggest Jesus probably rose from the dead.]

Southgate, Henry. *Christus Redemptor: Being the Life, Character, and Teachings of Our Blessed Lord and Saviour Jesus Christ; Illustrated in Many Passages from the Writings of Ancient and Modern Authors.* London: Cassell, Petter & Galpin, 1875. [Risen, See. 279–85; Ascended, See. 286–90; N.B. Google book]

Spencer, F. Scott. *What Did Jesus Do? Gospel Profiles of Jesus' Personal Conduct.* Harrisburg, PA: Trinity Press International, 2003. [Resurrection, See. 5, 13, 37–38, 69–70, 74–75, 178, 189, 209–11, 237, 244 n. 10, 245 n. 14, 257]

Sperow, Everett H. *The Silent Nazarene.* Boston: Gorham, 1917. [Chapter 6 How He Came Forth Again, See. 269–300]

Spoto, Donald. *The Hidden Jesus: A New Life.* New York: St. Martin's Press, 1998. [Chapter 14 Of Time and Eternity: The Resurrection, See. 231–49]

Spring, Gardiner. *The Glory of Christ: Illustrated in His Character and History, Including the Last Things of His Mediatorial Government.* Vol. 1. New York: M.W. Dodd, 1852. [Chapter 9 Christ Glorious In His Resurrection, See. 247–74; Chapter 10 Christ's Ascension Glorious, See. 275–301; N.B. Archive.org]

Sproul, R. C. *The Glory of Christ.* Wheaton, IL: Tyndale House, 1990. [Chapter 13 Glory In The Resurrection, See. 165–80]

———. *The Work of Christ: What the Events of Jesus' Life Mean For You*. Colorado Springs, CO: David C Cook, 2012. [Chapter 10 Resurrection, See. 163–79; Chapter 11 Ascension, See. 181–98]

Stalker, James. *The Life of Jesus Christ*. New York: Revell, 1909. [Chapter 7—The End. See. The Resurrection and Ascension, #198–203, See. 140–44; N.B. Google book]

Stamm, Frederick Keller. *The Conversations of Jesus*. New York: Harper & Brothers, 1939. [The Post-Resurrection Conversations. Chapters 29–30, See. 255–78]

Stapfer, Edmond. *The Death and Resurrection of Jesus Christ*. Translated by Louise Seymour Houghton. New York: Scribner's Sons, 1898. [277 pages; N.B. Google book]

Stauffer, Ethelbert. *Jesus and His Story*. Translated by Richard and Clara Winston. New York: Knopf, 1960. [Chapter 7 The Passover of Death 7. The Empty Tomb, See. 143–47; 8. The Appearances of Christ, See. 147–53]

Stein, Robert H. *Jesus the Messiah: A Survey of the Life of Christ*. Downers Grove, IL: InterVarsity, 1996. [Chapter 19 The Resurrection, See. 259–76]

Steinmann, Jean. *The Life of Jesus*. Translated by Peter Green. Boston: Atlantic Monthly Press Book, 1959. [Chapter 16 The Resurrection, See. 223–26]

Stephen, Thomas. *A Gospel History of our Lord and Saviour Jesus Christ: or, A Life of the Man of Sorrows*. London: Dean, 1853. [Chapters 49–52, See. 734–85]

Stevens, Clifford J. *A Life of Christ*. Huntington: Our Sunday Visitor, 1983. [The Resurrection, See. 94–97; N.B. Useless.]

Stevens, William Arnold, and Ernest DeWitt Burton. *An Outline Handbook of the Life of Christ From the Four Gospels*. Boston: Bible Study, 1892. [See. 19, 28, 33; N.B. Archive.org]

Stevenson, Margaret J. *The Life of Jesus*. Topeka, KS: Crane, 1904. [See. 36–37; N.B. Archive.org. This work is a 38-page book.]

Stewart, Desmond. *The Foreigner: A Search for the First-Century Jesus*. London: H. Hamilton, 1981. [Resurrection, See. 5, 152–56, 159, 162; Post-resurrection apparitions, See. 5, 153–58, 166]

Stewart, James S. *The Life and Teaching of Jesus Christ*. Edinburgh: Saint Andrew Press, 1995. [Chapter 20 The Triumph, See. 173–83]

Stewart, John. *When Did Our Lord Actually Live? New Light on an Old Problem, and a New Solution*. Edinburgh: T&T Clark, 1935. [Part 4 The Resurrection and the Order of Events Connected With It, See. 75–80]

Stewart, Robert B. *The Quest of the Hermeneutical Jesus: The Impact of Hermeneutics on the Jesus Research of John Dominic Crossan and N. T. Wright*. Lanham: University Press of America, 2008. [See. 51–55, 100–103; N.B. Stewart offers an analysis of Crossan's works.]

Stifler, James Madison. *The Christ of Christianity: A Series of Studies Based on the Writings of Luke: "The Gospel of Luke" and "the Acts."* New York: Revell, 1915. [Chapter 22 Sunday Morning He is Raised from the Tomb and Appears to His Disciples and to Others, See. 161–66; Chapter 23 He Shows Himself to His Friends for Forty Days and then Ascends to Heaven. His Friends Pray and Wait, See. 167–72; N.B. Google book]

Stiles, Wayne. *Walking in the Footsteps of Jesus: A Journey Through the Lands and Lessons of Christ*. Ventura, CA: Regel, 2008. [Chapter 8 A Tomb with a View, See. 159–78]

Stock, Eugene. *Lessons on the Life of Our Lord: For the Use of Sunday School Teachers and Other Religious Instructors*. 2nd ed. London: Church of England Sunday School Institute, 1871. [Chapters 98–103, See. 267–81; N.B. Google book]

Stout, Andrew P. *Chronology of Christ's Life*. Indianapolis: Hiram Hadley, 1885. [See. 387–403; N.B. Archive.org]

Stowe, Harriet Beecher. *Footsteps of the Master*. New York: J. B. Ford, 1877. [Chapter 29 The Resurrection of Jesus, See. 281–87; Chapter 30 The Ascension of our Lord, See. 289–90; N.B. Google book]

Strobel, Lee. *The Case for the Real Jesus: A Journalist Investigates Current Attacks on the Identity of Christ*. Grand Rapids: Zondervan, 2007. Challenge #3. Part 1. New Explanations Have Refuted Jesus' Resurrection, See. 101–26; Part 2. The Cross-Examination, See. 127–56]

Sullivan, Clayton. *Rescuing Jesus from the Christians*. Harrisburg, PA: Trinity Press International, 2002. [Chapter 8 Strategy One. Distinguish between the Pre-Resurrection Jesus and the Post-Resurrection Jesus, See. 73–84]

Sweeley, John W. *Jesus in the Gospels: Man, Myth, or God*. Lanham: University Press of America, 2000. [Chapter 7 The Resurrection of Jesus: Myth, Magic, or Miracle?, See. 163–94; N.B. This work should be explored.]

Sweet, Leonard I., and Frank Viola. *Jesus: A Theography*. Nashville: Nelson, 2012. [Chapter 15 The Resurrection, Ascension, and Pentecost, See. 259–80]

Swindoll, Charles R. *Jesus: The Greats Life of All*. Nashville: Nelson, 2008. [Part 4: The King, Chapters 16–20, See. 231–85]

Talbot, George F. *Jesus: His Opinions and Character: The New Testament Studies of a Layman*. Boston: Ellis, 1887. [Chapter 12 Legend of the Resurrection, See. 382–426; N.B. Google book]

Talmage, T. De Witt. *From Manger to Throne: Embracing a New Life of Jesus the Christ and a History of Palestine and Its People*. Philadelphia: Historical Pub., 1889. [Chapter 27 The Resurrection, See. 520–31; Chapter 28 The Ascension, See. 532–35; N.B. Archive.org, Google book, and HathiTrust]

Tambasco, Anthony J. *In the Days of Jesus: The Jewish Background and Unique Teaching of Jesus*. New York: Paulist, 1983. [Death and Afterward, See. 109–12]

Tatum, W. Barnes. *In Quest of Jesus*, Nashville: Abingdon, 1999. [Chapter 7 Resurrection and Virgin Birth, See. 143–51; Tatum offers a concise and objective overview of the literary traditions.]

Taylor, Jeremy. *The Great Exemplar of Sanctity and Holy Life: Described in the History of the Life and Death of our Ever-Blessed Saviour Jesus Christ*. London: William Pickering, 1849. [Section 16 Of the Resurrection and Ascension of Jesus, See. 789–810; N.B. Google book]

———. *The Life of Our Blessed Lord and Saviour Jesus Christ*. 1834 [Section 17 Of the Resurrection and Ascension of Jesus, See. 222–27; N.B. Google book]

Taylor, Kenneth Nathaniel. *Who Is This Man Jesus? The Complete Life of Jesus from the Living Bible*. Glendale, CA: Regal, 1974. [See. 250–70]

Taylor, Marion. *The Life of Christ: Also a Brief Story or History of My Life*. Louisville, KY: Pentecostal Publishing, 1910. [Chapters 49–55, See. 69–76; N.B. Google book]

Taylor, Thomas Eddy, S. Earl Taylor, and Charles Herbert Morgan. *Studies in the Life of Christ: A Year's Course of Thirty-Five Lessons, Providing a Daily Scheme for Personal Study; Adapted Also to Class-Work*. Cincinnati: Jennings & Pye, 1901. [Part 8 The Forty Days, See. 215–26; N.B. Google book]

Taylor, Vincent. *The Life and Ministry of Jesus*. Nashville: Abingdon, 1955. [Chapter 52 The Resurrection, See. 225–28]

Tenney, E. P. *Our Elder Brother: His Biography*. Springfield, MA: King-Richardson, 1897. [Book 8 Our Risen Redeemer, See. 357–401; N.B. Google book]

Thayer, E. W. *Sketches From The Life of Jesus: Historical and Doctrinal*. Chicago: Revell, 1891. [Chapter 37 The Resurrection, See. 395–406; Chapter 38 The Resurrection of Jesus. Tale of the Soldiers, See. 407–16; Chapter 39 The Resurrection of Jesus. The Witnesses, See. 417–28; Chapter 40 The Twelve Apostles, See. 429–40; Chapter 41 The Ascension, See. 441–53; N.B. Archive.org]

Theissen, Gerd, and Annette Merz. *The Historical Jesus: A Comprehensive Guide*. Minneapolis: Fortress, 1998. [Chapter 15 The Risen Jesus: Easter and Its Interpretations, See. 474–511; N.B. This text is a must read! Outstanding.]

Theodore, John T. *Who Was Jesus? A Historical Analysis of the Misinterpretations of His Life and Teachings*. New York: Exposition Press, 1961. [See. 185–99]

Thirlwall, Thomas. *Diatessaron, or, The History of Our Lord Jesus Christ*. London: J. Spragg, 1803. [Part 7 The Transactions of Forty Days, From the Day of the Resurrection to the Ascension, See. 269–90; N.B. Google book]

Thomas, W. H. Griffith. *Christianity Is Christ*. Grand Rapids: Zondervan, 1965. [Chapter 7 The Resurrection of Christ, See. 66–84]

Thompson, Joseph P. *The Life of Jesus of Nazareth: For Young People*. Norwich, CT: H. Bill, 1879. [Chapter 40 He Rose From the Dead, See. 532–53; Chapter 41 On Last Look and Word, See. 554–62; Chapter 42 In The Highest, See. 563–67; N.B. Google book]

Thomson, Charles. *A Synopsis of the Four Evangelists: or, A Regular History of the Conception, Birth, Doctrine, Miracles, Death, Resurrection, and Ascension of Jesus Christ, in the Words of the Evangelists*. Philadelphia: Published for the author, Wm. M'Culloch, printer, 1815. [Sections 49–52, See. 189–200; N.B. Archive.org]

Thomson, Ebenezer, and William Charles Price. *The History of Our Blessed Lord and Saviour Jesus Christ: With the Lives of the Holy Apostles, and Their Successors for Three Hundred Years after the Crucifixion*. London: Printed for John Pearmain, 1802. [Chapter 29, See. 401–7; N.B. Google book]

Thurman, William C. *Our Bible Chronology Established: The Sealed Book of Daniel Opened: or, A Book of Reference for Those Who Wish to Examine the "Sure Word of Prophecy."* Boston: Office of the World's Crisis, 1867. [See. 185–93; N.B. Google book]

Tidball, Charles S. *Holy Visions Sacred Stories: Realities from the Blessed Anne Catherine Emmerich*. Barrington, MA: Anthroposophic Press, 2012. [Chapter 21 Resurrection, See. 188–205; Chapter 22 The Ascension, See. 206–9]

Tiemeyer, T. N. *Jesus Christ: Super Psychic*. Washington: ESPress, 1976. [Chapter 13 The Case of the Missing Body, See. 138–49; Chapter 14 The Return from the Crypt, See. 150–60; N.B. This work is an interesting read.]

Tilden, Elwyn E. *Toward Understanding Jesus*. Englewood Cliffs, NJ: Prentice-Hall, 1956. [Resurrection of Jesus, See. 4, 5, 134–37, 144]

Tissot, James. *The Life of Our Saviour Jesus Christ: Three Hundred and Sixty-Five Compositions from the Four Gospels*. Translated by Arthur Bell. Vol. 4. Toronto: George N. Morang, 1899. [The Resurrection, See. 239–70; N.B. Archive.org and HathiTrust]

Torrey, R. A. *Studies in the Life and Teachings of our Lord*. Chicago: Bible Institute Colportage Association, 1909. [Lessons 135–140, See. 322–43; N.B. Archive.org]

———. *The Uplifted Christ*. Grand Rapids: Zondervan, 1965. [Chapter 4 The Resurrection of Jesus Christ, 1 Corinthians 15:14–17, See. 43–58; Chapter 5 The Best News The

World Ever Heard, Luke 24:34, See. 59–68; Chapter 6 Seven Easter Certainties John 20:31, See. 69–83]

Tucker, Joshua T. *The Sinless One, or, The Life Manifested*. Boston: S. K. Whipple, 1855. [Chapter 21 See. 293–305; N.B. Archive.org]

Turner, H. E. W. *Jesus, Master and Lord: A Study in the Historical Truth of the Gospels*. London: Mowbray, 1954. [Chapter 12 The Resurrection of Jesus Christ, See. 345–73]

Tuttle, Hudson. *The Career of the Christ-Idea in History*. Boston: Adams, 1870. [Chapter 11 Burial and Resurrection of Jesus, See. 104–10; N.B. Archive.org, Google book, and HathiTrust]

Uhlhorn, Gerhard. *The Modern Representations of the Life of Jesus: Four Discourses*. Translated by Charles E. Grinnell. Boston: Little, Brown, 1868. [Fourth Discourse. Miracles, See. 116–50; N.B. Google book]

Vallings, J. F. *Jesus Christ, the Divine Man: His Life and Times*. New York: Revell, 1889. [Chapter 20 The Resurrection and the Forty Days, See. 190–209; Chapter 21 The Ascension and After, See. 210–13; N.B. Archive.org]

Van Voorst, Robert E. *Jesus Outside the New Testament: An Introduction to the Ancient Evidence*. Grand Rapids: Eerdmans, 2000. [Resurrection, See. 11, 48, 53, 57, 65–67, 90, 92, 101, 102, 114, 119, 127, 128, 132, 136, 138, 142, 143, 151, 152, 154–56, 173, 174, 176, 177, 186, 202, 205, 214]

Vassilakos, Aristarchus. *The Trial of Jesus Christ*. Chicago: The Orthodox Christian Educational Society, 1950. [See. 41–62]

Vaughan, Bernard. *Society, Sin and The Saviour Addresses on the Passion of Our Lord*. London: Kegan Paul, Trench, Trübner, 1907. [Scene 8 Christ Risen From the Dead, See. 255–80; N.B. HathiTrust]

Veuillot, Louis. *The Life of Our Lord Jesus Christ*. Translated by Anthony Farley. New York: Peter F. Collier, 1875. [Book 9 Jesus Arisen, See. 458–72; N.B. Archive.org]

Vickers, John. *The Real Jesus: A Review of His Life, Character, and Death from a Jewish Standpoint. Addressed to Members of the Theistic Church*. London: Williams & Norgate, 1891. [Chapter 9 The Resurrection Drama, See. 240–68; N.B. Archive.org and Google book]

Vollmer, Philip. *The Modern Student's Life of Christ: A Textbook for Higher Institutions of Learning and Advanced Bible Classes*. New York: Revell, 1912. [Division 6 The Forty Days of Resurrection Life, Chapter 48 The Resurrection and Five Appearances, See. 268–74; Chapter 49 The Last Five Appearances of Christ and His Ascension, See. 275–82; N.B. Google book]

Vos, Howard F. *Beginnings in the Life of Christ*. Chicago: Moody Press, 1975. [The Resurrection and Post-Resurrection Ministry, See. 121–26]

Walker, Albert H. *Christ's Christianity: Being the Precepts and Doctrines Recorded in Matthew, Mark, Luke and John, as Taught by Jesus Christ, Analyzed and Arranged According to Subjects*. New York: Equity Press, 1911. [The Death and Resurrection of Jesus, See. 110–13; N.B. Archive.org and Google book]

Walker, Peter. *In the Steps of Jesus: An Illustrated Guide to the Places of the Holy Land*. Oxford: Lion, 2007. [Chapter 14 Emmaus, See. 200–206]

———. *Jesus and His World*. Downers Grove, IL: InterVarsity, 2003. [Chapter 11 The Following Sunday, See. 154–69]

Wallace, Catherine M. *The Confrontational Wit of Jesus: Christian Humanism and the Moral Imagination*. Eugene, OR: Cascade, 2016. [Chapter 13 Resurrection and the Moral Imagination, See. 138–49; Chapter 15 The Question I'm Not Avoiding, See. 154–61]

Wallace, O. C. S. *The Life of Jesus: Studies for Young People*. Philadelphia: American Baptist Publication Society, 1893. [Chapter 30 The Forty Days, See. 186–92; N.B. Archive.org and HathiTrust]

Walser, G. H. *The Life and Teachings of Jesus*. Boston: Sherman, French, 1909. [The Resurrection, 318–31; N.B. Archive.org and Google.com]

Walter, William W. *The Sweetest Story Ever Told*. Aurora, IL: Williams W. Walter, 1916. [Chapter 22 The Resurrection, See. 198–201; Chapter 23 The Fishing Trip, See. 202–8; N.B. Google book and HathiTrust]

Wand, J. W. C. *The Life of Jesus Christ*. London: Methuen, 1955. [Chapter 13 The Triumph, See. 163–70]

Ware, Henry. *The Life of the Saviour*. 7th ed. Boston: American Unitarian Association, 1873. [Chapter 22 The Resurrection and Ascension, See. 251–61; N.B. Archive.org and HathiTrust]

Warne, Francis Wesley. *The Sinless Incarnation*. New York: Methodist Book Concern, 1926. [Chapter 7 From Burial To Ascension, See. 79–84]

Warner, Richard. *A Chronological History of Our Lord and Saviour Jesus Christ*. Bath: R. Cruttwell, 1819. [Part 7 The Events of Forty Days, from the Day of the Resurrection to the Ascension, See. 369–87; N.B. Google book]

Warschauer, J. *The Historical Life of Christ*. London: Unwin, 1927. [Chapter 20 Lo, I Am With You Alway, See. 341–61]

Watkinson, Redford A. *Who Was Jesus*. New York: N. Tibbals, 1867. [Chapter 13 The Miracles of Jesus. See. One Fifty-Three Great Fishes, See. 574–75; Chapter 15 The Trial, Crucifixion, and Resurrection, See. 653–65; N.B. Archive.org and Google book]

Watson, John. *The Life of the Master*. New York: Declare, Phillips, 1901. [Epilogue: The Eternal Christ, See. 293–301; N.B. Archive.org]

Watson, Samuel, Mrs. *The Life of Jesus Christ the Saviour Retold From the Evangelists*. London: Religious Tract Society, 1885. [Chapter 41 The Resurrection and Ascension, See. 426–41; N.B. Google book]

Weatherhead, Leslie D. *His Life and Ours: The Significance for Us of the Life of Jesus*. New York: Abingdon-Cokesbury, 1933. [Chapter 15 Resurrection, See. 275–94; Chapter 16 Ascension, See. 295–311]

———. *It Happened in Palestine*. New York: Abingdon, 1936. [Chapter 18 In The Garden of the Resurrection, See. 311–16]

Weaver, S. Townsend. *The Biblical Life of Jesus Christ: A Standard Biography of Our Lord in the Words of the Gospels According to Matthew, Mark, Luke and John . . .* Philadelphia: The University Literature Extension, 1911. [The Third Division: Jesus The Ever-Living Savior, See. 287–304; N.B. Archive.org]

Weaver, Walter P. *The Historical Jesus in the Twentieth Century, 1900–1950*. Harrisburg, PA: Trinity Press International, 1999. [Chapter 4 Resurrection and Death: Jesus in the Twenties, See. 99–140; also 7, 21, 70, 89, 97, 153, 162, 166, 177, 187, 196–97, 216, 221–22, 235, 246, 266, 318, 325, 336, 344, 347, 350, 353]

Weed, George Ludington. *A Life of Christ for the Young*. Philadelphia: George W. Jacobs, 1898. [Chapters 66–72, See. 310–40; N.B. Archive.org and Google book]

Weiss, Bernhard. *The Life of Christ*. Translated by M. G. Hope. Vol. 3. Edinburgh: T&T Clark, 1884. [Chapter 10 The Third Day rose again from the Dead, See. 382–97; Chapter 11 Ascended into Heaven, See. 398–409; N.B. Archive.org]

Wernle, Paul. *The Sources of our Knowledge of the Life of Jesus*. Translated by Edward Lummis. London: Philip Green, 1907. [See. 77–79; N.B. HathiTrust]

Whipple, Wayne. *The Story-Life of The Son of Man: Nearly a Thousand Stories from Sacred and Secular Sources in a Continuous and Complete Chronicle of the Earth Life of the Saviour*. New York: Revell, 1913. [Chapters 38–39, See. 513–36; N.B. Archive.org and Google book]

White, Ellen Gould Harmon. *The Desire of Ages*. Oakland, CA: Pacific Press, 1898. [To The Father's Throne, See. Chapters 81–87, See. 779–835; N.B. Google book and HathiTrust]

Wierwille, Victor Paul. *Jesus Christ, Our Passover*. New Knoxville, Ohio: American Christian Press, 1980. [Chapter 12 The Resurrection Through the Ascension: The Forty Days, See. 349–78; Chapter 13 The Ascension Through Pentecost, See. 379–97; N.B. Wierwille was the founder of The Way International.]

Wieseler, Karl. *A Chronological Synopsis of the Four Gospels*. 2nd ed. Translated by Edmund Venerables. London: George Bell, 1877. [See. 402–19; N.B. Archive.org]

Wilkinson, William Cleaver. *Concerning Jesus Christ: The Son of Man*. Philadelphia: Griffith & Rowland Press, 1918. [Chapters 37–48, See. 256–327; N.B. Google book and HathiTrust]

Willam, Franz Michel. *The Life of Jesus Christ in the Land of Israel and Among Its People*. Edited by Newton Wayland Thompson. St. Louis: B. Herder, 1946. [Chapter 19 The Resurrection, See. 458–82]

Willett, Herbert L. *Life and Teachings of Jesus*. Chicago: Revell, 1898. [Part 1 Chapter 6 The Week of Tragedy and Triumph, See. 71–77, 156–58; N.B. Archive.org, Google book, and HathiTrust]

Williams, Henry Wilkinson. *The Incarnate Son of God: or, The History of the Life and Ministry of the Redeemer*. London, 1853. [Chapter 15 The Resurrection Of The Lord Jesus, And The Last Forty Days Spent By Him On Earth, See. 331–50]

Williams, Jay G. *Yeshua Buddha: An Interpretation of New Testament Theology as a Meaningful Myth*. Wheaton, IL: Theosophical Publishing House, 1978. [Chapter 7 Resurrection: Beyond the End, See. 110–16; N.B Theosophical interpretations.]

Williams, Peter S. *Getting at Jesus: A Comprehensive Critique of Neo-Atheist Nonsense about the Jesus of History*. Eugene, OR: Wipf & Stock, 2019. [Chapter 4 Getting at Evidence for the Resurrection, See. 233–300; N.B. This work should be examined.]

Wilson, A. N. *Jesus*. London: Sinclair-Stevenson, 1992. [Jesus Christ, See. 239–50]

Wilson, Ian. *Jesus: The Evidence. The Latest Research and Discoveries Investigated*. London: Weidenfeld & Nicolson, 1996. [Chapter 10 Did Jesus Really Rise From The Dead?, See. 137–53]

Wilson, P. Whitwell. *The Christ We Forget: A Life of Our Lord for Men of Today*. New York: Revell, 1917. [Chapter 42 From Sight To Faith, See. 304–10; N.B. Google book]

Wilson, William. *The Redeemer Being Four Lectures on the Nativity, the Baptism, the Crucifixion, and the Ascension of Our Lord*. Edinburgh: Andrew Elliot, 1874. [Lecture 4 The Redeemer—His Ascension, See. 113–54; N.B. Archive.org]

Winstanley, Edward William. *Jesus and the Future*. Edinburgh: T&T Clark, 1913. [Chapter 5 Resurrection and Life. (ii) The Resurrection of Jesus, See. 217–20; N.B. Archive.org]

Winter, David. *The Search for the Real Jesus*. Wilton, CT: Morehouse-Barlow, 1982. [Chapter 11 Resurrection, See. 112–21]

Wise, Daniel. *Our King and Saviour: or, The story of Our Lord's life on earth. In which its great events are arranged in their probable chronological order, and so set forth as to make their reality and meaning clear to the understandings and attractive to the imaginations and hearts of young persons and general readers*. New York: Nelson & Philip, 1875. [See. 347–67; N.B. Archive.org]

Witherington, Ben. *The Jesus Quest: The Third Search for the Jew of Nazareth*. Downers Grove, IL: InterVarsity, 1995. [Resurrection, See. 55, 75–77, 91–92, 96, 169, 227]

———. *What Have They Done With Jesus? Beyond Strange Theories and Bad History*. New York: HarperOne, 2006. [See. 6, 49–52, 174–76]

Woodhead, Abraham or R. H. *An Historical Narration of the Life and Death of our Lord Jesus Christ: In Two Parts*. Oxford: Printed at Theatre in Oxford, 1685. [See. 300–42; N.B. Archive.org and Google book]

———. *The History of the Life of our Lord Jesus Christ . . .* Translated by William Crathorne. 5th ed. Dublin: Printed by and for Bart Corcoran, 1763. [Chapters 43–54, See. 204–20; N.B. Google book has the author identified on page iii, To the English Reader as Mr. Woodhead. The 1685 text from Princeton Theological Seminary has penciled in on the cover page "By Abraham Woodhead, Roman Catholic."]

Workman, George Coulson. *Jesus the Man and Christ the Spirit*. New York: Macmillan, 1928. [Chapter 7 The Resurrection, See. 159–82]

Wright, N. T. *The Challenge of Jesus: Rediscovering Who Jesus Was and Is*. Downers Grove, IL: InterVarsity, 1999. [Chapter 6 The Challenge of Easter, See. 126–49]

———. *The Scriptures, the Cross and the Power of God: Reflections for Holy Week*. Louisville: Westminster John Knox, 2006. [Chapter 8 Easter Vigil: Come and see! Go and tell (Matthew 18:1–10), See. 68–74; Chapter 9 Easter morning: New temple, new creation (John 20.1–10), See. 76–82]

Wright, Paul. *A Complete Life of Our Blessed Lord and Saviour, Jesus Christ: That Great Example as Well as Saviour of Mankind: Containing a . . . Full Account of All the Real Facts Relating to the Exemplary Life, Meritorious Sufferings, and Death of Our Glorious Redeemer: To Which Is Added . . . the Lives, Transactions, Sufferings, & Deaths of His Holy Apostles, Evangelists, Disciples . . . : The Whole Interspersed with Practical Improvements and Useful Remarks . . .* Windham: Webb, 1814. [Chapters 40—43, See. 258–75; N.B. Archive.org, Google book, and HathiTrust]

Yost, Casper Salathiel. *The Carpenter of Nazareth: A Study of Jesus in the Light of His Environment and Background*. St. Louis: Bethany Press, 1938. [Chapter 26 Victory Over Death, See. 277–90]

Zahrnt, Heinz. *The Historical Jesus*. Translated by John S. Bowden. New York: Harper & Row, 1963. [Chapter 9 On the third day, See. 120–38; N.B. This text is worth examining.]

Chapter 12

Jesus's Life: Biographies and Historicity of Christ: Con Resurrection

Ajijola, Adeleke Dirisu. *Historical Jesus*. Delhi, India: Adam Publishers, 1999. [Part 6 Events After Crucifixion, See. 211–38; N.B. The author asserts that Jesus did not die in Jerusalem and lived at least until the age of seventy.]

Aruṇ. *The Untold Life of Jesus (What is the Truth)*. Meerut: Anu, 2007. [Chapter 9 Appendices—Long Interval Between the Resurrection and the Ascension, See. 106–7; N.B. The author claims that "Jesus died in Sringar and his tomb is situated in Rosabal."]

Aslan, Reza. *Zealot: The Life and Times of Jesus of Nazareth*. New York: Random House, 2013. [Resurrection, See. xxvi–xxvii, 29, 153, 164–66, 174–78; N.B. The author asserts, "these stories are not meant to be accounts of historical events . . ." (p. 177)]

Baigent, Michael. *The Jesus Papers: Exposing the Greatest Cover-up in History*. San Francisco: HarperSan Francisco, 2006. [Chapter 7 Surviving the Crucifixion; Chapter 8 Jesus in Egypt; Chapter 9 The Mysteries of Egypt; Chapter 10 Initiation; Chapter 11 Experiencing the Source, See. 115–224; N.B. Baigent claims that Jesus was taken down from the cross alive, smuggled to Egypt with his wife Mary Magdalene, and eventually moved to France.]

Besant, Annie. *Esoteric Christianity or The Lesser Mysteries*. London: Theosophical Publishing Society, 1901. [Chapter 8 Resurrection and Ascension, See. 231–52; N.B. Archive.org]

Borg, Marcus J. *Jesus: Uncovering the Life, the Teachings, and Relevance of a Religious Revolutionary*. New York: HarperSanFrancisco, 2006. [Chapter 10 Executed by Rome, Vindicated by God, See. 261–92; N.B. This text should be read.]

———. "The Truth of Easter." In *The Meaning of Jesus: Two Visions*. Marcus J. Borg and N. T. Wright. New York: HarperSanFrancisco, 2000. [Chapter 8 The Truth of Easter, See. 129–42; N.B. This work should be examined.]

Brodie, Thomas L. *Beyond the Quest for The Historical Jesus: Memoir of a Discovery*. Sheffield: Sheffield Phoenix, 2012. [See. 208–9; N.B. Brodie's thoughtful text is a must read. It challenges conservatives and liberals such as Bart Ehrman (See. 226–31).]

Cain, Marvin Fay. *Jesus the Man: An Introduction for People at Home in the Modern World*. Santa Rosa, CA: Polebridge, 1999. [The Resurrection of Jesus, See. 127–34]

Caine, Hall. *Life of Christ*. London: Collins, 1938. [See. 937–1041; N.B. This work is an absolute must read. Caine, a layman asks honest questions and honestly discusses multiple problems associated with the New Testament text.]

Capps, Donald. *Jesus: A Psychological Biography*. St. Louis: Chalice, 2000. [See. 30, 41, 263–65; N.B. Capps discusses the possibility that the appearances were dreams that served a quasi-therapeutic role.]

Carotta, Francesco. *Jesus Was Caesar: On the Julian Origin of Christianity An Investigative Report*. Translated by Tommie Hendriks, Joseph Horvath, and Manfred Junghardt. The Netherlands: Aspekt, 2005. [Jesus' Entombment and Resurrection, See. 313–16; Appearances of the Resurrected One—Ascension, See. 317–23]

Carrier, Richard. *On the Historicity of Jesus: Why We Might Have Reason to Doubt*. Sheffield: Sheffield Phoenix, 2014. [What Happened to the Body?, See. 368–71]

Casey, Maurice. *Jesus of Nazareth: An Independent Historian's Account of His Life and Teaching*. London: T&T Clark, 2010. [Chapter 12 Did Jesus Rise from the Dead?, See. 455–508; N.B. This is perhaps one of the best scholarly written works on Jesus. It is an absolute must to read.]

Cascioli, Luigi. *The Fable of Christ*. Author. 2002. [N.B. This work is by a former Catholic priest who became a militant atheist. Information about the author and text was found online.]

Choudhury, Paramesh. *From Kashmir to Palestine*. New Delhi: P. Choudhury, 1996. [Chapter 12 Jesus Did not Die on the Cross, See. 252–324; Notovitch's Discovery, See. 325–33; N.B. The author claims that Jesus did not die nor ascend to heaven, rather he moved to Kashmir.]

Crossan, John Dominic. *The Birth of Christianity*. New York: HarperCollins, 1998. [Chapter 25 The Other Passion-Resurrection Story, See. 481–525; N.B. This text should be explored.]

———. *The Historical Jesus: The Life of a Mediterranean Jewish Peasant*. San Francisco: HarperSanFrancisco, 1991. [Chapter 14 Death and Burial, See. 391–94; [Chapter 15 Resurrection and Authority, See. 395–426; N.B. This text should be read.]

———. *Jesus: A Revolutionary Biography*. San Francisco: HarperSanFrancisco, 1994. [Chapter 6, See. 124–27; Chapter 7, See. 181–92]

Crossan, John Dominic, and Richard G. Watts. *Who is Jesus?: Answers To Your Questions About the Historical Jesus*. New York: HarperPaperbacks, 1996. [Chapter 8 What Happened on Easter Sunday?, See. 149–67]

Cutner, Herbert. *Jesus: God, Man, or Myth? An Examination of the Evidence*. New York: Truth Seeker, 1950. [See. 18–24, 142, 218–19, 268–69]

Drews, Arthur. *The Christ Myth* 3rd ed. Translated by C. Delisle Burns. London: T. Fischer Unwin, 1910. [This famous, classic work advocates the Christ Myth; N.B. Archive.org, Gutenberg.org, and HathiTrust]

Ehrman, Bart D. *How Jesus Became God: The Exaltation of a Jewish Preacher From Galilee*. New York: HarperOne, 2014. [Chapter 4 The Jesus of Jesus: What We Cannot Know, See. 129–69; Chapter 5 The Resurrection of Jesus: What We Can Know, See. 171–210; N.B. Ehrman's work is a must read.]

———. *Jesus: Apocalyptic Prophet of the New Millennium*. Oxford: Oxford University Press, 1999. [Chapter 13 From apocalyptic prophet to lord of all: the afterlife of Jesus, See. 227–38]

Ellegård, Alvar. *Jesus: One Hundred Years Before Christ: A Study in Creative Mythology.* Woodstock, NY: Overlook Press, 1999. [Paul's life and his revelations, See. 14–19; Resurrection, See. 76–78]

Fida, Ahtisham, et al. *Jesus Lived in Japan.* Srinagar, Kashmir, India: Dastgir Publications Trust, 1996. [134 pages. N.B. The author postulates that Jesus survived the crucifixion.]

Fox, Robin Lane. *The Unauthorized Version: Truth and Fiction in the Bible.* London: Penguin, 2006.

Funk, Robert Walter. *Honest to Jesus: Jesus for a New Millennium.* San Francisco: HarperSanFrancisco, 1996. [Chapter 14 Resurrection and Return, See. 257–79; N.B. Funk was the founder of the Jesus Seminar. This work should be examined.]

Funk, Robert Walter, and the Jesus Seminar. *The Acts of Jesus: The Search for the Authentic Deeds of Jesus.* San Francisco: HarperSanFrancisco, 1998. [Empty Tomb, Appearances & Ascension, See. 449–96; N.B. This book is highly recommended.]

Graves, Robert, and Joshua Podro. *Jesus in Rome: A Historical Conjecture.* London: Cassell, 1957 [Chapter 1 The Crucifixion and Resurrection, See. 1–15; Chapter 5 The Tomb of Jesus, See. 68–87; N.B. This book speculates that Jesus survived his crucifixion.]

Harpur, Tom. *For Christ's Sake.* Boston: McClelland & Stewart, 1993. [The Resurrection of Jesus, See. 97–103]

Holbach, Paul Henri Thiry. *Ecce Homo!: An Eighteenth Century Life of Jesus: Critical Edition and Revision of George Houston's Translation from the French.* Edited by Andrew Hunwick. Berlin: Mouton De Gruyter, 1995. [Chapter 16 Resurrection of Jesus. His Conduct Until His Ascension. Examination of the Proofs of the Resurrection, See. 229–42]

———. *Ecce Homo: or, A Critical Enquiry into the History of Jesus Christ.* Translated by George Houston. 2nd ed. London: D. I. Eaton, 1813. [Chapter 17 Resurrection of Jesus; —His Conduct Until His Ascension; —Examination of the Proofs of the Resurrection, See. 256–76; N.B Archive.org, Google book, and Gutenberg.org]

Holtzmann, Oskar. *The Life of Jesus.* Translated by J. T. Bealby and Maurice A. Canney. London: Adams & Charles Black, 1904. [Chapter 14 Resurrection and Continued Life, See. 492–529; N.B. HathiTrust]

Keim, Theodor. *The History of Jesus of Nazara.* Translated by Arthur Ransom. Vol. 6. London: Williams & Norgate, 1883. [Part 3 Burial and Resurrection, See. 250–83; N.B. Google book and HathiTrust. This is an important, and must read dated work from a liberal-rationalist point of view.]

Klausner, Joseph. *Jesus of Nazareth: His Life, Times, and Teachings.* Translated by Herbert Danby. New York: Macmillan, 1943. [Seventh Book 4 The Account of the Resurrection, See. 356–59. This Jewish rabbi asserts that some of the disciples saw Jesus in visions.]

Lataster, Raphael. *Questioning the Historicity of Jesus: Why a Philosophical Analysis Elucidates the Historical Discourse.* Leiden: Brill. 2019. [See. 212, 230–31, 233, 247–49; N.B. An interesting work.]

Lüdemann, Gerd. *Jesus After Two Thousand Years: What He Really Said and Did.* Amherst, NY: Prometheus, 2001. [Mark, See. 111–16; Matthew, See. 251–56; Luke, See. 406–15; John, See. 575–88; N.B. This work is a recommended read.]

McComas, E. W. *A Rational View of Jesus and Religion.* New York: J. W. Lovell, 1880. [Chapters 19–22, See. 588–706; N.B. HathiTrust; This dated, detailed work should be read.]

Miller, Robert J. *The Jesus Seminar and its Critics*. Santa Rosa, CA: Polebridge, 1999. [Chapter 8 Apologetics and the Resurrection, See. 125–46; N.B. Miller's thoughtful work should be read.]

Mountcastle, William W. *The Secret Ministry of Jesus: Pioneer Prophet of Interfaith Dialogue*. Lahham: University Press of America, 2008 [112 pages; N.B. The author postulates that Jesus survived the crucifixion, moved to Srinagar, and then to India, Tibet and China.]

Murdock, D. M. *Who was Jesus? Fingerprints of the Christ*. Seattle, WA: Stellar House, 2011. [See. 20–21, 248–55]

Notovitch, Nicolas. *The Unknown Life of Jesus Christ*. Translated by Alexina Loranger Donovan. Chicago: Rand, McNally, 1894. [The author claims that during the unknown years of Jesus, he left Galilee for India and studied with Buddhists and Hindus there before returning to Judea. Eventually Jesus was crucified but Pilate ordered the body to be removed during the night. See.182–3; N.B. Archive.org, Google book, and Gutenberg.org]

Osman, Ahmed. *The House of the Messiah: Controversial Revelations on the Historical Jesus*. London: HarperCollins, 1992. [Chapter 32 Evidence From the Tomb, See. 169–74; N.B. The author proposes that Jesus and Joshua were one and the same.]

Pappas, Paul C. *Jesus' Tomb In India: The Debate on His Death and Resurrection*. Berkeley, CA: Asian Humanities Press, 1991. [Chapter 2 The Debate over Christ's Death and Resurrection, See. 31–58]

Pick, Bernhard. *The Life of Jesus According to Extra-Canonical Sources*. New York: J. B. Alden, 1887. [Section 88 Report of the Resurrection of Jesus, Sections 145–147; 90 Report of the Ascension of Jesus, See. 147–48; N.B. Google book]

Price, Robert M. *The Christ Myth Theory and Its Problems*. Cranford, NJ; American Atheist Press, 2011. [The Empty Tomb (Mark 16:1–8), See. 150–52; The Resurrection of Jesus (Matthew 27:62–28:20), See. 156–59; The Ascension (2 Kings 2:11; Luke 24:49–53), 235–38; Jesus Appears to Mary Magdalene (Tobit 12:14–2; John 20:1, 11–17), See. 244–45; N.B. This book is an interesting and useful read.]

———. *Deconstructing Jesus*. Amherst, NY: Prometheus, 2000. [See. 9, 10, 27, 34, 35, 43, 47, 54, 55, 56, 61, 93, 148, 149, 179, 215, 224, 228, 251, 260, 264: N.B. See Chapter 7 The Cruci-fiction?, See. 215–26]

———. *The Incredible Shrinking Son of Man: How Reliable is the Gospel Tradition?* Amherst, NY: Prometheus, 2003. [Chapter 14 The Resurrection, See. 333–48]

———. *Killing History: Jesus in the No-Spin Zone*. Amherst, NY: Prometheus, 2014. [The Missing Chapter: Raising Jesus, See. 205–14]

Remsburg, John E. *The Christ: A Critical Review and Analysis of the Evidences of His Existence*. New York: Truth Seeker, 1909. [Chapter 7 Resurrection of Christ, See. 296–339; N.B. Google book. This work is a classic, and dated source that employs a question and answer format. One major goal of this work was to prove that the accounts are contradictory.]

Renan, Ernest. *Renan's Life of Jesus*. Translated by William G. Hutchison. London: Scott, 1897. [Chapter 26 Jesus in the Tomb. See. 271–72; N.B. Google book; various translations.]

Robertson, Archibald. *Jesus: Myth or History?* London: Watts, 1946. [See. 3, 9, 15, 23, 28, 30, 45, 47–48, 62–63, 71–73, 81, 89, 99; N.B. Successfully, Robertson attempts to "bring out the strong points of each" (p. xiii) side of the argument.]

Salibi, Kamal. *Who Was Jesus? Conspiracy in Jerusalem*. London: Tauris Parke, 2007. [Chapter 12 The Treason of Judas, See. 177–86]

Schonfield, Hugh J. *Jesus A Biography*. London: Duckworth, 1939. [Epilogue: He is Not Here, See. 260–64]

———. *The Passover Plot: New Light on the History of Jesus*. London: Hutchinson of London, 1966. [Chapter 13 He is not Here, See. 170–82]

Smith, Arthur D. Howell. *Jesus Not A Myth*. London: Watts, 1942. [See 189–90]

Spong, John Shelby. *Jesus for the Non-Religious: Recovering the Divine at the Heart of the Human*. New York: HarperSanFrancisco, 2007. [Part 1 Separating the Human Jesus from the Myth. Chapter 11 The Eternal Truth Inside the Myths of Resurrection and Ascension, See. 117–29; Spong's work is a recommended read.]

Strauss, David Friedrich. *The Christ of Faith and the Jesus of History: A Critique of Schleiermacher's Life of Jesus*. Translated by Leander E. Keck. Philadelphia: Fortress, 1977. [The Resurrection and the Stories of the Empty Tomb, See. 127–39; Jesus' Postresurrection Life, See. 139–57]

———. *In Defense of My Life of Jesus Against the Hegelians*. Translated by Marilyn Chapin Massey. Hamden, CT: Archon, 1983. [See. xxvii, 6, 35, 57–58]

———. *The Life of Jesus Critically Examined*. Translated by George Eliot. 4th ed. London: Swan Sonnenechevin, 1902. [Third Part. Chapter 4 Death and Resurrection of Jesus, §137–140, See 709–44; Chapter 5 The Ascension, §141–143, See. 745–56; N.B. Archive.org; N.B. This work is a classic, dated source often cited and used as a foil by its opponents.]

Thompson, Thomas L. *The Messiah Myth: The Near Eastern Roots of Jesus and David*. New York: Basic Books, 2005. [Thompson argues that the biblical accounts of both King David and Jesus of Nazareth are mythical in nature and based on Mesopotamian, Egyptian, Babylonian, and Greek and Roman literature.]

Tobin, Paul. *The Rejection of Pascal's Wager: A Skeptic's Guide to the Bible and the Historical Jesus*. England: Authors OnLine, 2009. [Chapter 15 Burial and Resurrection, See. 539–79]

Vickers, John. *The Real Jesus: A Review of His Life, Character, and Death from a Jewish Standpoint. Addressed to Members of the Theistic Church*. London: Williams & Norgate, 1891. [Chapter 9 The Resurrection Drama, See. 240–68; N.B. Archive.org]

Wells, George Albert. *Did Jesus Exist?* 2nd ed. London: Pemberton, 1986. [on third day, See. 30–31, 67, 115, 165; of Jesus his appearances after, See. 21, 26, 30, 37, 67, 124, 144]

———. *The Historical Evidence for Jesus*. Buffalo, NY: Prometheus, 1982. [Chapter 8 Paul and the Resurrection, See. 43–45]

———. *A Study in Christian Origins of Early Christians*. London: Pemberton, 1971. [Resurrection, See. 40–49]

Zindler, Frank R. *The Jesus the Jews Never Knew*. Cranford, NJ: American Atheist Press, 2003. [N.B. This lengthy book asserts that the ancient Jews never heard of Jesus of Nazareth. If Jesus did not exist, there could not be a resurrection.]

Category VI

Jesus's Life: General Works and the Person of Jesus, the History of the Early Church, and the Shroud of Turin

CHAPTER 13

Jesus's Life: General Works the Person Jesus, the History of the Early Church, and the Shroud of Turin: Pro Resurrection

Aarde, Andries van. *Fatherless in Galilee: Jesus as Child of God*. Harrisburg, PA: Trinity Press International, 2001. [Resurrection, appearances, See. 26, 185–87]

Abbadie, James. *The Deity of Jesus Christ Essential to the Divinity of Our Lord Jesus Christ*. Burlington, NJ: S. C. Ustick, 1802. [Chapter 5 Section 6, See. 295–96; N.B. Google book]

Adams, Jonathan. *Lessons in Contempt: Poul Ræff's translation and publication in 1516 of Johannes Pfefferkorn's "The Confession of the Jews."* Odense: University Press of Southern Denmark, 2013. [The Resurrection of Christ, See. 11–14]

Adam, Karl. *The Christ of Faith: The Christology of the Church*. New York: Mentor Omega, 1957. [Chapter 25 The Reign of the Redeemer, See. 388–404]

———. *The Son of God*. Translated by Philip Hereford. Translated by Philip Hereford. Sheed & Ward: London, 1934. [Chapter 7 The Resurrection of Christ, See. 207–62; N.B. Archive.org]

Adams, Frank O. *Sindon: A Layman's Guide to the Shroud of Turin*. Patrick Walsh Press, 1982. [144 pages]

Adamson, Thomas. *Studies of the Mind in Christ*. Edinburgh: T&T Clark, 1898. [Chapter 12 The Mental Identity of Christ After His Resurrection, See. 285–96; N.B. Archive.org and Google book]

Akin, Daniel L. *Discovering the Biblical Jesus*. Nashville: Lifeway, 2003. [Chapter 5 Raised in Power and Glory, See. 97–118]

Aldwinckle, Russell F. *More than Man: A Study in Christology*. Grand Rapids: Eerdmans, 1976. [Resurrection, of Jesus, See. 50, 53, 63, 66, 194–95, 197–98, 206, 208]

Alexander, J. H. *Gleanings About Jesus Christ and Early Christianity*. London: James Nisbet, 1896. [Chapter 2 Our Lord's Crucifixion, Death, and Resurrection with Some Extracts from Various Apologists and Eminent Writers on these Subjects, See. 45–93]

Allen, Nicholas Peter Legh. *The Turin Shroud and the Crystal Lens*. Centrahil, Port Elizabeth, [South Africa]: Empowerment Technologies Pty. Ltd. 1998. [287 pages]

Ambruzi, Aloysius. *Jesus: "Yesterday and Today and Forever" (Heb. 13:8)*. Translated by Sister Gilda Dal Corso. Westminster, MD: Newman Press, 1962. [Book 4 From the Glory of the Resurrection to the Splendor of the Heavenly Jerusalem. See. 549–607]

Aulén, Gustaf. *Jesus in Contemporary Historical Research.* Translated by Ingalill H. Hjelm. Philadelphia: Fortress, 1976. [Chapter 6 The Earthly Jesus and Faith in Christ in the Primitive Church, See. 121–33]

Baggett, John. *Seeing Through the Eyes of Jesus: His Revolutionary View of Reality and His Transcendent Significance for Truth.* Grand Raids: Eerdmans, 2008. [Chapter 14 The Resurrected Life, See. 319–39]

Balabat, Janina. *Conversations with an Atheist.* Lake Mary, FL: Creation House, 2008. [Chapter 21 Jesus Has Risen, See. 228–33]

Barberis, Bruno. *The Holy Shroud.* Gorle, Italy: Velar, 2010. [48 pages]

Barclay, William. *The Mind of Jesus.* New York: Harper & Row, 1961. [Chapter 28 The Resurrection, See. 279–314; Chapter 29 The Ascension, See. 315–21]

Barnes, Arthur Stapylton. *The Holy Shroud of Turin.* London: Burns Oates & Washbourne, 1934. [70 pages]

Barton, William. *The Week Of Our Lord's Passion.* Chicago: Hope, 1907. [See. 62–72; N.B. Google book]

Bauckham, Richard. *Gospel Women Studies of the Named Women in the Gospels.* Grand Rapids: Eerdmans, 2002. [Chapter 8 The Women and the Resurrection: The Credibility of Their Stories, See. 257–310; N.B. This book should be examined.]

Beauchamp, William. *Essays on the Truth of the Christian Religion.* Marietta: Printed for the Author, by Joseph Israel, 1811. [Chapter 26 The miracles recorded in the New Testament, demonstrate the truth of the Christian Religion, because they are genuine, See. 155–66; N.B. Google book]

Beeck, Frans Josef van. *Christ Proclaimed: Christology as Rhetoric.* New York: Paulist, 1979. [Resurrection appearances, See. 253n69, 316–17, 318–20; Easter appearances Eschatological Christology—Wolfhart Pannenberg, See. 308–24; as historical event, See. 311–14; Objectivity of the, See. 196–98; Setting of recollection and recollection, See. 253–59]

Beke, Charles. *Jesus The Messiah.* London: Trübner, 1872. [Chapter 20 The Resurrection of the Messiah, See. 262–91; N.B. Google book and HathiTrust]

Bell, Nancy. *Legends of Our Lord and the Holy Family.* London: Kegan Paul, Trench, Trübner, 1910. [Chapters 15–16, See. 248–90]

Bernard, J. H. *Studia Sacra.* London: Hodder & Stoughton, 1917. [Chapter 6 The Evidence for the Resurrection of Christ, See. 126–69; N.B. This is a solid, dated work.]

Billon, B. M. *Man of the Turin Shroud.* Ilfracombe: Stockwell, 1977. [54 pages]

Bingham, Richard. *Immanuel; or God with Us: A Series of Lectures on the Divinity and Humanity of our Lord; as Well as on His Descent into Hell, Resurrection, Ascension, and Second Advent.* London: Printed For Seeley, Burnside & Seeley, 1843. [Lecture 13. The Resurrection and Ascension of Our Lord, 321–80; N.B. Google book]

Bird, Michael F. *Are You the One Who Is to Come? The Historical Jesus and the Messianic Question.* Grand Rapids: Baker Academic, 2009. [Messiah Inferred from the Resurrection, See. 64–66; also 73–74]

———. *Jesus is the Christ: The Messianic Testimony of the Gospels.* Downers Grove, IL: InterVarsity, 2012. [Resurrection, of Jesus See. 3, 6–7, 10–11, 18, 20–26, 29–30, 37, 45, 54, 56, 77, 79, 85, 87–91, 111, 114–15, 125, 132–33, 135, 139, 141–42, 173, 184]

Bird, Michael F., and James G. Crossley. *How Did Christianity Begin? A Believer and Non-Believer Examine the Evidence.* London: SPCK, 2008. [Chapter 2 The Resurrection, See.

38–50; Response from Michael F. Bird, See. 64–69; N.B. Bird presents the position of a believer. This work is a must read. See. 51–63 for Crossley's important refutation.]

Boers, Hendrikus. *Who was Jesus? The Historical Jesus and the Synoptic Gospels*. New York: Harper & Row, 1989. [Part 2 From Jesus to Primitive Christianity. Chapter 7 The Emergence of the Christian Faith, See. 102–11]

Boettner, Loraine. *The Person of Christ*. Grand Rapids: Eerdmans, 1943. [Chapter 14 The Exaltation of Christ, See. 93–100]

Boff, Leonardo. *Jesus Christ Liberator: A Critical Christology for Our Time*. Translated by Patrick Hughes. Maryknoll, NY: Orbis Books, 1978. [Chapter 7 Resurrection: The Realization of a Human Utopia, See. 121–38]

Borchert, Gerald L. *Jesus of Nazareth: Background, Witnesses, and Significance*. Macon, GA: Mercer University Press, 2011. [See. 141–42, 167–73; 233–35]

Boring, M. Eugene. *The Continuing Voice of Jesus: Christian Prophecy and the Gospel Tradition*. Louisville: Westminster John Knox, 1991. [Part 3 Prophetic Sayings of the Risen Jesus in Gospels, See. 189–268]

———. *Sayings of the Risen Jesus Christian Prophecy in the Synoptic Tradition*. Cambridge: Cambridge University Press, 1982. [Chapter 13 Christian Prophecy in Matthew, See. 204–18; Luke—Acts and the Sayings of the Risen Jesus, See. 226–29]

Boyd, Gregory A. *Cynic Sage 'or' Son of God?* Wheaton: BridgePoint, 1995. [Chapter 13 Devoured by Beasts or Raised From the Dead? A Critique of Crossan's and Mack's Explanations for the Resurrection Faith of the Early Church, See. 267–93]

Boyer, Mark G. *Christ our Passover has been Sacrificed: A Guide Through Paschal Mystery Spiritual, Mystical Theology in the Roman Missal*. Eugene, OR: Wipf & Stock, 2018. [Chapter 12 Easter Sunday of the Resurrection of the Lord, See. 86–92; Chapter 13 The Ascension of the Lord, See. 93–96]

Braaten, Carl E. *Who Is Jesus? Disputed Questions and Answers*. Grand Rapids: Eerdmans, 2011. [Chapter 3 Did Jesus Really Rise from the Dead?, See. 49–57]

Braden, Clark. *The Gross Errors of Popular Teaching in Regard to the Dates of the Birth of Christ and of Events Connected with His Early History, and in Regard to the Dates of His Arrest; the Trials; the Crucifixion; the Burial; the Resurrection, and the Ascension of Christ*. Cairo, IL: Author, 1902. [When did Jesus Arise from the Tomb?, See. 105–9; N.B. Archive.org. Advocates a Wednesday crucifixion.]

Briggs, Charles Augustus. *The Messiah of the Apostles*. New York: Scribner's Sons. 1895. [The Resurrection of Jesus, See. 534–38; N.B. Google book]

———. *The Messiah of the Gospels*. New York: Scribner's Sons, 1894. [The Resurrection and Second Advent, See. 94–100; N.B. Google book and HathiTrust]

Bright, Bill. *A Man Without Equal*. Orlando, FL: NewLife, 1992. [Chapter 6 Revolutionary Resurrection, See. 63–70]

Broadus, John A. *Jesus of Nazareth*. 2nd ed. New York: A. C. Armstrong, 1890. [Part 3 The Supernatural Works of Jesus, See. 85, 99–103; N.B. Archive.org and Google book]

Brookes, James H. *The Christ*. New York: Revell, 1893. [Chapter 11 Christ's Resurrection, See. 129–55]

Brown, Simon. *Evidence of the Crucifixion, Death and Resurrection of Jesus Christ*. CreateSpace, 2015. [256 pages]

———. *The Shroud Speaks for Itself: Evidence Proving the Authenticity of the Shroud*. CreateSpace, 2013. [98 pages]

Category VI— Jesus's Life: General Works and the Person of Jesus

Bruce, F. F. *Jesus: Lord & Savior*. Downers Grove, IL: InterVarsity, 1986. [Chapter 12 The Risen Lord, See. 115–27]

Bruggen, Jakob van. *Jesus the Son of God: The Gospel Narratives as Message*. Translated by Nancy Forrest-Flier. Grand Rapids: Baker, 1996. [Resurrection of Jesus, See. 219–22]

Buckham, John Wright. *Christ and the Eternal Order*. Boston: Pilgrim Press, 1906. [Chapter 18 Christ Risen, See. 142–50; N.B. Archive.org]

Bulst, Werner. *The Shroud of Turin*. Translated from the German by Stephen McKenna and James J. Galvin in co-operation with the Holy Shroud Guild, Esopus, New York, 1957.

Burrell, David James. *The Wonderful Teacher and What He Taught*. New York: Fleming, 1902. [Chapter 23 The Resurrection, See. 289–300; N.B. HathiTrust]

Burrows, Millar. *Jesus in the First Three Gospels*. Nashville: Abingdon, 1977. [Chapter 18 The Resurrection, See. 270–79]

Burton, Henry. *Gleanings in the Gospels*. London: Charles H. Kelly, 1896. [Chapter 14 The Christ of the Resurrection, See. 231–48; Chapter 15 The Christ on the Shore, See. 249–69; Chapter 16 The House of Mary, See. 270–76; N.B. Google book]

Canale, Andrew. *Understanding the Human Jesus: A Journey in Scripture and Imagination*. New York: Paulist, 1985. [Chapter 11 Resurrection, See. 188–98]

Carmody, John, et al. *Exploring the New Testament*. Englewood Cliffs, NJ: Prentice-Hall, 1986. [See. 173–75, 217, 232–33, 295–97]

Carpenter, Lant. *An Apostolical Harmony of the Gospels*. 2nd ed. London: Longman, Orme, Brown, Green, & Longmans, 1838. [Part 10 From the Burial of Our Lord in the Tomb of Joseph, to His Ascension into Heaven, See. 283–304; N.B. Google book]

Carpenter, Russell Lant, ed. *A Monotessaron, or, The Gospel Records of the Life of Christ, Combined into One Narrative, on the Basis of Dr. Carpenter's Apostolical Harmony*. London: E. T. Whitfield, 1851. Part 10. From the Burial of Our Lord in the Tomb of Joseph, to His Ascension into Heaven, See. 230–44; N.B. Google book]

Carroll, John. *The Existential Jesus*. Berkeley, CA: Counterpoint, 2009. [Chapter 6 The Empty Tomb, See. 125–34]

Carroll, Warren H. *Founding of Christendom*. Vol. 1. Front Royal, VA: Christendom Press, 1985. [Chapter 16 "I am the Resurrection and the Life" (29–30 AD), See. 351–93]

Carson, D. A. *God With Us: Themes from Matthew*. Ventura, CA: Regal, 1985. [Chapter 12 Death—and the Death of Death, See. 153–63]

Cassels, Louis. *This Fellow Jesus*. Anderson, IL: Warner Press, 1973. [Chapters 12–13, See. 84–93]

Cawley, Frederick. *The Transcendence of Jesus Christ*. Edinburgh: T&T Clark, 1936. [Chapter 4 The Finality of Jesus Christ, See. 232–39]

Chatham, Joshua G. *In the Midst Stands Jesus: A Pastoral Introduction to the New Testament*. Staten Island, NY, 1972. [Chapter 19 The Resurrection of Christ, See. 153–57]

Cinquemani, Nicolò. *The Double Images on the Shroud of Turin: A Medical Inquiry Into The Crucifixion*. Roma: Giovinezza, 1997. [60 pages]

Clarke, Rufus. *The True Prince of the Tribe of Judah or Life Scenes of the Messiah*. Boston: Albert Colby, 1859. [Chapter 23 Resurrection of the Messiah, See. 292–304; Chapter 24 The Walk to Emmaus, See. 305–17; Chapter 25 The Ascension, See. 318–30; N.B. Archive.org]

Clemen, Carl. *Primitive Christianity and its Non-Jewish Sources*. Translated by Robert G. Nisbet. Edinburgh: T&T Clark, 1912. [The Person of Christ, See. 188–99; The Passion and Resurrection, See. 333–35; N.B. Archive.org]

Cochrane, Charles C. *Jesus of Nazareth in Word and Deed*. Grand Rapids: Eerdmans, 1979. [Chapter 19 The Risen Christ, See. 114–20]

Cock, W. H. *Creation and Redemption*. London: Skeffington, 1933. [Chapter 27 The Resurrection, See. 272–78; Chapter 28 To the Ascension and After, See. 279–88]

Collingwood, C. *Christ as Found in The Evangelists Compared with Present-Day Teaching*. London: Elliot Stock, 1883. [See. 262–303; N.B. Archive.org]

Compton-Rickett, Joseph. *Origins and Faith: An Essay of Reconciliation*. New York: Revell, 1909. [Chapter 10 Jesus and the Miraculous, See. 163–72; N.B. Google book]

Cook, P. *Jesus of Nazareth: The Anointed of God or the Inner History of a Consecrated Life*. Chicago: Revell, 1904. [The Resurrection, See. 133–34; N.B. Archive.org, Google book, and HathiTrust]

Counts, Bill. *Once A Carpenter*. Irvine, CA: Harvest House, 1975. [Chapter 20 O Death, Where is Your Victory?, See. 246–54]

Craig, Clarence Tucker. *The Beginning of Christianity*. New York: Abingdon-Cokesbury, 1943. [Chapter 9 The Origin of Christian Belief, See. 133–37]

Crysdale, Cynthia S. W. *Embracing Travail Retrieving the Cross Today*. New York: Continuum, 1999. [See. 152]

Currer-Briggs, Noel. *The Holy Grail and the Shroud of Christ: The Quest Renewed*. Maulden, UK: ARA Publications, 1984. [179 pages]

Danin, Avinoam. *The Botany of the Shroud: The Story of Floral Images on the Shroud of Turin*. Durham, North Carolina: Council for Study of the Shroud of Turin, 2010. Jerusalem: Danin, 2010. [104 pages]

Dawe, Donald G. *Jesus: The Death and Resurrection of God*. Atlanta: John Knox, 1985. [Chapter 6 The Resurrection of Jesus as the Disclosure of the Human, See. 101–19]

Deane-Drummond, Celia. *Christ and Evolution: Wonder and Wisdom*. Minneapolis: Fortress, 2009. [Jesus Christ resurrection, See. 146]

De Bary, Richard. *The Mystical Personality of the Church*. London: Longmans, Green, 1913. [Chapter 3 The Results of Worship, See. 44–54, 59–63]

Demarest, Bruce A. *Who Is Jesus?* Wheaton, IL: Victor, 1978. [Chapter 11 Resurrected Lord, See. 113–22]

DeMent, Byron Hoover. *The Bible Reader's Life of Christ*. New York: Revell, 1928. [Chapter 11 The Period of Exaltation—Jesus Gaining the Victory Over Death, See. 311–32]

Denney, James. *Jesus and the Gospel: Christianity Justified in the Mind of Christ*. New York: A. C. Armstrong, 1909. [Book 2 The Historical Basis of the Christian Faith, See. 99–143; N.B. Archive.org and Google book]

De Wesselow, Thomas. *The Sign The Shroud of Turin and the Secret of the Resurrection*. New York: Dutton, 2012. [448 pages]

DeWitt, Dan. *Christ or Chaos*. Wheaton, IL: Crossway, 2016. [Jesus Christ, resurrection of, See. 103–11]

Dibelius, Martin. *From Tradition to Gospel*. New York: Scribner's Sons, 1965. [See. 189–92]

Dickerman, Benoni. *The Blood-Stained Cross: A Messianic Lyric, or, The Birth, Life, Death, Resurrection and Ascension of Jesus, the Christ*. Columbus, OH: Fred J. Heer, 1884. [To His Resurrection, See. 64–71; To His Ascension, See. 72–73; N.B. poetry]

Dodd, C. H. *The Founder of Christianity*. NY: Macmillan, 1970. [Chapter 9 The Sequel: (3) The sequel, See. 163–72]

Donaldson, John William. *Christian Orthodoxy Reconciled with the Conclusions of Modern Biblical Learning: A Theological Essay, with Critical and Controversial Supplements*.

London: Williams & Norgate, 1857. Appendix 4. See. 267–73; N.B. Archive.org and Google book]

Donehoo, James DeQuincey. *The Apocryphal and Legendary Life of Christ.* New York: Macmillan, 1903. [See. 396–448; N.B. Google book]

Dowling, Levi H. *The Aquarian Gospel of Jesus the Christ: The Philosophic and Practical Basis of the Religion of the Aquarian Age of the World and of the Universal Church.* Mineola, New York: Dover, 2008. [Sections 20–21, Chapters 172–80, See. 244–57; N.B. Reprint of the 1911 publication; Gutenberg.org. Dowling claims post-resurrection appearances in Egypt, Greece, and India.]

Drew, G. S. *The Son of Man His Life and Ministry.* London: Henry S. King, 1875. [Chapter 2 The Resurrection and Ascension, See. 223–38; N.B. Google book]

Drummond, Robert J. *Faith's Certainties* London: Hodder & Stoughton, 1909. [Chapter 6 The Crowning Fact of Christianity—The Resurrection, See. 101–21; N.B. Archive.org.]

DuBose, William Porcher. *The Gospel in the Gospels.* London: Longmans, Green, 1908. [Chapter 15 The Resurrection, See. 180–95; N.B. Google book]

Duncan, George S. *Jesus, Son of Man: Studies Contributory to a Modern Portrait.* London: Nisbet, 1947. [Chapter 13 The Triumph of the Son of Man, See. 172–78]

Dunkerley, Roderic. *The Unwritten Gospel.* London: George Allen & Unwin, 1925. [See. 189–203]

Dunn, James D. G. *The Evidence for Jesus.* Philadelphia: Westminster, 1985. [Chapter 3 What did the First Christians Believe about the Resurrection?, See. 53–78; N.B. This chapter is a recommended reading.]

———. *Jesus Remembered.* Grand Rapids: Eerdmans, 2003. [Chapter 18 *Et Resurrexit*, See. 825–79; N.B. This text should be examined.]

Dwyer, John C. *Church History: Twenty Centuries of Catholic Christianity.* New York: Paulist Press, 1985. [The Resurrection, See. 21–22; From Jesus' Death to the Conversion of Paul, See. 22–24]

Early, Joseph E. *A History of Christianity: An Introductory Survey.* Nashville: B&H Academic, 2015. [See. 10.]

Easterbrook, Gregg. *Beside Still Waters Search for Meaning in an Age of Doubt.* New York: William Morrow, 1998. [Resurrection of, See. 22, 98–99, 101, 237, 277, 287, 292, 294–96]

Ebbutt, A. J. *Who Do You Say that I Am?: Answers to Your Questions About Jesus.* Philadelphia: Westminster, 1957. [Question 13 Did Jesus Really Rise From the Dead?, See. 110–28]

Ebersol, Charles E. *The Four Gospels in One Made Plain.* New York: Fleming, 1937. [Chapter 6 The Risen Life, See. 171–81]

Ebrard, Johannes Heinrich August. *The Gospel History: A Compendium of Critical Investigations in Support of the Historical Character of the Four Gospels.* Translated by James Martin. Edinburgh: T&T Clark, 1863. [Chapter 10 Resurrection and Ascension of Jesus, 447–72; N.B. Archive.org and Google book]

Eckardt, A. Roy. *Jews and Christians: The Contemporary Meeting.* Bloomington: Indiana University Press, 1986. [See. 14, 16, 82–87, 90, 137–39, 144–45, 149, 150, 154, 155, 156, 168; N.B. Eckardt was a Methodist clergy and leading scholar of Christian-Jewish relations.]

Edwards, Douglas Allen. *The Shining Mystery of Jesus.* New York: Longmans, Green, 1928. [Chapter 8 The Resurrection of Jesus, See. 139–63; N.B. Archive.org]

Edwards, O. C. *Luke's Story of Jesus*. Philadelphia: Fortress, 1981. [Chapter 4 Climax in Jerusalem, See. He is Risen, See. 93–96]

Ellis, E. Earle. *Christ and the Future in New Testament History*. Boston: Brill, 2001. [Chapter 8 Resurrection: Jesus, the Sadducees and Qumran, See. 96–104]

Ellison, H. L. *Jesus as Man*. Grand Rapids: Eerdmans, 1978. [Chapter 9 The Resurrection and Ascension, See. 60–64]

Elwood, Douglas J., and Patricia I. Magdamo. *Christ in Philippine Context: A College Textbook in Theology and Religious Studies*. Quezon City: New Day, 1971. [Chapter 14 The Faith of First Century Christians, See. 261–72]

Erickson, Millard J. *The Word Became Flesh*. Grand Rapids: Baker, 1991. [Chapter 19 The Uniqueness of Christ: The Resurrection, See. 481–505; N.B. This work offers a good, concise reading.]

Evans, C. Stephen. *The Historical Christ & the Jesus of Faith: The Incarnational Narrative as History*. 1996. Oxford: Clarendon, 1996. [See. 37, 142, 156, 233, 239, 271, 309, 353–54]

Everett, J. N. *Behold The Man: The Life and Teaching of Jesus Christ*. London: Edward Arnold, 1969. [Chapter 12 The Empty Tomb, See. 131–41]

Felder, Hilarin. *Christ and the Critics*. Vol. 1. Translated by John L. Stoddard. London: Burnes Oates, 1925. [Part 3—The Divine Consciousness of Christ, Chapter 2—i. The Divinity of Christ After His Resurrection, See. 309–16]

———. *Christ and the Critics*. Vol. 2. Translated by John L. Stoddard. London: Burnes Oates, 1924. [Part 2—The Works of Christ, Chapter 3—Science and Christ's Resurrection, See. 370–416]

Ferguson, John. *Jesus in the Tide of Time: An Historical Study*. London: Routledge & Kegan Paul, 1980. [Jesus, resurrection of, See. 25, 52–53, 89]

Finlay, M. H. *Face the Facts Questions and Answers Concerning the Christian Faith*. 2nd ed. Bombay: Gospel Literature Service, 1968. [Did Jesus Really Die on the Cross?, See. 50–60]

First Fruits of Zion. *Chronicles of the Messiah*. Marshfield, MO: First Fruits of Zion, 2014. [See. 1683–780]

Fishback, James. *The Philosophy of the Human Mind in Respect to Religion: or, A Demonstration from the Necessity of Things that Religion Entered the World By Revelation*. Lexington, KT: Thomas T. Skillman, 1813. [See. 80, 161, 205, 208, 213; N.B. Google book and HathiTrust]

Fitzmyer, Joseph A. *A Christological Catechism: New Testament Answers*. New York: Paulist, 1991. [Chapter 18 How are References to the Resurrection of Jesus in the New Testament to be Interpreted?, See. 86–92; Chapter 19 How are New Testament References to the Ascension of Jesus to be Understood?, See. 93–96]

Flavel, John. *The Fountain of Life; or, A Display of Christ in His Essential and Meditorial Glory*. New York: American Tract Society, 1820. Reprint. [Chapter 39 The Resurrection of Christ, See. 482–96; Chapter 40 The Ascension, See. 496–508; N.B. Archive.org, the London edition of 1820. Original published in 1671.]

Foley, Leonard. *Believing in Jesus: A Popular Overview of the Catholic Faith*. 5th ed. Cincinnati, OH: St. Anthony Messenger Press, 2005. [Chapter 7 The Rising of Jesus from the Dead, See. 56–60]

Folliot, Katherine. *Jesus, Before He Was God*. Great Britain: Hazell Watson & Viney, 1978. [Chapter 8 The Resurrection, See. 106–23]

Ford, David F., and Mike Higton, eds. *Jesus*. Oxford: Oxford University Press, 2002. [See. 22–25]

Forrest, David W. *The Authority of Christ*. Edinburgh: T&T Clark, 1906. [Christ, His resurrection, See. 42–44; N.B. Archive.org and Google book]

———. *The Christ of History and of Experience*. Edinburgh: T&T Clark, 1897. [Lecture 4 The Transition From the Historical to the Spiritual Christ, See. 137–68; N.B. Google book]

Foster, George Burman. *The Finality of the Christian Religion*. Chicago: University of Chicago Press, 1906. [See. 80, 114, 135–37, 354–55, 373–74, 387; N.B. Archive.org, Google book, and HathiTrust]

Foster, R. C. *The Final Week*. Grand Rapids: Baker, 1962. [Chapter 19 The Resurrection, See. 251–67]

France, R. T. *I Came to Set the Earth on Fire*. Downers Grove, IL: InterVarsity, 1975. [See. 161–72]

Frederick, William. *Infallible Proof by Three Immutable Witnesses Proving Wednesday Crucifixion by the Literal Fulfillment of Many Types and Prophesies, in the Death and Resurrection of Jesus, and the Science of Astronomy*. Clyde, OH: Author. [336 pages; N.B. Google book and HathiTrust. This is an interesting work to better understand the viewpoint of Wednesday advocates.]

Fredriksen, Paula. *From Jesus to Christ: The Origins of the New Testament Images of Jesus*. New Haven: Yale University Press, 1988. [Resurrection: of Jesus, See. xii, 209]

Freeman, Charles. *A New History of Early Christianity*. New Haven: Yale University Press, 2009. [Chapter 3 Jesus before the Gospels, See. 22–30; Chapter 4 Breaking Away, See. 31–43]

Frei, Hans W. *The Identity of Jesus Christ: The Hermeneutical Bases of Dogmatic Theology*. Eugene, OR: Wipf & Stock, 1997. [Chapter 13 Jesus Identified in His resurrection, See. 174–83]

Fulton, John. *The Chalcedonian Decree: or, Historical Christianity, Misrepresented by Modern Theology, Confirmed by Modern Science, and Untouched by Modern Criticism*. [Lecture 6, See. 186, 188–93, New York: Thomas Whittaker, 1892. [N.B. Archive.org and HathiTrust]

Gall, James. *Good Friday a Chronological Mistake or The Real History of the Lord's Burial Recovered*. Edinburgh: Gall & Inglis, 1882. [Chapter 8 Raising Again the Third Day, 42–46; Eighth Day (Sunday), See. 86–88. Gall advocates a Thursday Crucifixion. N.B. Google book from the Bodleian library.]

Gallwey, Peter. *The Watches of the Sacred Passion with Before and After*. Vol. 2. 3rd ed. London: Art & Book, 1896. [Part 3 Chapter 4 After, Scenes 126–137, See. 616–722; N.B. Archive.org and Google book]

Gardner, Martin. *Urantia: The Great Cult Mystery*. Amherst, NY: Prometheus, 1995. [Appendix D The Story of Joseph of Arimathea, See. 419–22]

Garland, David E. *A Theology of Mark's Gospel*. Grand Rapids: Zondervan, 2015. [Chapter 14 The Ending of Mark's Gospel: A New Beginning, See. 535–58]

Garrett, Alfred Cope. *The Man from Heaven*. Philadelphia: Engle Press, 1939. [See. 426–41]

Garrigou-Lagrange, Reginald. *Christ The Savior: A Commentary on the Third part of St. Thomas' Theological Summa*. Translated by Bede Rose. St. Louis: B. Herder, 1957. [Chapter 38 Christ's Resurrection and Ascension, See. 663–73]

Garza-Valdes, Leoncio A. *The DNA of God?* New York: Doubleday, 1999. [256 pages]

Gifford, William Alva. *The Seekers Why Christian Orthodoxy Is Obsolete*. Boston: Beacon, 1954. [Chapter 6 Jesus Christ, See. 102–17; N.B. No real content about the resurrection is presented.]

Gilchrist, John. *The Crucifixion of Christ: Fact, Not Fiction*. 1994. [36 pages, Refutes Deedat; N.B. Available online]

Gill, Charles. *The Evolution of Christianity*. London: Williams & Norgate, 1883. [Book 3 Christianity 1. The Resurrection, See. 271–80; N.B. Google book]

Gill, John. *The Prophecies of the Old Testament Respecting the Messiah Considered: And Proved to be Literally Fulfilled in Jesus*. London: Printed for Aaron Ward, 1728. [Chapter 11 Concerning the Resurrection of the Messiah From the Dead, See. 178–88; Chapter 12 Concerning the Ascension of the Messiah to Heaven, See. 188–99; N.B. Google book]

Gilmore, James R., and Lyman Abbot. *The Life of Our Lord: Being a Complete Connected Account The Life of Our Lord Woven from the Text of the Four Evangelists*. New York: Fords, Howard & Hulbert, 1881. [Chapter 43 Christ's Resurrection and Ascension, See. 773–98; N.B. Archive.org and Google book]

Girdlestone, Robert Baker. *Why Do I Believe in Jesus Christ? Four Addresses to Business and Professional Men*. London: Hodder & Stoughton, 1904. [§11. His Resurrection, See. 55–57]

Godbey, W. B. *Life of Jesus and His Apostles*. Louisville: Pentecostal Publishing, 1904. [Chapter 17 The Resurrection, See. 402–24; Chapter 18 Ascension into Heaven, See. 425–31; N.B. Archive.org]

Goldberg, Michael. *Jews and Christians Getting Our Stories Straight: The Exodus and the Passion-Resurrection*. Philadelphia: Trinity Press International, 1991. [Chapter 14 Matthew 28, See. 201–12; N.B. The Rabbi presents the Jewish Master Story of Exodus from a Jewish perspective and Passion-Resurrection Master Story found in the Gospel of Matthew from a Christian point of view.]

Good, John Walter. *The Jesus of Our Fathers*. New York: Macmillan, 1923. [Part 7 The Exaltation and Sovereignty of Christ, See. 647–74]

Goodier, Alban. *Jesus Christ: The Son of God*. Grail, 1947. [The Resurrection, See. 73–80]

Goodwin, Daniel Reyes. *Syllabus or Skeleton of Dr. Goodwin's Lectures on Apologetics, or, The Evidences of Christianity*. Philadelphia: Caxton, 1874. [See. 1, 7, 9, 13, 17, 21, 27, 46; N.B. Google book]

Gorge, Charles. *The Incarnation of the Son of God: Being the Bampton Lectures for the Year 1891*. London: John Murray, 1891. [See. 15, 54–55, 57, 61, 62, 65; N.B. Archive.org]

Graham, Alfred. *The Christ of Catholicism: A Meditative Study*. Longmans, Green, 1947. [The Resurrection, See. 140–49]

Grant, Frederick C. *The Life and Times of Jesus*. New York: Abingdon, 1921. [Chapter 32 The Resurrection, See. 215–22]

Gregory, Andrew F., ed. *The Fourfold Commentary*. London: SPCK, 2006. [Matthew 28:1–20, See. 61–62 (David Bartlett); Mark 16.1–8, See. 103–4 (Morna D. Hooker); Luke 24:1–53, See 159–63 (Andrew F. Gregory); John 20–21, See. 205–8 (Henry Wansbury)]

Grensted, L. W. *The Person of Christ*. New York: Harper & Brothers, 1933. [Resurrection, See. 28, 64–65]

Griffiths, Douglas Allen. *Whose Image and Likeness?* [*Concerning the Authenticity of the Shroud in the Cathedral at Turin as being the one in which Christ was Wrapped After his Death on the Cross. With photographs*] Nottingham, 1964. [109 pages]

Grimbol, William R. *The Complete Idiot's Guide to the Life of Christ*. Indianapolis, IN: Alpha, 2001. [Chapter 19 It Is All About Appearances, See. 167–71]

Guignebert, Charles. *The Early History of Christianity*. NY: Twayne, 1927. [See. 44–50]

Haight, Roger. *The Future of Christology*. New York: Continuum, 2005. [Jesus Christ, resurrection of, See. 38, 44–45, 82–83, 89–90, 95–96, 102, 198, 201–3]

———. *Jesus: Symbol of God*. Maryknoll, NY: Orbis Books, 2000. [Chapter 5 Jesus' Resurrection, See. 119–51]

Hall, Charles Cuthbert. *The Universal Elements of the Christian Religion: An Attempt to Interpret Contemporary Religious Conditions*. New York: Fleming, 1905. [Lecture 4 The Saviour of the World, See. 153–203; N.B. Archive.org, Google book, and HathiTrust]

Hamilton, Laurentine. *A Reasonable Christianity*. San Francisco: Issued for the Author by Dewey, 1881. [Chapter 11 The Resurrection, See. 169–81; N.B. Google book]

Hanson, Richard Simon. *Journey to Resurrection: The Drama of Lent and Easter in the Gospel of John*. New York: Paulist. 1986. [Chapter 9 Resurrection Morn, See. 67–70]

Haralick, Robert M. *Analysis of Digital Images of the Shroud of Turin*. Spatial Data Analysis Laboratory, Virginia Polytechnic Institute and State University, 1984. [132 pages]

Hargis, Jeffrey W. *Against the Christians: The Rise of Early Anti-Christian Polemic*. New York: Peter Lang, 1999. [Resurrection of, See. 6, 45, 68, 73, 84]

Harold, Preston. *The Shining Stranger: An Unorthodox Interpretation of Jesus and His Mission*. New York: Wayfarer Press, 1967. [Chapter 15 The Resurrection, See. 311–32]

Harris, Murray J. *3 Crucial Questions About Jesus*. Grand Rapids: Baker, 1994. [Chapter 2 Did Jesus Rise from the Dead?, See. 31–64]

Harrison, Everett F. *A Short Life of Christ*. Grand Rapids: Eerdmans, 1968. [Chapter 16 The Resurrection, See. 231–46; Chapter 17 The Ascension, See. 247–53]

Headlam, Arthur C. *Jesus Christ In History and Faith*. London: John Murray, 1925. [Lecture 6 The Resurrection and the Virgin Birth, See. 159–80]

———. *St. Paul and Christianity*. New York: Longmans, Green, 1913. [See. 54–57; N.B. Archive.org.]

Hegel, Friedrich. *On Christianity: Early Theological Writings*. New York: Harper Torchbooks, 1948. [The Resurrection and the Commands Thereafter, See. 83–85]

Heisler, Charles W. *Passion of Our Lord: An Interwoven Narrative of the Sufferings, Death, Resurrection and Ascension of Our Lord and Saviour Jesus Christ in the Words of the Four Evangelists*. Albany, NY: Sabbath Literature, 1904. [See. 113–39; N.B. Archive.org]

Heller, John H. *Report on the Shroud of Turin*. Boston: Houghton Mifflin, 1983. [225 pages]

Hendrix, Eugene Russell. *The Religion of the Incarnation*. Nashville: Publishing House of the M.E Church, South, 1903. [See. 217–59; N.B. Google book and HathiTrust]

Hengel, Martin. *Studies in Early Christology*. London: T&T Clark, 2004. [Jesus, the Messiah of Israel, See. 1–73, especially 9–21. N.B. Hengel discusses when in the eyes of the disciples Jesus became the Messiah and the Son of God.]

Hennell, Charles C. *An Inquiry Concerning the Origin of Christianity*. London: Smallfield, 1838. [See. 35–37; N.B. Archive.org, Google book, and HathiTrust]

Hennrich, Kilian J. *Readings and Meditations on Christ: Victim and Victor*. Patterson, NJ: St. Anthony Guild Press, 1940. [Christ the Victor, See. 59–98]

Henriksen, Jan-Olav. *Desire, Gift, and Recognition: Christology and Postmodern Philosophy*. Grand Rapids: Eerdmans, 2009. [Part 4 Resurrection and Incarnation as Gift, See. 337–67]

Hick, John. *The Metaphor of God Incarnate: Christology in a Pluralistic Age.* Louisville: Westminster John Knox, 1993. [Chapter 2 Jesus' Life, Death and Resurrection, See. 15–26]

Hindmarsh, Robert. *A Seal Upon the Lips of the Unitarians, Trinitarians, and all Others Who Refuse to Acknowledge the Sole, Supreme, and Exclusive Divinity of Our Lord and Saviour Jesus Christ.* Manchester: F. Davis, 1814. [See. #46–48, 54, 118–20; N.B. Archive.org, Google book, and HathiTrust]

Hinson, E. Glenn. *A History of Christianity up to 1300.* Macon: Mercer University Press, 1995. [The Resurrection, See. 21]

Hoare, Rodney. *The Turin Shroud Is Genuine: The Irrefutable Evidence.* London: Souvenir Press, 1998. [188 pages]

Hodgkin, Henry T. *Jesus Among Men.* London: Student Christian Movement Press, 1930. [See. 155–56]

Hodgson, Peter C. *Jesus Word and Presence: An Essay in Christology.* Philadelphia: Fortress, 1971. [Jesus as Present, See. 220–91]

Holding, James Patrick. *Shattering the Christ Myth: Did Jesus Not Exist?* US: Xulon, 2008. [387 pages]

How, W. Walsham. *The New Testament of Our Lord and Saviour Jesus Christ: The Four Gospels.* London: SPCK, 1910. [No pagination: N.B. Google book]

Howard, Jeremy Royal. *Holman QuickSource Guide to Understanding Jesus.* Nashville: B&H, 2009. [Chapter 14 Up from Death, See. 213–37]

Hughes, Frederick Stephen. *Where is Christ? A Question for Christians.* Boston: Houghton Mifflin, 1919. [See. 38; N.B. Archive.org]

Huidekoper, Frederic. *Indirect Testimony of History to the Genuineness of the Gospels.* New York: James Miller, 1880. [See. 89, 140–45; N.B. Google book and HathiTrust]

Hunter, Archibald M. *The Work and Words of Jesus.* Philadelphia: Westminster, 1950. [Chapter 15 The Resurrection, See. 123–30]

Iannone, John. *The Three Cloths of Christ: The Emerging Treasures of Christianity.* US: North Star, 2010. [247 pages]

Inbody, Tyron L. *The Many Faces of Christology.* Nashville: Abingdon, 2002. [Chapter 7 Jesus, Judaism, and Christianity, Sect. 3 The Resurrection of Jesus, See. 176–80]

Ingraham, J. H. *The Prince of House of David; or, Three Years in the Holy City.* New York: Pudney & Russell, 1859. [Letter 27, See. 439–51; N.B. Archive.org. Fiction.]

Jack, J. W. *The Historic Christ: An Examination of Dr. Robert Eisler's Theory According to the Slavonic Version of Josephus and Other Sources.* London: James Clarke, 1933. [See. 75, 77, 79, 91, 163–67, 245]

Jennings, A. G. *The Last Days of Jesus Christ: or, The Gospel Account of the Great Atonement.* Philadelphia: American Sunday-School Union, 1893. [See. 83–112; N.B. Google book]

Jensen, David H. In *The Company of Others: A Dialogical Christology.* Cleveland: Pilgrim Press, 2001. [Chapter 4 the Absent Presence of the Risen Christ, See. 90–130]

Jeremias, Joachim. *New Testament Theology: The Proclamation of Jesus.* New York: Scribner's Sons, 1971. [Chapter 7 Easter, See. 300–11]

Johnston, J. Wesley. *The Master.* New York: Abingdon, 1923. [The Master's Easter Day, See. 167–84]

Jones, J. P. *The Teaching of Jesus our Lord.* London: Christian Literature Society, 1908. [Study 24 His Future Life and Work, See. 50–51; N.B. Archive.org.]

Kasper, Walter. *Jesus the Christ*. Mahwah, NJ: Paulist, 1985. [Part 2 The History and Destiny of Jesus Christ, B. Christ, Risen and Transcendent, See. 124–60]

Kaufman, Gordon D. *Jesus and Creativity*. Minneapolis: Fortress, 2006. [Jesus appearances after death, See. 5, 9–10, 19, 21, 49–50, 92, 94–95, 117n12; Resurrection, See. xii, xiv, 9–13, 15–18, 21, 23–24, 28, 36–38, 52, 55, 57, 92–95, 116n12]

Kaylor, R. David. *Jesus the Prophet: His Vision of the Kingdom on Earth*. Louisville: Westminster John Knox, 1994. [A Concluding Theological Postscript: This Jesus God Raised Up, See. 212–14]

Keehus, Magnus N. *Jesus, is He the Messiah of Israel? "Who will Declare His Generation?" A Dialogue Based on the Tanakh, Talmud, and Targumim; the Dead Sea Scrolls; and the New Testament*. Eugene, OR: Wipf & Stock, 2011. [Chapter 4 Resurrection and Skepticism: Jesus Rose from the Dead, See. 138–92]

Kennard, Douglas W. *Messiah Jesus: Christology in His Day and Ours*. New York: Peter Lang, 2008. [Chapter 13 Jesus' Resurrection, See. 333–52]

Kenrick, Francis Patrick. *The Four Gospels Translated from the Latin Vulgate with Critical Notes*. New York: Edward Dunigan, 1849. [Matthews, See. 208–11; Mark, See. 296–99; Luke, See. 445–50; John, See. 564–72; N.B. Archive.org, Google book, and HathiTrust]

Kent, Charles Foster. *The Life and Teachings of Jesus According to the Earliest Records*. New York: Scribner's Sons, 1913. [§144 The Living Christ, See. 297–310; N.B. Archive.org]

Keown, Mark J. *What's God Up To on Planet Earth? A No-Strings Attached Explanation of the Christian Message*. Eugene, OR: Wipf & Stock, 2011. [See. 54–55]

Kereszty, Roch A. *Jesus Christ: Fundamentals of Christology*. New York: Communio Book, 2002. [Chapter 2 The Death and Resurrection of Jesus, See. 32–71]

Kim, Yung Suk. *Resurrecting Jesus The Renewal of New Testament Theology*. Eugene, OR: Cascade, 2015. [Chapter 6 The Resurrection of Jesus, See. 91–107]

Kirtley, J. S. *The Disciple and His Lord: or, Twenty-six Days with Jesus*. Philadelphia: American Baptist Publication Society, 1906. [See. 225–43; N.B. Archive.org and Google book]

Klotz, John C. *The Coming of the Quantum Christ: The Shroud of Turin and the Apocalypse of Selfishness*. CreateSpace, 2014. [256 pages]

Knight, Jonathan. *Christian Origins*. London: T&T Clark, 2008. [Chapter 16 The Resurrection of Jesus, See. 148–56; N.B. This chapter is worth examining.]

———. *Jesus: An Historical and Theological Investigation*. London: T&T Clark, 2004. [Chapter 10 He Has Been Raised; He Is Not Here, See. 193–224]

Küng, Hans. *Judaism Between Yesterday and Tomorrow*. New York: Crossroads, 1992. [See. Resurrection of, See. 337–42, 364–67, 373, 378, 492, 505, 507–8, 570, 602, 606]

LaHaye, Tim. *Why Believe in Jesus?* Eugene, OR: Harvest House, 2004. [Part 4 Evidence for the Resurrection, See. 223–88]

Lake, Kirsopp. *The Stewardship of Faith: Our Heritage from Early Christianity*. New York: G. P. Putnam, 1915. [See. 58–61; N.B. Google book]

Lamsa, George M. *My Neighbor Jesus: In the Light of His Own Language, People, and Time*. New York: Harper & Brothers, 1932. [Chapter 16 The Resurrection, See. 140–48]

Lane Dermot A. *Christ at the Centre: Selected Issues in Christology*. New York: Paulist, 1990. [Chapter 4 The Resurrection of Jesus as Gift, See. 80–102]

———. *The Reality of Jesus: An Essay in Christology*. New York: Paulist, 1975. [Chapter 4 The Resurrection: A Survey of the Evidence, See. 44–65; Chapter 5 The Resurrection: A Theological Response, See. 66–81]

Larson, James Henry. *Meet the Man You Were Born to Love*. New York: Fortuny's, 1939. [Resurrection, Appearances, Ascension, See. 188-96]

Latourette, Kenneth Scott. *A History of Christianity*. NY: Harper & Row, 1953. [See. 57-59]

Lavoie, Gilbert R. *Unlocking the Secrets of the Shroud*. Allen, TX: Thomas More, 1998. [224 pages]

Leask, W. *The Footsteps of the Messiah: A Review of Passages on the History of Jesus Christ*. New York: William S. Martien, 1847. [Chapters 22-24, See. 308-51; N.B Archive.org]

Lenowitz, Harris. *The Jewish Messiahs From the Galilee to Crown Heights*. New York: Oxford University Press, 1998. [See. 47-49]

Lenwood, Frank. *Jesus Lord or Leader*. London: Constable, 1930. [See. 82-85]

Levison, N. *Passiontide or the Last Days of the Earthly Life of the Master*. Edinburgh: T&T Clark, 1927. [Chapter 12 The Resurrection, See. 159-74]

Lewis, Abram Herbert. *Biblical Teachings Concerning the Sabbath and the Sunday*. 2nd ed. Alfred Centre, NY: American Sabbath Tract Society, 1888. [Chapter 5 The Time of Christ's Resurrection, See. 50-63; Chapter 6 Christ's Example Concerning the First Day of the Week, See. 64-73; N.B. Google book]

Lewis, Peter. *The Glory of Christ*. Chicago: Moody, 1997. [Part 5 Christ the Exalted Lord, See. 357-400]

Licona, Michael R. *Why Are These Differences in the Gospels: What We Can Learn from Ancient Biography*. Oxford: Oxford University Press, 2017. [Appendix 3 Which Women Were Present at the Cross, Burial, and Empty Tomb?, See. 209-12]

Lightfoot, John. *A Commentary on the New Testament from the Talmud and Hebraica: Matthew, 1 Corinthians*. Grand Rapids: Baker, 1979. [Chapter 4 Emmaus Lk 24, See. 314-21; N.B. Reprint of the 1859 ed. published by Oxford University Press, Oxford, England, under title: *Horae Hebraicae et Talmudicae*]

Litwa, M. David. *Iesus Deus The Early Christian Depiction of Jesus as a Mediterranean God*. Mineapolis: Fortress, 2014. [Chapter 5 We Worship One who Rose from His Tomb, See. 141-56]

Litwiller, Kurt Dean. *Humble King to Conquering King: The Week That Changed Everything*. Apopka, FL: NewBookPublishing.com, 2011. [209 pages]

Loewe, William P. *The College Student's Introduction to Christology*. Collegeville, MN: Liturgical Press, 1996. [Part 2 Origin and Meaning of Belief in Jesus' Resurrection, See. 97-138]

Long, George. *An Inquiry Concerning Religion*. London: Longman, Brown, Green & Longmans, 1855. [The Testimony of the Apostles to the Resurrection of Jesus, See. 89-93; N.B. Google book]

Lorimer, George C. *Jesus the World's Savior: Who He Is, Why He Came, and What He Did*. Chicago: S. C. Griggs, 1883. [Chapter 19 The Resurrection of Jesus, See. 284-97; N.B. Google book and HathiTrust]

Luther, Martin. *Martin Luther's Easter Book*. Edited and translated by Roland H. Bainton. Minneapolis: Augsburg, 1997. [The Resurrection, See. 87-103]

Maas, A. J. *Christ In Type and Prophecy*. Vol. 2. New York: Benziger, 1893. [Part 8 The Glory of the Messias, See. 351-420; N.B. Archive.org. Not useful.]

Macartney, Clarence Edward Noble. *Christianity and Common Sense: A Dialogue of Faith*. Chicago: John C. Winston, 1927. [Chapter 7 Common Sense and the Resurrection, See. 161-91]

Category VI— Jesus's Life: General Works and the Person of Jesus

———. *Twelve Great Questions About Christ*. New York: Revell, 1923. [Chapter 7 Did Christ Rise from the Dead?, See. 114–29; Chapter 8 Did Christ Ascend Into Heaven?, See. 130–143]

Machovec, Milan. *A Marxist Looks at Jesus*. Philadelphia: Fortress, 1976. [Jesus Christ resurrection, See. 145, 160–71, 172, 181, 182, 209, 219; post-resurrection appearances, See. 160–61, 165–69, 188; Emmaus, See. 161, 181; exaltation, See. 163–64, 168]

Mackey, James P. *Jesus the Man & the Myth: A Contemporary Christology*. New York: Paulist. 1979. [Chapter 3 The Resurrection, See. 86–120]

Mackintosh, H. R. *The Doctrine of the Person of Jesus Christ*. New York: Scribner's Sons, 1912. [Book 3 Part 2 Chapter 5 The Exalted Lord, See. 363–82; N.B. Archive.org]

Macy, S. B. *The Prince of Peace*. London: Longmans, Green, 1913. [See. 527–48. N.B. Mrs. S. B. Macy was the wife of the Rev. Vincent Travers Macy]

Maher, Robert W. *Science, History, and the Shroud of Turin*. New York: Vantage, 1986. [106 pages]

Major, H. D. A., et al. *The Mission and Message of Jesus: An Exposition of the Gospels in the Light of Modern Research*. New York: E. P. Dutton, 1938. [The Resurrection of Jesus, See. 211–18; 292–97; 934–56]

Manson, T. W. *The Servant-Messiah: A Study of the Public Ministry of Jesus*. Grand Rapid: Baker, 1977. [Chapter 6 The Risen Christ and the Messianic Succession, See. 89–99]

Marino, Joseph. *Wrapped Up In The Shroud, Chronicle of a Passion*. St. Louis: Cradle Press, 2011. [340 pages]

Martensen, Hans Lassen. *Jacob Boehme, His Life and Teaching or Studies in Theosophy*. Translated by T. Rhys Evans. London: Hodder & Stoughton, 1885. [See. 275–81: N.B. Google book]

Mathews, George Martin. *Christ in the Life of To-Day*. Dayton, OH: Otterbein Press, 1916. [The Power of Christ's Resurrection, See. 180–86; N.B. Google book]

Mathews, Shailer. *The Gospel and the Modern Man*. New York: Macmillan, 1910. [Chapter 7 The Deliverance from Death, See. 223–38; N.B. Archive.org and Google book]

Maurice, Frederick Denison. *Theological Essays*. 2nd London ed. New York: Redfield, 1854. [Essay 8 Resurrection of the Son of God From the Death, the Grave, and Hell, See. 116–42; N.B. Archive.org, Google book, and HathiTrust]

Maus, Cynthia Pearl. *Christ and the Fine Arts: An Anthology of Pictures, Poetry, Music, and Stories Centering in the Life of Christ*. New York: Harper & Brothers, 1938. [Part 5 §1 The Resurrection, See. 427–64; §2 His Ascension, See. 465–95]

McClymond, Michael J. *Familiar Stranger: An Introduction to Jesus of Nazareth*. Grand Rapids: Eerdmans, 2004. [A New Beginning: The Resurrection, See. 129–32]

McCollister, John C. *The Christian Book of Why*. New York: J. David, 1983. [See. 35–38]

McCrone, Walter. *Judgement Day for the Turin Shroud*. Chicago: Microscope, 1997. [341 pages]

McCulloh, James M. *An Impartial Exposition of the Evidences and Doctrines of the Christian Religion*. Baltimore: Armstrong & Berry, 1836. [See. 216–17, 220, 225, N.B. Google book]

McDaniel, George White. *The Supernatural Jesus*. Nashville: Sunday School Board of the Southern Baptist Convention, 1924. [Chapter 7 The Resurrection of Jesus, See. 132–63]

McDowell, Josh. *More Than A Carpenter*. Wheaton, IL: Living Books, 1984. [Chapter 8 Can You Keep a Good Man Down?, See. 89–100]

McDowell, Josh, and Sean McDowell. *More Than a Carpenter*. Revised and updated. Carol Stream, IL: Tyndale House, 2009. [Chapter 19 Can You Keep a Good Man Down?, See. 125–40]

McKenzie, C. W. *The Throne of His Glory*. Ilfracombe, N. Devon: Stockwell, 1953. [Chapter 18 Death and Resurrection, See. 81–87]

McKim, Ralph Harrison. *Christ and Modern Unbelief*. Thomas Whittaker, 1893. [Chapter 7 Modern Theories of the Resurrection of Jesus, See. 125–46; N.B. Archive.org]

McKnight, Scot. *The Story of the Christ*. Grand Rapids: Baker Academic, 2006. [Chapter 7 Passion and Resurrection, See. 175–80]

McMahon, Christopher. *Our Salvation: An Introduction to Christology*. Winona, MN: Saint Mary's Press, 2007. [Chapter 3 The Resurrection, See. 82–95]

Meacham, William. *Turin Shroud, Image of Christ? : Symposium and Exhibition of Photographs, March 3–9, 1986: Proceedings*. Hong Kong: Turin Shroud Photographic Exhibition Organizing Committee, 1987. [65 pages]

Meier, John P. *The Mission of Christ and His Church: Studies in Christology and Ecclesiology*. Wilmington, DE: Michael Glazier, 1990. [Chapter 7 Two Disputed Questions in Matthew 28:16–20, See. 153–79]

Meldau, Fred John. *Messiah in Both Testaments*. Denver: Christian Victory, 1967. [Prophecies Concerning the Sufferings, Death and Resurrection of Messiah, See. 59–76; N.B. The author examines Psalm 22 and Isaiah 53.]

Meyer, Ben F. *The Aims of Jesus*. San Jose, CA: Pickwick, 2002. [The Gospel Literature: Data on Jesus, 1 Corinthians 15:3–5, See. 61–63]

Miles, Jack. *Christ: A Crisis in the Life of God*. New York: Random House, 2002. [He Rises to Life, Incorporates, Ascends to Heaven, and Marries, See. 236–45]

Miller, Lucius Hopkins. *Our Knowledge of Christ: An Historical Approach*. New York: Henry Holt, 1914. [The Resurrection, See. 80–84]

Milman, Henry Hart. *The History of Christianity from the Birth of Christ to the Abolition of Paganism in the Roman Empire*. Vol. 1. New York: Harper & Brothers, 1855. [Book 2 Chapter 1 The Resurrection and First Promulgation of Christianity, See. 145–49; N.B. Archive.org, Google book, and HathiTrust]

———. *The Character and Conduct of the Apostles considered as an Evidence of Christianity, in Eight Sermons preached before the University of Oxford*. Oxford: At the University Press, 1827. [Lecture 8, 1 Cor. 15. 19, See. 327–68; N.B. Archive.org and Google book]

Mimpriss, Robert. *A Continuous History of the Holy Gospel According to Greswell's Arrangement*. Cheltenham: Published by William Wight, 1838. [Part 5 Arranged in the Order of Time, Comprehending the Space of Forty Days' Time, See. 188–99; N.B. Google book]

———. *The Gospel Treasury, and Expository Harmony of the Four Evangelists*. 3rd ed. London: The Systematic Bible Teaching Mission Depository, 1885. [Part Fifth, See. 947–90; N.B. Archive.org]

Mitchell, W. R. *The Life of Jesus Christ*. London: Sampson Low, Marston, 1927. [Chapter 42 The Resurrection, See. 239–50]

Moltmann, Jürgen. *The Crucified God: The Cross of Christ as the Foundation and Criticism of Christian Theology*. Minneapolis: Fortress, 1993. [Jesus' Resurrection from the Dead, See. 166–78; The Significance of the Cross and Risen Christ, See. 178–87]

———. *The Way of Jesus Christ: Christology in Messianic Dimensions.* Translated by Margaret Kohl. New York: HarperSanFrancisco, 1990. [Chapter 5 The Eschatological Resurrection of Christ, See. 213–73]

Moment, John J. *Faith in Christ.* New York: Scribner's Sons, 1917. [Chapter 5 The Cross. See. 7 Easter, See. 253–55; N.B. HathiTrust]

Moore, Hight C. *From Bethlehem to Olivet.* Nashville: Sunday School Board of the Southern Baptist Convention, 1934. [Chapter 9 The Forty Days, See. 81–97]

Morgan, Rex. *Perpetual Miracle: An Account of the Holy Shroud of Turin.* Manly, Australia: Runciman, 1980. [185 pages]

Morris, Wingfield Scott. *Jesus, King of Kings.* Boston: Meador, 1933. [Chapter 25 The Resurrection and Ascension, See. 125–50]

Mosheim, Johann Lorenz. *Historical Commentaries on the State of Christianity during the First Three Hundred and Twenty-five Years from the Christian Era.* Vol. 1. Translated by Robert Studley Vidal. 1852. [See. 98–100; N.B. Archive.org, Google book, and HathiTrust. In 1753, the original Latin version was published.]

Murray, William D. *What Manner of Man is This? Studies in the Life of Christ.* New York: Young Men's Christian Association Press, 1907. [Chapter 18 He comes out of the graves, See. 77–80]

Nash, John F. *Christianity: The One, the Many. What Christianity Might Have Been and Could Still Become.* Vol. 1. US: Xlibris, 2007. [Resurrection and Ascension, See. 72–75, 85]

Nash, Ronald H. *Christianity and the Hellenistic World.* Grand Rapids: Zondervan, 1984. [See. 14, 20, 23, 61, 138, 197; N.B. Not useful.]

Navarante, Louis-Marie. *The Holy Shroud Why We Believe.* Nawala, Sri Lanka: MG Printer (PVT), 2014.

Navigators Ministry. *The Life & Ministry of Jesus Christ. Book 3. From His Last Entry into Jerusalem to the Resurrection and Ascension.* Colorado Springs, CO: NavPress, 1977. [Chapter 6 Jesus' Victory and Commission, See. 75–85]

Neville, Robert Cummings. *Symbols of Jesus: A Christology of Symbolic Engagement.* Cambridge: Cambridge University Press, 2001. [Resurrection, See. 61, 165–67, 198, 202–4, 238]

Newman, Albert Henry. *A Manual of Church History.* Judson Press, Revised ed. Vol. 1 1933. [The Resurrection and Ascension, See. 77–78; N.B. Google book, American Baptist Publication Society, 1899.]

Newman, Randy. *Engaging with the Jewish People.* United Kingdom: The Good Book Company, 2016. [See. 76–80]

Newman, T. C. *Follow the Light: The Shroud's Revelations.* T. C. Newman, 2013. [116 pages]

Nicoll, W. Robertson. *The Church's One Foundation: Christ and Recent Criticism.* London: Hodder & Stoughton, 1901. [Chapter 6 The Resurrection of Our Lord From the Dead, See. 130–49; N.B. Archive.org and HathiTrust]

Nolloth, Charles Frederick. *The Person of Our Lord and Recent Thought.* London: Macmillan, 1908. [Chapter 11 The Resurrection, See. 237–53; N.B. Archive.org and Google book]

O'Collins, Gerald. *Christology A Biblical, Historical, and Systematic Study of Jesus.* Oxford: Oxford University Press, 1995. [Chapter 4 The Resurrection, See. 82–112]

———. *Jesus Our Redeemer: A Christian Approach to Salvation.* Oxford: Oxford University Press, 2007. [Chapter 12 Bodily Resurrection and the Transformation, See. 238–67]

O'Grady, John F. *Models of Jesus*. Garden City, NY: Doubleday, 1981. [Resurrection, See. 50–51, 65–66, 107–10]

Osborne, Harold. *Christ and the Early Church*. London: University Tutorial Press, 1934. [Chapter 7 Resurrection, See. 107–21]

Ousler, Fulton. *The Greatest Story Ever Told: A Tale of the Greatest Life Ever Lived*. Garden City, NY: Doubleday, 1975. [See. 294–99]

Oxley, Mark. *The Challenge of the Shroud: History, Science and the Shroud of Turin*. AuthorHouse, 2010. [348 pages]

Pagliarino, Guido. *The Mysterious Shroud of Turin*. Morrisville, NC: Lulu, 2006. [80 pages]

Pannenberg, Wolfhart. *Jesus God and Man*. 2nd ed. Translated by Lewis L. Wilkins and Duane A. Priebe. Philadelphia: Westminster, 1977. [Chapter 2 Christology and Soteriology, #3 Jesus' Resurrection as the Ground of His Unity with God, See. 53–114]

Patzia, Arthur G. *The Emergence of the Church Context, Growth, Leadership & Worship*. Downers Grove, IL: InterVarsity Press, 2001. [Jesus: From Easter to Pentecost, See. 69–72]

Perkins, Pheme. *The Gnostic Dialogue the Early Church and the Crisis of Gnosticism*. New York: Paulist, 1979. [Resurrection, of Jesus, See. 38–40, 50–51, 55, 117, 179]

Petrelli, Giuseppe. *The Son of Man*. Trenton, NJ: Merlo's Publishing, 1943. [See. 350–97]

Petrosillo, Orazion, and Emanuela Marinelli. *The Enigma of the Shroud—A Challenge to Science*. San Gwann, Malta: Publishers Enterprises Group, 1996. [260 pages]

Pike, Diane Kennedy, and R. Scott Kennedy. *Wilderness Revolt: A New View of the Life and Death of Jesus*. Garden City, NY: Doubleday, 1972. [Chapter 13 Not the Messiah, Yet Raised from the Dead, See. 241–60]

Pitzer, Alexander White. *Ecce Deus-Homo or the Work and Kingdom of the Christ of Scripture*. Philadelphia: Lippincott, 1868. [Chapter 6 The Resurrection of Jesus, See. 83–104; N.B. Archive.org]

Placher, William C. *Jesus The Saviour: The Meaning of Jesus Christ for Christian Faith*. Louisville: Westminster John Knox, 2001. [Part 4 Resurrection, See. 157–81]

Platt, David. *Follow Me. A Call to Die. A Call to Live*. Carol Stream, IL: Tyndale House, 2013. [Chapter 4 Don't Make Jesus Your Personal Lord and Savior, See. 79–81]

Plumptre, E. H. *Christ and Christendom: The Boyle Lectures for the Year 1866*. London: Alexander Strahan, 1867. [Chapter 8 The Resurrection, See. 287–314; N.B. Google book]

Pokorný, Petr. *The Genesis of Christology: Foundations for a Theology of the New Testament*. Translated by Marcus Lefébure. Edinburgh: T&T Clark, 1987. [The empty tomb, See. 151–56]

Poling, Daniel A. *He Came From Galilee*. New York: Harper & Row, 1965. [See. 225–40]

Porter, J. R. *The Illustrated Guide to the Bible*. New York: Oxford University Press, 1995. [The Resurrection, See. 208–11; The Ascension, See. 212–13]

———. *Jesus Christ: The Jesus of History, the Church of Faith*. New York: Oxford University Press, 1999. [The Aftermath, See. 128–34; The Resurrection, See. 218–19]

Purinton, Herbert R., and Sadie Brackett Costello. *The Achievement of the Master*. New York: Scribner's Sons, 1926. [See. 190–94]

Purves, George T. *Christianity in the Apostolic Age*. New York: Scribner's Sons, 1902. [Chapter 2 The Origin of Christianity, See. 8–20; N.B. Archive.org]

Radner, Ephraim. *The World in the Shadow of God: An Introduction to Christian Natural Theology*. Eugene, OR: Cascade, 2010. [See. 104–62; N.B. This work consists of poetry.]

Räisänen, Heikki. *The Rise of Christian Beliefs: The Thought World of Early Christians*. Minneapolis: Fortress, 2010. [The Easter Experiences, See. 57–59]

Rausch, Thomas P. *Who Is Jesus? An Introduction to Christology*. Collegeville, MN: Liturgical Press, 2003. [Chapter 7 God Raised Him from the Dead, See. 111–24]

Reader's Digest. *The Story of Jesus*. Pleasantville, NY: Reader's Digest, 1993. [Dead—And Yet Alive Again, See. 296–301]

Reber, George. *The Christ of Paul or the Enigmas of Christianity*. New York: Charles P. Somerby, 1876. [Chapter 6 How the Four Gospels Originated, See. 72–80; N.B. Google book]

Reed, Charles E. B. *The Companions of the Lord: Chapters on the Lives of the Apostles*. London: Religious Tract Society, 1873. [Chapter 5 The Peter of the Gospels: From the Entry to the Ascension, See. 75–96; Thomas, See. 242–47; N.B. Archive.org and Google book]

Reiser, William. *An Unlikely Catechism Some Challenges for the Creedless Catholic*. Mahwah, NJ: Paulist, 1985. [Chapter 3 Who Owns the Future A Reflection on the Resurrection, See. 118–44]

Reynolds, Andrew, J. *Jesus of Nazareth: The Prince of Life*. Denver, CO: Fowler-Metzger-Aley, 1933. [Chapter 14 The Resurrection, See. 233–49]

Rice, John R. *Is Jesus God: An Answer to Infidels in the Church and Out*. Wheaton: Sword of the Lord, 1948. [Chapter 5 The Resurrection of Jesus Christ, See. 105–58]

Rinaldi, Peter M. *The Man in the Shroud: A Study of the Shroud of Christ*. London: Futa, 1974. [125 pages]

Robinson, Arthur W. *The Christ of the Gospels*. London: Student Christian Movement, 1924. [Chapter 14 The Fact of the Resurrection, See. 184–93]

Robinson, John A. T. *The Human Face of God*. Philadelphia: Westminster, 1973. [Resurrection, See. 27, 28, 127–42]

Rogers, Raymond N. *A Chemist's Perspective on the Shroud of Turin*. Edited by Barrie M. Schwortz. Florissant, CO: Barrie M. Schwortz, 2008. [149 pages]

Rose, Vincent. *Studies on the Gospels*. London: Longmans, Green, 1903. [Chapter 8 The Empty Tomb, See. 257–307; N.B. Archive.org]

Roukema, Riemer. *Jesus, Gnosis and Dogma*. New York: T&T Clark, 2010. [Chapter 4 Jesus' Death, Resurrection, and Exaltation, See. 88–113]

Rutter, Henry. *The Life, Doctrines, and Sufferings of Our Blessed Lord and Saviour Jesus Christ as Recorded by the Four Evangelists*. London: W. Clowes, 1830. [See. 447–56; N.B. Archive.org and HathiTrust]

Salstrand, George A. E. *What Jesus Began: The Life and Ministry of Christ*. Nashville: Broadman Press, 1976. [Chapter 17 Forty Unique and Momentous Days, See. 170–80]

Sanders, J. Oswald. *The Incomparable Christ: A Doctrinal and Devotional Study*. Chicago: Moody, 1971. [Chapter 32 The Resurrection of Christ, See. 223–29; Chapter 33 The Ministry of the Forty Days, See. 231–34; Chapter 34 The Ascension of Christ, See. 237–42]

Santala, Risto. *The Messiah In the New Testament In the Light of Rabbinical Writings*. Translated by William Kinnaird. Jerusalem: Karen Ahvah Meshihit, 1992. [Proofs of the Resurrection, See. 230–34]

Santayana, George. *The Idea of Christ in the Gospels or God in Man: A Critical Essay*. New York: Scribner's Sons, 1946. [Chapter 11 The Resurrection, See. 156–68]

Sawyer, Elbert H. *Biography of Jesus*. Chicago: John C. Winston, 1927. [Chapter 23 Resurrection and Ascension of Jesus, See. 166–76]

Schaff, Philip. *History of the Christian Church*. Vol. 1. New York: Scribner's, 1858. [The Resurrection of Christ, See. 172–86; N.B. CCEL.org and Google book]

———. *History of the Christian Church*. Vol. 4. New York: Scribner's, 1885. [See. 187; N.B. Archive.org and CCEL.org]

Schillebeeckx, Edward. *Jesus: An Experiment in Christology*. Translated by Hubert Hoskins. New York: Seabury, 1978. [Section 2 Direct hermeneusis of the resurrection in the New Testament, See. 516–44]

———. *Interim Report on the Books: Jesus & Christ*. New York: Crossroad, 1981. [Risen from the Dead, See. 134–39]

Schlatter, Adolf. *The History of the Christ: The Foundation for New Testament Theology*. Translated Andreas J. Köstenberger. Grand Rapids: Baker, 1997. [Chapter 5 The Easter Account, See. 375–89]

Schmidt, Nathaniel. *The Prophet of Nazareth*. London: Macmillan, 1905. [Excursus C. The Resurrection, See. 392–97; N.B. Archive.org]

Schönborn, Christoph Cardinal. *God Sent His Son: A Contemporary Christology*. Translated by Henry Taylor. San Francisco: Ignatius Press, 2010. [The Glorification of the Son, See. 312–37]

Schwager, Raymund. *Jesus in the Drama Salvation: Toward A Biblical Doctrine of Redemption*. Translated by James G. Williams and Paul Haddon. New York: Herder & Herder, 1999. [Fourth Act: Resurrection of the Son as Judgment of the Heavenly Father, See. 119–41]

Schwalbe, Larry, and Raymond N. Rogers. *Physics and Chemistry of the Shroud of Turin: A Summary of the 1978 Investigation*. New York; Amsterdam: Elsevier, 1982. [49 pages]

Schwarz, Hans. *Christology*. Grand Rapids: Eerdmans, 1998. [Chapter 3 See. 113–35; Chapter 6 Cross and Resurrection, See. 236–87]

Schweizer, Eduard. *Jesus*. Translated by David E. Green. Richmond, VA: John Knox, 1971. [Easter, See. 45–51]

Scott, Ernest F. *The First Age of Christianity*. New York: Macmillan, 1935. [See. 85–88]

Scrymgeour, William. *Lessons on the Life of Jesus*. Edinburgh: T&T Clark, 1883. [Lesson 32 From the Resurrection to the Ascension, See. 211–27; N.B. Archive.org]

Sensenig, Barton. *How Jesus Showed God to the People*. Philadelphia: Barton Sensenig, 1930. [See. 201–12]

Sharman, Henry Burton. *Jesus in the Records*. New York: Association Press, 1918. [Study 23 Events Subsequent to the Death of Jesus, See. 227–34; N.B. HathiTrust]

———. *Studies In the Life of Christ*. New York: Association Press, 1912. [Study 29 The Resurrection, Appearances and Ascension of Jesus, See. 212–18; N.B. Archive.org and Google book]

Sire, James W. *Why Good Arguments Often Fail: Making A More Persuasive Case For Christ*. Downers Grove, IL: InterVarsity, 2006. [The Resurrection of Jesus, See. 159–60]

Skelly, A. M. *Jesus and Mary*. St. Louis: B. Herder, 1930. [Eastertide, See. 215–22; The Resurrection of the Dead, See. 223–26]

Skinner, Conrad. *The Gospel of the Lord Jesus*. London: University of London Press, 1937. [Chapter 24 The Empty Tomb, See. 295–312]

Sloyan, Gerard S. *Jesus in Focus: A Life In Its Setting*. Mystic, CT: Twenty-Third Publications, 1983. [Chapter 20 The Man Raised from the Dead, See. 145–52]

Smith, Charles W. F. *The Paradox of Jesus in the Gospels*. Philadelphia: Westminster, 1969. [Chapter 8 The Paradox in Resurrection and Retrospect, See. 182–212]

Smith, Wilbur M. *The Supernaturalness of Christ*. Boston: W. A. Wilde, 1944. [Chapter 6 The Historical Reality of Christ's Resurrection, See. 189–228]

Sobrino, Jon. *Christology at the Crossroads: A Latin American Approach*. Translated by John Drury. Maryknoll, NY: Orbis Books, 1978. [Chapter 7 The Resurrection of Jesus: Hermaneutic Problem, See. 236–58; Chapter 8 The Resurrection of Jesus: Theological Problem, See. 259–72; Chapter 11 Theses for a Historical Christology, The Resurrection of Jesus, See. 374–81]

———. *Christ The Liberator; A View from the Victims*. Translated by Paul Burns. Maryknoll, NY: Orbis Books, 2001. [Chapter 4 The Historical Problem (1) The Reality of Jesus' Resurrection, See. 54–65; Chapter 5 The Historical Problem (2) The Analogy of "Easter Experiences" throughout History, See. 66–78]

Sox, H. David. *The Image on the Shroud: Is the Turin Shroud a Forgery?* London: Unwin Paperbacks, 1981. [175 pages]

Speer, Robert E. *The Meaning of Christ to Me*. New York: Revell, 1936. [Chapter 4 What the Resurrection of Christ Means to Me, See. 116–31]

Spring, Gardiner. *The Glory of Christ: Illustrated in His Character and History, Including the Last Things of His Mediatorial Government*. Volume 1. New York: M. W. Dodd, 1852. [Chapter 9 Christ Glorious in His Resurrection, See. 247–74; Chapter 10 Christ's Ascension Glorious, See. 275–432; N.B. Archive.org and HathiTrust]

Stackhouse, Thomas. *An History of the Holy Bible From the Beginning of the World to the Establishment of Christianity*. Vol. 2. London: William Aldard, 1788. [Book 8, See. 340–45; N.B. Google book. Two volumes in one.]

Stanton, Graham N. *Jesus and Gospel*. Cambridge: Cambridge University Press, 2004. [Chapter 7 Early objections to the resurrection of Jesus, See. 148–61]

Stanton, Vincent Henry. *The Jewish and the Christian Messiah*. Edinburgh: T&T Clark, 1886. [See. 252–55, 289–90, Resurrection the Third Day, See. 381; N.B. Archive.org and Google book]

Stegall, Thomas L. *The Gospel of the Christ: A Biblical Response to the Crossless Gospel Regarding the Contents of Saving Faith*. Milwaukee, WI: Grace Gospel Press, 2009. [Chapter 13 What Is the Gospel according to 1 Corinthians 15:1–2?, See. 479–528; Chapter 14 What Is the Gospel According to 1 Corinthians 15:3–11?, See. 529–91; N.B. Google book]

Stevenson, Kenneth E. *Proceedings of the 1977 United States Conference of Research on the Shroud of Turin*. (United States Conference of Research on the Shroud of Turin 1977, Albuquerque, NM), 1979. [243 pages]

Stevenson, Kenneth E., and Gary R. Habermas. *Verdict on the Shroud: Evidence for the Death and Resurrection of Jesus Christ*. London: Hale, 1982. [224 pages]

Stier, Rudolf. *The Words of the Risen Saviour and Commentary on the Epistle of St James*. Translated by William B. Pope. Edinburgh: T&T Clark, 1864. [Stier discusses Paul's three encounters with Jesus recorded in Acts, See. 1–61; N.B. Archive.org and Google book]

Storm, Harold. *Who Is Jesus: What did He Do and Why Did He Do It. Informational Lessons on Lutheran Doctrine*. Columbus, GA: Brentwood Christian Press, 1999. [Chapter 12 The Resurrection of Jesus, See. 81–85]

Strauss, Mark L. *Four Portraits, One Jesus*. Grand Rapids: Zondervan, 2007. [Chapter 20 The Resurrection of Jesus, See. 511–24]

Strobel, Lee. *The Case for Christ: A Journalist's Personal Investigation of the Evidence for Jesus*. Grand Rapids: Zondervan, 1998. [Part 3: Researching the Resurrection, Chapters 11–14, See. 191–257]

———. *The Case for Faith: A Journalist Investigates the Toughest Objections to Christianity*. Grand Rapids: Zondervan, 2000. [Resurrection of Jesus, See. 21, 22, 60, 151, 153, 251; evidence for the, See. 65–71]

———. *Lee Strobel's the Case for Christ: A Journalist's Personal Investigation of the Evidence for Jesus*. Grand Rapids: Zondervan, 2002. [Part 3 Can A Dead Man Come Back to Life?, See. 81–112]

Strong, Thomas B. *The Miraculous In Gospels and Creeds*. London: Longmans, Green, 1914. [See. 13–14]

Sutcliffe, Joseph. *An Introduction to Christianity Designed to Preserve Young People*. New York: N. Bangs & J. Emory, 1825. [Section 4 Of the Incarnation—the Ministry—the Death—and Ascension of our Blessed Lord and Saviour Jesus Christ, See. 65–67; N.B. Google book]

Tait, Arthur J. *The Heavenly Session of Our Lord: An Introduction to the History of the Doctrine*. London: Robert Scott, 1912. [247 pages; N.B. EBSCO]

Talmage, James E. *Jesus the Christ. A Study of the Messiah and His Mission According to Holy Scriptures both Ancient and Modern*. 3rd ed. Salt Lake City, UT: Deseret News, 1916. [Chapter 37 The Resurrection and the Ascension, See. 678–99; N.B. Archive.org]

Talmage, T. DeWitt. *From Manger to Throne: Embracing A New Life of Jesus Christ and A History of Palestine and Its People*. Philadelphia: Historical Publishing, 1890. [Chapter 37 The Resurrection, See. 617–34; Chapter 38 The Ascension, See. 635–39; N.B. Archive.org and HathiTrust]

Taylor, Isaac. *The Restoration of Belief*. Boston: E. P. Dutton, 1867. [The Second Intention of Christ's Mission As Attested By Miracles. See. 324–35; N.B. Archive.org and Google book]

Thaddeus, Sister Mary, et al. *Christ in Promise, in Person, and in His Church*. Milwaukee, Bruce, 1961. [Chapter 28 Christ's Victory, See. 373–83]

Theological-Historical Commission for the Greater Jubilee of the Year 2000, The. *Jesus Christ Word of the Father. Jesus Christ, Word of the Father & the Savior of the World*. Translated by Adrian Walker. New York: Crossroad, 1997. [Chapter 6 The Resurrection of Jesus, See. 89–105]

Thompson, William M. *The Jesus Debate: A Survey and Synthesis*. New York: Paulist, 1985. [Easter Experiences, See. 229–47]

Thomson, Ebenezer, and William Charles Price. *The History of Our Blessed Lord and Saviour Jesus Christ*. London: Printed for John Pearmain, 1802. [Chapter 39, See. 401–4; N.B. Archive.org and HathiTrust]

Tice, Rico. *Christianity Explored Study Guide, Leader's Edition*. Surrey, UK: Good Book Company, 2003. [Jesus—His Resurrection, See. 35–41]

Tidball, Thomas A. *Christ in the New Testament*. New York: Thomas Whittaker, 1891. [See. 19, 20, 52, 69, 94, 95, 97, 125, 138, 147, 169, 171, 172, 174, 176, 181, 182, 184, 185, 193, 195, 233, 234, 258, 279, 294, 295, 308, 309, 310, 349; N.B. Google book]

Torrance, Thomas F. *Atonement: The Person and Work of Christ*. Edited by Robert T. Walker. Downers Grove, IL: InterVarsity, 2009. [Chapter 7 The Resurrection of Jesus Christ,

Category VI— Jesus's Life: General Works and the Person of Jesus

See. 201–42; Chapter 8 The Nature of the Resurrection Event, See. 243–64; Chapter 9 The Ascension and Parousia of Jesus Christ, See. 265–70]

Torrey, R. A. *The Bible and Its Christ.* New York: Fleming, 1906. [Talk 5 Did Jesus Christ Really Rise From the Dead?, See. 58–69; Talk 6 The Self-Evident Truthfulness of the Gospel Stories of the Resurrection, See. 70–85; Talk 7 The Circumstantial Evidence of the Resurrection of Christ, See. 86–100; Talk 8 What the Resurrection of Jesus from the Dead Proves, See. 101–11; N.B. Archive.org]

Tribe, Frank C. *Portrait of Jesus? The Illustrated Story of the Shroud of Turin.* New York: Stein & Day, 1983. [281 pages]

Tripole, Martin R. *The Jesus Event and Our Response.* New York: Alba House, 1979. [Jesus' Resurrection, See. 172–83; Jesus' Exaltation, See. 180–82]

Tuck, William Powell. *The Compelling Faces of Jesus Christ.* Macon, GA: Mercer University Press, 2008. [Chapter 7 The Risen Christ, See. 119–38]

Turnbell, Robert. *Theophany; or, the Manifestation of God in the Life, Character, and Mission of Jesus Christ.* Hartford: Brockett, Fuller, 1849. [Chapter 5 The Resurrection of Christ: Its Reality and Import, See. 67–75; Chapter 6 The Ascension of Christ, See. 76–85; N.B. Google book and HathiTrust]

Valesio, Franco, and Peter M. Rinaldi. *The Cathedral of Turin and the Shroud.* Translated from the original Italian by P. M. Rinaldi. Turin, Italy: Cathedral of Turin, 1985.

Van Paassen, Pierre. *Why Jesus Died. New York*: Dial Press, 1949. [Chapter 7 What Happened to the Body of Jesus, See. 176–206]

Vardy, Peter, and Mary Mills. *The Puzzle of the Gospels.* London: M.E. Sharpe, 1997. [Resurrection, See. 200–204]

Vawter, Bruce. *This Man Jesus: An Essay Toward a New Testament Christology.* Garden City, NY: Doubleday, 1973. [Introduction: Paul on, See. 21–22; Chapter 1 He Has Been Raised, See. 33–51]

Veach, Robert Wells. *The King and His Kingdom. Constructive Studies in the Life of Christ for Classes and Private Use.* New York: Fleming, 1908. [Part 6 The Resurrection and the Coronation of the King, See. 137–50]

Vear, Eric. *The Life of the Messiah in His Jewish Context: Based Upon Dr. Arnold Fruchtenbaum.* n.p., 2015. [Chapter 10 The Resurrection and the Ascension of the King, §181–198, See. 751–84; N.B. Available online]

Vickers, John. *The Crucifixion Mystery: A Review of the Great Charge Against the Jews.* London: Williams & Norgate, 1895. The Resurrection, See. 67–83: N.B. Archive.org]

Vignon, Paul. *The Shroud of Christ.* New York: Dutton, 1902. [170 pages; N.B. Archive.org]

Wainwright, Elaine M. *Shall We Look for Another? A Feminist Rereading of the Matthean Jesus.* Maryknoll, NY: Orbis Books, 1998. [Chapter 7 The Liberator Liberated, the Crucified One Raised (Matthew 27:32–28:20), See. 112–18]

Walsh, John Evangelist. *The Shroud.* London: Allen, 1964. [152 pages]

Walvoord, John F. *Jesus Christ Our Lord.* Chicago: Moody, 1969. [Chapter 10 Christ in His Resurrection, See. 191–218]

Washington, Linda, et al. *Puzzlement & Predicaments of the Bible: The Weird, the Wacky, and the Wondrous.* New York: Howard, 2007. [Dead Man walking, See. 254–56]

Watchtower Bible and Tract Society of New York. *Reasoning from the Scriptures.* Brooklyn, NY: Watchtower Bible and Tract Society, 1985. [Resurrection, See. 333–35; N.B. Available online at Scribd.com]

Watson, Samuel, Mrs. *The Life of Jesus Christ the Saviour Retold From the Evangelists*. London: Religious Tract Society, 1885. [Chapter 41 The Resurrection and Ascension, See. 426–41; N.B. Google book]

Weinel, Heinrich, and Alban G. Widgery. *Jesus in the Nineteenth Century and After*. Edinburgh: T&T Clark, 1914. [See. 42–48, 87–88, 101, 132–33, 148, 170, 366, 414, 424; N.B. Archive.org]

Weiss, Johannes. *Earliest Christianity: A History of the Period AD 30–150*. Volume 1. Translated by Fredrick C. Grant. New York: Harper & Brothers, 1937. [Chapter 2 The Rise of the New Faith, See. 14–44; Chapter 4 The New Doctrine, See. 83–107]

Welker, Michael. *God the Revealed: Christology*. Translated by Douglas W. Stott. Grand Rapids: Eerdmans, 2013. [Part 2 The Resurrection, See. 104–43]

Wells, Edward. *A Treatise Concerning the Harmony of the Four Gospels*. London: Printed for James Knapton, 1718. [N.B. Archive.org and Google book]

Wessels, Cletus. *Jesus In the New Universe Story*. Maryknoll, NY: Orbis Books, 2003. [Part 3 The Biblical Stories, See. 85–140]

West, Thomas H. *Jesus and the Quest for Meaning: Entering Theology*. Minneapolis: Fortress, 2001. [Chapter 6 The Resurrection of Jesus, See. 107–18; Chapter 7 The Risen Christ Continues the Mission, See. 119–37]

White, Ellen G. *The Desire of Ages*. Mountain View, CA: Pacific Press, 1898. [Chapters 80–87, See. 779–833; N.B. Available online]

———. *The Spirit of Prophecy: The Great Controversy Between Christ and Satan from the Destruction of Jerusalem to the End of Time*. Battle Creek, MI: Steam Press, 1878. [Chapters 13–19, See. 191–263; N.B. Google book and Gutenberg.org]

Whitelaw, Thomas. *How is the Divinity of Jesus Depicted in the Gospels and Epistles?* London: Hodder & Stoughton, 1883 [Part 3 The Divinity of Jesus In Post-Incarnate Exaltation, See. 197–256; N.B. Archive.org]

Whitmer, John A. *Immanuel Jesus Christ: Cornerstone of Our Faith*. Nashville: Nelson, 1998. [Chapter 8 Christ's Ascension to the Right Hand of God the Father, See. 109–17]

Wieman, Henry Nelson, and Walter Marshall Horton. *The Growth of Religion*. Chicago: Willett, Clark, 1938. [The Message of the Apostles, See. 140–41.]

Wilcox, Robert K. *The Truth About the Shroud of Turin: Solving the Mystery*. Washington, DC: Regnery Publishing. 2010. [252 pages]

Williams, A. Lukyn. *The Hebrew-Christian Messiah; or, The Presentation of the Messiah to the Jews in the Gospel according to St. Matthew*. London, Society for Promoting Christian Knowledge, 1916. [Lecture Twelve The Messiah—The Victor, See. 397–410; N.B. Archive.org and HathiTrust]

Williams, Horace Blake. *Fundamentals of Faith in the Light of Modern Thought*. New York: Abingdon, 1922. [Chapter 12 The Risen Lord, See. 167–81; N.B. Archive.org and Google book]

Wilson, Clifford. *A Greater Than Jonah is Here*. Melbourne, Australia: The Australian Institute of Archaeology, 1968. [Chapter 5 Jonah—A Sign of Christ's Resurrection, See. 29–37; Chapter 6 The Early Disciples Doubt the Sign of Jonah, See. 37–48]

Wilson, Ian. *The Blood and the Shroud: New Evidence That the World's Most Sacred Relic is Real*. New York: Touchstone, 1998. [333 pages]

———. *Murder at Golgotha: Revisiting the Most Famous Crime Scene in History*. New York: St. Martin's Press, 2006. [Chapter 14 Grave Disturbances, See. 147–59; Chapter 15 Strange Sightings, See. 161–73]

Wilson, P. Whitwell. *A Layman's Confession of Faith*. New York: Revell, 1924. [Chapter 13 Did Christ Rise from the Dead?, See. 166–80]

Wives, E. W. *God In History*. United Kingdom: Lion, 1979. [Accounting for the Empty Tomb, See. 29–33]

Workman, George Coulson. *Jesus the Man and Christ the Spirit*. New York: MacMillan, 1928. [Chapter 7 The Resurrection, See. 159–82; N.B. Archive.org]

Worsley, F. W. *The Apocalypse of Jesus Being a Step in the Search for the Historical Christ*. London: J&J Bennett, 1912. [Jesus or Christ?, Section 2, See. 326–37; N.B. HathiTrust]

Wright, N. T. *Simply Jesus: A New Vision of Who He Was, What He Did, and Why He Matters*. New York: HarperOne, 2011. [Chapter 14 Under New Management: Easter and Beyond, See. 191–205]

———. "The Transforming Reality of the Bodily Resurrection." In *The Meaning of Jesus: Two Visions*. New York: HarperSanFrancisco, 1999. [See. 111–27]

Wuenschel, Edward. *Holy Shroud of Turin*. Esopus, NY: Holy Shroud Guild, 1953? [64 pages]

Yancey, Philip. *The Jesus I Never Knew*. Grand Rapids: Zondervan, 1995. [Chapter 11 Resurrection: A Morning Beyond Belief, See. 207–20]

Young, E. S. *The Life of Christ. A Harmony of the Four Gospels*. North Manchester, IN: Bible Student Publishing Company, 1898. [See. 327–42; N.B. Google book]

Young, John. *The Christ of History: An Argument Grounded in the Facts of His Life On Earth*. New York: R. Carter, 1866. [See. Conclusion, 253–60; N.B. Archive.org and Google book]

Zugibe, Frederick T. *The Cross and the Shroud: A Medical Inquiry into the Crucifixion*. New York: Paragon House, 1988. [236 pages]

Zwemer, Samuel M. *The Glory of the Cross*. London: Marshall Bros., 1935? [Chapter 9 He Showed Them His Hands, See. 109–18; Chapter 10 The Power of His Resurrection, See. 119–28; N.B. Available online]

Chapter 14

Jesus's Life: General Works the Person Jesus, the History of the Early Church, and the Shroud of Turin: Con Resurrection

Besant, Annie. *Esoteric Christianity or The Lesser Mysteries*. London: Theosophical Publishing Society, 1901. [Chapter 8 Resurrection and Ascension, See. 231–52; N.B. Archive.org. This work is an interesting, dated source.]

Borg, Marcus J. *Jesus: Uncovering the Life, the Teachings, and Relevance of a Religious Revolutionary*. New York: HarperSanFrancisco, 2006. [Chapter 10 Executed by Rome, Vindicated by God, See. 261–92; N.B. Borg's text is a recommended read.]

———. "The Truth of Easter." In *The Meaning of Jesus: Two Visions. Marcus J Borg and N. T. Wright*. New York: HarperSanFrancisco, 2000. [Chapter 8 The Truth of Easter, See. 129–42]

Carmichael, Joel. *The Unriddling of Christian Origins: A Secular Account*. Amherst, NY: Prometheus, 1995. [Chapter 6 The "Mother Church," See. 143–49; N.B. An interesting chapter to examine.]

Clarke, John. *A Critical Review of the Life Character, Miracles, and Resurrection of Jesus Christ in a Series of Letters to Dr. Adam Clarke*. London: J. Clarke, 1825. [Letter 15, See. 262–85; Letter 16, See. 286–315; N.B. Google book and HathiTrust. This classic, dated source is a must read!]

———. *A Critical Review of the Life, Character, Miracles, and Resurrection of Jesus Christ in a Series of Letters to Dr. Adam Clarke*. 2nd ed. Leeds: Printed by Joshua Hobson, 1839. [See. 372–76; N.B. Archive.org and Google book]

Conner, Robert P. *Jesus The Sorcerer Exorcist & Prophet of the Apocalypse*. Oxford: Mandrake of Oxford, 2006. [Chapter 4 The Resurrection as Ghost Story, See. 63–72]

Crossley, James G., and Michael F. Bird. *How Did Christianity Begin? A Believer and Non-Believer Examine the Evidence*. London: SPCK, 2008. [Chapter 2 The Resurrection, See. 51–63; Response to Michael F. Bird, See. 191–3; N.B. Bird presents the position of a believer and Crossley, a non-believer. This work is an absolute must read.]

Donehoo, James DeQuincey. *The Apocryphal and Legendary Life of Christ*. New York: Macmillan, 1903. [See. 396–448; N.B. Google book]

Dowling, Levi H. *The Aquarian Gospel of Jesus the Christ: The Philosophic and Practical Basis of the Religion of the Aquarian Age of the World and of the Universal Church.*. Mineola, New York: Dover, 2008. [Sections 20–21, Chapters 172–80, See. 244–57; N.B.

Category VI— Jesus's Life: General Works and the Person of Jesus

Reprint of the 1911 publication; Gutenberg.org. Dowling claims post-resurrection appearances occurred in Egypt, Greece, and India.]

Ehrman, Bart D. *Jesus, Interrupted: Revealing the Hidden Contradictions (and Why We Don't Know About Them)*. New York: HarperOne, 2009. [The Resurrection Narratives, See. 47–55; N.B. Another interesting and recommended work contributed by Ehrman.]

———. *Peter, Paul, and Mary Magdalene: The Followers of Jesus in History and Legend*. Oxford: Oxford University Press, 2006. [Peter and the Resurrection, See. 49–57; Paul and the Resurrection of Jesus, See. 111–13; The Women at the Tomb, 227–39; N.B. An excellent read.]

Gardner, Martin. *Urantia: The Great Cult Mystery*. Amherst, NY: Prometheus, 1995. [Appendix D The Story of Joseph of Arimathea, See. 419–22. N.B. Useless.]

Kalthoff, Albert. *The Rise of Christianity*. Translated by Joseph McCabe. London: Watts, 1907. [See. 137–41; N.B. Archive.org and Google book. Kalthoff was an early advocate of the Christ Myth.]

Kautsky, Karl. *Foundations of Christianity: A Study in Christian Origins*. New York: International Publishers, 1925. [The Resurrection of the Crucified, See. 371–78; N.B. Archive.org]

Küng, Hans. *Judaism Between Yesterday and Tomorrow*. New York: Crossroads, 1992. [Resurrection of, See. 337–42, 364–67, 373, 378, 492, 505, 507–8, 570, 602, 606; N.B. One should take time to examine Küng's text.]

Lewis, H. Spencer. *The Mystical Life of Jesus*. San Jose, CA: Rosicrucian Press, 1929. [Chapter 16 The Secret Facts of the Resurrection, See. 269–81; Chapter 17 The Unknown Life of Jesus, See. 283–92. Jesus survived the crucifixion; N.B. He was a Rosicrucian.]

———. *The Secret Doctrines of Jesus*. San Jose, CA: Grand Lodge of the English Language Jurisdiction, AMORC, 1998, 1995, 1937. [Chapter 8 The Greatest Miracle of Miracles, See. 71–79; Chapter 9 More Biblical Verification, See. 80–93; N.B. Available online]

Loisy, Alfred. *The Origins of the New Testament*. Translated by L. P. Jacks. New York: Collier, 1962. [See. 124–26, 158–61, 193–96, 266–71]

Mead, G. R. S. *Did Jesus Live 100 BC?* New Hyde Park, NY: University, 1968. [440 pages; N.B. Archive.org and available online from the Gnostic Society Library]

Moore, George. *The Brook Kerith: A Syrian Story*. New York: Macmillan, 1916. [This work is a fictional novel; N.B. Archive.org, Google book, and Gutenberg.org]

Nickell, Joe. *Inquest on the Shroud of Turin: Latest Scientific Findings*. Amherst, NY: Prometheus, 1998. [184 pages; N.B. Nickell's book is a recommended text to examine.]

Paine, Thomas. *Of the Evidence of Christ's Death, Burial and Resurrection, its Plainness to our Senses: a sermon preached at Braintree the Sabbath after the burial of that pious and valuable gentlewoman*. Boston: Printed by S. Kneeland & T. Green, 1732. [28 pages; N.B. Early American imprints. First series; no. 3586.]

Price, Robert M. *The Case Against the Case for Christ: A New Testament Scholar Refutes Lee Strobel*. Cranford, NJ: American Atheist Press, 2010. [Part 3 Rationalizing the Resurrection, See. 205–54; N.B. This text is a recommended read.]

Roberts, Jonathan M. *Antiquity Unveiled: Ancient Voices from the Spirit Realms Disclose the Most Startling Revelations Proving Christianity to be of Heathen Origin*, 3rd ed. Philadelphia: Oriental Publishing, 1912. [N.B. This work is an anthology of numerous ancient sources; N.B. Google book.]

Robertson, J. M. *Christianity and Mythology*. London: Watts, 1900. [The Burial and Resurrection, See. 381–82; The Banquet of Seven, See. 382–84; The Ascension, See. 384–85; N.B. Archive.org and Google book]

———. *The Jesus Problem: A Restatement of the Myth Theory*. London: Watts, 1917. [The Resurrection, See. 70–71; N.B. Archive.org]

———. *Pagan Christs Studies in Comparative Hierology*. London: Watts, 1903. [See. xii, 135, 141, 170, 180–81, 188, 193–94, 196–98, 359; Also see, The Christian Crucifixion, 114–18; N.B. Google book]

———. *Short History of Christianity*. 2nd ed. London: Watts, 1913. [The author advocates the Christ Myth; N.B. Archive.org]

Russell, John (Viscount Amberley). *An Analysis of Religious Belief*. Vol. 1. London: Trübner, 1876. [Resurrection, See. 353–64; N.B. Archive.org. Russell rejected Jesus's divinity and considered himself a deist.]

Schäfer, Peter. *Jesus in the Talmud*. Princeton: Princeton University Press, 2007. [This important work is a must read. It shows how over time the rabbis interpreted different aspects of Jesus's life, often polemical.]

Smith, William Benjamin. *The Birth of the Gospel: A Study of the Origin and Purport of the Primitive Allegory of Jesus*. Edited by Addison Gulick. NY: Philosophical Library, 1957. [See. 40, 112–16, 139, 189. Smith was a proponent of the Christ Myth and this work was published posthumously; N.B. HathiTrust]

———. *Ecce Deus: Studies of Primitive Christianity*. Chicago: Open Court, 1912. [Smith was a proponent of the Christ Myth; N.B. Archive.org]

Spong, John Shelby. *A New Christianity for the New World: Why Traditional Faith is Dying and How a New Faith is Being Born*. New York: HarperSanFrancisco, 2001. [See. 87–112]

———. *Unbelievable Why Neither Ancient Creed Nor The Reformation Can Produce a Living Faith Today*. New York: HarperSanFrancisco, 2018. [Part 9 Thesis 7: Easter, See. 169–88; Part 10 Thesis 8: The Ascension, See. 189–96]

Sylva [pseud.]. *Ecce Veritas: An Ultra Unitarian Review of the Life and Character of Jesus*. London: Trübner, 1874. [The Resurrection and Ascension, See. 140–47; Reducio Ad Absurdum, See. 147–52; N.B. Google book]

Tabor, James D. *Paul and Jesus: How the Apostle Transformed Christianity*. New York: Simon & Schuster, 2012. [Chapter 3 Reading the Gospels in the light of Paul, See. 68–90]

Thiering, Barbara. *Jesus & the Riddle of the Dead Sea Scrolls: Unlocking the Secrets of His Life Story*. New York: HarperSanFrancisco, 1992. [See. 126–53; N.B. Postulates that Jesus did not die on the cross.]

Vermes, Geza. *The Changing Faces of Jesus*. New York: Viking, 2000. [Resurrection of Jesus in Acts of the Apostles, See. 125–26, 129, 135–36; Jesus' predictions of, See. 184; in John's Gospel, See. 14, 185, 186; Paul on, 72, 83–84, 88, 89, 90, 96–100, 112, 129–30; significance, See. 96–100, 129–30, 132, 182; in Synoptic Gospels, See. 158, 161, 182–87]

———. *Jesus the Jew: A Historian's Reading of the Gospels*. Philadelphia: Fortress, 1981. [Resurrection, See. 35, 102, 150–51, 165, 235; empty tomb, See. 37–40, information of, in Gospels, See. 38–39; in John, See. 40–41, notion of, See. 37, 41, 234; predictions of, See. 37]

Wells, H. G. *The Outline of History: Being a Plain History of Life and Mankind*. Vol. 1 New York: Macmillan, 1921. [See. 584–88; N.B. Archive.org, Gutenberg.org, and HathiTrust]

Whittaker, Thomas. *The Origins of Christianity, with an Outline of Van Manen's Analysis of the Pauline Literature*. London: Watts, 1933. [N.B. Archive.org and Google book. He was an advocate of the Christ Myth.]

Zindler, Frank R., and Robert M. Price, eds. *Bart Ehrman and the Quest of the Historical Jesus of Nazareth*. Cranford, NJ: American Atheist Press, 2013. This multiple contributor text challenges the claim of New Testament scholar Bart Ehrman that Jesus of Nazareth existed. If Jesus did not exist, then there was no resurrection. This work is a must read.]

Category VII

Excerpts from Edited Books

CHAPTER 15

Excerpts from Edited Books: Pro Resurrection

Alston, William P. "Biblical Criticism and the Resurrection." In *The Resurrection: An Interdisciplinary Symposium on the Resurrection of Jesus*, edited by Stephen T. Davis, et al., 148–83. Oxford: University Press, 1997. [N.B. For a response by Sarah Coakley, See. 184–90]

Anderson, Charles. "Lukan Cosmology and the Ascension." In *Ascent into Heaven in Luke-Acts: New Explorations of Luke's Narrative Hinge*, edited by David K. Bryan and David W. Pao, 175–212. Minneapolis: Fortress, 2016.

Anderson, Norman. "The Resurrection: Fact or Legend?" In *Exploring the Christian Faith*, edited by Robin Keeley, 77–79. Nashville: Nelson, 1996.

Anderson, Paul N. "The Last Days of Jesus in John: An Introduction to the Issues." In *John, Jesus, and History*. Vol. 3 *Glimpses of Jesus through the Johannine Lens*, edited by Paul N. Anderson, et al., 29–42. Atlanta: SBL Press, 2016.

Ankerberg, John F. "The Church as Proof of the Resurrection and a Word about Alternate Critical Theories." In *Resurrected? An Atheist and Theist Dialogue: Gary R. Habermas and Antony G. N. Flew*, edited by John F. Ankerberg, 97–109. Lanham: Rowman & Littlefield, 2005.

Aquinas, Thomas. "The Resurrection of Jesus." In *Christian Apologetics: An Anthology of Primary Sources*, edited by Khaldoun A. Sweis and Chad V. Meister, 335–38. Grand Rapids: Zondervan, 2012. [Third Part; Question 53]

Armstrong, C. J., and Andrew R. D. DeLoach. "Un-Inevitable Easter Faith: Historical Contingency, Theological Consistency, and the Resurrection of Jesus Christ." In *The Resurrection Fact Responding to Modern Critics*, edited by John J. Bombaro and Adam S. Francisco, 177–206. Irvine, CA: NRP, 2016.

Attridge, Harold W. "From Discord Rises Meaning Resurrection Motifs in the Fourth Gospel." In *The Resurrection of Jesus in the Gospel of John*, edited by Craig R. Koester and Reimund Bieringer, 1–19. Tübingen: Mohr Siebeck, 2008.

Avis, Paul D. L. "The Resurrection of Jesus: Asking the Right Questions." In *The Resurrection of Jesus Christ*, edited by Paul D. L. Avis, 1–22. London: Darton, Longman and Todd, 1993.

Babcock, James F. "The Resurrection—A Credibility Gap." In *Christianity for the Tough-Minded; Essays in Support of an Intellectually Defensible Religious Commitment*, edited by John Warwick Montgomery, 245–51. Minneapolis: Bethany Fellowship, 1973.

Badham, Paul. "The Meaning of the Resurrection of Jesus." In *The Resurrection of Jesus Christ*, edited by Paul D. L. Avis, 23–38. London: Darton, Longman and Todd, 1993.

Baggett, David. "Resurrection Matters: Assessing the Habermas/Flew Discussion." In *Did the Resurrection Happen? A Conversation with Gary Habermas and Antony Flew*, edited by David Baggett, 107–66. Downers Grove, IL: InterVarsity, 2009.

Barclay, John M. G. "The Resurrection in Contemporary New Testament Scholarship." In *Resurrection Reconsidered*, edited by Gavin D'Costa, 13–30. Oxford: Oneworld, 1996.

Barker, Margaret. "Resurrection: Reflections on a New Approach." In *Resurrection*, edited by Stanley E. Porter, et al., 98–105. Sheffield: Sheffield Academic, 1999.

Barnett, Maurice. "Resurrection and the Cults." In *Resurrection! Essays in Honor of Homer Hailey*, edited by Edward Fudge, 81–96. Athens, AL: C.E.I. Publishing 1973.

Barnett, Paul. "Is the New Testament Historically Reliable?" In *In Defense of the Bible: A Comprehensive Apologetic for the Authority of Scripture*, edited by Steven B. Cowan and Terry L. Wilder, 223–66. Nashville: Broadman & Holman, 2013. [N.B. The Resurrection, See. 250–54]

Bauckham, Richard. "God Who Raises the Dead: The Resurrection of Jesus and Early Christian Faith in God." In *The Resurrection of Jesus Christ*, edited by Paul D. L. Avis, 136–54. London: Darton, Longman and Todd, 1993.

Beattie, Tina. "Sexuality and the Resurrection of the Body: Reflections in the Hall of Mirrors." In *Resurrection Reconsidered*, edited by Gavin D'Costa, 135–49. Oxford: Oneworld, 1996.

Bernard, John Henry. "The Evidence for the Resurrection of Christ." In *Studia Sacra*, edited by John Dublin, 126–69. London: Hodder & Stoughton, 1917. [N.B. Archive.org]

———. "The Miraculous in Early Christian Literature." In *Literature of the Second Century: Short Studies in Christian Evidences*, edited by F. R. Wynne, et al., 137–80. New York: James Pott, 1891. [N.B. Archive.org, Google book, and HathiTrust]

Betori, Giuseppe. "Luke 24:47: Jerusalem and the Beginning of the Preaching to the Pagans in the Acts of the Apostles." In *Luke and Acts*, edited by Gerald O'Collins and Gilberto Marconi, 103–20. New York: Paulist, 1993.

Beutler, Johannes. "Resurrection and the Forgiveness of Sins. John 20:23 Against its Traditional Background." In *The Resurrection of Jesus in the Gospel of John*, edited by Craig R. Koester and Reimund Bieringer, 237–51. Tübingen: Mohr Siebeck, 2008.

Bieringer, Reimund. "'I am Ascending to My Father and Your Father, to My God and Your God' (John 20:17). Resurrection and Ascension in the Gospel of John." In *The Resurrection of Jesus in the Gospel of John*, edited by Craig R. Koester and Reimund Bieringer, 209–35. Tübingen: Mohr Siebeck, 2008.

———. "'They Have Taken Away My Lord': Text-Immanent Repetitions and Variations in John 20,1–18." In *Repetitions and Variations in the Fourth Gospel: Style, Text, Interpretation*, edited by G. Van Belle, et al., 609–30. Leuven: Peeters, 2009.

Black, Allen. "Can We Still Believe in the Jesus of the Gospels?" In *Theology Matters: Answers for the Church Today In Honor of Harold Hazelip*, edited by Gary Holloway, et al., 142–52. Joplin, MO: College Press, 1998.

Black, David Alan. "Mark 16:9 as Markan Supplement." In *Perspectives on the Ending of Mark: 4 Views*, edited by David Alan Black, 103–23. Nashville: Broadman & Holman, 2008.

Bock, Darrell L. "The End of Mark: A Response to the Essays." In *Perspectives on the Ending of Mark: 4 Views*, edited by David Alan Black, 124–42. Nashville: Broadman & Holman, 2008.

———. "The Historical Jesus: An Evangelical View." In *The Historical Jesus: Five Views*, edited by James K. Beilby and Paul Rhodes Eddy, 249–81. Downers Grove, IL: InterVarsity, 1998.

———. "The Women Discover and Empty Tomb: Fabrication, Metaphor, or Something More." In *Who Is Jesus? Linking the Historical Jesus with the Christ of Faith*, 190–210. New York: Howard, 2012.

Bockmuehl, Markus. "Resurrection." In *The Cambridge Companion to Jesus*, edited by Markus Bockmuehl, 102–18. Cambridge: Cambridge University Press, 2001.

Bornkamm, Günther. "The Risen Lord and the Earthly Jesus: Matthew 28.16–20." In *The Future of Our Religious Past: Essays in Honour of Rudolf Bultman*, edited by James M. Robinson, 203–29. New York: Harper & Row, 1971.

Bowden, John. "The Miracles." In *A Basic Introduction to the New Testament*, edited by Robert C. Walton, 95–102. London: SCM, 1970.

Braaten, Carl E. "The Reality of the Resurrection." In *Nicene Christianity: The Future for a New Ecumenism*, edited by Christopher R. Seitz, 107–18. Grand Rapids: Brazos, 2004.

Bradshaw, Paul F. "The Origins of Easter." In *Passover and Easter: Origin and History to Modern Times*, edited by Paul Frederick Bradshaw and Lawrence A. Hoffman, 81–97. Notre Dame: University of Notre Dame Press, 2002.

Briere, Elizabeth. "The Resurrection in Liturgical Life in the Orthodox Church." In *"If Christ be not Risen": Essays in Resurrection and Survival*, edited by John Greenhalgh and Elizabeth Russell, 25–39. San Francisco: Collins Liturgical, 1988.

Brock, Ann Graham. "Peter, Paul, and Mary Cannical vs. Non-Canonical Portrayals of Apostolic Witnesses." In *Society of Biblical Literature 1999 Seminar Papers*, 173–202. Atlanta: Scholars Press, 1999.

Brown, Raymond E. "The Resurrection and Biblical Criticism." In *God, Jesus and Spirit*, edited by Daniel J. Callahan, 110–22. New York: Herder and Herder, 1969. [N.B. This is an interesting essay.]

Brown, Reagan. "The Inapplicability of Cognitive Dissonance as an Explanation for the Post-Crucifixion Behavior of the Disciples." In *Defending the Resurrection*, edited by J. P. Holding, 372–75. US: Xulon, 2010.

Brownell, Philip. "Personal Experience, Self-Reporting, and Hyperbole." In *Miracles: God, Science, and Psychology in the Paranormal. Vol. 3: Parapsychological Perspectives. Psychology, Religion, and Spirituality*, edited by J. Harold Ellens, 210–29. Westport, CT: Praeger, 2008.

Brownson, James V. "Neutralizing the Intimate Enemy: The Portrait of Judas in the Fourth Gospel." In *The Society of Biblical Literature 1992 Seminar Papers*, edited by Eugene H. Lovering, 49–60. Atlanta: Scholars Press, 1992.

Burge, Gary. "Session 6: The Death of Death. The Resurrection of Jesus (Matthew 28:1–10)." In *The Last Days of Jesus Participant's Guide*, edited by Matthew Williams, 107–28. Grand Rapids: Zondervan, 2009.

Burke, Christopher P. "What Would a Trial Lawyer Say About the Claims of the Gospels." In *The Harvest Handbook of Apologetics*, edited by Joseph M. Holden, 225–31. Eugene, OR: Harvest House, 2018.

Burridge, Richard A. "What Happened Next." In *Introduction to the Story of Christianity*. 3rd ed., edited by Tim Dowley, 14. Philadelphia: Fortress, 2018.

Butterworth, Mike. "Old Testament Antecedents to Jesus' Resurrection." In *Proclaiming the Resurrection: Papers from the First Oak Hill College Annual School of Theology*, edited by Peter M. Head, 1–28. Carlisle: Paternoster, 1998.

Campbell, Travis James. "Avalos contra Craig: A Historical, Theological, and Philosophical Assessment." In *Defending the Resurrection: Did Jesus Rise from the Dead?*, edited by J. P. Holding, 290–306. Xulon, 2010.

Carlson, Jason. "Jesus: Risen For a New Generation." In *Apologetics for a New Generation*, edited by Sean McDowell, 175–87. Eugene, OR: Harvest House, 2009.

Claussen, Carsten. "The Role of John 21: Discipleship in Retrospect and Redefinition." In *New Currents Through John: A Global Perspective*, edited by Francisco Lozada and Tom Thatcher, 55–68. Atlanta: Society of Biblical Literature, 2006.

Coakley, Sarah. "Is the Resurrection a 'Historical' Event? Some Muddles and Mysteries." In *The Resurrection of Jesus Christ*, edited by Paul D. L. Avis, 85–115. London: Darton, Longman and Todd, 1993.

Cole, Mary L. "'Behold the Lamb of God': John 1:29 and the Tamid Service." In *Rediscovering John: Essays on the Fourth Gospel in Honour of Frédéric Manns*, edited by Lesław Daniel. Chrupcała, 337–49. Milano, Italy: Edizioni Terra Santa, 2013.

Cooper, Henry. "Was Jesus Raised from the Dead?" In *The Messiahship of Jesus: What Jews and Jewish Christians Say*, compiled by Arthur W. Kac, 228–233. Chicago: Moody, 1980. [N.B. This writing originally appeared as "The Power of His Resurrection" in *The Hebrew Christian* 5, no. 2 (July 1932): 76–81]

Copan, Paul. "Why the World Is Not Religiously Ambiguous: A Critique of Religious Pluralism." In *Can Only One Religion Be True? Paul Knitter and Harold Netland in Dialogue*, edited by Robert B. Stewart, 139–62. Minneapolis: Fortress, 2013. [See. The Explanatory Power of Jesus' Bodily Resurrection, 148–49]

Cotes, Mary. "Women, Silence and Fear (Mark 16:8)." In *Women in the Biblical Tradition*, edited by G. J Brooke, 151–66. Lewiston, NY: Mellen, 1992.

Cotter, Wendy. "Greco-Roman Apotheosis Traditions and the Resurrection Appearances in Matthew." In *The Gospel of Matthew in Current Study: Studies in Memory of William G. Thompson*, edited by William G. Thompson and David E. Aune, 127–53. Grand Rapids: Eerdmans, 2001.

Cowan, Steven B. ed. *Five Views on Apologetics*. Grand Rapids: Zondervan, 2000. [Contributors include: William Lane Craig, Gary R. Habermas, Paul D. Feinberg, John M. Frame, and Kelly James Clark. See. Index]

———. "Is the Bible the Word of God?" In *In Defense of the Bible: A Comprehensive Apologetic for the Authority of Scripture*, edited by Steven B. Cowan, Terry L. Wilder, 429–63. Nashville: Broadman & Holman, 2013. [N.B. God Raised Jesus from the Dead, See. 445–46]

Cragg, Kenneth A. "Islamic Theology Limits and Bridges." In *The Gospel and Islam: A Compendium*, edited by Don M. McCurry, 160–168. Monrovia, CA: MARC, 1979 [See. 166]

Craig, William Lane. "The Bodily Resurrection of Jesus." In *Christian Apologetics: An Anthology of Primary Sources*, edited by Khaldoun A. Sweis and Chad V. Meister, 362–78. Grand Rapids: Zondervan, 2012.

———. "The Craig-Flew Debate." In *Does God Exist? The Craig-Flew Debate*, edited by Stan W. Wallace, 19–47. Aldershot: Ashgate, 2005. [Craig's Opening Statement, See. 19–23]

———. "Did Jesus Really Rise from the Dead?" In *If God Made the Universe Who Made God? 130 Arguments for Christian Faith*, edited by Holman Bible Editorial Staff, 91–93. Nashville: Holman Bible, 2012.

———. "Did Jesus Rise from the Dead?" In *Jesus Under Fire: Modern Scholarship Reinvents the Historical Jesus*, edited by Michael J. Wilkins and James Porter Moreland, 141–76. Grand Rapids: Zondervan, 1995.

———. "Did Jesus Rise from the Dead? 1 Corinthians 15." In *Apologetics Study Bible*, edited by Ted Cabal and the Holman Bible Staff, 1445–46. Nashville: Holman Bible, 2017.

———. "The Empty Tomb of Jesus." In *In Defense of Miracles: A Comprehensive Case for God's Action in History*, edited by Douglas R. Geivett and Gary R. Habermas, 247–61. Downers Grove, IL: InterVarsity, 1997.

———. "In Defense of Rational Theism." In *Does God Exist? The Debate Between Theists and Atheists*, edited by J. P. Moreland and Kai Nelsen, 139–61. Nashville: T. Nelson, 1990. [See. 140–41, 149–50; N.B. Reprinted by Prometheus, 1993.]

———. "John Dominic Crossan on the Resurrection of Jesus." In *The Resurrection: An Interdisciplinary Symposium on the Resurrection of Jesus*, edited by Davis, Stephen T., et al., 249–71. Oxford: University Press, 1997. [N.B. Response by Paul Rhodes Eddy, See. 272–86]

———. "A Reply to Objections." In *Does God Exist? The Craig-Flew Debate*, edited by Stan W. Wallace, 155–87. Aldershot: Ashgate, 2005. [The Argument from Miracles, See. 173–79]

———. "Resurrection and the Real Jesus." In *Will the Real Jesus Please Stand Up? A Debate Between William Lane Craig and John Dominic Crossan*, edited by Paul Copan, 156–79. Grand Rapids: Baker, 1998.

———. "Resurrection of Jesus." In *God: A Debate Between a Christian and an Atheist / William Lane Craig, Walter Sinnott-Armstrong*. Oxford: Oxford University Press, 2004. [See. 21–25, 69–73]

———. "Who Was Jesus? A Christian Perspective." In *Who Was Jesus? A Jewish-Christian Dialogue*, edited by Paul Copan and Craig A. Evans, 21–28. Louisville: Westminster John Knox, 2001.

———. "William Lane Craig's Rebuttal." In *Will the Real Jesus Please Stand Up? A Debate Between William Lane Craig and John Dominic Crossan*, edited by Paul Copan, 40–44. Grand Rapids: Baker, 1998.

———. "Wright and Crossan on the Historicity of the Resurrection of Jesus." In *The Resurrection of Jesus: John Dominic Crossan and N. T. Wright in Dialogue*, edited by Robert B. Stewart, 139–48. Minneapolis: Fortress, 2006.

Cranfield, C. E. B. "The Resurrection of Jesus Christ." In *The Historical Jesus in Recent Research*, edited by James D. G. Dunn and Scot McKnight, 382–91. Winona Lake, IN: Eisenbrauns, 2005.

Criswell, W. A. "The Literal Resurrection of Christ." In *Christ is Victor*, edited by W. Glyn Evans, 51–55. Valley Forge, PA: Judson, 1977.

Crockett, Clayton. "The Death of God, Death, and Resurrection." In *Resurrecting the Death of God: The Origins, Influence, and Return of Radical Theology*, edited by Daniel J. Peterson. Albany, NY: State University of New York Press, 2015. [See. 149–50]

Culpepper, R. Alan. "John 21:24–25: The Johannine *Sphragis*." In *John, Jesus, and History. Vol. 2. Aspects of Historicity in the Fourth Gospel*, edited by Paul N. Anderson, Felix S. J. Just, and Tom Thatcher, 349–64. Leiden: Brill, 2007.

Cumming, Joseph. "Did Jesus Die on the Cross? Reflections in Muslim Commentaries." In *Muslim and Christian Reflections on Peace: Divine and Human Dimensions*, edited by J. Dudley Woodberry, et al., 32–50. Lanham: University Press of America, 2005. [N.B. An important article to read.]

Davie, Martin. "The Resurrection of Jesus Christ in the Theology of Karl Barth." In *Proclaiming the Resurrection: Papers from the First Oak Hill College Annual School of Theology*, edited by Peter M. Head, 107–20. Carlisle: Paternoster, 1998.

Davies, Rupert E. "Study 5 The Work of Christ." In *An Approach to Christian Doctrine*, edited by Gerald Lewis, 72–90. London: Epworth, 1955. [N.B. The Cross of Jesus Must Not be Separated from His Resurrection, See. 74–75]

Davis, Stephen T. "Is It Rational for Christians to Believe in the Resurrection?" In *Contemporary Debates in Philosophy of Religion*, edited by Michael L. Peterson and Raymond J. VanArragon, 164–73. Oxford: Blackwell, 2004. [N.B. Reply by Martin, See. 184–86 and Reply to Davis, See. 186–87. This interchange is an informative reading.]

———. "James D. G. Dunn on the Resurrection of Jesus." In *Memories of Jesus: A Critical Appraisal of James D. G. Dunn's Jesus Remembered*, edited by Robert B. Stewart and Gary R. Habermas, 255–66. Nashville: B&H, 2010.

———. "'Seeing' the risen Jesus." In *The Resurrection: An Interdisciplinary Symposium on the Resurrection of Jesus*, edited by Davis, Stephen T., Daniel Kendall, and Gerald O'Collins, 126–47. Oxford: University Press, 1997.

D'Costa, Gavin. "The Resurrection, the Holy Spirit and the World Religions." In *Resurrection Reconsidered*, edited by Gavin D'Costa, 150–67. Oxford: Oneworld, 1996.

De Boer, Esther A. "The Lukan Mary Magdalene and the Other Women Following Jesus." In *A Feminist Companion to Luke*, edited by Amy-Jill Levine, 140–60. New York: Sheffield Academic, 2002.

De Boer, Martinus C. "Jesus' Departure to the Father in John Death or Resurrection." In *Theology and Christology in the Fourth Gospel: Essays by the Members of the SNTS Johannine Writings Seminar*, edited by Gilbert Van Belle, Van Der Watt J. G., and P. Maritz, 1–19. Leuven: Leuven University Press, 2005.

———. "Paul's Use of a Resurrection Tradition in 1 Cor 15, 20–28." In *The Corinthian Correspondence*, edited by R. Bieringer, 639–51. Leuven: Leuven University Press, 1996.

Delling, Gerhard. "The Significance of the Resurrection of Jesus for Faith in Jesus Christ." In *The Significance of the Message of the Resurrection for Faith in Jesus Christ*, edited by C. F. D. Moule, 77–104. London: SCM, 1968.

Delobel, Joël. "The Corinthians' (Un-)Belief in the Resurrection." In *Resurrection in the New Testament: Festschrift J. Lambrecht*, edited by Reimund Bieringer and Jan Lambrecht, 343–55. Leuven: Leuven University Press, 2002.

Delorme, Jean. "The Resurrection and Jesus' Tomb: Mark 16, 1–8 in the Gospel Tradition." In *The Resurrection and Modern Biblical Thought*. Translated by Charles Underhill Quinn, 74–106. New York: Corpus Books, 1970.

Denaux, Adelbert. "Matthew's Story of Jesus' Burial and Resurrection (Mt 27,57–28,20)." In *Resurrection in the New Testament: Festschrift J. Lambrecht*, edited by Reimund Bieringer and Jan Lambrecht, 123–45. Leuven: Leuven University Press, 2002.

Denaux, Adelbert, and Inge Van Wiele. "The Meaning of the Double Expression of Time in Luke 24,29." In *Miracles and Imagery in Luke and John: Festschrift Ulrich Busse*, edited by J. G. Verheyden et al., 67–88. Leuven: Peeters, 2008.

Dods, Marcus. "Did Christ Rise from the Dead?" In *Questions of Faith: A Series of Lectures on the Creed*, edited by Patrick Carnegie Simpson, 75–102. London: Hodder & Stoughton, 1904. [P. C. S. wrote the Prefactory Note; N.B. Google book]

———. "The Trustworthiness of the Gospels." In *The Supernatural in Christianity*, by Robert Rainy et al., 71–111. Edinburgh: T&T Clark, 1894. [Especially 96–108; N.B. Archive.org]

Draper, Paul. "Craig's Case for God's Existence." In *Does God Exist? The Craig-Flew Debate*, edited by Stan W. Wallace, 141–54. Burlington, VT: Ashgate, 2003. [See. Craig's Argument from Miracles, 149–50]

Dummelow, J. R. "The Resurrection." In *A Commentary on the Holy Bible By Various Writers*. New York: Macmillan, 1916. [The Resurrection, See. Cxxiii–xxviii; N.B. Google book]

Du Rand, Jan A. "The Creation Motif in the Fourth Gospel: Perspectives on its Narratological Function Within A Judaistic Background." In *Theology and Christology in the Fourth Gospel: Essays by the Members of the SNTS Johannine Writings Seminar*, edited by Gilbert Van Belle and J.G. Van Der Watt, 21–46. Leuven: Leuven University Press, 2005.

Dyer, Keith D. "Paul and Embodied Resurrection: Rethinking 1 Corinthians 15." In *Resurrection and Responsibility: Essays on Theology, Scripture, and Ethics in Honor of Thorwald Lorenzen*, edited by Thorwald Lorenzen and Keith D. Dyer, 136–164. Eugene, OR: Pickwick, 2009.

Dyer, Keith D., and David J. Neville, eds. *Resurrection and Responsibility: Essays on Theology, Scripture, and Ethics in Honor of Thorwald Lorenzen*. Eugene, OR: Pickwick, 2009. [275 pages; N.B. This work contains twelve essays.]

Earle, Ralph. "The Person of Christ: Death, Resurrection, Ascension." In *Basic Christian Doctrines*, edited by Carl F. H. Henry, 138–44. New York: Holt, Rinehart and Winston, 1962.

Edgar, R. McCheyne. "The Resurrection of Jesus Christ in its Historical, Doctrinal, Moral, and Spiritual Aspects." In *Living Papers on Present Day Themes Christian Evidences, Doctrines and Morals*. Vol. 8. New York: Fleming H. Revell, 1883. [Essay 45, See. 5–64; N.B. This is a good, dated source to examine.]

Edwards, Mark. "Markus Vincent on the Resurrection." In *If Christ has not been raised . . . : Studies on the Reception of the Resurrection Stories and the Belief in the Resurrection in the Early Church*, edited by Jozef Verheyden et al., 123–34. Göttingen: Vandenhoeck & Ruprecht, 2016.

Ellicott, C. J., ed. *Modern Scepticism: A Course of Lectures*. New York: Anson D. F. Randolph, 1871. [See. 181, 209, 216, 320, 337–42; 372–83, 388–89, 396–408; N.B. Google book]

Elliott, J. Keith. "The Last Twelve Verse of Mark: Original or Not?" In *Perspectives on the Ending of Mark: 4 Views*, edited by David Alan Black, 80–102. Nashville: Broadman & Holman, 2008.

Evans, Craig A. "The Christ of Faith is the Jesus of History." In *Debating Christian Theism*, edited by James Porter Moreland et al., 458–67. New York: Oxford University Press, 2013.

———. "Did Jesus Predict His Violent Death and Resurrection?" In *Evidence for God: 50 Arguments for Faith from the Bible, History, Philosophy*, edited by William A. Dembski and Michael R. Licona, 160–63. Grand Rapids: Baker, 2010.

———. "Did Jesus Predict His Death and Resurrection? In *Resurrection*, edited by Stanley E. Porter et al., 82–97. Sheffield: Sheffield Academic, 1999.

———. "Resurrection." In *The Routledge Companion to Philosophy of Religion*. 2nd ed., edited by Chad V. Meister and Paul Copan, 626–35. London: Routledge, 2013.

———. "What Do We Know for Sure about Jesus' Death?" In *Passionate Conviction: Contemporary Discourses on Christian Apologetics*, edited by Paul Copan and William Lane Craig, 109–22. Nashville: B&H, 2007.

Eynde, Sabine van den. "Love, Strong as Death? An Inter- and Intratextual Perspective on John 20, 1–18." In *The Death of Jesus in the Fourth Gospel*, edited by Gilbert Van Belle, 901–12. Leuven: Leuven University Press, 2007.

Fackre, Gabriel. "The Resurrection and the Uniqueness of Jesus Christ." In *Christ the One and Only: A Global Affirmation of the Uniqueness of Jesus Christ*, edited by Sung-Wook Chung, 67–89. Grand Rapids: Baker Academic, 2005.

Fenton, J. C. "The Ending of Mark's Gospel." In *Resurrection: Essays in Honour of Leslie Houlden*, edited by Stephen C. Barton and Graham Stanton, 1–7. London: SPCK, 1994.

———. "The Four Gospels: Four Perspectives on the Resurrection." In *The Resurrection of Jesus Christ*, edited by Paul D. L. Avis, 39–49. London: Darton, Longman & Todd, 1993.

Fernandes, Phil. "Did Jesus Really Rise From the Dead?" In *The Atheist Delusion: A Christian Response to Christopher Hitchens and Richard Dawkins*, 147–68. US: Xulon, 2009.

———. "Why Is It Important that Jesus Rose from the Dead." In *The Harvest Handbook of Apologetics*, edited by Joseph M. Holden, 157–60. Eugene, OR: Harvest House, 2018.

Fiorenza, Francis Schüssler. "The Resurrection of Jesus and Roman Catholic Fundamental Theology." In *The Resurrection: An Interdisciplinary Symposium on the Resurrection of Jesus*, edited by Stephen T. Davis et al., 213–48. Oxford: University Press, 1997.

Francisco, Adam S. "Can a Historian Explain the Empty Tomb with the Resurrection of Jesus?" In *The Resurrection Fact Responding to Modern Critics*, edited by John J. Bombaro and Adam S. Francisco, 43–58. Irvine, CA: NRP, 2016.

Fudge, Edward. "The Resurrection and the Life of the Christian." In *Resurrection! Essays in Honor of Homer Hailey*, edited by Edward Fudge, 51–64. Athens, AL: C.E.I. Publishing 1973.

Fuller, Reginald H. "The Passion, Death and Resurrection of Jesus according to St. John." In *The Passion, death and Resurrection of the Lord: A Commentary on the Four Gospels*, edited by Chicago Studies, 51–63. Mundelein, IL: Chicago Studies, 1980.

———. "Resurrection of Christ." In *The Oxford Companion to the Bible*, edited by Bruce M. Metzger and Michael D. Coogan, 647–49. New York: Oxford University Press, 1993.

Garcia, Jeffrey Paul. "See My Hands and Feet: Fresh Light on a Johannine Midrash." In *John, Jesus, and History*. Vol. 2. *Aspects of Historicity in the Fourth Gospel*, edited by Paul N. Anderson et al., 325–34. Leiden: Brill, 2007.

Gaventa, Beverly Roberts. "The Archive of Excess: John 21 and the Problem of Narrative Closure." In *Exploring the Gospel of John in Honor of D. Moody Smith*, edited by R. Alan Culpepper and Clifton C. Black, 240–52. Louisville: Westminster John Knox, 1996.

Geivett, R. Douglas. "The Epistemology of Resurrection Belief." In *The Resurrection of Jesus: John Dominic Crossan and N.T. Wright in Dialogue*, edited by Robert B. Stewart, 93–105. Minneapolis: Fortress, 2006.

———. "Reflections on the Explanatory Power of Theism." In *Does God Exist? The Craig-Flew Debate*, edited by Stan W. Wallace, 49–64. Aldershot: Ashgate, 2005. [The Resurrection of Jesus, See. 56–59]

———. "Religious Diversity and the Futility of Neutrality." In *Can Only One Religion Be True? Paul Knitter and Harold Netland in Dialogue*, edited by Robert B. Stewart, 181–202. Minneapolis: Fortress, 2013. [See. 196]

George, Augustin. "The Accounts of the Appearances to the Eleven From Luke 24, 36–53." In *The Resurrection and Modern Biblical Thought*. Translated by Charles Underhill Quinn, 50–73. New York: Corpus Books, 1970.

Gethin, Rupert. "The Resurrection and Buddhism." In *Resurrection Reconsidered*, edited by Gavin D'Costa, 201–16. Oxford: Oneworld, 1996.

Geyer, Hans-Georg. "The Resurrection of Jesus Christ: A Survey of the Debate in Present Day Theology." In *The Significance of the Message of the Resurrection for Faith in Jesus Christ*, edited by C. F. D. Moule, 105–35. London: SCM, 1968.

Gibson, Arthur. "Logic of the Resurrection. In *Resurrectio*n, edited by Stanley E. Porter et al., 166–94. Sheffield: Sheffield Academic, 1999.

Gillman, John. "The Emmaus Story in Luke-Acts Revisited." In *Resurrection in the New Testament: Festschrift J. Lambrecht*, edited by Reimund Bieringer and Jan Lambrecht, 165–88. Leuven: Leuven University Press, 2002.

Goodwin, Thomas. "Christ Set Forth, in His Death, Resurrection, Ascension, Sitting at God's Hand, and Intercession." In *Writings of the Doctrinal Puritans and the Divines of the Seventeenth Century*, edited by Religious Tract Society, 1846. [Chapter 3 Faith Supported by Christ's Resurrection, 51–91; Chapter 4 Faith Supported by Christ's Ascension and Sitting at the Right Hand of God, 92–116; N.B. Google book]

Graham, Nicolas. "The Resurrection." In *Mirfield Essays in Christian Belief: by Members of the Community of the Resurrection*. London: Faith Press, 1962. [See. 65–81; N.B. Nothing insightful.]

Green, H. Benedict. "Matthew 28:19, Eusebius, and the *lex orandi*." In *The Making of Orthodoxy: Essays in Honour of Henry Chadwick*, edited by Rowan Williams, 124–41. Cambridge: Cambridge University Press, 2002.

Green, Joel B. "'Witnesses of His Resurrection': Resurrection, Salvation, Discipleship, and Mission in the Acts of the Apostles." In *Life in the Face of Death: The Resurrection Message of the New Testament*, edited by Richard N. Longenecker, 227–46. Grand Rapids: Eerdmans, 1998.

Grelot, Pierre. "The Resurrection of Jesus: Its Biblical and Jewish Background." In *The Resurrection and Modern Biblical Thought*. Translated by Charles Underhill Quinn, 1–29. New York: Corpus Books, 1970.

Griffith-Jones, E. "The Second Miraculous Draught of Fishes." In *Miracles of Jesus*, 409–21. Cincinnati: Jennings & Graham, 191? [N.B. Archive.org]

Grobel, Kendrick. "Revelation and Resurrection." In *New Frontiers in Theology: Discussions Among Continental and American Theologians*, edited by James M. Robinson and John B. Cobb, 155–75. New York: Harper and Row, 1967.

Gundry, Robert H. "The Essential Physicality of Jesus' Resurrection according to the New Testament." In *Jesus of Nazareth Lord and Christ: Essays on the Historical Jesus and New*

Testament Christology, edited by Joel B. Green and Max Turner, 204–19. Grand Rapids: Eerdmans, 2014.

Habermas, Gary R. "Applying Resurrection Research and Closing Loopholes." In *Resurrected? An Atheist and Theist Dialogue: Gary R. Habermas and Antony G.N. Flew*, edited by John F. Ankerberg, 89–97. Lanham: Rowman & Littlefield, 2005.

———. "Can Naturalistic Theories Account for the Resurrection." In *The Apologetics Study Bible*, edited by Ted Cabal, 1621–622. Nashville: Holman Bible, 2003.

———. "Can Naturalistic Theories Account for the Resurrection?" In *If God Made the Universe, Who Made God? 130 Arguments for Christian Faith*, edited by Holman Bible Editorial Staff, 87–97. Nashville: Holman Reference, 2012.

———. "The Case for Christ's Resurrection." In *To Everyone an Answer: A Case for the Christian Worldview: Essays in Honor of Norman L. Geisler*, edited by Francis Beckwith and William Lane Craig, 180–98. Downers Grove, IL: InterVarsity, 2004.

———. "The Core Resurrection Data: The Minimal Facts Approach." In *Tough-minded Christianity: Honoring the Legacy of John Warwick Montgomery*, edited by William A. Dembski and Thomas Schirrmacher, 387–405. Nashville: B&H, 2008.

———. "The Disciples' Conviction and the Historicity of the Resurrection." In *If God Made the Universe Who Made God? 130 Arguments for Christian Faith*, edited by Holman Bible Editorial Staff, 89–91. Nashville: Holman Bible, 2012.

———. "The Empty Tomb of Jesus." In *Evidence for God: 50 Arguments for Faith from the Bible, History, Philosophy*, edited by William A. Dembski and Michael R. Licona, 168–71. Grand Rapids: Baker, 2010.

———. "Experiences of the Risen Jesus." In *Christian Apologetics: An Anthology of Primary Sources*, edited by Khaldoun A. Sweis and Chad V. Meister, 354–61. Grand Rapids: Zondervan, 2012.

———. "Jesus Did Rise from the Dead." In *Debating Christian Theism*, edited by James Porter Moreland et al, 484–94. New York: Oxford University Press, 2013.

———. "Jesus' Post-Resurrection Appearance to the Apostle Paul: Can It Withstand Critical Scrutiny?" In *Defending the Faith: Engaging the Culture. Essays Honoring L. Russ Bush*, edited by Bruce A. Little and Mark D. Liederbach, 101–18. Nashville: B&H, 2011.

———. "Mapping the Recent Trend Toward the Bodily Resurrection Appearances of Jesus in Light of Other Prominent Critical Positions." In *The Resurrection of Jesus: John Dominic Crossan and N.T. Wright in Dialogue*, edited by Robert B. Stewart, 78–92. Minneapolis: Fortress, 2006.

———. "Remembering Jesus' Resurrection: Responding to James D. G. Dunn." In *Memories of Jesus: A Critical Appraisal of James D. G. Dunn's Jesus Remembered*, edited by Robert B. Stewart and Gary R. Habermas, 267–85. Nashville: B&H, 2010.

———. "The Resurrection Appearances of Jesus." In *Evidence for God: 50 Arguments for Faith from the Bible, History, Philosophy*, edited by William A. Dembski, and Michael Licona, 172–75. Grand Rapids: Baker, 2010.

———. "The Resurrection Appearances of Jesus." In *In Defense of Miracles: A Comprehensive Case for God's Action in History*, edited by R. Douglas Geivett and Gary R. Habermas, 262–75. Downers Grove, IL: InterVarsity, 1997.

———. "The Resurrection of Christ." In *The Fundamentals for the Twenty-First Century*, edited by Mal Couch, 253–66. Grand Rapids: Kregel, 2000.

———. "The Resurrection of Jesus and Recent Agnosticism." In *Reasons for Faith: Making a Case for the Christian Faith: Essays in Honor of Bob Passantino and Gretchen*

Passantino Coburn, edited by Norman L. Geisler and Chad V. Meister, 281–96. Wheaton, IL: Crossway, 2007.

———. "The Resurrection of Jesus Time Line: The Convergence of Eyewitnesses and Early Proclamation." In *Contending With Christianity's Critics Answering New Atheists & Other Objectors*, edited by Paul Copan and William Lane Craig, 113–25. Nashville: B&H, 2009.

———. "Tracing Jesus' Resurrection to Its Earliest Eyewitness Accounts." In *God is Good, God is Great*, edited by Norman L. Geisler and Chad V. Meister 202–16. Downers Grove, IL: InterVarsity, 2009.

———. "Why I Believe the Miracles of Jesus Actually Happened." *Why I Am a Christian: Leading Thinkers Explain Why They Believe*, edited by Norman L. Geisler and Paul K. Hoffman, 120–34. Grand Rapids: Baker, 2006. [N.B. This article is a must read.]

Habermas, Gary R., and Benjamin C. F. Shaw. "Is There Evidence That Jesus Rose from the Dead?" In *The Harvest Handbook of Apologetics*, edited by Joseph M. Holden, 145–48. Eugene, OR: Harvest House, 2018.

Hagner, Donald A. "Gospel, Kingdom, and Resurrection in the Synoptic Gospels." In *Life in the Face of Death: The Resurrection Message of the New Testament*, edited by Richard N. Longenecker, 99–121. Grand Rapids: Eerdmans, 1998.

Hagner, Donald A., and Stephen E. Young. "The Historical-Critical Method and the Gospel of Matthew." In *Methods for Matthew*, edited by Mark Allan Powell, 11–43. Cambridge: Cambridge University Press, 2009. [Historical-Critical Method: Interpretation of Matthew 27:57–28:15, See. 31–43]

Hansen, Carolyn. "Tactile and True: The Physicality of the Resurrection." In *The Resurrection Fact Responding to Modern Critics*, edited by John J. Bombaro and Adam S. Francisco, 207–228. Irvine, CA: NRP, 2016.

Harbin, Michael A. "Historicity as Apologetic: The Cutting Edge." In *Evangelical Apologetics*, edited by Michael Bauman et al., 135–64. Camp Hill, PA: Christian Publishing, 1996.

Hasitschka, Martin. "The Significance of the Resurrection Appearance in John 21." In *The Resurrection of Jesus in the Gospel of John*, edited by Craig R. Koester and Reimund Bieringer, 311–28. Tübingen: Mohr Siebeck, 2008.

Head, Peter M. "Jesus' Resurrection in Pauline Thought: A Study in Romans." In *Proclaiming the Resurrection: Papers from the First Oak Hill College Annual School of Theology*, edited by Peter M. Head, 58–80. Carlisle: Paternoster, 1998.

Hebblethwaite, Brian. "The Resurrection and the Incarnation." In *The Resurrection of Jesus Christ*, edited by Paul D. L. Avis, 155–70. London: Darton, Longman and Todd, 1993.

Heinze, Rudi. "The Resurrection of Jesus in English Puritan Thought." In *Proclaiming the Resurrection: Papers from the First Oak Hill College Annual School of Theology*, edited by Peter M. Head, 81–106. Carlisle: Paternoster, 1998.

Heron, Alasdair. "The Person of Christ." In *Keeping The Faith: Essays to Mark the Centenary of Lux Mundi*, edited by Geoffrey Wainwright, 99–123. Philadelphia: Fortress, 1988. [Jesus of Nazareth, Crucified and Risen, See. 117–23]

Hinman, Joe. "The Oldest Resurrection Narrative (Part 1)." In *Defending the Resurrection*, edited by J. P. Holding, 96–102. US: Xulon, 2010.

Holding, James Patrick. "Hallucinations and Expectations." In *Defending the Resurrection: Did Jesus Rise from the Dead?*, edited by J. P. Holding, 369–71. US: Xulon, 2010.

Holland, Henry Scott. "The Power of the Resurrection." In *Miracles: Papers and Sermons Contributed to the Guardian* by W. Lock et al., prefatory note by H. S. Holland, 118–36. London: Longman, 1911. [N.B. Archive.org]

Holleman, Joost. "Jesus' Resurrection as the Beginning of the Eschatological Resurrection (1 Cor 15, 20)." In *The Corinthian Correspondence*, edited by R. Bieringer. 653–66. Leuven: Leuven University Press, 1996.

Holzapfel, Richard Neitzel, and Thomas A. Wayment. "The Resurrection." In *From the Last Supper Through the Resurrection*, edited by Richard Neitzel Holzapfel and Thomas A. Wayment, 378–97. Salt Lake City, UT: Deseret Book, 2003.

Hooker, Morna D. "Seeing and Believing John 20:1–18." In *Preaching John's Gospel: The World It Imagines*, edited by David Fleer and Dave Bland, 139–43. St. Louis: Chalice Press, 2008.

Horder, W. Garrett. "Article 2." In *Immortality: A Clerical Symposium on What are the Foundations of the Belief in the Immortality of Man*, edited by the Editor of "Homilectic Magazine," 30–62. London: James Nisbet, 1885. [Christ's own resurrection from the dead, See. 60–62; N.B. Google book]

Houlden, J. Leslie. "The Resurrection: History, Story and Belief." In *The Resurrection of Jesus Christ*, edited by Paul D. L. Avis, 50–67. London: Darton, Longman and Todd, 1993.

Howard, Jeremy Royal. "Is Jesus Alive Today? The Evidence and Why it Matters to You." In *Is Jesus Alive Today? The Evidence and Why it Matters to You*, edited by Holman Bible, 1–9. Nashville: Holman Bible, 2008.

Huebenthal, Sandra. "Luke 24:13–35, Collective Memory, and Cultural Frames." In *Biblical Interpretation in Early Christian Gospels. Vol. 3: The Gospel of Luke*, edited by Thomas R. Hatina, 85–95. London: T&T Clark, 2006.

Huffard, Everett W. "Culturally Relevant Themes about Christ." In *Muslims and Christians on the Emmaus Road*, edited by J. Dudley Woodberry, 161–74. Monrovia, CA: MARC. 1990.

Huffman, Douglas S. "Are There Contradictions in the Bible?" In *In Defense of the Bible: A Comprehensive Apologetic for the Authority of Scripture*, edited by Steven B. Cowan and Terry L. Wilder, 267–93. Nashville: B&H Academic, 2013. [Defending the Consistency of the New Testament Resurrection Narratives, See. 282–93]

Hurtado, Larry W. "The Women, the Tomb, and the Climax of Mark." In *A Wandering Galilean: Essays in Honour of Seán Freyne*, edited by Zuleika Rodgers et al., 427–450. Leiden: Brill, 2009.

Jenkins, Ferrell. "The Resurrection and the Deity of Christ." In *Resurrection! Essays in Honor of Homer Hailey*, edited by Edward Fudge, 41–48. Athens, AL: C.E.I. Publishing 1973.

Jones, Gareth. "The Resurrection in Contemporary Systematic Theology." In *Resurrection Reconsidered*, edited by Gavin D'Costa, 31–47. Oxford: Oneworld, 1996.

Judge, Peter J. "John 20, 24–29 More Than Doubt, Beyond Rebuke." In *The Death of Jesus in the Fourth Gospel*, edited by Gilbert Van Belle, 913–30. Leuven: University Press, 2007.

Kalman, Jason. "Job Denied the Resurrection of Jesus? A Rabbinic Critique of the Church Fathers' Use of Exegetical Traditions Found in the Septuagint and the Testament of Job." In *The Changing Face of Judaism, Christianity, and other Greco-Roman Religions in Antiquity*, edited by Ian H. Henderson and James H. Charlesworth, 371–97. Gütersloh: Gütersloher Verlagshaus, 2006.

Karris, Robert J. "Women and Discipleship in Luke." In *A Feminist Companion to Luke*, edited by Amy-Jill Levine and Marianne Blickenstaff, 23–43. London: Sheffield Academic, 2002.

Keener, Craig S. "Youthful Vigor and the Maturity of Age: Peter and the Beloved Disciple in John 20–21." In *Rediscovering John: Essays on the Fourth Gospel in Honour of Frédéric Manns*, edited by L. Daniel. Chrupcała, 559–75. Milano: Terra Santa, 2013.

Kendall, Jonathan. "Did Jesus Predict His Death and Resurrection?" In *Defending the Resurrection: Did Jesus Rise from the Dead?*, edited by J. P. Holding, 51–80. US: Xulon, 2010.

———. "'Hallucinations and Expectations.' The Vindication of the Messiah: Why Resurrection?" In *Defending the Resurrection: Did Jesus Rise from the Dead?*, edited by J. P. Holding, 369–71. US: Xulon, 2010.

———. "Hallucinations and the Risen Jesus." In *Defending the Resurrection: Did Jesus Rise from the Dead?*, edited by J. P. Holding, 134–81. US: Xulon, 2010.

———. "The Vindication of the Messiah: Why Resurrection?" In *Defending the Resurrection: Did Jesus Rise from the Dead?*, edited by J. P. Holding, 307–68. US: Xulon, 2010.

Kitzberger, Ingrid Rosa. "Transcending Gender Boundaries in John." In *A Feminist Companion to John*, edited by Amy-Jill Levine and Marianne Blickenstaff, 173–207. Cleveland: Pilgrim Press, 2003.

Koester, Craig R. "Jesus' Resurrection, the Signs, and the Dynamics of Faith in the Gospel of John." In *The Resurrection of Jesus in the Gospel of John*, edited by Craig A. Koester and Reimund Bieringer, 47–74. Tübingen, Germany: Mohr Siebeck, 2008.

Koester, Craig R., and R. Bieringer, eds. *The Resurrection of Jesus in the Gospel of John*. Tübingen, Germany: Mohr Siebeck, 2008. [358 pages; N.B. This work contains thirteen articles that should be examined.]

Labahn, Michael. "Peter's Rehabilitation (John 21:15–19) and the Adoption of Sinners: Remembering Jesus and Relecturing John." In *John, Jesus, and History*, Vol. 2. *Aspects of Historicity in the Fourth Gospel*, edited by Paul N. Anderson et al., 335–48. Leiden: Brill, 2007.

Larsson, Edvin. "The Resurrection of Jesus and the Rise." In *Texts and Contexts: Biblical Texts in Their Textual and Situational Contexts*, edited by Tord Fornberg and David Hellholm, 623–47. Oslo: Scandinavian University Press, 1995.

LaVerdiere, Eugene. "The Passion-Resurrection of Jesus according to St. Luke." In *The Passion, Death and Resurrection of the Lord: A Commentary on the Four Gospels*, edited by Chicago Studies, 35–50. Mundelein, IL: Chicago Studies, 1980.

Leaney, A. R. C. "The Resurrection of Christ." In *Difficulties for Christian Belief*, edited by R. P. C. Hanson, 56–71. London: Macmillan, 1967.

Leathes, Stanley. "The Evidential Value of St. Paul's Epistles." In *Modern Scepticism: A Course of Lectures: With an Explanatory Paper*, edited by Christian Evidence Society, 361–408. London: Hodder & Stoughton, 1871. [See. 367–78; 395–407; N.B. Google book and HathiTrust]

Léon-Dufour, X. "The Appearances of the Risen Lord and Hermaneutics." In *The Resurrection and Modern Biblical Thought*. Translated by Charles Underhill Quinn, 107–28. New York: Corpus Books, 1970.

Licona, Michael R. "Can We be Certain That Jesus Died on a Cross? A Look at the Ancient Practice of Crucifixion." In *Evidence for God: 50 Arguments for Faith from the Bible,*

History, Philosophy, edited by William A. Dembski and Michael R. Licona, 164–67. Grand Rapids: Baker, 2010.

———. "Did Jesus Really Rise from the Dead?" In *The Apologetics Study Bible for Students*, 1143–23. Nashville: Holman Bible, 2009. [N.B. idem. CSB Apologetics Study Bible for Students, 2017. See. 1299–308]

———. "Fish Tales: Bart Ehrman's Red Herrings and the Resurrection of Jesus." In *Come Let Us Reason: New Essays in Christian Apologetics*, edited by Paul Copan and William Lane. Craig, 137–50. Nashville: B&H Academic, 2012.

———. "A New Starting Point in Historical Jesus Research: The Easter Event." In *The Quest for the Real Jesus Radboud Prestige Lectures*, edited by Jan Van der. Watt, 99–127. Leiden: Brill, 2013.

———. "Were the Resurrection Appearances of Jesus Hallucinations?" In *Evidence for God: 50 Arguments for Faith from the Bible, History, Philosophy*, edited by William A. Dembski and Michael R. Licona, 176–78. Grand Rapids: Baker, 2010.

Lightfoot, Joseph Barber. "The Resurrection of Christ." In *Nineteenth Century Evangelical Theology*, edited by Fisher Humphreys, 177–81. Nashville: Broadman, 1984.

Lillie, William. "The Empty Tomb and the Resurrection." In *Historicity and Chronology in the New Testament*, edited by SPCK, 117–34. London: SPCK, 1965.

Lincoln, Andrew T. "'I am the Resurrection and the Life': The Resurrection Message of the Fourth Gospel." In *Life in the Face of Death: The Resurrection Message of the New Testament*, edited by Richard N. Longenecker, 122–44. Grand Rapids: Eerdmans, 1998.

Lindars, Barnabas. "The Resurrection and the Empty Tomb." In *The Resurrection of Jesus Christ*, edited by Paul D. L. Avis, 116–35. London: Darton, Longman and Todd, 1993.

Lodge, John C. "Matthew's Passion-Resurrection Narrative." In *The Passion, Death and Resurrection of the Lord: A Commentary on the Four Gospels*, edited by Chicago Studies, 3–20. Mundelein, IL: Chicago Studies, 1980?.

Longstaff, Thomas R.W. "What Are Those Women Doing at the Tomb of Jesus? Perspectives on Matthew 28:1." In *Feminist Companion to the New Testament and Early Christian Writings*, edited by Amy-Jill Levine and Marianne Blickenstaff, 196–204. Sheffield, England: Sheffield Academic, 2001.

Loughlin, Gerard. "Living in Christ: Resurrection and Salvation." In *Resurrection Reconsidered*, edited by Gavin D'Costa, 118–34. Oxford: Oneworld, 1996.

Mackay, D. M. "Can Anyone Believe That Jesus 'Ascended into Heaven'?" In *Hard Questions*, edited by Frank Colquhoun, 45–47. Downers Grove, IL: InterVarsity, 1976.

Maclear, G. F. "Difficulties on the Side of Unbelief In Accounting for Historical Christianity." In *Strivings for the Faith: A Course of Lectures*, edited by Christian Evidence Society, 1–36. London: Hodder & Stroughton, 1880. [Section 7 The Historical Fact of the Resurrection Alone an Adequate Ground for Celebrating the Rite, 25–32; Section 8 Difficulties to be Met, Supposing the Resurrection Not to be True, 32–36; N.B. Google book]

Macquarrie, John. "The Keystone of Christian Faith." In *"If Christ be not Risen": Essays in Resurrection and Survival*, edited by John Greenhalgh and Elizabeth Russell, 9–24. San Francisco: Collins Liturgical, 1988.

Marguerat, Daniel. "The Resurrection and Its Witnesses in the Book of Acts." In *Reading Acts Today: Essays in Honour of Loveday C. A. Alexander*, edited by Steve Walton and Thomas E. Phillips, 171–85. London: Bloomsbury, 2013.

Marshall, Christopher D. "Resurrexit: Lloyd Geering and the End of Resurrection." In *A Religious Atheist? Critical Essays on the Work of Lloyd Geering*, edited by Raymond Pelly and Peter Stuart, 77–95. Dunedin, New Zealand: Otago University Press, 2006. [Marshall critically rejects Geering's reading of Paul's theology of the resurrection and his claim of Paul's notion of the spiritual body.]

Marshall, David. "The Resurrection of Jesus and the Qur'an." In *Resurrection Reconsidered*, edited by Gavin D'Costa, 168–83. Oxford: Oneworld, 1996.

Marshall, I. H. "Raised for Our Justification: The Saving Significance of the Resurrection of Christ." In *Tough-Minded Christianity: Honoring the Legacy of John Warwick Montgomery*, edited by William A. Dembski and Thomas Schirrmacher, 244–71. Nashville: B&H Academic, 2008.

———. "The Resurrection in the Acts of the Apostles." In *Apostolic History and Gospel: Biblical and Historical Essays presented to F. F. Bruce on his 60th Birthday*, edited by W. Ward Gasque and Ralph P. Martin, 92–107. Grand Rapids: Eerdmans, 1970.

Mascall, Eric. "Did Jesus Really Rise from the Dead?" In *"If Christ be not Risen": Essays in Resurrection and Survival*, edited by John Greenhalgh and Elizabeth Russell, 56–66. San Francisco: Collins Liturgical, 1988.

Mather, P. Boyd. "Christian Prophecy and Matthew 28, 16–20." In *Society of Biblical Literature 1977 Seminar Papers*, edited by Paul J. Achtemeier, 103–115. Atlanta: Scholars Press, 1977.

Matthews, Robert J. "Resurrection: The Ultimate Triumph." *In Jesus Christ: Son of God, Savior*, edited by Paul H. Peterson, Gary L. Hatch, and Laura D. Card. Religious, 313–33. Studies Center, Brigham Young University, 2002. [N.B. This work represents a Mormon interpretation.]

Matzko, David McCarthy. "Christ's Body in its Fullness: Resurrection and the Lives of the Saints." In *Resurrection Reconsidered*, edited by Gavin D'Costa, 102–17. Oxford: Oneworld, 1996.

McCann, Justin. "The Resurrection of the Body." In *The Teaching of the Catholic Church: A Summary of Catholic Doctrine*. Vol. 2. Edited and arranged by George D. Smith. London: Burns Oates & Washbourne, 1948. [Chapter 34 The Resurrection of the Body, See. 1223–25]

McDowell, Sean. "Did Jesus Really Rise from the Dead?" In *Apologetics Study Bible for Students: Hard Questions, Straight Answers*, edited by Sean McDowell, 1114–15. Nashville: Holman Bible, 2009.

McGrew, Lydia. "Historical Inquiry." In *The Routledge Companion to Theism*, edited by Charles Taliaferro et al., 281–93. New York: Routledge, 2013.

McGrew, Timothy, and Lydia McGrew. "The Argument From: A Cumulative Case for the Resurrection of Jesus of Nazareth." In *The Blackwell Companion to Natural Theology*, edited by William Lane. Craig and J. P. Moreland, 593–662. West Sussex: Blackwell, 2009. [N.B. This essay is an absolute must read.]

McKnight, Scot. "Jesus and the Twelve." In *Key Events in the Life of the Historical Jesus: A Collaborative Exploration of Context and Coherence*, edited by Darrell L. Bock and Robert L. Webb, 181–214. Grand Rapids: Eerdmans, 2010.

Menken, Maarten J. J. "Interpretation of the Old Testament and the Resurrection of Jesus in John's Gospel." In *Resurrection in the New Testament: Festschrift J. Lambrecht*, edited by Reimund Bieringer and Jan Lambrecht, 189–205. Leuven: Leuven University Press, 2002.

Menuge, Angus. "Justified Belief in the Resurrection." In *The Resurrection Fact Responding to Modern Critics*, edited by John J. Bombaro and Adam S. Francisco, 147–176. Irvine, CA: NRP, 2016.

Meyer, Frederick. "The Resurrection." *In Bible Difficulties and How to Meet Them: A Symposium*, edited by Frederick A. Atkins, 79–94. New York: Revell, 1891. [N.B. Google book]

Meyer, Marvin. "Jesus, Judas Iscariot, and the Gospel of John." In *Jesus in Continuum*, edited by Tom Holmén, 115–32. Tübingen: Mohr Siebeck, 2012.

Michel, Otto. "The Conclusion of Matthew's Gospel: A Contribution to the History of the Easter Message." In *The Interpretation of Matthew*, edited by Graham Stanton, 39–51. 2nd ed. Edinburgh: T&T Clark, 1995.

Miller, W. R. "Legal Evidence for the Resurrection." In *Defending the Resurrection: Did Jesus Rise from the Dead?*, edited by J. P. Holding, 116–21. US: Xulon, 2010.

Moloney, Francis J. "John 21 and the Johannine Story." In *Anatomies of Narrative Criticism: The Past, Present, and Futures of the Fourth Gospel as Literature*, edited by Tom Thatcher and Stephen D. Moore, 237–52. Atlanta: Society of Biblical Literature, 2008.

Moltmann, Jürgen. "The Resurrection of Christ and the New Earth." In *Resurrection and Responsibility: Essays on Theology, Scripture, and Ethics in Honor of Thorwald Lorenzen*, edited by Keith D. Dyer and David J. Neville, 51–58. Eugene, OR: Pickwick, 2009.

———. "The Resurrection of Nature: An Aspect of Cosmic Christology." In *The Resurrection of the Dead*, edited by Andrés Torres Queiruga Luiz Carlos Susin, and Jon Sobrino, 81–89. London: SCM, 2006.

———. "The Resurrection of Christ: Hope for the World." In *Resurrection Reconsidered*, edited by Gavin D'Costa, 73–86. Oxford: Oneworld, 1996.

Montgomery, John Warwick. "A Juridical Defense of Jesus' Resurrection." In *Christian Apologetics: An Anthology of Primary Sources*, edited by Khaldoun A. Sweis and Chad V. Meister, 339–53. Grand Rapids: Zondervan, 2012.

Moore, Mark E. "Did Jesus Rise from the Dead?" In *A Humble Defense: Evidence for the Christian Faith*, edited by Mark E. Moore and Mark Scott, 145–64. Joplin, MO: College Press, 2004.

Moreland, J. P. "Yes! A Defense of Christianity." In *Does God Exist? The Great Debate: James Porter Moreland and Kai Nielsen*, 33–47. Nashville: Nelson, 1990. [See. 39–43]

Moritz, Joshua M. "Big Bang Cosmology and Christian Theology." In *Theology and Science: From Genesis to Astrobiology*, edited by Joseph Seckbach and Richard Gordon, 345–73. Singapore: World Scientific, 2019. [See. 362–66]

Moss, Charles. "The Rise of the Church of Christ: An Evidence of His Resurrection." In *Some Witnesses for the Faith: Six Sermons, Published by the Request of the Christian Evidence Society, at St. Stephens Church, South Kensington, on Sunday afternoons after Easter, 1877*, edited by SPCK, 51–73. London: SPCK, 1877. [The author was identified as "The Lord Bishop of Bath and Wells"; N.B. Google book]

Mott, L. A. "The Teaching of Jesus on His Resurrection." In *Resurrection! Essays in Honor of Homer Hailey*, edited by Edward Fudge, 29–38. Athens, AL: C.E.I. Publishing 1973.

Mourad, Suleiman A. "The Death of Jesus in Islam: Reality, Assumptions, and Implications." In *Engaging the Passion Perspectives on the Death of Jesus*, edited by Oliver Larry Yarbrough, 359–81. Minneapolis: Fortress, 2015.

———. "Does the Qur'an Deny or Assert Jesus's Crucifixion and Death." In *New Perspectives on the Qur'an: The Qur'an in its Historical Context* 2, edited by Gabriel Said Reynolds, 349–57. London: Routledge, 2011.

Neville, David J. "Creation Reclaimed: Resurrection and Responsibility in Mark 15:40–16:8." In *Resurrection and Responsibility: Essays on Theology, Scripture, and Ethics in Honor of Thorwald Lorenzen*, edited by Thorwald Lorenzen and Keith D. Dyer, 95–115. Eugene, OR: Pickwick, 2009.

Newman, Carey C. "Resurrection as Glory: Divine Presence and Christian Origins." In *The Resurrection: An Interdisciplinary Symposium on the Resurrection of Jesus*, edited by Stephen T. Davis et al., 59–89. Oxford: University Press, 1997.

Newman, Robert C. "Miracles and the Historicity of the Easter Week Narratives." In *Evidence for Faith: Deciding the God Question*, edited by John Warwick. Montgomery, 275–302. Dallas: Probe, 1991.

Neyrey, Jerome H. "'My Lord and My God': The Divinity of Jesus in Johns Gospel." In *Society of Biblical Literature 1986 Seminary Papers Series*, edited by Kent Harold Richards, 152–71. Atlanta: Scholars Press, 1986.

Nicklas, Tobias. "Resurrection in the Gospels of Matthew and Peter: Some Developments." In *Life Beyond Death in Matthews Gospel: Religious Metaphor or Bodily Reality?*, edited by Wim Weren, Huub Van De Sandt, and Jozef Verheyden, 27–41. Leuven: Peeters, 2011.

Niebuhr, R. R. "Resurrection." In *A Handbook of Christian Theology*, edited by Marvin Halverson and Arthur Allen Cohen, 323–26. New York: Living Age, 1958.

Nielsen, Jesper Tang. "Resurrection, Recognition, Reassuring: The Function of Jesus' Resurrection in the Fourth Gospel." In *The Resurrection of Jesus in the Gospel of John*, edited by Craig Koester and Riemund Bieringer, 134–78. Tübingen: Mohr Siebeck, 2008.

Novakovic, Lidija. "Jesus' Resurrection and Historiography." In *Jesus Research: New Methodologies and Perception: The Second Princeton-Prague Symposium on Jesus Research*, edited by James H. Charlesworth, 910–33. Grand Rapids: Eerdmans, 2014.

O'Collins, Gerald. "The Resurrection: The State of the Question." In *The Resurrection: An Interdisciplinary Symposium on the Resurrection of Jesus*, edited by Davis, Stephen T., Daniel Kendall, and Gerald O'Collins, 5–28. Oxford: University Press, 1997. [N.B. Response by Peter Carnley, See. 29–40]

———. "The Risen Jesus: Analogies and Presence." In *Resurrection*, edited by Stanley E. Porter, Michael A. Hayes, and David Tombs, 195–217. Sheffield: Sheffield Academic, 1999.

O'Day, Gail R. "Aspects of Historicity in John 13–21: A Response." In *John, Jesus, and History*. Vol. 2. *Aspects of Historicity in the Fourth Gospel*, edited by Paul N. Anderson et al., 365–78. Leiden: Brill, 2007.

———. "The Paraclete as Friend: Hope for the Future." In *Preaching John's Gospel: The World It Imagines*, edited by David Fleer and Dave Bland, 62–72. St. Louis: Chalice, 2008. [See. 70–72]

Okure, Teresa. "Jesus and Mary Magdalene." In *Feminism and Theology*, edited by Janet Martin Soskice and Diana Lipton, 312–26. Oxford: Oxford University Press, 2003.

O'Loughlin, Thomas. "Another Post-Resurrection Meal and its Implications for the Early Understanding of the Eucharist." In *A Wandering Galilean: Essays in Honour of Seán Freyne*, edited by Zuleika Rodgers et al., 485–503. Leiden: Brill, 2009.

O'Neill, J. C. "On the Resurrection as an Historical Question." In *Christ, Faith and History Cambridge Studies in Christology*, edited by Stephen Whitefield. Sykes and John Powell. Clayton, 205–19. Cambridge: Cambridge University Press, 1978.

Os, Bas van. "John's Last Supper and the Resurrection Dialogues." In *John, Jesus, and History*. Vol. 2. *Aspects of Historicity in the Fourth Gospel*, edited by Paul N. Anderson et al., 271–80. Atlanta: Society of Biblical Literature, 2007.

Osborne, Grant R. "Jesus' Empty Tomb and His Appearance in Jerusalem." In *Key Events in the Life of the Historical Jesus: A Collaborative Exploration of Context and Coherence*, edited by Darrell L. Bock and Robert L. Webb, 775–823. Grand Rapids: Eerdmans, 2010. [N.B. This text is a definite must to examine.]

Osiek, Carolyn. "The Women at the Tomb: What Are They Doing There?" In *Feminist Companion to the New Testament and Early Christian Writings*, edited by Amy-Jill Levine and Marianne Blickenstaff, 205–20. Sheffield, England: Sheffield Academic Press, 2001. [N.B. This is an interesting article.]

Padgett, Alan G. "Advice for Religious Historians: On the Myth of a Purely Historical Jesus." In *The Resurrection: An Interdisciplinary Symposium on the Resurrection of Jesus*, edited by Stephen T. Davis, Daniel Kendall, and Gerald O'Collins, 287–307. Oxford: Oxford University Press, 1997. [N.B. An interesting reading.]

Painter, John. "'The Light Shines in the Darkness . . .': Creation, Incarnation, and Resurrection in John." In *The Resurrection of Jesus in the Gospel of John*, edited by Craig R. Koester and Reimund Bieringer, 21–46. Tübingen, Germany: Mohr Siebeck, 2008.

Palmer, Sydney. "Repetition and the Art of Reading: 'on the third day' in John's Gospel." In *Repetitions and Variations in the Fourth Gospel: Style, Text, Interpretation*, edited by G. Van Belle et al., 403–18. Leuven: Peeters, 2009.

Pamplaniyil, Joseph Thomas. "Tupon tōn hēlōn . . . (JN 20,25) Johannine Double Entendre of Jesus' Wounds." In *The Death of Jesus in the Fourth Gospel*, edited by Gilbert Van Belle, 931–44. Leuven: University Press, 2007.

Pannenberg, Wolfhart. "Did Jess Really Rise from the Dead?" In *Exploring Christian Theology*, edited by Ronnie Littlejohn, 367–82. Lanham, MD: University Press of America, 1985.

———. "History and the Reality of the Resurrection." In *Resurrection Reconsidered*, edited by Gavin D'Costa, 62–72. Oxford: Oneworld, 1996.

Pao, David W. "Jesus's Ascension and the Lukan Account of the Restoration of Israel." In *Ascent into Heaven in Luke-Acts: New Explorations of Luke's Narrative Hinge*, edited by David K. Bryan and David W. Pao, 137–55. Minneapolis: Fortress, 2016.

Parton, Craig A. "The Case against The Case against Christianity: When Jerusalem Came to Athens." In *The Resurrection Fact Responding to Modern Critics*, edited by John J. Bombaro and Adam S. Francisco, 89–116. Irvine, CA: NRP, 2016.

Patterson, Paige. "The Work of Christ." In *A Theology for the Church*, edited by Daniel L. Akin, 545–602. Nashville: B&H Academic, 2007. [The Resurrection, See. 590–96]

Peake, A. S. "Did Jesus Rise Again?" In *Is Christianity True? A Series of Lectures Delivered In the Central Hall, Manchester*, edited by Anonymous, 56–76. Cincinnati: Jennings & Graham, 1904. [N.B. Archive.org]

Perkins, Pheme. "Matthew 28.16–20, Resurrection, Ecclesiology and Mission." In *Society of Biblical Literature 1993 Seminar Papers*, edited by Eugene H. Lovering, 574–588. Atlanta: Scholars Press, 1993.

———. "The Resurrection of Jesus." In *Handbook for the Study of the Historical Jesus: The Historical Jesus*, edited by Tom Holmén and Stanley E. Porter, 2409–32. Vol. 3. Leiden: Brill, 2011. [N.B. This essay is a solid reading.]

———. "The Resurrection of Jesus of Nazareth." In *Studying the Historical Jesus: Evaluations of the State of Current Research*, edited by Bruce Chilton and Craig A. Evans, 423–42. Leiden: Brill, 1994.

Perry, M. C. "Believing the Miracles and Preaching the Resurrection." In *The Miracles and the Resurrection*, 64–104. London: SPCK, 1964. [N.B. This work is a collection of essays by five contributors.]

Peters, Ted. "The Future of the Resurrection." In *The Resurrection of Jesus: John Dominic Crossan and N.T. Wright in Dialogue*, edited by Robert B. Stewart, 149–69. Minneapolis: Fortress, 2006.

Peterson, David. "Resurrection Apologetics and the Theology of Luke-Acts." In *Proclaiming the Resurrection: Papers from the First Oak Hill College Annual School of Theology*, edited by Peter M. Head, 29–57. Carlisle: Paternoster, 1998.

Pierson, Mark A. "Defending the Fundamental Facts of Good Friday and Easter Sunday." In *The Resurrection Fact Responding to Modern Critics*, edited by John J. Bombaro and Adam S. Francisco, 17–42. Irvine, CA: NRP, 2016.

Pokorny, Petr. "Burial Practices and Faith in Resurrection." In *The Tomb of Jesus and His Family: Exploring Ancient Jewish Tombs Near Jerusalem's Walls*, edited by James H. Charlesworth, 535–46. Grand Rapids: Eerdmans, 2013.

Porter, L. Aldin. "He Is Risen." In *Sperry Symposium Classics: The New Testament*, edited by Frank F. Judd and Gaye Strathearn, 36–45. Salt Lake City, UT: Deseret Book, 2006.

Porter, Stanley E. "Jesus and Resurrection." In *Jesus in Continuum*, edited by Tom Holmén, 323–53. Tübingen: Mohr Siebeck, 2012. [N.B. This work is an informative reading.]

———. "The Unity of Luke-Acts and the Ascension Narratives." In *Ascent into Heaven in Luke-Acts: New Explorations of Luke's Narrative Hinge*, edited by David K. Bryan and David W. Pao, 111–36. Minneapolis: Fortress, 2016. [N.B. This work is an informative reading.]

Powell, Mark Allan. "Literary Approaches and the Gospel of Matthew." In *Methods for Matthew*, edited by Mark Allan Powell, 44–82. Cambridge: Cambridge University Press, 2009. [The Resurrection and Commissioning of the Women (28:1–11), See. 73–77; The Report of the Guard, See. 77–80]

Priestley, Joseph. "On the Change which took place in the Character of the Apostles after the Resurrection of Jesus Christ." In *Dissertations and Discourses on the Evidences and Spirit of Christianity*. Boston: Samuel C. Simpkins, 1333 [1833]. [See. 121–84]

Quarles, Charles L. "The Gospel of Peter: Does It Contain a Precanonical Resurrection Narrative?" In *The Resurrection of Jesus: John Dominic Crossan and N. T. Wright in Dialogue*, edited by Robert B. Stewart, 106–20. Minneapolis: Fortress, 2006.

Ramsey, A. Michael. "What was the Ascension?" In *Historicity and Chronology in the New Testament*, edited by SPCK, 135–44. London: SPCK, 1965.

Rawlinson, A. E. and R. G. Parsons. "The Interpretation of the Christ in the New Testament." *In Foundations: A Statement of Christian Belief in Terms of Modern Thought: By Seven Oxford Men*, edited by Anonymous, 75–145. London: Macmillan, 1929. [The Primitive Community, See. 151–210]

Read, Jan A. du. "The Creation Motif in the Fourth Gospel: Perspectives on its Narratological Function with a Judaistic Background." In *Theology and Christology in the Fourth Gospel*, edited by G. Van Belle, et al., 21–46. Leuven: Leuven University Press, 2005.

Read-Heimerdinger, J. "Where is Emmaus? Clues in the Text of Luke 24 in Codex Bezae." In *Studies in the Early Text of the Gospels and Acts: The Papers of the First Birmingham Colloquium on the Textual Criticism of the New Testament*, edited by David G. K. Taylor, 229–44. Piscataway, NJ: Gorgias, 2013.

Reid, Robert Stephen. "Finishing the Story We Find Ourselves In (Mark 16:1–8)." In *Preaching Mark's Unsettling Messiah*, edited by David Fleer and Dave Bland, 175–81. Saint Louis: Chalice, 2006.

Reimer, Andy M. "A Biography of Motif: The Empty Tomb in the Gospels, the Greek Novels, and Shakespeare's Romeo and Juliet." In *Ancient Fiction: The Matrix of Early Christian and Jewish Narrative*, edited by Jo-Ann A. Bryant et al., 297–316. Atlanta: Society of Biblical Literature, 2005.

Rigato, Maria-Luisa. "'Remember . . . Then They Remembered': Luke 24:6–8." In *Luke and Acts*, edited by Gerald O'Collins and Gilberto Marconi, 93–102. New York: Paulist, 1993.

Roberts, Phil. "The Resurrection and Modern Theology." In *Resurrection! Essays in Honor of Homer Hailey*, edited by Edward Fudge, 99–126. Athens, AL: C.E.I. Publishing 1973.

Robinson, Maurice A. "The Long Ending of Mark as Canonical Verity." In *Perspectives on the Ending of Mark: 4 Views*, edited by David Alan Black, 40–79. Nashville: Broadman & Holman, 2008.

Row, C. A. "The Historical Evidence of the Resurrection of Jesus Christ." In *Living Papers on Present Day Themes: Christian Evidences, Doctrines And Morals*, 3–48. Vol. 1. New York: Fleming, 1873. [idem. *Present Day Tracts on Subjects of Christian Evidence, Doctrine, and Morals. By Various Writers*. Vol. 1. London: The Religious Tract Society. 1883. [See. 1–48]

———. "The Historical Evidence of the Resurrection of Jesus Christ." In *Popular Objections to Revealed Truths Considered in a Series of Lectures*, edited by Christian Evidence Society, 227–62. New York: A.D.F. Randolph, 1873. [N.B. Google book. This article is a classic, dated reading.]

———. "The Positive Evidence in Proof of the Historical Truth of the Miracles of the New Testament." In *Credentials of Christianity*. Preface by the Earl of Harrowby, 87–141. London: Christian Evidence Society, 1879. [That within the briefest interval after the Crucifixion, the Resurrection of Jesus was accepted as a fact . . . , See. 123–41; N.B. Google book]

Rowland, Christopher. "Interpreting the Resurrection." In *The Resurrection of Jesus Christ*, edited by Paul D. L. Avis, 68–84. London: Darton, Longman and Todd, 1993.

Ruffner, Henry. "Miracles, Considered as an Evidence of Christianity." In *Lectures on the Evidences of Christianity: Delivered at the University of Virginia, during the Session of 1850–1*, edited by W. H. Ruffner, 56–108. New York: Robert Carter, 1859. [See. 99–105; N.B. Google book]

Ryle, H. E. "The Resurrection of Our Lord Jesus Christ as an Historic Fact." In *The Faith of Centuries: Addresses and Essays on Subjects Connected with the Christian Religion*, edited by William Edward Bowen, 145–70. London: James Nisbet, 1897. [N.B. Archive.org]

Excerpts from Edited Books: Pro Resurrection

Samir Khalil Samir. "The Theological Christian Influence on the Qur'an: A Reflection." In *The Qur'an and its Biblical Subtext*, edited by Gabriel Said Reynolds, 141–62. New York: Routledge, 2010. [N.B. The author is an Egyptian Jesuit priest.]

Schaeffer, Susan E. "The Guard at the Tomb (*Gos. Pet* 8:28–11,49 and Matt 27:62–66; 28:2–4, 11–16): A Case of Intertextuality?" In *Society of Biblical Literature 1991 Seminar Papers*, edited by Eugene H. Lovering, 499–507. Atlanta: Scholars Press, 1993. [N.B. This interesting paper investigates two traditions of the guard at the tomb: the *Gospel of Peter* and Matthew.]

Schneiders, Sandra M. "Cross and Resurrection in the Gospel of John." In *The Resurrection of Jesus in the Gospel of John*, edited by Craig R. Koester and Reimund Bieringer, 153–76. Tübingen: Mohr Siebeck, 2008.

———. "John 20:11–18: The Encounter of Easter Jesus with Mary Magdalene—A Transformative Feminist Reading." In *What is John? Readers and Readings of the Fourth Gospel*, edited by Fernando F. Segovia, 155–68. Atlanta: Scholars Press, 1996.

———. "Touching the Risen Jesus: Mary Magdalene and Thomas the Twin in John 20." In *The Resurrection of Jesus in the Gospel of John*, edited by Craig R. Koester and Reimund Bieringer, 153–76. Tübingen: Mohr Siebeck, 2008.

Schnelle, Udo. "Cross and Resurrection in the Gospel of Johns." In *The Resurrection of Jesus in the Gospel of John*, edited by Craig R. Koester and Reimund Bieringer, 127–51. Tübingen: Mohr Siebeck, 2008.

Senior, Donald. "Crucible of Truth: Passion and Resurrection in the Gospel of Mark." In *The Passion, Death and Resurrection of the Lord: A Commentary on the Four Gospels*, edited by Chicago Studies, 21–34. Mundelein, IL: Chicago Studies, 1980?.

Setzer, Claudia. "Resurrection in the Gospels of Matthew: Reality and Symbol." In *Life Beyond Death in Matthews Gospel: Religious Metaphor or Bodily Reality?*, edited by Wim Weren, Huub Van De Sandt, and Jozef Verheyden, 43–55. Leuven: Peeters, 2011.

Sharp, Mary Jo. "Is the Story of Jesus Borrowed from Pagan Myths?" In *In Defense of the Bible: A Comprehensive Apologetic for the Authority of Scripture*, edited by Steven B. Cowan and Terry L. Wilder, 183–200 Nashville: Broadman & Holman, 2013. [Resurrection Stories, See. 194–200]

Shaw, Gregory. "Ascension of Christ." In *The Oxford Companion to the Bible*, edited by Bruce M. Metzger and Michael D. Coogan, 61–62. New York: Oxford University Press, 1993.

Sherlock, Thomas. "Sherlock's Trial of the Witnesses, with the Sequel to the Trial." In *Christian Literature: Evidences*. Prefatory Memoirs by J. S. Memes, 549–620. London: H.G. Bohn, 1847. [N.B. Google book]

Sleeman, Matthew. "The Ascension and Spatial Theory." In *Ascent into Heaven in Luke-Acts: New Explorations of Luke's Narrative Hinge*, edited by David K. Bryan and David W. Pao, 157–73. Minneapolis: Fortress, 2016. [N.B. This is an interesting chapter to read.]

Slenczka, Notger. "In What Sense has the Conviction that Jesus was Resurrected the 'Certainty of Facts'?" In *The Quest for the Real Jesus Radboud Prestige Lectures*, edited by Jan Van der Watt, 185–203. Leiden: Brill, 2013.

Smith, Robert Harry. "Matthew 28:16–20, Anticlimax or Key to the Gospel?" In *Society of Biblical Literature 1993 Seminary Papers*, edited by Eugene H. Lovering, 589–603. Atlanta: Scholars Press, 1993.

Smith, Wilbur M. "The Resurrection and Ascension of Our Lord." In *Things Most Surely Believed*, edited by Clarence Stonelynn Roddy, 49–62. Westwood, NJ: Revell, 1963.

———. "The Resurrection of Christ." In *Foundations of the Faith: Twelve Studies in the Basic Christian Revelation*, edited by David Jones Fant, 69–87. Westwood, NJ: Revell, 1951.

Stanley, David M. "The Risen Christ as Master of History." In *Theological Folia of Villanova University*, Vol. 2. edited by Joseph Papin. Villanova, PA: Villanova University Press, 1975.

Stevenson, Gregory. "Believing Is Seeing: The Dynamics of Faith in the Gospel of John." In *Preaching John's Gospel: The World It Imagines*, edited by David Fleer and Dave Bland, 111–22. St. Louis: Chalice, 2008. [The Resurrection and Belief (John 20), See. 120–21]

Stewart, Robert B. "The Hermeneutics of Resurrection: How N. T. Wright and John Dominic Crossan Read the Resurrection Narratives." In *The Resurrection of Jesus: John Dominic Crossan and N. T. Wright in Dialogue*, edited by Robert B. Stewart, 58–77. Minneapolis: Fortress, 2006.

Stoughton, John. "The Nature and Value of the Miraculous Testimony to Christianity." In *Modern Scepticism: A Course of Lectures: With an Explanatory Paper*, edited by Christian Evidence Society, 179–228. London: Hodder & Stoughton, 1871. [See. 208–10; N.B. Google book]

Streeter, Burnett Hillman. "Historic Christ: The Point of View of Modern Scholarship." In *Foundations: A Statement of Christian Belief in Terms of Modern Thought: By Seven Oxford Men*, edited by Anonymous, 75–145. London: Macmillan, 1929. [The Resurrection, See. 127–45]

Strobel, Lee. "Did Jesus Rise from the Dead?" In *Who Made God? And Answers to Over 100 Other Tough Questions of Faith*, edited by Ravi K. Zacharias and Norman L. Geisler, 97–104. Grand Rapids: Zondervan, 2003.

———. "More Tough Questions About Christ." In *Who Made God? And Answers to Over 100 Other Tough Questions on Faith*, edited by Ravi Zacharias and Norman Geisler, 87–102. Grand Rapids: Zondervan, 2003. [Did Jesus Rise From the Dead?, See. 97–102]

Swinburne, Richard. "Evidence for the Resurrection." In *The Resurrection: An Interdisciplinary Symposium on the Resurrection of Jesus*, edited by Stephen T. Davis et al, 191–212. Oxford: University Press, 1997.

———. "The Probability of the Resurrection." In *God and the Ethics of Belief: New Essays in Philosophy of Religion*, edited by Andrew Dole and Andrew Chignell, 117–130. Cambridge: Cambridge University Press, 2005. [N.B. An important essay to read.]

Syreeni, Kari. "Resurrection or Assumption? Matthew's View of the Post-Mortem Vindication of Jesus." In *Life Beyond Death in Matthews Gospel: Religious Metaphor or Bodily Reality?*, edited by Wim Weren, Huub Van De Sandt, and Jozef Verheyden, 57–77. Leuven: Peeters, 2011.

Tappenden, Frederick S. "Aural Performance, Conceptual Blending, and Intertextuality: The (Non-) Use of Scripture in Luke 24.45–48." In *Biblical Interpretation in Early Christian Gospels*. Vol. 3. *The Gospel of Luke*, edited by Thomas R. Hatina, 180–200. London: T &T Clark, 2010.

Taylor, Jerry. "The Empty Net Syndrome John 21:1–14." In *Preaching John's Gospel: The World It Imagines*, edited by David Fleer and Dave Bland, 26–31. St. Louis: Chalice, 2008.

Taylor, Marion Ann, and Heather E. Weir, eds. "Mary Magdalene: Receiving the Text." In *Women in the Story of Jesus: The Gospels Through the Eyes of Nineteenth-Century Female Biblical Interpreters*, 224–50. Grand Rapids: Eerdmans, 2016. [Chapter 8, Charlotte

Bickersteth Wheeler, "Carry the Glad Tidings," See. 224–27; Elizabeth Baxter, "Apostle of the Resurrection," See. 227–30; Elizabeth Lady Stanton, "Gullible Women," See. 230–32; Amelia Gillespie Smyth, Harmonizing Magdalene," See. 232–39; Elizabeth Rundle Charles, "Hidden Depths," See. 239–50]

Thatcher, Adrian. "Resurrection and Rationality." In *The Resurrection of Jesus Christ*, edited by Paul D. L. Avis, 171–86. London: Darton, Longman and Todd, 1993.

Thayer, Joseph Henry. "Criticism Confirmatory of the Gospels." In *Christianity and Skepticism Comprising A Treatment of Questions*, Edited by the Committee, 324–402. London: Hodder & Stoughton, 1872. [See 375–83; N.B. Google book]

Todd, John. "The Ascended Christ Interceding For Us." In *Talks To Boys And Girls About Jesus with Bible Links*, edited by W. F. Crafts, 363–70. New York: Funk & Wagnalls, 1887. [N.B. Archive.org and HathiTrust]

Torrey, R. A. "The Certainty and Importance of the Bodily Resurrection of Jesus Christ From the Dead." In *The Fundamentals: The Famous Sourcebook of Foundational Biblical Truths*, edited by Charles L. Feinberg and Reuben A. Torrey, 295–310. Grand Rapids: Kregel, 1990. [Updated edition of *Fundamentals for Today*, 1958]

Tuckett, C. M. "The Corinthians Who Say 'There is No Resurrection of the Dead' (1 Cor 15,12)." In *The Corinthian Correspondence*, edited by Reimund Bieringer, 247–75. Leuven: University Press, 1996.

Twining, Kinsley. "The Evidence of the Resurrection of Jesus Christ." In *Christianity and Scepticism: Embracing a Consideration of Important Traits of Christian Doctrine and Experience, and of Leading Facts in the Life of Christ*, edited by the Publisher, 223–53. Boston: Congregational Publishing Society, 1872. [N.B. Google book.]

Ullrich, Lothar. "Resurrection of Jesus." In *Handbook of Catholic Theology*, edited by Wolfgang Beinert and Francis Schüssler Fiorenza, 591–95. New York: Crossroad, 1995.

———. "Resurrection Narratives." In *Handbook of Catholic Theology*, edited by Wolfgang Beinert and Francis Schüssler Fiorenza, 586–91. New York: Crossroad, 1995.

Vaughan, James. "The Forty Days." In *Talks To Boys And Girls About Jesus with Bible Links*, edited by W. F. Crafts, 352–63. New York: Funk & Wagnalls, 1887. [N.B. Archive.org and HathiTrust]

Verheyden, Joseph. "The Great Escape: Some Comments on a Controversial Suggestion for Explaining Matt 28:2–4." In *Life Beyond Death in Matthews Gospel: Religious Metaphor or Bodily Reality?*, edited by Wim Weren et al., 201–16. Leuven: Peeters, 2011.

———. "Silent Witnesses: Mary Magdalene and the Women at the Tomb in the Gospel of Peter." In *Miracles and Imagery in Luke and John: Festschrift Ulrich Busse*, edited by J. G. Verheyden et al., 457–82. Leuven: Peeters, 2008.

Wainwright, Elaine M. "Feminist Criticism and the Gospel of Matthew." In *Methods for Matthew*, edited by Mark Allan Powell, 83–117. Cambridge: Cambridge University Press, 2009.

Wallace, Daniel B. "Mark 16:8 as the Conclusion to the Second Gospel." In *Perspectives on the Ending of Mark: 4 Views*, edited by David Alan Black, 1–39. Nashville: Broadman & Holman, 2008. [N.B. An interesting essay to examine.]

Walton, Steve. "Jesus's Ascension through Old Testament Narrative Traditions." In *Ascent into Heaven in Luke-Acts: New Explorations of Luke's Narrative Hinge*, edited by David K. Bryan and David W. Pao, 29–39. Minneapolis: Fortress, 2016.

Waterson, A. P. "Did Jesus Really Rise from the Dead?" In *Hard Questions*, edited by Frank Colquhoun, 41–44. Downers Grove, IL: InterVarsity, 1973.

Watson, Francis. "'I Received from the Lord . . .': Paul, Jesus, and the Last Supper." In *Jesus and Paul Reconnected: Fresh Pathways into an Old Debate*, edited by Todd D. Still, 103–24. Grand Rapids: Eerdmans, 2007. [See 108–10; N.B. Discusses the relationship with 1 Corinthian 15.]

———. "Must the Gospels Agree? In Dialogue with Augustine." In *Jesus Christ Today: Studies of Christology in Various Contexts*, edited by Stuart G. Hall, 63–87. Berlin: Walter de Gruyter GmbH, 2006. [See. 80–85]

Watson, Richard, bishop. "An Apology for the Bible; Abridged from Watson's Answer to the Second Part of Paine's Age of Reason." In *The Pleiad: A Series of Abridgements From Seven Distinguished Writers on the Evidences of Christianity*, edited by Francis Wrangham, 103–79. Edinburgh: Printed for Constable, 1828. [See. 158–68; N.B. Google book]

Weatherly, Jon A. "Eating and Drinking in the Kingdom of God: The Emmaus Episode and the Meal Motif in Luke-Acts." In *Christ's Victorious Church: Essays on Biblical Ecclesiology and Eschatology in Honor of Tom Friskney*, edited by Jon A. Weatherly, 18–33. Eugene, OR: Wipf & Stock, 2001.

Webb-Odell, R. "The Evidence of Christianity." In *The Christian Faith*, edited by Charles Frederick Nolloth, 91–114. London: Murray, 1922.

Webster, John. "Resurrection and Scripture." In *Christology and Scripture: Interdisciplinary Perspectives*, edited by Andrew T. Lincoln and Angus Paddison, 138–55. London: T&T Clark, 2008.

Wedderburn, A. J. M. "Resurrection." In *Jesus: The Complete Guide*, edited by James L. Houlden, 706–13. London: Continuum, 2005.

Welker, Michael. "Resurrection and the Eternal Life: The Canonic Memory of the Resurrected Christ, His Reality, and His Glory." In *The End of the World and the Ends of God: Science and Theology on Eschatology*, edited by John Polkinghorne and Michael Welker, 279–90. Harrisburg: Trinity Press International, 2000.

Weren, Wim J. C. "His Disciples Stole Him Away (Mt 28,13): A Rival Interpretation of Jesus' Resurrection." In *Resurrection in the New Testament: Festschrift J. Lambrecht*, edited by Reimund Bieringer and Jan Lambrecht, 147–63. Leuven: Leuven University Press, 2002.

———. "Matthew's Stories about Jesus' Burial and Resurrection (27:55–28:20) as the Climax of his Gospel." In *Life Beyond Death in Matthews Gospel: Religious Metaphor or Bodily Reality?*, edited by Wim Weren, Huub Van De Sandt, and Jozef Verheyden, 189–200. Leuven: Peeters, 2011.

———. "Matthew's View of Jesus' Resurrection: Transformations of a Current Eschatological Scenario." In *The Gospel of Matthew at the Crossroads of Early Christianity*, edited by Donald Senior, 701–11. Leuven: Peeters, 2011.

West, Gilbert. "Observations on the History and Evidence of the Resurrection of Jesus Christ." In *Christian Literature: Evidences*. Prefatory Memoirs by J. S. Memes, 621–713. London: Henry G. Bohn, 1847. [N.B. Google book. This is a classic, dated work.]

———. "The Resurrection: Order of Events, as Recorded by the Four Evangelists." In *Infidelity Comprising Jenyns' Internal Evidence*, edited by American Tract Society, 449–56. New York: American Tract Society, 1836. [N.B. Archive.org, Google book, and HathiTrust]

West, Nathaniel. "An Apologetic for the Resurrection of Christ." In *Defence and Confirmation of the Faith. Six Lectures*, edited by the Foundation of the Elliott Lectureship. 80–129. New York: Funk & Wagnalls, 1885. [N.B. Google book]

Wilckens, Ulrich. "The Tradition-History of the Resurrection of Jesus." In *The Significance of the Message of the Resurrection for Faith in Jesus Christ*, edited by C. F. D. Moule, 51–76. London: SCM, 1968.

Williams, Rowan. "Between the Cheribim: The Empty Tomb and the Empty Throne." In *Resurrection Reconsidered*, edited by Gavin D'Costa, 87–101. Oxford: Oneworld, 1996.

Wilson, C. W. "Some Evidence for the Resurrection." In *Christian Apologetics: A Series of Addresses Delivered before the Christian Association of University College, London*, edited by Walter W. Seton, 115–24; 132–33. New York: E.P. Dutton, 1903. [N.B. Google book]

Wilson, Gordon. "The Evidence for the Resurrection of Christ." In *Resurrection! Essays in Honor of Homer Hailey*, edited by Edward Fudge, 13–25. Athens, AL: C.E.I. Publishing 1973.

Witherington, Ben. "Resurrection Redux." In *Will the Real Jesus Please Stand Up? A Debate Between William Lane Craig and John Dominic Crossan*, edited by Paul Copan, 129–45. Grand Rapids: Baker, 1998.

Witmer, John A. "Jesus Christ: Know Jesus as Man and God." In *Understanding Christian Theology*, edited by Charles R. Swindoll and Roy B. Zuck, 291–385. Nashville: Nelson, 2003. [Christ's Ascension to the Right Hand of God the Father, See. 354–58]

Wood, David. "A Response to Dan Barker's 'Did Jesus Really Rise from the Dead?'" In *Defending the Resurrection: Did Jesus Rise from the Dead?*, edited by J. P. Holding, 81–95. US: Xulon, 2010.

Wright, C. J. "Jesus: The Revelation of God." In *The Mission and Message of Jesus: An Exposition of the Gospels in the Light of Modern Research*. By H. D. A. Major, T. W. Manson and C. J. Wright, 643–959. New York: E. P. Dutton, 1938. [Part 2 The Resurrection, See. 934–56]

Wright, N. T. "Jesus' Resurrection and Christian Origins." In *Passionate Conviction: Contemporary Discourses on Christian Apologetics*, edited by Paul Copan and William Lane Craig, 123–29. Nashville: B&H, 2007.

———. "Jesus and the Resurrection." In *Jesus Then & Now: Images of Jesus in History and Christology*, edited by Marvin W. Meyer and Charles Hughes, 54–71. Harrisburg, PA: Trinity Press International, 2001.

———. "The Surprise of Resurrection." In *Jesus, The Final Days: What Really Happened*, by Craig A. Evans and N. T. Wright, edited by Troy A. Miller, 75–107. Louisville: Westminster John Knox, 2009.

Wright, N.T., and John Dominic Crossan. "The Resurrection: Historical Event or Theological Explanation? A Dialogue." In *The Resurrection of Jesus: John Dominic Crossan and N. T. Wright in Dialogue*, edited by Robert B. Stewart, 16–47. Minneapolis: Fortress, 2006.

Yamauchi, Edwin M. "Did Christianity Copy Earlier Pagan Resurrection Stories." In *The Harvest Handbook of Apologetics*, edited by Joseph M. Holden, 149–55. Eugene, OR: Harvest House, 2018.

———. "Passover Plot or Easter Triumph? A Critical Review of H. Schonfield's Recent Theory." In *Christianity for the Tough Minded: Essays in Support of an Intellectually*

Defensible Religious Commitment, edited by John Warwick Montgomery, 261–71. Minneapolis: Bethany Fellowship, 1973.

Zangenberg, Jürgen. "'Bodily Resurrection' of Jesus in Matthew." In *Life Beyond Death in Matthews Gospel: Religious Metaphor or Bodily Reality?*, edited by Wim Weren et al., 217–30. Leuven: Peeters, 2011.

Zimmermann, Reuben. "Symbolic Communication between John and His Reader: The Garden Symbolism in John 19–20." In *Anatomies of Narrative Criticism: The Past, Present, and Futures of the Fourth Gospel as Literature*, edited by Tom Thatcher and Stephen D. Moore, 221–35. Atlanta: Society of Biblical Literature, 2008.

Zukeran, Patrick. "The Resurrection: Fact or Fiction?" In *Evidence, Answers & Christian Faith: Probing the Headlines That Impact Your Family*, edited by James F. Williams, 172–84. Grand Rapids: Kregel, 2002.

Zumstein, Jean. "Jesus' Resurrection in the Farewell Discourses." In *The Resurrection of Jesus in the Gospel of John*, edited by Craig R. Koester and Reimund Bieringer, 103–26. Wissenschaftliche Untersuchungen zum Neuen Testament 222. Tübingen: Mohr Siebeck, 2008.

Zwiep, Arie W. "Ascension Scholarship." In *Ascent into Heaven in Luke-Acts: New Explorations of Luke's Narrative Hinge*, edited by David K. Bryan and David W. Pao, 7–26. Minneapolis: Fortress, 2016.

CHAPTER 16

Excerpts from Edited Books: Con Resurrection

Allison, Dale C. "Thallus on the Crucifixion." In *The Historical Jesus In Context*, edited by Amy-Levine et al., 405–6. Princeton: Princeton University Press, 2006.

Avalos, Hector. "Resurrection." In *New Encyclopedia of Unbelief*, edited by Tom Flynn, 657–60. Amherst, NY: Prometheus, 2007.

Barker, Dan. "Did Jesus Really Rise From The Dead?" In *Abuse Your Illusions: The Disinformation Guide to Media Mirages and Establishment Lies*, edited by Russ Kick, 311–20. St. Paul: Consortium, 2003.

Berna, Kurt [pseud.]. "The International Foundation for the Holy Shroud." In *Truth About The Crucifixion Transcripts from the International Conference on Deliverance of Jesus from the Cross*, 151–64. London: Ascot, 1978.

Borg, Marcus. "The Gospels Are Reliable as Memory and Testimony." In *Debating Christian Theism*, edited by James Porter Moreland et al., 430–43. New York: Oxford University Press, 2013. [The Truth of the Easter Stories as Parabolic Testimony, See. 441–43]

———. "The Irrelevance of the Empty Tomb." In *Will the Real Jesus Please Stand Up? A Debate Between William Lane Craig and John Dominic Crossan*, edited by Paul Copan, 117–28. Grand Rapids: Baker, 1998.

Capps, Donald. "A Psychobiography of Jesus." In *Psychology and the Bible: A New Way to Read the Scriptures: From Christ to Jesus.* Vol. 4, edited by J. Harold Ellens and Wayne G. Rollins, 59–70. Westport, CT: Praeger, 2004. [The Resurrection Appears, See. 68]

———. "A Skeptic's Analysis." In *Resurrection: Faith or Fact? A Scholars' Debate Between a Skeptic and a Christian.* By Carl Stecher and Craig Blomberg, 195–219. Durham, NC: Pitchstone, 2019.

Carrier, Richard. "The Burial of Jesus in Light of Jewish Law." *The Empty Tomb: Jesus Beyond the Grave*, edited by Robert M. Price and Jeffrey Jay Lowder, 369–92. Amherst, NY: Prometheus, 2005. [N.B. Carrier's essay is an important work to examine.]

———. "The Plausibility of Theft." *The Empty Tomb: Jesus Beyond the Grave*, edited by Robert M. Price and Jeffrey Jay Lowder, 349–68. Amherst, NY: Prometheus, 2005. [N.B. This chapter is a significant reading.]

———. "The Spiritual Body of Christ and the Legend of the Empty Tomb." *The Empty Tomb: Jesus Beyond the Grave*, edited by Robert M. Price and Jeffrey Jay Lowder, 105–231. Amherst, NY: Prometheus, 2005c. [N.B. Carrier's lengthy article is a required reading.]

———. "Why the Resurrection Is Unbelievable." In *The Christian Delusion: Why Faith Fails*, edited by John W. Loftus, 291–315. Amherst, NY: Prometheus, 2010. [N.B. Carrier's major thesis is that there is a lack of sufficient evidence to warrant believing in Jesus's resurrection.]

Cavin, Robert Greg. "Is There Sufficient Historical Evidence to the Establish the Resurrection of Jesus?" *The Empty Tomb: Jesus Beyond the Grave*, edited by Robert M. Price and Jeffrey Jay Lowder, 9–41. Amherst, NY: Prometheus, 2005. [N.B. This required reading asserts that there is insufficient historical evidence to establish the resurrection hypothesis.]

Cohen-Sherbok, Dan. "The Resurrection of Jesus: A Jewish View." In *Resurrection Reconsidered*, edited by Gavin D'Costa, 184–200. Oxford: Oneworld, 1996. [N.B. At the end of the essay (p. 198), Cohen-Sherbok discusses what would be necessary to convince him of Jesus's resurrection.]

Cook, Michael J. "Gravitating to Luke's Historical Jesus: Help or Hindrance?" In *Teaching the Historical Jesus: Issues and Exegesis*, edited by Zev Garber, 195–206. New York: Routledge, 2015. [N.B. This is an interesting essay that should be examined.]

Crossan, John Dominic. "Bodily-Resurrection Faith." In *The Resurrection of Jesus: John Dominic Crossan and N. T. Wright in Dialogue*, edited by Robert B. Stewart, 171–86. Minneapolis: Fortress, 2006.

———. "Empty Tomb and Absent Lord (Mark 16:1–8)." In *The Passion in Mark: Studies on Mark 14–16*, edited by Werner H. Kelber, 135–52. Philadelphia: Fortress, 1976.

———. "Historical Jesus As Risen Lord." In *The Jesus Controversy Perspectives In Conflict: John Dominic Cross, Luke Timothy Johnson, Werner H. Keller*, edited by John Dominic Crossan, 1–47. Valley Forge, PA: Trinity Press International, 1999. [N.B. This essay is a recommended read.]

———. "John Dominic Crossan's Rebuttal." In *Will the Real Jesus Please Stand Up? A Debate Between William Lane Craig and John Dominic Crossan*, edited by Paul Copan, 45–47. Grand Rapids: Baker, 1998.

———. "The Resurrection: Historical Event or Theological Explanation? A Dialogue." In *The Resurrection of Jesus: John Dominic Crossan and N. T. Wright in Dialogue*, edited by Robert B. Stewart, 16–47. Minneapolis: Fortress, 2006. [N.B. See Crossan's response.]

Crossley, James G. "The Resurrection Probably Did Not Happen." In *Debating Christian Theism*, edited by James Porter Moreland et al., 484–94. New York: Oxford University Press, 2013. [N.B. Crossley discusses several topics that are well worth your time to examine.]

Cumming, Joseph L. "Did Jesus Die on the Cross: Reflections in Muslim Commentaries." In *Muslim and Christian Reflections on Peace: Divine and Human Dimensions*, edited by J. Dudley Woodberry, Osman Zümrüt, and Mustafa Köylü, 32–50. Yale University, 2005. [N.B. Available online]

Derrett, J. Duncan M. "Financial Aspects of the Resurrection." *The Empty Tomb: Jesus Beyond the Grave*, edited by Robert M. Price and Jeffrey Jay Lowder, 393–409. Amherst, NY: Prometheus, 2005. [N.B. Derrett investigates an intriguing topic: What happened to the Jesus's body and whom did any scenario profit?]

Dewey, Arthur J. "Resurrection Texts in the Gospel of Peter." In *The Resurrection of Jesus: A Sourcebook*, edited by Bernard Brandon Scott, 61–74. Santa Rosa, CA: Polebridge, 2008.

Drange, Theodore M. "Why Resurrect Jesus?" *The Empty Tomb: Jesus Beyond the Grave*, edited by Robert M. Price and Jeffrey Jay Lowder, 55–67. Amherst, NY: Prometheus, 2005. [N.B. This essay is an interesting reading that uses Christian theologian Charles Hodge as its intellectual foil.]

Ellens, J. Harold. "From Christ to Jesus: The Jesus Quest." In *Psychology and the Bible: A New Way to Read the Scriptures: From Christ to Jesus*. Vol. 4, edited by J. Harold Ellens and Wayne G. Rollins, 13–20. Westport, CT: Praeger, 2004. [See. 15]

Faber-Kaiser, Andreas. "He Did Not Die on the Cross." In *Truth About The Crucifixion Transcripts from the International Conference on Deliverance of Jesus from the Cross*, 69–78. London: Ascot, 1978.

Fales, Evan. "Reformed Epistemology and Biblical Hermeneutics." *The Empty Tomb: Jesus Beyond the Grave*, edited by Robert M. Price and Jeffrey Jay Lowder, 469–89. Amherst, NY: Prometheus, 2005.

———. "Taming the Tehom: The Sign of Jonah in Matthew." *The Empty Tomb: Jesus Beyond the Grave*, edited by Robert M. Price and Jeffrey Jay Lowder, 307–48. Amherst, NY: Prometheus, 2005. [N.B. This interesting work should be carefully examined.]

Flew, Antony G. N. "Theism, Revelation, and Jesus' Resurrection." In *Resurrected? An Atheist and Theist Dialogue: Gary R. Habermas and Antony G. N. Flew*, edited by John F. Ankerberg, 81–87. Lanham: Rowman & Littlefield, 2005.

Funk, Robert W. "The Resurrection of Jesus: Reports and Stories." In *The Resurrection of Jesus: A Sourcebook*, edited by Bernard Brandon Scott, 7–44. Santa Rosa, CA: Polebridge, 2008.

Goulder, Michael D. "A Baseless Fabric of a Vision." In *Resurrection Reconsidered*, edited by Gavin D'Costa, 48–64. Oxford: Oneworld, 1996.

Hoover, Roy W. "Was Jesus' Resurrection an Historical Event? A Debate Statement with Commentary." In *The Resurrection of Jesus: A Sourcebook*, edited by Bernard Brandon Scott, 75–92. Santa Rosa, CA: Polebridge, 2008. [N.B. Hoover's work should be carefully examined. His presentation is concise and logical.]

Hopkins, Brooke. "Jesus and Object Use: A Winnicottian Account of the Resurrection Myth." In *Freud and the Freudians on Religion: A Reader*, edited by Donald Capps, 230–40. New Haven: Yale University Press, 2001.

Jesus Seminar Spring Meeting, The. In *The Resurrection of Jesus: A Sourcebook*, edited by Bernard Brandon Scott, 45–48. Santa Rosa, CA: Polebridge, 2008. [Reprint from the *Fourth R*, 8(2): 12–17, 1995.]

Johnson, David, et. al. *Why After Listening to Christian Arguments We Are Still Skeptics*. Reason Press, 2018 [Resurrection (Ed Atkinson) Kindle]

Kirby, Peter. "The Case Against the Empty Tomb." *The Empty Tomb: Jesus Beyond the Grave*, edited by Robert M. Price and Jeffrey Jay Lowder, 233–60. Amherst, NY: Prometheus, 2005. [N.B. Kirby's article is a must read.]

Kirkhart, Bobbie. "Bridging the Leap of Faith." In *Everything You Know About God Is Wrong: The Disinformation Guide to Religion*, edited by Russ Kick, 120–25. New York: The Disinformation Company, 2007. [See. 124–25]

Loftus, John. "Resurrection of Jesus Never Took Place." In *The Case against Miracles*, edited by John Loftus. Hypatia, 2019. [Forthcoming]

Lowder, Jeffrey Jay. "Historical Evidence and the Empty Tomb Story: A Reply to William Lane Craig." *The Empty Tomb: Jesus Beyond the Grave*, edited by Robert M. Price and

Jeffrey Jay Lowder, 261–306. Amherst, NY: Prometheus, 2005. [N.B. This significant essay is a must read.]

Luedmann, Gerd. "The History and Nature of the Earliest Christian Belief in the Resurrection." In *The Historical Jesus in Recent Research*, edited by James D. G. Dunn and Scot McKnight, 413–19. Winona Lake, IN: Eisenbrauns, 2005. [N.B. The name of the contributor was misspelled. It should read: Lüdemann]

MacDonald, Dennis R. "Luke's Use of Papias for Narrating the Death of Judas." In *Reading Acts Today: Essays in Honour of Loveday C. A. Alexander*, edited by Steve Walton, 43–62. London: Bloomsbury, 2013.

Madsen, Abdus Salam. "Deliverance of Jesus from the Cross: Quranic and Islamic Evidence." In *Truth About The Crucifixion Transcripts from the International Conference on Deliverance of Jesus from the Cross*, 107–16. London: Ascot, 1978. [N.B. The author is a member of the Ahmadiyya Movement.]

Martin, Michael. "Is It Rational for Christians to Believe in the Resurrection?" In *Contemporary Debates in Philosophy of Religion*, edited by Michael L. Peterson and Raymond J. VanArragon, 174–83. Oxford: Blackwell, 2004. [N.B. Reply by Martin, See. 184–86 and Reply to Davis, See. 186–87. This interchange is an informative reading.]

———. "The Resurrection as Initially Improbable." *The Empty Tomb: Jesus Beyond the Grave*, edited by Robert M. Price and Jeffrey Jay Lowder, 43–54. Amherst, NY: Prometheus, 2005. [N.B. Martin employs Bayes's Theorem to demonstrate that the initial probability of the resurrection is very low. He is also refutes the probability of the incarnation, the resurrection of God, and Jesus being the incarnate God.]

———. "Swinburne on the Resurrection." *The Empty Tomb: Jesus Beyond the Grave*, edited by Robert M. Price and Jeffrey Jay Lowder, 453–68. Amherst, NY: Prometheus, 2005. [Martin employs Bayes's Theorem to demonstrate that the initial probability of the resurrection is very low.]

Marxsen, Willi. "The Resurrection of Jesus as a Historical and Theological Problem." In *The Significance of the Message of the Resurrection for Faith in Jesus Christ*, edited by C. F. D. Moule, 15–50. London: SCM, 1968. [N.B. This reading is a significant essay that should be examined.]

McCane, Byron R. "'Where No One Had Yet Been Laid': The Shame of Jesus' Burial." In *Authenticating the Activities of Jesus*, edited by Craig A. Evans and Bruce Chilton, 431–52. Leiden: Brill Academic, 2002. [N.B. This noteworthy essay demonstrates that the shame of Jesus's burial is consistent with the best evidence and explains why the tomb was not venerated.]

———. "'Where No One Had Yet Been Laid:' The Shame of Jesus' Burial." In *Society of Biblical Literature 1993 Seminar Papers Series*, edited by Eugene H. Lovering, 473–84. Atlanta: Scholars Press, 1993.

Miller, Robert J. "What Do Stories about Resurrection(s) Prove?" In *Will the Real Jesus Please Stand Up? A Debate Between William Lane Craig and John Dominic Crossan*, edited by Paul Copan, 77–98. Grand Rapids: Baker, 1998.

Nickell, Joe. "The Turin Shroud: A Postmortem." In *Christianity in the Light of Science: Critically Examining the World's Largest Religion*, edited by John W. Loftus. Amherst, NY: Prometheus, 2016. [N.B. Nickell presents a critical review of the literature exploring the purported authenticity of Shroud of Turin.]

Parsons, Keith. "Peter Kreeft and Ronald Tacelli on the Hallucination Theory." *The Empty Tomb: Jesus Beyond the Grave*, edited by Robert M. Price and Jeffrey Jay Lowder,

433–51. Amherst, NY: Prometheus, 2005. [N.B. This essay is an absolute must reading. Significantly, it refutes thirteen objections that Kreeft and Tacelli offer against the hallucination theory.]

———. "The Universe is Probable: The Resurrection is Not." In *Does God Exist? The Craig-Flew Debate*, edited by Stan W. Wallace, 115–30. Aldershot: Ashgate, 2005. [N.B. This work challenges two often-made assertions made by William Lane Craig and it is a must read.]

Price, Robert M. "Apocryphal Apparitions: 1 Corinthians 15:3–11 As A Post-Pauline Interpolation." *The Empty Tomb: Jesus Beyond the Grave*, edited by Robert M. Price and Jeffrey Jay Lowder, 69–104. Amherst, NY: Prometheus, 2005. [N.B. Price, a New Testament scholar challenges perhaps the most important verses from the Christian bible. This chapter is a must read.]

———. "Brand X Easters." In *The Resurrection of Jesus: A Sourcebook*, edited by Bernard Brandon Scott, 49–59. Santa Rosa, CA: Polebridge, 2008. [N.B. Price demonstrates that Easter stories of the gospels were typical and shares a resemblance to ancient Hellenistic myth and legend.]

———. "By This Time He Stinketh: The Attempts of William Lane Craig to Exhume Jesus." *The Empty Tomb: Jesus Beyond the Grave*, edited by Robert M. Price and Jeffrey Jay Lowder, 411–31. Amherst, NY: Prometheus, 2005. [N.B. Price, intriguingly refutes William Lane Craig's apologetic for the resurrection.]

Pyysiäinen, Ilkka. "The Mystery of the Stolen Body: Exploring Christian Origins." In *Exploring Christian Origins and Early Judaism: Contributions from Cognitive and Social Science*, edited by Petri Luomanen, Ilkka Pyysiäinen, and Risto Uro, 57–72. Leiden: Brill, 2007. [This essay employing cognitive psychology research is a must read.]

Qadir, Shaikh Abdul. "Jesus Travels to India and Kashmir: The Post Crucifixion Life of Jesus." In *Truth About The Crucifixion Transcripts from the International Conference on Deliverance of Jesus from the Cross*, 129–49. London: Ascot, 1978.

Rafiq, B. A. "Deliverance of Jesus from the Cross: Historical Evidence." In *Truth About The Crucifixion Transcripts from the International Conference on Deliverance of Jesus from the Cross*, 89–105. London: Ascot, 1978.

Rogers, John R. "An Examination of the Biblical Evidence for the Resurrection of Jesus." In *Resurrection, Sex and God: Essays on the Foundations of Faith*, edited by Arthur F. Ide, 17–46. Dallas: Minuteman, 1990. [N.B. This work presents a good summary of the reasons to doubt the historicity of the Jesus's resurrection.]

Segal, Alan F. "Life After Death: The Social Sources." In *The Resurrection: An Interdisciplinary Symposium on the Resurrection of Jesus*, edited by Stephen T. Davis et al., 90–125. Oxford: University Press, 1997. [See. 110–13]

———. "The Resurrection: Faith or History?" In *The Resurrection of Jesus: John Dominic Crossan and N. T. Wright in Dialogue*, edited by Robert B. Stewart, 121–48. Minneapolis: Fortress, 2006. [See. 131–34]

Sheehan, Thomas. "How Did Easter Originally Happen? An Hypothesis." In *The Resurrection of Jesus: A Sourcebook*, edited by Bernard Brandon Scott, 105–15. Santa Rosa, CA: Polebridge, 2008. [N.B. This essay offers a natural, and logical explanation for what occurred on Easter.]

———. "The Resurrection, an Obstacle to Faith?" In *The Resurrection of Jesus: A Sourcebook*, edited by Bernard Brandon Scott, 93–104. Santa Rosa, CA: Polebridge,

2008. [Sheehan's must read demonstrates how the resurrection accounts evolved and grew over time.]

Singer, Tovia. "The Resurrection: What is the Evidence?" In *The Book Your Church Doesn't Want You to Read: or Synagogue, Temple,* Mosque . . ., edited by Tim C. Leedom and Maria Muroy, 219–22. New York: Cambridge House Press, 2007.

Sinnott-Armstrong, Walter. *God? A Debate Between A Christian And An Atheist. William Lane Craig and Walter Sinnott-Armstrong.* Oxford: Oxford University Press, 2004. [Chapter 2 There Is No Good Reason to Believe in God. See. 2. Miracles, See. 36–38]

Skolfield, R. C. E. "Some Observations on the Life of Jesus." In *Truth About The Crucifixion Transcripts from the International Conference on Deliverance of Jesus from the Cross,* 117–28. London: Ascot, 1978.

Category VIII

The New Testament

Chapter 17

The Gospel of Mark

Abbott, Lyman. *An Illustrated Commentary on the Gospels According to Mark and Luke: For Family Use and Reference, and for the Great Body of Christian Workers of All Denominations.* Vol. 2. New York: A. S. Barnes, 1877. [See. 62–65; N.B. Archive.org, Google book, and Haititrust.org]

Achtemeier, Paul J. *Invitation to Mark: A Commentary on the Gospel of Mark with Complete Text from the Jerusalem Bible.* Garden City, NY: Image, 1978. [See. 227–34]

Adamczewski, Bartosz. *The Gospel of Mark: A Hypertextual Commentary.* New York: Peter Lang, 2014. [See. 193–96]

Adams, Jay Edward. *The Gospels of Matthew and Mark.* Woodruff, SC: Timeless Texts, 1999. [See. 328–29]

Akin, Daniel L. *Exalting Jesus in Mark.* Nashville: Holman, 2014. [See. 359–68]

Alexander, Joseph A. *The Gospel According to Mark: Explained.* New York: Charles Scribner, 1859. [See. 432–44; N.B. Archive.org and HathiTrust.]

Allen, Willoughby C., ed. *The Gospel According to Saint Mark: With Introduction, Notes and Map.* New York: Macmillan, 1915. [See. 188–96; N.B. HathiTrust]

Anderson, Hugh. *The Gospel of Mark.* London: Oliphants, 1976. [See. 351–62]

Bacon, Benjamin Wisner. *The Beginnings of the Gospel Story: A Historico-Critical Inquiry into the Sources and Structure of the Gospel According to Mark.* New Haven: Yale University Press, 1909. [See. 229–38; N.B. Archive.org]

Barbieri, Louis. *Mark.* Chicago: Moody, 1995. [See. 367–80]

Barclay, William. *The Gospel of Mark.* Philadelphia: Westminster, 1956. [See. 386–90]

Barnes, Albert. *Notes on the New Testament: Explanatory and Practical.* Vol. 1. *Matthew and Mark.* Edited by Robert Frew. London: Blackie & Son, 1868. [See. 390–94]

Barnett, Albert E. *Disciples to Such A Lord: The Gospel According to Mark.* New York: Women's Division of Christian Service Board of Missions, the Methodist Church, 1957. [See. 158–59]

Barnhouse, Donald Grey. *Mark: The Servant Gospel.* Edited by Susan T. Lutz. Wheaton, IL: Victor, 1988. [Chapter 12 The Resurrection and the Life, See. 145–56]

Beach, Curtis. *The Gospel of Mark: Its Making and Meaning.* New York: Harper, 1959. [Chapter 5 The Dénouement: The Easter Story (15:40–16:8), See. 115—19]

Beavis, Mary Ann. *Mark.* Grand Rapids: Baker Academic, 2011. [See. 239–50; N.B. General overview and discussion of the Appendix]

Bengel, Johann Albrecht, et al. *Gnomon of the New Testament*. Vol. 1. *Notes on St Mark*. Translated by Andrew Robert Fausset. Philadelphia: Smith, English, 1860. [See. 573–77; N.B. Google book]

Bennett, W. H. *The Life of Christ According to St Mark*. London: Hodder & Stoughton, 1907. [See. 270–72; 280–84; N.B. HathiTrust]

Benson, Dennis C. *Dennis Benson's Creative Bible Studies*. Loveland, CO: Group, 1985. [See. 267–69]

Berard, Wayne-Daniel. *When Christians were Jews (that is, now): Recovering the Lost Jewishness of Christianity with the Gospel of Mark*. Cambridge, MA: Cowley, 2006. [Chapter 15 Crucifixion, Resurrection, Redaction, Return, See. 228–33]

Best, Ernest. *Following Jesus: Discipleship in the Gospel of Mark*. Sheffield: JSOT Press, 1981. [Chapter 23 Mark 14.28; 16.7, See. 199–203; Chapter 31 A Note on the Risen Jesus in the Community, See. 237–42]

———. *Mark: The Gospel as Story*. Edinburgh: T&T Clark, 1985. [Chapter 12 The Resurrection, See. 72–78]

Bickersteth, Edward, and John Radford Thomson. *St. Mark*. Vol. 2. The Pulpit Commentary. New York: Funk & Wagnalls, 1913. [See. 346–71]

Binz, Stephen J. *Jesus, the Suffering Servant. Part 2, Mark 9–16*. New London, CT: TwentyThird Publications, 2012. [Lessons 29–30. See. 116–22]

Black, Allen. "Mark." In *The Transforming Word*. Edited by Mark W. Hamilton. Abilene, TX: Abilene Christian University Press, 2009. [See. 786–87]

Black, C. Clifton. *Mark*. Nashville: Abingdon, 2011. [See. 338–62; N.B. Black provides a good overview of the end of Mark.]

Blackburne, Gertrude Mary Ireland. *First Studies in S. Mark*. London: A. R. Mowbray, 1908. [See. 119–22]

Blight, Richard C. *An Exegetical Summary of Mark 9–16*. Dallas: SIL International, 2014. [See. 317–27; N.B. This work is a recommended read.]

Blount, Brian K., and Gary W. Charles. *Preaching Mark in Two Voices*. Louisville: Westminster John Knox, 2002. [See. 255–73; N.B. The authors provide a good discussion about Mark's controversial ending.]

Blunt, A. W. F. *The Gospel According to Saint Mark*. Oxford: Clarendon, 1929. [See. 265–70]

Bobertz, Charles A. *The Gospel of Mark: A Liturgical* Reading. Grand Rapids: Baker Academic, 2016. [Chapter 10 The Passion of Jesus: The Cross and Tomb (15:21–16:8), See. 195–98]

Bock, Darrell L. "The Gospel of Mark." In *Cornerstone Biblical Commentary*. Edited by Philip W. Comfort. Vol. 2. Carol Steam: IL: Tyndale House, 2005. [See. 552–58]

———. *Mark*. New York: Cambridge University Press, 2015. [See. 377–88; N.B. Bock presents a good overview.]

Bolt, Peter. *Jesus' Defeat of Death: Persuading Mark's Early Readers*. Cambridge: Cambridge University Press, 2003. [See. 260–68; N.B. This work is a good read.]

Boomershine, Thomas E. *The Messiah of Peace: A Performance-Criticism Commentary on Mark's Passion-Resurrection Narrative*. Eugene, OR: Cascade, 2015. [Chapter 8 The Resurrection (16:1–8), See. 327–58]

Borg, Marcus J. *Conversations with Scripture: The Gospel of Mark*. Harrisburg, PA: Morehouse, 2009. [See. 107–8]

Boring, M. Eugene. *Mark: A Commentary*. Louisville: Westminster John Knox, 2006. [See. 441–53; N.B. Boring offers a healthy text to read.]

Boring, M. Eugene, and Fred B. Craddock. *The People's New Testament Commentary*. Louisville: Westminster John Knox, 2004. [See. 171–73]

Bourdillon, Francis. *Family Readings: On the Gospel According to St. Mark: Consisting of Short Consecutive Portions, Comprising the Whole Gospel, with a Simple Exposition, for Daily Use in Christian Households*. London: Religious Tract Society, 1882. [See. 262–70; N.B. Google book]

Bowman, John. *The Gospel of Mark: The New Christian Jewish Passover Haggadah*. Leiden: Brill, 1965. [See. 308–13]

Branscomb, Bennett Harvie. *The Gospel of Mark*. New York: Harper & Brothers, 1937. [See. 304–14]

Bratcher, Robert G. *A Translator's Guide to the Gospel of Mark*. London: United Bible Societies, 1981. [See. 218–24; N.B. This work is an important text to read.]

Bratcher, Robert G., and Eugene A. Nida. *A Handbook on the Gospel of Mark*. New York: United Bible Societies, 1961. [See. 501–22; N.B. This work is an important text to read.]

Broadhead, Edwin Keith. *Mark*. Sheffield, England: Sheffield Academic, 2001. [See. 135–38]

———. *Prophet, Son, Messiah: Narrative Form and Function in Mark 14–16*. Sheffield, England: JSOT Press, 1994. [See. 232–96; N.B. This work is a recommended read.]

Broadus, John Albert. *Commentary on the Gospel of Mark*. Philadelphia: American Baptist Publication Society, 1905. [See. 139–48; N.B. Archive.org]

Brooks, James A. *Mark*. Nashville: Broadman, 1991. [See. 268–76; N.B. This work was recommended by D. A. Carson.]

Brower, Kent E. *Mark*. Kansas City, MO: Beacon Hill, 2012. [See. 411–16]

Brown, David. *A Commentary, Critical and Explanatory, on the Old and New Testaments Matthew—Romans*. Vol. 2. New York: Revell, 1878. [See. 94–95; N.B. Archive.org and Google book]

Burdon, Christopher. *Stumbling on God: Faith and Vision in Mark's Gospel*. Grand Rapids: Eerdmans, 1990. [See. 65–74, 97–108]

Burgon, John William. *The Last Twelve Verses of the Gospel According to S. Mark: Vindicated Against Recent Critical Objectors and Established*. Oxford: James Parker, 1871. [N.B. Archive.org, Google book, and Gutenberg.org. This dated source discusses the controversy of the last twelve verses of Mark.]

Burn, John Henry. *A Homiletical Commentary on the Gospel According to St. Mark*. New York: Funk & Wagnalls, 1896. [See. 602–25; N.B. Archive.org. This work is a good read.]

Burns, Cecil. *The Holy Gospel According to Saint Mark*. London: Catholic Truth Society, 1907. [See. 139–45]

Burton, Ernest DeWitt. *Studies in the Gospel According to Mark, for the Use of Classes in Secondary Schools and in the Secondary Division of the Sunday School*. Chicago: University of Chicago Press, 1904. [See. 220–25; N.B. Archive.org and Google book]

Byrne, Brendan. *A Costly Freedom: A Theological Reading of Mark's Gospel*. Collegeville, MN: Liturgical Press, 2008. [See. 251–62; N.B. This book is a healthy read.]

Cadoux, Arthur Temple. *The Sources of the Second Gospel*. New York: Macmillan, 1936. [Chapter 22 The Resurrection, See. 186–87; Chapter 23 The Lost Ending of the Second Gospel, See. 187–92; Note L. Analysis of Mark 15. 21–16. 8, See. 245–50]

Cahill, Michael. *The First Commentary on Mark: An Annotated Translation*. New York: Oxford University Press, 1998. [See. 127–31]

Calvin, John. *Commentary on a Harmony of the Evangelists, Matthew, Mark, and Luke.* Vol. 3. Translated by William Pringle. Edinburgh: Edinburgh Printing Company, 1846. [340–95; N.B. Available online. The author attempts to harmonize to the gospel narratives.]

Card, Michael. *Mark: The Gospel of Passion.* Downers Grove, IL: InterVarsity, 2012. [See. 187–91; Appendix E. The Additional Ending of Mark, See. 201–2]

Carlton, Matthew E. *The Translator's Reference Translation of the Gospel of Mark.* Dallas: SIL International, 2001. [See. 224–31; N.B. Carlton's book is a must to examine.]

Carmody, Timothy R. *Gospel of Mark, The: Question by Question.* New York, Paulist, 2010. [See. 114–18]

Carrington, Philip. *According to Mark: A Running Commentary on the Oldest Gospel.* Cambridge: Cambridge University Press, 1960. [See. 333–45]

———. *The Primitive Christian Calendar: A Study in the Making of the Marcan Gospel.* Cambridge: Cambridge University Press, 1952. [The Supplemental Resurrection and Ascension Section, See. 227–30]

Carter, Warren, and Amy-Jill Levine. *The New Testament: Methods and Meanings.* Nashville: Abingdon, 2013. [See. 50–54]

Chadwick, G. A., and Henry Burton. *The Gospel According to St. Mark.* New York: A. C. Armstrong, 1908. [See. 437–46; N.B. HathiTrust]

Choice Notes on the Gospel of S. Mark: Drawn From Old and New Sources. London: Macmillan, 1869. [See. 500–15; N.B. Google book]

Christian Foundation. *God Revealed in Mark.* US: Xlibris, 2010. [See. 249–56]

Clark, George W. *Notes on the Gospel of Mark: Explanatory and Practical: A Popular Commentary upon a Critical Basis, Especially Designed for Pastors and Sunday Schools. Also a Year in Mark Designed as a Special Study for Bible-Classes.* Philadelphia: American Baptist Publication Society, 1872. [See. 315–28; N.B. Archive.org and HathiTrust]

Clarke, William Newton. *Commentary on the Gospel of Mark.* Philadelphia: American Baptist Publication Society, 1881. [See. 243–95; N.B. Archive.org]

Clowes, J., and Emanuel Swedenborg. *The Gospel According to Mark.* 2nd ed. London: White, 1858. [See. 326–37; N.B. Archive.org]

Cobb, Laurel K. *Mark and Empire: Feminist Reflections.* Maryknoll, NY: Orbis Books, 2013. [See. 167–70]

Cole, R. A. *The Gospel According to St. Mark: An Introduction and Commentary.* Grand Rapids: Eerdmans, 1961. [See. 252–63; N.B. Cole provides a general overall review of the text.]

Committee of Publication for The American Sunday-School Union. *The Consecutive Union Question Book: Mark.* Philadelphia: American Sunday-School Union, 1847. [See. 108–12; N.B. Google book]

Cooper, Rodney L. *Mark: Holman New Testament Commentary.* Nashville: Broadman & Holman, 2000. [Chapter 16 He Is Risen . . . He Is Risen Indeed, See. 271–83]

Cowles, Henry. *Matthew and Mark: With Notes, Critical, Explanatory, and Practical.* New York: D. Appleton, 1881. [See. 351–56; N.B. Archive.org]

Cox, Steven Lynn. *A History and Critique of Scholarship Concerning the Markan Endings.* Lewiston: Mellen Biblical, 1993. [290 pages]

Crane, Steven A. *Marveling with Mark: A Homiletical Commentary on the Second Gospel.* Eugene, OR: Wipf & Stock, 2010. [Chapters 39–41, See. 351–78]

Cranfield, C. E. B. *The Gospel According to Saint Mark: An Introduction and Commentary.* Cambridge: University Press, 1963. [See. 462–76; N.B. Cranfield's text is a recommended read.]

Culpepper, R. Alan. *Mark.* Macon, GA: Smyth & Helwys, 2007. [See. 583–97; N.B. This work is a recommended source to examine.]

Cumming, John. *Sabbath Evening Readings on the New Testament: St. Mark.* Boston: J. P. Jewett, 1855. [Chapter 16 The Resurrection of Jesus, See. 261–68; Chapter 16 cont. The Great Commission, See. 269–88; N.B. Archive.org, Google book, and HathiTrust]

Cunningham, Phillip J. *Mark: The Good News Preached to the Romans.* New York: Paulist, 1995. [See. 155–57]

Dabney, J. P. *Annotations on the New Testament.* Part 1. *The Historical Books.* Cambridge: Hilliard & Brown, 1829. [See. 81; N.B. Google book and HathiTrust]

Danove, Paul L. *The End of Mark's Story: A Methodological Study.* Leiden: Brill, 1993. [8.1 The Textually Grounded, Readerly Guided Response at 16:8, See. 205–10; 8.4. The Textually Grounded Interpretation of the Ending, See. 221–22]

Darby, J. N. *Mark's Gospel.* London: G. Morrish, n.d. [See. 151–55; Author identified as J. N. D.]

Davies, J. *St. Mark's Gospel: The Text Divided into Paragraphs, and Arranged Chronologically, with Notes.* London: George Philip & Son, 1870. [Period 4 From Christ's Resurrection to His Ascension, See. 89–93; N.B. Google book]

Decker, Rodney J. *Mark: A Handbook on the Greek Text.* Waco, TX: Baylor University Press, 2014. [See. 270–91; N.B. This work is recommended to study.]

Deibert, Richard I. *Mark.* Louisville: Geneva Press, 1999. [See. 112–20]

Deppe, Dean B. *Theological Intentions of Mark's Literary Devices: Markan Intercalations, Frames, Allusionary Repetitions, Narrative Surprises, and The Types of Mirroring.* Eugene: OR: Wipf & Stock, 2015. [The Frame around the the Burial and Resurrection Narrative of 15:50–18.8, See. 194–97; 5c3. The Surprise Ending of Mark 16:8, See. 272–91]

Derrett, J. Duncan M. *The Making of Mark: The Scriptural Bases of the Earliest Gospel From the Transfiguration to the Anastasis*, Vol. 2. Shipston-on-Stour: Drinkwater, 1985. [§66 Anastasis: Mk. 16:1–8, See. 278–82; N.B. This is an interesting work to examine.]

Dewey, Joanna, and Elizabeth Struthers Malbon. "Mark." In *Theological Bible Commentary*, edited by Gail R. O'Day and David L. Petersen, 311–24. Louisville: WJK, 2009. [See. 323–24]

Donahue, John R., and Daniel J. Harrington. *The Gospel of Mark.* Collegeville, MN: Liturgical Press, 2002. [See. 457–64]

Dowd, Sharyn Echols. *Reading Mark: A Literary and Theological Commentary on the Second Gospel.* Macon, GA: Smyth & Helwys, 2000. [Epilogue: The Good News Begins Again (16:1–8), See. 167–71]

Driggers, Ira Brent. *Following God through Mark: Theological Tension in the Second Gospel.* Louisville: Westminster John Knox, 2007. [Chapter 5 God at/beyond the Ending (Mark 15:40–16:8), See. 85–98]

Dummelow, J. R., ed. *A Commentary on the Holy Bible.* New York: Macmillan, 1916. [See. 732–33; N.B. Archive.org, 1909]

Earle, Ralph. *The Gospel of Mark.* Grand Rapids: Baker, 1961. [See. 116–18]

———. *Mark: The Gospel of Action.* Chicago: Moody, 1970. [See. 125–26]

Eaton, Robert Ormston (compiler). *The Gospel according to Saint Mark*. London: Burns Oates & Washbourne, 1920. [See. 165-91; N.B. Archive.org]

Eby, Omar. *Markings, My Own: Musings on the Gospel of Mark*. Telford, PA: DreamSeeker, 2003. [See. 227-32]

Edwards, Douglas Allen. *The Defence of the Gospel*. London: Centenary Press, 1946. [See. 103-4]

Edwards, James R. *The Gospel According to Mark*. Grand Rapids: Eerdmans, 2002. [See. 490-508; N.B. Significantly, D. A. Carson rated this work as a best buy.]

English, Donald. *The Message of Mark: The Mystery of Faith*. Leicester, England: Inter-Varsity Press, 1992. [See. 238-43]

English, E. Schuyler. *Studies in the Gospel According to Mark: A Comprehensive Exposition of the Gospel of the Servant-Son of God*. New York: Publication Office "Our Hope" (Arno C. Gaebelein), 1943. [See. 490-505]

Erdman, Charles R. *The Gospel of Mark*. Philadelphia: Westminster, 1917. [See. 196-200; N.B. Archive.org and HathiTrust]

Evans, Craig A. *Mark 8:27–16:20*. Nashville: Nelson, 2001. [See. 522-51; N.B. This work is a must read.]

Exell, Joseph S. *The Biblical Illustrator Mark*. Grand Rapids: Baker, 1953. [See. 688-742; reprint; N.B. This classic, dated text is a must read.]

Farley, Lawrence R. *The Gospel of Mark: The Suffering Servant*. Ben Lomond, CA: Conciliar Press, 2004. [See. 267-74]

Farmer, William R. *The Last Twelve Verses of Mark*. London: Cambridge University Press, 1974. [123 pages; N.B. This commonly cited text is important to examine.]

Farrer, Austin. *St Matthew and St Mark*. 2nd ed. London: Dacre, 1966. [Chapter 9 The Marcan Ending, See. 144-59]

———. *A Study in St. Mark*. London: Dacre, 1951. [See. 172-81]

Fenton, J. C. *Finding the Way Through Mark*. London: Mowbray, 1995. [See. 114-16]

———. *More About Mark*. London: SPCK, 2001. [See. 71-78]

Ferguson, Sinclair B. *Let's Study Mark*. Edinburgh: Banner of Truth Trust, 1999. [72. Resurrection! (16:1-8), See. 269-72; 73. A Later Postscript (16:9-20), See. 273-76]

Flanagan, Patrick J. *The Gospel of Mark Made Easy*. New York: Paulist, 1997. [See. 16-70]

Focant, Camille. *The Gospel According to Mark: A Commentary*. Translated by Leslie R. Keylock. Eugene, OR: Pickwick Publications, 2012. [See. 653-76]

Fogarty, Philip. *Mark*. Blackrock, Dublin: Columba Press, 2011. [See. 91-93]

Ford, James. *The Gospel of St. Mark: Illustrated, Chiefly in the Doctrinal and Moral Sense, from Ancient and Modern Authors*. Joseph Masters: London, 1849. [See. 382-405; N.B. Google book]

France, R. T. *The Gospel of Mark*. New York: Doubleday, 1998. [See. 212-15]

———. *The Gospel of Mark: A Commentary on the Greek Text*. Grand Rapids: Eerdmans, 2002. [See. 670-88; N.B. Significantly, D. A. Carson recommends this work for advanced students.]

———. *Mark*. Peabody, MA: Hendrickson, 2007. [See. 222-25; cover states Dick France]

Francis, Leslie J. *Personality Type and Scripture: Exploring Mark's Gospel*. London: Mowbray, 1997. [See. 148-52]

Francis, Leslie J., and Peter Atkins. *Exploring Mark's Gospel: An Aid for Readers and Preachers Using Year B of the Revised Common Lectionary*. London: Continuum, 2002. [Chapter 34 Mark 16:1-8 Easter, See. 148-52]

Friel, Billie. *Manna from Mark: An Illustrative Pastoral Commentary on the Gospel of Mark*. Nashville: Broadman & Holman, 2004. [See. 186–91]

Fullmer, Paul M. *Resurrection in Mark's Literary-Historical Perspective*. London: T&T Clark, 2007.

Garland, David E. "Mark." In *Matthew–Mark*. Edited by Tremper Longman and David E. Garland. Grand Rapids: Zondervan, 2007. [See. 981–89; N.B. Garland offers a good overview.]

———. *Mark: The NIV Application Commentary*. Grand Rapids: Zondervan, 1996. [See. 610–30; N.B. Another good overview of the text.]

———. *Zondervan Illustrated Bible Backgrounds Commentary Matthew, Mark, Luke*. Edited by Clinton E. Arnold. Vol. 1. Grand Rapids: Zondervan, 2002. [Mark, See. 307–9]

Gavigan, James, and Brian McCarthy, eds. *The Navarre Bible: Saint Mark's Gospel in the Revised Standard Version and New Vulgate with a Commentary By Members of the Faculty of the University of Navarre*. Dublin, Ireland: Four Courts Press, 1999. [See. 196–202]

Geddert, Timothy J. *Mark*. Scottdale, PA: Herald Press, 2001. [See. 390–406]

Gill, John. *Gill's Commentary: Matthew to Acts*. Vol. 6. Grand Rapids: Baker, 1980. [See. 399–403; from the edition published by William Hill, London, 1852–1854; N.B. Available online.]

Girdlestone, Charles. *The New Testament of Our Lord and Saviour Jesus Christ: With a Commentary Consisting of Short Lectures for the Daily Use of Families*. Oxford: J. G. & F. Rivington, 1833. [See. 346–52; N.B. Google book]

Glover, Richard. *A Teachers Commentary on the Gospel of St. Mark*. Sunday School Union: London, 1884. [See. 310–22; N.B. Google book]

Godwin, Johnnie C. *Mark*, Vol. 16. Nashville: Broadman, 1979. [Salvation Symphony (15:42 to 16:20), See. 126–31]

Goodwin, Harvey. *A Commentary on the Gospel of S. Mark*. Cambridge: Deighton, Bell, 1860. [See. 248–61; N.B. Archive.org and Google book]

Gould, Ezra P. *A Critical and Exegetical Commentary on the Gospel of St. Mark*. New York: Scribner's Sons, 1903. [See. 299–309; N.B. Archive.org and Google book]

Grant, Frederick C. *The Earliest Gospel*. New York: Abingdon-Cokesbury, 1943. [See. 128–29, 133, 146–47, 153, 157, 170, 213, 253]

———. *The Gospel of Mark*. New York: Harper & Brothers, 1952. [See. 71–72]

Grant, Frederick W. *The Numerical Bible: The Gospels*. 3rd ed. New York: Loizeuax, 1904. [See. 339–42; N.B. Archive.org]

Green, S. W. *The Gospel According to St. Mark*. London: A. Melrose, 1908. [See. 237–42; N.B. Archive.org]

Groff, Randy, and Linda Neeley, eds. *Translator's Notes on Mark 9–16: Helps on Understanding and Translating the Gospel of Mark*. Dallas: SIL International, 2008.

Grogan, Geoffrey. *Mark*. Fearn, Scotland: Christian Focus, 1995. [See. 210–21]

Gundry, Robert H. *Commentary on the New Testament: Verse-by-Verse Explanations with a Literal Translation*. Peabody, MA: Hendrickson, 2010. [Mark. See. 219–20]

———. *Mark: A Commentary on His Apology for the Cross*. Grand Rapids: Eerdmans, 1993. [See. 988–1021; N.B. Gundry's work is a must read.]

Gutzke, Manford George. Go *Gospel: Daily Devotions and Bible Studies in the Gospel of Mark*. Glendale, CA: G/L Regal, 1968. [See. 170–81]

Guy, Harold A. *The Gospel of Mark*. London: Macmillan, 1968. [See. 185–89]

Haas, John A. W. *Annotations on the Gospel According to St. Mark*. New York: Christian Literature, 1895. [See. 276–83; N.B. Google book]

Hamilton, William. *The Modern Reader's Guide to Mark*. New York: Association Press, 1959. [See. 121–25]

Hare, Douglas R. A. *Mark*. Louisville: Westminster John Knox, 1996. [See. 222–28]

Hargreaves, John. *A Guide to Mark's Gospel*. London: SPCK, 1995. [See. 294–300]

Harrington, Daniel J. *The Gospel According to Mark*. New York: W. H. Sadlier, 1983. [See. 122–24]

Harrington, Wilfrid J. *What Was Mark At? The Gospel of Mark: A Commentary*. Blackrock, Co Dublin: Columba Press, 2008. [See. 153–59]

Hartman, Lars. *Mark for the Nations: A Text-and Reader-Oriented Commentary*. Eugene, OR: Pickwick, 2010. [See. 651–71]

Healy, Mary. *The Gospel of Mark*. Grand Rapids: Baker Academic, 2008. [See. 327–35]

Heil, John Paul. *The Gospel of Mark as a Model for Action: A Reader-Response Commentary*. New York: Paulist, 1992. [See. 345–55]

Hendriksen, William. *New Testament Commentary: Exposition of the Gospel According to Mark*. Grand Rapids: Baker, 1975. [See. 676–93]

Henry, Matthew. *Matthew. Commentary on the Whole Bible: Genesis to Revelation*. Edited by Leslie F. Church. Grand Rapids: Zondervan, 1960. [See. 1406–7; N.B. Available online.]

Hester, David W. *Does Mark 16:9–20 Belong in the New Testament?* Eugene, OR: Wipf & Stock, 2015. [N.B. An interesting work to peruse.]

Hewlett, John. *Commentaries and Annotations on the Holy Scriptures*. Vol. 4. London: Longman, Hurst, Rees, Orme, & Brown, 1816. [See. 179–80; N.B. Google book]

Hiebert, D. Edmond. *The Gospel of Mark: An Expositional Commentary*. Greenville, SC: Bob Jones University Press, 1994. [Part 4: The Resurrection of the Servant, See. 471–89]

———. *Mark: A Portrait of the Servant*. Chicago: Moody, 1974. [See. 407–22]

Hill, John Leonard. *Outline Studies in Mark*. New York: Abingdon-Cokesbury, 1945. [See. 168–81]

Hillard, A. E. *The Gospel According to St. Mark: With Introduction, Notes, and Maps*. London: Rivington, 1897. [See 101–2; N.B. Archive.org]

Hobbs, Herschel H. *An Exposition of the Gospel of Mark*. Grand Rapids: Baker, 1970. [See. 255–61]

Hooker, Morna Dorothy. *The Gospel According to St. Mark*. Peabody, MA: Hendrickson, 1991. [See. 582–94]

Hort, A. F., and Mary Dyson Hort. *St. Mark*. London: Cambridge University Press, 1928. [See. 113–17]

Horton, Robert F. *The Cartoons of St. Mark*. New York: Revell, 1894. [See. 291–306; N.B. Archive.org and HathiTrust]

Huat, Tan Kim. *The Gospel of Mark: A Commentary*. Manila, Philippines: Asia Theological Association, 2011. [See. 374–88]

Hughes, Albert. *Jesus According to* Mark. Philadelphia: American Bible Conference Association, 1936. [Chapter 12 The Servant Crowned At Last, See. 175–89]

Hughes, R. Kent. *Mark: Jesus, Servant and Savior*. Vol. 2. Westchester, IL: Crossway, 1989. [See. 215–20]

Humphrey, Hugh. *"He Is Risen!": A New Reading of Mark's Gospel*. New York: Paulist, 1992. [See. 148—59]

Hunter, A. M. *The Gospel According to Saint Mark*. London: SCM, 1949. [See. 147–53]

Hurtado, Larry W. *Mark*. San Francisco: Harper & Row, 1983. [See. 267–78]

Iersel, Bas M.F. van. *Mark: A Reader-Response Commentary*. Translated by W. H. Bisscheroux. Sheffield, England: Sheffield Academic, 1998. [See. 482–508]

Ironside, H. A. *Expository Notes on the Gospel of Mark*. New York: Loizeaux, 1948. [See. 242–51]

Jacobsen, David Schnasa. *Mark*. Minneapolis: Fortress, 2014. [See. 221–30]

Jacobus, Melancthon Williams. *A Commentary on the Gospel According to Mark*. New York: Macmillan, 1915. [See. 241–47; N.B. Archive.org and Google book]

———. *Notes on the Gospels, Critical and Explanatory. Mark and Luke*. New York: Robert Carter & Brothers, 1856. [See. 107–14; N.B. Google book]

Jarvis, Cynthia A., and E. Johnson, eds. *Feasting on the Gospels: Mark*. Louisville: Westminster John Knox, 2014. [See. 530–41]

Jennings, Theodore W. *The Insurrection of the Crucified: The "Gospel of Mark" as Theological Manifesto*. Chicago: Exploration Press, 2003. [See. 303–11]

Jensen, Irving L. *Mark: A Self-Study Guide*. Chicago: Moody, 1972. [Lesson 14 Resurrection and Final Appearances, See. 117–23]

Jensen, Richard A. *Preaching Mark's Gospel: A Narrative Approach*. Lima, OH: CSS Pub., 1996. [See. 195–200]

Johnson, B. W., and Don DeWelt. *The Gospel of Mark*. Joplin, MO: College Press, 1965. [See. 474–98]

Johnson, Sherman E. *A Commentary on the Gospel According to St. Mark*. London: Black, 1960. [See. 261–68]

Jones, Alexander. *The Gospel According to St. Mark: A Text and Commentary for Students*. New York: Sheed & Ward, 1963. [See. 245–50]

Jones, J. D. *The Gospel According to St Mark 14—End: A Devotional Commentary*. London: Religious Tract Society, 1921. [See. 248–356]

Juel, Donald. *The Gospel of Mark*. Nashville: Abingdon, 1999. [See. 167–76]

Kammrath, Luke. *"Follow Me" The Way of Jesus According to the Gospel of Mark*. Eugene, OR: Resource, 2012. [See. 114–16]

Keegan, Terence J. *A Commentary on the Gospel of Mark*. New York: Paulist, 1981. [See. 178–80]

Keenan, John P. *The Gospel of Mark: A Mahāyāna Reading*. Maryknoll, NY: Orbis Books, 1995. [See. 389–97]

Kelhoffer, James Anthony. *Miracle and Mission: The Authentication of Missionaries and Their Message in the Longer Ending of Mark*. Tübingen: Mohr Siebeck, 2000. [528 pages]

Kelly, William. *An Exposition of the Gospel of Mark . . .* Edited by E. E. Whitfield. Sunbury, PA: Believers Bookshelf, 1971. [See. 217–27; N.B. This exposition of Mark by Kelly was first printed in *The Bible Treasury* for the years 1864–66 (Vols. 5 and 6).]

Kent, Homer Austin. *Studies in the Gospel of Mark*. Winona Lake, IN: BMH, 1981. [Chapter 13 The Resurrection, See. 141–51]

Kernaghan, Ronald J. *Mark*. Downers Grove, IL: InterVarsity, 2007. [See. 338–44]

Kilgallen, John J. *A Brief Commentary on the Gospel of Mark*. New York: Paulist, 1989. [See. 297–311]

Killinger, John. *Hidden Mark: Exploring Christianity's Heretical Gospel*. Macon, GA: Mercer University Press, 2010. [See. 113–23]

———. *His Power In You*. Garden City: NY: Doubleday, 1978. [See. 148–52]

Kingsbury, Jack Dean. *Conflict in Mark: Jesus, Authorities, Disciples*. Minneapolis: Fortress, 1989. [See. 55–58]

Kinsler, F. Ross. *Inductive Study of the Book of Mark: The Gospel of Jesus Christ the Son of God*. South Pasadena, CA: William Carey Library, 1972. [See. 277–83]

Kinukawa, Hisako. *Women and Jesus in Mark: A Japanese Feminist Perspective*. Maryknoll, NY: Orbis Books, 1994. [See. 107–22]

Knapp, Charles. *St. Mark: With Introduction, Maps and Explanatory Notes Especially Intended for the Use of Schools and Theological Students*. London: Murby, 1912. [See. 180–82]

Kuruvilla, Abraham. *Mark: A Theological Commentary for Preachers*. Eugene, OR: Cascade, 2012. [Pericope 25 (15:40–16:8), See. 361–63]

Lachs, Samuel Tobias. *A Rabbinic Commentary on the New Testament: The Gospels of Matthew, Mark, and Luke*. Hoboken, NJ: Ktav, 1987. [See. 441–46]

Lagrange, Marie-Joseph. *The Gospel According to Saint Mark*. Burns, Oates: London, 1930. [See. 174–79]

Lane, William L. *The Gospel According to Mark*. Grand Rapids: Eerdmans, 1974. [See. 582–92; Lane's text is worth examining.]

Lange, Johann Peter. *Theological and Homiletical Commentary on the Gospels of St Matthew and St Mark Specially Designed and Adapted For the Use of Ministers and Students*. Vol. 3. Edinburgh: T&T Clark, 1842. [See. 493–523; N.B. Archive.org]

Lange, Johann Peter, and William G. T. Shedd. *The Gospel according to Mark*. New York: Charles Scribner, 1866. [See. 155–67; N.B. Google book]

Lapide, Cornelius Cornelii à. *The Great Commentary of Cornelius à Lapide: S. Matthew Gospel Chaps 22 to 28. S. Mark's Gospel-Complete*. Translated by Thomas Wimberly Mossman. Vol. 3. London: Hodges, 1887. [See. 442–48; N.B. Archive.org and Google book]

LaVerdiere, Eugene. *The Beginning of the Gospel: Introducing the Gospel According to Mark*. Collegeville, MN: Liturgical Press, 1999. [See. 316–59]

Lenski, R. C. H. *The Interpretation of St. Mark's Gospel*. Minneapolis: Augsburg, 1946. [See. 736–75; N.B. Another recommended text to explore.]

Lightfoot, R. H. *The Gospel Message of St. Mark*. Oxford: Clarendon, 1950. [Chapter 7 St. Mark's Gospel—Complete Or Incomplete?, See. 80–97]

Linden, Philip Van. *The Gospel According to Mark*. Collegeville, MN: Liturgical Press, 1983. [See. 83–85]

———. "Mark." In *Collegeville Bible Commentary*. Edited by Diane Bergant and Robert J. Karris. Collegeville, MN: Liturgical Press, 1989. [See. 934–35]

Lindsay, Thomas Martin. *The Gospel According to St. Mark*. London: T&T Clark, 1883. [See. 237–43; N.B. Archive.org]

Lohse, Eduard. *Mark's Witness to Jesus Christ*. New York: Association Press, 1955. [See. 90–93]

Lowrie, Walter. *Jesus According to St. Mark: An Interpretation of St. Mark's Gospel*. London: Longmans, Green and, 1929. [See. 550–54]

Luce, Harry Kenneth. *St Mark's Gospel In English*. 2nd ed. London: Black, 1931. [See. 75–77]

Luckock, Herbert Mortimer. *Footprints of the Son of Man: As Traced by Saint Mark, Being Eighty Portions for Private Study, Family Reading, and Instructions in Church*. 2nd ed. London: Rivingtons, 1885. [See. 316–41; N.B. Google book]

Lunn, Nicholas P. *The Original Ending of Mark: A New Case for the Authenticity of Mark 16:9–20*. Eugene, OR: Pickwick, 2014. [N.B. Lunn's work should be explored.]

Lyttelton, Edward. *The Gospel of St. Mark*. London: Longmans, Green, 1895. [See. 176–80; N.B. Archive.org]

MacArthur, John. *Mark 9–16*. Chicago: Moody, 2015. [See. 395–418]

———. *The MacArthur Bible Commentary: Unleashing God's Truth, One Verse at a Time*. Nashville: Nelson, 2005. [See. 1260–63]

MacDermott, George Martius. *The Gospel According to St. Mark*. London: Wells, Gardner, Darton, 1907. [See. 106–12; N.B. Archive.org]

MacDonald, Dennis Ronald. *The Gospels and Homer: Imitations of Greek Epic in Mark and Luke-Acts*. Lanham: Rowman & Littlefield, 2015. [See. 247–51; N.B. MacDonald's work is an intriguing contribution to research on Mark.]

———. *The Homeric Epics and the Gospel of Mark*. New Haven: Yale University Press, 2000. [Chapter 21 Tombs at Dawn, See. 162–68; N.B. MacDonald's work is an intriguing contribution to research on Mark.]

MacEvilly, John. *Exposition of the Gospels Consisting of an Analysis of Each Chapter and a Commentary . . . Matthew and Mark*. 4th ed. New York: Benzinger, 1898. [See. 661–72; N.B. Archive.org]

Maclaren, Alexander. *Expositions of Holy Scripture St. Mark Chaps. 9 to 16*. New York: Doran, 1915. [See. 248–311; N.B. Gutenberg.org]

Maclear, G. F., ed. *The Gospel According to St. Mark*. Cambridge: At the University Press, 1885. [See. 209–17 N.B. Archive.org]

Magness, J. Lee. *Sense and Absence: Structure and Suspension in the Ending of Mark's Gospel*. Atlanta: Scholars Press, 1986. [136 pages]

Malbon, Elizabeth Struthers. "Gospel of Mark." In *Women's Bible Commentary*. Edited by Carol A. Newsom, Sharon H. Ringe, and Jacqueline E. Lapsley. Louisville: Westminster John Knox, 2012. [See. 492]

———. *Hearing Mark: A Listener's Guide*. Harrisburg, PA: Trinity Press International, 2002. [See. 98–100]

Malina, Bruce J., and Richard L. Rohrbaugh. *Social Science Commentary on the Synoptic Gospels*. 2nd ed. Minneapolis: Fortress, 2003. [See. 219; N.B. This work is interesting and should be read.]

Mann, C. S. *Mark: A New Translation with Introduction and Commentary*. Garden City, NY: Doubleday, 1986. [See. 659–79]

Mansfield, M. Robert. "Spirit and Gospel." In *Mark*. Peabody, MA: Hendrickson, 1987. [See. 134–40]

Marcus, Joel. *Mark 8–16: A New Translation with Introduction and Commentary*. New Haven: Yale University Press, 2009. [See. 1079–96]

Marshall, F. *The Gospel according to St. Mark* (Revised Version). London: George Gill, 1903. [The Resurrection, See. 91–95; N.B. Archive.org]

Marshall, I. Howard. *St. Mark*. Scripture Union Bible Study Books. Grand Rapids: Eerdmans, 1968. [See. 62–64]

Martin, George. *The Gospel According to Mark: Meaning and Message*. Chicago: Loyola Press, 2005. [See. 448–60]

Martin, Ralph P. *Mark*. Atlanta: John Knox, 1981. [See. 94–96]

Martindale, C. C. *The Gospel According to Saint Mark*. Westminster, MD: Newman Press, 1956. [See. 169–75]

Masterman, J. H. B. *In the Footsteps of the Master: Sermon Outlines on St. Mark's Gospel.* London: Church Family Newspaper, 1922. [See. 117–25]

McBride, Alfred. *To Love and Be Loved by Jesus: Meditation and Commentary on the Gospel of Mark.* Huntington, IN: Our Sunday Visitor, 1992. [See. 141–44]

McCarren, Paul J. *A Simple Guide to Mark.* Lanham: Rowman & Littlefield, 2013. [See. 115–17]

McGarvey, J. W. *Matthew and Mark.* Vol. 1. Cincinnati: Chase & Hall, 1876. [See. 365–82; N.B. HathiTrust]

McGee, J. Venon. *Marching Through Mark.* Pasadena, CA: Thru The Bible Books, 1991. [See. 80–82]

McGowan, James A., and Mal Couch. *The Gospel of Mark: Christ the Servant.* Chattanooga, TN: AMG, 2006. [See. 227–33]

McKenna, David L. *The Communicator's Commentary: Mark.* Waco, TX: Word, 1982. [See. 322–29]

McKenna, Megan. *On Your Mark: Reading Mark in the Shadow of the Cross.* Maryknoll, NY: Orbis Books, 2006. [See. 215–29]

McLaughlin, G. A. *Commentary on the Gospel According to Saint Mark.* Salem, OH: Schmul, 1974. [See. 265–71]

McMillan, Earle. *The Gospel according to Mark.* Austin, TX: Sweet Publishing, 1973. [The Passion Narrative, 14:1–16:8, See. 187–90; Epilogue, 16:9–20, See. 190–92]

Medhurst, Phillip. *A Commentary on the Gospel According to Mark.* Bolton, England: Author, 2010. [See. 91–92; N.B. Archive.org]

Mellon, John C. *Mark as Recovery Story: Alcoholism and the Rhetoric of Gospel Mystery.* Urbana: University of Illinois Press, 1995. [The Empty Tomb, See. 81–86]

Menzies, Allan. *The Earliest Gospel: A Historical Study of the Gospel According to Mark.* London: Macmillan, 1901. [See. 284–97; N.B. Archive.org and Google book]

Meye, Robert P. *Jesus and the Twelve Discipleship and Revelation in Mark's Gospel.* Grand Rapids: Eerdmans, 1968. [Chapter 8 The Historicity of the Twelve, See. 192–209]

Meyer, Heinrich August Wilhelm. *Critical and Exegetical Hand-book to the Gospels of Mark and Luke.* Translated by Robert Ernest Wallis, et al. New York: Funk & Wagnalls, 1884. [See. 196–210; N.B. Archive.org]

Millard, F. L. H. *Handbook to the Gospel According to S. Mark for the Use of Teachers and Students.* London: Rivingtons, 1901. [See. 226–38; N.B. HathiTrust]

Miller, Susan. *Women in Mark's Gospel.* London: T&T Clark, 2004. [Chapter 11 The Women At the Tomb (16.1–8), See. 174–92]

Minear, Paul S. *Saint Mark.* London: SCM, 1963. [See. 132–36]

Minor, Mitzi. *The Power of Mark's Story.* St. Louis, MO: Chalice, 2001. [See. 91–110]

Mitchell, Joan L. *Beyond Fear and Silence: A Feminist-Literary Approach to the Gospel of Mark.* New York: Continuum, 2001. [Chapter 7 Silence, Secrets, and Speech, See. 76–82; Chapter 8 Calling a New Generation, See. 83–98]

Mitton, C. Leslie. *The Gospel According to St. Mark.* London: Epworth, 1957. [See. 135–40]

Moloney, Francis J. *The Gospel of Mark: A Commentary.* Peabody, MA: Hendrickson, 2002. [See. 339–62]

———. *Mark: Storyteller, Interpreter, Evangelist.* Peabody, MA: Hendrickson, 2004. [See. 111–12]

Montague, George T. *Mark, Good News for Hard Times: A Popular Commentary on the Earliest Gospel.* Ann Arbor, MI: Servant, 1981. [See. 185–97]

Montefiore, C. G., and Israel Abrahams. *The Synoptic Gospels*. Vol. 1. London: Macmillan, 1909. [Chapter 16 See. 383–85; Chapter 19 The Empty Tomb, See. 386–90; Chapter 20 Later Version of the Resurrection, See. 390–91; N.B. Archive.org]

Morgan, G. Campbell. *The Gospel According to Mark*. New York: Revell, 1927. [See. 338–50]

Morison, James. *A Practical Commentary on the Gospel According to St. Mark*. London: Hodder & Stoughton, 1884. [See. 441–70; Repr. by Klock & Klock, 1981; N.B. Archive.org and Google book]

———. *Mark's Commentary on the Gospel According to St. Mark*. London: Hamilton, Adams, 1873. [See. 462–92; N.B. Google book]

Moule, C. F. D. *The Gospel According to Mark*. Cambridge: At the University Press, 1965. [See. 130–34]

Moulton, Richard G. *St. Matthew and St. Mark and the General Epistles (Hebrews: St. Peter: St. Jude)*. New York & London: Macmillan, 1898. [See. 168–70; N.B. Google book and HathiTrust]

Mullins, Michael. *The Gospel of Mark: A Commentary*. Blackrock, Co Dublin: Columba Press, 2005. [See. 440–51]

Murray, William D. *The Life and Works of Jesus According to St. Mark*. New York: International Committee of Young Men's Christian Associations, 1906. [Twenty-Sixth Week. His Victory, See. 176–82; N.B. Archive.org and Google book]

Myers, Ched. *Binding the Strong Man: A Political Reading of Mark's Story of Jesus*. Maryknoll, NY: Orbis Books, 1988. [13D. The Discipleship Narrative Resumes (16:1–7), See. 397–99; 13X. "What Is The Meaning of Resurrection?" (16:8), See. 399–404]

Myers, Ched, and Karen Lattea. *Say to This Mountain: Mark's Story of Discipleship*. Maryknoll, NY: Orbis Books, 1996. [Chapter 25 The Third Call to Discipleship Mark 15:47–16:8, See. 205–10]

Nast, Johann William. *A Commentary on the Gospels of Matthew and Mark*. Cincinnati: Poe & Hitchcock, 1864. [Section 24, See. 752–60; N.B. Archive.org]

Navigators, The. *A NavPress Bible Study on the Book of Mark*. Colorado Springs, CO: NavPress, 1995. [See. 161–68]

Nichol, Francis D., ed. *The Seventh-day Adventist Bible Commentary: The Holy Bible with Exegetical and Expository Commentary Matthew to John*. Vol. 5. Washington, DC: Review and Herald, 1956. [See. 657–60]

Nineham, D. E. *The Gospel of St Mark*. Baltimore: Penguin, 1963. [See. 439–53]

Oden, Thomas C., ed. *Ancient Christian Commentary on Scripture: Mark*. Vol. 2. Downers Grove, IL: InterVarsity, 1998. [See. 239–56]

O'Flynn, J. A. "St Mark." In *A Catholic Commentary on Holy Scripture*. Edited by Bernard Orchard. London: Thomas Nelson, 1951. [See. 933–34]

Ogilvie, Lloyd John. *Life Without Limits: The Message of Mark's Gospel*. Waco, TX: Word, 1975. [See. 280–90]

Olivi, Pierre Jean. *Commentary on the Gospel of Mark/ Peter of John Olivi*. Translated by Robert J. Karris. Saint Bonaventure, NY: Franciscan Institute, 2011. [See. 57–61]

O'Malley, William J. *On Your Mark: Reading Scripture Without a Teacher*. Collegeville, MN: Liturgical Press, 2011. [See. 195–200]

Osborne, Grant R. *Mark*. Grand Rapids: Baker, 2014. [See. 316–25]

Owen, John J. *A Commentary, Critical, Expository and Practical, on the Gospels of Matthew and Mark*. New York: Leavitt & Allen, 1864. [See. 496–501; N.B. Archive.org and Google book]

Oyen, Geert van. *Reading the Gospel of Mark as a Novel*. Translated by Leslie R. Keylock. Eugene, OR: Cascade, 2014. [Chapter 9 Epilogue: Where Is Jesus?, See. 132–43]

Painter, John. *Mark's Gospel: Worlds in Conflict*. London: Routledge, 1997. [See. 210–17; N.B. Painter's text should be examined.]

Palmer, David G. *The Markan Matrix: A Literary-Structural Analysis of the Gospel of Mark*. Paisley: Ceridwen Press, 1999. [See. 284–331]

Parker, Joseph. *Preaching Through the Bible*. Vol. 21. *Mark—Luke*. Grand Rapids: Baker, 1959. [See. 195–200]

Paul, Geoffrey J. *The Gospel According to Saint Mark: Introduction and Commentary*. Madras: Published for the Senate of Serampore by the Christian Literature Society, 1957. [See. 262–66]

Peabody, David Barrett et al., eds. *One Gospel from Two: Mark's Use of Matthew and Luke: A Demonstration by the Research Team of the International Institute for Renewal of Gospel Studies*. Harrisburg, PA: Trinity Press International, 2002. [See. 324–43]

Peck, Edson Ruther. *"Jesus Christ, the Lion" and "Seeing with John."* New York: Vantage, 1995. [See. 218–23]

Perkins, Pheme. *The New Interpreter's Bible. General Articles on the New Testament, The Gospel of Matthew, The Gospel of Mark*. Edited by Leander E. Keck. Vol. 8. Nashville: Abingdon, 1995. [See. 726–33]

Perrin, Norman. *Christology and a Modern Pilgrimage: A Discussion with Norman Perrin*. Edited by Hans Dieter Betz. Missoula, MT: Society of Biblical Literature, 1971. [The Reference to "Killing" and to "Rising After Three Days," See. 26–28]

Phillips, Arnold Douglas. *The Son of God: An Explanation of St. Mark's Gospel*. Melbourne: Nelson, 1963. [See. 140–41]

Phillips, J. B. *Peter's Portrait of Jesus: A Commentary on the Gospel of Mark and the Letters of Peter*. London: Collins & World, 1976. [See. 138–41]

Phillips, John. *Exploring the Gospel of Mark: An Expository Commentary*. Grand Rapids: Kregel, 2004. [See. 341–49]

Picirilli, Robert E. *The Gospel of Mark*. Nashville: Randall House, 2003. [See. 428–41]

Placher, William C. *Mark*. Louisville: Westminster John Knox, 2010. [See. 239–48]

Plummer, Alfred. *The Gospel According to St. Mark*. Cambridge: University Press, 1920. [See. 198–205; N.B. Archive.org and HathiTrust]

Plumptre, E. H. *The Gospel According to St. Mark*. Edited by C. J. Ellicott. London: Cassell, 1890. [See. 262–67; N.B. HathiTrust]

Poole, Matthew. *Annotations Upon the Holy Bible Wherein the Sacred Text is Inserted and Various Readings . . .* Vol. 2. [Jeremiah—Rev] London: Printed for Thomas Parkhurst et al., 1700. [See. St. Mark, no pagination; N.B. Google book. Reprinted as *A Commentary on the Holy Bible*. Vol. 3. McLean, VA: MacDonald, 1962. See. 183–84]

Powell, Ivor. *Mark's Superb Gospel*. Grand Rapids: Kregel, 1985. [See. 417–30]

Powery, Emerson B. *Mark*. Nashville: Abingdon, 2011. [Chapter 8 Jesus' Burial and Resurrection, See. 75–81]

Prescott, John Eustace. *Every-Day Scripture Difficulties: Explained and Illustrated: The Gospels According to St. Matthew and St. Mark*. London: Parker, Son, and Bourn, 1863. [See. 299–338]

Rawlinson, A. E. J. *The Gospel According to St. Mark*. London: Methuen, 1925. [See. 242–49; 267–71]

Redlich, Edwin Basil. *St. Mark's Gospel: A Modern Commentary*. London: G. Duckworth, 1948. [See. 179–81]

Reid, Robert Stephen. *Preaching Mark*. St. Louis: Chalice, 1999. [See. 171–75]

Rice, Edwin Wilbur. *Commentary on the Gospel According to Mark, Giving the Texts of the Common Version (1611) and Revised Version (1881) (American Readings and Renderings) with Critical and Expository Notes and Illustrations and Maps and Engravings*. Philadelphia: American Sunday-School Union, 1917. [See. 240–50; N.B. Archive.org]

———. *People's Commentary on the Gospel According to Mark*. Philadelphia: American Sunday-School Union, 1892. [See. 203–13; N.B. Google book]

———. ed. *A Pictorial Commentary on the Gospel according to Mark*. 2nd ed. Philadelphia: American Sunday-School Union, 1881. [See. 203–13; N.B. Archive.org]

Riddle, Matthew B. *The Gospel According to Mark*. New York: Scribner's Sons, 1881. [See. 233–43; N.B. Google book]

Riley, Harold. *The Making of Mark: An Exploration*. Macon, GA: Mercer University Press, 1989. [See. 195–207]

Robertson, A. Irvine. *Lessons on the Gospel of St. Mark*. London: Black, 1904. [Lesson 22 The Lord's Resurrection and Ascension, See. 144–49; N.B. Archive.org]

Robertson, A. T. *Studies In Mark's Gospel*. New York: Doran, 1919. [See. 128–38]

———. *Word Pictures in the New Testament: Vol. 1. The Gospel according to Matthew. The Gospel According to Mark*. New York: Harper & Brothers, 1930. [See. 399–406]

Robinson, Charles S. *Studies in Mark's Gospel*. New York: American Tract Society, 1888. [Chapter 28 Lessons At The Sepulchre, See. 289–99; N.B. Google book]

Robinson, Cyril E. *The Gospel According to St. Mark*. London: Methuen, 1931. [See. 205–14]

Robinson, Theodore H. *St. Mark's Life of Jesus*. London: Student Christian Movement, 1922. [See. 113–30]

Rodd, Cyril S. *The Gospel of Mark*. London: Epworth, 2005. Print. [See. 184–88]

Rowlandson, William Henry. *The Gospel According to S. Mark*. Cambridge: J. Hall, 1869. [See 76–78, 92–95, 102; N.B. Google book]

Ryle, J. C. *Expository Thoughts on the Gospels: For Family and Private Use. St. Mark*. New York: Robert Carter & Brothers, 1858. [See. 353–70; N.B. Archive.org]

Sabin, Marie Noonan. *The Gospel According to Mark*. Collegeville, MN: Liturgical Press, 2006. [See. 151–65]

———. *Reopening the Word: Reading Mark as Theology in the Context of Early Judaism*. Oxford: Oxford University Press, 2002. [See. 196–222]

Sadler, M. F. *The Gospel According to St. Mark*. London: G. Bell, 1913. [See. 405–49; N.B. Archive.org and Google book]

Salmond, S. D. F., ed. *St. Mark*. Edinburgh: T.C. & E.C. Jack, 1922. [See. 434–54]

Sanner, A. Elwood. *The Gospel According to Mark*. [In *Beacon Bible Commentary*. Vol. 6. *Matthew Through Luke*. Kansas City, MO: Beacon Hill, 1964. [Section 8 The Resurrection Mark 16:1–20, See. 412–14]

———. *Mark*. Kansas City: Beacon Hill, 1978. [See. 251–55]

Sawyer, Leicester A. *First Gospel, Being the Gospel According to Mark*. Boston: Walker, Wise, 1864. [See. 166–69; N.B. Archive.org and HathiTrust]

Schmid, Josef. *The Gospel According to Mark*. Translated by Kevin Condon. Cork: Mercier, 1968. [See. 302–8]

Schmidt, Daryl Dean. *The Gospel of Mark*. Sonoma, CA: Polebridge, 1991. [See. 150–55]

Schnackenburg, Rudolf. *The Gospel According to St. Mark.* New York: Crossroad, 1981. [See. 161–69]

Schönborn, Christoph von. *Behold, God's Son! Reflections on the Gospel During the Year of Mark.* San Francisco: Ignatius Press, 2007. [Ascension of Our Lord, The Gospel of Mark 16:15–20, See. 195–97]

Schweizer, Eduard. *The Good News According to Matthew.* Atlanta: John Knox, 1975. [See. 363–79]

Scroggie, W. Graham. *St. Mark.* Grand Rapids: Zondervan, 1979. [See. 278–85]

Serendipity House. *Gospel of Mark Exploring the Life of Jesus.* Littleton, CO: Serendipity House, 1995. [Unit 26, See. 92–95]

Seymour, Jody. *Marking The Gospel. A Devotional Commentary on the Gospel of Mark.* Eugene, OR: Resources Publications, 2011. [Chapter 16 Mark 16:1–8 The Empty Tomb, See. 139–42]

Shiner, Whitney Taylor. *Proclaiming the Gospel: First-Century Performance of Mark.* Harrisburg, PA: Trinity Press International, 2003. [See. 188–89]

Sledd, Andrew. *Saint Mark's Life of Jesus.* Nashville: Cokesbury, 1927. [See. 209–10]

Sloyan, Gerard Stephen. *The Gospel of St. Mark.* Collegeville: Liturgical Press, 1960. [See. 120–22]

Slusser, Dorothy M., and Gerald H. Slusser. *The Jesus of Mark's Gospel.* Philadelphia: Westminster, 1967. [See. 148]

Smith, Chuck. *The Gospel of Mark For Growing Christians.* Old Tappan, NJ: Revell, 1973. [See. Chapter 16]

Smith, David. *Commentary on the Four Gospels.* Vol. 2. *Mark-Luke.* New York: Doubleday, Doran, 1928. [See. 147–50]

Smith, Hamilton. *The Gospel of Mark: An Expository Outline.* Coopies Way: Scripture Truth, 2007. [See. 136–41]

Smith, Sydney F. *The Gospel According to St. Mark.* London: Burns & Oates, 1901. [See 215–24]

Smith, Thomas Joseph. *Good News About Jesus as Told by Mark.* Atlanta: John Knox, 1977. [See. 87–95]

Solly, Henry Shaen. *The Gospel According to Mark: A Study in the Earliest Records of the Life of Jesus.* London: Sunday School Association, 1893. [See. 220–31; N.B. Google book and HathiTrust]

Sproul, R. C. *Mark.* Sanford, FL: Reformation Trust, 2011. [See. 411–24]

Stamm, Raymond T. "The Gospel According to Mark." In *New Testament Commentary A General Introduction to and a Commentary on the Books of the New Testament.* Edited by Herbert C. Alleman. Philadelphia: Muhlenberg Press, 1936. [See. 307–9]

Stein, Robert H. *Mark.* Grand Rapids: Baker Academic, 2008. [See. 727–38]

Stellhorn, F. W. *A Brief Commentary on the Four Gospels: For Study and Devotion: The Gospels.* Vol. 1. Columbus, OH: Lutheran Book Concern, 1891. [See. 170–71]

St. John, Harold. *An Analysis of the Gospel of Mark: The Son of God as Mark Portrayed Him.* London: Pickering & Inglis, 1956. [See. 167–73]

Stock, Augustine. *The Method and Message of Mark.* Wilmington, DE: Glazier, 1989. [A' The Tomb, 15:42–16:8 (Epilogue, 16:1–8), See. 418–39]

Stonehouse, Ned Bernard. *The Witness of Matthew and Mark to Christ.* Philadelphia: Presbyterian Guardian, 1944. [See. 86–118]

Story, Cullen I. K. *The Beginning of the Gospel of Jesus Christ According to Mark: From the Jordan River to the Open Tomb*. US: Xulon, 2004. [See. 278–83]

Strauss, Mark L. *Mark: Zondervan Exegetical Commentary on the New Testament*. Grand Rapids: Zondervan, 2014. [See. 714–31; N.B. This work is a definite read.]

Summers, Thos. O. *Commentary on the Gospels*. Vol. 2. *St. Mark*. Nashville: A. H. Redford, 1872. [See. 209–14; N.B. HathiTrust]

Sumner, John Bird. *A Practical Exposition of the Gospels of St. Matthew and St. Mark: In the Form of Lectures, Intended to Assist the Practice of Domestic Instruction and Devotion*. New York: Protestant Episcopal Press, 1831. [See. 405–8; N.B. Archive.org and Google book]

Swanson, Reuben J., ed. *New Testament Greek Manuscripts: Variant Readings Arranged in Horizontal Lines Against Codex Vaticanus*. Sheffield: Sheffield Academic, 1995. [See. 264–71]

Swartley, Willard M. *Mark: The Way for All Nations*. Scottdale, PA: Herald Press, 1979. [See. 196–205]

Sweat, Laura C. *Theological Role of Paradox in the Gospel of Mark*. Bloomsbury, 2013. [Chapter 8 The Promise Of Paradoxes: The Empty Tomb (16:1–8), See. 159–76]

Sweetland, Dennis M. *Mark: From Death to Life*. Hyde Park, NY: New City Press, 2007. [See. 202–14]

Swete, Henry Barclay. *The Gospel According to St. Mark*. London: Macmillan, 1905. [See. 394–408; N.B. Archive.org]

Swindoll, Charles R. *Insights on Mark*. Carol Stream, IL: Tyndale House, 2016. [See. 394–406]

Tan, Kim Huat. *Mark: A New Covenant Commentary*. Eugene, OR: Cascade, 2015. [The Resurrection of Jesus (16:1–8), See. 221–25]

Taylor, David Bruce. *Mark's Gospel as Literature and History*. London: SCM, 1992. [See. 347–64]

Taylor, J. J. *The Gospel According to Mark*. Nashville: Sunday School Board, Southern Baptist Convention, 1911. [See. 211–21; N.B. Archive.org]

Taylor, Vincent. *The Gospel According to St. Mark*. London: MacMillan, 1959. [See. 602–15; N.B. Taylor's text should be examined.]

Telford, W. R. *Writing on the Gospel of Mark*. Blandford Forum, Dorset, UK: Deo, 2009. [See. 528–33]

Theophylactus, of Orchida, Archbishop of Ochrida. *The Explanation by Blessed Theophylact, Archbishop of Ochrid and Bulgaria of the Holy Gospel According to St. Mark*. House Springs, MO: Chysostom Press, 1992. [See. 140–44]

Thompson, D. A. *The Controversy Concerning the Last Twelve Verses of the Gospel to Mark*. Walton-on-Thames, Surrey, UK: Bible Christian Unity Fellowship, between 1975 and 1979. [53 pages]

Thompson, Ernest Trice. *The Gospel According to Mark and Its Meaning for Today*. Richmond, VA: John Knox, 1954. [See. 238–45]

Thurston, Bonnie Bowman. *Preaching Mark*. Minneapolis: Fortress, 2002. [See. 185–90]

Tolar, William B., and Argile A. Smith. *Hope When Believers Struggle, Adult Leader Guide: Studies in Mark's Gospel*. Nashville: LifeWay Press, 2004. [See. 72–73]

Tolbert, Mary Ann. *Sowing the Gospel: Mark's World in Literary-Historical Perspective*. Minneapolis: Fortress, 1989. [See. 288–99]

———. "Mark." In *Women's Bible Commentary*. Edited by Carol A. Newsome and Sharon H. Ringe. Louisville: Westminster John Knox, 1998. [See. 410]

Trainor, Michael F. *The Quest for Home: The Household in Mark's Community*. Collegeville, MN: Liturgical Press, 2001. [See. 165–74]

Trueblood, Elton. *Confronting Christ*. New York: Harper, 1960. [Chapter 59 Resurrection of Christ, See. 175–77; Chapter 60 The Eternal Christ, See. 178–80]

Turner, C. H. *The Gospel According to St. Mark: Introduction and Commentary*. London: SPCK, 1900. [See. 82–85; N.B. Archive.org]

Turner, David L., and Darrell Bock. *The Gospel of Matthew the Gospel of Mark*. Carol Stream, IL: Tyndale House, 2005. [See. 552–58; N.B. Bock is the commentator on the Gospel of Mark.]

Upton, Bridget Gilfillan. *Hearing Mark's Endings: Listening to Ancient Popular Texts Through Speech Act Theory*. Leiden: Brill, 2006. [Chapter 7 A Speech Act Reading of Mark 16:1–8, See. 125–53; Chapter 8 A Speech Act Reading: The 'Longer Ending,' See. 154–95]

Vernon, Edward Thomson. *The Gospel of St. Mark: A New Translation in Simple English from the Nestlé Greek Text*. New York: Prentice-Hall, 1952. [See. 111–15]

Vines, Jerry. *Exploring the Gospels: Mark*. Neptune, NJ: Loizeaux, 1990. [See. 299–312]

Vos, Howard Frederic. *Mark: Bible Study Commentary*. Grand Rapids, Zondervan, 1983. [Chapter 17 The Resurrection of the Servant, See. 138–42]

Wadhams, Nellie Content Kimberly. *Project Lessons on the Gospel of Mark*. New York: Century, 1925. [See. 295–328]

Waetjen, Herman C. *A Reordering of Power: A Sociopolitical Reading of Mark's Gospel*. Minneapolis: Fortress, 1989. [Witness to the Resurrection and Final Instructions, See. 240–51; N.B. This book should be explored.]

Walton, Robert C. *A Gospel for Martyrs: Saint Mark's Gospel*. London: SCM, 1962. [See. 136–37]

Waterman, Mark M. W. *The Empty Tomb Tradition of Mark: Text, History, and Theological Struggles*. Los Angeles, CA: Agathos, 2006. [See. 1–212; N.B. This work is a must read.]

Watson, Richard, bishop. *An Exposition of the Gospels of St. Matthew and St. Mark, and of Some Other Detached Parts of Holy Scripture*. London: Published by John Mason, 1833. [See. 524–27; N.B. Google book]

Weaver, Walter P. *Mark*. Nashville: Graded Press, 1988. [See. 150–54]

Weber, Gerard P., and Robert L Miller. *Breaking Open the Gospel of Mark*. Cincinnati: St. Anthony Messenger Press, 1992. [Chapter 7 The End of Mark's Story, See. 117–23]

Weeden, Theodore J. *Mark-Traditions In Conflict*. Philadelphia: Fortress, 1971. [Chapter 4 The Empty-Grave Story and Mark's Polemic, See. 101–17; Chapter 5 The Opponents' Resurrection Story and Mark's View of the Exaltation, See. 118–37]

Weidner, Revere Franklin. *Commentary on the Gospel of Mark*. Allentown, PA: T. H. Diehl, 1888. [See. 293–301; N.B. Google book and HathiTrust]

Wessel, Walter W. *The Expositors Bible Commentary: with The New International Version of the Holy Bible (Matthew, Mark, Luke)*. Vol. 8. Grand Rapids: Zondervan, 1984. [See. 785–93]

Wessel, Walter W., and Mark L. Strauss. *Matthew & Mark*. Edited by Tremper Longman and David E. Garland. Grand Rapids: Zondervan, 2010. [See. 981–89]

Whedon, D. D. *A Popular Commentary on the New Testament The Gospels Matthew—Mark*. Vol. 1. London: Hodder & Stoughton, 1874. [See. 415–22; N.B. Google book]

Whiston, Lionel A. *Through Suffering to Victory: Relational Studies in Mark*. Waco, TX: Word, 1976. [Chapter 29 He Is Alive! Mark 16:1–8, See. 150–57]

Wilhelm, Dawn Ottoni. *Preaching the Gospel of Mark: Proclaiming the Power of God*. Louisville: Westminster John Knox, 2008. [See. 260–62]

Williams, Joel F. *Other Followers of Jesus: Minor Characters as Major Figures in Mark's Gospel*. Sheffield, England: JSOT Press, 1994. [See. 191–206]

Williamson, Lamar. *Mark*. Atlanta: John Knox, 1983. [See. 283–88]

Wilson, R. McL. "Mark." In *Peake's Commentary on the Bible*. Edited by Matthew Black. London: Nelson, 1962. [See. 818–19]

Witherington, Ben. *The Gospel of Mark: A Socio-Rhetorical Commentary*. Grand Rapids: Eerdmans, 2001. [See. 411–19; N.B. Witherington's book is a good read.]

Wolff, Richard. *The Gospel According to Mark*. Wheaton, IL: Tyndale House, 1969. [See. 134–37]

Wright, N. T. *New Testament for Everyone*. Lexington: Westminster John Knox, 2001. [See. 221–26]

Wuest, Kenneth Samuel. *Mark in the Greek New Testament for the English Reader*. Grand Rapids: Eerdmans, 1950. [See. 289–93]

Yarbo Collins, Adela. *The Beginning of the Gospel: Probings of Mark in Context*. Minneapolis: Fortress, 1992. [See. 119–48]

———. *Mark: A Commentary*. Edited by Harold W. Attridge. Minneapolis: Fortress, 2007. [See. 779–819; N.B. Yarbo's work is a must read.]

Zanchettin, Leo. *Mark: A Devotional Commentary: Meditations on the Gospel According to St. Mark*. Ijamsville, MD: Word Among Us, 1998. [See. 182–87]

Zenos, Andrew C. *Son of Man: Studies in the Gospel of Mark*. New York: Scribner's Sons, 1914. [The Resurrection of the Son of Man, See. 98–101; N.B. Archive.org]

Chapter 18

The Gospel of Matthew

Abbott, Lyman. *An Illustrated Commentary on the Gospel According to Matthew. For Family Use and Reference*. New York: A.S. Barnes, 1875. [See. 323–33; N.B. Archive.org, Google book, and HathiTrust]

Aborn, Thomas Lintill. *The Lectures of St. Matthew*. Milwaukee, WI: Morehouse, 1932. [See. 583–97]

Adamczewski, Bartosz. *The Gospel of Matthew: A Hypertextual Commentary*. New York: Peter Lang GmbH, 2017. [Section 6.8 Mt 28:1–15; cf. Acts 27:33–28:22, See. 195; Section 6.9 Mt 28:16–20; cf. Acts 28:23–31, See. 196–98]

Adams, Jay Edward. *The Gospels of Matthew and Mark*. Woodruff, SC: Timeless Texts, 1999. [See. 214–16]

Agnostic, An. *A Plain Commentary on the First Gospel by an Agnostic*. London: Williams & Norgate, 1891. [See. 629–52; N.B. Google book]

Albrecht, G. Jerome, and Michael J. Albrecht. *Matthew*. Milwaukee, WI: Northwestern Pub. House, 2000. [See. 434–44]

Albright, William Foxwell, and C. S. Mann. *Matthew*. Garden City, NY: Doubleday, 1971. [See. 357–63]

Alexander, Joseph A. *The Gospel According to Matthew*. New York: Charles Scribner, 1861. [See. 456; N.B. Archive.org.]

Allen, O. Wesley. *Matthew*. Minneapolis: Fortress, 2013. [See. 267–81]

Allen, Willoughby C. *A Critical and Exegetical Commentary on the Gospel According to S. Matthew*. New York: Scribner's Sons, 1907. [See. 300–308; N.B. Archive.org and HathiTrust]

Allison, Dale C. *Matthew: A Shorter Commentary*. London: T&T Clark 2004. [See. 539–49]

———. *The New Moses: A Matthean Typology*. Minneapolis: Fortress, 1993. [Matthew's Conclusion (28:16–20), See. 262–70]

———. *Studies in Matthew: Interpretation Past and Present*. Grand Rapids: Baker Academic, 2005. [See. 107–16]

Anderson, Edward E. *The Gospel According to St. Matthew*. Edinburgh: T&T Clark, 1909. [See. 222–26; N.B. Archive.org]

Anderson, William Angor. *The Gospel of Matthew: Proclaiming the Ministry of Jesus*. Liguori, MO: Liguori Publications, 2012. [Lesson 1 The Passion and Resurrection, See. 153–60]

Aquinas, Thomas, Saint. *Commentary on the Gospel of Matthew, Chapters 13-28*. Translated by Jeremy Holmes. Lander, WY: Aquinas Institute for the Study of Sacred Doctrine, 2013. [See. 455-71]

Argyle, A. W. *The Gospel According to Matthew*. Cambridge: Cambridge University Press, 1963. [See. 219-22]

Augsburger, Myron S. *The Communicator's Commentary: Matthew*. Waco, TX: Word, 1982. [See. 321-33]

Barclay, William. *The Gospel of Matthew:* Vol. 2. (*Chapters 11 to 28*). Louisville: Westminster John Knox, 1975. [See. 414-17]

Barker, William Pierson. *As Matthew Saw the Master*. Westwood, NJ: Revell, 1959. [Chapter 16 Jesus is Alive!, See. 148-54]

Barnes, Albert. *Notes on the New Testament Explanatory and Practical: Matthew and Mark*. Vol. 1. Edited by Robert Frew. London: Blackie & Son, 1868. [See. 317-27; N.B. Google book]

Barton, Bruce B., et al. *Matthew*. Wheaton, IL: Tyndale House, 1996. [See. 569-79]

Basser, Herbert, and Marsha B. Cohen. *Gospel of Matthew and Judaic Traditions*. Leiden: Brill, 2015. [See. 713-21]

Bauer, David R. *The Structure of Matthew's Gospel*. Decatur GA: Almond Press, 1988. [Chapter 6 The Structure of Matthew: Climax With Inclusion, See. 107-28]

Beare, Francis Wright. *The Gospel According to Matthew: Translation, Introduction, and Commentary*. San Francisco: Harper & Row, 1982. [See. 540-46]

Bendoraitis, Kristian A. *Behold the Angels Came and Served Him: A Compositional Analysis of Angels in Matthew*. London: Bloomsbury, 2016. [See. 186-99]

Bengel, Johann Albrecht, Ernest Bengel, and J. C. F. Steudel. *Gnomon of the New Testament: St Matthew*. 3rd ed. Vol. 1. Philadelphia: Smith, English, 1860. [See. 484-90; N.B. Google book]

Benson, Dennis C. *Dennis Benson's Creative Bible Studies*. Loveland, CO: Group, 1985. [See. 189-92]

Bertolini, Dewey M., and Rebecca Bertolini. *The Book of Matthew*. Nashville: Nelson, 2008. [Matthew 27:27-28:20—Crucified, Raised, And Praised, See. 327-31]

Bingham, Rowland V. *Matthew The Publican and His Gospel: Demonstrating the Rightful Place of this Gospel according to Matthew as the Initial Book of the New Covenant of Jesus Christ and a True Gospel of the Grace of God*. Toronto: Evangelical Publishers, 1900? [Chapter 11 The Great Commission to the Church, See. 117-26; N.B. Archive.org]

Blomberg, Craig L. *Matthew*. Nashville: Broadman, 1992. [See. 426-34]

Boice, James Montgomery. *The Gospel of Matthew*. Grand Rapids: Baker, 2006. [See. 637-52]

Boles, H. Leo. *A Commentary on the Gospel According to Matthew*. Nashville: Gospel Advocate, 1936. [See. 552-66]

Boring, M. Eugene, and Fred B. Craddock. *The People's New Testament Commentary*. Louisville: Westminster John Knox, 2004. [See. 101-4]

Boxall, Ian. *Discovering Matthew: Content, Interpretation, Reception*. Grand Rapids: Eerdmans, 2015. [See. 164-74]

Bradley, Marshell Carl. *Matthew: Poet, Historian, Dialectician*. New York: Peter Lang, 2007. [See. 167-69]

Category VIII—The New Testament

Brands, Michael. *The Life and Ministry of Jesus as Enactment of the Great Commission: A New Proposal for Interpreting Matthew 28:16-20 in Light of Matthew's Gospel.* Lewiston, NY: Mellen, 2015.

Bratcher, Robert G. *A Translator's Guide to the Gospel of Matthew.* London: United Bible Societies, 1981. [See. 371–76; N.B. This work must be carefully examined.]

Broadus, John Albert. *Commentary on the Gospel of Matthew.* Valley Forge, PA: American Baptist Publication Society, 1886. [See. 583–97; N.B. Archive.org, Google book, and HathiTrust]

Brown, Jeannine K. *Matthew.* Grand Rapids: Baker, 2015. [Matthew 28:1–20 The Resurrected Jesus Is Vindicated by God and Given All Authority, See. 316–21]

Bruce, F. F. *St. Matthew.* Grand Rapids: Eerdmans, 1970. [See. 93–95]

Bruce, William. *Commentary on the Gospel according to St. Matthew.* Boston: H. H. & T. W. Carter, 1870. [See. 668–82; N.B. HathiTrust]

Bruner, Frederick Dale. *The Churchbook: Matthew 13–28.* Dallas: Word, 1990. [See. 1072–107]

Buchanan, George Wesley. *The Gospel of Matthew.* Lewiston, NY: Mellen, 1996. [See. 1019–33]

Byrne, Brendan. *Lifting the Burden: Reading Matthew's Gospel in the Church Today.* Collegeville, MN: Liturgical Press, 2004. [See. 220–30]

Cabrido, John Arana. *The Portrayal of Jesus in the Gospel of Matthew: A Narrative-Critical and Theological Study.* Translated by Massimo Grilli. Lewiston, NY: Mellen, 2012. [See. 366–417]

Calvin, John. *Commentary on a Harmony of the Evangelists, Matthew, Mark, and Luke.* Vol. 3. Translated by William Pringle. Edinburgh: Edinburgh Printing Company, 1846. [See. 340–95; N.B. Available online.]

Cannon, William Ragsdale. *The Gospel of Matthew.* Nashville: Upper Room, 1983. [Chapter 6 The King of Glory Matthew 26–28, See. 124–27]

Card, Michael. *Matthew: The Gospel of Identity.* Downers Grove, IL: InterVarsity, 2013. [See. 247–52]

Carlston, Charles E., and Craig A. Evans. *From Synagogue to Ecclesia: Matthew's Community at the Crossroads.* Tübingen: Mohr Siebeck, 2014. [Passion and Resurrection, See. 458–75]

Carlton, Matthew E. *Translators Reference Translation of the Gospel of Matthew.* Dallas: SIL International, 2001. [See. 326–32; N.B. This work should be examined.]

Carr, Arthur. *The Gospel According to St. Matthew.* Cambridge: University Press, 1891. [See. 227–31; N.B Archive.org and HathiTrust]

———. *St. Matthew: The Revised Version.* Cambridge: University Press, 1939. [See. 162–64; First edition 1902]

Carson, D. A. *The Expositor's Bible Commentary: Revised Edition Matthew ~ Mark.* Edited by Tremper Longman and David E. Garland. Grand Rapids: Zondervan, 2010. [See. 656–70; N.B. This work should be examined.]

———. *The Expositor's Bible Commentary: With The New International Version of the Holy Bible Matthew, Mark, Luke.* Vol. 8. Grand Rapids: Zondervan, 1984. [Matthew, See. 586–99]

———. *God With Us: Themes from Matthew.* Ventura, CA: Regal, 1985. [Chapter 12 Death and the Death of Death, especially See. 162–64]

Carter, Warren. *Matthew and the Margins: A Sociopolitical and Religious Reading.* Maryknoll, NY: Orbis Books, 2000. [See. 543–54]

———. *Matthew: Storyteller, Interpreter, Evangelist.* Peabody, MA: Hendrickson, 2004. [See. 225]

Carter, Warren, and Amy-Jill Levine. *The New Testament: Methods and Meanings.* Nashville: Abingdon, 2013. [See. 34–35]

Case-Winters, Anna. *Matthew.* Louisville: Westminster John Knox, 2015. [See. 337–48]

Chamblin, J. Knox. *Matthew.* Fearn, Tain: Christian Focus, 2010. [See. 1455–501]

Choice Notes on the Gospel of S. Matthew Drawn from Old and New Sources. London: Macmillan, 1868. [See. 216–27; N.B Google book. The notes are selected from James Ford's "Illustrations of the Four Gospels" i.e., *The Gospel of S. Matthew Illustrated (Chiefly in the Doctrinal and Moral Sense) From Ancient and Modern Authors*]

Chrysostom, John. *The Homilies of S. John Chrysostom, Archbishop of Constantinople, on the Gospel of St. Matthew: Part 3. Hom. 59–90.* London: Walter Smith, 1885. [Homily 90, See. 1167–175; N.B. Google book]

Cladder, Herman J. *In the Fulness of Time: The Gospel of St. Matthew Explained.* Translated by Godfrey J. Schulte. St. Louis: B. Herder, 1925. [The Triumph, See. 375–82]

Clark, George W. *Notes on the Gospel of Matthew: Explanatory and Practical.* New York: Sheldon, 1870. [See. 396–410; N.B. Google book and HathiTrust]

Clarke, Howard W. *The Gospel of Matthew and Its Readers: A Historical Introduction to the First Gospel.* Bloomington, IN: Indiana University Press, 2003. [See. 244–53]

Clowes, J. *The Gospel According to Matthew: Translated from the Original Greek, and Illustrated by Extracts from the Theological Writings of That Eminent Servant of the Lord the Hon. Emanuel Swedenborg, Together with Notes and Observations of the Translator, Annexed to Each Chapter.* Manchester: Joseph Hayward, 1840. [See. 438–48; N.B. Archive.org and Google book]

Clymer, R. Swinburne. *The Illuminated Faith: The Christic Interpretation of the Gospel of St. Matthew.* Allentown, PA: Philosophical Publishing, 1912. [See. 263–67; N.B. Archive.org]

Conder, Eustace R. *A Commentary on St. Matthew's Gospel: Designed for Teachers, Preachers, and Educated English Readers Generally.* London: Elliot Stock, 1866. [See. 476–80]

Cowles, Henry. *Matthew and Mark: With Notes, Critical, Explanatory, and Practical.* New York: D. Appleton, 1881. [See. 257–63]

Cox, George Ernest Pritchard. *The Gospel According to Saint Matthew.* London: SCM, 1952. [See. 165–68]

Crain, Sellers S. *Matthew.* Searcy, AR: Resource Publications, 2010. [Chapter 28 Jesus' Resurrection and His Great Commission, See. 469–89]

Crissey, Clair M. *Layman's Bible Book Commentary: Matthew.* Nashville: Broadman, 1981. [See. 148–50]

Criswell, W. A. *Expository Notes on the Gospel of Matthew.* Grand Rapids: Zondervan, 1961. [See. 159–68]

Cumming, John. *Sabbath Evening Readings on the New Testament: St. Matthew.* Boston: J. P. Jewett, 1855. [See. 388–423; N.B. Archive.org]

Dabney, J. P. *Annotations on the New Testament.* Part 1. Cambridge: Hilliard & Brown, 1829. [See. 59–61; N.B. Google book]

Daniel, Monodeep. *The Gospel According to Matthew*. New Delhi: Centre for Dalit/Subaltern Studies, 2008. [See. 248–52]

Davies, J. (James, of Southport). *St. Matthew's Gospel: The Text Divided into Paragraphs and Arranged Chronologically, with Notes*. London: George Philip & Son, 1872. [See. 246–52; N.B. Google book]

Davies, Margaret. *Matthew*. Sheffield, England: JSOT Press, 1993. [See. 202–9]

Davies, W. D., and Dale C. Allison. *A Critical and Exegetical Commentary on The Gospel According to Saint Matthew*. Edinburgh: T&T Clark, 1997. [See. 659–91; N.B. This book is highly recommended by D. A. Carson.]

Davis, J. *St. Matthew's Gospel Text Divided Into Paragraphs, Arranged Chronologically, With Notes*. London: George Philip & Son, 1872. [See. 246–52; N.B. Google book]

Davis, William Hersey. *Notes on Matthew*. Nashville: Broadman, 1962. [The Resurrection (28:1–20), See. 105–9]

De Ridder, Richard R. *The Dispersion of the People of God: The Covenant Basis of Matthew 28:18-20 Against the Background of Jewish, Pre-Christian Proselyting and Diaspora, and the Apostleship of Jesus Christ*. Kampen, Netherlands: J. H. Kok, 1971. [See. 166–70; 175–96]

Dickson, David. *A Brief Exposition of the Evangel of Jesus Christ According to Matthew*. Edinburgh: Banner of Truth Trust, 1981. [See. 406–16; First published in 1647 "For Ralph Smith at the Sign of the Bible in Cornhill near the Royal Exchange."]

Dietrich, Suzanne de. *The Gospel According to Matthew*. Translated by Donald G. Miller. Richmond, VA: John Knox, 1961. [See. 149–52]

Doriani, Daniel M. *Matthew*. Phillipsburg, NJ: P & R Pub., 2008. [Chapter 97 The Resurrection of Jesus (27:62–28:15), See. 512–23; Chapter 98 The Resurrection: The Facts and Their Significance (28:16–20), See. 524–35]

Dummelow, J. R., ed. *A Commentary on the Holy Bible: Complete in One Volume, with General Articles and Maps*. New York: Macmillan, 1916. [See. 719–21; N.B. Archive.org]

Earle, Ralph. *Beacon Bible Commentary*. Vol. 6. *Matthew Through Luke*. Kansas City, MO: Beacon Hill, 1964. [Section 12 The Resurrection Matthew 28:1–20, See. 252–54]

Edwards, Richard Alan. *Matthew's Narrative Portrait of Disciples: How the Text-Connoted Reader Is Informed*. Harrisburg, PA: Trinity Press International, 1997. [See. 131–40]

———. *Matthew's Story of Jesus*. Philadelphia: Fortress, 1985. [Chapter 6 See. The Son's Obedience Vindicated (28:1–20), See. 92–95]

Ellis, Peter F. *Matthew: His Mind and His Message*. Collegeville, MN: Liturgical Press, 1974. [See. 97–98]

Elsley, Heneage. *Annotations on the Four Gospels and the Acts of the Apostles. Compiled and Abridged for the Use of Students*. Vol. 1. London: Printed for C. & J. Rivington, 1824. [See. 454–63; N.B. Google book]

English, E. Schuyler. *Studies in the Gospel According to Matthew*. New York: Revell, 1935. [See. 216–22]

Erdman, Charles R. *The Gospel of Matthew: An Exposition*. Philadelphia: Westminster, 1948. [See. 221–24]

Evans, Craig A. *Matthew*. New York: Cambridge University Press, 2012. [See. 475–87; N.B. This book should be examined.]

Exell, Joseph S. *The Biblical Illustrator: Matthew*. Grand Rapids: Baker, 1951. [See. 667–88; reprint]

Fenton, J. C. *The Gospel of St. Matthew*. Harmondsworth, UK: Penguin, 1963. [See. 449–53]

Filson, Floyd V. *A Commentary on the Gospel According to St. Matthew*. New York: Harper & Brothers, 1960. [See. 300–306]

Findlay, J. Alexander. *Jesus in the First Gospel*. London: Hodder & Stoughton, 1925. [See. 312–17]

Fogarty, Philip. *Matthew*. Dublin: Columba Press, 2010. [See. 117–25]

Ford, James. *The Gospel of S. Matthew: Illustrated (chiefly in the doctrinal and moral sense) from Ancient and Modern Authors*. London: J. Masters, 1859. [Chapter 28, See. 547–67; N.B. Google book]

Fortna, Robert Tomson. *The Gospel of Matthew: The Scholars Version Annotated with Introduction and Greek Text*. Santa Rosa, CA: Polebridge, 2005. [See. 242–45]

Foulkes, Francis. *A Guide to St Matthew's Gospel*. London: SPCK, 2001. [See. 259–63]

France, R. T. *The Gospel According to Matthew: An Introduction and Commentary*. Leicester: Inter-Varsity Press, 1985. [See. 405–16; N.B. This book was recommended by D. A. Carson as a best buy as the "Pride of the place."]

———. *The Gospel of Matthew*. Vol. 1. Grand Rapids: Eerdmans, 2010. [See. 1095–119]

———. *Matthew: Evangelist and Teacher*. Grand Rapids: Academie, 1989. [The Climax of the Gospel, See. 312–17]

Francis, Leslie J., and Peter Akins. *Exploring Matthew's Gospel: A Guide to the Gospel Readings in the Revised Common Lectionary*. London: Mowbray, 2001. [45. Easter Day, See. 213–17; Trinity Sunday, See. 217–21]

Franzmann, Martin H. *Follow Me: Discipleship According to Saint Matthew*. St. Louis: Concordia, 1961. [See. 215–26]

Fuller, Reginald H. "Matthew." In *Harper's Bible Commentary*. Edited by James L. Mays. San Francisco: Harper & Row, 1988. [See. 981–82]

Gaebelein, Arno Clemens. *The Gospel of Matthew: An Exposition*. Neptune, NJ: Loizeaux, 1961. [See. 611–24; Originally published by Our Hope Press, 1910; N.B. Archive.org, Google book, and HathiTrust]

Gardner, Richard B. *Matthew* (Believers Church Bible Commentary). Scottdale, PA: Herald Press, 1991. [See. 398–405]

Garland, David E. *Reading Matthew: A Literary and Theological Commentary on the First Gospel*. New York: Crossroad, 1993. [See. 262–69]

Gavigan, James, Brian McCarthy, and Thomas McGovern, eds. *The Navarre Bible: Saint Matthew's Gospel in the Revised Standard Version and New Vulgate*. 2nd ed. Dublin, Ireland: Four Courts, 2000. [See. 239–43]

Gibbs, Jeffrey A. *Jerusalem and Parousia: Jesus' Eschatological Discourse in Matthew's Commentary*. St. Louis: Concordia Academic, 2000. [Chapter 5 "To the End and Beyond": The End-Time Character of Jesus' Suffering, Death, and Resurrection, See. 139–66]

Gibson, John Monro. *The Gospel According to St. Matthew*. New York: C. Armstrong, 1890. [See. 433–50; N.B. Archive.org and Google book]

Gill, John. *Gill's Commentary: Matthew to Acts*. Vol. 6. Grand Rapids: Baker, 1980. [See. 300–306; Reprinted from the edition published by William Hill, London, 1852–1854]

Girdlestone, Charles. *The New Testament of Our Lord and Saviour Jesus Christ: With a Commentary Consisting of Short Lectures for the Daily Use of Families*. Vol. 1. Oxford: J. G. & F. Rivington, 1833. [See. 220–24; N.B. Google book]

Glasscock, Ed. *Matthew*. Chicago: Moody, 1997. [See. 547–57]

Glover, Richard. *A Teacher's Commentary on the Gospel of Matthew.* Grand Rapids: Zondervan, 1956. [See. 330–38]

Goldsmith, Martin. *Matthew and Mission: The Gospel Through Jewish Eyes.* Carlisle: Paternoster, 2001. [Chapter 14 The Resurrection and Great Commission, See. 195–207]

González, Justo L. *Three Months with Matthew.* Nashville: Abingdon, 2002. [See. 156–59]

Goodwin, Harvey. *A Commentary on the Gospel of S. Matthew.* Cambridge: Deighton, Bell, 1857. [See. 546–58; N.B. Google book]

Goulder, Michael D. *Midrash and Lection in Matthew: The Speaker's Lectures in Biblical Studies, 1969–71.* London: SPCK, 1974. [See. 448–49]

Grant, Frederick C. *The Gospel of Matthew, Chapter 13:53–28: in the King James Version with Introduction and Critical Notes.* Vol. 2. New York: Harper, 1955. [See. 58–61]

Grant, Frederick W. *The Numerical Bible: The Gospels.* 3rd ed. New York: Loizeuax, 1904. [See. 268–72; N.B. Archive.org]

Graves, Mike, and David M. May. *Preaching Matthew: Interpretation and Proclamation.* St. Louis, MO: Chalice, 2007. [See. 113–43]

Green, F. W. *The Gospel According to Saint Matthew, in the Revised Version.* Oxford: Clarendon, 1936. [See. 256–63]

Green, H. Benedict. *The Gospel According to Matthew in the Revised Standard Version: Introduction and Commentary.* Oxford: University Press, 1975. [See. 229–32]

Green, Michael. *Matthew for Today: A Running Commentary on the Gospel According to St. Matthew.* London: Hodder & Stoughton, 1988. [Chapter 21 The End of the Beginning (Matt. 28), See. 289–301]

———. *The Message of Matthew: The Kingdom of Heaven.* Downers Grove, IL: InterVarsity, 2000. [See. 311–23]

Guideposts Associates. *Matthew: The First Gospel.* Carmel, NY: Guideposts Associates, 1985. [The Resurrection of Jesus (28:1–20), See. 162–65]

Gundry, Robert H. *Commentary on the New Testament: Verse-By-Verse Explanations with a Literal Translation.* Peabody, MA: Hendrickson, 2010. [Matthew, See. 133–36]

———. *Matthew: A Commentary on His Handbook for a Mixed Church Under Persecution.* 2nd ed. Grand Rapids: Eerdmans, 1994. [See. 585–97; N.B. This book should be examined.]

———. *Matthew: A Commentary on His Literary and Theological Art.* Grand Rapids: Eerdmans, 1983. [See. The Resurrection of Jesus as a Demonstration of His Deity and Truthfulness, See. 585–91; The Contrast Between the Deceitfulness of the Jewish Leaders and the Truthfulness of Jesus (Continued) 28:11–15, See. 591–93; The Mission to All the Nations and Related Matthew Themes 28:16–20, See. 593–97]

Gutzke, Manford George. *Plain Talk on Matthew.* Grand Rapids: Zondervan, 1966. [Chapter 23 The Middle Cross and the Empty Tomb, See. 242–45]

Guy, Harold A. *The Gospel of Matthew.* London: Macmillan, 1971. [See. 148–49]

Hagner, Donald A. *Matthew.* Dallas: Word, 1995. [See. 865–89; Hagner's work should be read.]

Hahn, Scott, Curtis Mitch, and Dennis Walters. *The Gospel According to Saint Matthew.* San Francisco: Ignatius Press, 2000. [See. 69–71]

Hamm, Jeffery L. *Turning the Table on Apologetics.* Eugene, OR: Pickwick, 2018. [Empty-Tomb Empiricism, See. 110–18; N.B. The author presents a critical review of Helmut Thielicke's Reformation of Christian Conversation.]

Hamann, Henry Paul. *Chi Rho Commentary on the Gospel According to Matthew*. Adelaide, S. Aust.: Lutheran Pub. House, 1984. [See. 295–302]

Hare, Douglas R. A. *Matthew*. Louisville: John Knox, 1993. [See. 327–35]

Harrington, Daniel J. *The Gospel of Matthew*. Collegeville, MN: Liturgical Press, 1991. [See. 408–17]

———. "Matthew." In *The Collegeville Bible Commentary*. Edited by Dianne Bergant and Robert J. Karris. Collegeville, MN: Liturgical Press, 1989. [See. 902]

———. *Meeting St. Matthew Today: Understanding the Man, His Mission, and His Message*. Chicago: Loyola Press, 2010. [See. 81–83]

Harrington, Wilfrid J. *Reading Matthew for the First Time*. Mahwah, NJ: Paulist, 2014. [See. 138–40]

Harrison, R. L., and Sri Ponnambalam Rámanáthan. *The Gospel of Jesus According to St. Matthew, as Interpreted to R. L. Harrison by the Light of the Godly Experience of Sri Parânanda*. London: Kegan Paul, Trench, Trübner, 1898. [See. 254–56; N.B. Archive.org, Google book, and HathiTrust]

Hauerwas, Stanley. *Matthew*. Grand Rapids: Brazos, 2006. [See. 244–49]

Heil, John Paul. *The Death and Resurrection of Jesus: A Narrative-Critical Reading of Matthew 26–28*. Minneapolis: Fortress, 1991. [See. 97–112]

Henriksen, William. *New Testament Commentary Exposition of the Gospel According to Matthew*. Grand Rapids: Baker, 2007. [See. 987–1003]

Henry, Matthew. *Commentary on the Whole Bible: Genesis to Revelation*. Edited by Leslie F. Church. Grand Rapids: Zondervan, 1961. [See. 1358–63; N.B. biblestudytools.com]

Hewlett, John. *Commentaries and Annotations on the Holy Scriptures*. Vol. 4. London: Longman, Hurst, Rees, Orme, & Brown, 1816. [See. 155–56; N.B. Google book]

Hiliary, Saint, Bishop of Poitiers. *Commentary on Matthew*. Translated by Daniel H. Williams. Washington, DC: Catholic University of American Press, 2013. [See. 292–93]

Hill, David. *New Century Bible: The Gospel of Matthew*. London: Oliphants, 1972. [See. 358–62]

Hindson, Edward, and James Borland, eds. *Gospel of Matthew: The King is Coming*. Chattanooga, TN: AMG, 2007. [See. 245–51]

Hobbs, Herschel H. *Exposition of the Gospel of Matthew*. Grand Rapids: Baker, 1965. [See. 409–22]

Horton, Robert F. *A Devotional Commentary on the Gospel of St. Matthew*. New York: Revell, 1909. [See. 254–58; N.B. Archive.org]

Horton, Stanley M. *New Testament Study Bible: Matthew*. Edited by Thoralf Gilbrant and Ralph W. Harris. Springfield, MO: Complete Biblical Library in cooperation with the Gospel Publishing House, 1989. [See. 645–57]

Hostetler, Jonathan J. *Matthew Explained: The Gospel Story of Jesus as King*. Scottdale, PA: Herald Press, 1988, [Chapter 28 Confirmation of Jesus' Kingship, See. 171–75]

Howard, Fred D. *The Gospel of Matthew: A Study Manual*. Grand Rapids: Baker, 1961. [See. 97–98]

Howell, David B. *Matthew's Inclusive Story: A Study in the Narrative Rhetoric of the First Gospel*. Sheffield, Eng: Sheffield Academic Press, 1990. [See. 157–58; N.B. Useless.]

Hubbard, Benjamin Jerome. *The Matthean Redaction of a Primitive Apostolic Commissioning: An Exegesis of Matthew 28:16–20*. Missoula, MT: Society of Biblical Literature, 1974. [See. 1–187]

Ironside, H. A. *Expository Notes on the Gospel of Matthew*. New York: Loizeaux, 1948. [See. 393–407]

Jackson, Bernard Cecil, and Somerset Corry Lowry. *The Gospel according to St Matthew: A Devotional Commentary*. London: Religious Tract Society, 1931. [N.B. Chapters 15–28 were penned by Lowry. This work is located in the British Library.]

Jacobus, Melancthon W. *Notes on the Gospels: Critical and Explanatory . . . Incorporating with the Notes, on a New Plan, the Most Approved Harmony of the Four Gospels . . . Matthew*. New York: R. Carter, 1848. [Part 9 Our Lord's Resurrection. His Subsequent Appearances, and His Ascension, See. 305–13; N.B. Google book]

Jamieson, Robert, et al. *A Commentary, Critical and Explanatory, on the Old and New Testaments: Matthew—Romans*. Vol. 2. New York: Revell, 1878. [See. 61–64; N.B. Google book]

Jarvis, Cynthia A., and E. Johnson, eds. *Feasting on the Gospels: A Feasting on the Word Commentary. Matthew*, Vol. 2. Chapters 14–28. Louisville: Westminster John Knox, 2013. [See. 356–73]

Jensen, Irving L. *Matthew: A Self-Study Guide*. Chicago: Moody, 1974. [See. 106–10]

Jensen, Richard A. *Preaching Matthew's Gospel: A Narrative Approach*. Lima, OH: C.S.S., 1998. [See. 225–34]

Jerome, Saint. *Commentary on Matthew*. Translated by Thomas P. Scheck. Washington, DC: Catholic University of America Press, 2008. [See. 324–28]

Johnson, Benjamin A. *Matthew, the First Evangelist: A Reader's Commentary on the Gospel According to Matthew*. Lima, OH: C.S.S., 1977. [See. 173–74]

Jones, Alexander. *The Gospel According to St. Matthew: A Text and Commentary for Students*. New York: Sheed & Ward, 1965. [See. 317–21]

———. "St Matthew." In *A Catholic Commentary on Holy Scripture*, edited by Bernard Orchard. London: Thomas Nelson, 1953. [See. 903–4]

Jones, Ivor H. *The Gospel of Matthew*. London: Epworth, 1994. [See. 171–75]

Jones, J. Cynddylan. *Studies in the Gospel According to St. Matthew*. 2nd ed. Toronto: William Briggs, 1881. [See. 305–20; N.B Archive.org]

Kalas, J. Ellsworth. *Matthew*. Nashville: Abingdon, 2010. [Chapter 8 The Death and resurrection of Jesus, See. 83–91]

Kankaanniemi, Matti. *The Guards of the Tomb (Matt 27:62–66 and 28:11–15) Matthew's Apologetic Legend Revisited*. Biskopsgatan, Finland: Åbo Akademi University Press, 2010. [N.B. This is a significant work that must be read.]

Keener, Craig S. *A Commentary on the Gospel of Matthew*. Grand Rapids: Eerdmans, 1999. [See. 697–721; N.B. This text is a definite must read.]

———. *The Gospel of Matthew: A Socio-Rhetorical Commentary*. Grand Rapids: Eerdmans, 2009. [See. 697–721; N.B. Recommended by D. A. Carson for advanced students.]

———. *Matthew*. Downers Grove, IL: InterVarsity, 1997. [See. 393–401]

Kelly, William. *Lectures on the Gospel of Matthew*. New York: Loizeaux, 1911. [See. 509–19; N.B. Archive.org]

Kidder, Daniel P., ed. *Consecutive Questions on the Gospel of Matthew*. New York: Carlton & Phillips, 1855. [Lesson 41 The Resurrection, See. 177–80; N.B. Archive.org]

Kilgallen, John J. *A Brief Commentary on the Gospel of John*. Lewiston, NY: Mellen, 1992. [See. 223–27]

———. *A Sense of His Presence*. Garden City, NY: Doubleday, 1977. [See. 122–25]

Kingsbury, Jack Dean. *Matthew as Story*. Philadelphia: Fortress, 1988. [Chapter 4 The Resurrection of Jesus, See. 90–93]

———. *Matthew*. Philadelphia: Fortress, 1986. [See. 20–23, 25, 30, 32–33, 47, 53, 57, 66–67, 70, 79, 83, 84–85, 99, 101, 105, 108 n. 12, 111 n. 82, 111 n. 71, 112 n. 43, 113 n. 57, 58, 64, 66; 118 n. 85; 119 a. 99]

Kirk, Albert, and Robert E. Obach. *A Commentary on the Gospel of Matthew*. New York: Paulist, 1978. [See. 285–93]

Konradt, Matthias. *Israel, Church, and the Gentiles in the Gospel of Matthew*. Translated by Kathleen Ess. Waco, TX: Baylor University Press, 2014. [Chapter 5 Israel and the Gentiles, See. 265–325]

Kraszewski, Charles S. *The Gospel of Matthew with Patristic Commentaries = To Euangelion Kata Matthaion*. Lewiston: Mellen, 1999. [See. 376–82]

Kunkel, Fritz. *Creation Continues: A Psychological Interpretation of the First Gospel*. New York: Scribner's Sons, 1947. [See. 302–8]

Lachs, Samuel Tobias. *A Rabbinic Commentary on the New Testament: The Gospels of Matthew, Mark, and Luke*. Hoboken, NJ: Ktav, 1987. [See. 441–46. N.B. This work presents a Jewish examination of the text.]

Lange, Johann Peter. *Theological and Homiletical Commentary on the Gospels of St Matthew and St Mark*. Vol. 3. Edinburgh: T&T Clark, 1862. [See. 108–45; N.B. Archive.org]

Lapide, Cornelius Cornelii à. *The Great Commentary of Cornelius à Lapide: S. Matthew Gospel Chaps 22 to 28. S. Mark's Gospel-Complete*. Translated by Thomas Wimberly Mossman. Vol. 3. London: Hodges, 1887. [Chapter 28, See. 326–53; N.B. Google book]

Leavell, Roland Q. *Studies in Matthew: The King and the Kingdom*. Nashville: Convention, 1962. [See. 138–40]

Legg, John. *The King and His Kingdom: The Gospel of Matthew Simply Explained*. Darlington, UK: Evangelical Press, 2004. [See. 525–33]

Lenski, R. C. H. *Interpretation of St. Matthew's Gospel*. Columbus, OH: Lutheran Book Concern, 1932. [See. 1127–61; N.B. This work is a recommended text to examine.]

Levine, Amy-Jill. "Matthew." In *Women's Bible Commentary*, edited by Carol A. Newsom and Sharon H. Ringe. Louisville: Westminster John Knox, 1998. [See. 349; idem. 2012 Revised and Updated Version, See. 477]

Lewis, Jack P. *The Gospel according to Matthew*. Part 2. *13:53–28:20*. Austin, TX: Sweet, 1976. [The Resurrection, 28:1–20, See. 167–174]

Lewis, W. S., and Henry Matthias Booth. *The Preacher's Complete Homiletic Commentary on the Gospel According to St. Matthew*. New York: Funk & Wagnalls, 1910. [See. 642–60; N.B. Archive.org]

Livermore, Abiel Abbot. *The Four Gospels with a Commentary: Matthew*. Vol. 1. New York: James Miller, 1867. [Chapter 28, See. 340–47; N.B. Google book]

Long, Thomas G. *Matthew*. Louisville: Westminster John Knox, 1997. [See. 321–28]

Love, Stuart L. *Jesus and Marginal Women: The Gospel of Matthew in Social-Scientific Perspective*. Eugene, OR: Cascade, 2009. [Chapter 8 Jesus and the Women at the Cross and Tomb, See. 186–219]

Lowry, Somerset Corry, and Bernard Cecil Jackson. *The Gospel According to St. Matthew. Chapters 1–14 by . . . B. C. Jackson . . . Chapters 15–28 by . . . S. C. Lowry*. London: Religious Tract Society, 1931. [Chapter 52 Victory, See. 213–16; Chapter 53 Last Words, See. 217–20; N.B Lowry commented on the significant chapters.]

Luccock, Robert Edward. *Matthew*. Vol. 17. Nashville: Abingdon, 1994. [Chapter 16 Matthew 28, See. 137–42]

———. *Preaching through Matthew: Expository Reflections on the Gospel of Matthew*. Nashville: Abingdon, 1980. [See. 223–30]

Luce, Harry Kenneth. *St Matthew's Gospel in English-Revised Version. Edited with Introduction and Notes for the Use of Schools*. 3rd ed. A&C Black: London, 1938. [See. 112–14]

Luz, Ulrich. *Matthew 21-28: A Commentary*. Edited by Helmut Koester. Translated by James E. Crouch. Minneapolis: Fortress, 2005. [See. 590–637; N.B. This text is worth examining.]

———. *The Theology of the Gospel of Matthew*. Cambridge: Cambridge University Press, 1995. [Chapter 8 Passion and Easter (Matthew 26—28), See. 133–141]

Maas, A. J. *The Gospel According to Saint Matthew: With an Explanatory and Critical Commentary*. St. Louis: Herder, 1898. [See. 310–17; N.B. Archive.org]

MacArthur, John. *The MacArthur Bible Commentary*. Nashville: Nelson, 2005. [See. 1184]

———. *Matthew 24-28*. Chicago: Moody, 1989. [See. 303–47]

Macaulay, J. C. *Behold Your King*. Chicago: Moody, 1982. [Part 4 The King In His Power, See. 225–30]

MacDonald, William. *The Gospel of Matthew: Behold Your King*. Kansas City, KS: Walterick, 1974. [See. 319–24]

MacEvilly, John. *An Exposition of the Gospels Consisting of an Analysis of Each Chapter and a Commentary . . . Matthew and Mark*. 4th ed. New York: Benzinger, 1898. [See. 579–96; N.B. Archive.org]

Maclaren, Alexander. *The Gospel of St. Matthew*. Vol. 2. New York: A. C. Armstrong, 1894. [See. 200–20; N.B. Archive.org]

MacPhail, J. R. *The Gospel According to St Matthew*. Madras: Christian Literature Society, 1956. [Essay 11 The Resurrection, See. 280–84]

Maldonatus, Joannes. *A Commentary on the Holy Gospels . . . Translated . . . S. Matthew's Gospel, Chapters 15 to the End*. 2nd ed. Translated by George John Davie. Vol. 2. London: John Hodges, 1888. [See. 581–648; N.B. Archive.org]

Malina, Bruce J., and Richard L. Rohrbaugh. *Social Science Commentary on the Synoptic Gospels*. Minneapolis: Fortress, 1992. [See. 140–42]

———. *Social-Science Commentary on the Synoptic Gospels*, 2nd ed. Minneapolis: Fortress, 2003. [See. 322–24]

Marohi, Matthew J. *Unexpected New Life: Reading the Gospel of Matthew*. Eugene, OR: Cascade, 2012. [Chapter 8 Great Commission: The Continuing Story of Unexpected New Life, See. 79–86]

Marshall, F. *The Gospel of St. Matthew*. London: George Gill, 1900? [See. 99–107]

Martin, George. *Bringing the Gospel of Matthew to Life: Insight and Inspiration*. Ijamsville, MD: Word Among Us Press, 2008. [See. 657–69]

Martindale, C. C. *The Gospel According to Saint Matthew: With an Introduction and Commentary*. London: Longmans, Green, 1957. [See. 218–22]

McBride, Alfred. *The Kingdom and the Glory: The Gospel of St. Matthew*. New York: Arena Lettres, 1977. [See. 174–79]

McCarren, Paul J. *A Simple Guide to Mark*. Lanham: Rowman & Littlefield, 2013. [See. 115–17]

McCumber, William E. *Matthew*. Kansas City, MO: Beacon Hill, 1975. [See. 218–23]

McGarvey, J. W. Vol. 1. *Matthew and Mark*. Cincinnati: Chase & Hall, 1876. [See. 249–55; N.B. HathiTrust]

McKenna, Megan. *Matthew: The Book of Mercy*. Hyde Park, NY: New City Press, 2007. [See. 182–96]

McKenzie, Alyce M. *Matthew*. Louisville: Geneva Press, 1998. [See. 95–99]

McLaughlin, G. A. *Commentary on the Gospel According to Saint Matthew*. Boston: Christian Witness, 1909. [See. 387–92; Reprinted by Schmul Publishers, 1974; N.B. Archive.org]

McNeile, A. H. *The Gospel According to St. Matthew*. London: Macmillan, 1928. [See. 429–39; N.B. The author's name is also spelled M'Neile.]

McTernan, Oliver J. *A Call to Witness: Reflections on the Gospel of St Matthew*. Glasgow: William Collins Sons, 1988. [Chapter 13 Mission Made Possible A Reflection on Matt 28:16–20, See. 96–102]

Meier, John P. *Matthew*. Wilmington, DE: Michael Glazier, 1980. [See. 359–74]

———. *The Vision of Matthew: Christ, Church, and Morality in the First Gospel*. New York: Crossroad, 1991. [See. 35–39; 207–19]

Meyer, Heinrich August Wilhelm. *Critical and Exegetical Hand-Book to the Gospel of Matthew*. Translated by Peter Christie. Edited by William Stewart. Vol. 2. Edinburgh: T&T Clark, 1881. [See. 287–308; N.B. Archive.org]

Micklem, Philip Arthur. *St. Matthew*. London: Methuen, 1917. [See. 279–87; N.B. HathiTrust]

Miller, Adam William. *The Gospel of Matthew: An Exposition*. Anderson, IN: Warner, 1944. [See. 259–62]

Miller, Ron. *The Hidden Gospel of Matthew: Annotated & Explained*. Woodstock, VT: SkyLight Paths, 2004. [See. 221–25]

Minear, Paul S. *The Good News According to Matthew: A Training Manual for Prophets*. St. Louis: Chalice, 2000. [Chapter 9 Sheep Becoming Shepherds, See. 113–26]

———. *Matthew, the Teacher's Gospel*. New York: Pilgrim Press, 1982. [Final Mandate (27:55—28:20), See. 138–42; Supplement 5: The Covenant and Great Commission, See. 184–89]

Mitch, Curtis, and Edward P. Sri. *The Gospel of Matthew*. Grand Rapids: Baker Academic, 2010. [See. 365–73]

Montague, George T. *Companion God: A Cross-Cultural Commentary on the Gospel of Matthew*. New York: Paulist, 2010. [See. 353–60]

Montefiore, C. G., ed. *The Synoptic Gospels*. Vol. 2. London: Macmillan, 1909. [Chapter 24, The Empty Grave, See. 1087–99; N.B. Archive.org and HathiTrust]

Morgan, G. Campbell. *The Gospel According to Matthew*. Old Tappan, NJ: Revell, 1929. [See. 319–21]

Morison, James. *A Practical Commentary on the Gospel According to St. Matthew*. 9th ed. London: Hodder & Stoughton, 1895. [See. 612–26; N.B. Archive.org]

Morison, John Hopkins. *Disquisitions and Notes on the Gospels. Matthew*, 2nd ed. Boston: Walker, Wise, and Co., 1861. [See. 503–36; N.B. Archive.org]

Morris, Leon. *The Gospel According to Matthew*. Grand Rapids: Eerdmans, 1992. [See. 733–50]

———. *The Story of the Cross: A Devotional Study of St. Matthew*, Chapters 26–28. Grand Rapids: Eerdmans, 1957. [See. 112–28]

Moulton, Richard G. *St. Matthew and St. Mark and the General Epistles (Hebrews: St. Peter: St. Jude)*. New York & London: Macmillan, 1898. [See. 107-9; N.B. Google book]

Mounce, Robert H. *Matthew*. Peabody, MA: Hendrickson, 1991. [Chapter 28 The Resurrection, See. 264-69]

———. *Matthew: A Good News Commentary*. San Francisco: Harper & Row, 1985. [See. 273-78]

Mullins, Michael. *The Gospel of Matthew: A Commentary*. Dublin: Columba Press, 2007. [See. 613-20]

Mullooparambil, Sebastian. *Macrostructure of Matthew's Gospel*. Bangalore: Dharmaram, 2011. [4.5 The Second Main Section (21:12-28:15), See. 152-55; 4.6 The Concluding Part (28:16-20), See. 156-59]

Nast, Johann Wilhelm. *A Commentary on the Gospels of Matthew and Mark, Critical, Doctrinal, and Homiletical . . .* Poe & Hitchcock: Cincinnati, 1864. [See. 626-52; N.B. Archive.org]

Newman, Barclay Moon, and Philip C. Stine. *A Handbook on the Gospel of Matthew*. New York: United Bible Societies, 1992. [See. 875-87]

Nichol, Francis D., ed. *Seventh-day Adventist Bible Commentary: The Holy Bible with Exegetical and Expository Comment*. Vol. 5. Washington, DC: Review and Herald, 1956. [See. 553-60]

Nicholson, Edward Williams Byron. *New Commentary on the Gospel according to Matthew*. Vol. 1. London: C. Kegan Paul, 1881. [See. 239-41; N.B. Archive.org]

Nolland, John. *The Gospel of Matthew: A Commentary on the Greek Text*. Grand Rapid: Eerdmans, 2005. [See. 1244-72; N.B. This is a solid text to examine.]

O'Donnell, Douglas Sean. *Matthew: All Authority in Heaven and on Earth*. Wheaton, IL: Crossway, 2013. [Chapter 88 Behold Him That was Crucified (27:62-28:15), See. 894-904; Chapter 89 Operation Immanuel, (28:16-20), See. 905-19]

Offerman, Henry. "The Gospel According to Matthew." In *New Testament Commentary: A General Introduction to and a Commentary on the Books of the New Testament*. Edited by Herbert C. Alleman. Philadelphia: Muhlenberg Press, 1936. [See. 236-37]

O'Grady, John F. *The Gospel of Matthew: Question By Question*. New York: Paulist, 2007. [The Resurrection, See. 235-37; The Finale, 28:16-20, See. 239-41]

Osborne, Grant R. *Matthew*. Grand Rapids: Zondervan, 2010. [See. 1061-85; N.B. This is a book that should be examined.]

Overman, J. Andrew. *Church and Community in Crisis: The Gospel According to Matthew*. Valley Forge, PA: Trinity Press International, 1996. [See. 393-412]

Owen, John J. *A Commentary, Critical, Expository, and Practical, on the Gospels of Matthew and Mark: For the Use of Ministers, Theological Students, Private Christians, Bible Classes, and Sabbath Schools*. New York: Leavitt & Allen, 1864. [See. 405-15; N.B. Archive.org]

Pagola, José Antonio. *The Way Opened Up by Jesus: A Commentary on the Gospel of Matthew*. Miami: Convivium Press, 2012. [Chapter 41 Raised by God, See. 245-49; Chapter 42 I Am with You, See. 250-55]

Parambi, Baby. *The Discipleship of the Women in the Gospel According to Matthew: An Exegetical Theological Study of Matt. 27:51b-56, 57-61 and 28:1-10*. Rome: Pontificia Università Gregoriana, 2003. [See. 184-96]

Parker, Joseph. *A Homiletic Analysis of the Gospel by Matthew: With an Introductory Essay on the Life of Jesus Christ* ... Vol. 1. London: Hodder & Stoughton, 1870. [See. 328–33; N.B. Archive.org]

Parker, Pierson. *Good News in Matthew: Matthew in To-days English Version*. Glasgow: Collins, 1976. [Matthew 28, See. 281–83]

Patte, Daniel. *The Gospel According to Matthew: A Structural Commentary on Matthew's Faith*. Philadelphia: Fortress, 1987. [See. 392–405]

Patterson, Bob E. *Discovering Matthew: The Guideposts Home Bible Study Program*. Carmel, NY: Guideposts, 1985. [The Resurrection of Jesus (28:1–20), See. 162–65]

Peloubet, F. N. *Suggestive Illustrations on the Gospel According to Matthew; Illustrations from All Sources, Picturesque Greek Words, Library References to Further Illustrations, Photographs of Celebrated Pictures Referred To, for the Use of Leaders of Prayer-meetings, Christian Endeavorers, Sunday-school Teachers, Pastors*. New York: E. R. Herrick, 1897. [See. 450–63; N.B. Archive.org]

———. *The Teachers Commentary on the Gospel according to St. Matthew*. New York: Oxford University Press, 1901. [See. 360–69; N.B. Archive.org and HathiTrust]

Perlewitz, Miriam. *The Gospel of Matthew*. Wilmington, DE: M. Glazier, 1989. [Chapter 10, See. 17–179]

Pettingill, William L. *Simple Studies in Matthew*. 5th ed. Philadelphia: Philadelphia School of the Bible, 1910. [See. 316–30]

Phillips, John. *Exploring the Gospels: Matthew*. Neptune, NJ: Loizeaux, 1999. [See. 535–50]

Platt, David. *Exalting Jesus in Matthew*. Nashville: B&H, 2014. [See. 355–79]

Plummer, Alfred. *An Exegetical Commentary on the Gospel According to S. Matthew*, 2nd ed. London: E. Stock, 1910. [See. 411–39; N.B. Archive.org and HathiTrust]

Plumptre, E. H. *The Gospel According to St. Matthew, St. Mark, and St. Luke*, 2nd ed. Vol. 1. London: Cassell Petter & Galpin, 188? [See. 180–83; N.B. HathiTrust; *The Gospel According to St. Matthew*, 1880. See. 419–26]

Poole, Matthew. *Annotations Upon the Holy Bible Wherein the Sacred Text is Inserted and Various Readings* ... Vol. 2. [Jeremiah—Rev] London: Printed for Thomas Parkhurst et al., 1700. See. St. Matthew, no pagination; N.B. Google book. Reprinted as *A Commentary on the Holy Bible*. Vol. 3. McLean, VA: MacDonald, 1962. See. 144–47]

Poovey, W. A. *The Power of the Kingdom: Meditations on Matthew*. Minneapolis: Augsburg, 1974. [The Power of the Kingdom, See. 126–28]

Porteus, Beilby. *Lectures on the Gospel of St. Matthew; Delivered in the Parish Church of St. James, Westminster, in the Years 1798, 1799, 1800, and 1801*. Philadelphia: E. Littell, 1829. [See. 320–34; N.B. Archive.org]

Powell, Ivor. *Matthew's Majestic Gospel*. Grand Rapids: Kregel, 1987. [See. 514–24]

Powell, J. Enoch. *The Evolution of the Gospel: A New Translation of the First Gospel with Commentary and Introductory Essay*. New Haven: Yale University, 1994. [See. 218–21]

Pregeant, Russell. *Matthew*. St. Louis: Chalice, 2004. [See. 184–201]

Prescott, John Eustace. *Every-Day Scripture Difficulties: Explained and Illustrated: The Gospels According to St. Matthew and St. Mark*. London: Parker, Son, and Bourn, 1863. [See. 299–306]

Price, Charles. *Matthew*. Fearn: Christian Focus, 1998. [See. 323–30]

Proctor, John. *Matthew*. Peabody, MA: Hendrickson, 2007. [See. 240–45]

Racine, Jean-François. *The Text of Matthew in the Writings of Basil of Caesarea*. Atlanta: Society of Biblical Literature, 2004. [See. 235–37]

Reeves, Keith Howard. *The Resurrection Narrative in Matthew: A Literary-Critical Examination.* Lewiston: Mellen Biblical Press, 1993. [See. 52–81; N.B. Additional material is scattered throughout the text.]

Reid, Barbara E. *The Gospel According to Matthew.* Collegeville, MN: Liturgical Press, 2005. [See. 143–47]

Rice, Edwin Wilbur. *People's Commentary on the Gospel According to Matthew: Containing the Common Version, 1611, and the Revised Version, 1881 (American Readings and Renderings): With Critical, Exegetical and Applicative Notes, and Illustrations Drawn from Life and Thought in the East.* 3rd ed. Philadelphia: American Sunday-School Union, 1893. [See. 304–12; N.B. Archive.org]

Rice, John R. *The King of the Jews: A Verse by Verse Commentary on the Gospel According to Matthew.* Murfreesboro, TN: Sword of the Lord, 1955. [See. 488–504]

Richards, Larry. *The Servant King: The Life of Jesus on Earth: Studies in Matthew.* Elgin, IL: David C. Cook, 1976. [See. 265–67]

Rickaby, Joseph. *The Gospel According to St. Matthew.* London: Burns Oates & Washbourne, 1899. [See. 244–50]

Ridderbos, Herman N. *Matthew.* Grand Rapids: Regency, 1987. [See. 544–56]

———. *Matthew's Witness to Jesus Christ: the King and the Kingdom.* New York: Association Press, 1958. [Chapter 12 The Risen Christ, See. 92–94]

Rigaux, Béda. *The Testimony of St. Matthew.* Translated by Paul Joseph Oligny. Chicago: Franciscan Herald Press, 1968. [The Resurrection (28), See. 104–8]

Ritchie, Arthur. *Spiritual Studies in St. Matthew's Gospel.* Vol. 2. New York: Longmans, Green, 1902. [See. 366–74]

Robertson, Arthur K. *Matthew.* Chicago: Moody, 1983. [See. 161–66]

Robertson, A. T. *Commentary on the Gospel according to Matthew.* New York: Macmillan, 1911. [Chapter 11 The Triumph of Jesus, 28:1–20, See. 280–86; N.B. Google book]

———. *Word Pictures in the New Testament*: Vol. 1. *Matthew and Mark.* Nashville: Broadman Press, 1930. [See. 240–46]

Robinson, Theodore H. *The Gospel of Matthew.* New York: Harper, 1927. [See. 233–37]

Ross, Mark E. *Let's Study Matthew.* Edinburgh: Banner of Truth Trust, 2009. [The Third Day He Rose Again from the Dead (27:62–28:15), See. 289–93; 70. The All-Embracing Gospel (28:16–20), See. 294–97]

Ryle, J. C. *Expository Thoughts on the Gospels For Family and Private Use St. Matthew.* New York: Robert Carter, 1860. [See. 402–13; N.B. Archive.org]

Sabourin, Leopold. *The Gospel According to St. Matthew.* Bombay: St. Paul Publications, 1982. [See. 925–39]

Sadler, M. F. *The Gospel According to Saint Matthew: With Notes Critical and Practical.* London: G. Bell, 1890. [See. 465–94; N.B. Archive.org and Google book]

Sanders, J. Oswald. *Bible Studies in Matthews Gospel.* Grand Rapids: Zondervan, 1975. [See. 152–53; N.B. This book was formerly published as *100 Days With Matthew*, 1973.]

Saunders, Stanley P. *Preaching the Gospel of Matthew: Proclaiming God's Presence.* Louisville: Westminster John Knox, 2010. [See. 294–302]

Saunders, Stanley P., and David L. Petersen. "Matthew." In *Theological Bible Commentary.* Edited by Gail R. O'Day. Louisville: Westminster John Knox, 2009. [See. 309–10]

Schaberg, Jane. *The Father, the Son, and the Holy Spirit: The Triadic Phrase in Matthew 28:19b.* Chico, CA: Scholars Press, 1982. [N.B. This work was originally part of Schaberg's dissertation. It is a recommended read.]

Schaeffer, Charles Frederick. *Annotations on the Gospel According to St. Matthew: Part 2. Matthew 16 —28.* New York: Scribner's Sons, 1911. [See. 401–16; N.B. Google book]

Scaer, David P. *Discourses in Matthew: Jesus Teaches the Church.* Saint Louis: Concordia Publishing House, 2004. [Chapter 13 The Death and Resurrection as Apocalyptic Conclusion to the Catechesis, See. 395–408]

Schaff, Philip. *The Gospel According to Matthew.* New York: Scribner's Sons, 1882. [See 405–16; N.B. Google book]

Schmidt, Dan. *Follow the Leader.* Wheaton, IL: Victor, 1986. [See. 131–46]

Schnackenburg, Rudolf. *The Gospel of Matthew.* Grand Rapids: Eerdmans, 2002. [See. 293–300]

Schweizer, Eduard. *The Good News According to Matthew.* Atlanta: John Knox, 1975. [See. 521–36]

Scott, John P. *The Four Gospels Esoterically Interpreted.* Oceanside, CA: Langford Press, 1937. [See. 132–34; N.B. HathiTrust]

Scratton, George. *A Commentary on the Gospel According to St. Matthew.* London: Wyman & Sons, 1874. [See. 375–84; N.B. Archive.org and Google book]

Senior, Donald. *The Gospel of Matthew.* Nashville: Abingdon, 1997. [See. 173–77]

———. *Invitation to Matthew: A Commentary on the Gospel of Matthew with Complete Text from the Jerusalem Bible.* Garden City, NY: Image, 1977. [See. 270–76]

———. *Matthew.* Nashville: Abingdon, 1998. [See. 339–49]

Simcox, Carroll E. *The First Gospel: Its Meaning and Message.* Greenwich, CT: Seabury, 1963. [See. 306–11]

Simonetti, Manlio, ed. *Matthew 14-28.* Vol. 1b. Downers Grove, IL: InterVarsity, 2002. [See. 303–14]

Simpson, A. B. *The Gospel of Matthew.* Harrisburg, PA: Christian Publishing, 1886. [See. 297–339]

Slater, W. F. *St. Matthew: Introduction.* Edited by G. H. Box. New York: H. Frowde, Oxford University Press, 1922. [See. 354–57]

———. *St. Matthew: Introduction: Authorized Version: Revised Version with Notes, Index and Map.* Edinburgh: T.C. & E.C. Jack, 1901. [See. 324–29]

Smith, B. T. D. *The Gospel according to S. Matthew* [Cambridge Greek Testament]. Cambridge: Cambridge University Press, 1927. [The Discovery of the Empty Tomb, See. 211–15]

Smith, Chuck. *The Gospel of Matthew for Growing Christians.* Old Tappan, NJ: Revell, 1973. [See. 157–58]

Smith, David. *Commentary on the Four Gospels.* Garden City, NY: Doubleday, Doran, 1928. [See. 480–85]

———. *The Gospel According to St. Matthew.* London, E. C: Andrew Melrose, 1908. [See. 246–50; N.B. Google book]

Smith, Robert H. *Matthew.* Minneapolis, MN: Augsburg, 1989. [See. 331–41]

Spong, John Shelby. *Biblical Literalism: A Gentile Heresy: A Journey into a New Christianity Through the Doorway of Matthew's Gospel.* New York: HarperOne, 2016. [Part 10 Matthew's Easter Story: A New Perspective, See. 345–58; N.B. This critical review of the resurrection must be read. It details numerous contradictions and omissions that challenge the credulity of the New Testament accounts.]

Springer, Joseph Arthur. *Matthew: The Gospel of the King.* Chicago: Moody Correspondence School, 1954. [See. 182–87]

Sproul, R. C. *Matthew*. Wheaton: Crossway, 2013. [Chapter 128 The Resurrection Matthew 28:1-15, See. 813-19; Chapter 129 The Great Commission Matthew 28:16-20, See. 821-27]

Spurgeon, C. H. *An Exposition of the Gospel According to Matthew: The Gospel of the Kingdom*. Springfield, MO: Particular Baptist Press, 2015. [See. 254-58; Original title: *The Gospel of the Kingdom: A Popular Exposition of the Gospel According to Matthew*. London: Passmore and Alabaster, 1893; N.B. Archive.org]

———. *The Gospel of the Kingdom: A Popular Exposition of Matthew's Gospel*. New York: Revell, 1913. [See. 494-502; N.B. Archive.org, 1893, 254-58]

Stanley, David Michael. *The Gospel of St. Matthew*. Collegeville, MN: Liturgical Press, 1963. [See. 118-24]

Stanton, H. U. Weitbrecht. *The Gospel according to St. Matthew*. Madras: SPCK Depository, 1912. [See. 706-20; N.B. Archive.org]

Stellhorn, F. W. *A Brief Commentary on the Books of the New Testament: For Study and Devotion*. Vol. 1. *The Gospels*. Columbus, OH: Lutheran Book Concern, 1891. [See. 122-24]

Stevenson, Gregory M. "Matthew." In *The Transforming Word: One-Volume Commentary on the Bible*. Edited by Mark W. Hamilton. Abilene, TX: ACU Press, 2009. [See. 756-59]

Stock, Augustine. *The Method and Message of Matthew*. Collegeville, MN: Liturgical Press, 1994. [See. 434-41]

Stonehouse, Ned Bernard. *The Witness of Matthew and Mark to Christ*. Philadelphia: Presbyterian Guardian, 1944. [Chapter 6 The Resurrection Narrative in Matthew, See. 155-87]

Strohman, John M. *Application Commentary of the Gospel of Matthew*. Pierre, SD: Cross Centered Press, 2012. [See. 661-94]

Summers, Thos. O. *Commentary on the Gospels*. Vol. 1. *St. Matthew*. Nashville: Southern Methodist Publishing House, 1869. [See. 360-68; N.B. HathiTrust]

Sumner, John Bird. *A Practical Exposition of the Gospels of St. Matthew and St. Mark: In the Form of Lectures, Intended to Assist the Practice of Domestic Instruction and Devotion*. New York: Protestant Episcopal Press, 1831. [See. 265-69; N.B. Archive.org and Google book]

Swanson, Reuben J. *New Testament Greek Manuscripts: Variant Readings Arranged in Horizontal Lines Against Codex Vaticanus*. Sheffield: Sheffield Academic, 1995. [See. 292-96]

Talbert, Charles H. *Matthew*. Grand Rapids: Baker Academic, 2010. [See. 311-23]

Tasker, R. V. G. *The Gospel According to St. Matthew: An Introduction and Commentary*. Grand Rapids: Eerdmans, 1961. [See. 270-77]

Theology of Work Project (Boston, Mass.). *Theology of Work The Bible and Your Work Study Series: Matthew*. Peabody, MA: Hendrickson, 2015. [8. The Body of Christ at Work, Lesson #2: A Great Commission in Small Places (Matthew 28:16-20), See. 77-80]

Theophylactus. *The Explanation of the Holy Gospel According to Matthew*. House Springs, MO: Chrysostom Press, 1992. [See. 253-59]

Thomas, David. *The Genius of the Gospel: A Homiletical Commentary on the Gospel of St. Matthew*. Edited by William Webster. London: Dickinson & Higham, 1873. [See. 548-60; N.B. Google book]

Thomas, W. H. Griffith. *Outline Studies in the Gospel of Matthew*. Grand Rapids: Eerdmans, 1961. [See. 454-76]

Thompson, William G. *Matthew's Story: Good News for Uncertain Times.* New York: Paulist, 1989. [See. 142–45]

Thurston, Bonnie Bowman. *Wait Here and Watch: A Eucharistic Commentary on the Passion According to St. Matthew.* St. Louis, MO: CBP Press, 1989. [See. 82–91]

Tolbert, Malcolm. *Good News From Matthew.* Nashville: Broadman, 1975. [See. 242–48]

Toussaint, Stanley D. *Behold the King: A Study of Matthew.* Portland, OR: Multnomah Press, 1980. [See. 315–20]

Trapp, Joseph. *Explanatory Notes Upon the Four Gospels, and the Acts of the Apostles: In a New Method: For the Use of All, but Especially the Unlearned English Reader. In Two Parts. To Which Are Prefixed Three Discourses Relating to Both Parts: Of Which an Account is given in the Preface.* London: Printed for W. Russel, near St. Dunstan's Church in Fleetstreet, 1747. [See. 133–34; N.B. Google book]

Tresmontant, Claude. *The Gospel of Matthew.* Translated by K. D. Whitehead. Front Royal, VA: Christendom Press, 1996. [See. 595–98]

Trilling, Wolfgang. *The Gospel According to St. Matthew.* Vol. 2. New York: Crossroad, 1981. [See. 264–70]

Trollope, William. *The Gospel According to S. Matthew: With Prolegomena, Appendices, and Grammatical and Explanatory Notes.* Edited by William Henry. Rowlandson. Cambridge: J. Hall & Son, 1878. [See. 132–44; N.B. Google book]

Turner, David L. *Matthew.* Grand Rapids: Baker Academic, 2007. [See. 680–92]

Turner, David L., and Darrell L. Bock, The Gospel of Matthew. Carol Stream, IL: Tyndale House, 2005. [O. The Resurrection of Jesus, See. 369–73; P. Report of the Guard, See. 373–74; Q. The Commission of the Risen Lord, See. 374–78 (Turner)]

Upham, Francis W. *Saint Matthew's Witness to Words and Works of the Lord: or, Our Saviour's Life as Revealed in the Gospel of His Earliest Evangelist.* New York: Hunt & Eaton, 1891. [Chapter 34 The Resurrection, See. 400–15; N.B. Google book]

Valdés, Juan de. *Commentary upon the Gospel of St. Matthew: Now for the First Time Translated from the Spanish, and Never before Published in English.* Translated by John T. Betts. London: Trübner, 1882. [See. 494–508; N.B. Archive.org, Google book, and HathiTrust]

Vos, Howard Frederic. *Matthew: A Study Guide Commentary.* Grand Rapids: Zondervan, 1979. [See. 185–88]

Waetjen, Herman C. *The Origin and Destiny of Humanness: An Interpretation of the Gospel According to Matthew.* Corte Madera, CA: Omega, 1976. [See. 251–57]

Wainwright, Elaine Mary. *Towards a Feminist Critical Reading of the Gospel according to Matthew.* Berlin: De Gruyter, 1991. [See. 300–318]

Walvoord, John F. *Matthew: Thy Kingdom Come.* Chicago: Moody, 1974. [See. 239–44]

Walvoord, John F., and Charles H. Dyer. *Matthew.* Edited by Philip E. Rawley. Chicago: Moody, 2013. [Chapter 28 The Resurrection and Final Words of Jesus, See. 399–406]

Ward, Arthur Marcus. *The Gospel According to St Matthew.* London: Epworth, 1961. [See. 159–62]

Watson, Richard, bishop. *An Exposition of the Gospels of St. Matthew and St. Mark, and of Some Other Detached Parts of Holy Scripture.* London: Published by John Mason, 1833. [See. 436–42; N.B. Google book]

Weaver, Dorothy Jean. *Matthew's Missionary Discourse: A Literary Critical Analysis.* Sheffield: JSOT Press, 1990. [See. 150–53]

Category VIII—The New Testament

Weber, Hans-Rudi. *The Invitation Matthew on Mission.* New York: Joint Commission on Education and Cultivation Board of Missions of the United Methodist Church, 1971. [See. 121–23]

Weren, Wilhelmus Johannes Cornelis. *Studies in Matthew's Gospel: Literary Design, Intertextuality, and Social Setting.* Leiden: Brill, 2014. [Chapter 11 Matthew's View of Jesus' Resurrection: Transformation of a Current Eschatological Scenario, See. 210–21; Chapter 14 His Disciples Stole Him Away: (Mt 28:13): A Rival Interpretation of Jesus' Resurrection, See. 266–76]

Weston, Henry G. *Matthew: The Genesis of the New Testament: Its Purpose, Character, and Method.* New York: Revell, 1900. [See. 140—42; N.B. HathiTrust]

Whedon, D. D. *A Popular Commentary on the New Testament The Gospels Matthew—Mark.* Vol. 1. London: Hodder & Stoughton, 1874. [Matthew 28, See. 346–50; N.B. Google book]

Wiersbe, Warren W. *Meet Your King.* Wheaton, IL: Victor, 1980. [Chapter 26 The King's Victory (Matthew 28), See. 209–16]

Wilkins, Michael J. *Matthew.* Grand Rapids: Zondervan, 2004. [See. 932–72]

———. *Zondervan Illustrated Bible Backgrounds Commentary Matthew, Mark, Luke.* Edited by Clinton E. Arnold. Grand Rapids: Zondervan, 2002. [Matthew. See. 184–90]

Williams, A. Lukyn, et al. *The Pulpit Commentary, St Matthew.* Edited by H. D. M. Spence and Joseph S. Exell. Vol. 2. New York: Funk & Wagnalls, 1907. [See. 639–67; N.B. Google book)

Williams, Nathaniel Marshman. *The Gospel According to Matthew: With Notes: Intended for Sabbath Schools, Families, and Ministers.* Boston: Gould & Lincoln, 1873. [See. 319–32; N.B. Archive.org]

Willink, M. D. R. *The Gospel of St. Matthew: A Little Commentary.* Wallington, Surrey: Religious Education Press, 1959. [See. 118–20]

Winner, Lauren F. *The Voice of Matthew: The Gospel according to Matthew.* Nashville: Nelson, 2007. [See. 163–65]

Witherington, Ben. *Matthew.* Macon, GA: Smyth & Helwys, 2006. [See. 525–41]

Witherup, Ronald D. *Matthew: God with Us.* Hyde Park, NY: New City Press, 2000. [The Resurrection (28:1–15), 206–8; The Great Commission (28:16–20), See. 209–10]

Woodley, Matt. *The Gospel of Matthew: God with Us.* Downers Grove, IL: InterVarsity, 2011. [See. 259–70]

Woodward, James. *Journeying with Matthew: Reflections on the Gospel.* Louisville: Westminster John Knox, 2016. [Chapter 7 Easter, See. 76–85]

Wright, N. T. *Matthew for Everyone. Chapters 16–28.* London: SPCK, 2004. [See. 196–210]

Yeomans, William. *The Gospel of Matthew: A Spiritual Commentary.* Dublin: Dominican Publications, 1993. [See. 198–202]

Zanchettin, Leo, ed. *Matthew: A Devotional Commentary: Meditations on the Gospel According to St. Matthew.* Ijamsville, MD: Word Among Us, 1997. [See. 291–96]

Chapter 19

The Gospel of Luke

Abbott, Lyman. *An Illustrated Commentary on the Gospels According to Mark and Luke: For Family Use and Reference, and for the Great Body of Christian Workers of All Denominations*. Vol. 2. New York: A.S. Barnes, 1877. [See. 144–48; N.B. Archive.org]

Adamczewski, Bartosz. *The Gospel of Luke: A Hypertextual Commentary*. Frankfurt am Main: Peter Lang, 2016. [See. 195–202]

Adeney, Walter F., ed. *St. Luke: Introduction, Authorized Version, Revised Version with Notes, Illustrations*. Edinburgh: T.C. & E. C. Jack, 1901. [See. 387–97; N.B. HathiTrust]

Akaabiam, Terwase H. *The Proclamation of the Good News: A Study of Lk 24 in Tiv Context*. Frankfurt am Main, 1999. [184 pages]

Alleman, Herbert C., and John Aberly. *New Testament Commentary a General Introduction to and a Commentary on the Books of the New Testament*. Edited by Herbert C. Alleman. Philadelphia: Muhlenberg Press, 1944. [See. 356–58]

Allen, Jerry. *Translator's Notes on Luke: Helps on Understanding and Translating the Gospel of Luke*. Dallas, TX: SIL International, 2000. [See. 518–34]

Allen, O. Wesley, and David L. Petersen. "Luke." In *Theological Bible Commentary*. Edited by Gail R. O'Day. Louisville: Westminster John Knox, 2009. [See. 331–32]

Ambrose. *Commentary of Saint Ambrose on the Gospel According to Saint Luke*. Translated by Ide M. Ni Riain. Dublin: Halcyon, 2001. [See. 356–68]

———. *Exposition of the Holy Gospel According to Saint Luke: With, Fragments on the Prophecy of Esaias*. Translated by Theodosia Tomkinson. Etna, CA: Center for Traditionalist Orthodox Studies, 2003. [Book 10, See. 439–53]

Anderson, Kevin L. *'But God Raised Him from the Dead': The Theology of Jesus' Resurrection in Luke-Acts*. Bletchley, UK: Paternoster, 2006. [392 pages]

Applebury, T. R. *Studies in Luke*. Joplin, MO: College Press, 1971. [See. 386–97]

Arndt, William F. *Bible Commentary: The Gospel According to St. Luke*. Saint Louis: Concordia, 1956. [See. 480–504]

Ash, Anthony Lee. *The Gospel According to Luke*. Part 2. 9:51–24:53. Austin, TX: Sweet, 1973. [Chapter 7 The Resurrection and Ascension, 24:1–53, See. 147–56]

Baban, Octavian D. *On the Road Encounters in Luke-Acts: Hellenistic Mimesis and Luke's Theology of the Way*. Milton Keynes, UK: Paternoster, 2006. [See. 195–207]

Bailey, John Amedee. *The Traditions Common to the Gospels of Luke and John*. Leiden: Brill, 1963. [See. 85–102]

Ball, T. H. *Notes on Luke's Gospel*. Crown Point, IN: Donohue & Henneberry, 1889. [See. 112–20; N.B. Google book].

Balmforth, Henry. *The Gospel According to Saint Luke: In the Revised Version, with Introduction and Commentary*. Oxford: Clarendon, 1930. [See. 306–11]

Barclay, William. *The Gospel of Luke*. Philadelphia: Westminster, 1956. [See. 304–14]

Barnes, Albert. *Notes, Explanatory and Practical, on the Gospels: Designed for Sunday School Teachers and Bible Classes*. Vol. 2. New York: Harper and Brothers, 1843. [See. 167–75; N.B. Archive.org and Google book]

Barrell, E. V., and K. G. Barrell. *St. Luke's Gospel: An Introductory Study*. London: J. Murray, 1982. [See. 179–83]

Barton, Bruce B., et al. *Luke*. Wheaton, IL: Tyndale House, 1997. [See. 551–72]

Baugher, H. Louis. *Annotations on the Gospel According to St. Luke*. New York: Christian Literature, 1896. [See. 433–51; N.B. Google book]

Bengel, John Albert, and J. C. F Steudel. *Gnomon of the New Testament* Vol. 2. *Containing The Commentary on the Gospels According to St Luke and St John and the Acts of the Apostles*. Translated by A. R. Fausset. 3rd ed. Philadelphia: Smith, English &, 1860. [See. 218–25]

Benson, Dennis C. *Dennis Benson's Creative Bible Studies*. Loveland, CO: Group, 1985. [See. 396–400]

Bentley, Michael. *Saving a Fallen World: Luke Simply Explained*. Webster, NY: Evangelical Press US, 2007. [He has Risen! See. 316–28]

Benware, Paul N. *Luke, the Gospel of the Son of Man*. Chicago: Moody, 1985. [Chapter 5 The Final Authentication of Jesus the Son of Man, See. 144–47]

Blaiklock, E. M. *St. Luke*. Grand Rapids: Eerdmans, 1968. [See. 89–94]

Blight, Richard C. *An Exegetical Summary of Luke 12–24*. Dallas, TX: SIL International, 2007. [See. 534–81]

Bliss, George R. *Commentary on the Gospel of Luke*. Philadelphia: American Baptist Publication Society, 1884. [See. 344–55; N.B. Google book]

Bock, Darrell L. *Luke*. Grand Rapids: Baker, 1996. [E. Resurrection and Ascension of Jesus (24:1–53), 1879–950; N.B. This work was rated by D. A. Carson as "Pride of the place."]

———. *Luke*. Downers Grove, IL: InterVarsity, 1994. [See. 380–92]

———. *A Theology of Luke and Acts: Biblical Theology of the New Testament*. Edited by Andreas Köstenberger. Grand Rapids: Zondervan, 2012. [See. Jesus ascension of, 79, 204–5, 253–56; resurrection of, 79–80, 204–5, 253–56]

Boever, Richard A. *Good News From Luke: Practical Helps for Christian Living*. Liguori, MO: Liguori Publications, 1979. [See. 88–95]

Boles, H. Leo. *A Commentary on the Gospel by Luke*. Nashville: Gospel Advocate Company, 1974. [See. 460–80]

Bonaventure. *St. Bonaventure's Commentary on the Gospel of Luke, Chapters 17–24*. Translated by Robert J. Karris. St. Bonaventure, NY: Franciscan Institute, St. Bonaventure University, 2004. [See. 2189–249]

Bond, John. *The Gospel According to St. Luke: Being the Greek Text*. London: Macmillan, 1890. [See. 155–57; N.B. Archive.org]

Borgman, Paul. *The Way According to Luke: Hearing the Whole Story of Luke-Acts*. Grand Rapids: Eerdmans, 2006. [See. 243–46]

Boring, M. Eugene, and Fred B. Craddock. *The People's New Testament Commentary*. Louisville: Westminster John Knox, 2004. [See. 278–83]

Bovon, François. *Luke 3: A Commentary on the Gospel of Luke 19:28–24:53*. Edited by Helmut Koester. Translated by James E. Crouch. Minneapolis, MN: Fortress, 2012. [See. 321–421]

Bowie, Walter Russell. *The Compassionate Christ: Reflections from the Gospel of Luke*. New York: Abingdon, 1965. [See. 304–16]

Bratcher, Robert G. *A Translator's Guide to the Gospel of Luke*. London: United Bible Societies, 1982. [See. 380–94. N.B. This text is a definite read.]

Brown, David. *A Commentary, Critical and Explanatory, on the Old and New Testaments*. Vol. 2. *Matthew-Romans*. Edited by Robert Jamieson and A. R. Fausset. Vol. 2. New York: Revell, 1878. [See. 124–26; N.B. Archive.org and Google book]

Brown, Schuyler. *Apostasy and Perseverance in the Theology of Luke*. Rome: Pontifical Biblical Institute, 1969. [See. 74–81]

Browning, W. R. F. *The Gospel According to Saint Luke: Introduction and Commentary*. London: SCM, 1965. [See. 167–76]

Brownson, William Clarence. *Distinctive Lessons From Luke*. Grand Rapids: Baker, 1974. [Chapter 25 A Joyous Farewell, See. 126–28]

Burgon, John William. *A Plain Commentary on the Four Holy Gospels: Intended Chiefly for Devotional Reading: St. Luke-St. John*. Vol. 2. Philadelphia: Richard McCauley, 1868. [See. 615–25; N.B. Archive.org and Google book]

Burnham, David, and Sue Burnham. *Luke: A Doctor Examines the Life of Christ; A Discussion Guide for Home Bible Study*. Chicago: Moody, 1978. [The Living Christ, See. 94–96]

Burnside, W. F. *The Gospel According to St. Luke. The Greek Text, Edited with Introduction and Notes for the Use of Schools*. Cambridge: University Press, 1913. [See. 257–64; N.B. Archive.org]

Burton, Henry. *The Gospel According to St. Luke*. New York: A.C. Armstrong, 1897. [See. 400–415; N.B. Archive.org and Google book]

Butler, Trent C. *Luke*. Edited by Max E. Anders. Nashville: Holman Reference, 2000. [See. 411–28]

Byrne, Brendan. *The Hospitality of God: A Reading of Luke's Gospel*. Collegeville, MN: Liturgical Press, 2000. [See. 185–93]

Caird, G. B. *The Gospel of Saint Luke*. Harmondsworth, Mdsx., UK: Penguin, 1963. [See. 254–61; idem 1977]

Calvin, John. *Commentary on a Harmony of the Evangelists, Matthew, Mark, and Luke*. Vol. 3. Translated by William Pringle. Edinburgh: Edinburgh Printing Company, 1846. [340–95; N.B. Available online.]

Cannon, William Ragsdale. *A Disciple's Profile of Jesus: From the Gospel of Luke*. Nashville: Upper Room, 1975. [See. 113–17]

Card, Michael. *Luke: The Gospel of Amazement*. Downers Grove, IL: InterVarsity, 2011. [See. 259–66]

Carey, Greg. *The Gospel According to Luke: All Flesh Shall See God's Salvation*. Sheffield: Sheffield Phoenix Press, 2012. [See. 34–36]

Carlton, Matthew E. *The Translator's Reference Translation of the Gospel of Luke*. Dallas, TX: SIL International, 2008. [See. 456–89. N.B. This text is a must read.]

Carr, Arthur. *The Gospel According to St. Luke*. (*Notes on the Greek Testament*). London: Rivingtons, 1875. [See. 226–31; N.B. Google book]

Carroll, John T. *Luke: A Commentary*. Louisville: Westminster John Knox, 2012. [See. 474-97]

Cecilia, Madame. *The Gospel According to St. Luke (Books 1 and 2)*. New York: Benziger, 1906. [See. 510-28]

Childers, Charles L. *The Gospel According to St Luke: With Parallel Comments from Matthew and Mark*. [Beacon Bible Commentary. Vol. 6. Kansas City, MO: Beacon Hill, 1971. [Section 8 The Risen Christ Luke 24:1-53, See. 610-19]

Choice Notes on the Gospel of S. Luke: Drawn From Old and New Sources. London: Macmillan, 1869. [See. 364-84; N.B. Archive.org and Google book]

Clark, George W. *The Gospel of Luke: A Popular Commentary upon a Critical Basis, Especially Designed for Pastors and Sunday Schools*. Philadelphia: American Baptist Publication Society, 1896. [See. 492-504; N.B. Archive.org]

Clark, K. S. L. *The Gospel According to Saint Luke*. London: Darton, Longman & Todd, 1972. [See. 198-201]

Clowes, J., and Emanuel Swedenborg. *The Gospel According to Luke: Translated from the Original Greek, and Illustrated by Extracts from the Theological Writings of Emanuel Swedenborg, Together with Notes and Observations of the Translator, Annexed to Each Chapter*. London: J. S. Hodson, 1852. [See. 465-78; N.B. HathiTrust]

Clutterbuck, Ivan. *According to Luke: A Gospel for a New Millennium*. Leominster: Gracewing, 2000. [The Victorious Kingdom, See. 144-150]

Conzelmann, Hans. *The Theology of St. Luke*. Translated by Geoffrey Buswell. Philadelphia: Fortress, 1982. [See. 202-6]

Couch, Mal. *The Gospel of Luke: Christ, the Son of Man*. Chattanooga, TN: AMG, 2006. [See. 229-35]

Cowles, Henry. *Luke; Gospel History and Acts of the Apostles, With Notes, Critical, Explanatory, And Practical*. New York: D. Appleton, 1881. [See. 261-70; N.B. Google book]

Craddock, Fred B. *Luke*. Louisville: John Knox, 1990. [See. 279-95]

Creed, John Martin. *The Gospel According to St. Luke*. London: Macmillan, 1953. [See. 314-18]

Cukrowski, Kenneth L. "Luke." *The Transforming Word: One-Volume Commentary on the Bible*. Edited by Mark W. Hamilton. Abilene, TX: ACU Press, 2009. [See. 820-23]

Culpepper, R. Alan. "The Gospel of Luke." In *The New Interpreter's Bible. General Articles on the New Testament, The Gospel of Luke, The Gospel of John*. Vol. 9. Edited by Leander E. Keck. Nashville: Abingdon, 1995. [See. 446-90; N.B. Gail R. O'Day authored the Gospel of Mark.]

Culy, Martin M., et al. *Luke: A Handbook on the Greek Text*. Waco, TX: Baylor University Press, 2010. [See. 733-63]

Cumming, John. *Sabbath Evening Reading on the New Testament: St Luke*. Boston: John P. Jewett, 1855. [See. 454-76; N.B. Google book]

Cyril of Alexandria. *Commentary on the Gospel of Saint Luke*. Translated by R. Payne Smith. [United States]: Studion, 1983. [See. 614-20]

Dabney, J. P. *Annotations on the New Testament*. Part 1. Cambridge: Hilliard & Brown, 1829. [See. 137-42; N.B. Google book and HathiTrust]

Danker, Frederick W. *Jesus and the New Age: A Commentary on St. Luke's Gospel*. Philadelphia: Fortress, 1988. [See. 387-402]

Darby, J. N. *The Man of Sorrows: A Poem*. London: Pickering & Inglis, 1923. [See. 233-40]

———. *Notes of Addresses on the Gospel of Luke*. London: F.E. Race, 1922. [See. 247–55; N.B. The author is identified as JND.]

Davies, J. *St. Luke's Gospel: The Text Divided into Paragraphs and Arranged Chronologically, with Notes . . .* London: George Philip & Son, 1870. [Period 5 From Christ's Resurrection to his Ascension, See. 128–34; N.B. Google book]

Dean, Robert James. *Luke*. Nashville: Broadman Press, 1983. [The Lord Has Risen Indeed (24:1–53), See. 145–49]

Dillersberger, Josef. *The Gospel of Saint Luke Translated from the German*. Westminster: Newman Press, 1958. [See. 546–58]

Dillon, Richard J. *From Eye-Witnesses to Ministers of the World: Tradition and Composition in Luke 24*. Rome: Biblical Institute Press, 1978. [336 pages]

Dornisch, Loretta. *A Woman Reads the Gospel of Luke*. Collegeville, MN: Liturgical Press, 1996. [See. 222–38]

Drury, John. *Luke*. New York: Macmillan, 1973. [See. 212–20]

Dummelow, J. R., ed. *A Commentary on the Holy Bible By Various Writers*. New York: Macmillan, 1916. [See. 768–69; N.B. Archive.org]

Earle, Ralph. *The Gospel of Luke*. Grand Rapids: Baker, 1968. [See. 104–7]

Easton, Burton Scott. *The Gospel According to St. Luke: A Critical and Exegetical Commentary*. New York: Scribner's Sons, 1926. [See. 355–67]

Edwards, James R. *The Gospel According to Luke*. Apollos, 2015. [See. 707–42; N.B. This work is a healthy reading.]

Edwards, O. C. *Luke's Story of Jesus*. Philadelphia: Fortress, 1981. [He is Risen, See. 93–96]

Ellis, E. Earle. *The Gospel of Luke*. Grand Rapids: Eerdmans, 1981. [See. 273–80]

Erdman, Charles R. *The Gospel of Luke: An Exposition*. Philadelphia: Westminster, 1921. [See. 221–29]

Evans, C. F. *Saint Luke*. London: SCM, 1977. [See. 885–928]

Evans, Craig A. *Luke*. Peabody, MA: Hendrickson, 1990. [§57–60. See 346–62; N.B. This work is a solid reading.]

Exell, Joseph S. *The Biblical Illustrator: or, Anecdotes, Similes, Emblems, Illustrations; Expository, Scientific, Geographical, Historical, and Homiletic, Gathered from a Wide Range of Home and Foreign Literature, on the Verses of the Bible Saint Luke*. Vol. 3. New York: Revell, 188? [See. 615–84; N.B. Haithitrust.org. This text is a classic, dated source.]

Farrar, F. W. *The Gospel According to St. Luke*. Cambridge: University Press, 1899. [See. 357–67; N.B. Archive.org, Google book, and HathiTrust. This work is a dated, but detailed reading.]

Findlay, J. Alexander. *The Gospel According to St. Luke: A Commentary*. London: Student Christian Movement Press, 1937. [See. 240–47]

Fitzmyer, Joseph A. *The Gospel According to Luke (10–24)*. Garden City, NY: Doubleday, 1985. [See. 1532–91]

Fogarty, Philip. *Navigating the Gospels: Luke*. Dublin: Columba Press, 2009. [See. 125–29]

Foote, James. *Lectures on the Gospel According to Luke*. 3rd ed. Vol. 2. Edinburgh: Ogle & Murray, 1858. [See. 737–800; N.B. Archive.org and Google book]

Forbes, Greg W., and Scott D. Harrower. *Raised From Obscurity: A Narrative and Theological Study of the Characterization of Women in Luke-Acts*. Eugene, OR: Pickwick, 2015. [See. 128–38]

Ford, D. W. Cleverley. *A Reading of Saint Luke's Gospel*. London: Hodder & Stoughton, 1967. [See. 249-56]

Ford, James. *The Gospel of S. Luke Illustrated (Chiefly in the Doctrinal and Moral Sense)*. London: J. Masters, 1851. [See. 651-83; N.B. Archive.org]

France, R. T. *Luke*. Grand Rapids: Baker, 2013. [The Risen Jesus Revealed, See. 380-85; The Commissioning of the Disciples, See. 386-97]

Fuller, Reginald Horace. *Luke's Witness to Jesus Christ*. London: Lutterworth, 1963. [Chapter 5 The Passion and Resurrection of Jesus, See. 74-78; idem 1958]

Gadenz, Pablo T. *The Gospel of Luke*. Grand Rapids, Baker Academic, 2018. [Fulfillment in Jesus' Resurrection Luke 24:1-53, See. 389-403]

Garland, David E. *Luke*. Grand Rapids: Zondervan, 2011. [See. 739-60; 940-73; N.B. D. A. Carson rated this commentary as a best buy.]

Garvie, Alfred E., ed. *The Gospel According to St. Luke*. London: Andrew Melrose, 1911. [See. 368-81]

Gast, Gustave Carl. *Bible Study: The Gospel According to St. Luke*. Columbus, OH: Lutheran Book Concern, 1940. [See. 183-90]

Gavigan, James, and Brian McCarthy, eds. *The Navarre Bible: Saint Luke's Gospel in the Revised Standard Version and New Vulgate*. Dublin: Four Courts Press, 1991. [See. 258-68]

Geldenhuys, Norval. *Commentary on the Gospel of Luke*. Grand Rapids: Eerdmans, 1956. [See. 622-47]

Gettys, Joseph M. *How to Study Luke*. Richmond: John Knox, 1947. [See. 139-44]

Gibson, Joyce L. *Luke*. Lancaster, PA: Starburst, 2002. [Luke 24 A Bright Day Dawns, See. 311-22]

Gideon, Virtus E. *Luke: A Study Guide*. Grand Rapids: Zondervan, 1967. [See. 123-28]

Gill, John. *Gill's Commentary*. Vol. 5. *Matthew to Acts*. Grand Rapids: Baker, 1980. [See. 582-91; from the edition published by William Hill, London, 1852-54 reprint; N.B. Available online]

Gillman, John. *Luke: Stories of Joy and Salvation*. Hyde Park, NY: New City Press, 2002. [See. 202-12]

Gilmour, S. MacLean. "The Gospel According to St. Luke: Exegesis." In *Luke; John*. Vol. 8. *The Interpreter's Bible*. Nashville: Abingdon-Cokesbury, 1952. [See. 415-34]

Ginns, R. "St Luke." In *A Catholic Commentary on Holy Scripture*. Edited by Bernard Orchard. London: Nelson, 1953. [See. 969-70]

Girdlestone, Charles. *The New Testament of Our Lord and Saviour Jesus Christ: With a Commentary Consisting of Short Lectures for the Daily Use of Families*. Vol. 2. Oxford: J. G. & F. Rivington, 1833. [See. 544-52; N.B. Google book]

Godet, Frédéric Louis. *A Commentary on the Gospel of St. Luke*. 5th ed. Vol. 2. Edinburgh: T&T Clark, 1887. [See. 345-71; N.B. Archive.org and Google book]

González, Justo L. *Luke*. Louisville: Westminster John Knox, 2010. [See. 72-83]

Gooding, D. W. *According to Luke: A New Exposition of the Third Gospel*. Leicester, England: Inter-Varsity Press, 1987. [See. 347-56]

Goodloe, James C. *Preaching Through Luke: The Gospel as Catechism*. Eugene: Wipf & Stock, 2014. [See. 288-301]

Goodwin, Harvey. *A Commentary on the Gospel of S. Luke*. Cambridge: Deighton, Bell, 1865. [See. 373-92; N.B. Google book]

Goulder, Michael D. *Luke: A New Paradigm Part 2 (cont.). Commentary: Luke 9.51–24.53*. Vol. 2. Sheffield: JSOT Press, 1989. [See. 774–99; N.B. This book is a good read.]

Grant, Frederick W. *The Numerical Bible: The Gospels*. 3rd ed. New York: Loizeuax, 1904. [See. 465–69; N.B. Archive.org]

Green, Joel B. *The Gospel of Luke*. Grand Rapids: Eerdmans, 1997. [See. 832–64]

Grün, Anselm. *Jesus: The Image of Humanity Luke's Account*. New York: Continuum, 2001. [Chapter 9 Resurrection Stories, See. 103–13]

Gundry, Robert H. *Commentary on the New Testament: Verse-by-Verse Explanations with a Literal Translation*. Peabody, MA: Hendrickson, 2010. [Luke. See. 342–46]

Gutzke, Manford George. *Plain Talk on Luke*. Grand Rapids: Zondervan, 1966. [See. 168–80]

Guy, Harold Alfred. *The Gospel of Luke*. London: Macmillan, 1972. [Chapter 23 The Resurrection Story, See. 148–50]

Hannam, Wilfred L. *In The Things of My Father: A Study of the Purpose of Luke the Evangelist*. London: Hodder & Stoughton, 1935. [Chapter 21 As Though He Would Go Further, See. 243–50]

Harrington, Wilfrid J. *The Gospel According to St. Luke: A Commentary*. Westminster, MD: Newman Press, 1967. [See. 270–94]

———. *Luke: Gracious Theologian: The Jesus of Luke*. Blackrock: Columbia Press, 1997. [Chapter 8 Death and Vindication, See. 105–10]

Hendriksen, William. *New Testament Commentary: Exposition of the Gospel According to Luke*. Grand Rapids: Baker, 1978. [See. 1050–82]

Henry, Matthew. *Commentary on the Whole Bible: Genesis to Revelation*. Edited by Leslie F. Church. Grand Rapids: Zondervan, 1961. [See. 1500–1505; N.B. Available online.]

Hewlett, John. *Commentaries and Annotations on the Holy Scriptures*. Vol. 4. London: Longman, Hurst, Rees, Orme, & Brown, 1816. [See. 231; N.B. Google book]

Hill, John Leonard. *Outline Studies in Luke*. New York: Revell, 1937. [See. 170–82]

Hillard, A. E. *The Gospel According to St. Luke*. London: Rivingtons, 1905. [See. 126–29; N.B. Archive.org]

Hobbs, Herschel H. *An Exposition of the Gospel of Luke*. Grand Rapids: Baker, 1966. [See. 345–55]

Horton, Stanley M., ed. *New Testament Study Bible: Luke*. Springfield, MO: Complete Biblical Library in Cooperation with the Gospel Publishing House, 1986. [See. 695–726]

Hughes, R. Kent. *Luke: That You May Know the Truth*. Wheaton, IL: Crossway, 2015. [See. 833–66]

Hunt, Gladys M. *Luke: A Daily Dialog With God: 3 Months with the Life of Christ*. Wheaton, IL: Harold Shaw, 1986. [Chapter 8 The Resurrection, See. 168–75]

Hutchinson, Orion N. *Luke*. Vol. 19. Nashville: Abingdon, 1994. [See. 144–50]

Ironside, H. A. *Addresses on the Gospel of Luke*. Vol. 2. New York: Loizeaux, 1946. [See. 695–723]

Jacobsen, David Schnasa, and Günter Wasserberg. *Preaching Luke-Acts*. Nashville: Abingdon, 2001. [Chapter 3 Hope for Resurrection: A Learning Experience (Luke 24:13–49), See. 55–71]

Jacobus, Melancthon W. *Notes on the Gospels, Critical and Explanatory . . . Mark and Luke*. New York: R. Carter, 1866. [See. 309–19; N.B. Google book]

Category VIII—The New Testament

Jamieson, Robert. ed. *A Commentary, Critical And Explanatory on the Old And New Testaments*. Vol. 2. *Matthew—Romans* (David Brown)]. New York: Fleming, 1878. [See. 124–26; N.B. Google book]

Jarvis, Cynthia A., and E. Elizabeth Johnson, eds. *Feasting on the Gospels. A Feasting on the Word Commentary Luke*. Vol. 2. *Chapters 12–24*. Louisville: Westminster John Knox, 2014. [See. 344–61]

Jeffrey, David Lyle. *Luke*. Grand Rapids: Brazos, 2012. [See. 281–89]

Jensen, Irving L. *Luke: A Self-Study Guide*. Chicago: Moody Bible Institute, 1970. [See. 99–104]

Jensen, Richard A. *Preaching Luke's Gospel: A Narrative Approach*. Lima, OH: CSS Publishing, 1997. [See. 227–33]

Johnson, Timothy Luke. *The Gospel of Luke*. Edited by Daniel J. Harrington. Collegeville, MN: Liturgical Press, 1991. [See. 386–406]

Jones, Simon. *Luke: Crossway Bible Guide*. Leicester: Crossway, 1999. [See. 197–204]

Just, Arthur A. *Luke 9:51—24:53*. St. Louis: Concordia, 1997. [See. 963–1058. N.B. This text is a good read.]

Just, Arthur A., and Thomas C. Oden, eds. Luke: *Ancient Christian Commentary on Scripture New Testament 3*. Downers Grove: IL InterVarsity, 2003. [See. 373–93]

Karris, Robert J. *Invitation to Luke: A Commentary on the Gospel of Luke with Complete Text from the Jerusalem Bible*. Garden City, NY: Image, 1977. [See. 269–77]

Kealy, John P. *Luke's Gospel Today*. Denville, NJ: Dimension, 1979. [See. 445–68]

Kelly, William. *An Exposition of the Gospel of Luke*. Minneapolis: Klock & Klock Christian Publishers, 1981. [See. 365–76; reprint]

Kidder, Daniel P. ed. *Consecutive Questions on the Gospel of Luke*. 1856. New York: Carlton & Phillips, 1856. [Lesson 36, See. 126–30; N.B. Archive.org]

Kilgallen, John J. *A Brief Commentary on the Gospel of Luke*. New York: Paulist, 1988. [See. 222–29]

Killinger, John. *A Devotional Guide to the Gospels: 336 Meditations*. Waco, TX: Word, 1980. [See. 137–44]

Knapp, Charles. *St. Luke: With Introduction, Maps and Explanatory Notes Especially Intended for the Use of Schools and Theological Students*. London: Murby, 1917. [See. 298–319]

Knight, Jonathan. *Luke's Gospel*. London: Routledge, 1998. [See. 144–46]

Kodell, Jerome. "Luke." In *Collegeville Bible Commentary*. Edited by Dianne Bergant and Robert J. Karris. Collegeville, MN: Liturgical Press, 1989. [See. 978–80]

Kreitzer, Beth, ed. *Luke*. Vol. 3. Downers Grove, IL: InterVarsity, 2015. [See. 476–502]

Lachs, Samuel Tobias. *A Rabbinic Commentary on the New Testament: The Gospels of Matthew, Mark, and Luke*. Hoboken, NJ: Ktav, 1987. [See. 441–46]

Lamar, J. S. *Luke*. Vol. 2. Cincinnati: Chase & Hall, 1878. [See. 276–85]

Lampe, G. W. H. *Peake's Commentary on the Bible*. Edited by Matthew Black. London: Nelson, 1962. [See. 842–43]

Larkin, William J. *Acts*. Downers, IL: InterVarsity, 1995. [See. 37–48]

Larson, Bruce. *The Communicator's Commentary: Luke*. Waco, TX: Word, 1983. [See. 330–45]

LaVerdiere, Eugene. *Luke*. Wilmington, DE: Michael Glazier, 1980. [See. 280–92]

Leaney, A. R. C. *A Commentary on the Gospel According to St. Luke*. 2nd ed. London: Adam & Charles Black, 1966. [See. 28–31; 289–96]

Lee, Witness. *Life-Study of Luke*. Anaheim, CA: Living Stream Ministry, 1986. [See. 465–82]

Lenski, R. C. H. *The Interpretation of St. Luke's Gospel*. Minneapolis, MN: Augsburg, 1946. [See. 1168–212; N.B. This work is a healthy read.]

Liefeld, Walter L. "Luke." *The Expositor's Bible Commentary. Vol. 8. Matthew-Mark-Luke*. Edited by Frank Ely Gaebelein. Grand Rapids: Zondervan, 1984. [See. The Resurrection and Ascension, 1047–57]

Liefeld, Walter L., and David W. Pao. *Luke~Acts*. Edited by Tremper Longman and David E. Garland. Vol. 10. Grand Rapids: Zondervan, 2007. [See. 340–55]

Lieu, Judith. *The Gospel of Luke*. London: Epworth, 1997. [See. 200–10]

Lightfoot, John. *A Commentary on the New Testament From the Talmud and Hebraica, Matthew— 1 Corinthians*. Grand Rapids: Baker, 1979. [Exercitations Upon The Evangelist St. Luke, See. 218–31; Reprinted from the 1859 edition published by Oxford University Press. Formerly titled *Horae Hebraicae Et Talmudicae*. N.B. Available online]

Lindsay, Thomas M. *The Gospel According to St. Luke: With Introduction, Notes, and Maps. Chapters 13-24*. Edinburgh: T&T Clark, 1887. [See. 239–45; N.B. Available online]

Lucado, Max. *Life Lessons from the Inspired Word— Book of Luke*. Word, 1998. [Lesson Twelve, Seeing Jesus, See. 101–9]

Luce, H. K., ed. *The Gospel According to S. Luke*. Cambridge: University Press, 1949. [See. 356–67]

Luck, G. Coleman. *Luke: The Gospel of the Son of Man*. Chicago: Moody, 1960. [See. 120–25]

MacArthur, John. *Luke 18-24*. Chicago: Moody, 2014. [Chapters 36–40, See. 405–55]

———. *The MacArthur Bible Commentary: Unleashing God's Truth, One Verse at a Time*. Nashville: Nelson, 2005. [See. 1334–37]

MacEvilly, John. *An Exposition of the Gospel of St. Luke: Consisting of an Analysis of Each Chapter and of a Commentary, Critical, Exegetical, Doctrinal, and Moral*. Dublin: M. H. Gill, 1887. [See. 231–47; N.B. Archive.org]

Maclaren, Alexander. *Expositions of Holy Scripture*. New York: Doran, 1888? [See. 318–99; N.B. Archive.org and Gutenberg.org]

MacPherson, Duncan. *Luke*. Chicago: ACTA Foundation, 1971. [Chapter 7 The Resurrection of Jesus Lk 24:1–53, See. 105–10; N.B. Luke, by D. Macpherson.--Acts, by N. Lash.—1 Peter, by B. Robinson.]

Major, J. R. *The Gospel of St. Luke*. London: Printed by A. J. Valpy and sold by Bladwin, Cradock and Joy, 1826. [See. 359–68; N.B. Google book]

Malina, Bruce J., and Richard L. Rohrbaugh. *Social Science Commentary on the Synoptic Gospels*. Minneapolis: Fortress, 1992. [See 140–41]

Manson, William. *The Gospel of Luke*. New York: Harper, 1930. [See. 263–82]

Marshall, F. *The School and College: St. Luke*. London: George Gill, 1899. [See. 159–65]

Marshall, I. H. *The Gospel of Luke: A Commentary on the Greek Text*. Grand Rapids: Eerdmans, 1978. [See. 877–910]

Martin, Hugh. *"According to St. Luke": Studies in the Person and Teaching of Christ*. London: Student Christian Movement Press, 1936. [Week 12 The Risen Jesus, See. 91–97]

Martindale, C. C. *The Gospel According to Saint Luke*. Westminster, MD: Newman Press, 1957. [See. 193–201]

Massey, James. *Dalit Bible Commentary: New Testament*. Vol. 3. *The Gospel According to Luke*. New Delhi: Centre for Dalit/Subaltern Studies, 2007. [See. 222–29]

Mattill, A. J. *Luke and the Last Things: A Perspective for the Understanding of Lukan Thought.* Dillsboro, NC: Western North Carolina Press, 1979. [See. 124–29]

Maurice, F. D. *The Gospel of the Kingdom of Heaven: A Course of Lectures on the Gospel of St. Luke.* London: Macmillan, 1864. [Lecture 28 The King Triumphant, See. 357–68; N.B. Archive.org]

McBride, Alfred. *The Human Face of Jesus: Meditation and Commentary on the Gospel of Luke.* Huntington, IN: Our Sunday Visitor, 1992. [See. 208–16]

McBride, Denis. *Emmaus: The Gracious Visit of God According to Luke.* Dublin: Dominican Publications, 1991. [See. 121–74]

McCarren, Paul J. *A Simple Guide to Luke.* Lanham: Rowman & Littlefield, 2013. [See. 147–52]

McGee, J. Vernon. *Luke.* Nashville: Nelson, 1991. [See. 293–304]

McLaughlin, G. A. *Commentary on the Gospel According to Saint Luke.* Salem, OH: Schmul, 1974. [See. 451–65; Reprint, 1912, The Christian Witness]

McNicol, J. "The Gospel According to Luke." In *The New Bible Commentary.* Edited by F. Davidson. London: Inter-Varsity Fellowship, 1954. [See. 863–64]

Meyer, Heinrich August Wilhelm. *Critical and Exegetical Hand-Book to the Gospels of Mark and Luke.* Translated by Robert Ernest Wallis, William P. Dickson, and M. B. Riddle. New York: Funk and Wagnalls, 1884. [See. 571–90; N.B. Archive.org]

Miller, Donald G. *The Gospel According to Luke.* Richmond, VA: John Knox, 1959. [See. 168–75]

Milne, Douglas J. W. *Let's Study Luke.* Edinburgh: Banner of Truth Trust, 2005. [The Resurrection and Ascension (24:1–53], See. 378–95]

Montefiore, C. G., and Israel Abrahams. *The Synoptic Gospels.* Vol. 2. London: Macmillan, 1909. [See. 1087–99; N.B. Google book]

Moorman, John R. H. *The Path to Glory: Studies in the Gospel According to Saint Luke.* London: SPCK, 1960. [See. 289–300]

Morgan, G. Campbell. *The Gospel According to Luke.* New York: Revell, 1931. [See. 275–84]

Morris, Leon. *The Gospel According to St. Luke: An Introduction and Commentary.* Grand Rapids: Eerdmans, 1974. [See. 332–45]

Morrison, George H. *Morrison on Luke.* Vol. 2. Chattanooga, TN: AMG, 1978. [See. 113–46]

Mullins, Michael. *Gospel of Luke: A Commentary.* Blackrock, Co Dublin: Columba Press, 2010. [See. 511–18]

Navarre Bible, The: Saint Luke's Gospel in the Revised Standard Version and New Vulgate, with a Commentary by the Members of the Faculty of Theology of the University of Navarre. Dublin: Four Courts Press, 1993. [The Resurrection and Ascension of Jesus the Lord, See. 258–68]

Neale, David A. *Luke 9–24: A Commentary in the Wesleyan Tradition.* Kansas City: Beacon Hill, 2013. [See. 238–55]

Nevin, Alfred. *A Popular Commentary on the Gospel According to Luke.* Philadelphia: W. Flint, 1868. [Lessons 136—139, See. 677–700; N.B. Google book and HathiTrust]

Nichol, Francis D., ed. *Seventh-day Adventist Bible Commentary: The Holy Bible with Exegetical and Expository Comment.* Vol. 5. Washington, DC: Review & Herald, 1957. [See. 879–87]

Nickle, Keith Fullerton. *Preaching the Gospel of Luke: Proclaiming God's Royal Rule.* Louisville: Westminster John Knox, 2000. [See. 254–64]

Nolland, John. *Word Biblical Commentary: Luke 18:35–24:53*. Vol. 35c. Waco, TX: Word, 1982. [See. 1168–230. N.B. Nolland's text is a solid reading.]

Norwood, Fredrick William, and F. R. Barry. *St. Luke: A Little Library of Exposition*. London: Cassell, 1926. [See. 101–14]

Obach, Robert E., and Albert E. Kirk. *A Commentary on the Gospel of Luke*. New York: Paulist, 1986. [See. 253–66]

Oosterzee, Johannes Jacobus Van. *Theological and Homiletical Commentary on the Gospel of St Luke*. Edited by Johann Peter Lange. Translated by S. Taylor. Vol. 2. Edinburgh: T&T Clark, 1863. [See. 406–52; N.B. Google book]

Owen, John J. *A Commentary, Critical, Expository and Practical, on the Gospel of Luke: For the Use of Ministers, Theological Students, Private Christians, Bible Classes, and Sabbath Schools*. New York: Leavitt & Allen, 1859. [See. 376–400; N.B. Archive.org and Google book]

Pallis, Alexandros. *Notes on St. Luke and the Acts*. Edinburgh: Oxford University Press, 1928. [See. 46–47]

Parker, Joseph. *The People's Bible: Discourses Upon Holy Scripture*. Vol. 20. *Mark— Luke*. London: Hazell, Watson & Viney, 1902. [Part From Them, See. 450–56; N.B. Archive.org]

Parsons, Mikeal C. *Luke*. Grand Rapids: Baker Academic, 2015. [See. 348–57]

Pate, C. Marvin. *Luke*. Chicago: Moody, 1995. [See. 465–82]

Patella, Michael. *The Gospel According to Luke*. Collegeville, MN: Liturgical Press, 2005. [See. 153–58]

Perrotta, Kevin. *Luke: The Good News of Gods Mercy*. Chicago: Loyola Press, 2000. [Week 6 The Lord Has Risen Indeed, See. 72–80]

Phillips, John. *Exploring the Gospel of Luke: An Expository Commentary*. Grand Rapids: Kregel, 2005. [See. 296–304]

Pinfold, James T. *St. Luke and His Gospel: An introduction*. London: Epworth, 1923. [See. 6, 8, 11, 23, 46, 63, 75, 88, 94, 99, 115, 116, 174, 177, 178, 197; N.B. Archive.org]

Plummer, Alfred. *A Critical and Exegetical Commentary on the Gospel According to S. Luke*. 5th ed. Edinburgh: T&T Clark, 1922. [See. 546–71; Reprint; N.B. Archive.org, Google book, and HathiTrust]

Plumptre, E. H. *The Gospel According to St. Matthew, St. Mark, and St. Luke*. Edited by Charles John Ellicott. 2nd ed. Vol. 2. London: Cassell, Petter & Galpin, 1878? [See. 359–65; N.B. *The Gospel according to St. Luke*—Haithitrust.org]

Poole, Matthew. *Annotations Upon the Holy Bible Wherein the Sacred Text is Inserted and Various Readings . . .* Vol. 2. [Jeremiah—Rev] London: Printed for Thomas Parkhurst et al., 1700. See. St. Luke, no pagination; N.B. Google book. Reprinted as *A Commentary on the Holy Bible*. Vol. 3. McLean, VA: MacDonald, 1962. See. 272–76]

Powell, Ivor. *Luke's Thrilling Gospel*. Grand Rapids: Kregel, 1984. [See. 487–503]

Powell, Mark Allan. *What Are They Saying About Luke?* Mahawah, NJ: Paulist, 1989. [The Meaning of Jesus' Resurrection and Ascension, See. 71–76]

Prange, Victor H. *Luke*. Saint Louis: Concordia, 2004. [See. 258–66]

Ragg, Lonsdale. *St. Luke*. London: Methuen, 1922. [See. 308–22; N.B. Archive.org]

Reid, Barbara E. *Choosing the Better Part? Women in the Gospel of Luke*. Collegeville, MN: Liturgical Press, 1996. [See. 199–204]

Reiling, J., and J. L. Swellengrebel. *A Translator's Handbook on the Gospel of Luke*. Leiden: Brill, 1971. [See. 743–66. N.B. This source is an important text to read.]

Rice, Edwin Wilbur. *Commentary on the Gospel According to Luke: Giving Critical, Exegetical and Applicative Notes, and Illustrations Drawn from Life and Thought in the East: With the Common Version, 1611, and the Revised Version, 1881, American Readings and Renderings*. 6th ed. Philadelphia: Union Press, 1900. [See. 313–28; N.B. Archive.org]

Riddle, Matthew B. *The International Revision Commentary on the New Testament: The Gospel According to Luke*. Edited by Philipp Schaff. Vol. 3. New York: Scribner's Sons, 1882. [See. 352–69; N.B. Google book, 1899.]

Ringe, Sharon H. *Luke*. Louisville: Westminster John Knox, 1995. [See. 282–90]

Ritchie, Arthur. *Spiritual Studies in St. Luke's Gospel*. Vol. 2. Milwaukee: Young Churchman, 1906. [See. 399–421]

Robertson, A. T. *Word Pictures in the New Testament: The Gospel According to Luke*. Vol. 2. Grand Rapids: Baker, 1930. [See. 290–98]

Robinson, Chas. S. *Studies in Luke's Gospel Second Series*. New York: American Tract Society, 1889. [See. 283–319]

Rohr, Richard. *The Good News According to Luke: Spiritual Reflections*. New York: Crossroad, 1997. [See. 189–92]

Rose, V. *The Holy Gospel According to Saint Luke*. Translated by Newton Wayland Thompson. Baltimore: John Murphy, 1931. [See. 205–20]

Ross, J. M. E. *The Gospel According to St. Luke, 18–24: A Devotional Commentary*. London: Religious Tract Society, n.d. [See. 191–214]

Rowe, Christopher Kavin. *Early Narrative Christology: The Lord in the Gospel of Luke*. Grand Rapids: Baker, 2009. [See. 182–89]

Ryken, Philip Graham. *Luke 13–24*. Vol. 2. Phillipsburg, NJ: P&R, 2009. [See. 630–703]

Ryle, J. C. *Expository Thoughts on the Gospels. For Family and Private Use St. Luke*. Vol. 2. New York: Robert Carter, 1875. [See. 491–530; N.B. Google book]

Sabourin, Leopold. *The Gospel According to St Luke: Introduction and Commentary*. Bandra, Bombay: St Paul Publications, 1984. [See. 395–408]

Sadler, M. F. *The Gospel According to St. Luke: With Notes Critical and Practical*. London: George Bell, 1887. [See. 610–34; N.B. HathiTrust]

Schaberg, Jane D., and Sharon H. Ringe. "Gospel of Luke." In *Women's Bible Commentary*. Edited by Carol A. Newsom, Sharon H. Ringe, and Jacqueline E. Lapsley. 3rd ed. Louisville: Westminster John Knox, 2012. [See. 509–11]

Schleiermacher, Friedrich. *Luke: A Critical Study*. Translated by Connop Thirlwall. Edited by Terrence N. Tice. Lewiston, NY: Mellen, 1993. [See. 309–14]

Schönborn, Christoph Cardinal. *Jesus, the Divine Physician: Reflections on the Gospel During the Year of Luke*. Translated by Henry Taylor. San Francisco: Ignatius Press, 2008. [See. 188–215]

Schweizer, Eduard. *The Good News According to Luke*. Atlanta: John Knox, 1984. [See. 364–80]

Scott, John P. *The Four Gospels Esoterically Interpreted*. Oceanside, CA: Langford Press, 1937. [See. 154; N.B. HathiTrust]

Scott, Macrina. *Bible Stories Revisited: Discover Your Story in the Gospel of Luke and the Acts of the Apostles*. Cincinnati, OH: St. Anthony Messenger Press, 2004. [See. 135–47]

Scroggie, W. Graham. *Dr. W. Graham Scroggie on Luke & John*. London: Ark Pub., 1981. [See. 85–88]

Simpson, A. B. *The Gospel of Luke*. Harrisburg, PA: Christian Publications, 193? [See. 194–216]

Smith, David. *Commentary on the Four Gospels*. Garden City, NY: Doubleday, Doran, 1928. [See. 464–74]

Spaulding, Henry G. *Young Learners' Lesson-Book on the Gospel of Luke*. Boston: Unitarian Sunday-School Society, 1890. [Chapter 30 The Resurrection, See. 164–72; N.B. Google book]

Spence, H. D. M., and J. Marshall Lang. *St. Luke*. Vol. 2. Edited by H. D. M. Spence and Joseph S. Exell. London: Funk & Wagnalls, 1906. [See. 267–303; N.B. Christianclassiclibrary.com and Google book]

Spencer, F. Scott. *The Gospel of Luke and Acts of the Apostles*. Nashville: Abingdon, 2008. [Chapter 6 See Death and Life, See. 211–14]

Sproul, R. C. *A Walk with Jesus: Enjoying the Company of Christ*. Fearn: Christian Focus, 1999. [See. 363–70]

Stagg, Frank. *Studies in Luke's Gospel*. Nashville: Convention Press, 1967. [See. 135–37]

Stanley, Stephen. *Discovering Luke: The Guideposts Home Bible Study Program*. Carmel: Guideposts, 1985. [Lesson 8: Luke 24:1–53, Jesus Is Risen, See. 143–52]

Stark, James. *Commentary on the Gospel According to Luke: Showing the Doctrines Taught by Jesus Christ, and How Far These Agree with the Doctrines Taught by Paul and Other Apostles, and by Modern Churches*. Vol. 2. London: Longmans, Green, Reader, & Dyer, 1866. [See. 441–542; N.B. HathiTrust]

Stein, Robert H. *Luke*. Nashville: Broadman Press, 1992. [See. 602–25]

Stellhorn, F. W. *A Brief Commentary on the Four Gospels: For Study and Devotion*. Vol. 2. Columbus, OH: Lutheran Book Concern, 1891. [See. 262–66]

Stevenson, Morley. *Handbook to the Gospel According to S. Luke: For the Use of Teachers and Students*. London: Rivingtons, 1909. [See. 251–59]

Stifler, James Madison. *The Christ of Christianity: A Series of Studies Based on the Writings of Luke: "The Gospel of Luke" and "the Acts."* New York: Revell, 1915. [Chapters 23–25, See. 161–72; N.B. Google book]

Stock, Eugene. *Talks on St. Luke's Gospel*. London: Religious Tract Society, 1913. [See. 280–97; N.B. HathiTrust]

Stöger, Alois. *The Gospel According to St. Luke*. New York: Herder & Herder, 1969. [See. 252–78]

Stoll, Raymond F. *The Gospel According to St. Luke*. New York: Pustet, 1931. [See. 390–99]

Stonehouse, Ned Bernard. *The Witness of Luke to Christ*. Grand Rapids: Eerdmans, 1951. [See. 141–51]

Strauss, Mark L. *Zondervan Illustrated Bible Backgrounds Commentary*: Vol. 1. *Matthew, Mark, Luke*. Edited by Clinton E. Arnold. Grand Rapids: Zondervan, 2002. [Luke, See. 497–501]

Stuhlmueller, Carroll. *The Gospel of St. Luke*. Collegeville: Liturgical Press, 1964. [See. 155–60]

Summers, Ray. *Commentary on Luke: Jesus, the Universal Savior*. Waco, TX: Word, 1972. [See. 317–38]

Summers, Thos. O. *Commentary on the Gospels*. Vol. 3. *St. Luke*. Nashville: Publishing House of the Methodist Episcopal Church, South, 1872. [See. 362–75; N.B. HathiTrust]

Sumner, John Bird. *A Practical Exposition of the Gospel According to St. Luke*. London: T. Hatchard, 1850. [Lectures 90–92, See. 480–98; N.B. Google book]

Swanson, Richard W. *Provoking the Gospel of Luke: A Storyteller's Commentary, Year C*. Cleveland: Pilgrim Press, 2006. [See. 139–46]

Swindoll, Charles R. *Insights on Luke*. Grand Rapids: Zondervan, 2011. [See. 514–27]

Sydnor, William. *Jesus According to Luke*. New York: Seabury, 1982. [Chapter 9 The Resurrection Luke 24:1–52, See. 125–32]

Talbert, Charles H. *Reading Luke: A Literary and Theological Commentary on the Third Gospel*. New York: Crossroad, 1989. [See. 226–33]

Tannehill, Robert C. *The Narrative Unity of Luke-Acts: A Literary Interpretation*. Philadelphia: Fortress, 1986. [See. 275–301]

Taylor, Vincent. *Behind the Third Gospel: A Study of the Proto-Luke Hypothesis*. Oxford: Clarendon, 1926. [See. 63–75]

Tew, W. Mark. *Luke: Gospel to the Nameless and Faceless*. Eugene, OR: Wipf & Stock, 2012. [See. 305–12]

Theophylactus. *The Explanation by Blessed Theophylact of the Holy Gospel According to St. Luke / Translated from the Original Greek*. Translated by Christopher Stade. House Springs, MO: Chrysostom Press, 1997. [See. 316–28]

Thomas, M. M. *Crucified Jesus the Lord of the World: (Luke 19–24)*. Translated by T. M. Philip Tiruvalla: Christava Sahitya Samithy, 2008. [Risen Jesus, See. 106–17]

Thomas, W. H. Griffith. *Outline Studies in the Gospel of St. Luke*. Grand Rapids: Eerdmans, 1951. [See. 358–405]

Thompson, G. H. P. *The Gospel According to Luke in the Revised Standard Version*. Oxford: Clarendon, 1972. [See. 275–83]

Thomson, James. *Exposition of the Gospel According to St Luke, in a Series of Lectures Chapters 20–24*. Vol. 3. Edinburgh: Adam & Charles Black, 1851. [See. 194–241]

Tiede, David Lenz. *Luke*. Minneapolis, MN: Augsburg, 1988. [See. 427–44]

Tilborg, Sjef van, and Patrick Chatelion Counet. *Jesus' Appearances and Disappearances in Luke 24*. Leiden: Brill, 2000.

Tinsley, E. J. *The Gospel According to Luke*. Cambridge: Cambridge University Press, 1965. [See. 203–9]

Tittle, Ernest Fremont. *The Gospel According to Luke: Exposition & Application*. New York: Harper & Brothers, 1951. [See. 265–74]

Tolbert, Malcolm O. *The Broadman Bible Commentary*. Vol. 9. *Luke-John*. Edited by Clifton J. Allen. Nashville: Broadman Press, 1969. [See. 182–87]

Trainor, Michael F. *About Earth's Child: An Ecological Listening to the Gospel of Luke*. Sheffield, UK: Sheffield Phoenix Press, 2012. [See. 283–92]

Trites, Allison A. "The Gospel of Luke." In *Cornerstone Biblical Commentary*. Edited by Philip W. Comfort. Vol. 12. Carol Stream, IL: Tyndale House, 2006. [See. 316–28]

Trollope, William. *The Gospel According to S. Luke: With Prolegomena, Appendices and Grammatical and Explanatory Notes*. Edited by W. H. Rowlandson. 5th ed. Cambridge: J. Hall, 1883. [See. 142–48; N.B. Google book]

Turlington, Henry E. *Luke's Witness to Jesus*. Nashville: Broadman Press, 1967. [The Resurrection, See. 90–93]

Turpin, W. T. *"The Man Christ Jesus:" Being Addresses On The Gospel of Luke*. London: W. H. Broom & House, 1880. [Lecture 9 Luke 24.28–53, See. 1–30]

Van Doren, W. H. *A Suggestive Commentary on St. Luke: With Critical and Homiletical Notes on an Original Plan. St. Luke*. Vol. 2. London: R. D. Dickinson, 1867. [See. 518–58; N.B. Archive.org]

Vinson, Richard Bolling. *Luke*. Macon, GA: Smyth & Helwys, 2008. [See. 739–60]

Walker, Rollin Hough. *A Study of Luke's Gospel by the Questionnaire Method: A Handbook for Bible Classes and for Private Study*. New York: Methodist Book Concern, 1921. [See. 158–62; N.B. Archive.org, Google book, and HathiTrust]

Walker, Thomas W. *Luke*. Louisville: Geneva Press, 2001. [See. 94–101]

Walpole, A. S. *The Gospel According to Saint Luke in the Revised Version*. London: Oxford University Press, 1910. [See. 143–47]

Wansbrough, Henry. *The Gospel of Luke*. New York: Doubleday, 1998. [See. 192–201]

———. *The Lion and the Bull: The Gospels of Mark and Luke*. London: Darton, Longman & Todd, 1996. [See. 189–95]

Ward, Monsignor. *The Holy Gospel According to Luke*. London: Catholic Truth Society, 1915. [See. 272–83]

Weisiger, Cary N. *The Gospel of Luke: A Study Manual*. Grand Rapids: Baker, 1966. [See. 127–28]

Welch, Reuben. *Luke*. Kansas City, MO: Beacon Hill, 1974. [The Resurrection, See. 212–21]

Whedon, D. D. *Commentary on the Gospels: Intended for Popular Use: Luke—John*. New York: Nelson & Phillips, 1866. [See. 214–22; N.B. Google book]

Whitham, A. R. *The Gospel According to St. Luke*. London: Rivingtons, 1919. [Chapter 7 The Resurrection, See. 233–43]

Wiersbe, Warren W. *Be Courageous*. Wheaton, IL: Victor, 1989. [Chapter 12 The Son of Man Triumphs, See. 141–51]

Wilcock, Michael. *The Savior of the World: The Message of Luke's Gospel*. Downers Grove, IL: InterVarsity, 1979. [See. 205–15]

Wilkinson, Wilfred. *Good News in Luke: Luke in Today's English Version*. Cleveland: Collins World, 1977. [See. 248–51]

Willcock, J. *A Homilectical Commentary on the Gospel According to St. Luke*. New York: Funk & Wagnalls, 1896. [See. 600–16, N.B. Archive.org]

Willis, Wesley R. *Luke*. Wheaton: Victor, 1987. [Luke 24, See. 89–95]

Wright, N. T. *Luke for Everyone*. London: SPCK, 2004. [See. 288–302]

CHAPTER 20

The Gospel of John

Abbott, Lyman. *An Illustrated Commentary on the Gospel According to St. John: For Family Use and Reference, and for the Great Body of Christian Workers of All Denominations.* New York: A. S. Barnes, 1879. [See. 227–43; N.B HathiTrust]

Alleman, Herbert C. "The Gospel According to John." In *New Testament Commentary.* Edited by Herbert C. Alleman. Philadelphia: Muhlenberg Press, 1936. [See. 396–400]

Allen, Paul Marshall. *Notes on the Gospel of John.* Great Barrington, MA: SteinerBooks, 2013. [John 20, See. 250–63; John 21, See. 264–71]

Anderson, William A. *The Gospel of John.* Mission Hills, CA: Benziger, 1988. [See. 101–17]

Appleton, George. *John's Witness to Jesus.* New York: Association Press, 1955. [Chapter 11 Risen Lord, See. 87–93; Chapter 12 Savior of the World, See. 94–96]

Aquinas, Thomas. *Commentary on the Gospel of John: Chapters 13–21.* Translated by Fabian R. Larcher and James A. Weisheipl. Catholic University of America Press, 2010. [Chapter 20, See. 252–81; Chapter 21, See. 282–308]

Ashcraft, Janice, and Jay Ashcraft. *Creative Bible Lessons in John: Encounters with Jesus.* Grand Rapids: Zondervan, 1995. [Lesson, 12 See. 99–107]

Ashton, John. *Understanding the Fourth Gospel.* Oxford: Clarendon, 1991. [Chapter 13 Passion and Resurrection. [See. 493–97, 501–14]

Attridge, Harold W. *Essays on John and Hebrews.* Grand Rapids: Baker Academic, 2010. [11. "Don't Be Touching Me": Recent Feminist Scholarship on Mary Magdalene, See. 137–59; 12. From Discord Rises Meaning: Resurrection Motifs in the Fourth Gospel, See. 160–76]

Augsburger, Myron S. *Discovering John: The Guideposts Home Bible Study Program.* Carmel, NY: Guideposts, 1985. [Lesson 8, See. 136–50; N.B. The author is identified in WorldCat.]

Augustine, Aurelius. *The Works of Aurelius Augustine/ Lectures or Tractates on the Gospel . . .* Vol. 11. *Saint Augustine (of Hippo Tractates).* Translated by James Innes. Edinburgh: T&T Clark, 1874. [See. 120–24; 517–46; N.B. Google book]

Aus, Roger David. *Simon Peter's Denial and Jesus' Commissioning Him as His Successor in John 21:15–19. Studies in Their Judaic Background.* Lanham: University Press of America, 2013. [N.B. Interesting insights and a recommended reading.]

Bacon, Benjamin Wisner. *The Gospel of the Hellenists.* Edited by Carl H. Kraeling. New York: Henry Holt, 1933. [See. 229–36]

Bailey, John Amedee. *The Traditions Common to the Gospels of Luke and John*. Leiden: Brill, 1963. [See. 85–102]

Bailey, R. F. *The Gospel of S. John: An Introductory Commentary*. London: Student Christian Movement Press, 1940. [See. 222–35]

Barclay, William. *The Gospel of John*. Vol. 2 (Chapters 8 to 21). Philadelphia: Westminster, 1956. [See. 307–38]

Barnes, Albert. *Notes, Explanatory and Practical, on the Gospels: Designed for Sunday School Teachers and Bible Classes*. Vol. 3. New York: Harper & Brothers, 1843. [See. 388–98; N.B. Google book, Vol. 2 in two volumes, 1855.]

Barnhart, Bruno. *The Good Wine: Reading John from the Center*. New York: Paulist, 1993. [See. 216–74]

Barnhouse, Donald Grey. *Illustrating the Gospel of John*. Grand Rapids: Revel, 1998. [Chapter 22 God Put You Here "On Purpose," See. 283–99; Chapter 23 The Post Resurrection Ministry of Jesus, See. 301–8]

Barrett, C. K. *Essays on John*. Philadelphia: Westminster, 1982. [Chapter 10 John 21.15–25, See. 159–67]

———. *The Gospel According to St. John: An Introduction with Commentary and Notes on the Greek Text*. Vol. 2. Philadelphia: Westminster, 1978. [See. 560–88]

Bartholomew, Gilbert L. *Pass It On: Telling and Hearing Stories from John*. Cleveland, OH: United Church Press, 1992. [Chapter 5 Grief Turned to Joy: Mary Magdalene (John 20:1–18), See. 71–82; Chapter 6 Failure and Forgiveness: Peter, See. 83–95]

Barton, Bruce B., et al. *John: Life Application Bible Commentary*. Wheaton, IL: Tyndale House, 1995. [John 20, See. 385–400; John 21, See. 401–12]

Barton, V. Wayne. *The Gospel of John: A Study Manual*. Grand Rapids: Baker, 1960. [See. 89–95]

Bauckham, Richard. *The Testimony of the Beloved Disciple: Narrative, History, and Theology in the Gospel of John*. Grand Rapids: Baker Academic, 2007. [Chapter 13 The 153 Fish and the Unity of the Fourth Gospel, See. 271–84]

Baumler, Gary P. *John*. Saint Louis: Concordia, 2005. [Part 8 Jesus Rises from the Dead and Strengthens His Disciples Faith (20:1–21:25), See. 257–75]

Beasley-Murray, George Raymond. *Word Biblical Commentary: John*. Vol. 36. Waco, TX: Word, 1987. [See. 364–418; N.B. This work is a solid recommended read.]

Belle, Gilbert van. *Johannine Bibliography: 1966–1985: A Cumulative Bibliography on the Fourth Gospel*. Leuven: Leuven University Press, 1988. [See. 304–17]

Bengel, John Albert, and J. C. F Steudel. *Gnomon of the New Testament*. Vol. 2. *Containing The Commentary on the Gospels According to St Luke and St John and the Acts of the Apostles*. Translated by A. R. Fausset. 3rd ed. Philadelphia: Smith, English, 1860. [See. 487–509; N.B. Google book]

Bennema, Cornelis. *Encountering Jesus: Character Studies in the Gospel of John*. 2nd ed. Minneapolis: Fortress, 2014. [See. 330–37]

Benson, Dennis C. *Dennis Benson's Creative Bible Studies*. Loveland, CO: Group, 1985. [See. 504–10]

Berkeley, James P. *Reading the Gospel of John*. Chicago: Judson Press, 1958. [Chapter 20 The Son in the Midst of His Brothers (20:1–29), See. 220–235; Chapter 21 Love Me . . . Follow Me (21:1–25), See. 236–42; Chapter 24 The Holy Spirit in the Fourth Gospel (20:22), See. 263–80]

Bernard, J. H. *A Critical and Exegetical Commentary on the Gospel According to St. John.* Edited by A. H. McNeile. Vol. 2. New York: Scribner's Sons, 1929. [See. 656–714]

Blaine, Bradford B. *Peter in the Gospel of John: The Making of an Authentic Disciple.* Atlanta: Society of Biblical Literature. 2007. [Chapter 5 The Race to the Empty Tomb, See. 105–25; Chapter 6 John 21 as Gospel Supplement, See. 127–42; Chapter 7 The Fishing Expedition and the Miraculous Catch of Fish, See. 143–60; Chapter 8 Shepherd and Martyr, See. 161–82]

Blank, Josef. *The Gospel According to St. John.* New York: Crossroad, 1981. [The Story of Easter, See. 101–58]

Bligh, John. *The Sign of the Cross: The Passion and Resurrection of Jesus according to St John.* England: St. Paul Publications, 1974. [See. 63–112]

Blomberg, Craig L. *The Historical Reliability of John's Gospel: Issues & Commentary.* Downers Grove, IL: InterVarsity, 2002. [See. 258–81; N.B. Worth examining.]

Boice, James Montgomery. *The Gospel of John: An Expositional Commentary.* Vol. 5. Grand Rapids: Baker, 2001. [Sections 254–270, See. 1563–664]

———. *The Gospel of John: An Expositional Commentary John 18:1 — 21:25.* Vol. 5. Grand Rapids: Zondervan, 1979. [See. 268–393]

Bonaventure. *Commentary on the Gospel of John.* Edited and Translated by Robert J. Karris. Saint Bonaventure, NY: Franciscan Institute, Saint Bonaventure University, 2007. [John 20, See. 943–87; John 21, See. 989–1022]

Bonney, William. *Caused to Believe: The Doubting Thomas Story at the Climax of John's Christological Narrative.* Leiden: Brill, 2002. [192 pages]

Borchert, Gerald L. *John 12–21.* Nashville: Broadman & Holman, 2002. [Chapter 8 The Resurrection Stories (20:1–21:25), See. 287–343; N.B. This is a work worth reading.]

Boring, M. Eugene, and Fred B. Craddock. *The People's New Testament Commentary.* Louisville: Westminster John Knox, 2004. [See. 355–62]

Bouyer, Louis. *The Fourth Gospel.* Translated by Patrick Byrne. Westminster, MD: Newman Press, 1964. [See. 219–26]

Brant, Jo-Ann A. *John.* Grand Rapids: Baker Academic, 2011. [Part 4: Jesus's Resurrection: Endings and Epilogues, See. 263–90]

Bridger, Gordon. *The Man From Outside.* Leicester: Inter-Varsity, 1969. [Chapter 43 Evidence for the Resurrection 20:1–10, See. 177–80; Chapter 44 More Evidence for the Resurrection 20:11–31, See. 180–84; Chapter 45 The Challenge of Christian Discipleship 21:1–25, See. 185–90]

Brodie, Thomas L. *The Gospel According to John: A Literary and Theological Commentary.* New York: Oxford University Press, 1993. [See. 560–96; N.B. This work contains a good overview of the narrative.]

Brown, David. *A Commentary, Critical and Explanatory, on the Old and New Testaments.* Vol. 2. *Matthew—Romans.* Edited by Robert Jamieson and A. R. Fausset. New York: Revell, 1878. [See. 168–71; N.B. Google book]

Brown, George James. *Lectures on the Gospel According to St. John, Forming a Continuous Commentary.* Vol. 2. Oxford: Hammans, 1863. [See. 415–515; N.B. Google book]

Brown, Raymond E. *The Gospel According to John (13–21).* Garden City, NY: Doubleday, 1970. [Part 3: The Risen Jesus, See. 966–1065; The Epilogue, See. 1066–130; N.B. This work is a definite must to read.]

———. *The Gospel of St. John and the Johannine Epistles.* 3rd ed. Collegeville, MN: Liturgical Press, 1960. [See. 93–100]

Bruce, F. F. *The Gospel of John: Introduction, Exposition and Notes*. Grand Rapids: Eerdmans, 1983. [See. 383–411]

Bruner, Frederick Dale. *The Gospel of John: A Commentary*. Grand Rapids: Eerdmans, 2012. [See. 1137–99; N.B. This work is a healthy read.]

Bryant, Beauford H., and Mark S. Krause. *John*. Joplin, MO: College Press, 1998. [John 20, See. 387–402; John 21, See. 403–15]

Bultmann, Rudolf. *The Gospel of John: A Commentary*. Philadelphia: Westminster, 1971. [See. 681–718; N.B. This book from a liberal perspective is worth exploring.]

Burge, Gary M. *Interpreting the Gospel of John: A Practical Guide*. 2nd ed. Grand Rapids: Baker Academic, 2013. [See. 8, 43, 45, 51, 66, 76–86]

———. *John: The NIV Application Commentary*. Grand Rapids: Zondervan, 2000. [John 20:1–31, See. 549–77; John 21:1–25, See. 578–600]

Burgon, John William. *A Plain Commentary on the Four Holy Gospels: Intended Chiefly for Devotional Reading: St. Luke-St. John*. Vol. 2. Philadelphia: Richard McCauley, 1868. [Chapter 20, See. 907–23; Chapter 21, See. 923–38; N.B. Google book]

Burridge, Richard. *John: The People's Bible Commentary*. Abingdon: Bible Reading Fellowship, 2008. [See. 228–41]

Bussche, Henri Van den. *The Gospel of the Word*. Chicago: Priory Press, 1967. [See. 206–11]

Byrne, Brendan. *Life Abounding: A Reading of John's Gospel*. Collegeville, MN: Liturgical Press, 2014. [The Risen Life of Jesus: 20:1–21:25), See. 327–54]

Calvin, Jean. *The Gospel According to St. John 11 — 21 and the First Epistle of John*. Translated by T. H. L. Parker. Edited by David W. Torrance and Thomas F. Torrance. Grand Rapids: Eerdmans, 1959. [See. 192–226]

Candler, Warren A. *Practical Studies in the Fourth Gospel*. Nashville: Publishing House Methodist Episcopal Church, South, Lamar & Barton, Agents, 1914. [Chapters 20–22, See. 333–76; N.B. Archive.org and Google book]

Cannon, William Ragsdale. *The Gospel of John*. Nashville: The Upper Room, 1985. [See. 108–16]

Card, Michael. *John: The Gospel of Wisdom*. Downers Grove, IL: InterVarsity, 2014. [John 20, See. 203–10; John 21, See. 211–17]

Carlton, Matthew E. *The Translator's Reference Translation of the Gospel of John*. Dallas: SIL International, 2003. [See. 238–54; N.B. Carlton's work is a must read.]

Carson, D. A. *The Gospel According to John*. Leicester: Inter-Varsity Press, 1991. [See. 631–86; N.B. This work should be examined.]

Carter, James E. *Layman's Bible Book Commentary: John*. Vol. 18. Nashville: Broadman, 1984. [See. 148–60]

Carter, Warren. *John and Empire: Initial Explorations*. New York: T&T Clark, 2008. [See. 315–32]

Casey, Maurice. *Is John's Gospel True?* London: Routledge, 1996. [See. 191–98; N.B. Casey's writing is thoughtful and instructive.]

Cassidy, Richard J. *John's Gospel in New Perspective: Christology and the Realities of Roman Power*. Maryknoll, NY: Orbis Books, 1992. [Chapter 7 John 20–21 and Readers in Roman Surroundings, See. 69–79]

Cecilia, Madame. *The Gospel According to St. John*. New York: Benziger, 1923. [See. 351–78; 421–25]

Chennattu, Rekha M. *Johannine Discipleship as a Covenant Relationship*. Peabody: Hendrickson, 2006. [See. 140–79]

Choice Notes on the Gospel of S. John. Drawn From Old and New Sources. London: Macmillan, 1869. [See. 360–90; N.B. Google book]

Clark, George W. *Notes on the Gospel of John: Explanatory and Practical: A Popular Commentary Upon a Critical Basis, Especially Designed for Pastors and Sunday-Schools*. Philadelphia: American Baptist Publication Society, 1879. [See. 315–36; N.B. HathiTrust]

Clark, Henry W. *The Christ From Without and Within: A Study of the Gospel by St. John*. 2nd ed. New York: Revell, 1908. [Chapter 18 See. 220–24; N.B Archive.org]

———. *The Gospel According to St. John: Authorised Version*. New York: Revell, 1915. [See. 236–55; N.B. HathiTrust]

Clymer, R. Swinburne. *The Interpretation of St. John: An Exposition of the Divine Drama; the Nazarene's Life and What It Teaches to Man. The Glory or Tragedy of Man's Soul in the Exercise of Its Inherent Capability to Become Divine*. Quakertown, PA: Philosophical Publishing, 1953. [See. 239–66]

Comfort, Philip Wesley. *I Am the Way: A Spiritual Journey Through the Gospel of John*. Eugene, OR: Wipf & Stock, 1994. [Chapter 20 Raising from the Dead, See. 160–69; Chapter 21 The Conclusion and Epilogue to the Journey, See. 171–76; Previously published by Baker, 1994]

Comfort, Philip W., and Wendell C. Hawley. *Opening John's Gospel and Epistles*. Wheaton: Tyndale House, 1994. [John 20:1–31 Jesus' Resurrection, See. 311–25; John 21:1–25, The Epilogue: Jesus' Last Resurrection Appearance, See. 327–41]

Counet, Patrick Chatelion. *John, A Postmodern Gospel: Introduction to Deconstructive Exegesis Applied to the Fourth Gospel*. Leiden: Brill, 2000. [Chapter 8 The Last Word. The Logos in the Beginning: John 21, 24–25, See. 317–36]

Countryman, Louis William. *The Mystical Way in the Fourth Gospel: Crossing Over Into God*. Philadelphia: Fortress, 1987. [See. 122–35]

Cowles, Henry. *The Gospel and Epistles of John*. New York: D. Appleton, 1876. [See. 289–310; N.B. Archive.org]

Craddock, Fred B. *John*. Atlanta: John Knox, 1982. [See. 140–48]

Crosby, Michael. *Do You Love Me? Jesus Questions the Church*. Maryknoll, NY: Orbis Books, 2000. [See. 183–222]

Culpepper, R. Alan. *The Gospel and Letters of John*. Nashville: Abingdon, 1998. [See. 239–50]

Cyril of Alexandria. *Commentary on John*. Translated by David R. Maxwell and edited Joel C. Elowsky, Vol. 2. Downers Grove, IL: InterVarsity, 2015. [See. 356–86]

Dabney, J. P. *Annotations on the New Testament*. Part 1. Cambridge: Hilliard & Brown, 1829. [See. 216–21; N.B. Google book]

Darby, J. N. *Notes on the Gospel of John*. London: G. Morrish, 1900. [See. 276—88; Note: by J.N.D. on title page]

Darms, Anton. *The Abundant Gospel*. New York: Loizeaux Brothers, Bible Truth Depot, 1941. [See. 207–21]

Davies, J. *St. John's Gospel: The Text Divided Into Paragraphs, and Arranged Chronologically, with Notes*. London: George Philip, 1874. [Period 5 From Christ's Resurrection to His Ascension, See. 257–78; N.B. Google book]

Deems, Charles F. *The Gospel of Spiritual Insight: Being Studies in the Gospel of St. John*. New York: Wilbur B. Ketcham, 1891. [See. 332–65; N.B. Google book]

Deichmann, Hilda Elizabeth Greifrau von. *Notes on the Gospel and Revelation of St. John.* London: Published for the Author by Theosophical Publishing Society, 1910. [See. 132–61]

Derickson, Gary W., and Earl Radmacher. *The Disciplemaker: What Matters Most to Jesus.* Salem, OR: Charis Press, 2001. [Appendix 8 The Message of John and Belief In John 20:30–31, See. 330–31]

Diel, Paul and Jeanine Solotareff. *Symbolism in the Gospel of John.* Translated by Nelly Marans. San Francisco: Harper & Row, 1988. [Chapter 26 The Resurrection, See. 213–16]

Dodd, C. H. *Historical Tradition in the Fourth Gospel.* Cambridge: University Press, 1963. [Part 1 Chapter 7 The Reunion, See. 137–51]

Dods, Marcus. *The Gospel of St. John.* New York: A. C. Armstrong and Son, 1902. [Chapter 22 The Resurrection, See. 351–62; Chapter 23 Thomas Test, See. 363–79; Chapter 24 Appearance at Sea of Galilee, See. 381–96; Chapter 25 Restoration of Peter, See. 397–410; Chapter 26 Conclusion, See. 411–27; N.B. Archive.org]

Dongell, Joseph. *John: A Bible Commentary in the Wesleyan Tradition.* Indianapolis, IN: Wesleyan Publishing House, 1997. [Part 6—The Resurrection Appearances of Joy and Commission (20:1–21:25), See. 233–56]

Doohan, Leonard. *John: Gospel for a New Age.* Santa Fe, NM: Bear, 1988. [See. 125–27]

Drummond, D. T. K. *The Last Scenes in the Life of Our Lord and Saviour.* London: R. B. Seeley and W. Burnside, 1841. [See. 342–80; N.B. Google book]

Dummelow, J. R., ed. *A Commentary on the Holy Bible By Various Writers.* New York: Macmillan, 1916. [See. 808–12]

Dunwell, Francis Henry. *A Commentary on the Authorized English Version of the Gospel According to St. John: Compared with the Sinaitic, Vatican, and Alexandrine Manuscripts, and also with Dean Alford's Revised Translation.* London: J. T. Hayes, 1872. [See. 420–56; N.B. Archive.org and Google book]

Eckman, George P. *Studies in the Gospel of John: Prepared for Readers of the English New Testament. Designed for Use in Bible Classes, Prayer Meetings, and Private Study.* New York: Methodist Book Concern, 1907. [See. 255–336; N.B. Google book]

Edwards, Mark J. *John.* Malden, MA: Blackwell, 2004. [See. 189–208]

Edwards, R. A. *The Gospel According to St. John: Its Criticism and Interpretation.* London: Eyre & Spottiswoode, 1954. [Chapter 7 The Resurrection, See. 165–88]

Ellicott, C. J., ed. *A New Testament Commentary for English Readers.* 2nd ed. Vol. 1. London: Cassell, Petter, Galpin, 1878. [See. 540–51, H.W. Watkins, *The Gospel According to St. John*; N.B. Archive.org]

Ellis, Peter F. *The Genius of John: A Composition-Critical Commentary on the Fourth Gospel.* Collegeville, MN: Liturgical Press, 1984. [See. 280–312]

Ellis, Peter F., and Judith Monahan Ellis. *The Gospel According to John.* New York: W. H. Sadlier, 1983. [See. 155–71]

Elowsky, Joel C., and Thomas C. Oden, eds. *The Ancient Christian Commentary on Scripture.* Downers Grove, IL: InterVarsity, 2006. [See. 335–98]

Erdman, Charles R. *The Gospel of John.* Philadelphia: Westminster, 1944. [See. 165–78]

Evans, Owen E. *The Gospel According to St. John.* London: Epworth, 1965. [See. 208–25]

Exell, Joseph S. *The Biblical Illustrator; or, Anecdotes, Similes, Emblems, Illustrations: Expository, Scientific, Geographical, Historical, and Homiletic, Gathered from a Wide*

Range of Home and Foreign Literature, on the Verses of the Bible. Saint John. Vol. 3. New York: Revell, n.d. [See. 358–521; N.B. Dated, but an excellent read.]

Farley, Lawrence R. *The Gospel of John: Beholding the Glory.* Ben Lomond, CA: Conciliar Press, 2006. [Chapter 6 The Resurrection (20:1—21:24), See. 339–68; Chapter 7 Final Note (21:25), See. 369]

Fawcett, John. *An Exposition of the Gospel According to St. John.* Knaresborough: J. D. Hannam, 1856. [See. 206–67; N.B. Google book]

Fenton, J. C. *Finding the Way Through John.* 2nd ed. London: Mowbray, 1995. [See. 129–40]

———. *The Gospel According to John in the Revised Standard Version.* Oxford: Clarendon, 1970. [See. 200–12]

Filson, Floyd V. *The Gospel According to John.* Richmond, VA: John Knox, 1963. [See. 14–55]

Findlay, J. Alexander. *The Fourth Gospel: An Expository Commentary.* London: Epworth, 1956. [See. 138–55]

Flanagan, Neal M. "John." In *Collegeville Bible Commentary.* Edited by Dianne Bergant and Robert J. Karris. Collegeville, MN: Liturgical Press, 1989. [See. 1013–30]

Ford, James. *The Gospel of S. John: Illustrated (chiefly in the doctrinal and moral sense) from Ancient and Modern Authors.* London: J. Masters, 1852. [Chapter 20, See. 666–95; Chapter 21, See. 695–718; N.B. Google book]

Ford, W. Herschel. *Simple Sermons From the Gospel of John: John 10 to End.* Vol. 3. Grand Rapids: Zondervan, 1958. [See. 178–217]

Fortna, Robert Tomson. *The Fourth Gospel and Its Predecessor: From Narrative Source to Present Gospel.* Philadelphia: Fortress, 1988. [The Resurrection, See. 187–204]

———. *The Gospel of Signs: A Reconstruction of the Narrative Source Underlying the Fourth Gospel.* London: Cambridge University Press, 1970. [A Miraculous Draught of Fish (21:1–14), See. 87–98]; The Resurrection (20:1–20), See. 134–44]

Foster, Lewis. *John: Unlocking the Scriptures for You.* Cincinnati, OH: Standard Publishing, 1987. [See. 209–31]

Fredrikson, Roger L. *John.* Waco, TX: Word, 1985. [See. 281–97]

Gaebelein, Arno Clemens. *The Gospel of John: A Complete Analytical Exposition of the Gospel of John.* New York: Publication Office "Our Hope," 1936. [See. 379–414]

Gaebelein, Frank E. *The Expositor's Bible Commentary.* Vol. 9. *(John-Acts).* Grand Rapids: Zondervan, 1981. [See. 187–203]

Gangel, Kenneth O. *John.* Edited by Max E. Anders. Nashville: Holman Reference, 2000. [John 20 Sights of Super Sunday, See. 363–79; John 21 Jesus Is Lord!, See. 381–96]

Gardner-Smith, P. *Saint John and the Synoptic Gospels.* Cambridge: University Press, 1938. [See. 73–87]

Garvie, Alfred E. *The Beloved Disciple: Studies of the Fourth Gospel.* New York: Doran, 1922. [Part 3 The Appendix (John 21), See. 30–37; N.B. Archive.org and HathiTrust]

George, Larry Darnell. *Reading the Tapestry: A Literary-Rhetorical Analysis of the Johannine Resurrection Narrative (John 20-21).* New York: P. Lang, 2000. [195 pages]

Gerber, Edward H. *The Scriptural Tale in the Fourth Gospel: With Particular Reference to the Prologue and a Syncretic (Oral and Written) Poetics.* Leiden: Brill, 2017. [See. 280–83; 344–49]

Gilbert, T. W. *The Gospel According to St. John.* London: Religious Tract Society, 1930. [See. 207–50]

Gill, John. *An Exposition of the Gospel According to John*. Springfield, MO: Particular Baptist Press, 2003. [See. 606–42; Reprint of third edition, London: Matthews and Leigh, 1809]

Gill, William Hugh. *The Incarnate Word: Being the Fourth Gospel Elucidated by Interpolation for Popular Use*. Philadelphia: George W. Jacobs, 1900. [See. 252–73]

Girdlestone, Charles. *The New Testament of Our Lord and Saviour Jesus Christ: With a Commentary Consisting of Short Lectures for the Daily Use of Families*. Vol. 2. Oxford: J. G. & F. Rivington, 1833. [See. 700–12; N.B. Google book]

Godet, Frédéric Louis. *Commentary on the Gospel of St. John*. Translated by S. Taylor and M. D. Cusin. Vol. 3. Edinburgh: T&T Clark, 1877. [See. 304–66; N.B. Google book]

Gordon, S. D. *Quiet Talks on John's Gospel*. New York: Revell, 1915. [See. 223–56; N.B. HathiTrust]

Gore-Booth, Eva. *A Psychological and Poetic Approach to the Study of Christ in the Fourth Gospel*. London: Longmans, Green, 1923. [See. 341–61; N.B. Archive.org]

Govett, Robert. *Exposition of the Gospel of St. John*. Vol. 2. London: Bemrose, 1881. [See. 402–57; N.B. Google book]

Grant, Frederick C. *John, Ch. 13–21 and the Epistles of John; 1 John, 2 John, 3 John in the King James Version*. New York: Harper, 1956. [See. 34–40]

Grant, Frederick W. *The Numerical Bible: The Gospels*. 3rd ed. New York: Loizeuax, 1904. [See. 612–26; N.B. Archive.org]

Grayston, Kenneth. *The Gospel of John*. Philadelphia: Trinity Press International, 1990. [See. 165–77]

Greene, Oliver B. *The Gospel According to John (Chapters 15–21)*. Vol. 3. Greenville, SC: Gospel Hour, 1966. [See. 313–416]

Gregg, David. *Studies in John's Gospel: The Gospel of Christ's Deity*. New York: American Tract Society, 1891. [Christ Risen, See. 316–32; The Risen Christ and His Disciples, See. 333–48; N.B. Archive.org]

Grenier, Brian. *St. John's Gospel: A Self-Directed Retreat*. Homebush, N.S.W.: St. Paul Publications, 1991. [See. 199–208]

Gruenler, Royce Gordon. *The Trinity in the Gospel of John: A Thematic Commentary on the Fourth Gospel*. Grand Rapids: Baker, 1986. [See. 136–40]

Gundry, Robert H. *Commentary on the New Testament: Verse-by-Verse Explanations with a Literal Translation*. Peabody, MA: Hendrickson, 2010. [John, See. 455–63]

Guthrie, Donald. *Exploring God's Word: A Guide to John's Gospel*. Grand Rapids: Eerdmans, 1986. [See. 213–31]

Gutzke, Manford George. *Plain Talk On John*. Grand Rapids: Zondervan, 1968. [Chapter 21 The Resurrection, See. 197–204; Chapter 22 The Continuing Ministry of Jesus, See. 205–10]

Haenchen, Ernst. *John 2: A Commentary on the Gospel of John Chapters 7–21*. Translated by Robert W. Funk. Edited by Ulrich Busse. Philadelphia: Fortress, 1984. [Chapter 43 The Appearance of Jesus and the First Conclusion, See. 203–17; Chapter 44 The Epilogue, See. 218–34]

Hahn, Scott, and Curtis Mitch. *The Gospel of John*. San Francisco: Ignatius Press, 2003. [See. 55–57]

Halsey, Michael D. *The Gospel of Grace and Truth: A Theology of Grace From the Gospel of John*. Duluth, MN: Grace Gospel Press, 2015. [Chapter 3 But These Are Written

(20:31) The Narrative Form of John's Gospel, See. 51–64; Chapter 5 Jesus Is the Christ, the Son of God (20:31) John's Theology of Jesus Christ, See. 85–123]

Hanson, Anthony Tyrrell. *The Prophetic Gospel: A Study of John and the Old Testament.* Edinburgh: T&T Clark, 1991. [Chapter 13 Death and Resurrection, See. 229–33]

Harney, Kevin. *John: An Intimate Look at the Savior.* Grand Rapids: Zondervan, 1995. [Study 13 Victory Over Sin and Death, See. 88–90]

Harrington, Daniel J. *John's Thought and Theology: An Introduction.* Wilmington, DE: M. Glazier, 1990. [See. 107–12]

Harrington, Wilfred J. *John: Spiritual Theologian. The Jesus of John.* Blackrock, Co Dublin, Columbia Press, 2007. [See. 91–97]

Harrison, Everett Falconer. *John: The Gospel of Faith.* Chicago: Moody, 1962. [See. 117–26]

———. *Meditations on the Gospel of John: The Son of God among the Sons of Men.* Boston: Wilde, 1958. [See. 210–51]

Harrison, McVeigh. *A Devotional Commentary on the Gospel of St. John.* St. Andrew's P.O., TN: St. Andrews Book Shop, 1919. [St John 20, See. 234–50; St John 21, See. 251–77; N.B. Google book]

Harrison, Paul W. *The Light that Lighteth Every Man.* Grand Rapids: Eerdmans, 1960. [John 20: The Resurrection, See. 331–37; John 21: Appendix, See. 338]

Hart, J. Stephen. *A Companion to St. John's Gospel.* Melbourne: Melbourne University Press, 1952. [Chapter 23 Easter Day, See. 203–9; Chapter 24 The Epilogue, See. 210–15]

Hastings, Edward, ed. *The Speaker's Bible: The Gospel According to St John.* Vol. 2. Aberdeen, Scotland: Speaker's Bible Office, 1931. [See. 185–228]

Hayford, Jack W. *Living Beyond the Ordinary: Discovering the Keys to an Abundant Life A Study of John.* Nashville: Thomas Nelson, 1993. [Lesson 14: See. 149–51]

Heil, John Paul. *Blood and Water: The Death and Resurrection of Jesus in John 18–21.* Washington, DC: Catholic Biblical Association of America, 1995. [See. 121–71]

Henderson, Robert Arthur. *The Gospel of Fulfilment: A Study of St. John's Gospel.* London: Society for Promoting Christian Knowledge, 1936. [See. 244–61]

Hendriksen, William. *The Gospel of John.* London: Banner of Truth Trust, 1959. [See. 447–95]

Hengstenberg, E. W. *Commentary on the Gospel of St. John.* Minneapolis: Klock & Klock Christian Publishers, 1980. [See. 433–98; Originally published by T&T Clark Edinburgh 1865, reprint]

Henry, Matthew. *Commentary on the Whole Bible: Genesis to Revelation.* Edited by Leslie F. Church. Grand Rapids: Zondervan, 1961. [See. 1624–35; N.B. Reprint and online]

Herzog, Frederick. *Liberation Theology: Liberation in the Light of the Fourth Gospel.* New York: Seabury, 1972. [See. 243–53]

Hewlett, John. *Commentaries and Annotations on the Holy Scriptures.* Vol. 4. London: Longman, Hurst, Rees, Orme, & Brown, 1816. [See. 287–90; N.B. Google book]

Hibbert, Giles. *John.* Chicago: ACTA Foundation, 1972. [See. 152–76]

Hobbs, Herschel H. *An Exposition of The Gospel of John.* Grand Rapid: Baker, 1968. [See. 279–97]

Hole, F. B. *The Gospel of John: Briefly Expounded.* London: Central Bible Truth Depot, 1954? [See. 161–82]

Hoskyns, Edwyn Clement. *The Fourth Gospel.* Edited by Francis Noel Davey. London: Faber & Faber, 1947. [See. 538–62]

Hovey, Alvah. *Commentary on the Gospel of John*. Philadelphia: American Baptist Publication Society, 1885. [See. 393–419; N.B. Archive.org]

How, William Walsham. *The Gospel According to Saint John*. London: SPCK, 1878. [Chapters 20—21, no pagination; N.B. Google book]

Howard, Wilbert F., and Arthur John Gossip. "The Gospel According to John." In *The Interpreter's Bible Luke and John*. Edited by George A. Buttrick, Vol. 7 Nashville: Abingdon-Cokesbury, 1952. [See. 789–811]

Howard-Brook, Wes. *Becoming Children of God: John's Gospel and Radical Discipleship*. Maryknoll, NY: Orbis Books, 1994. [See. 437–82]

———. *John's Gospel & the Renewal of the Church*. Maryknoll, NY: Orbis Books, 1997. [Chapter 10 Easter and Beyond, See. 141–70]

Hughes, R. Kent. *Behold the Man*. Wheaton, IL: Victor, 1984. [Chapters 19–21, See. 156–80]

———. *John: That You May Believe*. Wheaton, IL: Crossway, 1999. [See. 451–83]

Hunt, B. P. W. Stather. *Some Johannine Problems*. London: Skeffington, 1958. [Chapter 13 The Forty Days, See. 144–56]

Hunter, A. M. *The Gospel According to John*. Cambridge: University Press, 1965. [See. 183–98]

Hutcheson, George. *An Exposition of the Gospel According to John*. Grand Rapids: Kregel, 1959. [See. 410–39]

———. *The Gospel of John*. Edinburgh: Banner of Truth Trust, 1972. [Chapter 20, See. 410–27; Chapter 21, See. 427–39; N.B. First published 1657]

Ironside, H. A. *Addresses on the Gospel of John*. Neptune, NJ: Loizeaux, 1942. [See. 856–92]

Irudaya, Raj. "The Gospel According to John." In *One Volume Dalit Bible Commentary New Testament*. Edited by T. K. John. New Delhi: Centre For Dalit / Subaltern Studies, 2010. [See. 307–10]

Jacobus, Melancthon W. *Notes on the Gospels, Critical and Explanatory, Incorporating with the Notes on a New Plan, the Most Approved Harmony of the Four Gospels: John*. New York: R. Carter, 1865. [See. 325–43; N.B. Google book]

Jarvis, Cynthia A., and E. Elizabeth Johnson, eds. *Feasting on the Gospels: A Feasting on the Gospels John*, Vol. 2. Chapters 10–21. Louisville: Westminster John Knox, 2013. [See. 308–55]

Jenkins, David L. *Windows on the Gospel of John*. Nashville: Broadman Press, 1988. [Chapter 12 John 20:1 to 21:25, See. 183–210]

John Chrysostom, Saint. *Commentary on Saint John the Apostle and Evangelist*. Translated by Thomas Aquinas Goggin. New York: Fathers of the Church, 1960. [Homilies 84–88, See. 417–78]

Johnson, B. W. *The New Testament Commentary: Vol. 3—John. A Commentary for the People*. St. Louis, MO: Christian Board of Publication, 1886. [See. 293–321; N.B. CCEL.org]

Johnston, Mark G. *Let's Study John*. Edinburgh: Banner of Truth Trust, 2003. [See. 250–74]

Kanagaraj, Jey J. *John: A New Covenant Commentary*. Eugene, OR: Cascade, 2013. [John 20: Visions of the Risen Jesus, See. 195–204; John 21: Epilogue, See. 205–14]

Kanagaraj, Jey J., and Ian S. Kemp. *The Gospel According to John*. Singapore: Asia Theological Association, 2000. [Chapter 20 The Risen Lord, See. 393–406; Chapter 21 The Call to Ongoing Commitment, See. 407–16]

Karris, Robert J. *Jesus and the Marginalized in John's Gospel*. Collegeville, MN: Liturgical Press, 1990. [See. 91–95]

———. *John: Stories of the Word and Faith*. Hyde Park, NY: New City Press, 2008. [See. 162–74]

Keddie, Gordon J. *A Study Commentary on John. Volume 2: John 13–21*. Darlington: Evangelical Press, 2001. [See. 354–429]

Keener, Craig S. *The Gospel of John: A Commentary*. Peabody, MA: Hendrickson, 2003. [See. 1167–242; N.B. This text is a solid work to examine and D. A. Carson recommends it for advanced students.]

Kelly, Anthony, and Francis J. Moloney. *Experiencing God in the Gospel of John*. New York: Paulist, 2003. [See. 372–87]

Kelly, William. *An Exposition of the Gospel of John*. London: T Weston, 1892. [See. 406–52; N.B. Google book, 1908]

Kilgallen, John J. *A Brief Commentary on the Gospel of John*. Lewiston, NY: Mellen Biblical Press, 1992. [Chapter 20, See. 233–42; Chapter 21, See. 243–53]

Kirk, Albert, and Robert E. Obach. *A Commentary on the Gospel of John*. New York: Paulist, 1981. [See. 249–66]

Klink, Edward W. *John: Zondervan Exegetical Commentary on the New Testament*. Grand Rapids: Zondervan, 2016. [See. 823–926; N.B. Klink's text should be examined.]

Knox, John. *A New Testament Commentary for English Readers*. Vol. 1. The Gospels. London: Burns Oates & Washbourne, 1953. [John 20, See. 267–70; John 21, See. 270–72]

Knox, W. H. *The Gospel of John*. Essex: S.P. Bookman, 1957. [See. 688–745]

Kobel, Esther. *Dining with John: Communal Meals and Identity Formation in the Fourth Gospel and Its Historical and Cultural Context*. Leiden: Brill, 2011. [See. 210–12, 311, 315]

Koester, Craig R., and Reimund Bieringer, eds. *The Resurrection of Jesus in the Gospel of John*. Tübingen: Mohr Siebeck, 2008. [358 pages; N.B. This text contains essays.]

———. *The Word of Life: A Theology of John's Gospel*. Grand Rapids: Eerdmans, 2008. [Chapter 5 Crucifixion and Resurrection, See. 123–32]

Köstenberger, Andreas J. *John*. Grand Rapids: Academic, 2004. [See. 558–606]

———. *A Theology of John's Gospel and Letters*. Grand Rapids: Zondervan, 2009. [Chapter 4 See. 257–62; Part 3B. The End (Purpose; 20:30–31), See. 329–35; N.B. This work is a good read.]

Kruse, Colin G. *The Gospel According to John: An Introduction and Commentary*. Grand Rapids: Eerdmans, 2003. [See. 375–95]

Kysar, Robert. *John*. Minneapolis: Augsburg, 1986. [See. 294–322]

———. *John's Story of Jesus*. Philadelphia: Fortress, 1984. [See. 85–96]

———. *Preaching John*. Minneapolis: Fortress, 2002. [The Resurrection Appearances, See. 155–74]

Lamont, Daniel. *Studies in the Johannine Writings*. London: J. Clarke, 1956. [Chapter 6 The Resurrection, See. 107–15]

Laney, J. Carl. *John*. Chicago: Moody, 1992. [See. 357–85]

Lange, Johann Peter. *The Gospel According to John*. Edited by Philip Schaff. Translated by Edward D. Yeomans and Evelina Moore. New York: Scribner's Sons, 1871. [See. 503–54; N.B. Archive.org]

Lapide, Cornelius à. *The Great Commentary of Cornelius à. Lapide. S. John's Gospel Chaps. 12 to 21 and Epistles 1, 2, and 3*. Translated by Thomas W. Mossman. 4th ed. Edinburgh: John Grant, 1908. [Chapter 20, See. 253–84; Chapter 21, See. 285–318; N.B. Google book]

La Potterie Ignace de. *The Hour of Jesus: The Passion and the Resurrection of Jesus According to John*. Translated by Gregory Murray. New York: Alba House, 1989. [Chapter 8 The Genesis of Easter Faith, 159–90]

Larsen, Kasper Bro. *Recognizing the Stranger: Recognition Scenes in the Gospel of John* (Biblical Interpretation Series, v. 93). Leiden: Brill, 2008. [Chapter 4 Recognition and Departure (John 20–21), See. 185–217]

Laurin, Roy L. *John, Life Eternal: A Devotional Commentary*. Chicago: Moody, 1972. [See. 250–87]

Lee, Robert. *Outline Studies in John*. Grand Rapids: Kregel, 1987. [See. 137–40; Reprint. *The Outlined John*. London: 1929]

Lenski, R. C. H. *The Interpretation of St. John's Gospel*. Minneapolis: Augsburg, 1961. [See. 1332–444; N.B. This book is a lengthy and detailed work.]

Leonard, W. "St John." In *A Catholic Commentary on Holy Scripture*. Edited by Bernard Orchard. London, 1953. [See. 1015–17]

Lewis, Karoline M. *John*. Minneapolis: Fortress, 2014. [See. 237–61]

Lewis, Scott M. *The Gospel According to John and the Johannine Letters*. Collegeville, MN: Liturgical Press, 2005. [Epilogue: The Resurrection Appearance in Galilee (21:1–25), See. 103–7]

Lightfoot, John. *A Commentary on the New Testament from the Talmud and Hebraica, Matthew—1 Corinthians*. Vol. 3. Grand Rapids: Baker, 1979. [See. 443–55]

Lightfoot, R. H. *St. John's Gospel: A Commentary*. Edited by C. F. Evans. Oxford: Clarendon, 1956. [See. 328–43]

Lincoln, Andrew T. *The Gospel According to Saint John*. Peabody, MA: Hendrickson, 2005. [See. 487–523]

Lindars, Barnabas, ed. *The Gospel of John*. London: Oliphants, 1972. [See. 594–642]

Linn, Otto F. *The Gospel of John: An Exposition*. Anderson, IN: Gospel Trumpet, 1942. [See. 149–60]

Lipscomb, David. *A Commentary to the Gospel according to John*. Edited by C. E. W. Dorris. Nashville: Gospel Advocate, 1976. [See. 306–26]

Lockyer, Thomas F. *The Gospel of St. John*. Edited by Arthur E. Gregory. London: C. H. Kelly, 1901. [See. 282–326]

Lovette, Roger. *Questions Jesus Raised*. Nashville: Broadman Press, 1986. [Chapters 18–21, See. 110–28]

Loyd, Philip Henry. *The Life According to S. John: Eighty-four Meditations*. London: Mowbray, 1936. [See. 271–314]

Lucado, Max. *Life Lessons from the Inspired Word of God— Book of John*. Word, 1996. [Lesson 11 The Risen Christ, See. 93–100; Lesson 12 Peter's Second Chance, See. 101–9]

Luthardt, Chr Ernst. *St John's Gospel Described And Explained According to Its Peculiar Character*. Translated by Caspar Gregory. Vol. 3. Edinburgh: T&T Clark, 1878. [See. 315–90; N.B. Archive.org]

Lüthi, Walter. *St. John's Gospel: An Exposition*. Translated by Kurt Schoenenberger. Richmond: John Knox, 1960. [See. 308–48]

Maahs, Kenneth H. *The John You Never Knew: Decoding the Fourth Gospel*. New York: Peter Lang, 2006. [Chapter 8 Fish That Won't Get Away: The Children of God, See. 159–77; N.B. Discusses the topic of numerology: the number 153.]

MacArthur, John. *The MacArthur Bible Commentary: Unleashing God's Truth, One Verse at a Time*. Nashville: Nelson, 2005. [See. 1423–28]

Macaulay, J. C. *Devotional Studies in St. John's Gospel*. Grand Rapids: Eerdmans, 1945. [See. 266–85]

———. *Expository Commentary on John*. Chicago: Moody, 1978. [See. 257–76]

MacEvilly, John. *An Exposition of the Gospel of St. John: Consisting of an Analysis of Each Chapter, and of a Commentary, Critical, Exegetical, Doctrinal, and Moral, Having the Text, English and Latin, Prefixed in Full to Each Chapter*. New York: Benziger, 1889. [See. 354–79; N.B. Google book]

MacGregor, G. H. C. *The Gospel of John*. New York: Harper & Brothers, 1928. [See. 354–78]

Maclaren, Alexander. *The Gospel of St. John*. London: Hodder & Stoughton, 1893. [See. 207–22; N.B. Archive.org and Google book, 1908]

MacRae, George W. *Invitation to John: A Commentary on the Gospel of John with Complete Text from the Jerusalem Bible*. Garden City, NY: Image, 1978. [See. 217–33]

MacRory, Joseph. *The Gospel of St. John*. Dublin: Browne & Nolan, 1897. [See. 356–86; N.B. HathiTrust]

Madsen, Norman P. *John*. Nashville: Abingdon, 1994. [Chapter 16 John 20, See. 141–47; Chapter 17 John 21, See. 148–54]

Mahoney, Robert. *Two Disciples at the Tomb: The Background and Message of John 20.1–10*. Bern: Lang, 1974. [See. 141–309]

Malina, Bruce J., and Richard L. Rohrbaugh. *Social-Science Commentary on the Gospel of John*. Minneapolis: Fortress, 1998. [See. 278–90]

Manson, William. *The Incarnate Glory. An Expository Study of the Gospel According to St. John*. London: J. Clarke, 1923. [Chapter 10 The Resurrection. Manifestations of the Risen Lord, See. 228–46]

Marrow, Stanley B. *The Gospel of John: A Reading*. New York: Paulist, 1995. [See. 352–77]

Marsh, John. *The Gospel of St John*. Baltimore: Penguin, 1968. [See. 624–78]

Martin, Francis, and William M. Wright. *The Gospel of John*. Grand Rapids: Baker Academic, 2015. [See. 331–56]

Martin, George. *Bringing the Gospel of John to Life: Insight and Inspiration*. Huntington, IN: Our Sunday Visitor, 2016. [See. 548–90]

Martindale, C. C. *The Gospel According to St. John: With an Introduction and Commentary*. Westminster, MD: New Press, 1956. [See. 156–70]

Matson, Mark A. "John." In *The Transforming Word: One-Volume Commentary on the Bible*. Edited by Mark W. Hamilton. Abilene, TX: ACU Press, 2009. [See. 851–54]

———. *John*. Louisville: Westminster John Knox, 2002. [Unit 10 John 20-21, See. 116–29].

Maurice, Frederick Denison. *The Gospel of St. John: A Series of Discourses*. Cambridge: Macmillan, 1893. [See. 443–68; N.B. Archive.org and HathiTrust]

Mayfield, Joseph H., and Ralph Earle. *John, Acts*. Vol. 7. Beacon Bible Commentary. Kansas City: Beacon Hill, 1965. [Section 8 Resurrection and Appearances, See. 226–43; N.B. Mayfield authored the commentary on John.]

McBride, Alfred. *The Divine Presence of Jesus: Meditation and Commentary on the Gospel of John*. Huntington, IN: Our Sunday Visitor, 1992. [See. 180–90]

McCarren, Paul J. *A Simple Guide to John*. Lanham: Rowman & Littlefield, 2013. [Chapter 20 See. 167–72; Chapter 21, See. 173–77]

McCarthy, Brian, ed. *The Navarre Bible: Saint Johns Gospel in the Revised Standard Version and New Vulgate, with a Commentary By the Faculty of Theology, University of Navarre*. Dublin, Ireland: Four Courts Press, 1989. [See. 233–45]

McGann, Diarmuid. *Journeying Within Transcendence: A Jungian Perspective on the Gospel of John*. New York: Paulist, 1988. [See. 181–99]

McIntyre, John. *The Holy Gospel according to St. John*. London: Catholic Truth Society, 1899. [See. 207–23; N.B. Archive.org].

McLaughlin, G. A. *Commentary on the Gospel According to Saint John*. Chicago: The Christian Witness Company, 1913. [Chapter 20, See. 271–81; Chapter 21, See. 283–90; N.B. Archive.org]

M'Clymont, J. A. *St. John. Revised*. New York: Henry Frowde, 1922. [See. 279–97]

McPolin, James. *John*. Wilmington, DE: Glazier, 1979. [See. 212–29]

Meldau, Fred John. *The More Abundant Life: The Gospel of John with Helpful Notes*. Denver, CO: Christian Victory, 1945. [See. 71–78]

Metzger, Paul Louis. *The Gospel of John: When Love Comes to Town*. Downers Grove, IL: Intervarsity, 2010. [See. 245–75]

Meyer, F. B. *Love to the Uttermost: Expositions of John 13—21*. New York: Revell, 1898–1899. [See. 258–93; N.B. Archive.org]

Meyer, Heinrich August Wilhelm. *Critical and Exegetical Handbook to the Gospel of John*. Translated by Frederick Crombie. Vol. 2. Edinburgh: T&T Clark, 1875. [Chapter 20, See. 366–87; Chapter 21, See. 388–412; N.B. Google book]

Michaels, J. Ramsey. *The Gospel of John*. Grand Rapids: Eerdmans, 2010. [See. 984–1058; N.B. This work is a healthy reading and it is recommended by D. A. Carson.]

———. *John*. Peabody, MA: Hendrickson, 1989. [See. 336–64; idem 1984, 1995]

Miller, Carol J. *That You Believe: The Gospel of John*. Vol. 1. Pittsburgh: The Kerygma Program, 2001. [Chapter 14 I am the Resurrection and the Life, See. 120–30]

Milligan, William, and William F. Moulton. *The Gospel According to John*. Edited by Philip Schaff. New York: Scribner's Sons, 1883. [See. 402–39; N.B. Archive.org, 1898]

Milne, Bruce. *The Message of John: Here Is Your King!: With Study Guide*. Leicester: Inter-Varsity Press, 1993. [See. 289–321]

Minear, Paul S. *John, the Martyr's Gospel*. New York: Pilgrim Press, 1984. [Chapter 15 Feed My Sheep, See. 153–62]

Moloney, Francis J. *Glory Not Dishonor: Reading John 13-21*. Minneapolis: Augsburg Fortress, 1998. [See. 153–92]

———. *The Gospel of John*. Edited by Daniel J. Harrington. Collegeville, MN: Liturgical Press, 1998. [See. 515–66]

Morgan, Charles Herbert. *John, the Interpreter of Christ: St. John and His Writings*. New York: Methodist Book Concern, 1921. [See. 12–14; N.B. Google book]

Morgan, G. Campbell. *The Gospel According to John*. Old Tappan, NJ: Revell, 1933. [See. 306—33]

Morris, Leon. *The Gospel According to John*. Grand Rapids: Eerdmans, 1995. [See. 731–77]

———. *Reflections on the Gospel of John*. Peabody, MA: Hendrickson, 2000. [See. 686–750]

Mounce, Robert H. *Luke~Acts [John]*. Edited by Tremper Longman and David E. Garland. Grand Rapids: Zondervan, 2007. [See. 642–61]

Muirhead, Lewis Andrew. *The Message of the Fourth Gospel.* London: Williams & Norgate, 1925. [See. 218–31]

Mullins, Michael. *The Gospel of John: A Commentary.* Blackrock, Co. Dublin: Columba Press, 2003. [The Risen And Glorified Lord Jn 20.1–21.25, See. 397–419]

Murray, J. O. F. *Jesus According to S. John.* London: Longmans, Green, 1938. [Chapter 25 The First Easter Day. 20:1–31, See. 358–69; Chapter 26 The Appearance by the Lake 21:1–25, See. 370–80]

Myers, Alicia D. *Characterizing Jesus: A Rhetorical Analysis on the Fourth Gospel's Use of Scripture in its Presentation of Jesus.* London: T&T Clark, 2012. [The New Creation (Jn 20.1–30), See. 172–77]

Navarre Bible, The. *Saint John's Gospel in the Revised Standard Version and New Vulgate, with a Commentary by the Members of the Faculty of Theology of the University of Navarre.* Dublin: Four Courts Press, 2003. [The Appearances of the Risen Christ, See. 192–201]

Newbigin, Lesslie. *The Light Has Come: An Exposition of the Fourth Gospel.* Grand Rapids: Eerdmans, 1982. [See. 261–81]

Newbolt, W. C. E. *Handbook to the Gospel According to S. John: For the Use of Teachers and Students.* London: Rivingtons, 1906. [See. 163–65]

Newheart, Michael Willett. *Word and Soul: A Psychological, Literary, and Cultural Reading of the Fourth Gospel.* Collegeville, MN: Liturgical Press, 2001. [See. 122–33]

Newman, Barclay Moon, and Eugene A. Nida. *A Translator's Handbook on the Gospel of John.* London: United Bible Societies, 1980. [Chapter 20, See. 601–21; Chapter 21, See. 622–39; N.B. This work is a must read.]

Neyrey, Jerome H. *The Gospel of John.* Cambridge: Cambridge University Press, 2007. [See. 315–43]

———. *The Gospel of John in Cultural and Rhetorical Perspective.* Grand Rapids: Eerdmans, 2009. [See. 441–53]

Nichol, Francis D., ed. *Seventh-day Adventist Bible Commentary: The Holy Bible with Exegetical and Expository Comment.* Vol. 5. Washington, DC: Review & Herald, 1957. [See. 1064–73]

Nolloth, Charles Frederick. *The Fourth Evangelist: His Place in the Development of Religious Thought.* London: John Murray, 1925. [See. 131–35]

Nonnus, of Nisibis. *Commentary on the Gospel of Saint John.* Translated by Robert W. Thomson. Atlanta: Society of Biblical Literature, 2014. [John 20, See. 411–28; John 21, See. 429–43]

O'Day, Gail R. "The Gospel of John." In *The New Interpreter's Bible. The Gospel of Luke, The Gospel of John.* Vol. 9. Nashville: Abingdon, 1995. [See. 838–65; N.B. Alan R. Culpepper authored *The Gospel of Luke*]

———. "Gospel of John." In *Women's Bible Commentary.* Edited by Carol A. Newsom, Sharon H. Ringe, and Jacqueline E. Lapsley. Louisville: Westminster John Knox, 2012. [See. 527–30]

———. "John." In *Women's Bible Commentary Expanded Edition.* Edited by Carol A. Newsom and Sharon H. Ringe. Louisville: Westminster John Knox, 1998. [See. 392–93]

———. *The Word Disclosed: Preaching the Gospel of John.* St. Louis, MO: Chalice, 2002. From Fear to Joy (John 20:19–23), See. 147–51]

O'Day, Gail R., and Susan Hylen. *John.* Louisville: Westminster John Knox, 2006. [See. 191–204]

Oglesby, Stuart R. *The Light is Still Shining: The Gospel of John for a Troubled World.* New York: Revell, 1944. [See. 166–82]

O'Grady, John F. *According to John: The Witness of the Beloved Disciple.* New York: Paulist, 1999. [The resurrection Appearances, See. 110–17]

———. *Preaching the Gospel of John.* New York: Paulist, 2009. [See. 100–107; 128–30]

Olsen, Erling C. *Walks with Our Lord Through John's Gospel.* Vol. 3. Grand Rapids: Zondervan, 1941. [See. 604–51]

Owen, John J. *A Commentary, Critical, Expository, and Practical, on the Gospel of John.* New York: Leavitt & Allen, 1860. [See. 472–502; N.B. Archive.org]

Painter, John. *The Quest for the Messiah: The History, Literature, and Theology of the Johannine Community.* 2nd ed. Nashville: Abingdon, 1993. [The Quest for the Body (20.1–18), See. 379–81]

Palmer, Earl F. *The Intimate Gospel: Studies in John.* Waco, TX: Word, 1978. [See. 166–78]

Papadopoulos, Gerasimos. *The Gospel of St. John: A Commentary.* Translated by Peter A. Chamberas. Brookline, MA: Holy Cross Orthodox Press, 2010. [Chapter 20:1–31, See. 321–33; Chapter 21:1–25, See. 334–42]

Paránanda, Sri. *An Eastern Exposition of the Gospel of Jesus According to St. John.* Edited by R. L. Harrison. London: W. Hutchinson, 1902. [See. 289–301; N.B. Archive.org, Google book, and HathiTrust]

Pate, C. Marvin. *The Writings of John: A Survey of the Gospel, Epistles, and Apocalypse.* Grand Rapids: Zondervan, 2011. [See. 207–22]

Paul, Geoffrey J. *St. John's Gospel: A Commentary.* Madras: Published for the Senate of Serampore College by the Christian Literature Society, 1965. [See. 256–73]

Peck, Edson Ruther. *"Jesus Christ the Lion" and "Seeing with John."* New York: Vantage Press, 1995. [See. 524–49]

Pentecost, Geo F. *Studies in the Gospel of St. John.* Cleveland, OH: Union Gospel Press, 1946. [See. 231–52]

Perkins, Pheme. *The Gospel According to St. John: A Theological Commentary.* Chicago: Franciscan Herald Press, 1978. [See. 231–46]

———. *Gospel of St. John.* Chicago: Franciscan Herald Press, 1975. [See. 92–98]

Petterson, Christina. *From Tomb to Text: The Body of Jesus in the Book of John.* London: Bloomsbury, 2017. [Resurrection, See. 72–75; Chapter 6 The Mediator, See. 114–35]

Phillips, John. *Exploring the Gospels.* Neptune, NJ: Loizeaux, 1988. [See. 373–401; idem 2001]

Pink, Arthur W. *Exposition of the Gospel of John.* Vol. 3. *John 15.7 to End.* Grand Rapids: Zondervan, 1975. [See. 253–333]

Plummer, Alfred, ed. *The Gospel According to St. John.* Cambridge: Cambridge University Press, 1913. [See. 337–57; N.B. Google book, 1886]

Poole, Matthew. *Annotations Upon the Holy Bible Wherein the Sacred Text is Inserted and Various Readings... Vol. 2.* [*Jeremiah—Rev*] London: Printed for Thomas Parkhurst et al., 1700. See. St. John, no pagination; N.B. Google book. Reprinted as *A Commentary on the Holy Bible.* Vol. 3 McLean, VA: MacDonald, 1962. See. 378–84]

Porter, Stanley E. *John, His Gospel, and Jesus: In Pursuit of the Johannine Voice.* Grand Rapids: Eerdmans, 2015. [Chapter 9 Jesus and the Ending of John's Gospel, See. 225–45]

Pryor, John W. *John, Evangelist of the Covenant People: The Narrative & Themes of the Fourth Gospel.* Downers Grove, IL: InterVarsity, 1992. [See. 20:1–29 The Risen Lord, See. 83–90; 20:30–31, See. 90–91; 21:1–25 Epilogue, See. 91–94]

Quast, Kevin. *Reading the Gospel of John: An Introduction.* New York: Paulist, 1991. [Chapter 15 The Resurrection Appearances: "That You May Believe" (John 20), See. 129–39; Chapter 16 The Epilogue (John 21), See. 140–46]

Quimby, Chester Warren. *John, the Universal Gospel.* New York: Macmillan, 1947. [See. 196–203]

Rainbow, Paul A. *Johannine Theology: The Gospel, the Epistles and the Apocalypse.* Downers Grove, IL: IVP Academic, 2014. [See. 31, 68–69, 82, 110, 146, 150–51, 181, 191, 202, 203, 222–25, 227, 233–34, 322, 385]

Raven, Frederick Edward. *Readings on the Gospel of John.* Vol. 3. London: G. Morrish, 1921. [See. 330–77; N.B. The title page reads "With F. E. R. at Greenwich, 1897."]

Ray, Stephen K. *St. John's Gospel: A Bible Study Guide and Commentary.* San Francisco, CA: Ignatius Press, 2002. [See. 366–400]

Reith, George. *The Gospel According to St. John: With Introduction and Notes.* Part 2. Edinburgh: T&T Clark, 1889. [See. 155–78; N.B. Archive.org]

Rensberger, Davis. "John." In *Theological Bible Commentary.* Edited by Gail R. O'Day and David L. Petersen. Louisville: Westminster John Knox, 2009. [See. 354–56]

Rheaume, Randy. *God the Son: What John's Portrait of Jesus Means and Why it Matters.* Eugene, OR: Wipf & Stock. 2018. [See. 146–49]

Rice, Edwin Wilbur. *Commentary on the Gospel According to John: Containing the Common Version, 1611, and the Revised Version, 1881 (American Readings and Renderings): With Critical, Exegetical and Applicative Notes and Illustrations Drawn from Life and Thought in the East.* Philadelphia: Union Press, 1900. [See. 310–31; N.B. Archive.org, 1891 and Google book, 1893]

Rice, John R. *The Son of God: A Verse-by-Verse Commentary on the Gospel According to John.* Murfreesboro, TN: Sword of the Lord, 1976. [See. 387–416]

Richardson, Alan. *The Gospel According to Saint John: Introduction and Commentary.* London: SCM, 1959. [Chapter 20 The Resurrection and Ascension of Christ 20.1–31, See. 206–13; Chapter 21 The Appendix 21.1–25, See. 214–20]

Rickaby, Joseph. *The Gospel According to St. John: Scripture Manuals for Catholic Schools.* Edited by Sydney F. Smith. London: Burns Oats & Washbourne, 1898. [See. 152–64]

Ridderbos, Herman N. *The Gospel According to John: A Theological Commentary.* Grand Rapids: Eerdmans, 1997. [See. 629–83]

Riggs, James Stevenson. *The Messages of Jesus According to the Gospel of John: The Discourses of Jesus in the Fourth Gospel.* New York: Scribner's Sons, 1907. [The Resurrection The Beginning of Exaltation. The Messiah Glorified. Faith Triumphant, See. 339–58; N.B. Google book]

Riley, Gregory J. *Resurrection Reconsidered: Thomas and John in Controversy.* Minneapolis: Fortress, 1995. [222 pages]

Robertson, A. T. *The Divinity of Christ in the Gospel of John.* New York: Revell, 1916. [See. 153–68; N.B. Archive.org]

———. *Word Pictures in the New Testament.* Vol. 5. *The Fourth Gospel, the Epistle to the Hebrews.* Nashville: Broadman, 1932. [Chapter 20, See. 308–17; Chapter 21, See. 318–23]

Robinson, Benjamin Willard. *The Gospel of John: A Handbook for Christian Leaders.* New York: Macmillan, 1925. [Chapter 16 The Last Hours, See. 247–65]

Robinson, John A. T. *The Priority of John.* Edited by J. F. Coakley. Oak Park, IL: Meyer Stone, 1987. [See. 288–95]

Royster, Dmitri. *The Holy Gospel According to Saint John: A Pastoral Commentary.* Yonkers, NY: St Vladimir's Seminary Press, 2015. [Chapter 20, See. 513–30; Chapter 21, See. 531–47]

Rushdoony, Rousas John. *The Gospel of John.* Vallecito, CA: Ross House, 2000. [See. 267–81]

Ryle, J. C. *Expository Thoughts on the Gospels: For Family and Private Use. St. John.* Vol. 3. New York: Revell, n.d. [See. 346–473; N.B. Archive.org, 1857]

Sadler, M. F. *The Gospel According to St. John: With Notes Critical and Practical.* London: George Bell & Sons, 1883. [See. 470–507; N.B. Google book]

Salier, Willis Hedley. *The Rhetorical Impact of the Sēmeia in the Gospel of John.* Tübingen: Mohr Siebeck, 2004. [See. 147–70]

Sanday, William. *The Authorship and Historical Character of the Fourth Gospel: Considered in Reference to the Contents of the Gospel Itself: A Critical Essay.* London: Macmillan, 1872. [See. 258–72; N.B. Archive.org]

Sanders, J. N. *A Commentary on the Gospel According to St. John.* Edited by Brian A. Mastin. New York: Harper & Row, 1968. [See. 416–58]

Sanford, John A. *Mystical Christianity: A Psychological Commentary on the Gospel of John.* New York: Crossroad, 1993. [See. 321–37]

Saunders, Ernest W. *John Celebrates the Gospel.* New York: Abingdon, 1968. [See. 152–64]

Schmid, U. B., et al., eds. *The New Testament in Greek 4 The Gospel According to St. John: Majuscule.* Vol. 2: New Testament Tools, Studies and Documents. New York: Brill, 1995. [See. 529–53]

Schmiedel, Paul Wilhelm. *The Johannine Writings.* Translated by Maurice A. Canney. London: A. & C. Black, 1908. [Chapter 3 Sect. 26 The Story of Jesus' Resurrection, See. 130–34; N.B. Archive.org and HathiTrust]

Schnackenburg, Rudolf. *The Gospel According to St. John Commentary on Chapters 13–21.* Translated by David Smith and G. A. Kon. Vol. 3. New York: Crossroad, 1982. [See. 300–74]

Schneiders, Sandra Marie. *Jesus Risen in our Midst: Essays on the Resurrection of Jesus in the Fourth Gospel.* Collegeville, MN: Liturgical Press, 2013. [Part 1 The Bodily Resurrection of Jesus, See. 3–96]

———. *Written that You May Believe: Encountering Jesus in the Fourth Gospel.* New York: Crossroad, 1999. [See. 180–207]

Scott, John P. *The Four Gospels Esoterically Interpreted.* Oceanside, CA: Langford Press, 1937. [See. 166–69; N.B. HathiTrust]

Scott, Martin. *Sophia and the Johannine Jesus.* Sheffield: JSOT Press, 1992. [Jesus Sophia and Mary Magdala (John 20.1–18), See. 222–34]

Scott, W. Frank. *A Homilectical Commentary on the Gospel According to St. John.* New York: Funk & Wagnalls, 1896. [Chapter 20, See. 553–76; Chapter 21, See. 577–99; N.B. Archive.org]

Scroggie, W. Graham. *Dr. W. Graham Scroggie on Luke & John.* London: Ark Publishing, 1981. [See. 152–55]

———. *St. John.* New York and London: Harper and Brothers, 1931. [See. 126–32]

Sears, Edmund H. *The Fourth Gospel: The Heart of Christ.* 2nd ed. Boston: Noyes, Holmes, 1872. [Part 3 Chapter 10 The Reappearings of Jesus, See. 394–403; N.B. Archive.org]

Setzer, Robert B. *Encounters with the Living Christ: Meeting Jesus in the Gospel of John.* Valley Forge, PA: Judson Press, 1999. [See. 144–68]

Simpson, A. B. *The Gospel of John.* Harrisburg, PA: Christian Publications, 193? [See. 91–99; N.B. Formerly published as *Christ in the Bible: Volume 15, The Gospel of John*, 1904.]

Sinclair, Scott Gambrill. *The Past from God's Perspective: A Commentary on John's Gospel.* North Richland Hills, TX: BIBAL Press, 2004. [Chapter 20, See. 337–60; Chapter 21, See. 361–81]

Sinclair, Scott G. *The Road and the Truth: The Editing of John's Gospel.* Vallejo, CA: Bibal Press, 1994. [Chapter 8 The Editor's Answer to How We Can Know the Gospel Is True (John 21:24–25), See. 71–77]

Skinner, Christopher W. *John and Thomas— Gospels in Conflict? Johannine Characterization and the Thomas Question.* Eugene, OR: Pickwick, 2009. [Chapter 4 Jesus and Peter in the Fourth Gospel. See. 121–38]

Sloyan, Gerard S. *John.* Atlanta: John Knox, 1988. [See. 219–33]

Smith, Dennis E., and Michael E. Williams, eds. *John: The Storyteller's Companion to the Bible.* Abingdon Press, 1996. [See. 170–93]

Smith, D. Moody. *John.* Nashville: Abingdon, 1999. [See. 370–406]

Smith, Robert H. *Wounded Lord Reading John Through the Eyes of Thomas: A Pastoral and Theological Commentary on the Fourth Gospel.* Edited by Donna Duensing. Eugene, OR: Cascade, 2009. [John 20:1–31, See. 179–92; John 21:1–25, See. 193–202]

Spaeth, Adolph. *Annotations on the Gospel According to St. John.* Vol. 5. New York: Christian Literature, 1896. [Chapter 20, See. 298–323; Chapter 21, See. 324–43; N.B. Google book]

Speer, Robert E. *John's Gospel: The Greatest Book in the World: Suggestions for the Study of the Gospel by Individuals and In Groups.* New York: Revell, 1915. [See. 185–208; N.B. HathiTrust]

Speyr, Adrienne von. *The Birth of the Church: Meditations on John 18–21.* Translated by David Kipp. San Francisco: Ignatius Press, 1991. [See. 159–443]

Spong, John Shelby. *The Fourth Gospel: Tales of a Jewish Mystic.* San Francisco: HarperOne, 2013. [Part 5 Resurrection: Mystical Oneness Revealed, See. 265–316; N.B. Written from a liberal point of view.]

Staley, Jeffrey Lloyd. *The Print's First Kiss: A Rhetorical Investigation of the Implied Reader in the Fourth Gospel.* Atlanta, GA: Scholars Press, 1988. [The Victimization of the Implied Reader: Example Five 20:30–21:25, See. 111–18]

Stallings, Jack Wilson. *The Randall House Bible Commentary: The Gospel of John.* Nashville: Randall House, 1989. [See. 276–94]

Stedman, Ray C., and Jim Denney. *God's Loving Word: Exploring the Gospel of John.* Grand Rapids: Discovery House, 1993. [See. 458–82]

Stellhorn, F. W. *A Brief Commentary on the Four Gospels: For Study and Devotion.* Vol. 1. Columbus, OH: Lutheran Book Concern, 1891. [See. 342–48]

St. Helen's Church, Bishopsgate. *John's Gospel.* London: Marshall Pickering, 1999. [Study Guide 26, See. 208–15; Study Guide 27, See. 216–22]

Stibbe, Mark W. G. *John.* Sheffield: JSOT Press, 1993. [See. 198—215]

Story, Cullen I. K. *The Fourth Gospel: Its Purpose, Pattern, and Power*. Shippensburg, PA: Ragged Edge Press, 1997. [See. 361–89]

Strachan, R. H. *The Fourth Gospel, Its Significance and Environment*. 3rd ed. London: Student Christian Movement Press, 1941. [See. 324–40]

Sueltz, Arthur Fay. *Deeper Into John's Gospel*. San Francisco: Harper & Row, 1979. [See. 134–56]

Summers, Ray. *Behold the Lamb: An Exposition of the Theological Themes in the Gospel of John*. Nashville: Broadman Press, 1979. [See. 262–92]

Sumner, John Bird. *A Practical Exposition of the Gospel According to St. John: In the Form of Lectures, Intended to Assist the Practice of Domestic Instruction and Devotion*. London: J. Hatchard and Son, 1835. [See. 503–26; N.B. Archive.org]

Swain, Lionel. *The Gospel According to St John*. London: Sheed & Ward, 1978. [Part 4 The Resurrection (20:1–21:25), See. 242–59]

Swartley, Willard M. *John: Believers Church Bible Commentary*. Harrisonburg, VA: Herald Press, 2013. [The Risen Jesus Ignites Mission and New Community, John 20, See. 452–74; New Horizons and Destinies, John 21, See. 475–96]

Sweeley, John W. *Jesus in the Gospels: Man, Myth, or God*. Lanham: University Press of America, 2000. [See. 163–97]

Sylva, Dennis D. *Thomas— Love As Strong As Death: Faith and Commitment in the Fourth Gospel*. London: Bloomsbury, 2013. [Chapter 3 There Is (No) More: God From Beyond The Limits Of Belief (John 20:24–29; 21.1–2), See. 82–107]

Talbert, Charles H. *Reading John: A Literary and Theological Commentary on the Fourth Gospel and the Johannine Epistles*. New York: Crossroad, 1992. [See. 248–64]

Tasker, R. V. G. *The Gospel According to St. John: An Introduction and Commentary*. Leicester: Inter-Varsity Press, 1960. [See. 220–37]

Taylor, Michael J. *John: The Different Gospel: A Reflective Commentary*. Staten Island, NY: Alba House, 1983. [See. 239–69]

Temple, Sydney. *The Core of the Fourth Gospel*. London: Mowbrays, 1975. [See. 250–51]

Temple, William. *Readings in St. John's Gospel (First And Second Series)*. London: Macmillan, 1949. [See. 375–412]

Tenney, Merrill C. *The Expositor's Bible Commentary*. Vol. 9. *(John-Acts)*. Grand Rapids: Regency Reference Library, 1981. [See. 187–203; N.B. Tenney penned the commentary on John.]

———. *John: The Gospel of Belief: An Analytic Study of the Text*. Grand Rapids: Eerdmans, 1948. [See. 272–94; idem 1989]

Thatcher, Floyd W., ed. *Discovering John: The Guideposts Home Bible Study Program*. Carmel, NY: Guideposts, 1985. [Lesson 8 John 20–21, See. 136–50]

Theodore of Mopsuestia. *Commentary on the Gospel of John*. Edited by Joel C. Elowsky. Translated by Marco Conti. Downers Grove, IL: InterVarsity, 2010. [See. 157–69]

Tholuck, A. *A Commentary on the Gospel of St. John*. Translated by Abram Kaufman. Boston: Perkins and Marvin, 1836. [See. 444–74; N.B. Archive.org and Hathitrust]

Thomas, David. *The Genius of the Fourth Gospel: The Gospel of St. John, Exegetically and Practically Considered. Extending From Chapter 14 To 21*. Vol. 3. London: R. D. Dickinson, 1885. [See. 352–69]

Thompson, Marianne Meye. *John: A Commentary*. Louisville: Westminster John Knox, 2015. [The Resurrection of Jesus, See. 408–47]

Titus, Eric Lane. *The Message of the Fourth Gospel*. New York: Abingdon, 1957. [See. 237–53]

Torrance, Thomas. *Expository Studies in St. John's Miracles*. London: James Clarke, 1938. [Chapter 10 The Second Miraculous Draught of Fishes, See. 18–205]

Towns, Elmer L. *The Gospel of John: Believe and Live*. Old Tappan, NJ: Revell, 1990. [See. 340–75]

Trench, George Henry. *A Study of St. John's Gospel, to Which Are Added: 1. The Julian and Jewish Calendars for AD 27–29. 2. A Diary of All the Events in Our Lord's Ministry Which Are Mentioned in the Gospels. 3. Tables Showing How the Fourth Gospel Dovetails with the Three Synoptics*. London: John Murray, 1918. [See. 412–540]

Turner, George Allen, and Julius R. Mantey. *The Gospel According to John*. Grand Rapids: Eerdmans, 1964. [See. 384–416]

Vanderlip, D. George. *John, the Gospel of Life*. Valley Forge, PA: Judson Press, 1979. [Chapter 10 Life Proclaimed, See. 127–34]

Van Doren W. H. *Gospel of John: Expository and Homiletical Commentary*. Grand Rapids: Kregel, 1981. [See. 1342–436; Reprint. Originally published: *A Suggestive Commentary on St. John*. London: R. D. Dickenson. 1872; N.B. HathiTrust]

Vanier, Jean. *Drawn Into the Mystery of Jesus Through the Gospel of John*. Ottawa: Novalis, 2004. [Chapter 25 Call to Forgive (John 20), See. 333–46; Chapter 26 Meeting Jesus every day (John 21), See. 347–59]

Vine, W. E. *John: His Record of Christ*. London: Oliphants, 1948. [Chapter 20, See. 181–84; Chapter 21, See. 185–90]

Waetjen, Herman C. *The Gospel of the Beloved Disciple: A Work in Two Editions*. New York: T&T Clark International, 2005. [See. 409–26]

Wahlde, Urban C. *Commentary on the Gospel and Letters of John*. Vol. 2. Grand Rapids: Eerdmans, 2010. [See. 836–907; N.B. This work is a detailed, healthy reading.]

Ward, Ronald A. *The Gospel of John*. Grand Rapids: Baker, 1961. [See. 129–39]

Watkins, H. W. *The Gospel According to St. John*. In *A New Testament Commentary for English Readers. By Various Writers*. 2nd ed. Vol. 1. Edited by C. J. Ellicott. London: Cassell Petter & Galpin, 1878. [See. 540–51; N.B. Archive.org and Google book]

Weber, Gerard P., and Robert Miller. *Breaking Open the Gospel of John*. Cincinnati, OH: St. Anthony Messenger Press, 1995. [See. 117–30]

Webster, Jane S. *Ingesting Jesus: Eating and Drinking in the Gospel of John*. Atlanta: Society of Biblical Literature, 2003. [Chapter 8 Resurrection Breakfast (21:1–25), See. 133–46]

Welch, Charles H. *Life Through His Name: Being an Exposition of the Gospel of John*. London: Berean, 1953. [See. 537–52]

Westcott, Brooke Foss. *The Gospel According to St John*: (Reprinted from "The Speaker's Commentary"). London: John Murray, 1882. [See. 288–307; N.B. Google book]

Whedon, D. D. *Commentary on the Gospels: intended for popular use: Luke—John*. New York: Nelson & Phillips, 1866. [John Chapter 20, See. 408–14; Chapter 21, See. 414–22; N.B. Google book]

Wheeler, Michael. *St. John and the Victorians*. Cambridge: Cambridge University Press, 2012. [Chapter 8 Touching the Risen Body: Mary Magdalene and Thomas, See. 199–235; Afterward, See. 236–38]

Whitacre, Rodney A. *John*. Downers Grove, IL: InterVarsity, 1999. [See. 470–501]

Whitelaw, Thomas. *The Gospel of St. John: An Exposition Exegetical and Homiletical*. Glasgow: J. Maclehose & Sons, 1888. [See. 421–61; N.B. Google book and HathiTrust]

Williamson, Lamar. *Preaching the Gospel of John: Proclaiming the Living Word.* Louisville: Westminster John Knox, 2004. [See. 274–303]

Witherington, Ben. *John's Wisdom: A Commentary on the Fourth Gospel.* Louisville: Westminster John Knox, 1995. [Part 6 The Resurrection Narratives: Including the Epilogue John 20:1—21:25, See. 323–61]

Worsley, F. W. *The Fourth Gospel and the Synoptists: Being a Contribution to the Study of the Johannine Problem.* Edinburgh: Clark, 1909. [See. 57–61; 148–50; N.B. Archive.org]

Wright, N. T. *John for Everyone.* Part 2 Chapters 11–21. London: SPCK, 2004. [See. 139–69]

Yarbrough, Robert W. *John.* Everyman's Bible Commentary. Chicago: Moody, 1991. [See. 197–213]

Young, Samuel. *John.* Edited by William M. Greathouse and Willard H. Taylor. Vol. 4. Kansas City, MO: Beacon Hill, 1979. [See. 160–78]

Zanchettin, Leo., ed. *John: A Devotional Commentary: Meditations on the Gospel According to St. John.* Ijamsville, MD: Word Among Us, 2000. [The Risen Christ— John 20:1-21:25, See. 211–26]

Chapter 21

The Acts of the Apostles

Abbott, Lyman. *An Illustrated Commentary on the Acts of the Apostles: For Family Use and Reference, and for the Great Body of Christian Workers of All Denominations.* Vol. 4. New York: A.S. Barnes, 1878. [See. 29–36; N.B. Archive.org, Google book, and HathiTrust]

Aberly, John. "The Acts." In *New Testament Commentary.* Edited by Herbert C. Alleman. Philadelphia: Muhlenberg Press, 1936. [See. 401–2]

Alexander, Joseph A. *The Acts of the Apostles.* New York: Scribner, 1857. [See. 1–38; N.B. Archive.org and Google book]

Alexander, Loveday. *Acts.* Peabody, MA: Hendrickson, 2007. [See. 22–27]

Allen, Andrew James Campbell. *The Acts of the Apostles.* London: James Nisbet, 1891. [See. 28–31]

Allen, Frank Emmett. *The Acts of the Apostles.* Boston: Christopher Publishing House, 1931. [See. 1–46]

Allen, Ronald J. *Acts of the Apostles.* Minneapolis: Fortress, 2013. [See. 15–27]

Anderson-Berry, David. *Pictures in the Book of Acts: or, the Unfinished Work of Jesus.* Glasgow: Pickering & Inglis, 193? [See. 9–51]

Andrews, H. T. *The Acts of the Apostles: With Introduction and Notes.* London: Andrew Melrose, 1908. [See. 32–44; N.B. Google book and HathiTrust]

Arnold, Clinton E. *Acts* (Zondervan Illustrated Bible Background). Grand Rapids: Zondervan, 2002. [See. 7–14]

Arnot, William. *Studies in Acts: The Church in the House.* Grand Rapids: Kregel, 1978. [See. 13–38]

Arrington, French L. *The Acts of the Apostles: An Introduction and Commentary.* Peabody, MA: Hendrickson, 1988. [See. 3–17]

Ash, Anthony Lee. *The Acts of the Apostles. Part 1. 1:1—12:25.* Austin, TX: Sweet Publishing, 1979. [See. 25–38]

Aymer, Margaret. "Acts of the Apostles." In *Women's Bible Commentary.* Edited by Carol A. Newsom, Sharon H. Ringe, and Jacqueline E. Lapsley. Louisville: Westminster John Knox, 2012. [See. 538–39]

Baker, Charles F. *Understanding the Book of Acts.* Grand Rapids: Grace Bible College Publications, 1981. [See. 15–18]

Balge, Richard D. *Acts.* Milwaukee, WI: Northwestern Publishing House, 1988. [See. 8–22]

Barclay, William. *The Acts of the Apostles*. 3rd ed. Louisville: Westminster John Knox, 2003. [See. 9–19]

———. *The Acts of the Apostles*. Philadelphia: Westminster, 1955. [See. 1–11]

Barker, Charles Joseph. *The Acts of the Apostles: A Study in Interpretation*. London: Epworth, 1969. [See. 15–18]

Barnes, Albert. *Notes, Explanatory and Practical, on the Acts of the Apostles: Designed for Bible Classes and Sunday Schools*. 12th ed. New York: Harper, 1854. [See. 7–23; N.B. Archive.org and HathiTrust]

Barnhouse, Donald Grey, and Herbert Henry Ehrenstein. *Acts: An Expositional Commentary*. Grand Rapids: Zondervan, 1979. [See. 13–25]

Barr, Beth Allison, et al., eds. *The Acts of the Apostles: Four Centuries of Baptist Interpretation: The Baptists' Bible*. Waco, TX: Baylor University Press, 2009. [See. 73–105]

Barrett, C. K. *The Acts of the Apostles: A Shorter Commentary*. London: T&T Clark, 2002. [See. 1–14]

———. *A Critical and Exegetical Commentary on the Acts of the Apostles*. Vol. 1. Edinburgh: T&T Clark, 1994. [See. 59–105; N.B. This book is worth examining.]

Bartlet, J. Vernon, ed. *The Acts: Introduction, Authorized Version, Revised Version with Notes, Index and Map*. Edinburgh: T. C. & E. C. Jack, 1901. [See. 35–37; N.B. HathiTrust]

Baumgarten, M. *The Acts of the Apostles: or, The History of the Church in the Apostolic Age*. Translated by A. J. W. Morrison. Vol. 1. Edinburgh: T&T Clark, 1854. [See. 9–23; N.B. Archive.org]

Beck, W. E. *The Acts of the Apostles*. London: University of Tutorial Press, 1937. [N.B. Located only in the Ayson Clifford Library, Carey Baptist College, Auckland, New Zealand.]

Bede, the Venerable, Saint. *The Venerable Bede Commentary on the Acts of the Apostles*. Translated by Lawrence T. Martin. Kalamazoo, MI: Cistercian Publications, 1989. [See. 9–25]

Bence, Philip A. *Acts: A Bible Commentary in the Wesleyan Tradition*. Indianapolis, IN: Wesleyan Publishing House, 1998. [Chapter 1 Background (1:1–26), See. 2–36]

Bengel, Johann Albrecht, Ernest Bengel, and J. C. F. Steudel. *Gnomon of the New Testament: Containing the Commentary On the Gospels According to St Luke and St John and the Acts of the Apostles*. Translated by A. R. Fausset. Vol. 2. Philadelphia: Smith, English, 1860. [See. 510–22; N.B. Google book]

Benham, William. "The Acts of the Apostles." In *The New Testament of Our Lord and Saviour Jesus Christ According to the Authorised Version. Containing the Acts, Epistles, and Revelation*. Vol. 2. Published Under the Direction of the Tract Committee. London: Society for Promoting Christian Knowledge, 1881. [No pagination; N.B. Google book]

Benson, Dennis C. *Dennis Benson's Creative Bible Studies*. Loveland, CO: Group, 1985. [See. 514–19]

Benson, Edward White. *Addresses on the Acts of the Apostles: Delivered to Ladies in Lambeth Palace Chapel during the Years 1887 to 1892*. London: Macmillan, 1901. [See. 1–21; N.B. Google book]

Bishop, Eric F. F. *Apostles of Palestine: The Local Background to the New Testament Church*. London: Lutterworth, 1958. [See. 21–30]

Category VIII—The New Testament

Blaiklock, E. M. *The Acts of the Apostles: An Historical Commentary*. Grand Rapids, Tyndale Press, 1974. [See. 49–53]

———. *Acts: The Birth of the Church*. Old Tappan, NJ: Revell, 1980. [See. 9–19]

Blair, Edward Payson. *A Study of the Book of Acts*. New York: Abingdon-Cokesbury, 1951. [See. 8–11]

Blunt, A. W. F. *The Acts of the Apostles in the Revised Version*. Oxford: Clarendon, 1922. [See. 53–54; N.B. Google book]

Bock, Darrell L. *Acts*. Grand Rapids: Baker Academic, 2007. [See. 49–91; N.B. Recommended by D. A. Carson for advanced student.]

———. *A Theology of Luke and Acts: Biblical Theology of the New Testament*. Edited by Andreas J. Köstenberger. Grand Rapids: Zondervan, 2012. [Introduction: Jesus Ascends to the Father and Gives a Mission (Acts 1:1–11), See. 79–80; Resurrection-Ascension, 204–5; The Work of Salvation: The Cross and Jesus' Resurrection-Ascension, 253–56]

Boice, James Montgomery. *Acts: An Expositional Commentary*. Grand Rapids: Baker, 1997. [See. 13–37]

Boring, M. Eugene, and Fred B. Craddock. *The People's New Testament Commentary*. Louisville: Westminster John Knox, 2004. [See. 366–69]

Bosworth, Edward I. *New Studies in Acts*. New York: Young Men's Christian Association Press, 1911. [See. 3–9; N.B. Archive.org, Google book, and HathiTrust]

———. *Studies in the Acts and Epistles: Based on the Records and Letters of the Apostolic Age by Ernest De Witt Burton*. New York: International Committee of Young Men's Christian Associations, 1900. [See. 10–13; N.B. Google book]

Brewster, John. *Lectures on the Acts of the Apostles: Delivered in the Parish Church of Stockton upon Tees, During Lent in the Years 1803, 1804, 1805, & 1806*. Vol. 2. London: G.J.G. & F. Rivington, 1830. [See. 41–60; N.B. Google book]

Brown, Charles. *The Acts of the Apostles*. London: The Religious Tract Society, 1925. [See. 9–30]

Brown, David. *A Commentary, Critical and Explanatory on the Old and New Testaments: Matthew—Romans*. Vol. 2. New York: Revell, 1878. [See. 174–77; N.B. Google book]

Browne, Laurence Edward. *The Acts of the Apostles: With Introduction and Notes*. London: Society for Promoting Christian Knowledge, 1925. [See. 1–25]

Bruce, F. F. *The Acts of the Apostles: The Greek Text with Introduction and Commentary*. Grand Rapids: Eerdmans, 1952. [See. 65–80]

———. *The Book of the Acts*. Grand Rapids: Eerdmans, 1988. [Chapter 1 The Birth of the Church, See. 28–48]

Burnham, David, and Sue Burnham. *Acts: The Body in Action: A Discussion Guide for Home Bible Study*. Chicago: Moody, 1978. [See. 9–14]

Burnside, W. F. *The Acts of the Apostles: The Greek Text*. Cambridge: Cambridge University Press, 1916. [See. 75–80; N.B. Archive.org]

Burrell, David James, and Joseph Dunn Burrell. *The Early Church Studies in the Acts of the Apostles*. New York: American Tract Society, 1897. [See. 7–18; N.B. Google book]

Calvin, John. *Calvin's Commentaries: The Acts of the Apostles 1–13*. Translated by John W. Fraser and William James Gilmour MacDonald. Edited by David W. Torrance and Thomas F. Torrance. Grand Rapids: Eerdmans, 1965. [See. 21–48]

Cannon, William Ragsdale. *The Book of Acts*. Nashville: Upper Room, 1989. [Chapter 1 The Risen Christ and His Disciple Acts 1:1–26, See. 15–23]

Carlton, Matthew E. *The Translator's Reference Translation of the Acts of the Apostles*. Dallas, TX: SIL International, 2001. [See. 1–14; N.B. This work is a definite read.]

Carter, Charles W., and Ralph Earle. *The Acts of the Apostles*. Grand Rapids: Zondervan, 1973. [See. 1–26; N.B. First printed in 1959.]

Carter, Warren, and Amy-Jill Levine. *The New Testament: Methods and Meanings*. Nashville: Abingdon, 2013. [See. 94–95]

Carver, William Owen. *The Acts of the Apostles*. Nashville: Broadman Press, 1916. [See. 11–22; N.B. Google book]

Cave, Sydney, and W. F. Howard. *The Acts of the Apostles*. London: Cassell, 1929. [See. 15–21]

Cecilia, Madame. *The Acts of the Apostles Books: 1 and 2*. London: K. Paul, Trench, Trübner, 1908. [See. 55–74; N.B. Archive.org]

Chance, J. Bradley. *Acts*. Macon, GA: Smyth & Helwys, 2007. [See. 33–45]

Chappell, Clovis G. *When the Church Was Young*. New York: Abingdon-Cokesbury, 1950. [See. 9–30]

Chrysostom, John. *The Homilies of S. John Chrysostom, Archbishop of Constantinople: On the Acts of the Apostles*. Part 1. Homilies 1–28. Oxford: J. H. Parker, 1851. [See. 1–52; N.B. Archive.org]

Chung-Kim, Esther, and Todd R. Hains, eds. *Acts*. Downers Grove, IL: InterVarsity, 2014. [See. 4–17]

Clark, Albert Curtis. *The Acts of the Apostles*. Oxford: Clarendon, 1933. [See. 336–38; Repr., 1970]

Clark, George W. *Harmony of the Acts of the Apostles: And Chronological Arrangement of the Epistles and Revelation, with Chronological and Explanatory Notes, and Valuable Tables*. Philadelphia: American Baptist Publication Society, 1897. [See. 21–25; N.B. EBSCO]

———. *Notes on the Acts of the Apostles, Explanatory and Practical: A Popular Commentary Upon a Critical Basis, Especially Designed for Pastors and Sunday-Schools*. Philadelphia: American Baptist Publication Society, 1892. [See. 17–26; N.B. Archive.org and HathiTrust]

Conzelmann, Hans. *Acts of the Epistles: A Commentary on the Acts of the Apostles*. Edited by Eldon Jay Epp and Christopher R. Matthews. Translated by Donald H. Juel, A. Thomas Kraabel, and James Limburg. Philadelphia: Fortress, 1987. [See. 3–12; N.B. Examine this text.]

Cook, David. *Teaching Acts: Unlocking the Book of Acts for the Bible Teacher*. London: PTMEDIA Christian Focus, 2007. [See. 55–65]

Cook, F. C. *The Acts of the Apostles: With a Commentary and Practical and Devotional Suggestions for Reader and Students of the English Bible*. London: Longmans, Green, and, 1866. [See. 1–13; N.B. Google book]

Couch, Mal, ed. *A Bible Handbook to the Acts of the Apostles*. Grand Rapids: Kregel, 1999. [See. 178–95]

Cowles, Henry. *Luke: Gospel History and Acts of the Apostles, with Notes, Critical, Explanatory, and Practical, Designed for Both Pastors and People*. New York: D. Appleton, 1881. [See. 277–85; N.B. Google book and HathitTrust]

Cox, Lilian E. "The Acts of the Apostles." In *The Twentieth Century Bible Commentary*. Edited by G. Henton Davies, Alan Richardson, and Charles L. Wallis. New York: Harper & Brothers, 1955. [See. 459–60]

Criswell, W. A. *Acts: In One Volume*. Grand Rapids: Zondervan, 1983. [See. 13–58]

Category VIII—The New Testament

Crowe, Jerome. *The Acts*. Wilmington, DE: Michael Glazier, 1979. [See. 3–8]

Cukrowski, Kenneth L. "Acts of the Apostles." In *The Transforming Word: One-Volume Commentary on the Bible*. Edited by Mark W. Hamilton. Abilene, TX: Abilene Christian University Press, 2009. [See. 856–57]

Culy, Martin M., and Mikeal C. Parsons. *Acts: A Handbook on the Greek Text*. Waco, TX: Baylor University Press, 2003. [See. 1–22]

Custer, Stewart. *Witness to Christ: A Commentary on Acts*. Greenville, SC: BJU Press, 2000. [See. 1–16]

Dabney, J. P. *Annotations on the New Testament*. Part 1. Cambridge: Hilliard and Brown, 1829. [See. 222–24; N.B. Google book]

Davies, J. *The Acts of the Apostles: The Text Divided into Paragraphs, with Notes*. London: George Philip & Son, 1871. [See. 4–10; N.B. Google book]

Demaray, Donald E. *The Book of Acts: A Study Manual*. Grand Rapids: Baker, 1959. [See. 13–14]

Denton, W. *A Commentary on the Acts of the Apostles*. Vol. 1. London: George Bell, 1874. [See. 1–40; N.B. Archive.org and Google book]

Dessain, C. S. "Acts of the Apostles." In *A Catholic Commentary on Holy Scripture*. Edited by Bernard Orchard. London: Nelson, 1953. [See. 1023–24]

De Welt, Don. *Acts Made Actual: A New Commentary, Workbook, Teaching Manual*. Joplin, MO: College Press, 1958. [See. 23–34]

Dick, John. *Lectures on the Acts of the Apostles*. 2nd ed. New York: Robert Carter, 1857. [Lecture 1, See. 1–19; N.B. Archive.org and HathiTrust]

Dummelow, J. R., ed. *A Commentary on the Holy Bible by Various Writers*. New York: Macmillan, 1916. [See. 817–19; N.B. Google book]

Dunn, James D. G. *The Acts of the Apostles*. Valley Forge, PA: Trinity Press International, 1996. [See. 1–21; N.B. Examine Dunn's text.]

Dunnett, Walter M. *The Book of Acts*. Grand Rapids: Baker, 1981. [See. 15–21]

Earle, Ralph. "Acts." The Acts of the Apostles. In *Beacon Bible Commentary*. Vol. 7. *John-Acts*. Kansas City, MO: Nazarene Publishing House, 1965. [See. 256–71; N.B. Joseph H. Mayfield authored "John"]

Eddleman, H. Leo. *An Exegetical and Practical Commentary on Acts: A Verse by Verse Study of the Fifth Book of the New Testament*. Dallas: Book of Life, 1974. [See. 1–11]

Edwards, David L. *Good News in Acts: The Acts of the Apostles in Today's English Version*. Glasgow: Fontana, 1974. [See. 97–98]

Erdman, Charles R. *The Acts*. Philadelphia: Westminster, 1919. [See. 15–27; N.B. Archive.org]

Exell, Joseph S. *The Biblical Illustrator: The Acts*. Vol. 1. New York: Revell, 1905. [See. 1–108; N.B. Archive.org; N.B. Definitely examine this dated source.]

Fallis, William Joseph. *Studies in Acts*. Nashville: Convention Press, 1949. [See. 1–10]

Faw, Chalmer Ernest. *Acts (Believers Church Bible Commentary)*. Scottdale, PA: Herald Press, 1993. [See. 28–38]

Fernando, Ajith. *Acts: The NIV Application Commentary From Biblical Text . . . to Contemporary Life*. Grand Rapids: Zondervan, 1998. [See. 49–85]

Findlay, James Alexander. *The Acts of the Apostles*. London: Student Christian Movement Press, 1934. [See. 57–62]

Fitzmyer, Joseph A. *The Acts of the Apostles*. New York: Doubleday, 1998. [See. 191–221]

Flanagan, Neal M. *The Acts of the Apostles: Introduction and Commentary.* Collegeville, MN: Liturgical Press, 1964. [See. 23–27]

Foakes-Jackson, F. J., and Kirsopp Lake. *The Beginnings of Christianity:* Part 1. *The Acts of the Apostles.* Vol. 1. *Prolegomena 1 The Jewish, Gentile and Christian Backgrounds.* Edited by F. J. Foakes Jackson and Kirsopp Lake. London: Macmillan, 1920. [Jesus Christ, Resurrection of, See. 303, 321, 322, 335, 381, 382; N.B. Archive.org]

Forbes, Greg W., and Scott D. Harrower. *Raised From Obscurity: A Narratival and Theological Study of the Characterization of Women in Luke-Acts.* Eugene, OR: Pickwick, 2015. [Chapter 8 The Birth of the Church (Acts 1–2), See. 149–53]

Ford, James. *The Acts of the Apostles, Illustrated (Chiefly in the Doctrinal and Moral Sense) From Ancient and Modern Authors.* London: Joseph Masters, 1856. [See. 7–35; N.B. Google book]

Ford, W. Herschel. *Simple Sermons From the Book of Acts.* Grand Rapids: Zondervan, 1950. [See. 13–23]

Fraser, Donald. *The Speeches of the Holy Apostles.* New York: Macmillan, 1882. [Chapter 1 St. Peter To The Brethren At Jerusalem, See. 7–19; N.B. Archive.org]

Furneaux, William Mordaunt. *The Acts of the Apostles: A Commentary for English Readers.* Oxford: Clarendon, 1912. [See. 1–26; N.B. Archive.org]

Gaebelein, A. C. *The Acts of the Apostles: An Exposition.* New York: Publication Office "Our Hope," 1912. [See. 13–27; N.B. Google book and HathiTrust]

———. *The Annotated Bible: The Holy Scriptures Analyzed and Annotated The Gospels and the Book of Acts.* Vol. 1. New York: Publication Office "Our Hope," 1913. [See. 256–58; N.B. Archive.org and HathiTrust]

Gangel, Kenneth O. *Acts.* Nashville: Broadman & Holman, 1998. [See. 5–19]

———. *Acts.* Wheaton, IL: Victor, 1987. [See. 13–20]

Gardiner, E. A. *The Acts of the Apostles: Text of the Revised Version.* London: Rivingtons, 1934. [See. 3–7]

Gaventa, Beverly Roberts. *The Acts of the Apostles.* Nashville: Abingdon, 2003. [See. 61–73]

Gavigan, James, Brian McCarthy, and Thomas McGovern, eds. *The Navarre Bible: The Acts of the Apostles in the Revised Standard Version and New Vulgate with a Commentary By Members of the Faculty of Theology of the University of Navarre.* Dublin, Ireland: Four Courts Press, 1992. [See. 29–40]

Geikie, Cunningham. *The Apostles, Their Lives and Letters.* New York: James Pott, 1897. [Chapter 1 The Days After Calvary, See. 1–19; N.B. Archive.org and HathiTrust]

Gettys, Joseph M. *How to Teach Acts.* Richmond: John Knox, 1959. [Lesson 3, See. 23–29]

Gill, John. *Gill's Commentary.* Vol. 5. *Matthew to Acts.* Grand Rapids: Baker, 1980. [See. 798–807; Reprinted from the edition published by William Hill. London. 1852–54; N.B. Archive.org]

Gloag, Paton James. *A Critical and Exegetical Commentary on the Acts of the Apostles.* Vol. 1. T&T Clark: Edinburgh, 1870. [See. 39–67; N.B. Archive.org and Google book]

González, Justo L. *Acts: The Gospel of the Spirit.* Maryknoll, NY: Orbis Books, 2001. [See. 13–31]

Gooding, D. W. *True to the Faith: Charting the Course Through the Acts of the Apostles.* Grand Rapids: Gospel Folio Press, 1995. [See. 33–55]

Grech, Prospero. *Acts of the Apostles Explained: A Doctrinal Commentary.* New York: Alba House, 1966. [Chapter 1, See. 19–23]

Green, Samuel G. *The Acts of the Apostles: An Exposition for English Readers, on the Basis of Professor Hackett's Commentary on the Original Text.* Vol. 1. London: J. Heaton, 1862. [See. 27–47]

Greene, Oliver B. *The Acts of the Apostles.* Greenville, SC: Gospel House, 1968. [See. 15–65]

Gundry, Robert H. *Commentary on the New Testament: Verse-by-Verse Explanations with a Literal Translation.* Peabody, MA: Hendrickson, 2010. [Acts. See. 464–68]

Guthrie, Donald. *The Apostles.* Grand Rapids: Zondervan, 1975. [See. 12–23]

Guy, Harold A. *The Acts of the Apostles.* London: Macmillan, 1953. [See. 33–37]

Hackett, Horatio B. *A Commentary on the Acts of the Apostles.* Edited by Alvah Hovey. Valley Forge, PA: American Baptist Publication Society, 1882. [See. 29–41; N.B. Archive.org and Google book, 1852]

Haenchen, Ernst. *The Acts of the Apostles: A Commentary.* Philadelphia: Westminster, 1971. [See. 148–65]

Hahn, Scott, Curtis Mitch, and Dennis Walters. *The Acts of the Apostles: With Introduction, Commentary, and Notes.* 2nd ed. San Francisco, CA: Ignatius Press, 2002. [See. 17–19]

Hamm, M. Dennis. *The Acts of the Apostles.* Collegeville, MN: Liturgical Press, 2005. [See. 11–16]

Hanson, R. P. C. *The Acts in the Revised Standard Version.* Oxford: Clarendon, 1967. [See. 57–61]

Harbour, Brian L. *Living Expectantly.* Nashville: Broadman Press, 1990. [See. 9–15]

Hargreaves, John. *A Guide to Acts.* London: SPCK, 1990. [See. 4–13]

Harrison, Everett Falconer. *Acts: The Expanding Church.* Chicago: Moody, 1975. [See. 35–48]

Henry, Matthew. *Commentary on the Whole Bible: Genesis to Revelation.* Edited by Leslie F. Church. Grand Rapids: Zondervan, 1961. [See. 1636–40; N.B. Available online.]

Henson, Hensley. *Apostolic Christianity: Notes and Inferences Mainly Based on S. Paul's Epistles to the Corinthians.* London: Methuen, 1898. [Part 3. Chapter 2 The Resurrection, 94–106; N.B. EBSCO]

Hervey, A. C. *The Acts of the Apostles.* Vol. 1. H. D. M. Spence and Joseph S. Exell. London: Funk & Wagnalls, 1909. [See. 1–40; N.B. The Pulpit Commentary; Archive.org and HathiTrust]

Hewlett, John. *Commentaries and Annotations on the Holy Scriptures.* Vol. 4. London: Longman, Hurst, Rees, Orme, & Brown, 1816. [See. 293–96; N.B. Google book]

Hills, O. A. *The Testimony of the Witnesses: A Devotional and Homiletical Exposition of the Acts of the Apostles.* New York: T. Nelson and Sons, 1913. [See. 1–21; N.B. Archive.org]

Hooton, Walter Stewart. *Turning-Points in the Primitive Church.* London: C. J. Thynne, 1919. [See. 6–15]

Horton, Stanley M. *Acts.* Springfield, MO: Complete Biblical Library, 1991. [See. 18–37]

———. *The Book of Acts.* Springfield, MO: Gospel Publishing House, 1981. [See. 15–28]

Howson, J. S. *The Evidential Value of the Acts of the Apostles.* New York: Dutton, 1880. [Lesson 2 The Relation of this Book to the Gospel of History, See. 49–95; N.B. Archive.org]

Howson, J. S., and H. D. M. Spence-Jones. *The Acts of the Apostles.* New York: Scribner's Sons, 1883. [See. 1–9]

Hughes, R. Kent. *Acts: The Church Afire.* Wheaton, IL: Crossway, 1996. [See. 13–28]

Humphry, William Gilson. *A Commentary on the Book of the Acts of the Apostles.* London: John W. Parker, 1854. [See. 1–13; N.B. Google book]

Ironside, H. A. *Lectures on the Book of Acts.* New York: Loizeaux, 1943. [See. 9–36]

Jacobsen, David Schnasa, and Günter Wasserberg. *Preaching Luke-Acts.* Nashville: Abingdon, 2001. [Chapter 3 Hope for Resurrection: A Learning Experience Luke 24:13–49, See. 55–71]

Jacobson, William. *The Acts of the Apostles.* In *The Holy Bible According to the Authorized Version (AD 1611) in 4 Volumes.* Vol. 2. *St John–The Acts of the Apostles.* Edited by F. C. Cook. New York: Scribner's Sons. 1880. [See. 351–60; N.B. Also known as the Speaker's Commentary.]

Jacobus, Melancthon W. *The Catechetical Question Book: Acts.* New York: Carter, 1859. [See. 5–11; N.B. Google book and HathiTrust]

Jensen, Irving L. *Acts: An Inductive Study: A Manual of Bible-Study-in-Depth.* Chicago: Moody, 1968. [See. 57–71]

Johnson, Timothy Luke. *The Acts of the Apostles.* Edited by Daniel J. Harrington. Collegeville, MN: Liturgical Press, 1992. [See. 23–41]

Jones, J. Cynddylan. *Studies in the Acts of the Apostles.* London: Houlston, 1878. [See. 1–17; N.B. Archive.org and Google book]

Jones, J. Estill. *Acts: Working Together in Christ's Mission.* Nashville: Convention Press, 1974. [See. 6–10]

Karris, Robert J. *Invitation to Acts: A Commentary on the Acts of the Apostles with Complete Text From the Jerusalem Bible.* Garden City, NY: Image, 1978. [See. 21–29]

Kee, Howard Clark. *To Every Nation Under Heaven: The Acts of the Apostles.* Harrisburg, PA: Trinity Press International, 1997. [See. 31–41]

Keener, Craig S. *Acts: An Exegetical Commentary: Introduction and 1:1 — 2:47.* Vol. 1. Grand Rapids: Baker Academic, 2012. [See. 646–779. N.B. This source is a solid work to examine.]

Kelly, William. *An Exposition of the Acts of the Apostles: Newly Translated from an Amended Text.* 3rd ed. London: C.A. Hammond, 1952. [See. 9–16]

Kent, Charles Foster. *The Work and Teachings of the Apostles.* New York: Scribner's Sons, 1916. [See. 21–27; N.B. Archive.org and HathiTrust]

Kent, Homer Austin. *Jerusalem to Rome: Studies in the Book of Acts.* Grand Rapids: Baker, 1972. [See. 21–29]

Kilgallen, John J. *A Brief Commentary on the Acts of the Apostles.* New York: Paulist, 1988. [See. 3–10]

Kistemaker, Simon. *New Testament Commentary: Exposition of the Acts of the Apostles.* Grand Rapids: Baker, 1990. [See. 43–69]

Knox, Ronald A. *A New Testament Commentary for English Readers: The Acts of the Apostles. St. Paul's Letters to the Churches.* Vol. 2. New York: Sheed & Ward, 1954. [See. 1–5]

Krodel, Gerhard. *Acts.* Minneapolis, MN: Augsburg, 1986. [See. 51–68]

Kürnizger, Josef. *The Acts of the Apostles.* Vol. 1. Translated by Anthony N. Fuerst. New York: Herder & Herder, 1969. [See. 1–27]

Kurz, William S. *Acts of the Apostles.* Grand Rapids: Baker Academic, 2013. [See. 25–42]

———. "The Acts of the Apostles." In *The Collegeville Bible Commentary.* Edited by Dianne Bergant and Robert J. Karris. Collegeville, MN: Liturgical Press, 1989. [See. 1037–39]

———. *The Acts of the Apostles.* Collegeville, MN: Liturgical Press, 1983. [See. 17–22]

Kwon, Yon-Gyong. *A Commentary on Acts.* London: SPCK, 2012. [See. 6–19]

Lake, Kirsopp, and Henry J. Cadbury. *The Beginnings of Christianity*: Part 1. *The Acts of the Apostles*. Vol. 4. Translated by Kirsopp Lake and Henry J. Cadbury. Edited by F. J. Foakes and Kirsopp Lake. London: Macmillan, 1933. [See. 1–15; Note 3. The Ascension, 16–22; Note 4. The Death of Judas, 22–29; Note 6. The Twelve and the Apostles, 37–46; N.B. This book is a classic, dated source.]

Lampe, G. W. H. "Acts." In *Peake's Bible Commentary*, Edited by Matthew Black and H. H. Rowley. London: Thomas Nelson, 1962. [See. 882–87]

Larkin, William J. *Acts*. Edited by D. Stuart. Briscoe and Haddon W. Robinson. Downers Grove, IL: InterVarsity, 1995. [See. 37–48]

———. *The Gospel of Luke—Acts*. Edited by Philip W. Comfort. Carol Stream, IL: Tyndale House, 2006. [See. 377–85]

Lash, Nicholas. "Acts." In *Luke*. Duncan Macpherson, Nicholas Lash, and Bernard Robinson. Chicago: ACTA Foundation, 1971. [See. 113–17]

LaSor, William Sanford. *Church Alive*. Glendale, CA: G/L Regal, 1972. [See. 18–41]

Lechler, Gotthard Victor. *The Acts of the Apostles: An Exegetical and Doctrinal Commentary*. Translated by Charles F. Schaeffer. New York: Scribner's Sons, 1867. [See. 7–25; N.B. Google book]

Le Cornu, Hilary. *A Commentary on the Jewish Roots of Acts*. Jerusalem: Academon, 2003. [See. 1–51]

Lee, Robert. *The Outlined Acts: Blackboard Outlines with Notes on the Acts of the Apostles, Etc*. London: Pickering & Inglis, 1931. [See. 5–11]

Lee, Witness. *Life-Study of Acts Messages 1–18*. Anaheim, CA: Living Stream Ministry, 1986. [See. 1–42]

Lenski, R. C. H. *The Interpretation of the Acts of the Apostles*. Columbus, OH: Lutheran Book Concern, 1934. [See. 17–54; N.B. Consider examining]

Liggins, Stephen S. *Many Convincing Proofs: Persuasive Phenomena Associated with Gospel Proclamation in Acts*. Berlin: de Gruyter, 2016. [See. 110–15]

Lightfoot, John. *A Commentary on the New Testament From the Talmud and Hebraica, Matthew — 1 Corinthians*. Vol. 4. *Acts — 1 Corinthians*. Vol. 4. Grand Rapids: Baker, 1979. [See. 5–20; Reprinted from the 1859 edition published by Oxford University Press]

———. *The Works of the Reverend & Learned John Lightfoot D.D. in Two Volumes*. Vol. 1. London: Printed by W. R., 1684. [The Chronicle and Order of the Acts of the Apostles: The Epistles and the Revelation. The Second Part. Acts 1, See. 275–76; N.B. Archive.org, Google book, and HathiTrust]

Lightfoot, Joseph Barber. *The Acts of the Apostles: A Newly Discovered Commentary*. Edited by Ben Witherington. Vol. 2. Downers Grove, IL: InterVarsity, 2014. [See. 75–85]

Lindsay, Thomas M. *The Acts of the Apostles*. Edinburgh: T&T Clark, 1884. [See. 37–47; N.B. Archive.org]

Livermore, Abiel Abbot. *The Acts of the Apostles: With a Commentary*. Boston: J. Munroe, 1844. [See. 13–24; N.B. Archive.org and Google book]

Longenecker, Richard N. *Acts*. Grand Rapids: Zondervan, 2007. [See. 48–64]

———. *The Expositor's Bible Commentary: Luke ~ Acts*. Edited by Tremper Longman and David E. Garland. Vol. 10. Grand Rapids: Zondervan, 2007. [See. 713–31]

Loomis, B. B. *Studies in the Acts of the Apostles*. New York: Eaton & Mains, 1896. [See. 22–25: N.B. Archive.org]

Lovett, C. S. *Acts*. Baldwin Park, CA: Personal Christianity, 1972. [See. 24–39]

Luccock, Halford E. *The Acts of the Apostles in Present-Day Preaching*. Chicago: Willett, Clark, 1938. [See. 1–45]

Lüdemann, Gerd. *The Acts of the Apostles: What Really Happened in the Earliest Days of the Church*. Amherst, NY: Prometheus, 2005. [See. 31–45; N.B. The author believes the ascension is ahistorical and many accounts found in the first chapter have nil historical value.]

———. *Early Christianity According to the Traditions in Acts: A Commentary*. Minneapolis: Fortress, 1989. [See. 25–37; N.B. The author asserts that many accounts recorded in Acts are ahistorical or derive from tradition.]

Lumby, J. Rawson. *The Acts of the Apostles*. Cambridge: University Press, 1904. [See. 80–92; N.B. Google book and HathiTrust]

Lynch, Denis. *The Story of the Acts of the Apostles: A Narrative of the Development of the Early Church*. New York: Benziger, 1917. [See. 23–31; N.B. Archive.org]

Lyttelton, George William. *The Four Gospels and the Acts of the Apostles*. London: Rivingtons, 1856. [See. 376–78; N.B. Archive.org]

MacArthur, John. *The MacArthur Bible Commentary: Unleashing God's Truth, One Verse at a Time*. Nashville: Nelson, 2005. [See. 1431–35]

Macaulay, J. C. *Devotional Commentary on the Acts of the Apostles*. Grand Rapids: Eerdmans, 1946. [See. 15–23]

MacDonald, William. *The Acts: Dynamic Christianity*. Kansas City, KS: Walterick, 1971. [See. 11–25]

MacEvilly, John. *Exposition of the Acts of the Apostles Consisting of an Analysis of Each Chapter and of a Commentary*. New York: Benziger, 1899. [See. 1–13; N.B. Archive.org]

Maddox, Robert L. *Acts*. Vol. 19. *Layman's Bible Book Commentary*. Nashville: Broadmen Press, 1979. [See. 15–25]

Malina, Bruce J., and John J. Pilch. *Social-Science Commentary on the Book of Acts*. Minneapolis: Fortress, 2008. [See. 19–27]

Marshall, I. Howard. *The Acts of the Apostles: An Introduction and Commentary*. Grand Rapids: Eerdmans, 2000. [See. 55–67]

Martin, Francis, and Thomas C. Oden, eds. *Ancient Christian Commentary on Scripture: Acts*. Vol. 5. Downers Grove, IL: InterVarsity, 2006. [See. 1–19]

Martin, Ralph P. *Acts*. London: Scripture Union, 1967. [See. 5–7]

Martindale, C. C. *The Acts of the Apostles*. Westminster, MD: Newman Press, 1958. [See. 1–7]

Maskew, T. R. *Annotations on the Acts of the Apostles, Original and Selected: Designed Principally for the Use of Candidates for the Ordinary B.A. Degree, Students for Holy Orders, &c. with College and Senate-House Examination Papers*. Cambridge: J. & J.J. Deighton, 1847. [See. 15–24; N.B. Google book]

Massey, James. "Acts of the Apostles." In *One Volume Dalit Bible Commentary New Testament*. Edited by T. K. John. New Delhi: Centre For Dalit / Subaltern Studies, 2010. [See. 313–14]

Matthews, Shelly. *The Acts of the Apostles: Taming the Tongues of Fire*. Sheffield: Sheffield Phoenix Press, 2013. [See. 25–26]

Mauck, John W. *Paul on Trial: The Book of Acts as a Defense of Christianity*. Nashville: Nelson, 2001. [Acts 1—By Many Infallible Proofs, See. 49–54]

McBride, Alfred. *The Gospel of the Holy Spirit: A Commentary on the Acts of the Apostles*. New York: Hawthorn, 1975. [See. 24–25]

McBride, Denis. *Emmaus: The Gracious Visit of God According to Luke*. Dublin: Dominican Publications, 1991. [See. 175–201]

McGarvey, J. W. *A Commentary on Acts of Apostles: With a Revised Version of the Text*. Cincinnati: Wrightson, 1863. [See. 9–23; N.B. Archive.org and HathiTrust]

McLaughlin, G. A. *Commentary on the Acts of the Apostles*. Chicago: Christian Witness, 1915. [See. 7–18]

Meyer, Heinrich August Wilhelm. *Critical and Exegetical Handbook to the Acts of the Apostles*. 2nd ed. Translated by Paton J. Gloag and William P. Dickson. Edited by William Ormiston. New York: Funk & Wagnalls, 1883. [See. 23–39; N.B. Archive.org and Google book, 1889]

Mimpriss, Robert. *The Teacher's Manual; Grades 1 and 2. Acts of the Apostles Fifty-Two Lesson*. London: The British and Colonial Educational Association, 1864. [See. 2–5; N.B. Google book]

Morgan, G. Campbell. *The Acts of the Apostles*. New York, Chicago: Revell, 1924. [See. 7–23; N.B. Archive.org]

Morrison, Thomas. *The Acts of the Apostles and the Epistles of Paul*. 3rd ed. Edinburgh: Oliphant, Anderson & Ferrier, 1888. [See. 10–12; N.B. Archive.org]

Moulton, H. K. *The Acts of the Apostles: Introduction and Commentary*. Madras: Published for the Senate of Serampore by the Christian Literature Society, 1957. [See. 66–79]

Mullins, Michael. *The Acts of the Apostles: A Commentary*. Blackrock, Co. Dublin: Columba Press, 2013. [See. 59–68]

Munck, Johannes. *The Anchor Bible: The Acts of the Apostles*. Edited by William F. Albright and Christopher Stephen Mann. New York: Doubleday, 1967. [See. 3–12]

Neil, William. *The Acts of the Apostles*. London: Oliphants, 1973. [See. 63–71]

Newman, Barclay Moon, and Eugene A. Nida. *A Translator's Handbook on the Acts of the Apostles*. London: United Bible Societies, 1972. [See. 11–32; N.B. This work is a definite must read.]

Nichol, Francis D., ed. *Seventh-day Adventist Bible Commentary: The Holy Bible with Exegetical and Expository Comment*. Vol. 6. Washington, DC: Review and Herald, 1957. [See. 118–32]

O'Day, Gail R. "Acts." In *Women's Bible Commentary*. Edited by Carol A. Newsom, Sharon H. Ringe, and Jacqueline E. Lapsley. Louisville: Westminster John Knox, 1998. [See. 395–96]

Ogilvie, Lloyd John. *The Communicator's Commentary: Acts*. Waco, TX: Word, 1983. [See. 23–53]

Olshausen, Hermann. *Biblical Commentary on the Gospels, and on the Acts of the Apostles*. Translated by John Gill, Richard Garvey, and William Lindsay. Vol. 4. Edinburgh: T&T Clark, 1850. [See. 347–67; N.B. Archive.org]

Owen, John J. *Acts of the Apostles: According to the Text of Augustus Hahn: With Notes and a Lexicon: For the Use of Schools, Colleges, and Theological Seminaries*. New York: Leavitt & Allen, 1856. [See. 91–97; N.B. Archive.org]

Packer, J. W. *Acts of the Apostles: Commentary*. Cambridge: Cambridge University Press, 1966. [See. 20–26]

Page, T. E., and A. S. Walpole. *The Acts of the Apostles*. London: Macmillan, 1895. [See. 1–11: N.B. Archive.org]

Pallis, Alexandros. *Notes on St. Luke and the Acts*. Edinburgh: Oxford University Press, 1928. [See. 49–50]

Parker, Joseph. *Apostolic Life: As Revealed in the Acts of the Apostles*. New York: Funk & Wagnalls, 1883. [See. 1–39; N.B. Archive.org, Google book, and HathiTrust]

Parsons, Mikeal C. *Acts*. Grand Rapids: Baker Academic, 2008. [See. 25–35]

———. "Acts." In *Mercer Commentary on the Bible*: Vol. 7. *Acts and Pauline Writings*. Edited by Watson E. Mills and Richard F. Wilson. Macon, GA: Mercer University Press, 1997. [See. 3–5]

Peirce, Bradford K. *Notes on Acts of the Apostles*. Edited by D. P. Kidder. New York: Lane & Scott, 1848. [See. 5–18; N.B. Archive.org]

Pelikan, Jaroslav. *Acts*. Grand Rapids: Brazos, 2005. [See. 37–47]

Peloubet, F. N. *Suggestive Illustrations on the Acts of the Apostles*. Philadelphia: A. J. Holman, 1901. [See. 1–33; N.B. Archive.org]

———. *The Teachers' Commentary on the Acts of the Apostles*. New York: Oxford University Press, 1901. [See. 1–16; N.B. Google book and HathiTrust]

Perdue, Cary Milburn. *Acts Analyzed and Explained*. Manila, Republic of the Philippines: O.M.F., 1983. [See. 24–35]

Pervo, Richard I. *Acts: A Commentary*. Edited by Harold W. Attridge. Minneapolis: Fortress, 2009. [See. 31–60; N.B. Pervo's text is highly recommended.]

———. *Luke's Story of Paul*. Minneapolis: Fortress, 1990. [See. 15–18]

Peterson, David G. *The Acts of the Apostles*. Grand Rapids: Eerdmans, 2009. [See. 100–29; N.B. This work has been rated by D. A. Carson as a best buy.]

Phillips, John. *Exploring Acts*. Chicago: Moody, 1986. [See. 11–32]

Pierson, Paul Everett. *Themes from Acts*. Ventura, CA: Regal, 1982. [See. 8–22]

Pilch, John J. *Visions and Healing in the Acts of the Apostles: How the Early Believers Experienced God*. Collegeville, MN: Liturgical Press, 2004. [See. 13–25]

Polhill, John B. *Acts*. Vol. 26. Nashville: Broadman Press, 1992. [See. 77–95]

Poole, Matthew. *Annotations Upon the Holy Bible Wherein the Sacred Text is Inserted and Various Readings . . . Vol. 2. [Jeremiah—Rev]* London: Printed for Thomas Parkhurst et al., 1700. See. The Acts of the Apostles, no pagination; N.B. Google book. Reprinted as *A Commentary on the Holy Bible*. McLean, VA: MacDonald, 1962. See. 384–87]

Powell, Ivor. *The Amazing Acts*. Grand Rapids: Kregel, 1987. [See. 18–33]

Price, Eugenia. *Learning to Live From the Acts*. Philadelphia: Lippincott, 1970. [See. 9–14]

Pyle, Thomas. *A Paraphrase with Notes on the Acts of the Apostles and Upon the Epistles of the New Testament*. 3rd ed. London: Printed for D. Midwinter et al., 1737. [See. 1–9; N.B. Google book and HathiTrust]

Rackham, Richard Belward. *The Acts of the Apostles: An Exposition*. London: Methuen, 1901. [See. 3–14; N.B. Archive.org and HathiTrust]

Ramsay, William M. *Pictures of the Apostolic Church Studies in the Book of Acts*. London: Hodder & Stoughton, 1910. [See. 1–4; Repr., Grand Rapids: Baker, 1959]

Reese, Gareth L. *New Testament History: A Critical and Exegetical Commentary on the Book of Acts*. Joplin, MO: College Press, 1986. [See. 1–33]

Renan, Ernest. *The Apostles*. New York: Carleton, 1869. [See. 54–90; N.B. Archive.org and Gutenberg.org]

Ricciotti, Giuseppe. *The Acts of the Apostles: Texts and Commentary*. Translated by Laurence E. Byrne. Milwaukee: Bruce, 1958. [See. 43–57]

Rice, Edwin Wilbur. *People's Commentary on the Acts:*. Philadelphia: American Sunday-School Union, 1896. [See. 25–38; N.B. Google book]

Category VIII—The New Testament

Rice, John R. *Filled with the Spirit: The Book of Acts A Verse-by-Verse Commentary*. Murfreesboro, TN: Sword of the Lord, 1963. [See. 23–60]

Ripley, Henry J. *The Acts of the Apostles*. Boston: Gould and Lincoln, 1867. [See. 7–19; N.B. Google book and HathiTrust]

Robertson, A. T. *Word Pictures in the New Testament: Volume 3: The Acts of the Apostles*. Grand Rapids: Baker, 1930. [See. 3–19]

Robertson, William. *Studies in the Acts of the Apostles*. New York: Revell, 1901. [See. 6–12]

Robinson, Anthony B., and Robert W. Wall. *Called to be Church: The Book of Acts for a New Day*. Grand Rapids: Eerdmans, 2006. [See. 29–48]

Ryn, August Van. *Acts of the Apostles: The Unfinished Work of Christ*. New York: Loizeaux, 1961. [See. 19–31]

Ryrie, Charles Caldwell. *The Acts of the Apostles*. Chicago: Moody, 1961. [See. 12–16]

Sadler, M. F. *The Acts of the Apostles: With Notes Critical and Practical*. London: George Bell, 1904. [See. 1–19]

Sargent, James E. *Acts*. Nashville: Abingdon, 1994. [See. 13–16]

Schnabel, Eckhard J. *Acts*. Grand Rapids: Zondervan, 2012. [See. 63–107; N.B. This is a great read and D. A. Carson also recommends it for advanced students.]

Scroggie, W. Graham. *The Acts of the Apostles*. Grand Rapids: Zondervan, 1976. [See. 25–30]

Shade, W. Robert, and Bruce Nicholls. *Acts*. Singapore: Asia Theological Association, 2007. [See. 19–36]

Shepherd, William. *Horæ Apostolicæ: A Digested Narrative of the Acts and Writings of the Apostles of Jesus Christ. Arranged According to Townsend*. London: Longman, Brown, Green, & Longmans, 1846. [See. 1–10; N.B. Google book]

Sitterly, Charles Fremont. *Jerusalem to Rome: The Acts of the Apostles*. New York: Abingdon, 1915. [40–45; N.B. Google book]

Sledd, Andrew. *His Witnesses: A Study of the Book of Acts*. Nashville: Cokesbury, 1935. [Chapter 1 From the Resurrection to Pentecost, See. 19–32]

Smith, James Hamblin. *Short Notes on the Greek Text of the Acts of the Apostles*. 4th ed. London: Rivingtons, 1890. [See. 3–7; N.B. Google book and HathiTrust]

Smith, Miles Woodward. *On Whom the Spirit Came: A Study of the Acts of the Apostles*. Philadelphia: Judson Press, 1948. [See. 11–17]

Smith, Robert H. *Concordia Commentary: Acts*. Saint Louis: Concordia, 1970. [See. 37–49]

Soards, Marion L. *The Speeches in Acts: Their Content, Context, and Concerns*. Louisville: Westminster John Knox, 1994. [See. 21–31]

Södergren, Carl J. *The Acts*. Rock Island, IL: Augustana Book Concern, 1927. [See. 19–28]

Spencer, F. Scott. *Acts*. Sheffield: Sheffield Academic Press, 1997. [See. 23–31]

———. *The Gospel of Luke and Acts of the Apostles*. Nashville: Abingdon, 2008. [Chapter 7 See. 215–16]

———. *Journeying through Acts: A Literary-Cultural Reading*. Peabody, MA: Hendrickson, 2004. [See. 33–41]

Stack, Richard. *Lectures on the Acts of the Apostles: Explanatory and Practical*. 2nd ed. London: T. Cadell & W. Davies, 1805. [See. 1–26; N.B. Archive.org, Google book, and HathiTrust]

Stagg, Frank. *The Book of Acts: The Early Struggle for an Unhindered Gospel*. Nashville: Broadman Press, 1955. [See. 28–50]

Stam, Cornelius Richard. *Acts: Dispensationally Considered.* Chicago: Berean Bible Society, 1954. [See. 25–67]

Stellhorn, F. W. *Annotations on the Acts of the Apostles.* New York: Christian Literature, 1896. [See. 1–17; N.B. Archive.org]

Stier, Rudolf. *The Words of the Risen Saviour, and Commentary on the Epistle of St James.* Translated by William B. Pope. 1859. [To Saul the Persecutor, Acts 9:4–6, 22:7–10; 26:14–16. See. 1–27, N.B. Google book]

Stifler, James M. *An Introduction to the Study of the Acts of the Apostles.* New York: Revell, 1892. [See. 3–13; N.B. Google book]

Stokes, George Thomas. *The Acts of the Apostles.* London: Hodder & Stoughton, 1893. [See. 23–81; N.B. Archive.org, Google book, Gutenberg.org, and HathiTrust]

Stott, John R. W. *The Spirit, the Church, and the World.* Downers Grove: InterVarsity, 1990. [See. 32–59]

Summers, Thos O. *Commentary on the Acts of the Apostles.* Nashville: Publishing House of the Methodist Episcopal Church, South, 1882. [See. 11–28]

Talbert, Charles H. *Acts.* Atlanta: John Knox, 1984. [See. 6–17]

———. *Reading Acts: A Literary and Theological Commentary on the Acts of the Apostles.* New York: Crossroad, 1997. [See. 19–39]

Tannehill, Robert C. *The Narrative Unity of Luke-Acts: A Literary Interpretation: The Acts of the Apostles.* Vol. 2. Philadelphia: Fortress, 1991. [See. 9–25]

Taylor, Justin. "Acts of the Apostles." In *International Bible Commentary.* Edited by William R. Farmer. Collegeville, MN: Liturgical Press, 1998. [See. 1509–11]

Thomas, David. *A Homiletic Commentary on the Acts of the Apostles: The Second Gospel of St. Luke.* London: Richard D. Dickinson, 1870. [See. 1–23; N.B. Google book]

Thomas, Derek W. H. *Acts.* Phillipsburg, NJ: P&R Publishing, 2011. [See 3–26]

Thomas, W. H. Griffith. *Outline Studies in the Acts of the Apostles.* Grand Rapids: Eerdmans, 1956. [See. 25–46]

Thompson, Alan J. *The Acts of the Risen Lord Jesus: Luke's Account of God's Unfolding Plan.* Nottingham, England: Apollos, 2011. [See. 73–108]

Thompson, Richard P. *Keeping the Church in its Place: The Church as Narrative Character in Acts.* London: T&T Clark, 2006. [See. 29–37]

Tourville, Robert E. *The Acts of the Apostles: A Verse-by-Verse Commentary from the Classical Pentecostal Perspective.* New Wilmington, PA: House of Bon Giovanni, 1983. [See. 1–23]

Trollope, William. *A Commentary on the Acts of the Apostles: With Examination Questions, and a Series of Examination Papers, Accompanied by References to the Text at the Foot of Each Page.* Cambridge: Printed by and for J. Hall, 1847. [See. 15–37; N.B. Google book]

Turnbull, Ralph G. *The Acts of the Apostles.* Grand Rapids: Baker, 1961. [See. 11–13]

Vaughan, C. J. *The Church of the First Days: Lectures on the Acts of the Apostles.* Vol. 1. Cambridge: Macmillan, 1864. [See. 1–36; N.B. Google book and HathiTrust]

Vaughan, Curtis. *Acts: A Study Guide.* Grand Rapids: Zondervan, 1974. [See. 13–18]

Veil, Charles-Marie du. *A Commentary on the Acts of the Apostles.* Edited by F. A. Cox. London: Printed for the Society, by J. Haddon, 1851. [See. 5–32; N.B. HathiTrust]

Venkataraman, Babu Immanuel. *Acts of the Apostles: An Exegetical and Contextual Commentary.* Bangalore, India: Primalogue, 2016. [See. 11–21]

Wagner, C. Peter. *Spreading the Fire: A New Look at Acts—God's Training Manual for Every Christian.* Ventura, CA: Regal, 1994. [See. 9–31]

Walaskay, Paul W. *Acts*. Louisville: Westminster John Knox, 1998. [See. 25–32]

Walker, Thomas. *The Acts of the Apostles*. Chicago: Moody, 1965. [See. 1–25]

Wall, Robert W. "The Acts of the Apostles." In *The New Interpreter's Bible*. Vol. 10. *Acts, Introduction to Epistolary Literature, Letter to the Romans, First Letter to the Corinthians*. Nashville: Abingdon, 2002. [See. 37–52]

Whedon, D. D. *Commentary on the New Testament: Acts—Romans*. Vol. 3. New York: Phillips & Hunt, 1871. [Acts, See. 15– 26; N.B. Google book]

White, Ellen Gould Harmon. *The Acts of the Apostles in the Proclamation of the Gospel of Jesus Christ*. Mountain View, California: Pacific Press, 1911. [See. 9–34; N.B. HathiTrust]

Whitelaw, Thomas. *A Homiletical Commentary on the Acts of the Apostles*. New York: Funk & Wagnalls, 1896. [See. 13–42; N.B. Archive.org. This work is a must read.]

Williams, C. S. C. *A Commentary on the Acts of the Apostles*. New York: Harper & Brothers, 1957. [See. 54–61]

Williams, David John. *Acts*. Peabody, MA: Hendrickson, 1990. [See. 19–38]

Williams, John, Bishop of Connecticut. *Studies in the Book of Acts*. New York: T. Whittaker, 1888. [3–19; N.B. Archive.org and Google book]

Williams, R. R. *The Acts of the Apostles: Introduction and Commentary*. London: SCM, 1953. [See. 34–38]

Williamson, Charles C. *Acts*. Louisville: Westminster John Knox, 2000. [See. 6–13]

Willimon, William H. *Acts*. Atlanta: John Knox, 1988. [See. 19–25]

Winn, Albert Curry. *The Acts of the Apostles: Layman's Bible Commentary*. Vol. 20. Richmond, VA: John Knox, 1960. [See. 19–28]

Wise, Isaac Mayer. *The Origin of Christianity and a Commentary to the Acts of the Apostles*. Cincinnati: Bloch, 1868. [See. 16–23; N.B. americanjewisharchives.org, Archive.org, Google book, and HathiTrust. An interesting point of view written by a Jewish detractor.]

Witherington, Ben. *The Acts of the Apostles: A Socio-Rhetorical Commentary*. Grand Rapids: Eerdmans, 1998. [See. 105–27; N.B. Definitely examine Witherington's text.]

Witherspoon, Jet. *Acts: The Amazing History of the Early Churc*h. Hazelwood, MO: Pentecostal Publishing House, 1972. [See. 9–15]

Woodbridge, Charles J. *A Study of the Book of Acts: "Standing on the Promises."* Grand Rapids: Baker, 1955. [See. 11–13]

Wordsworth, Chr. *The New Testament of Our Lord and Saviour Jesus Christ: In the Original Greek with Introduction and Notes: The Acts of the Apostles*. London: Rivingtons, 1877. [See. 35–42; N.B. Archive.org, 1891]

Wright, N. T. *Acts For Everyone. Chapters 1–12*. Louisville: Westminster John Knox, 2008. [See. 1–20]

Young, E. S. *Acts of the Apostles: The Teaching of the Holy Scriptures*. Elgin, IL: Bible Student Company, 1915. [See. 19–27; N.B. Archive.org and EBESCO]

Yrigoyen, Charles. *Acts For Our Time*. Nashville: Abingdon, 1992. [See. 16–22]

Zeller, Eduard. *The Contents and Origin of the Acts of the Apostles, Critically Investigated*. Translated by Joseph Dare and Franz Overbeck. Vol. 1. London: Williams & Norgate, 1875. [See. 165–71; N.B. Archive.org and Google book]

Zwiep, Arie W. *Judas and the Choice of Matthias: A Study on Context and Concern of Acts 1:15–26*. Tübingen: Mohr Siebeck, 2004. [270 pages]

CHAPTER 22

1 Corinthians 15

Abogunrin, Samuel Oyinloye. *The First Letter of Paul to the Corinthians*. Ibadan: Daystar, 1991. [See. 162–69]

Ackerman, David A. *Lo, I Tell You a Mystery: Cross, Resurrection, and Paraenesis in the Rhetoric of 1 Corinthians*. Eugene, OR: Pickwick, 2006. [Paul's Ideology of Resurrection, See. 85–89]

Ambrosiaster. *Commentaries on Romans and 1–2 Corinthians*. Translated by Gerald Lewis Bray. Downers Grove, IL: InterVarsity, 2009. [See. 191–94]

Applebury, T. R. *Studies in First Corinthians*. Joplin, MO: College Press, 1963. [See. 268–77]

Arrington, French L. *Divine Order in the Church: A Study of 1 Corinthians*. Grand Rapids: Baker, 1978. [See. 161–68]

Asher, Jeffrey R. *Polarity and Change in 1 Corinthians 15: A Study of Metaphysics, Rhetoric, and Resurrection*. Tübingen: Mohr Siebeck, 2000. [See. 58–60]

Avery, Margaret. *Romans, 1 and 2 Corinthians, Galatians and Hebrews*. Denville, NJ: Dimension, 1972. [See. 29–30]

Bailey, Kenneth E. *Paul Through Mediterranean Eyes: Cultural Studies in 1 Corinthians*. Downers Grove, IL: InterVarsity, 2011. [See. 419–47]

Baird, William. *The Corinthian Church: A Biblical Approach to Urban Culture*. New York: Abingdon, 1964. [Chapter 6 The Problem of Death, See. 169–78]

———. *1 Corinthians, 2 Corinthians*. Atlanta: John Knox, 1980. [See. 62–64]

Baker, William R. *1 Corinthians. 2 Corinthians*. Edited by Philip Wesley Comfort. Carol Stream, IL: Tyndale House, 2009. [See. 209–19; N.B. Ralph P. Martin with Carl N. Toney wrote 2 Corinthians.]

Barclay, William. *The Letters to the Corinthians*. Philadelphia: Westminster, 1975. [See. 137–49]

Barnes, Albert. *Notes, Explanatory and Practical, on the First Epistle of Paul to the Corinthians*. New York: Harper, 1864. [See. 998–1011; N.B. Archive.org, 1837, Google book, 1857, 1858, and HathiTrust, 1847]

Barnett, Paul. *1 Corinthians*. Fearn, Ross-shire: Christian Focus, 2000. [See. 267–83]

Barrett, C. K. *The Acts of the Apostles: A Shorter Commentary*. London: T&T Clark, 2002. [See. 1–14]

———. *A Commentary on the First Epistle to the Corinthians*. New York: Harper & Row, 1968. [See. 334–50; N.B. Worth examining.]

Barton, Bruce B. *1 & 2 Corinthians: Life Application Commentary*. Edited by Grant Osborne. Wheaton, IL: Tyndale House, 1999. [See. 217–27]

Bassler, Jouette. "1 Corinthians." In *Women's Bible Commentary*. Edited by Carol A. Newsom, Sharon H. Ringe, and Jacqueline E. Lapsley. Louisville: Westminster John Knox, 2012. [See. 565]

Beardslee, William A. *First Corinthians: A Commentary for Today*. St. Louis: Chalice, 1994. [See. 143–55]

Beet, Joseph Agar. *A Commentary on St. Paul's Epistles to the Corinthians*. Hodder & Stoughton: London, 1882. [See. 263–73; N.B. Archive.org and Google book]

Bengel, Johann Albrecht, and James Bryce. *Gnomon of the New Testament*. Vol. 3. 3rd ed. Translated by James Bryce. Philadelphia: Smith, English, 1860. [See. 316–20; N.B. Google book]

Benson, Joseph. *The Holy Bible Containing the Old and New Testament of Our Lord and Saviour Jesus Christ. Vol. 2. Romans to the Revelation*. New York: Lane & Tippett, 1847. [See. 198–201; N.B. Google book]

Berquist, Millard J. *Studies in First Corinthians*. Nashville: Convention Press, 1960. [See. 115–22]

Bertolini, Dewey M., and Larry Richards. *1 & 2 Corinthians*. Nashville: Nelson, 2009. [1 Corinthians 15—The Resurrection: Hoax or History?, See. 183–91]

Bickel, Stan, and Stan Jantz. *1 & 2 Corinthians: Finding Your Unique Place in God's Plan*. Eugene, OR: Harvest House, 2004. [Chapter 9 The Resurrection: There's No Denying It, 1 Corinthians 15–16, See. 109–13]

Billroth, Gustav. *A Commentary on the Epistles of Paul to the Corinthians*. Translated by W. Lindsay Alexander. Vol. 2. Edinburgh: Thomas Clark, 1837. [See. 72–90; N.B. Archive.org and Google book]

Blair, J. Allen. *Living Wisely: A Devotional Study of the First Epistle to the Corinthians*. Neptune, NJ: Loizeaux, 1969. [See. 298–315]

Blenkinsopp, Joseph. *Corinthian Mirror: A Study of Contemporary Themes in a Pauline Epistle*. London: Sheed & Ward, 1964. [Resurrection of Christ, See. 37, 57, 61, 113, 221, 226]

Blomberg, Craig. *1 Corinthians*. Grand Rapids: Zondervan, 1995. [See. 293–97]

Boring, M. Eugene, and Fred B. Craddock. *The People's New Testament Commentary*. Louisville: Westminster John Knox, 2004. [See. 541–43]

Boyer, James L. *For a World like Ours: Studies in 1 Corinthians*. Grand Rapids: Baker, 1971. [See. 138–40]

Branick, Vincent P. *First Corinthians: Building up the Church*. Hyde Park, NY: New City Press, 2001. [See. 127–33]

Bratcher, Robert G. *A Translator's Guide to Paul's First Letter to the Corinthians*. London: United Bible Societies, 1982. [See. 142–47; N.B. This work is a must read.]

Braxton, Brad R. "1 Corinthians." In *Theological Bible Commentary*. Edited by Gail R. O'Day and David L. Petersen. Louisville: Westminster John Knox, 2009. [See. 390–91]

Bray, Gerald, and Thomas C. Oden, eds. *Ancient Christian Commentary on Scripture—1–2 Corinthians*. Downers Grove, IL: InterVarsity, 1999. [See. 148–56]

Bridger, Gordon F. *Corinthians-Galatians*. London: Scripture Union, 1985. [See. 47–48]

Briscoe, D. Stuart. *Expository Nuggets From 1 Corinthians*. Grand Rapids: Baker, 1995. [See. 105–10]

Brookins, Timothy A., and Bruce W. Longenecker. *1 Corinthians 10–16: A Handbook on the Greek Text*. Waco, TX: Baylor University Press, 2016. [See. 134–53]

Brown, E. F. *The First Epistle of Paul the Apostle to the Corinthians*. London: SPCK, 1923. [See. 248–59]

Brown, John. *The Resurrection of Life: An Exposition of First Corinthians 15 with a Discourse on Our Lord's Resurrection*. Oliphant: Edinburgh, 1866. [See. 87–114; N.B. Google book]

Brown, Paul J. *Bodily Resurrection and Ethics in 1 Cor 15: Connecting Faith and Morality in the Context of Greco-Roman Mythology*. Tübingen: Mohr Siebeck, 2014. [See. 108–73]

Brown, Raymond Bryan. "1 Corinthians." In *The Broadman Bible Commentary Acts— 1 Corinthians*. Edited by Clifton J. Allen. Vol. 10. Nashville: Broadman, 1970. [See. 383–88]

Bruce, F. F. *1 and 2 Corinthians*. London: Oliphants, 1971. [See. 137–45]

———. *The New International Commentary on the New Testament*. Grand Rapids: Eerdmans, 1953. [See. 346–60]

Bullinger, E. W. *The Companion Bible: Being the Authorized Version of 1611 with the Structures and Notes, Critical, Explanatory and Suggestive and with 198 Appendixes*. London: Oxford University Press, 1922. [See. 1721–22]

Butler, Paul T. *Studies in First Corinthians*. Joplin, MO: College Press, 1985. [Chapter 15 The Problem of The Resurrection. See. 320–32]

Caldwell, John R. *The Charter of the Church: Revised Notes of an Exposition of the First Epistle to the Corinthians*. Vol. 2. Chapters 9 to 16. Glasgow: Pickering & Inglis, 1900. [See. 220–31]

Callan, Charles Jerome. *The Epistles of St. Paul: With Introduction and Commentary for Priests and Students*. Vol. 1. J. F. Wagner: New York, 1922. [See. 412–20; N.B. Archive. org]

Calvin, Jean. *Commentary on the Epistles of Paul the Apostle to the Corinthians*. Translated by John Pringle. Vol. 2. Grand Rapids: Eerdmans, 1948. [See. 5–23]

Candlish, Robert S. *Life in a Risen Saviour: Being Discourses on the Argument of the Fifteenth Chapter of First Corinthians*. Edinburgh: Black, 1858. [Discourses 1–3. See. 1–46; N.B. Archive.org]

Carpenter, S. C. ed. *Corinthians 1 & 2*. Cambridge: At the University Press, 1936. [See. 57–61]

Carter, Warren, and Amy-Jill Levine. *The New Testament: Methods and Meanings*. Nashville: Abingdon, 2013. [See. 143–44]

Caudill, R. Paul. *First Corinthians: A Translation with Notes*. Nashville: Broadman, 1983. [See. 95–97]

Chafin, Kenneth. *Mastering the New Testament: 1, 2 Corinthians*. Waco, TX: Word, 1985. [See. 178–84]

Chauke, E., et al. *First Corinthians*. Kisumu, Kenya: Evangel Publishing House, 1976. [See. 209–18]

Chrysostom. *1 Corinthians: A Commentary*. Translated by Paul Nadim Tarazi. St. Paul, MN: OCABS Press, 2011. [See. 259–77]

Chrysostom, John. *The Homilies of S. John Chrysostom, Archbishop of Constantinople, on the First Epistle of St. Paul the Apostle to the Corinthians. Part 1. Hom. 1.—24*. Oxford: Parker, 1839. [See. 529–52; N.B. Google book]

Ciampa, Roy E., and Brian S. Rosner. *The First Letter to the Corinthians*. Grand Rapids: Eerdmans, 2010. [See. 736–60]

Clark, George W. *Romans and 1 and 2 Corinthians: A Popular Commentary Upon a Critical Basis, Especially Designed for Pastors and Sunday Schools*. Philadelphia: American Baptist Publication Society, 1897. [See. 303–8; N.B. Archive.org]

Clark, Gordon H. *First Corinthians: A Contemporary Commentary*. 2nd ed. Jefferson, MD: Trinity Foundation, 1991. [See. 250–60]

Clarke, Adam. *Adam Clarke's Commentary on the Bible*. Edited by Ralph Earle. Grand Rapids: Baker, 1967. [See. 1120–21]

Cochrane, James. *The Resurrection of the Dead: Its Design, Manner, and Results, in an Exposition of the Fifteenth Chapter of First Corinthians*. Edinburgh: W. Blackwood, 1869. [Discourse 2 The Resurrection of Christ the Grand Proof of the Truth of Christianity, See. 33–51; N.B. Google book and HathiTrust]

Coleman, Lyman, and Richard Peace. *1 Corinthians: A Pastor Directed Study Course for Small Groups Combining Expository Teaching, Small Group Sharing, Personal Application*. Vol. 2. Littleton, CO: Serendipity House, 1986. [See. 73–76]

Colet, John. *John Colet's Commentary on First Corinthians*. Edited by Bernard O'Kelly and Catherine Anna Louise Jarrott. Binghamton, NY: Medieval & Renaissance Texts & Studies, 1985. [See. 277–79]

Collins, Raymond F. *First Corinthians*. Collegeville, MN: Liturgical Press, 1999. [See. 525–43]

Conzelmann, Hans. *1 Corinthians: A Commentary on the First Epistle to the Corinthians*. Philadelphia: Fortress, 1975. [See. 248–67; N.B. Examine Conzelman's text.]

Cowles, Henry. *The Longer Epistles of Paul: Viz: Romans, 1 Corinthians, 2 Corinthians*. New York: D. Appleton, 1880. [See. 269–73; N.B. HathiTrust]

Cox, Samuel. *The Resurrection: Twelve Expository Essays on the Fifteenth Chapter of St. Paul's First Epistle to the Corinthians*. London: Richard D. Dickinson, 1881. [See. 1–59; N.B. Google book]

Dabney, J. P. *Annotations on the New Testament*. Part 1. Cambridge: Hilliard & Brown, 1829. [See. 371–72; N.B. Google book and HathiTrust]

Daniel, Monodeep. "First Letter of Paul to the Corinthians." In *One Volume Dalit Bible Commentary New Testament*. Edited by T. K. John. New Delhi: Centre For Dalit, 2010. [See. 415–16]

Darby, John. *Notes of Readings on the Epistles to the Corinthians*. London: G. Morrish, 1825. [See. 134–53; N.B. The abbreviation J. N. D. is the pseudonym for the author.]

Dahl, M. E. *The Resurrection of the Body: A Study of 1 Corinthians 15*. London: SCM, 1962. [Chapter 2 Difficulties of the Accepted Exegesis, See. 20–33; Additional Note A. Christ's Resurrection the Cause of Ours, St Thomas Aquinas, See. 96–100; N.B. Dahl's work should be examined.]

Davies, Rupert E. *Studies in 1 Corinthians*. London: Epworth, 1962. [See. 85–88]

Dean, Robert James. *First Corinthians for Today*. Nashville: Broadman, 1972. [See. 135–45]

DeHaan, M. R. *Studies in First Corinthians: Messages on Practical Christian Living*. Grand Rapids: Zondervan, 1956. [See. 167–73]

Deluz, Gaston. *A Companion to 1 Corinthians*. Translated by Grace E. Watt. Darton, Longman & Todd: London, 1963. [See. 220–30]

Dods, Marcus. *The First Epistle to the Corinthians*. New York: C Armstrong, 1896. [See. 327–40; N.B. Archive.org, 1889 and Google book, 1891]

Drummond, James. *The Epistles of Paul, the Apostle, to the Thessalonians, Corinthians, Galatians, Romans, and Philippians*. New York: G. P. Putnam's Sons, 1899. [See. 119-22; N.B. Archive.org and Google book]

Dummelow, J. R., ed. *A Commentary on the Holy Bible by Various Writers*. New York: Macmillan, 1920. [See. 916-18; N.B Archive.org]

Dunn, James D. G. *1 Corinthians*. Sheffield: Sheffield Academic Press, 1995. [See. 10-107; N.B. Definitely read Dunn's work.]

Edwards, Thomas Charles. *A Commentary on the First Epistle to the Corinthians*. New York: A. C. Armstrong, 1886. [See. 385-408; N.B. Archive.org and Google book]

Elkins, Garland. "The Resurrection of Christ—Foundation of Our Hope." In *Studies in 1 Corinthians*. Edited by Dub McClish, Valid Publications, 1982. [See. 200-208]

Ellicott, C. J. *A Critical and Grammatical Commentary on St. Paul's First Epistle to the Corinthians*. Andover: W. F. Draper, 1889. [See. 288-300; N.B. Archive.org, Google book, and HathiTrust]

Ellingworth, Paul, and Howard Hatton. *A Translator's Handbook on Paul's First Letter to the Corinthians*. London: United Bible Societies, 1985. [See. 289-302; N.B. This work is a good read.]

Erdman, Charles R. *The First Epistle of Paul to the Corinthians; an Exposition*. Philadelphia: Westminster, 1928. [See. 135-41]

Eriksson, Anders. *Traditions as Rhetorical Proof: Pauline Argumentation in 1 Corinthians*. Stockholm: Almqvist & Wiksell, 1998. [See. 86-97; 232-59]

Evans, Canon. "1 Corinthians." In *The Holy Bible, According to the Authorized Version (AD 1611), with an Explanatory and Critical Commentary and a Revision of the Translation Romans to Philemon*. Vol. 3. Edited by F. C. Cook. New York: Scribner's Sons, 1892. [See. 352-60; N.B. Google book]

Evans, Ernest. *The Epistles of Paul the Apostle to the Corinthians: In the Revised Version, with Introduction and Commentary*. Oxford: Clarendon, 1930. [See. 140-43]

Evans, James L. *1 and 2 Corinthians*. Nashville: Abingdon, 2011. [Hopes Really Does Float 1 Corinthians 15-16, See. 85-86]

Evans, William. *Romans, and 1 and 2 Corinthians*. New York: Revell, 1918. [Chapter 8 Doctrinal Discussion—The Resurrection (Chapter 15), See. 180-90; N.B. Google book and HathiTrust]

Exell, Joseph S. *The Biblical Illustrator: or, Anecdotes, Similes, Emblems, Illustrations; Expository, Scientific, Geographical, Historical, and Homiletic, Gathered from a Wide Range of Home and Foreign Literature, on the Verses of the Bible The First Corinthians*. Vol. 2. New York: Revell, 1887. [See. 380-427; N.B. This book is a healthy, dated source.]

Farley, Lawrence R. *First and Second Corinthians: Straight From the Heart*. Ben Lomond, CA: Conciliar Press, 2005. [See. 165-72]

Farrar, F. W., and David Thomas. *1 Corinthians. The Pulpit Commentary*. Edited by H. D. M. Spence and Joseph S. Excel. London: Funk & Wagnalls, 1913. [See. 483-86]

Fausset, A. R. "The First Epistle of Paul The Apostle to the Corinthians." In *A Commentary, Critical, Experimental, and Practical, on the Old and New Testaments 1 Corinthians-Revelation*. Vol. 2. New York: Revell, 1878. [See. 291-94; N.B. Reprint: *A Commentary, Critical, Experimental, and Practical, on the Old and New Testaments 1 Corinthians-Revelation*. Vol. 6. Grand Rapids: Eerdmans, 1948. See. 325-28. Available online]

Fee, Gordon D. *The First Epistle to the Corinthians*. Grand Rapids: Eerdmans, 1987. [See. 713–45; N.B. This work D. A. Carson co-ranked as a best general commentary.]

Fisher, Fred L. *Commentary on 1 & 2 Corinthians*. Toronto: Word, 1975. [See. 234–43]

Fitzmyer, Joseph A. *First Corinthians: A New Translation with Introduction and Commentary*. New Haven: Yale University Press, 2008. [See. 539–67]

Fitzwater, P. B. *The Church and Modern Problems in the Light of the Teachings of Paul in First Corinthians*. Chicago: Bible Institute Colportage Ass'n, 1914. [See. 112–17; N.B. Archive.org]

Frick, Philip Louis. *The Resurrection and Paul's Argument: A Study of First Corinthians Fifteenth Chapter*. Cincinnati: Jennings & Graham, 1912. [348 pages; N.B. This lengthy work should be explored.]

Furnish, Victor Paul. *The Theology of the First Letter to the Corinthians*. Cambridge: Cambridge University Press, 1999. [See. 4, 17, 41, 56, 110–12, 120, 132]

Gaebelein, Arno Clemens. *The Annotated Bible: The Holy Scriptures Analysed and Annotated: The New Testament Romans-Ephesians*. Vol. 2. New York: Publication Office "Our Hope," 1916. [See. 135–42; N.B. Archive.org]

Gaffin, Richard B. *The Centrality of the Resurrection: A Study in Paul's Soteriology*. Grand Rapids: Baker, 1978. [1 Corinthians 15:12–19, 36–38; The Resurrection of Christ. See. 114–25]

Garland, David E. *1 Corinthians*. Grand Rapids: Baker Academic, 2003. [See. 678–704; N.B. This book was co-ranked by D. A. Carson as a best general commentary.]

Gavigan, James, and Brian McCarthy, eds. *The Navarre Bible St Paul's Epistles to the Corinthians in the Revised Standard Version and New Vulgate / with a commentary by members of the Faculty of Theology of the University of Navarre*. Dublin: Four Courts Press, 1991. [See. 33; The Resurrection of the Dead, See. 141–45]

Getty, Mary Ann. "1 Corinthians." In *The Collegeville Bible Commentary*. Edited by Dianne Bergant and Robert J. Karris. Collegeville, MN: Liturgical Press, 1989. [See. 1129–30]

Getty-Sullivan, Mary Ann. *First Corinthians, Second Corinthians*. Collegeville, MN: Liturgical Press, 1983. [See. 70–73]

Gill, David. *Zondervan Illustrated Bible Backgrounds Commentary: Romans to Philemon*. Edited by Clinton E. Arnold. Vol. 3. Grand Rapids: Zondervan, 2002. [1 Corinthians, See. 174–77]

Glen, J. Stanley. *Pastoral Problems in First Corinthians*. Philadelphia: Westminster, 1964. [See. 188–98]

Godbey, W. B. *Corinthians-Galatians: Paul, the Champion Theologian*. Vol. 4. Cincinnati: Knapp, 1898. [See. 243–48]

Godet, Frédéric Louis. *Commentary on St. Paul's First Epistle to the Corinthians*. Edinburgh: T&T Clark, 1890. [See. 321–50; N.B. Archive.org and Google book]

Gorder, Paul R. van. *The Church Stands Corrected*. Wheaton, IL: Victor, 1976. [Chapter 14 Resurrection Reality (1 Corinthians 15), See. 143–50]

Gorman, Michael J. *Apostle of the Crucified Lord: A Theological Introduction to Paul & His Letters*. 2nd ed. Grand Rapids: Eerdmans, 2017. [The Gospel In Creed and Verse, See. 121–24; Chapter 10 Chaos, the Cross, and the Spirit in Corinth, See. 331–36]

Goudge, Henry Leighton. *The First Epistle to the Corinthians*. London: Methuen, 1903. [See. 135–44; N.B. Archive.com]

Gould, Dana. *1 Corinthians*. Nashville: Broadman & Holman, 1998. [See. 88–90]

Gould, Ezra P. *Commentary on the Epistles to the Corinthians*. Philadelphia: American Baptist Publication Society, 1887. [See. 127–31; N.B. Archive.org]

Goulder, Michael D. *Paul and the Competing Mission in Corinth*. Peabody, MA: Hendrickson, 2001. [See. 177–83]

Govett, Robert. *Christ's Resurrection and Ours: or, 1 Corinthians 15 Expounded*. Miami Springs, FL: Conley & Schoettle, 1985. [See. 1–30; N.B. Google book, 1876 printing]

Gray, James M. *A Picture of the Resurrection: An Exposition of the Fifteenth Chapter of First Corinthians*. New York, Revell, 1917 [43 pages; The Resurrection of Christ, See. 12–17; N.B. Google book]

Grayston, Kenneth. "1 and 2 Corinthians." In *The Twentieth Century Bible Commentary*. Edited by G. Henton Davies, Alan Richardson, and Charles L. Wallis. New York: Harper & Brothers, 1955. [See. 478–82.]

Greene, Oliver B. *The First Epistle of Paul the Apostle to the Corinthians*. Greenville, SC: Gospel Hour, 1965. [See. 478–98]

Gromacki, Robert Glenn. *Called to Be Saints: An Exposition of 1 Corinthians*. Grand Rapids: Baker, 1977. [See. 181–87]

Grosheide, F. W. *Commentary on the First Epistle to the Corinthians*. Grand Rapids: Eerdmans, 1953. [See. 346–60]

Gundry, Robert H. *Commentary on the New Testament: Verse-by-Verse Explanations with a Literal Translation*. Peabody, MA: Hendrickson, 2010. [On Resurrection, 1 Corinthians 15:1–58, See. 679–82]

Gutzke, Manford George. *Plain Talk on First and Second Corinthians*. Grand Rapids: Zondervan, 1978. [See. 140–45; N.B. Not useful.]

Halley, Henry H. *Halley's Bible Handbook with the New International Version*. Grand Rapids: Zondervan, 2000. [See. 786–87]

Hamar, Paul A. *New Testament Study Bible: Romans-Corinthians*. Edited by Ralph W. Harris and Stanley M. Horton. Vol. 7. Springfield, MO: Complete Biblical Library, 1989. [See. 454–63]

Hannah, Darrell D. *The Text of 1 Corinthians in the Writings of Origen*. Atlanta: Scholars Press, 1997. [See. 145–50]

Harbour, Brian L. *Contextualizing the Gospel: A Homiletic Commentary on 1 Corinthians*. Macon, GA: Smyth & Helwys, 2011. [See. 197–201]

Hargreaves, John. *A Guide to 1 Corinthians*. London: SPCK, 1978. [See. 189–200]

Harris, John Tindall. *The Writings of the Apostle Paul: With Notes, Critical and Explanatory*. London: Headley, 1901. [See. 163–69; N.B. Google book]

Harris, W. B. *The First Epistle of St. Paul to the Corinthians: Introduction and Commentary*. Madras: Published for the Senate of Serampore College by the Christian Literature Society, 1958. [See. 188–94]

Harrisville, Roy A. *1 Corinthians*. Minneapolis: Augsburg, 1987. [See. 247–64]

Hays, Richard B. *First Corinthians*. Louisville: John Knox, 1997. [See. 252–62]

Heading, John. *First Epistle to the Corinthians*. Kansas City: Walterick, 1965. [See. 241–52]

Henry, Matthew. *An Exposition of All the Books of the Old and New Testaments*. Vol. 5. Acts—Revelation. London: W. Lochhead, 1806. [See. 343–45; N.B. Google book. Reprinted as *Commentary on the Whole Bible: Genesis to Revelation*. Edited by Leslie F. Church. Grand Rapids: Zondervan, 1961. See. 1822–23]

Henry, Matthew, and Thomas Scott. *The Pocket Bible Commentary: John—1 Corinthians*. Vol. 8. Lincoln, NE: Back to the Bible, n.d. [See. 124–25]

Henson, Hensley. *Apostolic Christianity: Notes and Inferences Mainly Based on S. Paul's Epistles to the Corinthians.* London: Methuen, 1898. [Chapter 2 The Resurrection, 94–106; N.B. Archive.org]

Héring, Jean. *The First Epistle of Saint Paul to the Corinthians.* Translated by A. W. Heathcote and P. J. Allcock. London: Epworth, 1962. [See. 156–64]

Hewlett, John. *Commentaries and Annotations on the Holy Scriptures.* Vol. 4. London: Longman, Hurst, Rees, Orme, & Brown, 1816. [See. 458–60; N.B. Google book]

Hillyer, Norman. *1 and 2 Corinthians.* In *New Bible Century.* Edited by D. Guthrie & J. A. Motyer. Grand Rapids: Eerdmans, 1970. [See. 1070–71]

Hobbs, Herschel H. *The Epistles to the Corinthians: A Study Manual.* Grand Rapids: Baker, 1960. [See. 69–71]

Hodge, Charles. *A Commentary on the First Epistle to the Corinthians.* Grand Rapids: Eerdmans, 1953. [See. 308–23]

Hoh, Paul Jacob. *Studies in First Corinthians / Prepared Under the Auspices of the Parish and Church School Board of the United Lutheran Church in America.* Philadelphia: United Lutheran Publishing House, 1937. [See. 82–84]

Holladay, Carl R. *The First Letter of Paul to the Corinthians.* Austin, TX: Sweet Publishing, 1979. [See. 191–200]

Holleman, Joost. *Resurrection and Parousia: A Traditio-Historical Study of Paul's Eschatology in 1 Corinthians 15.* Leiden: Brill, 1996. [233 pages; N.B. A definite text to examine.]

Horsley, Richard A. *1 Corinthians.* Nashville: Abingdon, 1998. [See. 197–203]

Horton, Stanley M. *1 & 2 Corinthians.* Springfield, MO: Logion Press, 1999. [See. 145–51]

Howard, Fred D. *1 Corinthians: Guidelines for God's People.* Nashville: Convention Press, 1983. [See. 122–25]

Hughes, Albert. *Studies in First Corinthians.* Toronto: Crusader Press, 1945. [See. 267–84]

Hughes, Robert B. *First Corinthians.* Chicago: Moody, 1985. [See. 138–43]

Hurd, John Coolidge. *The Origin of 1 Corinthians.* Macon, GA: Mercer University Press, 1983. [Concerning the Resurrection (1 Cor. 15), See. 195–200]

Hutson, Christopher R. "1 Corinthians." In *The Transforming Word: One-Volume Commentary on the Bible.* Edited by Mark W. Hamilton. Abilene, TX: ACU Press, 2009. [See. 932]

Ironside, H. A. *Addresses on the First Epistle to the Corinthians.* New York: Loizeaux, 1938. [See. 459–77]

Jackman, David. *Let's Study 1 Corinthians.* Edinburgh: Banner of Truth Trust, 2004. [See. 241–51]

Jacobs, Henry Eyster, et al. *Annotations on the Epistles of Paul to 1 Corinthians 7—16, 2 Corinthians and Galatians.* New York: Christian Literature, 1897. [See. 121–27; N.B. Google book]

Jensen, Irving L. *1 Corinthians: A Self-Study Guide.* Chicago: Moody Bible Institute, 1972. [See. 100–103]

Johnson, Alan F. *1 Corinthians.* Downers Grove, IL: InterVarsity, 2004. [See. 279–89]

Keener, Craig S. *1—2 Corinthians.* Cambridge: Cambridge University Press, 2005. [See. 121–26]

Kelly, William. *Notes on the First Epistle of Paul the Apostle to the Corinthians: With a New Translation.* London: G. Morrish, 1878. [See. 246–60; N.B. HathiTrust]

Kilgallen, John J. *First Corinthians: An Introduction and Study Guide.* New York: Paulist, 1987. [See. 127–34]

Kim, Yung Suk. *Christ's Body in Corinth: The Politics of a Metaphor*. Minneapolis: Fortress, 2008. [See. 77–78]

Kistemaker, Simon. *New Testament Commentary: Exposition of the First Epistle to the Corinthians*. Grand Rapids: Baker, 1993. [See. 521–47]

Kling, Christian Friedrich. *The First Epistle of Paul to the Corinthians*. Translated by Daniel W. Poor. New York: Scribner's Sons, 1900. [See. 306–15; N.B. Google book]

Knowling, R. J. *The Testimony of St. Paul to Christ Viewed in Some of its Aspects*. 3rd ed. London: Hodder & Stoughton, 1911. [Lecture 13 Epistles to the Corinthians, See. 266–310, especially, 300–309; N.B. HathiTrust]

Knox, Ronald A. *A New Testament Commentary for English Readers: The Acts of the Apostles. St. Paul's Letters to the Churches*. Vol. 2. New York: Sheed & Ward, 1954. [See. 166–70]

Kovacs, Judith L., ed. *1 Corinthians: Interpreted by Early Christian Commentators*. Grand Rapids: Eerdmans, 2005. [See. 242–49]

Lambrecht, Jan. "1 Corinthians." In *The International Bible Commentary: A Catholic Commentary for the Twenty-first Century*. Edited by William R. Farmer. Collegeville, MN: Liturgical Press, 1998. [See. 1601–29]

Lapide, Cornelius à. *The Great Commentary of Cornelius à Lapide*. Translated by W. F. Cobb. Vol. 7. Edinburgh: J. Grant, 1908. [See. 363–73; N.B. Google book]

Laurin, Roy L. *Where Life Matures: 1 Corinthians*. Wheaton, IL: Van Kampen, 1950. [See. 268–80]

Lee, Robert G. *Beds of Pearls Messages on Basic Christian Truth*. Grand Rapids: Zondervan, 1960. [Chapter 6 The Complement, See. 75–84]

Lenski, R. C. H. *The Interpretation of St. Paul's First and Second Epistles to the Corinthians*. Minneapolis: Augsburg, 1937. [See. 623–60; N.B. This text is a healthy read.]

Lewis, Scott Martin. *"So that God May be all in All": The Apocalyptic Message of 1 Corinthians 15, 1–34*. Rome: Editrice Pontificia Università Gregoriana, 1998. [See. 27–44]

Lewis, Steve. *First Corinthians Verse-by-Verse*. Parker, CO: Eagle Trail Press, 2012. [See. 308–17]

Linton, Henry. *"Jesus and the Resurrection:" Being an Exposition, in Twelve Sermons, of 1 Corinthians 15*. London: William Macintosh, 1865. [See. 1–73; N.B. Bodleian Libraries]

Locke, John. *A Paraphrase and Notes on the Epistles of St. Paul to the Galatians, 1 and 2 Corinthians, Romans, Ephesians*. Edited by Arthur William. Wainwright. Oxford: Clarendon, 1987. [See. 246–50; Reprint, 1707; N.B. Archive.org, 1707]

Lockwood, Gregory J. *1 Corinthians*. Saint Louis: Concordia, 2000. [See. 547–65]

Luck, G. Coleman. *First Corinthians*. Chicago: Moody, 1958. [See. 113–16]

Lull, David John, and William A. Beardslee. *1 Corinthians*. St. Louis: Chalice, 2007. [See. 130–33]

Luther, Martin. *Luther's Works Commentaries on 1 Corinthians 7, 1 Corinthians 15; Lectures on 1 Timothy*. Edited by Hilton C. Oswald. Translated by Martin H. Bertram. Vol. 28. St. Louis: Concordia, 1973. [See. 59–107]

MacArthur, John. *1 Corinthians*. Chicago: Moody, 1984. [See. 397–414]

———. *The MacArthur Bible Commentary: Unleashing God's Truth, One Verse at a Time*. Nashville: Nelson, 2005. [See. 1604–6]

MacEvilly, John. *An Exposition of the Epistles of St. Paul, and of the Catholic Epistles: Consisting of an Introduction to each Epistle, and Analysis of Each Chapter, a Paraphrase of the Sacred Text, and a Commentary, Embracing Notes, Critical, Explanatory, and Dogmatical*. Vol. 1. Dublin: M.H. Gill, 1898. [See. 262–66; N.B. Archive.org]

MacGorman, J. W. *Romans, 1 Corinthians*. Nashville: Broadman, 1980. [See. 143–45]

MacKintosh, R. *Thessalonians and Corinthians: The Westminster New Testament*. Edited by Alfred E. Garvie. London: Andrew Melrose. 1909/1858. [See. 172–76; N.B. Archive.org]

Macknight, James. *A New Literal Translation from the Original Greek of All the Apostolical Epistles*. Vol. 2. London: Printed for Longman et al., 1821. [See. 246–62; N.B. Christianclassiclibrary.org]

MacRory, Joseph. *The Epistles of St. Paul to the Corinthians*. Dublin: M. H. Gill, 1935. [See 225–34]

Malcolm, Matthew R. *Paul and the Rhetoric of Reversal in 1 Corinthians: The Impact of Paul's Gospel on His Macro-Rhetoric*. New York: Cambridge University Press, 2013. [Chapter 5 See. 231–66]

———. *The World of 1 Corinthians: An Exegetical Source Book of Literary and Visual Backgrounds*. Eugene, OR: Cascade, 2013. [Present Death and Future Resurrection, 132–59]

Malina, Bruce J., and John J. Pilch. *Social-Science Commentary on the Letters of Paul*. Minneapolis: Fortress, 2006. [See. 122–25]

Manetsch, Scott M. ed. *Reformation Commentary on Scripture 1 Corinthians*. Downers Grove, IL: IVP Academic, 2017. [See. 350–69; N.B. This book is a collection of numerous writers.]

Mare, W. Harold. *The Expositor's Bible Commentary with the New International Version of The Holy Bible Romans— Galatians*. Edited by Frank E. Gaebelein. Vol. 10. Grand Rapids: Zondervan, 1976. [See. 281–85]

Mare, W. Harold, and Murray J. Harris. *1, 2 Corinthians*. Grand Rapids: Zondervan, 1995. [See. 109–12]

Marrow, Stanley B. *Paul for Today's Church: A Commentary on First Corinthians*. New York: Paulist, 2013. [See. 185–95]

Martin, Alfred. *First Corinthians*. Neptune, NJ: Loizeaux, 1989. [See. 128–33]

Martin, Dale B. *The Corinthian Body*. New Haven: Yale University Press, 1995. [See 123–26; N.B. Three important pages that must be read.]

Martin, Ralph P. *1 and 2 Corinthians*, Galatians. Grand Rapids: Eerdmans, 1968. [See. 46–47]

———. *The Spirit and the Congregation: Studies in 1 Corinthians 12–15*. Grand Rapids: Eerdmans, 1984. [Chapter 6 The Risen Lord, See. 91–105]

Massie, J. *Corinthians: Introduction, Authorized Version, Revised Version with Notes*. London: Caxton, 1903. [See. 241–45]

McFadyen, John Edgar. *The Epistles to the Corinthians*. London: Hodder & Stoughton, 1911. [See. 203–12; N.B. HathiTrust]

McGee, J. Vernon. *1 Corinthians*. Pasadena, CA: Thru the Bible Books, 1981. [See. 163–73]

McPheeters, Julian C. *The Epistles to the Corinthians*. Grand Rapids: Baker, 1964. [See. 69–71]

Melanchthon, Philipp. *Annotations on the First Epistle to the Corinthians*. Translated by John Patrick Donnelly. Milwaukee: Marquette University Press, 1995. [See. 163–67]

Metz, Donald S. *The First Epistle of Paul to the Corinthians*. Vol. 8. *Romans, 1 Corinthians 2 Corinthians*. Kansas City, MO: Beacon Hill, 1968. [See. 456–63]

Meyer, Heinrich August Wilhelm. *Critical and Exegetical Hand-book to the Epistles to the Corinthians*. Translated by D. Douglas Bannerman and William P. Dickson. Winona Lake, IN: Alpha Greek Library, 1980. [See. 337–52; exact reprint of the 6th edition of 1884; N.B. Archive.org]

Micklem, Nathaniel. *A First Century Letter: Being an Exposition of Paul's First Epistle to the Corinthians*. London: Student Christian Movement, 1920. [See. 87–90; N.B. HathiTrust]

Milinovich, Timothy. *Beyond What Is Written: The Performative Structure of 1 Corinthians*. Eugene, OR: Pickwick, 2013. [See. 186–96]

Milligan, William. *The Resurrection of the Dead: An Exposition of 1 Corinthians 15*. 2nd ed. Edinburgh: T&T Clark, 1895. [See. 3–39; N.B. Archive.org and Google book]

Mitchell, Dan. *The Book of First Corinthians: Christianity in a Hostile Culture*. Chattanooga, TN: AMG, 2004. [See. 207–17]

Mitchell, Margaret Mary. *Paul and the Rhetoric of Reconciliation: An Exegetical Investigation of the Language and Composition of 1 Corinthians*. Louisville: Westminster John Knox, 1993. [See. 283–88]

Moffatt, James. *The First Epistle of Paul to Corinthians*. New York: Harper & Brothers, 1938. [See. 234–44]

Montague, George T. *First Corinthians*. Grand Rapids: Baker Academic, 2011. [See. 260–71]

Moorehead, William G. *Outline Studies in Acts, Romans, First and Second Corinthians, Galatians and Ephesians*. Chicago: Revell, 1902. [Chapter 8 The Resurrection of the Body, See. 155–58; N.B. Google book]

Morgan, G. Campbell. *The Corinthian Letters of Paul: An Exposition of 1 and 2 Corinthians*. New York: Revell, 1946. [See. 182–90]

Morris, Leon. *The First Epistle of Paul to the Corinthians*. Grand Rapids: Eerdmans, 1958. [See. 203–12]

Murphy-O'Connor, Jerome. *Keys to First Corinthians: Revisiting the Major Issues*. Oxford: Oxford University Press, 2009. [See. 230–41]

———. *1 Corinthians*. New York: Doubleday, 1998. [See. 154–63]

———. *1 Corinthians*. Wilmington, DE: Glazier, 1979. [See. 137–41]

Nash, Robert Scott. *1 Corinthians*. Macon, GA: Smyth & Helwys, 2009. [See. 393–404]

Nasrallah, Laura S. "1 Corinthians." In *Fortress Commentary on the Bible The New Testament*. Edited by Margaret Aymer, Cynthia Briggs Kittredge, and David A. Sánchez. Minneapolis: Fortress, 2014. [See. 460–63]

Naylor, Peter. *A Study Commentary on 1 Corinthians*. Darlington: Evangelical Press, 2004. [See. 413–31]

Neil, William. *Good News in Corinthians 1 & 2: Paul's First and Second Letters to the Corinthians in Today's English Version*. Cleveland, OH: Collins World, 1977. [See. 101–4]

Nelson Teacher's Resource on First Corinthians. Nashville: Nelson, 2002. [See. 167–70]

Nichol, Francis D., ed. *Seventh-day Adventist Bible Commentary: The Holy Bible with Exegetical and Expository Comment*. Vol. 6. Washington, DC: Review & Herald, 1957. [See. 797–804]

Nicholes, Lou. *1 & 2 Corinthians: Letters of Correction*. US: Xulon, 2004. [See. 105–7]

Nicoll, W. Robertson, ed. *The Expositor's Greek Testament: The Acts of the Apostles*. Vol. 2. London: Hodder & Stoughton, 1897. [See. 917–25; N.B. Archive.org]

Category VIII—The New Testament

Nowell-Rostron, S. *St Paul's First Epistle to the Corinthians*. London: Religious Tract Society, 1931. [See. 202–13]

Nystrom, Carolyn and Margaret Fromer. *People in Turmoil: A Woman's Workshop on First Corinthians*. Grand Rapids: Lamplighter, 1985. [How Will It End, See. 88–90]

Olshausen, Hermann. *Biblical Commentary on St. Paul's First and Second Epistles to the Corinthians*. Edinburgh: T&T Clark, 1855. [See. 235–42; N.B. Archive.org and Google book]

Orr, William F., and James Arthur Walther. *1 Corinthians: A New Translation. The Anchor Bible*. Garden City: Doubleday, 1976. [See. 316–27]

Oster, Richard E. *1 Corinthians*. Joplin, MO: College Press, 1995. [See. 349–64]

Parker, Joseph. *The People's Bible: Discourses Upon Holy Scripture. Vol. 26. Romans—Galatians*. New York: Funk & Wagnalls, 1886. [The Resurrection of Christ, See. 311–18; N.B. Archive.org]

Parry, R. St. John, ed. *The First Epistle of Paul the Apostle to the Corinthians: In the Revised Version*. Cambridge: University Press, 1916. [See. 213–23; N.B. Google book]

Pascuzzi, Maria. *First and Second Corinthians*. Collegeville, MN: Liturgical Press, 2005. [See. 83–85]

Peifer, Claude J. *The First and Second Epistles of St. Paul to the Corinthians: Introduction and Commentary*. Collegeville, MN: Liturgical Press, 1960. [See. 53–55]

Perkins, Pheme. *First Corinthians*. Grand Rapids: Baker Academic, 2012. [See. 172–83]

Pettingill, William L. *Simple Studies in First and Second Corinthians*. Findlay, OH: Fundamental Truth, 1943. [See. 34–36]

Phillips, John. *Exploring 1 Corinthians: An Expository Commentary*. Grand Rapids: Kregel, 2002. [See. 329–51]

Picirilli, Robert E. *The Randall House Bible Commentary: 1, 2 Corinthians*. Nashville: Randall House, 1987. [See. 213–21]

Piconio, Bernardine à. *An Exposition of the Epistles of St. Paul*. Translated by A. H. Prichard. London: John Hodges, 1889. [See. 344–51; N.B. Archive.org]

Poole, Matthew. *Annotations Upon the Holy Bible Wherein the Sacred Text is Inserted and Various Readings . . . Vol. 2. [Jeremiah—Revelation]* London: Printed for Thomas Parkhurst et al., 1700. [no pagination; N.B. Google book. Reprinted as *A Commentary on the Holy Bible*. McLean, VA: MacDonald, 1962. See. 592–94]

Powers, B. Ward. *First Corinthians: An Exegetical and Explanatory Commentary: A Consideration of Some Views Ancient and Modern in the Light of a Verse-by-Verse Look at What the Text Actually Says: A Somewhat Traditional Interpretation Plus Contemporary Application*. Eugene, OR: Wipf & Stock, 2008. [See. 443–50]

Practical Christianity Foundation. *1st and 2nd Corinthians: Correcting the Church*. Canada: Practical Christianity Foundation, 2013. [See. 297–312]

Pratt, Richard L. *1 & 2 Corinthians*. Edited by Max E. Anders. Nashville: Holman, 2000. [Controversy Over the Resurrection, See. 257–63]

Pridham, Arthur. *Notes and Reflections on the First Epistle to the Corinthians*. London, Plymouth: Longmans, Green, Reader, & Dyer, 1866. [See. 368–86; N.B. Google book]

Prior, David. *The Message of 1 Corinthians: Life in the Local Church*. Leicester: Inter-Varsity Press, 1985. [See. 256–66]

Proctor, John. *First and Second Corinthians*. Louisville: Westminster John Knox, 2015. [See. 115–20]

Quast, Kevin. *Reading the Corinthian Correspondence: An Introduction*. New York: Paulist, 1994. [See. 88–94]

Redpath, Alan. *Royal Route to Heaven: Studies in the First Corinthians*. Westwood, NJ: Revell, 1960. [See. 194–205]

Reed, Oscar F. *Corinthians*. Beacon Bible Expositions Vol. 7. Edited by William M. Greathouse & Willard H. Taylor. Kansas City, MO: Beacon Hill, 1976. [See. 155–61]

Rees, W. "1 & 2 Corinthians." In *A Catholic Commentary on Holy Scripture*. Edited by Bernard Orchard. London: Nelson, 1951. [See. 1081–97]

Rice, John R. *The Church of God at Corinth: A Verse-by-Verse Commentary on 1 and 2 Corinthians*. Murfreesboro, TN: Sword of the Lord, 1973. [See. 141–46]

Rickaby, Joseph. *Notes on St. Paul: Corinthians, Galatians, Romans*. 1898. [See. 112–20; N.B. Archive.org and HathiTrust]

Riggs, James Stevenson. *Epistles to the Corinthians: 1 Corinthians*. New York: Macmillan, 1922. [See. 122–30; N.B. Google book]

Robertson, A. T. *Word Pictures in the New Testament: The Epistles of Paul*. Vol. 4. Nashville: Broadman, 1931. [See. 186–90]

Robertson, Archibald (Bishop), and Alfred Plummer. *A Critical and Exegetical Commentary on the First Epistle of St. Paul to the Corinthians*. 2nd ed. Edinburgh: T&T Clark, 1914. [See. 330–51; N.B. Archive.org]

Robertson, E. H. *Corinthians 1 and 2*. New York: Macmillan, 1973. [See. 91–93]

Robertson, F. W. *Expository Lectures on St. Paul's Epistles to the Corinthians: Delivered at Trinity Chapel, Brighton*. London: Smith, Elder, 1856. [See. 241–64; N.B. Archive.org]

Ruef, J. S. *Paul's First Letter to Corinth*. Baltimore: Penguin, 1971. [See. 157–64]

Sadler, M.F. *The First and Second Epistles to the Corinthians*. London: George Bell, 1898. [See. 258–71; N.B. Archive.org and HathiTrust]

Sampley, J. Paul. "The First Letter to the Corinthians." In *Acts of the Apostles, Introduction to Epistolary Literature, Letter to the Romans, First Letter to the Corinthians*. Vol. 10 of *The New Interpreter's Bible*. Edited by Leander E. Keck. Nashville: Abingdon, 2002. [See. 973–83]

Shore, T. Teignmouth. *St. Paul's Epistles to the Corinthians: The First Epistle to the Corinthians, with Commentary*. Edited by C. J. Ellicott. London: Cassell, 1879. [See. 139–44; N.B. Archive.org and HathiTrust]

Simon, W. G. H. *The First Epistle to the Corinthians: Introduction and Commentary*. London: SCM, 1959. [See. 138–44]

Snyder, Graydon F. *First Corinthians: A Faith Commentary*. Macon, GA: Mercer University Press, 1992. [See. 189–200]

Snyder, Russell D. "The First Epistle to the Corinthians." In *New Testament Commentary*. Edited by Herbert C. Alleman. Philadelphia: Muhlenberg Press, 1936. [See. 480–81]

Soards, Marion L. *1 Corinthians*. New International Biblical Commentary. Peabody, MA: Hendrickson, 1999. [See. 314–30]

Spittler, Russell P. *The Corinthian Correspondence*. Springfield, MO: Gospel Publishing House, 1976. [Chapter 9 Destroying the Last Enemy, See. 78–86; N.B. This chapter primarily deals with resurrection of the body.]

Spurgeon, Andrew B. *1 Corinthians: An Exegetical and Contextual Commentary*. Bangalore, India: Primalogue. 2012. [See. 173–76]

Stam, Cornelius Richard. *Commentary on the First Epistle of Paul to the Corinthians*. Chicago: Berean Bible Society, 1988. [See. 245–57]

Stanley, Arthur Penrhyn. *The Epistles of St. Paul to the Corinthians: With Critical Notes and Dissertations*. 4th ed. London: John Murray, 1876. [See. 283–300; N.B. Archive.org and Google book]

Staton, Knofel. *First Corinthians: Unlocking the Scriptures for You*. Cincinnati, OH: Standard Publishing, 1987. [See. 245–54]

Stedman, Ray C. *Letters to a Troubled Church: 1 and 2 Corinthians*. Grand Rapids: Discovery House, 2007. [See. 217–31]

Stratemeier, Klaas Jacob. *Preaching Christ in Corinth: Exegetical—Homiletical Sermon Outlines on First Corinthians*. Grand Rapids: Zondervan, 1936. [See. 87–98]

Talbert, Charles H. *Reading Corinthians: A Literary and Theological Commentary on 1 and 2 Corinthians*. New York: Crossroad, 1987. [See. 96–99]

Tarazi, Paul Nadim. *1 Corinthians: A Commentary*. Translated by Paul Nadim Tarazi. St. Paul, MN: OCABS Press, 2011. [See. 259–77]

Taylor, Mark Edward. *1 Corinthians*. Nashville: B&H, 2014. [See. 365–82]

Thiselton, Anthony C. *First Corinthians: A Shorter Exegetical and Pastoral Commentary*. Grand Rapids: Eerdmans, 2006. [See. 253–68; N.B. This work is a must reading.]

———. *The First Epistle to the Corinthians: A Commentary on the Greek Text*. Grand Rapids: Eerdmans, 2000. [See. 1169–22; N.B. This work was ranked by D. A. Carson as the best commentary on the Greek text.]

Thom, John Hamilton. *St. Paul's Epistles to the Corinthians: An Attempt to Convey Their Spirit and Significance*. Boston: Crosby, Nichols, 1852. [See. 217–30; N.B. Archive.org]

Thrall, Margaret E. *The First and Second Letters of Paul to the Corinthians*. Cambridge: University Press, 1965. [See. 102–8]

Toppe, Carleton. *1 Corinthians*. St. Louis: Concordia, 2005. [Chapter 4 The bodily resurrection (15:1–58), See. 140–46]

Trail, Ronald L. *An Exegetical Summary of 1 Corinthians 10—16*. Dallas, TX: SIL International, 2001. [See. 272–303; N.B. This text is a recommended read.]

Um, Stephen T. *1 Corinthians: The Word of the Cross*. Wheaton, IL: Crossway, 2015. [See. 255–72]

Valdés, Juan de. *Juan de Valdés' Commentary Upon St. Paul's First Epistle to the Church at Corinth*. Translated by John T. Betts. London: Trübner, 1883. [See. 264–76; N.B. Google book and HathiTrust]

Van Buren, Paul M. *According to the Scriptures: The Origins of the Gospel and of the Church's Old Testament*. Grand Rapids: Eerdmans, 1998. [Chapter 1 The Gospel Before Paul, See. 10–22]

Vang, Preben. *1 Corinthians*. Grand Rapids: Baker, 2014. [1 Corinthians 15:1–11, Resurrection and History, See. 200–15 and 1 Corinthians 15:12–34, Resurrection and Christian Living, See. 206–11]

Vaughan, Curtis, and Thomas D. Lea. *1 Corinthians*. Grand Rapids: Lamplighter, 1983. [See. 150–55]

Verbrugge, Verlyn D. "1 Corinthians." In *The Expositor's Bible Commentary Romans—Galatians*. Edited by Tremper Longman and David E. Garland. Vol. 11. Grand Rapids: Zondervan, 2008. [See. 390–95]

Vine, W. E. *1 Corinthians*. London: Oliphants, 1951. [See. 202–10]

Vines, Jerry. *God Speaks Today: A Study of 1 Corinthians*. Grand Rapids: Zondervan, 1979. [See. 229–43]

Walter, Eugen. *The Epistles to the Corinthians*. London: Sheed & Ward, 1971. [See. 156–69]

Warden, Duane. *1 Corinthians*. Searcy, AR: Resource Publications, 2016. [See. 431–50]

Watson, Nigel. *The First Epistle to the Corinthians*. 2nd ed. London: Epworth, 1992. [See. 155–64]

Welch, J. Wilbert. *Conduct Becoming Saints: The Book of 1 Corinthians*. Schaumburg, IL: Regular Baptist Press, 1978. [Chapter 11 The Christian and Resurrection Proofs, See. 98–107]

Whedon, D. D. *Commentary on the New Testament 1 Corinthians—2 Timothy*. Vol. 4. New York: Phillips & Hunt, 1880. [The First Epistle to the Corinthians, See. 11–19; N.B. Google book and HathiTrust]

Whitby, Daniel. *A Paraphrase and Commentary on the New Testament: Vol. 2. Containing All the Epistles, with a Discourse on the Millennium*. London: Printed by W. Bowyer, for Awnsham & John Churchill, 1703. [Annotations on Chapter 15, See. 186–88; N.B. Google book and HathiTrust]

Wiersbe, Warren W. *Be Wise: An Expository Study of 1 Corinthians*. Wheaton, IL: Victor, 1983. [See. 148–51]

Williams, C. S. C. "1 and 2 Corinthians." In *Peake's Commentary on the Bible*. Edited by Matthew Black. London: Nelson, 1962. [See. 963–64]

Willis, Wesley R. *1 Corinthians*. Wheaton, IL: Victor, 1989. [See. 82–87]

Willis, Wesley, and Elaine Willis. *Loving God in a Hostile World: A Study of 1 Corinthians*. Colorado Springs, CO: Accent, 1993. [Chapter 11 Assured of Resurrection I Corinthians 15:1–34, See. 98–104]

Wilson, Geoffrey B. *1 Corinthians: A Digest of Reformed Comment*. London: Banner of Truth Trust, 1971. [See. 215–24]

Wingard, Robert W. *Paul and the Corinthians*. Nashville: Abingdon, 1999. [Chapter 5 The Resurrection and Other Essentials, See. 83–91]

Witham, Robert. *Annotations on the New Testament of Jesus Christ*. Vol. 2. Douay, 1733. [See. 126–30; N.B. Google book. The title page states by R.W.D.D.]

Witherington, Ben. *Conflict and Community in Corinth: A Socio-Rhetorical Commentary on 1 and 2 Corinthians*. Grand Rapids: Eerdmans, 1995. [See. 291–303; N.B. Examine this work.]

Woodford, J. R. "Acts of the Apostles." In *The New Testament of Our Lord and Saviour Jesus Christ According to the Authorised Version: Containing the Acts, Epistles, and Revelation*. Vol. 3. Edited by J. Massie. London: SPCK, 1881. [See. The Epistle to the Corinthians, no pagination; N.B. Google book]

Wordsworth, Chr. *The New Testament of Our Lord and Saviour Jesus Christ in the Original Greek with Introductions and Notes: St. Paul's Epistles; The General Epistles; The Book of Revelation, and Indexes*. Vol. 2. London: Rivingtons, 1872. [See. 135–37; N.B. Archive.org and HathiTrust]

Wright, N. T. *Paul for Everyone: 1 Corinthians*. London: SPCK, 2003. [See. 201–11]

Zodhiates, Spiros. *Conquering the Fear of Death: An Exposition of 1 Corinthians 15, Based upon the Original Greek Text*. Grand Rapids: Eerdmans, 1970. [See. 1–242; N.B. This book should be read.]

Category IX

*Creeds, Religion, Doctrinal,
Sermons, Commentaries*

Chapter 23

The Apostles' Creed

Abbey, Merrill R. *Creed Of Our Hope*. Nashville: Abingdon, 1954. [Chapter 4 Resurrection— A Mighty Challenge, See. 49-61]

Abernethy, Arthur Talmage. *The Apostles' Creed: A Romance in Religion*. Nashville, Cokesbury, 1925. [Chapter 8 He Rose Again, See. 47-53; Chapter 9 He Ascended into Heaven, See. 54-60]

Ashwin-Siejkowski, Piotr. *The Apostles' Creed: The Apostles' Creed and Its Early Christian Context*. Vol. 1. London: T&T Clark, 2009. [Chapter 6 He Descended into Hell; on the Third Day He Rose Again from the Dead, See. 56-66; Chapter 7 He Ascended into Heaven, and Sits at the Right Hand of God the Father Almighty, See. 67-75]

Ayo, Nicholas. *The Creed as Symbol*. Notre Dame: University of Notre Dame Press, 1989. [Chapter 5 On the Third Day He Rose Again, See. 81-87; Chapter 6 He Ascended into Heaven, and is Seated at the Right Hand of the Father, See. 89-94]

Backemeyer, Frederick William. *This Abiding Creed: An Unconventional Approach to the Apostles' Creed*. Grand Rapids: Zondervan, 1940. [Chapter 5 The World Needs Easter!, See. 55-61; Chapter 6 Ascended Into Heaven, See. 62-73]

Baggott, L. J. *The Faith for the Faithful*. London: Nisbet, 1928. [Chapter 6 Dead. Buried. Risen, See. 121-54; Chapter 7 Descent Into Hell, See. 155-67; Chapter 8 The Ascent Into Heaven, See. 168-84]

Baird, Andrew Cumming. *Christian Fundamentals: A Modern Apology for the Apostles' Creed*. Edinburgh: T&T Clark, 1926. [Chapter 8 The Resurrection and Ascension, See. 129-51; N.B. Google book].

Baker, Charles Richard. *The Apostles' Creed: Tested By Experience: Lectures Delivered in the Church of the Messiah, Brooklyn*. New York: T. Whittaker, 1884. [The Resurrection of the Christ, See. 49-57; N.B. Archive.org and Google book]

Balthasar, Hans Urs von. *Credo: Meditations on the Apostles' Creed*. Translated by David Kipp. New York: Crossroad, 1990. [Chapter 5 The Third Day Arose Again from the Dead, See. 57-60; Chapter 6 Ascended into Heaven, He Sits at the Right Hand of God Almighty, See. 61-65]

Barclay, William. *The Apostles' Creed for Everyman*. New York: Harper & Row, 1967. [Chapter 11 The Third Day He Rose Again From the Dead, See. 134-61; Chapter 12 He Ascended into Heaven, See. 162-73]

Category IX—Creeds, Religion, Doctrinal, Sermons, Commentaries

Baring-Gould, S. *Village Conferences on The Creed*. London: Joseph Master, 1873. [Chapter 15 The Resurrection, See. 89–94; Chapter 16 The Great Forty Days, See. 95–102; Chapter 17 The Ascension, See. 103–9; N.B. Google.com]

Barkway, Lumsden. *The Creed and Its Credentials*. London: SPCK, 1935. [Chapter 5 The Resurrection of Our Lord, See. 43–54]

Barr, O. Sydney. *From the Apostles' Faith to the Apostles' Creed*. New York: Oxford University Press, 1964. [Chapter 8 The Third Day He Rose Again From the Dead, See. 101–17; Chapter 12 He Ascended into Heaven, See. 141–42]

Barry, J. G. H. *Meditations on the Apostles' Creed*. New York: E. S. Gorham, 1912. [The Fifteenth Meditation. The Third Day He Rose Again From the Dead, See. 305–26; The Sixteenth Meditation. And Ascended Into Heaven, See. 329–48]

Barth, Karl. *Credo*. New York: Scribner's Sons, 1962. [Chapter 10 The Third Day He Rose Again From the Dead, See. 95–104; Chapter 11 He Ascended Into Heaven and Sitteth On the Right Hand of God the Father Almighty, See. 105–16]

———. *The Faith of the Church: A Commentary on the Apostles' Creed According to Calvin's Catechism*. Translated by Gabriel Vahanian. New York: Meridian, 1960. [Chapter 8 Doctrine of the Exaltation (Questions 73–87), See. 96–119]

Bayes, Jonathan F. *The Apostles' Creed: Truth with Passion*. Eugene, OR: Wipf & Stock, 2010. [Chapter 11 On the Third Day He Rose From the Dead, See. 108–18; Chapter 12 He Ascended to the heavens, See. 119–32]

Beeching, H. C. *The Apostles' Creed: Six Lectures Given In Westminster Abbey*. London: J. Murray, 1905. [Lecture 4 See. He Ascended into Heaven, See. 64–68; N.B. Google book and HathiTrust]

Beets, Henry, and M. J. Bosma. *Catechism of Reformed Doctrine: For Advanced Classes*. 5th ed. Grand Rapids: Eerdmans, 1928. [Lesson 17 The States of the Mediation-continued, See. 48–51]

Bell, G. K. A. *The Meaning of the Creed: Papers on the Apostles' Creed*. New York: Macmillan, 1917. [Chapter 6 The Resurrection of Jesus Christ, See. 97–110; Chapter 7 The Ascension of Jesus Christ, See. 111–30; N.B. Google book]

Berger, Peter L. *Questions of Faith: A Skeptical Affirmation of Christianity*. Malden, MA: Blackwell, 2004. [Chapter 8 He Descended into Hell. On the Third Day He Rose Again. He Ascended into Heaven, See. 103–14]

Bethune-Baker, James Franklin. *The Faith of the Apostles' Creed: An Essay in Adjustment of Belief and Faith*. London: Macmillan, 1918. [Chapter 6 The Third Day He Rose Again from the Dead, He Ascended Into Heaven, See. 130–39; N.B. Archive.org]

Bird, Charles John. *A Practical Exposition of the Apostles' Creed in the Form of Question and Answer Designed for the Use of Children*. Hereford: Printed By E. G. Wright, 1827. [See. 9; N.B. Google book. Title page states "By A Clergyman."]

Bodington, Eric James. *A Short History and Exposition of the Apostles' Creed and of the First Eight of the Thirty-Nine Articles of Religion*. With an introduction by the Lord Bishop of Salisbury. Oxford: Blackwell, 1897. [Article 5, See. 81–82; Article 6, See. 83–85; N.B. Google book and HathiTrust]

Bosworth, Thomas. *The Apostles' Creed and the Nicene Creed. With Explanations and Illustrations From the Holy Scriptures*. London: Thomas Bosworth, 1868. [See. 10–11; N.B. Google book]

Briggs, Charles A. *The Fundamental Christian Faith: The Origin, History and Interpretation of the Apostles' and Nicene Creeds*. New York: Scribner's Sons, 1913. [Chapter 7 Risen

From The Dead, See. 137–54; Chapter 8 Ascended Into Heaven, See. 155–57; N.B. Google book and Hathitrust]

Briscoe, D. Stuart. *The Apostles' Creed: Beliefs That Matter*. Wheaton, IL: Harold Shaw, 1994. [Chapter 7 Rose Again From the Dead, See. 99–112; Chapter 8 He Ascended into Heaven, See. 113–26]

Brock, Isaac. *Sermons on the Apostles' Creed: Preached in the Autumn of 1863, at the Episcopal Jews' Chapel of the London Society for Promoting Christianity amongst the Jews*. William Macintosh: London, 1864. [Sermon 7 Christ's Resurrection, See. 68–79; Sermon 8 Christ's Exaltation, See. 80–90; N.B. Archive.org and Google book]

Bruce, Michael. *No Empty Creed*. New York: Seabury, 1964. [Chapter 6 Was there an Empty Tomb, See. 57–65; Chapter 7 Did Christ Ascend to Heaven?, See. 66–74]

Brunner, Emil. *I Believe In The Living God. Sermons on the Apostles' Creed*. Translated by John Holden. Philadelphia: Westminster, 1966. [Chapter 7 Easter Certainty, See. 86–97; Chapter 8 The Living Lord, See. 98–110]

Burn, A. E. *The Apostles' Creed*. London: Rivingtons, 1906. [The Third Day He Rose From the Dead, 77–81; Ascended into Heaven, See. 81–83; N.B. Archive.org]

Burnaby, John. *The Belief of Christendom: A Commentary on the Nicene Creed*. London: National Society, 1959. [Chapter 11 He Rose Again, See. 97–105; Chapter 12 Ascended Into Heaven, See. 106–14]

Burrell, David James. *The Apostles' Creed*. New York: American Tract Society, 1915. [Section 5 The Third Day He Rose Again from the Dead, See. 117–24; Section 6 He Ascended into Heaven, See. 125–29; N.B. Archive.org and Google book]

Campbell, Ross Turner. *Class-Room Lectures on the Apostles Creed*. Sterling, KS: Sterling Bulletin Print, 1931. [Eighth Lecture. The Third Day, See. 84–91; Ninth Lecture. He Rose from the Dead, See. 92–104; Tenth Lecture. He Ascended into Heaven, See. 105–7]

Campbell, W. Hume. *Lessons on the Apostles' Creed*. London: Church of England Sunday School Institute, 192? [Chapter 23 Easter.—The Resurrection, See. 83–86; Chapter 28 The Ascension, See. 106–8]

Candler, Warren Akin. *The Christ and The Creed*. Nashville: Cokesbury, 1927. [Chapter 5 The Christ in the Creed: His Resurrection, See. 83–100]

Chambré, A. St. John. *Sermons on the Apostles' Creed*. New York: Whitaker, 1898. [Chapter 6 The Third Day He Rose Again From The Dead, See. 93–102; Chapter 7 Ascension-Session, See. 103–18; N.B. Archive.org]

Chase, Frederic Henry. *Belief And Creed: Being an Examination of Portions of "The Faith of a Modern Churchman" Dealing with the Apostles' Creed*. London: Macmillan, 1919. [Chapter 4 The Resurrection on the Third Day, See. 81–158]

Clare, Maurice [pseud.]. *The Creed in Human Life: A Devotional Commentary For Everyday Use*. New York: Hodder & Stoughton, 1912. [Chapter 11 The Likeness of His Resurrection, See. 209–22; Chapter 12 The Ascent of Man, See. 223–38]

Claudel, Paul. *I Believe in God: A Meditation on the Apostles' Creed*. Translated by Helen Weaver. New York: Holt, Rinehart & Winston, 1963. [The Third Day He Rose Again from the Dead, 137–43; He Ascended into Heaven, See. 144–48]

Cobb, William. F. *Mysticism and the Creed*. London: Macmillan, 1914. [Chapter 14 The Third Day He Rose Again, See. 229–40; Chapter 15 The Third Day He Rose Again (continued), See. 241–61; Chapter 16 He Ascended into Heaven, See. 262–72; N.B. Archive.org]

Cole, C. Donald. *"I Believe..."* Chicago: Moody, 1983. [Chapter 16 The Third Day He Rose From the Dead, See. 89–94; Chapter 17 He Ascended into Heaven, See. 95–101]

Coyle, Robert Francis. *Rocks and Flowers; Seven Discourses on the Apostles' Creed*. Denver, Fisher Book & Stationery, 1910. [The Stone Rolled Away: On the Third Day He Rose Again From the Dead, See. 25–35; The Ascension and Judgment, See. 37–45]

Cranfield, C. E. B. *The Apostles' Creed: A Faith to Live By*. Grand Rapids: Eerdmans, 2004. [Chapter 8 On the Third Day He Rose Again, See. 36–42; Chapter 9 He Ascended into Heaven, and is Seated at the Right Hand of the Father, See. 43–48]

Davies, Rupert Eric. *Making Sense of the Creeds*. London: Epworth, 1987. [Chapter 4 For us men and for our salvation he came down from heaven, See. On the Third Day He Rose Again, See. 51–52; He Ascended into Heaven and is Seated on the Right Hand of the Father, See. 52–54]

Day, Gardiner M. *The Apostles' Creed; An Interpretation For Today*. New York: Scribner's Sons, 1963. [Chapter 9 The Third Day He Rose Again from the Dead, See. 85–94; Chapter 10 He Ascended into Heaven, and Sitteth on the Right Hand of God the Father Almighty, See. 95–103]

Devine, Arthur. *The Creed Explained, or, An Exposition of Catholic Doctrine According to the Creeds of Faith and the Constitutions and Definitions of the Church*. London: R. & T. Washbourne, 1892. [Article 5 He Descended into Hell; the Third Day He Rose Again From the Dead, See. 204–21; Article 6 He Ascended into Heaven, and Sitteth at the Right Hand of God, the Father Almighty, See. 222–27; N.B. Google book]

Dodds, James. *Exposition of the Apostles' Creed*. Philadelphia: Westminster, 1896. [Chapter 5 He Descended Into Hell; The Third Day He Rose Again from the Dead, See. 54–65; Chapter 6 He Ascended Into Heaven, and Sitteth on the Right Hand of God the Father Almighty, See. 66–70; N.B. Archive.org, Google book, Gutenberg.org, and HathiTrust]

Dods, Marcus. "Lecture 3 Did Christ Rise From The Dead?" In *Questions of Faith: A Series of Lectures on the Creed*. Edited by P. Carnegie Simpson. London: Hodder & Stoughton, 1904. [See. 75–102; N.B. Google book]

Douglass, Earl L. *The Faith We Live By: An Exposition of the Apostles' Creed*. Nashville, Cokesbury, 1937. [Chapter 7 He Descended Into Hell; The Third Day He Rose Again from the Dead, See. 99–118; Chapter 8 He Ascended into Heaven, and Sitteth on the Right Hand of God the Father Almighty, See. 119–30]

Downes, J. Cyril. *The Facts of the Faith: A Commentary on the Apostles' Creed*. London: Epworth, 1949. [Part 2 God the Son. See. The Third Day He Rose Again, See. 78–87; He Ascended Into Heaven, and Sitteth On the Right Hand of God the Father Almighty, See. 88–95]

Drown, Edward S. *The Apostles' Creed To-Day*. New York: Macmillan, 1917. [Chapter 4 The Interpretation of the Apostles' Creed To-Day, See. 6 The Third Day He Rose from the Dead, See. 101–7; N.B. Archive.org]

DuBose, Henry Wade. *We Believe: A Study of the Apostles' Creed*. Richmond: John Knox Press, 1960. [Chapter 7 The Risen Lord, See. 48–54]

Duffy, Eamon. *The Creed In The Catechism: The Life of God for Us*. London: Continuum, 1996. [Resurrection and Ascension, See. 72–79]

Edwards, Mark J., ed. *We Believe in the Crucified and Risen Lord*. Downers Grove, IL: InterVarsity, 2009. [On the Third Day He Rose Again, See. 139–44; In Accordance with the Scriptures, See. 145–54; He Ascended into Heaven, See. 155–64]

Ellens, J. Harold. *Honest Faith for Our Time: Truth-Telling About the Bible, the Creed, and the Church*. Eugene, OR: Pickwick, 2010. [Chapter 6 He Rose from the Dead, See. 31–36; Ascended and Enthroned Judge, See. 37–43]

Eyton, Robert. *The Apostles' Creed: Sermons*. London: Kegan Paul, Trench: Trübner, 1890. [Sermon 9 The Resurrection, See. 81–88; Sermon 10 The Ascension, See. 89–96; N.B. Google book]

Ferrin, Howard W. *I Believe—Addresses on The Apostles' Creed*. New York: Revell, 1938. [Chapter 12 The Third Day He Rose Again From the Dead, See. 98–106; Chapter 13 He Ascended Into Heaven, See. 107–13]

Finegan, Joseph. *What Do You Believe? Catholics Believe The Apostles' Creed*. New York: Paulist, 1938. [The Third Day He Arose Again From the Dead; He Ascended into Heaven, See. 9–10; N.B. Archive.org]

Forell, George Wolfgang. *Understanding the Nicene Creed*. Philadelphia: Fortress, 1965. [And the Third Day He Arose Again . . . According to the Scriptures . . . Ascended into Heaven, See. 52–65]

Foster, John McGaw. *To Know and Believe: Studies in the Apostles' Creed*. London, Longmans, Green, 1908. [Chapter 9 The Supreme Miracle, See. 70–78; Chapter 10 The Ascended Lord—The Judge, See. 79–86; N.B. Google book]

Franklin, B. *The Creed and Modern Thought*. New York: E. & J. B. Young, 1881. [The Third Day He Rose From The Dead and The Third Day He Rose Again, According To The Scriptures, See. 256–65; He Ascended Into Heaven, and Sitteth On The Right Hand Of God, The Father Almighty, See. 266–74; N.B. Archive.org and Google book]

Gibson, R. C. *The Apostles' Creed: Collated Chiefly From The Works of Bishop Pearson, Dr. Barrow and Dr. Hammond, Etc*. London: William Macintosh, 1875. [The Third Day He Rose Again from the Dead, See. 84–89; He Rose Again from the Dead, See. 89–94; He Ascended into Heaven, See. 95–97; N.B. Google book]

Goodwin, Harvey. *The Foundations of the Creed*. London: J. Murray, 1889. [Chapter 6 He Descended Into Hell; The Third Day He Rose again from the Dead, See. 166–92; Chapter 7 He Ascended Into Heaven, and Sitteth on the Right Hand of God the Father Almighty, See. 193–215; N.B. Google book]

Gorle, J. *An Analysis of Pearson on the Creed: With Examination Questions*. Cambridge: J. Hall, 1849. [Art. 5 He Descended into Hell; the Third Day He Rose Again from the Dead, See. 231–69; Art. 6 He Ascended into Heaven, and Sitteth on the Right Hand of God, the Father Almighty, See. 270–306; N.B. Google book]

Graham, William. "The Resurrection and Ascension." In *A Pulpit Commentary on Catholic Teaching:* Vol. 1. *Creed*. New York: Joseph F. Wagner, 1908. [See. 154–60; N.B. Google book]

Hall, Arthur C. A. *Meditations on the Creed*. New York: James Pott, 1879? [Meditation 12 The Third Day He Rose from the Dead, See. 92–99; Meditation 13 He Ascended into Heaven, See. 100–102; N.B. Google book and Hathitrust]

Harn, Roger E. Van ed. *Exploring And Proclaiming The Apostles' Creed*. Grand Rapids: Eerdmans, 2004. [The Third Day He Rose Again from the Dead (George Hunsiger), See. 136–53; He Ascended into Heaven and Is Seated at the Right Hand of God the Father Almighty (Lois Malcolm), See. 161–72]

Harned, David Baily. *Creed and Personality Identity: The Meaning of the Apostles' Creed*. Philadelphia: Fortress, 1981. [Chapter 6 The Third Day, See. 73–84]

Harrison, McVeigh. *Common Sense About Religion: Being a Synopsis of the Evidence of Reason, Revelation and Experience as to the Truth of the Apostles' Creed*. West Park, NY: Holy Cross, 1931. [Chapter 20 The Third Day He Rose Again from the Dead, See. 320–34; Chapter 21 He Ascended Into Heaven, and Sitteth on the Right Hand of God the Father Almighty—The Ascended Christ Essential to Modern Thought, See. 335–46]

Hayes, Charles H. *Bible Lessons on the Creed*. New York: Edwin S. Gorham, 1906. [Lesson 26 The Third Day He Rose Again, 124–27; Lessons 27–30, See. 127–40; N.B. Google book and Hathitrust]

Hedley, George. *The Symbol of the Faith: A Study of the Apostles' Creed*. New York: Macmillan, 1948. [Chapter 9 He Rose Again, See. 75–82; Chapter 10 He Ascended Into Heaven, See. 83–91]

Heywood, Bernard Oliver Francis. *This Is Our Faith: An Explanation of the Articles of the Christian Faith as Contained in the Apostles' Creed*. Hodder & Stoughton: London, 1938. [Chapter 9 The Third Day He Rose Again from the Dead, See. 124–37; Chapter 10 He Ascended into Heaven, and Sitteth on the Right Hand of God the Father Almighty, See. 138–48]

Hopkins, Archibald. *The Apostles' Creed: An Analysis of its Clauses, with Reference to their Credibility*. Boston: American Unitarian Association, 1900. [The Third Day He Rose from the Dead, He Ascended into Heaven, and Sitteth on the Right Hand of God the Father Almighty, See. 51–98; N.B. Google book]

Hopkins, John Henry. *The Primitive Creed, Examined and Explained: In Two Parts*. Burlington: Edward Smith, 1834. [Discourse 7 The Resurrection of Christ, See. 91–104; Discourse 8 Types of the Ascension, See. 105–19; N.B. Google book]

Hornyold, John Joseph. *The Grounds of the Christian's Belief; or, The Apostles Creed Explained: In A Concise, Easy, and Familiar Manner. In Twenty-Three Moral Discourses*. Birmingham: Printed and Sold by T. Holliwell, 1771. [Article 5 Discourse 1 He Descended into Hell, the Third Day He Rose Again from the Dead, See. 134–46; Discourse 2 The Third Day He Rose Again from the Dead, See. 147–60; Article 6 Discourse 2 He Ascended into Heaven and Sits at the Right Hand of God, the Father Almighty, See. 161–72; Discourse 2 He Ascended into Heaven and Sits at the Right Hand of God, the Father Almighty, See. 173–85; N.B. Google book. The Author is identified as J-H-C].

Horton, Michael Scott. *We Believe: Recovering the Essentials of the Apostles' Creed*. Nashville: Word, 1998. [Chapter 6 Can We Still Believe in the Resurrection?, See. 105–28; Chapter 7 Ascended in Glory, Returning in Judgment, See. 129–54]

Howell, James C. *The Life We Claim: The Apostles' Creed For Preaching, Teaching, And Worship*. Nashville: Abingdon, 2005. [Chapter 8 The Third Day He Rose from the Dead, See. 81–90; Chapter 9 From Thence Shall Come to Judge the Quick and the Dead, See. 91–92]

Hunsinger, George. "The Third Day He Rose Again From the Dead." In *Exploring and Proclaiming The Apostles' Creed*. Edited by Roger E. Van Harn. Grand Rapids: Eerdmans, 2004. [See. 136–53]

Hunton, William Lee. *I Believe: Meditations on the Creed*. Philadelphia: United Lutheran Publication House, 1922. [Rose Again From The Dead, See. 50–52; Ascended Into Heaven, See. 53–57; N.B. Google book]

Hutchins, James. *A Series of Plain and Familiar Discourses on the Apostles' Creed.* London: W. Watson, 1827. [Chapter 15 The Resurrection of Christ, See. 244–62; Chapter 16 The Ascension, See. 263–80; N.B. Google book]

Ihmels, L. "On the Third Day He Rose Again from the Dead." In *The Truth of the Apostles' Creed An Exposition by Twelve Theologians of Germany.* Edited by William Laible. Translated by Charles E. Hay. Philadelphia: Lutheran Publication Society, 1916. [See. 97–110; N.B. Google book]

Ince, G. J. *A Year's Course On The Creed.* London: Faith Press, 1940. [Lessons 19–21, See. 79–88]

Jacobs, Charles M. *The Faith of the Church: Addresses on the Apostles' Creed.* Philadelphia: Board of Publication of the United Lutheran Church in America, 1938. [Chapter 9 The Resurrection, See. 63–72; Chapter 10 The Exaltation, See. 73–80]

James, Ron. *Creed and Christ: A Devotional Approach to the Apostles' Creed.* Nashville: Upper Room, 1986. [Chapter 6 The Third Day He Rose Again from the Dead, See. 57–66; Chapter 7 He Ascended into Heaven, and Sitteth at the Right Hand of God the Father Almighty, See. 67–74]

Jennings, Theodore W. *Loyalty To God: The Apostles' Creed in Life and Liturgy.* Nashville: Abingdon, 1992. [Chapter 13 Rose from the Dead, See. 129–43; Chapter 14 Ascended into Heaven, See. 144–49]

Johnson, Cliff Ross. *Every Moment An Easter.* Alexandria, VA: Privately Published for the Friends and Members of Westminster Presbyterian Church, 1962. [He Ascended Into Heaven, See. 59–68]

Johnson, Timothy Luke. *The Creed: What Christians Believe and Why It Matters.* New York: Doubleday, 2003. [Chapter 6 He Ascended . . . and Will Come Again, See. 176–215]

Johnston, J. Wesley. *The Creed and the Prayer.* New York: Eaton & Mains, 1896. [Chapter 6 The Third Day He Rose From the Dead, See. 81–96; Chapter 7 He Ascended into Heaven, and Sitteth at the Right Hand of God the Father Almighty, See. 81–107; N.B. Google book]

Johnston, Mark G. *Our Creed: For Every Culture and for Every Generation.* Phillipsburg, NJ: P & R Pub., 2012. [Chapter 5 Jesus Christ: Risen, Ascended, and Enthroned, See. 61–70]

Kemmer, Alfons. *The Creed in the Gospels.* Translated by Urban Schnaus. New York: Paulist, 1986. [Article 5 On The Third Day He Rose from the Dead, See. 63–79; Article 6 He Ascended Into Heaven and is Seated at the Right Hand of God the Almighty Father, See. 80–86]

Ken, Bishop (Thomas). *Exposition of the Apostles' Creed.* London: William Pickering, 1852. [The Third Day He Rose Again from the Dead, See. 50–57; N.B. Google book]

Kennedy, G. A. Studdert. *I Believe: Sermons on the Apostles' Creed.* New York: Doran, 1928. [Chapter 11 The Third Day He Rose Again From The Dead, See. 252–69; Chapter 12 He Ascended Into Heaven, See. 270–89; N.B. First published as *Food for the Fed-up* (London: Hodder & Stoughton, 1921); N.B. HathiTrust]

Kennett, Basil. *A Brief Exposition of the Apostles' Creed According to Bishop Pearson, In a New Method by Way of Paraphrase and Annotation By B. Kennett.* London: Printed for James Knapton, 1721. [Article 5 He Defended into Hell, the Third Day He Rose Again from the Dead, See. 94–112; Article 6 He Ascended into Heaven, and Sittieth on the Right Hand of God the Father Almighty, See. 113–23; N.B. Archive.org and Google book]

King, Peter. *The History of the Apostles Creed: With Critical Observations on Its Several Articles*. 3rd ed. London: Printed by W.B. for Jonathan Robinson at the Golden Lion, and John Wyat at the Rose, in St. Paul's Church-Yard, 1711. [See. 271-81; N.B. Archive. org and Google book]

Knox, Ronald A. *The Creed In Slow Motion*. New York: Sheed & Ward, 1949. [Chapter 14 The Third Day He Rose Again from the Dead, See. 116-24; Chapter 15 He Ascended Into Heaven, Sitteth at the Right Hand of God, See. 125-33]

Kuiper, Henry J. *Sermons on the Apostles' Creed, Lords Days: 8-24*. Vol. 2. Grand Rapids: Zondervan, 1937. [Chapter 17 The Resurrection of Christ (Edward J. Messelink), See. 181-91; Chapter 18 The Ascension of Christ (Anthony Karreman), See. 191-202]

Küng, Hans. *Credo: The Apostles' Creed Explained For Today*. Translated by John Bowden. New York: Doubleday, 1993. [Part 4 Descent into Hell—Resurrection—Ascension, See. 95-121]

Laible, Wilhelm, ed. *The Truth of the Apostles Creed: An Exposition By Twelve Theologians Of Germany*. Translated by Charles E. Hay. Philadelphia: The Lutheran Publication Society, 1916. [Chapter 7 On the Third Day He Rose Again from the Dead (L. Ihmels), See. 97-110; N.B. Google book]

Langford, William. *A Series of Familiar Discourses on the Apostles' Creed, the Lord's Prayer and the Litany: With a Treatise on Confirmation and the Sacrament*. London: Published by C. & J. Rivington, 1824. [Sermon 8, See. 137-56, especially 146-51; N.B. Archive. org and Google book]

Leathes, Stanley. *The Christian Creed: Its Theory and Practice with A Preface on Some Present Dangers of the English Church*. New York: Dutton, 1878. [Chapter 16 The Third Day He Rose Again from the Dead, See. 179-90; Chapter 17 The Third Day He Rose Again from the Dead (Continued), See. 191-203; Chapter 18 The Third Day He Rose Again from the Dead, See. 205-16; Chapter 19 He Ascended Into Heaven, See. 217-28; N.B. Google book]

Leighton, Robert, Abp. of Glasgow. *Expositions on the Creed, the Lord's Prayer, and the Ten Commandments*. London: Joseph Rickerby, 1836. [See. 22-25; N.B. Google book and HathiTrust]

Lias, J. J. *The Nicene Creed: A Manual for the use of Candidates for Holy Orders*. London: Sonnenschein, 1897. [Chapter 5 The Redemptive Work of Jesus Christ, See. 140-253; esp. Section 3, 223-36; N.B. Google book]

Lochman, Jan Milič. *The Faith We Confess: An Ecumenical Dogmatics*. Translated by David Lewis. Philadelphia: Fortress, 1984. [Chapter 12 On the Third Day He Rose Again from the Dead, See. 147-62; Chapter 13 Ascended to Heaven, See. 163-76]

Lockerbie, D. Bruce. *The Apostles' Creed: Do You Really Believe It?* Wheaton, IL: Victor, 1977. [Chapter 5 He Rose Again from the Dead, See. 55-66; Chapter 6 He Ascended into Heaven, See. 67-78]

Macartney, Clarence Edward. *Things Most Surely Believed: A Series of Sermons on the Apostles' Creed*. Nashville: Cokesbury, 1930. [Chapter 5 He Rose Again from the Dead, See. 68-84; Chapter 6 He Ascended Into Heaven, See. 85-100]

Maclear, G. F. *An Introduction to the Creeds*. London: Macmillan, 1889. [Chapter 5 The Fifth Article, See. 137-61; Chapter 6 The Sixth Article, See. 162-79; N.B. Archive.org and HathiTrust]

MacDonald, Alexander. *The Symbol of the Apostles: A Vindication of the Apostolic Authorship of The Creed on the Lines of Catholic Tradition*. New York: Christian Press

Association, 1903. [Chapter 12 The Articles of the Creed. 4, See. 302–3; N.B. Archive.org and HathiTrust]

MacGregor, Geddes. *The Nicene Creed: Illumined By Modern Thought*. Grand Rapids: Eerdmans, 1980. [Chapter 9 Resurrection, See. 80–89; Chapter 10 Ascension, See. 90–97]

Malden, R. H. *Christian Belief: A Short Exposition of the Apostles' Creed*. London: SPCK, 1958. [Chapter 5 The Risen Master, See. 31–36; Chapter 6 The Ascended Christ, See. 37–42]

Marthaler, Bernard L. *The Creed*. Mystic, CT: Twenty-Third Publications, 1987. [Chapter 11 Life Is Changed, Not Taken Away, See. 177–90; Chapter 12 If I Be Lifted Up . . . See. 191–201]

McClure, Walter Emerson. *"Lord, I Believe": Sermons on the Apostles' Creed*. Grand Rapids: Eerdmans, 1937. [Chapter 8 The Third Day He Arose Again from the Dead, See. 99–109; Chapter 9 He Ascended Into Heaven and Sitteth at the Right Hand of God the Father Almighty, See. 110–19]

McEwen, James Stevenson. *Why We Are Christians: An Interpretation of the Apostles' Creed*. Edinburgh: Saint Andrew Press, 1970. [The Third Day He Rose Again from the Dead, See. 46–48; He Ascended into Heaven, and Sitteth on the Right Hand of God the Father Almighty, See. 48–49]

McGrath, Alister E. *"I Believe": Exploring the Apostles' Creed*. Downers Grove, IL: InterVarsity, 1997. [Chapter 4 God the Son: His Death and Resurrection, See. 55–72; Chapter 5 God the Son His Present Activity and Future Role God the Holy Spirit, See. 73–90]

———. *I Believe: Understanding and Applying the Apostles' Creed*. Grand Rapids: Zondervan, 1991. [On the Third Day He Rose Again, See. 85–92; He Ascended into Heaven, and is Seated at the Right hand of the Father, See. 93–100]

Meulen, John M. Vander. *The Faith of Christendom: A Series of Studies on the Apostles' Creed*. Richmond, VA: Presbyterian Committee of Publication, 1936. [Chapter 6 What Became of the Body?, See. 109–27; Chapter 7 Why the Ascension?, See. 128–43]

Meyer, F. B. *The Creed of Creeds: A Series of Short Expositions of the Apostles' Creed*. London: Sir Isaac Pitman & Sons, 1906. [Chapter 19 He Descended into Hell, the Third Day He Rose Again from the Dead, See. 93–96; Chapter 20 The Third Day He Rose Again from the Dead, See. 97–100; Chapter 21 The Third Day He Rose Again, See. 101–4; Chapter 22 He Ascended, See. 105–8; Chapter 23 He Ascended into Heaven, See. 109–12; Chapter 24 He Ascended into Heaven, See. 113–16; Chapter 25 He Ascended into Heaven, See. 117–20; Chapter 26 He Ascended into Heaven, See. 121–24; N.B. Archive.org]

Mill, William Hodge. *An Analysis of the Exposition of the Creed written by the Right Rev. . . . John Pearson*. 3rd English ed. Cambridge: Gilbert & Rivington, 1853. [The Third Day He Rose Again, See. 89–93; He Ascended Into Heaven, See. 93–95; N.B. Google book and HathiTrust]

Mortimer, Alfred G. *The Creeds: An Historical and Doctrinal Exposition of the Apostles', Nicene, and Athanasian Creeds*. London: Longmans, Green, 1902. [Article 5, 2. Of Our Lord's Resurrection, See. 181–89; Article 6 Of the Ascension, Session, and Reign of Our Lord, See. 190–99; N.B. Google book]

Mozley, J. K. *Historic Christianity and the Apostles' Creed*. London: Longmans, Green, 1920. [See. 80–81; N.B. Archive.org]

Mueller, John Theodore. *Faith of Our Fathers: A Review of Our Holy Christian Faith As Set Forth In the Apostles' Creed*. Grand Rapids: Eerdmans, 1939. [Section 8 I Believe In Jesus Christ . . . the Third Day He Rose again from the Dead, See. 80–81]

Müller, Michael. *God The Teacher of Mankind: A Plain, Comprehensive Explanation of Christian Doctrine. The Apostles' Creed*. New York: Benziger, 1880. [Christ's Resurrection, See. 332–56; Christ's Ascension into Heaven, See. 357–60; N.B. Google book]

Nares, Edward. *Discourses on the Three Creeds: And on the Homage Offered to Our Saviour, on Certain and Particular Occasions during His Ministry, as Expressed in the Evangelical Writings . . .* London: Printed for Baldwin, Cradock and Joy, 1819. [Sermon 5, See. 159–93; N.B. Google book]

Neumann, R. *Credo (I Believe) or, The Apostles' Creed Viewed in a Series of Sermons*. Burlington, IA: German Literary Board, 1916. [Chapter 5 The Resurrection and Ascension, with Accompanying Events, See. 65–80; N.B. Arnold Johannes Robert, 1872–]

Newland-Smith, J. N. *The Creed of Christendom as Expressed in the Nicene Creed: Short Instructions for Bible Classes, the Senior Classes in Secondary Schools, and Others*. London: Mowbray, 1920. [Chapter 8 The Resurrection of Christ, See. 93–104; Chapter 9 The Ascension and Second Advent, See. 115–26]

O'Collins, Gerald, and Mary Venturini. *Believing: Understanding the Creed*. New York: Paulist, 1991. [Chapter 11 On the Third Day He Rose Again, See. 102–12; Chapter 12 He Ascended into Heaven, See. 113–20]

———. *Friends in Faith: Living the Creed Day by Day*. New York: Paulist, 1989. [Chapter 7 On the Third day He Rose Again, See. 40–44]

Ogden, John. *Believing the Creed: A Metaphorical Approach*. London: Epworth, 2009. [Chapter 6 Jesus See. On the Third Day He Rose Again, See. 110–19; He Ascended into Heaven, See. 119–21]

Olevianus, Caspar. *An Exposition of the Apostles' Creed: or The Articles of the Faith, in Which the Main Points of the Gracious Eternal Covenant between God and Believers Are Briefly and Clearly Treated*. Translated by Lyle D. Bierma. Grand Rapids: Reformation Heritage, 2009. [The Third Day He Rose Again from the Dead, See. 92–99; He Ascended into Heaven, See. 100–106]

O'Rafferty, Nicholas. *Instructions on Christian Doctrine: The Apostles' Creed*. New York: Bruce, 1941. [Chapter 25 Resurrection of Jesus Christ from the Dead, See. 183–89; Chapter 26 Lessons from the Resurrection, See. 190–95; Chapter 27 Ascension of Jesus Christ into Heaven, See. 196–202; Chapter 28 Motives for the Ascension of Jesus Christ, See. 203–10; N.B. Adapted from the Italian of Francesco Vicentini, 1696–1777.]

Ottley, Robert Lawrence. *The Rule of Faith and Hope: A Brief Exposition of the Apostles' Creed*. London: R. Scott, 1912. [Chapter 5 The Glorified Savior, See. 72–90; N.B. Google book and HathiTrust]

Packer, J. I. *Affirming The Apostles' Creed*. Wheaton, IL: Crossway, 2008. [Chapter 11 The Third Day, See. 91–96; Chapter 12 He Ascended Into Heaven, See. 97–102]

———. *Growing In Christ*. Wheaton, IL: Crossway, 1994. [Chapter 11 The Third Day, See. 59–61; Chapter 12 He Ascended into Heaven, See. 63–66]

———. *I Want To Be A Christian*. Wheaton, IL: Tyndale House, 1977. [Chapter 11 The Third Day, See. 50–52; Chapter 12 He Ascended into Heaven, See. 53–56]

Page, James R. *An Exposition of the Thirty-Nine Articles of the Church of England.* New York: Appleton, 1845. [Article 4 On the Resurrection of Christ, See. 73–83; N.B. Archive.org]

Palmer, Roland F. *Good News.* Toronto: Supplies Dept., Church of England in Canada, 1943. [Chapter 5 He Descended Into Hell; The Third Day He Rose Again from the Dead; He Ascended Into Heaven, See. 44–49]

Pannenberg, Wolfhart. *The Apostles' Creed in the Light of Today's Questions.* Philadelphia: Westminster, 1972. [The Third Day He Rose Again from the Dead, He Ascended into Heaven, See. 96–115]

Pearson, John. *An Analysis of the Exposition of the Creed.* Compiled by W. H. Mill. Cambridge: Cambridge University Press, 1884. [Article 5 He Rose Again, See. 84–96; Article 6 He Ascended Into Heaven, and Sitteth on the Right Hand of God the Father Almighty, See. 93–94; N.B. Google book]

———. *An Exposition of the Creed.* Revised by Temple Chevallier and Robert Sinker. Cambridge: At The University Press, 1882. [Article 5 He Rose Again, See. 479–90; the Third Day, See. 491–509; Article 6 He Ascended into Heaven, See. 510–20; N.B. Archive.org and HathiTrust]

Perkins, Pheme. *What We Believe: A Biblical Catechism of the Apostles' Creed.* New York: Paulist, 1986. [Chapter 4 Jesus: Risen and Exalted, See. 57–69]

Polkinghorne, John C. *The Faith of a Physicist: Reflections of a Bottom-up Thinker: The Gifford Lectures for 1993–4.* Princeton: Princeton University Press, 1994. [Chapter 6 Crucifixion and Resurrection, See. 106–23]

Poole, George Ayliffe. *Sermons on the Apostles' Creed.* R. Grant & Son: Edinburgh, 1837. [Sermon 9 He Was Buried—The Third Day He Rose Again from the Dead, See. 151–71; Sermon 10 He Ascended Into Heaven, and Sitteth on the Right Hand of God the Father Almighty, See. 172–88; N.B. Google book]

Rankin, James. *The Creed in Scotland: An Exposition of the Apostles' Creed. With Extracts from Archbishop Hamilton's Catechism of 1552, John Calvin's Catechism of 1556 and a Catena of Ancient Latin and Other Hymns.* Edinburgh: William Blackwood & Sons, 1890. [Article 5 He Descended into Hell; the Third Day He Rose Again from the Dead, See. 165–88; Article 6 He Ascended into Heaven, and Sitteth at the Right Hand of God the Father Almighty, See. 189–208; N.B. Google book]

Ratzinger, Cardinal Joseph. *Credo For Today: What Christians Believe.* Translated by Michael J. Miller. San Francisco: Ignatius Press, 2009. [Descended into Hell—Ascension—Resurrection of the Body: Difficulties of the Apostles' Creed, See. 82–102]

———. *Introduction to Christianity.* Translated by Michael J. Miller and J. R Foster. San Francisco, CA: Communio, 2004. [Part Two. 2. 4. Rose Again [from the dead], See. 301–9; 5. He Ascended into Heaven and is Seated at the Right Hand of the Father, See. 310–18]

Rein, Gerhard, ed. *A New Look at the Apostles' Creed.* Minneapolis: Augsburg, 1969. [The Third Day He Rose Again from the Dead (Günther Bornkamm), See. 45–50; He Ascended into Heaven (Anton Vögtle), See. 51–56]

Richards, William Rogers. *The Apostles' Creed in Modern Worship.* New York: Scribner's Sons, 1906. [Chapter 5 The Exaltation of Our Lord, See. 75–104; N.B. Archive.org and Google book]

Ricker, George M. *The Faith Once Given: The Apostles' Creed Interpreted for Today.* Philadelphia: Westminster, 1978. [Chapter 7 The Victory Through Faith, See. 67–73]

Robinson, John A. T. *But That I Can't Believe!* New York: New American Library, 1967. [Chapter 7 The Resurrection, See. 57–60]

Rolfus, H. *Explanation of the Apostles' Creed: A Thorough Exposition of Catholic Faith.* New York: Benziger, 1902. [The Third Day He Arose Again from the Dead, See. 186–91; He Ascended Into Heaven—The Ascension Of Christ, See. 191–96; N.B. Google book]

Ross, George Alexander Johnston. *The God We Trust; Studies In The Devotional Use of the Apostles' Creed.* New York: Revell, 1913. Lecture 4 Through Death to God, See. 97–115; N.B. Google book]

Ross, John A. *This We Believe: Meditations on the Apostles' Creed.* Nashville: Abingdon, 1966. [He Rose Again From the Dead, See. 88–94; He Ascended, See. 94–106]

Rufinus, Aquileinsis. *Rufinus: A Commentary on the Apostles' Creed.* Translated by John Norman Davidson Kelly. Westminster: Newman Press, 1955. [Christ's Crucifixion, See. 62–65; The Ascension and Session, See. 65–67]

Russell-Caley, W. B. *The Creed In Daily Life.* London: Marshall Bros., 1915. [Chapter 7 The Third Day He Rose Again from the Dead, See. 75–86; Chapter 8 He Ascended Into Heaven, See. 87–98]

Sanderson, Edgar. *The Creed and the Church: A Hand-Book of Theology, Being a Synopsis of Pearson on the Creed, and of Hooker's Ecclesiastical Polity, Book 5 . . . the History of the Book of Common Prayer, the Thirty-nine Articles, Etc.* 3rd ed. Cambridge: J. Hall & Son, 1880. [Article 5 Section 2 The Third Day He Rose Again from the Dead, See. 43–47; Article 6 Section 1 He Ascended into Heaven, See. 48–49; N.B. Google book]

Satterlee, Henry Yates. *A Creedless Gospel and the Gospel Creed.* New York: Scribners' Sons, 1895. [Chapter 12 The Resurrection in Relation to Historical Evidence, See. 293–323; Chapter 13 The Ascension in Relation to the Problem of the Destiny of Man, See. 324–48; N.B. Archive.org and Google book]

Schenck, Ferdinand Schureman. *The Apostles' Creed in the Twentieth Century.* New York: Revell, 1918. [Chapter 7 The Third Day He Rose from the Dead, See. 89–100; Chapter 8 He Ascended Into Heaven and Sitteth at the Right Hand of God the Father Almighty, See. 101–11; N.B. Google book]

Schlatter, A. "He Ascended into Heaven, and Sitteth on the Right Hand of God, the Father Almighty." In *The Truth of the Apostles' Creed An Exposition by Twelve Theologians of Germany.* Edited by William Laible. Translated by Charles E. Hay. Philadelphia: Lutheran Publication Society, 1916. [See. 111–21; N.B. Google book]

Scott, A. Boyd *Nevertheless We Believe (a Scottish Minister's Belief).* London: Hodder & Stoughton, 1923. [Chapter 6 The Resurrection Of Jesus, See. 39–44]

Scott, W. A. *The Christ of the Apostles' Creed: The Voice of the Church Against Arianism, Strauss and Renan, With An Appendix.* New York: A.D.F. Randolph, 1867. [Chapter 11 Christ Rose The Third Day, See. 224–48; Chapter 12 The Resurrection Historically Demonstrated, See. 249–73; Chapter 13 Christ Ascended Into Heaven, See. 274–95; N.B. Google book]

Scroggie, W. Graham. *Christ in the Creed.* London: Marshall, Morgan & Scott, n.d. [Chapter 7 The Resurrection of Christ, See. 72–81; Chapter 8 The Ascension of Christ, See. 82–93]

Secker, Thomas. *Lectures on The Catechism of the Church of England: With A Discourse on Confirmation.* Dublin: Printed For A. & W. Watson, 1825. [Lecture 10 Article 5 The Third Day He Rose Again from the Dead, See. 82–91; N.B. Archive.org, Google book, and HathiTrust]

Seilhamer, Frank H. *We Believe: An Historical and Spiritual Guide to the Nicene Creed.* Lima, OH: C.S.S. Pub., 1993. [Nicene Creed 8 We Believe In the Resurrection of the Body, See. 67–76]

Shideler, Mary McDermott. *A Creed for a Christian Skeptic.* Grand Rapids: Eerdmans, 1968. [Chapter 14 The Third Day He Rose Again From The Dead, See. 116–20; Chapter 15 He Ascended Into Heaven, See. 121–23]

Simcox, Carroll E. *Living The Creed; A Study of the Apostles' Creed.* New York: Morehouse-Gorham, 1950. [Chapter 9 The Third Day He Rose Again from the Dead, See. 80–89; Chapter 10 He Ascended into Heaven, and Sitteth on the Right Hand of God the Father Almighty, See. 90–99]

Simmons, Alfred Henry. *But This I Can Believe.* London: Faith Press, 1968. [Chapter 4 He Descended Into Hell: The Third Day He Rose Again from the Dead, See. 39–48; Chapter 5 He Ascended Into Heaven, and Sitteth On The Right Hand of God the Father Almighty, See. 49–52]

Skrine, John Huntley. *Creed and the Creeds: Their Function in Religion.* London: Longmans, Green, 1911. [See. 102–4; N.B. Google book]

Sloan, Harold Paul. *The Apostles' Creed.* New York: Methodist Book Concern, 1930. [Chapter 6 The Third Day He Rose from the Dead, See. 123–38]

Smart, James D. *The Creed in Christian Teaching.* Philadelphia: Westminster, 1962. [Chapter 11 The Third Day He Rose Again from the Dead, See. 145–58; Chapter 12 He Ascended Into Heaven and Sitteth at the Right Hand of God the Father Almighty, See. 159–69]

Smith, Dana Prom. *An Old Creed for a New Day.* Philadelphia: Fortress, 1975. [Chapter 8 He Rose Again from the Dead; He Ascended into Heaven, See. 69–81]

Smith, Harold. *The Creed Their History, Nature and Use.* London: Robert Scott, 1962. [Article 5 Decent And Resurrection, See. 80–98; Article 6 The Ascension And Session, See. 99–107]

Smith, Judith F. *Faith and Duty: A Course of Lessons on the Apostles' Creed and the Ten Commandments for Children of Eight to Ten Years.* New York: Benziger, 1920. [Lesson 30 The Resurrection of our Blessed Lords, See. 88–93; Lesson 31 To Believe (St. Thomas and Others, See. 93–97; Lesson 32 To Work (St. Peter), See. 97–100; Lesson 33 To Wait (St. John), See. 100–104; Lesson 34 To Teach, See. 104–9; Lesson 35 Christ's Ascension into Heaven, See. 109–12; N.B. Google book and HathiTrust]

Snaith, Norman H. *I Believe in . . .* London: SCM, 1949. [Chapter 10 The Resurrection, See. 78–81; Chapter 11 The Ascension, See. 82–83]

Spencer, Thomas. *The Faith of the Ages. A Series of Meditations Devotional and Practical, on the Apostles' Creed.* Petersburg, VA: Franklin Press, 1900. [No. 13 The Third Day He rose again from the dead, See. 83–89; No. 14 He Ascended into Heaven, See. 90–96; N.B. Google book and HathiTrust]

Spirago, Francis. *The Catechism Explained: An Exhaustive Exposition of the Christian Religion.* New York: Benziger, 1899. [The Exaltation of Christ, See. 188–92; N.B. Archive.org and Google book]

Sproul, R. C. *The Symbol.* Nutley, NJ: Presbyterian and Reformed Publishing, 1975. [Chapter 8 On the Third Day He Rose Again from the Dead, See. 89–97; Chapter 9 He Ascended into Heaven and Sits on the Right Hand of God, See. 98–109]

Stimson, Henry Albert. *The Apostles' Creed in the Light of Modern Discussion.* Boston: Pilgrim Press, 1898. [Chapter 8 The Affirmation of the Resurrection of Christ, See. 119–35; N.B. Archive.org and Google book]

Stockwood, Mervyn. *There Is A Tide.* London: George Allen & Unwin, 1945. [Chapter 5 Jesus Christ—His Resurrection, See. 45–51; Chapter 6 Jesus Christ—His Ascension, See. 52–58]

Stone, S. J. *Lyra Fidelium: Twelve Hymns on Twelve Articles of the Apostles' Creed.* London: SPCK, 1870. [Article 5, See. 20–23; Article 6, See. 24–26; N.B. Google book]

Swete, Henry Barclay. *The Apostles' Creed: Its Relation To Primitive Christ*ianity. London: C.J. Clay & Sons, 1894. [Chapter 6 The Ascension . . . See. 64–72; N.B. Google book and HathiTrust]

Tait, Arthur J. *Lecture Outlines on the Thirty-Nine Articles.* London: Elliot Stock, 1910. [Article 4 The Resurrection of Christ, See. 42–45; N.B. Archive.org]

Thielicke, Helmut. *I Believe: The Christian's Creed.* Translated by John W. Doberstein and H. George Anderson. Philadelphia: Fortress, 1968. [Rose Again from the Dead, See. 148–87; Ascended Into Heaven, and Sitteth at the Right Hand of God, See. 188–200]

Trevor, John William. *A Catechism on the Apostles' Creed.* London: Rivingtons, 1859. [Article 5 He Descended into Hell; The Third Day He Rose Again from the Dead, See. 46–53; Article 6 He Ascended in Heaven, and Sitteth on the Right Hand of God the Father Almighty, See. 53–57; N.B. Archive.org and Google book]

Tupper, William George. *Ten Sermons in Illustration of the Creed.* Oxford: John Henry Parker, 1853. [Sermon 7 Human Nature (1) Purified, (2) Humbled, and (3) Exalted In Christ. See. 105–13; N.B. Google book]

Twining, Agatha G. *The Children's Creed. Being A Simple Explanation of the Apostles' Creed.* London, 1906. [Chapter 10 The Third Day He Rose Again from the Dead, See. 53–58; Chapter 11 He Ascended Into Heaven, See. 59–64]

Underhill, Evelyn. *The School of Charity; Meditations on the Christian Creed.* London: Longmans, Green, 1934. [Chapter 6 Glorified, See. 63–73]

Van Wyke, William P. *My Sermon Notes On Doctrinal Themes, 1st Series, including 24 Sermons on the Apostles' Creed.* Grand Rapids: Baker, 1947. [Chapter 21 The Resurrection of Christ, See. 125–29; Chapter 22 Our Savior's Ascension, See. 131–36]

Waddams, Herbert W. *Believing.* New York: Morehouse-Gorham, 1958. [Resurrection, See. 56–62; Ascension, See. 62–65]

Walton, Alfred Grant. *This I Can Believe: An Outline of Essentials of the Christian Faith.* Freeport, NY: Books for Libraries Press, 1971. [Chapter 6 Did Jesus Rise from the Dead?, See. 112–29]

Warner, Beverley E. *The Facts and the Faith: A Study In the Rationalism of the Apostles' Creed.* New York: T. Whittaker, 1897. [Chapter 6 The Resurrection the Prime Historical Fact of Christianity etc., See. 83–101]

Westcott, Brooke Foss. *The Historic Faith: Short Lectures on the Apostles' Creed.* London: Macmillan, 1883. [Chapter 6 He Descended Into Hell: The Third Day He Rose Again from the Dead; He Ascended Into Heaven and Sitteth on the Right Hand of God the Father Almighty, See. 78–83; N.B. Archive.org]

Wheeler, Henry. *The Apostles' Creed; An Examination of its History and an Exposition of its Contents.* New York: Eaton & Mains, 1912. [Article 5 He Descended Into Hell; The Third Day He Rose Again from the Dead, See. 87–97; Article 6 He Ascended Into

Heaven, and Sitteth on the Right Hand of God the Father Almighty, See. 98–104; N.B. Archive.org]

Williamson, Elbert M. *A Layman's Guide to the Apostles' Creed: A Devotional Study.* Danville, VA: McCain Printing, 1989. [Chapter 6 Our Risen Lord, See. 45–52]

Willis, David. *Clues To The Nicene Creed: A Brief Outline of the Faith.* Grand Rapids: Eerdmans, 2005. [Chapter 5 The Work of Christ, See. Rose Again according to the Scriptures, See. 97–101]

Wilson, Henry Albert. *The Faith of a Little Child: Talks with Little Children on the Apostles' Creed.* Philadelphia: George W. Jacobs, 1913. [Chapter 3 The Greatest Victory In the World's History, See. 25–35; Chapter 4 How Our Elder Brother Went Home Again, See. 36–46; N.B. Google book]

Wingren, Gustaf. *Credo, The Christian View of Faith and Life.* Translated by Edgar M. Carlson. Minneapolis: Augsburg, 1981. [Chapter 5 The Resurrection, See. 113–27; Chapter 6 The Gospel, See. 128–32]

Winn, Albert Curry. *A Christian Primer: The Prayer, the Creed, the Commandments.* Louisville: Westminster John Knox, 1990. [Chapter 18 The Third Day He Rose again from the Dead, See. 134–38; Chapter 19 He Ascended Into Heaven and Sitteth on the Right Hand of God the Father Almighty, See. 139–45]

Witsius, Herman. *Sacred Dissertations on What Is Commonly Called the Apostles' Creed.* Translated by Donald Fraser. Vol. 2. Glasgow: Khull, Blackie, 1823. [Dissertation 19 On the Resurrection of Christ, See. 166–97; Dissertation 20 On Christ's Ascension into Heaven, See. 198–236; N.B. Archive.org and Google book]

Wordsworth, Elizabeth. *Illustrations of the Creed.* 2nd edition. London: Longman, Green, 1894. [Chapter 14 The Third Day He Rose Again From The Dead, See. 194–207; Chapter 15 He Ascended Into Heaven, and Sitteth On the Right Hand Of God the Father Almighty, See. 208–18]

World Council of Churches Commission On Faith and Order. *Confessing One Faith: Towards an Ecumenical Explication of the Apostolic Faith as Expressed in the Nicene-Constantinopolitan Creed (381).* Geneva: World Council of Churches, Commission on Faith and Order, 1987. [Explication for Today, He Rose and Ascended into Heaven, See. 58–63]

Wuerl, Donald. *Faith That Transforms Us: Reflections on the Creed.* Frederick, MD: Word Among Us Press, 2013. [Chapter 5 Jesus' Passion, Death, and Resurrection, See. 63–74; Chapter 6 Jesus' Ascension and Second Coming, See. 75–78]

Yonge, John Eyre. *An Exposition of the Apostles' Creed.* London: Hodder & Stoughton, 1888. [Article 5 He Descended Into Hell: The Third Day He Rose Again from the Dead, See. 85–100; Article 6 He Ascended Into Heaven, and Sitteth on the Right Hand of God the Father Almighty, See. 101–7; N.B. Archive.org and Google book]

Zahn, Theodor. *The Apostles' Creed: A Sketch of its History and an Examination of its Contents.* Translated by C. S. Burn and A. E. Burn. London: Hodder & Stoughton, 1899. [Chapter 6 The Third Day He Rose Again from the Dead, See. 159–61; Chapter 7 Ascended into Heaven, Sitteth at the Right Hand of God, the Father Almighty, See. 162–66; N.B. Google book]

Chapter 24

Philosophy, Psychology, Religion
e.g., Catholic, Protestant, Mormon

Barrow, Isaac. *The Works of Isaac Barrow*. Vol. 2. New York: John C. Riker, 1845. [He Rose from the Dead, See. 481–94; He Rose from the Dead &c, See. 494–501; He Ascended into Heaven, See. 501–3; N.B. Archive.org]

Bauerschmidt, Frederick Christian, and James J. Buckley. *Catholic Theology: An Introduction*. Walden, MA: Wiley Blackwell, 2017. [Death and Resurrection, See. 119–22; The Claim of Jesus, See. 119–22]

Beaven, James. *A Catechism on the Thirty-nine Articles of the Church of England with Additions and Alterations Adapting it to the Book of Common Prayer of the Protestant Episcopal Church in the United States*. New York: General Protestant Episcopal Sunday School Union, 1853. [Article 4 See. 18–19; N.B. Archive.org]

Beinert, Wolfgang, and Francis Schüssler Fiorenza, eds. *Handbook of Catholic Theology*. New York: Herder & Herder, 2000. [Resurrection Narratives, See. 586–91 (Lothar Ullrich); Resurrection of Jesus, See. 591–95 (Lothar Ullrich)]

Benson, Robert Hugh. *Christ In The Church: A Volume of Religious Essays*. St Louis: Herder, 1911. [Part 4 Failure and Triumph. 3. The Resurrection, See. 210–31; N.B. Archive.org]

Beveridge, William. *An Exposition of the Thirty-nine Articles of the Church of England*. 1825. London: James Duncan, 1830. [Article 4. See. 151–87; N.B. Google book]

Bickersteth, Edward. *Questions Illustrating the Thirty-nine Articles of the Church of England*. 2nd ed. London: Francis & John Rivington, 1846. [Article 4 Of the Resurrection of Christ, See. 15–18. N.B. Archive.org and Google book]

Bokenkotter, Thomas. *Essential Catholicism*. Garden City, New York: Doubleday, 1985. [Part 2 Jesus the Christ. 6 Death and Resurrection, See. 62–66]

Brooke, Stopford A. *God and Christ Sermons*. London: Philip Green, 1894. [Chapter 15 The Resurrection of Jesus, See. 218–35; N.B. Google Book and HathiTrust]

Brown, John. *An Essay Towards an Easy, Plain, Practical, and Extensive Explication of the Assembly's Shorter Catechism*. New York: Robert Carter, 1845. [of Christ's Exaltation, See. 130–35; N.B. Archive.org, Google book, and HathiTrust]

Browne, Edward Harold. *An Exposition on the Thirty-Nine Articles Historical and Doctrinal*. New York; Dutton, 1883. [Article 4 Of the Resurrection of Christ, See. 104–18; N.B. Archive.org and Google book]

Burke, John J. *The Doctrine of the Mystical Body of Christ According to the Principles of the Theology of St. Thomas.* Translated by Joseph Anger. New York: Benziger, 1931. [The Glorification of Christ and the Doctrine of the Mystical Body, See. 53–59]

Burnett, Gilbert. *An Exposition of the 39 Articles of the Church of England.* Oxford: University Press, 1831. [Article 4 Of the Resurrection of Christ, See. 75–86; N.B. Archive.org and HathiTrust]

Callan, Charles J., and John A. McHugh. *A Parochial Course of Doctrinal Instructions For All Sundays and Holydays of the Year.* Vol. 1. Dogmatic series. New York: Joseph A Wagner, 1921. [Easter Sunday: The Resurrection of Christ, See. 353–70; Feast of Ascension: The Ascension of Christ, See. 462–78; N.B. Archive.org and HathiTrust]

Carpenter, Lant. *Sermons on Practical Subjects.* Edited by Mary Carpenter. Bristol: Philip & Evans, 1840. [Sermon 19, See. 273–86; N.B. Google book and HathiTrust]

Catholic Church. *Catechism of the Catholic Church.* 2nd ed. Città del Vaticano: Libreria Editrice Vaticana, 1997. [Article 5 He Descended into Hell on the Third Day He Rose Again, See. 164–72; Article 6 He Ascended into Heaven and is Seated at the Right Hand of the Father, See. 172–74]

Cavanaugh, Joseph H. *Evidence For Our Faith.* 3rd ed. Notre Dame, IN: University of Notre Dame Press, 1959. [Chapter 5 Christ's Claims Are Credible. See. Resurrection, See. 73–74, 87–103]

Chrysostom, John, Brother. *Manual of Christian Doctrine Comprising Dogma, Moral, and Worship.* Philadelphia: John Joseph McVey, 1923. [Chapter 14 Christ's Descent into Hell, His Resurrection, See. 100–104; Chapter 15 The Ascension of Our Lord, See. 105–7; N.B. Archive.org]

Church of Jesus Christ of Latter-day Saints. *A Hand-Book of Reference to the History the Chronology, Religion and Country of the Latter-day Saints.* Salt Lake City: Juvenile Instructor Office, 1884. [See. 95; N.B. Google book]

Cooper, John M. *Religion Outlines For Colleges: Course 3. Christ and His Church.* Vol. 3. Washington, DC: Catholic Education Press, 1930. [Chapter 25 The Credentials of Christ. 6. The Resurrection, See. 477–88]

Cory, Catherine A., and David T. Landry, eds. *The Christian Theological Tradition* 2nd ed. Upper Saddle River: NJ, 2003. [Chapter 6 Jesus and the Gospels. The Death and Resurrection of Jesus, See. 77–78 (Catherine Cory)]

Coverdale, Myles. *Remains of Myles Coverdale, Bishop of Exeter.* Edited by George Pearson. Cambridge: University Press, 1846. [The Hope of the Faithful, Which Entreateth of the Resurrection, and Ascension of Christ, with the Fruit and Commodity Thereof, See. 141–52; N.B. Archive.org and Google book]

Devivier, W. *Christian Apologetics: A Defense of the Catholic Faith.* Edited by S. G. Messmer. New York: Benziger, 1908. [Art. 3 Ten Proofs of the Divinity of the Mission of Jesus . . . 2. The Second Proof. The Resurrection of Jesus Christ, See. 187–99; N.B. Archive.org and Google book]

Donovan, C. F. (compiler). *Our Faith and Facts.* Chicago: Patrick L. Baine, 1925. [See. 17, 678]

Duggan, G. H. *Beyond Reasonable Doubt.* Boston: Daughters of St. Paul Press, 1987. [Chapter 6 The Resurrection of Jesus Christ, See. 141–65; N.B. This work reviews six alternative explanations for the resurrection narratives.]

Eddowes, Ralph. *Sermons Delivered Before the First Society of Unitarian Christians.* Philadelphia: Abraham Small, 1817. [Sermon 5 Christ raised by the Power of God, See. 87–102; Sermon 6 Ascension and Exaltation of Christ, See. 103–19; N.B. Google book]

Farrelly, M. John. *Faith in God Through Jesus Christ: Foundational Theology 2.* Collegeville, MN: Liturgical Press, 1997. [Chapter 5 The Resurrection of Jesus, and Early Christian Understanding of Salvation and Revelation, See. 162–207]

Fenton, Joseph Clifford. *Laying the Foundation: A Handbook of Catholic Apologetics.* 2016. [Chapter 16 The Resurrection. See. 319–56; N.B. This source should be examined. It was originally published in 1942 under the title *We Stand with Christ: An Essay in Catholic Apologetics.*]

Fichter, Joseph Henry. *Textbook in Apologetics.* Milwaukee: Bruce, 1947. [Chapter 8 Miracles Prove the Divinity of Christ. See. The Supreme Miracle: the Resurrection, See. 72–78]

Finlay, Peter. *The Church of Christ: Its Foundation and Constitution.* London: Longmans, Green, 1922. [Lecture 2 The Divinity of Christ. See 53–60; N.B. Google book]

Fiorenza, Francis, and John P. Galvin. *Systematic Theology: Roman Catholic Perspectives.* 2nd ed. Minneapolis: Fortress, 2011. [Resurrection, See. 291–303]

Flint, Robert. *Sermons and Addresses.* New York: Charles Scribner's Sons, 1899. [Sermon and Address 18 Ends of Christ's Death and Resurrection, See. 204–12; N.B. Google book]

Flynn, Eileen P., and Gloria Blanchfield Thomas. *Living Faith: An Introduction to Theology.* Kansas City, MO: Sheed & Ward, 1989. [Chapter 3 Jesus the Christ, Resurrection, See. 84–86]

Furness, William Henry. *The Gospels, Historical: Address Delivered at the Unitarian Conference in Washington, DC, October, 1895* and Other Sermons. Privately printed, 1895. [The Resurrection of Jesus. See. 41–57; N.B. Google book]

Gibbons, James Cardinal. *Our Christian Heritage.* Baltimore: John Murphy, 1889. [Chapter 16 Our Lord's Divinity Confirmed by His Miracles, and Especially by His Resurrection, See. 240–51; N.B. Google book]

Gibson, Edgar C. S. *The Thirty-Nine Articles of the Church of England Explained with an Introduction.* Vol. 1. London: Methuen, 1896. [See. 181–88; N.B. Archive.org and HathiTrust]

Gilbert, Bishop of Sarum. *An Exposition of the Thirty-Nine Articles of the Church of England.* Revised and Corrected by James R. Page. New York: D. Appleton, 1845. [Art. 4 Of the Resurrection of Christ, See. 73–83; N.B. HathiTrust]

Green, Ashbel. *Lectures on the Short Catechism of the Presbyterian Church in the United States of America* Vol. 1. Philadelphia: Presbyterian Board of Publication, 1841. [Chapter 25 Wherein Consists Christ's Exaltation?, See 365–70; Chapter 26 Wherein Consists Christ's Exaltation?—Continued, See. 370–79; N.B. Archive.org and Google book]

Gregg, David. *Facts that Call for Faith: A Series of Discourses.* New York: E. B. Treat, 1898. [The Resurrection of Jesus Christ, See. 195–212; N.B. Google book]

Hammer, Bonaventure. *God, Christ, And the Church: Catholic Doctrine and Practice Explained.* New York: Benziger, 1911. [Part 2 Jesus Christ, See 2. Christ's resurrection cannot be proved: it is a legend of later times, See. 172–75, 200–202]

Harper, James. *An Exposition in the Form of Question and Answer of the Westminster Assembly's Shorter Catechism.* Pittsburgh: United Presbyterian Board of Publication,

Philosophy, Psychology, Religion e.g., Catholic, Protestant, Mormon

1905. [Question 28 Wherein consisteth Christ's exaltation?, See. 146–50; N.B. Archive.org and Google book]

Heenan, John Carmel. *The Faith Makes Sense*. New York: Sheed & Ward, 1948. [See. 183–90]

Hellwig, Monika K. *Understanding Catholicism*. 2nd ed. [New York: Paulist, 2002. [The Resurrection, Foundation for Our Hope, See. 103–11]

Henry, A.-M. ed. *The Historical and Mystical Christ*. Vol. 5. Translated by Angeline Bouchard. Chicago: Fides, 1958. [Chapter 4 The Glorious Epic of Jesus Christ (A.-M. Henry), The Resurrection of Christ, See. 213–17; The Ascension, See. 217–19]

Heydon, J. K. *The God of Love*. New York: Sheed & Ward, 1944. [Chapter 9 The Resurrection, See. 172–84]

Hill, Brennan, R. *Exploring Catholic Theology: God, Jesus, Church, and Sacraments*. Mystic: Connecticut: Twenty-Third Publication, 2003. [The Mystery of Jesus's Resurrection, See. 148–56]

Holmes, Robert. *Four Tracts*. Oxford: Printed for D. Prince and J. Cooke, 1788. [Tract 4 Resurrection of the Body. As Inferred from that of Christ, and Exemplified by Scriptural Cases, See. 219–27; N.B. Google book]

Hugueny, Père Etienne. *Catholicism and Criticism*. Translated by Stanislaus M. Hogan. New York: Longmans, Green, 1922. [First Part Apologetics Chapter 1 The Christ-fact, See. 22–35; N.B. Archive.org]

Hunt, David. *Essays on Religious Subjects including the Ordinances, Deity of Our Lord and Savior Jesus Christ, Resurrection of the Dead, etc.* New Vienna, OH: Friends' Publishing House, 1874. [See. 119–20; N.B. Google book]

Hunter, Sylvester Joseph. *Outlines of Dogmatic Theology*. 2nd ed. Vol. 2. London: Longmans, Green, 1895. [#552 The Resurrection, See. 541–43; N.B. Archive.org and Google book]

Lake, John G. *John G. Lake: The Complete Collection of His Life Teachings*. Compiled by Roberts Liardon. Tulsa, OK: Albury, 1999. [The Resurrection #1, See. 794–806; Resurrection #2, See. 807–12]

Lardner, Nathaniel. *The Works of Nathaniel Lardner*. Vol. 10. London: William Ball, 1838. [See. 369–92; N.B. Archive.org]

Leavitt, Dennis H. & Richard O. Christensen. *Scripture Study for Latter-Day Saint Families: the New Testament*. Salt Lake City, UT: Desert, 2006. [See. 53–54, 77–78, 111–12, 141–44, 145–46, 211–12; N.B. This work presents a Mormon interpretation.]

Lewis, John. *The Church Catechism Explained and Supported by Scriptural Proofs*. Dublin: Printed for A&W Watson, 1828. [Section 6 Of Christ's Exaltation, See. 19–21; N.B. Google book]

MacBride, John David. *Lectures on the Articles of the United Church of England and Ireland*. Oxford: John Henry Parker, 1853. [Article 4, See. 136–43; N.B. Google book]

Martinelli, Anthony. *The Word Made Flesh: An Overview of the Catholic Faith*. New York: Paulist, 1993. [Chapter 7 The Death and Resurrection of Jesus, See. 103–18]

McBrien, Richard P. *Catholicism*. New York: Harper SanFrancisco, 1966. [The Resurrection, See. 428–40]

Miller, J. R. *Devotional Hours with the Bible Readings in the Synoptic Gospels on the Life of Christ*. London: Hodder & Stoughton, 1911. [See. 307–26, N.B. Google book. Not useful.]

Morgan, G. Campbell. *The Westminster Pulpit: The Preaching of G. Campbell Morgan*. Vol. 3. Westwood, NJ: Revell, 1954. [Chapter 7 The Value and Proof of the Resurrection, See. 89–101]

Muir, Robert H. *Parish Tracts for the Perilous Times of the Last Days: Memorials of a Closed Ministry in the Church of Scotland*. Edinburgh: Religious Tract & Book Society of Scotland, 1903. [Third Address, Christ's Resurrection is Life from the Dead to All His Members: An Exposition of Mark 16, See. 43–62]

New Catechism: Catholic Faith for Adults, A. Translated by Kevin Smyth. New York: Herder and Herder, 1967. [Risen and Still with You, See. 178–85; The Celebration of Easter, See. 185–90]

Nichols, Aidan. *Epiphany: A Theological Introduction to Catholicism*. Collegeville, MN: Liturgical Press, 1996. [Jesus Christ, Ascension of, See. 146–48; Resurrection of, See. 101–3, 142–46]

Noble, Samuel. *Important Doctrines of the True Christian Religion, Explained, Demonstrated and Vindicated From Vulgar Errors*. London: J. S. Hodson, 1846. [Lecture 8 The Resurrection of the Lord Jesus Christ, and the Divine Nature of His Resurrection-Body, See. 113–29; N.B. Google book]

Noort, G. Van. *Dogmatic Theology*. Vol. 1. *The True Religion*. Translated by John J. Castelot and William R. Murphy from the 5th ed. Westminster, MD: Newman Press, 1955. [Section 2 The Truth of the Christian-Catholic Religion; Article 4 Christ's Resurrection Proves His Divine Mission, See. 165–87]

Nowell, Alexander. *A Catechism, or First Instruction and Learning of Christian Religion*. London: Printed for the Prayer-Book and Homily Society, 1846. [See. 58–63; N.B. Archive.org]

O'Collins, Gerald. *Rethinking Fundamental Theology: Toward a New Fundamental Theology*. Oxford: Oxford University Press, 2011. [Chapter 6 The Crucified and Resurrected Revealer, See. 136–65]

O'Grady, John F. *Catholic Beliefs and Traditions: Ancient and Ever*. New York: Paulist, 2001. [Jesus, resurrection, See. 55–56, 69, 70, 71–72]

Ott, Ludwig. *Fundamentals of Catholic Dogma*. 5th ed. Book Three The Doctrine of God the Redeemer. Part 2 The Doctrine of the Work of the Redeemer. Translated by Patrick Lynch. St Louis: Herder, 1962. [§13 Christ's Resurrection, See. 192–93; §14 Christ's Ascension into Heaven, See. 194–95]

Pasco, Rowanne, and John Redford, eds. *Faith Alive: A New Presentation of Catholic Belief and Practice*. Mystic, CT: Twenty-Third Publications, 1990. [Chapter 20 Death and Resurrection of Christ, See 113–16]

Paterson, Alexander Smith. *A Concise System of Theology on the Basis of the Shorter Catechism*. Edinburgh: Robert Carter, 1848. [Of Christ's State of Exaltation, See. 107–10; N.B. Archive.org and Google book]

Pilch, John J. *The Triduum and Easter Sunday: Breaking Open the Scriptures*. Collegeville, MN: Liturgical Press, 2000. [Chapter 3 Easter Vigil, See. 25–33; Chapter 4 Easter Sunday, See. 45–50]

Potts, John Faulkner. *The Swedenborg Concordance: A Complete Work of Reference to the Theological Writings of Emanuel Swedenborg*. Vol. 5. London: Swedenborg Society, 1898. [Resurrection, See. 538–41; N.B. Archive.org]

Ratzinger, Joseph Cardinal. *God and the World: A Conversation with Peter Seewald*.

Philosophy, Psychology, Religion e.g., Catholic, Protestant, Mormon

San Francisco: Ignatius Press, 2002. [Part 1 God, 14. The Cross, See. The Resurrection, See. 336–39]

Rausch, Thomas P. *Catholicism in the Third Millennium*. 2nd ed. Collegeville, MN: Liturgical Press, 2003. [Jesus, death and resurrection, See. 33–34, 235]

———. *This Is Our Faith: An Introduction to Catholicism*. New York: Paulist, 2014. [See. 70–75]

Rodgers, John H. *Essential Truths for Christians: A Commentary on the Anglican Thirty-Nine Articles and an Introduction to Systematic Theology*. Blue Bell, PA: Classical Anglican Press, 2011. [Art. 4 Of the Resurrection of Christ, See. 115–44]

Rogers, Thomas. *The Catholic Doctrine of the Church of England: An Exposition of the Thirty-Nine Articles*. Edited by J. J. S. Perowne. Cambridge: University Press, 1854. 1854. [Article 4 Of the Resurrection of Christ, See. 62–64; N.B. Archive.org]

Rollock, Robert. *Select Works of Robert Rollock*. Vol. 2. Edited by William M. Gunn. Edinburgh: Printed for the Wodrow Society, 1844. [Of the Resurrection of Christ, See. 330–705; N.B. Archive.org and Google book]

Russell, Charles Taze. *The Time Is At Hand*. Brooklyn, New York: Watch Tower Bible & Tract Society, 1889 [See. 103–42, especially 124–37; N.B. Archive.org and HathiTrust. Vol. 2 of *Millennial Dawn*. First published in 1889 by the Watch Tower Society. The series was later re-titled *Studies in the Scriptures*.]

Salter, James. *An Exposition, or Practical Treatise on the Church Catechism*. London: Andrew Brice, 1753. [See. 7–8; N.B. Google book]

Secker, Thomas. *The Works of Thomas Secker*. Vol. 6. London: Printed for C.C & J. Rivington, 1811. [Lecture 10 Creed. Article 5 The Third Day He Rose Again from the Dead, See. 92–101; N.B. HathiTrust]

Sheed, F. J. *Theology and Sanity*. New York: Sheed & Ward 1946. [Chapter 18 The Redeemer (4) Resurrection and Ascension, See. 215–37]

Sheehan, Michael. *Apologetics and Catholic Doctrine*. 6th ed. London: Saint Austin Press, 2001. [Resurrection of Jesus Christ, See. 104, 110–11, 338, 390, 396, 405–9, 463, 516

Smith, George D., arranged and edited. *The Teaching of the Catholic Church: A Summary of Catholic Doctrine*. Vol. 2. New York: Macmillan, 1950 [1927]. [The Resurrection of the Body (Justin McCann), See. 1218–227]

Smith, Joseph. *The Teachings of Joseph Smith*. Edited by Larry E. Dahl and Donald Q. Cannon. South Salt Lake City, UT: Bookcraft, 1997. [Resurrection, See. 558–62]

Talmage, James E. *The Articles of Faith: A Series of Lectures on the Principal Doctrines of Latter-Day Saints*. 11th ed. Salt Lake City, UT: Deseret News, 1919. [Lecture 21 Article 10, See. 395–97; N.B. Archive.org]

Thomas, W. H. Griffith. *The Principles of Theology: An Introduction to the Thirty-Nine Articles*. London: Longmans, Green, 1930. [Article 4, See. 73–89]

Tillotson, John. *The Works of Dr. John Tillotson*. Vol. 6. London, Printed by J. F. Dove, for R. Priestley, 1820. [Sermons 119 Jesus the Son of God, proved by His Resurrection, See. 48–64; N.B. HathiTrust]

Townson, Thomas. *The Works of the Reverend Thomas Townson . . . To which is Prefixed an Account of the Author with an Introduction to the Discourses on the Gospel . . .* Vol. 1. London: Printed for F. C. & J. Rivington, 1810. [See. 91–92, 114–15, 226; N.B. Archive.org and Google book]

———. *The Works of the Reverend Thomas Townson . . . To which is Prefixed an Account of the Author with an Introduction to the Discourses on the Gospels . . .* Vol. 2. Discourse on the Evangelical History from the Interment to the Ascension of our Lord. London: Printed for F. C. & J. Rivington, 1810. [See. 1–181; N.B. Archive.org and Google book]

Twisleton, Frederick. *The Principles of the Christian Religion Explained, in a Brief Commentary Upon the Church Catechism.* London: Printed for T. Cadell, 1827. [Section 12 Of His resurrection, the Third Day, from the Dead, See. 111–20; N.B. Archive.org]

Tyrrell, George. *Oil And Wine.* London: Longmans, Green, 1911. [The Resurrection, See. 126–34; The Ascension, See. 134–46; N.B. Archive.org and Google book]

Veneer, John. *An Exposition on the Thirty-nine Articles of the Church of England.* London: Printed for C. Rivington, 1725. [Article 4, See. 22–25; N.B. Google book]

Walsh, Milton. *Into All Truth: What Catholics Believe—and Why.* San Francisco: Ignatius Press, 2013. [Chapter 1 The Resurrection of Jesus, See. 9–22]

Watchtower Bible and Tract Society of New York. *You Can Live Forever in Paradise on Earth.* Brooklyn, NY: Watch Tower Bible and Tract Society of New York, 1982. [See. 172; N.B. "He was the first raised as a spirit person."]

Watson, Thomas. *A Body of Practical Divinity.* Philadelphia: Thomas Wardle, 1833. [Christ's Exaltation, See. 137–40; N.B. Archive.org]

Wilhelm, Joseph, and Thomas B. Scannell. *A Manual of Catholic Theology.* Vol. 2. New York: Benziger, 1899. [Section §204 Christ's Glorification—His Resurrection and Ascension, See. 179–80; also See. 298–301, 466; N.B. Archive.org]

Wilmers, W. *Handbook of the Christian Religion for the Use of Advanced Students and the Educated Laity.* Edited by James Conway. New York: Benziger, 1892. [The divine mission of Christ is proved in particular by His resurrection from the dead, See. 41–44; N.B. Archive.org]

Wilson, John. *Physicist Examines Hope in the Resurrection: Examination of the Significance of the Work of John C. Polkinghorne for the Mission of the Church.* Eugene, OR: Wipf & Stock, 2017. [Chapter 7 Resurrection, See. 110–35]

Chapter 25

Doctrines, Dogmatics, and Systematic Theology

Aaron, Daryl. *Understanding Theology in 15 Minutes a Day*. Minneapolis: Bethany House, 2012. [Chapter 21 Is the Resurrection of Jesus Really That Important?, See. 113–17]

Alexander, Archibald. *A Brief Compend of Bible Truth*. Philadelphia: Presbyterian Board of Publication, 1846. [Chapter 20 Resurrection and Ascension of Christ, See. 114–16; N.B. Archive.org and Google book]

Alington, Cyril. *Sense and Non-Sense: Being a Study in Basic Christianity*. Oxford: Blackwell, 1949. [Appendix C The Empty Tomb, See. 95–96; Appendix D The Ascension, See. 96]

Allen, Diogenes. *Finding Our Father*. Atlanta: John Knox, 1974. [Chapter 6 Faith In the Resurrection: How We Can Believe, See. 95–105]

———. *Theology for a Troubled Believer: An Introduction to the Christian Faith*. Louisville: Westminster John Knox, 2010. [Chapter 13 The Resurrection of Jesus and Eternal Life, See. 131–46]

Allen, E. L. *Divine and Human*. London: Epworth, 1952. [Chapter 3 The Christ, Pt. 4 Resurrection, See. 69–73]

Allison, Gregg R. *Historical Theology: An Introduction to Christian Doctrine: A Companion to Wayne Grudem's Systematic Theology*. Grand Rapids: Zondervan, 2011. [Chapter 19 Resurrection and Ascension, See. 411–29; N.B. Informative.]

Altizer, Thomas J. J. *Genesis and Apocalypse: A Theological Voyage Toward Authentic Christianity*. Louisville: Westminster John Knox, 1990. [Chapter 5 The Resurrection of God, See. 81–92]

———. *The Genesis of God: A Theological Genealogy*. Louisville: Westminster John Knox, 1993. [Resurrection of God. See. 32, 34, 37, 40, 89, 163, 169]

Ames, William. *The Marrow of Theology*. Translated by John Dykstra Eusden. Boston: Pilgrim Press, 1968. [Translated from the third Latin edition, 1629. Book One. Section 23 The Exaltation of Christ, See. 144–49; N.B. Archive.org provides the 1639 publication: *The Marrow of Sacred Divinity*, See. 91–99]

Anders, Max E. *New Christian's Handbook: Everything New Believers Need to Know*. Nashville: Nelson, 1999. [If the Resurrection Is True, Jesus Is God, See. 214–16]

Anderson, Robert T., and Peter B. Fischer. *An Introduction to Christianity*. New York: Harper & Row, 1966. [Chapter 6 Jesus the Christ, See. 175–82, 185]

Category IX—Creeds, Religion, Doctrinal, Sermons, Commentaries

Andrews, Samuel J. *Man and the Incarnation: or, Man's Place in the Universe as Determined by His Relations to the Incarnate Son.* New York: G. P. Putnam's Sons, 1905. [Chapter 12 Supernature, the Supernatural, See. 129–33; N.B. Google book]

Ankerberg, John, and Dillon Burroughs. *God in 60 Seconds.* Eugene, OR: Harvest House, 2010. [Part 2 Questions About Jesus, See. 16–17, 19–20, 24–25]

Arndt, William F. *Fundamental Christian Beliefs: A Survey of Christian Doctrine.* St. Louis: Concordia, 1964. [The Savior in Exaltation, See. 41–42]

Arnold, Thomas. *Literature and Dogma: An Essay Towards A Better Apprehension of the Bible.* New York: Macmillan, 1914. [See. 132, 147–49, 218–23, 234–37, 260; N.B. Google book]

Arrington, French L. *Christian Doctrine: A Pentecostal Perspective.* Vol. 2. Cleveland: Pathway, 1993. [Chapter 4 The Exaltation of Christ, See. 83–100; N.B. Arrington's work provides a good overview.]

Astley, Jeff. *SCM Studyguide to Christian Doctrine.* London: SCM Press, 2010. [Resurrection of Christ, See. 37, 70, 106, 115, 121, 122–23, 125, 130, 133, 135, 136, 138, 210, 213]

Athanasius, Saint, Patriarch of Alexandria. *Athanasius on the Incarnation of the Word.* Translated by Philip Schaff. New York: Christian Literature Publishing, 1892. [See online: Christian Classics Ethereal Library, Chapter 5 The Resurrection. See. 21–25]

Auberlen, Carl August. *The Divine Revelation: An Essay in Defence of the Faith.* Translated by A. B. Paton. Edinburgh: T&T Clark, 1874. [The Resurrection of Jesus, See. 56–68; N.B. Google book]

Aulén, Gustaf. *The Drama and the Symbols: A Book on Images of God and the Problems They Raise.* Translated by Sydney Linton. Philadelphia: Fortress, 1970. [Resurrection, See. 178–82]

———. *The Faith of the Christian Church.* Fifth Swedish edition, Translated by Eric Herbert Wahlstrom. Philadelphia: Fortress, 1960. [Christ, resurrection of, See. 72, 154–55, 195, 213, 216–21, 347]

Badham, Paul. *The Contemporary Challenge of Modernist Theology.* Cardiff: University of Wales Press, 1998. [Chapter 8 The Modernist Understanding of the Resurrection of Jesus Christ, See. 101–13]

Badke, William B. *The Hitchhiker's Guide to the Meaning of Everything.* Grand Rapids: Kregel, 2005. [Chapter 34 Not the End, See. 151–55]

Baker, Charles F. *A Dispensational Theology.* Grand Rapids: Grace Bible College Publications, 1971. [The Resurrection of Christ, See. 371–77; The Ascension and Exaltation of Christ, See. 377–82]

Baker, John Austin. *The Faith of A Christian.* London: Darton, Longman and Todd, 1996. [Appendix A, See. 172 The Nature of Jesus' Resurrection; N.B. Available online. See. Evidence for the Resurrection]

Baly, Denis, and Royal W. Rhodes. *The Faith of Christians.* Philadelphia: Fortress, 1984. [Chapter 7 Resurrection, See. 87–99]

Bancroft, Emery H. *Christian Theology, Systematic and Biblical.* 2nd ed. Grand Rapids: Zondervan, 1976. [The Resurrection of Jesus Christ, See. 127–52]

———. *Elemental Theology, Doctrinal and Conservative.* Grand Rapids: Zondervan, 1965. [Chapter 3 The Doctrine of Jesus Christ. The Resurrection of Jesus Christ, See. 138–49]

Banks, John S. *A Manual of Christian Doctrine.* 4th ed. Cincinnati: Jennings & Graham, 1897. [The Miracle of the Resurrection, See. 64–66; N.B. Archive.org]

Barackman, Floyd H. *Practical Christian Theology: Examining the Great Doctrines of the Faith*. 4th ed. Grand Rapids: Kregel, 2001. [His Exaltation, See. 171–75]

Barrett, B. F. *A Course of Lectures on the Doctrines of the New Jerusalem Church as Revealed in the Theological Writings of Emanuel Swedenborg*. New York: Joseph Snowden, 1842. [Lecture 10 The Doctrine of the New Jerusalem Church Concerning the Resurrection, with a Brief View of the Spiritual World, See. 348–53; N.B. Google book]

Barth, Karl. *Church Dogmatics*. Translated by G. T. Thomson. London: SCM, 1949. [Chapter 18 The Third Day He Rose Again From The Dead, See. 121–23; Chapter 19 He Ascended Into Heaven, and Sitteth On the Right Hand of God the Father Almighty, See. 124–28; N.B. portions are idem. *Dogmatics In Outline*. 1947]

———. *God Here and Now*. Translated by Paul M. van Buren. London: Routledge, 2003. [Jesus of Nazareth, resurrection, See. 39, 45–46, 57, 77, 108]

———. *The Göttingen Dogmatics: Instruction in the Christian Religion*. Edited by Hannelotte Reiffen. Translated by Geoffrey W. Bromily. Vol. 1. Grand Rapids: Eerdmans, 1991. [Jesus Christ, resurrection, See. 123, 143, 149–50, 160–61, 164, 196, 233]

Bartholomew, David J. *Uncertain Belief: Is It Rational to be a Christian?* Oxford: Clarendon, 1996. [See. 67–68, 105, 110–12, 205]

Bavinck, H. *Our Reasonable Faith*. Grand Rapids: Eerdmans, 1956. [Chapter 18 The Work of Christ in His Exaltation, See. 357–85; 1909 reprint]

———. *Reformed Dogmatics: Sin and Salvation in Christ*. Edited by John Bolt. Translated by John Vriend. Vol. 3. Grand Rapids: Baker Academic, 2004. [Christ's Exaltation, See. 418–84; N.B. This text is worth examining.]

Bawer, Bruce. *Stealing Jesus: How Fundamentalism Betrays Christianity*. New York: Crown, 1997. [See. 43–45, 48, 74, 88–89, 99–100, 324]

Beard, J. R. *A Manual of Christian Evidence Containing, as an Antidote to Current Materialistic Tendencies, Particularly as Found in the Writings of Ernest Renan, An Outline of the Manifestation of God in the Bible, In Providence, In History, In the Universe, and In the Lord and Saviour Jesus Christ*. London: Simpkin, Marshall, 1868. [Natural Circumstances Attending The Resurrection of Jesus Attest Its Reality, See. 428–37; Natural Circumstances Following the Resurrection of Jesus Attest Its Reality, See. 437–45; N.B. Archive.org and Google book]

Beckwith, Clarence Augustine. *Realities of Christian Theology: An Interpretation of Christian Experience*. New York: Houghton, Mifflin, 1906. [The first corner-stone of their belief-his self-revelation after his burial, See. 307–8; N.B. Archive.org and Google book]

Beet, Joseph Agar. *The Credentials of the Gospel; A Statement of the Reason of the Christian Hope*. London: Wesleyan Methodist Book-Room, 1895. [This claim was conceded to Christ by the Apostles, in spite of His death, because they believed that He had risen from the dead, See. 111–15; N.B. Achieve.org]

———. *A Manual of Theology*. New York: A. C. Armstrong, 1906. [Chapter 26 Christ Is Risen, 204–7; Chapter 27 Proof That He Actually Rose, 208–17; Chapter 28 Objections, 218–28; N.B. Google.com]

———. *Through Christ to God: A Study in Scientific Theology*. London: Hodder & Stoughton, 1895. [The Resurrection of Christ, See. 301–73; N.B. Archive.org; N.B. This is a good, dated source to read.]

Benson, Clarence H., and Robert J. Morgan. *Exploring Theology: A Guide for Systematic Theology and Apologetics: Three Books in One.* Wheaton, IL: Crossway, 2007. [The Resurrection of Christ, See. 85-93]

Berkhof, Hendrikus. *Christian Faith: An Introduction to the Study of the Faith.* Revised edition. Translated by Sierd Woudstra. Grand Rapids: Eerdmans, 1986. [Chapter 36 Resurrection and Glorification, See. 312-24]

Berkhof, Louis. *Manual of Christian Doctrine.* Grand Rapids: Eerdmans, 1933. [The State of Exaltation, See. 193-99]

———. *Reformed Dogmatics.* Vol. 1. Grand Rapids: Eerdmans, 1932. [The State of Exaltation, See. 348-62]

———. *Summary of Christian Doctrine for Senior Classes.* Grand Rapids: Eerdmans, 1947. [Chapter 15 The States of Christ. See. 101-5]

———. *Systematic Theology.* 2nd edition. Grand Rapids: Eerdmans, 1941. [The State of Exaltation, See. 344-55]

Berkouwer, G. C. *Studies in Dogmatics: The Return of Christ.* Grand Rapids: Eerdmans, 1972. [The resurrection of Christ and the resurrection of the dead, See. 180-90]

Bernard, David K. *The Apostolic Life.* Hazelwood MO: Word Aflame, 2006. [Chapter 35 After the Passion of the Christ (Easter), See. 263-65]

Bickel, Bruce, and Stan Jantz. *Bruce & Stan's Guide to God: A User-Friendly Approach.* Eugene, OR: Harvest House, 1997. [Chapter 8 Jesus Christ: Son of God—Born to Die. 6 Jesus Came Back From the Dead, See. 187-90; 7 Jesus Ascended into Heaven, See. 190]

Bilezikian, Gilbert G. *Christianity 101: Your Guide to Eight Basic Christian Beliefs.* Grand Rapids: Zondervan, 1993. [Christ In His Exaltation, 73-81]

Binney, Amos, and Daniel Steele. *Binney's Theological Compend Improved: Containing a Synopsis of the Evidences, Doctrines, Morals and Institutions of Christianity: Designed for Bible Classes, Theological Students, and Young Preachers.* New York: Nelson & Phillips, 1875. [Resurrection of Jesus, See. 43-48; N.B. Archive.org]

Bird, Michael F. *Evangelical Theology: A Biblical and Systematic Introduction.* Grand Rapids: Zondervan, 2013. [The Resurrection of Jesus, See. 435-48; The Ascension and Session of Jesus, See. 449-59; N.B. This text is recommended to examine.]

Birks, Thomas Rawson. *Supernatural Revelation, or, First Principles of Moral Theology.* London: Macmillan, 1879. [See. 46, 47, 53, 99, 138, 156, 157, 160, 161, 176, 192, 224; N.B. Archive.org and Google book]

Bloesch, Donald G. *Christian Foundations in 7 Volumes: The Last Things: Resurrection, Judgment, Glory.* Downers Grove, IL: InterVarsity, 2004. [The Resurrection of Jesus, See. 115-19]

———. *A Theology of Word & Spirit: Authority & Method in Theology.* Downers Grove, IL: InterVarsity, 1992. [See pages 13, 53, 60, 101, 115, 169, 183, 195, 216, 241, 272]

Boa, Kenneth. *God, I Don't Understand: Answers to Difficult Questions of the Christian Faith.* Eugene, OR: Wipf & Stock, 2012. [Chapter 6 The Resurrection Body, See. 113-15, 120]

Boettner, Loraine. *Studies in Theology.* Vol. 7. Philadelphia: Presbyterian and Reformed Publishing Company, 1970. [The Exaltation of Christ, See. 190-95]

Boice, James Montgomery. *Foundations of the Christian Faith: A Comprehensive & Readable Theology.* Downers Grove, IL: InterVarsity, 1986. [Chapter 16 The Pivotal Doctrine of the Resurrection, See. 340-48; Chapter 17 Verifying the Resurrection, See. 349-60;

Chapter 18 He Ascended Into Heaven, See. 361–67; N.B. This book presents a healthy read.]

Borg, Marcus J. *Speaking Christian: Why Christian Words Have Lost their Meaning and Power—And How they Can Be Restored*. New York: HarperOne, 2011. [Chapter 9 Easter, See. 107–13; N.B. This work offers a liberal insight.]

Boston, Thomas. *An Illustration of the Doctrines of the Christian Religion, with Respect to Faith and Practice, Upon the Plan of the Assembly's Shorter Catechism, Comprehending a Complete Body of Divinity*. Vol. 2. Berwick: Printed by and for W. Gracie, and J. Rennison, 1804. [Of Christ's Exaltation, See. 80–107; N.B. Google book]

Bowers, G. M. *Faith and Doctrines of the Early Church*. Altadena, CA: Triumph, 1978. [Chapter 3 Does Easter Commemorate the Resurrection?, See. 43–58]

Bowker, John. *God: A Very Short Introduction*. Oxford: Oxford University Press, 2014. [The Crucifixion and the Resurrection, See. 59–64]

Boyd, Gregory A., and Edward K. Boyd. *Letters from a Skeptic*. Colorado Springs, CO: Chariot Victor, 1994. [Correspondence 16 How can you believe that a man rose from the dead?, See. 99–109]

Braaten, Carl E. *Christian Dogmatics*. Edited by Carl E. Braaten and Robert W. Jenson. Vol. 1. Philadelphia: Fortress, 1984. [The Humiliation and Exaltation of Jesus Christ, See. 545–56]

———. *The Future of God; The Revolutionary Dynamics of Hope*. New York: Harper & Row, 1969. [God's Self-Definition in Jesus' Resurrection, See. 73–78]

———. *That All May Believe: A Theology of the Gospel and the Mission of the Church*. Grand Rapids: Eerdmans, 2008. [Chapter 7 The Resurrection Debate Revisited, See. 92–106; N.B. Insightful.]

Bray, Gerald. *God is Love: A Biblical and Systematic Theology*. Wheaton, IL: Crossway, 2012. [Chapter 26 Sending the Son, See. 593–98]

Breckinridge, Robert J. *The Knowledge of God, Objectively Considered, Being the First Part of Theology Considered as a Science of Positive Truth, Both Inductive and Deductive*. New York: R. Carter, 1858. [Crucifixion and Resurrection of Christ, See. 79–80; N.B. Archive.org, Google book, and HathiTrust]

Brock, Rita Nakashima, and Rebecca Ann Parker. *Saving Paradise: How Christianity Traded Love of this World for Crucifixion and Empire*. Boston: Beacon, 2008. [Resurrection of Jesus Christ, See. 53–55, 57, 115–16, 132–33, 145–46, 158, 160, 161, 166, 244–45]

Broeke, James Ten. *A Constructive Basis for Theology*. London: Macmillan, 1914. [See. 56, 77–79, 317; N.B. Archive.org]

Broocks, Rice. *God's Not Dead*. 2013. Nashville: Nelson, 2015. [Chapter 7 Jesus and the Resurrection, See. 139–62]

———. *Man, Myth, Messiah: Answering History's Greatest Question*. Nashville: W Publishing Group, 2016. [Chapter 5 The Resurrection: The Event that Changed Everything, See. 91–115]

Brown, Archibald G. *The Face of Jesus Christ: Sermons on the Person and Work of our Lord*. Edinburgh: Banner of Truth Trust, 2012. [The Death, Resurrection, and Revelation of Jesus Christ, See. 131–43; N.B. reprint]

Brown, Colin. *That You May Believe: Miracles and Faith-then and Now*. Grand Rapids: Eerdmans, 1985. [Miracles and the Resurrection, See. 104–7]

Brown, David. *Discipleship and Imagination: Christian Tradition and Truth*. Oxford: Oxford University Press, 2000. [Resurrection of Christ, See. 111–15, 392]

Brown, David. *Jesus and God in the Christian Scriptures.* London: Sheldon Press, 1967. [Qur'anic References to the Death of Jesus, See. 35–36]

Brown, Henry Clay. *Reason of Christian Doctrines.* Chicago: Winona, 1907. [Christ's Resurrection, See. 210–29]

Brown, John. *A Compendious View of Natural and Revealed Religion.* Philadelphia: David Hogan, 1819. [Of Christ's States of Humiliation and Exaltation, See. 324–35; N.B. Archive.org and Google book]

Brown, Michael B. *Bottom Line Beliefs: Twelve Doctrines All Christians Hold In Common (Sort Of).* Macon, GA: Smyth & Helwys, 2009. [Chapter 3 Jesus' Resurrection, See. 21–27]

Brown, William Adams. *Christian Theology in Outline.* London: T&T Clark, 1906. [Judgment after death, See. 253–54, 336, 346, 370; N.B. Google books]

Brunner, Emil. *The Christian Doctrine of Creation and Redemption: Dogmatics.* Translated by Oliver Wyon. Vol. 2. London: Lutterworth, 1952. [Chapter 12 (E). The Risen and Exalted Lord, See. 363–78]

———. *The Christian Doctrine of the Church, Faith, and the Consummation Dogmatics*: Vol. 3. Translated by David Cairus. Philadelphia: Westminster, 1962. [Part 3 Chapter 10 Universalism and World Judgment, See. 167–75; Part 4 Chapter 9 The Resurrection, See. 408–14]

———. *The Scandal of Christianity.* London: SCM, 1951. [Chapter 5 Resurrection, See. 94–115]

Bryan, William Jennings. *Seven Questions In Dispute.* New York: Revell, 1924. [Chapter 5 The Bodily Resurrection of Jesus, See. 85–102]

Buel, Samuel. *A Treatise of Dogmatic Theology.* Vol. 2. New York: T. Whittaker, 1890. [Chapter 22 The Resurrection of Christ and the Resurrection of the Body, See. 383–400]

Buhring, Kurt. *Conceptions of God, Freedom, and Ethics in African American and Jewish Theology.* New York: Palgrave Macmillan, 2008. [Jesus, resurrection of, 23, 25, 27, 30–32, 35–36, 38, 41, 46, 48, 59, 63, 67, 76, 81, 173, 175–76, 182, 195]

Bultmann, Rudolf. *Theology of the New Testament.* Translated by Kendrick Grobel. Vol. 1. New York: Scribner, 1951. [See. 26–32, 36, 43, 45, 49, 60, 80–83, 92, 123, 127, 140–47, 188; also #33 Christ's Death and Resurrection as Salvation-Occurrence, See. 292–313, 318, 328, 345; N.B. Worth examining.]

Burrell, Maurice C. *My Belief: The Faith of an Anglican.* London: Marshall, Morgan & Scott, 1970. [Part 1 Christian Faith 8. Christ's Resurrection, See. 44–49]

Burrows, Millar. *An Outline of Biblical Theology.* Philadelphia: Westminster, 1946. [See. 66, 93]

Buswell, J. Oliver. *A Systematic Theology of the Christian Religion.* Vol. 2 Part 3 and Part 4. Grand Rapids: Zondervan, 1962. [J. 1 Corinthians, Chapter 15, Verses 1–19, See. 333–34; Evidence From the Resurrection Appearances of Christ, See. 343]

Butler, John J. *Natural and Revealed Theology: A System of Lectures, Embracing the Divine Existence and Attributes; Authority of the Scriptures; Scriptural Doctrine; Institutions and Ordinances of the Christian Church.* Dover, NH: Freewill Baptist Printing, 1861. [Lecture 31 The Resurrection, See. 326–33; N.B. Google book]

Buttrick, George Arthur. *So We Believe, So We Pray.* New York: Abingdon-Cokesbury, 1951. [Chapter 7 Faith in Life Eternal, See. 102–18]

Byrum, Russell R. *Christian Theology: A Systematic Statement of Christian Doctrine for the Use of Theological Students*. Anderson, IN: Gospel Trumpet, 1925. [Proof of the Resurrection of Christ, See. 125–27]

Cadoux, Cecil John. *The Case For Evangelical Modernism: A Study of the Relation Between Christian Faith and Traditional Theology*. Chicago: Clark, 1939. [See. 154–59]

———. *A Pilgrim's Further Progress: Dialogues on Christian Teaching*. Oxford: Blackwell, 1943. [Predictions of the Resurrection, See. 29–30; The Nature of the Resurrection Appearances, See. 30–31].

Caird, G. B. *A Primer of Christianity: Part 3. The Truth Of The Gospel*. London: Oxford University Press, 1950. [The Resurrection, See. 85–87]

Calvin, Jean, and John Allen. *Institutes of the Christian Religion*. New-Haven: Hezekiah Howe, 1816. [Book 2 Chapter 16 Christ's Execution of the Office of a Redeemer to Procure our Salvation; His Death, Resurrection, and Ascension to Heaven, See. 539–66; N.B. Google book]

Cambon, Mark G. *Bible Doctrines: Beliefs That Matter*. Grand Rapids: Zondervan, 1970. [Chapter 9 Eschatology. See. 255, 257–59]

Campbell, R. J. *The New Theology*. New York: Macmillan, 1907. [Chapter 12 The resurrection of Jesus, See. 214–17; Theories of Resurrection, See. 217–22; N.B. Archive.org]

Carmody, John. *The Heart of the Christian Matter: An Ecumenical Approach*. Nashville: Abingdon, 1983. [Resurrection Jesus', See. 57–60, 84, 146, 164, 165, 219, 253, 273]

Carnell, Edward John. *The Case for Biblical Christianity*. Grand Rapids: Eerdmans, 1969. [Chapter 16 The Fear of Death and the Hope of the Resurrection, See. 174–82; N.B. Nothing useful.]

Cassels, Louis. *Christian Primer*. Garden City, NY: Doubleday, 1964. [Can you believe in the Resurrection?, See. 23–26]

Cauthen, Kenneth. *Systematic Theology: A Modern Protestant Approach*. Lewiston, NY: Mellen, 1986. [Resurrection of Jesus, See. 91, 159, 233–34, 251, 260, 393, 421]

Chadwick, Henry. *Lessing's Theological Writings: Selections in Translation with an Introductory Essay*. Translated by Henry Chadwick. Stanford: Stanford University Press, 1957. [See. 17, 26, 49–51, 54, 55]

Chafer, Lewis Sperry. *Major Bible Themes: 52 Vital Doctrines of the Scripture Simplified and Explained*. Edited by John F. Walvoord. Grand Rapids: Zondervan, 1974. [Chapter 10 God the Son: His Resurrection, See. 65–69; Chapter 11 God the Son: His Ascension and Priestly Ministry, See. 70–72]

———. *Systematic Theology. Christology*. Vol. 5. Dallas: Dallas Seminary Press, 1947. [Chapter 10 The Resurrection of Christ Incarnate, See. 231–60; Chapter 11 The Ascension of Christ, See. 261–79]

———. *Systematic Theology: Doctrinal Summarization*. Vol. 7. Dallas: Dallas Theological Seminary, 1948. [Resurrection, See. 266–68]

———. *Systematic Theology: Ecclesiology—Eschatology*. Vol. 4. Dallas: Dallas Theological Seminary, 1948. [The Resurrected Christ, See. 79–93]

———. *Systematic Theology: Soteriology* Vol. 3. Dallas: Dallas Theological Seminary, 1948. [The Resurrected Christ, See. 16]

Chalmers, R. C. *A Faith for You*. Richmond, VA: John Knox. 1962. [Chapter 4 Resurrection, See. 59–73]

Chamberlain, Paul. *Why People Don't Believe: Confronting Seven Challenges to Christian Faith*. Grand Rapids: Baker, 2011. [Resurrection, of Jesus, See. 75–76]

Chapman, Colin. *An Eerdmans' Handbook: The Case For Christianity*. Grand Rapids: Eerdmans, 1981. [Did Jesus Rise From The Dead?, See. 278–90]

Charry, Ellen T. *By the Renewing of Your Minds: The Pastoral Function of Christian Doctrine*. New York: Oxford University Press, 1997. [See. 18, 92, 93–94]

Chumbley, Kenneth L. *The Gospel Argument for God: Revised*. Temple Terrace, FL: Florida College Press, 2014. [Chapter 13 Remember that Jesus Christ was Raised from the Dead, See. 93–95]

Clarke, Adam. *Christian Theology*. New York: G. Lane & P. P. Sandford, 1842. [Christ, See. 120; N.B. Google book]

Clarke, William Newton. *An Outline of Christian Theology*. New York: Scribner's Sons, 1898. [Resurrection, See. 272–75; N.B. Archive.org and Google book]

Close, Henry T. *Reasons For Our Faith*. Richmond, VA: John Knox, 1962. [The Resurrection, See. 47–52]

Cole, C. Donald. *Basic Christian Faith*. Westchester, IL: Crossway, 1985. [Chapter 23 Christ's Exaltation, See. 179–84]

Coleman, Michael Edward. *Faith Under Fire*. New York: Scribner's Sons, 1943. [Chapter 8 Sect. Resurrection, See. 95–100]

Conder, Eustace R. *The Basis Of Faith: A Critical Survey of the Grounds of Christian Theism*. London: Hodder & Stoughton, 1877. [Lecture 8 Jesus, See. 369–70; N.B. Google book]

Conner, J. M. *Outlines of Christian Theology: or, Theological Hints*. Little Rock, AR: Brown Print. 1896. [Chapter 17 Resurrection, See. 161–63; N.B. Archive.org]

Conner, W. T. *Christian Doctrine*. Nashville: Broadman, 1937. [Resurrection, of Jesus, 53–55, 65–67, 178–79]

———. *The Gospel of Redemption*. Nashville: Broadman, 1945. [Victory manifest in the resurrection, See. 119–27]

———. *Revelation and God: An Introduction to Christian Doctrine*. Nashville: Broadman, 1936. [The Resurrection of Jesus, See. 160–64]

———. *A System of Christian Doctrine*. Nashville: Sunday School Board of the Southern Baptist Convention, 1924. [See. 41, 135–37]

Cooke, William. *Christian Theology: Its Doctrines and Ordinances Explained and Defended*. London: Hamilton, Adams, 1879. [The Resurrection, See. 588; N.B. Google book]

Copenhaver, Martin B. *To Begin at the Beginning: An Introduction to the Christian Faith*. Cleveland: United Church Press, 1994. [Chapter 3 The Jesus of the Resurrection, See. 41–62]

Cottam, Joseph Almond. *Know The Truth*. New York: American Tract Society, 1940. [Chapter 13 Know The Power of Christ's Resurrection, See. 183–99]

Cottrell, Jack. *The Faith Once For All: Bible Doctrine For Today*. Joplin, MO: College Press, 2003. [Chapter 14 The Work of Christ, The Resurrection, See. 272–83]

Cousar, Charles B. *A Theology of the Cross: The Death of Jesus in the Pauline Letters*. Minneapolis: Fortress, 1990. [Chapter 3 Jesus' Death and Resurrection, See. 88–108]

Cowley, Matthias F. *Cowley's Talks on Doctrine*. Chattanooga, TN: B. E. Rich, 1902. [The Resurrection, See. 162–69; N.B. Google book]

Cox, David. *What Christians Believe*. London: Darton, Longman & Todd, 1963. [The Resurrection, See. 56–61]

Crawford, C. C. *Survey Course in Christian Doctrine*. Vol. 3. Joplin, MO: College Press, 1964. [Lesson 93 The Resurrection of Jesus, See. 302–8; Lesson 94 The Resurrection of Jesus Concluded), See. 308–19]

Creager, John A. *Theodynamics: NeoChristian Perspectives for the Modern World*. Lanham, MD: University Press of America, 1994. [See. 292–95]

Culver, Robert Duncan. *Systematic Theology: Biblical and Historical*. Fearn, Ross-shire: Mentor, 2005. [Part 4 Christology: Person and Work of Christ. 20. The Resurrection of Christ (1), See. 601–7; 21. The Resurrection of Christ (2), See. 608–15; 22. The Ascension of Christ, See. 616–22]

Curtis, Olin Alfred. *The Christian Faith Personally Given in a System of Doctrine*. New York: Eaton & Mains, 1905. [Founding the New Race, See. 329–30; N.B. Archive.org and Google book]

———. *Elective Course of Lectures in Systematic Theology*. Madison, NJ: Drew Theological Seminary, 1901. [Thirty-First Discussion 3. Our Lords Resurrection, See. 54; 4. Our Lord's Ascension and Session, See. 54; N.B. Ebscohost.com]

Custance, Arthur C. *The Doorway Papers*. Vol. 5. Grand Rapids: Zondervan, 1975. [Part 8 The Resurrection of Jesus Christ, See. 334–65; N.B. Between 1957 and 1972 Custance wrote the ten volume "Doorway Papers" that attempt to bridge the gap between a scientific and a Christian worldview. Available online]

Dabney, R. L. *Syllabus and Notes of the Course of Systematic and Polemic Theology*. 5th ed. Richmond, VA: Presbyterian Committee of Publication, 1878. [Lecture 45 Christ's Humiliation and Exaltation, See. 546–48]

Dagg, J. L. *A Manual of Theology*. Charleston, SC: Southern Baptist Pub. Soc., 1857. [Exaltation, See. 206–7; N.B. Google book]

Dalferth, Ingolf U. *Crucified and Resurrected: Restructuring the Grammar of Christology*. Translated by Jo Bennett. Grand Rapids: Baker Academic, 2015. [Resurrection, the. See Jesus and, See. 24–37; Cross and Resurrection: The Word of the Cross, See esp. 52–71; 106n54; The Verbal Format of the Resurrection Confession, See. 154–55]

Daniélou, Jean. *The Development of Christian Doctrine Before the Council of Nicaea*. Vol. 1. *The Theology of Jewish Christianity*. Translated by John A. Baker. London: Darton, Longman & Todd, 1964. [Ascension, See. 247–63; Resurrection of Christ, 1, 21, 27, 88, 127–29, 179, 226, 245, 249, 344]

Davies, Brian. *Thinking About God*. London: Chapman, 1985. [Resurrection, as proof of Divinity of Christ, See. 248, 263, 266, 269–70]

Davis, Charles. *Theology for Today*. New York: Sheed & Ward, 1963. [Resurrection of Christ, See. 204, 243, 271]

Davis, Stephen T. *Christian Philosophical Theology*. Oxford University Press, 2006. [Part 2 Chapter 7 Was Jesus Raised Bodily?, See. 111–28; Chapter 8 Seeing the Risen Jesus, See. 129–48; N.B. This work is a good read.]

Dawson, Robert Dale. *The Resurrection in Karl Barth*. Aldershot: Ashgate, 2007. [256 pages]

Denney, James. *Studies in Theology*. 4th ed. London: Houghton & Stoughton, 1895. [Lecture 7 Christ in His Exaltation, See. 152–72; N.B. Archive.org]

Dewar, Daniel. *Elements of Systematic Divinity*. Glasgow: T. Murray, 1867. [Chapter 13 The Exaltation of the Mediator— His Resurrection, See. 196–211; Chapter 14 The Resurrection—The Expediency of His Ascension, See. 212–24; Chapter 15 The Exaltation of Christ—Ascension and Sitting at the Right Hand of God, See. 225–40; N.B. Google book]

Category IX—Creeds, Religion, Doctrinal, Sermons, Commentaries

Dick, John. *Lectures on Theology*. Cincinnati: Applegate, 1856. [Lecture 61 Christ's State of Exaltation, See. 328–43; N.B. Archive.org. Dick's work is a good, dated reading.]

Dickie, John. *The Organism of Christian Truth: A Modern Positive Dogmatic*. Edinburgh: James Clark &, 1930. [The Resurrection, See. 325–30]

Dorner, I. A. *A System of Christian Doctrine*. Translated by Alfred Cave and J. S. Banks. Vol. 4. Edinburgh: T&T Clark, 1890. [Sect. 125 The Resurrection of Christ, See. 132–37; Sect. 126 The Ascension, See. 138–42; N.B. Google book]

Driscoll, Mark and Gerry Breshears. *Doctrine: What Christians Should Believe*. Wheaton: Crossway, 2010. [Chapter 9 Resurrection: God Saves. See. 279–303]

Dunning, H. Ray. *Grace, Faith, and Holiness: A Wesleyan Systematic Theology*. Kansas City: Beacon Hill, 1988. [See. 434–35, 476–77]

Durant, Will. *The Story of Civilization: Caesar and Christ*. New York: Simon & Schuster, 1944. [Death and Transfiguration, See. 573–74]

Dwight, Timothy. *Theology: Explained and Defended in a Series of Sermons*. Vol. 2. New York: Harper, 1850. [Sermon 61 Resurrection of Christ, See. 264–73; Sermon 62 The Resurrection of Christ cont., See. 274–86; N.B. Archive.org]

Easton, W. Burnet. *Basic Christian Beliefs*. Philadelphia: Westminster, 1957. [Chapter 5 Jesus, Who Is the Christ, C. His Resurrection, See. 110–16]

———. *The Faith of a Protestant*. New York: Macmillan, 1946. [Chapter 6 The Resurrection, See. 40–47]

Edwards, Richard Alan. *The Sign of Jonah in the Theology of the Evangelists and Q*. Naperville, IL: A. R. Allenson, 1971. [122 pages]

Ellingsen, Mark. *A Common Sense Theology: The Bible, Faith, and American Society*. Macon, GA: Mercer University Press, 1995. [See. 28, 39–42, 44, 46–48, 165, 188]

Ely, Ezra Stiles. *A Synopsis of Didactic Theology*. Philadelphia: J. Crissy, 1822. [Part 2 Chapter 5 He arose from the dead and ascended into heaven, See. 66–69; N.B. Archive.org, Google book, and HathiTrust]

Emesowum, Charles K. *Doctrinal Conflicts in Christendom: Which Way Out? A Survey of Doctrinal Divergences and Conflicting Beliefs Among Christian Churches and Denominations*. Imo State: Atlantica, 2007. [Chapter 6 Did Jesus return back to the earth after ascending to heaven? Christian groups differ on this, See. 43–50]

Enns, Paul P. *Approaching God: Daily Readings in Systematic Theology*. Chicago: Moody, 1991. [Part 3 Christ, See. April 30–May 7; N.B. This text does not contain pagination.]

———. *The Moody Handbook of Theology*. Chicago: Moody, 1989. [Resurrection of Christ, See. 234–35; Ascension of Christ, See. 235; also, 95, 264]

Erickson, Millard J. *Christian Theology*. 2nd ed. Grand Rapids: Baker, 1998. [Part 7: The Person of Christ, See. 686–87; 708–10; 794–97; The Exaltation, The Last Things, See. 1204–5]

———. *Christian Theology*. 3rd ed. Grand Rapids: Baker, 2013. [Part 7 Evidence of the Resurrection, See. 631–33; Part 8 The Exaltation, See. 70912; N.B. Erickson's work is a definite read.]

———. *Introducing Christian Doctrine*. 2nd. ed. Edited by L. Arnold. Grand Rapids: Baker Academic, 2001. [The Evidence of the Resurrection, See. 219–20; The Exaltation, See. 246–48]

———. *Where Is Theology Going? Issues and Perspectives on the Future of Theology*. Grand Rapids: Baker, 1994. [Resurrection, historicity of, See. 171]

Evans, Tony. *Theology You Can Count On: Experiencing What the Bible Says About . . . God the Father, God the Son, God the Holy Spirit, Angels, Salvation, the Church, the Bible, the Last Things.* Chicago: Moody, 2008. [The Uniqueness in Christ in His Resurrection, See. 245–55]

Evans, William. *The Great Doctrines of the Bible.* Chicago: Moody, 1974. [Part One. 2, The Resurrection of Jesus Christ, See. 84–96; 3, The Ascension and Exaltation of Jesus Christ, See. 96–101. N.B. 1912, 1939 and 1949]

———. *What Every Christian Should Believe.* Chicago: Bible Institute Colportage, 1922. [See. 41, 42, 91–96; N.B. Google book]

Fabricius, Kim. *Propositions on Christian Theology: A Pilgrim Walks the Plank.* Durham: Carolina Academic Press, 2008. [Ten Propositions on the Resurrection, 35–39]

Fackre, Gabriel. *The Christian Story: A Narrative Interpretation of Basic Christian Doctrine.* 3rd ed. Grand Rapids: Eerdmans, 1996. [See. 127, 129, 144–47, 165, 215–16, 264]

Farrelly, John. *Faith In God Through Jesus Christ: Foundational Theology 2.* Collegeville, MN: Liturgical Press, 1997. [Chapter 5 The Resurrection of Jesus, and Early Christian Understanding of Salvation and Revelation, See. 162–207]

Farrow, Douglas. *Ascension Theology.* London: Bloomsbury, 2013. [177 pages]

Ferré, Nels F. S. *The Christian Understanding of God.* New York: Harper & Brothers, 1951. [The Resurrection, See. 211–16]

Fessenden, Thomas. *A Theoretic Explanation of the Science of Sanctity According to Reason, Scripture, Common Sense, and the Analogy of Things, Containing an Idea of God, of His Creations and Kingdoms, of the Holy Scriptures, of the Christian Trinity, and of the Gospel System.* Brattleboro: Printed by William Fessenden, for the Author, 1804. [Chapter 6 Of the Incarnation, Humiliation, and Mission of Christ 3. Exaltation to the Throne of God, See. 154–61; N.B. Archive.org and Google book]

Field, Benjamin. *The Student's Handbook of Christian Theology.* London: Hodder & Stoughton, 1870. [Section 3 #5. Is there any confirmation of this view arising out of the history of our Lord's death and resurrection?, See. 94–95; N.B. Archive.org and Google book]

Finegan, Jack. *First Steps in Theology.* New York: Association Press, 1960. [Part 2 Christ, See. 71–74]

Finger, Thomas N. *Christian Theology: An Eschatological Approach.* Scottdale, PA: Herald Press, 1985. [Chapter 18 The Resurrection of Jesus Christ, See. 349–67]

Fiorenza, Francis Schüssler. *Foundational Theology: Jesus and the Church.* New York: Crossroad, 1984. [The Resurrection of Jesus, See. 1–55]

Fisher, William Edgar. *Sound Doctrine: A Scriptural Treatise on the Statement of Doctrine as Set Forth in the Manual of the Pentecostal Church of the Nazarene, and Contained in the Word of God.* Kansas City, MO: Pentecostal Nazarene Publishing House, 1918. [Chapter 8 The Resurrection of Christ, See. 63–66; Chapter 9 The Ascension, See. 69–72; N.B. Archive.org]

Fitzwater, P. B. *Christian Theology: A Systematic Presentation.* 2nd ed. Grand Rapids. Eerdmans, 1948. [Section 8 The Resurrection of Jesus Christ, See. 159–65; Section 9 The Exaltation of Jesus Christ, See. 163–66]

Fleming, M. R. *A Confession of Faith for the Average Christian.* Boston: Gorham Press, 1916. [He Arose From the Tomb to Guarantee Our Resurrection, See. 59–60; N.B. Google book]

Ford, David. *Theology: A Very Short Introduction.* 2nd ed. Oxford: Oxford University Press, 2000. [The Resurrection of Jesus Christ, See. 91–93]

Foster, Randolph S. *Beyond the Grave: Being Three Lectures Before Chautauqua Assembly in 1878.* New York: Phillips & Hunt, 1882. [See. 163, 164, 165; N.B. Google book and HathiTrust. This work challenges the conservative Church line about Jesus's resurrection, See 163–65. It was harshly criticized in James E. Lake's *Bishop Foster's Heresy,* 1889.]

———. *Evidences of Christianity: The Supernatural Book.* Vol. 3. New York: Hunt & Eaton, 1890. [See. 67, 85, 234, 236, 239, 244, 264, 265, 270, 272, 273, 289, 294, 302, 303, 346, 394; N.B. Google book and HathiTrust]

Foster, Robert V. *Systematic Theology.* Nashville: Cumberland Presbyterian Publishing House, 1898. [Chapter 3 The Christ of Exaltation, See. 489–506; N.B. Google book]

Frame, John M. *Systematic Theology: An Introduction to Christian Belief.* Phillipsburg, NJ: P & R Publishing, 2013. [Questions 51–53, See. 912]

Fries, Heinrich. *Fundamental Theology.* Translated by Robert J. Daly. Washington, DC: Catholic University of America Press, 1996. [The Resurrection (Raising) Of Jesus From The Dead, See. 354–61]

Frost, Bede. *The Christian Mysteries.* London: A. R. Mowbray, 1950. [Chapter 8 Of the Resurrection, See. 86–93]

Gamertsfelder, Solomon J. *Systematic Theology.* Cleveland C. Hauser, 1913. [The Witness of Miracles, See. 253–54; N.B. Ebscohost]

Garrett, James Leo. *Systematic Theology: Biblical, Historical, and Evangelical.* Vol. 2. Grand Rapids: Eerdmans, 1995. [Chapter 50 The Resurrection of Jesus, See. 76–107; Chapter 51 The Ascension and the Heavenly Session of Jesus, See. 108–22; N.B. This text is worth examining.]

Garvie, Alfred E. *The Christian Doctrine of the Godhead; or, The Apostolic Benediction as the Christian Creed.* London: Hodder & Stoughton, 1926. [The Lordship: The Resurrection, See. 87–91]

Gaybba, Brian. *God Is A Community: A General Survey of Christian Theology.* Pretoria: University of South Africa Press, 2004. [Chapter 14 The Work of Christ, 14.2.5 The role of the resurrection, See. 195–200]

Geering, Lloyd. *Christianity Without God.* Wellington: Bridget Williams, 2002. [Chapter 6 How Did Jesus Become God?, See. 73–86]

———. *Tomorrow's God: How We Create Our Worlds.* Wellington: Bridget Williams, 1994. [See. 152–53, 165, 220]

Geffré, Claude. *A New Age in Theology.* Translated by Robert Shillenn. New York: Paulist, 1974. [Chapter 6 The Resurrection as the Center of Christian Theology, See. 97–110]

Geisler, Norman L., and Ronald Rhodes. *Conviction Without Compromise. Standing Strong In the Core Beliefs of the Christian Faith.* Eugene, OR: Harvest House, 2008. [See The Bodily Resurrection of Christ, See. 109–20; The Bodily Ascension of Christ, See. 145–56]

Gerhart, Emanuel V. *Institutes of the Christian Religion.* Translated by Philip Schaff. Vol. 2. New York: Funk & Wagnalls, 1894. [Chapter 11 His Resurrection, See. 379–402; Chapter 12 Ascension and Glorification, See. 403–13; N.B. Archive.org, Google book, and HathiTrust]

Gill, John. *A Body of Doctrinal and Practical Divinity: or, A System of Practical Truths Deduced from the Sacred Scriptures.* London: Printed by Whittingham & Rowland,

1815. [Book 5 Chapter 6 Of the Resurrection of Christ from the Dead, See. 293–96; Chapter 7 Of the Ascension of Christ, See. 296–300; N.B. Archive.org. This book is a classic, dated source.]

Gillespie, William. *The Truth of the Evangelical History of our Lord Jesus Christ: Proved, In Opposition to D. F. Strauss, the Chief of Modern Disbelievers in Revelation.* Edinburgh: A. and C. Black, 1856. [See. 13, 18, 121, 123, 141; N.B. Archive.org]

Goodwin, John. *Christian Theology.* London: Thomas Tegg, 1836. [Chapter 4 Christ. See. Resurrection, See. 129–30; N.B. Google book]

Gore, Charles. *The New Theology and the Old Religion: Being Eight Lectures, Together with Five Sermons.* New York: E. P. Dutton, 1907. [See. 101, 109–23, 134, 154, 157, 176, 190, 199, 212, 220; N.B. Archive.org and Google book]

Gould, Ezra P. *The Biblical Theology of the New Testament.* London: MacMillan, 1901. [The Teaching of the Twelve, See. 53–57; N.B. Archive.org and Google book]

Gräbner, A. L. *Outlines of Doctrinal Theology.* St. Louis: Concordia, 1898. [Christology. #118 Christ's Resurrection, See. 146–50; #119 Christ's Ascension Into Heaven, See. 150–54; N.B. Google book]

Graham, Billy. *The Faithful Christian: An Anthology of Bill Graham.* Compiled by William Griffin and Ruth Graham. New York: McCracken Press, 1994. [Chapter 18 Resurrection, See. 211–16]

Gray, Albert F. *Christian Theology.* Vol. 2. Anderson, IN: Warner Press, 1946. [The Resurrection of the Dead, See. 229–34]

Greeley, Andrew M. *The Great Mysteries: Experiencing Catholic Faith From the Inside Out.* Lanham, MD: Sheed & Ward, 2003. [Chapter 4 The Mystery of the Cross and Resurrection, See. 39–49]

Green, Peter. *I Believe In God.* London: Longmans, Green, 1934. [Chapter 9 The Resurrection, See. 93–102; Chapter 10 The Ascended Christ and the Sacraments, See. 103–10]

Greig, Gary S., and Kevin N. Springer, eds. *The Kingdom and the Power: Are Healing and the Spiritual Gifts Used by Jesus and the Early Church Meant for the Church Today?* Ventura, CA: Regal, 1993. [Appendix 3: Matthew 28:18-20 The Great Commission and Jesus' Commands to Preach and Heal, See. 399–403]

Grenz, Stanley J. *Reason for Hope: The Systematic Theology of Wolfhart Pannenberg.* Grand Rapids: Eerdmans, 2005. [Resurrection of, See. 157–59, 188–97]

———. *Theology for the Community of God.* Nashville: Broadman & Holman, 1994. [Jesus' resurrection, See. 334–39]

———. *What Christians Really Believe—And Why.* Louisville: Westminster John Knox, 1998. [Jesus and the Resurrection, See. 98–100]

Grider, J. Kenneth. *A Wesleyan-Holiness Theology.* Kansas City: Beacon Hill, 1994. [Chapter 13 The Empty Tomb, See. 336–49]

Grudem, Wayne A. *Bible Doctrine: Essential Teachings of the Christian Faith.* Edited by Jeff Purswell. Grand Rapids: Zondervan, 1999. [Chapter 16 Resurrection and Ascension, See. 261–69]

———. *Christian Beliefs: Twenty Basics Every Christian Should Know.* Grand Rapids: Zondervan, 2005. [Chapter 11 What is the Resurrection?, See. 76–78; N.B. Not useful]

———. *Making Sense of Christ and the Spirit: One of Seven Parts from Grudem's Systematic Theology* (Making Sense of Series). Grand Rapids: Zondervan, 2011. [Chapter 4 Resurrection and Ascension, See. 124–132]

———. *Systematic Theology: An Introduction to Biblical Doctrine*. Leicester: Inter-Varsity, 2000. [Chapter 28 Resurrection and Ascension, See. 608–21; N.B. This text offers a concise presentation.]

Gulley, Norman R. *Systematic Theology: Creation, Christ, Salvation*. Berrien Springs, MI: Andrews University Press, 2012. [Resurrection, See. 470–73]

Guthrie, Shirley C. *Christian Doctrine*. Revised Edition Atlanta: Westminster John Knox, 1994. [Who's in Charge Here? The Doctrine of the Resurrection, See. 244, 252, 270–74; 370, 393–94]

Gutzke, Manford George. *Plain Talk About Christian Words*. Grand Rapids: Zondervan, 1964. [His Resurrection, See. 107–10; His Ascension, See. 110–13]

Haering, Theodor. *The Christian Faith: A System of Dogmatics*. 2nd ed. Translated by John Dickie and George Ferries. Vol. 2. London: Hodder & Stoughton, 1913. [Resurrection of Jesus, See. 627, 629, 751; N.B. Archive.org. The author's name is also spelled Häring.]

Hall, Douglas John. *The Cross in Our Context: Jesus and the Suffering Word*. Minneapolis: Fortress, 2003. [See. 31, 40, 101]

———. *Professing the Faith: Christian Theology in a North American Context*. Minneapolis: Fortress, 1993. [Ascension, See. 434; Resurrection of, See. 387, 403, 406, 421, 493, 521, 527, 549]

Hall, Francis J. *The Passion and Exaltation of Christ*. New York: Longmans, Green, 1918. [323 pages; N.B. HathiTrust. A dated, but interesting read.]

———. *Theological Outlines*. 3rd ed. Edited by Frank Hudson Hallock. New York: Morehouse-Barlow, 1961. [Chapter 21 Mysteries of Christ's Exaltation, See. 205–13; idem. 1933]

Halsey, Leroy J. *Living Christianity: or, Old Truths Restated*. Philadelphia: Presbyterian Board of Publication, 1881. [Chapter 12 The Resurrection of Christ, See. 93–100; N.B. Archive.org]

Halverson, Marvin, ed. *A Handbook of Christian Theology*. New York: Meridian, 1958. [Resurrection, See. 323–26 (Richard R. Niebuhr)]

Hamilton, Peter N. *The Living God and the Modern World; Christian Theology Based on the Thought of A. N. Whitehead*. Philadelphia: United Church Press, 1967. [Chapter 7 The Livingness of Jesus Christ. See. "Christ is Risen," See. 214–28; Jesus is Lord, See. 229–34]

Hanson, Anthony Tyrrell, and R. P. C. Hanson. *Reasonable Belief: A Survey of the Christian Faith*. Oxford: Oxford University Press, 1980. [The Resurrection, See. 72–77]

Hanson, Bradley C. *Introduction to Christian Theology*. Minneapolis: Fortress, 1997. [Chapter 6 The Person of Jesus Christ, See. 131–40]

Harkness, Georgia Elma. *Understanding the Christian Faith*. New York: Abingdon-Cokesbury, 1947. [The Resurrection, See. 85–88]

Härle, Wilfried. *Outline of Christian Doctrine: An Evangelical Dogmatics*. Translated by Nicholas Sagovsky and Ruth Yule. Grand Rapids: Eerdmans, 2015. [The Raising of Jesus from the Dead, See. 264–66]

Harnack, Adolf von. *History of Dogma*. Translated by Neil Buchanan. Vol. 1. New York: Dover, 1961. [The Common Preaching concerning Jesus Christ in the First Generation of Believers, See. 76–85; Reprinted circa 1900 edition with corrections; N.B. Archive.org]

Harris, Harriet A. *Fundamentalism and Evangelicals*. Oxford: Clarendon, 1998. [See. 315, 323–24]

Harris, John Glyndwr. *Christian Theology: The Spiritual Tradition*. Brighton: Sussex Academic Press, 2001. [The Resurrection of Christ, See. 49]

Hascall, Daniel. *The Elements of Theology: or, The Leading Topics of Christian Theology: Plainly and Scripturally Set Forth: With the Principal Evidences of Divine Revelation Concisely Stated, with Questions: For the Use of Families, Bible Classes, and Seminaries of Learning*. New York: Lewis Colby, 1847. [Section 5 The Resurrection of Christ, See. 202–8, N.B. Google book and HathiTrust]

Haughton, Rosemary. *The Passionate God*. New York: Paulist, 1981. [Chapter 4 Resurrection, See. 129–73; also See 1, 64, 79, 197, 206, 208–11, 254, 273, 274–75]

Hayes, Hopton. *The Scripture-Account of the Attributes and Worship of God; and of the Character and Offices of Jesus Christ*. 4th ed. Hackney: D. Eaton, 1815. [Chapter 55 Of the Resurrection of Jesus Christ, See. 237–45; Chapter 56 Of the Ascension of Jesus Christ, See. 246–48; N.B. Google book]

Headlam, Arthur C. *Christian Theology: The Doctrine of God*. Oxford: Clarendon, 1934. [Chapter 12 The Miraculous Elements in the Life of Jesus. The Evidence of St. Paul the Resurrection, See. 277–86]

Hebert, Arthur Gabriel. *Fundamentalism and the Church*. Philadelphia: Westminster, 1957. [See. 75, 80–83]

Hege, Brent A. R. *Myth, History, and the Resurrection in German Protestant Theology*. Eugene, OR: Pickwick, 2017. [172 pages]

Hegel, Georg Wilhelm Friedrich. *Early Theological Writings*. Translated by T.M. Knox. New York: Harper& Brothers, 1963. [The Spirit of Christianity and Its Fate, See. 281–301]

Helffenstein, Samuel. *The Doctrines of Divine Revelation: As Taught in the Holy Scriptures, Exhibited, Illustrated, and Vindicated. Designed for the Use of Christians Generally, and for Young Men, Preparing for the Gospel Ministry, in Particular*. Philadelphia: James Kay, Jun. & Brother, 1842. [Chapter 45 The Exaltation of Christ, See. 290–97; Chapter 46 On the Exaltation of Christ, See. 298–302; N.B. Archive.org]

Hey, John. *Lectures in Divinity: Delivered in the University of Cambridge*. Vol. 4. Cambridge: Printed by John Smith, Printer to the University, 1822. [Article 4 Of the Resurrection of Christ, See. 31–32; also see 188, 194, 279; N.B. Google book]

Higgins, Gregory C. *The Tapestry of Christian Theology: Modern Minds on the Biblical Narrative*. Mahwah, NJ: Paulist, 2003. [Chapter 7 The Resurrection and Hans Küng's *On Being a Christian*, See. 135–54]

———. *Wrestling with the Questions: An Introduction to Contemporary Theologies*. Minneapolis: Fortress, 2009. [Chapter 8 Resurrection: Stanley Hauerwas and Postliberal Theology. What does the resurrection mean for Christian life?, See. 139–48]

Hill, George, and Alexander Hill. *Lectures In Divinity*. 3rd ed. Vol. 1. Edinburgh: Waugh & Innes, 1833. [Chapter 8 Resurrection of Christ, See. 180–92; N.B. Archive.org and Google book]

Hinlicky, Paul R. Divine *Complexity: The Rise of Creedal Christianity*. Minneapolis, MN: Fortress, 2011. [Chapter 2 From Resurrection Kerygma to Gospel Narrative, See. 25–68]

Hobbs, Herschel H. *Fundamentals of our Faith*. Nashville: Broadman, 1960. [Chapter 4 Jesus Christ. See. 47–50]

Hodge, Archibald Alexander. *Outlines of Theology*. New York: Robert Carter, 1876. [Chapter 23 The Intercession of Christ, See. 329–31; N.B. Archive.org]

———. *Questions on the Text of the Systematic Theology of Dr. Charles Hodge: Together with an Exhibition of Various Schemes Illustrating the Principles of Theological Construction.* New York: Scribner's Sons, 1885. [Chapter 13 The Exaltation of Christ, See. 111; N.B. Archive.org]

Hodge, Charles. *Systematic Theology.* Vol. 2. New York: Scribner, Armstrong, 1876. [Chapter 13 The Exaltation of Christ, See. 626-38; N.B. CCEL.org and Google book]

Hodgson, Leonard. *Christian Faith and Practice: Seven Lectures.* Oxford: Basil Blackwell, 1952. [See. 54-55]

Hodgson, Peter Crafts. *Winds of the Spirit: A Constructive Christian Theology.* Louisville: Westminster John Knox, 1994. [Chapter 16 Christ Risen: The Shape of Reconciliatory Emancipation, See. 267-75]

Hoeksema, Herman. *Reformed Dogmatics.* Grandville, MI: Reformed Free Pub. Association, 2004. [The State of Exaltation, See. 412-26; N.B. Hoeksema provides a concise overview.]

Holmes, Robert. *Treatises on Religious and Scriptural Subjects.* Oxford: University Press, 1806. [Chapter 6 On the Resurrection of Christ and of the Body, Sect. 1, See. 399-406; Chapter 7 The Resurrection of the Body Deduced from the Resurrection of Christ, and Illustrated from His Transfiguration, See. 425-56; N.B. Google book]

Horton, Michael Scott. *The Christian Faith: A Systematic Theology for Pilgrims on the Way.* Grand Rapids: Zondervan, 2011. [Chapter 16 The State of Exaltation: The Servant Who is Lord, See. 521-47]

———. *Pilgrim Theology: Core Doctrines for Christian Disciples.* Grand Rapids: Zondervan, 2012. [Resurrection of Jesus Christ, See. 44, 48-50, 216-28, 338]

House, H. Wayne, and Gordon Carle. *Doctrine Twisting: How Core Biblical Truths are Distorted.* Downers Grove, IL: InterVarsity, 2003. [Chapter 5 Jesus' Resurrection: Was It His Actual Body?, See. 83-101]

Houtepen, Anton W. J. *God: An Open Question.* Translated by John Bowden. London: Continuum, 2002. [Jesus, the Risen One?, See. 207; The Living From the Dead, See. 208-13]

Hove, E. *Christian Doctrine.* Minneapolis: Augsburg, 1930. [The Two States of Christ §109-113, See. 196-204]

Hovey, Alvah. *Manual of Systematic Theology, and Christian Ethics.* Boston: Author, 1877. [See. 65, 193-94, 290; N.B. Archive.org and Google book]

Huffer, Alva G. *Systematic Theology.* Oregon: Restitution Press, 1960. [Chapter 47 The Resurrection of Christ, See. 298-306; Chapter 48 The Heavenly Ministry of Christ, See. 307-8]

Hughes, Albert. *In the Garden: Messages That Minister.* Toronto, Canada: Evangelical Publishers, 1933. [164 pages]

Hughes, H. Maldwyn. *Basic Beliefs; An Introduction to Christian Doctrine.* New York: Abingdon, 1929. [The Resurrection of Jesus, See. 28]

———. *Christian Foundations: An Introduction to Christian Doctrine.* London: Epworth, 1928. [Note B. The Theological Significance of the Empty Tomb, See. 59-60]

Hunter, Sylvester Joseph. *Outlines of Dogmatic Theology.* 2nd ed. Vol. 2. London: Longmans, Green 1895. [Chapter 5 Mysteries of the Life of Christ. See. #552 The Resurrection, See. 541-43; N.B. Google book and HathiTrust]

Hutton, Richard Holt. *Essays Theological and Literary.* 2nd ed. Vol. 1. London: Macmillan, 1880. [Essay 6 Christian Evidences, Popular and Critical, See. 116–49; N.B. Archive.org and Google book]

Ignatius IV Patriarch of Antioch. *The Resurrection and Modern Man.* Crestwood, NY: St. Vladimir's Seminary Press, 1985. [96 pages]

Illingworth, J. R. *The Doctrine of the Trinity, Apologetically Considered.* London: Macmillan, 1907. [See. 37, 39–42, 55, 57; N.B. Archive.org]

Jacobs, Henry Eyster. *Elements of Religion.* Philadelphia: The Board of Publication of the Council of the Evangelical Lutheran Church in North America, 1898. [Chapter 12 The State of Exaltation, See. 97–115; N.B Archive.org]

———. *A Summary of the Christian Faith.* Philadelphia: United Lutheran Publication House, 1905. [Resurrection of Christ, See. 84, 123, 152–57, 175; N.B. Archive.org]

James, Edwin O. *The Christian Faith in the Modern World: A Study in Scientific Theology.* London: A.R. Mowbray, 1930. [Chapter 7 Resurrection and Immortality, See. 117–33]

Jenson, Robert W. *Systematic Theology.* Vol. 1. New York: Oxford University Press, 1997. [Chapter 12 Resurrection, See. 194–206]

———. *A Theology In Outline: Can These Bones Live?* New York: Oxford University Press, 2016. [Chapter 3 Jesus and Resurrection, See. 26–39]

Jinkins, Michael. *Invitation To Theology.* Downers Grove, IL: InterVarsity, 2001. [Resurrection of Jesus Christ, See. 103–14, 138–39, 149–52, 248–60]

Johnson, Derek. *A Brief History of Theology: From the New Testament to Feminist Theology.* London: Continuum, 2008. [Resurrection, See. 9, 12, 16, 24, 59, 111, 194, 195, 243]

Johnson, E. H., and Henry G. Weston. *An Outline of Systematic Theology and of Ecclesiology.* Philadelphia: American Baptist Publication Society, 1895. [His Exaltation, See. 179–80; N.B. Archive.org and Google book]

Johnston, Mark. *Saving God: Religion After Idolatry.* Princeton: Princeton University Press, 2011. [Jesus Christ, Resurrection of, See. 166, 174, 175–76]

Jones, Beth Felker. *Practicing Christian Doctrine: An Introduction to Thinking and Living Theologically.* Grand Rapids: Baker Academic, 2014. [See. 187–88; Easter, See. 227–28]

Jones, Joe R. *A Grammar of Christian Faith: Systematic Explorations in Christian Life and Doctrine.* Vol. 2. Lanham, MD: Rowman & Littlefield, 2002. [Chapter 8 The Work of Jesus Christ. See. 463–76]

Kaufman, Edmund G. *Basic Christian Convictions.* North Newton, KS: Bethel College, 1972. [B10 The Resurrection and its Mystery, See. 136–45; B11 The Ascension, See. 144–45]

Kaufman, Gordon D. *Systematic Theology; A Historicist Perspective.* New York: Scribner' Sons, 1968. [The Resurrection, See. 411–34; N.B. An interesting, liberal point of view.]

Kedney, John Steinfort. *Christian Doctrine Harmonized and Its Rationality Vindicated.* Vol. 2. New York: G. P. Putnam's Sons, 1889. [Chapter 24 Eschatology,—The Resurrection and Glorification of Jesus Christ, See. 279–85; N.B. Archive.org and Google book]

Kendall, R. T. *Understanding Theology.* Vol. 2. Fearn, Great Britain: Christian Focus, 2000. [See. 199–201]

Killinger, John. *Ten Things I Learned Wrong From A Conservative Church.* New York: Crossroad, 2002. [See. 139–41, 143, 144, 146]

Knapp, Georg Christian. *Lectures On Christian Theology.* Translated by Leonard Woods. 6th American ed. Philadelphia: J. W. Moore, 1856. [Article 10 Of Jesus Christ. Chapter 2

Section 97 History of Christ considered as a man, in his state of exaltation, See. 346–49; N.B. Archive.org and Google book]

Knight, Henry H. *A Future For Truth: Evangelical Theology in a Postmodern World.* Nashville: Abingdon, 1997. [Chapter 4 The Resurrection of the Crucified Jesus, See. 70–84]

Knight, Jonathan. *Jesus: An Historical and Theological Investigation.* London: T&T Clark, 2004. [Chapter 10 He Has Been Raised; He Is Not Here, See. 193–223]

Knitter, Paul F. *Without Buddha I Could not be a Christian.* Richmond: Oneworld, 2013. [Risen from the dead, See. 102–3]

Knox, Ronald A. *Some Loose Stones: Being a Consideration of Certain Tendencies in Modern Theology Illustrated by Reference to the Book Called "Foundations."* London: Longmans, Green, 1914. [Chapter 4 Cui Bono? An Enquiry About the Empty Tomb, See. 68–85; N.B. Archive.org, Google book, and HathiTrust]

Knudson, Albert C. *The Doctrine of Redemption.* New York: Abingdon-Cokesbury, 1933. [Resurrection of Jesus, See. 325, 489]

Köstenberger, Andreas J., and Peter T. O'Brien. *Salvation to the Ends of the Earth: A Biblical Theology of Mission.* Downers Grove, IL: InterVarsity, 2001. [Jesus' resurrection and the 'Great Commission' (Matt 28), See. 101–9]

Kraus, C. Norman. *God Our Savior: Theology In A Christological Mode.* Scottsdale, PA: Herald Press, 1991. [See. 23, 217, 222–23]

Küng, Hans. *On Being a Christian.* Translated by Edward Quinn. Garden City, NY: Doubleday, 1976. [Chapter 5 The New Life, See. 347–410; N.B. This book is written from a frank, liberal point of view.]

Ladd, George Eldon. *A Theology of the New Testament.* Grand Rapids: Eerdmans, 1974. [Chapter 24 The Resurrection, See. 315–27; N.B. Ladd offers a good, short overview.]

LaGrand, James. *The Earliest Christian Mission to 'All Nations' In The Light of Matthew's Gospel.* Atlanta: Scholars Press, 1995. [The Resurrection of the Lord, See. 225–33; The Great Commission, See. 234–47]

Lampe, G. W. H. *God as Spirit.* Oxford: Clarendon, 1977. [See. 3, 4, 85, 128, 98–99, 147–53, 156–57, 160–61.]

Lampe, Peter. *New Testament Theology in a Secular World: A Constructivist Work in Philosophical Epistemology and Christian Apologetics.* London: T&T Clark, 2012. [The Resurrection of Jesus, See. 79–89; Easter, See. 227–34]

Lanier, John J. *Kinship of God and Man.* Vol. 2. New York: T. Whittaker, 1902. [Chapter 5 Which Exalted Divine Activities Is Ascension Into Heaven, See. 165–86; N.B. Google book and HathiTrust]

Lathrop, Joseph. *A View of the Doctrines and Duties of the Christian Religion in Fortynine Discourses on St. Paul's Epistle to the Ephesians: With a Preliminary Discourse on the Evidence of the Gospel, Especially Those Derived from the Conversion, Ministry and Writings of That Apostle.* Worcester: Isaiah Thomas, 1801. [Lesson 9 See. 110–22; N.B. Archive.org, Google book, and HathiTrust]

Lawler, Michael G. *Raid on the Inarticulate: An Invitation to Adult Religion.* Washington, DC: University Press of America, 1980. [Chapter 5 Stories and Myths, See. 116–19]

Lawson, John. *Comprehensive Handbook of Christian Doctrine.* Englewood Cliffs, NJ: Prentice-Hall, 1967. [He Rose Again, etc., See. 96–110]

Lee, Jung Young. *The Theology of Change: A Christian Concept of God in an Eastern Perspective.* Maryknoll, NY: Orbis Books, 1979. [The Crucifixion and Resurrection of Christ, See. 100–101]

Leitch, Addison H. *Interpreting Basic Theology.* New York Meredith Press, 1967. [Chapter 14 The Resurrection: His And Ours, See. 183–95]

Leith, John H. *Basic Christian Doctrine.* Louisville: Westminster John Knox, 1993. [The Resurrection of Jesus Christ, See. 140–42; The Ascension, See. 143–44]

Lewis, Gordon R., and Bruce A. Demarest. *Integrative Theology: Historical, Biblical, Systematic, Apologetic, Practical.* Vol. 2. Grand Rapids: Zondervan, 1996. [Christ's Resurrection, Ascension, and Present Exaltation, See. 437–96; idem. 1987; N.B. This work is a must read.]

Lidgett, J. Scott. *The Christian Religion: Its Meaning and Proof.* New York: Eaton & Mains, 1907. [Book 2. Chapter 1 The Content of the Christian Religion, See. 131–37; N.B. Archive.org and Google book]

———. *The Fatherhood of God in Christian Truth and Life.* Edinburgh: T&T Clark, 1902. [Chapter 9 The Consummation of All Things, See. 409–20; N.B. Google book and HathiTrust]

Lightner, Robert P. *Evangelical Theology A Survey and Revi*ew. Grand Rapids: Baker, 1987. [Christ's Resurrection from the Dead, See. 88–90]

Limbaugh, David. *Jesus on Trial: A Lawyer Affirms the Truth of the Gospel.* Washington, DC: Regnery, 2014. [Chapter 11 Truth, Miracles, and the Resurrection of Christ, See. 108–19]

Lindberg, Conrad Emil. *Christian Dogmatics and Notes on the History of Dogma.* Translated by Conrad Emanuel Hoffsten. Rock Island, IL: Augustana Book Concern, 1922. [The State of Exaltation, See. 238–44; N.B. Archive.org and Google book]

Lindsell, Harold, and Charles J. Woodbridge. *A Handbook of Christian Truth.* Westwood, NJ: Revell, 1953. [Part 4 The Person and Ministry of Jesus Christ. Chapter 9 The Deity of Jesus, See. 132–36; Chapter 23 The Resurrection of Christ, See. 154–59; Chapter 24 The Ascension, 160–65]

Linn, Jan G. *How To Be An Open-Minded Christian Without Losing Your Faith.* St. Louis: Chalice Press, 2002. [Chapter 2 What You Can Believe about Jesus, The Resurrection is more than an Empty Tomb, See. 29–34]

Litton, Edward Arthur. *Introduction to Dogmatic Theology.* London: J. Clarke, 1960. [Resurrection, Ascension, Session at the Right Hand of God, See. 195–96]

Livingston, James C. *Modern Christian Thought: From the Enlightenment to Vatican II.* New York: Macmillan, 1971. [See. 154, 185, 378–79]

Lockyer, Herbert. *All the Doctrines of the Bible: A Study and Analysis of Major Bible Doctrines.* Marshall Pickering (HarperCollins), 1991. [His Resurrection, See. 53–54; His Ascension, See. 54–56]

Lodahl, Michael. *The Story of God: Wesleyan Theology and Biblical Narrative.* Kansas City: Beacon Hill, 1994. [Chapter 19 Jesus Christ, Resurrected One, See. 153–57]

Lohse, Bernhard. *A Short History of Christian Doctrine.* Translated by F. Ernest Stoeffler. Philadelphia: Fortress, 1966. [See. 9, 25, 39, 72, 80]

Long, Abram M. *Pillars of the Christian Faith.* New York: Revell, 1947. [Chapter 6 Christ The Risen Redeemer, See. 147–61]

Lord, Willis. *Christian Theology for the People.* New York: R. Carter, 1875. [The Resurrection of Christ, See. 308–13; N.B. Google book]

Lowrey, Asbury. *Positive Theology: Being a Series of Dissertations on the Fundamental Doctrines of the Bible.* Cincinnati: Methodist Book Concern, 1853. [Dissertation 10 The Fact and Results of the Resurrection of Christ, See. 139–50; Dissertation 11 The Fact and Objects of Our Lord's Ascension, See. 151–67; N.B. Archive.org and Google book]

Ludow, William L. *What It Means To Be A Christian.* Norwell, MA: Christopher Pub. House, 1988. [Chapter 7 The Resurrection of Jesus Christ, See. 39–42]

MacArthur, John, and Richard Mayhue, eds. *Biblical Doctrine: A Systematic Summary of Bible Truth.* Wheaton: Crossway, 2017. [Resurrection and Ascension, See. 315–21]

Mackenzie, W. Douglas. *The Final Faith: A Statement of the Nature and Authority of Christianity as the Religion of the World.* New York: Macmillan, 1910. [The Cross and the Resurrection, See. 43–45; N.B. Google book]

Mackey, James P. *Modern Theology: A Sense of Direction.* Oxford: Oxford University Press, 1987. [The resurrection of Jesus, See. 66–74; Eucharist, See. 75–79, 81–83]

MacPherson, John. *Christian Dogmatics.* Edinburgh: T&T Clark, 1898. [Part 3 The Doctrine of Redemption. §53. State of Exaltation, See. 326–27; N.B. Archive.org]

Macquarrie, John. *Principles of Christian Theology.* 2nd ed. New York: Scribner's Sons, 1977. [Chapter 12 The Person of Jesus Christ. See. 286, 289–303, 305]

Manley, Basil. *The Bible Doctrine of Inspiration Explained and Vindicated.* New York: A. C. Armstrong, 1888. [See. 156–58; N.B. Archive.org, Google book, and HathiTrust]

Mansini, Guy. "What Is A Dogma?" *The Meaning and Truth of Dogma in Edouard Le Roy and His Scholastic Opponents.* Rome: Pontifica Università Gregoria, 1985. [Dogma as Material for Speculation (e.g., the Resurrection), See. 193–99]

Markham, Ian S. *Understanding Christian Doctrine.* Malden: Blackwell, 2008. [The Resurrection of Jesus, See. 199–200]

Marsh, Herbert. *A Course of Lectures Containing a Description and Systematic Arrangement of the Several Branches of Divinity.* Vol. 1. Cambridge: William Hilliard, 1812. [See. 22, 25–26, 38, 56, 63; N.B. Archive.org and Google book]

Martensen, Hans. *Christian Dogmatics: A Compendium of the Doctrines of Christianity.* Translated by W. Urwick. Edinburgh: T&T Clark, 1898. [Part 4 The Doctrine of the Son. §172 On the Third Day the King Rose from the Dead, See. 318–21; §173 The Ascension of the Lord, See. 321–22; N.B. Archive.org and HathiTrust]

Martin, Walter. *Essential Christianity: A Handbook of Basic Christian Doctrines.* Grand Rapids: Zondervan, 1962. [Chapter 5 The Gospel of Resurrection, See. 55–61]

Mascall, E. L. *The Secularization of Christianity: An Analysis and a Critique.* New York: Holt, Rinehart & Winston, 1965. [Chapter 5 Facts of the Gospels. Part 7, See. 266–82]

Mason, Arthur James. *The Faith of the Gospel: A Manual of Christian Doctrine.* London: Longman, Green, 1894. [Chapter 7 The Risen Lord and the Gift of the Spirit. (2) His Resurrection, See. 213–16; (3) His Ascension, See. 216; N.B. Archive.org and HathiTrust]

Mathews, Shailer. *The Faith of Modernism.* New York: Macmillan, 1924. [The Resurrection of Jesus, See. 152–55; N.B. HathiTrust]

Matthews, W. R. *God and This Troubled World: Essays in Spiritual Construction.* New York: E. P. Dutton, 1934. [Chapter 20 The Truth of the Resurrection, See. 223–29]

Maurice, Frederick Denison. *Theological Essays.* 2nd ed. Cambridge: Macmillan, 1853. [Essay 8 The Resurrection of the Son of God From Death, the Grave, and Hell, See. 152–88; Essay 11 On the Ascension of Christ, See. 254–86; N.B. Archive.org]

May, Melanie A. *A Body Knows: A Theopoetics of Death and Resurrection*. New York: Continuum, 1995. [Resurrection of Jesus. See. 37–38, 39]

McCarty, W. A., and T. R. McCarty. *Doctrines for the Times*. Atlanta: Foote & Davies, 1895. [Chapter 3 The Resurrection, See. 31–45]

McClendon, James William. *Systematic Theology: Doctrine*. Vol. 2. Nashville: Abingdon, 1994. [Chapter 6 Jesus the Risen Christ, See. 238–79; N.B. This is an interesting work to read.]

———. *Systematic Theology: Ethics*. 2nd ed. Vol. 1. Nashville: Abingdon, 2002. [Resurrection Ethics, See. 245–77]

McCrossan, Thomas J. *The Bible: Its Christ and Modernism*. Seattle, WA: T. J. McCrossan, 1929. [The Physical Resurrection of our Lord, See. 121–31]

McDowell, John. *Theology: In a Series of Sermons in the Order of the Westminster Shorter Catechism*. Vol. 1. Elizabeth-town: Mervin Hale, 1825. [Sermon 37 The Resurrection of Christ, See. 351–62; Sermon 38 The Ascension and Session of Christ, See. 362–69; N.B. Google book; In the book the author's name is spelled M'Dowell.]

McDowell, Josh, and Sean McDowell. *The Unshakable Truth*. Eugene: OR: Harvest House, 2010. [Truth Eight: Jesus' Bodily Resurrection, See. 277–96; N.B. This work refutes several alternative theories.]

McGiffert, Arthur Cushman. *A History of Christian Thought: From Jesus to John of Damascus*. Vol. 1. New York: Scribner's Sons, 1932. [See. 10–11, 13, 20, 22, 39, 94, 107, 118, 136]

McGrath, Alister E. *Christian Theology: An Introduction*. 2nd ed. Malden, MA: Blackwell, 2007. [Chapter 10 Faith and History: A New Histological Agenda, See. 376–85]

———. *Studies in Doctrine*. Grand Rapids: Zondervan, 1997. [Chapter 4 The Resurrection Event, See. 44–55]

———. *Theology: The Basics*. Malden, MA: Blackwell, 2004. [Resurrection of Christ. See. 53, 78, 79, 98, 99, 100, 135]

McGrath, Alister E., and J. I. Packer, eds. *Zondervan Handbook of Christian Beliefs*. Grand Rapids: Zondervan, 2005. [The Resurrection and Kingship of Jesus, See. 156–58; Did Jesus Really Rise From the Dead? etc., See. 266–85; also See. How Muslims See Jesus, 165–66]

McInerny, Ralph M. *Miracles: A Catholic View*. Huntington, IN: Our Sunday Visitor, 1986. [The Resurrection, See. 57–59]

McKown, Edgar Monroe, and Carl J. Scherzer. *Understanding Christianity: A Study of Our Christian Heritage*. New York: Ronald Press, 1949. [See. 27, 28, 84, 112]

Mellenbruch, Parl Leslie. *The Doctrines of Christianity: A Handbook of Evangelical Theology*. New York: Revell, 1931. [Chapter 5 The Preparation of Redemption 1. 2. (2) Exaltation, See. 79–84]

Memes, T. S., ed. *The Christian Treasury: A Selection of Standard Treatises on Subjects of Doctrinal and Practical Christianity: Containing Magee's Discourses and Dissertations on the Scriptural Doctrines of Atonement and Sacrifice; Witherspoon's Practical Treatise on Regeneration; Boston's Crook in the Lot; Stuart's Letters on the Divinity of Christ ; Guild's Moses Unveiled ; Guild's Harmony of All the Prophets ; Less's Authenticity, Uncorrupted Preservation, and Credibility of the New Testament*. London: Henry G. Bohn, 1844. [See. 10, 36, 54, 58, 61, 212, 213, 225, 231; N.B. Archive.org and Google book]

Micklem, Nathaniel. *The Creed of a Christian: Being Monologues Upon Great Themes of the Christian Faith*. London: Student Christian Movement Press, 1940. [Chapter 8 He Is Risen, See. 74–81]

———. *Faith and Reason*. London: Duckworth, 1963. [Resurrection, See. 86–89]

———. *What Is the Faith!* London: Hodder & Stoughton, 1936. [Chapter 9 The Resurrection, See. 170–87]

Micks, Marianne H. *Introduction To Theology*. New York: Seabury, 1964. [Chapter 3 From Resurrection to Incarnation, See. 30–42]

Migliore, Daniel L. *Faith Seeking Understanding: An Introduction to Christian Theology*. 2nd ed. Grand Rapids: Eerdmans, 2004. [Chapter 8 The Person and Work of Jesus Christ. Dimensions of the Resurrection of Christ, See. 191–96; Appendix B: The Resurrection: A Dialogue, See. 370–83]

Miley, John. *Systematic Theology*. Vol. 2. New York: Hunt & Eaton, 1894. [Part 6 Eschatology. Chapter 4 The Resurrection, See. 448–57; N.B. Archive.org]

Milne, Bruce. *Know the Truth: A Handbook of Christian Belief*. 3rd ed. Downers Grove, IL: InterVarsity, 1999. [Post-Resurrection, See. 176–77; Other Gospel Evidence: the Resurrection, See. 181–87]

Ministerial Association, General Conference of Seventh-day Adventists. *Seventh-day Adventists Believe: A Biblical Exposition of 27 Fundamental Doctrines*. Washington, DC: Ministerial Association, General Conference of Seventh-day Adventists, 1988. [Resurrection, Christ's, See. 115, 356, 357]

Mitchell, Thomas. *The Gospel Crown of Life: A System of Philosophical Theology*. Albany: J. Munsell, Printer, 1851. [Chapter 1 The Resurrection of the Dead, See. 12–15; N.B. Google book and HathiTrust]

Mohler, J. S. *The Resurrection*. Elgin, IL: Brethren Publishing House, 1901. [128 pages; N.B. Google book]

Monfort, F. C. *Applied Theology*. Cincinnati: Monfort, 1904. [The Risen Savior, See. 103–6; N.B. Archive.org]

Montgomery, John Warwick. *The Suicide of Christian Theology*. Minneapolis: Bethany Fellowship, 1970. [See. 76–174]

Moody, Dale. *The Word of Truth: A Summary of Christian Doctrine Based on Biblical Revelation*. Grand Rapids: Eerdmans, 1981. [He Rose Again on the Third Day, See. 388–91; He Ascended into Heaven, See. 391]

Moore, Daniel F. *Jesus, an Emerging Jewish Mosaic Jewish Perspectives, Post-Holocaust*. New York: T&T Clark, 2008. [Resurrection of, See. 179–83, 218–20; N.B. Moore interacts with Rabbi Pinchas Lapide regarding Jesus's resurrection.]

Morse, Christopher. *Not Every Spirit: A Dogmatics of Christian Disbelief*. Valley Forge, PA: Trinity Press International, 1994. [The Resurrection, See. 155–61]

Moss, Claude Beaufort. *The Christian Faith: An Introduction to Dogmatic Theology*. London: Society for Promoting Christian Knowledge, 1944. [Chapter 20 The Resurrection of Our Lord, 115–20; Chapter 21 The Doctrine of the Resurrection, See. 120–23; Chapter 22 The Ascension and Heavenly Session, See. 123–25]

Moule, H. C. G. *Outlines of Christian Doctrine*. New York: Thomas Whittaker, 1923. [Chapter 6 The Resurrection, Ascension, Session, and Return, See. 99–104; N.B. Google book and HathiTrust]

Mueller, David L. *Foundation of Karl Barth's Doctrine of Reconciliation: Jesus Christ Crucified and Risen*. Lewiston, NY: Mellen, 1990. [See. 88–103; 145–51; 336–67]

Mueller, John Theodore. *Christian Dogmatics; A Handbook of Doctrinal Theology for Pastors, Teachers, and Laymen.* St. Louis: Concordia, 1934. [The State of Exaltation, See. 295–96; The Several Stages of Christ's Exaltation, See. 296–301]

Mullins, Edgar Young. *The Christian Religion in Its Doctrinal Expression.* Philadelphia: Roger Williams Press, 1917. [Chapter 17 Last things. See. (3) Resurrection of Christ an apocalyptic stage, See. 450; also See 45–46, 149, 160, 169, 261, 272; N.B. Google book]

———. *Christianity at the Cross Roads.* New York: George H. Doran, 1924. [See. 29, 192]

Musser, Donald W., and Joseph L. Price, eds. *A New Handbook of Christian Theology.* Nashville: Abingdon, 1992. [Resurrection. See. 402–8 (Eduard Schweizer)]

Nash, Ronald H. *Faith & Reason: Searching for a Rational Faith.* Grand Rapids: Academie, 1988. [Chapter 19 Two Indispensable Miracles ... The Resurrection, See. 266–72]

Neander, Johann August Wilhelm. *Lectures on the History of Christian Dogmas.* Translated by J. E. Ryland. Vol. 2. London: Henry G. Bohn, 1858. [See. 168, 205, 213, 326, 339, 440, 459, 469, 651; N.B. Google book]

Nelson's Introduction to Christian Faith. Nashville: Thomas Nelson, 1992. [See. 77–81]

Newlands, George. *God in Christian Perspective.* Edinburgh: T&T Clark, 1994. [Chapter 20 Death and Resurrection, 270–81]

Nichol, C. R., and Robertson L. Whiteside. *Sound Doctrine: A Series of Bible Studies For Sunday School Classes, Prayer Meetings, Private Study, College Classes, etc.* Vol. 1. Clifton, TX: Mrs. C. R. Nichol, 1920. [The Great Commission, See. 97–107; N.B. Google book]

Nichol, Francis D. *Answers to Objections: An Examination of the Major Objections Raised Against the Teachings of Seventh-Day Adventists.* Washington, DC: Review & Herald, 1952. [Objection 45. See. 230–31]

Nicholls, William. *Systematic and Philosophical Theology.* Harmondsworth, England: Penguin, 1969. [See. 341–46]

Noebel, David A. *Understanding the Times: The Collision of Today's Competing Worldviews.* 2nd ed. Manitou Springs, CO: Summit Ministries, 2006. [5.2.10 Rejection of Jesus as Savior, See. 224; 10.1.4 Resurrection and History, See. 393–95; 11.2.9 Jesus Ascended Bodily Into Heaven and Muhammad Did Not, See. 435–36]

Noort, G. van. *Dogmatic Theology.* Vol. I. *The True Religion.* Translated and revised by John J. Castelot and William R. Murphy. Westminster: Newman Press, 1955. [Article 4 Christ's Resurrection Proves His Divine Mission, See. 165–87]

Norris, Richard A. *Understanding the Faith of the Church.* San Francisco: HarperSanFrancisco, 1979. [Chapter 6 Died ... Rose ... Ascended, See. 125–41]

Nunn, Henry Preston Vaughan. *What Is Modernism?* London: SPCK, 1932. [The Resurrection, See. 67–124]

Oden, Thomas C. *After Modernity ... What? Agenda for Theology.* Grand Rapids: Zondervan, 1990 [Chapter 9 Resurrection: Christ's and Ours, See. 133–38]

———. *Agenda for Theology.* San Francisco: Harper & Row, 1979. [Resurrection, See. 123–27]

———. *Classic Christianity: A Systematic Theology.* New York: HarperOne, 2009. [The Risen Lord, See. 457–81; Ascension and Session, See. 483–500]

———. *Systematic Theology: The Word of Life.* Vol. 2. Peabody, MA: Hendrickson, 1989. [The Risen Lord, See. 451–501; idem. 2006]

Ogden, Schubert Miles. *The Reality of God, and Other Essays.* New York: Harper & Row, 1966. [See. 109, 202, 217–18]

Oosterzee, Johannes Jacobus van. *Christian Dogmatics: A Text Book for Academical Instruction and Private Study*. Translated by John Watson and Maurice J. Evans. Vol. 2. New York: Scribner, Armstrong, 1874. [Section 105 The Resurrection, See. 563–71; Section 106 The Exaltation to Heaven, See. 571–76; N.B. Archive.org and HathiTrust. This book is a good, dated source.]

Orchard, W. E. *Foundations of Faith*. 2. *Christological*. London: Doran, 1925. [Chapter 7 The Resurrection, See. 97–112]

Orr, James. *The Christian View of God and the World: As Centring in the Incarnation*. 8th ed. Edinburgh: Andrew Elliot, 1907. [Lecture 6 The Resurrection of Christ and the Reality of His Divine Claim, See. 453–55; N.B. Archive.org]

Ottati, Douglas F. *Hopeful Realism: Reclaiming the Poetry of Theology*. Cleveland: Pilgrim Press, 1999. [Meaning and Mystery of Resurrection, See. 51–68]

Otto, Randall E. *Coming in the Clouds: An Evangelical Case for the Invisibility of Christ at His Second Coming*. Lanham, MD: University Press of America, 1994. [The Resurrection of Christ, See. 238–48; The Ascension, See. 249–58]

Owen, Robert. *A Treatise of Dogmatic Theology*. 2nd ed. London: J. T. Hayes, 1887. [Chapter 16 Of Christ's Descent Into Hell, Of His Resurrection, and Ascension, See. 289–94; N.B. Archive.org and Google book]

Packer, J. I. *Concise Theology: A Guide to Historic Christian Beliefs*. Carol Stream, IL: Tyndale House, 1993. [Resurrection, See. 125–26; Ascension See. 127–28]

Palmer, Albert W. *The Light of Faith: An Outline of Religious Thought for Laymen*. New York: Macmillan, 1946. [Chapter 6 Three Possible Views of the Resurrection, See. 61–72]

Pannenberg, Wolfhart. *Systematic Theology*. Translated by Geoffrey W. Bromiley. Vol. 1. Grand Rapids: Eerdmans, 1991. [See. 211, 264–65, 306–8, 314–15, 442]

———. *Systematic Theology*. Translated by Geoffrey W. Bromiley. Vol. 3. Grand Rapids: Eerdmans, 1998. [Resurrection of Jesus Christ, See. 10–11, 144–45, 200, 241–42, 258, 261, 274, 277, 281–82, 306, 323, 347, 474, 533]

Pardington, George P. *Outline Studies in Christian Doctrine*. Harrisburg, PA: Christian Publications, 1926. [The Exaltation of Christ, See. 244–47]

Parks, Leighton. *What Is Modernism?* New York: Scribner's Sons, 1924. [The Resurrection of Jesus, See. 40–47]

Passmore, William. *A Compendium of Evangelical Theology, Given in the Words of Holy Scripture*. New York: A. D. F. Randolph, 1873. [See. 410–19; N.B. Archive.org and Google book]

Patton, Francis Landey. *Fundamental Christianity*. New York: Macmillan, 1926. [Chapter 4 The Person of Christ, See. 233–41]

Peake, Arthur S. *Christianity: Its Nature and Its Truth*. New York: Thomas Y. Crowell, 1908. [Chapter 12 The Resurrection of Jesus, See. 192–208; N.B. Archive.org]

Pelikan, Jaroslav. *The Christian Tradition: A History of the Development of Doctrine*. Vol.1, *The Emergence of the Catholic Tradition: (100–600)*. Chicago: University of Chicago Press, 1971. [See. 30, 47–48, 149–52]

———. *The Christian Tradition: A History of the Development of Doctrine*. Vol 3, *The Growth of Medieval Theology (600–1300)*. Chicago: University of Chicago Press, 1978. [See. 75, 132–34, 152–54, 192, 193–94, 302]

———. *The Christian Tradition: A History of the Development of Doctrine*. Vol. 2, *The Spirit of Eastern Christendom (600–1700)*. Chicago: University of Chicago Press, 1974. [See. 61, 138–39, 225, 257]

Doctrines, Dogmatics, and Systematic Theology

Percival, Henry R. *A Digest of Theology Being a Brief Statement of Christian Doctrine According to the Consensus of the Great Theologians of the One, Holy, Catholic and Apostolic Church: Together with an Appendix Containing, among Other Things, in English, the Doctrinal Decrees of the Ecumenical Synods*. Philadelphia: J. J. McVey, 1893. [Book 2 Of the Incarnation of the World 3. Of the Resurrection of Christ, See. 87–88; 5. Of the Ascension of Our Lord, and of His Session at the Right Hand of the Father, See. 89–90; N.B. Google book and HathiTrust]

Peters, Ted. *God—The World's Future: Systematic Theology for a New Era*. 3rd ed. Minneapolis: Fortress, 2015. [The Significance of the Resurrection, See. 367–73; The Historicity of the Resurrection, See. 373–78; also See 36, 86–88, 91, 93–94, 245, 272, 282, 294, 347, 388, 425, 435, 480, 484, 487, 496, 525, 535, 552–54, 589n71, 602–3, 608, 612, 626, 686]

Phillips, J. B. *Your God Is Too Small*. New York: Macmillan, 1969. [Chapter 13 Demonstration with the Enemy, 2. If the Resurrection did not happen, who was Christ?, See. 125–28]

Pictet, Benedict. *Christian Theology*. Translated by Frederick Reyroux. London: R. B. Seeley & W. Burnside, 1834. [Book 6 Chapter 12 Of the Resurrection and Ascension of Christ, See. 302–9; N.B. Google book]

Pieper, Francis. *Christian Dogmatics*. Vol. 2. Saint Louis: Concordia, 1951. [The Several Stages of Christ's Humiliation and Exaltation, See. 323–30]

Pinnock, Clark H. *Tracking the Maze: Finding Our Way Through Modern Theology From An Evangelical Perspective*. San Francisco: Harper & Row, 1990. [The Resurrection of Christ, See. 202–3]

Pohier, Jacques Marie. *God—In Fragments*. New York: Crossroad, 1986. [The resurrection of Christ makes him pass into the transcendence of God, See. 49–52]

Pohle, Joseph. *Soteriology; A Dogmatic Treatise on the Redemption*. Edited by Arthur Preuss. 3rd ed. St. Louis: Herder, 1919. [The Resurrection, See. 101–9; N.B. Archive.org]

Polkinghorne, John C. *The God of Hope and the End of the World*. New Haven: Yale University Press, 2002. [Chapter 6 The Resurrection of Jesus, See. 66–78]

Polkinghorne, John C., and Nicholas Beale. *Questions of Truth: Fifty-one Responses to Questions About God, Science, and Belief*. Louisville: Westminster John Knox, 2009. [Chapter 47 Why Believe Jesus Rose from the Dead?, See. 88–89]

Polkinghorne, John C., and Michael Welker. *Faith in the Living God: A Dialogue*. Minneapolis: Fortress, 2001. [Chapter 3 Faith in Christ (by) John Polkinghorne. See. The Resurrection, See. 46–48]

Pope, William Burt. *A Compendium of Christian Theology: Being Analytical Outlines of a Course of Theological Study, Biblical, Dogmatic, Historical*. 2nd ed. Vol. 2. New York: Phillips & Hunt, 1882. [The State of Exaltation, See. 166–84; N.B. Google book]

Porteous, Alvin C. *Prophetic Voices in Contemporary Theology: The Theological Renaissance and the Renewal of the Church*. Nashville: Abingdon, 1966. [See. 90–91]

Portier, William L. *Tradition and Incarnation: Foundations of Christian Theology*. New York: Paulist, 1994. [Chapter 14 Resurrection, See. 326–58]

Powers, Joseph M. *Spirit and Sacrament: The Humanizing Experience*. New York: Seabury, 1973. [The Risen Lord, See. 63–84]

Prenter, Regin. *Creation and Redemption*. Translated by Theodor I. Jensen. Philadelphia: Fortress, 1967. [The Resurrection, See. 424–29]

Prozesky, Martin. *A New Guide to the Debate About God*. London: SCM, 1992. [Resurrection of Christ, See. 36–42, 124-26, 162, 164–65.]

Purkiser, W. T., ed. *Exploring Our Christian Faith*. Kansas City: Beacon Hill, 1960. [Jesus' Burial and Resurrection, See. 169–70; The Ascension, See. 170–71]

Quick, Oliver Chase. *Doctrines of the Creed: Their Basis in Scripture and Their Meaning Today*. New York: Scribner's Sons, 1960. [The Different Presuppositions of the Believer and of the Critic, See. 146–50]

Rae, Murray. *Christian Theology: The Basics*. London: Routledge, 2015. [Resurrection, See. 110–12]

Rahner, Karl. *Foundations of Christian Faith: An Introduction to the Idea of Christianity*. Translated by William V. Dych. New York: Seabury, 1978. [Chapter 6 The Theology of the Death and the Resurrection of Jesus, See. 264–72]

Ralston, Thomas N. *Elements of Divinity, or, A Concise and Comprehensive View of Bible Theology Comprising the Doctrines, Evidences, Morals, and Institutions of Christianity: With Appropriate Questions Appended to Each Chapter*. Vol. 2. Cincinnati: Hitchcock & Walden, 1878. [Chapter 13 Miracles of the New Testament, See. 637–45; N.B. HathiTrust. The author claims that sixty soldiers watched the tomb.]

Ramm, Bernard L. *A Handbook of Contemporary Theology*. Grand Rapids: Eerdmans, 1974. [Resurrection of Christ, See. 105–7]

Ramsey, Michael. *To Believe Is To Pray: Readings From Michael Ramsey*. Edited by James E. Griffiss. Cambridge, MA: Cowley, 1996. [Chapter 6 The Resurrection, See. 94–109]

Raymond, Bradford Paul. *Christianity and the Christ: A Study of Christian Evidences*. New York: Hunt & Eaton, 1894. [Chapter 6 Christ and the Resurrection, See. 125–44; N.B. Google book and HathiTrust. The author interacts with Reimarus and Renan.]

Raymond, Miner. *Systematic Theology*. Vol. 1. Cincinnati: Hitchcock & Walden, 1877. [Apologetics 2. Argument First-Miracles, See. 82–100; N.B. Google book and HathiTrust]

———. *Systematic Theology*. Vol. 2. Cincinnati: Hitchcock & Walden, 1877. [Resurrection, See. 457–66; N.B. Google book and HathiTrust]

Rhein, Francis Bayard. *Understanding the New Testament*. Woodbury, NY: Barron's Educational Series, 1974. [The Resurrection, See. 141–44]

Rice, Richard. *The Reign of God: An Introduction to Christian Theology From a Seventh-day Adventist Perspective*. 2nd edition. Berrien Springs, MI: Andrews University Press, 1997. [Jesus' Resurrection, See. 168–72]

Richardson, Alan. *The Gospel and Modern Thought*. London: Oxford University Press, 1950. [Did Jesus Really Rise from the Dead?, See. 55–64]

Richardson, Robert D. *The Gospel of Modernism*. London: Skeffington, 1935. [The Life of Jesus . . . See. 145–47; Appendix 2 The Resurrection of Jesus, See. 247–72]

Richey, Thomas. *Truth and Counter Truth*. New York: Potts & Amery, 1869. [Essay 7 The Death and Resurrection of Christ: Reconciliation and Justification, See. 73–84; N.B. Archive.org]

Ridgeley, Thomas. *A Body of Divinity Wherein the Doctrines of the Christian Religion Are Explained and Defended*. Vol. 1. Revised and corrected by John M. Wilson. New York: Robert Carter, 1855. [Questions 53, 54 Christ's Exaltation In and After His Ascension, See. 606–23; N.B. Archive.org, Google book, and HathiTrust; This dated source is worth examining.]

Robinson, Godfrey Clive, and Stephen F. Winward. *Here Is The Answer*. Valley Forge: Judson Press, 1970. [Chapter 7 Did Jesus Rise from the Dead?, See. 46–50]

Robinson, John A. T. *But That I Can't Believe!* New York: New American Library, 1967. [Chapter 7 The Resurrection, See. 57–60]

Robinson, Thomas. *The Christian System: Unfolded in a Course of Practical Essays on the Principal Doctrines and Duties of Christianity*. London: Printed for the Author. 1805. [Essay 30 On The Resurrection and Intercession of Christ, See. 424–37; N.B. Archive.org and Google book]

Ross, C. Randolph. *Common Sense Christianity*. Cortland, NY: Occam, 1989. [Chapter 6 The Resurrection: Historically Probable, Religiously Insignificant, See. 67–76]

Rota, Michael. *Taking Pascal's Wager: Faith, Evidence, and the Abundant Life*. Downers Grove, IL: InterVarsity, 2016. [Chapter 11 Historical Evidence For Christianity: The Resurrection, See. 154–64; N.B. This work is a short, concise read.]

Russell, C. Allyn. *Voices of American Fundamentalism: Seven Biographical Studies*. Philadelphia: Westminster, 1976. [See. 16, 85, 98, 140, 145, 170, 180, 198, 213]

Ryrie, Charles Caldwell. *Basic Theology: A Popular Systemic Guide to Understanding Biblical Truth*. Chicago: Moody, 1999. [Chapter 46 The Resurrection and Ascension of Christ, See. 308–12]

Sailhamer, John H. *Christian Theology*. Grand Rapids: Zondervan, 1998. [The Person of Christ: His Exaltation, See. 59]

Samples, Kenneth R. *Without a Doubt: Answering the 20 Toughest Faith Questions*. Grand Rapids: Baker, 2004. [Chapter 10 Did Jesus Christ Actually Rise from the Dead?, See. 134–47]

Sarrels, Elder R. V. *Systematic Theology*. Azle, TX: Harmony Hill, a Primitive Baptist Foundation, 1978. [The State of Exaltation, See. 248–52]

Schilling, S. Paul. *Contemporary Continental Theologians*. Nashville: Abingdon, 1966. [See. 86–87, 131]

Schleiermacher, Friedrich, and James S. Stewart. *The Christian Faith*. Edited by H. R. Mackintosh. Philadelphia: Fortress, 1928. [The Facts of the Resurrection and the Ascension of Christ, and the Prediction of His Return to Judgment Cannot be Laid Down as Properly Constituent Parts of the Doctrine of His Person, See. 417–24]

Schmaus, Michael. *Dogma: 3, God and His Christ*. Sheed & Ward, Kansas City, 1971. [Chapter 3 The Salvific Activity of Jesus . . . Risen or Raised?, See. 60–61; Resurrection and Ascension, See. 61–66]

Schmid, Heinrich. *The Doctrinal Theology of the Evangelical Lutheran Church*. Translated by Charles A. Hay and Henry E. Jacobs. 5th ed. Philadelphia: Lutheran Publication Society, 1876. [See. 396–98, 417–20; N.B. Archive.org and Google book]

Schultze, Augustus. *Christian Doctrine and Systematic Theology*. 2nd ed. Bethlehem, PA: Bethlehem Printing Company, 1914. [Chapter 23 The State of Exaltation, See. 126–30; N.B. Archive.org and Google book]

Schwarz, Hans. *Responsible Faith: Christian Theology in the Light of 20th-century Questions*. Minneapolis: Augsburg, 1986. [Resurrection of Jesus Christ, See. 38, 48, 122, 177, 179, 180, 183, 205, 208–14, 221, 244, 248, 254, 257–58, 278–82, 381–85]

Scott, John. *The Works of the Learned and Reverend John Scott, D.D., Sometime Rector of St. Giles's in the Fields*. Vol. 3. Oxford: Clarendon, 1826. [Christ proved the Mediator, See. 265–306; N.B. Google book. The author emphasizes that the testimony was highly credible.]

Seaton, Thomas. *A Compendious View of the Grounds of Religion Both Natural and Revealed in Two Dissertations.* London: Printed for J&J Knapton, 1729. [See. 23–33; N.B. Google book]

Selwyn, Edward Gordon. *The Approach to Christianity.* New York: Longmans, Green, 1925 [Chapter 6 The Risen and Ascended Lord, See. 190–219]

Shaw, A. R. *Theology for the People.* Richmond, VA: Whittet & Shepperson, 1902. [Chapter 7 See. 101–10; N.B. Archive.org]

Shaw, John Mackintosh. *Christian Doctrine: A One-Volume Outline of Christian Belief.* New York: Philosophical Library, 1954. [Resurrection of Jesus, See. 221, 224, 317, 324 n.]

Shedd, William G. T. *Dogmatic Theology.* Vol. 1. New York: Scribner's Sons, 1888. [Chapter 3 Credibility of the Scriptures. See. 121–22; N.B. Google book and HathiTrust]

———. *Dogmatic Theology.* Vol. 2. New York: Scribner's Sons, 1888. [Chapter 3 The Resurrection, See. 647–58; N.B. Archive.org and HathiTrust]

Sheldon, Henry C. *System of Christian Doctrine.* New York: Methodist Book Concern, 1886. [Appendix 1 The Miracle of Christ's Resurrection, See. 581–90; N.B. Archive.org, Google book, and HathiTrust]

Simpson, A. B. *The Cross of Christ.* Brooklyn, NY: Christian Alliance, 1910. [Chapters 7–10, See. 91–157; N.B. Google book and HathiTrust. This is a recommended, dated source.]

Singmaster, J. A. *A Handbook of Christian Theology.* Philadelphia: United Lutheran Publication House, 1927. [The State of Exaltation, See. 200–206]

Sire, James W. *Why Good Arguments Often Fail Making A More Persuasive Case For Christ.* Downers Grove, IL: InterVarsity, 2006. [See. 159–60]

Smart, James D. *The ABC's of Christian Faith.* Philadelphia: Westminster, 1968. [Chapter 6 Resurrection, See. 44–49]

Smith, James. *Essays on the First Principles of Christianity: On the Proper Method of Establishing Sound Doctrine from the Sacred Oracles; and on the Difference Senses of Scriptural Terms.* London: R. Ogle, 1808. [Essay 11 Christ's Resurrection—Important Facts Admitted—The Witnesses, etc., See. 217–49; N.B. Google book]

Smith, Samuel Stanhope. *A Comprehensive View of the Leading and Most Important Principles of Natural and Revealed Religion: Digested in Such Order as to Present to the Pious and Reflecting Mind, a Basis for the Superstructure of the Entire System of the Doctrines of the Gospel.* New Brunswick: Deare & Myer, 1816. [The Credibility of the Witnesses of the Miracles and Resurrection of Christ, See. 89–99; N.B. Archive.org, Google book, and HathiTrust. The author emphasizes the credibility of the witnesses.]

Smyth, Julian Kennedy. *Christian Certainties Of Belief; The Christ, The Bible, Salvation, Immortality.* New York: New-Church Press, 1916. [See. 107–10; N.B. Google book]

Snowden, James Henry. *The Basal Beliefs of Christianity.* New York: Macmillan, 1911. [Chapter 20 The Resurrection of Christ, See. 133–42; N.B. Google book, and HathiTrust]

———. *What Do Present Day Christians Believe?* New York: Macmillan, 1930. [Chapter 65 Why Do We Believe in the Resurrection of Jesus?, See. 225–29; Chapter 66 What Is the Great Commission of Jesus?, See. 229–32; Chapter 67 What Was the Ascension of Jesus, See. 233–36]

Somerset, Edward Adolphus. *Christian Theology and Modern Scepticism.* London: James Bain, 1872. [See. 36, 44, 121; N.B. Archive.org, Google book, and HathiTrust]

Song, Choan-Seng. *Tracing The Footsteps of God: Discovering What You Really Believe*. Minneapolis: 2007. [Chapter 2 Did Jesus Rise from the Dead and Does It Matter?, See. 25–37]

Sproul, R. C. *Basic Training, Plain Talk on the Key Truths of the Faith*. Grand Rapids: Zondervan, 1982. [Chapter 8 On the Third Day He Rose Again From the Dead, See. 110–19]

———. *Essential Truths of the Christian Faith*. Wheaton, IL: Tyndale House, 1992. [Chapter 33 The Ascension of Christ, See. 95–97]

———. *Renewing Your Mind: Basic Christian Beliefs You Need To Know*. Grand Rapids: Baker, 1998. [Chapter 8 Grave with a View, 129–40; Chapter 9 There for Us, See. 141–52]

———. *What We Believe: Understanding and Confessing the Apostles' Creed*. Grand Rapids: Baker, 2015. [Chapter 8 Grave with a View, See. 133–44; Chapter 9 There for Us, See. 145–58; Previous edition published in 1998 as *Renewing Your Mind*]

Sproull, Thomas. *Prelections on Theology*. Pittsburgh: Myers, Shinkle, 1882. [Prelection 17 The Exaltation of Christ, See. 200–12]

Spurrier, William A. *Guide to the Christian Faith: An Introduction to Christian Doctrine*. New York: Scribner's Sons, 1952. [Chapter 8 Doctrine of the Resurrection, See. 136–51]

Stacey, John. *Groundwork of Theology*. London: Epworth, 1987. [Chapter 6 The Death and Resurrection of Jesus Christ, See. 146–58]

Stackhouse, John G. *Can God Be Trusted? Faith and the Challenge of Evil*. New York: Oxford University Press, 1998. [See. 142–46]

Stafford, T. P. *A Study of Christian Doctrines*. Kansas City, MO: Western Baptist, 1936. [Chapter 40 The Resurrection, See. 587–606]

Stanfield, James Monroe. *Corner Stones of Faith: Being the Witness of the Bible Brought to Bear on the Vital Questions of the Christian Religion*. Grand Rapids: Eerdmans, 1938. [The Resurrection, See. 166; Jesus the Resurrection and the Life, See. 198–208]

Stearns, Lewis French, and George Lewis. Prentiss. *Present Day Theology: A Popular Discussion of Leading Doctrines of the Christian Faith with a Biographical Sketch by G. L. Prentiss*. New York: Scribner's Sons, 1893. [See. 95, 138, 143–45, 383, 409; N.B. Google book and HathiTrust]

Steinmann, Jean. *A Christian Faith For Today*. Translated by Edmond Bonin. Paramus, NJ: Newman Press, 1969. [Jesus' Resurrection, See. 43–46]

Stevens, William Wilson. *Doctrines of the Christian Religion*. Grand Rapids: Eerdmans, 1967. [The Resurrection of Christ, 192–96]

Stillingfleet, Edward. *Origines Sacrae: or, a Rational Account of the Grounds of the Christian Faith as to the Truth and Divine Authority of the Scriptures*. Cambridge: Printed at the University-Press, for Henry Mortlock, 1701. [Book 2 Chapter 9 The Rational Evidence of the Truth of the Christian Religion from Miracles, See. 13. The Apostles Evidence of the Truth of their Doctrine Lay in Being Eye-witnesses of our Savior's Miracles and Resurrection, See. 189–204; N.B. Google book]

Stone, Darwell. *Outlines of Christian Dogma*. London: Longmans, Green, 1900. [Chapter 8 The Resurrection and Ascension of our Lord and the Coming of the Holy Ghost, See. 99–106; N.B. Archive.org and HathiTrust]

Stoney, James Butler. *The Circle of Truth: Being Notes of Lectures*. London: G. Morrish, n.d. [Chapter 1 The Death and Resurrection of Christ, See. 1–23; N.B. The title page reads by J. B. S. with no date of publication.]

Storr, Gottlieb Konrad Christian, Carl Christian Von Flatt, and Samuel Simon Schmucker. *An Elementary Course of Biblical Theology, Translated from the Work of Professors Storr and Flatt, with additions by S. S. Schmucker*. 2nd ed. New York: Printed and Published by Gould & Newman, 1836. [Section 78 The Exaltation of the Man Jesus Presupposes His Intimate Union with the Godhead, See. 421–28; Section 83 Description of Christ's State of Exaltation, See. 434–38; N.B. Google book and HathiTrust]

Stott, John R. W. *Basic Christianity*. Grand Rapids: Eerdmans, 2008. [Chapter 4 The Resurrection of Christ, See. 57–72; N.B. This is a classic text first published in 1958.]

Strobel, Lee. *The Case for a Creator: A Journalist Investigates Scientific Evidence that Points Toward God*. Grand Rapids: Zondervan, 2004. [Appendix: A Summary of the Case for Christ, See. 297–98]

Strong, Augustus Hopkins. *Outlines of Systematic Theology: Designed for the Use of Theological Students*. Philadelphia: Griffith & Rowland, 1908. [The State of Exaltation, See. 190–91; N.B. Archive.org, Google book, and HathiTrust]

———. *Systematic Theology. A Compendium, Etc*. Vol. 1, 3. E.R. Andrews: Rochester, 1886. [Resurrection. See. 66, 77, 79, 227, 385, 577; N.B. Google book]

Strong, Thomas B. *A Manual of Theology*. 2nd ed. London: A. and C. Black, 1903. [Chapter 2, See. 85–90; N.B. The 1892 printing is available as a Google book.]

Stroup, George W. *The Promise of Narrative Theology: Recovering the Gospel in the Church*. Atlanta: John Knox, 1982. [See. 260]

Stump, Joseph. *The Christian Faith. A System of Christian Dogmatics*. Macmillan: New York, 1932. [Chapter 11 The States of Christ. See. The Exaltation, See. 170–79]

Summers, Thomas O. *Systematic Theology: A Complete Body of Wesleyan Arminian Divinity, Consisting of Lectures on the Twenty-five Articles of Religion*. Nashville: Publ. House of the Methodist Episcopal Church, South, 1888. [Book 3 Part 1. Chapter 1 The Nature of Christ's Resurrection Body, See. 302–7; Chapter 2 The Certainty of Christ's Resurrection, See. 308–16; Chapter 3 The Ascension and Session of Christ, See. 317–21; N.B. Archive.org and Google book]

Swinburne, Richard. *Is There a God?* Oxford: Oxford University Press, 1996. [Resurrection of, See. 126–29]

———. *Was Jesus God?* Oxford: Oxford University Press, 2014. [Chapter 8 The Resurrection of Jesus, See. 114–27]

Swindoll, Charles R., and Roy B. Zuck. *Understanding Christian Theology*. Nashville: Thomas Nelson, 2003. [Part 3 Jesus Christ, 8. Christ's Ascension to the Right Hand of God the Father, See. 354–58; Part 10 End Times, 12. The Order of Resurrections, See. 1331–38]

Tacey, David J. *Religion As Metaphor: Beyond Literal Belief*. New Brunswick (US): Transaction Publishers, 2015. [Chapter 9 Resurrection: Ascending to Where?, See. 167–86]

Talling, Marshall P. *The Science of Spiritual Life: An Application of Scientific Method in the Exploration of Spiritual Experience*. New York: Revell, 1912. [Resurrection, or Translation?, See. 220–23 N.B. Google book]

Taylor, Vincent. *Doctrine and Evangelism*. London: Epworth, 1953. [Chapter 15 The Exalted Christ, See. 64–67]

Terry, Milton Spenser. *Biblical Dogmatics; An Exposition of the Principal Doctrines of the Holy Scriptures*. New York: Eaton & Mains, 1907. [The Resurrection and Ascension, See. 278–79; N.B. Archive.org, Google book, and HathiTrust]

Thielen, Martin. *What's the Least I Can Believe and Still be a Christian: A Guide to What Matters Most*. Louisville: Westminster John Knox, 2011. [Chapter 17 Jesus' Resurrection: Is there Hope?, See. 116–26]

Thielicke, Helmut. *The Evangelical Faith*. Vol. 2. Edited and translated by Geoffrey W. Bromiley. Grand Rapids: Eerdmans, 1977. [Chapter 30 Kingly Office, See. 421–52; N.B. This work is a must read.]

Thiessen, Henry Clarence. *Introductory Lectures in Systematic Theology*. Grand Rapids: Eerdmans, 1956. [Chapter 27 The Work of Christ: His Resurrection and Ascension, See. 331–40]

———. *Lectures in Systematic Theology*. Revised ed. Grand Rapids: Eerdmans, 1979. [Chapter 26 The Work of Christ: His Resurrection, Ascension, and Exaltation, See. 243–50]

Thiselton, Anthony C. *Systematic Theology*. Grand Rapids: Eerdmans, 2015. [Chapter 14 See. The Resurrection of Jesus Christ, See. 354–58]

Thomas, Owen C. *Introduction To Theology*. Wilton, CT: Morehouse-Barlow, 1983. [See. 211–12, The Resurrection of Christ, See. 225–26]

Thomas, W. H. Griffith. *Christianity is Christianity*. London: Longmans, Green, 1916. [Chapter 7 The Resurrection of Christ, See. 52–67; N.B. Google book. This work is a good, dated read.]

———. *The Principles of Theology: An Introduction to the Thirty-nine Articles*. London: Longmans, Green, 1930. [Article 4, See. 73–89]

Thorsen, Donald A. D. *An Exploration of Christian Theology*. Peabody, MA: Hendrickson, 2008. [The Resurrection of Jesus, See. 181–83]

Thurian, Max. *Love And Truth Meet*. Translated by C. Edward Hopkin. Philadelphia: Pilgrim Press, 1968. [Chapter 15 The Resurrection, See. 52–55; Chapter 16 The Ascension, See. 56–57]

———. *Our Faith, Basic Christian Belief*. New York: Crossroad, 1982. [Chapter 16 See. 77–80]

Tillich, Paul. *Systematic Theology: Existence and The Christ*. Vol. 2. Chicago: University of Chicago Press, 1957. [The Reality of Christ, See. 150–65]

Toon, Peter. *Our Triune God: A Biblical Portrayal of the Trinity*. Vancouver: Regent College Publishing, 1996. [The Impact of the Resurrection, See. 158–60; The Resurrection of Jesus, See. 203–6]

Torrey, R. A. *The Higher Criticism and the New Theology: Unscientific, Unscriptural, and Unwholesome*. New York: Gospel Publishing House, 1911. [Chapter 9 The Certainty and Importance of the Real and Bodily Resurrection of Jesus Christ, See. 241–48; N.B. Archive.org and HathiTrust]

Towey, Anthony. *An Introduction to Christian Theology: Biblical, Classical, Contemporary*. London: Bloomsbury, 2013. [See. 121–27]

Tracey, David. *Religion As Metaphor Beyond Literal Belief*. New Brunswick, Transaction Publishers, 2015. [Chapter 9 Resurrection: Ascending to Where?, See. 167–68; N.B. This is an interesting work worth examining.]

Tsoukalas, Steven. *Christian Faith 101: The Basics and Beyond*. Valley Forge, PA: Judson Press, 2000. [Chapter 6 The Resurrection and Ascension of Christ, See. 55–63]

Ungar, Paul. *The Mystery of Christian Faith: A Tangible Union with the Invisible God: An Apologetic on the Borderline of Theology, Medicine, and* Philosophy. Lanham, MD: University Press of America, 2008. [Controversy over John 20:29, See. 88–90; St. Thomas, See. 85–90, 91–106]

Urban, Linwood. *A Short History of Christian Thought*. New York: Oxford University Press, 1986. [See. 29, 31, 34, 76, 198–99, 201, 205, 220–23, 226, 239]

Usher, James, and Hastings Robinson. *A Body of Divinity: Or the Sum and Substance of Christian Religion*. London: R. B. Seeley & W. Burnside, 1841. [Of the Resurrection of Christ, See. 222–23; Of Christ's Ascension, See. 223–24; N.B. Archive.org and Google.com]

Valentine, Mary Hester. *Miracles: Guidelines For Contemporary Catholics*. Chicago: Thomas More Press, 1988. [The Great Miracle: The Resurrection, See. 55–71]

Valentine, Milton. *Christian Theology*. Vol. 2. Philadelphia: Lutheran Publication Society, 1906. [Division 3 The States of Christ. The State of Exaltation, See. 91–95; N.B. Google book]

Van Buren, Paul Matthews. *A Theology of the Jewish-Christian Reality*. Lanham: University Press of America, 1995. [Chapter 5 Christ Risen: Easter, See. 107–30; N.B. This book is an interesting, short read.]

Vanderlaan, Eldred Cornelius. *Fundamentalism Versus Modernism*. New York: H. W. Wilson, 1925. [Bodily Resurrection, See. 333–49; N.B. Archive.org]

Vanhoozer, Kevin J. *First Theology: God, Scripture & Hermeneutics*. Downers Grove, IL: InterVarsity, 2002. [Chapter 9 The Hermeneutics of I-Witness Testimony John 21:20–24 & the Death of the Author, See. 257–74]

Van Winkle, Peter. *The Christophanies*. New York: Loizeaux, 1977. [254 pages]

Voigt, Andrew George. *Biblical Dogmatics*. Columbia, SC: Press of Lutheran Board of Publication, 1917. [The Exaltation of Christ and Redemption, See. 140–45; N.B. Google book]

Wagner, James Edgar. *Incarnation to Ascension: A Pastoral Interpretation*. Philadelphia: Christian Education Press, 1962. [Chapter 4 If In This Life Only: The Resurrection, See. 64–84; Chapter 5 The Same also that Ascended: The Ascension, See. 85–102]

Wainwright, Geoffrey. *Doxology: The Praise of God in Worship, Doctrine, and Life: A Systematic Theology*. New York: Oxford University Press, 1980. [See. 47, 56, 282, 451]

Wakefield, Samuel. *A Complete System of Christian Theology: or, A Concise, Comprehensive, and Systematic View of the Evidences, Doctrines, Morals, and Institutions of Christianity*. Cincinnati: Walden & Stowe, 1869. [See. 87–88; N.B. Google book and HathiTrust]

Walton, Alfred Grant. *This I Can Believe: An Outline of Essentials of the Christian Faith*. New York: Harper & Brothers, 1935. [Chapter 6 Did Jesus Rise from the Dead?, See. 112–29]

Ward, Keith. *God, Faith & the New Millennium: Christian Belief in an Age of Science*. Oxford, England: Oneworld, 1998. [The Gospel of the Resurrection, See. 182–84]

Ward, William B. *Beliefs That Live*. Richmond: John Knox, 1963. [Chapter 5 The Victorious Christ, See. 55–62; Chapter 6 The Doctrine of the Ascension, See. 63–70]

Warden, John. *Scripture Exhibited in Its Purity and Simplicity: Being a System of Revealed Religion*. 3rd ed. London: Printed for Thomas Tegg, 1843. [Of the Resurrection of Christ and His Ascension, See. 207–19; N.B. HathiTrust]

Wardlaw, Ralph. *Systematic Theology*. Edited by James Robinson Campbell. Vol. 1. Edinburgh: A. and C. Black, 1856. [Chapter 13 External Evidences of Christianity.

Miracles, See. 286–311; N.B. Google book and HathiTrust. This book is a healthy, dated source.]

Ware, Bruce A. *Big Truths For Young Hearts: Teaching and Learning the Greatness of God.* Wheaton, IL: Crossway, 2009. [Jesus' Resurrection: The Proof that Christ's Death for Sin Worked, See. 135–38]

Waterhouse, Steven. *Not By Bread Alone: An Outlined Guide to Bible Doctrine.* Amarillo, TX: Westcliff Press, 2003. [Chapter 8 Christology, See. 97–98]

Watson, Richard, bishop. *Theological Institutes: or, A View of the Evidences, Doctrines, Morals, and Institutions of Christianity.* Edited by J. M. M'Clintock. New York: Carlton & Porter, 1857. [Chapter 15 The Miracles of Scripture, See. 60–61; N.B. Archive.org, Google book, and HathiTrust]

Weatherhead, Leslie D. *The Christian Agnostic.* New York: Abingdon, 1965. [Resurrection of Christ, See. 127–41]

Weaver, Jonathan. *Christian Doctrine, A Comprehensive Treatise on Systematic and Practical Theology.* Dayton, OH: United Brethren Publishing House, 1889. [See. 273, 275, 294–95]

———. *A Practical Comment on the Confession of Faith of the Church of the United Brethren in Christ.* Dayton, OH: United Brethren, 1892. [Chapter 5 See. The Resurrection and Ascension of Christ, See. 70–72; N.B. Google book]

Webber, Christopher. *Welcome to the Christian Faith.* New York: Morehouse, 2011. [Resurrection, See. 56–58]

Weber, Otto. *Foundations of Dogmatics.* Translated by Darrell L. Guder. Vol. 2. Grand Rapids: Eerdmans, 1983. [Raised Again for Our Justification, See. 67–75]

Weiss, Bernhard. *Biblical Theology of the New Testament.* Vol. 1. Translated by David Eaton. Edinburgh: T&T Clark, 1892. [The Death and Resurrection of Christ, See. 430–37; N.B. Archive.org]

Welch, Claude, ed. *God and Incarnation in Mid-Nineteenth Century German Theology: G. Thomasius, I. A. Dorner, A. E. Biedermann.* New York: Oxford University Press, 1965. [See. 75–80]

Wellcome, I. C., and Clarkson Goud. *The Plan of Redemption By Our Lord Jesus Christ: Carefully Examined and Argued by Inquiring into God's Revealed Purpose in the Creation of Man, the Adamic Law.* Boston: Advent Christian Publication Society, 1867. [See. 184, 312; N.B. Archive.org and Google book]

Werner, Martin. *The Formation of Christian Dogma: An Historical Study of Its Problem . . .* Translated by Samuel George Frederick Brandon. New York: Harper & Brothers, 1957. [Jesus Resurrection, Eschatological Significance, See. 20, 23, 31, 36, 44, 46–47, 127, 165, 282]

Whale, J. S. *Christian Doctrine: Eight Lectures Delivered in the University of Cambridge to Undergraduates of All Faculties.* Cambridge: University Press, 1961. [Chapter 4 See. 68–73]

Wickes, Thomas. *The Economy of the Ages.* New York: Revell, 1875. [Chapter 35 The First Resurrection, 493–521; N.B. HathiTrust. This work is a healthy, dated source.]

Wilder, Amos Niven. *Otherworldliness and the New Testament.* New York, Harper & Brothers, 1954. [Chapter 4 The Resurrection Faith and a Relevant Salvation, See. 94–122]

Wiles, Maurice F. *Reason To* Believe. Harrisburg, PA: Trinity Press International, 2000. [Chapter 4 The Birth, Death and Resurrection: Did They All Really Happen?, See. 30–37]

Wiley, H. Orton. *Christian Theology*. Vol. 2. Kansas City: Beacon Hill, 1947. [The State of Exaltation, See. 201–10]

Wiley, H. Orton, and Paul T. Culbertson. *Introduction to Christian Theology*. Kansas City: Beacon Hill, 1946. [The Exaltation, See. 209–13]

Wilhelm, Joseph, and Thomas B Scannell. *A Manual of Catholic Theology: Based on Scheeben's Dogmatik*. Vol. 2. 3rd ed. London: Kegan, Paul, Trench, Trübner, 1908. [Section 204 Christ's Glorification—His Resurrection and Ascension, See. 179–80; also See. 298–301, 466; N.B. Archive.org]

Williams, Ernest Swing. *Systematic Theology* Vol. 2. Springfield, MO: Gospel Publishing House, 1953. [Chapter 11 The Resurrection and Ascension, See. 81–85]

Williams, J. Rodman. *Renewal Theology*. Grand Rapids: Zondervan, 1988. [Chapter 15 The Exaltation of Christ, See. 381–413; N.B. This is a definite work worth examining.]

Williams, Rowan. *On Christian Theology*. Oxford: Blackwell, 2000. [Chapter 12 Between The Cherubim: The Empty Tomb and the Empty Throne, See. 183–96]

Williamson, Clark M. *Way of Blessing, Way of Life: A Christian Theology*. St. Louis: Chalice Press, 1999. [See. 200–202]

Wilmers, W. *Handbook of the Christian Religion: For the Use of Advanced Students and the Educated Laity*. Edited by James Conway. New York: Benziger, 1891. [The divine mission of Christ is proved in particular by His resurrection from the dead, See. 41–44; N.B. Archive.org and Google book]

Wilson, James. *A Treasury of Biblical and Theological Knowledge*. Book 1. London: Hamilton, Adams, 1845. [Essay 7 On the Resurrection of Jesus Christ, See. 69–88; N.B. Google book]

Wilson, Jonathan R. *A Primer For Christian Doctrine*. Grand Rapids: Eerdmans, 2005. [The Resurrection of Christ, See. 52–55]

Wingren, Gustaf. *Gospel and Church*. Translated by Ross Mackenzie. Edinburgh: Oliver & Boyd, 1964. [Chapter 3 Christ and the Renewal of Creation, The Resurrection, See. 85–101]

Winward, Stephen F. *A Modern ABECEDARY for Protestants*. New York: Association Press, 1964. [The Resurrection, See. 54–55; The Evidence for the Resurrection, See. 55; The Ascension, See. 55]

Wood, Charles James. *Survivals In Christianity: Studies in the Theology of Divine Immanence*. New York: Macmillan, 1893. [Lecture 5 The Resurrection, See. 199–206; N.B. Google book and HathiTrust]

Wright, Charles James. *Miracle in History and in Modern Thought; or, Miracle and Christian Apologetic*. New York: H. Holt, 1930. [Chapter 7 The Resurrection of Christ and Miracle, See. 344–65; N.B. Wright's work is a recommended reading.]

Yoder, John Howard. *Preface To Theology: Christology and Theological Method*. Grand Rapids: Brazos, 2002. [Jesus, resurrection of, See. 56, 73, 77, 87, 96, 105, 109, 119, 126–27, 134, 141, 170, 215, 237, 268, 320]

Chapter 26

Jesus Christ Resurrection Sermons

Alcock, George Augustus. *The Resurrection of Christ: Its Evidential Value, and Its Doctrinal Significance. A Sermon.* Dublin, 1884.

Algar, H. *Notes on the Sermon on the Mount and A Harmony of the Accounts of the Resurrection.* London: W. Kent; Newcastle-under-Lyme: Thos. Peake, 1884. [See. 45–51; N.B. Google book]

Andrewes, Lancelot. *Two Sermons of the Resurrection.* Cambridge: Cambridge University Press, 1932. [N.B. Two Easter sermons by the Anglican bishop and scholar Lancelot Andrewes (1555–1626).]

Arnold, Thomas. *Christian Life and Doctrine: Sermons.* London: Longmans, Green, 1878. [Sermon 12 Certainty of Christ's Resurrection, See 94–102; N.B. Archive.org and Google book]

———. *Sermons Chiefly on the Interpretation of Scripture.* 2nd ed. London: B. Fellowes, 1845. [Sermon 23 Christ's Resurrection—The Confession of Thomas, See. 231–40; N.B. Google book]

Atterbury, Lewis, and Edward Yardley. *Sermons on Select Subjects.* Vol. 1. London: T. Osborne, 1743. [Sermon 13 Of the Resurrection of Christ, and Our Own Resurrection, See. 266–87; N.B. Google book]

Baker, Daniel. *Rival Sermons: Second Series.* Philadelphia: William S. Martien, 1854. [Sermon 9 The Tomb of Jesus, See. 230–53; N.B. Archive.org]

Barrow, Isaac. "He Rose Again From the Dead." In *Sacred Classics: or, Cabinet Library of Divinity: Sermons on the Resurrection.* Vol. 16. Edited by R. Cattermole and H. Stebbing. London: John Hatchard, 1835. [Sermon 2, See. 26–61; N.B. Google book]

———. "The Third Day He Rose Again, &c." In *Sacred Classics: or, Cabinet Library of Divinity: Sermons on the Resurrection.* Vol. 16. Edited by R. Cattermole and H. Stebbing. London: John Hatchard, 1835. [Sermon 3, See. 65–84; N.B. Google book]

Beasley-Murray, George Raymond. *The Resurrection of Jesus Christ.* London: Oliphants, 1964. [48 pages]

Betzer, Dan. *He's Alive.* Springfield, MO: General Council of the Assemblies of God: Revivaltime, 1979. [30 pages]

Beveridge, William. "Christ's Resurrection A Proof of Ours." In *Sacred Classics: or, Cabinet Library of Divinity: Sermons on the Resurrection.* Vol. 16. Edited by R. Cattermole and H. Stebbing. London: John Hatchard, 1835. [See. 139–52; N.B. Google book]

———. "Christ the First Fruits." In *Sacred Classics: or, Cabinet Library of Divinity: Sermons on the Resurrection*. Vol. 16. Edited by R. Cattermole and H. Stebbing. London: John Hatchard, 1835. [See. 137–35; N.B. Google book]

———. *Sermons Concerning the Death, Resurrection, and Ascension of Christ, and the Mission of the Holy Ghost*. 2nd ed. Vol. 6. London: Printed by W. Bowyer, for Richard Smith in Exeter Change in the Strand. 1712. [390 pages; N.B. Google book]

Bourn, Samuel. *A Sermon on the Resurrection*. Newark: Printed and sold by Allin and Ridge, 1793. [16 pages; N.B. Google book]

Bradlee, C. D. *Jesus Christ, Eternally Alive: A Sermon*. Boston: Eustis Towle, 1888. [11 pages; Caleb D. Bradlee, senior pastor of the Church at Harrison Square, Boston, Mass., preached April 1, 1888, Easter Sunday. Boston: Eustis Towle, 1888.

Bramley, Henry Ramsden. *Christ's Resurrection A Moral Certainty: A Sermon Preached before the University of Oxford, on St. Mark's Day, 1889, in the Chapel of St. Mary Magdalen College*. Oxford: Mowbray, 1889? [40 pages]

Branham, William. *Proof of His Resurrection*. Jeffersonville, IN: Voice of God Recordings, 1991.

Bray, John L. *The Three Appearings of Christ*. Plant City, FL: n.p., 197? [20 pages]

Broadus, John R. "The Resurrection of the Body." In *Great Sermons on the Resurrection of Christ*. Compiled by Wilbur M. Smith. Grand Rapids: Baker, 1996. [See. 257–68]

Brooke, Stopford A. *The Resurrection of Jesus*. London: Philip Green, 1884. [12 pages]

Brooks, Phillip. *An Easter Sermon*. London: H. R. Allenson, 1905? [44 pages; N.B. HathiTrust]

Brown, Abner. *The Resurrection of Christ*. In *Practical Sermons by Dignitaries and other Clergymen*. Vol. 3. London: John Parker. 1846. [See. 241–58; N.B. Google book]

Bruce, A. B. "The Doubt of Thomas. (John 20:24–29)." In *Great Sermons on the Resurrection of Christ*. Compiled by Wilbur M. Smith. Grand Rapids: Baker, 1996. [See. 145–53]

Bryant, Al. *Sermon Outlines on the Death, Resurrection, and Return of Christ*. Grand Rapids: Kregel, 1998. [64 pages]

Budd, Leonard H., and Roger H. Talbott. *Resurrection Promises*. Lima, Ohio: C.S.S., 1987. [84 pages]

Burder, George. *Village Sermons: or Sixty-Five Plain and Short Discourses on the Principal Doctrines of the Gospel*. Vol. 2. Philadelphia: W. W. Woodward, 1817. [Chapter 46 The Resurrection of Christ, See. 136–45; N.B. Google book]

Butcher, Henry W. *Sermons Preached at Margate*. London: Hodder & Stoughton, 1879. [Chapter 9 The Place of the Resurrection in the Gospel, See. 119–29; N.B. Google book]

Candlish, Robert S. "The Pious Dead are Lost, Living Believers are Miserable (1 Corinthians 15:18–46)." In *Great Sermons on the Resurrection of Christ*. Compiled by Wilbur M. Smith. Grand Rapids: Baker, 1996. [See. 235–53]

Cattermole, Richard, and Henry Stebbing, eds. *Sermons on the Resurrection, Particularly Adapted for Christian Consideration During Easter, Selected from the Works of the Most Eminent English Divines*. London, Hatchard, 1835. [333 pages, 14 sermons; N.B. Google book]

Chamberlain, Thomas. "Touch Me Not." In *Sermons for Sundays, Festivals, and Fasts, and Other Liturgical Occasions*. Vol. 2. Edited by Alexander Watson, 201–12. London: Joseph Masters, 1846. [N.B. Google book]

Chappell, Wallace D. *When Jesus Rose*. Nashville, Broadman, 1972. [127 pages]

Corwin, Edward Tanjore. *The Resurrection of Christ: An Easter Dialogue*. New York: Board of Publication of the Reformed Church in America 189-?

Coughlin, Charles E. *The Story of the Resurrection*. Royal Oak, MI: n.p., 1940. [16 pages; N.B. HathiTrust]

Cronk, Malcolm R. *Resurrection Realities*. Los Angeles, CA: Church of the Open Door, 1972. [14 pages; N.B. Located only at Biola University.]

DeHaan, Richard W. *From Time to Eternity*. Grand Rapids: Radio Bible Class, 1970. [36 pages]

Disney, John. *Sermons by John Disney*, in Two Volumes. Vol. 2. London: Printed for J. Johnson, 1793. [Sermon 23 The Resurrection of Jesus, See. 379–96; N.B. Google book]

Dix, Morgan. *Two Sermons on the Resurrection of Christ Our Lord*: Preached in Trinity Church New York: April 29th and May 6th. New York: Edwin S. Gorham, 1906. [30 pages]

Donne, John. "Christ's Triumph in the Resurrection." In *Sacred Classics: or, Cabinet Library of Divinity: Sermons on the Resurrection*. Vol. 16. Edited by R. Cattermole and H. Stebbing, 154–78. London: John Hatchard, 1835. [N.B. Google book]

Duncan, Alexander. *The Evidence of the Resurrection of Jesus as Recorded in the New Testament; A Sermon Preached before The Society in Scotland for Propagating Christian Knowledge at their Anniversary Meeting, in the High Church of Edinburgh*. Edinburgh, Printed for the Society, 1783. [80 pages; N.B. Google book]

Emmons, Nathanael. *The Works of Nathanael Emmons*. Vol. 4. Edited by Jacob Ide. Boston: Crocker & Brewster, 1842. [Sermon 4 The Resurrection of Jesus Christ, See. 60–73; N.B. HathiTrust]

Evans, Thomas. *A Sermon on the Evidences and the Lessons of the Resurrection of Christ*. Calcutta: Printed by J. W. Thomas, Baptist Mission Press, 1881. [20 pages; N.B. Located only at the University of Oxford.]

Everest, Quinton J. *Resurrection: Sermons*. South Bend, IN: Your Worship Hour, 1973. [48 pages]

Expository Sermons on the New Testament. New York: Hodder & Stoughton, n.d. [A collection of sermons from thirteen authors; N.B. Archive.org]

Faber, A. H. *The Resurrection of Christ Considered in Its Bearing upon this Life: A Sermon Preached in the Chapel of New College, Oxford, on Easter-day, 1860*. Oxford: Parker. Printed for private circulation, 1860. [18 pages; N.B. Google book]

Falconer, Thomas. *The Resurrection of our Saviour Asserted from an Examination of the Proofs of the Identity of his Character After that Event, in a Letter to the Reverend L. R. Bath, 1798*. Oxford: At the University Press for the author, 1817. [32 pages; N.B. Only in the British Library, St. Pancras.]

Findlay, George G. "The Ascension of Jesus." In *Great Sermons on the Resurrection of Christ*. Compiled by Wilbur M. Smith. Grand Rapids: Baker, 1996. [See. 184–94]

Fitzgerald, John H. *The Body of Jesus was Cremated: An Easter Sermon*. Brooklyn: Christ Church Bay Ridge, 1959. [20 pages]

Ford, D. W. Cleverley. *Preaching the Risen Christ*. Peabody, MA: Hendrickson, 1994. [128 pages]

Foster, James. *The Resurrection of Christ Prov'd and Vindicated*. London: Printed for John Clark, 1720. [31 pages; N.B. Available online at select universities.]

Frothingham, Octavius Brooks. *The Resurrection of the Son of Man: A Sermon*. New York: D. G. Francis, 17 Astor Place, 1874. [27 pages; N.B. HathiTrust]

Furness, William H. *The "Power of His Resurrection": Easter 1884*. Philadelphia?: n.p., 1884? [23 pages; N.B. Located at Harvard University.]

Gaddy, C. Welton. *Easter Proclamation Remembrance and Renewal*. Nashville, Broadman Press, 1974. [96 pages]

Gill, John. "The Doctrine of the Resurrection, Stated and Defended; in Two Sermons from Acts 2." In *A Defence of Some Important Doctrines of the Gospel in Twenty-six Sermons*. Glasgow: Andrew Young, 1826. [Sermon 1, See. 515–38; Sermon 2, See. 538–76; N.B. Google book]

Gospel of the Resurrection: A Course of Sermons Preached in the Chapel of Pusey House, Oxford, The. London, A.R. Mowbray, 1962.

Gregg, David. *The Immortality of the Child of God: As Seen Through the Resurrection of Jesus Christ*. New York: Apex, n.d. [17 pages]

Grove, Henry. *The Evidence for our Saviour's Resurrection Consider'd: with the Improvement of this Important Doctrine*. London: Printed for John Gray, 1730. [4 pages. Reproduction of the original housed in the British Library. N.B. Available via the World Wide Web. Access limited by licensing agreements.]

Gurney, Thomas A. "The Church of the Resurrection (John 20:17)." In *Great Sermons on the Resurrection of Christ*. Compiled by Wilbur M. Smith. Grand Rapids: Baker, 1996. [See. 127–43]

Gwynne, J. Harold. *Easter Lilies*. Grand Rapids: Eerdmans, 1940. [142 pages]

Haines, Herbert. *St. Paul a Witness to the Resurrection: A Sermon on Acts 22. 7, 8*. Oxford: James Parker and Co., 1867. [21 pages; N.B. Google book]

Haldeman, I. M. *The Sevenfold Glory of the Risen Christ*. New York: I. M. Haldeman, 1933. [Sermon preached in the meeting house of the First Baptist Church, Broadway and seventy-ninth street, New York City, N.Y., Easter morning, April 16th, 1933.]

Harris, John Andrews. *Principles of Agnosticism Applied to Evidences of Christianity: Nine Sermons*. New York: Thomas Whittaker, 1883. [Sermon 9 The Resurrection of Christ, See. 100–113; N.B. Google book]

Hart, Levi. *The Resurrection of Jesus Christ Considered and Proved: And the Consequent Truth and Divinity of the Christian System Briefly Illustrated*, 1786. Newport Books. Book 14. [Newport Collection at Digital Commons @ Salve Regina.]

Hay, Alexander. *Sermon on the Resurrection of Christ*. Lynchburg: Printed by Carter & Weaver, 1803. [20 pages]

Hayes, Doremus, A. "The Resurrection Appearances of Christ." In *Great Sermons on the Resurrection of Christ*. Compiled by Wilbur M. Smith. Grand Rapids: Baker, 1996. [See. 58–71]

Hobbs, Herschel H. *Messages on the Resurrection*. Grand Rapids: Baker, 1959. [87 pages]

Hocking, David L. *The Power of the Resurrection*. La Mirada, CA: Biola Hour Ministries, Biola University, 1991. [24 pages; N.B. This work is available online.]

Holmes, Robert. *The Resurrection of the Body, Deduced from the Resurrection of Christ, and Illustrated from His Transfiguration: A Sermon Preached before the University of Oxford, at St. Mary's, on Easter-Monday, March 31, 1777*. Oxford: Printed for D. Prince and J. Cooke. Sold by Mess. Rivington, London, 1779. [36 pages; N.B. Google book]

Holyday, Barten. *Three Sermons upon the Passion, Resurrection and Ascension of our Saviour*. Oxford: Printed for D. Prince and J. Cooke. And sold by Mess. Rivington, London, 1779. [36 pages]

Hook, Walter Farquhar. *Sermons Suggested by the Miracles of our Lord and Saviour Jesus Christ*. Vol. 2. London: George Bell, 1848. [Sermon 35 The Second Miraculous Draught of Fishes, See. 262–80; Sermon 36 The Miraculous Signs of Faith, See. 281–95; N.B. Google book]

Horne, Chevis F. *Basic Bible Sermons on Easter*. Nashville: Broadman Press, 1990. [127 pages]

Horne, George. "Jesus Risen." In *Sacred Classics: or, Cabinet Library of Divinity: Sermons on the Resurrection*. Vol. 16. Edited by R. Cattermole and H. Stebbing. London: John Hatchard, 1835. [See. 241–56; N.B. Google book]

Horsley, Samuel. *Nine Sermons on the Nature of the Evidence by which the Fact of our Lord's Resurrection is Established*. New York: T&J Swords; Boston, Wells & Lilly, 1816. [250 pages; N.B. HathiTrust]

Houghton, Alexander. *Observations on the Evidence of Christ's Resurrection: the Principal Objections Answered, and the Divine Origin of the Christian Religion Clearly Proved: Two Sermons, Preached at the Octagon Chapel*. London: Printed for J. Johnson, 1798. [58 pages; N.B. Google book]

Howe, Thomas. *The Christian's Triumph in the Death of Christ. A Sermon, Preached at Yarmouth, January 14, 1770; on occasion of the death of Mrs. Persis Eldridge, who died January 3d, in the 77th year of her age*. London: Printed for J. Buckland, at No. 57. in Pater-Noster Row, 1770. [25 pages; N.B. Eighteenth century collection online.]

Hutson, Curtis. *Great Preaching on the Resurrection*. Murfreesboro, TN: Sword of the Lord, 1984. [266 pages]

Jenkins, J. (James of Castle-Douglas). *The Death, Burial, and Resurrection of Jesus Christ: A Sermon Preached in the U.P. Church, Newton Stewart, on the occasion of the death of the Rev. W. Reid, Pastor of the Congregation*. Castle Douglas: Printed at the Advertiser Office, 1864. [28 pages; N.B. Located at the National Library of Scotland]

Johnson, Albert G. *The Fragrance of the Empty Tomb: A Pulpit Discourse*. Portland, OR: Durham, Ryan & Downey, 1940. [28 pages]

Jones, J. D. *The Gospel of Grace*. London: J. Clarke, 1907. [Chapter 8 Easter Triumph, See. 117–33]

Keble, John. "The Two Ascensions of Christ." In *Sermons for Sundays, Festivals, and Fasts, and Other Liturgical Occasions*. Vol. 2. Edited by Alexander Watson, 255–63. London: Joseph Masters, 1846. [N.B. Google book]

Kee, Alistair. *From Bad Faith to Good News: Reflections on Good Friday and Easter*. London: SCM, 1991. [147 pages]

Lawson, Charles. *Sermons Preached Chiefly in the Chapel of the Founding Hospital, London*. London: John Parker, 1838. [Sermon 8 The Journey to Emmaus, See. 102–16; N.B. Google book]

Layman, A. *A Sermon on the Resurrection, by a Layman: Wherein 'tis shew'd, that the incarnation and suffering of our Saviour on the cross, was in order to put the truth of his resurrection out of doubt, to prove the Certainty of a Future State, and to induce every individual Man seriously to consider, and piously to prepare himself for another World*. Printed by J. W. and sold by T. Cooper in Pater-Noster-Row, and by the Booksellers of London and Westminster, 1738. [N.B. Reproduction of original from British Library]

Liddon, H. P. "Jesus on the Evening of Easter Day." In *Great Sermons on the Resurrection of Christ*. Compiled by Wilbur M. Smith. Grand Rapids: Baker, 1996. [See. 111–24]

———. *The Power of Christ's Resurrection*. London: Rivingtons, 1869. [23 pages; N.B. Project Canterbury]

———. "The Resurrection Inevitable (Acts 2:24)." In *Great Sermons on the Resurrection of Christ*. Compiled by Wilbur M. Smith. Grand Rapids: Baker, 1996. [See. 206–19]

———. "The Undying One (Romans 6:9)." In *Great Sermons on the Resurrection of Christ*. Compiled by Wilbur M. Smith. Grand Rapids: Baker, 1996. [See. 221–34]

Locke, F. M. *Sermon on the Resurrection*. Edgewood, TX: Enterprise Print, 1914. [109 pages]

Lushington, Thomas. *The Resurrection Rescued from the Soldiers Calumnies: In Two Sermons Preached at St. Maries in Oxon*. London: Printed for Richard Lownds at the White Lion in Paul's Church-yard, 1659. [100 pages; N.B. Early English Books Online]

MacGregor, James. *The Resurrection of Jesus: As a Doctrine, and as a Fact*. Edinburgh, n.d. [130 pages]

Maclaren, Alexander. "Witnesses of the Resurrection." In *Great Sermons on The Resurrection*. Grand Rapids: Baker, 1963. [See. 51–60; N.B First published in 1896 by Fleming H. Revell under the title, *Resurrection*.]

Maclaren, William. *Christ's Resurrection; Principal Geering's Views Exposed*. Preached and recorded at the Prayer Meeting in the Free Presbyterian Church of Scotland, Gisborne, NZ on Wednesday, 8th November, 1967. Gisborne: Westminster Standard, 1968. [16 pages]

MacPherson, Alexander. *A Sermon on the Evidence of the Resurrection of our Lord Jesus Christ*. London: printed by J. Bradley, 1839. [16 pages]

Mason, Richard. *The Resurrection Proved from Reason as Well as Scriptures: A Sermon preached at Faversham in the County of Kent Sunday afternoon May the 2d, 1742*. London, 1742. [22 pages]

Mather, Cotton. *Reason Satisfied: And Faith Established: The Resurrection of a Glorious Jesus Demonstrated by many Infallible Proofs: and the Holy Religion of a risen Jesus, Victorious over all Cavils of the Blasphemous Adversaries*. Boston, 1712. [47 pages; N.B. Early American imprints: 1639–1800]

May, Joseph. *The Myth of the Resurrection of Jesus: A Sermon*. Boston, G. H. Ellis, 1893. [22 pages; The Weekly Exchange. Ser. 2, no. 22]

McCaleb, John Moody. *Facts About the Resurrection*. "Delivered at Cornell Ave. Church of Christ, Chicago." Cincinnati, Ohio: F.L. Rowe, 1937. [16 pages]

McCaul, Alexander. "*The Power of Christianity A Perpetual Evidence of Christ's Resurrection: The Spital Sermon for Easter Tuesday, 1845: preached before the Lord Mayor and sheriffs, and other governors of the royal hospitals.*" In *Practical Sermons*. Vol. 1. Edited by A. Watson and J. C. Crosthwaite. London: John Parker, 1845. [See. 359–73 pages; N.B. Google book.]

McGee, Vernon J. *The Power of the Resurrection*. Los Angeles, CA: Church of the Open Door, n.d. [23 pages]

McIlvaine, Charles Pettit. "The Resurrection of Christ (Luke 24:34)." In *Great Sermons on the Resurrection of Christ*. Compiled by Wilbur M. Smith. Grand Rapids: Baker, 1996. [See. 17–37]

Means, Alexander. *Sermons on the Resurrection*. Macon, GA: J. W. Burke, 1871. [45 pages]

Meyer, F. B. "Death a Parenthesis in Life (Revelation 1:17–18)." In *Great Sermons on the Resurrection of Christ*. Compiled by Wilbur M. Smith. Grand Rapids: Baker, 1996. [See. 247–54]

Miller, George Frazier. *The Resurrection a Witnessed Fact*. Sermon delivered Easter morning, April 7, 1912. Brooklyn, 1912. [8 pages]

Moody, D. L. "The Fifteenth Chapter of First Corinthians." In *Great Sermons on The Resurrection*. Grand Rapids: Baker, 1963. [See. 61–75; N.B. First published in 1896 by Fleming H. Revell under the title, *Resurrection*.]

Moody, Paul D. *The First Easter Sermon: An Address*. Northfield, Mass., Northfield Press, 1910. [37 pages]

Morgan, G. Campbell. "Led Out, Led In (Luke 24:50)." In *Great Sermons on the Resurrection of Christ*. Compiled by Wilbur M. Smith. Grand Rapids: Baker, 1996. [See. 173–83]

———. "The Rekindled Fire (Luke 24:32)." In *Great Sermons on the Resurrection of Christ*. Compiled by Wilbur M. Smith. Grand Rapids: Baker, 1996. [See. 98–107]

———. *The Westminster Pulpit*. Vol. 9. *The Preaching of G. Campbell Morgan*. Westwood, NJ: Revell, 1954. [Chapter 10 The Resurrection, See. 134–46]

Mortimer, Alfred G. *Jesus and the Resurrection Thirty Addresses for Good Friday and Easter*. London: Longmans, Green, 1907. [298 pages; N.B. Google book]

Motter, Alton M., ed. *Preaching the Resurrection: 22 Great Easter Sermons*. Philadelphia: Muhlenberg Press, 1959. [186 pages]

Newton, John. *The Works of the Rev. John Newton*. Edinburgh: University Press, 1827. [Sermon 25 Messiah's rising from the Dead, See. 727–31; Sermon 26 The Ascension of the Messiah to Glory, See. 731–34; N.B. Google book]

Nott, Abner Kingman. *Jesus and the Resurrection*. "A Sermon Delivered Sabbath Evening, February 13th, 1859, at the Academy of Music, New York." New York, 1859. [116 pages; N.B. Archive.org]

Nott, Eliphalet. *The Resurrection of Christ: A Series of Discourse*. New York: Scribner, Armstrong, 1872. [157 pages; N.B. Google book]

Ockenga, Harold John. *The Resurrection of Christ: 1 Corinthians 15:1–20*. 197-? [6 pages]

Paine, Thomas. *Of the Evidence of Christ's Death, Burial and Resurrection; it's plainness to our senses &c.: a sermon preached at Braintree the Sabbath after the burial of that pious and valuable gentlewoman, Mrs. Ann Niles, the virtuous consort of the Reverend Mr. Samuel Niles, of that town. Who died October 25th, 1732. In the fifty-fifth year of her age*. Boston: Printed by S. Kneeland & T. Green, M, 1732. [27 pages; N.B. Early American imprints]

Peabody, Andrew P. *The Power of the Resurrection: A Sermon Preached at King's Chapel*, on Easter Sunday, April 21, 1867, on the dedication of a monument in memory of the young men of the parish who fell during the recent war. Boston: J. H. Eastburn's Press, 1867. [22 pages]

Philip, James. *The Death and Resurrection of Christ*. Dundee: Geo. E. Findlay, n.d. [88 pages]

Pierce, Samuel Eyles. *Discourses Designed as Preparatory to the Administration of The Lord's Supper with Several Sermons*. London: Ebenezer Palmer, 1827. [Sermon 14 On the Resurrection of Christ; See. 339–74; N.B. Google book]

Proud, J. *On the Resurrection of Jesus Christ: A Sermon Delivered in York-Street Chapel, St. James Square, Westminster, on April the 14th, 1805*. London: J&E Hodson, 1805. [17 pages]

Ramsay, D. M. *The Resurrection of our Lord: A Sermon Preached by the Rev. D. M. Ramsay, pastor of Knox Church, Ottawa, on Sunday, the 2nd April, 1899 (Easter Sunday)*. Ottawa: n.p., 1899. [CIHM/ICH microfiche series, no 12299; N.B. Hathitrst.org]

Rattray, Thomas. *The Regal Advent and the Resurrection of the Past: A Sermon, the sixth of a series on these subjects*. Toronto?: D. K. Winder, 1878. [CIHM/ICH microfiche series, no. 91638; N.B. HathiTrust]

Reichel, Charles Parsons. *The Spiritual Body of Christ a Proof of His Resurrection: A Sermon Preached before the University of Dublin, in the Chapel of Trinity College, on Easter Sunday, 1853*. Dublin: Hodges & Smith, 1853. [36 pages]

Reynell, Carew. *The Resurrection of our Saviour tim'd, Saviour Rightly 1726*. London: Printed for Tho. Combes, 1726. [31 pages; N.B. Eighteenth Century Collections online]

Rice, Daniel. *The Resurrection of Christ, the Divine Seal to the Truth of Christianity: A Synodical Sermon preached before the Synod of Wabash, in session at Crawfordsville, Indiana, November 21, 1869*. Lafayette, IN: Rosser, Spring, 1869. [22 pages]

Robertson, Archibald (Bishop). "The Resurrection of Our Lord Jesus Christ." In *Critical Questions: Being a Course of Sermons Delivered in St. Mark's Church*. 2nd ed. London: Masters, 1906. [See. 97–120; N.B. Google book]

Saphir, Adolph. "The Church of the World (Matthew 28:18–20)." In *Great Sermons on the Resurrection of Christ*. Compiled by Wilbur M. Smith. Grand Rapids: Baker, 1996. [See. 156–70]

Saurin, James. *Eleven Select Sermons by Jacques Saurin on Various Important Subjects*. Concord: George Hough, 1806. [Sermon 7 The Resurrection of Jesus Christ, See. 170–196; N.B. Google book]

———. *Sermons of the Rev. James Saurin*. Edited by Samuel Burder. Translated by Robert Robinson, Henry Hunter and Joseph Sutcliffe. Vol. 2. New York: Harper & Brothers, 1836. [Sermon 74 Obscure Faith; or, the Blessedness of Believing Without Having Seen, See. 173–77; N.B. Google book]

Schmalenberger, Jerry L. *Resurrection, Checking the Vital Signs: Sermons for the Easter Season, Series B*. Lima, OH: C.S.S. Publishing, 1981. [59 pages]

Schmidt, Martin J. *The Proclamation of the Risen Jesus Christ in Lutheran Preaching: A Content Analysis of Selected Sermons, Representing Ninety-Seven years of Preaching within the Lutheran Church—Missouri Synod, as found in Magazin fuer Ev.-Luth. Homiletik und Pastoraltheologie (1877–1929) and The Concordia Pulpit (1930–1973)*. Ed. D. Teachers College, Columbia University, 1974. [310 leaves]

Schroeder, Frederick W. "The Impact of Resurrection." In *Preaching the Resurrection" Twenty-two Great Easter Sermons*. Edited by Alton M. Motter. Philadelphia: Fortress, 1959. [See. 152–58]

Seamands, Stephen. *Give Them Christ Preaching His Incarnation, Crucifixion, Resurrection, Ascension and Return*. Downers Grove, IL: InterVarsity, 2012. [See. 99–157]

Seelye, Julius H. *The Resurrection of Christ the Justification of Missions: A Sermon Preached at the sixty-fourth annual meeting of the American Board of Commissioners for Foreign Missions*, Minneapolis, September 23, 1873. Cambridge, MA: Riverside Press, 1873. [16 pages; N.B. Google book]

Seidenspinner, Charles. *Believest Thou This? : A Meditation Concerning the Resurrection of Jesus*. Birmingham, AL: Southeastern Bible School, 1946 [5 unnumbered pages]

Sermon Preached Against Quakerism: Being a Discourse of the Resurrection and Ascension of the Body of the Holy Jesus of Nazareth, A. Preach'd at Whitehaven, January the 1st, 1709–10. London: Printed and sold by H. Hills, 1711. [Also available on microfilm.—Woodbridge, CT: Research Publications, Inc., 1986.—1 reel; 35mm.—(The Eighteenth Century; reel 5466, no. 7)]

Sharp, John. *Sermons Preached on Several Occasions with Two Discourses of Conscience*. Vol. 2. 3rd ed. London: William Parker, 1738. [Sermon 3, See. 65–93; Sermon 8, See. 200–24; N.B. Archive.org and Google book]

Shelton, Lee Roy. *The Resurrection*. New Orleans, LA: Old Puritan Press, 19—? [46 pages]

Shepherd, William H. *If A Sermon Falls in the Forrest Preaching* Resurrection Texts. Lima, OH: CSS, 2002. [254 pages]

Sherman, Henry. *The Certainty of Christ's Resurrection*. Grand Rapids: Inheritance, 1972. [31 pages; N.B. Early American imprints. Second series; no. 23931]

Sibbes, Richard. *Two Sermons*. London: Printed by T. Cotes, sold by Andr. Kembe, 1638. [83 pages; Puritan Collection of English and American Literature]

Sibly, Manoah. *The Resurrection of the Lord: A Sermon Preached at the New Jerusalem Temple, in Red Cross Street, near Cripplegate, London: on Easter Day, March 24, 1799*. London: Printed by the author, 1799. [26 pages]

Simpson, Matthew. *The Triumphant Christ*. Waukesha, WI: Metropolitan Church Assn., n.d. [26 pages]

Slattery, Charles Lewis. *The Fact of Christ's Resurrection; A Sermon Preached in Grace Church in New York . . . April 30, 1916*. New York: Irving Press, 1916. [20 pages]

Smith, Wilbur M. [compiler]. *Great Sermons on the Resurrection of Christ*. Grand Rapids: Baker, 1996. [289 pages]

Sockman, Ralph W. "Too Great for the Grave." In *Preaching the Resurrection Twenty-two Great Easter Sermons*. Edited by Alton M. Motter. Philadelphia: Fortress, 1959. [See. 165–72]

South, Robert. "For Easter-Day." In *Sacred Classics: or, Cabinet Library of Divinity: Sermons on the Resurrection*. Vol. 16. Edited by R. Cattermole and H. Stebbing. London: John Hatchard, 1835. [See. 1–25; N.B. Google book]

Spurgeon, C. H. "All Hail." In *Great Sermons on the Resurrection of Christ*. Compiled by Wilbur M. Smith. Grand Rapids: Baker, 1996. [See. 87–86]

———. *Spurgeon's Sermons on the Death and Resurrection of Jesus*. Compiled by Patricia S. Klein. Peabody, MA: Hendrickson, 2015. [159 pages]

———. "The Stone Rolled away (Matthew 28:2)." In *Great Sermons on the Resurrection of Christ*. Compiled by Wilbur M. Smith. Grand Rapids: Baker, 1996. [See. 73–86]

Stebbing, Henry, ed. *Sermons on the Resurrection Particularly Adapted for Christian Consideration During Easter Selected from the Works of the most Eminent English Divines*. London: John Hatchard, 1835. [The Google book states Richard Cattermole was an additional editor; N.B. Google book and HathiTrust]

Stevenson, Dwight E. "The Power of His Resurrection." In *Preaching the Resurrection Twenty-two Great Easter Sermons*. Edited by Alton M. Motter. Philadelphia: Fortress, 1959. [See. 173–79]

Still, William, and George Ewen. *Studies on the Resurrection*. Aberdeen: Author, 1971. [43 pages]

Stone, Francis. *Jewish Prophecy the Sole Criterion to Distinguish between Genuinine and Spurious Christian Scripture . . . A Discourse*. 4th ed. London: Printed for the author, 1806. [A Discourse Preached: John 1, 45, See. 50–52; N.B. Google book.]

Struthers, Gavin. *The Resurrection, its Certainty and Mode: a sermon; preached in the Relief Church, Campbell St., Glasgow, August 16th, 1846 on the occasion of the death of the Rev. Robert Brodie, A.M.* Glasgow: Robert Jackson Edinburgh: W. Oliphant, 1846. [61 pages]

Taverner, Richard. "Homily: An Homily of the Resurrection of our Saviour Jesus Christ; for Easter-Day." In *Sermons or Homilies Appointed to be Read in Churches in the Time of Queen Elizabeth of Famous Memory*. 4th ed. Oxford: Clarendon Press, 1817. [First published in 1593; N.B. Google book; numerous copies available online. The author was identified in the 1852 printing.]

Taylor, Myron J. *The Resurrection: A Study in the History of Preaching*. PhD, School of Theology at Claremont, 1980. [Thesis 290 pages]

Thompson, Henry. "The Walk to Emmaus." In *Sermons for Sundays, Festivals, and Fasts, and Other Liturgical Occasions*. Vol. 2. Edited by Alexander Watson. London: Joseph Masters, 1846. [See. 123–35; N.B. Google book]

Thoresby, Francis. *Four Sermons on the Resurrection of Christ*. Devonport: Printed by W. Byers, 1824. [35 pages; N.B. Located only at the University of Cambridge.]

Tillotson, John. "Jesus, The Son of God, Proved by His Resurrection." In *Sacred Classics: or, Cabinet Library of Divinity: Sermons on the Resurrection*. Vol. 16, edited by R. Cattermole and H. Stebbing, 87–104. London: John Hatchard, 1835. [N.B. Google book]

———. *Several Discourses of the Life, Sufferings, Resurrection, and Ascension of Christ; and the Operations of the Holy Ghost. Being the Tenth Volume, published from the originals, by Ralph Barker*, . . . London: Printed for Ri. Chiswell, 1704. [Sermon 5 The Evidence of our Saviour's Resurrection, See. 133–64; Sermon 7 The Resurrection of our Saviour Considered, as an Argument, See. 197–223]

———. *The Works of Dr. John Tillotson. In Ten Volumes—Vol. 8*. London: J. F. Dove, 1820. [Sermon 192 The Evidence of Our Saviour's Resurrection, See. 308–25; Sermon 193 The Possibility of the Resurrection Asserted and Proved, See. 326–43; Sermon 194 The Resurrection of Our Saviour Considered, As an Argument for Seeking Things Above, See. 344–58; N.B. Archive.org]

———. *The Works of the most Reverend Dr. John Tillotson, Late Archbishop of Canterbury: Containing Two Hundred Sermons and Discourses*. Vol. 2. 2nd ed. London: John Nicholson, 1717. [Sermon 89, See. 251–58; N.B. Google book and HathiTrust]

Tilly, William. *The Power, Vertue, and Influence of Christ's Resurrection; and the Excellency of Knowing that Above, and Beyond all other Knowledge. : a sermon preach'd before the University of Oxford, at St. Mary's, on Easter-Tuesday, 1718*. Oxford: Printed by L. Lichfield, for Edw. Whistler; and are to be sold by J. Knapton, and H. Clements, Booksellers . . . London, 1718. [31 pages]

Torrey, R. A. *The Bible and its Christ; Being Noonday Talks with Businessmen on Faith and Unbelief*. Reprint *Talks to Men about the Bible and the Christ of the Bible*. Grand Rapids: Zondervan, 1955. [139 pages; N.B. Archive.org]

Tóth, Tihamér. *The Risen Christ: Sermons on the Resurrection and on the Blessed Virgin*. Translated by V. G. Agotai and edited by Rev. Newton Thompson. St Louis: Herder, 1955. [213 pages]

Wallis, John. *The Resurrection Asserted: In a Sermon Preached to the University of Oxford on Easter-day, 1679*. Oxford: Printed by Hen. Hall for James Good, 1679. [37 pages]

Watson, Alexander., ed *Sermons for Sundays, Festivals and Fasts* and Other Liturgical Occasions contributed. Vol. 2, Part 2. London: Joseph Masters, 1846. [N.B. This work contains three sermons dealing with the resurrection; N.B. Google]

Wentworth, E. *Christ's Resurrection: The Pledge and Pattern of the Resurrection of Believers: A Sermon, Delivered at the Funeral of Julia Harriot Kellogg, third daughter of Gen. John*

Kellogg, of Benson, VT. April 27th, 1846. Whitehall, NY: William S. Southmayd, printer, 1846. [11 pages]

West, J., and Richard Binkley. *Four Discourses on the Miracles Attending the Death of Christ: The Effects produced upon the Spectators; the Solemnities Attending His Burial; and the Evidence of His Resurrection*. London: Published by Richard Baynes, 1826. [153 pages; Lecture 4 The Resurrection of Jesus]

Westcott, Brooke Foss. "The Great Commission (John 20:21–22)." In *Great Sermons on the Resurrection of Christ*. Compiled by Wilbur M. Smith. Grand Rapids: Baker, 1996. [See. 195–201]

Wiersbe, Warren W. [compiler]. *Classic Sermons on the Resurrection of Christ*. Grand Rapids: Kregel, 1991. [155 pages; N.B. Eighteenth Century Collections online]

Williams, John. *A Sermon Upon the Resurrection Preached before the Right Honourable Sir Edward Clark, Lord-Mayor, the Aldermen, and Governors of the several hospitals of the city, at St. Bridget's Church, on Easter-Monday, April 5, 1697: being one of the anniversary spittal-sermons*. London: Printed for Ri. Chiswell and Tho. Cockerill, 1697. [32 pages; N.B. Early English Books]

Wright, John J. *The Resurrection Fact or Myth. An Easter Pastoral Addressed to the Diocese of Pittsburgh*. 1969. [9 pages; N.B. Archive.org]

Young, Dinsdale T. "Three Phases of the Risen Christ." In *Great Sermons on the Resurrection of Christ*. Compiled by Wilbur M. Smith, Grand Rapids: Baker, 1996. [See. 87–96]

Chapter 27

New Testament Commentaries and Annotations by One Person

Adam, Thomas. *An Exposition of the Four Gospels*. Vol. 2. Edited by A. Westoby. London: J. Hatchard, 1837. [Mark, See. 144–50; Luke, See. 353–64; John, See. 534–47; N.B. Google book]

Asimov, Isaac. *Asimov's Guide to the Bible*. Vol. 2. New York: Random House, 1981. [See. 897–902; N.B. Archive.org.]

Barclay, William. *The Acts of the Apostles*. Daily Study Bible. Philadelphia: Westminster, 1955. [Acts, See. 1–11]

———. *The Gospel of Mark*. Daily Study Bible. Philadelphia: Westminster, 1956. [See. 386–90]

———. *The Gospel of Matthew*. Vol. 2 (Chapters 11 to 28). Daily Study Bible. Philadelphia: Westminster, 1976. [See. 375–78]

———. *The Gospel of John*. Vol. 2. Daily Study Bible. Philadelphia: Westminster, 1956. [See. 307–38]

———. *The Gospel of Luke*. Daily Study Bible. Philadelphia: Westminster, 1956. [See. 304–14]

———. *The Letters to the Corinthians*. Daily Study Bible. Philadelphia: Westminster, 1975. [See. 1–11]

Barnes, Albert. *Notes on the Explanatory and Practical on the Acts of the Apostles*. New York: Harper & Brothers, 1854. [Acts, See. 7–23; N.B. Archive.org, Google book, and HathiTrust]

———. *Notes on the Explanatory and Practical on the First Epistle of Paul to the Corinthians*. New York: Harper & Brothers, 1864. [1 Cor 15, See. 137–48; N.B. Archive.org, Google book, and HathiTrust]

———. *Notes, Explanatory and Practical, on the Gospels. In Two Volumes*. Vol. 2. *John*. New York: Leavitt, Lord, 1836. [John, See. 354–64; N.B. Google book]

———. *Notes, Explanatory and Practical, on the Gospels. In Two Volumes*. Vol. 2. *Luke*. New York: Leavitt, Lord, 1836. [See. 151–59; N.B. Google Book]

———. *Notes on the New Testament Explanatory and Practical*. Vol. 1. *Matthew and Mark*. London: Blackie, 1868. [Matthew, See. 317–27, 457–58; Mark, See. 390–94; N.B. Google book.]

New Testament Commentaries and Annotations by One Person

Barth, C. G. *The Bible Manual: An Expository and Practical Commentary on the Books of Scripture, Arranged in Chronological Order.* London: James Nisbet, 1865. [The New Testament Eighth Section. From Resurrection to the Ascension of Jesus, See. 734–44; The Acts of the Apostles, First Section. Review of the Life and Ascension of Jesus, See. 745–46; N.B. Google book]

Bellett, J. G. *The Evangelists: Papers on the Four Gospels.* New York: Loizeaux, 1800?]. [Matthew, See. 72; Mark, See. 39–44; Luke, See. 163–81; John, See. 169–84]

Benson, Dennis C. *Dennis Benson's Creative Bible Studies.* Loveland, CO: Group, 1985. [Matthew, See. 189–92; Mark, See. 267–69; Luke, 396–400; John, See. 504–10; Acts, See. 514–19]

Binney, Amos, and Daniel Steele. *The People's New Testament Including Brief Notes on the New Testament with Notes.* New York: Nelson & Philips, 1879. [Available online without pagination.]

Butler, J. Glentworth. *The Bible Readers' Commentary. The New Testament: The Four Fold Gospel.* Vol. 1. New York: D. Appleton, 1878. [Sections 160–66, See. 557–87 N.B. Google book]

Calvin, John. *Commentary on a Harmony of the Evangelists, Matthew, Mark, and Luke.* Volume 3. Translated by William Pringle. Grand Rapids: Baker, 1989. [337–95;
———. *Commentary on the Gospel According to John.* Vol. 2. Translated by William Pringle. Grand Rapids: Baker, 1989. See. 247–300; *Commentary upon the Acts of the Apostles,* Vol. 1 See. 31–72; Calvin's Commentary 22-Volume Set Reprinted by Baker. Originally printed for the Calvin Translation Society Edinburgh, Scotland.]

Carroll, B. H. *An Interpretation of the English Bible: The Four Gospels.* Edited by J. B. Cranfill. Grand Rapids: Baker, 1976. Sections 30–32, See. 402–50; Reprinted with permission from Broadman Press, 1948]

Challoner, Richard, and H. J. Ganass. *The New Testament of Our Lord and Saviour Jesus Christ.* Turnhout, Belgium: Henri Proost, 1914. [Matthew, See. 104–5; Mark, See. 154–55; Luke, See. 234–37; John, See. 298–302; Acts, See. 304–6; 1 Cor 15, See. 446–47; N.B. Archive.org]

Chalmers, Thomas. *Posthumous Works of the Rev. Thomas Chalmers.* Edited by William Hanna. Vol. 1. New York: Harper & Brothers, 1848. [Matthew, See. 47–48; Mark, See. 76–77; Luke, See. 112–13; John, See. 144–47; Acts, See. 147–49; 1 Cor 15, See. 238–40; N.B. Google book]

Chase, Frederic Henry. *The Gospels In the Light of Historical Criticism.* London: MacMillan, 1914. [Preface (2) The Resurrection of Our Lord, See. 20–34]

Clarke, Adam, and Daniel Curry. *The New Testament of our Lord and Saviour Jesus Christ: The Text in the Authorized Translation, with a Commentary and Critical Notes.* Vol. 1. New York: Phillips & Hunt, 1883. [See. 169–72; 210–12; 298–302; 399–406; 411–14; N.B. Google book]

Cobb, Sylvanus. *The New Testament of our Lord and Saviour Jesus Christ: With Explanatory Notes and Practical Observations.* Boston: Published by the Commentator, 1864. [See. 91–92; 132–35; 212–15; 279–84; 284–86; 447–49; N.B. Archive.org]

Comfort, Philip Wesley. *A Commentary on the Manuscripts and Text of the New Testament.* Grand Rapids: Kregel, 2015. [See. 177, 197–206, 240–45, 274–76, 278–79]

Cook, F. C. *Romans to Philemon.* Vol. 3. New York: Scribner's Sons, 1881. [See. 352–60; N.B. Archive.org]

Category IX—Creeds, Religion, Doctrinal, Sermons, Commentaries

———. *St. John-The Acts of the Apostles*. Vol. 2. New York: Scribner's Sons, 1880. [See. 287–307; 351–60; N.B. Acts is available at Archive.org]

———. *St. Matthew—St. Mark—St. Luke*. Vol. 1. New York: Scribner's, Sons, 1878. [See. 191–97; 293–308; 464–72]

Corrigan, Michael Augustine. *The New Testament of Our Lord and Saviour Jesus Christ*. New York: Benziger, 1897. [See. 58–59; 91–92; 147–49; 189–93; 193–94; 291–92; N.B. Google book]

Cummings, J. A. *The New Testament of our Lord and Saviour Jesus Christ*. 2nd ed. Boston: Hilliard, Gray, Little, and Wilkins, 1832. [See. 43–46; 69; 107–9; 135–37; 138–39; 205–6; N.B. Google book]

Dake, Finis. *Dake's Annotated Reference Bible: New Testament*. Grand Rapids: Zondervan, 1961. [See. 33–34; 54–55; 90–91; 118–20; 122; 187–88]

Darby, John Nelson. *The Gospels, Acts, Epistles, and Book of Revelation: Commonly Called The New Testament*. London: G. Moorish, 1884. [N.B. Archive.org and elsewhere online.]

Diodati, Giovanni. *Pious Annotations Upon the Holy Bible*. London: Printed for Nicholas Fussell, 1643. [N.B. Early English Books online]

D'Oyly, George, and Richard Mant. *The Holy Bible, according to the Authorized Version with Notes, Explanatory and Practical*. Vol. 3. Matthew—Revelation. London: SPCK, 1889. [No pagination; N.B. Archive.org]

Dunwell, Francis Henry. *The Four Gospels As Interpreted by the Early Church*. London: William Clowes, 1876. [Matthew, See. 489–509; Mark, See. 569–70; Luke, See. 691–98; John, See. 911–24; N.B. Archive.org and Google book]

Elsley, Heneage. *Annotations on the Four Gospels and the Acts of the Apostles*. Edited by R. Walker. Oxford: J. Vincent, 1844. [Matthew, See. 247–52; Mark, See. 293–95; Luke, 407–10; John, See. 486–93; Acts, See. 503–5; N.B. Google book]

Exell, Joseph S. *The Biblical Illustrator*. Grand Rapids: Baker, 1953. [N.B. 23 volume set reprint. The original (1888–1902) spanned 56 volumes; N.B. Archive.org has scanned Luke and 1 Corinthians. These dated works are a recommended read.]

Fraser, Donald. *Synoptical Lectures on the Books of Holy Scripture*. London: J. Nisbet, 1886. [N.B. Archive.org]

Furness, W. H. *Remarks on the Four Gospels*. London: Charles Fox, 1837. [Chapter 12 The Death and Resurrection of Jesus, 246–88; N.B. Google book]

Gaebelein, A.C. *The Annotated Bible: The Holy Scriptures Analyzed and Annotated The New Testament*. Vol. 1. *The Gospels and the Book of Acts*. New York: Publication Office "Our Hope," 1913. [Matthew, See. 60–62; Mark, See. 106–8; Luke, See. 173–74; John, See. 242–46; Acts, See. 256–58; N.B. Archive.org]

———. *The Holy Scriptures Analysed and Annotated*. Vol. 11. Romans—Ephesians. New York: Publication Office "Our Hope," 1913. [See. 135–42; N.B. Archive.org]

Grant, Frederick C. *Nelson's Bible Commentary*. Vol. 6. Matthew–Acts. New York: Thomas Nelson, 1962. [Matthew, See. 134–36; Mark, See. 206–8; Luke, See. 319–23; John, See. 407–13; Acts, See. 420–22]

———. *Nelson's Bible Commentary*. Vol. 7. Romans-Revelation. New York: Thomas Nelson, 1962. [7. The Basic Christian Doctrine, the Resurrection, 15.1–58; See. 103–5]

Grant, Frederick W. *The Numerical Bible*. Vol. 5. The Gospels. 3rd ed. New York: Loizeaux, 1897. [Matthew, See. 268–72; Mark, See. 339–42; Luke, See. 465–69; John, See. 612–26; N.B. Archive.org]

Gray, James M. *Home Bible Study Commentary.* Grand Rapids: Kregel, 1985. [Matthew, See. 312–13; Mark, See. 319–20; Luke, See. 332–33; John, See. 334–35; Acts, See. 345–46; 1 Cor. 15, See. 374]

Greswell, Edward. *Dissertations Upon the Principles and Arrangement of a Harmony of the Gospels.* Vol. 3. Oxford: University Press, 1830. [Dissertation 6, See. 169–218; N.B. Google book]

Gundry, Robert H. *Commentary on the New Testament: Verse-by-Verse Explanations with a Literal Translation.* Hendricksen, 2010. [Matthew, See. 133–36; Mark, 219–20; Luke, See. 341–46; John, See. 455–63; Acts, See. 466–68; 1 Cor 15, See. 679–81]

Hall, Thomas Cuming. *The Messages of Jesus According to the Synoptists.* New York: Scribner's Sons, 1901. [The Resurrection of the Christ, See. 218–22; N.B. Google book]

Hammond, Henry. *A Paraphrase and Annotations Upon All of the Books of the New Testament.* Vol. 3. [*Matthew–Acts*]. Oxford: University Press, 1845. [Matthew, See. 181–83; Mark, See. 215; Luke, See. 297; John, See. 339–44; Acts, See. 345–52; N.B. Google book]

Haweis, Thomas. *The Evangelical Expositor: or, a Commentary on the Holy Bible.* London: Printed for Edward and Charles Dilly, 1765. [N.B. World Wide Web. Access limited by licensing agreements.]

Hayford, Jack W. ed. *The Hayford Bible Handbook.* Nashville: Nelson, 1995. [Matthew, See. 310; Mark, See. 297; Luke, See. 309–10; John, See. 322–23; Acts, See. 328–29]

Hendriksen, William. *A Commentary on the Gospel of John.* London: Banner of Truth Trust, 1964. [John, See. 447–94; N.B. Worthy of consulting.]

———. *New Testament Commentary: Exposition of the Gospel According to Luke.* Grand Rapids: Baker, 1978. [Luke, See. 1050–82]

———. *New Testament Commentary: Exposition of the Gospel According to Mark.* Grand Rapids: Baker, 1975. [Mark, See. 676–93]

———. *New Testament Commentary: Exposition of the Gospel According to Matthew.* Grand Rapids: Baker, 1973. [Matthew, See. 986–1003]

Henry, Matthew. *An Exposition of All the Books of the Old and New Testament.* Vol. 5 Acts–Revelation. London: W. Gracie, 1806. [Acts, See. 4–10; 1 Cor 15, See. 343–46; N.B. Google book. Henry's must read work is a classic, dated source.]

———. *An Exposition of All the Books of the Old and New Testament.* Vol. 4 Matthew–John. London: W. Gracie, 1806. [Matthew, See. 251–57; Mark, See. 325–28; Luke, See. 475–83; John, See. 687–707; N.B. Google book. Henry's must read work is a classic, dated source.]

Hewlett, John. *Commentaries and Annotations on the Holy Scriptures*, Volume 4. [*Matt–Rev*]. London: Longman et al., 1816. [Matthew, See. 155–56; Mark, See. 179–80; Luke, See. 231; John, See. 287–90; Acts, See. 293–96; 1 Cor 15, See. 455–56; N.B. Google book]

Hitchcock, Roswell, ed. *Hitchcock's New and Complete Analysis of the Holy Bible: or, The Whole of the Old and New Testaments Arranged According to Subjects.* New York: A. J. Johnson, 1871. [Book 3 Jesus Christ. Chapter 2 Prophecies Concerning Christ, #23 Resurrection, See. 37; Chapter 8 The Burial and Resurrection of Christ, See. 59–61; Chapter 9 Christ's Subsequent Appearances, See. 61–62; Chapter 10 Christ's Ascension: Christ in Heaven, See. 62–63; N.B. Archive.org and Google book]

Holden, George. *The Christian Expositor or Practical Guide to the Study of the New Testament Intended for the Use of General Readers.* London: Gilbert & Rivington, 1830.

Category IX—Creeds, Religion, Doctrinal, Sermons, Commentaries

[Matthew, See. 123–26; Mark, See. 144–46; Luke, See. 202–4; John, See. 278–81; Acts, See. 283–85; 1 Corinthians, See. 438–39; N.B. Google book]

Howell, Laurence. *A Complete History of the Holy Bible; as contained in the Old and New Testaments, including also the occurrences of four hundred years, from the last of the prophets to the birth if Christ, and the life of our Blessed Saviour and his apostles, &c. With copious notes, critical and explanatory, practical and devotional.* Vol. 2. Philadelphia: W. W. Woodward, 1808. [See. 421–442; N.B. Google book; See. 249–70; N.B. HathiTrust]

Jamieson, Robert. *Commentary Critical and Explanatory on the Whole Bible.* Grand Rapids: Christian Classics Ethereal Library, 1871. [N.B. Online CCEL]

Jenks, William. *The Comprehensive Commentary on the Holy Bible.* Matt—John. Vol. 1. Brattleboro: Fessenden, 1834. [Matthew, See. 302–6; Mark, See. 396–400; Luke, See. 591–99; John, See. 820–37; N.B. Google book]

Johnson, B. W. *The People's New Testament with Notes.* Grand Rapids: Christian Classics Ethereal Library, 1891. [N.B. Available online]

Jones, Joel. *Notes on Scriptures.* Philadelphia: William S. & Alfred Martien, 1861. [Chapter 12 The Resurrection, See. 446–90; Chapter 13 Walk to Emmaus, etc. See. 490–517; Chapter 14 Events that Followed the Lord's Resurrection, See. 517–48; N.B. Google book]

Keener, Craig S. *The IVP Bible Background Commentary*: New Testament. 2nd ed. Downers Grove, IL: InterVarsity, 1994. [Matthew, See 124–25; Mark, See 174–75; Luke, See. 242–44; John, See. 309–13; Acts, See. 319–21; 1 Corinthians 15, See. 491–92]

Knox, Ronald A. *A Commentary on the Gospels.* New York: Sheed & Ward, 1952. [Matthew, See. 70–72; Mark, See. 114–17; Luke, See. 196–99; John, See. 272–77]

Lee, Witness. *The New Testament Recovery Vers*ion. Translated by the Editorial Section Living Stream Ministry. Anaheim, CA: Living Stream Ministry, 1991. [See. 162–64; 239–42; 353–58; 457–67; 474–79; 744–47]

Lenski, R. C. H. *The Interpretation of the Acts of the Apostles.* Minneapolis: Augsburg, 1964. [See. 17–53]

———. *The Interpretation of St. John's Gospel.* Minneapolis: Augsburg, 1961. [See. 1332–444]

———. *The Interpretation of St. Luke.* Columbus, OH: Wartburg Press, 1951. [See. 1168–212]

———. *The Interpretation of St. Mark's Gospel.* Minneapolis: Augsburg, 1964. [See. 736–75]

———. *The Interpretation of St. Matthew's Gospel.* Columbus, Ohio: Lutheran Book Concern, 1932. [See. 1127–61]

———. *The Interpretation of St. Paul's First and Second Epistles to the Corinthians.* Minneapolis: Augsburg, 1963. [See. 623–61]

Lightfoot, Bishop John. *A Commentary of the New Testament from the Talmud and Hebraica.* 2 Volumes. 1684. [N.B. Available online at various sites such as preteristarchive.com and CCEL.org]

———. *The Works of the Reverend & Learned John Lightfoot D.D. in two Volumes.* Volume 1. London: Printed by W. R., 1684. N.B. Archive.org, Google book, and HathiTrust]

Livermore, Abiel Abbot. *The Four Gospels with a Commentary. Vol. 1. Matthew.* Boston: James Munroe, 1843. [Matthew, See. 340–47; N.B. Google book]

———. *The Four Gospels with a Commentary.* Vol. 2. *Mark, Luke and John.* Boston: James Munroe, 1844. [Mark, See. 57–58; Luke, See. 176–81; John, See. 347–58; N.B. Google book]

Longking, Joseph. *Notes Illustrative and Explanatory on the Holy Gospels.* Vol. 4 New York: G. Lane & P. P. Sandford, 1844. [Lessons 25–27, See. 481–510; N.B. Google book]

Lonsdale, John and William Hale Hale. *The Four Gospels with Annotations.* London: Francis & Rivington, 1849. [Matthew, See. 108–9; Mark, See. 146–47; Luke, See. 226–29; John, See. 295–300; N.B. Google book]

Luther, Martin. *Luther's Works.* Philadelphia: Fortress Press and Concordia, 1957. [N.B. This work is part of a 55-volume collection that contains John and 1 Corinthians.]

MacArthur, John. *The MacArthur Bible Commentary.* Nashville: Nelson, 2005. [Matthew, See. 1184–86; Mark, See. 1260–63; Luke, See. 1334–37; John, See. 1423–30; Acts, See. 1431–35; 1 Cor 15, See. 1604–7]

MacEvilly, John. *An Exposition of the Gospel Consisting of an Analysis of Each Chapter and of a Commentary Critical, Exegetical, Doctrinal, and Moral.* 4th ed. Dublin: M. H. Gill, 1898. [Matthew, 579–96; Mark, See. 666–72; N.B. Archive.org]

———. *An Exposition of the Gospel of St. John Consisting of an Analysis of Each Chapter and of a Commentary Critical, Exegetical, Doctrinal, and Moral.* 2nd ed. revised. Dublin: Gill, 1902. [See. 357–79; N.B. Archive.org]

———. *An Exposition of the Gospel of St. Luke Consisting of an Analysis of Each Chapter and of a Commentary Critical, Exegetical, Doctrinal, and Moral.* 2nd ed. revised. Dublin: Gill, 1887. [See. 231–47; N.B. Archive.org]

Makrakes, Apostolos. *Interpretation of the Entire New Testament.* Translated by Albert George Alexander. 2 Volumes. Chicago: Orthodox Christian Education Society, 1949–1950. [Volume 1 The Gospels and Volume 2 Matthew, See. 457–72; Mark, See. 616–23; Luke, See. 817–28; John, See. 1090–105; The Acts of the Apostles, See. 1126–36]

McGee, J. Vernon. *Thru the Bible with J. Vernon McGee.* Vol. 4 *Matthew—Romans.* Nashville: Nelson, 1983. [Matthew, See. 151–54; Mark, See. 23–36; Luke, See. 356–61; John, See. 494–506; Acts, See. 510–15]

McGrath, Alister. *The NIV Bible Companion: A Basic Commentary on the Old and New Testaments.* Grand Rapids: Zondervan, 1997. [Matthew, See. 283; Mark, See. 300–301; Luke, See. 324–25; John, See. 348–49; Acts, See. 351–52; 1 Corinthians, See. 386–87]

Meyer, Heinrich August Wilhelm. *Critical And Exegetical Hand-Book to the Acts of the Apostles.* Translated by Paton J. Gloag and William P. Dickson. New York: Funk & Wagnalls, 1883. [Acts, See. 337–53; N.B. Archive.org and HathiTrust.]

———. *Critical And Exegetical Hand-Book to the Epistles to the Corinthians.* Translated by Paton J. Gloag and William P. Dickson. New York: Funk & Wagnalls, 1877. [1 Cor 15, See. 337–53; N.B. Google book and HathiTrust]

———. *Critical and Exegetical Handbook to the Gospel of John.* Vol. 2. Translated by William P. Dickson and Frederick Crombie, Edinburgh: T&T Clark, 1875. [See. 366–412; N.B. Archive.org and Google book]

———. *Critical And Exegetical Hand-Book to the Gospels of Mark and Luke.* Translated by Robert Ernest Wallis and William P. Dickson. New York: Funk & Wagnalls, 1884. [Mark, See. 196–210; Luke, See. 571–93; N.B. Archive.org and Hathitrust]

———. *Critical and Exegetical Handbook to the Gospel of Matthew.* Vol. 2. Translated by Peter Christie and William Stewart, Edinburgh: T&T Clark, 1881. [See. 287–308; N.B. Archive.org and HathiTrust]

Category IX—Creeds, Religion, Doctrinal, Sermons, Commentaries

Moody, D. L. *Notes from my Bible: From Genesis to Revelation*. Chicago: Revell, 1895. [Matthew, See. 111; Luke, See. 132; John, See. 144; Acts, See. 144–45; 1 Cor 15, See. 160–61; N.B. Archive.org]

Morgan, G. Campbell. *An Exposition of the Whole Bible Chapter By Chapter In One Volume*. Old Tappan, NJ: Revell, 1959. [Matthew, See. 422–23; Mark, See. 430–31; Luke, See. 441; John, See. 448–49; Acts, See. 450; 1 Cor 15, See. 476]

Ness, Christopher. *History and Mystery of the Old and New Testament. The Fourth Volume of the Sacred History and Mystery of the New Testament, Logically Difficult and Theologically Improved: beginning at the birth of Christ, and ending at the last of the Revelations, wherein is held forth the life of Christ, and the lives of all the Apostles*. London: Printed by Thomas Snowden, for the Author, 1696. [Chapter 35 Of Christ's Resurrection, See. 260–76; Chapter 37 Of Christ's Ten Appearances, See. 277–90; Chapter 38 Of Christ's Fourth Appearance. See. 290–301; Chapter 39 Of Christ's Sixth Appearance, 301–7; Chapter 40 Of Christ's Seventh Appearance, See. 307–21; The Second Part of the New Testament. Chapter 1 Of the Antecedents of Christ's Ascension, 322–35; [N.B. Digitalpuritan.net. This is a detailed work.]

Nevin, Alfred. *Popular Expositor of the Gospels and Acts for Pulpit, Sunday-School, and Family: Matthew, Mark, John*. Philadelphia: Ziegler & McCurdy, 1872. [Archive.org]

Olshausen, Hermann. *Biblical Commentary on the New Testament*. Vol. 3. Translated by David Fosdick. New York: Sheldon, 1866. [On The Resurrection of Jesus, See. 114–58; Acts, See. 173–88; N.B. CCEL]

Patton, William, ed. *The Cottage Bible and Family Expositor: Containing the Old and New Testaments*. Vol. 2. Hartford: Case. Tiffany & Burnham, 1837. [See. 1063–65; 1087–88; 1135–38; 1182–85; 1186–88; N.B. Archive.org]

Poole, Matthew. *Annotations Upon the Holy Bible Wherein the Sacred Text is Inserted and Various Readings*. Vol. 2. Jeremiah—Revelation. London: Printed for Thomas Parkhurst, 1700. [no pagination; N.B. Google book]

Porter, J. L. *The Pew and Study Bible: Containing the Old and New Testaments*. London: Blackie, 1876. [Matthew, See. 1074; Mark, See. 1099–1100; Luke, See. 1142–44; John, See. 1174–77; Acts, See. 1178–79; 1 Cor 15, See. 1251–52; N.B. Google book]

Richards, Lawrence O. *The Bible Reader's Companion*. Wheaton: Victor, 1991. [Matthew, See. 629; Mark, See. 648; Luke, See. 674; John, See. 697–98; Acts, See. 708; 1 Cor 15, See. 771]

Riley, W. B. *The Bible of the Expositor and the Evangelist*. Vols. 1–10. Cleveland: Union Gospel Press, 1926–1928. [Vol. 3 Matthew, Chapter 15 Christ's Resurrection and Ascension Certain, See. 312–26; Vol. 4. Mark and Luke, Chapter 14 The Resurrection of Jesus Christ, See. 229–43; Vol. 5. John, Chapter 15 Christ's Deity and Man's Salvation, John 20:30, 31, See 241–55; Vol. 6 Acts, Chapter 1 The Ascension Promises, See. 9–25; Vol. 10 1 Corinthians, Chapter 10 The Pillars of an Apostle's Gospel 1 Corinthians 15:1–34, See. 151–73]

Robertson, A. T. *Word Pictures of the New Testament*. Vol. 5. *The Fourth Gospel and The Epistle to the Hebrews*. Grand Rapids: Baker, 1930. [The Fourth Gospel, See. 308–23]

———. *Word Pictures of the New Testament*. Vol. 4. *The Epistles of Paul*. Grand Rapids: Baker, 1930. [1 Cor 15, See. 186–90]

———. *Word Pictures of the New Testament*. Vol. 1. *The Gospel According to Matthew; The Gospel According to Mark*. Grand Rapids: Baker, 1930. [Matthew, See. 240–46; Mark, See. 399–406]

———. *Word Pictures of the New Testament*. Vol. 3. *The Acts of the Apostles*. Grand Rapids: Baker, 1930. [Acts, See. 3–19]

———. *Word Pictures of the New Testament*. Vol. 2. *The Gospel According to Luke*. Grand Rapids: Baker, 1930. [Luke, See. 290–98]

Robinson, Thomas. *Scripture Characters; or, A Practical Improvement of the Principal Histories in the Old and New Testament*. Vol. 4. London: W. Clowes, 1814. [Section 42 Jesus Christ, See. 126–41; Section 43 Jesus Christ, See. 142–54; Section 44 Jesus Christ, See. 155–57; N.B. Google book]

Roustaing, J. B. ed. *The Four Gospels Explained by their Writers*. Vol. 2. Translated by W. F. Kirby. London: Trübner, 1881. [See. 416–48; N.B. Google book]

Ryle, J. C. *Expository Thoughts on the Gospels: St. Luke*. New York: Robert Carter, 1875. [See. 491–530; N.B. Archive.org]

———. *Expository Thoughts on the Gospels: St. John*. New York: Revell, 1875. [See. 346–473; N.B. Archive.org]

———. *Expository Thoughts on the Gospels: St. Mark*. New York: Robert Carter, 1858. [See. 353–70; N.B. Archive.org]

———. *Expository Thoughts on the Gospels: St. Matthew*. New York: Robert Carter, 1860. [See. 402–13; N.B. Archive.org]

Sadler, Gilbert T. *The Inner Meaning of the Four Gospels Reinterpreted in the Light of Modern Research, and in Relation to Spiritual and Social Needs*. London: C. W. Daniel, 1920. [Matt. 28, 1–15 The Resurrection, See. 100–101; Matt. 28, 16–20 The Commission, See. 101; N.B. HathiTrust]

Sailhamer, John. *The NIV Compact Bible Commentary*. Grand Rapids: Zondervan, 1999. [Matt., See. 45; Mark, See. 469; Luke, See. 483–84; John, See. 495–96; Acts, See. 497–98; 1 Cor. 15, See. 538.]

Sargent, Frederick. *A Compendium of Biblical Criticism on the Canonical Books of the Holy Scriptures*. London: Longman, Green, Longman & Roberts, 1860. [Matthew, See. 260; Mark, See. 274; Luke, See. 289; John, See. 299; Acts, See. 300; 1 Cor 15, See. 399; N.B. Google book]

Schmidt, Paul Wilhelm, ed. *A Short Protestant Commentary on the Books of the New Testament*. Vol. 1. Translated by Francis Henry Jones. London: Williams & Norgate, 1882. [Archive.org]

Scott, John P. *The Four Gospels Esoterically Interpreted*. Oceanside, CA: Langford Press, 1937. [Matt 28, See. 132–34; Mark, See. 138; Luke, See. 154; John, See. 166–67; N.B. Haithitrust.org]

Scott, Thomas. *The New Testament of Our Lord and Saviour Jesus Christ with Original Notes, Practical Observations*, Vol. 1. New York: Dodge & Sayee, 1816. [no pagination; N.B. Archive.org]

———. *The New Testament of Our Lord and Saviour Jesus Christ with Original Notes, Practical Observations*, Vol. 2. St Paul's Epistles. New York: Dodge & Sayee, 1816. [no pagination; N.B. Archive.org]

Shaw, Fernando. *A Summary of the Bible; or the Principal Heads of Natural and Revealed Religion*. London: Richard Fox, 1730. [See. 269–71; N.B. Google book]

Simpson, A. B. *Christ in the Bible*. Vol. 9. *Matthew, Mark & Luke*. New York: Christian Alliance Publishing, 1889. [N.B. EBSCO]

Skinner, Matthew, L. *A Companion to the New Testament The Gospels and Act*. Waco, TX: Baylor University Press, 2017. [Mark, See. 156–58; Luke, See. 186–88; John, See. 218–20; Acts, See. 235]

Sutcliffe, Joseph. *A Commentary on the Old and New Testament*. Vol. 2. 2nd ed. London: John Mason, 1838. [Matthew, See. 278–80; Mark, See. 300–301; Luke, See. 337–39; John, See. 381–85; Acts, See. 388–90; 1 Cor 15, See. 492–93; N.B. Google book]

Swaggart, Jimmy. *Jimmy Swaggart Bible Commentary*. Volumes 8–13. Baton Rouge, LA: World Evangelism Press, 1995–1998.

Swihart, Stephen D. ed. *Logos International Bible Commentary: Acts–John*. Vol. 2. Plainfield, NJ: Logos International, 1981.

———. *Logos International Bible Commentary: The Gospels of Matthew, Mark and Luke*. Plainfield, NJ: Logos International, 1981. [Matthew, See. 326–30; Mark, See. 414–17; Luke, See. 585–90]

Swindoll, Charles R. *The Swindoll Study Bible: New Living Translation*. Carol Stream, IL: Tyndale House, 2017. [Matt, See. 1184–85; Mark, 1220–222; Luke, See. 1270–272; John, See. 1313–316; Acts, See. 1321–323; 1 Cor 15, See. 1428–429]

Thomas, Mack. *The Complete Bible Discussion Guide: Group Discussion Questions for Every Chapter in the Bible*. Sisters, OR: Questar, 1992. [See. 425–26, 449, 481–82, 511–13, 515–16, 579]

Thompson, Charles. *A Synopsis of the Four Evangelists*. Philadelphia: Wm. M'Culloch, 1815. [Section 49–52, See. 189–200; N.B. Archive.org]

Thorburn, Thomas James. *The Mystical Interpretation of the Gospels: Critical Studies in the Historic Narratives*. New York: Scribner's Sons, 1916. [Chapter 15 The Descension to Hades. The Resurrection and Ascension to Heaven, See. 302–29; N.B. Google Book]

Toy, Crawford Howell. *Quotations in the New Testament*. New York: Scribner's Sons 1884. [Acts, See. 95; N.B. Google book]

Trapp, John. *A Commentary or Exposition Upon All the Books of the New Testament*. 2nd ed. London: R.W., 1656. [Matthew, See. 336–40; Mark, See. 368–69; Luke, See. 423–25; John, See. 516–24; Acts, See. 527–29; 1 Cor 15, See. 697–98; N.B. Google book]

Wayne, Thomas. *The General View of the Holy Scriptures; or, the Times, Places, and Persons*. 2nd ed. London: I. B and S. B., 1640 [Of Christ's Death, Resurrection, etc., See. 345–47; N.B. Google Books]

Weiss, Bernhard. *A Commentary on the New Testament [Matthew— Mark]*. Vol. 1. Translated by George H. Schodde and Epiphanius Wilson. New York: Funk & Wagnalls, 1906. [Matthew, See. 248–51; Mark, See. 371–75; N.B. Google book and HathiTrust]

———. *A Commentary on the New Testament [Romans–Colossians]*. Vol. 3. Translated by George H. Schodde and Epiphanius Wilson. New York: Funk & Wagnalls, 1906. [HathiTrust]

———. *A Commentary on the New Testament [Luke and Acts]*. Vol. 2. Translated by George H. Schodde and Epiphanius Wilson. New York: Funk & Wagnalls, 1906. [Luke, See. 205–12; Acts, See. 416–23; N.B. Archive.org and HathiTrust]

Wells, Edward. *A Treatise Concerning Harmony of the Four Gospels*. London: Printed for James Knapton, 1718. [See. 216–25; N.B. Google book]

Wesley, John. *The New Testament with Explanatory Notes*. Halifax: William Nicholson, 1869. [Matthew, See. 98–99; Mark, See. 137–38; Luke, See. 208–11; John, See. 271–75; Acts, See. 276–78; 1 Cor 15, See. 431–33; N.B. Google book]

New Testament Commentaries and Annotations by One Person

West, Nathaniel. *The Complete Analysis of the Holy Bible*. New York: A. J. Johnson, 1869. [Chapter 13 Christ's Resurrection and Ascension, Section 242–275, See. 248–53; N.B. Archive.org, Google book, and HathiTrust]

Whitby, Daniel. *A Commentary on the Gospels and Epistles of the New Testament*. Vol. 4. London: William Tegg, 1843. [Matthew, See. 184–91; Mark, See. 242–45; Luke, See. 319–21; John, See. 407–12; Acts, See. 421–25; N.B. Archive.org]

Wiersbe, Waren W. *Wiersbe's Expository Outlines on the New Testament*. Colorado Springs, CO: Chariot Victor. 1992. [Matt, See. 99–102; Mark, See. 141–43; Luke, See. 204–6; John, See. 208–10; Acts, See. 278–80; 1 Cor 15, See. 465–66]

Wordsworth, Chr. *The New Testament of Our Lord and Saviour Jesus Christ. Vol. 1. The Four Gospels and Acts of the Apostles*, 1872. [Matthew, See. 107–10; Mark, See. 153–56; Luke, See. 252–55; John, See. 358–66; Acts, See. 35–42; N.B. Archive.org]

———. *The New Testament of Our Lord and Saviour Jesus Christ, in the Original Greek, with Introductions and Notes, St Paul's Epistles; The General Epistles; The Book of Revelation, and Indexes*. Vol. 2. London: Rivingtons, 1872. [See. 135–37; N.B. Archive.org]

Yeager, Ralph O. *Renaissance New Testament* [18 Volumes]. Powhatan, VA: Firebird Press, 1998.

Ylvisaker, Joh. *The Gospels: A Synoptic Presentation of the Text in Matthew, Mark, Luke and John*. Minneapolis: Augsburg, [original 1907] 1932. [Jesus' Exaltation, 151–60, See. 758–90]

CATEGORY X

Islamic Interpretations of the Crucifixion

CHAPTER 28

Jesus's Crucifixion: Pro Resurrection

Abdul-Haqq, Abdiyah Akbar. *Sharing Your Faith With a Muslim*. Bloomington, MN: Bethany, 1980. [Chapter 11 The Suffering Servant, See. 131–39]

Abraham, A. J. *Another Look: One God and Three Faiths*. Lanham, MD: UPA, 2014 [See. 20, 282–88]

———. *Islam and Christianity: Crossroads in Faith*. Bloomington, Bristol, IN: Wyndham Hall Press, 1987. [See. 131–40]

Accad, Foud Elias. *Building Bridges Christianity and Islam*. Colorado Springs, CO: Navpress, 1997. [Chapter 16 Does the Qur'an Support Jesus' Crucifixion?, See. 138–41]

Addison, James Thayer. *The Christian Approach to the Moslem: A Historical Study*. NY: AMS Press, 1966. [See. 6]

African Christian Press. *Christian Witness Among Muslims*. Bartlesville, OK: Living Sacrifice Book, 1994. [Chapter 7 The Sacrifice of Jesus Christ, See. 55–62]

Ali, Daniel, and Robert Spencer. *Inside Islam: A Guide for Catholics 100 Questions and Answers*. West Chest, PA: Ascension Press, 2003. [Question 38 Why Don't Muslims Believe that Jesus Died on the Cross?; Question 39 How then do Muslims Explain the Biblical Accounts of Jesus' Passion and Death?; N.B. No pagination]

Ali, Maulvi Muhammad. *Muhammad and Christ*. Madras: SPCK, 1921. [Chapter 5 Circumstances Relating to Death, See. 118–46]

Al Kindy, Abd al Masih ibn Ishak. *The Apology of Al Kindy, Written at the Court of Al Mâmûn (AH 215; AD 830) In Defense of Christianity Against Islam*. Reprint of 2nd ed. Translated by William Muir. London: SPCK, 1911. [See. 118–19; N.B. Archive.org and HathiTrust]

Ankerberg, John, and Emil Caner. *The Truth about Islam and Jesus*. Eugene, OR: Harvest House, 2009. [Does Islam deny the death of Christ?—According to Islam, did Jesus go to heaven?, See. 66–67]

Ankerberg, John, and John Weldon. *The Fast Facts on Islam*. Eugene, OR: Harvest House, 2001. [Jesus' Crucifixion and Resurrection, See. 30–31]

———. *The Facts on Islam*. Eugene, OR: Harvest House, 2003. [Islam teaches that Jesus Christ was neither crucified nor resurrected; therefore, salvation cannot possibly be had through faith in Christ, See. 27; N.B. Copyright 1991 and revised 1998]

Category X—Islamic Interpretations of the Crucifixion

Anyabwile, Thabiti. *The Gospel for Muslims: Simple Ways to Share Christ with Confidence.* Chicago: Moody, 2010. [Chapter 4 Jesus Christ: The Lamb Slain—and Resurrected!, See. 67–78]

Arnold, John Muehleisen. *Islam: Its History, Character, and Relation to Christianity.* 3rd ed. London: Longmans, Green, 1874. [See 158–61; N.B. Google book]

———. *The Koran and the Bible or, Islam and Christianity.* 2nd ed. London: Longmans, Green, Reader, & Dyer, 1866. [See. 189–92, 466–68; N.B. Archive.org]

Azunah, John. *My Neighbour's Faith: Islam Explained for Christians.* Nairobi, Kenya: Hippo, 2008. [Jesus' Passion, See. 112–17]

Barton, James L. *The Christian Approach to Islam.* Boston: Pilgrim Press, 1918. [Chapter 19 The Christian Message to Muslims, See. 267–68; N.B. Archive.org and HathiTrust]

Basetti-Sani, Giulio. *The Koran in the Light of Christ: A Christian Interpretation of the Sacred Book of Islam.* Chicago: Franciscan Herald Press, 1977. [The Text Which Seems to Deny the Death of Christ on the Cross, See. 158–79]

Beaumont, I. Mark. *Christology in Dialogue with Muslims: A Critical Analysis of Christian Presentations of Christ for Muslims from the Ninth and Twentieth Centuries.* Translated by H. J. Chaytor. Colorado Springs, CO: Paternoster, 2005. [Christ did not Die on the Cross, See. 9–11]

Becker, C. H. *Christianity and Islam.* London: Harper & Brothers, 1909. [Muhammad's Knowledge of Christianity, See. 20–25; N.B. Google book]

Benedict, David. *History of All Religions, as Divided into Paganism, Mahometanism, Judaism and Christianity with an Account of Literary and Theological Institutions.* Providence: John Miller, 1824. [Mahometanism, See. 29–33; N.B. Archive.org and HathiTrust]

Bennett, Clinton. *Understanding Christian-Muslim Relations.* New York: Continuum, 2008. [The Crucifixion, See. 51–52; Deedat on Jesus' Crucifixion, See. 169–71; Was Jesus Crucified?, See. 219–221]

Bickel, Bruce, and Stan Jantz. *Bruce & Stan's Pocket Guide to Islam.* Eugene, OR Harvest House, 2002. [See. 73]

Bin Shamoon, Yahya. *Islam and its Militants Conquerable with the Pen: Through the Quran and Hadith: Irrefutable Proofs of False Beliefs of Muslims.* Philadelphia: Xlibris, 2002. [Death and Resurrection of Jesus on the Third Day according to the Gospels, See. 26–27; also 126]

Board of Missionary Preparation. *The Presentation of Christianity to Moslems: The Report of a Committee Appointed by the Board of Missionary Preparation: Presented at the Sixth Annual Meeting in New York, December, 1916.* New York: Board of Missionary Preparation, 1917. [Jesus and the Mahdi, See. 42–43]

Braswell, George E. *Islam: Its Prophet, Peoples, Politics and Power.* Nashville: B&H, 1996. [Crucifixion and Death of Jesus, See. 282–84]

Bridger, J. Scott. *Christian Exegesis of the Qurʾān: A Critical Analysis of the Apologetic Use of the Qurʾān in Select Medieval and Contemporary Arabic Texts.* Eugene, OR: Pickwick, 2016. [The Crucifixion and Resurrection of Christ, See. 121–28]

Brown, Brian Arthur. *Three Testaments Torah, Gospel, and Quran.* Lanham, MD: Rowman & Littlefield, 2012. [Chapter 8 Gospel and Quran, See. 216–17]

Brown, David. *The Cross of the Messiah.* London: Sheldon Press, 1969. [Part 1 The Records of the Crucifixion, See. 23–27; Part 2 The Theology of the Crucifixion, See. 28–41; N.B. This work is a good reading.]

———. *Jesus and God in the Christian Scriptures*. London: Sheldon Press, 1967. [Qur'anic References to the Death of Jesus, See. 35–36]

Burns, Robert A. *Christianity, Islam, and the West*. Lanham, MD: University Press of America, 2011. [Chapter 6 The Islamic Jesus, See. 32–36]

Busse, Heribert. *Islam, Judaism and Christianity: The Theological and Historical Affiliations*. Princeton, NJ: Markus Wiener, 1998. [The Crucifixion (Sura 4:156–157), See. 132–35]

Caner, Emir Fethi, and Ergun Mehmet Caner. *More than a Prophet: An Insider's Response to Muslim Beliefs about Jesus and Christianity*. Grand Rapids: Kregel, 2003. [Was Jesus Christ Crucified?, See. 50, 52, 62–63, 84–85, 95]

Caner, Ergun Mehmet, and Emir Fethi Caner. *Unveiling Islam: An Insider's Look at Muslim Life and Beliefs*. Grand Rapids: Kregel, 2009. [Christ's Death and Ascension, See. 219–20]

Carlson, Norman E. "Swede." *Fantasies From the Arabian Knights Or Strange Tails By A False Prophet Or Muslim Evangelism: A Christian Apologetic*. 2nd ed. n.p., 2014. [The Prophets of Islam, #24 Jesus—Issa, See. 100–101; A Prophetic Passage Concerning the Crucifiction [sic] of Jesus (Issa/Isa), See. 118–21; Our Lord's Resurrection (And Ours), See. 159–66]

Cassini, Charles. *Islam Claims and Counterclaims*. Revised. San Jose: Writers Club Press, 2002. [See. 53–54]

Chapman, Colin. *Cross and Crescent: Responding to the Challenge of Islam*. 2nd ed. Downers Grove, IL: InterVarsity, 2008. [Chapter 26 The Islamic View of Jesus, See. 253–54]

Christian Witness Among Muslims: A Handbook Written Especially for Christians of Africa (south of Sahara). Accra, Ghana: Africa Christian Press, 1977. [Lesson 7 The Sacrifice of Jesus Christ, See. 44–49; Lesson 8 The Victory of Jesus Christ, See. 50–53]

Clark, Malcolm. *Islam For Dummies*. New York: John Wiley, 2011. [See. The Death of Jesus]

Collyer, William Bengo. *Lectures on Scripture Comparison: or, Christianity Compared with Hinduism, Mohammedanism, the Ancient Philosophy, and Deism*. London: S&R Bentley, 1823. [See. 330–31, 356–57, 376; N.B. Google book]

Cooper, Anne, comp. *Ishmael My Brother: A Christian Introduction*. Edited and updated by Elsie A. Maxwell. London: Monarch, 2003. [Jesus' Death, See. 61–63]

Coplestone, F. S. *Jesus Christ or Muhammad? The Bible or the Koran?* Great Britain: Christian Focus, 2000. [The Resurrection of Christ, See. 150–59]

Cornell, Vincent J. ed. *Voices of Islam*. Westport, CT: Praeger, 2007. [Chapter 10 The Passion of 'Ashura in Shiite Islam (Kamran Scot Aghaie), See. 118]

Cragg, Kenneth. *The Call of the Minaret*. 3rd ed. Oxford: Oneworld, 2000. [Jesus Christ, death of in Muslim Thought, See. 224, 226; Interpreting the Cross, See. 265–68]

———. *Jesus and the Muslims: An Exploration*. London: Allen & Unwin, 1985. [Chapter 6 Gethsemane and Beyond, See. 166–88]

Cragg, Kenneth, and R. Marston Speight. *The House of Islam*. 3rd ed. Belmont, CA: Wadsworth, 1988. [Chapter 3 Qur'an, See. 31–32, 36]

Crossley, John. *Explaining the Gospel to Muslims*. London: Lutterworth, 1960. [See. 18–21]

Cumming, Joseph L. *Did Jesus Die on the Cross? The History of Reflection on the End of His Earthly Life in Sunni Tafsir Literature*. Yale University, 2001. [N.B. This work, available online is a must read.]

Daniel, Norman. *Islam and the West: The Making of an Image*. Edinburgh: Edinburgh University Press, 1960. [Crucifixion denied, See. 171–77, 277; Defended, See. 168, 70 82, 286]

Dardess, George. *Do We Worship the Same God? Comparing the Bible and the Qur'an.* Cincinnati: St. Anthony Messenger Press, 2006. [Chapter 9 What Do We Each Believe About the Crucifixion and Resurrection?, See. 89–96; N.B. This work provides concise opinions from both faiths.]

Deshmukh, Ibrahimkhan O. *The Gospel and Islam.* Bombay: Gospel Literature Service, 1982. [See. 201–14, 232]

Dharmaraj, Glory E., and Jacob S. Dharmaraj. *Christianity and Islam: A Missiological Encounter.* Delhi: ISPCK, 1998. [Jesus and Crucifixion, See. 159–61]

Dirks, Jerald. *The Cross & The Crescent: An Interfaith Dialogue between Christianity and Islam.* Beltsville, MD: Amana, 2001. [Chapter 5 The Crucifixion—A Question of Identity, See. 77–111]

Dretke, James P. *A Christian Approach to Muslims: Reflections From West Africa.* Pasadena, CA: William Carey Library, 1979. [See. 73–75]

Ebied, Rifaat Y., and David Thomas, eds. *Muslim-Christian Polemic During the Crusades: The Letter From the People of Cyprus and Ibn Abī; Ṭālib al-Dimashqī's Response.* Leiden: Brill, 2005. [See. 247, 261–63, 319, 405]

Elass, Mateen. *Understanding the Koran: A Quick Christian Guide to the Muslim Holy Book.* Grand Rapids: Zondervan, 2004. [Denying the Redeemer, See. 64–66]

Elder, John. *The Biblical Approach to the Muslim Apologetics.* Fort Washington, PA: Worldwide Evangelization Crusade, 1978. [The Death of Jesus, See. 71–72]

Ellul, Jacques. *Islam and Judeo-Christianity: A Critique of Their Commonality.* Eugene, OR: Wipf & Stock, 2015. [See 30, 90]

Esposito, John L. *What Everyone Needs to Know about Islam.* Oxford: Oxford University Press, 2011. [What do Muslims Believe about Mary and Jesus?, See. 33–35]

Evans, Jack. *The Cross or the Crescent? An Exposé of Islam.* Wichita Falls, TX: Western Christian Foundation, 1977. [See. 75–79]

Garlow, James L. *A Christian's Response to Islam.* 2nd ed. Colorado Springs, CO: Victor, 2005. [See. 64–65, 158]

Gatje, Helmut. *The Qur'an and its Exegesis.* Translated and edited by Alford T. Welch. London: Routledge, 1976. [The Death of Jesus, See. 127–29]

Geisler, Norman L., and Abdul Saleeb. *Answering Islam: The Crescent in Light of the Cross.* Grand Rapids: Baker, 1993. [Chapter 11 A Defense of the Deity of Christ, See. 242–55; N.B. A recommended reading.]

———. *Answering Islam: The Crescent in Light of the Cross.* 2nd ed. Grand Rapids: Baker, 2002. [Chapter 3 The Prophets, See. 66–69; Chapter 13 A Defense of Salvation by the Cross, See. 278–93; N.B. This work is a recommended reading.]

George, Timothy. *Is the Father of Jesus the God of Muhammad?* Grand Rapids: Zondervan, 2002. [The Crucial Difference, See. 97–103]

Ghattas, Raouf, and Carol Ghattas. *A Christian Guide to the Qur'an: Building Bridges In Muslim Evangelism.* Grand Rapids: Kregel, 2009. [Jesus' Crucifixion: Verse 157, See. 66–67; Jesus' Death and Resurrection: Verse 33, See. 174–75; N.B. This work explains Muslim arguments against Jesus's resurrection.]

Gilchrist, John. *The Christian Witness to the Muslim.* Vol. 2. Benoni, South Africa, 1988. [Comparing Biblical and Qur'anic Tenets, C. The Crucifixion in Islam and Christianity, See. 246–46; N.B. Available online]

———. *Facing the Muslim Challenge: A Handbook of Christian—Muslim Apologetics.* Cape Town, South Africa: Life Challenge Africa, 2002. [The Substitution Theory in the

Qur'an, See. 108–11; The Swooning theory of Muslim Apologists, See. 111–13; What Really was the Sign of Jonah?, See. 114–16; N.B. Available on the internet.]

———. *Sharing the Gospel with Muslims: A Handbook for Bible-Based Muslim Evangelism.* Nairobi, Kenya: Life Challenge Assistance Network, 2009. [David: Prophecies of Death and resurrection, See. 81–89; The Ascension of Jesus to Heaven, See. 109–10]

Goddard, Hugh. *Muslim Perceptions of Christianity.* London: Grey Seal, 1996. [See. 24–25, 96–107, 13–39]

Goldmann, David. *Islam and the Bible: Why Two Faiths Collide.* Chicago: Moody, 2004. [Death, See. 38]

Goldsack, William. *The Bible in Islam.* Madras: Christian Literature Society for India. 1922. [Chapter 6 Bible Doctrine in Islam, See. 59–61; N.B. Google book]

Goldsmith, Martin. *Islam & Christian Witness: Sharing the Faith with Muslims.* Downers Gove, IL: InterVarsity, 1982. [The Resurrection, See. 86–88]

Greear, J. D. *Breaking the Islam Code.* Eugene, OR: Harvest House, 2010. [Chapter 8 The Objections, Part One. About God, Jesus, and the Cross, See. 115–17]

Grypeou, Emmanouela, Mark N. Swanson and David Thomas, eds. *The Encounter of Eastern Christianity with Early Islam.* Leiden: Brill, 2006. ["Folly to the Hunafa': The Crucifixion in Early Christian-Muslim Controversy," See. 237–56 (Mark N. Swanson)]

Guillaume, Alfred. *Islam.* 2nd ed. Middlesex, Eng., 1956. [See. 196–97]

Hahn, Ernest. *Jesus in Islam: A Christian View.* I.E.L.C. Board for Literature, 1975. [Chapter 4 The Death of Jesus, See. 19–24]

Haines, John. *Good News for Muslims: Tools for Proclaiming Jesus to Your Neighbor.* Philadelphia: Middle East Resources, 1998. [Jesus Did Not Die On The Cross, See. 64–66]

Halliday, G. Y. *Islam and Christianity or The Quran and the Bible: A Letter to A Muslim Friend By a Missionary.* New York: American Tract Society, 1901. [Self-Contradictions in the Quran, See. 56–57; Christ's Death and Resurrection, See. 155–61; N.B. HathiTrust]

Hanegraaff, Hank. *Muslim: What You Need to Know About the Word's Fastest-Growing Religion.* Nashville: W Publishing Group, 2017. [Resurrection, See. 159–62]

Hardt, Doug. *Who Was Muhammad? An Analysis of the Prophet of Islam in Light of the Bible and the Quran.* Rinffold, GA: TEACH Services, 2016. [Chapter 7 Jesus in the Quran]

Harris, George K. *How to Lead Moslems to Christ.* Philadelphia, China Inland Mission, 1947? [Chapter 4 Apparently Unbridgeable Chasms, See. 43–49]

Heck, Paul L. *Common Ground: Islam, Christianity, and Religious Pluralism.* Washington, DC: Georgetown University Press, 2009. [Crucifixion of Jesus, See. 7–9, 32, 37, 38]

Hedges, Paul, ed. *Contemporary Muslim-Christian Encounters: Developments, Diversity and Dialogue.* London: Bloomsbury, 2015. [Jesus, crucifixion/cross, See. 3, 14, 24, 25, 28, 66]

Hewer, C. T. R. *Understanding Islam: An Introduction.* Minneapolis: Fortress, 2006. [Jesus in the Qur'an, See. 184–85]

Hicham, E. C. *Your Questions Answered: A Reply to Muslim Friends.* Carlisle, PA: EP, 2008. [Chapter 6 Did Jesus really die on the cross?, See. 67–78. N.B. This is a short, informative reading.]

Hummel, Daniel. *Jesus and Muhammad Commonalities of Two Great Religions.* Clifton, NJ: Blue Dome Press, 2017. [See. 10.5 The Death of Jesus]

Ibn Warraq. *Why I Am Not a Muslim*. Amherst, NY: Prometheus, 1995. [Jesus, See. 29, 63–64]

'Isá Abd Allāh Muḥammad al-Mahdī. *Was Christ Really Crucified?* Villach, Austria: Light of Kife, 1994. [N.B. Available on the internet.]

Ives, E. W. *God In History*. Tring, Herts, UK: Lion Publishing, 1979. [Accounting for the empty tomb, See. 29–33]

Jabbour, Nabeel T. *The Crescent Through the Eyes of the Cross: Insights from an Arab Christian*. Colorado Springs, CO: NAV Press, 2008. [See. 187; N.B. Arabic spelling: Jabbūr, Nabīl.]

———. *Unshackled & Growing: Muslims and Christians on the Journey to Freedom*. Colorado Springs, CO: Dawson Media, 2006. [Chapter 3 The Proofs About Jesus, See. 39–43; N.B. Arabic spelling: Jabbūr, Nabīl.]

Jadeed, Iskander. *The Cross in the Gospel and the Quran*. Colorado Springs, CO: Voice of Preaching the Gospel, 198-? [The Resurrection of Christ, See. 5–41]

Jessup, Henry Harris. *The Mohammedan Missionary Problem*. Philadelphia: Presbyterian Board of Publication, 1880. [See. 51–58; N.B. Google book]

Jones, L. Bevan. *Christianity Explained to Muslims: A Manual for Christian Workers*. Calcutta: YMCA Publishing House, 1938. [Chapter 5 The Historicity of the Crucifixion, See. 99–119; N.B. Available online]

———. *The People of the Mosque An Introduction to the Study of Islam* with Special Reference to India. London: Student Christian Movement Press, 1932. [The Crucifixion, See. 272–74, 293–95; N.B. Archive.org]

Kateregga, Badru D., and David W. Shenk. *Islam and Christianity: A Muslim and a Christian in Dialogue*. Nairobi: Uzima, 1980. [See. 140–41, 160–61]

Keating, Sandra Toenies. *What Catholics Should Know About Islam*. New Haven, CT: Knights of Columbus Supreme Council Catholic Information Center, 2008. [See. 25]

Kindī, Muḥammad ibn Yūsuf, 897–961 [Muḥammad ibn Yūsuf al-Kindī. *The Apology of al Kindy, written at the court of al Mâmûn (circa AH 215; AD 830), in Defence of Christianity against Islam*. 2nd ed. Translated by William Muir. SPCK, 1911. *The Life of Christ*. See. 118–22; N.B. This is a polemical work against Islam and it is attributed to an unknown person, Al-Kindi. Archive.org and HathiTrust]

Koelle, S. W. *The Death of Christ upon the Cross: A Fact, not a Fiction. Being a Word in Defence of Christianity against Mohammedan Attacks*. London: Church Missionary House, 1885. [80-page tract]

———. *Mohammed and Mohammedanism: Critically Considered*. London: Rivingtons, 1889. [Chapter 50 The death of both these prophets was no less wonderful than their birth and life, See. 372–74; N.B. Google book]

Küng, Hans. *Islam: Past Present and Future*. Translated by John Bowden. Oxford: Oneworld, 2007. [Jesus, crucifixion, See. 497–99, 511]

Lausanne Committee for World Evangelism. *Ministry in Islamic Contexts*. US: Lausanne Committee for World Evangelism, 1996. [See. 33]

Lawrence, Chellaian. *Jesus as Prophet in Christianity and Islam: A Model for Interfaith Dialogue*. Delhi: ISPCK, 1997. [Chapter 5 Jesus the Christ: The Decisiveness of the Crucifixion, See. 235–304; N.B. This work is a detailed reading.]

Lawson, Todd. *The Crucifixion and the Qur'an: A Study in the History of Muslim Thought*. Oxford: Oneworld, 2013. [See. 22–23, 26–41, 120–35; N.B. Lawson belongs to the Bahia community.]

Leirvik, Oddbiøm. *Images of Jesus Christ in Islam: Introduction, Survey of Research, Issues of Dialogue*. 2nd ed. London: Continuum, 2010. [See. 2, 31, 67–68, 129, 130, 150, 165, 176–83]

Licona, Michael R. *Paul Meets Muhammad: A Christian-Muslim Debate on the Resurrection*. Grand Rapids: Baker, 2006 [N.B. An interesting 175-page text!]

Madany, Bassam M. *The Bible and Islam: Sharing God's Word With a Muslim: A Basic Guide*. 4th ed. US: Author. 2003. [Online without pagination. See. The Crucifixion]

Mallon, Elias D. *Islam: What Catholics Need to Know*. Washington, DC: National Catholic Educational Association, 2006. [See. 123]

Marsh, Charles R. *Share Your Faith with a Muslim*. Chicago: Moody, 1980. [Chapter 9 Jesus Christ and His Atoning Death, See. 5458]

Martinson, Paul Varo. *Islam: An Introduction For Christians*. Translated by Stefanie O. Cox. Minneapolis: Augsburg, 1994. [Death and Resurrection of Jesus According to the Qur'an, See. 187]

Masood, Steven. *Jesus and the Indian Messiah: Modern Muslim Polemics re-examined*. Eng: Word of Life, 1994. [Chapter 5 A New Discovery, 47–54; Chapter 6 The Crucifixion Factor, See. 55–66; Chapter 7 Death and the Resurrection, See. 67–83; Chapter 8 The Ascension of Jesus, See. 84–92]

——— . *Why Follow Jesus?* UK: OM Publishing, 1997. [Chapter 9 The Crucifixion Factor, See. 45–49; Chapter 10 The Risen Jesus!, See. 52–57]

Masri, Fouad. *Connecting with Muslims: A Guide to Communicating Effectively*. Downers Grove, IL: InterVarsity, 2014. [Chapter 8 Who Actually Died on the Cross?, See. 129–46]

Maurer, Andreas, and John Gilchrist. *Great Gospel Concepts for Your Muslim Friends: Eight Gospel Concepts for Personal Study*. Mondeor, South Africa: Mercsca, 1994. [8. The crucifixion in Islam and Christianity; N.B. These study outlines are summaries of the material from "The Christian Witness to the Muslim" by John Gilchrist, pages 114–265, edition 1988. Located in one library: Ashbury Theological Seminary]

McCurry, Don, ed. *The Gospel and Islam: A 1978 Compendium*. Monrovia, CA: Missions Advanced Research and Communication Center, 1979. [Islamic Theology: Limits and Bridges (Kenneth A. Cragg), See. 196–204]

——— . *Healing the Broken Family of Abraham New Life for Muslims*. Colorado Springs, CO: Ministries to Muslims, 2001. [Chapter 31 Muslim Questioning of Christian Doctrine, See. 238, 246, The Denial of the Crucifixion, See. 253–56]

McDowell, Bruce A., and Anees Zaka. *Muslims and Christians at the Table: Promoting Biblical Understanding Among North American Muslims*. Philipsburg, NJ: P&R, 1999. [Chapter 6 The Person and Mission of 'Isa Ibn Maryam . . . Jesus' Crucifixion, See. 116–21]

McDowell, Josh, and John Gilchrist. *The Islam Debate*. San Bernardino, CA: Here's Life, 1983. [See 103–32; N.B. McDowell and Gilchrist debate Ahmed Deedat. A good reading.]

McDowell, Josh, and Jim Walker. *Understanding Islam & Christianity*. Eugene, OR: Harvest House, 2013. [Chapter 7 Jesus' Crucifixion, See. 125–46; N.B. A good reading.]

Miller, Dave. *The Quran Unveiled*. Montgomery, AL: Apologetics Press, 2005. [The Death and Resurrection of Jesus: Atonement, Sin, and Redemption, See. 158–60]

Miller, Roland E. *Muslims and the Gospel: Bridging the Gap: A Reflection on Christian Sharing.* Minneapolis: Lutheran University Press, 2005. [Chapter 15 Dealing with the Hard Questions, See. Crucifixion, See. 365–67]

Miller, William McElwee. *A Christian's Response to Islam.* Philipsburg, NJ: Presbyterian and Reformed Publishing, 1976. [See. 77]

Milot, Jean-René. *Muslims and Christians Enemies of Brothers.* Translated by Sr. Mary Thomas Noble. New York: Alba House, 1997. [Doctrinal differences, See. 12]

Morey, Robert A. *Islam Unveiled The True Desert Storm.* Shermans Dale, PA: Scholars Press, 1991. [See. 97–98]

Moucarry, Chawkat. *Faith to Faith: Christianity & Islam in Dialogue.* Leicester: Inter-Varsity Press, 2001. [See. 20, 40, 108–9; Chapter 10 The Crucifixion: Illusion or Reality, See. 127–44; Death, Resurrection, Ascension, See. 151–53; Preach the Death and Resurrection of Jesus, See. 153. This work is an important reading.]

———. *The Prophet and the Messiah: An Arab Christian Perspective on Islam & Christianity.* Downers Grove, IL: InterVarsity, 2002. [Part 3: Jesus Christ, See. 127–66; N.B. This work is a recommended reading.]

Mourad, Suleiman A. "The Death of Jesus in Islam: Reality, Assumptions, and Implications." In *Engaging the Passion Perspectives on the Death of Jesus.* Edited by Oliver Yarbrough. Minneapolis: Fortress, 2015. [Chapter 19, See. 359–81]

Muir, William. *The Beacon of Truth or Testimony of the Coran to the Truth of the Christian Religion.* London: Religious Tract Society, 1894. [See. 134–44; N.B. Archive.org]

———. *The Coran: Its Composition and Teaching And the Testimony It Bears to the Holy Scriptures.* London: SPCK, 1903. [See. 20; N.B. Google book]

———. *The Identity of Christ in Islam From the Perspective of Thomas Aquinas.* Nairobi: Paulines Publications Africa, 2008. [The Qur'anic View of the Death of Jesus, See. 100–102]

Mvumbi, Frederic Ntedika. *Journey Into Islam: An Attempt to Awaken Christians in Africa.* Nairobi: Paulines, 2008. [Qur'anic Perspectives of Jesus' Death, See. 94–99]

Nehls, Gerhard, and Water Eric. *The Islamic Christian Controversy: A Trainer's Textbook for Muslim Evangelism.* Nairobi, Kenya: Life Challenge Africa, 1996. [Islamic Objections to the Crucifixion, See. 66–71]

Nichols, Laurie Fortunak, and Gary R. Corwin, eds. *Envisioning Effective Ministry Evangelism in a Muslim Context.* Wheaton, IL: EMIS, 2010. [A Muslim Theology of Jesus' Birth and His Death, See. 81–83 (Gerald Wiens)]

North Africa Mission. *A Short Handbook.* Darby, PA: North Africa Mission, 1976. [Chapter 4 Jesus Christ—How Could He Have Died?, See. 33–38]

Parrinder, Geoffrey. *Jesus in the Qur'an.* London: Faber & Faber. 1965. [Chapter 11 The Death of Jesus, See. 105–21; N.B. This is a useful text to examine.]

Parshall, Phil. *Beyond the Mosque: Christians Within Muslim Community.* Grand Rapids: Baker, 1991. [See. 62, 205]

———. *The Cross and the Crescent: Understanding the Muslim Heart and Mind.* Waynesboro, GA: Gabriel, 2002. [Savior Jesus, See. 261–64]

———. *Muslim Evangelism.* Waynesboro, GA: Gabriel Publishing, 2003 [See. 153]

———. *New Paths in Muslim Evangelism.* Grand Rapids: Baker, 1980. [See. 138–39]

Paterson, Andrea C. *Three Monotheistic Faiths—Judaism, Christianity, Islam: An Analysis and Brief History.* Bloomington, IN: AuthorHouse, 2009. [See. 156]

Perkins, Mitali. *Islam and Christianity.* Louisville: Congregational Ministries Publishing, Presbyterian Church (US), 2003. [See. 9–13]

Peters, F. E. *Jesus & Muhammad: Parallel Tracks, Parallel Lives.* New York: Oxford University Press, 2011. [Chapter 8 A New Dawn: The Aftermath, the Legacy, See. 143–51]

———. *The Monotheists: Jews, Christians, and Muslims in Conflict and Competition. The Peoples of God.* Vol. 1. Princeton, NJ: Princeton University Press, 2003. [See. 57–58, 61, 66–67]

———. *A Reader on Classical Islam.* Princeton, NJ: Princeton University Press, 1994. [Jesus crucifixion, See. 31–32]

Phillips, Walter. *Brothers Kept Apart Examining the Christian and Islamic Barriers that have Divided Christians and Muslims for over 1,300 years.* iUniverse, 2009. [Chapter 6 What do the Bible and the Qur'an Commonly Teach about Jesus' Crucifixion, Death, and Resurrection?, See. 23–34]

Qureshi, Nabeel. *No God But One: Allah or Jesus? A Former Muslim Investigates the Evidence for Islam and Christianity.* Grand Rapids: Zondervan, 2016. [Part 6 Did Jesus Die on the Cross?, See. 149–210]

———. *Seeking Allah Finding Jesus: A Devout Muslim Encounters* Christianity. Grand Rapids: Zondervan, 2014. [Chapter 25 Crucifying the Swoon Theory, See. 147–54]

Rao, Bandi Sreenivasa. *Christ in the Qur'an and Bible: (was he crucified?).* Godavari, India: Bandbrothers, 1975. [Chapter 6 Was Jesus Crucified?, See. 58–83]

Register, Ray G. *Dialogue and Interfaith Witness with Muslims.* Spanish Fort, AL: Nall Printing, 1979. [On the Cross, See. 43–51]

Rhodes, Ron. *The 10 Things You Need to Know About Islam.* Eugene, OR: Harvest House, 2007. [Jesus' crucifixion, See. 113–14; Jesus' Resurrection, See. 114–15; Jesus' Death on the Cross, See. 119–23]

———. *Reasoning From the Scriptures with Muslims.* Eugene, OR: Harvest House, 2002. [Jesus was Not Crucified, but was Taken into Heaven by Allah, See. 136–39]

Richardson, Don. *Secrets of the Koran.* Ventura, CA: Regal, 2003 [See. 143, 149, 233]

Richardson, Joel. *Antichrist: Islam's Awaited Messiah.* Enumclaw, WA: Pleasant Word, 2006. [See. 125–27]

Richter, Rick. *Comparing the Qur'an and the Bible: What They Really Say About Jesus, Jihad, and More.* Grand Rapids: Baker, 2011. [The Crucifixion, See. 66–70]

Riddell, Peter G., and Peter Cotterell. *Islam in Context Past Present Future.* Grand Rapids: Baker Academic, 2003. [Qur'an and Crucifixion, See. 77–80]

Ridgeon, Lloyd V. J. *Crescents on the Cross Islamic Visions of Christianity.* Oxford: Oxford University Press, 2001. [See. 9–10, Jesus' Ascent, See. 39–40]

Robinson, Neal. *Christ in Islam and Christianity.* Albany: State University of New York Press, 1991. [Muhammad and the Christians, See. 111–16; The Crucifixion, See. 171–74]

Saal, William J. *Reaching Muslims for Christ.* Chicago: Moody, 1993. [The Crucifixion of Jesus, See. 140–41]

Sadr-Ud Din. *Fundamentals of the Christian Faith in the Light of the Gospels.* Columbus, OH: Ahmadiyyah Anjuman Isha'at Islam Lahore, 1997. [See. 88, 91–92]

Safa, Reza F. *Inside Islam: Exposing and Reaching the World of Islam.* Orlando, FL: Creation House, 1996. [Islam Denies the Death of Jesus, See. 62–64]

Category X—Islamic Interpretations of the Crucifixion

Sahas, Daniel J. *John of Damascus on Islam: The "Heresy of the Ishmaelites."* Leiden: Brill, 1972. [See. 84–85]

Sarker, Abraham. *Understand My Muslim People: By a Former Muslim.* Newberg, OR: Barclay, 2004. [Was Jesus Really Crucified?, See. 129–30; also See. 134–37, 157, 227, 258–59]

Schirrmacher, Christine. *The Islamic View of Major Christian Teachings: the Role of Jesus Christ, Sin, Faith and Forgiveness: Essays.* Hamburg: RVB International, 2001. [Chapter 13 The Crucifixion of Jesus in View if Moslem Theology, See. 69–78]

Schmidt, Alvin J. *The Great Divide: The Future of Islam and the Triumph of the West.* Boston: Regina Orthodox Press, 2004. [Chapter 1 Jesus and Muhammad: Polar Opposites . . . Their Deaths, See. 34–36]

Schumann, Olaf H. *Jesus the Messiah in Muslim Thought.* Delhi: ISPCK, 2002. [The Death of Jesus, See. 27–28]

Scott, Robert. *Questions Muslims Ask: What Christians Actually and Don't Believe.* Downers Grove, IL: InterVarsity, 2011. [Chapter 3 What Sort of God Can Be Murdered? The Certain Victory of Jesus the Messiah, See. 51–67]

Shedinger, Robert F. *Was Jesus a Muslim Questioning: Categories in the Study of Religion.* Minneapolis: Fortress, 2009. [See. 131–33]

Shem, G. *Understanding Some Muslim Misunderstandings.* Krishnagiri Concordia Press, 1977. [See. 4–6]

Shenk, David W. *Journeys of the Muslim Nation and the Christian Church: Exploring the Mission of Two Communities.* Scottdale, PA: Herald Press, 2003. [The Offense of the Cross, 136–37]

Shorrosh, Anis A. *Islam Revealed: A Christian Arab's View of Islam.* Nashville: Nelson, 1988. [Chapter 4 The Crucifixion: Fact or Fiction?, See. 107–37]

Siddiqui, Mona. *Christians, Muslims, and Jesus.* New Haven: Yale University Press, 2013. [See. 54, 55, 226–37]

Singh, David Emmanuel, ed. *Jesus and the Cross: Reflections of Christians from Islamic Contexts.* Waynesboro, GA: Regnum, 2008. [Five essays]

———, ed. *Jesus and the Resurrection: Reflections of Christians from Islamic Contexts.* Eugene, OR: Wipf & Stock, 2014. [203 pages]

Smith, Shelton L. *Islam: A Raging Storm.* Murfreesboro: Sword of the Lord, 2002 [Islam Incompatible with Christianity, See. 44–45]

Sookhdeo, Patrick. *Understanding Islamic Theology.* McLean, VA: Isaac Publishing, 2013. [N.B. unpaginated]

Spencer, Robert. *The Complete Infidel's Guide to the Koran.* Washington, DC: Regnery Pub.; New York: Distributed to the trade by Perseus Distribution, 2009. [The Uncrucified Christ, See. 143–44; The True Christians and Those False Worshippers of Christ, See. 151–52]

———. *Did Muhammad Exist? An Inquiry into Islam's Origins.* Wilmington, Delaware: Intercollegiate Studies Institute, 2012. [See. 25, 34, 47, 53]

———. *The Truth about Muhammad: Founder of the World's Most Intolerant Religion.* Washington, DC: Regnery, 2006. [crucifixion of, See. 55–56, 177–78]

Sproul, R. C., and Abdul Saleeb. *The Dark Side of Islam.* Wheaton: Crossway, 2003. [Chapter 6 Islam and Christianity on the Death of Christ, 65–71]

Steenbrink, Karel. *The Jesus Verses of the Qur'an.* Delhi, India: Henry Martyn Institute, 2011. [Saved from the Cross, See. 74–80]

Sudworth, Richard. *Encountering Islam: Christian-Muslim Relations in the Public Square*. London: SCM, 2017. [See. 80–81, 128]

Swanson, Mark N. "Debating According to the Rule: A Conversation about the Resurrection." In *The Character of Christian-Muslim Encounter: Essays in Honour of David Thomas*. Edited by Douglas Pratt, et al. Leiden: Brill, 2015. [See. 186–204]

Swartley, Keith E., ed. *Encountering the World of Islam*. Littleton, CO: Authentic Media, 2005. [Crucifixion, Muslim View of, See. 36, 106, 232, 283, 312

Sweetman, J. Windrow. *Islam and Christian Theology: The Medieval Developments Significant for Comparative Study*. Vol. 2. Pt. 2. London: Lutterworth, 1955. [See. 251–53]

———. *Islam and Christian Theology: Preparatory Historical Survey of the Early Period*. Vol. 1. Part 1. London: Lutterworth, 1947. [The Death and Crucifixion of Jesus, See. 79–80]

Tanagho, Samy. *Glad News! God Loves You My Muslim Friend*. Chicago: Moody, 2017. [Section 7 The Crucifixion and Resurrection of Jesus Christ, See. 173–96; Section 8 The Ascension and Return of Jesus Christ, See. 197–99; N.B. Self-published in 1999]

Thompson, Andrew. *Jesus of Arabia*. London: Motivate Press, 2016. [Appendix B: Islamic Views of the Crucifixion, See. 153–62]

Tisdall, William St. Clair. *A Manual of the Leading Muhammadan Objections to Christianity*. London: SPCK, 1904. [See. 113–19; N.B. Archive.org and Google book]

Titus, Murray T. *The Religious Quest of India: Indian Islam*. London: Oxford University Press, 1930. [Against Jesus Christ, See. 224–25; N.B. Discussed the Ahmadiyya movement.]

Troll, Christian W. *Dialogue and Difference: Clarity in Christian-Muslim Relations* Maryknoll, NY: Orbis Books, 2009. [See. 17, 149–50]

———. *Muslims Ask, Christians Answer*. Translated by David Marshall. Hyde Park, NY: New City Press, 2012. [Chapter 3 Cross, Sin, Redemption, See. 29–31]

Van Gorder, A. Christian. *No God But God: A Path to Muslim-Christian Dialogue on God's Nature*. Maryknoll, NY: Orbis Books, 2003. [Islam and the Cross of Jesus, See. 133–39]

Waardenburg, Jacques, ed. *Muslim Perceptions of Other Religions: A Historical Survey*. New York: Oxford University Press, 1999. [See. 230, 234, 273, 274]

Waddy, Charis. *The Muslim Mind*. New York: New Amsterdam Books, 1990. [See. 127–28]

Wagner, Walter H. *Opening the Qur'an: Introducing Islam's Holy Book*. Notre Dame: University of Notre Dame Press, 2008. [Jesus Raised to God's Presence, See. 333–34]

Walker, James K. *What the Quran Really Teaches About Jesus*. Eugene: OR: Harvest House, 2018. [Chapter 12 Jesus of the Qur'an Was Not Crucified on the Cross, See. 83–88; Chapter 13 Jesus of the Qur'an Did Not Rise from the Dead, See. 89–94]

Walter, H. A. *The Religious Life of India: The Ahmadiya Movement*. London: Oxford University Press, 1918. [N.B. Archive.org. The author, a member of the YMCA of India and Madras investigates the development and beliefs of the Ahmadiya movement.]

Watt, William Montgomery. *Islam and Christianity Today: A Contribution to Dialogue*. London: Routledge & Kegan Paul, 1983. [The Resurrection of Jesus, See. 102–3]

———. *Muslim-Christian Encounters; Perceptions and Misperceptions*. London: Routledge, 1991. [See. 21–22, 116–17, 126–29]

Wenisch, Fritz. *Judaism, Christianity, and Islam: Differences, Commonalities, and Community*. San Diego, CA: Cognella, 2015. [Who do Christians say that Jesus is? – Two controversial Muslim beliefs]

Wessels, Anton. *Understanding the Qur'an.* Translated by John Bowden. London: SCM, 2000. [The Crucifixion of Jesus, See. 149–51]

White, James R. *What Every Christian Needs to Know about the Qur'an.* Bloomington, IN: Bethany House, 2013. [Chapter 6 The Qur'an and the Cross, See. 129–43; N.B. White's publication is a concise read.]

Wilson, Billy. *Informed on Islam: Study Guide 2—Excerpt* [World Impact booklet] 2011.

Wilson, John W. *Christianity Alongside Islam.* Victoria, Australia: Acorn Press, 2010. [Chapter 5 Jesus in the Bible and the Qur'an, See. 61–73]

Wood, Simon A. *Christian Criticisms, Islamic Proofs: Rashid Rida's Modernist Defense of Islam.* Translated and analyzed by Simon A. Wood. Oxford: Oneworld, 2012. [137, 41]

Woodberry, J. Dudley, ed. *Muslims and Christians on the Emmaus Road.* Monrovia, CA: MARC, 1989. [Everett W. Huffard, Culturally Relevant Themes About Christ, See. 165]

Zafar, Harris. *Demystifying Islam: Tackling the Tough Questions.* Lanham: Rowman & Littlefield, 2017. [Demystifying Islam's view of Jesus Christ, Crucifixion, See. 153–62]

Zahniser, A. H. Mathias. *The Mission and Death of Jesus in Islam and Christianity.* Maryknoll, NY: Orbis Books, 2008. [259 pages; N.B. Zahniser's work is a definite must read.]

Zaka, Anees, and Diane Coleman. *The Truth About Islam: The Noble Qur'an's Teachings in Light of the Holy Bi*ble. Phillipsburg, NJ: P & R, 2004. [The Islamic View of Jesus Christ, 59–60; Denial of Crucifixion, See. 60–61]

Zayn, M. Faruk. *Christianity, Islam and Orientalism.* London: Saqi, 2003. [Chapter 8 The Crucifixion?, See. 145–58]

Zebiri, Kate. *Muslims and Christians Face to Face.* London: Oneworld, 2000. [See. 21, 45, 62, 163, 216, 217]

Zwemer, Samuel M. *Islam and the Cross: Selections from the "Apostle to Islam."* Arranged and edited by Roger S. Greenway. Philipsburg, NJ: P&R, 2002. [Jesus Christ, death of, See. 25, 41, 47–48]

———. *Mohammed or Christ.* London: Seeley, 1916. [See. 227–42; N.B. Archive.org]

———. *The Moslem Christ: An Essay on the Life, Character, and Teachings of Jesus Christ According to the Koran and Orthodox Tradition.* New York: American Tract Society, 1912. [Chapter 2 The Koran Account of His Life, Death, and Translation, See. 49–50; N.B. This work explains the views of Islam. Archive.org]

Chapter 29

Jesus's Crucifixion: Con Resurrection

'Abd al 'Ātī, Hammūda. *Islam in Focus*. Beltsville, MD: Amana, 1998. [Jesus the Son of Mary, See. 157–61]

Adeleke Dirisu Ajijola. *The Myth of the Cross*. Adam Publishers, 1994. [Chapter 1 The First Basic Doctrine of Modern Christianity, See. 38–63]

Ahmad, Ghulām. *Jesus in India: Being an Account of Jesus' Escape from Death on the Cross and of His Journey to India*. London: Islam International, 1989. [N.B. This book reflects the view of the Ahmadiyya community i.e., that Jesus escaped death on the cross and journeyed to India.]

———. *A Review of Christianity from a New Point of View*. Punjab: Nazir Daewat-O-Tabligh, 1976. [Jesus Did Not Die Upon the Cross, See. 10–26; N.B Jesus was buried in India. This book reflects the views of the Ahmadiyya.]

Ahmad, Khwaja Nazir. *Jesus in Heaven on Earth: Journey of Jesus to Kashmir, His Preaching to the Lost Tribes of Israel, and Death and Burial in Sringar*. Columbus, OH: Ahmadiyya Anjuman Isha 'at Islam Lahore, 1998. [This 427-page book reflects the views of the Ahmadiyya i.e., that Jesus escaped death on the cross and journeyed to India.]

Ahmad, Tahir. *Christianity: A Journey from Facts to Fiction*. 4th ed. Tilford, UK: Islam International, 2006. [Crucifixion, See. 67–83; Reviva; or Resurrection?, See. 85–111; N.B. Available online.]

Ahmed Hamoud Maamiry. *Jesus Christ as Known by Muslims*. New Delhi: Lancers, 1989. [Chapter 4 The Legend of Crucifixion, See. 45–69]

Ajijola, Adeleke Dirisu. *The Myth of the Cross*. Adam Publishers, 1994. [Chapter 2 The Second Basic Doctrine of Modern Christianity, See. 43–63; N.B. Available online.]

Akyol, Mustafa. *Islamic Jesus: How the King of the Jews Became a Prophet of the Muslims*. New York: St. Martin's Press, 2017. [Chapter 6 The Qur'anic Jesus, See. 151–57]

Albahri, Yaser. *Jesus Resuscitated! The Story Behind Who Saved the Life of Jesus and Why*. Pittsburgh: Dorrance, 2014. [160 pages; N.B. Claims that Jesus did not die on the cross. Free download available online.]

Algar, Hamid. *Jesus in the Qur'an: His Reality Expounded in the Qur'an*. Oneonta, NY: Islamic Publications International, 1999. [See. 29–40]

Ali, Maulana Muhammad. *Introduction to the Study of The Holy Qur'an*. Columbus, OH: Ahmadiyya Anjuman, 1992. [See. 106–12; N.B. First published in 1936.]

———. *The Religion of Islam: A Comprehensive Discussion of the Sources, Principles and Practices of Islam*. Lahore, Pakistan: Ripon Printing Press, 1950. [See. 262]

Alkhuli, Muhammad Ali. *Islam and Christianity*. Swailch, Jordan: Dar Alfalah, 2007. [See. 25, 36–67]

———. *The Truth about Jesus Christ*. Riyadh, Saudi Arabia: International Islamic Publishing House, 1990. [See. 43–45, 48]

Ansari, Muhammad Fazl-ur-Rahman. *Islam and Christianity in the Modern World: Being an Exposition of the Qur'anic View of Christianity in the Light of Modern Research*. Selangor: Thinkers Library, 1999. [See. 41]

Asad, Muhammad. *The Message of the Qur'an*. Bristol, England: Book Foundation, 2008. [See. 153–54]

Assfy, Zaid H. *Islam and Christianity: Connections and Contrasts, Together with the Stories of the Prophets and Imams*. York: Sessions, 1977. [See. 56–57]

Ataie, Ali. *In Defense of Islam: Confronting the Christians with Their Own Scriptures*. No publisher, 2004. [Chapter 4 Refuting the Crucifixion and Resurrection, See. 110–52; Jesus was neither killed nor crucified by his enemies, See. 316; N.B. An interesting reading available online.]

'Ataur-Rahim, Muhammad, and Ahmad Thomson. *Jesus: A Prophet of Islam*. India: Chaudhry, 1996. [Jesus in the Qur'an, See 266–67; N.B. Archive.org]

Aykol, Mustafa. *The Islamic Jesus: How the King of the Jews Became a Prophet of the Muslims*. New York: St. Martin's Press, 2017. [See. 152–55]

Ayoub, Mahmoud. *A Muslim View of Christianity: Essays on Dialogue by Mahmoud Ayoub*. Edited by Irfan A. Omar. Maryknoll, NY: Orbis, 2007. [Toward an Islamic Christology 2: The Death of Jesus, Reality or Delusion—A Study of the Death of Jesus in Tafsir Literature, See. 156–70; N.B. This essay is a recommended read.]

Badre-i-Alam, Muhammad. *Nuzul-e-Isa = Descension of Jesus Christ*. Translated by Syed Aqil Mohammed. Delhi: Dini Book Depot, 1974? [Jesus Christ, See. 45–51; Crucifixion and Natural Death, See. 71–78]

Badre, Muhammad. *The Truth About Islam*. Cairo: Al-Maaref, 1910. [See. 95–96]

Bengalee, Mutiur Rahman. *Tomb of Jesus*. Qadian. 3rd ed. Nazir Dawato Tabligh, Ahmadiyya Muslim Association, UK, 2001 [Chapter 1 Jesus Did Not Die on the Cross, See. 8–26; Chapter 2 Resurrection and Ascension of Jesus, See. 27–32; Chapter 3 Where Did Jesus Go?, See. 33–43; Chapter 4 Jesus' Journey to India According to Buddhist Records, See. 44–56]

Bucaille, Maurice. *The Bible The Quran and Science the Holy Scriptures Examined in the Light of Modern Knowledge*. Translated from the French by Alastair D. Pannell and the Author. 2014. [See. 41–42; 50, 56, 72, 76–77; no pagination; N.B. Archive.org]

Buckridan, Rakib. *The Bible and Christianity: Their Impending Demise and a Forward-Looking Plea*. 2nd ed. Tacarigua, Trinidad & Tobago: Rakib Buckridan, 2011. [Chapter 10 Death, Resurrection, and Ascension of Jesus, See. 280–91]

Choudhury, Parmesh. *From Kashmir To Palestine*. New Delhi: P. Choudhury, 1996. [Chapter 12 Jesus Did not Die on the Cross, See. 252–324; Notovitch's Discovery, 325–33; N.B. The author claims that Jesus did not die nor ascend to heaven, rather he moved to Kashmir.]

Cishtī, Yū' suf Salīm. *What is Christianity: Being a Critical Examination of Fundamental Doctrines of the Christian Faith*. Karachi, World Federation of Islamic Missions, 1970.

Cucarella, Diego R. Sarrió. *Muslim-Christian Polemics across the Mediterranean: The Splendid Replies of Shihab al-Din al-Qarafi (d. 684/1285)*. Leiden: Brill, 2015. [Jesus the Messiah, the Prophet Who Did Not Die, See. 142–47]

Cumming, Joseph L. *Did Jesus Die on the Cross? The History of Reflection on the End of His Earthly Life in Sunni Tafsir Literature*. Yale University, 2001. [N.B. This work is a must read and it is available online]

Deedat, Ahmed. *Crucifixion or Cruci-fiction*. Doha, Qatar: Dar El-Ulum Foundation; Doha, Qatar: Distributed by the Ministry of Awqaf and Islamic Affairs, 1984. [Also titled *Crucifixion* or *Cruci-fiction; Resurrection or Resuscitation; The God that never was*; N.B. Available online]

Dialogue Between Islam and Christianity: Discussion of Religious Dogma Between Intellectuals from the Two Religions. Translated by The Institute of Islamic and Arabic Sciences in America. Fairfax, VA: IIASA, 2000. [The Crucifixion, See. 60–120; The Resurrection, See. 121–58; N.B. This work is an interesting read.]

Dimashkiah, Abdul Rahman. *Let the Bible Speak*. Riyadh, Saudi Arabia: International Islamic Publishing House, 1997. [Contradictory narrations about crucifixion, See. 61–62; N.B Available online]

Emerick, Yahiya. *The Complete Idiot's Guide to Understanding Islam*. 2nd Edition. Indianapolis, IN: Alpha, 2004. [See. 46, 224, 230]

Esack, Farid. *The Qur'an: A User's Guide*. Oxford: Oneworld, 2005. [Jesus, See. 154–55]

Faber-Kaiser, Andreas. *Jesus Died in Kashmir: Jesus, Moses and the Ten Lost Tribes of Israel*. London: Gordon Cremonesi, 1977. [N.B. The author of this book postulates that Jesus survived his crucifixion and afterward traveled to Kashmir.]

Faris-al-Qayrawani. *Was Christ Really Crucified?* Colorado Springs, CO: Al-Noor, 1992. [42 pages; N.B. Available online; Goodway Publishing, 2010]

Fatoohi, Louay. *The Mystery of the Crucifixion: The Attempt to Kill Jesus in the Qur'an, the New Testament, and Historical Sources*. Birmingham, UK: Luna Plena, 2008. [147 pages]

Glassé, Cyril. *Jesus, Son of Mary: An Islamic Perspective*. London: Altajir World of Islam 1998. [The text of this pamphlet is taken from the entry under 'Jesus: Son of Mary' by Cyril Glassé from *The Concise Encyclopedia of Islam*, published by Stacey International in 1989.]

———. *The New Encyclopedia of Islam*. Laham, MD: Rowman & Littlefield, 2002. [Jesus, Son of Mary, See. 239–40]

Goddard, Hugh. *Muslim Perceptions of Christianity*. London: Grey Seal, 1996. [See. 2, 24, 105]

Goldman, David. *Islam and the Bible Why Two Faiths Collide*. Chicago: Moody, 2004. [Death, 38]

Gümüş, M. Siddik. *Islam and Christianity*. Hakîkat Kitâbevi, 2004. [See. 16, 17, 20, 108, 152, 290, 291, 292]

Hálid, Halil. *The Crescent Versus the Cross*. London: Luzac, 1907. [See. 16–17] N.B. Archive.org]

Haneef, Suzanne. *What Everyone Should Know About Islam and Muslims*. Chicago: Kazi, 1982. [See. 175–76]

Hanish, Otoman Zar-Adusht. *Yehoshua Nazir Jesus the Nazarite: Life of Christ*. Los Angeles: Mazdaznan Press, 1917. [230 pages; N.B. Archive.org]

Category X—Islamic Interpretations of the Crucifixion

Harputlu, İshak. *Could Not Answer*. Waqf Ikhlas publications, no. 13. Istanbul, Turkey: Hakîkat Kitabevi, 2004 [1891 or 2]. [N.B. Available online without pagination]

Hassnain, Fida M., and Daniel Levi. *The Fifth Gospel: New Evidence from the Tibetan, Sanskrit, Arabic, Persian, and Urdu Sources about the Historical Life of Jesus Christ after the Crucifixion*. Edited by Ahtisham Fida. Nevada City, CA: Blue Dolphin, 2006. [Chapter 4 Ministry and Crucifixion, See. 186–98; Chapter 5 Jesus Christ in the East, 199–289; N.B. The fundamental claim by the author is that Jesus survived the crucifixion and traveled to India.]

Hicham, E. M. *Your Questions Answered: a Reply to Muslim Friends*. Carlisle, PA: EP, 2009. [Chapter 6 Did Jesus Really Die on the Cross?, See. 67–78]

Hummel, Daniel. *Jesus and Muhammad Commonalities of Two Great Religions*. Clifton, NJ: Blue Dome Press, 2017. [See. 10.5 The Death of Jesus, no pagination]

Hussein, M. Kamel. *City of Wrong: A Friday*. Translated by Kenneth Cragg. Amsterdam: N.V. Djambatan, 1959. [234 pages; N.B. This is an often-cited text.]

Ibn Taimīya, Ahmad ibn 'Abd al-Halīm. *A Muslim Theologian's Response to Christianity*: Ibn Taymiyya's al-Jawab al-sahih. Edited and translated by Thomas Frank Michel. Delmar, NY: Caravan, 1984. [See. 195, 235–36, 303–12]

Ikhlas, Waqf. *Islam and Christianity*. İstanbul: Hakikat Kitabevi, 1998. [See 184, fn 1; N.B. Publication No: 12 is available online.]

Imran, Adil Nizamuddin. *Christ Jesus, the Son of Mary: A Muslim Perspective*. Lombard, IL: Book of Signs Foundation, 2009. [Section 16 The False Crucifixion, See. 242–49]

Imran, Muhammad. *Distortions about Islam in the West*. 2nd rev. & enlarged ed. Karachi: Islamic Research and Publication Bureau, 2009. [See. 11, 57–58]

Isik, Hüseyn Hilmi. *Islam and Christianity*. Istanbul: Hakîkat Kitâbevi, 2014.

Kairanvi, Maulana M. *Rahmatullah. Izhar-Ul-Haq The Truth Revealed*. London: Ta-Ha, 1989. [Book 3 God is Immune to Death, See. #208–10; A debate between Inman Raazi and a Priest, Book 3, 222–23; N.B. This work is available online.]

Kamauddin, Al-Hajj Khwaja. *Islam and Christianity*. 1932 [1977 2nd reprint]. Ballimaran, Delhi: Bharat Press, 1977. [Chapter 1 Muhammad and Jesus, See. 1–10]

Khalidi, Tarif. *The Muslim Jesus Sayings and Stories in Islamic Literature*. Cambridge, MA: Harvard University Press, 2001. [#282, See. 205]

Khan, Md. Irshad Anwar. *Christ Jesus in the Gospels and the Quran*. Huma Khurshid, 2008. [Chapter 8 Resurrection, See. 40–44; Chapter 9 Appearance, See. 45–47; Chapter 10 Ascension, See. 48; Chapter 11 The Quran Rejects Crucifixion, See. 49–53]

Khan, Muhammad Zafrulla. *Deliverance from the Cross*. London: London Mosque, 1978. [Chapter 3 Death, See. 24–41; Chapter 4 Shroud, See. 42–58; Chapter 5 Resurrection, See. 59–65]

Mabera, Hussein Y. *Anatomy of the Qur'an; Fact or Fallacy. A Rejoinder to GJO Moshay*. Lagos, Nigeria: Ibrash Islamic Publication Centre, 1998. [See. 201]

Maqsood, Ruqaiyyah Waris. *The Mysteries of Jesus: A Muslim Study of the Origins and Doctrines of the Christian Church*. Oxford: Sakina, 2000. [Chapter 20 Did the Crucifixion Kill Jesus?, See. 169–80; Chapter 21 Was Jesus Buried Alive?, See. 181–91]

Matlock, Gene D. *Jesus and Moses are Buried in India!* Adelanto, CA: Geo-Mind Publications, 1991. [Chapter 11 Is Jesus Buried in India?, See. 356–422]

Mish'al Ibn Abdullah al-Kahdi. *What Did Jesus Really Say?* Ann Arbor, MI: Islamic Assembly of North America, 1996. [See. 492–93]

Mohammad, Maulana Hafiz Sher. *The Death of Jesus: A Compilation of the Evidence of Islamic Sources and Authorities and Muslim Scholars and Writers*. Translated by Zahid Aziz. Ohio, US: Ahmadiyya Anjuman Isha'at Islam Lahore, 2003. [82 pages]

Mohammed, Ovey N. *Muslim-Christian Relations: Past, Present, Future*. Eugene, OR: Wipf & Stock, 2008. [See. 61–64. Previously published by Orbis Books, 1999]

Mohammed, Waffie. *Christianity According to Islamic Beliefs*. Kula Lumpur: A. S. Noordeen, 2008. [Crucifixion, The Qur'an Denies Crucifixion of Jesus, See. 88–89; N.B. Originally published: Trinidad and Tobago: Markaz Al Ihsaan, 2007.]

Muhammad, Maulana Hafiz Sher. *The Death of Jesus: A Compilation of the Evidence of Islamic Sources and Authorities and Muslim Scholars and Writers*. Translated by Zahid Aziz. Ohio: Ahmadiyya Anjuman Isha'at at Islam Lahore, 2003. [N.B. This work represents the view of the Ahmadiyya Association.]

Muḥammad Rashīd Riḍā. *Christian Criticisms, Islamic Proofs: Rashid Rida's Modernist Defense of Islam*. Translated and analyzed by Simon A. Wood. Oxford: Oneworld, 2012. [See. 137, 141]

Naik, Zakir. *Similiarities Between Islam & Christianity*. New Delhi: Adam Publishers, 2012. [See. 21–22, 38]

Pappas, Paul Constantine. *Jesus' Tomb in India: The Debate on His Death and Resurrection*. Berkeley, CA: Asian Humanities Press, 1991. [202 pages; N.B. This work claims to "critically review the Ahmadi thesis i.e., that Jesus did not die on the cross and it seeks to assess the facts on which they base their contention."]

Qasem, Mohamed. *A Closer Look at Christianity* | Books on Islam and Muslims | Al-Islam. org. [N.B. Available online without pagination.]

Salibi, Kamal S. *Who Was Jesus? Conspiracy in Jerusalem*. London: Tauris Parke, 2007. [Chapter 12 The Treason of Judas, See. 177–86]

Saritoprak, Zeki. *Islam's Jesus*. Gainesville, FL: University Press of Florida, 2015. [Jesus: ascension of, See. 20–21; crucifixion and resurrection of, See. 16–19, 17–33, 105–7]

Shams, J. D. (Hazrat Maulana Jala-ud-Din). *Where did Jesus Die?* 12th ed. Punjab, India: Nazarat Nashro Isha'at Qadian, 2017. [244 pages; N.B. This work is available online]

Shittu, Abdur-Raheem Adebayo. *Islam and Christianity: Why the Conflict?* Ibadan, Nigeria: Al-Faurqa'an, 1992. [The Crucifixion of Jesus, See. 62–64]

Siddiqi, Muzammil H. "Jesus in the Qur'an: Some Similarities and Differences with the New Testament." In *Muslims and Christians, Muslims and Jews: A Common Past, A Hopeful Future*. Edited by Marilyn Robinson Waldman. Columbus, OH: Islamic Foundation of Central Ohio, 1992. [See. 35–46]

Sultan, Sohaib. *The Koran for Dummies*. Indianapolis, IN: Wiley, 2004. [Jesus and the Cross, See. 128]

Truth About The Crucifixion Transcripts from the International Conference on Deliverance of Jesus from the Cross. London: Ascot Press, 1978. [N.B. This work contains a series of essays that discuss the view that Jesus did not die on the cross. The Ahmadiyya Community in the United Kingdom organized the conference.]

Ulfat Aziz-us-Samad. *A Comparative Study of Christianity & Islam*. Delhi: Noor, 1986. [See. 20, 23, 29]

———. *Islam and Christianity*. Lahore: Ahmadiyyah Anjuman Isha'at Islam, 1970. [Chapter 7 The Death of Jesus, See. 126–41]

Usmani, Muhammad Taqi. *What is Christianity?* Translated by Muhammad Shoaib Omar. Karachi, Pakistan: Siddiqi Trust, 1987. [See. 33–34; N.B. Archive.org]

Category X—Islamic Interpretations of the Crucifixion

Wheeler, Brandon M. *Prophets in the Quran: An Introduction to the Quran and Muslim Exegesis.* London: Continuum, 2002. [Jesus, Crucifixion and Ascension, See. 314–17; N.B. Wheeler has selected excerpts and translated passages from the Quran.]

Zein, M. Faru *Christianity, Islam and Orientalism.* London: Saqi, 2003 [Chapter 8 The Crucifixion, See. 145–63]

Category XI

*Judaic Interpretations
of Jesus's Resurrection*

CHAPTER 30

Jewish Converts: Pro Resurrection

Baron, David. *Rays of the Messiah: Christ in the Old Testament*. Eugene, OR: Wipf & Stock, 2001. [See. 42–43, 48–50; N.B. reprint of 1886 edition.]

Benedict, George. *Christ Finds A Rabbi: An Autobiography*. Philadelphia: Author, 1932. [Chapter 20 Resurrection, See. 251–62]

Bernis, Jonathan. *A Rabbi Looks at Jesus of Nazareth*. Grand Rapids: Chosen, 2011. [Chapter 12 Resurrection: Fact or Fiction?, See. 181–203]

Brown, Michael L. *Answering Jewish Objections to Jesus*. Vol. 3. *Messianic Prophecy Objections*. Grand Rapids, Baker, 2003. Resurrection of Jesus, See. 76–77, 114–17]

Chosen People Ministries. *How to Introduce Your Friends to the Messiah*. Charlotte, NC: Chosen People Ministries, 1991. [See. 41; N.B. Chosen People Ministries is a Messianic Jewish organization which engages in evangelism to Jews.]

Dushaw, Amos I. *The Man Called Jesus*. London: Revell, 1939. [Chapter 20 Christus Victor, See. 358–79]

Edersheim, Alfred. *The Life and Times of Jesus the Messiah*. Vol. 2. New York: Longmans, Green, 1907. [Chapter 16 On the Resurrection of Christ from the Dead, See. 630–52; N.B. Archive.org. This classic, dated work is worth examining.]

Fisher, John. *The Olive Tree Connection: Sharing Messiah with Israel*. Downers Grove, IL: InterVarsity, 1978. [The Case of the Empty Tomb, See. 162–68]

Frey, Joseph Samuel C. F. *A Course of Lectures on the Messiahship*. New York: Vincent L. Dill, 1844. [Chapter 13 The Resurrection of the Messiah, See. 267–82; Second Part. The Resurrection of the Messiah, See. 283–99; N.B. Google book]

———. *Joseph and Benjamin: A Series of Letters on the Controversy Between Jews and Christians: Comprising the Most Important Doctrines of the Christian Religion*. Vol. 2. New York: Reter Hill, 1837. [Letters 2–6 Resurrection of Christ, etc., See. 19–75; N.B. Google book]

Fruchtenbaum, Arnold G. *The Resurrection of the Messiah*. Ariel Ministries, 2005. [This 38 page booklet is available online.]

Gartenhaus, Jacob. *Winning Jews to Christ: A Handbook to Aid Christians in their Approach to the Jews*. Gartenhaus, 1963. [Chapter 17 N.B This unpaginated work is available online.]

Category XI—Judaic Interpretations of Jesus's Resurrection

Jocz, Jakob. *The Jewish People and Jesus Christ: The Relationship Between Church and Synagogue*. 3rd ed. Grand Rapids: Baker, 1979. [The Resurrection-Faith and Its Effects, See. 149–52]

Levison, N. *Passiontide or the Last Days of the Earthly Life of the Master*. Edinburgh: T&T Clark, 1927. [Chapter 12 The Resurrection, See. 159–74]

Maass, Eliezer. *Stand Firm: A Survival Guide for the New Jewish Believer*. Lansing, IL: AMF International, 1995. [Chapter 5 The Resurrection Makes the Difference, See. 37–45]

Mishkin, David. *Jewish Scholarship on the Resurrection of Jesus*. Eugene, OR: Pickwick, 2017. [N.B. This recommended work is a comprehensive overview of the topic from the viewpoint of a Messianic Jew. His dissertation on this topic is available online.]

Montefiore, Hugh. *The Womb and the Tomb The Mystery of the Birth and Resurrection of Jesus*. London: Fount, 1992. [Chapter 10 The Empty tomb in the Gospels, See. 111–21; Chapter 11 The Gospel Appearances, See. 122–33; Chapter 12 The Rest of the New Testament, 134–47; Chapter 13 The Resurrection of Jesus, See. 148–66]

Neander, Augustus. *The Life of Jesus Christ in Its Historical Connexion and Historical Development*. Translated by John M'Clintock and Charles E. Blumenthal. London: George Bell, 1888. [Chapter 8 The Resurrection, See. 468–84; Chapter 9 The Ascension, See. 484–87; N.B. Google book]

Rambsel, Yacov. *Yeshua: The Name of Jesus Revealed in the Old Testament*. Toronto: Frontier Research, 1996. [See. 136–37]

Rosen, Moishe. *Y'shua: The Jewish Way to Say Jesus*. Chicago: Moody Bible Institute, 1982. [Chapter 12 Resurrection, See. 53–57; N.B. Rosen was the founder of Jews for Jesus.]

Rosen, Moishe, and Ceil Rosen. *Witnessing to Jews: Practical Ways to Relate the Love of Jesus*. San Francisco: Purple Pomegrante, 1998. [Christ's Resurrection!, See. 137–40]

Rubin, Barry. *You Bring the Bagels, I'll Bring the Gospel*. Old Tappan, NJ: Chosen, 1989. [See. 161–62]

Stern, David H. *Jewish New Testament Commentary: A Companion to the Jewish New Testament*. 6th ed. Clarksville, MD: Jewish New Testament Publication, 1999. [See. 85–86; 101–2; 150–52; 211–14; 215–18; 484–88]

Triestman, Mitch. *To the Jew First: A Textbook on Jewish Evangelism*, Philadelphia: Lifeline, 1998. [The Resurrection Accounts, See. 184–86]

Chapter 31

Jewish Detractors: Con Resurrection

Alter, Michael J. *The Resurrection: A Critical Inquiry*. Bloomington, IN: Xlibris, 2015. [N.B. This 912-page text explores 113 issues that analyze 120 contradictions and 217 speculations. It is the most detailed analysis of Jesus's resurrection by a Jewish researcher.]

Ben-Chorin, Schalom. *Brother Jesus: The Nazarene Through Jewish Eyes*. Atlanta: University of Georgia Press, 2001. [See. 186–88]

Berger, Alan L., and David Patterson. *Jewish Christian Dialogue: Drawing Honey from the Rock*. St. Paul, MN: Paragon House, 2008. [resurrection of, See. 3, 55, 186, 231–32]

Berger, David, trans. *The Jewish-Christian Debate in the High Middle Ages: A Critical Edition of the "Niẓẓaḥon Vetus."* Philadelphia: The Jewish Publication Society of America, 1979. [#29, See. 62–63; #145, See. 151–52; #201, See. 202; He should have done so openly, See. 298]

Bickerman, E. J. "The Empty Tomb." In *Studies in Jewish Christian History*. Vol. 2. Edited by Amram Tropper, 712–25. Leiden: Brill, 2007.

Bokser, Ben Zion. *Judaism and Christian Predicament*. NY: Alfred A. Knopf, 1967. [Resurrection of, See. 188, 202, 44–47, 249, 263, 98–99]

Boyarin, Daniel. *The Jewish Gospels: The Story of the Jewish Christ*. New York: New Press, 2012. [Epilog, See. 19–60; N.B. He writes, "The exaltation and resurrection experiences of his followers are a product of the narrative, not a cause of it."]

Cohen, Joseph. *The Deicides: Analysis of the Life of Jesus, and of the Several Phases of the Christian Church in their Relation to Judaism*. Translated by Anna Maria Goldsmid. Baltimore: Deutsch, 1873. [Resurrection of Jesus, See. 113–24; N.B. Google book]

———. *The Existence of Christ Disproved by Irresistible Evidence, in a Series of Letters, from a German Jew*. London: Henry Hetherington, 1873. [See. 4, 96, 101, 104; N.B. Google book. Superficial references to Jesus's resurrection.]

Cohn-Sherbok, Dan. *The Jewish Messiah*. Edinburgh: T & T Clark, 1997. [Death and Resurrection, See. 66–71; N.B. Nothing useful.]

———. *Rabbinic Perspectives on the New Testament*. Lewiston: Edwin Mellen, 1990. [Chapter 6 Jesus' Burial Garment, See. 57–65; N.B. The author asserts that the Gospels themselves "seriously call into question the view that Jesus was buried in the Shroud of Turin."]

———. "The Resurrection of Jesus: A Jewish View." In *Resurrection Reconsidered*. Edited by Gavin D'Costa. Oxford: Oneworld, 1996. [See. 184–200]

Cohon, Beryl D. *Men at the Crossroads Between Jerusalem and Rome*. New York: Thomas Yoseloff, 1970. [Jesus the Resurrected Christ, See. 115–20]

Cook, Michael J. "Evolving Jewish Views of Jesus." In *Jesus Through Jewish Eyes*. Compiled and edited by Beatrice Bruteau. Maryknoll, NY: Orbis Books, 2001. [See. 10]

———. *Modern Jews Engage the New Testament: Enhancing Jewish Well-Being in a Christian Environment*. Woodstock, VT: Jewish Lights, 2012. [resurrected of reported, See. 58, 149–50, 158, 179–80, 228, 254, 260; cognitive dissonance and?, 324n.323]

Cresson, Warder. *The Key of David: David the True Messiah*. Philadelphia, 1852. [Third Pillar.—Resurrection of Jesus, See. 181–83; N.B. Archive.org. Cresson was a Quaker who converted to Judaism and became Michoel Boaz Yisroel ben Avraham!]

Dimont, Max I. *Appointment in Jerusalem: A Search for the Historical Jesus*. New York: St. Martin's Press, 1991. [Chapter 7 A Concerto of Faith and Doubt, See. 113–24]

———. *Jews, God, and History*. New York: Simon & Schuster, 1962. [See. 139–43]

Dubnov, Simon. *History of the Jews: From the Beginning to Early Christianity*. Vol. 1. Translated by Moshe Spiegel. New York: Thomas Yoseloff, 1967. [Original Judeo-Christian Community, See. 853]

Enelow, Hyman Gerson. *A Jewish View of Jesus*. New York: Macmillan, 1920. [See. 159–60; N.B. Archive.org]

Fluegel, Maurice. *The Messiah-Ideal: Comparative Religious Legislations, Doctrines and Forms Unfolding that Ideal*. Vol. 1. Jesus of Nazareth. Baltimore: Theo. Kroh, 1896. [See. 105–7; N.B. Google book]

Flusser, David. *Jesus*. Jerusalem: Magnes, 1997. [See. 20, 35, 155, Epilogue, 175–77]

———. *The Sage from Galilee: Rediscovering Jesus' Genius*. Grand Rapids: Eerdmans, 2008. [Resurrection of Jesus, See. 2, 163]

Fredriksen, Paula. *Jesus of Nazareth, King of the Jews: A Jewish Life and the Emergence of Christianity*. New York: Knopf, 2000. [Afterward: Jesus, Christianity, and History, See. 261–68]

Freud, Sigmund. *The Standard Edition of the Complete Psychological Works of Sigmund Freud : Transl. from the German. 23. 1937–1939. Moses and Monotheism. An Outline of Psycho-Analysis and Other Works*. London: Hogarth Press; Institute of Psychoanalysis, 1939. [Essay 3 Part 1 D. Application, See. 89–90; N.B. *The Origins of Religion*. Penguin, 1960, See. 334]

Golding, Shmuel. *The Light of Reason. New Testament Fallacies: A Critical Criticism of the Gospels and Acts*. Vol. 3. Jerusalem: Author, 1992. [Mark, See. 46–48; Acts, See. 69; Fiction or Crucifixion, See. 82–88]

Goldstein, Morris. *Jesus in the Jewish Tradition*. New York: Macmillan, 1950. [Resurrection, See. 92, 120, 153, 158–59, 186, 204, 232]

Goodman, Paul. *The Synagogue and the Church: Being A Contribution to the Apologetics of Judaism*. London: Routledge, 1906. [See. 251–63; N.B. Archive.org and HathiTrust]

Grayzel, Solomon. *A History of the Jews*. Philadelphia: JPS, 1963. [See. 135–36]

Greenberg, Irving. "Religious Values After the Holocaust: A Jewish View." In *Jews and Christians after the Holocaust*. Edited by Abraham J. Peck. Philadelphia: Fortress, 1982. [See. 85]

Hart, Lewis A. *A Jewish Reply to Christian Evangelists*. New York: Bloch, 1906. [See. 27, 31, 110; N. B. Google book]

Homolka, Walter. New York: *Jesus Reclaimed: Jewish Perspectives on the Nazarene.* Translated by Ingrid Shafer. New York: Berghahn, 2015. [See. 43, 76–77]

Itzkoff, Seymour W. *Who Are the Jews?* Ashfield, MA: Paideia, 2004. [See. 126]

Joseph, Simon J. *Jesus and the Temple: The Crucifixion in its Jewish Context.* Cambridge: Cambridge University Press, 2016. [Chapter 7 The Dying Savior, See. 210–37; esp. 210–15 discusses 1 Corinthians 15:3–8; N.B. An excellent chapter to examine.]

Kalisch, Isidor. *A Guide for Rational Inquiries into the Biblical Writings: Being an Examination of the Doctrinal Difference Between Judaism and Primitive Christianity, Based Upon a Critical Exposition of the Book of Matthew.* Translated by M. Meyer. Cincinnati: Bloch, 1857. [See. 102, 142–45, 178–82; N.B. Archive.org]

Kaufmann, Yehezkel. *Christianity and Judaism: Two Covenants.* Translated by C. W. Efroymson. Jerusalem: Magnes Press, 1988. [See. 132–35]

Klausner, Joseph. *Jesus of Nazareth: His Life, Times and Teaching.* Translated by Herbert Danby. New York: Macmillan, 1943. [Seventh Book: The Trial, and Crucifixion of Jesus 4. The Account of the Resurrection, See. 356–59]

Klinghoffer, David. *Why the Jews Rejected Jesus: The Turning Point in Western History.* New York: Doubleday, 2006. [See. 77, 86–89]

Kohler, Kaufmann. *The Origins of the Synagogue and the Church.* Edited by H. G. Enelow. New York: Macmillan, 1929. [See. 227–37; 262; N.B. Haithitrust.org]

Krauskopf, Joseph. *Jesus, Man or God? Five Discourses.* Philadelphia: Rayner, 1911. [See. 4, 26, 44, 46]

Lapide, Pinchas. *Jesus in Two Perspectives: A Jewish-Christian Dialog.* Pinchas Lapide & Ulrich Luz. Translated by Lawrence W. Denef. Minneapolis: Augsburg, 1985. [See. 31]

———. *Jewish Monotheism and Christian Trinitarian Doctrine.* Translated by Leonard Swidler. Philadelphia: Fortress, 1981. [Dialogue, See. 59–80; N.B. Lapide states: "I accept the resurrection of Easter Sunday not as an invention of the community of disciples, but as a historical event." Significantly, he adds, "For details, I can only refer to my book *Auferstehung—ein judisches Glaubenserlebnis* ("Resurrection: A Jewish Faith Experience.")

———. *The Resurrection of Jesus: A Jewish Perspective.* Minneapolis: Augsburg, 1983. [160-page text]

Leidner, Harold. *The Fabrication of the Christ Myth.* Tampa, FL: Survey, 1999. [N.B. Leidner was an American patent attorney and advocate of the Christ Myth.]

Levine, Amy-Jill. *The Misunderstood Jew: The Church and the Scandal of the Jewish Jesus.* New York: HarperSanFrancisco, 2006. [Chapter 2 From Jewish Sect to Gentile Church, See. 56–62]

Levine, Samuel. *You Take Jesus, I'll Take God: How to Refute Christian Missionaries.* Los Angeles: Hamoroh Press, 1980. [A2. Why should anyone believe in the supposed resurrection of Jesus when some of the apostles themselves did not believe it?, See. 70; A3. If Jesus really did return from the dead, and if he really came in the name of grace and kindness, then why didn't he reveal himself to everyone?, See. 70–72]

Ludwig, Emil. *The Son of Man: The Story of Jesus.* Translated by Eden and Cedar Paul. New York: Boni & Liveright, 1928. [See. 313–15; N.B. Originally Emil Cohn was raised as a non-Jew but he was not baptized.]

Marks, Stanley J. and Ethel Marks. *Judaism Looks at Christianity, 7 B.C.E–1986 C.E.* Newell, IA: Bireline, 1986. [Chapter 10 The Chart of Irreconcilable Resurrection, See. 131–32; Chapter 11 Lies by St. Matthew The Ascension: Dilemma, See. 133–37]

Category XI—Judaic Interpretations of Jesus's Resurrection

Mendelssohn, Moses. "From 'Counter-Reflections to Bonnet's Palingenesis' (1770)." In *Moses Mendelssohn: Writings on Judaism, Christianity, and the Bible*. Edited by Michah Gottlieb, Translated by Curtis Bowman, Elias Sacks and Allan Arkush. Leonon, NH: University Press of New England, 2011. [See. 18; N.B. Excerpt from "Counter-Reflections to Bonnet's *Palingenesis*," Jub A 7:90–106 (in German)]

Moffic, Eric. *What Every Christian Needs to Know About the Jewishness of Jesus: A New Way of See the Most Influential Rabbi in History*. Nashville: Abingdon Press, 2015. [e-book. See: Resurrection]

Montefiore, C. G. *The Synoptic Gospels*. Edited by Israel Abrahams. Vol. 2. London: Macmillan, 1909. [Chapter 34 See. 1087–99]

Philippson, Ludwig. *The Crucifixion and the Jews*. Translated by Maurice Mayer. Philadelphia: Jones & Hamilton, printers, 5626. [See. 15; N.B. Archive.org. The year 5626 corresponds to the year 1866.]

Pittsburgh Conference, The. "The Pittsburgh Platform"—1885. Pittsburgh, PA: The Conference, 1885. [Platform 7 "We reassert the doctrine of Judaism that the soul is immortal, grounding the belief on the divine nature of human spirit, which forever finds bliss in righteousness and misery in wickedness. We reject as ideas not rooted in Judaism, the beliefs both in bodily resurrection and in Gehenna and Eden (Hell and Paradise) as abodes for everlasting punishment and reward." N.B. Given that there is no bodily resurrection, Jesus was not bodily resurrected. Available online.]

Roffman, Etomar Ben. *The Great Christ Debate: A Quest for the Theological Reconciliation of Judaism, Christianity, and Islam*. Hicksville, NY: Exposition Press, 1978. [See. 8–12, 21, 133; N.B. The author writes: "I [Barry S. Roffman] wrote this book under the pen name of Etomar Ben Roffman back in 1978 when I was married to a Christian. At the time I didn't even know how to correctly spelling my first Hebrew name—Itamar. THE GREAT CHRIST DEBATE was an attempt to gather into one place all the key arguments of Judaism, Christianity and Islam about who Jesus really was . . . Eventually, as that book makes clear, I turned to Orthodox Judaism."]

Rosenberg, Roy A. *The Concise Guide to Judaism History, Practice, Faith*. New York: Nal, 1990. [See. 53]

Rosenberg, Stuart E. *Secrets of the Jews*. Buffalo, NY: Sundial, 1994. [Death and Resurrection, See. 33]

Roth, Cecil. *A Short History of the Jewish People*. New York: Schocken, 1961. [See. 140. N.B. No content.]

Sachar, Abram Leon. *A History of the Jews*. New York: Alfred A. Knopf, 1965. [See. 134–35]

Sandmel, Samuel. *A Jewish Understanding of the New Testament: Augmented Edition*. KTAV: New York, 1956. [Resurrection, Acts 261; John, 270, 276–77; Luke, 189; Mark, 122; disputed over in Matthew, 164; Paul, 57–59, 85]

———. *Judaism and Christian Beginnings*. New York: Oxford University Press, 1978. [See. 307, 323–24, 350–51, 368–69, 387–89, 395]

———. *We Jews and Jesus*. New York: Oxford University Press, 1973. [Chapter 2 Early Christianity and Its Jewish Background, See. 17–29; Chapter 3 The Divine Christ, See. 35–36]

Schlesinger, Max Shlezinger. *The Historical Jesus of Nazareth*. New York: Charles P. Somerby, 1876. [See. 86–87; N.B. Google book]

Schwartz, G. David. *A Jewish Appraisal of Dialogue: Between Talk and Theology.* Lanham, MD: University Press of America, 1994. [N.B. Two Popular Jewish Interpretations of Jesus. Pinchas Lapide on the Resurrection of Jesus, See. 61–68]

Segal, F. Alan. *Life After Death: A History of the Afterlife in Western Religion.* New York: Doubleday, 2005. [See. The Scandal of the Resurrection, 447–63; N.B. This book is an important source to examine.]

———. "Life and Death: The Social Sources" in *The Resurrection, An Interdisciplinary Symposium on the Resurrection of Jesus,* ed. Stephen Davis, Daniel Kendall, and Gerald O'Collins. Oxford: Oxford University Press, 1997. [See. 90–125]

Shapiro, Rami M. "Listening to Jesus with an Ear for God." In *Jesus Through Jesus Eyes.* Compiled and edited by Beatrice Bruteau. Maryknoll, NY: Orbis Books, 2001. [See. 160]

Sigal, Gerald. *The Jew and the Christian Missionary: A Jewish Response to Missionary Christianity.* New York: Ktav, 1981. [The Resurrection, See. 238–53; N.B. This text is a must to read.]

———. *The Jewish Response to Missionary Christianity: Why Jews Don't Believe in Jesus.* Createspace, 2015. [Chapter 68 A Resurrection Tale, See. 389–411; N.B. Awesome! Sigal's work is a definite, must read.]

———. *The Resurrection Fantasy: Reinventing Jesus.* US: Xlibris, 2012. [314 pages; N.B. This work is an absolute must to read.]

Silver, Abba Hillel. *Where Judaism Differed: An Inquiry into the Distinctiveness of Judaism.* New York: Macmillan, 1956. [See. 97–98; N.B. Silver explains why, from a Christian perspective that Jesus died.]

Singer, Tovia. *Let's Get Biblical.* Monsey, NY: Outreach Judaism. [Can These Two Stories Both Be True? Matthew 28:1–10 and John 20:1–18, See. 92–97; Questions About the Resurrection, See. 98–99; N.B. Singer has an accompanying CD]

Solomon, George. *The Jesus of History and the Jesus of Tradition Identified.* London: Reeves & Turner, 1880. [See. 73, 109, 120; N.B. Google book]

Spinoza, Benedictus de. *The Chief Works of Benedict de Spinoza.* Translated by R. H. M. Elwes. Vol. 2. London: G. Bell, 1891. [Letter 24, January 14, 1676, See. 304–5; Letter 25 February 7, 1876, See. 305–9; N.B. Archive.org]

Steinberg, Milton. *Basic Judaism.* New York: Harcourt, Brace, & World, 1947. [See. 112]

Talmage, Frank Ephraim. *Disputation and Dialogue: Reading in the Jewish-Christian Encounter.* New York: Ktav, 1975. [Jesus, resurrection of, See. 30, 42, 45, 46 48, 66, 136, 178, 197; N.B. Talmage assembles a collection of readings about the Jewish-Christian encounter.]

Trattner, Ernest R. *As A Jew Sees Jesus.* New York: Scribner's Sons, 1931. [Chapter 11 The Character of the New Testament, See. 134–49; N.B. Rabbi Trattner does not specifically discuss Jesus's resurrection. Rather, he attempts to explain how the stories about Jesus developed and evolved.]

Troki, Isaac Ben Abraham. *Faith Strengthened.* New York: Ktav, 1970. [Matthew 28:18, See. 248–49; John 20:17, See. 268; Acts 1, 6–7, See. 40–41, 268–69; N.B. Archive.org., 1851 printing]

Trypho, the Jew. *Dialogue with Trypho. From Ante-Nicene Fathers,* Vol. 1. Edited by Alexander Roberts, James Donaldson, and A. Cleveland Coxe. Translated by Marcus Dodds and George Reith. Buffalo, NY: Christian Literature publishing, 1885. [Chapter 108 The Resurrection of Christ did Not Convert the Jews. But Through the Whole

World They Have Sent Men to Accuse Christ; N.B. Available online. Trypho was a fictional character invented by Justin Martyr.]

Vermès, Géza. *Jesus In His Jewish Context*. Minneapolis: Fortress, 2003. [See. 21–23]

———. *The Resurrection: History and Myth*. New York: Doubleday, 2008. [See. 143]

Walker, Thomas T. *Jewish Views of Jesus*. London: George Allen & Unwin, 1931. [See. 21–22, 28, 29, 64, 89–90, 102, 106, 114–15, 132, 135–36; N.B. Reprinted by Arno, 1973; N.B. A Christian who surveyed Jewish views of Jesus wrote this work.]

Weiss, Louis. *Some Burning Questions: An Exegetical Treatise on Christianizing of Judaism*. Columbus, OH, 1893. [See. 42–43, 76; N.B. Google book]

Wise, Isaac Mayer. *The Martyrdom of Jesus of Nazareth*. 3rd ed. Cincinnati and Chicago, 1874. [See. 126 N.B. Archive.org. Wise refutes the crucifixion story and resurrection. This entire text should be examined.]

———. *The Origin of Christianity and a Commentary to the Acts of the Apostles*. Cincinnati: Bloch, 1868. [See. 16–23; N.B. Google book. This book should be examined.]

Yisrael, Rav-Zuridan. *Let's Talk About Jesus: A Critical Look at Common Beliefs on Jesus & Christianity*. 2008. [The Resurrection, See. 17–24]

Zeitlin, Irving M. *Jesus and the Judaism of His Time*. Cambridge: Polity Press, 1988. [Chapter 12 The Resurrection Appearance, See. 163–67]

Zeitlin, Solomon. *Solomon Zeitlin's Studies in the Early History of Judaism*. Vol 1. New York: Ktav, 1973. [The Christ Passage in Josephus, See. 407–31]

Category XII

Reference Sources, Dissertations and Theses, and Introduction to the New Testament

CHAPTER 32

Dictionaries, Encyclopedia, and Glossaries

Abbott, Lyman, and Thomas Jefferson Conant, eds. *A Dictionary of Religious Knowledge, for Popular and Professional Use; Comprising Full Information on Biblical, Theological, and Ecclesiastical Subjects.* New York: Harper, 1875. [Ascension Day, See. 75; Resurrection of Jesus Christ, See. 803–4; N.B. Archive.org]

Achtemeier, Paul J., ed. *Harpers Bible Dictionary.* New York: Harper & Row, 1985. [Ascension of Christ, See. 73 (James M. Efird); Resurrection, See. 864–65 (Reginald H. Fuller)]

Compendious Dictionary of the Holy Bible, A.: Containing a Biographical History of the Persons: A Geographical-Historical Account of the Places . . . London: Printed for W. Button by S. Rousseau, 1796. [Ascension of Our Lord, See. 39; Jesus, See. 263–65 N.B. Google book]

Addis, William E., and Thomas Arnold. *A Catholic Dictionary or the Universal Christian Educator and Popular Encyclopedia of Religious Information.* New York: Christian Press Association, 1896. [Ascension of Christ, See. 62; Easter, Feast of, See. 283–85; N.B. Archive.org and Google book]

Alexander, Archibald. *A Pocket Dictionary of the Holy Bible . . .* Philadelphia: American Sunday School Union, 1830. [Ascension of Christ, See. 74; N.B. Google book]

Alexander, David, and Pat Alexander, eds. *Eerdmans' Handbook to the Bible.* Grand Rapids: Eerdmans, 1984. [Resurrection, See. 493, 513, 529–30; The Accounts of the Resurrection (David Wheaton), See. 548, 550, 595]

Alexander, T. Desmond, and Brian S. Rosner, eds. *New Dictionary of Biblical Theology.* Downers Grove, IL: InterVarsity, 2000. [Exaltation, See. 467–70 (B. M. Fanning)]

Allen, Clifton Judson, et al., eds. *Encyclopedia of Southern Baptists.* Vol. 1. Nashville: Broadman, 1958. [Resurrection, See. 705–6 (Ray Summers); Ascension, See. 706 (V. E. Gideon)]

Angeles, Peter A. *Dictionary of Christian Theology.* San Francisco: Harper & Row, 1985. [Resurrection, See. 173]

Anthony, Michael J., ed. *Evangelical Dictionary of Christian Education.* Grand Rapids: Baker Academic, 2001. [Resurrection of Jesus Christ, See. 596–98 (Jerry Root)]

Apostolos-Cappadona, Diane. *Dictionary of Christian Art.* New York: Continuum, 1994. [Ascension of Christ, See. 40; Resurrection of Jesus Christ, See. 290]

Atkinson, David John, ed. *New Dictionary of Christian Ethics and Pastoral Theology.* Leicester: Inter-Varsity Press, 1995. [Resurrection, See. 737–38 (D. B. Garlington)]

Attridge, Harold W., and Richard P. McBrien, eds. *The HarperCollins Encyclopedia of Catholicism.* New York: HarperCollins, 1995. [Resurrection of Christ, See. 1108–10 (Pheme Perkins)]

Attwater, Donald, ed. *A Catholic Dictionary.* 31st ed. New York: Macmillan, 1961. [Ascension, See. 35; Resurrection of Christ, See. 429; N.B. Earlier editions 1931, 1949, 1958.]

Ayre, John. *The Treasury of Bible Knowledge.* New York: Appleton, 1866. [Ascension, See. 62; Resurrection, See. 758–60; N.B. Archive.org and Google book]

Balentine, Samuel Eugene, ed. *The Oxford Encyclopedia of the Bible and Theology.* Vol. 2. Oxford: Oxford University Press, 2015. [Resurrection in the New Testament, see. 236–43 (Steven J. Kraftchick)]

Balz, Horst Robert, and Gerhard Schneider, eds. *Exegetical Dictionary of the New Testament.* Vol. 1. Grand Rapids: Eerdmans, 1990. [Anastasis resurrection, See. 88–92 (J. Kremer)]

Barnes, Charles Randall, ed. *Barnes's Bible Encyclopedia: Biographical, Geographical, Historical, and Doctrinal.* Vol. 3. New York: Eaton & Mains, 1900. [Resurrection of Christ, See. 932–33]

———. *Dictionary of the Bible: Biographical, Geographical, Historical, and Doctrinal.* New York: Eaton & Mains, 1900. [Resurrection of Christ, See. 932–33; N.B. Also *The People's Bible Encyclopedia*, Vol. 2. Chicago: People's Publication Society, 1912. Google book]

Barr, John. *Barr's Complete Index and Concise Dictionary of the Holy Bible.* New York: Lane & Scott, 1851. [Ascension, See. 14; Resurrection of Christ, See. 131; N.B. Google book]

Bastow, James Austin. *A Biblical Dictionary.* London: Longman, Brown, Green, Longmans & Roberts, 1859. [Ascension, See. 99; Resurrection of Christ, See. 579–80; N.B. Google book]

Bauer, Johannes Baptist. *Encyclopedia of Biblical Theology: The Complete Sacramentum Verbi.* Vol. 1. New York: Crossroad, 1981. [Ascension, See. 37–42 (Robert Koch)]

Beavis, Mary Ann., and Michael J. Gilmour, eds. *Dictionary of the Bible and Western Culture.* Sheffield: Sheffield Phoenix Press, 2012. [Ascension, See. 33 (Joshua N. Rhone); Resurrection, See. 441–42 (Eliot Tofa)]

Beinert, Wolfgang, and Francis Schüssler Fiorenza, eds. *Handbook of Catholic Theology.* New York: Crossroad, 1995. [Ascension of Christ, See. 29–33 (Lothar Ullrich); Resurrection Narratives, See. 586–91 (Lothar Ullrich)]

Benedetto, Robert. *Encyclopedia of the Reformed Faith.* Edited by Donald K. McKim. Louisville: Westminster/John Knox, 1992. [Ascension, See. 12 (Peter Toon); Resurrection, See. 319–20 (Richard B. Gaffin)]

Benham, William, ed. *The Dictionary of Religion: An Encyclopaedia of Christian and Other Religious Doctrines, Denominations, Sects, Heresies, Ecclesiastical Terms, History, Biography . . .* London: Cassell, 1887. [Ascension, See. 77–78; Resurrection, See. 893–96; N.B. Archive.org]

Benton, Angelo Ames, ed. *The Church Cyclopædia: A Dictionary of Church Doctrine, History, Organization and Ritual.* New York: James Pott, 1883. [Ascension, See. 77; Resurrection of Christ, See. 656–57; N.B. Archive.org and Google book]

Berardino, Angelo Di, ed. *Encyclopedia of the Early Church.* Translated by Adrian Walford. Vol. 1. New York: Oxford University Press, 1992. [Ascension, See. 83 (V. Saxer)]

Dictionaries, Encyclopedia, and Glossaries

Bercot, David W., ed. *A Dictionary of Early Christian Beliefs: A Reference Guide to More than 700 Topics Discussed by the Early Church Fathers*. Peabody, MA: Hendrickson, 2012. [Resurrection of Christ]

Betz, Hans Dieter, ed. *Religion Past & Present. Encyclopedia of Theology and Religion*. Vol. 11. Leiden: Brill, 2012. [Resurrection of Jesus Christ, See. 148–49 (Jürgen Becker); Dogmatics, See. 149–50 (Christoph Schwöbel)]

———, ed. *Religion Past & Present. Encyclopedia of Theology and Religion*. Vol. 1. Leiden: Brill, 2007. [Ascension of Christ, New Testament, See. 429–30 (M. Eugene Boring)]

Blanchard, W. *A Dictionary of Scripture Words, &c.* York: Printed by W. Blanchard, 1808. [Ascension, See. 4; Resurrection, See. 18; N.B. Available by the British Library]

Blunt, John Henry, ed. *Dictionary of Doctrinal and Historical Theology*. London: Longmans, Green, 1892. [Ascension, See. 50; Resurrection of Christ, See. 646–49; N.B. Google book and HathiTrust]

Bodensieck, Julius, ed. *The Encyclopedia of the Lutheran Church*. Vol. 1. Minneapolis: Augsburg, 1965. [Christology, See. 483–86 (Ernst Kinder)]

Born, Adrianus Van den. *Encyclopedic Dictionary of the Bible: A Translation and Adaptation of A. van den Borns Bijbels Woordenboek*, 2nd revised edition, 1954–1957. Translated by Louis Francis. New York: McGraw-Hill, 1963. [Ascension of Jesus, See. 146–50; Resurrection of Jesus Christ, See. 2011–22]

Bouyer, Louis. *Dictionary of Theology*. Translated by Charles Underhill. Quinn. Desclée, 1965. [Ascension of Christ, See. 40–42; Resurrection, See. 388–90]

Bowden, John, ed. *Encyclopedia of Christianity*. New York: Oxford University Press, 2005. [Resurrection, See. 1029–32 (John Bowden)]

Bowker, John, ed. *The Oxford Dictionary of World Religions*. Oxford: Oxford University Press, 1999. [Ascension, See. 96; Resurrection of Christ, See. 813]

Brand, Chad, et al., eds. *Holman illustrated Bible Dictionary*. Nashville: Holman Reference, 2003. [Ascension, See. 233 (Mark M. Overstreet); Resurrection of Jesus Christ, 1381–82 (Bill Cook)]

Brandon, Samuel George Frederick, ed. *A Dictionary of Comparative Religion*. London: Weidenfeld and Nicolson, 1970. [Ascension of Christ, See. 104 (S. G. F. Brandon); Jesus of Nazareth, See 372–73 (S. G. F. Brandon)]

Bradshaw, Paul F., ed. *The New Westminster Dictionary of Liturgy and Worship*. Louisville: Westminster John Knox, 2002. [Ascension Day, See. 29–30 (Martin F. Connell)]

Brasher, Brenda E., ed. *Encyclopedia of Fundamentalism*. New York: Routledge, 2001. [Ascension, See. 39–40 (Donald S. Armentrout); Resurrection (Christ), See. 413–15 (Thomas Kinsell Carr)]

Broderick, Robert C., comp. *Catholic Concise Dictionary*. Edited by Placid Hermann and Marion Alphonse Habig. Chicago: Franciscan Herald Press, 1966. [Ascension (of Christ), See. 25; Resurrection, See. 232]

———., ed. *The Catholic Encyclopedia*. Nashville: Nelson, 1987. [Ascension of Christ, See. 54; Resurrection of Christ, See. 524]

Bromiley, Geoffrey W., ed. *The International Standard Bible Encyclopedia*. Vol. 4. Grand Rapids: Eerdmans, 1988. [Resurrection of Jesus Christ, See. 150–54 (Leon Morris)]

Brown, Colin, ed. *The New International Dictionary of New Testament Theology*. Grand Rapids: Zondervan, 1986. [The Resurrection in Contemporary Theology, See. 281–309 (C. Brown). N.B. Worth examining.]

Brown, J. Newton, ed. *Fessenden & Co.'s Encyclopedia of Religious Knowledge, or, Dictionary of the Bible, Theology, Religious Biography, All Religions, Ecclesiastical History, and Missions*. Brattleboro, VT: Fessenden and Co., 1835. [Ascension of Christ, See. 128–29; Exaltation of Christ, See. 517; Resurrection of Christ, See. 1020–21; N.B. HathiTrust]

Brown, John. *A Dictionary of the Holy Bible: Containing an Historical Account of the Person; a Geographical and Historical Account of the Persons and Places; a Literal, Critical, and Systematical Description of Other Objects* . . . London: William Tegg, 1848. [Christ, See. 156–57; N.B. Google book]

Browning, W. R. F. *A Dictionary of the Bible*. Oxford: Oxford University Press, 1996. [Ascension, See. 26–27; Resurrection of Jesus, See. 320–21]

Bryant, Al, ed. *The Compact Bible Dictionary*. Grand Rapids: Regency Reference Library, 1967. [Ascension of Christ, See. 58; Resurrection of Jesus, See. 498]

———, comp. *Today's Dictionary of the Bible*. Minneapolis, MN: Bethany House, 1982. [Restoration of Christ, See. 525–26]

Buck, Charles. *A Theological Dictionary: Containing Definitions of All Religious Terms* . . . London: Printed for James Duncan et al., 1833. [Ascension of Christ, See. 70; Resurrection of Christ, See. 826–28; N.B. Archive.org and Google book]

Buckland, Augustus Robert, and A. Lukyn Williams, eds. *The Universal Bible Dictionary*. New York: Revell, 1914. [Resurrection of Christ, See. 413; N.B. Archive.org]

Butler, Trent C., ed. *Holman Bible Dictionary*. Nashville: Holman Bible, 1991. [Ascension, See. 109–10 (Charles R. Wade); Resurrection of Jesus Christ, See. 1179–80 (William L. Hendricks)]

Buttrick, George Arthur. *The Interpreter's Dictionary of the Bible*. Vol. 4. New York: Abingdon, 1962. [Resurrection in the NT, See. 43–53 (J. A. T. Robinson)]

———. *The Interpreter's Dictionary of the Bible*. Vol. 1. New York: Abingdon, 1962. [Ascension, See. 245–47 (J. M. Robinson)]

Byrne, Peter, and Leslie Houlden, eds. *Companion Encyclopedia of Theology*. London: Routledge, Taylor & Francis, 1995. [Jesus in History and Belief, See. 177–80 (Leslie Holden); The Triune God of the Bible and the Emergence of Orthodoxy, See. 196–97 (Robert L. Wilken)]

Cairns, Alan. *Dictionary of Theological Terms*. Greenville, SC: Ambassador Emerald International, 2002. [Resurrection, See. 380–83]

Calmet, Augustin. *Calmet's Great Dictionary of the Holy Bible: Historical*. Volume 1. Charlestown: Samuel Etheridge, 1812. [Ascension, no pagination; Jesus, no pagination; N.B. Google book]

Campbell-Jack, Campbell, ed. *New Dictionary of Christian Apologetics*. Downers Grove, IL: InterVarsity, 2006. [Resurrection of Jesus, See. 614–17 (Gary R. Habermas); resurrection of Jesus, Implications of, See. 617–19 (Gary R. Habermas)]

Carr, Wesley A., ed. *The New Dictionary of Pastoral Studies*. Grand Rapids: Eerdmans, 2002. [Resurrection, See. 315–16]

Carter, Charles Sydney, and G. E. Alison Weeks, eds. *The Protestant Dictionary*. London: Harrison Trust, 1933. Resurrection Body of Christ, See. 588–90 (C. H. H. Wright)]

Charley, Julian. *50 Key Words The Bible*. Richmond: John Knox, 1971. [Resurrection, See. 52–53]

Cloud, David W. *Way of Life Encyclopedia of the Bible & Christianity*. 4th ed. Port Huron, MI: Way of Life, 2002. [Resurrection, See. 476–78]

Coggins, R. J., and J. Leslie Houlden, eds. *A Dictionary of Biblical Interpretation*. London: SCM, 1990. [Resurrection Narratives, See. 589-91 (J. C. Fenton)]

Cohn-Sherbok, Dan. *Blackwell Dictionary of Judaica*. Cambridge, MA: Blackwell Reference, 1992. [Jesus, See. 262-63]

———. *A Dictionary of Judaism and Christianity*. Philadelphia: Trinity Press International, 1991. [Ascension Day, See. 11; Resurrection, See. 145-46]

Collinge, William J. *The A to Z of Catholicism*. Lanham: Scarecrow Press, 2001. [Resurrection, See. 453-55]

———. *Historical Dictionary of Catholicism*. 2nd ed. Lanham: Scarecrow Press, 2012. [Ascension, See. 52; Resurrection, See. 380-81]

Collins, John J., and Daniel C. Harlow, eds. *The Eerdmans Dictionary of Early Judaism*. Grand Rapids: Eerdmans, 2010. [Resurrection, New Testament, See. 1143-44 (George W. E. Nickelsburg)]

Collins, Mary, Joseph A. Komonchak, and Dermot A. Lane, eds. *The New Dictionary of Theology*. Collegeville, MN: Liturgical Press, 1993. [Ascension of Christ, See. 63-64 (Lionel Swain); The Resurrection of Christ, See. 880-84 (Gerald O'Collins)]

Common English Bible. *Bible Dictionary*. Nashville: Common English Bible, 2011. [Resurrection, See. 321-22]

Concise Routledge Encyclopedia of Philosophy. London: Routledge. 2000. [Resurrection, See. 769 (Peter Van Inwagen)]

Concordia Publishing House. *Companion Dictionary of the Bible*. St. Louis: Concordia, 1985. [Ascension, See. 28; Resurrection, See. 172]

Copan, Paul, and Tremper Longman, eds. *Dictionary of Christianity and Science: The Definitive Reference for the Intersection of Christian Faith and Contemporary Science*. Grand Rapids: Zondervan, 2017. [Resurrection of Jesus, See. 573-75 (Gary R. Habermas)]

Cornfeld, Gaalyahu, ed. *Pictorial Biblical Encyclopedia*. New York: MacMillan, 1964. [Transfiguration and Resurrection, See. 691]

Counsell, Michael, comp. *A Basic Bible Dictionary*. Norwich: Canterbury Press, 2004. [Ascension of Christ, See. 13; Resurrection, See. 100]

Covel, James. *A Concise Dictionary of the Holy Bible: Designed for the use of Sunday-School Teachers and Families . . .* New York: Carlton & Phillips, 1854. [Ascension of Christ, See. 42; N.B. Google book and HathiTrust]

Crim, Keith R., Roger Aubrey Bullard, and Larry D. Shinn, eds. *Abingdon Dictionary of Living Religions*. Nashville: Abingdon, 1981. [Ascension of Christ, See. 65 (T. O. Hall); Resurrection, See. 619-20 (L. E. Keck)]

Cross, Frank Leslie, ed. *The Oxford Dictionary of the Christian Church*. London: Oxford University Press, 1966. [Ascension of Christ, See. 92; Resurrection of Christ, See. 1157-58; N.B. idem. 1957 printing]

Cross, Frank Leslie, and E. A. Livingstone, eds. *The Oxford Dictionary of the Christian Church*. 2nd ed. London: Oxford University Press, 1974. [Ascension of Christ, See. 94-95; Resurrection of Christ, See. 1177-78]

Cully, Iris V., and Kendig Brubaker Cully, eds. *Harper's Encyclopedia of Religious Education*. San Francisco: Harper & Row, 1990. [Resurrection, See. 556-57; V. L. Wimbush)]

Davie, Martin, ed. *New Dictionary of Theology: Historical and Systematic*. 2nd ed. Downers Grove, IL: IVP Academic, 2016. [Ascension and Heavenly Session of Christ, See. 66-68 (M. Ovey); Resurrection of Christ, See. 765-69 (J. R. A. Merrick)]

Davies, J. G., ed. *A Dictionary of Liturgy and Worship*. New York: Macmillan, 1972. [Ascension Day, See 41 (A. A. McArthur); Easter, See. 166–68 (J. G. Davies)]

Davis, John D. *Davis Dictionary of the Bible*: 4th rev. ed. Grand Rapids: Baker, 1972. [Jesus Christ, See. 412–13]

———. *A Dictionary of the Bible*. Philadelphia: Westminster, 1898. [Jesus Christ, See. 374–75; N.B. Archive.org]

Deist, Ferdinand. *A Concise Dictionary of Theological Terms with an English-Afrikaans and an Afrikaans-English List*. Pretoria: Sigma Press, 1984. [Ascension, See. 14; Resurrection Narratives, See. 145]

DeMoss, Matthew S., and J. Edward Miller, eds. *Zondervan Dictionary of Bible and Theology Words*. Grand Rapids: Zondervan, 2002. [Ascension, See. 29; Resurrection, See. 208–9]

Dodd, Debbie. *Dictionary of Theological Terms in Simplified English: A Resource for English Language Learners*. Wheaton, IL: EMIS (Evangelism and Missions Information Service), 2003. [Ascension, See. 22; Resurrection, See. 121–22; Resurrection of Christ, See. 122]

Doniger, Wendy, ed. *Merriam-Webster's Encyclopedia of World Religions*. Springfield, MA: Merriam-Webster, 2000. [Ascension, See. 80; Resurrection, See. 925]

Donzel, E. Van, B. Lewis, and Ch. Pellat, eds. *Encyclopedia of Islam*. Vol. 4. Leiden: E. J. Brill, 1973. ʿĪsā, 11. See. 83–84 (G. C. Anawati)]

Douglas, J. D., ed. *The New Bible Dictionary*. Grand Rapids: Eerdmans, 1962. [Ascension, See. 94; 2. The Resurrection of Christ, See. 1086–88]

———. *New 20th-Century Encyclopedia of Religious Knowledge*. 2nd ed. Grand Rapids: Baker, 1991. [Resurrection of Christ, See. 710–12 (Robert W. Yarbrough)]

Douglas, J. D., and Earle E. Cairns, eds. *The New International Dictionary of the Christian Church*. 2nd ed. Grand Rapids: Zondervan, 1996. [Ascension, See. 76 (R. E. Nixon); Resurrection of Christ, See. 839–40 (R. E. Nixon)]

Douglas, J. D., Walter A. Elwell, and Peter Toon, eds. *The Concise Dictionary of the Christian Tradition: Doctrine, Liturgy, History*. London: Marshall Pickering, 1989. [Resurrection of Christ, See. 324]

Douglas, J. D., and N. Hillyer, eds. *The Illustrated Bible Dictionary*: Part 1. Leicester: Inter-Varsity, 1980. [Ascension, See. See. 129 (K.A. Kitchen)]

———, eds. *The Illustrated Bible Dictionary*: Part 3. Leicester: Inter-Varsity, 1980. [Resurrection, See. 1330–33 (L. L. Morris)]

———, eds. *New Bible Dictionary*. 2nd ed. Downers Grove, IL: InterVarsity, 1993. [Ascension, See. 93 (J. S. Wright); Resurrection, See. 1020–23 (L. L. Morris)]

Douglas, James D., and Merrill C. Tenney, eds. *The New International Dictionary of the Bible*. Grand Rapids: Zondervan, 1987. [Ascension of Christ, See. 97 (Peter Toon); Resurrection of Jesus Christ, See. 855–58 (Peter Toon)]

Durnbaugh, Donald F., ed. *The Brethren Encyclopedia*. Vol. 2. Philadelphia, Pa: Brethren Encyclopedia, 1983. [Resurrection, See. 1102]

Dyck, Cornelius J., and Dennis D. Martin, eds. *The Mennonite Encyclopedia: A Comprehensive Reference Work on the Anabaptist-Mennonite Movement*. Vol. 5. Hillsboro, KS: Mennonite Brethren Pub. House, 1990. [Resurrection, See. 768–69 (D. Schroed)]

Dyrness, William A., and Veli-Matti Kärkkäinen, eds. *Global Dictionary of Theology: A Resource for the Worldwide Church*. Downers Grove, IL: IVP Academic, 2008. [Resurrection, See. 754–58 (D. L. Stubbs)]

Eadie, John, ed. *A Biblical Cyclopædia; or, Dictionary of Eastern Antiquities, Geography, Natural History* ... London: Charles Griffin, 1868. [Jesus, Jesus Christ, See. 371–74; Resurrection, See. 550–51; N.B. The 6th edition (1860) is a Google book]

Easton, M. G. *Illustrated Bible Dictionary*. New York: Harper & Brothers, 1893. [Resurrection of Christ, See. 581–82; N.B. CCEL]

Ekstrom, Reynolds R. *The New Concise Catholic Dictionary for Parents and Religion Teachers*. Mystic, CT: Twenty-Third Publications, 1995. [Resurrection, See. 218–19]

Eliade, Mircea, ed. *Encyclopedia Religion*. Vol. 12. New York: Macmillan, 1987. [Resurrection, Christianity, See. 347–48 (Helmer Ringgren)]

Elwell, Walter A., ed. *Baker Encyclopedia of the Bible*. Vol. 2. Grand Rapids: Baker, 1995. [Resurrection, See. 1841–43 (Gerald L. Borchert)]

———., ed. *Baker Theological Dictionary of the Bible*. Grand Rapids: Baker, 2000. [Ascension of Jesus Christ, See. 38–40; Exaltation, See. 225–26 (Herbert M. Wolf); Resurrection, The New Testament, See. 677–79 (Eric W. Adams)]

———., ed. *The Concise Evangelical Dictionary of Theology*. 2nd ed. Grand Rapids: Baker Academic, 2001. [Ascension of Christ, See. 103–4 (A. Ross); Resurrection of Christ, See. 1014–17 (Gary R. Habermas)]

———., ed. *Topical Analysis of the Bible: A Survey of Essential Christian Doctrines*. Peabody, MA: Hendrickson, 2012. [Circumstances Related to Christ's Resurrection and Return, See. 86–87; The Meaning of the Resurrection of Christ, 469–72]

Engles, William Morrison, ed. *Bible Dictionary for the Use of Bible Classes, Schools and Families*. 3rd ed. Philadelphia: Presbyterian Board of Publication, 1851. [Resurrection, See. 303; N.B. Google book.]

Erickson, Millard J. *The Concise Dictionary of Christian Theology*. Wheaton, IL: Crossway, 2001. [Ascension of Christ, See. 17; Christ, Exaltation of, See. 62; Resurrection of Christ, See. 170]

———. *Concise Dictionary of Christian Theology Revised Edition*. Wheaton, IL: Crossway, 1986. [Ascension of Christ, See. 14; Christ, Exaltation of, See. 29; Resurrection of Christ, See. 143]

Espín, Orlando O., and James B. Nickoloff, eds. *An Introductory Dictionary of Theology and Religious Studies*. Collegeville, MN: Liturgical Press, 2007. [Ascension, See. 86–87 (Regina A. Boisclair); Resurrection in Christianity, See. 1163–64 (F. M. Gillman); Resurrection of Christ, See. 1164–65 (William Reiser)]

Evans, Craig A., ed. *Encyclopedia of the Historical Jesus*. New York: Routledge, 2010. [Ascension, See. 41–43 (James D. G. Dunn); Resurrection of Jesus, See. 498–505 (Pheme Perkins)]

Evans, Craig A., and Stanley E. Porter, eds. *Dictionary of New Testament Background*. Downer Grove, IL: InterVarsity, 2000. [Resurrection, See. 931–36 (G. R. Osborne). N.B. This article is a good read.]

Ewing, W., and J. E. H. Thomson. *The Temple Dictionary of the Bible*. London: J. M. Dent & Sons, 1910. [Resurrection of Our Lord, See. 661–62; N.B. Archive.org and Haithrust.org]

Fahlbusch, Erwin, and G. W. Bromiley, eds. *The Encyclopedia of Christianity*. Vol. 4. Grand Rapids: Eerdmans, 2005. [Resurrection, See. 664–72 (Cynthia L. Rigby)]

———. *The Encyclopedia of Christianity*. Vol. 1. Grand Rapids: Eerdmans, 1999. [Ascension of Christ, See. 130–31 (François Bovon)]

Fairbairn, Patrick, ed. *The Imperial Bible Dictionary, Historical, Biographical, Geographical and Doctrinal.* London: Blackie & Son, 1872. [Resurrection of Christ, See. 763–70 (William Milligan); N.B. HathiTrust]

Fallows, Samuel, ed. *The Popular and Critical Bible Encyclopedia and Scriptural Dictionary Fully Defining and Explaining All Religious Terms.* Vol. 3. Chicago: Howard-Severance, 1913. [Resurrection of Christ, See. 1452–53; N.B. Archive.org and Google book]

Farrar, John. *A Biblical and Theological Dictionary: Illustrative of the Old and New Testaments.* 2nd ed. London: John Mason, 1852. [Ascension, See. 43; Resurrection, See. 542–43; N.B. Google book]

Fausset, A. R., comp. *The Critical and Expository Bible Cyclopædia* Hartford, CT: S. S. Scranton, 1908. [Jesus Christ, See. 374–77; N.B. Archive.org]

Ferguson, Everett, Michael P. McHugh, and Frederick W. Norris, eds. *Encyclopedia of Early Christianity.* 2nd ed. New York: Garland, 1999. [Resurrection, See. 978–81 (Pheme Perkins)]

Ferguson, Sinclair B., et al., eds. *New Dictionary of Theology.* Downers Grove, IL: IVP Academic, 1988. [Resurrection of Christ, See. 582–83 (D. Garlington)]

Ferm, Vergilius, ed. *The Encyclopedia of Religion.* Paterson, NJ: Littlefield, Adams, 1964. [Ascension, See. 41 (R. E. E. Harkness); Resurrection of Jesus, See. 658–59 (Ernest Findlay Scott)]

Finney, Paul Corby, ed. *The Eerdmans Encyclopedia of Early Christian Art and Archaeology.* Vol. 1. Grand Rapids: Eerdmans, 2017. [Ascension, See. 127–29 (Alison C. Poe)]

———, ed. *The Eerdmans Encyclopedia of Early Christian Art and Archaeology.* Vol. 2. Grand Rapids: Eerdmans, 2017. [Resurrection, See. 414 (Paul Corby Finney)]

Flinn, Frank K. *Encyclopedia of Catholicism.* Edited by J. Gordon. Melton, New York: Facts On File, 2008. [Ascension, See. 61–62; Resurrection (of Christ), See. 548–50]

Flynn, Tom, ed. *The New Encyclopedia of Unbelief.* Amherst, NY: Prometheus, 2007. [Resurrection, See. 657–60 (Hector Avalos)]

Fodor, Nandor. *Encyclopedia of Psychic Science.* New Hyde Park New York: University, 1974. [Resurrection, See. 328]

Freedman, David Noel, ed. *The Anchor Bible Dictionary.* Vol. 5. New York: Doubleday, 1992. [Resurrection in Early Christianity, See. 688–91 (George W. E. Nickelsburg).]

———, ed. *The Anchor Bible Dictionary.* Vol. 1. New York: Doubleday, 1992. [Ascension of Christ, See. 472–74 (Norman R. Gulley)]

———, ed. *Eerdmans Dictionary of the Bible.* Grand Rapids: Eerdmans, 2000. [Ascension, See. 109–10 (Philip Munoa; Resurrection, See. 1120–22 (David Ralph Seely)]

Fuerbringer, L., et al., eds. *The Concordia Cyclopedia; A Handbook of Religious Information, with Special Reference to the History, Doctrine, Work, and Usages of the Lutheran Church.* St. Louis: Concordia, 1927. [Ascension, See. 41–42; Resurrection, See. 134–35; N.B. Archive.org]

Gaskell, G. A. *Dictionary of All Scriptures and Myths.* New York: Dorset Press, 1988. [Ascension of Jesus, See. 70; Resurrection From the Dead, See. 626–27; reprint, 1960.]

Gassmann, Günther. *Historical Dictionary of Lutheranism.* Lanham, MD: Scarecrow Press, 2001. [Resurrection, See. 290–91]

Geaves, Ron. *Continuum Glossary of Religious Terms.* New York: Continuum, 2002. [Ascension (Christianity), See. 37; Resurrection (Christianity), See. 337]

Gehman, Henry Snyder, ed. *The New Westminster Dictionary of the Bible.* Philadelphia: Westminster, 1970. [Ascension, See. 67; Resurrection, See. 799]

Geisler, Norman L. *Baker Encyclopedia of Christian Apologetics*. Grand Rapids: Baker, 2006. [Resurrection, Alternate Theories of. See. 644–47; Resurrection of Christ, See. 648–49; Resurrection Claims in Non-Christian Religions, See. 649–51; Resurrection, Evidence for, See. 651–56; Resurrection, Objections to, See. 657–64; Resurrection, Physical Nature of, See. 664–70; N.B. Geisler's work is a must read!]

Gentz, William H. ed. *The Dictionary of Bible and Religion*. Nashville: Abingdon, 1986. [Resurrection of Jesus, See. 886–87 (Howard Clark Kee)]

Glassé, Cyril. *The New Encyclopedia of Islam*. 4th ed., Lanham: Rowman & Littlefield, 2013. [Jesus, son of Mary, See. 268–69]

Glazier, Michael, and Monika Hellwig, eds. *The Modern Catholic Encyclopedia*. Collegeville, MN: Liturgical Press, 1994. [Ascension of Christ, See. 52–54 (Bríd Long); Resurrection of Christ, See. 741–45 (Wilfrid J. Harrington)]

González, Justo L. *Essential Theological Terms*. Louisville: Westminster, 2005. [Ascension, See. 19; Resurrection, See. 152]

Goodhugh, W., ed. *The Bible Cyclopaedia: or, Illustrations of the Civil and Natural History of the Sacred Writing*. Vol. 1. London: J. W. Parker, 1841–43. [Ascension of Christ, See. 123–24; N.B. HathiTrust]

Goring, Rosemary, ed. *Larousse Dictionary of Beliefs and Religions*. New York: Larousse, 1994. [Ascension, 38; Resurrection, See. 439]

Gowan, Donald E., ed. *The Westminster Theological Wordbook of the Bible*. Louisville: Westminster John Knox, 2003. [Ascend, See. 20–21 (Douglas R. A. Hare); The Resurrection of Jesus, See. 433–35 (Richard N. Longenecker)]

Granbery, J. C. *A Bible Dictionary for Sunday Schools & Families*. Nashville: Publishing House M.E. Church, South, 1921. [Resurrection, See. 347; N.B. Archive.org (1914)]

Green, Joel B., ed. *Dictionary of Scripture and Ethics*. Grand Rapids: Baker Academic, 2011. [Resurrection, See. 677–80 (Richard N. Longenecker)]

Green, Joel B., Jeannine K. Brown, and Nicholas Perrin, eds. *Dictionary of Jesus and the Gospels*. 2nd ed. Downers Grove, IL: InterVarsity, 2013. [Ascension of Jesus, See. 59–61 (S. Walton); Resurrection, See. 774–89 (K. L. Anderson); N.B. This dictionary article is a healthy reading.]

Green, Joel B., and Scot McKnight, eds. *Dictionary of Jesus and the Gospels*. Downers Grove, IL: InterVarsity, 1992. [Resurrection, See. 673–88 (G. R. Osborne); N.B. This article is a detailed reading!]

Green, Samuel G. *A Biblical and Theological Dictionary: Designed as an Illustrative Commentary on the Sacred Scriptures*. 28th ed. London: Elliot Stock, 1868. [See: Ascension of Our Lord; Resurrection of Christ; no pagination; N.B. Google book]

Hahn, Scott, ed. *Catholic Bible Dictionary*. New York: Doubleday, 2009. [Ascension of Christ, See. 72–74; The Resurrection of Christ, See. 767–69]

Hardon, John A. *Modern Catholic Dictionary*. Garden City, NY: Doubleday, 1980. [Ascension, See. 43; Resurrection of Christ, See. 466]

Harrison, Everett Falconer, ed. *Bakers Dictionary of Theology*. Grand Rapids: Baker, 1960. [Ascension, See. 67–68 (Alexander Ross); Resurrection, See. 448–56 (Wilbur M. Smith)]

Harrison, Everett Falconer, Geoffrey William. Bromiley, and Carl F. H. Henry, eds. *Wycliffe Dictionary of Theology*. Peabody, MA: Hendrickson, 1999. [The Ascension, See. 67–68 (Alexander Ross); Resurrection, See. 448–56 (Wilbur M. Smith); idem. *Baker's Dictionary of Theology*, 1960. N.B. This article should be examined.]

Harvey, Van A. *A Handbook of Theological Terms*. New York: Macmillan, 1964. [Ascension, See. 30–31; Resurrection of Christ, See. 203–6]

Hastings, James, Frederick C. Grant, and H. H. Rowley, eds. *Dictionary of the Bible* Revised edition. New York: Scribner's Sons, 1963. [Ascension, See. 60–91; Jesus Christ, See. 490–91; Resurrection, See. 845]

Hastings, James, John A. Selbie, and Louis H. Gray, eds. *A Dictionary of Christ and the Gospels*. Vol. 1. Edinburgh: T&T Clark, 1906. [Ascension, See. 124–28 (P. Dearmer); N.B. Google book]

———, eds. *A Dictionary of Christ and the Gospels*. Vol. 2. Edinburgh: T&T Clark, 1908. [Resurrection of Christ, See. 505–14 (W. J. Sparrow-Simpson); N.B. Archive.org. This article should be examined.]

———, eds. *Dictionary of the Apostolic Church*: Vol. 1. Aaron-Lystra. Edinburgh: T&T Clark, 1915. [Ascension, See. 95–99 (A. J. Maclean); N.B. Archive.org]

———, eds. *Dictionary of the Apostolic Church*: Vol. 2. Macedonia-Zion. Edinburgh: T&T Clark, 1918. [Resurrection of Christ, See. 329–67 (J. M. Shaw); N.B. Archive.org]

———, eds. *Encyclopedia of Religion and Ethics*. Vol. 7. New York: Scribner's Sons, 1910. [Jesus, 2. The Experience of the Disciples after the Resurrection, See. 523–24 (W. Douglas Mackenzie)]

Hawthorne, Gerald F., Ralph P. Martin, and Daniel G. Reid, eds. *Dictionary of Paul and His Letters*. Downers Grove, IL: InterVarsity, 1993. [Resurrection, See. 805–12 (L. J. Kreitzer)]

Hayes, Patrick J., ed. *Miracles: An Encyclopedia of People, Places, and Supernatural Events from Antiquity to the Present*. Santa Barbara, CA: ABC-CLIO, 2016. [Resurrection/Resuscitation, See. 343–44 (Patrick J. Hayes)]

Herbermann, Charles G., ed. *The Catholic Encyclopedia: An International Work of Reference*. Vol. 1. New York: Encyclopedia Press, 1907. [Ascension, See. 767 (John J. Wynne); N.B. online]

———., *The Catholic Encyclopedia: An International Work of Reference*. Vol. 12. New York: Encyclopedia Press, 1911. [Resurrection, See. 789–93 A. J. Maas); N.B. Available online]

Hindson, Edward E., and Ergun Mehmet. Caner, eds. *The Popular Encyclopedia of Apologetics*. Eugene, OR: Harvest House, 2008. [Christ, Resurrection of, See. 135–38 (Gary Habermas)]

Holder, R. Ward, ed. *The Westminster Handbook to Theologies of the Reformation*. Louisville: Westminster John Knox, 2010. [Resurrection, See. 136 (Gregory J. Miller)]

Hook, Walter Farquhar. *A Church Dictionary: A Practical Manual of Reference for Clergyman and Students*. Edited by Walter J. Hook and W. R. W. Stephens. 15th ed. London: John Murray, 1896. [Ascension Day, See. 64; Resurrection, See. 653–64; N.B. Google book and HathiTrust]

Horn, Siegfried H., ed. *Seventh-day Adventist Bible Dictionary*. Washington, DC: Review and Herald Publ. Association, 1960. [Ascension, See. 80]

Houlden, J. Leslie, and R. J. Coggins, eds. *The SCM Dictionary of Biblical Interpretation*. London: SCM, 1990. [Resurrection of Christ, See. 505–14 (C. F. Evans); Resurrection Narratives, See. 589–91 (J. C. Fenton)]

Hughes, Thomas Patrick, ed. *A Dictionary of Islam*. New York: Scribner, Welford, 1885. [Jesus Christ, See. 232; N.B. Archive.org and Google book]

Dictionaries, Encyclopedia, and Glossaries

Hutchinson Dictionary of Ideas, The. Santa Barbara, CA: ABC-CLIO, 1994. [Ascension Day, See. 36; Jesus, See. 281; Resurrection, See. 446–47]

Inglis, James. *A Topical Dictionary of Bible Texts*. Grand Rapids: Baker, 1977. [Resurrection, See. 394]

Jackson, Samuel Macauley, ed. *The Concise Dictionary of Religious Knowledge*. New York: Christian Literature, 1889. [Resurrection, See. 804–5 (Talbot Wilson Chambers); N.B. Archive.org and HathiTrust]

Jacobus, Melancthon Williams, and Elbert Clarence Lane, eds. *A New Standard Bible Dictionary*. 3d rev. ed. ed. New York: Funk & Wagnalls, 1936. [Jesus Christ, 4. Resurrection, See. 451–52 (James Denney and Alfred E. Garvie); Resurrection, See. 769–70 (Andrew C. Zenos); N.B. Also known as *Funk & Wagnalls New Standard Bible Dictionary*]

Jones, Lindsay, ed. *Encyclopedia of Religion*. 2nd ed. Vol. 7. Detroit: Thomson Gale, 2005. [Jesus, Resurrection, See. 4851–52 (Dale C. Allison)]

———, ed. *Encyclopedia of Religion*. 2nd ed. Vol. 11. Detroit: Thomson Gale, 2005. [Resurrection, See. 7762–68 (Helmer Ringgren)]

Jones, William. *The Biblical Cyclopædia: or, Dictionary of the Holy Scriptures*. London: J. Haddon, 1841. [Ascension of Christ, See. 88–89; Resurrection of Christ, See. 772–77; N.B. Google book]

Keeley, Robin, ed. *Eerdmans' Handbook to Christian Belief*. Grand Rapids: Eerdmans, 1982. [Jesus Christ, See. 113–18; The Resurrection: Fact or Legend? (Norman Anderson), See. 114–15]

Kelly, Gabrielle. *Bible Dictionary: A Dictionary of Biblical and Theological*. Hindmarsh, S. Australia: ATF, 2008. [Ascension, See. 19; Resurrection, See. 223]

Kennedy, Richard. *The International Dictionary of Religion*. New York: Crossroad, 1984. [Resurrection, See. 155]

Kerr, James S., and Charles Lutz. *A Christian's Dictionary 1,600 Names, Words and Phrases*. Philadelphia: Fortress, 1969. [Ascension and Ascension Day, See. 12; The Resurrection, See. 136]

Kessler, Edward, and Neil Wenborn, eds. *A Dictionary of Jewish-Christian Relations*. Cambridge: Cambridge University Press, 2008. [Resurrection Narratives, See. 376]

Kittel, Gerhard, ed. *Theological Dictionary of the New Testament*. Translated by Geoffrey W. Bromiley. Vol. 1. Grand Rapids: Eerdmans, 1995. [Resurrection in the NT, See. 370–71 (Oepke)]

———, ed. *Theological Dictionary of the New Testament*. Translated by Geoffrey W. Bromiley. Vol. 2. Grand Rapids: Eerdmans, 1995. [See. 333–39 (Oepke)]

Kitto, John F. *A Cyclopaedia of Biblical Literature In Three Volumes*. 3rd ed. Vol. 2, edited by William Lindsay Alexander. Edinburgh: Adam and Charles Black, 1876. [Jesus Christ, See. 582–91; N.B. Various publications online at HathiTrust]

———, ed. *The New Sunday School Teachers' Biblical Dictionary*. London: Elliot Stock, 1882. [Ascend, See. 93; Jesus, See. 730; N.B. Google book]

Kurian, George Thomas., ed. *The Encyclopedia of Christian Civilization*. Vol. 1. Malden, MA: Wiley-Blackwell, 2011. [Ascension, See. 145 (Alvin J. Schmidt)]

———, ed. *The Encyclopedia of Christian Civilization*. Vol. 3. Malden, MA: Wiley-Blackwell, 2011. [Resurrection, See. 1967–74 (Gary R. Habermas) This article should be examined; Risen Christ, See. 1996–98 (Alvin J. Schmidt)]

———, ed. *Nelson's New Christian Dictionary: The Authoritative Resource on the Christian World.* Nashville: Nelson, 2001. [Ascension, See. 55–56; Jesus Christ, See. 408]

Lacoste, Jean-Yves, ed. *Encyclopedia of Christian Theology.* P–Z. Vol. 3. New York: Routledge, 2005. [Resurrection of Christ, See. 1370–76 (Christian Duquoc)]

LaHaye, Tim, et al., eds. *The Popular Encyclopedia of Bible Prophecy.* Eugene, OR: Harvest House, 2004. [Resurrection, See. 326–31 (Gary R. Habermas)]

Landman, Isaac, Louis Rittenberg, and Simon Cohen, eds. *The Universal Jewish Encyclopedia.* New York: Ktav, 1969. [Jesus of Nazareth, See. 85]

Lang, Jovian P. *Dictionary of the Liturgy.* New York: Catholic Book Publ., 1989. [Ascension, See. 43; Easter, See. 172]

Latourelle, Rene, and Rino Fisichella, eds. *Dictionary of Fundamental Theology.* New York: Crossroad, 2000. [Paschal Mystery 2: The Resurrection of Jesus, See. 769–76 (Gerald O'Collins)]

Léon-Dufour, Xavier. *Dictionary of Biblical Theology.* Translated by Joseph Cahill. Edited by Edward Malcolm. Stewart. 2nd ed. New York: Seabury, 1973. [Ascension, See. 33–36 (Pierre Benoit); Resurrection, See. 494–99 (Jean Radermakers)]

———. *Dictionary of the New Testament.* Translated by Terrence Prendergast. New York: Harper & Row, 1983. [Appearances of Christ, See. 100–101; Ascension, See. 104; Resurrection, See. 349–50]

Livingstone, Elizabeth A., ed. *The Concise Oxford Dictionary of the Christian Church.* Oxford: Oxford University Press, 1977. [Ascension of Christ, See: 36; Resurrection of Christ, See. 436–37]

———, ed. *The Concise Oxford Dictionary of the Christian Church.* 3rd ed. Oxford: Oxford University Press, 1997. [Ascension of Christ, See: 112–13; Resurrection of Christ, See. 1387–86]

Lockyer, Herbert, ed. *Nelson's Illustrated Bible Dictionary: An Authoritative One-Volume Reference work on the Bible.* Nashville: Nelson, 1986. [Ascension of Christ, See. 107–8; Resurrection of Jesus Christ, See. 910–11]

Longman, Tremper, ed. *The Baker Compact Bible Dictionary.* Grand Rapids: Baker, 2014. [Ascension, See. 21; Resurrection, See. 286–87]

Ludlow, Daniel H., ed. *Encyclopedia of Mormonism: The History, Scripture, Doctrine, and Procedure of the Church of Latter-day Saints.* Vol. 2. New York: Macmillan, 1992. [Easter, See. 433 (Mary Ellen Stewart Jamison); Resurrection of Jesus Christ, See. 733–34 (Tad R. Callister); Forty-Day Ministry and Other Post-Resurrection Appearances of Jesus Christ, See. 734–36 (John Gee); Latter-Day Appearances of Jesus Christ, See. 736–37 (Joel A. Flake)]

Lueker, Erwin Louis, ed. *The Concordia Bible Dictionary.* St. Louis: Concordia, 1963. [Ascension, See. 15; Resurrection, See. 116]

———. *Lutheran Cyclopedia.* St. Louis: Concordia, 1975. [Ascension, See. 53]

Malcolm, Howard. *A Dictionary of the Most Important Names, Objects, and Terms.* Boston: Gould, Kendall & Lincoln, 1843. [Resurrection, See. 210–11; N.B. HathiTrust]

Manser, Martin H., ed. *The Hodder Dictionary of Bible Themes.* London: Hodder & Stoughton, 1988. [#2555 Jesus Christ, Resurrection appearances of, See. 86; #2560 Jesus Christ, resurrection of, See. 87]

Marijnen, P. A., ed. *The Encyclopedia of the Bible.* Englewood Cliffs, NJ: Prentice-Hall, 1965. [Ascension, Christ's, See. 19; Resurrection, See. 206–7]

Dictionaries, Encyclopedia, and Glossaries

Marthaler, Bernard L., ed. *New Catholic Encyclopedia*. 2nd ed. Vol. 1. Detroit: Gale, 2003. [Ascension of Jesus Christ, See. 768–71 (J. D. Quinn)]

———. ed. *New Catholic Encyclopedia*. 2nd ed. Vol. 12. Detroit: Gale, 2003. [Resurrection of Christ, See. 145–65 (F. X. Durrwell)]

Martin, Ralph, and Peter H. Davids, eds. *Dictionary of the Later New Testament & Its Developments*. Downers Grove, IL: InterVarsity, 1997. [Ascension, See. 95–100 (W. J. Larkin); Resurrection, See. 1015–20 (S. H. Travis)]

Mateo-Seco, Lucas Francisco, and Giulio Maspero, eds. *The Brill Dictionary of Gregory of Nyssa* (Supplements to Vigiliae Christianae, v. 99). Translated by Seth Cherney. Leiden: Koninklijke Brill NV, 2010. [Resurrection, See. 668–71 (Lucas Francisco Mateo-Seco)]

Mathews, Shailer, and Gerald Birney Smith, eds. Smith. *A Dictionary of Religion and Ethics*. New York: Macmillan, 1923. [Ascension, See. 30; Jesus Christ, See. 236]

McAuliffe, Jane Dammen, ed. *Encyclopedia of the Qur'an*. Vol. 1. Leiden: Brill, 2001. [The non-crucifixion of Jesus, See. 488]

McCabe, Joseph. *A Rationalist Encyclopedia: A Book of Reference on Religion, Philosophy, Ethics, and Science*. London: Watts, 1950. [The Resurrection, See. 496–97]

McClintock, John, and James Strong. *Cyclopedia of Biblical, Theological, and Ecclesiastical Literature*. Vol. 8. New York: Harper, 1879. [Resurrection of Christ, See. 1055–56; N.B. Archive.org]

McElrath, William N. *A Bible Dictionary for Young Readers*. Nashville: Broadman, 1965. [Ascension, See. 15; Resurrection]

McFarland, Ian A., David Fergusson, Karen Kilby, and Iain R. Torrance, eds. *The Cambridge Dictionary of Christian Theology*. Cambridge: Cambridge University Press, 2011. [Ascension and Session, See. 35–37 (Douglas Farrow); Resurrection, See. 444–45 (N. T. Wright)]

McGrath, Alister E., ed. *The Blackwell Encyclopedia of Modern Christian Thought*. Oxford: Blackwell, 1993. [Resurrection, See. 553–57 (Gerald O'Collins)]

McGuckin, John Anthony, ed. *The Encyclopedia of Eastern Orthodox Christianity*. Vol. 2. Oxford: Wiley-Blackwell, 2011. [Resurrection, See. 469–71 (Theodore G. Stylianopoulos)]

———, ed. *The Westminster Handbook to Patristic Theology*. Louisville: Westminster John, 2004. [Resurrection, See. 292–95]

McKenzie, John L. *Dictionary of the Bible*. New York: Bruce, 1965. [Ascension, 59–60; Resurrection, See. 731–34]

McKim, Donald K. *The Westminster Dictionary of Theological Terms*. Louisville: Westminster John Knox, 2014. [Ascension of Jesus, See. 21; Resurrection of Jesus Christ, See. 270]

Meagher, Paul K. *Encyclopedic Dictionary of Religion*: Volume A–E. Washington, DC: Corpus Publ., 1979. [Ascension of Christ, See. 279–80 (R. L. Stewart)]

Metford, John C. *Dictionary of Christian Lore and Legend*. London: Thames and Hudson, 1983. [Ascension of Christ, See. 35; Resurrection of Christ, See. 212]

Metzger, Bruce M., and Michael David. Coogan, eds. *The Oxford Guide to Ideas & Issues of the Bible*. Oxford: Oxford University Press, 2001. [Ascension of Christ, See. 49–51 (Gregory Shaw); Resurrection of Christ, See. 437–40 (Reginald H. Fuller)]

Miller, Madeleine (Sweeny), and John Lane Miller. *Harper's Bible Dictionary*. New York: Harper & Row, 1973. [Ascension of Christ, See. 46; Resurrection, See. 612–13 (Edwin Lewis and Robert C. Danton)]

Category XII—Reference Sources, Dissertations and Theses, and Introduction to the New Testament

Mills, Watson E., ed. *Mercer Dictionary of the Bible.* Macon, GA: Mercer University Press, 1990. [Resurrection in the New Testament, See. 755–56 (Richard R. Wilson)]

Mounce, William D., ed. *Mounce's Complete Expository Dictionary of Old & New Testament Words.* Grand Rapids: Zondervan, 2006. [Resurrection New Testament, See. 587]

Muller, Richard A. *Dictionary of Latin and Greek Theological Terms: Drawn Principally from Protestant Scholastic Theology.* Grand Rapids: Baker, 1985. [Resurrectio, See. 265]

Musser, Donald W., and Joseph L. Price, eds. *New and Enlarged Handbook of Christian Theology.* Nashville: Abingdon, 2003. [Resurrection, See. 422–27 (Eduard Schweizer)]

Myers, Allen C., ed. *The Eerdmans Bible Dictionary.* Grand Rapids: Eerdmans, 1987. [Ascension, See. 90–91; Jesus Christ, See. 576; Resurrection of Jesus, See. 858–60]

Nave, Orville J. *Topical Bible: A Digest of the Holy Scriptures . . .* Lincoln, NE: Topical Bible, 1905. [Ascension, See. 78; Jesus Christ, Resurrection of, See. 726–28; N.B. Google book]

Neill, Stephen, ed. *Concise Dictionary of the Bible.* Part 2. L–Z. London: Lutterworth, 1966. [Resurrection of Christ, See. 267–68]

Neill, Stephen, John Goodwin, and Arthur Dowle, eds. *The Modern Reader's Dictionary of the Bible.* New York: Association Press, 1966. [Ascension, See. 23; Resurrection of Christ, See. 267–68]

Netton, Ian Richard. *A Popular Dictionary of Islam.* Atlantic Highlands, NJ: Humanities Press, 1992. [Isa, See. 124–25]

Neusner, Jacob, Alan J. Avery-Peck, and William Scot Green, eds. *The Encyclopaedia of Judaism.* Vol. 2. 2nd ed. Leiden: Brill, 2005. [Jesus and Judaism, See. 1221–22 (Bruce Chilton)]

Neusner, Jacob, and William Scott Green, eds. *Dictionary of Judaism in the Biblical Period: 450 BCE to 600 CE.* Vol. 2. New York: Macmillan, 1996. [Jesus of Nazareth, See. 344]

Nevins, Albert J., ed. *The Maryknoll Catholic Dictionary.* Wilkes-Barre, PA: Dimension, 1965. [Ascension of Christ, See. 53–54; Resurrection of Christ, See. 492]

New World Dictionary-Concordance to the New American Bible, The. New York: World Publishing, 1970. [Resurrection of Christ, See. 574–76; N.B. Archive.org]

Nicholson, William. *Bible Student's Companion or The Bible Explainer.* New York: Revell, 1870. [Resurrection, See. 726–27; N.B. Archive.org]

O'Carroll, Michael. *Theotokos: A Theological Encyclopedia of the Blessed Virgin Mary.* Wilmington, Delaware: Glazier, 1982. [Resurrection of Christ, See. 310]

O'Collins, Gerald, and Edward G. Farrugia. *A Concise Dictionary of Theology.* New York: Paulist, 2000. [Appearances of the Risen Lord, See. 17; Ascension, See. 19; Resurrection, See. 226–27]

Olson, Roger E. *The SCM Press A–Z of Evangelical Theology.* London: SCM, 2005. [Resurrection, See. 251–53]

———. *The Westminster Handbook to Evangelical Theology.* Louisville: Westminster John Knox, 2004. [Resurrection, See. 251–53]

Orr, James, ed. *The International Standard Bible Encyclopedia.* Chicago: Howard-Severance Company, 1925. [Resurrection of Jesus Christ, See. 2565–69 (W. H. Griffith Thomas). This article is a must read.]

Packard, Frederick A. *The Union Bible Dictionary*: Prepared for the American Sunday-School Union and revised by the Committee of Publication. Philadelphia: American Sunday-School Union, 1838. [Resurrection, See. 527; N.B. Google book. The title page reads "By The Author Of 'The Teacher Taught.'"]

Dictionaries, Encyclopedia, and Glossaries

Palmer, Edwin H., ed. *The Encyclopedia of Christianity*. Wilmington, DE: National Foundation for Christian Education, 1964. [Ascension, See. 427–31 (George W. Knight)]

Parente, Pietro, et al. *Dictionary of Dogmatic Theology*. Translated by Emmanuel Doronzo. Milwaukee: Bruce, 1951. [Resurrection of Christ, See. 241–42]

Patrinacos, Nicon D. *A Dictionary of Greek Orthodoxy*. Minneapolis, MN: Light & Life, 2001. [Ascension, See. 42; Resurrection of Christ, See. 318–19]

Patte, Daniel, ed. *The Cambridge Dictionary of Christianity*. New York: Cambridge University Press, 2010. [Ascension, See. 76; Resurrection of Jesus, See. 1073–74]

Piercy, William C., ed. *Murray's Illustrated Bible Dictionary*. London: John Murray, 1908. [Ascension, See. 62–63 (W. J. Sparrow Simpson); Jesus Christ, See. 413–14 (W. J. Sparrow Simpson); Resurrection of Our Lord, See. 743 (W. J. Sparrow Simpson); N.B. Archive.org]

Pike, E. Royston. *Encyclopaedia of Religion and Religions*. London: George Allen & Unwin, 1951. [Jesus, See. 209–10; Jesus Myth, See. 210; Resurrection, See. 322–23]

Powell, Mark Allan, and Barry L. Bandstra, eds. *The HarperCollins Bible Dictionary*. New York: HarperCollins, 2011. [Ascension of Christ, See. 60 (James M. Efird); Resurrection of Jesus, See. 876–77 (W. Sibley Towner and Mark Allan Powell)]

Presbyterian Board of Publication. *Bible Dictionary for the Use of Bible Classes, Schools and Families*. Philadelphia: Presbyterian Board of Publication, 1851. [Ascension, See. 47–48; Resurrection, See. 371; N.B. HathiTrust]

Rahner, Karl, ed. *Sacramentum Mundi: An Encyclopedia of Theology*. Vol. 5. New York: Herder & Herder, 1968. [Resurrection of Christ, See. 323–24 (Karl Rahner)]

———, ed. *Sacramentum Mundi: An Encyclopedia of Theology*. Vol. 1. New York: Herder & Herder, 1968. [Ascension of Christ, See. 109–10 (Joseph Ratzinger)]

Rahner, Karl, and Herbert Vorgrimler. *Dictionary of Theology*. 2nd ed. New York: Crossroad, 1985. [Ascension, See. 27–28; Resurrection of Jesus, See. 440–43]

Rand, William W. *Dictionary of the Holy Bible*. New York: American Tract Society, 1914. [Ascension, See. 41; Resurrection of Christ, See. 370–71; N.B. Archive.org. Also published in 1859 under the title *A Dictionary of the Holy Bible For General Use in the Study of the Scriptures*]

———. *Dictionary of the Holy Bible for General Use in the Study of the Scriptures*. New York: American Tract Society, 1886. [Resurrection of Christ, See. 475–76; N.B Archive.org]

Rees, Abraham. *The Cyclopaedia; or, Universal Dictionary of Arts, Sciences, and Literature*. Vol. 30. London: Longman, Hurst, Rees, Orme, & Brown, 1819. [Resurrection, no pagination; N.B. Archive.org]

Reese, William L. *Dictionary of Philosophy and Religion: Eastern and Western Thought*. Atlantic Highlands, NJ: Humanities Press, 1996. [Resurrection, See. 651]

Reid, Daniel G., ed. *The IVP Dictionary of the New Testament: A One-Volume Compendium of Contemporary Biblical Scholarship*. Downers Grove, IL: InterVarsity, 2004. [Jesus; Resurrection in the Four Gospels, See. 901–13 (G. R. Osborne); N.B. This article contains a good overall review on the topic.]

Richards, Lawrence O., ed. *Expository Dictionary of Bible Words*. Grand Rapids: Regency Reference Library, 1985. [Appear/Appearance, See. 61–65; Ascend, See. 77–78; Resurrection, See. 527–30]

———., ed. *The Revell Bible Dictionary.* Old Tappan, NJ: Revell, 1990. [Ascension of Christ, See. 99; Resurrection, See. 857–60]

Richardson, Alan, ed. *A Theological Word Book of the Bible.* New York: MacMillan, 1951. [Ascension, See. 22–23 (A. M. Ramsey); Resurrection, See. 193–95 (Alan Richardson)]

———, ed. *The Westminster Dictionary of Christian Theology.* Philadelphia: Westminster, 1969. [Ascension of Christ, See. 15–16 (J. G. Davies); Resurrection of Christ, See. 290–91 (Alan Richardson)]

Richardson, Alan, and John Bowden, eds. *The Westminster Dictionary of Christian Theology.* Philadelphia: Westminster, 1983. [Ascension of Christ, See. 44–45 (Rowan Williams); Resurrection, See. 501–3 (C. F. Evans)]

Robinson, Edward, ed. *The Comprehensive Critical and Explanatory Bible Encyclopedia . . .* Toledo, OH: OA. Browning, 1881. [Resurrection, See. 785–86; N.B. Archive.org]

Robinson, John. *A Theological, Biblical, and Ecclesiastical Dictionary.* London: G. Sidney, 1815. [Ascension of Our Lord, no pagination; Jesus, no pagination; Resurrection, no pagination; N.B. Google book]

Roth, Cecil, ed. *Encyclopaedia Judaica.* Vol. 10. Jerusalem: Encyclopaedia Judaica, 1971. [Jesus, See. 12]

Rowley, H. H. *Short Dictionary of Bible Themes.* New York: Basic, 1968. [Ascension of Jesus, See. 6–7; Resurrection of Jesus, See. 82–83]

Russell, Letty, and J. Shannon Clarkson, eds. *Dictionary of Feminist Theologies.* Louisville: Westminster John Knox, 1996. [Resurrection, See. 242–43 (Margaret M. Campbell)]

Ryken, LeLand, et al., eds. *Dictionary of Biblical Imagery.* Downers, Grove, IL: InterVarsity, 1998. [Ascension, See. 49; Resurrection, See. 711–12]

Sakenfeld, Katharine Doob, ed. *The New Interpreter's Dictionary of the Bible.* Vol. 1. Nashville: Abingdon, 2006. [Ascension, See. 290–91 (A. W. Zwiep)]

———, ed. *The New Interpreter's Dictionary of the Bible.* Vol. 3. Nashville: Abingdon, 2008. [Jesus Christ, J. After Death, See. 290–93 (Dale C. Allison)]

Sanford, Elias B. *A Concise Cyclopedia of Religious Knowledge: Biblical, Biographical, Geographical, Historical, Practical and Theological.* Hartford, CT: S.S. Scranton, 1909. [Jesus Christ, See. 479; N.B. Archive.org and HathiTrust]

Sawyer, John F. A. *A Concise Dictionary of the Bible and its Reception.* Louisville: Westminster John Knox, 2009. [Ascension, See. 23–24; Resurrection, See. 222–23]

Schaff, Philip, ed. *A Dictionary of the Bible.* Philadelphia: American Sunday-School Union, 1880. [Resurrection, See. 733–34; N.B. Archive.org]

Scorgie, Glen G., ed. *Dictionary of Christian Spirituality.* Grand Rapids: Zondervan, 2011. [Resurrection, See. 716–17 (Cynthia Cheshire)]

Simpson, Matthew, ed. *Cyclopaedia of Methodism: Embracing Sketches of its Rise, Progress, and Present Condition, with Biographical Notices and Numerous Illustrations.* 4th ed. Philadelphia: L. H. Everts, 1881. [Resurrection, See. 751–52; N.B. Archive.org]

Singer, Isadore, ed. *The Jewish Encyclopedia.* Vol. 8. New York: Funk and Wagnalls, 1904. [Jesus of Nazareth, See. 169, 172 (Samuel Krauss); N.B. Available online]

Skolnik, Fred, ed. *Encyclopaedia Judaica.* 2nd ed. Vol. 11. Detroit: Thompson-Gale, 2007. [Jesus, See. 248 (David Flusser)]

Sleigh, W. W. *The Christians Defensive Dictionary Being an Alphabetical Refutation of the General Objections to the Bible.* Philadelphia: Edward C. Biddle, 1837. [Resurrection, See. 333–38; Resurrection of Christ, See. 338–42; N.B. HathiTrust]

Smith, William, ed. *A Concise Dictionary of the Bible . . .* Boston: Little, Brown, and Co., 1865. [Jesus Christ, See. 404; N.B. HathiTrust]

———, ed. *A Dictionary of the Bible Comprising Its Antiquity, Biography, Geography and Natural History.* Hartford, CT: S. S. Scranton, 1896. [Jesus Christ, See. 410; N.B. Google book]

Smith, William, and Samuel Cheetham, eds. *Dictionary of Christian Antiquities.* Vol. 2. London: John Murray, 1880. [Resurrection of Our Lord, See. 1790–91 (Richard John Tyrwhitt); N.B. Google book and Archive.org]

Steinmueller, John E., and Katheryn Sullivan. *Catholic Biblical Encyclopedia, New Testament.* New York: Joseph F. Wagner, 1949. [Ascension of Christ, See. 47–48; Resurrection of Christ, See. 547–48]

Stuhlmueller, Carroll, and Dianne Bergant, eds. *The Collegeville Pastoral Dictionary of Biblical Theology.* Collegeville, MN: Liturgical Press, 1996. [Ascension, See. 49–52 (M. Dennis Hamm); Resurrection, See. 835–39 (Pheme Perkins)]

Taliaferro, Charles, and Elsa J. Marty, eds. *A Dictionary of Philosophy of Religion.* New York: Bloomsbury Academic, 2018. [Resurrection, See. 198–99]

Tanzella-Nitti, Giuseppe, et al., eds. *Interdisciplinary Encyclopedia of Religion and Science.* Rome: Advanced School for Interdisciplinary Research (ADSIR), 2002. [Resurrection (Paul O'Callaghan); N.B. Available online]

Taylor, Richard S., ed. *Beacon Dictionary of Theology.* Kansas City, Mo: Beacon Hill, 1983. [Ascension, See. 52 (Alex R. G. Deasley; Resurrection of Christ, See. 452–53 (W. T. Purkiser)]

Tenney, Merrill C., ed. *Handy Dictionary of the Bible.* Zondervan, 1965. [Ascension of Christ, See. 15; Resurrection of Jesus Christ, See. 128]

Tenney, Merrill C., and Steven Barabas, eds. *The Zondervan Pictorial Encyclopedia of the Bible.* Vol. 5. Grand Rapids: Zondervan, 1976. [Resurrection of Jesus Christ, See. 75–83 (J. A. Schep)]

Tenney, Merrill C., and Moisés Silva, eds. *The Zondervan Encyclopedia of the Bible.* Vol. 5. Grand Rapids: Zondervan, 2009. [Resurrection of Jesus Christ, See. 95–103 (J. A. Schep)]

———, eds. *The Zondervan Encyclopedia of the Bible.* Vol. 1. Grand Rapids: Zondervan, 2009. [Ascension of Christ, See. 380–82]

Thiselton, Anthony C. *A Concise Encyclopedia of the Philosophy of Religion.* Grand Rapids: Baker Academic, 2005. [Resurrection, See. 262–63]

Timpson, Thomas. *A Key to the Bible Containing A Summary of Biblical Knowledge, and a Dictionary of All the Principal Words in the Old and New Testaments.* London: William Smith, 1840. [Resurrection of Christ, See. 292; N.B. Archive.org]

Tischler, Nancy M., ed. *All Things in the Bible: An Encyclopedia of the Biblical World.* Vol. 2. Westport, CT: Greenwood Press, 2006. [Resurrection, See. 530–32]

Trier, Daniel and Walter A. Elwell, eds. *Evangelical Dictionary Theology.* 3rd ed. Grand Rapids: Baker Academic, 2017. [Ascension of Christ, See. 87–88 (M. A. Bowald); Resurrection of Christ, See. 742–45 (Gary R. Habermas)]

Unity School of Christianity. *Metaphysical Bible Dictionary.* Lee's Summit, MO: Unity School of Christianity, 1950. [Resurrection, See. 553–55; N.B. Library of Congress Catalogue identifies Charles Fillmore, 1854–1948 as a related name.]

Vanhoozer, Kevin J., ed. *Dictionary for Theological Interpretation of the Bible.* London: Society for Promoting Christian Knowledge, 2006. [Ascension, See. 65–68 (Douglas Farrow); Resurrection Narratives, See. 675–76 (N. T. Wright)]

Category XII—Reference Sources, Dissertations and Theses, and Introduction to the New Testament

Verbrugge, Verlyn D., ed. *The NIV Theological Dictionary of New Testament Words*. Grand Rapids: Zondervan, 2000. [Anastasis, See. 117–25]

Viening, Edward, ed. *The Zondervan Topical Bible*. Grand Rapids: Zondervan, 1971. [Ascension of Christ, See. 34; Christ, Exaltation, See. 523–24; Resurrection, See. 854–57]

Water, Mark, comp. *The New Encyclopedia of Christian Quotations*. Grand Rapids: Baker, 2000. [Ascension, See. 79; Resurrection, See. 864–66]

Watson, Richard, bishop. *A Biblical and Theological Dictionary: Explanatory of the History, Manners, and Customs of the Jews and Neighboring Nations*. New York: T. Mason & G. Lane, 1840. [Resurrection, See. 820–22; N.B. Google book]

Werblowsky, Raphael Jehudah Zwi, and Geoffrey Wigoder, eds. *The Oxford Dictionary of the Jewish Religion*. New York: Oxford University Press, 1997. [Jesus, See. 368]

Wiener, Philip P., ed. *Dictionary of the History of Ideas: Studies of Selected Pivotal Ideas*. New York: Scribner's Sons, 1974. [Ascension, See 2, 411a; Resurrection, See. 1, 21b–22b; 2, 155b, 335a, 335b, 342a, 411a, 413a, 470b; 3, 223a–23b, 277a, 282a, 283a, 284a]

Wigoder, Geoffrey, et al., eds. *Illustrated Dictionary & Concordance of the Bible*. New York: Readers Digest Association, 1986. [Ascension, See. 122–24; Resurrection, See. 856–57]

Williams, Albert Nathaniel, ed. *Key Words of the Bible: A New Guide to Better Understanding of the Scriptures*. New York: Duell, Sloan & Pearce, 1956. [Ascension of Jesus, See. 29–30]

Wright, Charles H. H., and Charles Neil, eds. *The Protestant Dictionary: Containing Articles on the History and Practices of the Christian Church*. London: Hodder & Stoughton, 1904. [Ascension Day, See. 47; Resurrection of Christ, See. 595–602 (George Hanson); N.B. Google book]

Wright, William. *The Illustrated Bible Treasury*. London: Thomas Nelson, 1899. [Ascension, See. 379; Resurrection of Christ, See. 610–11; N.B. Archive.org and HathiTrust]

Youngblood, Ronald F., ed. *Nelson's Illustrated Bible Dictionary*. Nashville: Nelson, 1995. [Ascension of Christ, See. 125–26; Resurrection of Jesus Christ, See. 1080–82]

Chapter 33

Dissertations, Theses, and Papers

Acker, Jones Miles. "An Inquiry Into the Values for Dialogic Preaching in the Resurrection of Jesus Christ for the Work of Man." Thesis, Claremont School of Theology, 1966. [117 leaves]

Aggett, Michael John. "'Jesus' Resurrection: A Story of Its Interpretation from Reimarus to the Present." Master's thesis, University of Cape Town, 2006. [112 pages]

Ahurwendeire, Athanasius Mugarra. "The Will of the Risen Lord: An Exegetical-Theological Analysis of Matthew 28:16—20." Pont. Univ. Lateranense, Diss., Città del Vaticano, 2005. [670 pages]

Alfors, Quinten Hans Peter. "The Evidence of the Physical Resurrection of Christ in the Language of John Twenty." Master's thesis, Wheaton College, IL.,1953. [79 pages]

Allen, Nicholas Peter Legh. "Methods and Techniques Employed in the Manufacture of the Shroud of Turin." PhD diss., University of Durban-Westville, 1994. [277 leaves]

Allison, Dale. C. "The End of the Ages Has Come: An Early Interpretation of the Passion and Resurrection of Jesus." PhD diss., Duke University, 1982. [485 pages; AAT 8302427]

Alumkal, Jacob Paxy. "The Death and Resurrection of Jesus Christ Implied in the Image of the Paschal Lamb in 1 Cor 5:7 : An Intertextual, Exegetical and Theological Study." PhD diss., Université de Lucerne: 2013. [414 pages]

Anderson, Douglas W. "The Origin and Purpose of Matthew 27, 51b–53." PhD diss., University of Otago, Dunedin, New Zealand, 2013. [501 pages; Available online]

Anderson, Kathy Lorraine. "Recognizing the Risen Christ: A Study of the Non-Recognition/Recognition Motif in the Post-resurrection Appearance Narratives (Luke 24:13–35; John 20:22–18 and John 21:1–14)." Master's thesis, Pittsburgh Theological Seminary, 2004. [113 pages]

Anderson, Kevin L. "The Resurrection of Jesus in Luke-Acts." PhD diss., Brunei University, 2000.

Anderson, Tawa Jon. "The Myth of the Metaphorical Resurrection: A Critical Analysis of John Dominic Crossan's Methodology, Presuppositions, and Conclusions." PhD diss., Southern Baptist Theological Seminary, 2011. [303 pages. (UMI no.: 3454173)]

Andjelic, Milenko A. "The Resurrection and Pannenberg's Reality as History." Master's thesis, Wheaton College, Wheaton, IL., 1987. [123 leaves]

Arenobine, Robert D. "The Resurrection of the Saints in Matthew 27:52–53." Master's thesis, Grace Theological Seminary. [57 pages]

Atkins, J. D. "The Doubt of the Apostles and the Resurrection Faith of the Early Church." PhD diss., Marquette University, 2010. [510 pages; Available online]

Atkinson, Amanda Catherine. "Pauline Conversion and the Resurrection Narrative: A Psychological Case Study." Master's thesis, University of Georgia, 2012. [73 pages]

Aye, Noel Saw Naw. "The Passion and Resurrection Predictions According to Mark (8:31, 9:31, 10:33–34)." Master's thesis, St. Joseph's Seminary (Yonkers, NY), 2002. [71 leaves]

Bae, Sungjin. "Jesus' Resurrection as the Climactic Semeion in the Fourth Gospel." PhD diss., The Southern Baptist Theological Seminary, 2008. [185 pages; AAT 3357124]

Balasundaram, Sunil. "The Resurrection Predictions in the Synoptic Gospels as an Indication of Incipient Knowledge in Jesus' Self-understanding, with Special Reference to N. T. Wright." Master's thesis (Theology), Westminster Theological Seminary, Philadelphia, 2002. [77 leaves]

Balchin, Frank Kenneth. "The Significance of the Resurrection of Jesus Christ in New Testament Thought." PhD diss., Union Theological Seminary, 1958. [172 pages; AAT 0215190]

Ball, Richard J. "The Shroud of Turin and its Alchemic Probability Circa AD 1350." ALM., History of Science, Harvard University 2005. [98 leaves]

Ballentine, Elodie. "A Preliminary Study of the Ending of Mark's Gospel." Masters thesis, Denver Conservative Baptist Seminary, 1984. [87 leaves; N.B. Theological Research Exchange Network (Series), #090–0270.]

Bang, S. S. "The Eschatological Meaning of Jesus' Resurrection as a Historical Event: A Comparison of the Views of Wolfhart Pannenberg and N.T. Wright." ETD., Amsterdam Vrije Universiteit, 2014. [275 pages]

Barber, Cyril J. "Theology of the Resurrection in John's Gospel." Master's thesis, Dallas Theological Seminary, 1967. [55 leaves]

Barnhill, Gregory M. "The Role of Paul's Quotations From the Jewish Scriptures In First Corinthians 15." Master's thesis, Dallas Theological Seminary, 2014. [64 pages]

Bayer, H. F. "Synoptic Predictions of the Vindication and Resurrection of Jesus: Their Provenance, Meaning and Correlation." PhD diss., University of Aberdeen, 1984.

Beechler, Donald J. "The Centrality of the Resurrection and its Relation to the Revelatory Presence of God in Jesus, in the Christology of Wolfhart Pannenberg." PhD diss., Pontificia Studiorum Universitas a S. Thomas d'Aquin (Rome), 1973. [490 pages]

Benjamin, David Eugene. "The Identification of the Genre 'gospel' and Its Hermeneutical Significance for the Canonical Gospels." PhD diss., Southwestern Baptist Theological Seminary, 1995. [284 pages; AAT 9707439]

Bergesen, David E. "The Great Commission: A Study of the Meaning, Form, and Signficiance of St. Matthew 28:18–20." Master's Thesis (STM), General Theological Seminary, 1968. [90 leaves]

Bergquist, James Alan. "The Resurrection of Jesus in the New Testament: An Exegetical Study." PhD diss., University of Southern California, 1962. [504 pages; AAT 6302140]

Best, Alexander. "The Resurrection of Jesus." Master's thesis, Baptist Bible Institute, 1932. [36 pages]

Bevan, Hubert Basil Henry. "The Significance of the Resurrection Narrative in the Fourth Gospel." Master's thesis, University of Wales Aberystwyth, 1975. [226 leaves]

Bibza, James. "A Critical Analysis of the Publications of D. P. Fuller, G. E. Ladd, I. H. Marshall and M. C. Tenney on the Resurrection of Jesus Christ with Special Attention to the Problem of the Locale of the Post-Resurrection Appearances (Conservative Evangelicals)." PhD diss., Princeton Theological Seminary, 1985. [300 pages; AAT 8517384]

Blanchard, Leo. "A Consideration of the Cross and Resurrection of Jesus Christ in the Theology of Jurgen Moltmann." Master's thesis, Oblate College, Washington, DC., 1972. [57 leaves]

Blank, Reiner. "The Resurrection Appearances of Christ in the Light of Recent and Contemporary Criticism." Master's thesis, Trinity Evangelical Divinity School, 1972. [110 leaves]

Blumenfeld, Donald E. "Easter Encounters an Examination of the Resurrection Appearances in the Gospels of Luke and John." PhD diss., Graduate Theological Foundation, 1996.

Blumenstein, John Max. "An Exegetical Study of Matthew 27:38–54." PhD diss., Union Theological Seminary in Virginia, 1991. [178 pages; AAT 9226628]

Boateng, Kwasi. "The Resurrection of Jesus and the Believer in 1 Corinthians 15:1–18." Master's thesis, Melbourne College of Divinity, 2007. [99 leaves]

Bonney, William L. "Why the Risen Jesus Appeared to Thomas: An Analysis of John 20:24–29 in the Context of a Synchronic Reading of the Gospel." PhD diss., Fordham University, 1998. [299 pages; AAT 9816342]

Boomershine, Thomas Eugene. "Mark the Storyteller: A Rhetorical-Critical Investigation of Mark's Passion and Resurrection Narrative." PhD diss., Union Theological Seminary, 1974. [395 pages; AAT 7418837]

Bradley, Mark Alan. "The Functions of Questions in the Fourth Gospel: A Narrative-Critical Inquiry." PhD diss., Golden Gate Baptist Theological Seminary, 1994. [281 pages; AAT 9431756]

Bragg, Paul DeWitte. "The Resurrection of Jesus in the light of Criticism." Master's thesis, Baptist Bible Institute, 1933. [29 leaves]

Brands, Michael. "The Kingdom Commission, Light for the Nations: the Expanding Mission of Matthew 28:16–20 in Its Literary Context Within Matthew's Gospel." PhD diss., Luther Seminary, 2007. [288 pages]

Bray, James Seddon. "The Date of the Crucifixion and Resurrection Investigated: Did It Really Happen." Master's thesis, St. Stephen's College, 2000. [159 pages]

Brighton, Louis A. "The Ending on Mark 16:9–20." Master's thesis (STM), Concordia Seminary, St. Louis 1964. [98 leaves;]

Brunk, George Rowland. "The Concept of the Resurrection According to the Emmaus Account in Luke's Gospel." ThD diss., Union Theological Seminary in Virginia, 1975. [442 pages]

Buglass, Anthony E. "The Historicity of the Resurrection of Jesus: A Study of the New Testament Evidence." Master's thesis, North-West University Potchefstroom Campus South Africa, 2008. [174 pages online]

Burke, Albert Carswell. "The Resurrection in the Acts of the Apostles." Master's thesis, Princeton Theological Seminary, 1952. [142 Leaves]

Butler, Daniel L. "'Go into all the World' : A Study of the Great Commission Texts and the Church's Response in Acts." Master's thesis, Vanguard University of Southern California, 2002. [172 leaves]

Category XII—Reference Sources, Dissertations and Theses, and Introduction to the New Testament

Campbell, W. Thomas. "The Relationship of the Thomas Pericope to Signs and Belief in the Fourth Gospel." PhD diss., Southwestern Baptist Theological Seminary, 2000. [224 pages; AAT 9968722]

Carmichael, Lawrence Garten. "An Apologetic for the Death, Burial, and Bodily Resurrection of Jesus Christ." Master's thesis, Western Evangelical Seminary, 1980. [118 leaves]

Carson, Mary Catherine. "And They Said Nothing To Anyone: a Redaction-Critical Study of the Role and Status of Women in the Crucifixion, Burial and Resurrection Stories of the Canonical and Apocryphal Gospels." PhD diss., University of Newcastle Upon Tyne (United Kingdom), 1990. [404 pages; AAT DX96298; N.B. Available online]

Cauthron, Halbert A. "The Meaning of Kingship In Johannine Christology: A Structuralist Exegesis of John 18.1–20.18." PhD diss., Vanderbilt University, 1984. [214 pages]

Cavin, Robert Gregory. "Miracles, Probability, and the Resurrection of Jesus: A Philosophical, Mathematical, and Historical Study." PhD diss., University of California, Irvine, 1993. [389 leaves; AAT 9323907; N.B. An interesting thesis.]

Cecil, Douglas M. "The Emphasis of the Resurrection in the Apostles' Preaching in the Book of Acts Compared to Current Evangelistic Emphases." Master's thesis, Dallas Theological Seminary, 1984. [83 leaves]

Chalakkal, Sebastian. "The Post-resurrection Appearances in Contemporary Catholic Christology: A Study of Hans Küng (1928-), Walter Kasper (1933-) and Hans Kessler (1938-)." PhD diss., Pontificia Universitas Gregoriana, Facultas Theologiae. 2004. [85 leaves]

Childs, Hal. "The Myth of the Historical Jesus and the Evolution of Consciousness." PhD diss., Graduate Theological Union, 1998. [263 pages]

Chitavath, Babu. "Paul's Exceptional Easter-experience: An Exegetical-Theological Study of 1 Cor 15, 8 in Relation to Acts 9, 3–19 ; 22, 6–21, 26, 12–18." PhD diss., Pontificia Universita Urbaniana, 2002. [215 pages[

Cho, James. "Karl Barth's teaching on the resurrection and parousia of Jesus Christ according to the Church dogmatics." Master's thesis, Fuller Theological Seminary, 1998. [55 leaves]

Chun, Kyung-Yun. "The Resurrection of Jesus in Luke-Acts and in the Fifteenth Chapter of First Corinthians." PhD diss., Boston University School of Theology, 1952. [222 pages; AAT 0178303]

Churchill, A. D. "The Resurrection of Christ: The Relation of the Historical Event to the New Testament Conception of Resurrection." PhD diss., University of Oxford, 1968. [405 leaves]

Chute, Wayne. "Go Make Disciples: A Clarification of the Command in the Great Commission according to Matthew." Master's thesis, Western Conservative Baptist Seminary, 1977. [Trens]

Cloud, Gilbert A. "Echoes of Scripture in the Emmaus Road Encounter of Luke 24:1–35." Master's thesis, George Fox University, 2004. [76 leaves]

Cobb, Jimmy Hickman. "The Resurrection of Jesus in the Theology of Wolfhart Pannenberg." ThD., Southwestern Baptist Theological Seminary, 1971. [268 leaves]

Conley, Toney A. "The Authenticity of the Witnesses Concerning the Resurrection." Master's thesis, Cincinatti Bible Seminary, 1947. [88 leaves]

Connelly, Douglas. "The Old Testament Predictions of the Resurrection of Jesus." Master's thesis (ThM), Grace Theological Seminary, 1981. [68 leaves]

Cooney, James Matthew. "Theological Implications of the Shroud of Turin." STL., St. Mary's Seminary (Baltimore, Md.), 1957. [71 leaves]

Cory, John Ream. "The Resurrection of Jesus Compared in the Thought of Rudolf Bultmann and Karl Barth." Master's thesis, Northwestern University, 1968.

Cortes Fuentes, David. "Eyes to See and Ears to Hear: Echoes of Moses in Matthew's Portrayal of Jesus." PhD diss., Northwestern University, 1999. [222 pages; AAT 9953258]

Crotty, Nicholas. "The Development in St. Thomas's Teaching on the Soteriological Role of Christ's Resurrection." Pars diss. ad lauream, Pontificium Atheneum Angelicum de Urbe, 1962. [58 pages]

Dammrose, Gary L. "The Relation of the Resurrection Appearances to Christian Faith in the New Testament." Master's thesis, Phillips University Graduate Seminary, 1967. [87 leaves]

Daniel, Elinor Perkins. "A Rhetorical Analysis of the Resurrection Appearance Narratives in the Christian Gospels." PhD diss., Georgia State University, 1994. [125 pages; AAT 9503500]

Davis, Patricia L. "Remembering: The Tomb as a Site of Memory in the Gospel of Luke." Master's thesis, Flinders University of South Australia, School of Theology. No date. [47 leaves]

Day, Jim. "The Emmaus Journey Narrative (Luke 24:13–35): A Study in Theological Purpose and Literary Intention." Master's thesis, Holy Apostles College and Seminary, Cromwell, CT, 2005.

Decker, Donald F. "The Historical and Literary Evidence for the Resurrection of Christ." Master's thesis, Butler University, 1957. [91 leaves]

De Freitas, Elizabeth A. "Resurrection in the Fourth Gospel." Master's thesis, St. John's University, 1983. [68 pages]

Dijkhuizen, Pieternella. "An Investigation Into the Historical, Hermeneutical and Gospel-Critical Parameters for the Interpretation of the Symbol of Resurrection." Master's thesis, University of South Africa, 2007. [217 pages; N.B. Available online.]

Donathan, Jerry Leon. "The Significance of Luke's Resurrection Narrative for a Contemporary Study of the Historical Jesus." ThD., Southwestern Baptist Theological Seminary, 1976. [206 leaves; AAT 0327586]

Drury, John L. "The Resurrected God: Karl Barth's Trinitarian Theology of Easter." PhD diss., Princeton Theological Seminary, 2011. [249 leaves]

Elledge, Casey Deryl. "Resurrection and the End of History: The Resurrection Motif in Paul's Preaching and Defense in the Acts of the Apostles." PhD diss., Princeton Theological Seminary 2001. [379 leaves]

Enyioha, Bennett Uche. "Nonrecognition as a Motif in the Post-Resurrection Appearance Narratives (Presence)." PhD diss., The Southern Baptist Theological Seminary, 1985. [336 pages; AAT 8604436]

Ezeogu, Ernest Munachi. "The Purpose of the Great Commission: A Historical-Critical Exegesis of Matthew 28:16–20." PhD diss., University of St. Michael's College (Canada), 2004. [221 pages; AAT NQ97495]

Farrier, Daniell E. "The Realization of the Resurrection of the Dead in 1 Corinthians 15: the Consummate Redemption of the Church as a Function of Covenantal Union with the Resurrected Christ." Master's thesis, Gordon-Conwell Theological Seminary, 2005. [169 leaves]

Fazio, James I. "Two Commissions: Theological Implications of Matthew's Gospel." Master's thesis, Southern California Seminary, 2013. [57 leaves; Theological Research Exchange Network (Series), #129–0011]

Fenimore, Randolph C. "The Resurrection of Jesus." BD thesis, Bethany Theological Seminary 1964. [69 pages]

Fernando, Samuel Andrew. "Resurrection and Reality: In Dialogue with T. F. Torrance." [Master's thesis, 2014. University of Otago, Dunedin, New Zealand, 2014. [131 pages]

Fianu, Emmanuel Kofi. "A Narrative-Critical and Theological Study of Luke 24,13—35." PhD diss., Pont. Univ. Gregoriana, Rome 2000.

Fischer, David Hickman. "The Resurrection In A Process Theological Perspective." [PhD diss., Vanderbilt University, 1976. [321 leaves]

Fleming, Peter James. "The Resurrection of Jesus in Recent Form Criticism." PhD diss., Southwestern Baptist Theological Seminary, 1964. [AAT 0258168]

Fournier, Susan M. "Matthew 28:16–20 : A Key to the Theology of the First Gospel." Master's thesis, Catholic University of America, 1983. [91 pages]

Francis, Dan R. "A Critical Survey of Contemporary Literature Concerning the Empty Tomb in Mark." Master's thesis, Southern Baptist Theological Seminary, 1980. [122 leaves]

Frazier, John C. "On the Road to Emmaus." Master's thesis, Concordia University, 1993.

Fuller, Daniel P. "Easter Faith and History." PhD diss., Basel University. 1964. [279 pages]

Fuller, Luther M. "The Resurrection of Jesus." Master's thesis, Gordon College, 1935. [51 pages]

Fullmer, Paul M. "Resurrection in Mark's Literary-Historical Context." PhD diss., Graduate Theological Union, 2005. [317 pages; AAT 3173123]

Gear, Spencer Douglas. "Crossan and the Resurrection of Jesus: Rethinking Presuppositions, Methods and Models." PhD diss., University of Pretoria, 2015. [482 pages; N.B. Available online]

Gentry, Norman John. "The Great Commission." Master's thesis, Dallas Theological Seminary, 1954. [55 leaves]

Geoff, Richard G. "The Resurrection of Jesus as a Basis of Hope for the Future in the Theologies of Wolfhart Pannenberg and Jürgen Moltmann: A Theological Dialogue." PhD diss.,Wesley Theological Seminary, 1974. [113 leaves]

George, James Wesley. "Significance of the Original Audience of Matthew: A Comparison of the General-Audience Approach and the Critical-Consensus Approach." PhD diss., Mid-America Baptist Theological Seminary, 2000. [225 pages; AAT 9989309]

George, Larry Darnell. "The Narrative Unity of the Fourth Gospel's Resurrection: A Literary-Rhetorical Reading of John 20–21." PhD diss., Vanderbilt University, 1997. [246 pages; AAT 9815593]

Gibbs, Jeffrey A. "The Synoptic Problem: Basic Arguments Examined with the Burial-Resurrection Narratives as a Test Case." Master's thesis, Concordia Theological Seminary, Ft. Wayne, 1988. [130 leaves. Tren Dissertations. 3090]

Glasow, David B. "The Threefold Contribution of Gerald O'Collins's Fundamental Theology: Its Christocentric Outlook, its Focus on the Resurrection and its Groundwork for Ecumenism." PhD diss., Catholic University of America, 2015. [221 pages]

Goldsmith, Dale. "The Function of Jesus' Resurrection in Ignatius and the Early Church." PhD diss., University of Chicago, 1973. [225 leaves]

Graieg, David Jonathan. "The Resurrection and Western Culture." Master's thesis, Dallas Theological Seminary, 2012. [63 pages]

Gray, Robert D. "The Objective Nature of the Resurrection Body of Christ." Master's thesis, Wheaton College, 1967. [158 pages]

Greenway, Leonard. "The Resurrection of Our Lord." PhD diss., Pikes Peak Bible Seminary and Burton College, 1938. [80 pages]

Gutierrez, Juan Eliezer de Leon. "The Historical Reliability of the Resurrection Account Presented in the Emmaus Story." Master's thesis, Kentucky Christian University, 2010. [114 pages]

Gwynne, Paul. "The Tradition of the Empty Tomb: Historical Evidence and Theological Presupposition in the Writings of Gerald O'Collins." Master's thesis, Melbourne College of Divinity, 1989. [176 leaves]

Habermas, Gary Robert. "The Resurrection of Jesus: A Rational Inquiry." Ph.D diss., Michigan State University, 1976. [363 pages; AAT 7627101; N.B. Available online.]

Hall, James LeLand. "A Study of the Significance of the Appearances of Christ After the Resurrection." Master's thesis. Southern Baptist Theological Seminary, 1949. [65 leaves]

Hamann, Henry Paul. "The Ending of St. Mark's Gospel: A Study in Textual Criticism." Master's thesis (STM), Concordia Seminary, St. Louis, 1949. [98 leaves]

Hancock, Thomas. "Historic and Psychologic Aspects of the Resurrection of Jesus." Master's thesis, Clark University, 1916. [109 pages]

Hankins, John Eric. "Meal, Martyrdom, and Mimesis: The Theology of Jesus at the Last Supper." PhD diss., Southwestern Baptist Theological Seminary, 2007. [166 pages; AAT 3289558]

Hearon, Holly Elizabeth. "Witness and Counter-Witness: The Function of the Mary Magdalene Tradition in Early Christian Communities." PhD diss., Graduate Theological Union, 1998. [283 pages; AAT 9910261].

Hege, Brent A. R. "The Resurrection of Jesus: A Study in Myth and History." Master's thesis, Lutheran Theological Seminary at Gettysburg, 2001. [148 leaves]

Heller, James John. "The Resurrection of the Dead in the Light of the Biblical View of Life." PhD diss., Princeton Theological Seminary, 1955. [426 leaves]

Henderson, Timothy P. "The People Believe That He Has Risen from the Dead": The Gospel of Peter and Early Christian Apologetics." PhD diss., Marquette University, 2010. [N.B. Available online]

Hickcox, Percy Merriman. "The Historicity of the Resurrection of Jesus." Master's thesis, Boston University, 1922. [56 pages; N.B. Available online]

Hickling, S. R. "An Evidentiary Analysis of Doctor Richard Carrier's Objections to the Resurrection of Jesus Christ." PhD diss., Potchefstroom Campus of the North-West University, 2017. [322 pages; N.B. Available online]

Hitchcock, Ronald Lee. "A Study of the Resurrection of Jesus, with a Survey of Representative Viewpoints on the Subject." Master's thesis, Abilene Christian College, 1967. [136 leaves]

Holloman, Henry W. "Exposition of the Post-Resurrection Appearances of Our Lord." PhD diss., Dallas Theological Seminary, 1967. [261 leaves]

Holmyard, Harold R. "Preparation of Israel for Messiah with Regard to Resurrection as Epitomized by Psalm 16 in Acts 2." Master's thesis, Grace Theological Seminary, 1981. [146 leaves]

Holsinger, Madra E. "The Doctrine of the Resurrection of Jesus Christ Its Significance in Apostolic Teaching." Master's thesis, Wheaton College, 1948. [134 leaves]

Hook, Peter. "A Study of the Problem Passages Relating to the Ascension." Master's thesis, Dallas Theological Seminary, 1978. [48 pages]

Hoskins, Paul M. "Jesus as the Replacement of the Temple in the Gospel of John." PhD diss., Trinity Evangelical Divinity School, 2002. [344 pages; AAT 3068017]

Hubbard, Benjamin Jerome. "The Matthean Redaction of a Primitive Apostolic Commissioning: An Exegesis of Matthew 28:16–20." PhD diss., The University of Iowa, 1973. [189 pages; AAT 7330929]

Hughes, Kelly A. "Shroud of Turin: A Review of the Current Evidence and Data." MFS, National University, San Diego 2006. [61 leaves]

Hunter, JoAnn Heaney. "Communicating the Message of the Resurrection to a Crucified World." Master's thesis, St. John's University, 1981. [60 leaves]

Hutton, Delvin Dwayne. "The Resurrection of the Holy Ones (Matthew 27: 51B–53): A Study of the Theology of the Matthean Passion Narrative." PhD diss., Harvard University, 1970. [198 leaves; AAT 0217434]

Inboden, Scott W. "The Scope of Christian Mission Mandated by Matthew 28:19–20." Master's thesis, Grace Theological Seminary, 1984. [68 leaves]

Iverson, Kelly Ryan. "Irony in the End: A Textual and Literary Analysis of Mark 16:7–8." Master's thesis (ThM), Dallas Theological Seminary 2001. [97 leaves]

Jackson, Dalen Craig. "The Apocalyptic Orientation of Mark 14:26–16:8." PhD diss., The Southern Baptist Theological Seminary, 1991. [257 pages; AAT 9205769]

Janes, Harold T. "The Resurrection of Jesus In Light of the Mystery Religions." BA Divinity, Chicago Theological Seminary, 1929. [91 pages]

Jeanes, Samuel Arthur. "The Authenticity and Significance of the Great Commission." Master's thesis, Eastern Baptist Theological Seminary, 1945. [87 leaves]

Johnson, Benjamin A. "Empty Tomb Tradition in the Gospel of Peter." PhD diss., Harvard University, 1965. [132 leaves]

Jones, Beth Felker. "The Marks of His Wounds: On the Bodily Resurrection in Augustine and Calvin." PhD diss., Duke University, 2004. [298 pages; AAT 3177869]

Jovanovic, Mihailo. "Christ's Resurrection According to St. Paul." Master's thesis, St. Vladimir's Orthodox Catholic Theological Seminary, 1954. [58 leaves; TREN thesis, no. 015-0089]

Just, Arthur A. "Table Fellowship and the Eschatological Kingdom in the Emmaus Narrative of Luke 24." PhD diss., Durham University, 1989. [279 pages; N.B. Available at Durham E-Theses Online: http://etheses.dur.ac.uk/10486/]

Kamaleson, Samuel. "An Analysis of the Interpretative Methodology of Rudolf Bultmann's Exegesis of the Resurrection Event." Master's thesis, Ashbury Theological Seminary, 1971. [178 leaves]

Kankaanniemi, Matti. "The Guards of the Tomb: Matt 27, 62–66 and 28,11–15: Matthew's Apologetic Legend Revisited." PhD diss., Åbo: Åbo Akademi, 2010. [486 pages]

Keaty, Anthony W. "The Bodily Resurrection of Jesus in the Christology of Edward Schillebeeckx." Master's thesis (STM), Jesuit School of Theology at Berkeley, 1988. [100 pages]

Kelhoffer, James Anthony. "Miracle and Mission: The Authentication of Missionaries and Their Message in the Longer Ending of Mark (Mark 16:9–20)." PhD diss., University of Chicago, 1999. [689 pages; AAT 9920148]

Kensinger, Keith Arnold. "Resurrection as a Beginning: A Redactional Analysis of Mark 16:1–8." PhD diss., Aquinas Institute of Theology, 1977. [266 pages; AAT 7914147]

Kessler, Wm. Thomas. "Peter as the First Witness of the Risen Lord: An Historical and Theological Investigation." ThD., Pontificia Universita Gregoriana (Vatican City), 1995. [331 pages; AAT C638738]

Kieffer, James Shiffer. "The Necessity of the Resurrection of Jesus Christ." Master's thesis, Dallas Theological Seminary, 1944. [40 pages]

Kim, Benjamin M. H. "Disciples and Discipleship in the Fourth Gospel in Light of the Shift in Christological Understanding Resulting from the Resurrection of Jesus." PhD diss., Trinity Evangelical Divinity School, 2003. [234 pages; AAT 3087176]

Kim, Dae Gee. "The Trinitarian Relationship of the Holy Spirit in the Resurrection of Christ and of Believers." Master's thesis, Covenant Theological Seminary, 1979. [112 leaves]

Kirk, James Ernest. "The Resurrection of Christ as a Theological Ground for Ethics in the New Testament." Master's thesis, Abilene Christian College, 1973. [123 leaves]

Klausli, Markus T. "The Significance of the Resurrection of Christ for the Sanctification of the Believer: A Theological Study of Romans 6:1–14." Master's thesis (STM), Dallas Theological Seminary, 2001. [64 leaves; Theological Research Exchange Network (Series), 001–0772]

Knapp, Richard. "The Resurrection Narratives: How Might We Approach Them?" Master's thesis, Fairfield University, 1988. [122 leaves]

Konis, Polyvios. "From the Resurrection to the Ascension: Christ's Post Resurrection Appearances in Byzantine Art." PhD diss., University of Birmingham, 2010.

Kosanke, Charles. "Encounter with the Risen Jesus in Luke-Acts." ThD diss., Pontificia Universita Gregoriana (Vatican City), 1993. [233 pages; AAT C438392]

Kounter, Jacob. "The 'Minimal Facts of the Resurrection' Argument Applied to Islam." Senior Thesis, Liberty University, 2017. [36 pages; Available online]

Larson, John Theodore. "The Application of Redaction Criticism to the Resurrection Accounts of the Synoptic Gospels." Master's thesis, Graduate Theological Union, 1971. [82 leaves]

LaVerdiere, Eugene A. "The Emmaus Journey Narrative (LK 24:13–35): A Study in Lukan Redaction and Composition." PhD diss., University of Chicago, 1977. [247 leaves; AAT T-26426]

Laverdière, H. "The Socio-Politic of a Relic: Carbon Dating the Turin Shroud." PhD diss., University of Bath, 1989.

Lawson, Benjamin T. "The Crucifixion of Jesus in the Qur'an and Quranic Commentary: An Historical Survey." Master's thesis, Institute of Islamic Studies, McGill University, 1980. [147 pages]

Lee, Yong-Won. "Resurrection vs. Hallucination: An Argument for the Historicity of the Resurrection of Jesus in Terms of Probabilistic Analysis." PhD diss., The Southern Baptist Theological Seminary, 2009. [182 pages; AAT 3401800]

Lewis, David Isaac Melvin. "Suspended Endings in Ancient Literature: A Context for the Evaluation of the Ending of Mark's Gospel." Master's thesis (STM), Concordia Seminary, St. Louis, 1998. [49 leaves]

Licona, Michael R. "The Historicity of the Resurrection of Jesus: Historiographical Considerations in the Light of Recent Debates." PhD diss., University of Pretoria, 2008. [502 pages; N.B. Available online. This thesis is a must read.]

———. "Pursuing the Resurrection of Jesus from a Different Perspective." Master's thesis, Liberty University, 2000. [162 leaves]

Llagas, Carlos Manuel Maria A. "Resurrection Before Christ: An Exegesis of Old Testament and Intertestamental Literature." Master's thesis, Catholic Theological Union, 1988. [84 pages]

Luck, William F. "The Resurrectional Argument for the Existence of God: An Analysis." Master's thesis, Trinity Evangelical Divinity School, 1973. [110 leaves]

Lygre, John Gerhard. "Exaltation: Considered with Reference to the Resurrection and Ascension in Luke-Acts." PhD diss., Princeton Theological Seminary, 1975. [215 leaves]

MacDonald, D. B. "Resurrection, A Fact in History." Master's thesis, University of Toronto, 1896.

MacMillan, Patricia Helene. "Science, Conflict and the Devotional Artifact: A Social Cartography of the Turin Shroud Controversy." PhD diss., York University, 2013. [Ottawa: Library and Archives Canada = Bibliothèque et Archives Canada, 2013]

Mahoney, Robert P. "Two Disciples At the Tomb." PhD diss., Theological Faculty of the Bavarian Julius-Maximilian University of Würzburg, 1973. [344 pages]

Maldonado, Robert D. "Scripture, Tradition, and Theology in the Lucan Resurrection and Infancy Narratives." Master's thesis, Graduate Theological Union, 1982. [123 leaves]

Malesky, Charles Adam. "The Crucifixion and Resurrection of Jesus Christ in the Theology of Rudolf Bultmann." Master's thesis, Southern Methodist University, 1961. [99 leaves]

Maples, Kenneth. "The Function of Paschal Allusions in John's Crucifixion Narrative: An Examination of John's Typological Depiction of the Death of Jesus." Master's thesis, Southeastern Baptist Theological Seminary, 2007. [105 pages]

Marco, Anthony. "1 Corinthians 15 as a Lens for Interpreting the Appearance Narratives." Master's thesis, Holy Apostles College & Seminary, 2014.

Marlow, John Thomas Arthur. "A Narrative Analysis of Acts 1–2." PhD diss., Golden Gate Baptist Theological Seminary, 1988. [106 pages; AAT 8815837]

Mather, Paul Boyd. "The Appearances of the Risen Lord and Prophetic Utterance in Early Christianity." PhD diss., University of Chicago, 1972. [328 pages; AAT T-23791]

Mathew, Parackel Kuriakose. "The Setting of the Resurrection Narrative in the Gospel According to St. Matthew." PhD diss., McGill University (Canada), 1979. [261 leaves; AAT 0531653]

McCament, David A. "The Science of the Shroud: Constructing Effective Curriculum in Undergraduate Forensic Science Education Utilizing Research on the Shroud of Turin." MFS., National University, San Diego, 2000. [87 leaves]

McCasland, S. Vernon. "The Genesis of the New Testament Narratives of the Resurrection of Jesus." PhD diss., University of Chicago, 1926. [370 leaves; AAT T-11914]

McDonald, Lee. "The Resurrection of Jesus in History and Faith: An Investigation of Two Critical Approaches to the Easter Kerygma in the New Testament." PhD diss., University of Edinburgh, 1976. [413 leaves]

McDowall, David. "A Study of the Angelic Appearances and Their Ministry in the Resurrection Narratives." Master's thesis, Capital Bible Seminary, 1981. [113 leaves]

McGillicuddy, T. P. "The Resurrection and the Empty Tomb: Insights into the New Creation." Master's thesis, St. Vladimir's Serminary, 1991.

McGraw, Larry Ray. "An Examination of the literary Context of the Great Commission in Matthew 28:16–20." PhD diss., Southwestern Baptist Theological Seminary, 1983. [235 leaves; AAT 0553566]

McIntyre, Don Virgil. "The Resurrection of Jesus as Related to Pastoral Counseling." Thesis, Claremont School of Theology, 1977. [133 pages]

McLeay, Simon. "What did Paul of Tarsus Believe about the Resurrection of Jesus of Nazareth?" Master's thesis, University of Otago, 1993. [55 leaves]

McMahon, Edward John. "The Death and Resurrection of Jesus in Luke 23:26–24:53: A Greimassian Analysis." PhD diss., Vanderbilt University, 1984. [397 pages; AAT 8503897]

Medina, Nestor. "Resurrection and Discipleship Implications in the Christological Thought of Jon Sobrino." Master's thesis, University of St. Michael's College, 2000. [107 pages]

Meehan, Sister Thomas More. "John 19:32–35 and 1 John 5:6–8: A Study in the History of Interpretation." PhD diss., Drew University, 1985. [225 pages; AAT 8601972]

Mekkattukunnel, Andrew George. "The Priestly Blessing of the Risen Christ: An Exegetico-Theological Analysis of Luke 24, 50—53." PhD diss., Pontificia Univ. Gregoriana, Rome, 2000. [261 pages]

Meyer, Benjamin J. "How did the Resurrection Influence the Life of Peter?" Master's thesis, Dallas Theological Seminary, 1971. [51 leaves]

Miller, Malcolm. "The Resurrection of Jesus Christ and Its Relation to the Teachings of the New Testament." BD thesis, Chicago Theological Seminary, 1908. [65 leaves]

Miller, Willard Gene. "The Resurrection of Christ In Peter's Speeches." ThD diss., Dallas Theological Seminary, 1948. [273 leaves]

Mirecki, Paul Allan. "Mark 16: 9–20: Composition, Tradition and Redaction." ThD diss., Harvard University, 1986. [172 pages; AAT 8619014]

Mishkin, David. "Jewish Scholarship on the Resurrection of Jesus." PhD diss., University of Pretoria, 2015. [223 pages; N.B. Available online.]

Moeser, Annelies G. "Death of Judas Iscariot." Master's thesis, Catholic Theological Union Seminary, 1990. [116 pages; TREN thesis, no. 033–0249]

Moginot, Albert F. "Petrine Theology Relative to the Death and Resurrection of Christ." Master's thesis, Dallas Theological Seminary, 1947. [70 leaves]

Molina, Franscico J. "A Literary and Rhetorical Analysis of the Longer Ending of the Gospel of Mark (Mark 16:9–20)." STL., Catholic University of America 1997. [145 leaves; N.B. Theological Research Exchange Network (Series), #029–0400.]

Monette, Greg. "Resurrecting a Marginal Jew: A Study on the Resurrection Narratives in the New Testament Using John P. Meier's Criteria for Determining Historical Authenticity." Master's thesis, Acadia Divinity College, 2011. [141 leaves]

Mugarra Ahurwendeire, Athanasius. "The Will of the Risen Lord: An Exegetical-Theological Analysis of Matthew 28:16–20." PhD diss., Pont. Univ. Lateranense, 2005. [670 pages]

Mulder, Frederik Sewerus. "The Resurrection of Jesus: Recent Major Figures in the Debate." Master's thesis, University of Pretoria, 2006. [217 pages; N.B. Available online.]

Mull, Andrew B. "A Comparative Study of a Debate Over Authenticity: Matthew 28:18–20." Master's thesis, Dallas Theological Seminary, 2001. [Theological Research Exchange Network (Series), 001–0793]

Category XII—Reference Sources, Dissertations and Theses, and Introduction to the New Testament

Mumley, William E. "The Great Commission in Kingdom Context: An Integrated Theological Analysis of Matthew 24:14 and 28:18–20." Master's thesis, Western Seminary, 2007. [156 leaves; Theological Research Exchange Network #002–0815]

Munro, Don W. "The Resurrection of our Lord Jesus Christ." Master's thesis, San Francisco Theological Seminary, 1976. [134 leaves]

Murphy, Larry Edwin. "The Concept of the Twelve in Luke-Acts as a Key to the Lukan Perspective on the Restoration of Israel." PhD diss., The Southern Baptist Theological Seminary, 1988. [272 pages; AAT 8818526]

Nathan, Bruce A. "An Isogogical and Exegetical Study of Mark 16:9–20." Master's thesis, Concordia Theological Seminary, 1980. [43 leaves]

Noyalis, Walter Jerome. "The Resurrection of Jesus as Metaphor in the Theology of Wolfhart Pannenberg." PhD diss., University of Notre Dame, 1979. [179 leaves]

O'Leary, Finbarr. "The Significance of the Empty Tomb for the Christian Faith." Master's thesis, Pontifical University, St. Patrick's College, Maynooth, 2004. [85 leaves]

Oliver, Isaac Wilk. "Torah Praxis After 70 CE Reading Matthew and Luke-Acts as Jewish Texts." PhD diss., University of Michigan, 2012. [589 pages, N.B. See. 246–48, 252]

Olson, Raymond M. "The Importance of the Resurrection in the Witness of Peter." Master's thesis, Luther Theological Seminary, 1943. [57 leaves]

Oluwafemi, Titus. "Jesus' Resurrection as the Ultimate 'Sign' of His Messianic Authority: (A Special Reference Study of the Jonah-Sign in Matthew-Luke and the Temple-Sign in John)." PhD diss., Baylor University, 1979. [164 pages]

Onuoha, Anselm E. "The Curious Character of Mark's Gospel Ending: Reading Mark 16:1–8, Master's thesis, St. John's University, 1998. [80 pages]

O'Reilly, Laurie M. "The Chiastic Structure of Luke 23:26–53 : A Literary-Critical Analysis." Master's thesis, Vanderbilt University, 1984. [61 pages]

Osborne, Grant R. "History and Theology in the Resurrection Narratives: A Redactional Study." PhD diss., University of Aberdeen, 1975. [N.B. Available online]

Oyer, Linda "Interpreting the New in Light of the Old: A Comparative Study of the Post-Resurrection Commissioning Stories in Matthew and John." PhD diss., Institut Catholique de Paris, Faculte de Theologie et de Sciences Religieuses, 1997. [490 pages]

Pannozzi, Frank J. "Resurrection Language of 1 Cor. 15:3–8 and its Theological Background." Master's thesis, Catholic University of America, 1975. [127 pages]

Pappas, Thomas C. "'Go and make disciples!': Matthew 28:19." Master's thesis, Grace Theological Seminary, 1980. [47 pages]

Parambi, Baby. "The Discipleship of the Women in the Gospel According to Matthew: An Exegetical Theological Study of Matt. 27:51b–56, 57–61 and 28:1–10." STD thesis, Roma: Pontificia Università Gregoriana, 2003. [270 pages]

Parris, David. "A Study on the History of the Interpretation of Matthew 28:18–20." Master's thesis, Fuller Theological Seminary, 1994. [86 leaves]

Parsons, Elmer E. "Psychological Evidences of the Resurrection of Jesus Christ: A Study in Biblical Theology." Master's thesis, Ashbury Theological Seminary, 1955. [185 leaves]

Parsons, Mikeal Carl. "The Ascension Narratives in Luke-Acts." PhD diss., The Southern Baptist Theological Seminary, 1985. [313 pages; AAT 8527907]

Perkins, Daniel Elinor. "A Rhetorical Analysis of the Resurrection Appearances in the Christian Gospels." PhD diss., Georgia State University, 1994. [120 leaves]

Perschbacher, Wesley J. "An Examination of the Data of John 20 Regarding the Empty Tomb and the Resurrection Appearances of Jesus Christ." Master's thesis, Trinity Evangelical Divinity School, 1973. [112 leaves]

Petersen, Harry Frederick. "The Testimony to the Resurrection in the Gospel of Luke." Master's thesis, Princeton Theological Seminary, 1959. [135 leaves]

Petersen, William L. "The Text of the Resurrection Narratives According to Greek, Vetus Latina and Vetus Syra Sources." Master's thesis, Lutheran Theological Seminary (Saskatoon, Sask.), McGill University. [178 leaves]

Phelps, Ryan Kendall. "The Great Commissioning: An Exegesis of Matthew 28.16–20." Master's thesis, Liberty Baptist Theological Seminary, 2011. [87 pages; N.B. Available online.]

Phillips, Vicki Cass. "Women's Speech and Silence in the Gospel According to Mark." PhD diss., Vanderbilt University, 1997. [264 pages; AAT 9724981]

Playoust, Catherine Anne. "Lifted up from Earth: The Ascension of Jesus and the Heavenly Ascents of Early Christians." PhD diss., Harvard. 2006. [309 pages; AAT 3239143]

Prevallet, Elaine Marie. "Luke 24:26 : A Passover Christology." PhD diss., Marquette University, 1967. [233 pages; AAT 6800496]

Prince, Deborah Thompson. "Visions of the Risen Jesus: The Rhetoric of Certainty in Luke 24 and Acts 1." PhD diss., University of Notre Dame, 2005. [330 leaves; AAT 3165187]

Purim, Reynaldo. "An Introduction to the Philosophy of the Death and Resurrection of Jesus Christ." PhD diss., Southern Baptist Theological Seminary, 1934. [222 leaves]

Puskas, Charles B., Jr. "The Conclusion of Luke-Acts: An Investigation of the Literary Function and Theological Significance of Acts 28:16–31." PhD diss., Saint Louis University, 1980. [188 pages; AAT 8101271]

Ray, Jerry Lynn. "Narrative Irony in Luke-Acts." PhD diss., University of Virginia, 1991. [267 pages; AAT 9208905]

Reeves, Keith Howard. "The Resurrection Narrative in Matthew: A Literary-Critical Examination." PhD diss., Union Theological Seminary in Virginia, 1988. [195 pages; AAT 8819785]

Reinhartz, Adele. "John 20:30–31 and the Purpose of the Fourth Gospel." PhD diss., McMaster University (Canada), 1983. [254 frames; AAT NK65454]

Rellstab, Theodore L. "The Shroud of Turin as Historical and Theological Factor." Master's thesis, Concordia Theological Seminary, 1980. [54 leaves]

Rendell, James. "The Significance of the Ascension." Master's thesis, Dallas Theological Seminary, 1958. [68 pages]

Rensburg, Hanré Janse van. "The Resurrection Revived: A Critical Examination." Master's thesis, University of Pretoria, 2010. [176 pages; N.B. Available online.]

Richardson, Robert Lee. "The Function of the Scriptures in the Rise of the Easter Faith." PhD diss., Vanderbilt University. 1972. [335 leaves]

Riegel, Joseph. "An Inductive Analysis of the Argument of 1 Corinthians 15." Master's thesis, Dallas Theological Seminary, 1980. [85 pages]

Riley, Gregory John. "Doubting Thomas: Controversy between the communities of Thomas and John." PhD diss., Harvard University, 1990. [199 pages; AAT 9113248]

Roberts, T. A. "The Historical Appeal of Christian Theology as Illustrated by the Passion and Resurrection Narratives of the Four Gospels." PhD diss., University of Oxford, 1956. [289 leaves]

Category XII—Reference Sources, Dissertations and Theses, and Introduction to the New Testament

Rylander, Mark Allen. "The Significance of the Resurrection, Ascension, and Session of the Lord Jesus in the Speeches and Letters of Peter." Master's thesis (ThM), Dallas Theological Seminary, 1983. [44 pages]

San, Myat Shwe. "The Significance of the Resurrection of Jesus for Systematic Theology: A Comparative Study of Karl Barth's and Wolfhart Pannenberg's Understanding of Jesus' Resurrection." PhD diss., Regensburg University, 2004. [220 pages]

Savarino, Joseph. "Toward an Adequate Understanding of Christ's Resurrection." Master's thesis, Marquette University, 1968. [109 leaves]

Sawyer, Karen Elaine. "The Resurrection of Our Lord: A Study and Dual-Text Edition." PhD diss., University of Toronto, 2001. [332 pages; AAT NQ58970]

Schaberg, Jane. "The Father, the Son and the Holy Spirit: An Investigation of the Origin and Meaning of the Triadic Phrase in Matt 28:19B." PhD diss., Union Theological Seminary, 1980. [487 pages; AAT 8019618]

Schiotz, Fredik Axel. "Grounds for Belief in the Bodily Resurrection of Jesus Christ." Master's thesis, Luther Theological Seminary, 1933. [142 leaves]

Schmidt, Martin J. "The Proclamation of the Risen Jesus Christ in Lutheran Preaching: a content analysis of selected sermons, representing ninety-seven years of preaching within the Lutheran Church—Missouri Synod, as found in Magazin fuer Ev.-Luth. Homiletik und Pastoraltheologie (1877–1929) and The Concordia Pulpit (1930–1973)." Ed. D. Teachers College, Columbia University, 1974. [310 leaves]

Schnaus, Edward Urban. "The Doctrine of Saint Thomas Aquinas on the Resurrection of Christ as the Meritorious and Exemplary Cause of the Resurrection of our Bodies." Master's thesis, Catholic University of America, 1941. [60 leaves]

Schneiders, Sandra Marie. "The Johannine Resurrection Narrative: An Exegetical and Theological Study of John 20 as a Synthesis of Johannine Spirituality. (Volumes 1 and 2)." STD diss., Pontificia Universita Gregoriana (Vatican City), 1975. [925 pages; AAT 8302749]

Seal, Welton Ollie, Jr. "The Parousia in Mark: A Debate with Norman Perrin and His "School." PhD diss., Union Theological Seminary, 1982. [215 pages; AAT 8228204]

See, Steven H. "The Resurrection of Jesus Christ in the Writings of St. Irenaeus and in the Contemporary Thought of Richard R. Niebuhr: A Study in the Historical Problem of Interpreting the Resurrection of Christ." BD thesis, Episcopal Theological School, 1961. [89 pages]

Selby, Peter Stephen Maurice. "Belief in the Resurrection of Jesus Christ." PhD diss., King's College London, 1974. [238 leaves]

Sexton, Charnel Sterling. "The Resurrection and its Significance According to I Corinthians 15." Master's thesis, Columbia Theological Seminary, 1963. [174 leaves]

Shank, Douglas H. "The Great Commission to 'Make Disciples': Its Interpretation and Application to Mission Strategy." Master's thesis, Trinity Evangelical Divinity School, 1985. [139 leaves; N.B. TREN thesis, no. 006–0188.]

Shaw, Benjamin C. "Jesus' Resurrection: A Historical Investigation." Master's thesis, Liberty University, 2011. [113 pages; N.B. Available online.]

Shepard, Robert Burpo, Jr. "'My Name is Pontius Pilate': A New Understanding for Christians of the Tragic Roots of Anti-Semitism in the Gospels Through the Voices of Simon of Cyrene, Joseph of Arimathea, Pontius Pilate, Herod Antipas, Caiphas, and Barabbas." D. Min., School of Theology at Claremont, 1983. [111 pages; AAT 8316125]

Sherwood, Thomas E. "Resurrection and Redemption: An Exegetical and Historical Study of the Soteriological Force of Christ's Resurrection." PhD diss., Pontifical University, Maynooth, 1958. [184 leaves]

Shimodate, Madao. "The Significance of the Emmaus Pericope in Luke-Acts." Master's thesis, Concordia Seminary, 1973. [117 leaves]

Silverstein, Philip. "A Talmudist's Reading of Matthew." Thesis (D. Min.), Lutheran Theological Seminary at Philadelphia, 2008. [137 leaves; Theological Research Exchange Network 001-0793]

Sleeper, Charles Freeman. "Resurrection, History, and Interpretation." PhD diss., Vanderbilt University, 1963. [309 leaves]

Smith, Daniel Alan. "The Post-Mortem Vindication of Jesus in the Sayings Gospel Q." PhD diss., University of St. Michael's College, 2001. [346 pages; AAT NQ64784]

Smith, Daniel Evans. "A Harmony of the Great Commission in the Gospels." Master's thesis, Dallas Theological Seminary, 1978. [66 leaves]

Smith, Kenneth. "A Series of Bible Lessons on First Corinthians." Master's thesis, Dallas Theological Seminary, 1976. [85 pages]

Smith, Mahon T. "The Effect of Philosophical Presuppositions Upon Interpretations of The Resurrection." PhD diss., Southern Baptist Theological Seminary, Diss., 1978. [331 pages]

Smith, Robert Houston. "The Episode of Peter's Confession in Tradition and Gospel." PhD diss., Yale University, 1960. [342 pages; AAT 8009381]

Sniatyunskyi, Leslee. "Mark's Empty Tomb, Discipleship and Grief." Master's thesis, Flinders University, 2015. [113 leaves]

Snyder, Francis Clark. "The Reality of the Resurrection of Jesus." BD thesis, Chicago Theological Seminary 1924. [42 pages]

Sorensen, Robert Allen. "The Literary Function of Acts' Vision Narratives." PhD diss., Loyola University of Chicago, 2005. [440 pages; AAT 3175772]

Specht, Walter F. "An Examination of the Time Elements Pertaining to the Death, Burial and Resurrection of Christ Used in the New Testament." Master's thesis, Seventh-day Adventist Theological Seminary, 1946. [93 leaves]

Speciale, Stephen E. "Lk. 1:5-45 and 24:13-35 : Luke as Easter Witness." Master's thesis, Jesuit School of Theology at Berkeley, 1985. [104 pages]

Stankus, Pat. "The Problem of the Resurrection." Master's thesis, Fairfield University, 1986. [107 leaves]

Stanley, David Michael. "Christ's Resurrection in Pauline Soteriology." PhD diss., Rome, 1952. [N.B. Published by Analecta Biblica]

Starkey, John C. M. "The Easter Experiences: An Interdisciplinary Investigation of Religious Experience in Theology, Philosophy, and Psychology." PhD diss., Boston University, 1998. [755 pages; AAT 9825414]

Staudt, Calvin K. "The Idea of the Resurrection in the Ante-Nicene Period." PhD diss., University of Chicago, 1909. [82 pages]

Stephens, Gregory D. "Mark 16:9-20 : Is It Valid." Master's thesis, Capital Bible Seminary, 2000. [71 leaves; N.B. Theological Research Exchange Network (Series), #014-0128.]

Stobart, Andrew J. "A Constructive Analysis of the Place and Role of the Doctrine of Jesus' Resurrection within the Theologies of Rowan Williams and Robert Jenson." PhD diss., University of Aberdeen, 2007. [668 pages]

Strand, Ahlert J. C. "The Morning of the Lord's Resurrection." Master's thesis, Concordia Theological Seminary, Ft. Wayne, 1978. [28 leaves]

Sullivan, Roger W. "The Christology of the Johannine Passion and Resurrection Narratives." ThD diss., New Orleans Baptist Theological Seminary, 1986. [161 pages; AAT 8706825]

Surrey, Cameron. "Forgiveness and the Risen-Wounded Christ: In Dialogue with Karl Barth and Hans Urs von Balthasar." PhD diss., University of Otago, Dunedin, New Zealand, 2014. [241 pages; N.B. Available online]

Swanson, Mark Nathaniel. "'FOLLY TO THE HUNAFA' The Cross of Christ in Arabic Christian-Muslim Controversy in the Eighth and Ninth Centuries AD." PhD diss., Pontificio Istituto di Studi Arabi e d'Islamistica (Rome), 1992. [N.B. Archive.org. Especially read Chapters 3 and 5.]

Szymansk, Mary Reginette. "The Crucifixion in the Light of the Shroud of Turin." Master's thesis, St. Bonaventure University, 1959. [75 pages]

Taylor, Birgit. "Outrageous Women: A Comparison of Five Passages Within the Canonical Passion and Empty Tomb Narratives Emphasizing the Role of Women." Master's thesis, University of Cape Town, 2004. [120 leaves]

Taylor, Warren Francis. "The Resurrection: A Study in the History of Preaching." PhD diss., School of Theology at Claremont, 1980. [290 leaves]

Tham, Po Wing. "The Rhetorical Function of the Feast of Passover in the Gospel of John." PhD diss., Dallas Theological Seminary, 2005. [244 pages; AAT 3217227]

Thayil, Philip. "Witness Mandate of the Risen Jesus in Luke 24,48 and Acts 1,8 : Its Theological and Juridical Implications." ThD diss., Pontificia Universita Gregoriana (Vatican City), 1993. [283 pages; AAT C439186]

Thompson, Timothy J. "Resurrection Witness: A Christian Claim to Uniqueness in a Religiously Plural World." Lincoln Christian Seminary, 1993. [144 leaves]

Thorpe, Mary Brennan. "Make Disciples of all Nations: Jesus' Shifting Mission in the Gospel of Matthew." Master's thesis, Virginia Theological Seminary, 2009. [84 pages]

Tiffin, John M. "The Meaning of Matthew 28:17 in Light of the Author's Theological Purpose." Master's thesis, Western Conservative Baptist Seminary, 1980. [126 pages]

Torstrick, Melvin E. "The Post-Resurrection Missionary Commissions of Jesus." Master's thesis, New Orleans Baptist Theological Seminary, 1965. [96 leaves]

VanBeek, Lawrence H. "John 20:22: An Interpretation." Master's thesis, Providence College and Seminary (Canada), 1990. [110 pages; AAT MM67027]

Virtue, Willis W. "The Believer's Identification with Christ in His Resurrection." Master's thesis, Evangelical Theological College (Dallas, TX), 1935. [70 leaves]

Vistar, Deolito V. "The Supreme Σημεῖον of Jesus' Death-and-Resurrection in the Fourth Gospel." PhD diss., University of Otago, Dunedin, New Zealand, 2017. [374 pages]

Vorass, Steven L. "The Function of the Emmaus Passage within the Structure of Luke-Acts: A Literary Study of Luke 24:13–35." Master's thesis, Northern Baptist Theological Seminary, 1989.

Waldo, W. A. "The Resurrection of Jesus Christ As A Fact." DB (Bachelor of Divinity). University of Chicago, 1899. [14 pages]

Wallace, George Lynn. "The New Testament Resurrection Narratives: History and Metaphor." Master's thesis, Amridge University, 2000. [138 pages; AAT EP25807]

Warner, David W. "'Go' Verbs in Matthew: Implications for the Interpretation of Matthew 28:16–20." Master's thesis, Concordia Theological Seminary, Fort Wayne, 2003. [106 leaves]

Warren, Paul F. "The Resurrection Problematic: A Discussion of the Resurrection of Jesus in the Christology of Wolfhart Pannenberg." Master's thesis, Graduate Theological Seminary, 1975. [156 leaves]

Watanabe, Masataka Mark. "The Empty Tomb Tradition of Mark: Text, History, and Theological Struggles." PhD diss., Fuller Theological Seminary, School of Theology, 2005. [314 pages; AAT 3191345]

Watson, Richard. "The Shroud of Turin." Master's thesis, Wartburg Theological Seminary, 1977. [142 pages]

Weiss, Lyle K. "The Public Significance of the Bodily Resurrection of Jesus Christ." Master's thesis, St. Mary's Seminary and University, 2007. [252 pages; AAT 3297744]

Wessel, Herman August. "The Place of the Resurrection of Jesus Christ in the Book of Acts." Master's thesis, Louisville Presbyterian Theological Seminary, 1935. [65 leaves]

Whitaker, Max. "Is Jesus Athene or Odysseus? Investigating the Unrecognizability and Metamorphosis of Jesus in his Post-Resurrection Appearances." PhD diss., University of Otago, Dunedin, New Zealand, 2016. [329 pages; Available online]

Williams, Jeremy. "Ecclesiastes Revisited: Does the Resurrection of Christ Affect Qoheleth's Biblical Theology of Death?" Master's thesis (ThM), Dallas Theological Seminary, 2007. [60 leaves, Theological Research Exchange Network (Series), #001–1164.]

Williams, Richard W. "Historicity of the Resurrection in Contemporary Theology." Master's thesis, Hamline University, 1978. [86 leaves]

Wilton, Murray Ross. "Witness as a Theme in the Fourth Gospel." PhD diss., New Orleans Baptist Theological Seminary, 1992. [205 pages; AAT 9311809]

Witherup, Ronald David. "The Cross of Jesus: A Literary-Critical Study of Matthew 27 (Passion Narrative Criticism)." PhD diss., Union Theological Seminary in Virginia, 1985. [409 pages; AAT 8613771]

Woleng, Aylwin. "A Study on the Four Views of the Ending of Mark." Master's thesis, Southern California Seminary, 2009. [54 leaves]

Wolf, William James. "The Marcan Resurrection Account in Light of Current Studies with a Special Emphasis on Existential Hermeneutics." Master's thesis, Emmanuel School of Religion, 1974. [138 leaves]

Woodcock, Eldon. "The Significance of the Resurrection of Christ in the Writings of Paul." PhD diss., Duke University, 1967. [313 leaves]

Woodring, Richard C. "Signs for Those Who Believe: A Critical Study of Mark 16:18." Master's thesis, Grace Theological Seminary, 1970. [82 pages]

Wortham, Thomas Emerson. "Paul's doctrine of the resurrection of Jesus Christ." PhD diss., Southern Baptist Theological Seminary, 1938. [172 leaves]

Wright, George Clarence. "The Resurrection of Christ." BD (Bachelor of Divinity), University of Chicago, 1897. [19 pages]

Wright, George H. "The Death and Resurrection of Christ in the Soteriology of St. John Chrysostom." Master's thesis, Marquette University, 1966. [71 leaves]

Wyper, Stephen A. "An Examination of Myth and the Resurrection." Master's thesis, Talbot, 1977. [110 leaves]

Yeboah-Amoako, Anthony K. "The Lord has Risen Indeed (Luke 24:34): An Examination of the Question of the Historicity of the Resurrection of Jesus Christ." Master's thesis, Andrews University, Seventh-day Adventist Theological Seminary, 1988. [176 leaves]

Yingling, M. F. "Christ's Bodily Resurrection: An Historical Reality." Master's thesis, Catholic University of America, 1900? [113 leaves]

Category XII—Reference Sources, Dissertations and Theses, and Introduction to the New Testament

Zolondek, Michael V. "The Christology of Jesus' Disciples." Master's thesis, Florida International University, 2010. [70 pages]

Zwiep, Arie W. "The Ascension of the Messiah: An Inquiry Into the Ascension and Exaltation of Jesus in Lukan Christology." University of Durham, 1996. [337 pages]

Chapter 34

Introduction to the New Testament and Biblical Criticism

Achtemeier, Paul J., et al. *Introducing the New Testament: Its Literature and Theology.* Grand Rapids: Eerdmans, 2001. [4.2.6 The Death and Resurrection of Jesus the Messiah, Son of God (26.1–28:20), See. 115–16; 8.7 The Resurrection of Jesus, See. 241–44; 6.3.8 The Exaltation of Jesus (24:1–53), See. 171–72; 7.3.3; also See. 196–97]

Barclay, William. *Barclay's Guide to the New Testament.* Louisville: Westminster John Knox, 2008. [Resurrection of Jesus Christ, See. 178–79, 209–10]

Barnett, Paul. *Is The New Testament Reliable?* 2nd ed. Downers Grove, IL: InterVarsity, 2003. [Chapter 12 The Resurrection of Jesus, See. 111–35]

Beck, Dwight Marion. *Through the Gospels to Jesus.* New York: Harper & Brothers, 1954. [Chapter 38 The Empty Tomb. The Resurrection Appearances, See. 324–33; Chapter 55 The Resurrection Appearances, See. 445–49; Chapter 56 Epilogue. The Appearances at the Sea of Tiberias, See. 450–53]

Bergh van Eysinga, G. A. van den. *Radical Views About the New Testament.* Translated by S. B. Slack. Chicago: Open Court, 1912. [See. 26, 46, 96, 122; N.B. Archive.org.]

Bishop, Eric F. F. *Jesus of Palestine: The Local Background to the Gospel Documents.* London: Lutterworth, 1955. [#106 He Is Risen: He Is Not Here, See. 253–54; #108 Olivet and the Master's Trysting Place, See. 257–58; #110 After the Crucifixion the Resurrection, See. 265–68; #111 The Place of the Ascension, See. 269–70; #131 The Resurrection Scenes, See. 312–15]

Blair, Joe. *Introducing the New Testament.* Nashville: B&H, 1994. [See. 66, 79–80, 89, 99–100, 104–5, 140]

Blomberg, Craig L. *Jesus and the Gospels: An Introduction and Survey.* 2nd ed. Nashville: B&H Publishing, 2009. [Chapter 17 Passion, Crucifixion, and Resurrection, See. Resurrection, See. 409–18]

Boyd, Gregory A. *The Crucifixion of the Warrior God: Interpreting the Old Testament's Violent Portraits of God in Light of the Cross.* Vol. 1. Minneapolis: Fortress, 2017. [The Cross and Resurrection, See. 167–71]

Brown, Raymond E. *An Introduction to the New Testament.* New York: Doubleday, 1997. [Resurrection (and appearances) of Jesus, See. 110, 147–49, 202–3, 260–62, 281, 298, 367, 524–25, 534–35, 688, 694, 763, 821, 823, 829, 835]

Category XII—Reference Sources, Dissertations and Theses, and Introduction to the New Testament

———. *An Introduction to the New Testament: The Abridged Edition.* Edited and abridged by Marion L. Soards. New Haven: Yale University Press, 2016. [See. 55–57; 91–97; 98–100; 191–92]

Chatham, Josiah G. *In the Midst Stands Jesus: A Pastoral Introduction to the New Testament.* Staten Island, NY: Alba House, 1972. [Chapter 19 The Resurrection, See. 153–57]

Childs, Brevard S. *The New Testament as Canon: An Introduction.* Minneapolis: Fortress, 1984. [See. 92–95; 140–42]

Clarke, William Kemp Lowther. *New Testament Problems: Essays—Essays—Reviews—Interpretations.* London: SPCK, 1929. [Chapter 12 What Became of Our Lord's Body?, See. 102–7]

Connick, C. Milo. *The New Testament: An Introduction to Its History, Literature, and Thought.* 2nd ed. Belmont, CA: Wadsworth, 1978. [See. 214–19]

Cousar, Charles B. *An Introduction to the New Testament: Witnesses to God's New Work.* Louisville: Westminster John Knox, 2006. [See. 38–39, 116, 130, 133–34, 141]

Crapps, Robert W., et al. *Introducing the New Testament.* New York: Ronald Press, 1969. [Chapter 5 Jerusalem: Ministry, Crucifixion, Resurrection, See. 181–83]

Davies, W. D. *Invitation to the New Testament: A Guide to Its Main Witness.* Garden City, NY: Doubleday, 1966. [Chapter 40 The Return of Jesus: The Resurrection, See. 495–501]

DeSilva, David A. *An Introduction to the New Testament: Context, Methods and Ministry.* Downers Grove, IL: InterVarsity, 2004. [Resurrection (of Jesus), See. 54, 149, 151, 153, 155, 158, 165–66, 173, 177, 179–81, 188, 198, 201, 203–4, 211–12, 224–26, 239, 245, 283, 309, 311–13, 315, 319–20, 328, 332, 353–54, 356, 361, 363, 389, 393, 414–15, 420, 425, 431, 454, 458, 460, 482–85, 500, 515, 525, 587–89, 618, 623–24, 661, 717–18, 755, 817, 846, 852, 854]

Detzler, Wayne A. *New Testament Words in Today's Language.* Wheaton, IL: Victor, 1986. [Resurrection, See. 328–29]

Drane, John. *Introducing the New Testament.* Minneapolis: Fortress, 2001. [Chapter 5 The Resurrection, See. 98–110]

Duling, Dennis C., and Norman Perrin. *The New Testament Proclamation and Parenesis, Myth and History.* 3rd ed. Fort Worth: Harcourt Brace, 1994. [Resurrection appearances, See. 188, 382, 392, 410, 458]

Ehrman, Bart D. *The Bible: A Historical and Literary Introduction.* 2nd ed. Oxford: Oxford University Press, 2018. [Jesus the Vindicated Son of God, See. 268–69; What the Resurrection Confirmed for Paul, See. 319–20; What the Resurrection Changed for Paul, See. 320–21]

———. *The New Testament: A Historical Introduction to the Early Christian Writings.* 2nd. ed. New York: Oxford University Press, 2000. [Resurrection of Jesus, See. 72–74, 133, 135, 183–84, 188, 253–55, 270–72, 294–97, 324–31]

———. *The New Testament A Historical Introduction to the Early Christian Writings.* 6th ed. New York: Oxford University Press, 2016. [See. 117–18; Jesus' Resurrection From An Apocalyptic Perspective, 303–5]

Elwell, Walter A., and Robert W. Yarbrough. *Encountering the New Testament: A Historical and Theological Survey.* 3rd ed. Grand Rapids: Baker, 2013. [Resurrection, See. 247–48]

Farrar, F. W. *Texts Explained or, Helps to Understand the New Testament.* Cleveland, OH: F. M. Barton, 1899. [See. 45, 61–62, 83–84, 120–25, 127, 203–4]

Fiensy, David A. *The College Press NIV Commentary New Testament Introduction.* Joplin, MO: College Press, 1994. [Jesus' Resurrection, See. 115–17]

Fox, Robin Lane. *The Unauthorized Version: Truth and Fiction in the Bible.* London: Penguin, 2006.

Freed, Edwin D. *The New Testament: A Critical Introduction.* 2nd ed. Belmont, CA: Wadsworth, 1991. [Resurrection of Jesus, See. 114, 154, 201–5; in John's gospel, See. 337, 338, 341, 346, 350; in Paul, See. 228, 229–30, 239–42, 271, 282–83, 321]

———. *The New Testament: A Critical Introduction.* 3rd ed. Belmont, CA: Wadsworth, 2001. [Death and Resurrection of Jesus, See. 118–21]

Grassi, Joseph A. *Jesus is Shalom: A Vision of Peace from the Gospels.* Mahwah, NJ: Paulist, 2006. [The Message of Peace in the Resurrection Appearances, See. 123–26; The Resurrection Stories, Jesus' Final Triple Greeting of Peace, and Last Blessing, See. 153–55]

Gromacki, Robert G. *New Testament Survey.* Grand Rapids: Baker, 1974. [See. 107–8, 128–29, 147–48, 160–61, 214]

Gundry, Robert H. *A Survey of the New Testament.* 5th ed. Grand Rapids: Zondervan, 2012. [Excursus: The Miracles and Resurrection of Jesus; See. 139–41]

Harris, Stephen L. *The New Testament: A Student's Introduction* 6th ed. New York: McGraw-Hill, 2009. [See. 130–31, 149–51 (Mark); 160–61, 179–80 (Matt); 336–37 (in Paul's letters)]

Harrison, H. D., ed. *A Survey of the New Testament.* 1983. [See. 15, 33–34, 51, 65–66, 67–70, 105–6]

Heard, Richard. *An Introduction to the New Testament.* New York: Harper & Brothers, 1950. [See. 38–39, 62]

Hester, H. I. *The Heart of the New Testament.* Liberty, MO: Quality Press, 1963. [Chapter 10 Victory Over Death, See. 223–32; N.B. Traces the reported events and reviews four attempted explanations.]

Jensen, Irving L. *The Layman's Bible Study Notebook: An Inductive Bible Study.* Irvine, CA: Harvest House, 1978. [See. 133, 209, 334–39, 441–49, 452–55, 692–95]

Johnson, Jeremiah J. *The Resurrection of Jesus in the Gospel of Peter: A Tradition-Historical Study of the Akhîm Gospel Fragment.* London: Bloomsbury, 2016. [Chapter 6 Resurrection in New Testament Texts, 5. Jesus' Resurrection, etc. See. 106–110].

Johnson, Timothy Luke. *The Writings of the New Testament.* 3rd ed. Minneapolis: Fortress, 2010. [Chapter 5 The Resurrection Faith, See. 95–109]

Juel, Donald. *An Introduction to New Testament Literature.* Nashville: Abingdon, 1978. [Chapter 7 Resurrection Stories in the Synoptics, See. 166–75]

Kelly, Joseph F. *An Introduction to the New Testament for Catholics.* Collegeville, MN: Liturgical Press, 2006. [See. 34–35, 107–9, 154–56, 177–78]

Knowling, R. J. *Witness of the Epistles: A Study in Modern Criticism.* London: Longman, Green, and Co., 1892. [Chapter 7 The Resurrection, See. 365–96; N.B. Archive.org]

Köstenberger, Andreas J., et al. *The Cradle, the Cross, the Crown: An Introduction to the New Testament.* 2nd ed. Nashville: B&H Academic, 2016. [Jesus the Risen Messiah, See. 137–39; also See. 333, 371–73, 422, 569]

Kruger, Michael J., ed. *A Biblical Theological Introduction to the New Testament: The Gospel Realized.* Wheaton: Crossway, 2016. [655 pages]

Lea, Thomas, and David Alan Black. *The New Testament: Its Background and Message*. 2nd ed. Nashville: B&H, 2003. [Chapter 11 The Final Week of Jesus' Life—Crucifixion and Resurrection, See. 270–78]

Loader, William. *The New Testament with Imagination: A Fresh Approach to its Writings and Themes*. Grand Rapids: Eerdmans, 2007. [Mark 16:1–8 and 1 Corinthians 15:1–11, See. 54–62]

Machen, J. Gresham. *The New Testament: An Introduction to its Literature and History*. Edited by W. John Cook. Carlisle, PA: Banner of Trust, 1976. [The Cross and the Resurrection as the Foundation of Apostolic Preaching, See. 57–62]

Marsh, F. E. *1000 Bible Study Outlines*. London: Pickering & Inglis, 1925. [Section 117, See. 53; Sections 180–188, See. 83–90]

Martin, Dale B. *Biblical Truth: The Meaning of Scripture in the Twenty-First Century*. New Haven: Yale University Press, 2017. [The Resurrection of Christ, See. 198–215; N.B. The author asserts that "All we need to confess . . . is that what ever they experienced, which is forever inaccessible to us as history or science was caused by God." p. 213]

McDonald, Lee Martin, and Stanley Porter. *Early Christianity and Its Sacred Literature*. Peabody, MA: Hendrickson, 2000. [Chapter 6 The Story of Jesus, Part B: Easter Faith and the Resurrection Narratives, See. 178–224; N.B. This work is one of the best introductions to the New Testament.]

Merz, Philip Paul. *Thesaurus Biblicus, or Handbook of Scripture Reference compiled from the Latin of Philip Paul Merz*. Waterloo: Observer Book Publication, 1880. [Christ Rose on the Third Day from the Dead, See. 128–29; Christ Ascended into Heaven, See. 129; N.B. Google book. By L. A. Lambert.]

Metzger, Bruce M. *The New Testament: Its Background, Growth, and Content*. Nashville: Abingdon, 1965. [The Resurrection and Ascension of Jesus Christ, See. 126–32]

Moffatt, James. *An Introduction to the Literature of the New Testament*. New York: Scribner's Sons, 1927. [Mark, See. 252–53; Resurrection—narratives in Matthew, See. 254–55; in the Fourth gospel, See. 536]

Neill, Stephen. *The Interpretation of the New Testament 1861–1961*. Oxford: Oxford University Press, 1966. [Resurrection of, See. 136, 181, 190, 226, 233–34, 249, 262, 267, 270–82, 286, 287]

Ochs, Christoph. *Matthaeus Adversus Christianos: The Use of the Gospel of Matthew in Jewish Polemics Against the Divinity of Jesus*. Tübingen: Mohr Siebeck. 2013. [See. 121–23; 164–65; 206; 312; N.B. This important work presents a survey of Jewish polemics refuting Jesus's claimed deity.]

Perrin, Norman. *The New Testament Proclamation and Parenesis, Myth and History*. 1974. New York: Harcourt Brace Jovanovich, 1974. [See 23, 32, 42, 94, 176, 199, 203]

Porter, J. R. *The Illustrated Guide to the Bible*. New York: Oxford University Press, 1995. [See. 208–12]

Pregeant, Russell. *Encounter with the New Testament An Interdisciplinary Approach*. Minneapolis: Fortress, 2009. [See. 4, 54, 94, 96, 122–23, 136–37, 156, 184–85]

———. *Engaging the New Testament An Interdisciplinary Approach*. Minneapolis: Fortress, 1995. [Chapter 4 The Resurrection Faith and the Expanded Tradition, 137–44]

Price, James L. *The New Testament: Its History and Theology*. Revised ed. New York: MacMillan, 1987. [The Resurrection of Jesus, See. 239–42]

Rae, Murray A. *History and Hermaneutics*. London: T&T Clark, 2005. [Chapter 4 The Resurrection, See. 68–91; N.B. This excellent chapter is a must read!]

Rall, Harris Franklin. *New Testament History: A Study of the Beginnings of Christianity.* New York: Abingdon, 1914. [Chapter 21 The Beginnings of the Church, See. 139–42; N.B. Archive.org, Google book, and HathiTrust]

Richardson, Alan. *An Introduction to the Theology of the New Testament.* New York: Harper & Brothers, 1958. [Chapter 9 The Resurrection, Ascension and Victory of Christ, See. 190–200]

Robertson, A. T. *Studies in the New Testament.* Nashville: Broadman, 1949. [Chapter 7 The Resurrection of Jesus, 89–99; N.B. Robertson provides a brief review of the resurrection narratives.]

Schreiner, Thomas R. *New Testament Theology: Magnifying God in Christ.* Grand Rapids: Baker Academic, 2008. [The Resurrection of Jesus, See. 104–8; also See. 274–76; Jesus as Resurrected Lord, See. 291–94]

Selby, Donald J. *Introduction to the New Testament: The Word Became Flesh.* New York: Macmillan, 1971. [See. 109–10, 147–48, 193–94, 260–61, 291–92]

Sell, Henry T. *Studies in the Four Gospels, the Master Books of the World.* 1917 [See. 20, 60–61, 87, 122–23, 156; N.B. Google book. Very superficial material.]

Smith, William, ed. *A Smaller Scripture History in Three Parts.* New York: Harper & Brothers, 1871. [Chapter 26 The Resurrection and Ascension of Christ, See. 299–306; N.B. Google book]

Spivey, Robert A., and D. Moody Smith. *Anatomy of the New Testament: A Guide to Its Structure and Meaning.* 2nd ed. New York: Macmillan, 1974. [The Resurrection of Jesus of Nazareth. See. 237–48]

Stauffer, Ethelbert. *New Testament Theology.* Translated by John Marsh. London: SCM, 1955. [Chapter 32 The Resurrection, See. 135–37; Chapter 33 The Ascension, See. 137–39]

Strauss, Mark L. *Four Portraits, One Jesus: A Survey of Jesus and the Gospels.* Grand Rapids: Zondervan, 2007. [Chapter 20 The Resurrection of Jesus, See. 511–23]

Strong, Augustus H. *Popular Lectures on the Books of the New Testament.* Philadelphia: Griffith & Rowland, 1914. [See. 56–57, 64, 99, 139–40, 166; N.B. Archive.org and Google book]

Tanner, Obert C., et al. *Toward Understanding the New Testament.* Salt Lake City: Signature, 1990. [Chapter 10 The Passion and the Resurrection, See. 240–51]

Towns, Elmer L., and Ben Gutierrez, eds. *The Essence of the New Testament: A Survey.* Nashville: B&H, 2012. [Resurrection, See. 103, 154; Resurrection appearances, See. 109–10, 114, 277, 304]

Wendt, Hans Hinrich. *The Teaching of Jesus.* Vol. 2. Translated by John Wilson. New York: Scribner's Sons, 1892. [Resurrection After Three Days, See. 265–69; N.B. Archive.org]

Wenham, David, and Steve Walton. *Exploring the New Testament A Guide to the Gospels & Acts.* 2nd ed. Downers Grove, IL: IVP Academic, 2011. [See. 51, 53, 57, 61, 85, 137, 138, 140, 144, 145, 146, 162–63, 175, 178, 184, 186–87, 194, 195, 203, 207, 211, 213, 223, 225, 237, 247, 283, 288, 308, 309]

Names Index

A

Aarde, Andries van, 211
Aaron, Daryl, 405
Abanes, Richard, 85
Abbadie, James, 211
Abbey, Merrill R., 383
Abbott, Lyman, 85, 161, 275, 294, 313, 328, 350, 493
'Abd al 'Ātī, Hammūda, 475
Abdul-Haqq, Abdiyah Akbar, 463
Abell, Dave, 85
Aberly, John, 350
Abernethy, Arthur Talmage, 383
Abogunrin, Samuel Oyinloye, 365
Aborn, Thomas Lintill, 294
Abraham, A. J., 463
Accad, Foud Elias, 463
Acharya, S. (pseud. M. Murdock), 47
Achtemeier, Paul J., 275, 493, 529
Acker, Jones Miles, 511
Ackerman, David A., 365
Adam, Karl, 211
Adam, Thomas, 450
Adamczewski, Bartosz, 275, 294, 313
Adams, Alice Dana, 85
Adams, Charles C., 161
Adams, Frank O., 211
Adams, Hannah, 85
Adams, Jay Edward, 275
Adams, Jonathan, 211
Adams, Michelle Medlock, 65
Adamson, Thomas, 211
Adeney, Walter F., 313
Addis, William E., 493
Addison, James Thayer, 463
Addison, Joseph, 85
African Christian Press, 463
Aggett, Michael John, 511
Agnostic, An, 294
Ahmad, Ghulām, 475
Ahmad, Khwaja Nazir, 475
Ahmad, Tahir, 475
Ahmed, Hamoud Maamiry, 475
Ahurwendeire, Athanasius Mugarra, 511
Aiken, Charles Augustus, 85
Aikman, David, 85
Ajijola, Adeleke Dirisu, 204, 475
Akaabiam, Terwase H., 313
Akin, Daniel L., 211, 275
Akyol, Mustafa, 475
Albahri, Yasser, 475
Albrecht, G. Jerome, 294
Albright, William Foxwell, 294
Albro, John A., 147
Alcock, George Augustus, 439
Alden, Isabella McDonald, 161
Alden, Joseph, 85
Aldrich, J. K., 3
Aldwinckle, Russell F., 211
Aletheia, M. D. (pseud.), 47
Alexander, Archibald, 85, 405, 493
Alexander, David, 493
Alexander, Dennis, 147
Alexander, Gross, 161
Alexander, J. H., 211
Alexander, Joseph A., 275, 294, 350
Alexander, Loveday, 350
Alexander, T. Desmond, 493
Alexander, William, 86
Alfors, Quinten Hans Peter, 511
Algar, H., 439
Algar, Hamid, 475
Alger, William Rounseville, 75
Ali, Daniel, 463
Ali, Maulana Muhammad, 475–76
Ali, Maulvi Muhammad, 463
Alington, Cyril, 405
Alkhuli, Muhammad Ali, 476
Alkier, Stefan, 3
Al Kindy, Abd al Masih ibn Ishak, 463
Allard, Daniel, 161

Names Index

Allberry, Sam, 3
Alleman, Herbert C., 313, 328
Allen, Andrew James Campbell, 350
Allen, Charles Livingstone, 161
Allen, Charlotte, 161
Allen, Clifton Judson, 493
Allen, David M., 161
Allen, Diogenes, 405
Allen, Don (pseud. Hiram L. True), 43
Allen, E. L., 405
Allen, Ethan, 47, 127
Allen, Frank Emmett, 350
Allen, Jerry, 313
Allen, Nicholas Peter Legh, 211, 511
Allen, O. Wesley, 3, 294, 313
Allen, Paul Marshall, 328
Allen, Ronald J., 161, 350
Allen, Thomas, 161
Allen, Willoughby C., 275, 294
Allison, Dale C., 3, 161, 267, 294, 511
Allison, Gregg R., 405
Allix, Pierre, 86
Alston, William P., 241
Alsup, John E., 3
Alter, Michael J., 43, 485
Altizer, Thomas J. J., 405
Amberley, John Russell, viscount, 127
Ambrose, 313
Ambrosiaster, 365
Ambruzi, Aloysius, 211
Amery, Heather, 65
Ames, William, 405
Anders, Isabel, 65
Anders, Max E., 405
Anderson-Berry, David, 350
Anderson, Charles, 241
Anderson, Charles C., 162
Anderson, Don, 3
Anderson, Douglas W., 511
Anderson, Edward, 294
Anderson, Hugh, 162, 275
Anderson, J. N. D., 86
Anderson, Kevin L., 3, 313
Anderson, Norman, 86, 241
Anderson, Paul N., 241
Anderson, Robert T., 405
Anderson, Tawa Jon, 511
Anderson, William A., 294, 328
Andjelic, Milenko A., 511
Andrewes, Lancelot, 3, 439
Andrews, H. T., 350
Andrews, Richard, 127
Andrews, Samuel J., 162, 406
Andrews, Thomas, 86
Angeles, Peter A., 493

Angus, Joseph, 162
Angus, William, 162
Ankerberg, John F., 3, 86, 241, 406, 463
Annet, Peter, 43, 47, 127
Ansari, Muhammad Fazl-ur-Rahman, 476
Anthony, Michael J., 493
Anyabwile, Thabiti, 464
Apostolos-Cappadona, Diane, 493
Applebury, T. R., 313, 365
Appleton, George, 328
Aquinas, Thomas, 241, 295, 328
Aradi, Zsolt, 147
Archer, Gleason L., 86
Archer-Shepherd, E. H., 4
Arenobine, Robert D., 512
Argyle, A. W., 295
Armstrong, C. B., 86
Armstrong, C. J., 241
Armstrong, Garner Ted, 162
Armstrong, William Park, 4
Arndt, William F., 313, 406
Arnold, Clinton E., 350
Arnold, John Muehleisen, 464
Arnold, Thomas, 406, 439
Arnot, William, 350
Arraj, Jim, 4
Arrington, French L., 350, 365, 406
Aruṇ, 204
Asad, Muhammad, 476
Ash, Anthony Lee, 313, 350
Ashcraft, Janice, 328
Asher, Jeffrey R., 365
Ashton, John, 328
Ashwin-Siejkowski, Piotr, 383
Asimov, Isaac, 127, 450
Aslan, Reza, 204
Assfy, Zaid H., 476
Astley, Jeff, 406
Ataie, Ali, 476
⊠Ataur-Rahim, Muhammad, 476
Athanasius, Saint, 406
Atkins, J. D., 512
Atkins, Peter, 4
Atkinson, Amanda Catherine, 512
Atkinson, David John, 494
Atrott, Hans, 127
Atterbury, Lewis, 439
Attridge, Harold W., 241, 328, 494
Attwater, Donald, 494
Atwater, John Birdseye, 162
Atwill, Joseph, 47
Auberlen, Carl August, 406
Augsburger, Myron S., 4, 295, 328
Augustine, Aurelius, 328
Aulén, Gustaf, 212, 406

Aurelio, John, 75, 162
Aus, Roger David, 43, 328
Austin, B. F., 4
Austin, E. L. C., 4
Austin, Mary, 162
Avalos, Hector, 48, 127, 267
Avant, John, 65
Avery, Margaret, 365
Avis, Paul D. L., 4, 241
Aye, Noel Saw Naw, 512
Aykol, Mustafa, 476
Aymer, Margaret, 350
Ayo, Nicholas, 383
Ayoub, Mahmoud, 476
Ayre, John, 494
Azunah, John, 464

B

Baban, Octavian D., 313
Babcock, James F., 241
Bacchiocchi, Samuele, 4
Bachelard, Sarah, 65
Backemeyer, Frederick William, 383
Bacon, Benjamin Wisner, 275, 328
Baden, Robert, 65
Bader, Joanne, 65
Badham, Paul, 242, 406
Badke, William B., 406
Badre-i-Alam, Muhammad, 476
Badre, Muhammad, 476
Bae, Sungjin, 512
Baggett, David, 242
Baggett, John, 212
Baggott, L. J., 87, 383
Bahnsen, Greg L., 87
Baigent, Michael, 48, 127, 204
Bailey, John Amedee, 313, 329
Bailey, Kenneth E., 365
Bailey, R. F., 329
Bailie, Gil, 87
Baird, Andrew Cumming, 383
Baird, William, 365
Baker, Charles F., 350, 406
Baker, Charles Richard, 383
Baker, Daniel, 439
Baker, John Austin, 406
Baker, Septina, 162
Baker, William R., 365
Balabat, Janina, 212
Balasundaram, Sunil, 512
Balchin, Frank Kenneth, 512
Baldwin, Louis J., 162
Balentine, Samuel Eugene, 212
Balfour, Frederic H., 48, 128
Balge, Richard D., 350
Ball, Richard J., 512
Ball, T. H., 314
Ballard, Frank, 87, 147
Ballentine, Elodie, 512
Ballou, Robert O., 48, 128
Balmforth, Henry, 314
Balsiger, David W., 4
Balthasar, Hans Urs von, 4, 383
Baly, Denis, 406
Balz, Horst Robert, 494
Bancroft, Emery H., 406
Bang, S. S., 512
Banks, John S., 406
Banks, William L., 4
Bannerman, James, 4
Barackman, Floyd H., 407
Barber, Cyril J., 512
Barberis, Bruno, 212
Barbieri, Louis, 275
Barclay, John M. G., 242
Barclay, Oliver R., 87
Barclay, Robert, 87
Barclay, William, 87, 147, 162, 212, 275, 295, 314, 329, 351, 365, 383, 450, 529
Bard, Andreas, 61
Baring-Gould, S., 4, 48, 128, 384
Barker, Charles Joseph, 351
Barker, Dan, 48, 128
Barker, Gregory A., 162
Barker, Margaret, 4, 242
Barker, William Pierson, 295
Barkway, Lumsden, 384
Barnes, Albert, 275, 295, 314, 329, 351, 365, 450
Barnes, Arthur Stapylton, 211
Barnes, Charles Randall, 494
Barnett, Albert E., 275
Barnett, Henry C., 4
Barnett, Maurice, 242
Barnett, Paul, 61, 87, 163, 242, 365, 529
Barnett, Walter, 163
Barnhart, Bruno, 329
Barnhill, Gregory M., 512
Barnhouse, Donald Grey, 4, 275, 329, 351
Baron, David, 483
Barr, Beth Allison, 351
Barr, John, 494
Barr, O. Sydney, 384
Barrell, E. V., 314
Barrett, B. F., 407
Barrett, C. K., 329, 351, 365

Names Index

Barrow, Isaac, 398, 439
Barrows, Charles H., 163
Barry, Alfred, 87
Barry, F. R., 87
Barry, J. G. H., 384
Barsness, Todd, 65
Barth, C. G., 451
Barth, Karl, 75, 384, 407
Barth, Markus, 4
Bartholomew, David J., 87, 407
Bartholomew, Gilbert L., 329
Bartlet, J. Vernon, 351
Bartlett, Clarence, 163
Bartlett, David Lyon, 5, 147
Barton, Bruce B., 295, 314, 329, 366
Barton, George A., 163
Barton, James L., 464
Barton, John, 4
Barton, Stephen C., 4
Barton, V. Wayne, 329
Barton, William E., 5, 163
Basetti-Sani, Giulio, 464
Bass, John, 163
Basser, Herbert, 295
Bassler, Jouette, 366
Bast, David, 5
Bastow, James Austin, 494
Bate, George, 87
Battenhouse, Henry Martin, 163
Bauckham, Richard, 212, 242
Bauer, David R., 295
Bauer, Johannes Baptist, 494
Bauerschmidt, Frederick Christian, 398
Baugher, H. Louis, 314
Bauman, Edward W., 163
Baumgarten, M., 351
Baumler, Gary P., 329
Bavinck, Herman, 407
Bawer, Bruce, 407
Bayer, Hans F., 286, 512
Bayes, Jonathan F., 384
Baxter, Batsell Barrett, 87
Baxter, Margaret, 163
Baxter, Richard, 87
Beach, Curtis, 275
Beard, Arthur, 5
Beard, J. R., 87, 407
Beardslee, William A., 365
Beardsley, Frank Grenville, 147
Beare, Francis Wright, 295
Beasley-Murray, George Raymond, 5, 329, 439
Beattie, James, 88
Beattie, Tina, 242
Beauchamp, William, 88, 212
Beaumont, I. Mark, 464

Beaven, James, 398
Beavis, Mary Ann, 275, 494
Beck, Dwight Marion, 529
Beck, W. E., 351
Beck, William F., 61, 163
Becker, C. H., 464
Beckman, Beverly Ann, 65
Beckwith, Clarence Augustine, 407
Beckwith, Francis J., 88, 147
Bede, the Venerable, Saint, 351
Beeching, H. C., 384
Beechler, Donald J., 512
Beeck, Frans Josef van, 212
Beers, V. Gilbert, 65
Beet, Joseph Agar, 88, 366, 407
Beets, Henry, 384
Beiler, Irwin Ross, 163
Beinert, Wolfgang, 398, 494
Beisner, E. Calvin, 88
Beke, Charles, 212
Belknap, Jeremy, 5
Bell, B. Clayton, 88
Bell, G. K. A., 384
Bell, Nancy, 212
Bell, William S., 43, 48, 128
Belle, Gilbert van, 329
Bellett, J. G., 451
Belser, Joh Evang, 5, 163
Bence, Philip A., 351
Ben-Chorin, Schalom, 485
Bendoraitis, Kristian A., 295
Benedetto, Robert, 494
Benedict, David, 464
Benedict, George, 483
Benedict XVI (pope), 5, 163
Benesch, Friedrich, 5
Bengalee, Mutiur Rahman, 476
Bengel, Johann Albrecht, 276, 295, 314, 329, 351, 366
Benham, William, 351, 494
Benjamin, David Eugene, 512
Benjamin, Joshua M., 48
Bennema, Cornelis, 329
Bennett, Clinton, 464
Bennett, D. M., 48, 128
Bennett, James, 156, 164
Bennett, W. H., 276
Benoit, Pierre, 5
Benson, C., 88, 164
Benson, Clarence H., 407
Benson, Dennis C., 276, 295, 314, 329, 351, 451
Benson, Edward White, 351
Benson, George, 5
Benson, Joseph, 365

Names Index

Benson, Richard Meux, 5
Benson, Robert Hugh, 398
Bentham, Jeremy, 48
Bentley, Michael, 314
Benton, Angelo Ames, 494
Benware, Paul N., 314
Berard, Wayne-Daniel, 276
Berardino, Angelo Di, 494
Bercot, David W., 495
Bergen, John Tallmadge, 88
Berger, Alan L., 485
Berger, David, 485
Berger, Peter L., 384
Bergesen, David E., 512
Bergh van Eysinga, G. A. van den, 529
Bergquist, James Alan, 512
Bergt, Carolyn S., 65
Berguer, Georges, 164
Berkeley, James P., 329
Berkhof, Hendrikus, 407
Berkhof, Louis, 407
Berkouwer, G. C., 407
Berna, Kurt (pseud.), 43, 267
Bernard, David K., 407
Bernard, Henry Norris, 164
Bernard, J. H., 212, 242, 330
Bernard, Pierre R., 5, 164
Bernis, Jonathan, 483
Berquist, Millard J., 366
Berthe, Augustin, 164
Bertolini, Dewey M., 295, 366
Berwick, G. J. *See* Indian Officer., 134
Besant, Annie, 48, 128–29, 204, 235
Bessler, Joseph A., 164
Best, Alexander, 512
Best, Ernest, 276
Best, John H., 147
Bethune-Baker, James Franklin, 164, 384
Betori, Giuseppe, 242
Betz, Hans Dieter, 495
Betzer, Dan, 439
Beutler, Johannes, 242
Bevan, Hubert Basil Henry, 512
Bevan, William, 6
Beveridge, William, 398, 439
Bewes, Richard, 6
Bible, Andrew F., 6
Bibza, James, 513
Bickel, Bruce, 88, 408, 464
Bickel, Stan, 366
Bickerman, E. J., 485
Bickersteth, Edward, 276, 398
Bieringer, Reimund, 6, 242
Biffi, Inos, 65
Bigland, John, 6
Bilezikian, Gilbert G., 408
Billington, Rachel, 65
Billon, B. M., 212
Billroth, Gustav, 366
Binder, Amy, 65
Bingham, Richard, 212
Bingham, Rowland V., 295
Binney, Amos, 408, 451
Bin Shamoon, Yahya, 464
Binz, Stephen J., 6, 276
Bird, Charles John, 384
Bird, Michael F., 164, 212, 408
Bird, Robert, 164
Birks, Thomas Rawson, 408
Biser, Eugen, 6
Bishop, Eric F. F., 351, 529
Bishop, Hugh, 6
Bisset, William, 164
Black, Allen, 242, 276
Black, C. Clifton, 276
Black, David Alan, 242
Blackaby, Henry T., 65
Blackburne, Gertrude Mary Ireland, 276
Blackford, Russell, 49, 129
Blaiklock, E. M., 88, 314, 351
Blaine, Bradford B., 329
Blair, Edward Payson, 351
Blair, J. Allen, 366
Blair, Joe, 529
Blanchard, John, 61, 88
Blanchard, Leo, 513
Blanchard, W., 495
Blank, Josef, 329
Blank, Reiner, 513
Blatchford, Robert, 48, 129
Blenkinsopp, Joseph, 366
Bligh, John, 6, 330
Blight, Richard C., 276, 314
Bliss, George R., 314
Bloesch, Donald G., 75, 408
Blomberg, Craig, 88, 295, 330, 366, 529
Blomfield, Ezekiel, 164
Blount, Brian K., 276
Blumenfeld, Donald E., 513
Blumenstein, John Max., 513
Blunt, A. W. F., 276, 352
Blunt, Henry, 164
Blunt, John Henry, 495
Blunt, John J., 6
Blythe, Catherine, 65
Blyton, Enid, 66
Boa, Kenneth, 89, 408
Boardman, George Dana, 6
Board of Missionary Preparation, 464
Boateng, Kwasi, 513

Bobertz, Charles A., 276
Bock, Darrell L., 164-65, 243, 276, 314, 352
Bock, Emil, 165
Bockmuehl, Markus N. A., 165, 243
Bode, Edward Lynn, 6
Bodensieck, Julius, 495
Bodington, Eric James, 384
Body, George, 6
Boers, Hendrikus, 213
Boettner, Loraine, 212, 408
Boever, Richard A., 314
Boff, Leonardo, 6, 213
Bohnet, Eric C., 66
Boice, James Montgomery, 6, 295, 330, 352, 408
Boismard, Marie-Emile, 75
Bokenkotter, Thomas, 398
Bokser, Ben Zion, 485
Bold, T. A., 6
Boles, H. Leo., 295, 314
Bolt, Peter, 276
Bombaro, John J., 7
Bomford, Rodney, 89
Bonaventure, 165, 314, 330
Bond, B. W., 89
Bond, Helen K., 165
Bond, John, 314
Bonforte, John, 165
Bonnet, M. Charles, 89
Bonney, William, 330
Bonney, William L., 513
Bookhart, C. Franklin, 7
Bonnke, Reinhard, 7
Boomershine, Thomas E., 276, 513
Boomsma, Clarence, 89
Boon, Fiona, 66
Borchert, Gerald L., 213, 330
Borg, Marcus J., 7, 204, 235, 267, 276, 409
Borgman, Paul, 314
Boring M. Eugene, 213, 276-77, 295, 314, 330, 352, 366
Born, Adrianus Van den, 495
Bornhäeuser, Karl, 7, 165
Bornkamm, Günther, 165, 24
Bose, Ram Chandra, 89
Bosley, Harold A., 165
Boston, Thomas, 409
Bosworth, E. I. (Edward Increase), 165, 352
Bosworth, Thomas, 384
Bottome, Margaret, 61
Boully, James, 89
Bounds, Edward McKendree, 7
Bourdillon, Francis, 277
Bourgeault, Cynthia, 165
Bourgy, Paul, 7, 75

Bourke, Myles M., 61
Bourn, Samuel, 89, 440
Bouyer, Louis, 330, 495
Bovon, François, 165, 315
Bowden, Joan Chase, 66
Bowden, John, 243, 495
Bowen, Clayton Ray, 7, 75, 165
Bowers, G. M., 409
Bowie, Walter Russell, 166, 315
Bowker, John, 409, 495
Bowman, John, 277
Bowman, S. L., 89
Boxall, Ian, 295
Boyarin, Daniel, 485
Boyd, Gregory A., 89, 166, 213, 409, 529
Boyd, Robert T., 89
Boyer, James L., 366
Boyer, Mark G., 213
Boyse, Christopher, 61
Braaten, Carl E., 89, 213, 243, 409
Braden, Clark, 89, 166, 213
Bradlaugh, Charles, 49, 129
Bradlee, C. D., 440
Bradley, Mark Alan, 513
Bradley, Marshell Carl, 295
Bradley, Samuel Carlyle, 166
Bradshaw, Paul F., 243, 495
Bragg, Paul DeWitte, 513
Bragge, Francis, 147
Bramley, Henry Ramsden, 440
Brand, Chad, 495
Brandon, Samuel George Frederick, 495
Brands, Michael, 296, 513
Bradshaw, Paul F., 495
Branham, William, 440
Branick, Vincent P., 366
Branscomb, Bennett Harvie, 277
Brant, Jo-Ann A., 330
Brasher, Brenda E., 495
Braswell, George E., 464
Bratcher, Robert G., 277, 296, 315, 366
Braxton, Brad R., 366
Bray, Gerald, 366, 409
Bray, James Seddon, 513
Bray, John L., 440
Breckinridge, Robert J., 409
Brewster, John, 352
Bridger, Gordon, 330, 366
Bridger, J. Scott, 464
Briere, Elizabeth, 243
Brierley, Justin, 90
Briggs, Charles Augustus, 166, 213, 384
Bright, Bill, 213
Brighton, Louis A., 513
Briscoe, D. Stuart, 366, 385

Names Index

Broadhead, Edwin Keith, 277
Broadus, John A., 213, 277, 296
Broadus, John R., 440
Brock, Ann Graham, 243
Brock, Isaac, 385
Brock, Rita Nakashima, 409
Broderick, Robert C., 495
Brodie, Thomas L., 204, 330
Broeke, James Ten, 409
Bromiley, Geoffrey W., 495
Broocks, Rice, 409
Brooke, John Hanley, 155
Brooke, Stopford A., 398, 440
Brookes, James H., 7, 213
Brookins, Timothy A., 367
Brooks, James A., 277
Brooks, Phillip, 440
Brot, Keith A. La, 166
Broughton, William P., 7
Brouwer, Sigmund, 155
Brower, Kent E., 277
Brown, Abner, 440
Brown, Archibald G., 409
Brown, Brian Arthur, 464
Brown, Charles, 352
Brown, Colin, 148, 409, 495
Brown, David 1803–1897, 277, 315, 330, 352
Brown, David 1948–, 409
Brown, David 1922–1982, 410, 464–65
Brown, E. F., 367
Brown, George James, 330
Brown, Henry Clay, 409
Brown, J. Newton (John Newton), 496
Brown, James Baldwin, 7
Brown, Jeannine K., 296
Brown, John 1722–1787, 90, 166, 366, 398, 410, 496
Brown, Michael B., 410
Brown, Michael L., 483
Brown, Paul J., 75, 367
Brown, Raymond Bryan, 367
Brown, Raymond E., 7, 90, 243, 330, 529–30
Brown, Reagan, 243
Brown, Schuyler, 315
Brown, Simon, 213
Brown, S. Kent, 166
Brown, Thomas, 166
Brown, Thomas, Gent. of Blackheath, 166
Brown, William Adams, 409
Brown, William E., 90
Browne, Edward Harold, 398
Browne, Laurence Edward, 352
Browne, Sylvia, 49, 129, 166
Brownell, Philip, 243
Browning, W. R. F., 315, 496

Brownson, James V., 243
Brownson, O. A., 90
Brownson, William Clarence, 315
Bruce, Alexander Balmain, 90, 148, 440
Bruce, David, 7
Bruce, F. F., 214, 296, 331, 352, 367
Bruce, Michael, 385
Bruce, William, 296
Bruckberger, R. L., 166
Bruggen, Jakob van, 166, 214
Brumback, Carl, 8
Brundage, George, 66
Brundrit, Daniel Fernley, 8
Bruner, Frederick Dale, 296, 331
Brunk, George Rowland, 513
Brunner, Emil, 385, 410
Bryan, Christopher, 8
Bryan, David, 8
Bryan, Lyman, 8
Bryan, William Jennings, 90, 166, 410
Bryant, Al, 440, 496
Bryant, Beauford H., 331
Bryant, Robert A., 8
Bryant, Wilbur Franklin, 166
Bucaille, Maurice, 476
Buchanan, George Wesley, 296
Buck, Charles, 496
Buck, D. D., 8, 167
Buck, Deanna Draper, 66
Buckham, Allan, 66
Buckham, John Wright, 214
Buckland, Augustus Robert, 496
Buckridan, Rakib, 476
Budd, Leonard H., 8, 440
Buehner, Caralyn, 66
Buel, Samuel, 410
Buglass, Anthony E., 513
Buhring, Kurt, 410
Bulfinch, Stephen G., 90
Bullinger, E. W., 367
Bulst, Werner, 214
Bultmann, Rudolf, 331, 410
Burder, George, 440
Burdon, Christopher, 277
Burge, Gary, 243, 331
Burge, Ted, 148
Bürgener, Karsten, 8
Burgess, Andrew R., 8
Burgess, Beverly Capps, 66
Burgess, George, 75
Burgess, Isaac B., 167
Burgon, John William, 277, 315, 331
Burkart, Jeffrey E., 66
Burke, Albert Carswell, 513
Burke, Christopher P., 243

Burke, John J., 399
Burkitt, F. C., 167
Burn, A. E., 385
Burn, John Henry, 277
Burnaby, John, 385
Burnett, Gilbert, 399
Burnham, David, 315, 352
Burns, Cecil, 277
Burns, J., 167
Burns, Robert A., 465
Burnside, W. F. (Walter Fletcher), 315, 352
Burr, William Henry, 49, 129
Burrell, David James, 8, 214, 352, 385
Burrell, Maurice C., 410
Burridge, Richard, 244, 331
Burrows, Millar, 214, 410
Burton, Ernest DeWitt, 167, 277
Burton, Henry, 214, 315
Busenitz, Nathan, 90
Bush, George, 8, 76
Businger, L. C., 167
Bussche, Henri Van den, 331
Busse, Heribert, 465
Buswell, J. Oliver, 410
Butcher, Geoffrey, 66
Butcher, Henry W., 440
Butcher, John Beverley, 8
Butler, Daniel L., 513
Butler, J. Glentworth, 167, 451
Butler, John J., 410
Butler, Paul T., 367
Butler, Trent C., 315, 496
Butt, Kyle, 90
Butterworth, Mike, 244
Buttrick, David G., 8, 167
Buttrick, George Arthur, 90, 410, 496
By A Teacher, 189
Bynum, Caroline Walker, 75
Byrne, Brendan, 277, 296, 315, 331
Byrne, Pete, 496
Byrum, Russell R., 411
Byung-Mu, Ahn, 167

C

Cable, John H., 167
Cabrido, John Arana, 296
Cadman, Jas P., 167
Cadoux, Arthur Temple, 277
Cadoux, Cecil John, 49, 129, 167, 411
Cahill, Michael, 277
Cahill, Thomas, 167
Cain, Marvin Fay, 204
Caine, Hall, 205
Caird, G. B., 315, 411
Cairns, Alan, 496
Cairns, D. S., 148
Cairns, John, 90
Caldwell, John R., 367
Callan, Charles Jerome, 367, 399
Calmet, Augustin, 496
Calvin, John, 278, 296, 315, 352, 451
Cambon, Mark G., 411
Camp, Norman Harvey, 75
Campbell, Archibald, 90
Campbell, Charlie, 90
Campbell, Douglas, 49, 129
Campbell, George, 148
Campbell-Jack, Campbell, 496
Campbell, R. J., 167, 411
Campbell, Robert Allen, 167
Campbell, Ross Turner, 385
Campbell, Steuart, 49, 129
Campbell, Travis James, 244
Campbell, W. Hume, 385
Campbell, W. Thomas, 514
Campbell, William A., 49, 129
Canale, Andrew, 214
Candler, Warren Akin, 8, 90, 331, 385
Candlish, Robert S., 367, 440
Caner, Emir Fethi, 465
Caner, Ergun Mehmet, 91, 465
Cannon, Delores, 49, 130, 168
Cannon, William Ragsdale, 296, 315, 331, 352
Cantalamessa, Raniero, 9
Capps, Donald, 205, 267
Capt, E. Raymond, 9
Card, Michael, 168, 278, 296, 315, 331
Carey, Greg, 315
Carey, P. M., 91
Carey, S. Pearce, 168
Carlson, Jason, 244
Carlson, Norman E., 465
Carlston, Charles E., 296
Carlton, Matthew E., 278, 296, 315, 331, 353
Carmichael, Joel, 235
Carmichael, Lawrence Garten, 514
Carmody, John, 214, 411
Carmody, Timothy R., 278
Carnell, Edward John, 91, 411
Carnley, Peter, 9
Carotta, Francesco, 49, 130, 205
Carpenter, Boyd, 9
Carpenter, Lant, 214, 399
Carpenter, Russell Lant, 214
Carpenter, S. C., 367
Carr, Arthur, 296, 315

Names Index

Carr, Wesley A., 496
Carrier, Richard, 49, 130, 205, 267
Carrington, Philip, 168, 278
Carroll, B. H., 451
Carroll, John, 214, 316
Carroll, Patrick J., 168
Carroll, Warren H., 214
Carson, D. A., 9, 214, 296 331
Carson, Mary Catherine, 514
Carter, Charles Sydney, 496
Carter, Charles W., 353
Carter, James E., 331
Carter, Warren, 278, 297, 331, 353, 367
Cartledge, Samuel A., 168
Carver, William Owen, 353
Cascioli, Luigi, 205
Case, Shirley Jackson, 168
Case-Winters, Anna, 297
Casey, Maurice, 168, 204, 331
Caspari, Charles Edward, 168
Cassels, Louis, 168, 214, 411
Cassels, Walter R., 50, 130, 156
Cassidy, Richard J., 331
Cassini, Charles, 465
Catchpole, David , 9
Catholic Church, 399
Cattermole, R., 9, 440
Caudill, R. Paul, 367
Cauthen, Kenneth, 411
Cauthron, Halbert A., 514
Cavanaugh, Joseph H., 399
Cave, Sydney, 353
Cavin, Robert Greg, 50, 268, 514
Cawley, Frederick, 214
Cecil, Douglas M., 514
Cecilia, Madame, 9, 316, 331, 353
Cell, Charles W., 168
Celsus. *See* Origen., 50, 56, 112
Chadwick, G. A., 278
Chadwick, Henry, 411
Chadwick, John White, 168
Chafer, Lewis Sperry, 411
Chaffey, Tim, 9
Chafin, Kenneth, 367
Chalakkal, Sebastian, 9, 514
Challoner, Richard, 451
Chalmers, R. C. , 411
Chalmers, Thomas, 91, 451
Chamberlain, Paul , 91, 412
Chamberlain, Thomas, 440
Chambers, Catherine, 60
Chamblin, J. Knox, 297
Chambré, A., 385
Chance, J. Bradley, 353
Chandler, Samuel, 9
Chapman, Colin, 91, 412, 465
Chapman, Edwin, 168
Chapman, Raymond, 9, 61
Chappell, Clovis G., 353
Chappell, Wallace D., 1, 26
Charles, Elizabeth Rundle, 9
Charlesworth, James H., 10, 168
Charley, Julian, 496
Charry, Ellen T., 412
Chase, Frederic Henry, 61, 385, 451
Chatham, Joshua G., 214, 530
Chauke, E., 367
Cheney, Johnston M., 168
Chennattu, Rekha M., 331
Chevrot, Georges, 10
Chew, J. A., 66
Childers, Charles L., 316
Childs, Brevard S., 530
Childs, Hal, 514
Chitavath, Babu, 514
Cho, James, 514
Choice Notes on the Gospel of S. John, 332
Choice Notes on the Gospel of S. Luke, 316
Choice Notes on the Gospel of S. Mark, 278
Choice Notes on the Gospel of S. Matthew, 297
Chojnacki, Stanislaw, 10
Chosen People Ministries, 483
Choudhury, Paramesh, 205, 476
Chrispin, Gerald, 10
Christian Foundation, 278
Christian Witness Among Muslims, 465
Christlieb, Theodore, 91
Chrysostom, John, 297, 353, 367
Chrysostom, John, Brother, 399
Chubb, Thomas, 50, 130, 156
Chumbley, Kenneth L., 412
Chun, Kyung-Yun, 514
Chung, Chi, 66
Chung-Kim, Esther, 353
Chun, Kyung-Yun, 514
Churchill, A. D., 514
Church, Leslie F., 169
Church of Jesus Christ of Latter-Day Saints, The, 169, 399
Chute, Wayne, 514
Ciampa, Roy E., 368
Cinquemani, Nicolò, 214
Cishtī, Yūsuf Salīm, 385, 476
Cladder, Herman J., 297
Clare, Maurice (pseud.), 385
Clark, Albert Curtis, 353
Clark, Braden, 169
Clark, Daniel, 10
Clark, Dennis E., 169
Clark, George W., 278, 297, 316, 332, 353, 368

Clark, Gordon H., 368
Clark, Henry W., 332
Clark, Horace, 169
Clark, K. S. L., 316
Clark, Malcolm, 465
Clark, Mark, 91
Clark, Neville, 10
Clark, William R., 91
Clarke, Adam, 169, 368, 412, 451
Clarke, Howard W., 297
Clarke, James Freeman, 50, 91, 130
Clarke, John, 44, 50, 130, 235
Clarke, Laurence, 169
Clarke, Richard F., 61
Clarke, Rufus, 214
Clarke, William Kemp Lowther, 530
Clarke, William Newton, 278, 412
Claudel, Paul, 385
Claussen, Carsten, 244
Clayton, Philip, 148
Clemen, Carl, 214
Clements, Tad S., 156
Clergy Centre (London), 91
Cleveland, Rich, 10
Clifford, Ross, 10, 91
Close, Henry T., 412
Cloud, David W., 496
Cloud, Gilbert A., 514
Clow, W. M., 169
Clowes, J., 148, 278, 297, 316
Clutterbuck, Ivan, 316
Clymer, R. Swinburne, 297, 332
Coakley, Sarah, 244
Cobb, Jimmy Hickman, 514
Cobb, Laurel K., 278
Cobb, Sylvanus, 451
Cobb, William. F., 385
Cochrane, Charles C., 215
Cochrane, James, 76, 368
Cock, W. H., 215
Cockin, George S., 169
Coggins, R. J., 497
Cogitans, John, 91
Cohen, Joseph, 485
Cohn-Sherbok, Dan, 268, 485–86, 497
Cohon, Beryl D., 486
Cole, C. Donald, 386, 412
Cole, Mary L., 244
Cole, R. A., 278
Coleman, Lyman, 368
Coleman, Michael Edward, 412
Coleman, Sheila Schuller, 66
Coleridge, Henry James, 169
Coles, George, 92
Colet, John, 368

Colgrave, Bertram, 92
Collinge, William J., 497
Collingwood, C., 215
Collins, Anthony, 10
Collins, Francis S., 148
Collins, John J., 497
Collins, Mary, 497
Collins, Raymond F., 368
Collyer, William Bengo, 148, 465
Colquhoun, Frank, 92
Columbine, William Brailsford, 50, 130
Comblin, Joseph, 10
Comfort, Philip Wesley, 332, 451
Committee of Publication for The American Sunday-School Union, 278
Common English Bible, 497
Compendious Dictionary of the Holy Bible, A, 493
Compton-Rickett, Joseph, 215
Conaty, Thomas James, 169
Concise Routledge Encyclopedia of Philosophy, 497
Concordia Publishing House, 497
Conder, Eustace Rogers, 169, 297, 412
Conley, Toney A., 514
Connelly, Douglas, 514
Conner, J. M., 412
Conner, Robert P., 44, 130, 235
Conner, W. T., 10, 412
Cooney, James Matthew, 515
Connick, C. Milo, 169, 530
Considine, Thomas, 61
Conway, Bobby, 92
Conzelmann, Hans, 316, 353, 368
Cook, David, 92, 353
Cook, F. C., 353, 451–52
Cook, George, 10, 61
Cook, Michael J., 268, 486
Cook, Michael L., 169
Cook, P. (Peter), 215
Cook, Richard B., 169
Cooke, Greville, 170
Cooke, Richard Joseph, 76
Cooke, William, 412
Cooley, William Forbes, 170
Cooney, James Matthew, 515
Cooper, Anne, 465
Cooper, Charles D., 170
Cooper, Henry, 244
Cooper, John M., 399
Cooper, Robert, 50, 130
Cooper, Rodney L., 278
Cooper, Thomas, 10, 92
Copan, Paul, 92, 244, 497
Copenhaver, Martin B., 412

Coplestone, F. S., 465
Cordelier, John, 170
Cornélis, H., 76
Cornell, George W., 170
Cornell, Vincent J., 465
Corner, David, 148
Corner, Mark, 148
Cornfeld, Gaalyahu, 170, 497
Cornish, Rick, 92
Corrigan, Michael Augustine, 451
Cortes Fuentes, David, 515
Corwin, Edward Tanjore, 441
Cory, Catherine A., 399
Cory, John Ream, 515
Cotes, Mary, 244
Cottam, Joseph Almond, 412
Cotter, Wendy, 244
Cottrell, Jack, 412
Couch, Mal, 316, 353
Coughlin, Charles E., 441
Counet, Patrick Chatelion, 332
Counsell, Michael, 497
Countryman, Louis William, 332
Counts, Bill, 170, 215
Courduan, Winfried, 92
Cousar, Charles B., 412, 530
Courtney, Claudia, 66
Covel, James, 497
Coverdale, Myles, 399
Covington, Nicholas, 44
Cowan, Steven B., 92, 244
Cowgill, Frank Brooks, 170
Cowles, Henry, 278, 297, 316, 332, 353
Cowley-Brown, George James, 170
Cowley, Joy, 66
Cowley, Matthias F., 412
Cox, David, 412
Cox, George Ernest Pritchard, 297
Cox, Harvey, 170
Cox, Jennifer Ann, 76
Cox, Lilian E., 353
Cox, Ronald J., 170
Cox, Samuel, 10, 368
Cox, Steven Lynn, 278
Coyle, Robert Francis, 385
Coyne, Jerry A., 130, 156
Craddock, Fred B., 316, 332
Cragg, Kenneth A., 244, 465
Craig, Clarence Tucker, 215
Craig, William Lane, 10–11, 50, 92–93, 131
Crain, Sellers S., 297
Crane, Steven A., 278
Cranfield, C. E. B., 245, 279, 386
Cranfield, Thomas, 11
Crapps, Robert W., 530

Craveri, Marcello, 170
Crawford, C. C., 413
Crawford, Dan R., 11
Crawford, Robert G., 148
Creager, John A., 413
Crean, Thomas, 93
Cree, Robert, 93
Creed, John Martin, 316
Cresson, Warder, 486
Cresswell, Peter, 50, 131
Crim, Keith R., 497
Crissey, Clair M., 297
Criswell, W. A., 245, 297, 353
Crockett, Clayton, 245
Cromie, Richard M., 11
Cronk, Malcolm R., 441
Crooker, Joseph Henry, 50, 131, 170
Crooll, Rabbi Joseph, 93
Crosby, Howard, 170
Crosby, Michael, 332
Croscup, George E., 170
Cross, Frank Leslie, 497
Crossan, John Dominic, 11, 50–51, 131, 205, 268
Crosse, Charles H., 93
Crossley, James G., 235, 268
Crossley, John, 465
Croswell, Laurence, 11
Crotty, Nicholas, 515
Crowder, Bill, 11
Crowe, Jerome, 354
Cruz, Arthur, 51
Crysdale, Cynthia S. W., 215
Cucarella, Diego R. Sarrió, 477
Cukrowski, Kenneth L., 316, 354
Cully, Iris V., 497
Culpepper, R. Alan, 246, 279, 316, 332
Culver, Robert Duncan, 11, 170, 413
Culy, Martin M., 316, 354
Cumming, John, 279, 297, 316
Cumming, Joseph L., 246, 268, 465, 477
Cummings, Brad, 11
Cummings, J. A., 452
Cumo, Christopher, 170
Cunningham, Phillip J., 171, 279
Currer-Briggs, Noel, 215
Curtis, Arthur Herbert, 171
Curtis, Olin Alfred, 413
Custance, Arthur C., 413
Custer, Stewart, 354
Cutner, Herbert, 50, 131, 205
Cutts, Edward Lewes, 171
Cyril of Alexandria, 316, 332

D

Dabney, J. P., 279, 297, 316, 332, 354, 368
Dabney, R. L., 413
Dagg, J. L., 413
Dahl, M. E., 368
Dake, Finis, 452
Dale, Alan T., 66, 171
Dale, Robert William, 76
Daleiden, Joseph L., 51, 131
Dalferth, Ingolf U., 413
Dallas, H. A., 171
Dallmann, William, 171
Dammrose, Gary L., 515
Damon, Louis A., 171
Daniel, Elinor Perkins, 515
Daniel, Monodeep, 298, 368
Daniel, Norman, 465
Daniélou, Jean, 413
Daniel-Rops, Henri, 171
Daniels, Kenneth W., 51, 131
Danin, Avinoam, 215
Danker, Frederick W., 316
Danove, Paul L., 279
Darby, J. N., 279, 316, 332, 368, 452
Darden, Bob, 171
Dardess, George, 466
Darlison, Bill, 76
Darms, Anton, 332
Darrow, Floyd L., 156
David, Juliet, 66
Davidson, Alice Joyce, 66
Davie, Martin, 246, 497
Davies, Brian, 413
Davies, E. O., 148
Davies, J., 279, 298, 317, 332, 354
Davies, J. G., 11, 498
Davies, Margaret, 298
Davies, Rupert E., 246, 368, 386
Davies, W. D., 298, 530
Davis, Charles, 413
Davis, J. D., 93
Davis, John, 66
Davis, John D., 498
Davis, Joy Morgan, 66
Davis, Noah K., 171
Davis, Patricia L., 515
Davis, Robert, 66
Davis, Singleton Water, 76
Davis, Stephen T., 12, 93, 246, 413
Davis, Will, 93
Davis, William Hersey, 298
Dawe, Donald G., 12, 215
Dawes, Gregory W., 51, 131, 171
Dawson, Gerrit Scott, 12

Dawson, Ralph, 12
Dawson, R. Dale, 12, 413
Dawson, William J., 171
Day, E. Hermitage, 12
Day, Gardiner M., 386
Day, Jim, 515
Daybell, Chad, 66
D'Costa, Gavin, 11, 246
Dean, David A., 76
Dean, Robert James, 93, 317, 368
Deane, Anthony C., 171
Deane-Drummond, Celia, 215
De Bary, Richard, 215
De Broer, Esther A., 246
De Boer, Martinus C., 246
De Candole, H. L. C. V., 93
Decker, Donald F., 515
Decker, Rodney J., 279
Deedat, Ahmed, 51, 61, 477
Deems, Charles F., 171, 332
Defence of Natural and Revealed Religion, A, 93
De Freitas, Elizabeth A., 515
DeHaan, M. R., 368
DeHaan, Richard W., 441
Deibert, Richard I., 279
Deichmann, Hilda Elizabeth Greifrau von, 333
Deigloriam, A. M., 148
Deist, Ferdinand, 498
Dell, J. A., 93
Delling, Gerhard, 246
Delobel, Joël, 246
Delorme, Jean, 246
Deluz, Gaston, 368
Demaray, Donald E., 354
Demarest, Bruce A., 215
DeMent, Byron Hoover, 215
DeMoss, Matthew S., 498
Denaux, Adelbert, 246
Denney, James, 171, 215, 413
Denny, Walter Bell, 171
Denton, W., 354
Deppe, Dean B., 279
Derickson, Gary W., 333
De Ridder, Richard R., 298
Derrett, J. Duncan M., 12, 268, 279
Deshmukh, Ibrahimkhan O., 466
DeSilva, David A., 530
Dessain, C. S., 354
Detzler, Wayne A., 530
Devine, Arthur, 386
Devivier, Walter, 93, 399
Dewar, Daniel, 93, 413

Names Index

De Welt, Don, 354
De Wesselow, Thomas, 215
Dewey, Arthur J., 268
Dewey, Joanna, 279
DeWitt, Dan, 215
De Wohl, Louis, 93
Dhanis, Édouard, 12
Dharmaraj, Glory E., 466
Dialogue Between Islam and Christianity, 477
Dibble, Charles Lemuel, 93
Dibelius, Martin, 215
Dick, John, 354, 414
Dickens, Charles, 172
Dickerman, Benoni, 215
Dickie, John, 414
Dickinson, Richard William, 12
Dickson, David, 298
Dickson, John P., 172
Didon, père (Henri), 172
Diel, Paul, 333
Dietrich, Suzanne de, 298
Dietz, Thos G., 172
Dijkhuizen, Pieternella, 515
Dillersberger, Josef, 317
Dillion, Richard J., 317
Dimashkiah, Abdul Rahman, 477
Dimont, Max I., 486
Diodati, Giovanni, 452
Dirks, Jerald, 466
Dirksen, Aloys Herman, 172
Disney, John, 441
Divine of the Church of England, 12
Dix, Morgan, 94, 441
Doane, T. W., 51, 131
Doane, William Croswell, 12
Dobson, Cyril Comyn, 12
Docker, Ernest Brougham, 44, 51, 131
Dockeray, Norman R. C., 149
Dodd, C. H., 215, 333
Dodd, Debbie, 498
Dodd, Thomas J., 94, 149
Dodds, James, 386
Dodge, Ebenezer, 94
Dods, Marcus, 247, 333, 368, 386
Dodson, Jonathan K., 12
Doherty, Earl, 51, 131
Donahue, John R., 279
Donaldson, John William, 215
Donathan, Jerry Leon, 515
Donehoo, James DeQuincey, 216
Dongell, Joseph, 333
Doniger, Wendy, 498
Donne, Brian K., 13
Donne, John, 441
Donovan, C. F., 399

Donzel, E. van, 498
Doohan, Leonard, 333
Dore, James, 13
Doriani, Daniel M., 298
Dorner, I. A., 414
Dornisch, Loretta, 317
Dougherty, Robert Lee, 172
Douglas, J. D., 498
Douglass, Earl L., 386
Dow, John, 172
Dowd, Sharyn Echols, 279
Dowling, Levi H., 216
Downes, J. Cyril., 386
Downie, Robert Mager, 76
Dowse, Edgar, 13
Doyle, Christopher, 67
D'Oyly, George, 452
Drake, Durant, 51, 131
Drane, John William, 172, 530
Drange, Theodore M., 131, 269
Draper, Deanna, 67
Draper, George Otis, 51, 132
Draper, Paul, 247
Dretke, James P., 466
Drew, G. S., 216
Drews, Arthur, 51, 205
Dreyer, Nicole E., 67
Driggers, Ira Brent, 279
Drinkwater, F. H., 13
Driscoll, Mark, 414
Drohan, Francis Burke, 51, 132
Drown, Edward S., 386
Drummond, D. T. K., 333
Drummond, James, 369
Drummond, Richard Henry, 172
Drummond, Robert J., 216
Drury, John, 317
Drury, John L., 515
Dryden, D. A., 76
Dubnov, Simon, 486
DuBose, Henry Wade, 386
Du Bose, Horace M., 13
DuBose, William Porcher, 216
Dudley, Thomas Underwood, 94
Duff, Edward Macomb, 149
Duffy, Eamon, 386
Duggan, G. H., 399
Duke, Doyle E., 51, 132
Duling, Dennis C., 530
Dulles, Avery, 94
Dummelow, J. R., 247, 279, 298, 317, 333, 354, 369
Duncan, Alexander, 94, 441
Duncan, George S., 172, 216
Dunkerley, Roderic, 216

Dunn, James D. G., 216, 354, 369
Dunnett, Walter M., 354
Dunning, H. Ray, 414
Dunwell, Francis Henry, 333, 452
Du Pin, Louis Ellies, 172
Dupuis, Charles-François, 132
Duquesne, Jacques, 172
Du Rand, Jan A., 247
Durant, Will, 414
Duriez, Colin, 172
Durnbaugh, Donald F., 498
Durrwell, F.-X. (François-Xavier), 13
Dushaw, Amos I., 483
Dwight, Timothy, 414
Dwyer, John C., 216
Dyck, Cornelius J., 498
Dyer, Keith D., 13, 247
Dymski, J. Daniel, 13
Dyrness, William A., 498

E

Eadie, John, 499
Earle, Ralph, 247, 279, 298, 317, 354
Earman, John, 149
Easterbrook, Gregg, 216
Easton, Burton Scott, 317
Easton, M. G., 499
Easton, W. Burnet, 414
Eaton, Robert, 13, 280
Ebbutt, A. J., 216
Ebersol, Charles E., 216
Ebied, Rifaat Y., 466
Ebrard, Johannes Heinrich August, 94, 216
Eby, Omar, 280
Eckhardt, A. Roy, 216
Eckman, George P., 13, 333
Eddleman, H. Leo, 354
Eddowes, Ralph, 400
Eddy, Sherwood, 172
Eddy, Zachary, 172
Edersheim, Alfred, 172, 483
Edgar, R. McCheyne, 13, 247
Edinger, Edward F., 173
Edis, Taner, 156
Edmunds, Albert J., 13
Edwards, David L., 354
Edwards, Douglas Allen, 216, 280
Edwards, F. Henry, 173
Edwards, James R., 280, 317
Edwards, Mark J., 13, 247, 333, 386
Edwards, Martin Luther, 94
Edwards, O. C., 217, 317
Edwards, R. A., 333
Edwards, Richard Alan, 298, 414
Edwards, Thomas Charles, 369
Eggleston, Edward, 173
Ehrman, Bart D., 51, 132, 205, 236, 530
Eikamp, Arthur R., 173
Eisler, Robert, 173
Ekstrom, Reynolds R., 499
Elass, Mateen, 466
Elder, John, 466
Elder, Karen Childs, 67
Eliade, Mircea, 499
Elkins, Garland, 369
Elledge, Casey Deryl, 515
Ellegård, Alvar, 52, 132, 206
Ellens, J. Harold, 269, 387
Ellicott, C. J., 94, 173, 247, 333, 369
Ellingsen, Mark, 414
Ellingworth, Paul, 369
Elliot, Rachel, 67
Elliott, E. K., 13
Elliott, J. Keith, 247
Elliott, Walter, 173
Ellis, E. Earle, 217, 317
Ellis, Eric Kent, 13
Ellis, Gwen, 67
Ellis, Peter F., 298, 333
Ellison, H. L., 217
Ellul, Jacques, 466
Elowsky, Joel C., 333
Elsley, Heneage, 298, 452
Elson, Edward L. R., 13
Elwell, Walter A., 499, 530
Elwood, Douglas J., 217
Ely, Ezra Stiles, 414
Emerick, Yahiya, 477
Emerson, William A., 173
Emerton, Ephraim, 156
Emesowum, Charles K., 414
Emmerich, Anna Catherine, 173
Emmons, Nathanael, 441
Endō, Shūsaku, 173
Endsjø, Dag Øistein, 14, 77
Enelow, Hyman Gerson, 486
Engles, William Morrison, 499
English, Donald, 280
English, E. Schuyler, 280, 298
English, George Bethune, 52, 132
Enns, Paul P., 414
Enyioha, Bennett Uche, 515
Erdman, Charles R., 173, 280, 298, 317, 333, 354, 369
Erickson, David, 67

Erickson, Mary E., 67
Erickson, Millard J., 217, 414, 499
Eriksson, Anders, 369
Erlandson, E. J., 61
Erskine, John, 173
E. S. A. (Earnest S. Appleyard), 173
Esack, Farid, 477
Espín, Orlando O., 499
Esposito, John L., 466
Essay on the Evidence of the Truth of Christianity, An, 94
Estborn, Sigfrid, 94
Evans, Canon, 369
Evans, C. F., 14, 317
Evans, C. Stephen, 94
Evans, Craig A., 14, 173, 247–48, 280, 298, 317, 499
Evans, Elizabeth Edson, 52, 132
Evans, Ernest, 369
Evans, Jack, 466

Evans, James L., 369
Evans, Owen E., 333
Evans, Thomas, 441
Evans, Tony, 414
Evans, William, 14, 173, 369, 415
Evanson, Edward, 174
Évely, Louis, 414
Everard, Elizabeth, 67
Everest, Harvey W., 94
Everest, Quinton J., 441
Everett, J. N., 217
Ewald, H., 174
Ewen, Pamela Binnings, 414
Ewing, W., 499
Exell, Joseph S., 280, 298, 317, 333, 354, 369, 452
Expository Sermons on the New Testament, 441
Eynde, Sabine van den, 248
Eyton, Robert, 387
Ezeogu, Ernest Munachi, 515

F

Faber, A. H., 441
Faber, George Stanley, 94
Faber-Kaiser, Andreas, 269, 477
Fabricius, Kim, 415
Fackre, Gabriel, 248, 415
Fahlbusch, Erwin, 499
Fahling, Adam, 174
Faid, Robert W., 94
Fairbairn, A. M., 174
Fairbairn, Patrick, 500
Falconer, Thomas, 61, 441
Fales, Evan, 269
Fallis, William Joseph, 354
Fallows, Samuel, 500
Faris-al-Qayrawani, 477
Farley, Benjamin Wirt, 174
Farley, Lawrence R., 280, 334, 369
Farmer, William R., 280
Farrar, F. W., 174, 317, 369, 530
Farrar, John, 500
Farrell, Walter, 174
Farrelly, John, 94, 415
Farrelly, M. John, 400
Farrer, Austin, 280
Farrier, Daniell E., 515
Farrow, Douglas, 14, 415
Fatoohi, Louay, 477
Faunce, Daniel Worcester, 14, 174
Fausset, A. R., 369, 500
Faust, David, 94
Faw, Chalmer Ernest, 354
Fawcett, John, 334

Fazio, James I., 516
Fee, Gordon D., 370
Feeney, Robert, 174
Feinberg, John S., 95
Felder, Hilarin, 149, 217
Fell, John, 95
Fenimore, Randolph C., 516
Fenton, J. C., 14, 248, 280, 299, 334
Fenton, Joseph Clifford, 95, 400
Ferbeck, Guillaume, 95
Ferguson, Everett, 500
Ferguson, John, 217
Ferguson, Sinclair B., 280, 500
Ferm, Vergilius, 500
Fernandes, Phil, 95, 248
Fernández, Andrés, 174
Fernando, Ajith, 95, 354
Fernando, Mark, 14
Fernando, Samuel Andrew, 516
Ferré, Nels F. S., 415
Ferrin, Howard W., 387
Ferris, Theodore Parker, 174
Fessenden, Thomas, 415
Feuerbach, Ludwig, 95
Fianu, Emmanuel Kofi, 516
Fichter, Joseph Henry, 95, 400
Fida, Ahtisham, 52, 132, 206
Field, Benjamin, 415
Field, Frank McCoy, 174
Fiensy, David A., 531
Figgs, John Neville, 95
Fillion, L.-Cl., 174

Names Index

Fillmore, Charles (*See* Unity School of Christianity), 509
Filson, Floyd V., 14, 299, 334
Findlay, George G., 441
Findlay, J. Alexander, 299, 317, 334
Finegan, Jack, 175, 415
Finegan, Joseph, 387
Finger, Thomas N., 415
Finlay, M. H., 217
Finlay, Peter, 400
Finney, Paul Corby, 500
Fiorenza, Francis Schüssler, 248, 400, 415
First Fruits of Zion, 217
Fischer, David Hickman, 516
Fischer, M. Hadwin, 175
Fishback, James, 217
Fishel, Kent M., 14
Fisher, Aileen, 67
Fisher, Fred L., 370
Fisher, George Park, 95
Fisher, John, 483
Fisher, William Edgar, 415
Fiske, Charles, 175
Fitzgerald, David, 52
Fitzgerald, John H., 441
Fitzmyer, Joseph A., 217, 317, 354, 370
Fitzwater, P. B., 370, 415
Flanagan, Neal M., 334, 355
Flanagan, Patrick J., 280
Flavel, John, 217
Fleetwood, John, 175
Fleming, Caleb, 132
Fleming, M. R., 415
Fleming, Peter James, 516
Flew, Antony G. N., 269
Flinn, Frank K., 500
Flinn, Lisa, 67
Flint, Robert, 400
Flood, Edmund, 14, 175
Fluegel, Maurice, 486
Flusser, David, 486
Flynn, Eileen P., 400
Flynn, Leslie B., 14
Flynn, Tom, 500
Foakes-Jackson, F. J., 355
Focant, Camille, 280
Fodor, James, 52, 132
Fodor, Nandor, 500
Fogarty, Philip, 280, 299, 317
Foley, Leonard, 217
Folliot, Katherine, 217
Foote, G. W., 133
Foote, James, 317
Footman, Henry, 95
Forbes, Greg W., 317, 355

Ford, D. W. Cleverley, 14, 318, 441
Ford, David F., 218, 416
Ford-Grabowsky, Mary, 14
Ford, James, 280, 299, 318, 334, 355
Ford, W. Herschel, 334, 355
Forell, George Wolfgang, 387
Forrest, David W., 218
Fortna, Robert Tomson, 299, 334
Forward, Martin, 175
Foster, Chad, 95
Foster, Charles A., 14
Foster, George Burman, 218
Foster, James, 62, 441
Foster, John McGaw, 387
Foster, Lewis, 334
Foster, Randolph S., 96, 416
Foster, R. C., 175, 218
Foster, Robert V., 416
Fouard, Constant, 175
Foulkes, Francis, 299
Fournier, Susan M., 516
Fowle, T. W., 96
Fox, Robin Lane, 205, 530
Frame, Hugh Fulton, 175
Frame, John M., 96, 416
France, R. T., 175, 218, 280, 299, 318
Francis, Dan R., 516
Francis, Leslie J., 280, 299
Francisco, Adam S., 248
Frank, Penny, 67
Franklin, B., 387
Franks, James Clarke, 96
Franzmann, Majella, 96
Franzmann, Martin H., 299
Fraser, Donald, 355, 452
Fraser, Neil McCormick, 15
Frazier, John C., 516
Frede, Victoria, 52, 133
Frederick, William, 15, 218
Fredriksen, Paula, 175, 218, 486
Fredrikson, Roger L., 334
Freed, Edwin D., 531
Freedman, David Noel, 500
Freeman, Charles, 218
Freemantle, W. H., 96
Frei, Hans W., 218
French, Fiona, 67
Freud, Sigmund, 133, 486
Frey, Joseph Samuel C. F., 96, 483
Frick, Philip Louis, 15, 370
Friedrich, Elizabeth, 67
Friel, Billie, 281
Fries, Heinrich, 416
Frost, Bede, 416
Frothingham, Octavius Brooks, 441

Fruchtenbaum, Arnold G., 483
Fry, Thomas Charles, 96
Fryar, Jane L., 67
Frye, Edwin Gibson, 15
Fudge, Edward, 15, 248
Fuerbringer, L., 500
Fuller, Daniel P., 15, 516
Fuller, Luther M., 516
Fuller, Reginald H., 15, 149, 248, 299, 318
Fullmer, Paul M., 15, 281, 516
Fulton, John, 218
Funk, Robert W., 52, 133, 206, 269
Furches, Joel, 96
Furneaux, Rupert, 44
Furneaux, William Mordaunt, 355
Furness, William Henry, 15, 175, 400, 442
Furnish, Victor Paul, 370
Furst, Jeffrey, 175
Fysh, Frederic, 77

G

Gaddy, C. Welton, 15, 442
Gadenz, Pablo T., 318
Gaebelein, A. C., 299, 334, 355, 370, 452
Gaebelein, Frank E., 334
Gaffin, Richard B., 370
Gall, James, 218
Gallwey, Peter, 218
Gamertsfelder, Solomon J., 416
Ganeri, Anita, 67
Gangel, Kenneth O., 334, 355
Gansky, Alton, 15
Garbett, C. F., 96, 175
Garbutt, Richard, 15
Garcia, Jeffrey Paul, 248
Gardiner, E. A., 355
Gardiner, Frederic, 176
Gardner, James, 52, 133, 176
Gardner, Laurence, 52, 133
Gardner, Martin, 218
Gardner, Richard B., 299
Gardner-Smith, P., 15, 176, 334
Garland, David E., 218, 281, 299, 318, 370
Garlow, James L., 466
Garman, W. O. H., 176
Garnett, Nathan, 96
Garrett, Alfred Cope, 218
Garrett, James Leo, 416
Garrigou-Lagrange, Réginald, 218
Garrott, John, 15
Gartenhaus, Jacob, 483
Garvie, Alfred E., 96, 176, 318, 334, 416
Garza-Valdes, Leoncio A., 218
Gaskell, G. A., 500
Gaskill, Alonzo L., 149
Gassmann, Günther, 500
Gast, Gustave Carl, 318
Gatje, Helmut, 466
Gault, C. W., 15
Gauvin, Marshall J., 133
Gaventa, Beverly Roberts, 248, 355
Gavigan, James, 281, 299, 318, 355, 370
Gaybba, Brian, 416
Gear, Spencer Douglas, 516
Geaves, Ron, 500
Geddert, Timothy J., 516
Geering, Lloyd, 15, 416
Geffré, Claude, 416
Gehman, Henry Snyder, 500
Geikie, Cunningham, 176, 355
Geil, William Edgar, 176
Geis, Robert J., 16
Geisler, Norman L., 16, 96–97, 149, 416, 466, 501
Geivett, R. Douglas, 149, 249
Geldenhuys, Norval, 318
Genesis Project Inc., 176
Gentry, Norman John, 516
Gentz, William H., 501
Geoff, Richard G., 516
George, Augustin, 249
George, James Wesley, 516
George, Larry Darnell, 334, 516
George, N. D., 77
George, Timothy, 466
Gerber, Edward H., 334
Gerdtell, Ludwig von, 149
Gere, George W., 62
Gerhard, Calvin S., 77
Gerhart, Emanuel V., 416
Gestefeld, Ursula N., 176
Gethin, Rupert, 249
Getty, George Albert, 97
Getty, Mary Ann, 370
Gettys, Joseph M., 318, 355
Getty-Sullivan, Mary Ann, 370
Geyer, Hans-Georg, 249
Ghattas, Raouf G., 97, 466
Gibbins, Ronald C., 16
Gibbons, James, 97, 400
Gibbs, Jeffrey A., 299, 516
Gibson, Arthur, 249
Gibson, Edgar C. S., 400
Gibson, John Monro, 97, 299
Gibson, Joseph Thompson, 176

Gibson, Joyce L., 318
Gibson, R. C., 387
Gibson, Shimon, 176
Gideon, Virtus E., 318
Gifford, William Alva, 219
Gift of the Holy Ghost to the Apostles and First Christians, The, 97
Gigot, Francis E., 176
Gilbert, Bishop of Sarum, 400
Gilbert, George Holley, 176
Gilbert, Levi, 176
Gilbert, T. W., 334
Gilchrist, John, 219, 466–67
Gill, Charles, 219
Gill, David, 370
Gill, John, 219, 281, 299, 318, 335, 355, 416, 442
Gill, William Hugh, 335
Gillespie, William, 417
Gillie, R. C., 176
Gilliom, James O., 149
Gillman, John, 249, 318
Gillmore, Hiram, 98
Gilmore, Albert Field, 176
Gilmore, James R., 219
Gilmour, S. MacLean, 318
Ginder, Richard, 62
Ginns, R., 318
Girdlestone, A. G., 98
Girdlestone, Charles, 281, 299, 318, 335
Girdlestone, Robert Baker, 62, 219
Girzone, Joseph F., 176
Glaser, Rebecca Stromstad, 67
Glasow, David B., 516
Glasscock, Ed, 299
Glassé, Cyril, 477, 501
Glazier, Michael, 501
Glen, J. Stanley, 370
Glenn, Paul J., 98
Gloag, Paton James, 355
Glover, Richard, 281, 300
Glover, T. R., 177
Gnilka, Joachim, 177
Godbey, J. E., 98
Godbey, W. B., 219, 370
Goddard, Hugh, 467, 477
Goddard, Jerome, 149
Godet, Frédéric Louis, 98, 318, 335, 370
Godfrey, Jan, 67
Godwin, Johnnie C., 281
Goergen, Donald, 16
Goguel, Maurice, 177
Goldberg, Michael, 219
Golding, Shmuel, 486
Goldman, David, 467, 477
Goldsack, William, 467
Goldsmith, Dale, 516
Goldsmith, Martin, 300, 467
Goldstein, Morris, 486
González, Justo L., 300, 318, 355, 501
Good, John Walter, 219
Gooder, Paula, 16
Goodhugh, W., 501
Goodier, Alban, 16, 219
Gooding, Christina, 67
Gooding, D. W., 318, 355
Goodloe, James C., 318
Goodman, Paul, 486
Goodspeed, Edgar J., 177
Goodwin, Daniel Raynes, 219
Goodwin, Harvey, 281, 300, 318, 387
Goodwin, John, 417
Goodwin, Thomas, 16, 177, 249
Goppelt, Leonhard, 16
Gorder, Paul R. van, 370
Gordon, A. J., 62
Gordon, George A., 150, 177
Gordon, S. D., 335
Gore, Charles, 98, 177, 417
Gore-Booth, Eva, 335
Gorham, Charles T., 44
Goring, Rosemary, 501
Gorle, J., 387
Gorman, Michael J., 370
Gospel of the Resurrection, The, 442
Goudge, Elizabeth, 177
Goudge, Henry Leighton, 370
Goulburn, Edward Meyrick, 77
Gould, Dana, 370
Gould, Ezra P., 271, 371, 417
Goulder, Michael D., 269, 300, 319, 371
Govett, R., 335, 371
Gowan, Donald E., 501
Gräbner, A. L., 417
Graham, Alfred, 219
Graham, Billy, 417
Graham, Lloyd, 52, 133
Graham, Nicolas, 249
Graham, William, 387
Graieg, David Jonathan, 517
Granbery, J. C, 501
Grant, Frederick C., 219, 281, 300, 335, 452
Grant, Frederick W., 319, 335
Grant, Malcolm, 98, 150
Grant, Michael, 177
Grant, Robert M., 150
Grassi, Joseph A., 177, 531
Graves, Kersey, 52, 133
Graves, Mike, 300
Graves, Robert, 52

Gray, Albert F., 417
Gray, Arthur R., 98
Gray, James M., 77, 371, 453
Gray, Robert D., 517
Grayston, Kenneth, 335, 371
Grayzel, Solomon, 486
Grech, Prospero, 355
Greear, J. D., 467
Greeley, Andrew M., 417
Green, Ashbel, 400
Green, F. W., 300
Green, H. Benedict, 249, 300
Green, Joel B., 249, 319, 501
Green, Michael, 16, 98, 300
Green, Peter, 417
Green, Samuel G., 356, 501
Green, S. W., 281
Greenberg, Irving, 486
Greene, Carol, 67
Greene, Oliver B., 98, 335, 356, 371
Greenhalgh, John, 16
Greenway, Leonard, 517
Greg, Samuel, 177
Greg, William R., 98
Gregg, David , 335, 400, 442
Gregory, Andrew F., 219
Gregory, Olinthus, 98
Greig, Gary S., 417
Grelot, Pierre, 249
Grenier, Brian, 335
Grensted, L. W., 219
Grenz, Stanley J., 417
Greswell, Edward, 453
Grey, Mary C., 16
Grider, J. Kenneth, 417
Grierson, Herbert , 16
Grierson, James, 16
Grieve, Val, 17
Griffin, George, 99
Griffin, James A., 17
Griffith, Gwilym O., 177
Griffith-Jones, E., 249
Griffiths, Douglas Allen, 219
Grimbol, William R., 177

Grimes, Nikki, 67
Grist, William Alexander, 177
Griswold, Rufus W., 177
Grobel, Kendrick, 249
Groff, Randy, 281
Grogan, Geoffrey, 281
Gromacki, Robert Glenn, 371, 531
Groothuis, Douglas R., 99, 177
Grosheide, F. W. , 371
Grotius, Hugo, 99
Grove, Henry, 17, 442
Grubb, Edward, 99, 177
Grudem, Wayne A., 417
Gruenler, Royce Gordon, 335
Grün, Anselm, 319
Grypeou, Emmanouela, 467
Guardini, Romano, 177
Guerber, H. A., 53, 133
Guest, John, 99
Guideposts Associates, 300
Guignebert, Charles, 178, 220
Guild, E. E., 53, 133
Guillaume, Alfred, 467
Guinness, H. Grattan, 99
Guinness, Howard, 17
Guinness, Paul Grattan, 177
Guitton, Jean, 99
Gulley, Norman R., 418
Gümüş, M. Sıddık, 477
Gundry, Robert H., 249, 281, 300, 319, 335, 356, 371, 453, 531
Gunsaulus, Frank Wakeley, 177
Gunter, W. Stephen, 17
Gurney, Joseph John, 99
Gurney, T. A., 17, 442
Guthrie, Donald, 178, 335, 356
Guthrie, Shirley C., 418
Gutierrez, Juan Eliezer de Leon, 517
Gutteridge, Don J., 99
Gutzke, Manford George, 77, 281, 300, 319, 335, 371, 418
Guy, Harold A., 178, 281, 300, 319, 356
Gwynne, J. Harold, 442
Gwynne, Paul, 517

H

Haas, John A. W., 281
Habermas, Gary R., 17, 77, 99, 178, 250, 251, 517
Habershon, Ada R., 150
Hackett, Horatio B., 356
Hadnut, Robert K., 99
Haenchen, Ernst, 335, 356
Haering, Theodor, 418

Hagner, Donald A., 251, 300
Hahn, Ernest, 467
Hahn, Scott, 300, 335, 356, 501 32
Haidle, Helen, 67
Haight, Roger, 220
Hailey, O. L., 17
Haines, Herbert, 442
Haines, John, 467

Names Index

Haldeman, I. M., 62, 442
Hales, B. D., 17
Hálid, Halil, 477
Hall, A. W., 17
Hall, Arthur C. A., 387
Hall, Charles Cuthbert, 220
Hall, Douglas John, 418
Hall, Francis J., 18, 418
Hall, G. Stanley, 178
Hall, James LeLand, 517
Hall, Jean, 18
Hall, John, 77
Hall, Joseph, 99
Hall, Thomas Cuming, 453
Haller, Karl Ludwig von, 99
Hallett, Joseph, 18
Halley, Henry H., 371
Halliday, G. Y., 467
Hallquist, Chris, 44, 133
Halsey, Leroy J., 178, 418
Halsey, Michael D., 335
Halverson, Marvin, 418
Hamann, Henry Paul, 301, 517
Hamar, Paul A., 371
Hamilton, Edward John, 99
Hamilton, Floyd Eugene, 99
Hamilton, Frank, 99
Hamilton, James, 178
Hamilton, Laurentine, 220
Hamilton, Peter N., 418
Hamilton, William, 281
Hamm, Jeffery L., 300
Hamm, M. Dennis, 356
Hammer, Bonaventure, 178, 400
Hammond, Henry, 453
Han, Cheon-Seol, 18
Hancock, Thomas, 517
Haneef, Suzanne, 477
Hanegraaff, Hank, 18, 100, 467
Hanhart, Karel, 44
Hanish, Otoman Zar-Adusht, 477
Hankins, John Eric, 517
Hanna, William, 18, 77, 178
Hannah, Darrell D., 371
Hannam, Wilfred L., 319
Hansen, Carolyn, 251
Hanson, Anthony Tyrrell, 336, 418
Hanson, Bradley C., 418
Hanson, Delbert James, 100
Hanson, George, 18
Hanson, Richard S., 18, 220
Hanson, R. P. C., 356
Haralick, Robert M., 356
Harbin, Michael A., 251
Harbour, Brian L., 356, 371

Harden, Ralph William, 18
Harden, William Dearing, 134
Hardesty, Susan, 67
Hardman, Oscar, 77
Hardon, John A., 501
Hardt, Doug, 467
Hare, Augustus, 18, 100
Hare, Douglas R. A., 282, 301
Hargis, Jeffrey W., 220
Hargreaves, Cecil, 150
Hargreaves, John, 282, 356, 371
Harington, Joy, 178
Harkness, Georgia Elma, 100, 418
Härle, Wilfried, 418
Harmon, George Milford, 62
Harmony of the Gospel Narratives of Holy Week, 18, 178
Harn, Roger E. Van, 387
Harnack, Adolf von, 418
Harned, David Baily, 387
Harney, Kevin, 336
Harold, Preston, 220
Harper, James, 400
Harpur, James, 150
Harpur, Tom, 53, 134, 206
Harputlu, İshak, 478
Harrast, Tracy L., 67
Harries, Richard, 18
Harrington, Daniel J., 282, 301, 336
Harrington, Wilfrid J., 178, 282, 301, 319, 336
Harris, Charles, 100
Harris, George K., 467
Harris, Greg, 18
Harris, Harriet A., 418
Harris, Henry, 77
Harris, John Andrews, 442
Harris, John Glyndwr, 419
Harris, John Tindall, 371
Harris, Murray J., 18, 62, 220
Harris, Sam, 53
Harris, Stephen L., 531
Harris, W. B., 371
Harrison, Everett Falconer, 178, 220, 336, 356, 501
Harrison, H. D., 531
Harrison, John, of the Inner Temple, 100
Harrison, McVeigh, 336, 388
Harrison, Paul W., 336
Harrison, R. L., 301
Harrisville, Roy A., 371
Hart, J. Stephen, 336
Hart, Levi, 62, 442
Hart, Lewis A., 486
Hartill, Isaac, 18
Hartman, Bob, 68

Names Index

Hartman, Lars, 282
Hartman, Sara, 68
Harvey, A. E., 179
Harvey, Nicholas Peter, 18
Harvey, Van A., 502
Harwood, Philip, 156, 179
Hascall, Daniel, 419
Hase, Karl von, 179
Hasitschka, Martin, 251
Hassnain, Fida M., 478
Hastings, Edward, 336
Hastings, James, 502
Hauerwas, Stanley, 301
Haughton, Rosemary, 419
Haweis, Thomas, 453
Hawthorne, Gerald F., 502
Hay, Alexander, 442
Hay, William, 100
Hayes, Charles H., 388
Hayes, Doremus A., 18, 442
Hayes, Hopton, 419
Hayes, Patrick J., 150, 502
Hayford, Jack W., 336, 453
Hays, Richard B., 371
Hays, Steve, 19
Healy, Mary, 282
Head, E. D., 371
Head, Peter M., 19, 251
Heading, John, 371
Headlam, Arthur C., 150, 220, 419
Heard, Richard, 531
Hearon, Holly Elizabeth, 517
Heath, Dale E., 19
Hebblethwaite, Brian, 100, 251
Hebert, Arthur Gabriel, 419
Heck, Paul L., 467
Hedges, Paul, 467
Hedley, George, 388
Heenan, John Carmel, 401
Heffern, Andrew Duff, 100
Hege, Brent A. R., 419, 517
Hegel, Georg Wilhelm Friedrich, 419
Hegemann, Werner, 44
Heikkinen, Jacob W., 77
Heil, John Paul, 282, 301, 336
Heinze, Rudi, 251
Heisler, Charles W., 220
Helffenstein, Samuel, 419
Hellen, John, 100
Heller, James John, 517
Hellwig, Monika K., 401
Helm, Nellie Lathrop, 179
Helms, Randel, 53, 134
Henderson, Robert Arthur, 336
Henderson, Timothy P., 100, 517
Hendrickx, Herman, 19
Hendriksen, William, 282, 319, 336, 453
Hendrix, Eugene Russell, 220
Hengel, Martin, 220
Hengstenberg, E. W., 336
Hennell, Charles C., 220
Hennell, S. S., 100
Henriksen, Jan-Olav, 220
Henry, A. M., 179
Henry, Matthew, 282, 301, 319, 336, 356, 371, 453
Henson, Hensley, 356, 371
Herbermann, Charles G., 502
Héring, Jean, 372
Hernandez, David, 53, 133
Heron, Alasdair, 251
Hervey, A. C., 356
Herzog, Frederick, 336
Herzog, William R., 179
Hession, Brian, 179
Hester, David W., 282
Hester, H. I., 531
Hetherington, William M., 100
Heuschen, J., 19
Hewer, C. T. R., 467
Hewlett, John, 282, 301, 319, 336, 356, 372, 453
Hewson, John, 19
Hey, John, 419
Heydon, J. K., 401
Heyer, Carol, 68
Heywood, Bernard Oliver Francis, 388
Hibbert, Giles, 336
Hicham, E. M., 467, 478
Hick, John, 100
Hickcox, Percy Merriman, 517
Hickling, S. Ross, 19, 517
Hiebert, D. Edmond, 282
Higgins, Gregory C., 419
Hiliary, Saint, Bishop of Poitiers, 301
Hill, Brennan, R., 401
Hill, David, 301
Hill, George, 101, 419
Hill, John Leonard, 282, 319
Hill, William Bancroft, 19, 179
Hillard, A. E., 179, 282, 319
Hills, O. A., 356
Hillyer, Norman, 372
Hindmarsh, Robert, 19, 221
Hindson, Edward E., 301, 502
Hinlicky, Paul R., 419
Hinman, Joe, 251
Hinson, E. Glenn, 221
Hitchcock, Albert Wellman, 179
Hitchcock, F. R. Montgomery, 150

Names Index

Hitchcock, Ronald Lee, 517
Hitchcock, Roswell, 453
Hittell, John S., 134
Hoadley, Burton James, 19
Hoare, Rodney, 19, 221
Hobbs, Herschel H., 19, 179, 282, 301, 319, 336, 372, 419, 442
Hocking, David L., 442
Hodge, Archibald Alexander, 419
Hodge, Charles, 372, 420
Hodge, Richard Morse, 179
Hodgetts, Albert William, 62
Hodgkin, Henry T., 221
Hodgson, Ch., 179
Hodgson, George, 78
Hodgson, Leonard, 420
Hodgson, Peter C., 221, 420
Hoehner, Harold W., 179
Hoeksema, Herman, 420
Hoffman, Reuben F., 179
Hoh, Paul Jacob, 372
Holbach, Paul Henri Thiry, 53, 134, 206
Holder, R. Ward, 502
Holding, James Patrick, 19, 101, 221, 251
Hole, F. B., 336
Holladay, Carl R., 372
Holland, Henry Scott, 62, 252
Holleman, Joost, 252, 372
Hollis, Gertrude, 19
Holloman, Henry W., 517
Holloway, David, 20
Holloway, Gary, 150
Holloway, Richard, 101
Holmes, Andy, 68
Holmes, Robert, 401, 420, 442
Holmyard, Harold R., 517
Holsinger, Madra E., 518
Holtzmann, Oskar, 206
Holy Bible Explained, 101
Holyday, Barten, 442
Holzapfel, Richard Neitzel, 20, 252
Homolka, Walter, 487
Hook, Peter, 518
Hook, Walter Farquhar, 443, 502
Hooke, S. H., 20
Hooker, Morna D., 252, 282
Hooton, Walter Stewart, 356
Hoover, Arlie J., 101
Hoover, Roy W., 269
Hopkins, Archibald, 388
Hopkins, Brooke, 269
Hopkins, John Henry, 388
Hopkins, Keith, 53, 134
Hopkins, Mark, 101
Hopp, Kenneth Harvey, 101

Horbury, William, 53, 134
Horder, W. Garrett, 252
Horn, Siegfried H., 502
Horne, Chevis F., 443
Horne, Thomas Hartwell, 101
Hornsby, Sarah, 20
Hornyold, John Joseph, 388
Horsley, John, 62
Horsley, Richard A., 372
Horsley, Samuel, 20, 443
Hort, A. F., 282
Hort, Fenton John Anthony, 101
Horton, Michael Scott, 388, 420
Horton, Robert F., 282, 301
Horton, Stanley M., 301, 319, 356, 372
Horváth, Tibor, 101
Hosie, Lady, 180
Hosking, John, 101
Hoskins, Paul M., 518
Hoskyns, Edwyn Clement, 20, 336
Hostetler, Jonathan J., 301
Houdmann, S. Michael, 101
Houghton, Alexander, 443
Houghton, Louise Seymour, 180
Houlden, J. Leslie, 20, 252, 502
House, H. Wayne, 101, 420
Houselander, Caryll, 20
Houston, George (?), 134
Houston, J., 150
Houtepen, Anton W. J., 420
Hove, E., 420
Hovey, Alvah, 150, 337, 420
How, W. Walsham, 221, 337
Howard, Fred D., 301, 372
Howard, Jeremy Royal, 221, 252
Howard, Thomas, 102
Howard, Wilbert F., 337
Howard-Brook, Wes, 337
Howe, Fisher, 20
Howe, Frederic R., 102
Howe, Thomas, 443
Howell, David B., 301
Howell, James C., 388
Howell, Laurence, 454
Howick, E. Keith, 150
Howie, Vicki, 67
Howson, J. S., 356
Hoyland, Geoffrey, 78
Huat, Tan Kim, 282
Hubbard, Benjamin Jerome, 301, 518
Hubbard, George Henry, 150
Hudnut, Robert K., 102
Huebenthal, Sandra, 252
Huelster, A., 150
Huffaker, Alice, 150

Huffard, Everett W., 252
Huffer, Alva G., 429
Huffman, Douglas S., 252
Hughes, Albert, 282, 372, 420
Hughes, Frederick Stephen, 221
Hughes-Games, Joshua, 78
Hughes, H. Maldwyn, 420
Hughes, Kelly A., 518
Hughes, R. Kent, 282, 319, 337, 356
Hughes, Robert B., 372
Hughes, Thomas Patrick, 502
Hugueny, Père Etienne, 401
Huidekoper, Frederic, 221
Hume, David, 156
Hummel, Daniel, 467, 478
Humphrey, Hugh, 282
Humphreys, Kenneth, 53
Humphry, William Gilson, 78
Hunkin, J. W., 62
Hunsinger, George, 388
Hunt, B. P. W. Stather, 337
Hunt, David (c. 1870), 401
Hunt, David (1926–2013), 102
Hunt, Gladys M., 319
Hunt, T. W., 180

Hunter, A. M. (Archibald Macbride), 180, 221, 282, 337
Hunter, Henry, 102
Hunter, JoAnn Heaney, 518
Hunter, Sylvester Joseph, 401, 420
Hunton, William Lee, 388
Hurd, John Coolidge, 372
Hurlbut, Jesse Lyman, 180
Hurst, John F., 134
Hurtado, Larry W., 252, 283
Hussein, M. Kamel, 478
Hutcheson, George, 337
Hutchins, James, 389
Hutchinson Dictionary of Ideas, The, 502
Hutchinson, Orion N., 319
Hutchinson, Robert J., 180
Hutchinson, Samuel, 78
Hutchison, John, 150
Hutson, Christopher R., 372
Hutson, Curtis, 20, 443
Hutton, Delvin Dwayne, 518
Hutton, Richard Holt, 421
Hutton, Vernon Wollaston, 180
Huxley, Thomas H., 157
Hyslop, James H., 157

I

Iannone, John, 221
Ibn Taimīya, Aḥmad ibn ʿAbd al-Halīm, 478
Ibn Warraq, 468
Ide, Arthur Frederick, 20
Iersel, Bas M. F. van, 283
Ignatius IV Patriarch of Antioch, 421
Ihmels, L., 389
Ikhlas, Waqf, 478
Illingworth, J. R., 150, 421
Impartial Examination and Full Confutation of the Argument Brought by Mr. Woolston's Pretended Rabbi, 62
Imran, Adil Nizamuddin, 478
Imran, Muhammad, 478
Inboden, Scott W., 518
Inbody, Tyron L., 221
Ince, G. J., 389
Indian Officer. *See* Berwick, G. J., 134
Ing, Paul Tan Chee, 102

Ingalls, Marilyn F., 68
Ingersoll, Robert G., 53, 134
Inglis, James, 503
Ingraham, J. H., 221
Ingram, Chip, 102
Ingram, Joseph Edward, 20
Instone-Brewer, David, 102
Inwagen, Peter van, 102
Ireland, John, 102
Ireson, Gordon W., 20
Ironside, H. A., 283, 302, 319, 337, 357, 372
Irudaya, Raj, 337
Irvine, Alexander, 180
ʿĪsá ʿAbd Allāh Muḥammad al-Mahdī, 468
Isik, Hüseyn Hilmi. *See* Harputlu Ishak., 478
Itzkoff, Seymour W., 487
Iverson, Kelly Ryan, 518
Ives, E. W., 468

J

Jabbour, Nabeel T. or Jabbūr, Nabīl, 102, 468
Jack, J. W., 221
Jackman, David, 372
Jackson, Antonia, 68
Jackson, Bernard Cecil, 302

Jackson, Dalen Craig, 518
Jackson, John, 102
Jackson, Samuel Macauley, 503
Jacob, of Serug, 20
Jacobovici, Simcha, 20

Jacobs, Charles M., 389
Jacobs, Henry Eyster, 372, 421
Jacobsen, David Schnasa, 283, 319, 357
Jacobson, William, 357
Jacobus, Melancthon Williams, 107, 283, 302, 319, 337, 357, 503
Jacoby, Douglas A., 102
Jadeed, Iskander, 468
Jaimson, David Lee, 62
Jaki, Stanley L., 20
James, C. C., 180
James, Edwin O., 421
James, Rick, 180
James, Ron, 389
Jamieson, Robert, 302, 320, 454
Janes Harold T., 518
Jansen, John Frederick, 20
Jarvis, Cynthia A., 283, 302, 320, 337, 283
Jarvis, F. Washington, 180
Jarvis, Samuel Farmar, 180
Jeanes, Samuel Arthur, 518
Jefferson, Charles Edward, 102
Jeffrey, David Lyle, 320
Jeffrey, Grant R., 102
Jeffs, Stephanie, 68
Jenkin, Robert, 102
Jenkins, David L., 337
Jenkins, Ferrell, 252
Jenkins, J. (James of Castle-Douglas), 443
Jenks, William, 454
Jennings, A. G., 21, 180, 221
Jennings, Theodore W., 283, 389
Jensen, David H., 221
Jensen, Irving L., 180, 283, 302, 320, 357, 372, 531
Jensen, Matthew D., 21
Jensen, Richard A., 283, 302, 320
Jenson, Robert W., 421
Jeon, Paul S., 180
Jeremias, Joachim, 221
Jerome, Saint, 302
Jersild, Paul T., 103
Jesse, William, 103
Jessup, Henry Harris, 468
Jesus Seminar Spring Meeting, The, 269
Jinkins, Michael, 421
Jocz, Jakob, 484
John-Charles, Peter, 21
John Chrysostom, Saint, 337
John, Jeffrey, 151
John, Paul, 53, 134
John Paul II, pope, 21
Johnson, Alan F., 372
Johnson, Albert G., 443
Johnson, Alice W., 68

Johnson, B. C., 53, 134
Johnson, B. W., 283, 337, 454
Johnson, Ben Campbell, 180
Johnson, Benjamin A., 302, 518
Johnson, Cathy Ann, 68
Johnson, Cliff R., 21, 389
Johnson, David, 269
Johnson, Derek, 421
Johnson, E. H., 421
Johnson, G. Timothy, 103
Johnson, Harry, 181
Johnson, Jeremiah, 531
Johnson, John J., 103
Johnson, Kim Allan, 21
Johnson, Paul, 181
Johnson, Sherman E., 181, 283
Johnson, Timothy Luke, 21, 151, 320, 357, 389, 531
Johnston, Howard Agnew, 103, 151
Johnston, J. Wesley, 221, 389
Johnston, Mark, 421
Johnston, Mark G., 337, 389
Johnston, Robert Dougall, 78
Johnstone, T. Boston, 181
Jones, Alexander, 283, 302
Jones, Beth Felker, 421, 518
Jones, Dennis G., 68
Jones, Gareth, 252
Jones, Ivor H., 302
Jones, J. Cynddylan, 302, 357
Jones, J. D., 103, 283, 443
Jones, J. Estill, 357
Jones, J. P., 221
Jones, Joe R., 421
Jones, Joel, 181, 454
Jones, John Benjamin, 103
Jones, L. Bevan, 468
Jones, Lindsay, 503
Jones, Simon, 320
Jones, William, 503
Jortin, John, 103
Joseph, Simon J., 487
Joshi, S. T., 134
Joslin, Mary, 68
Jovanovic, Mihailo, 518
Joyce, Donovan, 181
Judge, Peter J., 252
Judson, Albert, 21
Juel, Donald, 283, 531
Jung, C. G., 134
Just, Arthur A., 320, 518
Juster, Daniel C., 103

K

Kadlecek, Jo, 21
Kähler, Martin, 181
Kairanvi, Maulana M. Rahmatullah, 478
Kalas, J. Ellsworth, 302
Kalisch, Isidor, 487
Kallas, James G., 181
Kallenbach, Walter D., 103
Kalman, Jason, 252
Kalthoff, Albert, 236
Kamaleson, Samuel, 518
Kamauddin, Al-Hajj Khwaja, 478
Kamecke, Fred von, 103
Kammrath, Luke, 283
Kanagaraj, Jey J., 337
Kankaanniemi, Matti, 21, 302, 518
Karris, Robert J., 253, 320, 338, 357
Kartsonis, Anna D., 21
Kasper, Walter, 222
Kateregga, Badru D., 468
Kates, Frederick Ward, 62
Kaufman, Edmund G., 421
Kaufman, Gordon D., 222, 421
Kaufmann, Yehezkel, 487
Kautsky, Karl, 236
Kaye, Bruce, 151
Kaylor, R. David, 222
Kealy, John P., 320
Kean, Leah, 68
Kearney, Milo, 53, 135
Keating, Sandra Toenies, 468
Keaty, Anthony W., 518
Keble, John, 443
Keddie, Gordon J., 338
Kedney, John Steinfort, 103, 421
Kee, Alistair, 21, 443
Kee, Howard Clark, 357
Keegan, Terence J., 283
Keehus, Magnus N., 222
Keeley, Robin, 503
Keenan, John P., 283
Keener, Craig S., 151, 181, 253, 302, 338, 357, 372, 454
Keener, J. C., 103
Keffer, Lois, 68
Keigwin, John, 21
Keim, Theodor, 135, 206
Keith, Alexander, 103
Kelhoffer, James Anthony, 283, 518
Keller, Timothy, 103
Kelly, Anthony, 21, 338
Kelly, Gabrielle, 503
Kelly, Joseph F., 531
Kelly, William, 283, 302, 320, 338, 357, 372

Kelsey, Morton T., 21
Kemmer, Alfons, 389
Ken, Bishop (Thomas), 389
Kena, Kwasi Issa, 22
Kendall, Jonathan, 253
Kendall, R. T., 421
Kennard, Douglas W., 222
Kennedy, D. James, 22
Kennedy, Geoffrey Anketell Studdert, 389
Kennedy, John, 22, 104
Kennedy, Ludovic, 54, 135
Kennedy, Richard, 503
Kennett, Basil, 389
Kenrick, Francis Patrick, 222
Kensinger, Keith Arnold, 519
Kent, Charles Foster, 181, 222, 357
Kent, Homer Austin, 283, 357
Kent, Jack A., 44
Keown, Mark J., 222
Kephart, Cyrus Jeffries, 181
Kephart, Ezekiel Boring, 104
Kepler, Thomas S., 22
Kereszty, Roch A., 222
Kernaghan, Ronald J., 283
Kerr, Hugh Thomson, 22
Kerr, James S., 503
Kersten, Holger, 44, 54, 135
Kesich, Veselin, 22
Kessler, Edward, 503
Kessler, William Thomas, 22, 519
Kevan, Ernest F., 62
Keyser, Leander S., 104
Khalidi, Tarif, 478
Khan, Md. Irshad Anwar, 478
Khan, Muhammad Zafrulla, 478
Kidder, Daniel P., 151, 302, 320
Kidder, Richard, 104
Kieffer, James Shiffer, 519
Kiehl, Erich H., 181
Kilgallen, John J., 283, 302, 320, 338, 357, 372
Killinger, John, 283, 320, 421
Killingworth, Grantham, 78
Kim, Benjamin M. H., 519
Kim, Dae Gee, 519
Kim, Stephen S., 151
Kim, Yung Suk, 222, 373
Kindī, Muhammad ibn Yūsuf, (Muhammad ibn Yūsuf al-Kindī), 104, 468
King, Geoffrey R., 22
King, Peter, 390
Kingsbury, Jack Dean, 284, 303
Kingsland, John P., 181
Kingsley, Calvin, 78

Names Index

Kinsler, F. Ross, 284
Kinukawa, Hisako, 284
Kirby, Peter, 269
Kirk, Albert, 303, 338
Kirk, James Ernest, 519
Kirke, Edmund (pseud. Gilmore, James Roberts), 181
Kirkhart, Bobbie, 269
Kirkland, Winifred, 22, 181
Kirkpatrick, Kathy Newell, 22
Kirtley, J. S., 222
Kistemaker, Simon J., 151, 357, 373
Kittel, Gerhard, 503
Kitto, John F., 181, 503
Kitzberger, Ingrid Rosa, 253
Klausli, Markus T., 519
Klausner, Joseph, 206, 487
Klein, Felix, 181
Kling, Christian Friedrich, 373
Klinghoffer, David, 487
Klink, Edward W., 338
Klopstock, Friedrich Gottlieb, 22, 182
Klotz, John C., 222
Knapp, Charles, 284, 320
Knapp, Georg Christian, 421
Knapp, Richard, 519
Knechtle, Cliffe, 104
Knight, Henry H., 422
Knight, Jonathan, 222, 320, 422
Knitter, Paul F., 422
Knowles, Archibald Campbell, 22
Knowling, R. J., 373, 531
Knox, John, 104, 182, 338
Knox, Ronald A., 357, 373, 390, 422, 454
Knox, W. H., 338
Knudson, Albert C., 422
Kobel, Esther, 338
Koch, Franz Xavier Jos, 104
Kodell, Jerome, 320
Koelle, S. W., 468
Koester, Craig R., 22, 253, 338
Koestler-Grack, Rachael A., 68
Kohler, Kaufmann, 487
Komarnitsky, Kris D., 44, 135
Komoszewski, J. Ed, 104
Komroff, Manuel, 182
Konis, Polyvios, 519
Konradt, Matthias, 303
Kopp, Clemens, 182
Kosanke, Charles, 519
Köstenberger, Andrea J., 104, 182, 338, 422, 531
Kounter, Jacob, 519
Kovacs, Judith L, 373
Kovcs, Victoria, 68
Kraus, C. Norman, 422
Krauskopf, Joseph, 487
Kreeft, Peter, 104
Kreitzer, Beth, 320
Krenzer, Rolf, 68
Krodel, Gerhard, 357
Kruger, Michael J., 531
Krummacher, Friedrich W., 22, 182
Kruse, Colin G., 338
Kryvelev, Iosif Aronovic, 54, 135
Kueker, Donald, 68
Kuhn, Alvin Boyd, 54, 135
Kuhn, Clyde L., 182
Kuiper, Henry J., 390
Kumar, Steve, 105
Küng, Hans, 78, 105, 222, 236, 390, 422, 468
Kunkel, Fritz, 303
Künneth, Walter, 22
Kurian, George Thomas, 503
Kürnizger, Josef, 357
Kurtz, Paul, 54
Kuruvilla, Abraham, 284
Kurz, William S., 357
Kuyper, Abraham, 23
Kwon, Yon-Gyong, 357
Kysar, Robert, 338

L

Labahn, Michael, 253
Lacey, T. A., 182
Lachs, Samuel Tobias, 284, 303, 320
Lacoste, Jean-Yves, 504
Ladd, George Eldon, 23, 422
LaGrand, James, 422
Lagrange, Marie-Joseph, 182, 284
LaHaye, Tim, 504
Laible, Wilhelm, 390
Laidlaw, John, 151
Lake, James E., 105
Lake, John, 401
Lake, Kirsopp, 23, 222, 358
Lamar, J. S., 320
Lamb, Francis Jones, 151
Lambrecht, Jan, 373
Lamont, Daniel, 338
Lampe, G. W. H., 23, 320, 358, 422
Lampe, Peter, 422
Lamsa, George M., 182, 222
Landels, William, 23
Landers, Caleb Marshall, 135

Landis, Robert W., 78
Landman, Isaac, 504
Lane Fox, Robin, 54, 135
Lane, William L., 284
Laney, J. Carl, 105, 338
Lang, Jovian P., 504
Lang, J. Stephen, 105
Lange, Johann Peter, 182, 284, 303, 338
Lange, Reinhold, 23
Langford, William, 390
Langley, Andrew, 68
Lanier, John J., 422
Lanier, W. Mark, 105
Lapide, Cornelius Cornelii à, 284, 303, 339, 373
Lapide, Pinchas, 44, 487
La Potterie, Ignace de, 23, 339
Lardner, Nathaniel, 401
Larkin, William J., 320, 358
Larmer, Robert A., 151
Larned, C. W., 182
Larsen, Kasper Bro., 339
Larson, Bruce, 320
Larson, James Henry, 223
Larson, John Theodore, 519
Larsson, Edvin, 253
Lash, Nicholas, 358
LaSor, William Sanford, 358
Latham, Henry, 23
Lathrop, Joseph, 422
La Touche Boesnier, Pierre de, 105
La Touche, Digges E., 105
Latourelle, René, 151, 504
Latourette, Kenneth Scott, 223
Laubach, Frank Charles, 182
Laurie, Greg, 23
Laurin, Roy L., 339, 373
Lausanne Committee for World Evangelism, 468
LaVerdiere, Eugene, 284, 320, 519
Laverdière, H., 519
Lavoie, Gilbert R., 23, 223
Lawler, Michael G., 422
Lawrence, Chellaian, 468
Lawrence, John J., 105
Lawson, Benjamin T., 519
Lawson, Charles, 443
Lawson, John, 422
Lawson, McEwan, 182
Lawson, Todd, 468
Lawton, John Stewart, 151
Layman, A., 62, 182, 443
Laymon, Charles M., 182
Layton, Bentley, 23
Lea, Thomas, 532

Leaney, A. R. C., 253, 320
Leask, William, 183, 223
Leathes, Stanley, 105, 253, 390
Leavell, Roland Q., 303
Leavitt, Dennis H., 401
Leavitt, John McDowell, 105
Lebreton, Jules, 183
Le Camus, Émile, 183
Lechler, Gotthard Victor, 358
Le Cornu, Hilary, 358
Lee, John David, 183
Lee, Jung Young, 423
Lee, Laurel, 68
Lee, Robert Greene, 23, 62, 339, 358, 373
Lee, Umphrey, 183
Lee, William, 54, 135
Lee, Witness, 321, 358, 454
Lee, Yong-Won, 519
Leeper, Wayne D., 23
Lees, G. Robinson, 183
Le Feuvre, Amy, 183
Legg, John, 303
Lehtipuu, Outi, 78
Leidner, Harold, 135, 487
Leigh, Susan K., 68
Leighton, Robert, Abp. of Glasgow, 390
Leirvik, Oddbiøm, 469
Leitch, Addison H., 423
Leitch, Ian, 106
Leland, John, 54, 106, 136
Lemcio, Eugene E., 183
Lennox, John C., 106
Lenowitz, Harris, 223
Lenski, R. C. H, 284, 303, 321, 339, 358, 373, 454
Lenwood, Frank, 223
Leonard, W., 339
Léon-Dufour, Xavier, 23, 183, 253, 504
Leslie, Charles, 106
Leslie, Rolla J., 54, 136
Lessing, Erich, 183
Lester, Charles Stanley, 183
Levering, Matthew, 78
Levett, Arthur, 54, 136
Levine, Amy-Jill, 303, 487
Levine, Samuel, 487
Levison, N., 223, 484
Lewis, Abram Herbert, 54, 136, 223
Lewis, Alan E., 23
Lewis, C. S., 152
Lewis, David Isaac Melvin, 519
Lewis, Edwin, 106
Lewis, F. Warburton, 183
Lewis, Gordon R., 106, 423
Lewis, H. Spencer, 54, 136, 236

Lewis, Jack P., 303
Lewis, Jason, 79
Lewis, John, 401
Lewis, Karoline M., 339
Lewis, Lorna, 68
Lewis, Paul, 106
Lewis, Peter, 223
Lewis, Scott M., 339, 373
Lewis, W. S., 106, 303
Lias, J. J., 152, 390
Licona, Michael R., 23, 223, 253, 254, 469, 519
Liddon, H. P., 23, 443
Liderbach, Daniel, 183
Lidgett, J. Scott, 423
Liefeld, Walter L., 321
Lieu, Judith, 321
Life of Christ and his Apostles, 183
Life of Our Saviour Jesus Christ, The, 183
Liggins, Stephen S., 358
Lightfoot, John, 223, 321, 339, 358, 454
Lightfoot, Joseph Barber, 254, 358
Lightfoot, R. H., 284, 339
Lightner, Robert P., 423
Ligny, François de, 183
Lilley, James Samuel, 24
Lillie, William, 254
Limbaugh, David, 184, 423
Lincoln, Andrew T., 254, 339
Lindars, Barnabas, 254, 339
Lindberg, Conrad Emil, 106, 423
Linden, Philip Van, 284
Lindsay, Thomas Martin, 284, 321, 358
Lindsell, Harold, 423
Lindvall, Michael L., 184
Linn, Jan G., 423
Linn, Otto F., 339
Linton, Henry, 24, 373
Linton, Irwin H., 106
Lipscomb, A. A., 24
Lipscomb, David, 339
Lisle, Lionel, 106
Little, Paul E., 106
Little, Sophia L., 24
Litton, E. A. (Edward Arthur), 152, 423
Litwa, M. David, 223
Litwiller, Kurt Dean, 223
Livermore, Abiel Abbot, 303, 358, 454
Livingston, James C., 423
Livingstone, Elizabeth A., 504
Llagas, Carlos Manuel Maria A., 520
Lloyd, Mary Edna, 68
Loader, William, 532
Loane, Marcus L., 24
Lochman, Jan Milič, 390
Locke, F. M., 444

Locke, John, 106, 373
Lockerbie, D. Bruce, 390
Lockhart, Douglas, 54, 136, 184
Lockton, W., 24
Lockwood, Gregory J., 373
Lockyer, Herbert, 152, 184, 423, 504
Lockyer, Thomas F., 339
Lodahl, Michael, 423
Lodge, John C., 254
Lodge, Oliver, 152
Loewe, William P., 223
Loftus, John W., 54, 136
Lohfink, Gerhard, 184
Lohse, Bernhard, 423
Lohse, Eduard, 284
Loisy, Alfred, 236
Loken, John, 24
London Religious Tract Society, 152
Long, Abram M., 423
Long, George, 223
Long, Thomas G., 303
Longenecker, Richard N., 24, 358
Longford, Frank Pakenham, 184
Longking, Joseph, 184, 455
Longman, Tremper, 504
Longstaff, Thomas R. W., 254
Lonsdale, John, 455
Loomis, B. B., 358
Loos, H. van der, 152
Loots, Barbara Kunz, 68
Lopez, René A., 24
Lord, Charles E., 106
Lord, Willis, 423
Lorenzen, Thorwald, 24
Lorimer, George Claude, 107, 184, 223
Lorimer, William, 24
Losch, Henry, 184
Loughlin, Gerard, 254
Loughry, J. N., 24
Love, Stuart L., 303
Lovett, C. S., 358
Lovette, Roger, 339
Lowber, James William, 107
Lowder, Jeffrey Jay, 269–70
Lowrey, Asbury, 424
Lowrie, Walter, 184, 284
Lowry, Somerset Corry, 303
Loyd, Philip Henry, 339
Loysen, Jacobus A. St. Morilyon, 107
Lucado, Max, 184, 321, 339
Luccock, Robert Edward, 304
Luce, Harry Kenneth, 284, 304, 321
Luck, G. Coleman, 321, 373
Luck, William F., 520
Luckhoo, Lionel, 62

Luckock, Herbert Mortimer, 284
Lüdemann, Gerd, 44–45, 206, 270, 359
Ludington, James, 25
Ludlow, Daniel H., 504
Ludow, William L., 424
Ludwig, Emil, 184, 487
Lüedmann, Gerd. *See* Lüdemann, Gerd., 270
Lueker, Erwin L., 504
Lull, David John, 373
Lumby, J. Rawson, 359
Lunn, Arnold, 25, 55, 107, 136, 152
Lunn, Nicholas P., 285
Lunny, William J., 25, 107
Lushington, Thomas, 62, 444
Luthardt, Chr Ernst, 107, 339
Luther, Martin, 25, 223, 373, 455
Lüthi, Walter, 339
Luz, Ulrich, 304
Lygre, John Gerhard, 520
Lynch, Denis, 359
Lyttelton, A. T., 152
Lyttelton, Edward, 285
Lyttelton, George William, 359

M

Maahs, Kenneth H., 340
Maas, A. J., 184, 223, 304
Maass, Eliezer, 484
Mabera, Hussein Y., 478
Macan, Reginald Walter, 25
MacArthur, John, 25, 184, 285, 304, 321, 340, 359, 373, 424, 455
Macartney, Clarence Edward, 107, 223, 390
Macaulay, J. C., 304, 340, 359
Macbride, John David, 184, 401
MacDermott, George Martius, 285
MacDonald, Alexander, 390
MacDonald, D. B., 520
MacDonald, Dennis Ronald, 55, 136, 270, 285
MacDonald, George, 152
MacDonald, William, 304, 359
MacEvilly, John, 285, 304, 321, 340, 359, 373, 455
MacGorman, J. W., 374
MacGregor, Geddes, 391
MacGregor, G. H. C., 340
MacGregor, James, 107, 444
Machen, J. Gresham, 532
Machovec, Milan, 224
Mackall, Dandi Daley, 68
Mackay, D. M., 254
Mackenzie, Carine, 69
Mackenzie, Mary Jane, 152
Mackenzie, W. Douglas, 185, 424
Mackey, James P., 224, 424
Mackinnon, James, 185
Mackintosh, H. R., 224
Mackintosh, Robert, 107, 374
Macknight, James, 374
Maclaren, Alexander, 25, 285, 304, 321, 340, 444
Maclaren, William, 444
Maclear, G. F., 254, 285
MacMillan, Patricia Helene, 520
MacMunn, Vivian Charles, 25
MacPhail, J. R., 304
MacPherson, Alexander, 444
MacPherson, Duncan, 321
MacPherson, John, 424
MacPherson, Robert, 25
Macquarrie, John, 254, 424
MacRae, George W., 340
MacRory, Joseph, 340, 374
Macy, S. B., 224
Madany, Bassam M., 469
Madden, Richard C., 185
Maddox, Robert L., 359
Madgett, A. Patrick, 107
Madigan, Kevin J., 79, 107
Madison, David, 55
Madsen, Abdus Salam, 270
Madsen, Norman P., 340
Magness, J. Lee, 285
Maher, Robert W., 224
Mahoney, Robert P., 25, 340, 520
Maier, Paul L., 69, 185
Mair, Alexander, 107
Maitland, Brownlow, 152
Major, H. D. A., 224
Major, J. R., 321
Makrakes, Apostolos, 455
Malbon, Elizabeth Struthers, 285
Malcolm, Howard, 504
Malcolm, Matthew R., 374
Malden, R. H., 391
Maldonado, Robert D., 520
Maldonatus, Joannes, 304
Malesky, Charles Adam, 520
Malham, John, 107
Malina, Bruce J., 285, 304, 321, 340, 359, 374
Malleson, Frederick Amadeus, 185
Mallon, Elias D., 469
Maloney, George A., 25
Maltby, Edward, 107
Maltby, William Russell, 63

Names Index

Manetsch, Scott M., 374
Mangasar M. M., 55, 136
Manley, Basil, 424
Mann, C. S., 185, 285
Manning, Samuel, 63
Manser, Martin H., 504
Mansfield, M. Robert, 285
Mansini, Guy, 424
Manson, T. W., 185, 224
Manson, William, 321, 340
Maples, Kenneth, 520
Maqsood, Ruqaiyyah Waris, 478
March, Daniel, 185
Marchant, James, 25, 185
Marco, Anthony, 520
Marcus, Joel, 285
Mardon, Benjamin, 63
Mare, W. Harold, 374
Marguerat, Daniel, 254
Marijnen, P. A., 504
Marino, Joseph, 224
Markham, Ian S., 424
Markos, Louis, 107
Marks, Stanley J., 487
Marlow, John Thomas Arthur, 520
Marnas, Mélanie, 185
Marohi, Matthew J., 304
Marrow, Stanley B., 340, 374
Marsh, Charles R., 469
Marsh, Clive, 185
Marsh, F. E., 25, 532
Marsh, Gideon W. B., 26, 185
Marsh, Herbert, 424
Marsh, John, 185, 340
Marshall, Christopher D., 255
Marshall, David, 255
Marshall, F., 285, 304, 321
Marshall, I. H., 255, 285, 321, 359
Marshall, Martha, 69
Marshall, Peter, 26, 69
Martelet, Gustave, 26
Martensen, Hans, 224, 424
Marthaler, Bernard L., 391, 505
Martin, A. D., 185
Martin, Aleck, 63
Martin, Alfred W., 185, 374
Martin, Cecil, 107
Martin, Dale B., 374, 532
Martin, Francis, 340
Martin, George, 285, 304, 340
Martin, Hugh, 185, 321
Martin, James, 26, 185
Martin, James Alfred, 108
Martin, J. Walter, 26
Martin, Michael, 55, 137, 270

Martin, Ralph P., 285, 359, 374, 505
Martin, von Cochem, 186
Martin, Walter Ralston, 108, 424
Martindale, C. C., 285, 304, 321, 340, 359
Martinelli, Anthony, 401
Martinson, Paul Varo, 469
Marxsen, Willi, 26, 270
Mascall, Eric Lionel, 255, 424
Maskew, T. R., 359
Mason, Arthur James, 424
Mason, Richard, 444
Masood, Steven, 469
Masri, Fouad, 469
Massee, J. C., 26
Massey, James, 321, 359
Massie, Edward, 26
Massie, J., 374
Masson, Robert, 107
Masterman, J. H. B., 286
Mateo-Seco, Lucas Francisco, 505
Matera, Frank J., 26
Mather, Cotton, 444
Mather, Paul Boyd, 255, 520
Matheson, George, 185
Mathew, Parackel Kuriakose, 520
Mathews, Basil Joseph, 185
Mathews, George Martin, 224
Mathews, Shailer, 224, 424, 505
Mathewson, Steven D., 26
Matlock, Gene D., 478
Matson, Mark A., 340
Matthews, Leonard, 68
Matthews, Robert J., 255
Matthews, Shelly, 359
Matthews, W. R., 424
Mattill, A. J., 322
Mattison, Hiram, 79
Matzko, David McCarthy, 255
Mauck, John W., 359
Maurer, Andreas, 469
Mauriac, François, 186
Maurice, Frederick Denison, 224, 322, 340, 424
Maus, Cynthia Pearl, 224
Maxwell-Stuart, P. G., 79
May, Joseph, 55, 137, 157, 444
May, Melanie A., 425
Mayfield, Joseph H., 340
Maylone, W. Edgar, 55, 137
McAllister, Dawson, 26
McAteer, Michael R., 186
McAuliffe, Jane Dammen, 505
McBirnie, William Steuart, 186
McBride, Alfred, 286, 304, 322, 340, 359
McBride, Denis, 321

Names Index

McBrien, Richard P., 401
McBurnie, David, 108
McCabe, Joseph, 44, 55, 137, 505
McCaleb, John Moody, 444
McCament, David A., 520
McCane, Byron R., 270
McCann, Justin, 79, 255
McCarren, Paul J., 286, 304, 322, 341
McCarthy, Brian, 340
McCarty, W. A., 425
McCasland, S. Vernon, 26, 186, 520
McCaul, Alexander, 444
McClelland, Adam, 186
McClendon, James William, 425
McClintock, John, 505
McClure, Walter Emerson, 391
McClymond, Michael J., 224
McCollister, John C., 224
McComas, E. W., 55, 137, 206
McConaughy, James, 186
McConnachie, James, 55, 137
McConnell, T. M., 186
McCormick, Matthew S., 55, 137
McCosh, James, 108
McCrone, Walter, 224
McCrossan, Thomas J., 425
McCrum, Michael, 186
McCulloh, James M., 224
McCumber, William E., 304
McCurry, Don, 469
McDaniel, George White, 224
McDonald, James I. H., 26
McDonald, Lee Martin, 186, 520, 532
McDonough, Andrew, 69
McDowall, David, 520
McDowell, Bruce A., 469
McDowell, John, 108, 425
McDowell, Josh, 26–27, 108–9, 186, 224–25, 425, 469
McDowell, Sean, 255
McElrath, William N., 505
McEwen, James Stevenson, 391
McFadyen, John Edgar, 374
McFarland, Alex, 109
McFarland, Ian A., 505
McFarland, John Thomas, 186
McGann, Diarmuid, 341
McGarvey, J. W., 27, 109, 286, 305, 360
McGee, J. Vernon, 27, 63, 286, 322, 374, 455
McGiffert, Arthur Cushman, 425
McGillicuddy, T. P., 520
McGowan, James A., 286
McGrath, Alister E., 27, 109, 391, 425, 455, 505
McGrath, James F., 186
McGraw, Larry Ray, 520

McGrew, Lydia, 255
McGrew, Timothy, 255
McGuckin, John Anthony, 505
McIlvaine, Charles Pettit, 109, 444
McInerny, Ralph M., 152, 425
McIntyre, Don Virgil, 521
McIntyre, John, 341
McKay, Johnston R., 27
McKenna, David L., 286
McKenna, Megan, 27, 286, 305
McKenzie, Alyce M., 305
McKenzie, John L., 505
McKenzie, Leon, 27
McKenzie, Robert A., 27
McKibbon, W. Stan, 27
McKinley, J. L., 27
McKinsey, C. Dennis, 55, 137
McKenzie, C. W., 225
McKim, Donald K., 505
McKim, Ralph Harrison, 225
McKnight, Edgar V., 186
McKnight, Scot, 225, 255
McKown, Edgar Monroe, 425
McLaren, Robert Bruce, 186
McLaughlin, G. A., 286, 305, 322, 341, 360
McLeay, Simon, 521
McLeman, James, 27, 79
McLennan, William E., 187
McLeskey, James Meadows, 109
M'Clymont, J. A., 341
McMahon, Christopher, 225
McMahon, Edward John, 521
McMillan, Earle, 286
McNabb, Vincent, 187
McNeile, A. H., 305
McNicol, J., 322
McPheeters, Julian C., 374
McPolin, James, 341
McRoberts, Kerry D., 109
McTernan, Oliver J., 305
McWherter, Leroy, 187
McWhinney, Thomas M., 109
Meacham, William, 225
Mead, Charles Marsh, 109
Mead, G. R. S., 236
Meadows, W. S. H., 27
Meagher, Jas L., 187
Meagher, Paul K., 505
Means, Alexander, 441
Medhurst, Phillip, 286
Medina, Nestor, 521
Meehan, Sister Thomas More, 521
Meighan, Thomas (Londres), 109
Meier, John P., 225, 305
Meister, Chad V., 109

Mekkattukunnel, Andrew George, 521
Melanchthon, Philipp, 374
Meldau, Fred John, 110, 152, 225, 341
Mellenbruch, Parl Leslie, 425
Mellon, John C., 386
Memes, T. S., 425
Men, Alexander, 187
Mendelssohn, Moses, 488
Mendon Associates, 110
Menken, Maarten J. J., 255
Menuge, Angus, 256
Menzies, Allan, 286
Meredith, Evan Powell, 55, 137, 187
Merezhkovsky, Dmitry Sergeyevich, 187
Merrick, Mary Virginia, 187
Merrill, George E., 187
Merton, Thomas, 27
Merz, Philip Paul, 532
Meslier, Jean, 55
Messori, Vittorio, 187
Metaxas, Eric, 152
Metford, John C., 505
Mettinger, Tryggve, 79
Metz, Donald S., 374
Metzger, Bruce M., 505, 532
Metzger, Paul Louis, 341
Meulen, John M. Vander, 391
Meye, Robert P., 286
Meyer, Ben F., 187, 225
Meyer, Benjamin J., 521
Meyer, F. B., 187, 341, 391, 444
Meyer, Frank Herman, 187
Meyer, Heinrich August Wilhelm, 286, 305, 322, 341, 360, 375, 455
Meyer, Marvin, 256
Miall, Edward, 110
Michaelis, Johann David, 27
Michaels, J. Ramsey, 341
Michel, Otto, 256
Micklem, E. R., 187
Micklem, Nathaniel, 110, 375, 426
Micklem, Philip Arthur, 305
Micks, Marianne H., 426
Micou, Richard Wilde, 110
Miethe, Terry L., 110
Migliore, Daniel L., 426
Miles, Jack, 225
Miles, Leland Weber, 137
Miles, W. J., 56, 137
Miley, John, 426
Milinovich, Timothy, 375
Mill, William Hodge, 391
Millard, F. L. H., 286
Miller, Adam William, 305
Miller, Calvin, 69, 110, 152

Miller, Carol J., 341
Miller, Dave, 469
Miller, Donald G., 322
Miller, George Frazier, 444
Miller, Herbert Sumner, 110
Miller, J. R., 187, 401
Miller, Jean, 69
Miller, Laurence W., 27
Miller, Lucius Hopkins, 225
Miller, Madeleine (Sweeny), 505
Miller, Malcolm, 521
Miller, Randolph Crump, 110
Miller, Richard C., 28
Miller, Robert J., 56, 137, 207, 270
Miller, Roland E., 470
Miller, Ron, 305
Miller, Susan, 286
Miller, Thomas A., 28
Miller, Willard Gene, 521
Miller, William McElwee, 470
Miller, W. R., 256
Milligan, William, 28, 341, 375
Mills, David, 56, 137
Mills, Watson E., 28, 506
Milman, Henry Hart, 225
Milne, Bruce, 341, 426
Milne, Douglas J. W., 322
Milot, Jean-René, 470
Mimpriss, Robert, 225, 360
Minear, Paul S., 28, 286, 305, 341
Ministerial Association, General Conference of Seventh-day Adventists, 426
Minor, Mitzi, 286
Minton, Henry Colin, 110
Mirecki, Paul Allan, 521
Mirsch, David, 45
Mish'al Ibn Abdullah al-Kahdi, 478
Mishkin, David, 28, 484, 521
Mitch, Curtis, 305
Mitchell, Dan, 375
Mitchell, Joan L., 286
Mitchell, Margaret Mary, 375
Mitchell, Thomas, 79, 426
Mitchell, W. R., 225
Mitton, C. Leslie, 286
M'Neile, Hugh. *See* McNeile, 28
Moberly, George, 28
Moeser, Annelies G., 521
Moffatt, James, 188, 375, 532
Moffic, Eric, 488
Moginot, Albert F., 521
Mohammad, Maulana Hafiz Sher, 479
Mohammed, Ovey N., 479
Mohammed, Waffie, 479
Mohler, J. S., 28, 426

Molina, Franscico J., 521
Molnar, Paul D., 28
Moloney, Francis J., 28, 256, 286, 341
Moltmann, Jürgen, 110, 225–26, 256
Molyneux, Reginald E., 110
Moment, John J., 226
Monette, Greg, 521
Monfort, F. C., 426
Mongar, Thomas M., 56, 137
Montague, George T., 286, 305, 375
Montefiore, C. G., 287, 305, 322, 488
Montefiore, Hugh, 28, 153, 484
Montgomery, John Warwick, 110, 256, 426
Moody, Dale, 426
Moody, D. L., 445, 456
Moody, Paul D., 445
Moore, Aubrey Lackington, 110
Moore, Daniel F., 426
Moore, George, 236
Moore, Hight C., 226
Moore, Mark E., 256
Moore, T. V., 28
Moorehead, William G., 375
Moorman, John R. H, 322
More, Paul Elmer, 188
Moreland, J. P., 111, 256
Morell, Thomas, 188
Morey, Robert A., 470
Morgan, Charles Herbert, 341
Morgan, G. Campbell, 188, 287, 305, 322, 341,
    360, 375, 402, 445, 456
Morgan, Rex, 226
Morgan, Richard, 188
Morgan, Robert J., 111
Morison, Frank (pseud. Albert Henry Ross),
    28
Morison, James, 287, 305
Morison, John, 111
Morison, John Hopkins, 188, 305
Moritz, Joshua M., 256
Morley, Brian, 111
Morris, Henry M., 111
Morris, Leon, 305, 322, 341, 375
Morris, Wingfield Scott, 226
Morrison, Charles R., 28
Morrison, George H., 322
Morrison, John Douglas, 111
Morrison, Thomas, 360
Morrow, Jonathan, 111
Morse, Christopher, 426
Mortimer, Alfred G., 28, 391, 445
Moser, Julie, 69
Mosheim, Johann Lorenz, 226
Moss, Charles, 29, 256
Moss, Claude Beaufort, 426

Mott, George Scudder, 79
Mott, L. A., 256
Motter, Alton M., 29, 445
Moucarry, Chawkat, 111, 470
Moule, Arthur Evans, 112
Moule, C. F. D., 29, 287
Moule, H. C. G., 29, 426
Moulton, H. K., 360
Moulton, Richard G., 287, 306
Mounce, Robert H., 306, 341
Mounce, William D., 506
Mountcastle, William W., 56, 137, 207
Mountford, William, 153
Mourad, Suleiman A., 256, 470
Mowat, Oliver, 112
Mozley, J. K., 391
Mudge, Zachariah Atwell, 112
Mueller, David L., 426
Mueller, John Theodore, 392, 427
Mugarra Ahurwendeire, Athanasius, 521
Muggeridge, Malcolm, 188
Muhammad, Maulana Hafiz Sher, 479
Muḥammad Rashīd Ridā, 479
Muir, Robert H., 402
Muir, William, 470
Muirhead, Lewis Andrew, 342
Mulder, Frederik Sewerus, 521
Mull, Andrew B., 521
Müller, Michael, 392
Muller, Richard A., 506
Mullin, Robert Bruce, 153
Mullins, Edgar Young, 112, 427
Mullins, Michael, 287, 306, 322, 342, 360
Mullooparambil, Sebastian, 306
Mumaw, John R., 28
Mumley, William E., 522
Muncaster, Ralph O., 29, 112, 188
Munck, Johannes, 360
Mundt, Phil, 153
Munk, Arthur W., 112
Munro, Don W., 522
Murdock, D. M., 206
Murphy, Catherine M., 188
Murphy, Elspeth Campbell, 69
Murphy, John, 188
Murphy, Larry Edwin, 522
Murphy, Richard Thomas Aquinas, 28
Murphy-O'Connor, Jerome, 375
Murray, J. O. F., 342
Murray, William D., 226, 287
Murry, J. Middleton, 188
Musser, Donald W., 427, 506
Muzzey, Artemas Bowers, 112
Mvumbi, Frederic Ntedika, 470
Myers, Alicia D., 342

Names Index

Myers, Allen C., 506

N

Naik, Zakir, 479
Nairne, Charles Murray, 112
Nappa, Mike, 188
Nares, Edward, 392
Nash, John, 226
Nash, Robert Scott, 375
Nash, Ronald H., 112, 153, 226, 427
Nasrallah, Laura S., 375
Nast, Johann William, 287, 306
Nathan, Bruce A., 522
Navarante, Louis-Marie, 226
Navarre Bible, The, 322, 342
Nave, Orville J., 506
Navigators Ministry, 226
Navigators, The, 287
Naylor, Peter, 375
Neale, David A., 322
Neander, August, 188, 484
Neander, Johann August Wilhelm, 427
Nederveld, Patricia L., 69
Neff, LaVonne, 69
Nehls, Gerhard, 470
Neil, William, 360, 375
Neill, Stephen, 506, 532
Nelson, W. H., 188
Nelson's Introduction to Christian Faith, 427
Nelson's Teacher's Resource on First Corinthians, 375
Ness, Christopher, 455
Netton, Ian Richard, 506
Neufeld, Thomas R., 188
Neumann, Arno, 188
Neumann, R., 392
Neusner, Jacob, 506
Neville, David J., 257
Neville, Robert Cummings, 226
Nevin, Alfred, 322, 456
Nevins, Albert J., 506
Newbigin, Lesslie, 342
Newbolt, W. C. E., 342
New Catechism Catholic Faith for Adults, A, 402
Newcomb, Harvey, 112
Newcome, William, 188
Newheart, Michael Willett, 342
Newlands, George, 427
Newland-Smith, J. N., 392
Newman, Albert Henry, 226
Newman, Barclay Moon, 306, 342, 360
Newman, Carey C., 257
Newman, John Henry Cardinal, 153

Myers, Ched, 287

Newman, Randy, 226
Newman, Robert C., 257
Newman, T. C., 226
Newton, Benjamin Wills, 63
Newton, John, 445
Newton, Michael, 56, 138
Newton, Richard, 189
New Trial of the Witnesses, The, 29
New World Dictionary-Concordance to the New American Bible, The, 506
Neyrey, Jerome H., 29, 257, 342
Nichol, C. R., 427
Nichol, Francis D., 287, 306, 322, 342, 360, 375, 427
Nicholes, Lou, 375
Nicoll, W. Robertson, 189, 226, 375
Nicholls, William, 427
Nichols, Aidan, 402
Nichols, Ichabod, 112
Nichols, Laurie Fortunak, 470
Nicholson, Edward Williams Byron, 306
Nicholson, William, 506
Nicholson, William R., 153
Nickell, Joe, 45, 157, 236, 270
Nicklas, Tobias, 257
Nickle, Keith Fullerton, 332
Niebuhr, Richard R., 29, 257
Nielsen, Jesper Tang, 257
Niemojewski, Andrzej, 138
Nietzsche, Friedrich W., 138
Niles, Daniel T., 189
Nineham, D. E., 287
Nisbet, E., 79
Noble, Samuel, 29, 112, 402
Nodet, Etienne, 189
Noebel, David A., 427
Noel, Conrad, 189
Nolland, John, 306, 323
Nolloth, Charles Frederick, 189, 226, 342
Nonnus, of Nisibis, 342
Noort, G. Van, 402, 427
Norborg, C. Sverre, 189
Norris, Richard A., 427
North Africa Mission, 470
Norwood, Fredrick William, 323
Notovitch, Nicolas, 56, 138, 207
Nott, Abner Kingman, 445
Nott, Eliphalet, 29, 445
Nouet, Jacques, 29
Novakovic, Lidija, 29, 257
Nowell, Alexander, 402

Names Index

Nowell-Rostron, S., 376
Noyalis, Walter Jerome, 522
Nseka, Christian Kita, 29

Nunn, Henry Preston Vaughan, 427
Nystrom, Carolyn, 376

O

Obach, Robert E., 323
O'Brien, John A., 112, 189
O'Carroll, Michael, 506
Ochs, Christoph, 532
Ochsenford, S. E., 30
Ockenga, Harold John, 445
O'Collins, Gerald, 30, 189, 226, 257, 392, 402, 506
O'Connell, John P., 189
O'Day, Gail R., 257, 342, 360
Oden, Thomas C., 287, 427
O'Donnell, Douglas Sean, 306
Odor, Ruth Shannon, 69
Offerman, Henry, 306
O'Flynn, J. A., 287
Ogden, John, 392
Ogden, Schubert Miles, 427
Ogilvie, Lloyd John, 287, 360
Oglesby, Stuart R., 342
O'Grady, John F., 227, 306, 343, 402
Okure, Teresa, 257
O'Leary, Finbarr, 522
Olevianus, Caspar, 392
Oliver, Isaac Wilk, 522
Olivi, Pierre Jean, 287
Olmstead, A. T., 189
O'Loughlin, Thomas, 257
Olsen, Erling C., 343
Olshausen, Hermann, 30, 360, 376, 456
Olson, Carl E., 30
Olson, Raymond M., 522
Olson, Roger E., 506
Oluwafemi, Titus, 522
O'Malley, William J., 287
O'Neill, J. C., 258

Onesimus, Captain (pseud. John Hewson), 30
Onuoha, Anselm E., 522
Oosterzee, Johannes Jacobus van, 323, 428
O'Rafferty, Nicholas, 392
Orchard, Bernard, 189
Orchard, W. E., 428
Ordal, Z. J., 30
O'Reilly, Laurie M., 522
Origen, 56, 112, 138
Orr, J. Edwin, 112
Orr, James, 30, 112, 428, 506
Orr, William F., 376
Os, Bas van, 257
Osborn, Edwin Faxon, 189
Osborne, Cecil G., 112
Osborne, Grant R., 30, 258, 287, 306, 522
Osborne, Harold, 227
Osborne, Kenan B., 30
Osiek, Carolyn, 258
Osman, Ahmed, 56, 138, 207
Oster, Richard, 376
Ott, Ludwig, 402
Ottati, Douglas F., 428
Ottley, Robert Lawrence, 392
Otto, Randall E., 428
Ousler, Fulton, 227
Overman, J. Andrew, 306
Owen, John J., 287, 306, 323, 343, 360
Owen, John Pickard (pseud. Samuel Butler), 56
Owen, Robert, 113, 428
Oxford Layman, 30
Oxley, Mark, 227
Oyen, Geert van, 288
Oyer, Linda, 522

P

Paassen, Pierre van, 56, 138, 189, 232
Packard, Frederick A., 506
Packer, J. I., 392, 428
Packer, J. W., 360
Padgett, Alan G., 153, 258
Page, Charles R., 189
Page, James R., 393
Page, Kirby, 189
Page, Nick, 190
Page, T. E., 360
Pagels, Elaine, 56, 138

Pagliarino, Guido, 227
Pagola, Jose Antonio, 190, 306
Paine, Thomas, 57, 138, 236, 445
Painter, John, 258, 288, 343
Paley, William, 113
Pallis, Alexandros, 323, 360
Palmer, Albert W., 428
Palmer, David G., 288
Palmer, Earl F., 343
Palmer, Edwin H., 507
Palmer, Francis B., 153

Names Index

Palmer, Joseph, 31
Palmer, Roland F., 393
Palmer, Sydney, 258
Pamplaniyil, Joseph Thomas, 258
Pannenberg, Wolfhart, 227, 258, 393, 428
Pannozzi, Frank J., 522
Panton, D. M., 63
Pao, David W., 258
Papadopoulos, Gerasimos, 343
Papini, Giovanni, 190
Pappas, Paul C., 207, 479
Pappas, Thomas C., 522
Paradise, Frank Ilsley, 190
Parambi, Baby, 306, 522
Parānanda, Sri, 343
Pardington, George P., 428
Parente, Pietro, 507
Parini, Jay, 190
Parker, Joseph, 288, 307, 323, 361, 376
Parker, Pierson, 307
Parks, Leighton, 428
Parrinder, Geoffrey, 470
Parris, David, 522
Parry, R. St. John, 376
Parshall, Phil, 470
Parsons, Elmer E., 522
Parsons, Keith, 270
Parsons, Lawrence (Earl of Rosse), 113
Parsons, Mikeal C., 31, 323, 361, 522
Parton, Craig A., 113, 258
Pascal, Blaise, 113
Pasco, Rowanne, 402
Pascuzzi, Maria, 376
Passmore, William, 428
Pate, C. Marvin, 190, 323, 343
Patella, Michael, 323
Paternoster, Michael, 31
Paterson, Alexander Smith, 402
Paterson, Andrea C., 113, 470
Patey, Edward H., 113
Paton, James, 31
Patrick, John, 113
Patrick, Simon, 31
Patrinacos, Nicon D., 507
Patte, Daniel, 307, 507
Patterson, Alexander, 190
Patterson, Bob E., 307
Patterson, Paige, 258
Patterson, Robert, 113
Patterson, Stephen J., 190
Patton, Francis Landey, 428
Patton, William, 190, 456
Patzia, Arthur G., 227
Paul, Geoffrey J., 288, 343
Paul, Leslie Allen, 190

Pawlitz, Gail, 69
Pawson, David, 31
Pax, Wolfgang E., 190
Paxy, Alumkal Jacob, 31
Paynter, H. M., 31
Peabody, Andrew P., 113, 445
Peabody, David Barrett, 288
Peacocke, Arthur, 153
Peake, Arthur S., 258, 428
Pearce, Zachary, 31, 153
Pearson, Charles William, 190
Pearson, John, 393
Peck, Edson Ruther, 288, 343
Peifer, Claude J., 376
Peirce, Bradford K., 361
Pelikan, Jaroslav, 361, 428
Peloubet, F. N., 307, 361
Penrose, John , 153
Pentecost, Geo F., 343
Pentecost, J. Dwight, 153
Perakh, Mark, 138, 157
Percival, Henry R., 429
Perdue, Cary Milburn, 361
Perkins, Daniel Elinor, 522
Perkins, Mitali, 471
Perkins, Pheme, 31, 227, 258, 288, 343, 376, 393
Perkins, Rufus Lord, 31
Perlewitz, Miriam, 307
Perrin, Norman, 31, 288, 532
Perrotta, Kevin, 323
Perry, Charles Austin, 31
Perry, John M., 31
Perry, Michael C., 31, 79, 153, 259
Perschbacher, Wesley J., 523
Pervo, Richard I., 361
Peters, F. E., 190, 471
Peters, G. M., 190
Peters, Ted, 32, 79, 153, 259, 429
Petersen, Harry Frederick., 523
Petersen, William L., 523
Peterson, David, 259
Peterson, David G., 361
Peterson, Eugene H., 32
Peterson, Paul K., 32
Petrelli, Giuseppe, 227
Petrosillo, Orazion, 227
Petterson, Christina, 343
Pettingill, William L., 307, 376
Petty, Daniel W., 32
Pfeiffer, C. Boyd, 138
Phelps, Elizabeth Stuart, 190
Phelps, Ryan Kendall, 523
Phelps, William Lyon, 63
Philip, James, 445

Names Index

Philip, Robert, 113
Philippson, Ludwig, 488
Philipse, Herman, 138
Phillips, Arnold Douglas, 288
Phillips, Forbes Alexander, 32
Phillips, J. B., 288, 429
Phillips, John, 288, 307, 323, 343, 361, 376
Phillips, Vicki Cass, 523
Phillips, Walter, 471
Phillips, Wendell, 190
Phipps, William E., 153
Piatt, Christian, 191
Pictet, Bénédict, 113, 429
Picirilli, Robert E., 288, 376
Pick, Bernhard, 207
Pickering, David, 113
Pickl, Josef, 191
Piconio, Bernadine à, 376
Piepenbring, Charles, 191
Pieper, Francis, 429
Pierce, Samuel Eyles, 445
Piercy, William C., 507
Pierson, Arthur Tappan, 114
Pierson, Mark A., 259
Pierson, Paul Everett, 361
Pieters, Albertus, 114
Pike, Diane Kennedy, 227
Pike, E. Royston, 507
Pilch, John J., 361, 402
Pilcher, Charles Venn, 79
Pine, Thomas, 32
Pinfold, James T., 323
Pingry, Patricia A., 69
Pink, Arthur W., 343
Pinnock, Clark H., 113, 429
Pipe, Rhona, 69
Piper, Sophia, 69
Pitre, Brant James, 191
Pittsburgh Conference, The, 488
Pitzer, Alexander White, 227
Placher, William C., 227, 288
Plantinga, Alvin, 114
Platt, David, 227, 307
Playoust, Catherine Anne, 523
Plummer, Alfred, 288, 307, 323, 343
Plumptre, E. H., 288, 307, 323, 191, 227
Pöelzl, Franz Xaver, 32
Pohier, Jacques Marie, 429
Pohle, Joseph, 429
Pokorný, Petr, 227, 259
Polhill, John B., 361
Poling, Daniel A., 191, 227
Poling, Judson, 114
Polkinghorne, John C., 153–54, 393, 429
Pollard, George Frederick, 32

Pollock, A. J., 32
Pollock, John, 191
Ponsonby, Reginald G., 191
Poole, Garry, 114
Poole, George Ayliffe, 393
Poole, Matthew, 288, 307, 323, 343, 361, 376, 456
Poole, Michael, 114
Poole, Susie, 69
Poovey, W. A., 307
Pope, William Burt, 429
Porcupine, Peter, 138
Porter, J. L., 456
Porter, J. R., 191, 227, 532
Porter, L. Aldin, 259
Porter, Stanley E., 32, 191, 259, 343
Porteous, Alvin C., 429
Porteus, Beilby, 114, 307
Portier, William L., 429
Poteat, Edwin McNeill, 32
Potin, Jacques, 191
Potts, James Henry, 114
Potts, John Faulkner, 402
Powell, Baden, 157
Powell, Doug, 114
Powell, Ivor, 288, 307, 323, 361
Powell, J. Enoch, 307
Powell, Mark Allan, 259, 323, 507
Power, Philip Bennett, 32, 191
Powers, B. Ward, 376
Powers, Joseph M., 429
Powery, Emerson B., 288
Powys, Llewelyn, 57, 138
Poynter, William, 114
Poythress, Vern S., 154
Practical Christianity Foundation, 376
Prange, Victor H., 323
Prat, Ferdinand, 191
Pratt, Richard L., 376
Pregeant, Russell, 307, 532
Prenter, Regin, 429
Presbyterian Board of Publication, 507
Prescott, John Eustace, 288, 307
Pressensé, Edmond de, 191
Prevallet, Elaine Marie, 523
Price, Charles, 307
Price, Eugenia, 361
Price, James L., 532
Price, Nelson L., 32
Price, R. G., 139
Price, Robert M., 45, 57, 139, 207, 236, 271
Priceless Pearls for All Christians, 32
Pridham, Arthur, 376
Pries, Mitchell Peter, 63
Priestley, Joseph, 32, 114, 259

571

Prince, Deborah Thompson, 523
Prince, Nathan, 63
Prior, David, 376
Prior, Kenneth Francis William, 115
Pritchard, John, 32, 115
Proctor, John, 307, 376
Proctor, William, 33
Prokofieff, Sergei O., 45
Protestant Episcopal Society for the Promotion of Evangelical Knowledge, 115
Proud, J., 445
Prozesky, Martin, 430
Pryor, John W., 344
Puig i Tàrrech, Armand, 191
Puiseux, J., 191
Pulley, Kelly, 69
Pullman, Philip, 139
Pulsford, W. Hanson, 191
Punter, Russell, 69
Purim, Reynaldo, 523
Purinton, Herbert R., 191, 227
Purkiser, W. T., 430
Purves, Andrew, 33
Purves, George T., 227
Puskas, Charles B., 523
Pyle, Thomas, 361
Pyysiäinen, Ilkka, 271

Q

Qadir, Shaikh Abdul, 271
Qasem, Mohamed, 479
Quackenbos, John D., 115
Quarles, Charles L., 33, 259
Quast, Kevin, 344, 377
Quattlebaum, Mary, 69
Quenot, Michel, 33
Queripel, John Henry, 33
Quick, Oliver Chase, 115, 430
Quimby, Chester Warren, 344
Quist, Allen, 115
Qureshi, Nabeel, 471

R

Racine, Jean-François, 307
Rackham, Richard Belward, 361
Radner, Ephraim, 227
Rae, Murray, 430, 532
Rafiq, B. A., 271
Ragg, Lonsdale, 115, 323
Rahner, Karl, 79, 115, 430, 507
Rainbow, Paul A., 344
Räisänen, Heikki, 228
Rall, Harris Franklin, 192, 533
Ralston, Thomas N., 430
Rambsel, Yacov, 484
Ramm, Bernard L., 115, 430
Ramsay, D. M., 63, 115, 445
Ramsay, William M., 361
Ramsbottom, B. A., 69
Ramsey, A. Michael, 33, 259, 430
Ramsey, Russ, 192
Rand, William W., 507
Randolph, B. W., 33
Randolph, Thomas, 192
Ranke-Heinemann, Uta, 57, 139
Rankin, James, 393
Rankin, John Chambers, 192
Rao, Bandi Sreenivasa, 471
Rattray, Thomas, 446
Ratzinger, Cardinal Joseph, 393, 402
Rausch, Thomas P., 228, 403
Rauser, Randal, 115
Raven, Frederick Edward, 344
Rawlinson, A. E. J., 259, 288
Rawson, Christopher, 69
Ray, Jerry Lynn, 523
Ray, Stephen K., 344
Rayburn, Cherie, 70
Raymond, Bradford Paul, 115, 430
Raymond, Miner, 430
Read, Jan A. du, 259
Reader's Digest, 228
Read-Heimerdinger, J., 260
Reading, William, 192
Real Dialogues on the Evidences of Christianity, 115
Reams, William, 192
Reardon, Patrick Henry, 192
Reber, George, 228
Redford, R. A., 116
Redlich, Edwin Basil, 289
Redpath, Alan, 377
Reed, Charles E. B., 228
Reed, Elizabeth A., 116
Reed, Oscar F., 377
Rees, Abraham, 507
Rees, W., 377
Reese, Gareth L., 351
Reese, William L., 507
Reeves, Keith Howard, 33, 308, 523
Register, Ray G., 471

Names Index

Reichel, Charles Parsons, 446
Reichenbach, Bruce R., 79
Reid, Barbara E., 308, 323
Reid, Daniel G., 507
Reid, Louis Arnaud, 116
Reid, Robert Stephen, 260, 289
Reiling, J., 323
Reimarus, Hermann Samuel, 57, 139
Reimer, Andy M., 260
Rein, Gerhard, 393
Reinhartz, Adele, 523
Reiser, William, 228
Reiss, Robert, 116
Reith, George, 344
Religious Tract Society, The, 154
Rellstab, Theodore L., 523
Remsburg, John E., 139, 207
Renan, Ernest, 57, 139, 207, 361
Rendell, James, 523
Rensberger, Davis, 344
Rensburg, Hanré Janse van, 523
Reumann, John, 192
Rex, H. H., 33
Reymond, Robert L., 116
Reynell, Carew, 446
Reynolds, Andrew, J., 228
Rheaume, Randy, 344
Rhees, Rush, 192
Rhein, Francis Bayard, 430
Rhodes, Ron, 116, 471
Rhymer, Joseph, 192
Rhys, Jocelyn, 45, 57, 139
Ricciotti, Giuseppe, 192, 361
Rice, Daniel, 446
Rice, Edwin Wilbur, 289, 361, 308, 324, 344, 361
Rice, John R., 33, 228, 308, 362, 377
Rice, Richard, 430
Richards, Hubert J., 33
Richards, Larry, 308
Richards, Lawrence O., 456, 507
Richards, William Rogers, 393
Richardson, Alan, 116, 154, 344, 430, 508, 533
Richardson, Don, 471
Richardson, Joel, 471
Richardson, Robert D., 430
Richardson, Robert Lee, 523
Richey, Thomas, 430
Richter, Rick, 471
Rickaby, Joseph, 308, 344, 377
Ricker, George M., 393
Riddell, Peter G., 471
Ridderbos, Herman N., 308, 344
Riddle, Matthew B., 289, 324
Riddle, T. Wilkinson, 33

Ridgeley, Thomas, 430
Ridgeon, Lloyd V. J., 471
Riegel, Joseph, 523
Riga, Peter J., 33
Rigato, Maria-Luisa, 260
Rigaux, Béda, 308
Riggenbach, Eduard, 33
Riggs, James Stevenson, 344, 377
Riggs, Ollie L., 33
Riley, Gregory J., 33, 344, 523
Riley, Harold, 289
Riley, W. B., 456
Rinaldi, Peter M., 228
Ring, T. P., 33
Ringe, Sharon H., 324
Riper, David Van, 33
Ripley, Henry J., 361
Rishell, Charles W., 116
Riss, Richard M., 33
Ritchie, Arthur, 308, 324
Robbins, Wilford L., 116
Roberson, Carroll, 192
Roberts, A. Wayne, 116
Roberts, Griffith, 34
Roberts, Jonathan M., 236
Roberts, Michael Symmons, 154
Roberts, Phil, 260
Roberts, Robert, 34
Roberts, T. A., 523
Robertson, A. Irvine, 289
Robertson, Archibald (1886–1961, atheist), 207
Robertson, Archibald (1853–1931, bishop), 377, 446
Robertson, Arthur K., 308
Robertson, A. T., 192, 289, 308, 324, 344, 362, 377, 456, 533
Robertson, Cindy, 70
Robertson, E. H., 377
Robertson, F. W., 377
Robertson, Jenny, 70
Robertson, J. M., 57, 139, 237
Robertson, William, 362
Robinette, Brian DuWayne, 34
Robinson, Anthony B., 362
Robinson, Arthur W., 228
Robinson, Benjamin Willard, 345
Robinson, Charles H., 34, 289
Robinson, Chas. S., 324
Robinson, Cyril E., 289
Robinson, Donald F., 192
Robinson, Edward, 117, 508
Robinson, Ezekiel Gilman, 117
Robinson, Frank B., 289
Robinson, Godfrey Clive, 431

Robinson, John, 508
Robinson, John A. T., 117, 228, 345, 394, 431
Robinson, Maurice A., 260
Robinson, Neal, 471
Robinson, Neil, 57, 139
Robinson, Sandra E., 70
Robinson, Theodore H., 289, 308
Robinson, Thomas, 431, 457
Robson, John, 34
Rock, Lois, 70
Rodd, Cyril S., 289
Rodgers, John H., 403
Rodriguez, K. S., 70
Roffman, Etomar Ben, 488
Rogers, Arthur Kenyon, 192
Rogers, Clement F., 63, 117, 154
Rogers, James Edwin Thorold, 192
Rogers, John R., 271
Rogers, Raymond N., 228
Rogers, Thomas, 403
Rogerson, John, 154
Rohr, Richard, 324
Rolfe, Eugene, 117
Rolfus, H., 394
Rollins, Wallace Eugene, 192
Rollock, Robert, 34, 403
Rolt, C. E., 80
Roop, Hervin Ulysses, 117
Roper, Albert L., 34
Roscamp, R. G., 193
Rose, V. (Vincent), 228, 324
Rosen, Moishe, 484
Rosenberg, Roy A., 488
Rosenberg, Stuart E., 488
Ross, Alexander Wendell, 193
Ross, C. Randolph, 431
Ross, George Alexander Johnston, 394
Ross, Hugh, 154
Ross, J. M. E., 324
Ross, John A., 394
Ross, Mark E., 308
Ross, William Stewart. *See* Saladin., 45, 140
Rota, Michael, 154, 431
Roth, Cecil, 488, 508
Roth, Timothy Dean, 34, 193
Rottmann, Erik, 70
Roukema, Riemer, 228
Roustaing, J. B., 457
Row, C. A., 117, 193, 260
Rowe, Christopher Kavin, 324
Rowe, Samuel, 117
Rowland, Christopher, 260
Rowlandson, William Henry, 289
Rowley, H. H., 508
Rowlingson, Donald Taggart, 193
Royster, Dmitri, 345
Rubin, Barry, 484
Ruch, Velma, 34
Ruef, J. S., 377
Ruffner, Henry, 260
Rufinus Aquileinsis, 394
Runcorn, David, 34
Rushdoony, Rousas John, 345
Russell, C. Allyn, 431
Russell-Caley, W. B., 394
Russell, Charles Taze, 403
Russell, Jeffrey Burton, 117
Russell, John (Viscount Amberley), 237
Russell, Letty, 508
Rustomjee, Framroz, 193
Rutland, Mark, 34
Rutter, Henry, 228
Ryken, LeLand, 508
Ryken, Philip Graham, 324
Ryland, John, 193
Rylander, Mark Allen, 524
Rylands, L. Gordon, 57, 140
Ryle, H. E., 260
Ryle, J. C., 289, 308, 324, 345, 457
Ryn, August Van, 362
Ryrie, Charles Caldwell, 362, 431

S

Saal, William J., 471
Sabin, Marie Noonan, 289
Sabourin, Leopold, 308, 324
Sachar, Abram Leon, 488
Sackman, Lana, 193
Sadler, Gilbert T., 457
Sadler, I. A., 34
Sadler, J. of Stoke-upon-Trent, 193
Sadler, M. F., 289, 308, 324, 345, 362, 377
Sadr-ud-Din, 471
Safa, Reza F., 471
Sagebeer, Joseph Evans, 117
Sahas, Daniel J., 472
Sailhamer, John H., 193, 431, 457
Sakenfeld, Katharine Doob, 508
Saladin (pseud. William Stewart Ross), 45
Salibi, Kamal, 208, 479
Salier, Willis Hedley, 345
Sallmon, William H., 193
Salmon, Edgar Frank, 118
Salmond, S. D. F., 193, 289
Salter, James, 403

Sampley, J. Paul, 377
Salstrand, George A. E., 228
Samir Khalil Samir, 261
Samples, Kenneth R., 431
San, Myat Shwe, 524
Sancken, Joni S., 34
Sanday, William, 193, 345
Sanders, E. P., 193
Sanders, Frank Knight, 193
Sanders, J. N., 345
Sanders, J. Oswald, 228, 308
Sanders, Nancy I., 70
Sanders, Phil, 118
Sanderson, Edgar, 394
Sandison, Geo H., 118
Sandlin, P. Andrew, 63
Sandmel, Samuel, 488
Sandoval, Chris, 45
Sanford, Elias B., 508
Sanford, John A., 345
Sanner, A. Elwood, 289
Santala, Risto, 228
Santayana, George, 228
Santucci, Luigi, 198
Saphir, Adolph, 446
Sargent, Frederick, 457
Sargent, James E., 362
Saritoprak, Zeki, 479
Sarker, Abraham, 472
Sarrels, Elder R. V., 431
Satta, Ronald F., 118
Satterlee, Henry Yates, 394
Saunders, Daniel J., 118
Saunders, Ernest W., 194, 345
Saunders, Stanley P., 308
Saurin, James, 446
Savage, Minot Judson, 194
Savarino, Joseph, 524
Sawicki, Marianne, 34
Sawyer, Elbert H., 229
Sawyer, John F. A., 508
Sawyer, Karen Elaine, 524
Sawyer, Leicester, 289
Sayers, Dorothy L., 63, 70, 118
Sayers, Stanley E., 34
Schaaffs, Werner, 154
Schaberg, Jane D., 308, 324, 524
Schaeffer, Charles Frederick, 309
Schaeffer, Susan E., 261
Scaer, David P., 309
Scarborough, Lee Rutland, 34
Scepticism Credulity, 118
Schäfer, Peter, 237
Schaff, Philip, 229, 309, 508
Schanz, Paul, 118

Schauffler, William G., 194
Scheffczk, Leo, 118
Schenck, Ferdinand Schureman, 394
Schep, J. A., 80
Schermerham, Martin Kellogg, 118
Schidlovsky, Dimitry, 70
Schillebeeckx, Edward, 229
Schilling, S. Paul, 431
Schiotz, Fredik Axel, 524
Schirrmacher, Christine, 472
Schlagel, Richard H., 57, 140, 157
Schlatter, Adolf, 229, 394
Schleiermacher, Friedrich, 194, 324, 431
Schlesinger, Max Shlezinger, 488
Schlier, Heinrich, 34
Schlink, Edmund, 194
Schmalenberger, Jerry L., 446
Schmaus, Michael, 431
Schmid, Heinrich, 431
Schmid, Josef, 289
Schmid, U. B., 345
Schmidt, Alvin J., 472
Schmidt, Austin G., 118
Schmidt, Dan, 309
Schmidt, Daryl Dean, 289
Schmidt, Martin J., 446, 524
Schmidt, Nathaniel, 194, 229
Schmiedel, Paul Wilhelm, 345
Schmisek, Brian, 80
Schnabel, Eckhard J., 194, 362
Schnackenburg, Rudolf, 290, 309, 345
Schnaus, Edward Urban, 524
Schneiders, Sandra Marie, 35, 261, 345, 524
Schnelle, Udo, 261
Schönborn, Christoph Cardinal, 229, 290, 324
Schonfield, Hugh J., 45, 57, 140, 208
Schreiner, Thomas R., 533
Schroeder, Frederick W., 446
Schröter, Jens, 194
Schultz, Emil, 118
Schultz, Hermann, 118
Schultze, Augustus, 431
Schumann, Olaf H., 472
Schutte, Flip, 35
Schwager, Raymund, 229
Schwalbe, Larry, 229
Schwartz, G. David, 489
Schwartzkopff, Paul, 35, 194
Schwarz, Hans, 229, 431
Schwarzwäller, Klaus, 35
Schweitzer, Albert, 194
Schweitzer, Don, 194
Schweizer, Eduard, 194, 229, 290, 309, 324
Scorgie, Glen G., 508
Scott, A. Boyd, 394

Scott, Bernard Brandon, 45
Scott, Ernest F., 118, 229
Scott, Kevin F., 118
Scott, John, 431
Scott, John P., 309, 324, 345, 457
Scott, Joseph John, 194
Scott, Macrina, 324
Scott, Martin, 345
Scott, Martin J., 118
Scott, Robert, 118, 472
Scott, Thomas (1808–1878), 57, 64, 140, 194, 457
Scott, Thomas (1747–1821), 119
Scott, W. A., 394
Scott, W. Frank, 345
Scratton, George, 309
Scroggie, W. Graham, 290, 324, 345, 362, 394
Scrymgeour, William, 195, 229
Seabury, William Jones, 64
Seal, Welton Ollie, Jr., 524
Seamands, Stephen, 446
Sears, Edmund H., 80, 346
Seaton, Thomas, 432
Seaver, Richard W., 119, 194
Seber, G. A. F., 119
Séché, Alphonse, 195
Secker, Thomas, 394, 403
See, Steven H., 524
Seelye, Julius H., 446
Segal, Alan F., 271, 489
Segundo, Juan Luis, 195
Seidenspinner, Charles, 446
Seilhamer, Frank H., 395
Selbie, W. B., 195
Selby, Donald J., 533
Selby, Peter, 35
Selby, Peter Stephen Maurice, 524
Selecman, Charles C., 119
Sell, Henry T., 195, 533
Selwyn, Edward Gordon, 64, 432
Senior, Donald, 261, 309
Sensenig, Barton, 229
Serendipity House, 290
Sermon preach'd against Quakerism, A, 446
Setzer, Claudia, 80, 261
Setzer, Robert B., 346
Sewall, Frank, 119
Sexton, Charnel Sterling, 524
Sexton, George, 119
Seymour, Jody, 290
Shade, W. Robert, 362
Shafto, G. R. H., 35
Shams, J. D., 479
Shank, Douglas H., 524
Shannon, Foster H., 119

Shapiro, Lawrence, 157
Shapiro, Rami M., 489
Sharman, Henry Burton, 229
Sharp, John, 447
Sharp, Mary Jo, 261
Sharpe, Kevin, 154
Shaw, A. R., 432
Shaw, Benjamin C., 524
Shaw, Elton Raymond, 195
Shaw, Fernando, 457
Shaw, Gregory, 261
Shaw, John Mackintosh, 35, 432
Sheaffer, Robert, 140
Shearer, J. B., 195
Shearer, James W., 195
Shedinger, Robert F., 472
Shedd, William G. T., 432
Sheed, F. J., 195, 403
Sheehan, Michael, 119, 403
Sheehan, Thomas, 45, 58, 140, 271
Sheen, F. J. (Francis J.), 195
Sheldon, Henry C., 58, 140, 432
Shelly, Rubel, 119
Shelton, Lee Roy, 447
Shem, G., 472
Shenk, David W., 472
Shepard, John Watson, 195
Shepard, Robert Burpo, 524
Shepherd, William, 362
Shepherd, William Henry, 35, 447
Sheppard, John, 119
Sherlock, Thomas, 35, 261
Sherman, Henry, 447
Sherman, Loren Albert, 80
Sherwood, Thomas E., 525
Shideler, Mary McDermott, 395
Shields, Charles Woodward, 119
Shimodate, Madao, 525
Shiner, Whitney Taylor, 290
Shittu, Abdur-Raheem Adebayo, 479
Shore, T. Teignmouth, 377
Shorrosh, Anis A., 119, 472
Short, Frank B., 119
Shorto, Russell, 195
Sibbes, Richard, 447
Sibly, Manoah, 447
Siddiqi, Muzammil H., 479
Siddiqui, Mona, 472
Sieker, Adolphus Theodore, 119
Sigal, Gerald, 45, 489
Silver, Abba Hillel, 489
Silverstein, Philip, 525
Silvester, Tipping, 35
Simcox, Carroll E., 309, 395
Simmons, Alfred Henry, 395

Names Index

Simon, Mary Manz, 70
Simon, Ulrich E., 35
Simon, W. G. H. (William Glyn Hughes), 377
Simonetti, Manlio, 309
Simonson, Louisie, 70
Simpson, A. B., 35, 309, 325, 346, 432, 457
Simpson, John, 119
Simpson, Matthew, 447, 508
Sinclair, Scott G., 346
Sinclair, Upton, 195
Singer, Isadore, 508
Singer, Tovia, 272, 489
Singh, Bakht, 64
Singh, David Emmanuel, 472
Singmaster, J. A., 432
Siniscalchi, Glenn B., 119
Sinkinson, Chris, 120
Sinnott-Armstrong, Walter, 58, 140, 272
Sire, James W., 120, 229, 432
Sirr, Joh D'Arcy, 35
Sitterly, Charles Fremont, 362
Skarmeas Nancy J., 70
Skelly, A. M., 229
Skinner, Andrew C., 35
Skinner, Christopher W., 346
Skinner, Conrad, 229
Skinner, Matthew L., 458
Skolfield, R. C. E., 272
Skolnik, Fred, 508
Skrine, John Huntley, 35, 395
Slack, Elvira J., 195
Slater, W. F., 309
Slattery, Charles Lewis, 80, 447
Sledd, Andrew, 290, 362
Sleeman, Matthew, 35, 261
Sleeper, Charles Freeman, 525
Sleigh, W. W., 120, 508
Slenczka, Notger, 261
Sloan, Harold Paul, 36, 395
Sloyan, Gerard S., 195, 229, 290, 346
Slusser, Dorothy M., 290
Smalbroke, Richard, 154
Smart, James D., 395, 432
Smart, J. J. C., 58, 140
Smith, Arthur D. Howell, 208
Smith, B. T. D., 309
Smith, Charles W. F., 230
Smith, Christian, 140
Smith, Chuck, 290, 309
Smith, D. Moody, 346
Smith, Dana Prom, 395
Smith, Daniel Alan, 36, 525
Smith, Daniel Evans, 525
Smith, David, 196, 290, 309, 325
Smith, Dennis E., 346
Smith, Elias, 64
Smith, George D., 403
Smith, George H., 58
Smith, George Williamson, 120
Smith, Graeme, 36, 120
Smith, Hamilton, 290
Smith, Harold, 395
Smith, Homer, 140
Smith, James, 362
Smith, James Hamblin, 362
Smith, Joseph, 403
Smith, Judith F., 395
Smith, Kenneth, 525
Smith, Mahon T., 525
Smith, Martina, 70
Smith, Miles Woodward, 362
Smith, Paul, 196
Smith, Robert H., 36, 309, 346, 362, 525
Smith, Robert Ora, 196
Smith, Samuel, 120
Smith, Samuel Stanhope, 120, 432
Smith, Shelton L., 472
Smith, Sydney F., 290
Smith, Terrell D., 70
Smith, Thomas Joseph, 290
Smith, Wilbur M., 36, 64, 120, 230, 261, 447
Smith, William, 509, 533
Smith, William A. M., 196
Smith, William Benjamin, 237
Smyth, John Paterson, 196
Smyth, Julian Kennedy, 432
Smyth, William, 120
Snaith, Norman H., 395
Sniatyunskyi, Leslee, 525
Snow, Eric V., 120
Snowden, James Henry, 36, 196, 432
Synder, Francis Clark, 526
Snyder, Graydon F., 377
Snyder, Russell D., 377
Soards, Marion L., 362, 377
Sobrino, Jon, 230
Sockman, Ralph W., 447
Söderblom, Nathan, 36
Södergren, Carl J., 362
Soelle, Dorothee, 196
Solly, Henry Shaen, 290
Solomon, George, 489
Soltau, George, 196
Some Doubts Respecting the Death, Resurrection, and Ascension of Jesus Christ, 64
Somerset, Edward Adolphus, 432
Song, Choan-Seng, 433
Sookhdeo, Patrick, 472
Sorensen, Robert Allen, 525
South, James T., 196

South, Robert, 447
Southgate, Henry, 196
Sox, H. David, 230
Spaeth, Adolph, 346
Sparrow-Simpson, W. J., 36
Spaulding, Henry G., 325
Specht, Walter F., 525
Speciale, Stephen E., 525
Speer, Robert E., 230, 346
Spence, H. D. M., 325
Spencer, Bonnell, 36
Spencer, Claudius B., 36
Spencer, F. Scott, 196, 325, 362
Spencer, Robert, 472
Spencer, Thomas, 395
Sperow, Everett H., 196
Speyr, Adrienne von, 346
Spinoza, Benedictus de, 489
Spirago, Francis, 395
Spittler, Russell P., 377
Spivey, Robert A., 533
Spong, John Shelby, 46, 58, 140, 208, 237, 309, 346
Spooner, Lysander, 58, 140, 157
Spoto, Donald, 196
Spring, Gardiner, 196, 230
Springer, Joseph Arthur, 309
Sproul, R. C., 120, 196–97, 290, 310, 325, 395, 433, 472
Sproull, Thomas, 433
Spurgeon, Andrew B., 377
Spurgeon, C. H., 36, 310, 447
Spurrier, William A., 433
Stacey, John, 433
Stack, Richard, 362
Stackhouse, John G., 120, 433
Stackhouse, Thomas, 154, 230
Stafford, T. P., 433
Stagg, Frank, 325, 362
Staley, Jeffrey Lloyd, 346
Stalker, James, 197
Stallings, Jack Wilson, 346
Stam, Cornelius Richard, 363, 377
Stamm, Frederick Keller, 197
Stamm, Raymond T., 290
Stanfield, James Monroe, 433
Stanford, Charles, 36
Stanford, Shane, 36
Stankus, Pat, 525
Stanley, Arthur Penrhyn, 378
Stanley, David Michael, 36, 262, 310, 525
Stanley, Stephen, 325
Stansbury, Hubert, 58, 140
Stanton, Graham N., 230
Stanton, H. U. Weitbrecht, 310

Stapfer, Edmond, 197
Stark, James, 325
Starkey, John C. M., 525
Staton, Knofel, 378
Staudt, Calvin Klopp, 380, 525
Stauffer, Ethelbert, 197, 533
Stearns, Lewis French, 433
Stebbing, Henry, 447
Stecher, Richard C., 36, 46, 140
Stedman, Ray C., 346, 378
Steele, David Ramsey, 58, 141
Steele, James, 120
Steenbrink, Karel, 472
Stegall, Thomas L., 230
Stein, Robert H., 197, 290, 325
Steinberg, Milton, 489
Steiner, Rudolf, 58, 141
Steinmann, Jean, 197, 433
Steinmeyer, F. L., 37
Steinmueller, John E., 509
Stellhorn, F. W., 290, 310, 325, 346, 363
Stenger, Victor J., 141
Stephen, Thomas, 197
Stephens, Gregory D., 525
Stern, David H., 484
Sterrett, James Macbride, 121
Stevens, A. T., 64
Stevens, Clifford J., 197
Stevens, William Arnold, 197
Stevens, William Wilson, 433
Stevenson, Dwight E., 447
Stevenson, Gregory M., 262, 310
Stevenson, Kenneth E., 37, 230
Stevenson, Margaret J., 197
Stevenson, Morley, 325
Stevenson, William, 154
Stewart, Alexander, 121
Stewart, Desmond, 197
Stewart, George, 37
Stewart, James S., 197
Stewart, John, 197
Stewart, John J., 37
Stewart, Robert B., 197, 262
St. Helen's Church, Bishopsgate, 346
Stibbe, Mark W. G., 346
Stiegemeyer, Julie, 70
Stier, Rudolf, 230, 363
Stifler, James Madison, 197, 325, 363
Stiles, Wayne, 197
Still, William, 447
Stillingfleet, Edward, 121, 433
Stimson, Henry Albert, 396
Stitt, Frederick H., 58, 141
St. John, Harold, 290
St. John, Patricia, 70

Stobart, Andrew J., 525
Stock, Augustine, 290, 310
Stock, Eugene, 197, 325
Stockwood, Mervyn, 396
Stokes, George Thomas, 363
Stoffel, Ernest Lee, 37
Stöger, Alois, 325
Stoll, Raymond F., 325
Stone, Darwell, 433
Stone, David Reuben, 121
Stone, Francis, 447
Stone, James S., 37
Stone, S. J., 396
Stonehouse, Ned Bernard, 290, 310, 325
Stoney, James Butler, 434
Storm, Harold, 230
Storr, Catherine, 70
Storr, Gottlieb Konrad Christian, 434
Storrs, Richard S., 121
Story, Cullen I. K., 291, 347
Story, Dan, 121
Stott, John R. W., 363, 434
Stoughton, John, 262
Stout, Andrew P., 198
Stowe, Harriet Beecher, 198
Stowell, Gordon, 70
Strachan, R. H., 347
Strand, Ahlert J. C., 526
Stratemeier, Klaas Jacob, 378
Strauss, David Friedrich, 58, 141, 208
Strauss, Mark L., 231, 291, 325, 533
Streeter, Burnett Hillman, 262
Strobel, Lee, 37, 198, 231, 262, 434
Strohman, John M., 310
Strong, Augustus Hopkins, 434, 533
Strong, Cynda, 70
Strong, Thomas B., 231, 434
Stroup, George W., 434
Struthers, Gavin, 447

Stuhlmueller, Carroll, 325, 509
Stump, Joseph, 434
Sudworth, Richard, 473
Sueltz, Arthur Fay, 347
Sullivan, Clayton, 198
Sullivan, James, 37
Sullivan, Roger W., 526
Sultan, Sohaib, 479
Summers, Ray, 325, 347
Summers, Thomas O., 291, 310, 325, 363, 434
Sumner, John Bird, 291, 310, 325, 347
Surgy, Paul de, 37
Surrey, Cameron, 526
Sutcliffe, Joseph, 231, 458
Swaggart, Jimmy, 458
Swain, Lionel, 37, 347
Swanson, Mark N., 473, 526
Swanson, Reuben J., 291, 310
Swanson, Richard W., 326
Swartley, Keith E., 473
Swartley, Willard M., 291, 347
Sweat, Laura C., 291
Sweeley, John W., 58, 141, 198, 347
Sweet, Leonard I., 198
Sweetland, Dennis M., 291
Sweetman, J., 473
Sweis, Khaldoun A., 121
Swete, Henry Barclay, 37, 80, 291, 396
Swihart, Stephen D., 458
Swinburne, Richard, 37, 262, 434
Swindoll, Charles R., 198, 291, 326, 434, 458
Synder, Francis Clark, 526
Sydnor, William, 326
Sykes, Arthur Ashley, 121
Sylva (pseud.), 237
Sylva, Dennis D., 347
Syreeni, Kari, 262
Szymansk, Mary Reginette, 526

T

Tabor, Britton H., 121
Tabor, James D., 237
Tacey, David J., 58, 141, 434
Taggart, Samuel, 121
Tait, Arthur J., 37, 231, 396
Talbert, Charles H., 310, 326, 347, 363, 378
Talbot, George F., 58, 141, 198
Taliaferro, Charles, 509
Talling, Marshall P., 434
Talmage, Frank Ephraim, 489
Talmage, James E., 231, 403
Talmage, T. De Witt, 198, 231
Tambasco, Anthony J., 198

Tan, Kim Huat, 291
Tanagho, Samy, 473
Tannehill, Robert C., 326, 363
Tanner, Obert C., 533
Tanzella-Nitti, Giuseppe, 509
Tappenden, Frederick S., 262
Tarazi, Paul Nadim, 378
Tarico, Valerie, 141
Tasker, John Greenwood, 121
Tasker, R. V. G., 310, 347
Tatham, C. Ernest, 37
Tatum, W. Barnes, 198
Taverner, Richard, 448

Names Index

Taylor, Birgit, 526
Taylor, David Bruce, 121, 291
Taylor, H. B., 121
Taylor, Isaac, 231
Taylor, J. J., 291
Taylor, James E., 121
Taylor, Jeremy, 198
Taylor, Jerry, 262
Taylor, John V., 37
Taylor, Justin, 363
Taylor, Kenneth Nathaniel, 198
Taylor, Marion, 198
Taylor, Marion Ann, 262
Taylor, Mark A., 70
Taylor, Mark Edward, 378
Taylor, Michael J., 347
Taylor, Myron J., 37, 448
Taylor, Richard S., 509
Taylor, Robert, 58, 141
Taylor, Thomas Eddy, 198
Taylor, Vincent, 198, 291, 326, 434
Taylor, Warren Francis, 526
Taylor, William Francis, 154
Taylor, William M., 155
Tebo, Mary Elizabeth, 70
Telford, W. R., 191
Temple, Sydney, 347
Temple, William, 347
Templeton, Charles, 59, 141
Tenney, E. P., 199
Tenney, Merrill C., 38, 80, 347, 509
Terry, Milton Spencer, 122, 435
Tertullian, 59, 122
Tess, Fries, 70
Tew, W. Mark, 326
Thaddeus, Sister Mary, 231
Tham, Po Wing, 526
Thatcher, Adrian, 263
Thatcher, Floyd W., 38, 347
Thayer, E. W., 199
Thayer, Joseph Henry, 263
Thayer, Thomas B., 122
Thayil, Philip, 526
Theissen, Gerd, 199
Theisz, George Elmer, 38
Theodore, John T., 199
Theodore of Mopsuestia, 347
Theological-Historical Commission for the Greater Jubilee of the Year 2000, The, 231
Theology of Work Project, 310
Theophylactus, of Orchida, Archbishop of Ochrida, 291, 310, 326
Thielen, Martin, 435
Thielicke, Helmut, 122, 396, 435
Thiering, Barbara, 46, 59, 141, 237
Thiessen, Henry Clarence, 435
Thirlwall, Thomas, 199
Thiselton, Anthony C., 378, 435, 509
Tholuck, A., 347
Thom, John Hamilton, 378
Thomas, David, 310, 347, 363
Thomas, Derek W. H., 363
Thomas, George Ernest, 38
Thomas, M. M., 326
Thomas, Mack, 458
Thomas, Owen C., 435
Thomas, Reuen, 80
Thomas, W. H. Griffith, 199, 310, 326, 363, 403, 435
Thomason, Jean, 71
Thompson, Alan J., 38, 363
Thompson, Andrew, 473
Thompson, Charles, 458
Thompson, D. A., 291
Thompson, Edward, 122
Thompson, Ernest Trice, 291
Thompson, G. H. P., 326
Thompson, Gordon G., 38
Thompson, Henry, 448
Thompson, J. M., 155
Thompson, Joseph P., 199
Thompson, K. C., 38
Thompson, Marianne Meye, 347
Thompson, Richard P., 363
Thompson, Thomas L., 208
Thompson, Timothy J., 526
Thompson, William G., 311
Thompson, William M., 231
Thomson, Alexander, 38
Thomson, Charles, 199
Thomson, Ebenezer, 199, 231
Thomson, James, 59, 141, 326
Thorburn, Thomas James, 38, 59, 141, 458
Thoresby, Francis, 448
Thornton, Norman, 122
Thorogood, Bernard, 38
Thorpe, Mary Brennan, 526
Thorsen, Donald A. D., 435
Thrall, Margaret E., 378
Thurian, Max, 435
Thurman, William C., 199
Thurston, Bonnie Bowman, 291, 311
Tice, Rico, 231
Tidball, Charles S., 199
Tidball, Thomas A., 231
Tiede, David Lenz, 326
Tiemeyer, T. N., 199
Tiffin, John M., 526
Tilborg, Sjef van, 326
Tilden, Elwyn E., 199

Tillich, Paul, 435
Tillotson, John, 403, 448
Tilly, William, 448
Timpson, Thomas, 509
Tinsley, E. J., 326
Tischler, Nancy M., 509
Tisdall, William St. Clair, 473
Tissot, James, 199
Tittle, E. J. (Ernest Fremont), 326
Titus, Eric Lane, 348
Titus, Murray T., 473
Toast, Sarah, 71
Tobey, Alvan, 122
Tobin, Paul, 59, 141, 208
Todd, John, 263
Tolar, William B., 291
Tolbert, Malcolm, 311, 326
Tolbert, Mary Ann, 291, 292
Toon, Peter, 38, 435
Toppe, Carleton, 378
Torrance, Thomas F., 38, 155, 231, 348
Torrey, R. A., 38, 122, 199, 232, 263, 435, 448
Torstrick, Melvin E., 526
Tóth, Tihamér, 38, 448
Touche, Everard Digges, 122
Tourville, Robert E., 363
Toussaint, Stanley D., 311
Towey, Anthony, 435
Towns, Elmer L., 348, 533
Townson, Thomas, 38, 403
Toy, Crawford Howell, 458
Tracey, David, 435
Trail, Ronald L., 378
Trainor, Michael F., 292, 326
Trapp, John, 458
Trapp, Joseph, 311
Trattner, Ernest R., 489
Trayil, Philip, 526
Treffry, Richard, 122
Trench, George Henry, 38, 348
Trench, Richard Chenevix, 155
Tresmontant, Claude, 311
Trevor, John William, 396
Tribe, Frank C., 232
Trice, Rico, 122

Trier, Daniel, 509
Triestman, Mitch, 484
Trilling, Wolfgang, 311
Tripole, Martin R., 232
Trites, Allison A., 326
Troki, Isaac Ben Abraham, 489
Troll, Christian W., 473
Trollope, William, 311, 326, 363
True, Hiram L. *See* Allen, Don., 43
Trueblood, Elton, 292
Truitt, Gloria A., 71
Trull, Joe E., 38
Trumper, Peter, 39
Truth About The Crucifixion Transcripts from the International Conference on Deliverance of Jesus from the Cross, 479
Trypho, the Jew, 489
Tsoukalas, Steven, 435
Tuck, Robert, 122
Tuck, William Powell, 232
Tucker, Joshua T., 200
Tuckett, C. M., 263
Tuckett, Ivor, 157
Tulga, Chester E., 398
Tullidge, Henry, 123
Tupper, William George, 396
Turlington, Henry E., 326
Turnbell, Robert, 232
Turnbull, Ralph G., 363
Turner, C. H., 292
Turner, David L., 292, 311
Turner, George Allen, 348
Turner, H. E. W., 200
Turpin, W. T., 326
Turrentine, Charles P., 80
Turton, William Harry, 123
Tuttle, Emily, 71
Tuttle, H. E. W., 200
Twelftree, Graham H., 155
Twining, Agatha G., 396
Twining, Kinsley, 263
Twisleton, Frederick, 404
Twyman, Tracy R., 46
Tymms, T. Vincent, 123
Tyrrell, George, 404

U

Uhlhorn, Gerhard, 123, 200
Ulfat Aziz-us-Samad, 479
Ullrich, Lothar, 263
Um, Stephen T., 378
Underhill, Evelyn, 396
Ungar, Paul, 436
Unitheist, 46, 141

Unity School of Christianity. *See* Fillmore, Charles, 509
Upham, Francis W., 39, 311
Upton, Bridget Gilfillan, 292
Urban, Linwood, 436
Usher, James, 436
Usmani, Muhammad Taqi, 479

V

Vaiden, Thomas J., 59, 142
Valdés, Juan de, 311, 378
Valentine, Mary Hester, 155, 436
Valentine, Milton, 436
Valesio, Franco, 232
Vallings, J. F., 200
VanBeek, Lawrence H., 526
Van Buren, Paul Matthews, 378, 436
Van Daalen, David H., 39
Vander, Ray Laan, 39
Vanderlaan, Eldred Cornelius, 123, 436
Vanderlip, D. George, 348
Van Doren, W. H., 326, 348
Vang, Preben, 378
Van Gorder, A. Christian, 473
Vanhoozer, Kevin J., 436, 509
Vanier, Jean, 348
Van Kempen, Case, 123
Van Paassen, Pierre, 232
Van Til, Cornelius, 123
Van Voorst, Robert E., 200
Van Winkle, Peter, 436
Van Wyke, William P., 396
Vardy, Peter, 232
Varley, Henry, 39
Vassilakos, Aristarchus, 200
Vaughan, Bernard, 200
Vaughan, C. J., 363
Vaughan, Curtis, 363, 378
Vaughan, David James, 123
Vaughan, Edward T., 123
Vaughan, James, 263
Vawter, Bruce, 232
Veach, Robert Wells, 232
Vear, Eric, 232
Veil, Charles-Marie du, 363
Veneer, John, 404
Venkataraman, Babu Immanuel, 363
Verbrugge, Verlyn D., 378, 510
Verheyden, Joseph, 263
Vermès, Géza, 237, 490
Vernon, Edward Thomson, 292
Veuillot, Louis, 200
Vickers, John, 200, 208, 232
Viening, Edward, 510
Vignon, Paul, 232
Villars, I., 80
Vine, W. E., 348, 378
Vines, Jerry, 292, 378
Vining, Teresa, 123
Vinson, Richard Bolling, 327
Vinzent, Markus, 39
Violette, E. E., 39
Virtue, Willis W., 526
Vischer, Phil, 71
Vistar, Deolito V., 526
Vivian, Philip, 142
Voigt, Andrew George, 436
Vollmer, Philip, 200
Volney, C. F., 142
Vorass, Steven L., 526
Vos, Howard F., 200, 292, 311
Vredenburgh, Charles Edwin, 142

W

Waardenburg, Jacques, 473
Wace, Henry, 39
Waddams, Herbert W., 396
Waddy, Charis, 473
Wade, George, 39
Wadhams, Nellie Content Kimberly, 292
Waetjen, Herman C., 292, 311, 348
Wagner, C. Peter, 363
Wagner, James Edgar, 436
Wagner, Walter H., 473
Wahlde, Urban C., 348
Wainwright, Elaine M., 232, 263, 311
Wainwright, Geoffrey, 436
Waite, Charles B., 59, 142
Wakefield, Samuel, 436
Walaskay, Paul W., 364
Waldie, Lance, 123
Waldo, W. A., 526
Walker, Albert H., 200
Walker, James K., 473
Walker, Joni, 71
Walker, Peter W. L., 39, 200
Walker, Rollin Hough, 327
Walker, Thomas, 1881–, 490
Walker, Thomas 1859–1912, 364
Walker, Thomas W. (Thomas Worth), 327
Wall, Robert W., 364
Wallace, Catherine M., 201
Wallace, Daniel B., 263
Wallace, George Lynn, 525
Wallace, J. Warner, 123
Wallace, O. C. S., 201
Wallis, John, 448
Walpole, A. S., 327
Walser, G. H., 201
Walsh, Chad, 123

Walsh, John Evangelist, 232
Walsh, Milton, 404
Walshe, Thomas Joseph, 123
Walter, Eugen, 378
Walter, H. A., 473
Walter, William W., 201
Walton, Alfred Grant, 123, 396, 436
Walton, Robert C., 292
Walton, Steve, 263
Walvoord, John F., 232, 311
Wand, J. W. C., 201
Wansbrough, Henry, 39, 327
Warburton, William, 123
Ward, Arthur Marcus, 311
Ward, Keith, 124, 155, 436
Ward, Monsignor, 327
Ward, Nelson W., 39
Ward, Ronald A., 348
Ward, Verlie, 71
Ward, William B., 436
Ward, William Hayes, 123
Warden, Duane, 379
Warden, John, 436
Wardlaw, Ralph, 155, 436
Ware, Augustus William, 39, 124
Ware, Bruce A., 437
Ware, Henry, 201
Warne, Floyd Lawrence, 142
Warne, Francis Wesley, 201
Warner, Beverley E., 396
Warner, David W., 526
Warner, Richard, 201
Warnock, Adrian, 39
Warren, Elizabeth, 39
Warren, Paul F., 527
Warschauer, J., 124, 201
Washburn, Lemuel Kelley, 59, 142, 157
Washington, Linda, 232
Watanabe, Masataka Mark, 527
Watchtower Bible and Tract Society of New York, 232, 404
Water, Mark, 40, 510
Waterhouse, Steven, 437
Waterman, Mark M. W., 40, 292
Waterson, A. P., 263
Watkins, H. W., 348
Watkinson, Redford A., 201
Watson, Alexander, 448
Watson, David C. K., 124
Watson, Francis, 263
Watson, John, 40, 201
Watson, Nigel, 40, 379
Watson, Rhonda, 71
Watson, Richard, 527

Watson, Richard, bishop, 124, 264, 292, 311, 437, 510
Watson, Samuel, Mrs., 201, 233
Watson, Thomas, 124, 404
Watt, William Montgomery, 124, 473
Watts, Charles, 59
Wayne, Thomas, 458
Weatherhead, Leslie D., 40, 201, 437
Weatherly, Jon A., 264
Weaver, Dorothy Jean, 311
Weaver, Jonathan, 437
Weaver, S. Townsend, 201
Weaver, Walter P., 201, 292
Webb, Guilford Polly, 40
Webb-Odell, R., 264
Webber, Christopher, 437
Weber, Gerard P., 292, 348
Weber, Hans-Rudi, 312
Weber, Otto, 437
Webster, Douglas D., 124
Webster, Jane S., 348
Webster, John, 264
Webster, William, 64
Wedderburn, A. J. M., 40, 264
Wedeven, Carol, 71
Weed, George Ludington, 201
Weeden, Theodore J., 292
Weghe, Rob Van de, 124
Weidner, Revere Franklin, 292
Weigall, Arthur, 59, 142
Weinel, Heinric, 233
Weir, John Ferguson, 124
Weir, Wilbert Walter, 124
Weisiger, Cary N., 327
Weiss, Bernhard, 202, 437, 458
Weiss, Louis, 490
Weiss, Lyle K., 527
Welch, Charles H., 348
Welch, Claude, 437
Welch, J. Wilbert, 379
Welch, Reuben, 327
Welker, Michael, 233, 264
Wellcome, I. C., 437
Wellman, Jack, 124
Wells, Edward, 233, 458
Wells, George Albert, 59, 142–43, 208
Wells, H. G., 59, 238
Wells, James, 124
Welsh, Robert Ethol, 124
Wendland, Johannes, 155
Wendt, Hans Hinrich, 533
Wenham, David, 533
Wenham, John William, 40
Wenisch, Fritz, 473
Wentworth, E., 449

Werblowsky, Raphael Jehudah Zwi, 510
Weren, Wim, H. Van De Sandt, 40
Weren, Wim J. C, 264
Werner, Martin, 437
Wernle, Paul, 202
Wesley, John, 458
Wessel, Herman August, 527
Wessel, Walter W., 292
Wessels, Anton, 474
Wessels, Cletus, 233
West, Gilbert, 40, 264
West, J., 449
West, J. R., 40
West, Nathaniel, 265, 459
West, Steven D., 124
West, Thomas H., 233
Westcott, Brooke Foss, 40, 80, 348, 396, 449
Weston, Henry G., 312
Whale, J. S., 437
Wharton, Edward C., 64
Whately, Richard, 125
Whatmore, George Bernard, 125
Whatmore, Leonard E., 40
Whedon, D. D., 292, 312, 327, 348, 364, 379
Wheeler, Brandon M., 480
Wheeler, Henry, 396
Wheeler, Michael, 348
Whipple, Wayne, 202
Whiston, Lionel A., 125
Whiston, William, 125
Whitacre, Rodney A., 348
Whitaker, Max, 527
Whitbie or Whitby, Daniel, 125, 379, 459
White, Ellen Gould Harmon, 40, 202, 233, 364
White, James Emery, 125
White, James R., 125, 474
White, Wilbert W., 81
Whitelaw, Thomas, 233, 348, 364
Whitham, A. R., 327
Whitmer, John A., 233
Whitney, Loren Harper, 60, 143, 157
Whiton, James Morris, 41, 81, 155
Whittaker, Thomas, 238
Whitworth, John F., 81
Wickes, Thomas, 437
Wiebe, Phillip H., 41
Wieman, Henry Nelson, 233
Wiener, Philip P., 510
Wiersbe, Warren W., 41, 312, 327, 379, 449, 459
Wieseler, Karl, 202
Wigoder, Geoffrey, 510
Wilckens, Ulrich, 41, 265
Wilcock, Michael, 327
Wilcox, Robert K., 233

Wilder, Amos Niven, 437
Wildsmith, Brian, 71
Wierwille, Victor Paul, 202
Wiles, Maurice F., 438
Wiley, H. Orton, 438
Wilhelm, Dawn Ottoni, 292
Wilhelm, Joseph, 404, 438
Wilkins, Michael J., 312
Wilkinson, Wilfred, 327
Wilkinson, William Cleaver, 202
Willam, Franz Michel, 202
Willcock, J., 327
Willett, Herbert Lockwood, 125, 202
Williams, A. Lukyn, 125, 233, 312
Williams, Albert Nathaniel, 510
Williams, C. S. C., 364, 379
Williams, David John, 364
Williams, Ernest Swing, 438
Williams, Henry Wilkinson, 202
Williams, Horace Blake, 155, 233
Williams, Isaac, 41
Williams, J. Rodman, 438
Williams, Jay G., 202
Williams, Jeremy, 527
Williams, Joel F., 293
Williams, John, 449
Williams, John, Bishop of Connecticut, 364
Williams, N. P., 41
Williams, Nathaniel Marshman, 312
Williams, Peter S., 202
Williams, R. R., 364
Williams, Rheinallt Nantlais, 125
Williams, Richard W., 527
Williams, Rowan, 41, 265, 438
Williams, Roy, 125
Williams, Stephen Douglas, 125
Williams, Stephen Joseph, 125
Williams, T. C., 155
Williamson, Charles C., 364
Williamson, Clark M., 438
Williamson, Elbert M., 397
Williamson, I. D., 125
Williamson, Karen, 71
Williamson, Lamar, 293, 349
Willimon, William H., 364
Willink, M. D. R., 312
Willis, David, 397
Willis, Wesley R., 327, 379
Willits, A. A., 155
Willitt, Herbert L., 202
Willoughby, R., 71
Wilmers, W., 125, 404, 438
Wilson, A. N., 202
Wilson, Billy, 474
Wilson, Clifford A., 126, 233

Wilson, C. W., 265
Wilson, Daniel, 126
Wilson, Etta, 71
Wilson, Geoffrey B., 379
Wilson, Gordon, 265
Wilson, Henry Albert, 397
Wilson, Ian, 202, 233
Wilson, James, 438
Wilson, John, 404
Wilson, John W., 473
Wilson, Jonathan R., 438
Wilson, P. Whitwell, 202, 234
Wilson, R. McL., 193
Wilson, W. D., 155
Wilson, William, 1874, 202
Wilson, William, Rector of Morley, 1694, 41
Wilton, Murray Ross, 527
Winchester, Elhanan, 126
Wingard, Robert W, 379
Wingeier, Douglas E., 41
Wingren, Gustaf, 397, 438
Winn, Albert Curry, 364, 397
Winner, Lauren F., 312
Winnington-Ingram, A. F., 126
Winstanley, Edward William, 202
Winter, David, 203
Witherup, Ronald David, 527
Winthrop, Elizabeth, 71
Winward, Stephen F., 438
Wise, Daniel, 203
Wise, Isaac Mayer, 364, 490
Wise, Robert L., 41
Witcher, W. C., 41, 126
Witham, Robert, 379
Witherington, Ben, 203, 265, 293, 312, 349, 364, 379
Witherspoon, Jet, 364
Witherup, Ronald D., 312
Witmer, John A., 265
Witness Lee. *See* Lee, Witness., 321, 358, 454
Witsius, Herman, 397
Wives, E. W., 234
Woleng, Aylwin, 527
Wolf, Beth Rowland, 71

Wolf, William James, 527
Wolfe, Charles E., 41
Wolfe, Rolland, 41, 46, 143
Wolff, Richard, 293
Wong, John B., 81
Wood, Charles James, 438
Wood, David, 265
Wood, James, 143
Wood, Simon A., 474
Wood, William, 41
Woodberry, J. Dudley, 474
Woodbridge, Charles J., 364
Woodcock, Eldon, 527
Woodford, J. R., 379
Woodhead, Abraham, 203
Woodley, Matt, 312
Woodring, Richard C., 527
Woodrow, Ralph E., 42
Woodward, James, 312
Woolston, Thomas, 157
Wordsworth, Chr., 364, 379, 459
Wordsworth, Elizabeth, 397
Workman, George Coulson, 203, 234
World Council of Churches Commission On Faith and Order, 397
Worsley, F. W., 234, 349
Worth, Roland H., 60, 143
Wortham, Thomas Emerson, 527
Wrangham, Francis, 126
Wright, C. J. (Charles James), 126, 155, 438
Wright, Charles H. H., 510
Wright, George Clarence, 527
Wright, George H., 527
Wright, G. Frederick, 126
Wright, John J., 64, 449
Wright, N. T., 42, 81, 126, 203, 234, 265, 293, 312, 327, 349, 364, 379
Wright, Paul, 203
Wright, William, 510
Wuellner, Bernard J., 42
Wuenschel, Edward, 234
Wuerl, Donald, 397
Wuest, Kenneth Samuel, 293
Wyper, Stephen A., 527

Y

Yamauchi, Edwin M., 265
Yancey, Philip, 234
Yarbo Collins, Adela, 293
Yarbrough, Robert W., 349
Yarnold, Greville Dennis, 42
Yarrington, W. H. H., 42
Yeager, Ralph O., 459
Yeboah-Amoako, Anthony K., 527

Yenne, Bill, 71
Yeomans, William, 312
Yingling, M. F., 527
Yisrael, Rav-Zurdian, 490
Ylvisaker, Joh, 459
Yoder, John Howard, 438
Yohe, Lou, 71
Yoho, Walter Allan, 64

Yonge, John Eyre, 397
Yost, Casper Salathiel, 203
Youd, Pauline, 71
Young, Dinsdale T., 449
Young, E. S., 234, 364
Young, John, 126, 234
Young, Matt, 158
Young, Samuel, 349
Youngblood, Ronald F., 510
Yrigoyen, Charles, 364

Z

Zacharias, Ravi K., 126
Zafar, Harris, 474
Zahn, Theodor, 397
Zahniser, A. H. Mathias, 474
Zahrnt, Heinz, 203
Zaka, Anees, 126, 474
Zanchettin, Leo, 293, 312, 349
Zangenberg, Jürgen, 266
Zayn, M. Faruk, 474
Zebiri, Kate, 474
Zein, M. Faruk, 480
Zeitlin, Irving M., 490
Zeitlin, Solomon, 490
Zeller, Eduard, 364
Zenos, Andrew C., 293
Zepa, 143
Zimmermann, Eleanor, 71
Zimmermann, Reuben, 266
Zindler, Frank R., 143, 208, 238
Zobel-Nolan, Allia, 71
Zodhiates, Spiros, 379
Zolondek, Michael V., 528
Zugibe, Frederick T., 234
Zukeran, Patrick, 126, 266
Zumstein, Jean, 266
Zwemer, Samuel Marinus, 42, 234, 474
Zwiep, Arie W., 42, 266, 364, 528

www.ingramcontent.com/pod-product-compliance
Lightning Source LLC
Chambersburg PA
CBHW080528300426
44111CB00017B/2650